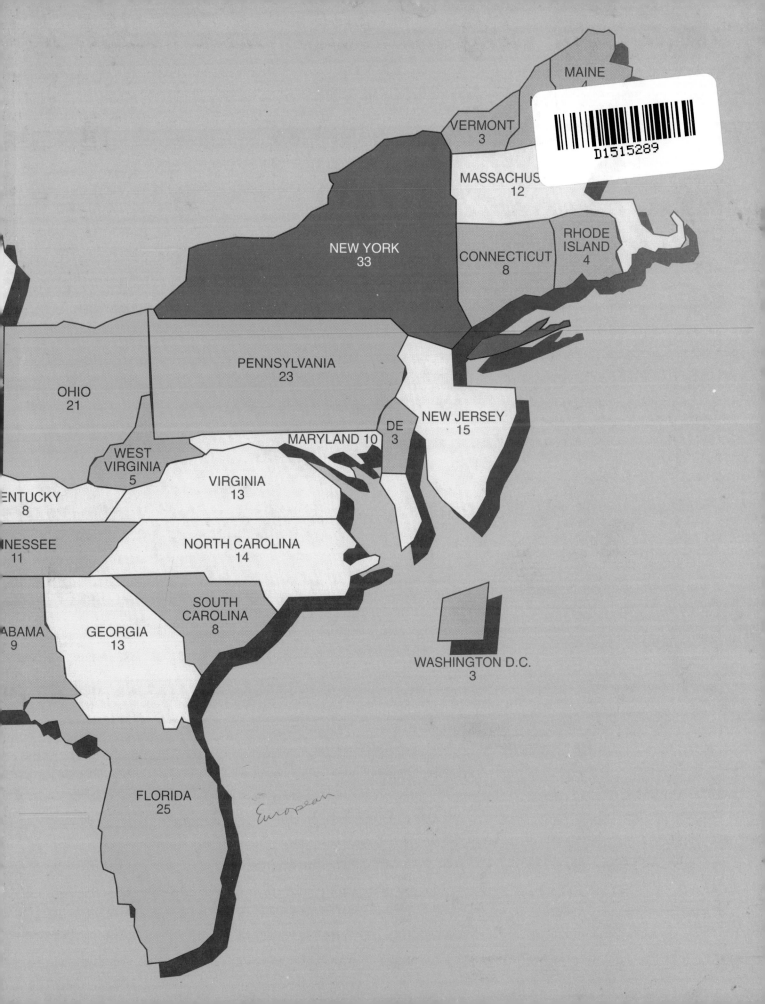

MAINE
4

VERMONT
3

MASSACHUS
12

NEW YORK
33

CONNECTICUT
8

RHODE
ISLAND
4

PENNSYLVANIA
23

OHIO
21

NEW JERSEY
15

WEST
VIRGINIA
5

MARYLAND 10

DE
3

KENTUCKY
8

VIRGINIA
13

NESSEE
11

NORTH CAROLINA
14

ALABAMA
9

GEORGIA
13

SOUTH
CAROLINA
8

WASHINGTON D.C.
3

FLORIDA
25

European

Government By The People

NATIONAL VERSION

Seventeenth Edition

James MacGregor Burns
*University of Maryland, College Park
and Williams College*

J.W. Peltason
University of California

Thomas E. Cronin
Whitman College

David B. Magleby
Brigham Young University

Prentice Hall, Upper Saddle River, New Jersey 07458

Library of Congress Cataloging-in-Publication Data

Government by the People : national version/ James MacGregor Burns
... [et al.]. — 17th ed.
    p. cm.
    Includes bibliographical references and index.
    ISBN 0-13-287160-2
    1. United States—Politics and government. I. Burns, James
MacGregor.
    JK274.G66 1998
    320.473—dc21
                            97-24095
                            CIP

Editorial Director: *Charlyce Jones Owen*
Editor in Chief: *Nancy Roberts*
Acquisitions Editor: *Michael Bickerstaff*
Marketing Manager: *Christopher DeJohn*
Development Editor and Project Manager: *Serena Hoffman*
Copy Editor: *Ann Hofstra Grogg*
Director of Production and Manufacturing: *Barbara Kittle*
Manufacturing Manager: *Nick Sklitsis*
Prepress and Manufacturing Buyer: *Bob Anderson*
Creative Design Director: *Leslie Osher*
Interior Designers: *Anne Bonanno Nieglos and Maria Lange*
Line Art Coordinator: *Michele Giusti*
Illustrations: *Mirella Signoretto and Maria Piper*
Director, Image Resource Center: *Lori Morris-Nantz*
Photo Research Supervisor: *Melinda Lee Reo*
Image Permission Supervisor: *Kay Dellosa*
Photo Researcher: *Joelle Burrows*
Supervisor of Production Services: *Lori Clinton*
Electronic Page Layout: *Joh Lisa*
Electronic Graphic Assistance: *Nancy Camuso Wells*
Cover art: © *Jane Sterrett*
Cover Design: *Anne Bonanno Nieglos and Nancy Camuso Wells*
Title Page Photograph: *Max Mackenzie/Uniphoto Picture Agency*

This book was set in 11/12 Garamond
by Prentice Hall Production Services and was
printed and bound by R R Donnelley & Sons.
The cover was printed by The Lehigh Press, Inc.

© 1998, 1995, 1993, 1990, 1989, 1987, 1985, 1984, 1981, 1978, 1975,
1972, 1969, 1966, 1963, 1960, 1957, 1954, 1952 by Prentice-Hall, Inc.
Simon & Schuster/A Viacom Company
Upper Saddle River, New Jersey 07458

Printed in the United States of America
10 9 8 7 6 5 4 3 2 1

ISBN 0-13-287160-2

Prentice-Hall International (UK) Limited, London
Prentice-Hall of Australia Pty. Limited, Sydney
Prentice-Hall Canada Inc., Toronto
Prentice-Hall Hispanoamericana, S.A., Mexico
Prentice-Hall of India Private Limited, New Delhi
Prentice-Hall of Japan, Inc., Tokyo
Simon & Schuster Asia Pte. Ltd., Singapore
Editora Prentice-Hall do Brasil, Ltda., Rio de Janeiro

BRIEF CONTENTS

CONTENTS

Contents

Contents

FEATURES

A Closer Look

We the People

You Decide!

From Coast to Coast

A MESSAGE FROM THE AUTHORS

Constitutional democracy—the kind we have in the United States—is exceedingly hard to win, equally hard to sustain, and often hard to understand without rigorous study. The form of constitutional democracy that has emerged in the United States requires continual participation by caring, tolerant, and informed citizens. The framers of our Constitution warned that we must be vigilant in safeguarding our rights, liberties, and political institutions. But to do this, we first have to understand these institutions and the forces that have shaped our political and constitutional systems.

American politics is now in a volatile period, with voters willing to switch back and forth between parties, and with the parties trying to find a basis for a new and lasting majority coalition. Although our defense policy changed with the collapse of communism, the world has not suddenly become a safe place in which to live. Regional strife and terrorism continue, and the United States has entered a period of reassessment of its role in the world, in the United Nations, in regional defense organizations like NATO, and in its economic relations with other countries.

President Bill Clinton and the Republicans who control Congress in the late 1990s both cooperate and clash over domestic and economic priorities. Americans have never liked political parties, yet our parties do work, and they do offer choices. Campaign financing is the center of endless debate and reform initiatives, and it remains one of our biggest challenges. Also hotly debated are how to improve educational opportunity, lessen crime and racism, promote trade, and encourage better paying jobs.

Although we constantly turn to government and elected officials with problems and requests, we are still highly critical of their shortcomings. A recurrent theme of this book is the absolute need for politics and politicians, despite the widespread tendency to criticize nearly everything political.

In the past, constitutional democracy has been the exception rather than the rule. Most people lived under autocratic or tyrannical regimes in which a small group imposed their will on everyone else. And even today, less than half of the nation-states around the globe exist as viable, healthy democracies. This is a testing time for new democracies as well as old ones. Contempt for government and politics is expressed here in the United States and abroad, yet politics and partisan competition are the life blood by which free people can achieve the ideals of a government by the people.

We hope you will come away from reading this book with a richer understanding of American politics, government, and the job of politicians, and we hope you will participate actively in making your constitutional democracy more vital and responsive to the urgent problems of the twenty-first century.

Reviewers

The writing of this book has profited from the informed professional, and often sharp, critical suggestions of our colleagues around the country. This and previous editions have been considerably improved as a result of reviews by the following individuals, for which we thank them all:

David Gray Adler, Idaho State University

James Anderson, Tulane University

David Barnum, De Paul University

Robert Bartlett, Purdue University

Robert C. Benedict, University of Utah

Thad Beyle, University of North Carolina

Gary Bryner, Brigham Young University

Jeanne Clarke, University of Arizona

Leif Carter, University of Georgia

Morgan Chawawa, De Kalb College

Richard Chesteen, University of Tennessee

Peggy J. Connally, North Central Texas College

Gary Cornia, Brigham Young University

Gary Covington, University of Iowa

Douglas Crane, De Kalb College

Richard Davis, Brigham Young University

James D. Decker, Macon College

Robert DiClerico, West Virginia University

Lois Lovelace Duke, Georgia Southern University

Pat Dunham, Duquesne University

Robert Elias, University of San Francisco

Larry Elowitz, Georgia State College

Steven Finkel, University of Virginia

Amy Fried, Colgate University

Mark Gibney, Purdue University

L. Tucker Gibson, Trinity University

Eugene Goss, Long Beach City College

James A. Graves, Kentucky State University

Eugene R. Grosso, Long Beach City College

Gail Harrison, Georgia Southern University

Paul Herrnson, University of Maryland

Marjorie Hershey, Indiana University

Michael J. Horan, University of Wyoming

Ronald J. Hrebenar, University of Utah

Diane P. Jennings, De Kalb College

Loch K. Johnson, University of Georgia

Bill Kelly, Auburn University

Janet M. Kelly, Clemson University

J. Landrum Kelly, Georgia Southern University

Donald F. Kettl, University of Wisconsin

Dwight Kiel, Central Florida University

Ron King, Tulane University

Michael E. Kraft, University of Wisconsin

Fred A. Kramer, University of Massachusetts

William Lammers, University of Southern California

Ned Lebow, Ohio State University

Paul Light, University of Minnesota

William Louthan, Ohio Weslyan University

Vincent N. Mancini, Delaware County Community College

Richard Matthews, Lehigh University

Robert McCalla, University of Wisconsin

Theodore R. Mosch, University of Tennessee-Martin

Max Neiman, University of California

David Nice, Washington State University

Richard Pacelle, University of Missouri

Glen Parker, Florida State University

Kelly D. Patterson, Brigham Young University

Richard Pious, Barnard College

George Pippin, Jones County College

John Portz, Northeastern University

Pamela Rodgers, University of Wisconsin

David Rosenbloom, American University

Alan Rosenthal, Rutgers University

H.E. Scruggs, Brigham Young University

Henry Shockely, Boston University

Steven Shull, University of New Orleans

Christine Marie Sierra, University of New Mexico

Robert W. Small, Massasoit Community College

Gregory W. Smith, Gettysburg College

Richard Smolka, American University

Neil Snortland, University of Arkansas at Little Rock

Michael W. Sonnleitner, Portland Community College

Thaddeus J. Tocza, University of Colorado at Boulder

Roy Thoman, West Texas A&M University

John Tierney, Boston College

Richard Valelly, Massachusetts Institute of Technology

R. Lawson Veasey, University of Arkansas

Cheryl D. Young, Texas Technical University

Joseph F. Zimmerman, State University of New York at Albany

Acknowledgments

We are grateful for the help we have received from our colleagues, research assistants, and support staff, who have helped each of us in the preparation of this new edition of *Government By The People*. We thank Elizabeth Schiller at the University of California at Irvine for her assistance. At Whitman College, special thanks to JoAnn Collins, Donna Jones, Adrianne Ralph, and Ken Singer for their assistance. At Brigham Young University, we give particular thanks to research assistants Jason R. Beal, Hilarie H. Robison, Jeremy C. Pope, Derall Riley, and Eric A. Smith.

Our special thanks go to our superb production editor, Serena Hoffman, who once again guided us in the rewriting of this book. She is as close to being a coauthor as a production editor can be. We also thank our Prentice Hall friends: Phil Miller, Charlyce Jones Owen, Nancy Roberts, and Mike Bickerstaff. And we want to thank the many other skilled professionals at Prentice Hall who assisted in the publication of this edition: Joh Lisa and Lori Clinton for excellent page layouts, Joelle Burrows for photo research, Mirella Signoretto and Maria Piper for the fine illustrations, Michelle Giusti for art coordination, and Anne Nieglos for the handsome interior and cover design.

Finally, we thank the students and professors who have sent us letters with suggestions for improving *Government By The People*. We welcome your notes, calls, and e-mail concerning any errors or ways we can further improve the book. Please write us care of the Political Science Editor at Prentice Hall, 1 Lake Street, Upper Saddle River, New Jersey 07458, or to us directly:

James MacGregor Burns
Academy of Leadership
University of Maryland
College Park, MD 20742

J.W. Peltason
School of Social Sciences
University of California
Irvine, CA 92717-5700
jwpeltas@uci.edu

Thomas E. Cronin
Whitman College
Walla Walla, WA 99362
cronin@whitman.edu

David B. Magleby
Department of Political Science
Brigham Young University
Provo, UT 84602
maglebyd@fhss.byu.edu

A MESSAGE FROM THE PUBLISHER

The gratifying success *Government By The People* has enjoyed over the years results from a distinguished authorship team who always write a superb book with a distinctive combination of features. Treating each new edition as a fresh challenge—and, in many ways, a virtually new book—the authors capture American government and politics as the dynamic ventures they are.

Comprehensive and Balanced Presentation

Known for its balanced coverage of constitutional principles, political processes, and political institutions, this latest edition offers the best of previous editions and exciting changes in content that include:

- A thematic examination of constitutional democracy—its ideals, its conditions, and the American struggle to realize its possibilities and potential. The American political experiment is frequently assessed in comparison with other nations.

- A unique chapter, "Making Social Policy" (Chapter 20), covers past policy initiatives, such as the New Deal and the Great Society, as well as current debates over welfare reform, health care, crime control, and education policies, and whether the responsibility belongs in Washington or in the states and local communities.

- A informative chapter, "The American Political Landscape" (Chapter 8), examines social and economic diversity in American society and some of the political consequences of living in an increasingly multicultural nation. This chapter provides the framework of the social fabric of our nation, which needs to be put in context before students can fully appreciate the role that public opinion, interest group politics, and voting behavior play in the United States.

- Extensive coverage of the 1996 election, including data from the National Election Study, analysis of the presidential race, and further interpretation of the revolutionary 1994 election.

- Discussion of the current Supreme Court (Chapter 16), including the politics of selection and confirmation, with full updates and integrated analysis of recent Supreme Court decisions.

- Substantially revised policy chapters reflect current policy initiatives and the priorities of the president and Congress.

- Complete incorporation of 1990 census data. Once a decade we get a thorough examination of the American polity, and these data are integrated where appropriate throughout the book.

- Much revised treatment of the presidency (Chapter 15), Congress (Chapter 14), and the bureaucracy (Chapter 17) to reflect current issues, including Bill Clinton's second term initiatives, the rise and decline of Newt Gingrich, and the emphasis on downsizing and privatization of government functions.

- Innovative treatment of political ideology and culture, political participation, voting turnout, voting behavior, and campaign financing.

- Expanded coverage of state and local politics in the *National, State, and Local Version* and the *Texas Version*, including full updates on 1996 election results and, in the *Texas Version*, eight chapters devoted to government and politics in the state of Texas.

- The examples in *Government By The People* are drawn from a wide range of current and historical sources. While fully reflecting recent political events, examples are also included from earlier eras to provide the important historical context within which current events can be better understood. Complete lists of suggested readings at the end of each chapter and detailed footnotes at the back of the book highlight sources of lasting and recent importance.

New Internet Activities

- **Politics Online** New end-of-chapter Internet exercises are designed to engage and educate students about the vast potential of the Internet. The exercises present information, pose questions, and provide guidance on accessing Internat resources that offer information and solve problems.

- **Prentice Hall Web Companion Site**

  http://www.prenhall.com/burns

  This free site allows students to fully access the power of the World Wide Web. Available to the students are interactive multiple choice, true/false, and essay questions. Also, we have a bulletin board and an area for breaking news to help the book and the students stay current.

Accessible and Engaging Features for the Student

Written with the student in mind by experienced scholars and teachers, *Government By The People* has always been admired for its elegant, yet engaging narrative style. To assist comprehension, key terms appear on first use in the text in boldfaced type, with a precise definition. These terms are also listed in the full Glossary at the end of the book.

Of particular appeal to students will be the wealth of boxed features. Boxes in the margins provide amusing anecdotes and historical, biographical, and demographic facts of interest about American politics that will enhance student learning.

You Decide! This participatory question-and-answer feature is designed to strengthen students' critical thinking skills as well as introduce interesting and challenging issues and ideas about American politics for students to ponder. A question is presented on the left page, and on the facing page a Thinking It Through discussion examines possible answers (although, as in real life, not all questions have definitive answers). This unique feature has long been a favorite among the many students who have used it.

A Closer Look These journalistic-style boxes combine text, tables, photographs, and art on relevant issues of high student appeal. Like a good lecture, they provide a pause in the narrative where appropriate, to allow the pursuit of a particular topic beyond the scope of the text. Some of the topics include: "Rap Lyrics and Free Speech," "Juries on Trial," "The New African American Electorate," "Religion and Politics," "Money and Congressional Campaigns," and "How Americans Define Their Ideology."

We the People These unique boxes are designed to reflect the concerns and experiences of ethnic and minority groups in American politics. Some of the topics include: "How Representative Are Our Presidents?" "Portrait of the Electorate," "Distribution of Education in the United States," "Problems Faced by Women Bureaucrats," and "Equal Justice." The We the People feature, plus Chapter 8 on "The American Political Landscape" and the many instances in the text where ethnic and minority concerns, histories, and stories are told have made *Government By The People* the strongest and most complete text available that integrates all Americans into the story of American politics.

From Coast to Coast This collection of four-color maps provides state-by-state comparisons on a broad range of topics, such as "The Uninsured," " Average Turnout in General Elections," "Party Control of State Legislatures," "Fiscal Capacity to Raise Revenue Through Taxes," and "Unequal Welfare Benefits in the States." The comparisons give students the opportunity to understand the different factors that affect state functions and performance.

Supplements for the Instructor

Government By The People is the core of a complete learning package that includes a wide range of proven as well as new instructional aids. The supplements have been completely revised, not only to incorporate material new to this edition, but also to ensure the highest quality and accuracy possible.

Instructor's Resource Manual This supplement provides the following resources for each chapter of the text: summary, review of major concepts, lecture suggestions and topic outlines, suggestions for classroom discussions, additional resource materials, and a detailed content outline for lecture planning. A guide to media resources section in each chapter identifies specific transparencies, video clips, laserdisk segments, and/or simulations available with the text that are appropriate for the content of that chapter. The Instructor's Resource Manual was prepared by Michael F. Digby and Larry Elowitz, both of Georgia College.

Strategies for Teaching American Government: A Guide for the New Instructor This unique guide offers a wealth of practical advice and information to help new instructors face the challenges of teaching courses in American Government. From setting course goals, conducting the class, constructing and evaluating tests or written assignments, to advising students, many of the issues and questions related to teaching are covered. The guide was written by Fred Whitford, Montana State University.

Test Item File The seventeenth edition test item file has been thoroughly reviewed and revised to ensure the highest level of quality and accuracy. Over 2,000 questions in multiple choice, true/false, and essay format are provided, covering factual, conceptual, and applied material from the text.

Prentice Hall Custom Test A computerized version of the test item file, this program allows full editing of questions and the addition of instructor-generated items. Other special features include random generation, scrambling question order, and test preview before printing. Available for IBM and Macintosh computers.

American Government Transparencies, Series III, IV, and V These sets of 75 to 100 four-color transparency acetates reproduce illustrations, charts, and maps from the text as well as from additional sources.

Instructor's Guide to American Government Transparencies, Series III, IV, and V This brief guide provides descriptions, teaching suggestions, and discussion questions for each transparency. There is a separate guide for each set of transparencies.

ABC News/Prentice Hall Video Libraries Prentice Hall and ABC News bring this innovative video collection to your classroom. This video library brings chapter concepts to life by illustrating them with newsworthy videos.

ABCNEWS

- *Images in American Government* shows the conflicts of past presidential campaigns and elections plus segments on current issues.
- *Issues in American Government* provides multiple segments on issues such as health care and welfare reform, environment, crime and violence, foreign policy, the federal budget, and government waste.

Instructor's Guide to ABC News/Prentice Hall Video Libraries Provides a brief synopsis and discussion questions for each segment in the video libraries.

ABCNEWS

Supplements for the Student

Study Guide Each chapter includes outlines, study notes, a glossary, practice tests, Political Science Today study assignments, and data analysis worksheets that reinforce student learning. The guide was prepared by Dorothy Palmer of Indiana University of Pennsylvania.

Government By The People **on CD-ROM** Through the Power CD technology of Zane Publishing, this CD will be compatible with both Mac and IBM. It will contain the complete text, multimedia chapter overviews, video, Multimedia Study Guide, glossary, and a full dictionary.

Multimedia Guide to American Government This unique resource provides text, video, simulations, images, and study guide tools in a CD-ROM format. Available on Windows and Macintosh platforms. Prepared by G. David Garson, North Carolina State University.

American Government Simulation Games, Series II Seven unique simulations engage students in various role-playing situations: Bill of Rights, House of Representatives, Presidential Budget, Secretary of State, Supreme Court, Washington Ethics, and Crime and Social Policy. Available for DOS, Windows, and Macintosh platforms and in CD-ROM format. The simulations were created by G. David Garson, North Carolina State University, and programmed by Electronic Courseware Systems, Inc., Champaign, Illinois.

A Guide to Civic Literacy This brief booklet provides suggestions for getting students involved in politics. It includes nine political activities for individuals or groups on agenda building, coalition building, registering and mobilizing voters, education, and increasing accountability. The guide was written by James Chesney and Otto Feinstein, both of Wayne State University.

The Write Stuff: Writing as a Performing and Political Art, Second Edition This brief booklet, written by Thomas E. Cronin, provides ideas and suggestions on writing style and methods in Political Science.

Themes of the Times **Supplement** Prentice Hall and *The New York Times* expand students' knowledge beyond the classroom and into the world we live in. Users of *Government By The People* can receive a complimentary newspaper supplement containing recent articles pertinent to American Government. These articles, featuring the best in reporting and journalistic integrity associated with *The New York Times*, update the text material and contribute real-world applications to the topics covered in the course.

Political Science on the Internet This timely supplement provides an introduction to the Internet and the numerous political sites on the World Wide Web. Describes e-mail, list servers, browsers, and how to document sources. It also includes Web addresses for the most current and useful political Web sites. Can be shrinkwrapped to the text free of charge.

ABOUT THE AUTHORS

James MacGregor Burns

James MacGregor Burns is a Senior Scholar, Academy of Leadership, University of Maryland, College Park, and Woodrow Wilson Professor Emeritus of Government at Williams College. He has written numerous books, including *The Power to Lead* (1984), *The Vineyard of Liberty* (1982), *Leadership* (1979), *Roosevelt: The Soldier of Freedom* (1970), *The Deadlock of Democracy: Four-Party Politics in America* (1963), and *Roosevelt: The Lion and the Fox* (1956). His most recent book is *A People's Charter: The Pursuit of Rights in America* (1991), which he wrote with his son, Stewart Burns. Burns is a past president of the American Political Science Association and winner of numerous prizes, including the Pulitzer Prize in History.

J.W. Peltason

J.W. Peltason is a leading scholar on the judicial process and public law. He is Professor Emeritus of Political Science at the University of California, Irvine. As past president of the American Council on Education, Peltason has represented higher education before Congress and state legislatures. His writings include *Federal Courts in the Political Process* (1955), *Fifty-Eight Lonely Men: Southern Federal Judges and School Desegration* (1961), and *Understanding the Constitution* (1997). Among his awards are the James Madison Medal from Princeton University and the American Political Science Association's Charles E. Merriam Award.

Thomas E. Cronin

Thomas E. Cronin is a leading student of the American presidency, leadership, and policy-making processes. He served recently as president of the Western Political Science Association. He teaches at and serves as president of Whitman College. He served as a White House Fellow and a White House aide. His writings include *The State of the Presidency* (1980), *U.S. v. Crime in the Streets* (1981), *Direct Democracy: The Politics of Initiative, Referendum, and Recall* (1989), *Colorado Politics and Government* (1993), and *The Paradoxes of the American Presidency* (1997). Cronin is a past recipient of the American Political Science Association's Charles E. Merriam Award.

David B. Magleby

David B. Magleby is nationally recognized for his expertise on direct democracy, voting behavior, and campaign finance. He is Professor of Political Science and department chair at Brigham Young University. He has taught at the University of California, Santa Cruz, and the University of Virginia. His writings include *Direct Legislation* (1984), *The Money Chase: Congressional Campaign Finance Reform* (1990), and *The Myth of the Independent Voter* (1992). He has been president of Pi Sigma Alpha, the national political science honor society, has received numerous teaching awards, and during 1996 was a Fulbright Scholar at Nuffield College, Oxford University.

1

Constitutional Democracy

*A*s we enter the twenty-first century, our Republic will have survived for two hundred and twelve years (longer than that if you date our origins from the Declaration of Independence in 1776 rather than from the adoption of the Constitution in 1788). During that time we have held—even in the midst of a civil war, depressions, and world wars—53 presidential elections and the peaceful transfer of power from one party to another scores of times. The most glorious moment for the new democracy was in 1800, when President John Adams and his Federalists yielded the presidency to the Jeffersonians, whom they hated and feared, without a fight. The only time our democracy failed was in 1861, when the people of eleven southern states, or more precisely when the white male voters in those states, decided they would rather fight than allow Abraham Lincoln and the new Republican Party to govern them.

Not many democracies have survived this long. We made it through the centuries for many reasons, but a major one has been that all Americans—Republicans and Democrats; business leaders and labor leaders; Protestants, Catholics, and Jews; Northerners and Southerners; New Yorkers and Peorians; Whites, African Americans, and Chicanos; rich and poor—all have shared a common commitment to our Constitution, to each other, and to the belief that our differences are best reconciled by debate, compromise, and voting, and that politicians who get the most votes in an election govern better than do generals who win wars, or businesspeople who produce wealth, or college professors who produce knowledge, or clergy who teach religion.

As we move into our third century, there are some disquieting signs, some widespread concerns about the vitality of our democratic system. Politician bashing has always been part of our tradition; now, however, Americans tend to be especially critical of public officials and disillusioned with our political system. We have always been skeptical about politics and politicians, and that is healthy. Even our greatest presidents (by common consent Washington, Lincoln, and Franklin Roosevelt) were roasted by the press and opposition leaders. Yet today criticism seems to be more relentless and intense. Radio and television talk show personalities and popular entertainers—ranging from Jay Leno, David Letterman, Rush Limbaugh, and Pat Robertson to *Nightline*, *60 Minutes*, and *20/20*—routinely mock our leaders.

There is growing evidence that this criticism is having an effect. Americans are becoming critical not just of public officials but of our political system itself. This skepticism about democracy is not limited to the United States. Harvard University political scientist Robert D. Putnam opens his seminal study of democracy, "Ironically, the philosophical ascendancy of liberal democracy is accompanied by growing discontent with its practical operations. From Moscow to East St. Louis, from Mexico City to Cairo, despair about public institutions deepens. As American democratic institutions begin their third century, a sense is abroad in the land that our national experiment in self-government is faltering."[1] As has happened in other nations, "weakening ties to the political community in a democratic system might foretell eventual revolution, civil war, or the loss of democracy."[2]

There is reason for concern about this hostility toward politics and politicians. A central tenet of democracy is that those who hold power can only do so by winning an election. *Government by the people is necessarily government by politicians.* In our political system, the fragmentation of powers requires politicians to mediate among factions, build coalitions, and work out compromises among and within the branches of our government to produce policy and action.

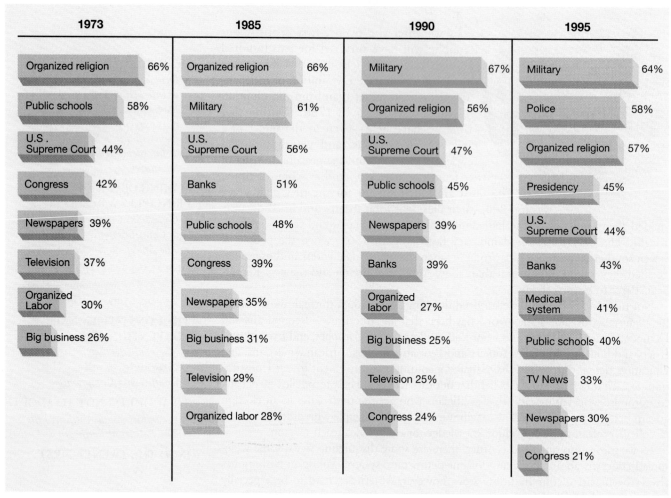

FIGURE 1-1 Confidence in Institutions

SOURCE: Surveys by the Gallup Organization.

We expect a lot from our politicians. They must operate within the rules of democracy, be honest, humble, patriotic, compassionate, sensitive to the needs of others, well-informed, competent, fair-minded, self-confident, and inspiriting. They must be candidates of the people, not of the money, courageous enough to stand up to special interests. They must not want power for itself, but lead because of their concern for the public good. And finally, they must be willing to do the job and get out when finished. Yet as we close out this century, Americans have generally negative views about politicians. They realize that at best politicians are skillful at compromising, mediating, negotiating, and brokering—and that governing requires these qualities. Yet Americans also suspect politicians of being ambitious, conniving, unprincipled, opportunistic, and corrupt. Compared to people in other professions, Americans hold politicians in low esteem (see Figure 1-1).

Why the gap between expectations about the actual and the ideal politician? The gap exists in part because we have such high expectations. We want politicians to be like us, yet better than us. We want politicians to be perfect, to have all the answers, and to have all the correct (in our minds) values. We want politicians to do what we want but ignore what other people want. We want politicians to solve our problems, yet we also want them to serve as scapegoats for the things we dislike about government: taxes, regulations, hard times, and limits on our freedom.

It is impossible for anyone to live up to these ideals. Like all individuals, politicians live in a world in which perfection may be the goal, yet compromise, ambition, fund raising, and self-promotion are necessary. "Ideal" leaders are usually dead. Ideal politicians could exist only in a community in which conflict did not exist—and probably where liberty and rights did not exist. But our love of liberty and diversity are too much a part of our culture for us to want to live in a community in which everybody agrees about every issue. In the real world, in the world in which we live, there is no freedom without politics and politicians.

This book is about how our democracy works. When you finish reading it, we hope you will come to see that politicians are essential to making democracy work and to recognize that to get rid of politics from public affairs would be to get rid of democracy.

DEFINING DEMOCRACY

We begin our exploration of this unique American experiment by examining the meaning of democracy and the historical events that created the constitutional democracy of the United States. **Constitutional democracy*** as used here refers to a government that enforces recognized limits on those who govern and allows the voice of the people to be heard through free and fair elections. **Constitutionalism** refers to how power is granted, dispersed, and limited.

The word "democracy" is nowhere to be found in the Declaration of Independence or in the U.S. Constitution, nor was it a term used by the founders of the Republic. Democracy is hard to define. It is both a very old term and a new one. It was used in a loose sense to refer to various undesirable things: "the masses," mobs, lack of standards, and a system that encourages **demagogues** (leaders who gain power by appealing to the emotions and prejudices of the rabble).

Because we are using the term in its political sense, we will be more precise. The distinguishing feature of democracy is that government derives its authority from its citizens. In fact, the word comes from two Greek words: *demos* (the people) and *kratos* (authority or power). Thus **democracy** means government by the people, not government by one person (a monarch, a dictator, a priest) or government by the few (an oligarchy or aristocracy).

Ancient Athens and a few other Greek cities had a **direct democracy**, in which citizens came together to discuss and pass laws and select their rulers by lot. These Greek city-states did not last, and most turned to mob rule and then resorted to dictators. When the word "democracy" came into English usage in the seventeenth century, it denoted this kind of direct democracy. It was a term of derision, a negative word, usually used to refer to mob rule.

James Madison, writing in *The Federalist*, No. 10, reflected the view of many of the framers of the U.S. Constitution when he wrote, "Such democracies [as the Greek and Roman] . . . have ever been found incompatible with personal security, or the rights of property; and have in general been as short in their lives, as they have been violent in their deaths" (*The Federalist*, No. 10 appears in the Appendix at the back of this book). Democracy has taken on a positive meaning only in the last one hundred years.

These days it is no longer possible, even if desirable, to assemble the citizens of any but the smallest towns to make their laws or to select their officials directly from among the citizenry. Rather, we have invented a system of representation.

"The Athenians are here, Sire, with an offer to back us with ships, money, arms, and men—and, of course, their usual lectures about democracy."

Drawing by Ed Fisher. © 1983 The New Yorker Magazine, Inc.

*Words that appear in boldfaced type throughout the text are defined in the Glossary at the end of this book.

Democracy today means **representative democracy**, or, to use Plato's term, a **republic**, in which those who have governmental authority get and retain authority directly or indirectly as a result of winning free elections in which all adult citizens are allowed to participate.

The framers preferred to use the term "republic" to avoid any confusion between direct democracy, which they disliked, and representative democracy, which they liked and thought secured all the advantages of a direct democracy while curing its weaknesses. Today, and in this book, *democracy* and *republic* are often used interchangeably.

Like most political concepts, democracy encompasses many ideas and has many meanings. Democracy is a way of life, a form of government, a way of governing, a type of nation, a state of mind, and a variety of processes. We can divide these many meanings into three broad categories: democracy as a system of interacting values, a system of interrelated political processes, and a system of interdependent political structures.

Democracy as a System of Interacting Values

As we enter the twenty-first century, the democratic faith may be as near a universal faith as the world has. A belief in human dignity, freedom, liberty, individual rights, and other democratic values is widely shared in most corners of the world. The essence of democratic values is contained in the ideas of popular consent, respect for the individual, equality of opportunity, and personal liberty.

POPULAR CONSENT The animating principle of the American Revolution, the Declaration of Independence, and the resulting new nation was **popular consent**, the idea that a just government must derive its powers from the consent of the people it governs. A commitment to democracy thus entails a community's willingness to participate and make decisions in government. These principles sound unobjectionable intellectually, but in practice they mean that certain individuals or groups may not get their way. A commitment to popular consent must involve a willingness to lose when most people vote the other way.

RESPECT FOR THE INDIVIDUAL Popular rule in a democracy flows from a belief that every individual has the potential for common sense, rationality, and fairness. Individuals have important rights; collectively, those rights are the source of all legitimate governmental authority and power. These concepts pervade all democratic thought. They are woven into the writings of Thomas Jefferson, especially in the Declaration of Independence: "All men . . . are endowed by their Creator with certain unalienable rights" (the Declaration of Independence appears in the Appendix). Constitutional democracies make the *person*—rich or poor, black or white, male or female—the central measure of value. The state, the union, and the corporation are measured in terms of their usefulness to individuals. Not all political systems, of course, put the individual first. Some promote **statism**, considering the state supreme. Democrats, however, believe that the state, or even the community, is less important than are the individuals who compose it.

EQUALITY OF OPPORTUNITY The importance of the individual is enhanced by the democratic value of *equality*: "All men are created equal and from that equal creation they derive rights inherent and unalienable, among which are the preservation of liberty and the pursuit of happiness." So reads Jefferson's first draft of the Declaration of Independence, and the words indicate the primacy of the concept. Alexis de Tocqueville, James Bryce, and other international visitors who studied American democracy were all struck by the strength of egalitarian thought and practice in both our political and our social lives.

But what does equality mean? What kind of equality? Economic, political, legal, social, or some other kind of equality? Equality for whom? For blacks as well as whites? For women as well as men? For Native Americans, descendants of the Pilgrims, and recent immigrants? And what kind of equality? *Equality of opportunity?* Almost all Americans say they want that. But also *equality of condition?* This last question is the toughest. Does equality of opportunity simply mean that everyone should have the same place at the starting line? Or does it mean an effort should be made to equalize the factors that during the course of a person's life determine how well he or she fares economically or socially?

President Herbert Hoover posed the issue this way: "We, through free and universal education, provide the training of the runners; we give to them an equal start; we provide in government the umpire of fairness in the race."[3] Franklin D. Roosevelt also sought to answer the question by proclaiming a "second Bill of Rights" that announced **Four Freedoms**—freedom of speech and expression, freedom of worship, freedom from want, and freedom from fear. Roosevelt's New Deal and its successor programs tried to advance the egalitarian notions and basic security that he asserted were the rights of human beings everywhere. (We return to the question of equal rights in Chapter 5.)

The ideal of liberty still inspires people today, enabling this one man to defy the tanks in Tiananmen Square during the brutal repression of the student democracy movement by the Chinese government.

PERSONAL LIBERTY Liberty has been the single most powerful value in American history. It was for "life, liberty, and the pursuit of happiness" that independence was declared; it was to "secure the Blessings of Liberty" that the Constitution was drawn up and adopted. Even our patriotic songs extol the "sweet land of liberty." *Liberty* or *freedom* (used interchangeably here) means that all individuals must have the opportunity to realize their own goals. The essence of liberty is *self-determination*. Liberty is not simply the absence of external restraint on a person (freedom from); it is the individual's freedom to act positively to reach his or her goals. Moreover, both history and reason suggest that individual liberty is the key to social progress. The greater the people's freedom, the greater the chance of discovering better ways of life.

DEMOCRATIC VALUES IN CONFLICT The basic values of democracy do not always coexist happily. Individualism may conflict with the collective welfare or the public good. Freedom as liberation may become freedom as alienation. Self-determination may conflict with equal opportunity. The right of General Motors to run its automobile factories to maximize profit, as compared to the right of automobile workers to join unions or to share in the running of the plants, illustrates this type of conflict in everyday life.

Liberty and equality interlock and stimulate each other at some points and oppose each other at others. Sometimes they do not relate at all. At one extreme, the pursuit of liberty might become license for unbridled selfishness or anarchy; at the other extreme, the pursuit of equality might become a leveling to dull mediocrity and even the erosion of liberty. Much of our political combat revolves around how to strike a balance among democratic values—how to protect the Declaration of Independence's unalienable rights of life, liberty, and the pursuit of happiness while permitting government to "form," as the Constitution announces, "a more perfect Union, establish Justice, insure domestic Tranquility, provide for the common defence, promote the general Welfare, and secure the Blessings of Liberty to ourselves and our Posterity" (see the Preamble to the Constitution).

Over the years the American political system has moved, despite occasional setbacks, toward greater freedom and more democracy. A commitment to democracy is in many ways a twentieth-century idea. People throughout the world are more attracted to democracy today than ever before. Recent events in China, Germany, Poland, the Czech Republic, Slovakia, Russia, and South Africa are evidence that the dream of freedom and democratic government is universal.

The Declaration of Independence committee set down on paper the ideas and goals that would later be incorporated in the Constitution. Shown here are (left to right) Thomas Jefferson, Roger Sherman, Benjamin Franklin, Robert Livingston, and John Adams.

Far more people dream about democracy than ever experience it, and many new democracies fail. To be successful, democratic government requires a political process as well as a governmental structure. In both areas, the American experiment is instructive.

Democracy as a System of Interrelated Political Processes

To become reality, democratic values must be incorporated into a political process, a set of arrangements for making decisions and managing the public's business. The essence of the democratic process is respect for the rules of fair play, which can be seen in the tradition of free and fair elections, majority rule, freedom of expression, and the right to assemble and protest.

FREE AND FAIR ELECTIONS DECIDED BY MAJORITY (PLURALITY) RULE Democratic government is based on free and fair elections held at intervals frequent enough to make them relevant to policy choices. Elections are one of the most important devices for keeping officials and representatives accountable.

We previously defined *representative democracy* to mean a system of government in which those who have the authority to make decisions with the force of law acquire and retain this authority either directly or indirectly as the result of winning free elections in which the great majority of adult citizens are allowed to participate. Crucial to modern-day definitions of democracy is the idea that *opposition political parties can exist,* can run candidates in elections, and can at least have a chance to replace those who are currently holding public office. Thus political competition and choice are crucial to the existence of democracy.

Although all citizens should have equal voting power, free and fair elections do not imply everyone must or will have equal political influence. Some people, because of wealth, talent, or position, have more influence than others. How much extra influence key figures should be allowed to exercise in a democracy is an ongoing question. But at the polls, a president or a pick-and-shovel laborer, a newspaper publisher or a lettuce picker, casts only one vote.

MAJORITY (PLURALITY) RULE Majority rule is one of the procedures that make elections free and fair. The basic rule of a democracy is that those with the most votes take charge of the government, at least until the next election, when a new majority may be voted in to take charge. In practice, *majority rule is often plurality rule*, in which the largest bloc takes charge, even though it may not constitute a true majority, which would be more than half the votes. Those elected do not have the right to curtail attempts of political minorities to use all peaceful means to become a majority. So even as the winners take power, the losers can go to work to try to get it back at the next election.[4]

Should the will of the majority prevail in all cases? Americans answer this question in a variety of ways. Some insist majority views should be enacted into laws and regulations. However, an effective representative democracy involves far more than simply ascertaining and applying the statistical will of most of the people. It is a more complicated and often untidy process by which the people and their agents debate, compromise, and arrive at a decision only after thoughtful deliberation.

The Constitution reflects the framers' fear of tyranny by majorities, especially momentary majorities that spring from temporary passion. The framers wanted to guard society against any one part acting unjustly toward any other part. To accomplish this end, they insulated certain rights and institutions from popular choice. The effective representation of the people, the framers insisted, could not and should not be an unthinking mouthpiece for parochial interests or for each shifting breeze of opinion.

FREEDOM OF EXPRESSION Free and fair elections depend on access to information relevant to voting choices. Voters must have access to facts, competing ideas, and the views of candidates. Free and fair elections require a climate in which competing, nongovernment-owned newspapers, radio stations, and television stations can flourish. If the government controls what will be said and how it will be said, then there is no democracy. Without free speech there are no free and fair elections.

THE RIGHT TO ASSEMBLE AND PROTEST Citizens must be free to organize for political purposes. Obviously, individuals can be more effective if they join with others in a party, a pressure group, a protest movement, or a demonstration. The right to oppose the government, to form opposition parties, and to have a chance of defeating incumbents is not only vital; it is a defining characteristic of a democracy.

Democracy as a System of Interdependent Political Structures

Democracy is, of course, more than values and processes. It also entails a system of political structures that safeguard these values and processes. In this country, the Constitution and the Bill of Rights create an ingenious structure—one that both grants and checks government power. This constitutional structure is reinforced by a political system of parties, interest groups, media, and other institutions that mediate between the electorate and those who govern and thus help to maintain democratic stability.

This constitutional system is remarkable for four elements: One is *federalism*, the division of powers between the national and state governments. Another is the *separation of powers* among the legislative, executive, and judicial branches. Liberty is further safeguarded by a system of *checks and balances*, which gives each branch its own powers as well as the "necessary constitutional means and personal motives to resist the encroachments of the others."[5] This combination of separation of powers and checks and balances was the supreme creation of the framers in 1787.

A TYPICAL ELECTION

It is the week before an American election for governor, the culmination of an intense, year-long campaign. During this last week, television and the newspapers are full of political ads: "A vote for Gabrillino is a vote for the people!" says one under a picture of Frank Gabrillino, the Democratic candidate. He is shown with Mrs. Gabrillino, a successful real-estate broker, and the Gabrillinos' three children. Gabrillino's campaign themes have stressed that he is not a politician, just a man of the people. He accuses his opponent, Sarah Wong, who has been governor for one term, of being soft on criminals, and he blames her for the state's economic downturn. Gabrillino insists that if Wong is reelected, the state is doomed. Wong—behind in the polls, although recently catching up—emphasizes her experience, her concern for all the people, and her willingness to fight the special interests. She is a Republican, but she plays down her party affiliation, since a majority of the voters in this state are Democrats.

The two candidates are accusing each other of all kinds of misdeeds. As the campaign progresses, their ads become more negative, more focused on personality than on political issues and positions. Gabrillino makes much of the fact that 20 years ago Wong indicated she had doubts about the morality and efficacy of the death penalty, but as governor she has not commuted any death sentences and has allowed two people to be executed. Wong's supporters charge that Gabrillino lacks compassion for the less fortunate and is in the hands of a group of extreme religious conservatives who are backing him. There are endorsements in the newspapers: Professors for Wong, Teachers for Gabrillino, Police Chiefs for Gabrillino, Sheriffs for Wong, Students for Wong, Chicanos for Gabrillino, Asians for Gabrillino. Each candidate plants letters to the editor in the newspapers. Local radio and television talk shows feature both candidates, and the candidates' organizations supply callers to attack their opponent.

Now it is election day. Less than half the eligible voters bother to vote, and exit polls indicate that the election is too close to call. Projections based on 25 percent of the vote make it clear that Gabrillino will get 48 percent of the vote, Wong 46 percent, and minor parties the rest. At 11:00 P.M., Wong calls Gabrillino, congratulates him on his victory, makes a concession speech before her disappointed workers, and thanks them for their support. Gabrillino speaks on TV to his cheering supporters, stating that his election was a great victory for the people.

Elections are such a familiar process that Americans take them for granted.

A final element is the *Bill of Rights*, a *written, explicit, enforceable* guarantee of individual liberties and due process before the law. The chapters that follow explain the principles and the architectural features of American-style democracy in more detail.

MAKING DEMOCRATIC PRINCIPLES A REALITY

New democracies often fail. It is one thing to espouse democratic values, another to put them into practice. Some people, for instance, believe in democracy until they lose power in an election. Or the citizens grow weary of the political wrangling that comes with democracy and long for a strong charismatic leader with simple solutions for complex problems. Such a leader, sometimes referred to as

Many people look upon elections with disdain, saying, "It's all politics." In fact, American elections are remarkable. They conclude with what is a rare event in the course of human history: the peaceful transfer of political power. What is unusual is what is *not* happening. Even though the day before the election Wong and her followers were insisting that if Gabrillino became governor there would be chaos and corruption, once the vote was counted there was never any possibility that Gabrillino would not become governor. When her term was up, Wong did not resist turning power over to the man she had called dangerous. It never crossed her mind to try to stay in office by calling on the state police to keep Gabrillino from taking power. None of Wong's supporters considered taking up arms, or going underground, or leaving the country. (Actually, they began to concentrate on how to win the next election.) Nor did Gabrillino or his followers ever give any thought to punishing Sarah Wong and her supporters. The Democrats fought to throw the Republicans out of office, not into jail.

It was just another routine American election—democracy at work. Most of the time in most nations, people in power got there either because they were born to the right family or because they killed or jailed their opponents. During most of human history, opposition political parties did not exist, and a political opponent was an enemy, to be eliminated at any cost.

At the conclusion of a hard-fought election in the United States, the loser, Robert Dole, is presented with the Award of Freedom by the winner, Bill Clinton. At the conclusion of a hard-fought election in Serbia, the loser, Slobodan Milosovic, turns his troops on the winners, the democracy movement. Daily street demonstrations eventually forced Milosovic to recognize the winners of the local elections.

the "man on horseback," is usually a military leader of heroic proportions. Leaders like Napoleon or Adolf Hitler promise to make the country work more smoothly, often by disbanding democratic institutions. Citizens may turn to such leaders when they face economic difficulties or are under threat from a foreign power. Sectional differences can also pull apart the fabric of democracy. Parts of a country that have a distinctive racial, religious, or ethnic composition often distrust the national majority and seek guarantees or special concessions—as French-speaking residents of Quebec have in Canada.

Because democracies are so difficult to sustain, comparatively few have lasted long (see Figure 1-2). More than half the world's constitutions have been written in the past four decades. On the entire continent of Asia, no democracy predates

■ Not Free ■ Partly Free □ Free

FIGURE 1-2   Map of Freedom

SOURCE: *Freedom Review*, January/February 1995. © 1995 by Freedom House.

World War II, when a democratic constitution was imposed on Japan. In Africa, the oldest democracy is Botswana, which has had free elections and a multiparty system since 1966.

Conditions Conducive to Constitutional Democracy

How do we explain the relatively small number of long-lived, strong democracies? Although it is hard to specify the precise conditions that are essential for the establishment and maintenance of a democracy, here are a few things we have learned.

EDUCATIONAL CONDITIONS   Clearly, the exercise of voting privileges takes some level of education on the part of the citizenry. But a word of caution: A high level of education does not "cause" or "guarantee" democratic government, as the example of Nazi Germany readily illustrates, and there are some democracies, such as India, where large numbers of people are illiterate. Still, voting makes little sense unless a considerable number of the voters can read and write and express their interests and opinions. The poorly educated and illiterate get left out in a democracy.

ECONOMIC CONDITIONS   A relatively prosperous nation, with an equitable distribution of wealth, provides the best context for democracy. Starving people are more interested in food than in voting. Where economic power is concentrated, political power is likely to be concentrated. Well-to-do nations have a greater chance of sustaining democratic governments than do those with widespread poverty. The reality is that extremes of wealth and poverty undermine the possibilities for a healthy constitutional democracy. Thus the prospects for an enduring democracy are greater in a Canada or France than a Rwanda or Russia.

Some measure of private ownership of property and a relatively favorable role for the market economy are also related to the creation and maintenance of democratic institutions. Democracies can range from heavily regulated economies with public ownership of many enterprises, such as Sweden, to those in which there is little government regulation of the marketplace. But there are no democracies with a command economy and little private ownership of property, although there are many nations with a market economy and no democracy. There are no truly democratic communist states, nor have there ever been any.

SOCIAL CONDITIONS Economic development generally makes democracy possible, yet political leadership and proper social conditions are necessary to make it real.[6] In a society fragmented into warring groups that differ fiercely on fundamental issues, government by discussion and compromise is difficult, as we have learned in Bosnia. When ideologically separated groups consider the issues at stake to be vital, they may prefer to fight rather than accept the verdict of the ballot box. But in a society that consists of many overlapping associations and groupings, individuals are not as likely to identify completely with a single group and give their allegiance to it. For example, Joe Brown is a Baptist, an African American, a southerner, a Democrat, an electrician, and a member of the National Rifle Association, and he makes $50,000 a year. On some issues Joe thinks as a Baptist, on others as a southerner, and on still others as an African American. Sue Jones is a Catholic, a Republican, an auto dealer, and a member of the National Organization for Women; she comes from a Polish background, and she makes $150,000 a year. Sometimes she acts as a Republican, sometimes as an American of Polish descent, and sometimes as a member of NOW. Jones and Brown differ on some issues yet agree on others. In general, the differences between them are not likely to be greater than their common interest in maintaining a democracy.[7]

Democracy is more likely to survive where a rich variety of associations and social institutions bind people together and get them accustomed to solve their differences by debate and discussion. Participation in these social institutions helps build and reinforce democratic habits. Such activities create what is coming to be called a nation's "social capital."[8] The family, the church, the school, and other associations of civic life all regulate important areas of life affected by and affecting government. If these institutions support and reinforce the idea of government by democratic procedures, then the habits of discussion, compromise, and respect for differences are strengthened by constant use.

IDEOLOGICAL CONDITIONS **Ideology** refers to basic beliefs about power and government and political practices—beliefs that arise out of the educational, economic, and social conditions we experience. Out of these educational, economic, and social conditions must also develop a general acceptance of the ideals of democracy, the willingness of a substantial portion of the people to agree to proceed democratically. This quality is sometimes called the *democratic consensus*. Robert Dahl, a well-known student of democratic ideas, writes:

> Prior to politics, beneath it, enveloping it, restricting it, conditioning it, is the underlying consensus on policy that usually exists in a society among a predominant portion of the politically active members. Without such a consensus, no democratic system would long survive the endless irritations and frustrations of elections and party competition.[9]

You Decide!

In sum, a society with the best chance for democratic success is one with an educated and fairly prosperous electorate, without extreme concentrations of wealth, relatively free from intense class, ethnic, religious, or sectional antagonisms, with many private loyalties and associations, and with other social institutions that buttress the principles and practices of democracy, all tending to produce a democratic consensus. Civilian control over the military is also essential. But no one of these conditions—or even all of them—guarantees democracy. There is no foolproof, double-your-money-back guarantee for freedom.

The American Example

Most Americans take democracy for granted. We somehow consider it inevitable. We take pride in our ability to make it work, yet we have essentially inherited a functioning system. Its establishment was the work of others, ten or more generations ago. The challenge for us is not just to keep it going but to improve it. But first we must understand it, and this requires careful consideration of our democratic and constitutional roots.

The United States provides an important contrast to dictatorship, tyranny, and anarchy. It also contradicts the general tendency of democracies to fail. There were many reasons one might have expected our system to fail. The thirteen states (formerly colonies) were independent and could have gone their separate ways. Critical sectional differences based on economics and slavery were an obvious problem. Religious, ethnic, and racial diversity, which poses so many challenges to governments around the world today, existed in substantial degree in the United States during its formative years. The driving ambition of the "man on the white horse" to solve the country's problems is a constant in any society, and our country has had its share.

Given these potential problems, how has our democracy survived? How did this nation establish democratic principles for its government? How did it limit potential abuses? These questions are of importance not only to Americans but to all who value freedom and democracy everywhere. To begin to answer them, we now turn to our country's formative period of nation building.

OUR CONSTITUTIONAL ROOTS

The framers of the U.S. Constitution had experience to guide them. For almost two centuries, Europeans had been sailing to the New World in search of liberty—especially religious liberty—as well as land and work. While still aboard the *Mayflower*, the Pilgrims drew up a compact to protect their religious freedom and to make possible "just and equal laws." In the American colonies, editors found they could speak freely in their newspapers, dissenters could distribute leaflets, and agitators could protest in taverns or in the streets. But the picture of freedom in the colonies was a mixed one. The Puritans in Massachusetts soon established a **theocracy**, a system of government in which religious leaders claimed divine guidance, and not all religious sects were granted equal religious liberty. Dissenters were occasionally chased out of town, and some printers had their shops closed or were even physically attacked.

In short, the colonists in those early centuries were struggling with the balance of unity and diversity, stability and dissent, order and liberty. Puritan theocrats continued to worry "about what would maintain order in a society lacking an established church, an attachment to place, and the uncontested leadership of men of merit."[10] Nine of the thirteen colonies eventually set up a state church. Throughout the 1700s Puritans in Massachusetts barred certain men from voting on the basis of church membership. To the Anglican establishment in Virginia, campaigns for toleration were in themselves subversive. Women could not vote at all.

The Pilgrims signing the Mayflower Compact aboard their ship on November 11, 1620.

Still, most colonial Americans enjoyed a wide array of liberties. When John Peter Zenger, a New York newspaper printer, was jailed in 1734 by royal authority on the charge of seditious libel, Zenger's attorney appealed to a jury and won a "not guilty" verdict. The case helped establish freedom of the press. Increasingly, questions arose about how people could secure their liberties, rather than leave them in the hands of mobs, sheriffs, or religious establishments. The answer was to bind liberties tightly into colonial laws and constitutions. The Maryland Act for the Liberties of the People legislated that "all the inhabitants of this Province being Christians [slaves excepted] should have such rights, liberties, immunities, privileges, and free customs" as any natural-born subject of England. The Massachusetts Body of Liberties of 1641, which served as a model for later New York and Pennsylvania charters, guaranteed freedom of speech and petition at public meetings, right of counsel, trial by jury, and "the same justice and law" for every person.[11]

The Rise of Revolutionary Fervor

As resentment against the British mounted during the 1770s and revolutionary fervor rose, Americans became determined to fight the British to win their rights and liberties. A year after the fighting broke out in Lexington, Concord, and other areas, the Declaration of Independence proclaimed in ringing tones that all men are created equal, endowed by their Creator with certain unalienable rights; that among them are "life, liberty, and the pursuit of happiness"; that to secure those rights governments are instituted among men; and that whenever a government becomes destructive of those ends, it is the right of the people to alter or abolish it. (Read the Declaration of Independence in the Appendix.)

We all have heard these great ideals so often that we take them for granted. Revolutionary leaders did not. They were deadly serious about these rights and willing to fight and pledge their lives, fortunes, and sacred honor for them. They determinedly set about guaranteeing liberty in the constitutions the states adopted as they broke away from the Crown. Bills of rights in the new state constitutions guaranteed free speech, freedom of religion, and the natural rights to life, liberty, and property. All the declarations spelled out the rights of persons accused of crime,

Thinking It Through

While more Americans may be bowling alone, what about the growth of new organizations such as the Sierra Club, the National Organization for Women, the American Association of Retired Persons, and so on? Doesn't that show a counter trend? Putnam found that the vast majority of the members of these associations only write a check or read a newsletter; few ever attend meetings or have any connection to other members. He acknowledges the growth of "support groups" as offsetting the erosion of conventional civic organizations.

Americans still rank high compared with other countries in social capital, but if there has been a deterioration in social capital, it could have consequences for the stability of our political system. What has caused this decline? Putnam discounts the movement of women into the labor force or the increasing mobility of our population as causes of this decline, but suggests that television—and, it may be assumed, the computer—have made our communities wider but shallower.

Putnam's work has its critics who believe that there has not been a serious decline in social involvement. Anyone living and working on an American college campus certainly finds active student participation in all kinds of organizations and associations. Others challenge his conclusion that television is largely responsible for this decline in political participation. The growth of radio talk shows, C-SPAN, CNN, Fox News, and Internet chat groups may be new ways to build social capital.

Do you think Putnam's arguments are convincing? How would you gather evidence to test his hypothesis? You might begin with a look at Sidney Verba, Kay Leman Scholzman, and Henry E. Brady, *Voice and Equality: Civic Volunteerism in American Politics* (Harvard University Press, 1995) and Pippa Norris, "Does Television Erode Social Capital? A Reply to Putnam," *P.S.: Political Science & Politics* 29 (September 1996), pp. 474–79.

Weaknesses of the Articles of Confederation

1. Congress had no direct authority over citizens but had to work through the states; it could not pass laws or levy taxes in order to carry out its responsibilities to defend the nation and promote its well-being.

2. Congress could not regulate trade between the states or with other nations. States taxed each others' goods and even negotiated their own trade agreements with other nations.

3. Congress could not forbid the states from issuing their own currencies, further complicating interstate trade and travel.

4. Congress had to handle all administrative duties because there was no executive branch.

5. The lack of a judiciary system meant that the national government had to rely on state courts to enforce national laws and settle disputes between the states. In practice, state courts could overturn national laws.

Under the leadership of Daniel Shays, a group of farmers took possession of the courthouse in Northampton, Massachusetts in 1786.

American colonists, resentful of crushing taxes and the denial of their basic liberties by the British, flung boxes of tea into Boston harbor in what we now know as "The Boston Tea Party."

such as knowing the nature of the accusation, being confronted by their accusers, and receiving a timely and public trial by jury.[12] Moreover, these guarantees were in *written* form, a sharp contrast to the unwritten British constitution.

Toward Unity and Order

As the war against the British widened, the need arose for a stronger central government that could pull the colonies together and conduct a revolutionary war. For a time the Continental Congress, which had led the way toward revolution, tried to direct hostilities against the British, but it took a man of George Washington's iron resolve to unify and direct the war effort. Sensing the need for more unity, Congress established a new national government under a written document called the **Articles of Confederation**. At first hardly worthy of the term "government," the Articles were not approved by all the state legislatures until 1781, after Washington's troops had been fighting for six years.

This new Confederation was a move toward a stronger central government, but a limited and inadequate one. Having fought a war against a strong central government in London, Americans were understandably reluctant to create another one, so the Articles established a fragile league of friendship rather than a national government. From 1777 to 1788, Americans made progress under this Confederation, but with the end of the war in 1783, the sense of urgency that had produced unity began to fade. Within the states, conflict between creditors and debtors grew intense. Foreign threats continued; territories ruled by England and Spain surrounded the new nation, which—internally divided and lacking a strong central government—made a tempting prize.

As pressures on the Confederation mounted, many leaders became convinced it would not be enough merely to revise the Articles of Confederation. To create a union strong enough to deal with internal diversity and factionalism as well as resist external threats, a stronger central government was needed. Although many Americans recognized the need to give Congress greater authority to regulate commerce and collect limited taxes, they were still suspicious of strong central government.

In August 1786, under the leadership of Alexander Hamilton, those who favored a truly national government took advantage of the **Annapolis Convention**, a meeting in Annapolis, Maryland, on problems of trade and navigation attended by delegates from five states, to issue a call for a convention that would have full authority to consider basic amendments to the Articles of Confederation. The delegates in Annapolis asked the legislatures of their states to appoint commissioners to meet in Philadelphia on the second Monday of May 1787, "to devise such further provisions as shall appear to them necessary to render the Constitution of the Federal Government adequate to the exigencies of the Union." The convention they called for became the **Constitutional Convention**.

For a short time all was quiet. Then, late in 1786, messengers rode into George Washington's plantation at Mount Vernon with the kind of news he and other leaders had dreaded. Farmers in western Massachusetts, crushed by debts and taxes, were rebelling against foreclosures, forcing judges out of their courtrooms, and freeing debtors from jails. Washington was appalled. Ten years before, he had been leading Americans in a patriotic war against the British, and now Americans were fighting Americans!

"What, gracious God, is man?" Washington exclaimed. Clearly, liberty—as license—had been allowed to go too far. Indeed, such disorder was a threat to liberty itself. If government could not check such disorders, Washington wrote to his friend James Madison, "what security has a man for life, liberty or property?" Without a stronger central government, "thirteen Sovereignties pulling against each other, and all tugging at the federal head will soon bring ruin on the whole."

Not all Americans reacted as Washington did to what became known as **Shays' Rebellion**, after its leader, Daniel Shays. When Abigail Adams, the politically knowledgeable wife of John Adams, sent news of the rebellion to Thomas Jefferson, the Virginian replied, "I like a little rebellion now and then," noting also that the "tree of liberty must be refreshed from time to time" with "the natural manure" of the blood of patriots and tyrants.

Shays' Rebellion petered out after the farmers attacked an arsenal and were cut down by cannon fire. Yet this "little rebellion" sent a stab of fear into the established leadership. It also acted as a catalyst. The message now was plain: Action must be taken to strengthen the machinery of government. Spurred on by Shays' Rebellion, seven states appointed commissioners to attend a convention in Philadelphia to strengthen the Articles of Confederation. Congress finally issued a cautiously worded call to the states to appoint delegates for the "sole and express purpose of revising the Articles of Confederation." The suspicious legislators specified that no recommendation would be effective unless approved by Congress and confirmed by all the state legislatures, as provided by the Articles.

At this point in the long American search for the balance between liberty and order, between diversity and unity, the impulse was decidedly toward order and unity.

THE CONSTITUTIONAL CONVENTION, 1787

The delegates who assembled in Philadelphia that May were presented with a condition, not a theory. They had to establish a national government powerful enough to prevent the young nation from dissolving. What these men did continues to have a major impact on how we are governed. It also provides an outstanding lesson in political science for the world.

The Delegates

Seventy-four delegates were appointed by the various states, but only 55 arrived in Philadelphia. Of these, approximately 40 took a real part in the work of the convention. It was a distinguished gathering. Many of the most important men of the nation were there: successful merchants, planters, bankers, lawyers, and former and present governors and congressional representatives (39 of the delegates had served in Congress). Most had read the classics of political thought. Most had participated

Shays' Rebellion

After the American Revolution, the young nation was torn by unsettled economic conditions and a severe depression. Paper money was in circulation, but little of it was honored at face value. Merchants and other "sound money" men wanted currencies with gold backing. In Massachusetts the "sound money" men controlled the government. Most of those who were harmed by the depression were propertyless and thus unable to vote. The quarrel grew until thousands of men in the western counties rose in armed revolt. They were led by Daniel Shays (1747–1825), a captain during the American Revolution. Shays' Rebellion lasted from August 1786 to February 1787.

The agitators objected to heavy land and poll taxes, the high cost of lawsuits, high salaries of state officials, oppressive court decisions, and dictatorial rulings of the state senate. In Northampton on August 29 the mob succeeded in keeping the courts closed so debtors could not be tried and put into prison. Fearful of being tried for treason for this action, Shays and his men broke up the state Supreme Court session at Springfield the following month. The revolt took a more serious turn when Shays and a force of 1,200 men returned to Springfield in January to capture the arsenal. Action by the national government prevented the attack on January 25. Most of the insurgents were captured in early February, ending the rebellion. The leaders were condemned to death for treason but were later pardoned. Shays himself later received a war pension for his service in the American Revolution.

SOURCE: © 1996 The Shay Group, P.O. Box 398, Amherst, MA.

The Framers: Hamilton and Madison

In the Constitution the framers offered perhaps the most brilliant example of collective intellectual genius—of combining both theory and practice—in the history of the Western world. How could a country 70 times smaller in population than it is today produce several dozen men of genius in Philadelphia, and probably another hundred or so equally talented political thinkers who did not attend? The lives of two prominent delegates, Alexander Hamilton and James Madison, help explain the origins of this collective genius.

Like most of the other framers, Hamilton and Madison were superbly educated. Both had extensive private tutoring—a one-to-one teacher-student ratio. Like scores of other thinkers of the day, both combined extensive practical experience with their schooling. Both were active in their political and religious groups; both took part in political contests and electoral struggles; both helped build political coalitions.

Both men were "moral philosophers" as well as political thinkers. They had strong views on the supreme value—liberty—as well as on current issues. Instead of simply sermonizing about liberty, they analyzed it; they debated what kind of liberty, how to protect it, how to expand it. They also thought hard about other values enshrined in the Declaration of Independence, such as the virtues and dangers of equality and what kind of "happiness" Americans should pursue.

vigorously in the practical task of constructing local and state governments. Many had also worked hard to create and direct the national Confederation of the states.

The convention was as representative as most political gatherings at the time: the participants were all white male landowners. These well-read, well-fed, well-bred, and often well-wed delegates were mainly state or national leaders, for in the 1780s ordinary people were not likely to participate in politics. (Even today farm laborers, factory workers, and truck drivers are seldom found in Congress, although a haberdasher, a peanut farmer, and a movie actor have made their way to the White House.) While most of those in attendance eventually supported the Constitution in the ratification debates, only 8 of the 56 signers of the Declaration of Independence were present at the Constitutional Convention.

Several of the participants at the convention stand out as the prime movers. Alexander Hamilton had been the engineer of the Annapolis Convention, and as early as 1778 he had been urging that the national government be made stronger. Hamilton had come to the United States from the West Indies and while still a college student had won national attention for his brilliant pamphlets in defense of the Revolutionary cause. During the war he served as General Washington's aide, and his experiences confirmed his distaste for a Congress so weak it could not even supply the Revolution's troops with enough food or arms.

From Virginia came two of the leading delegates: George Washington and James Madison. Although active in the movement to revise the Articles of Confederation, Washington had been reluctant to attend the convention. He accepted only when persuaded that his prestige was needed for its success. He was selected unanimously to preside over the meetings. According to the records, he spoke only twice during the deliberations, yet his influence was felt in the informal gatherings as well as during the sessions. The assumption that Washington would become the first president under the new constitution inspired confidence in it. James Madison was only 36 years old at the time of the convention, yet he was one of its most learned members. He had helped frame Virginia's first constitution and had served both in the Virginia Assembly and in the Confederation's Congress. Madison was also a leader of those who favored the establishment of a stronger national government.[13]

The proceedings of the convention were kept secret. To encourage everyone to speak freely, delegates were forbidden to discuss the debates with outsiders. It was feared that if a delegate publicly took a firm stand on an issue, it would be harder for him to change his mind after debate and discussion. The delegates also knew that if word of the inevitable disagreements got out, it would provide ammunition for the many enemies of the convention. There were critics of this secrecy rule, but without it, agreement might not have been possible.

Consensus

The Constitutional Convention is usually discussed in terms of its three famous compromises: the compromise between large and small states over representation in Congress, the compromise between North and South over the regulation and taxation of foreign commerce, and the compromise between North and South over the counting of slaves for taxation and representation. There were many other important compromises; yet on many significant issues, most of the delegates were in agreement.

Although a few delegates might have personally favored a limited monarchy, all supported a republican form of government. This was the only form seriously considered and the only form acceptable to the nation. Equally important, all the delegates were constitutionalists who opposed arbitrary and unrestrained government.

The common philosophy accepted by most of the delegates was that of *balanced government*. They wanted to construct a national government in which no single interest would dominate. Because most of the delegates represented citizens who were alarmed by the tendencies of desperate farmers to interfere with or abuse the property rights of others, they were primarily concerned with balancing the government in the direction of protection for property and business. Most of them respected the remark of Elbridge Gerry, delegate from Massachusetts: "The evils we experience flow from the excess of democracy. The people do not want virtue, but are dupes of pretended patriots." Likewise, there was substantial agreement with Gouverneur Morris's statement that property was the "principal object of government."

Benjamin Franklin, the 81-year-old delegate from Pennsylvania, favored extending the right to vote to all white males, but most of the delegates believed that owners of land were the best guardians of liberty. James Madison voiced the fear that those without property, if given the right to vote, would either combine to deprive property owners of their rights or would become the "tools of demagogues." The delegates agreed in principle on limited voting rights, but differed over the kind and amount of property one must own in order to vote. Because the states were in the process of relaxing qualifications for the vote, the framers recognized they would jeopardize approval of the constitution if they made the right to vote in federal elections more restricted than the franchises within the states. As a result, each state was left to determine the qualifications for electing members of the House of Representatives, the only branch of the national government in which the electorate was given a direct voice.

Within five days of its opening, the convention—with only Connecticut dissenting—voted that "a national government ought to be established consisting of a supreme legislative, executive, and judiciary." This decision to establish a national government that rested on and exercised power over individuals profoundly altered the nature of the central government and changed it from a loose league of states to a national government.

Few dissented from proposals to give the new Congress all the powers of the old Congress plus all other powers necessary to ensure that the harmony of the United States would not be challenged by state legislation. The framers agreed that a strong executive, which had been lacking under the Articles of Confederation, was necessary to provide energy and direction. An independent judiciary was also accepted without much debate. Other issues, however, sparked considerable conflict.

Conflict and Compromise

There were serious differences among the various groups, especially between the delegates of the large and small states. One of the most contentious issues was the distribution of the land extending westward to the Mississippi, land that had been secured through the Revolution. Several large states asserted claims to these western lands, but the small states generally objected. The large states also favored a strong national government (which they expected they could dominate), while the delegates from the small states were anxious to avoid being dominated.

This tension surfaced in the first discussions of representation in Congress. Franklin favored a single-house national legislature, but most states had had two-chamber legislatures since colonial times, and the delegates were used to the system. **Bicameralism**—the principle of the two-house legislature—implemented the delegates' belief in the need for balanced government. The smaller chamber would represent the aristocracy and offset the larger, more democratic House of Representatives.

THE VIRGINIA PLAN The Virginia delegation took the initiative. They had met during the delay before the convention, and as soon as the convention was organized, they presented 15 resolutions. These resolutions, the **Virginia Plan**, called for a strong central government with a legislature composed of two chambers. The members of the more representative chamber were to be elected by the voters; those of the smaller and more aristocratic chamber were to be chosen by the larger chamber from nominees submitted by the state legislatures. Representation in both houses was to be on the basis

James Madison

Alexander Hamilton

"Remember, gentlemen, we aren't here just to draft a constitution. We're here to draft the best damn constitution in the world."

Drawing by Steiner. © 1982 The New Yorker Magazine, Inc.

of either wealth or numbers. This gave the more populous and wealthier states—Massachusetts, Pennsylvania, and Virginia—a majority in the national legislature.

The Congress thus created was to be given all the legislative power of its predecessor under the Articles of Confederation, as well as the right "to legislate in all cases in which the separate States are incompetent." Further, it was to have the authority to veto state legislation that conflicted with the proposed constitution. The Virginia Plan also called for a national executive to be chosen by the legislature and a national judiciary with rather extensive jurisdiction. The national Supreme Court, along with the executive, was to have a qualified veto over acts of Congress.

THE NEW JERSEY PLAN The Virginia Plan dominated the discussion for the first few weeks. But by June 15 additional delegates from the small states had arrived, and they began a counterattack. They rallied around William Paterson of New Jersey, who presented a series of resolutions known as the **New Jersey Plan**. Paterson did not question the need for a strengthened central government, but he was concerned about how this strength might be used. The New Jersey Plan would give Congress the right to tax and regulate commerce and to coerce states, yet it would retain the single-house legislature (as under the Articles of Confederation) in which each state, regardless of size, would have the same vote. The plan contained the germ of what eventually came to be a key provision of our Constitution: the *supremacy clause*. The national Supreme Court was to hear appeals from state judges, and the supremacy clause would require all judges—state and national—to treat laws of the national government and the treaties of the United States as superior to the constitutions and laws of each of the states.

Paterson maneuvered to force concessions from the larger states. He favored a strong central government, but not one the big states could control. Further, he raised the issue of practical politics. To adopt the Virginia Plan—which would create a powerful national government dominated by Massachusetts, Pennsylvania, and Virginia and eliminate the states as important units of government—would all but guarantee that the states would reject the new constitution. Still, the large states resisted, and for a time the convention was deadlocked. The small states believed all states should be represented equally in Congress, at least in the upper house. The large states insisted representation in both houses be based on population or wealth, and that national legislators be elected by the voters rather than by state legislatures. Finally, a Committee of Eleven was elected to devise a compromise. On July 5 it presented its proposals.

THE CONNECTICUT COMPROMISE Because of the prominent role of the Connecticut delegation, this plan has since been known as the **Connecticut Compromise**, or as it is sometimes called, the Great Compromise. It called for one house in which each state would have an equal vote and a second house in which representation would be based on population and in which all bills for raising or appropriating money would originate. This proposal was a setback for the large states, which agreed to it only when the smaller states made it clear this was their price for union. After equality of state representation in the Senate was accepted, most objections to a strong national government dissolved.

NORTH-SOUTH COMPROMISES Other issues at the convention split the delegates North and South. Southerners were afraid a northern majority in Congress might discriminate against southern trade. They had some basis for this concern. John Jay, secretary of foreign affairs for the Confederation, had proposed a treaty with Great Britain that would have given advantages to northern merchants at the expense of southern exporters. To protect themselves, the southern delegates insisted a two-thirds majority be required in the Senate before presidents could ratify treaties.

Differences between the North and South were also evident on the issue of representation in the House of Representatives. The question was whether to count slaves for purposes of apportioning seats in the House. The South wanted to count slaves, thereby enlarging its number of representatives; the North resisted. After heated debate, the delegates agreed on the **three-fifths compromise**. Each slave would be counted as three-fifths of a free person for the purposes of apportionment in the House and of direct taxation. The explanation for "three-fifths," as opposed to some other fraction, was that it maintained a balance of power between the North and South. The issue of "balance" would recur in the early history of our nation as territorial governments were established and territories applied for statehood.

OTHER ISSUES   The delegates found other issues about which to argue. Should the national government have lower courts, or would one federal Supreme Court be enough? This issue was resolved by postponing the decision; the Constitution states that there shall be one Supreme Court and that Congress *may* establish inferior courts.

How should the president be selected? For a long time the convention accepted the idea that the president should be chosen by Congress. Yet the delegates feared Congress would dominate the president, or vice versa. Election by the state legislatures was also rejected because these bodies were distrusted. Finally, the electoral college system was devised. This was perhaps the most novel and contrived contribution of the delegates, and today it is one of the most criticized provisions in the Constitution.[14] (Consult Article II, Section 1, of the Constitution.)

After three months the delegates stopped debating. On September 17, 1787, they assembled for the impressive ceremony of signing the document they were recommending to the nation. All but three of those still present signed; others who opposed the general drift of the convention had already left. Their work well done, delegates adjourned to the nearby City Tavern to relax and celebrate.

TO ADOPT OR NOT TO ADOPT?

The delegates had gone far. They had disregarded Congress's instruction to do no more than revise the Articles. They had ignored Article XIII of the Articles of Confederation, which declared the Union to be perpetual and prohibited any alteration of the Articles unless agreed to by Congress and by *every one of the state legislatures*, a provision that had made it impossible to amend the Articles. The convention delegates, however, boldly declared that their newly proposed Constitution should go into effect when ratified by popularly elected conventions in nine states. They turned to this method of ratification for practical considerations as well as for reasons of principle. Not only were the delegates aware that there was little chance of securing approval of the new Constitution in all state legislatures; many also believed the Constitution should be ratified by an authority higher than a legislature. A constitution based on popular approval would have higher legal and moral status. The Articles of Confederation had been a compact of state governments, but the Constitution was based on "We the People." Nevertheless, even this method of ratification would not be easy. The nation was not ready to adopt the Constitution without a thorough debate.

Federalists versus Antifederalists

Supporters of the new government, by cleverly appropriating the name **Federalists**, took some of the sting out of charges they were trying to destroy the states and establish an all-powerful central government. By calling their opponents **Antifederalists**, they pointed up the negative character of the arguments of those who opposed ratification.

The split was in part geographical. Seaboard and city regions tended to be Federalist strongholds; backcountry regions from Maine (a part of Massachusetts)

Creating the Republic

April 1775 American Revolution begins at Lexington and Concord

June 1775 George Washington assumes command of Continental forces

July 1776 Declaration of Independence approved

November 1777 Articles of Confederation adopted by Continental Congress

March 1781 Articles of Confederation ratified by the states

October 1781 British defeated at Yorktown

April 1784 Congress ratifies peace treaty with British

August 1786 to February 1787 Shays' Rebellion in western Massachusetts

May 1787 Constitutional Convention opens in Philadelphia

September 1787 Constitution of the United States adopted by Convention

June 1788 Constitution ratified by nine states

Early 1789 First national elections

March 1789 United States Congress meets for the first time in New York

April 1789 George Washington inaugurated as first president

September 1789 John Jay becomes first chief justice of the United States

September 1789 Congress proposes Bill of Rights

December 1791 Bill of Rights (first 10 amendments) ratified as part of the U.S. Constitution

Note: It took about 15 years to win independence, form an interim government that tried to govern, fashion a "more perfect union," and actually get a national government, with functioning legislative, executive, and judicial branches.

1. *"All men are created equal"*: What kinds of equality are—and should be—protected by the Constitution, and by what means?

2. *"Government by the people"*: Does the evolving constitutional system, including political parties and interest groups, strengthen fair and effective representation of the people?

3. *Federalism*: Does the Constitution provide an efficient and realistic balance between national and state power?

4. *Checks and balances*: Does the constitutional separation of powers between the president and Congress lead to gridlock and delay?

5. *Minority rights*: Does the Constitution adequately protect the rights of women, African Americans, Native Americans, Hispanic Americans, other ethnic groups, and recent immigrants?

6. *Suspects' rights*: Can representative government uphold the rights of the criminally accused and yet protect its citizens?

7. *Individual liberties*: Are they adequately protected in the Constitution? Do big government and big business diminish the freedom of the individual?

8. *The judicial branch*: Is it too powerful? Are the federal courts exceeding their proper powers as interpreters of the Constitution?

9. *War and peace*: What are the responsibilities of the United States as the only superpower?

10. *Constitutional responsibilities*: Are Americans participating adequately in our democratic system? Do citizens take civic responsibilities too lightly? Is our democracy in jeopardy?

through Georgia, inhabited by farmers and other relatively poor people, were generally Antifederalists. But as in most political contests, no single factor completely accounted for the division between Federalists and Antifederalists. Thus in Virginia the leaders of both sides came from the same general social and economic class. New York City and Philadelphia strongly supported the Constitution, yet so did predominantly rural New Jersey.

The great debate was conducted through pamphlets, papers, letters to the editor, and speeches. The issues were important, but with few exceptions the argument about the merits of the Constitution was carried on in a quiet and calm manner. Out of the debate came a series of essays known as **The Federalist**, written by Alexander Hamilton, James Madison, and John Jay to persuade the voters of New York to ratify the Constitution. *The Federalist* is still, said Charles Beard, "widely regarded as the most profound single treatise on the Constitution ever written and as among the few masterly works in political science produced in all the centuries of history."[15] (Three of the most important *Federalist* essays, Nos. 10, 51, and 78, are found in the Appendix of this book. We urge you to read them.) The great debate stands even today as an outstanding example of free people using public discussion to determine the nature of their fundamental laws.

The Antifederalists' most telling criticism of the proposed Constitution was its failure to include a bill of rights.[16] The Federalists believed a bill of rights unnecessary. They contended that the proposed national government had only the specific powers delegated to it by the states and the people, so there was no need to specify that Congress could not, for example, abridge freedom of the press because it had no power to regulate the press. Moreover, the Federalists argued, to guarantee *some* rights might be dangerous, because it would then be thought that rights not listed could be denied. The Constitution already protected some important rights—trial by jury in federal criminal cases, for example. Hamilton and others also insisted that paper guarantees were weak supports on which to depend for protection against governmental tyranny.

The Antifederalists were unconvinced. If some rights were protected, what could be the objection to providing constitutional protection for others? Without a bill of rights, what was to prevent Congress from using one of its delegated powers to abridge free speech? If bills of rights were needed in state constitutions to limit state governments, why was a bill of rights not needed in the national constitution to limit the national government? This was a government farther from the people, they contended, with a greater tendency to subvert natural rights.

The Politics of Ratification

The absence of a bill of rights in the proposed constitution dominated the struggle over its adoption. "There is no Declaration of Rights" was the first sentence of an attack on the document by Virginia delegate George Mason. In taverns and church gatherings and newspaper offices up and down the eastern seaboard, people were muttering, "No bill of rights—no constitution!" This feeling was so strong that some Antifederalists, who were far more concerned with states' rights than individual rights, joined forces with bill of rights advocates in an effort to defeat the proposed Constitution.

The Federalists were first off the mark in the struggle over the Constitution that opened as soon as the delegates left Philadelphia in mid-September 1787. The Federalists' immediate tactic was to secure ratification in as many states as possible before the opposition had time to organize. The Antifederalists were handicapped. Most newspapers were owned by supporters of ratification. Moreover, Antifederalist strength was concentrated in rural areas, which were underrepresented in some state legislatures and difficult to arouse to political action. They needed time to perfect their organization and collect their strength. The Federalists, composed of a more closely knit group of leaders throughout the colonies, moved in a hurry.

In most of the small states, now satisfied by equal Senate representation, ratification was gained without difficulty. Delaware was the first state to ratify. By early 1788, Pennsylvania, New Jersey, Georgia, and Connecticut had also ratified. In the view of a grass-roots political observer, Mercy Warren of Massachusetts, there seemed to be few Americans who did not "unite in the general wish for the restoration of public faith, the revival of commerce, arts, agriculture, and industry, under a lenient, peaceable and energetic government."[17]

Reports were coming in from Massachusetts, however, that opposition was broadening, especially in the hinterland of the state. The position of such key leaders as John Hancock and Samuel Adams was in doubt. The debate in the ratifying convention in Boston pitched some of the most polished Federalist speakers against an array of eloquent but plainspoken Antifederalists. The debate raged for most of January 1788 into February. At times it looked as though the Constitution would lose, as Antifederalists raised the cry of "Why no Bill of Rights?" and other objections. But in the end the Constitution was narrowly ratified in Massachusetts, by 187 to 168 (see Table 1-1).

The Federalists were elated, yet, in fact, both sides had won. To gain votes for the Constitution, the Federalists had had to make a deal, one of the most important compromises in U.S. history. The Federalists adopted the strategy of accepting their opponents' most convincing argument—the lack of a bill of rights—and offered to add a bill of rights to the Constitution, but only *after* the new government under the Constitution was set up. Thus the Federalists sidetracked proposals for a second convention, which might have turned into a "runaway" gathering. In turn, the Antifederalists, led by such notables as Samuel Adams, won a promise for a bill of rights—a promise later honored by Madison and his fellow Federalist leaders. John Hancock, it was said, came over to the Federalist side after hints he might be selected vice-president under the new government.

The struggle over ratification of the Constitution continued through the spring of 1788. By June 21, Maryland, South Carolina, and New Hampshire had ratified, putting the Constitution over the top in the number (nine) required for ratification. But two big hurdles remained: Virginia and New York. Virginia was crucial, as the most populous state, the home of Washington and other heroes, a link between North and South. The Virginia ratifying convention rivaled the Constitutional Convention in the caliber of its delegates. Madison, who had only recently switched to favoring the bill of rights position after saying earlier it was unnecessary, captained the Federalist forces. The fiery Patrick Henry led the opposition. In an epic debate, Henry cried that liberty was the issue: "Liberty, the greatest of earthly possessions . . . that precious jewel!" But Madison quietly rebutted him and then played his trump card, a promise that a bill of rights embracing the freedoms of religion and speech and assembly would be added to the Constitution as the first order of business once the new government was established. At a critical moment, Washington himself tipped the balance with a letter urging ratification. News of the Virginia vote, 89 for the Constitution and 79 opposed, was rushed to New York.[18]

The great landowners along the Hudson, unlike their southern planter friends, were opposed to the Constitution. They feared federal taxation of their holdings, and they did not want to abolish the profitable tax New York had been levying on trade and commerce with other states. When the convention assembled, the Federalists were greatly outnumbered, but they were aided by the strategy and skill of Hamilton and by word of Virginia's ratification. New York approved by a margin of three votes. Although North Carolina and Rhode Island still remained outside the Union (the former ratified in November 1789, and the latter six months later), the new nation was created. In New York, a few members of the old Congress assembled to issue the call for elections under the new Constitution. Then Congress adjourned without setting a date for reconvening.

TABLE 1-1
Ratification of the U.S. Constitution

State	Date
Delaware	Dec. 7, 1787
Pennsylvania	Dec. 12, 1787
New Jersey	Dec. 19, 1787
Georgia	Jan. 2, 1788
Connecticut	Jan. 9, 1788
Massachusetts	Feb. 6, 1788
Maryland	April 28, 1788
South Carolina	May 23, 1788
New Hampshire	June 21, 1788
Virginia	June 25, 1788
New York	July 26, 1788
North Carolina	Nov. 21, 1789
Rhode Island	May 29, 1790

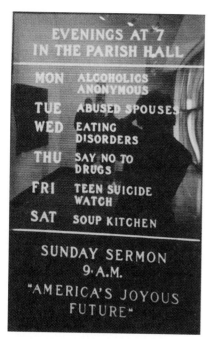

Despite the many serious problems facing our country, a spirit of optimism is still evident in our hopes for the future, as this church bulletin testifies.

INTO THE TWENTY-FIRST CENTURY

A constitution that is to endure must reflect both the hard experiences and high hopes of the people for whom it is written. Those who framed our Constitution did not, of course, complete the task of constitution making. That process began long before the Constitutional Convention, and it continues still. Constitutions, even written ones, are growing and evolving organisms.

In recent decades this nation celebrated the two-hundredth anniversary of the Constitution and of the Bill of Rights. This period of commemoration and celebration has also been a period of questioning. Questions about constitutional democracy have no easy answers, no single logical response. They are basic questions that deal with value choices. The questions in the box on page 20 may help stimulate your thinking as you proceed to a more detailed investigation of our Republic. You must remember, as you consider these questions, that the framers did not favor a government in which the mass of people would participate directly, or one that would always be responsive to the people at large. Rather, they sought to control both the spirit of faction and the emotional or ill-considered domination by majorities. Their prime concern was how to design a viable yet limited government. The framers had not seen a political party in the modern sense, and they probably would not have liked it if they had. They did not favor an arousing, mobilizing kind of leadership, but preferred instead a stabilizing, balancing, magisterial leadership, the kind George Washington was expected to (and generally did) supply.

According to an old story, Benjamin Franklin was confronted by a woman as he left the last session of the Constitutional Convention in Philadelphia in September 1787.

"What kind of government have you given us, Dr. Franklin?" she asked. "A Republic or a Monarchy?"

"A Republic, Madam," he answered, "if you can keep it."

 POLITICS ONLINE

The Internet and American Government

The study of American government has been made more accessible through the Internet. Original documents, library catalogs, news reports, interviews, and research by public and private agencies are now at your fingertips, and some services are free of charge. We have prepared a brief section for each chapter that illustrates ways the Internet can facilitate your study of politics. We provide Internet addresses and invite you to access the *Government by the People* home page at:

http://www.prenhall.com/burns

This home page will provide helpful links to other home pages plus constantly updated addresses for useful sources of information.

A great first stop in your political surfing would be "The Jefferson Project," which provides a catalog of Internet sites with useful information on current events, political parties, campaigns, and jokes:

http://www.voxpop.org/jefferson

If you are looking for information about the U.S. Constitution or other historical documents try:

http://www.law.emory.edu/FEDERAL.

Other examples of resources relating to the U.S. Constitution can be found on the "Founding Fathers Page" maintained by the National Archives and Records Administration at:

http://dolley.nara.gov/exhall/charters/constitution/confath.html

More generally, the National Archives and Records Administration is a good place to check for documents on our national government:

http://www.nara.gov

SUMMARY

1. Americans have long been skeptical of politicians and politics. Yet politics is a necessary activity for a democracy. Indeed politics and politicians are indispensable to making our system of separated institutions and checks and balances work.

2. Democracy is an often misused term, and it has many different meanings. We use it here to refer to a system of interacting values, interrelated political processes, and interdependent political structures. The vital principle of democracy is that a just government must derive its powers from the consent of the people, and that this consent must be regularly renewed at free and fair elections.

3. Stable constitutional democracy is encouraged by various conditions, such as an educated citizenry, a healthy economy, and overlapping associations and groupings within a society in which major institutions interact to create a certain degree of consensus. Civilian control over the military and a general acceptance of the ideals of democracy are also essential.

4. There has recently been some concern about what may be a decline in *social capital*—the experiences people gain

in working together in community groups. Lessons about compromise, accommodation, and participation are important building blocks for democracy.

5. Democracy developed gradually. A revolution had to be fought before a system of representative democracy could be tried and tested. It took several years before a national constitution could be written, and almost another year to be ratified. It took still another two years before a Bill of Rights could be adopted and ratified. It has taken more than two hundred years for democratic institutions to be refined and for systems of competition and choice to be hammered out. Democratic institutions in the United States are still evolving.

6. Constitutionalism is a general label we apply to arrangements such as checks and balances, federalism, separation of powers, due process, and the Bill of Rights that force our leaders and representatives to listen, think, deliberate, bargain, and explain before they act and make laws. A constitutional government enforces recognized and regularly applied limits on the powers of those who govern.

FURTHER READING

THORTON ANDERSON, *Creating the Constitution: The Convention of 1787 and the First Congress* (Pennsylvania State University Press, 1994).

BERNARD BAILYN, ED., *The Debate on the Constitution: Federalist and Antifederalist Speeches, Articles, and Letters During the Struggle over Ratification*, 2 vols. (Library of America, 1993).

LANCE BANNING, *The Sacred Fire of Liberty: James Madison and the Founding of the Republic* (Cornell University Press, 1995).

JAMES MACGREGOR BURNS, *The Vineyard of Liberty* (Knopf, 1982).

JAMES MACGREGOR BURNS AND STEWART BURNS, *The People's Charter* (Knopf, 1991).

THOMAS E. CRONIN, *Direct Democracy: The Politics of the Initiative, Referendum, and Recall* (Harvard University Press, 1989).

ROBERT A. DAHL, *Democracy and Its Critics* (Yale University Press, 1989).

AMY GUTMANN AND DENNIS THOMPSON, *Democracy and Disagreement* (Belknap, 1996).

ALEXANDER HAMILTON, JAMES MADISON, AND JOHN JAY, *The Federalist Papers*, ed. Clinton Rossiter (New American Library, 1961). Also in several other editions.

SAMUEL P. HUNTINGTON, *The Third Wave: Democratization in the Late Twentieth Century* (University of Oklahoma Press, 1991).

DREW R. MCCOY, *The Last of the Fathers: James Madison and the Republican Legacy* (Columbia University Press, 1989).

RICHARD B. MORRIS, *Witnesses at the Creation: Hamilton, Madison, and Jay and the Constitution* (Holt, Rinehart and Winston, 1985).

ROBERT D. PUTNAM, *Making Democracy Work: Civic Traditions in Modern Italy* (Princeton University Press, 1993).

ROBERT D. PUTNAM, "Bowling Alone: America's Declining Social Capital," *Journal of Democracy* 6, no. 1 (January 1995).

ALEXIS DE TOCQUEVILLE, *Democracy in America*, 2 vols., 1835 (Vintage, 1955).

SIDNEY VERBA, KAY LEMAN SCHOLZMAN, AND HENRY E. BRADY, *Voice and Equality: Civic Volunteerism in American Politics* (Harvard University Press, 1995).

GORDON S. WOOD, *The Creation of the American Republic, 1776–1787* (University of North Carolina Press, 1969).

See also the *Journal of Democracy*, published quarterly for the National Endowment for Democracy by the Johns Hopkins University Press.

2

The Living Constitution

$\mathcal{T}$he original, unamended Constitution in 1789 was a skinny document of some 4,543 words (you can carry it around in your coat pocket), yet it packed a powerful punch. It was intended to be only a framework for governing; it was a document into which citizens of the early Republic could, if optimistic, read their hopes, or, if pessimistic, their fears. Most of them would be surprised to learn that more than two hundred years later, we still have not written another constitution—let alone two or three!

Soon after the adoption of the Constitution, economic prosperity returned. Markets for American goods were opening in Europe, and business was pulling out of its postwar slump. Such developments seemed to justify Federalist claims that adoption of the Constitution would correct the nation's problems. Within a surprisingly short time the Constitution lost its partisan character; both Antifederalists and Federalists honored it. Politicians differed less and less over whether the Constitution was good; they began to argue over what it meant.

The adoption of the Bill of Rights in 1791 made the Constitution more popular than ever.[1] As the Constitution won the support of Americans, it began to take on the aura of **natural law,** law that defines right from wrong, law that is higher than human law. "The Fathers grew ever larger in stature as they receded from view; the era in which they lived and fought became a Golden Age; in that age there had been a fresh dawn for the world, and its men were giants against the sky."[2]

This early Constitution worship helped bring unity to the diverse new nation. Like the Crown in Great Britain, the Constitution became a symbol of national loyalty, evoking both emotional and intellectual support from all Americans, regardless of their differences. The framers' work became part of the American creed.[3] It stood for liberty, equality before the law, limited government—indeed, for just about whatever anyone wanted to read into it.

The Constitution, however, is more than a symbol. It is also a _supreme and binding law that both grants and limits powers_. "In framing a government which is to be administered by men over men," wrote James Madison in _The Federalist_, No. 51, "the great difficulty lies in this: you must first enable the government to control the governed; and in the next place oblige it to control itself." (Take a look at _The Federalist_, No. 51, which appears in the Appendix of this book.) The Constitution is both a positive instrument of government, which enables the governors to control the governed, and a restraint on government, which enables the ruled to check the rulers.

In what ways does the Constitution limit the power of the government? In what ways does it create governmental power? How has it managed to serve as a great symbol of national unity and at the same time a somewhat adaptable and changing instrument of government? The secret is an ingenious separation of powers and a system of checks and balances that combine to check power with power.

CHECKING POWER WITH POWER

It may seem strange to begin by stressing the ways in which the Constitution _limits_ governmental power, but we must keep in mind the dilemma the framers faced. They wanted a stronger and more effective national government than they had under the Articles of Confederation; at the same time, they were keenly aware that the people would not accept too much central control. Efficiency and order were important concerns, but they were not as important as _liberty_. The framers wanted to ensure domestic tranquillity and prevent future rebellions, but they also wanted

25

to forestall the emergence of a homegrown King George III. Accordingly, they allotted certain powers to the national government and reserved the rest for the states, thus establishing a system of *federalism* (whose nature and problems we take up in Chapter 3). Even this was not enough. They believed they needed additional means to limit the national government.

The most important way to make public officials observe the constitutional limits on their powers is through *regular and fair elections*; voters have the ability to throw out of office those who abuse power. Yet the framers were not willing to depend solely on such political controls, because they did not fully trust the people's judgment. "Free government is founded on jealousy, and not in confidence," said Thomas Jefferson. "In questions of power, then, let no more be heard of confidence in man, but bind him down from mischief by the chains of the Constitution."[4]

Even more important, the framers feared that a majority faction might use the new central government to deprive minorities of their rights. "A dependence on the people is, no doubt, the primary control on the government," Madison admitted in *The Federalist*, No. 51, "but experience has taught mankind the necessity of auxiliary precautions." What were these "auxiliary precautions" against popular tyranny?

Separation of Powers

The first step was the **separation of powers**, that is, the allocation of constitutional authority to each of the three branches of the national government. In *The Federalist*, No. 47, Madison wrote, "No political truth is certainly of greater intrinsic value, or is stamped with the authority of more enlightened patrons of liberty, than that . . . the accumulation of all powers, legislative, executive, and judiciary, in the same hands . . . may justly be pronounced the very definition of tyranny." (Chief among the "enlightened patrons of liberty" to whose authority Madison was appealing were John Locke and Montesquieu, whose works were subscribed to by most educated Americans.)

The intrinsic value of the principle of dispersion of power does not by itself account for its incorporation into our Constitution. Such dispersion of power had been the general practice in the colonies for more than one hundred years. Only during the Revolutionary period did some of the states and the Articles of Confederation concentrate authority in the hands of the legislature, and that unhappy experience confirmed the framers' belief in the merits of separation of powers. Many attributed the evils of state government and the lack of energy in the central government to the fact that there was no strong executive both to check legislative abuses and to give energy and direction to administration.

Still, separating power was not enough. There was always the danger—from the framers' point of view—that different officials with different powers might pool their authority and act together. Separation of powers by itself might not prevent governmental branches and officials from responding to the same pressures— from the demand of an overwhelming majority of the voters to suppress an offensive book, for example, or to impose confiscatory taxes on rich people. If separating power was not enough, what else could be done?

Checks and Balances: Ambition to Counteract Ambition

The framers' answer was a system of **checks and balances**. "The great security against a gradual concentration of the several powers in the same department," wrote Madison in *The Federalist*, No. 51, "consists in giving to those who administer each department the necessary constitutional means and personal motives to resist encroachments of the others. . . . Ambition must be made to counteract ambition."

Each branch therefore has a role in the actions of the others (see Figure 2-1). We have a "government of separated institutions sharing powers."[5] Congress enacts laws, yet the president can veto them. The Supreme Court can declare laws passed

"And there are three branches of government, so that each branch has the other two to blame everything on."

Dunagin's People by Ralph Dunagin. © 1978 Field Newspaper Syndicate. By permission of the News America Syndicate.

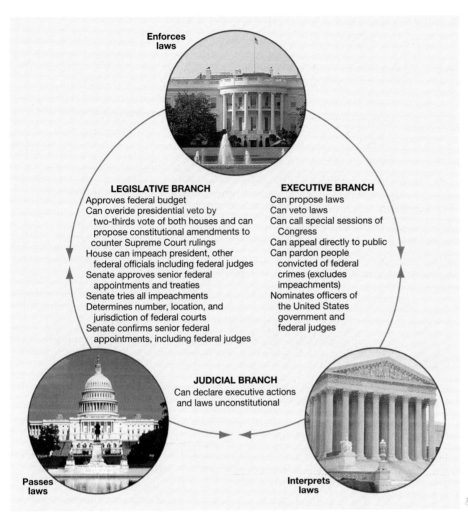

FIGURE 2-1 The Separation of Powers and Checks and Balances

by Congress and signed by the president unconstitutional, but the president appoints the justices and all the other federal judges with the Senate's approval. The president administers the laws, but Congress provides the money. Moreover, the Senate and the House of Representatives have an absolute veto over each other in the enactment of a law, because bills must be approved by both houses.

Not only does each branch have some authority over the others, but each is politically independent of the others. The president is selected by electors (now popularly elected). Senators are now chosen by the voters in each state, and members of the House are chosen by voters in their districts. And although federal judges are appointed by the president with the consent of the Senate, once in office they hold terms virtually for life.

The framers also ensured that a majority of the voters could win control over only part of the government at one time. Although a popular majority might take control of the House of Representatives in an off-year (nonpresidential) election, the president, representing a previous popular majority, would still have at least two years to go, as was the case in 1994, when Republicans took over the House and Bill Clinton continued as president. Further, senators are chosen for six years. Finally, independent national courts, which have developed their own powerful checks, were also provided. In fact, judges have become so important in our system of checks and balances that they deserve special attention.

JUDICIAL REVIEW AND THE "GUARDIANS OF THE CONSTITUTION"

Judges did not claim the power of **judicial review**—the power of a court to refuse to enforce a law or a government regulation that in the opinion of the judges conflicts with the Constitution—until some years after the Constitution was in operation. From the beginning, however, judges were expected to restrain legislative majorities. "The independence of judges," wrote Alexander Hamilton in *The Federalist*, No. 78 (which appears in the Appendix), "may be an essential safeguard against the effects of occasional ill humors in the society."

Judicial review is a contribution of the United States to the art of government, a contribution adapted in part in recent years in other nations such as Canada and Germany. (The Canadian constitution's "notwithstanding" provision allows either a provincial legislature or the national parliament to override certain sections of the Charter of Rights for a renewable period of six years.)[6] If British or American citizens are thrown into prison without cause, they can appeal to the courts of their respective countries for protection. But a British judge may *not* declare a law duly enacted by Parliament null and void because the judge believes it violates the British constitution; Parliament is the guardian of the British constitution. In the United States it is the courts, ultimately the Supreme Court, that are the keepers of the constitutional conscience—not Congress and not the president. How did judges get this tremendous responsibility?

Origins of Judicial Review

The Constitution says nothing about who should have the final word in disputes that might arise over its meaning. Whether the delegates to the Constitutional Convention of 1787 intended to give the courts the power of judicial review is a question long debated. The framers clearly intended for the Supreme Court to have the power to declare state legislation unconstitutional, but whether they intended to give it the same power over national legislation is not clear. The late Edward S. Corwin, the outstanding authority on the American Constitution, concluded that unquestionably "the framers anticipated some sort of judicial review. . . . But it is equally without question that the ideas generally current in 1787 were far from presaging the present vast role of the court."[7] Why, then, did the framers not specifically provide for judicial review? Probably because they believed the power could readily be inferred from certain general provisions.

The Federalists—those who wrote the Constitution and controlled the national government until 1801—generally supported a strong role for federal courts and favored judicial review. Their opponents, the Jeffersonian Republicans (called Democrats after 1832), were less enthusiastic. In 1798 and 1799 Jefferson and Madison (who by this time had left the Federalist camp), with the Virginia and Kentucky Resolutions, came close to the position that state legislatures—and not the Supreme Court—had the ultimate power to interpret the Constitution. These resolutions seemed to question whether the Supreme Court even had the final authority to review state legislation, something about which there had been little doubt.

When the Jeffersonians defeated the Federalists in the election of 1800, it was still undecided whether the Supreme Court would actually exercise the power of judicial review. The idea was in the air, logical reasons to support a doctrine of judicial review were at hand, and some precedents could even be cited; nevertheless judicial review was not an established power. Then in 1803 came *Marbury v Madison*, one of the most famous Supreme Court decisions of all time.[8]

Marbury versus Madison

The election of 1800 marked the rise to power of the Jeffersonian Republicans. President John Adams and fellow Federalists did not take their defeat easily. Indeed, they were greatly alarmed at what they considered to be the "enthronement of the rabble." Yet there was nothing much they could do about it before leaving office—or was there? The Constitution gives the president, with the consent of the Senate, the power to appoint federal judges to hold office during "good Behaviour." With the judiciary in the hands of good Federalists, thought Adams and his associates, they could stave off the worst consequences of Jefferson's victory.

The lame duck Federalist Congress created dozens of new federal judicial posts. (**Lame duck** is the term applied to elected officials who have recently been defeated for office but are serving out the rest of their term before being replaced by their successors.) By March 3, 1801, Adams had appointed, and the Senate had confirmed, loyal Federalists to all these new positions. Adams signed the commissions and turned them over to John Marshall, his secretary of state, to be sealed and delivered. Marshall had just received his own commission as chief justice of the United States, but he was continuing to serve as secretary of state until Adams's term as president expired. Working right up until nine o'clock on the evening of March 3, Marshall sealed, but was unable to deliver, all the commissions. The important ones were taken care of, however, and the only ones left were for the justices of the peace for the District of Columbia. The newly appointed chief justice left these commissions for his successor to deliver.

Jefferson, now inaugurated as president, was angered by this "packing" of the judiciary. When he discovered that some of the commissions were still lying on a table in the Department of State, he instructed a clerk not to deliver them. Jefferson could see no reason why the District needed so many justices of the peace, especially Federalist justices.[9]

Among the commissions not delivered was one for William Marbury. After waiting in vain, Marbury decided to seek action from the courts. Searching through the statute books, he came across Section 13 of the Judiciary Act of 1789, which authorized the Supreme Court "to issue writs of *mandamus*, in cases warranted by the principles and usages of law, to . . . persons holding office under the authority of the United States." A **writ of mandamus** is a court order directing an official, such as the secretary of state, to perform a ministerial duty, a duty about which the official has no discretion, such as delivering a commission. So, thought Marbury, why not ask the Supreme Court to issue a writ of *mandamus* to force James Madison, the new secretary of state, to deliver the commission? Marbury and his companions went directly to the Supreme Court, and, citing Section 13, they made the request.

What could Marshall do? If the Court issued the writ, Madison and Jefferson would probably ignore it. The Court would be powerless, and its prestige, already low, might suffer a fatal blow. On the other hand, by refusing to issue the writ, the judges would appear to support the Jeffersonian Republicans' claim that the Court had no authority to interfere with the executive. Would Marshall issue the writ? Most people thought so; angry Republicans even threatened impeachment if he did so.

On February 24, 1803, the Supreme Court delivered its opinion. The first part was as expected. Marbury was entitled to his commission, said Marshall, and Madison should have delivered it to him. Moreover, a writ of *mandamus* could be issued by the proper court against even so high an officer as the secretary of state, the president of the United States' own agent.

Then came the surprise. Although Section 13 of the Judiciary Act seems to give the Supreme Court original jurisdiction in cases such as that in question, this section, said Marshall, is contrary to Article III of the Constitution, which gives the Supreme Court original jurisdiction only when an ambassador or other foreign minister is affected or when a state is a party. Even though this is a case of original jurisdiction, Marbury is neither a state nor a foreign minister. If we follow Section 13, wrote Marshall, we have jurisdiction; if we follow the Constitution, we have no jurisdiction.

Marshall then posed the question in a more pointed way: Should the Supreme Court enforce an unconstitutional law? Of course not, he concluded. The

Chief Justice John Marshall (1755–1835), our most influential Supreme Court justice. Appointed in 1801, Marshall served until 1835. Earlier he had been a staunch defender of the U.S. Constitution at the Virginia ratifying convention, a member of Congress, and a secretary of state. He is one of those rare people who served in all three branches of government.

Constitution is the supreme and binding law, and the courts cannot enforce any action of Congress that conflicts with it.

The real question remained unanswered. Congress and the president had also read the Constitution, and according to their interpretation, which was also reasonable, Section 13 was compatible with Article III. Where did the Supreme Court get the right to say they were wrong? Why should the Supreme Court's interpretation of the Constitution be preferred to that of Congress and the president?

Paralleling Hamilton's argument in *The Federalist*, No. 78, Marshall reasoned: The Constitution is law: judges—not legislators or executives—interpret law. Therefore, judges should interpret the Constitution. "If two laws conflict with each other, the courts must decide on the operation of each," he said. Case dismissed.

Jefferson fumed. For one thing, Marshall had said that a court with the proper jurisdiction could issue a writ of *mandamus*, even against the secretary of state, one of the president's closest advisers. Yet there was little Jefferson could do about what he thought was Marshall's arrogance. There was not even a court order he could refuse to obey. In a single stroke, Marshall had lectured the Jeffersonian Republicans for failing to perform their duties, and he had gone a long way toward acquiring the power for the Supreme Court to review acts of Congress. And he had done it in a manner that made it difficult for the Republicans to challenge.

Marbury v Madison is a masterpiece of judicial strategy. Marshall went out of his way to declare Section 13 unconstitutional. He could have interpreted the section to mean that the Supreme Court could issue writs of *mandamus* in those cases in which it did have jurisdiction. He could have interpreted Article III to mean that Congress could add to, though not subtract from, the original jurisdiction the Constitution gives to the Supreme Court. He could have dismissed the case for want of jurisdiction without discussing Marbury's right to his commission. But none of these would have suited his purpose. Marshall was fearful for the Supreme Court's future; unless the Court spoke out, he reasoned, it would become subordinate to the president and Congress.

Marshall's decision, important as it was, did not by itself establish the Supreme Court's power to review and declare acts of Congress unconstitutional. Not until the *Dred Scott* case in 1857 did the Supreme Court declare another act of Congress unconstitutional,[10] and not until after the Civil War did the modern use of judicial review become established.

Marbury v Madison might have been interpreted by subsequent generations in a very limited way, so that the Supreme Court had the right to determine the scope of its own powers under Article III, but that Congress and the president had the authority to interpret their own powers under Articles I and II, respectively. One scholar insists that is what Marshall intended, and that the more expansive interpretation of *Marbury v Madison* is part of a myth designed to perpetuate judicial dominance.[11] However, Marshall's decision has not been interpreted in this way. On the contrary, building on Marshall's precedent over the decades, the Court has taken the commanding position as the authoritative interpreter of the Constitution.

Perhaps if Marshall had not spoken when he did, the Court might not have been able to assume the power of judicial review. He created the precedent. This is a classic example of constitutional development through judicial interpretation. The Constitution gives no specific authorization for the Court to declare congressional enactments null and void; yet today this practice is a vital part of our constitutional system.

Several important consequences follow from the acceptance of Marshall's argument that judges are the official interpreters of the Constitution. The most important is that even a law enacted by Congress and approved by the president may, under many circumstances, be challenged by a single person. Simply by bringing a lawsuit, those who lack the clout to get a bill through Congress or influence a federal agency may often secure a judicial hearing. And organized interest groups often find that policy goals unattainable by legislation can be achieved by litigation. Litigation thus supplements, and at times takes precedence over, legislation as a way to make public policy.[12]

CHECKS AND BALANCES: DOES IT WORK?

What if a majority of the people gain control of all branches of government and force through radical measures? If a great majority of the voters want to take a certain step, the framers knew that nothing could stop them. They reasoned that all they could do—and this is quite a lot—is to prevent, temporarily, full control by the popular majority.

Distrustful of both the elites and the masses, the framers deliberately *built inefficiency into our political system.* They designed the decision-making process so that the national government can act decisively only when there is general agreement, a consensus, among most of the interest groups and after all sides have had a chance to have their say.

More than two hundred years after the ratification of the Constitution, Americans continue to debate the desirability of these limits under the vastly different conditions of our times. Crucial questions remain: Are these checks necessary or sufficient to prevent abuses of political power? Do these limitations work to prevent abuses, or do they result in a "deadlock of democracy," making coherent governmental action for the general welfare difficult, if not impossible?

Modifications of Checks and Balances

Even though fragmentation of political power remains, several developments have modified the way the system of checks and balances works.

THE RISE OF NATIONAL POLITICAL PARTIES   Political parties can serve as unifying factors—at times drawing together the president, senators, representatives, and sometimes even judges behind common programs. Yet the parties, in turn, can be splintered and weakened by having to work through a system of fragmented governmental power, so they never become strong or cohesive. Moreover, when one party controls the Congress and the other the White House, as has generally been the case since the end of World War II, parties may intensify checks and balances, rather than moderate them, to the point that definitive action on some major issues may be difficult.[13]

Divided government may lead to such competition between the two branches that we find "each institution protecting and promoting itself through a broad interpretation of its constitutional and political status, even usurping the other's power when the opportunity presents itself."[14] Thus we have had battles over presidential **impoundment** of funds appropriated by Congress, budget deadlocks, and unseemly and angry confirmation hearings for the appointment of federal judges, especially for justices of the Supreme Court. Divided government also makes it difficult for the voters to hold anybody or any party accountable. "Presidents blame Congress . . . while members of Congress attack the president. . . . Citizens genuinely cannot tell who is to blame."[15]

Yet when all the shouting dies down, concluded David R. Mayhew after a careful review of the evidence, "control by one party has not made all that much difference." There have been just as many congressional investigations and just as much important legislation passed when one party controls Congress and another controls the presidency as when the same party controls both branches.[16] This conclusion is confirmed by President Clinton's first term, when there was more major legislation signed into law during his second two years (104th Congress, 1995–1996) when the Republicans controlled both houses, than during his first two years (103rd Congress, 1993–1995), when President Clinton worked with a Congress both chambers of which were under Democratic control. As Charles Jones, a noted scholar of Congress and the presidency has recently concluded, not

In 1857 the Supreme Court denied Dred Scott his freedom by ruling that slaves were property and protected as such by the Constitution. This decision declared an act of Congress—the Missouri Compromise—to be unconstitutional. This decision was later overruled by the Fourteenth Amendment.

The Exercise of Checks and Balances, 1789–1994

Vetoes

The president has vetoed over 2,500 acts of Congress.

Congress has overridden presidential vetoes over 100 times.

Judicial Review

The Supreme Court has ruled close to 150 congressional acts or parts thereof unconstitutional. Its 1983 decision on legislative vetoes (*INS v Chadha*) affects another 200 provisions.

Impeachment

The House of Representatives has impeached 16 federal officials, including 13 federal judges; of these, the Senate has convicted 7.

Confirmation

The Senate has refused to confirm 9 cabinet nominations, and many other cabinet and subcabinet appointments were withdrawn because of likely Senate rejection.

only is divided government not that important in determining how our government responds to crises, but divided government is precisely what the voters have wanted through much of our history.[17]

EXPANSION OF THE ELECTORATE AND CHANGES IN ELECTORAL METHODS The framers wanted the president to be chosen by the Electoral College—wise, independent citizens free from popular passions and hero worship—rather than by ordinary citizens. Almost from the beginning, however, presidential electors have pledged prior to elections to cast their votes for their parties' presidential candidates. Senators, originally elected by state legislatures, are today chosen directly by the people.

The "people" entitled to vote has expanded from white property-owning males to all citizens over 18 years of age. During the past century, American states have expanded the role of the electorate within the states by adopting **direct primaries**, in which the voters select party nominees, and by permitting the voters in about half the states to vote directly on laws (**initiative** and **referendum**) and even to remove elected state and local officials from office (**recall**). At the national level, the electorate has been given a major voice in choosing party nominees not merely for the House and the Senate but even for president.

ESTABLISHMENT OF AGENCIES DELIBERATELY DESIGNED TO EXERCISE LEGISLATIVE, EXECUTIVE, AND JUDICIAL FUNCTIONS When the national government began to regulate the economy seriously, it issued detailed rules on such complex matters as railroad safety, bank and stock exchange practices, employment conditions, union negotiations, and automobile emissions. It is impossible to assign regulatory responsibilities without providing the power to make and apply rules and to decide disputes. Beginning in 1887, Congress created independent regulatory commissions such as the Interstate Commerce Commission (which went out of business in 1995) and the Federal Communications Commission. In this century it established independent executive agencies such as the Environmental Protection Agency.

CHANGES IN TECHNOLOGY The system of checks and balances operates differently today from the way it did in 1787. Back then there were no televised congressional committee hearings, no electronic listening devices, no *Larry King Live* or *Rush Limbaugh* talk shows, no *New York Times*, *Wall Street Journal*, *USA Today*, CNN, or C-Span, no nightly news programs with national audiences, no presidential press conferences, and no live coverage of wars and of Americans being held hostage in foreign lands. Nuclear bombs, television, computers, cellular telephones, fax machines, public opinion polls, the World Wide Web—these and other innovations create conditions very different from those of two centuries ago. We also live in a time of instant polls that reliably tell us what people think about public issues.

In some ways these new technologies have added to the powers of presidents by, among other things, permitting them to appeal directly to millions of people and giving them immediate access to public opinion. These new technologies have also added leverage to organized interests by making it easy for them to target thousands of letters and calls at Congress, to organize letters to the editor, and to stage media events. New technologies have also given greater independence and influence to nongovernmental agencies such as the press. They have made it possible for rich people like Ross Perot and Steve Forbes and religious leaders like Pat Robertson, who have access to large resources, to bypass political parties and carry their message directly to the electorate.

THE EMERGENCE OF THE UNITED STATES AS A WORLD POWER AND THE EXISTENCE OF RECURRENT CRISES Today, problems anywhere in the world—China, Bosnia, the Persian Gulf—often become crises for the United States. The need to deal with perpetual emergencies has concentrated power in the hands of the chief executive and the presidential staff. The president's role as the most significant player on the world stage and the immediate coverage of summit conferences with foreign leaders enhance his status as domestic leader. Headline-producing ceremonial, as well as substantive, events give the president a visibility no congressional leader can achieve. The office of the president has on occasion served to impose some measure of national unity. Drawing on constitutional, political, and emergency powers, the president is sometimes able to overcome the restraints imposed by the Constitution on the exercise of governmental power—to the applause of some and the alarm of others.

The British and American Systems: A Study in Contrasts

Although many Americans question the usefulness and functions of some government institutions, we tend to take our system of checks and balances for granted, considering it necessary for constitutional government. Like Madison, we view the amassing of power by any one branch of government as leading to tyranny, especially since scandals such as Watergate, in which President Richard Nixon tried to use federal agencies to suppress evidence of his administration's involvement in a break-in at Democratic party headquarters, and the Iran-Contra affair, in which the Reagan administration worked covertly to sell arms to Iran, using the funds thus raised to get around congressional limitations on giving aid to the Nicaraguan government.

Yet it is quite possible for a government to be constitutional without these checks and balances. The British system is a good example (see Figure 2-2). Under the British system, voters elect members of Parliament from districts throughout the nation, much as we elect members of the House of Representatives. Members of the House of Commons have almost complete constitutional power. Leaders of the majority party serve as executive ministers who collectively form the cabinet, with the prime minister as its head. The prime minister is chosen by the majority party. Like the other cabinet members, he or she represents a *constituency* (a district). When the ruling party loses the support of the majority in the Commons on a major issue, it must resign or call for new elections. Formerly, the House of Lords could check the Commons, but it is now almost powerless. There is no high court in Great Britain with the power to declare acts of Parliament unconstitutional. The prime minister cannot veto them, although he or she may ask the Crown to dissolve Parliament and call new elections for members of the House of Commons.

The British system is based on *majority* (51 percent) or *plurality rule* (largest number); that is, a plurality of the voters elects a parliamentary majority. Like us, the British elect legislators from districts, and the party with the most votes in a district wins the seat, so that even with three or more parties, a plurality of the popular vote usually results in a majority of the parliamentary seats. So long as the parliamentary majority stays together, it can enact into law the majority party's program. British parties are cohesive and disciplined; party members vote together and support their parliamentary leaders. In Britain the party that wins an election has a very good chance of seeing its policy goals enacted.

Our system usually depends on the agreement of many elements of society. The party that wins a presidential or congressional election or even one that controls both these branches will still have a tough time carrying out its platform promises. The British system *concentrates* control and responsibility in the legislature; ours *diffuses* control and responsibility among several organs of government.

We have a written document called the Constitution; Britain has no such single document. Yet both systems are constitutional in the sense that the rulers are subject to defined restraints. The limits in our written Constitution and the conventions in the unwritten British constitution rest on underlying national values and attitudes.

British Labour party candidate Tony Blair's election in 1997 brought an end to 18 years of Conservative party control of the government. In a parliamentary system, the prime minister is the leader of the political party that wins the most seats in the House of Commons.

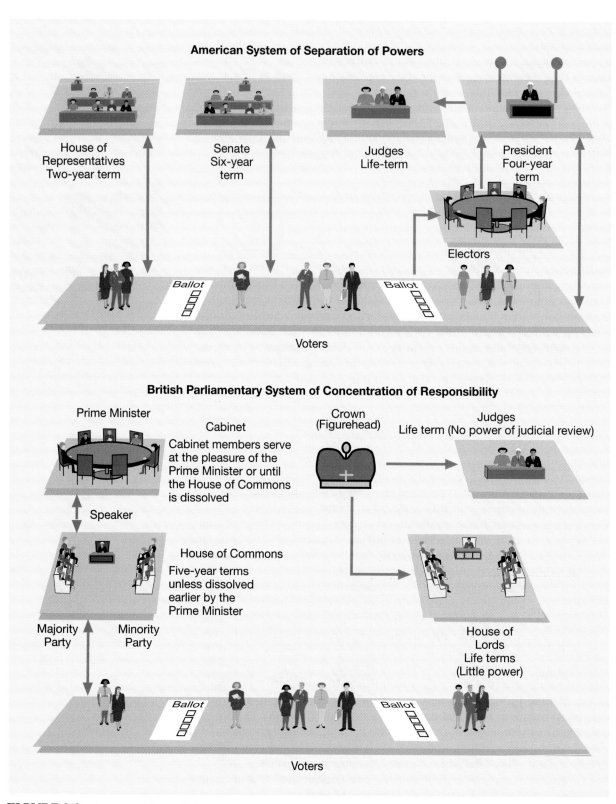

FIGURE 2-2 A Comparison of the British and American Systems

As careful as the Constitution's framers were to limit the powers they gave the national government, the main reason they had assembled in Philadelphia was to create a stronger national government. Having learned that a weak central government, incapable of governing, was a danger to liberty, they wished to establish a national government within the framework of a federal system with enough authority to meet the needs of all times. They made general grants of power, leaving it to succeeding generations to fill in the details and organize the structure of government in accordance with experience.

Hence our formal, written Constitution is only the skeleton of our system. It is filled out by numerous rules that must be considered part of our constitutional system in its larger sense. In fact, it is primarily through changes in our informal, unwritten Constitution that our system is kept up to date. These changes are found in certain basic statutes and historical practices of Congress, presidential practices, customs and usages of the nation, and decisions of the Supreme Court.

Congressional Elaboration

Because the framers gave Congress authority over many of the structural details of the national government, it is not necessary to amend the Constitution every time a change is needed. Rather, Congress can create legislation to meet the need. Examples of congressional elaboration appear in such legislation as the Judiciary Act of 1789, which laid the foundations of our national judicial system; in the laws establishing the organization and functions of all federal executive officials subordinate to the president; and in the rules of procedure, internal organization, and practices of Congress.

IMPEACHMENT AND REMOVAL POWER A dramatic example of congressional elaboration of our constitutional system is the use of the impeachment and removal power. An **impeachment** is a formal accusation against a public official and the first step in removal from office. Constitutional language is sparse. Look at your copy of the Constitution, and note that according to Article I—the Legislative Article—it is up to Congress to give meaning to that language. Article I gives the House of Representatives the sole power of impeachment, and the Senate the sole power to try all impeachments. When sitting for that purpose, senators "shall be on Oath or Affirmation." In the event the president is being tried, the chief justice of the United States presides. Article I also requires conviction on impeachment charges to have the agreement of two-thirds of the senators present. Judgments shall extend no further than removal from office and disqualification from holding any office under the United States, but a person convicted shall also be liable to indictment, trial, judgment, and punishment according to the law. In Article II—the Executive Article—the Constitution provides that the "President, Vice President and all civil Officers of the United States, shall be removed from Office on Impeachment for, and Conviction of, Treason, Bribery, or other High Crimes and Misdemeanors." This article also exempts cases of impeachment from the president's pardoning power. Article III—the Judicial Article—exempts cases of impeachment from the jury trial requirement. That is all the relevant constitutional language. We must look to history to answer most questions about the proper exercise of these powers.[18]

Fortunately, our experiences have triggered few acute constitutional disputes about the interpretation of impeachment procedures, and there is little history to go on. The House of Representatives has investigated 66 individuals for possible impeachment and has impeached 16 (one resigned after the impeachment resolutions were adopted, so the House voted on articles of impeachment for only 15); the Senate has convicted 7 (all federal judges). The recent spate of impeachment

Andrew Johnson is the only American president to be impeached, but the charges failed to receive the necessary two-thirds vote in the Senate.

proceedings—three since 1986—caused the Senate to decide, not without controversy, that the responsibility to hear evidence can be delegated to a committee. The Supreme Court has ruled that the Senate may so delegate and, in fact, that the House and Senate possess the constitutional authority to decide what the impeachment process shall be, subject to little, if any, judicial review.[19]

Only one president—Andrew Johnson—was impeached, in 1868, but the Senate failed by one vote to muster the two-thirds necessary to support the charges. Another president—Richard Nixon—resigned on August 9, 1974, to avoid impeachment after the House Judiciary Committee recommended three articles of impeachment against him. The House did not press the matter further, but the articles of impeachment were submitted by the committee and were "accepted" by the House.

Congressional precedents have rejected the broadest view: that the Constitution authorizes removal of officers by impeachment because of political objections to them or because of their unpopularity (a view that might have moved us more in the direction of a parliamentary type of government). Congress has also rejected the narrowest construction: that impeachable offenses are only those that involve violations of the criminal laws. Rather, the firmly established position is that impeachment and conviction are justified only if there have been serious violations of constitutional responsibilities and a clear dereliction of duty.[20]

Presidential Practices

Although the president's formal constitutional powers have not changed, the office is dramatically more important and more central today than it was in 1789. Vigorous presidents—George Washington, Thomas Jefferson, Andrew Jackson, Abraham Lincoln, Theodore Roosevelt, Woodrow Wilson, Franklin Roosevelt, Harry Truman, Lyndon Johnson, Bill Clinton—have boldly exercised their political and constitutional powers, especially during times of national crisis. Their presidential practices have become important precedents, building the power and influence of the office. Even John Tyler made his contribution to constitutional elaboration. Upon becoming president through vice-presidential succession, Tyler established the precedent that the vice-president becomes the president, not merely the acting president.

Presidential practices include **executive privilege** (the right of the president to withhold information), the impoundment of funds previously appropriated by Congress, the right to send our armed forces into hostilities, and, most important, the right to propose legislation and work actively to secure its passage by Congress. President Clinton, for example, placed health care reform on the national agenda as a priority for legislative action in his first term in office. After the defeat of his complex health plan, he pursued reform incrementally in his second term.

Foreign and economic crises as well as nuclear age realities add force to the president's role as the nation's "final arbiter." Political scientist Richard Neustadt says, "When it comes to action risking nuclear war, technology has modified the Constitution: the President, perforce, becomes the only such man in the system capable of exercising judgment under the extraordinary limits now imposed by secrecy, complexity, and time."[21] The presidency has also become the pivotal office for regulating the economy and protecting the general welfare. Plainly, the president has also become our chief legislator as well as our chief executive.

Custom and Usage

Custom and usage round out our governmental system. The development of structures *outside* the formal Constitution—such as national political parties and the extension of the suffrage within the states—have democratized our Constitution. Another example is presidential and vice-presidential debates under the sponsorship of the independent and nonprofit Commission on Presidential Debates. Through such developments, the president has become responsive to the people and has a political base different from that of Congress. Consequently, the constitutional relationship between the branches today is considerably different from that envisioned by the framers.

What is the difference between a custom and a usage? Not much. One could distinguish between them by reserving **custom** to refer to practices of nongovernmental institutions, such as political parties or of the electorate—not nominating or voting for persons who are not residents of the district they wish to represent—and reserving **usage** to refer to long-standing practices of Congress, the president, and the courts. In practice, the two terms are used interchangeably to refer both to customs of nongovernmental agencies and usages of governmental institutions, a practice we adopt here.

Judicial Interpretation

Judicial interpretation of the Constitution, especially by the Supreme Court, has played an important part in keeping the constitutional system up to date. As social and economic conditions have changed and new national demands have developed, the Supreme Court has changed its interpretation of the Constitution accordingly. In the words of Woodrow Wilson, "The Supreme Court is a constitutional convention in continuous session." Because the Constitution adapts to changing times, it does not require frequent formal amendment.

The advantages of this flexibility may be appreciated by comparing the national Constitution with the rigid and often overly specific state constitutions. Many state constitutions are so detailed that they tie the hands of the public officials. Such constitutions must be amended frequently or replaced every generation or so.

A Rigid or a Flexible Constitution?

The idea of a constantly changing system disturbs many people. How, they contend, can you have a constitutional government when the Constitution is constantly being twisted by interpretation and changed by informal methods? This view fails to distinguish between two aspects of the Constitution. As an expression of *basic and timeless personal liberties*, the Constitution does not, and should not, change. For example, a government cannot destroy free speech and still remain a constitutional government. In this sense the Constitution is unchanging. But when we con-

Presidential nominating conventions are not mentioned in the Constitution, but they are a fundamental custom of our political system today.

How should we change our Constitution?

Of the more than 170 constitutions in the world, the Constitution of the United States is the oldest and one of the most admired, yet it is constantly being updated and amended. Do you have any amendments you would like to see become part of the Constitution?

sider the Constitution as an *instrument of government* and a positive grant of power, we realize that if it does not grow with the nation it serves it will soon be pushed aside. The framers could not have conceived of the problems faced by a government of a large, powerful, and wealthy nation of about 270 million people in the last decade of the twentieth century. Although the general purposes of government remain the same—to establish liberty, promote justice, ensure domestic tranquillity, and provide for the common defense—the powers of government adequate to accomplish these purposes in 1787 are simply insufficient two hundred years later.

"We the people"—the people of today and tomorrow, not just the people of 1787—ordain and establish the Constitution. The Constitution, according to Thomas Jefferson, belongs to the living and not to the dead. So firmly did he believe this that he suggested there might be a new constitution for every generation. New constitutions have not been necessary, however, because in a less formal way, each generation has taken part in the process of developing and changing the original Constitution. Through its remarkable adaptability, our Constitution has survived democratic and industrial revolutions, the turmoil of civil war, the tensions of major depressions, and the dislocations of world wars.

CHANGING THE LETTER OF THE CONSTITUTION

The framers knew that future experiences would call for changes in the text of the Constitution and that some means for formal amendment was necessary. In Article V they gave responsibility for amending the Constitution to Congress and to the states; the president has no formal authority over constitutional amendments. Presidential veto power does not extend to them, although presidential political influence is often crucial in getting amendments proposed by Congress and ratified by the states. Nor may governors veto ratification of amendments by either state legislatures or state ratifying conventions.

Proposing Amendments

The first method for proposing amendments—and the only one used so far—is by a two-thirds vote of both houses of Congress. Dozens of resolutions proposing amendments are introduced in every session. Thousands have been introduced since 1789, most of them during the last two decades.[22] Few make any headway. Throughout our history Congress has proposed only 32 amendments, and only 21 plus the Bill of Rights have passed, including the Twenty-seventh, which was originally part of the Bill of Rights but took more than two hundred years for ratification.

In recent decades there has been a flurry of congressional attempts at constitutional amendments. None has been formally proposed by both chambers; many are currently under consideration. One being given serious consideration is the Balanced Budget Amendment. Public opinion polls show strong public support for such an amendment. It stands "unrivaled as a unifier of discontent with contemporary government. . . . No other constitutional reform emerging in this era [appeals] to such a broad spectrum of citizens."[23]

The amendment has several times secured the two-thirds vote it needs in the House but failed to do so in the Senate in 1986, 1994, and 1995. In 1996 it fell one short of the 67 needed. As a result of the 1996 elections, Republicans increased their majority in the Senate to 55 seats, and those Republican all favored such an amendment. Despite strong Democratic opposition, 1996 election increased the prospect of approval for the amendment. But when it came to vote in 1997, it again fell one short.

Nevertheless, in view of strong public support, debate is likely to continue and be centered on the details. Recent versions call for a balanced budget starting in 2002 unless three-fifths of both houses vote to suspend the requirement. The proposed amendment also contains a clause limiting the role of the courts by specifying: "The judicial power of the United States shall not extend to any case or controversy arising under this article, unless Congress specifically authorizes such judicial intervention."

Why has proposing amendments to the Constitution become such a popular pastime? In part because interest groups unhappy with Supreme Court decisions seek to overturn them. In part because groups frustrated by their inability to get things done in Congress—balancing the budget, for example—hope to bypass Congress. And in part because scholars or interest groups (not necessarily mutually exclusive categories) seek to change the procedures and processes of government to make the system more responsive.[24]

The second method for proposing amendments—by a convention called by Congress at the request of the legislatures in two-thirds of the states—has never been used. This method presents some difficult questions.[25] First, can state legislatures apply for a convention to propose specific amendments on one topic, or must they request a convention with full powers to revise the entire Constitution?[26] How long do state petitions remain alive? How should delegates be chosen? How should a convention be run?

Congress has considered bills to answer some of these questions but has not passed any, in part because most members do not wish to encourage a constitutional convention for fear that once in session it might propose amendments on any and all topics. Most proposals call for Congress to set the date and place for a convention whenever both chambers conclude that legislatures in two-thirds of the states have petitioned about a particular subject closely enough in time to one another to reflect a "contemporaneous national request" for action, variously defined as four to seven years.

Under Article V of the Constitution, Congress could call for such a convention without the concurrence of the president, who is not part of the amendatory process. Under most proposals, each state would have as many delegates to the convention as it has representatives and senators in Congress. Finally—a crucial point—the convention would be limited to considering only the subject specified in the state legislative petitions and described in the congressional call for the convention. Scholars are divided, however, on whether Congress has the authority to limit what a constitutional convention might propose.[27]

Despite several organized efforts to force Congress to call a constitutional convention (or else to propose the amendment itself), Congress has never done so.[28] We came close to a convention in 1967, when the thirty-third state legislature—only one short of the required number—petitioned Congress to call a convention to propose an amendment to set aside a Supreme Court ruling that both chambers of a state legislature must be apportioned on the basis of population. A thirty-fourth state never petitioned for a convention, and as state legislatures completed the process of reapportionment, pressure for an amendment abated.

Ratifying Amendments

After an amendment has been proposed, it must be ratified by the states. Again, two methods are provided by the Constitution: approval by the legislatures in three-fourths of the states, or approval by specially called ratifying conventions in three-fourths of the states. Congress determines which method is used. All amendments except one—the Twenty-first (to repeal the Eighteenth, the Prohibition Amendment)—have been submitted to the state legislatures for ratification.

Seven state constitutions specify that their state legislatures must ratify a proposed amendment to the U.S. Constitution by majorities of three-fifths or two-thirds of each chamber. Although a state legislature may change its mind and ratify an amendment after it has voted against ratification, the weight of opinion is that once a state has ratified an amendment, it cannot "unratify" it.[29]

AMENDING THE CONSTITUTION

The framers set up two ways to propose amendments and two ways to ratify them, and they saw to it that amendments could not be adopted by simple majorities. Each amendment must be both proposed and ratified.

Four Methods of Amending the Constitution

Methods of Proposal → **Methods of Ratification**

By two-thirds vote in both houses of Congress

- Usual method used → **3/4** By legislatures in three-fourths of the states
- Method still unused

By national constitutional convention called by Congress at the request of two-thirds of the state legislatures

- Used only once for Twenty-first Amendment → **3/4** By ratifying conventions in three-fourths of the states
- Method still unused

The Thirteenth, Fourteenth, and Fifteenth Amendments put an end to slave auctions like this and granted basic rights to all races.

The Nineteenth Amendment extended the right to vote to women.

The 27 Constitutional Amendments and Their Times for Ratification

	Amendment	Time to Ratify	Ratified		Amendment	Time to Ratify	Ratified
1–10.	Bill of Rights	2 years, 2½ months	1791	19.	Women's suffrage	1 year, 2½ months	1920
11.	Lawsuits against states	3 years, 10 months	1795	20.	Terms of office	11 months	1933
12.	Presidential elections	8½ months	1804	21.	Repeal of prohibition	9½ months	1933
13.	Abolition of slavery	10½ months	1865	22.	Limit on presidential terms	3 years, 11½ months	1951
14.	Civil rights laws	2 years, 11½ months	1868	23.	Washington, D.C., vote	9 months	1961
15.	Suffrage for all races	1 year, 1 month	1870	24.	Abolition of poll taxes	1 year, 5½ months	1964
16.	Income tax	3 years, 7½ months	1913	25.	Presidential succession	1 year, 6½ months	1967
17.	Senatorial elections	1 year, ½ month	1913	26.	18-year-old suffrage	4 months	1971
18.	Prohibition	1 year, 1½ months	1919	27.	Congressional salaries	202 years, 7½ months	1992

Submitting amendments to state legislatures rather than to ratifying conventions allows changes to be made in the Constitution without any direct expression by the voters. Legislators may have been elected before the proposed amendments were submitted to the states. In any event, state legislators are chosen because of their views on schools, taxation, or other matters, or because of their personal popularity. They are almost never elected because of their stand on proposed constitutional amendments, although in the 1970s the candidates' position on the Equal Rights Amendment (ERA) did surface as a key issue in several state legislative elections.

Procedures can make a difference. The decision to submit the Twenty-first Amendment repealing Prohibition to ratifying conventions came about because the "wets" rightly believed that repeal had a better chance of success with conventions than with the rural-dominated state legislatures. Since no convention had ever been held before, scholars debated whether Congress or the state legislatures had the authority to set up conventions. State legislatures went ahead and did so. Since voters selected delegates based on their pledge for or against ratification, the conventions were brief affairs (New Hampshire's lasted 17 minutes), so that this method amounted in essence to a direct referendum by the voters.[30] Also for tactical reasons, southern Democrats joined with eastern Republican conservatives in an unsuccessful effort to submit the Nineteenth Amendment to give women the vote, also called the Susan B. Anthony Amendment, to ratifying conventions.

The Supreme Court has said that ratification must take place within a "reasonable time" and has suggested that Congress should police this requirement. When Congress proclaims an amendment to be part of the Constitution, it must decide whether the amendment has been ratified within a reasonable time so that it is "sufficiently contemporaneous to reflect the will of the people."[31] However, Congress approved ratification of the Twenty-seventh Amendment, which had been before the nation for almost 203 years, so there seems to be no limit to what it will consider to be a "reasonable time." It is conceivable, but not likely, the Supreme Court could some day rule that the Twenty-seventh Amendment was not properly ratified.[32]

The question of reasonableness of time for ratification is not likely to become an issue with respect to future amendments. Because of their experience with the Twenty-seventh Amendment, Congress will probably be sure to continue the current practice of stipulating right in the text of proposed amendments that they will not become part of the Constitution unless ratified by the necessary number of states *within seven years* from the date of submission by Congress to the states for ratification. In fact, ratification ordinarily takes place rather quickly.[33]

Ratification Politics

Before the submission of the Equal Rights Amendment (ERA) and the D.C. Amendment, the Child Labor Amendment was the only formally proposed amendment since the Civil War that failed to be ratified. Ordinarily the existence of a political coalition sufficient to get an amendment proposed by Congress reflects enough support in the nation to ensure ratification. The failure of the ERA and the D.C. amendments to be ratified makes it clear this is not always the case.

THE EQUAL RIGHTS AMENDMENT   First introduced in 1923 and regularly thereafter, the Equal Rights Amendment (ERA) did not get much support until the 1960s. An influential book by Betty Friedan, *The Feminine Mystique* (1963), challenged stereotypes about the role of women. The National Organization for Women (NOW), formed in 1966, made ERA its central mission. By the 1970s the ERA had overwhelming support in both houses of Congress and in both national party platforms; not until 1980 did one party (the Republican) adopt a stance of neutrality. Every president from Harry Truman to Ronald Reagan, and many of their wives, endorsed the amendment. By the end of the campaign for

The Twenty-seventh Amendment: Is 203 Years a Reasonable Time?

In March 1982, Gregory Watson, a student at the University of Texas writing a paper on the Equal Rights Amendment, came across an amendment proposed in 1789 as part of the Bill of Rights that would prohibit a pay raise for members of Congress until the intervention of an election for members of the House. He found that only 6 of the original 13 states had ratified it, and that during the intervening years only 3 more states had done so.

Watson decided to start a ratification movement. He got some publicity for his efforts and, with the help of Texas Republican State Representative Don Mielke, persuaded 6 more state legislatures to ratify this long-forgotten proposed amendment. (By the way, Watson got only a C on his paper, although he "is credited with influencing 26 state legislatures to ratify the Twenty-seventh Amendment.")*

After Congress tried unsuccessfully in 1989 to avoid public anger by delegating their decision to increase congressional salaries to an independent commission, anti-Congress sentiment began to grow, and the ratification movement picked up steam. On May 7, 1992, the Michigan legislature became the thirty-eighth state to ratify the amendment, and on May 18, 1992, the United States archivist certified that it was part of the Constitution and had it printed in the *Federal Register*.

The first reaction of some congressional leaders was to question this action because the Supreme Court had made it clear that amendments must be ratified within a "reasonable time." However, when members of Congress realized that the issue could be used against them in the next election, they declared the Twenty-seventh Amendment to be "valid as part of the Constitution of the United States." The vote was 99 to 0 in the Senate, 414 to 3 in the House. Only the representative from Iowa spoke against ratification. He told his colleagues, "The principle of contemporary consensus . . . is just too important to ever waive just because it appears popular at the moment."

*Ruth Ann Strickland, "The Twenty-seventh Amendment and Constitutional Change by Stealth," *PS: Political Science and Politics* (December 1993), p. 720.

How the Amending Power Has Been Used

To Add or Subtract National Government Power

The Eleventh took some jurisdiction away from the national courts.

The Thirteenth abolished slavery and authorized Congress to legislate against it.

The Sixteenth enabled Congress to levy an income tax.

The Eighteenth authorized Congress to prohibit the manufacture, sale, or transportation of liquor.

The Twenty-first repealed the Eighteenth and gave states the authority to regulate liquor sales.

The Twenty-seventh limited the power of Congress to set members' salaries.

To Expand the Electorate and Its Power

The Fifteenth extended the suffrage to all male African Americans.

The Seventeenth took the right to elect their United States senators away from state legislatures and gave it to the voters in each state.

The Nineteenth extended suffrage to women.

The Twenty-third gave voters of the District of Columbia the right to vote for president and vice-president.

The Twenty-fourth prohibited any state from taxing the right to vote (the poll tax).

The Twenty-sixth extended the suffrage to otherwise qualified persons 18 years of age or older.

To Reduce the Electorate's Power

The Twenty-second took away from the electorate the right to elect any person to the office of president for more than two full terms.

---

ratification, more than 450 organizations with a total membership of more than 50 million were on record in support of the ERA.[34]

Soon after passage of the amendment by Congress in 1972 and submission to the states, many legislatures ratified quickly—sometimes without hearings—and by overwhelming majorities. By the end of 1972, 22 states had ratified the amendment.[35] It appeared that the ERA would soon become part of the Constitution. Then the opposition organized under the articulate leadership of Phyllis Schlafly, a prominent spokesperson for conservative causes, and the ERA became controversial.

Opponents argued that "women would not only be subject to the military draft but also assigned to combat duty. Full-time housewives and mothers would be forced to join the labor force. Furthermore, women would no longer enjoy existing advantages under state domestic relations codes and under labor law."[36] The ERA also became embroiled in the controversy over abortion. Many opponents contended that its ratification would jeopardize the power of states and Congress to regulate abortion and would compel public funding of abortions.[37]

After the ERA became controversial, state legislatures held lengthy hearings, and floor debates became heated. Legislators hid behind parliamentary procedures and avoided making a decision for as long as possible. Opposition to ratification arose chiefly in the same cluster of southern states that had opposed ratification of the Nineteenth Amendment.

As the opposition grew more active, proponents redoubled their efforts. The National Organization for Women (NOW) called for an economic boycott of cities in nonratifying states, and many organizations refused to hold their conventions in Chicago, Kansas City, Las Vegas, Miami, Atlanta, and New Orleans. In the autumn of 1978 it appeared that the ERA would fall three short of the necessary number of ratifying states before the expiration of the seven-year limit—March 22, 1979. After an extended debate, and after voting down provisions that would have authorized state legislatures to change their minds and rescind prior ratification, Congress, by a simple majority vote, extended the time limit until June 30, 1982. It was argued that because the seven-year time limit was in the accompanying enabling legislation, not in the body of the ERA amendment, it was subject to congressional modification by simple majority. Nonetheless, by the final deadline the amendment was still three state legislatures short. Its failure to be ratified made moot the pending court test of the extension's constitutionality.

The framers intended that amending the Constitution should be difficult. The ERA ratification battle demonstrated how well they planned.[38]

THE D.C. AMENDMENT The Constitution vests in Congress the right to exercise exclusive legislation over the seat of the government of the United States, that is, the District of Columbia. Congress has delegated some home rule powers, now subject to considerable supervision by a presidentially appointed control board, to those who live in Washington, D.C., or the District, as it is usually called. People who live in Washington pay federal and city taxes and are subject to federal laws.

Under the Twenty-third Amendment, the District has three electoral votes. The District's only congressional voice is a nonvoting delegate who serves on committees, attends sessions, and may participate in all debates. In 1993 a Democrat-controlled House of Representatives allowed the District delegate to vote in committees and on the floor but stipulated that the delegate's vote could never make the decisive difference on any issue. In 1995 the Republican-controlled House took that vote away.

An amendment proposed in 1978 would have given the 543,000 people of the District of Columbia two senators and the same number of representatives (one, under current law) in the House of Representatives it would have if it were a state. It would also have given the District a vote in the ratification of constitutional amendments and made possible the addition of electoral votes should an increase in population warrant it. In contrast to what it did with ERA, Congress pointedly reverted to earlier practice and placed the seven-year limit for ratification in the text of the amendment, thus precluding extending the time limit by a simple majority of both houses.

Although their initial hopes for ratification were high, advocates of the amendment knew that ratification would be difficult. Many people viewed the District as "too urban, too liberal, and too Democratic." Moreover, the coalition that pushed the D.C. Amendment through Congress failed to maintain its cohesion during the ratification struggle. Even though the D.C. Amendment passed both chambers of Congress by large margins and with impressive bipartisan support in 1978, it had been ratified by only 16 states by its deadline of August 22, 1985.

Proponents of the amendment next turned their attention to persuading Congress to admit the District to the Union as a state—except for a small portion that would remain the "seat of the Government of the United States." Statehood for the District of Columbia would accomplish all that the D.C. Amendment could have done, and more. Moreover, it would require only a simple majority vote of both houses of Congress and the approval of the president. As the Democrats stood to gain the District's senators, the Democratic party platform of 1992 and 1996 pledged support for statehood for the District, and President Clinton declared, "It is fundamentally unfair that residents of the District are denied full representation and participation in our national life."[39]

On November 21, 1993, the House of Representatives voted 227 to 153 against statehood, but Eleanor Holmes Norton, the District's nonvoting delegate, and other statehood proponents declared a victory in that they got committee hearings, a floor debate, and a vote on the bill. They consider that the "issue now has national visibility." However, any immediate hope for statehood was dashed by the 1994 and 1996 elections, when Republicans won congressional majorities. Furthermore, the District in effect lost even its home rule powers for at least eight years when in 1995, as a result of the city's financial crisis, Congress created a Board of Control consisting of five members appointed by the president. The Board has authority over the District's spending, financial planning, and borrowing, and is mandated to bring the District's budget into balance.[40]

How the Amending Power Has Been Used (continued)

To Limit State Government Power

The Thirteenth abolished slavery.

The Fourteenth granted national citizenship and prohibited states from abridging privileges of national citizenship; from denying persons life, liberty, and property without due process; and from denying persons equal protection of the laws. This amendment has come to be interpreted as imposing restraints on state powers in every area of public life.

To Make Structural Changes in Government

The Twelfth corrected deficiencies in the operation of the Electoral College that were revealed by the development of a two-party national system.

The Twentieth altered the calendar for congressional sessions and shortened the time between the election of presidents and their assumption of office.

The Twenty-fifth provided procedures for filling vacancies in the vice-presidency and for determining whether presidents are unable to perform their duties.

POLITICS ONLINE

Using the Internet to Amend the Constitution

One of the strengths of our Constitution is that it can be amended. Today, various groups use the Internet to propose constitutional amendments and circulate petitions to be delivered to Congress. The agenda of the Internet constitutional amendments reflects both conservative and liberal positions. Examples of proposed constitutional changes include the elimination of federal taxes, the elimination of lawyers in public office, the elimination of the death penalty, the establishment of world peace, and term limits for public officials.

One home page begins by saying, "Dear American, We live in the only industrialized nation in the world that still supports capital punishment." The letter ends by saying, "Join me in *signing* this petition on the Web."

http://www-unix.oit.umass.edu/-mellis/dp/frontpage.html

Two other resources on the Web related to *The Federalist* essays are:

http://www.mcs.net/knautz/fed/fedpaper.html

and a page with links to the historical archives of the University of Illinois:

knautzer@mcs.net

SUMMARY

1. Our Constitution both grants and limits powers. The framers established a government by ordinary people. They did not anticipate Americans would be so virtuous and civic minded that they could be trusted to operate a government without checks and balances. The framers were suspicious of people, especially of those having political power, so they separated and distributed the powers of the newly created national government in a variety of ways.

2. The framers were also concerned to create a national government strong enough to solve national problems. Thus they gave the national government substantial grants of power, but these grants were made with such broad strokes that it has been possible for the constitutional system to remain flexible and adapt to changing conditions.

3. Although the American governmental system has its roots in British traditions, our separation of powers and checks and balances systems differ sharply from the British system of concentrated responsibility. It is also different because our courts have the power of judicial review.

4. The constitutional system has been modified over time, adapting to new conditions through congressional elaboration, presidential practices, customs and usages, and judicial interpretation.

5. Although adaptable, the Constitution itself needs to be altered from time to time, and the document provides a procedure for its own amendment. An amendment must be both proposed and ratified: proposed by either a two-thirds vote in each chamber of Congress or by a national convention called by Congress on petition of the legislatures in two-thirds of the states; ratified either by the legislatures in three-fourths of the states or by specially called ratifying conventions in three-fourths of the states. The Constitution has been formally amended 27 times. The usual method has been proposal by a two-thirds vote in both houses of Congress and ratification by the legislatures in three-fourths of the states.

FURTHER READING

BRUCE A. ACKERMAN, *We the People* (Harvard University Press, Belknap Press, 1991).

LANCE BANNING, *The Sacred Fire of Liberty: James Madison and the Founding of the Federal Republic* (Cornell University Press, 1995).

WILBOURN E. BENTON, ED., *1787: Drafting the U.S. Constitution* (Texas A&M Press, 1986).

RICHARD B. BERNSTEIN, *Amending America: If We Love the Constitution So Much Why Do We Keep Trying to Change It?* (Time, 1993).

JAMES BRYCE, *The American Commonwealth*, vols. 1 and 2 (Macmillan, 1889).

JAMES MACGREGOR BURNS, *The Vineyard of Liberty* (Knopf, 1982).

RUSSELL L. CAPLAN, *Constitutional Brinkmanship: Amending the Constitution by National Convention* (Oxford University Press, 1988).

ROBERT LOWRY CLINTON, *Marbury v. Madison and Judicial Review* (University Press of Kansas, 1989).

SCOTT DOUGLAS GERBER, *To Secure These Rights: The Declaration of Independence and Constitutional Interpretation* (New York University Press, 1995).

CHARLES HARDIN, *Constitutional Reform in America: Essays on the Separation of Powers* (Iowa State University Press, 1989).

BARBARA B. KNIGHT, *Separation of Powers in the American Political System* (George Mason University Press, 1989).

DAVID E. KYVIG, *Explicit and Authentic Acts: Amending the U.S. Constitution, 1776–1995* (University Press of Kansas, 1996).

LIBRARY OF CONGRESS, CONGRESSIONAL RESEARCH SERVICE, *The Constitution of the United States of America: Analysis and Interpretation*, Senate Document 100-9 (U.S. Government Printing Office, 1991).

DONALD G. MATHEWS AND JANE SHERRON DE HART, *Sex, Gender, and the Politics of ERA: North Carolina and the Nation* (Oxford University Press, 1990).

DREW R. MCCOY, *The Last of the Fathers: James Madison and the Republican Legacy* (Columbia University Press, 1989).

FORREST MCDONALD, *Novus Ordo Seclorum: The Intellectual Origins of the Constitution* (University Press of Kansas, 1985).

J. W. PELTASON, *Understanding the Constitution*, 14 ed. (Harcourt Brace, 1997).

BARBARA A. PERRY, *Unfounded Fears: Myths and Realities of a Constitutional Convention* (Greenwood Press, 1989).

JAMES L. SUNDQUIST, *Constitutional Reform and Effective Government* (Brookings Institution, 1986).

JOHN R. VILE, *The Constitutional Amending Process in American Political Thought* (Praeger, 1992).

JOHN R. VILE, *Rewriting the United States Constitution: An Examination of Proposals from Reconstruction to the Present* (Praeger, 1991).

On Reading the Constitution

More than two hundred years after its ratification, our Constitution remains the operating charter of our republic. It is neither self-explanatory nor a comprehensive description of our constitutional rules. Still, it remains the starting point. Many Americans who swear by the Constitution have never read it seriously, although copies can be found in the back of most American government and American history textbooks.

Justice Hugo Black, who served on the Supreme Court for 34 years, kept a copy of the Constitution with him at all times. He read it often. Reading the Constitution would be a good way for you to begin (and then reread again to end) your study of the government of the United States. Thus, we have included a copy of it at this point in the book. Please read it carefully.

The Constitution
of the
United States

The Preamble

We the People of the United States, in Order to form a more perfect Union, establish Justice, insure domestic Tranquility, provide for the common defense, promote the general Welfare, and secure the Blessings of Liberty to ourselves and our Posterity, do ordain and establish this Constitution for the United States of America.

Article I—The Legislative Article

Legislative Power

Section 1 All legislative Powers herein granted shall be vested in a Congress of the United States, which shall consist of a Senate and House of Representatives.

House of Representatives: Composition; Qualifications; Apportionment; Impeachment Power

Section 2 The House of Representatives shall be composed of Members chosen every second Year by the People of the several States, and the Electors in each State shall have the Qualifications requisite for Electors of the most numerous Branch of the State Legislature.

No Person shall be a Representative who shall not have attained to the Age of twenty five Years, and been seven Years a Citizen of the United States, and who shall not, when elected, be an Inhabitant of that State in which he shall be chosen.

Representatives and direct Taxes[1] shall be apportioned among the several States which may be included within this Union, according to their respective Numbers, *which shall be determined by adding to the whole Number of free Persons, including those bound to Service for a Term of Years, and excluding Indians not taxed, three fifths of all other Persons.*[2] The actual Enumeration shall be made within three Years after the first Meeting of the Congress of the United States, and within every subsequent Term of ten Years, in such Manner as they shall by Law direct. The Number of Representatives shall not exceed one for every thirty Thousand, but each State shall have at least one Representative; and until each enumeration shall be made, the State of New Hampshire shall be entitled to chuse three, Massachusetts eight, Rhode-Island and Providence Plantations one, Connecticut five, New-York six, New Jersey four, Pennsylvania eight, Delaware one, Maryland six, Virginia ten, North Carolina five, South Carolina five, and Georgia three.

When vacancies happen in the Representation from any State, the Executive Authority thereof shall issue Writs of Election to fill such Vacancies.

The House of Representatives shall chuse their Speaker and other Officers; and shall have the sole Power of Impeachment.

Senate Composition: Qualifications, Impeachment Trials

Section 3 The Senate of the United States shall be composed of two Senators from each State, *chosen by the Legislature thereof,*[3] for six Years; and each Senator shall have one Vote.

Immediately after they shall be assembled in Consequence of the first Election, they shall be divided as equally as may be into three Classes. The Seats of the Senators of the first Class shall be vacated at the Expiration of the second Year, of the second Class at the Expiration of the fourth Year, and of the third Class at the Expiration of the sixth Year, so that one third may be chosen every second Year; *and if Vacancies happen by Resignation, or otherwise, during the Recess of the Legislature of any State, the Executive thereof may make temporary Appointments until the next Meeting of the Legislature, which shall then fill such Vacancies.*[4]

No person shall be a Senator who shall not have attained to the Age of thirty Years, and been nine Years a Citizen of the United States, and who shall not, when elected, be an inhabitant of that State for which he shall be chosen.

The Vice President of the United States shall be President of the Senate, but shall have no Vote, unless they be equally divided.

The Senate shall chuse their other Officers, and also a President pro tempore, in the Absence of the Vice President, or when he shall exercise the Office of President of the United States.

The Senate shall have the sole Power to try all Impeachments. When sitting for that Purpose, they shall be on Oath or Affirmation. When the President of the United States is tried, the Chief Justice shall preside: And no Person shall be convicted without the Concurrence of two thirds of the Members present.

Judgment in Cases of Impeachment shall not extend further than to removal from Office, and disqualification to hold and enjoy any Office of honor, Trust or Profit under the United States; but the Party convicted shall nevertheless be liable and subject to Indictment, Trial, Judgment and Punishment, according to law.

Congressional Elections: Times, Places, Manner

Section 4 The Times, Places and Manner of holding Elections for Senators and Representatives, shall be prescribed in each State by the Legislature thereof; but the Congress may at any time by Law make or alter such Regulations, except as to the Places of chusing Senators.

The Congress shall assemble at least once in every Year, *and such Meeting shall be on the first Monday in December, unless they shall by Law appoint a different Day.*[5]

---

[1]Modified by the 16th Amendment
[2]Replaced by Section 2, 14th Amendment

[3]Repealed by the 17th Amendment
[4]Modified by the 17th Amendment
[5]Changed by the 20th Amendment

Powers and Duties of the Houses

Section 5   Each House shall be the Judge of the Elections, Returns and Qualifications of its own Members, and a Majority of each shall constitute a Quorum to do Business; but a smaller Number may adjourn from day to day, and may be authorized to compel the Attendance of absent Members, in such Manner, and under the Penalties as each House may provide.

Each House may determine the Rules of its Proceedings, punish its Members for disorderly Behaviour, and, with the Concurrence of two thirds, expel a Member.

Each House shall keep a Journal of its Proceedings, and from time to time publish the same, excepting such Parts as may in their Judgment require Secrecy; and the Yeas and Nays of the Members of either House on any question shall, at the Desire of one fifth of those Present, be entered on the Journal.

Neither House, during the Session of Congress, shall, without the Consent of the other, adjourn for more than three days, nor to any other place than that in which the two Houses shall be sitting.

Rights of Members

Section 6   The Senators and Representatives shall receive a Compensation for their Services, to be ascertained by Law, and paid out of the Treasury of the United States. They shall in all Cases, except Treason, Felony and Breach of the Peace, be privileged from Arrest during their Attendance at the Session of their respective Houses, and in going to and returning from the same; and for any Speech or Debate in either House, they shall not be questioned in any other Place.

No Senator or Representative, shall, during the time for which he was elected, be appointed to any civil Office under the Authority of the United States, which shall have been created, or the Emoluments whereof shall have been encreased during such time; and no Person holding any Office under the United States, shall be a Member of either House during his Continuance in Office.

Legislative Powers: Bills and Resolutions

Section 7   All Bills for raising Revenue shall originate in the House of Representatives; but the Senate may propose or concur with Amendments as on other Bills.

Every Bill which shall have passed the House of Representatives and the Senate, shall, before it becomes a Law, be presented to the President of the United States; if he approve he shall sign it, but if not he shall return it, with his Objections to that House in which it shall have originated, who shall enter the Objections at large on their Journal, and proceed to reconsider it. If after such Reconsideration two thirds of that House shall agree to pass the Bill, it shall be sent, together with the Objections, to the other House, by which it shall likewise be reconsidered, and if approved by two thirds of that House, it shall become a Law. But in all such Cases the Votes of both Houses shall be determined by yeas and Nays, and the Names of the Persons voting for and against the Bill shall be entered on the Journal of each House respectively. If any Bill shall not be returned by the President within ten Days (Sundays excepted) after it shall have been presented to him, the Same shall be a Law, in like Manner as if he had signed it, unless the Congress by their Adjournment prevent its Return, in which Case it shall not be a Law.

Every Order, Resolution, or Vote to which the Concurrence of the Senate and House of Representatives may be necessary (except on a question of Adjournment) shall be presented to the President of the United States; and before the Same shall take Effect, shall be approved by him, or being disapproved by him, shall be repassed by two thirds of the Senate and House of Representatives, according to the Rules and Limitations prescribed in the Case of a Bill.

Powers of Congress

Section 8   The Congress shall have Power To lay and collect Taxes, Duties, Imposts and Excises, to pay the Debts and provide for the common Defence and general Welfare of the United States; but all Duties, Imposts and Excises shall be uniform throughout the United States.

To borrow Money on the Credit of the United States;

To regulate Commerce with foreign Nations, and among the several States, and with the Indian Tribes;

To establish an uniform Rule of Naturalization, and uniform Laws on the subject of Bankruptcies throughout the United States;

To coin Money, regulate the Value thereof, and of foreign Coin, and fix the Standard of Weights and Measures;

To provide for the Punishment of counterfeiting the Securities and current Coin of the United States;

To establish Post Offices and post Roads;

To promote the Progress of Science and useful Arts, by securing for limited Times to Authors and Inventors the exclusive Right to their respective Writings and Discoveries;

To constitute Tribunals inferior to the supreme Court;

To define and punish Piracies and Felonies committed on the high Seas, and Offences against the Law of Nations;

To declare War, grant Letters of Marque and Reprisal, and make Rules concerning Captures on Land and Water;

To raise and support Armies, but no Appropriation of Money to that Use shall be for a longer Term than two Years;

To provide and maintain a Navy;

To make Rules for the Government and Regulation of the land and naval Forces;

To provide for calling for the Militia to execute the Laws of the Union, suppress Insurrections and repel Invasions;

To provide for organizing, arming, and disciplining, the Militia, and for governing such Part of them as may be employed in the Service of the United States, reserving to the States respectively, the Appointment of the Officers, and the Authority of training the Militia according to the discipline prescribed by Congress;

To exercise exclusive Legislation in all Cases whatsoever, over such District (not exceeding ten Miles square) as may, by Cession of particular States, and the Acceptance of Congress, become the Seat of the Government of the United States, and to exercise like Authority over all Places purchased by the Consent of the Legislature of the State in which the Same shall be, for the Erection of Forts, Magazines, Arsenals, dock-Yards, and other needful Buildings;—And

To make all Laws which shall be necessary and proper for carrying into Execution the foregoing Powers, and all other Powers vested by this Constitution in the Government of the United States, or in any Department or Officer thereof.

Powers Denied to Congress

Section 9   The Migration of Importation of such Persons as any of the States now existing shall think proper to admit, shall not be prohibited by the Congress prior to the Year one thousand eight hundred and eight, but a Tax or Duty may be imposed on such Importation, not exceeding ten dollars for each Person.

The privilege of the Writ of Habeas Corpus shall not be suspended, unless when in Cases of Rebellion or Invasion the public Safety may require it.

No Bill of Attainder or ex post facto Laws shall be passed.

No Capitation, or other direct, Tax shall be laid, unless in Proportion to the Census or Enumeration herein before directed to be taken.[6]

No Tax or Duty shall be laid on Articles exported from any State.

No Preference shall be given by any Regulation of Commerce or Revenue to the Ports of one State over those of another; nor shall Vessels bound to, or from, one State, be obliged to enter, clear, or pay Duties in another.

---

[6]Modified by the 16th Amendment

No Money shall be drawn from the Treasury, but in Consequence of Appropriations made by Law; and a regular Statement and Account of the Receipts and Expenditures of all public Money shall be published from time to time.

No Title of Nobility shall be granted by the United States; And no Person holding any Office of Profit or Trust under them, shall, without the Consent of Congress, accept of any present, Emolument, Office, or Title, of any kind whatever, from any King, Prince, or foreign State.

Powers Denied to the States

Section 10   No State shall enter into any Treaty, Alliance, or Confederation; grant Letters of Marque and Reprisal; coin Money; emit Bills of Credit; make any Thing but gold and silver Coin a Tender in Payment of Debts; pass any Bill of Attainder, ex post facto Law, or Law impairing the Obligation of Contracts, or grant any Title of Nobility.

No State shall, without the Consent of the Congress, lay any Imposts or Duties on Imports or Exports, except what may be absolutely necessary for executing its inspection Laws: and the net Produce of all Duties and Imposts, laid by any State on Imports or Exports, shall be for the Use of the Treasury of the United States; and all such Laws shall be subject to the Revision and Controul of the Congress.

No State shall, without the Consent of Congress, lay any Duty of Tonnage, keep Troops, or Ships of War in time of Peace, enter into any Agreement or Compact with another State, or with a foreign Power, or engage in War, unless actually invaded, or in such imminent Danger as will not admit of Delay.

ARTICLE II—THE EXECUTIVE ARTICLE

Nature and Scope of Presidential Power

Section 1   The executive Power shall be vested in a President of the United States of America. He shall hold his Office during the Term of four Years and, together with the Vice President, chosen for the same Term, be elected as follows:

Each State shall appoint, in such Manner as the Legislature thereof may direct, a Number of Electors, equal to the whole Number of Senators and Representatives to which the State may be entitled in the Congress: but no Senator or Representative, or Person holding an Office of Trust or Profit under the United States, shall be appointed an Elector.

The Electors shall meet in their respective States, and vote by Ballot for two Persons, of whom one at least shall not be an Inhabitant of the same State with themselves. And they shall make a List of all the Persons voted for, and of the Number of Votes for each; which List they shall sign and certify, and transmit sealed to the Seat of the Government of the United States, directed to the President of the Senate. The President of the Senate shall, in the Presence of the Senate and House of Representatives, open all the Certificates, and the Votes shall then be counted. The Person having the greatest Number of Votes shall be the President, if such Number be a Majority of the whole Number of Electors appointed; and if there be more than one who have such Majority and have an equal Number of Votes, then the House of Representatives shall immediately chuse by Ballot one of them for President; and if no person have a Majority, then from the five highest on the List the said House shall in like Manner chuse the President. But in chusing the President, the Votes shall be taken by States, the Representation from each State having one Vote; A quorum for this Purpose shall consist of a Member or Members from two thirds of the States, and a Majority of all the States shall be necessary to a Choice. In every Case, after the Choice of the President, the person having the greatest Number of Votes of the Electors shall be the Vice President. But if there should remain two or more who have equal Vote, the Senate shall chuse from them by Ballot the Vice President.[7]

The Congress may determine the Time of chusing the Electors, and the Day on which they shall give their Votes; which Day shall be the same throughout the United States.

No Person except a natural born Citizen, or a Citizen of the United States, at the time of the Adoption of this Constitution, shall be eligible to the Office of President; neither shall any Person be eligible to that Office who shall not have attained to the Age of thirty five Years, and been fourteen Years a Resident within the United States.

In Case of the Removal of the President from Office, or of his Death, Resignation, or Inability to discharge the Powers and Duties of the said Office, the same shall devolve on the Vice President, and the Congress may by Law provide for the Case of Removal, Death, Resignation, or Inability, both of the President and Vice President, declaring what Officer shall then act as President, and such Officer shall act accordingly, until the Disability be removed, or a President shall be elected.[8]

The President shall, at stated Times, receive for his Services, a Compensation, which shall neither be encreased nor diminished during the Period of which he shall have been elected, and he shall not receive within that Period any other Emolument from the United States, or any of them.

Before he enter on the Execution of his Office, he shall take the following Oath or Affirmation:—"I do solemnly swear (or affirm) that I will faithfully execute the Office of President of the United States, and will to the best of my Ability, preserve, protect and defend the Constitution of the United States."

Powers and Duties of the President

Section 2   The President shall be the Commander in Chief of the Army and Navy of the United States, and of the Militia of the several States, when called into the actual Service of the United States, he may require the Opinion, in writing, of the principal Officer in each of the executive Departments, upon any Subject relating to the Duties of their respective Offices, and he shall have the Power to grant Reprieves and Pardons for Offences against the United States, except in Cases of Impeachment.

He shall have Power, by and with the Advice and Consent of the Senate to make Treaties, provided two thirds of the Senators present concur; and he shall nominate, and by and with the Advice and Consent of the Senate, shall appoint Ambassadors, other public Ministers and Consuls, Judges of the supreme Court, and all other Officers of the United States, whose Appointments are not herein otherwise provided for, and which shall be established by Law: but the Congress may by Law vest the Appointment of such inferior Officers, as they think proper, in the President alone, in the Courts of Law, or in the Heads of Departments.

The President shall have Power to fill up all Vacancies that may happen during the Recess of the Senate, by granting Commissions which shall expire at the End of their next Session.

Section 3   He shall from time to time give to the Congress Information of the State of the Union, and recommend to their Consideration such Measures as he shall judge necessary and expedient; he may, on extraordinary Occasions, convene both Houses, or either of them, and in Case of Disagreement between them, with Respect to the Time of Adjournment, he may adjourn them to such Time as he shall think proper; he shall receive Ambassadors and other public Ministers; he shall take Care that the Laws be faithfully executed, and shall Commission all the Officers of the United States.

Section 4   The President, Vice President and all civil Officers of the United States, shall be removed from Office on Impeachment for, and Conviction of, Treason, Bribery, or other High Crimes and Misdemeanors.

ARTICLE III—THE JUDICIAL ARTICLE

Judicial Power, Courts, Judges

Section 1   The judicial Power of the United States, shall be vested in one supreme Court, and in such inferior Courts as the Congress may from time to time ordain and establish. The Judges, both the supreme and inferior Courts,

---

[7]Changed by the 12th and 20th Amendments

[8]Modified by the 25th Amendment

shall hold their Offices during good Behaviour, and shall, at stated Times, receive for their Services, a Compensation, which shall not be diminished during their Continuance in Office.

Jurisdiction

Section 2   The judicial Power shall extend to all Cases, in Law and Equity, arising under this Constitution, the Laws of the United States, and Treaties made, or which shall be made, under their Authority;—to all Cases affecting Ambassadors, other public Ministers and Consuls;—to all Cases of admiralty and maritime Jurisdiction;—to Controversies to which the United States shall be a Party;—to Controversies between two or more States; *between a State and Citizens of another State;*[9]—between Citizens of different States;—between Citizens of the same State claiming Lands under Grants of different States, and between a State, or the Citizens thereof, and foreign States, Citizens, or Subjects.

In all Cases affecting Ambassadors, other public Ministers and Consuls, and those in which a State shall be Party, the supreme Court shall have original Jurisdiction. In all the other Cases before mentioned, the supreme Court shall have appellate Jurisdiction, both as to Law and Fact, with such Exceptions, and under such Regulations as Congress shall make.

The Trial of all Crimes, except in Cases of Impeachment, shall be by Jury; and such Trial shall be held in the State where the said Crimes shall have been committed; but when not committed within any State, the Trial shall be at such Place or Places as the Congress may by Law have directed.

Treason

Section 3   Treason against the United States, shall consist only in levying War against them, or in adhering to their Enemies, giving them Aid and Comfort. No Persons shall be convicted of Treason unless on the Testimony of two Witnesses to the same overt Act, or on Confession in open Court.

The Congress shall have Power to declare the Punishment of Treason, but no Attainder of Treason shall work Corruption of Blood, or Forfeiture except during the Life of the Person attainted.

ARTICLE IV—INTERSTATE RELATIONS

Full Faith and Credit Clause

Section 1   Full Faith and Credit shall be given in each State to the public Acts, Records, and judicial Proceedings of every other State. And the Congress may by general Laws prescribe the Manner in which such Acts, Records and Proceedings shall be proved, and the Effect thereof.

Privileges and Immunities; Interstate Extradition

Section 2   The Citizens of each State shall be entitled to all Privileges and Immunities of Citizens in the several States.

A person charged in any State with Treason, Felony or other Crime, who shall flee from Justice, and be found in another State, shall on Demand of the executive Authority of the State from which he fled, be delivered up, to be removed to the State having jurisdiction of the Crime.

No person held to Service or Labour in one State, under the Laws thereof, escaping into another, shall, in Consequence of any Law or Regulation therein, be discharged from such Service or Labour, but shall be delivered up on Claim of the Party to whom such Service or Labour may be due.[10]

Admission of States

Section 3   New States may be admitted by the Congress into this Union; but no new State shall be formed or erected within the Jurisdiction of any other State; nor any State to be formed by the Junction of two or more States, or Parts of States, without the Consent of the Legislatures of the States concerned as well as of the Congress.

The Congress shall have Power to dispose of and make all needful Rules and Regulations respecting the Territory or other Property belonging to the United States; and nothing in this Constitution shall be so construed as to Prejudice any Claims of the United States, or of any particular State.

Republican Form of Government

Section 4   The United States shall guarantee to every State in this Union a Republican Form of Government, and shall protect each of them against Invasion; and on Application of the Legislature, or of the Executive (when the Legislature cannot be convened) against domestic Violence.

ARTICLE V—THE AMENDING POWER

The Congress, whenever two thirds of both Houses shall deem it necessary, shall propose Amendments to this Constitution, or, on the Application of the Legislatures of two thirds of several States, shall call a Convention for proposing Amendments, which, in either Case, shall be valid to all Intents and Purposes, as Part of this Constitution, when ratified by the Legislatures of three fourths of the several States, or by Conventions in three fourths thereof, as the one or the other Mode of Ratification may be proposed by the Congress; Provided that no Amendment which may be made prior to the Year One thousand eight hundred and eight shall in any Manner affect the first and fourth Clauses in the Ninth Section of the first Article; and that no State, without its Consent, shall be deprived of its equal Suffrage in the Senate.

ARTICLE VI—THE SUPREMACY ACT

All Debts contracted and Engagements entered into, before the Adoption of this Constitution, shall be as valid against the United States under the Constitution, as under the Confederation.

This Constitution, and the Laws of the United States which shall be made in Pursuance thereof; and all Treaties made, or which shall be made, under the Authority of the United States, shall be the supreme Law of the Land; and the Judges in every State shall be bound thereby, any Thing in the Constitution or Laws of any State to the Contrary notwithstanding.

The Senators and Representatives before mentioned, and the Members of the several State Legislatures, and all executive and judicial Officers, both of the United States and of the several States, shall be bound by Oath or Affirmation, to support this Constitution; but no religious Test shall ever be required as a Qualification to any Office or public Trust under the United States.

ARTICLE VII—RATIFICATION

The Ratification of the Conventions of nine States, shall be sufficient for the Establishment of this Constitution between the States so ratifying the Same.

Done in Convention by the Unanimous Consent of the States present the Seventeenth Day of September in the Year of our Lord one thousand seven hundred and Eighty seven and of the Independence of the United States of America the Twelfth *In Witness whereof We have hereunto subscribed our Names.*

AMENDMENTS

The Bill of Rights

[The first ten amendments were ratified on December 15, 1791, and form what is known as the "Bill of Rights."]

AMENDMENT 1—RELIGION, SPEECH, ASSEMBLY, AND POLITICS

Congress shall make no law respecting an establishment of religion, or prohibiting the free exercise thereof; or abridging the freedom of speech, or of the press; or the right of the people peaceably to assemble, and to petition the government for a redress of grievances.

---

[9]Modified by the 11th Amendment
[10]Repealed by the 13th Amendment

AMENDMENT 2—MILITIA AND THE RIGHT TO BEAR ARMS

A well regulated Militia, being necessary to the security of a free State, the right of the people to keep and bear Arms, shall not be infringed.

AMENDMENT 3—QUARTERING OF SOLDIERS

No Soldier shall, in time of peace be quartered in any house, without the consent of the Owner, nor in time of war, but in manner to be prescribed by law.

AMENDMENT 4—SEARCHES AND SEIZURES

The right of the people to be secure in their persons, houses, papers, and effects, against unreasonable searches and seizures, shall not be violated, and no Warrants shall issue, but upon probable cause, supported by Oath or affirmation, and particularly describing the place to be searched, and the persons or things to be seized.

AMENDMENT 5—GRAND JURIES, SELF-INCRIMINATION, DOUBLE JEOPARDY, DUE PROCESS, AND EMINENT DOMAIN

No person shall be held to answer for a capital, or otherwise infamous crime, unless on a presentment or indictment of a Grand jury, except in cases arising in the land or naval forces, or in the Militia, when in actual service in time of War or public danger; nor shall any person be subject for the same offence to be twice put in jeopardy of life or limb; nor shall be compelled in any criminal case to be a witness against himself, nor be deprived of life, liberty, or property, without due process of law; nor shall private property be taken for public use, without just compensation.

AMENDMENT 6—CRIMINAL COURT PROCEDURES

In all criminal prosecutions, the accused shall enjoy the right to a speedy and public trial, by an impartial jury of the State and district wherein the crime shall have been committed, which district shall have been previously ascertained by law, and to be informed of the nature and cause of the accusation; to be confronted with the witnesses against him; to have compulsory process for obtaining Witnesses in his favor, and to have the Assistance of Counsel for his defense.

AMENDMENT 7—TRIAL BY JURY IN COMMON LAW CASES

In Suits at common law, where the value in controversy shall exceed twenty dollars, the right of trial by jury shall be preserved, and no fact tried by a jury shall be otherwise re-examined in any Court of the United States, than according to the rules of the common law.

AMENDMENT 8—BAIL, CRUEL AND UNUSUAL PUNISHMENT

Excessive bail shall not be required, nor excessive fines imposed, nor cruel and unusual punishments inflicted.

AMENDMENT 9—RIGHTS RETAINED BY THE PEOPLE

The enumeration in the Constitution, of certain rights, shall not be construed to deny or disparage others retained by the people.

AMENDMENT 10—RESERVED POWERS OF THE STATES

The powers not delegated to the United States by the Constitution, nor prohibited by it to the States, are reserved to the States respectively, or to the people.

AMENDMENT 11—SUITS AGAINST THE STATES
[Ratified February 7, 1795]

The Judicial power of the United States shall not be construed to extend to any suit in law or equity, commenced or prosecuted against one of the United States by Citizens of another State, or by Citizens or Subjects of any Foreign State.

AMENDMENT 12—ELECTION OF THE PRESIDENT
[Ratified June 15, 1804]

The Electors shall meet in their respective states, and vote by ballot for President and Vice-President, one of whom, at least, shall not be an inhabitant of the same state with themselves; they shall name in their ballots the person voted for as President, and in distinct ballots the person voted for as Vice-President, and they shall make distinct lists of all persons voted for as President, and of all persons voted for as Vice-President, and of the number of votes for each, which lists they shall sign and certify, and transmit sealed to the seat of the government of the United States, directed to the President of the Senate;—The President of the Senate shall, in presence of the Senate and House of Representatives, open all the certificates and the votes shall then be counted;—The person having the greatest number of votes for President, shall be the President, if such number be a majority of the whole number of Electors appointed; and if no person have such majority, then from the persons having the highest numbers not exceeding three on the list of those voted for as President, the House of Representatives shall choose immediately, by ballot, the President. But in choosing the President, the votes shall be taken by states, the representation from each state having one vote; a quorum for this purpose shall consist of a member or members from two-thirds of the states, and a majority of all states shall be necessary to a choice. And if the House of Representatives shall not choose a President whenever the right of choice shall devolve upon them, *before the fourth day of March next following*, then the Vice-President shall act as President, as in the case of the death or other constitutional disability of the President.[11] The person having the greatest number of votes as Vice-President, shall be the Vice-President, if such a number be a majority of the whole numbers of Electors appointed, and if no person have a majority, then from the two highest numbers on the list, the Senate shall choose the Vice-President; a quorum for the purpose shall consist of two-thirds of the whole number of Senators, and a majority of the whole number shall be necessary to a choice. But no person constitutionally ineligible to the office of President shall be eligible to that of Vice-President of the United States.

AMENDMENT 13—PROHIBITION OF SLAVERY
[Ratified December 6, 1865]

Section 1   Neither slavery nor involuntary servitude, except as a punishment for crime whereof the party shall have been duly convicted, shall exist within the United States, or any place subject to their jurisdiction.

Section 2   Congress shall have power to enforce this article by appropriate legislation.

AMENDMENT 14—CITIZENSHIP, DUE PROCESS, AND EQUAL PROTECTION OF THE LAWS
[Ratified July 9, 1868]

Section 1   All persons born or naturalized in the United States, and subject to the jurisdiction thereof, are citizens of the United States and of the State wherein they reside. No State shall make or enforce any law which shall abridge the privileges or immunities of citizens of the United States; nor shall

---

[11]Changed by the 20th Amendment

any State deprive any person of life, liberty, or property, without due process of law; nor deny to any person within its jurisdiction the equal protection of the laws.

Section 2 Representatives shall be apportioned among the several States according to their respective numbers, counting the whole number of persons in each State, excluding Indians not taxed. But when the right to vote at any election for the choice of electors for President and Vice President of the United States, Representatives in Congress, the Executive and Judicial officers of a State, or the members of the Legislature thereof, is denied to any of the male inhabitants of such State, being twenty-one[12] years of age, and citizens of the United States, or in any way abridged, except for participation in rebellion, or other crime, the basis of representation therein shall be reduced in the proportion which the number of such male citizens shall bear to the whole number of male citizens twenty-one years of age in such State.

Section 3 No person shall be a Senator or Representative in Congress, or elector of President and Vice President, or hold any office, civil or military, under the United States, or under any State, who, having previously taken an oath, as a member of Congress, or as an officer of the United States, or as a member of any State legislature, or as an executive or judicial officer of any State, to support the Constitution of the United States, shall have engaged in insurrection or rebellion against the same, or given aid or comfort to the enemies thereof. But Congress may by a vote of two-thirds of each House, remove such disability.

Section 4 The validity of the public debt of the United States, authorized by law, including debts incurred for payment of pensions and bounties for services in suppressing insurrection or rebellion, shall not be questioned. But neither the United States nor any State shall assume or pay any debt or obligation incurred in aid of insurrection or rebellion against the United States, or any claim for the loss or emancipation of any slave; but all such debts, obligations and claims shall be held illegal and void.

Section 5 The Congress shall have power to enforce, by appropriate legislation, the provisions of this article.

AMENDMENT 15—THE RIGHT TO VOTE
[Ratified February 3, 1870]

Section 1 The right of citizens of the United States to vote shall not be denied or abridged by the United States or by any State on account of race, color, or previous condition of servitude.

Section 2 The Congress shall have power to enforce this article by appropriate legislation.

AMENDMENT 16—INCOME TAXES
[Ratified February 3, 1913]

The Congress shall have power to lay and collect taxes on incomes, from whatever source derived, without apportionment among the several States, and without regard to any census or enumeration.

AMENDMENT 17—DIRECT ELECTION OF SENATORS
[Ratified April 8, 1913]

The Senate of the United States shall be composed of two Senators from each State, elected by the people thereof, for six years; and each Senator shall have one vote. The electors in each State shall have the qualifications requisite for electors of the most numerous branch of the State legislatures.

When vacancies happen in the representation of any State in the Senate, the executive authority of such State shall issue writs of election to fill such vacancies: *Provided*, That the Legislature of any State may empower the executive thereof to make temporary appointment until the people fill the vacancies by election as the legislature may direct.

This amendment shall not be so construed as to affect the election or term of any Senator chosen before it becomes valid as part of the Constitution.

AMENDMENT 18—PROHIBITION
[Ratified January 16, 1919. Repealed December 5, 1933 by Amendment 21]

Section 1 After one year from the ratification of this article the manufacture, sale, or transportation of intoxicating liquors within, the importation thereof into, or the exportation thereof from the United States and all territory subject to the jurisdiction thereof for beverage purposes is hereby prohibited.

Section 2 The Congress and the several states shall have concurrent power to enforce this article by appropriate legislation.

Section 3 This article shall be inoperative unless it shall have been ratified as an amendment to the Constitution by the legislatures of the several states, as provided in the Constitution, within seven years from the date of the submission hereof to the States by the Congress.[13]

AMENDMENT 19—FOR WOMEN'S SUFFRAGE
[Ratified August 18, 1920]

The right of the citizens of the United States to vote shall not be denied or abridged by the United States or by any State on account of sex.

Congress shall have power, by appropriate legislation, to enforce the provision of this article.

AMENDMENT 20—THE LAME DUCK AMENDMENT
[Ratified January 23, 1933]

Section 1 The terms of the President and Vice President shall end at noon on the 20th day of January, and the terms of the Senators and Representatives at noon on the 3rd day of January, of the years in which such terms would have ended if this article had not been ratified; and the terms of their successors shall then begin.

Section 2 The Congress shall assemble at least once in every year, and such meeting shall begin at noon on the 3rd day of January, unless they shall by law appoint a different day.

Section 3 If, at the time fixed for the beginning of the term of the President, the President elect shall have died, the Vice President elect shall become President. If a President shall not have been chosen before the time fixed for the beginning of his term, or if the President elect shall have failed to qualify, then the Vice President elect shall act as President until a President shall have qualified; and the Congress may by law provide for the case wherein neither a President elect nor a Vice President elect shall have qualified, declaring who shall then act as President, or the manner in which one who is to act shall be selected, and such person shall act accordingly until a President or Vice President shall have qualified.

Section 4 The Congress may by law provide for the case of the death of any of the persons from whom the House of Representatives may choose a President whenever the right of choice shall have developed upon them, and for the case of the death of any of the persons from whom the Senate may choose a Vice President whenever the right of choice shall have devolved upon them.

---

[12]Changed by the 26th Amendment

[13]Repealed by the 21st Amendment

Section 5 Sections 1 and 2 shall take effect on the 15th day of October following the ratification of this article.

Section 6 This article shall be inoperative unless it shall have been ratified as an amendment to the Constitution by the legislatures of three-fourths of the several States within seven years from the date of its submission.

AMENDMENT 21—REPEAL OF PROHIBITION
[Ratified December 5, 1933]

Section 1 The eighteenth article of amendment to the Constitution of the United States is hereby repealed.

Section 2 The transportation or importation into any State, Territory, or Possession of the United States for delivery or use therein of intoxicating liquors, in violation of the laws thereof, is hereby prohibited.

Section 3 This article shall be inoperative unless it shall have been ratified as an amendment to the Constitution by conventions in the several States, as provided in the Constitution, within seven years from the date of the submission hereof to the States by the Congress.

AMENDMENT 22—NUMBER OF PRESIDENTIAL TERMS
[Ratified February 27, 1951]

Section 1 No person shall be elected to the office of the President more than twice, and no person who has held the office of President, or acted as President, for more than two years of a term to which some other person was elected President shall be elected to the Office of the President more than once. But this Article shall not apply to any person holding the office of President when this article was proposed by the Congress, and shall not prevent any person who may be holding the office of President, or acting as President, during the term within which this Article becomes operative from holding the office of President or acting as President during the remainder of such term.

Section 2 This Article shall be inoperative unless it shall have been ratified as an amendment to the Constitution by the legislatures of three-fourths of the several states within seven years from the date of its submission to the States by the Congress.

AMENDMENT 23—PRESIDENTIAL ELECTORS FOR THE DISTRICT OF COLUMBIA
[Ratified March 29, 1961]

Section 1 The District constituting the seat of Government of the United States shall appoint in such manner as the Congress may direct:

A number of electors of President and Vice President equal to the whole number of Senators and Representatives in Congress to which the District would be entitled if it were a State, but in no event more than the least populous State; they shall be in addition to those appointed by the States, but they shall be considered, for the purposes of the election of President and Vice President, to be electors appointed by a State; and they shall meet in the District and perform such duties as provided by the twelfth article of amendment.

Section 2 The Congress shall have power to enforce this article by appropriate legislation.

AMENDMENT 24—THE ANTI-POLL TAX AMENDMENT
[Ratified January 23, 1964]

Section 1 The right of citizens of the United States to vote in any primary or other election for President or Vice President, for electors for President or Vice President, or for Senator or Representative in Congress, shall not be denied or abridged by the United States or any State by reason of failure to pay any poll tax or other tax.

Section 2 The Congress shall have power to enforce this article by appropriate legislation.

AMENDMENT 25—PRESIDENTIAL DISABILITY, VICE PRESIDENTIAL VACANCIES
[Ratified February 10, 1967]

Section 1 In case of the removal of the President from office or his death or resignation, the Vice President shall become President.

Section 2 Whenever there is a vacancy in the office of the Vice President, the President shall nominate a Vice President who shall take the office upon confirmation by a majority vote of both houses of Congress.

Section 3 Whenever the President transmits to the President pro tempore of the Senate and the Speaker of the House of Representatives his written declaration that he is unable to discharge the powers and duties of his office, and until he transmits to them a written declaration to the contrary, such powers and duties shall be discharged by the Vice President as Acting President.

Section 4 Whenever the Vice-President and a majority of either the principal officers of the executive departments, or of such other body as Congress may by law provide, transmit to the President pro tempore of the Senate and the Speaker of the House of Representatives their written declaration that the President is unable to discharge the powers and duties of his office, the Vice President shall immediately assume the powers and duties of the office as Acting President.

Thereafter, when the President transmits to the President pro tempore of the Senate and the Speaker of the House of Representatives his written declaration that no inability exists, he shall resume the powers and duties of his office unless the Vice President and a majority of either the principal officers of the executive departments, or of such other body as Congress may by law provide, transmit within four days to the President pro tempore of the Senate and the Speaker of the House of Representatives their written declaration that the President is unable to discharge the powers and duties of his office. Thereupon Congress shall decide the issue, assembling within forty-eight hours for that purpose if not in session. If the Congress, within twenty-one days after receipt of the latter written declaration, or, if Congress is not in session, within twenty-one days after Congress is required to assemble, determines by two-thirds vote of both houses that the President is unable to discharge the powers and duties of his office, the Vice President shall continue to discharge the same as Acting President; otherwise, the President shall resume the powers and duties of his office.

AMENDMENT 26—EIGHTEEN-YEAR-OLD VOTE
[Ratified July 1, 1971]

Section 1 The right of citizens of the United States, who are eighteen years of age, or older, to vote shall not be denied or abridged by the United States or by any State on account of age.

Section 2 The Congress shall have power to enforce this article by appropriate legislation.

AMENDMENT 27—CONGRESSIONAL SALARIES
[Ratified May 7, 1992]

No law, varying the compensation for the services of the Senators and Representatives, shall take effect, until an election of Representative shall be intervened.

3

American Federalism

As is true of Americans today, Americans at the time of the founding of this nation put at the top of their worry list a fear that governments might threaten their liberties. Questions about how powers were to be divided between the new national government and the states were much on their minds. *Federalism*—the constitutional division of powers between the national government and the states—has from our beginnings been hailed as a potent barrier against tyranny.[1]

Questions about the relations between the national government and the states did not end with the founding period. In 1861, men and women fought and died for Virginia or for Texas or for the Union (although it would be a mistake to think of the Civil War as merely a particularly heated debate over the principles of federalism). Today questions about the relations between the national government and the states have again become a hot issue for Americans. This debate was one of the central themes of the 1994 congressional and the 1996 presidential elections, with Republicans leading the charge against the national government and urging a massive return of powers and responsibilities to the states. Antigovernment themes, most particularly those directed against entitlements, were part of the campaign rhetoric of candidates from both political parties.

But it is not just in the United States that federalism issues have come to the top of the political agenda. In Canada the very nature of their federal system is at stake as the French-speaking province of Quebec demands special status and a considerable measure of autonomy.[2] The former Soviet Union—a highly centralized government that was federal only in form but not in fact—broke apart into 15 independent nations. Russia (or more precisely, the Russian Federation) is going through a struggle to redefine its federal relationship to its 21 autonomous republics, with the breakaway republic of Chechnya being the most severe test. Throughout Central Europe tensions erupt into violence as nations divide and subdivide. And even in the United Kingdom there are calls for rethinking the relationship between England and Scotland and Wales. "In the last few years sentiment for independence for Scotland has grown by leaps and bounds."[3] There are similar calls in Wales for a local parliament.

In the United States, from the days of the New Deal in the 1930s to today, there has been a steady drift of power and responsibility from the states to the national government. Presidents Nixon, Reagan, and Bush tried to slow down the growth of the national government under the banner of New Federalism. Richard Nixon declared, "For a third of a century, power and responsibility have flowed toward Washington. We intend to reverse this tide." "It is my intention to curb the size and influence of the federal establishment," Ronald Reagan vowed in 1981."[4] But although Presidents Carter and Clinton put some brakes on the growth of the national government, it was not until the elections of 1994, when the Republicans took control of both houses of Congress, that a major, almost revolutionary, attempt to return many functions back to the states—the "devolution revolution"[5]—occurred, at least at the level of the rhetoric.

Although in 1995, to the surprise of most observers, some Supreme Court justices reopened *constitutional* questions about the powers of the national government,[6] debates today are not likely to be about the constitutional division of authority between the national government and the states. Despite the Court's declaring that congressional attempts to regulate firearms around schools was unconstitutional,[7] the national government's constitutional authority over an

Interpretations of Federalism

Federalism is a powerful but elusive concept, leading both scholars and politicians to add adjectives that reflect their ideas:

Dual Federalism interprets the Constitution as giving a limited list of powers—primarily foreign policy and national defense—to the national government, leaving most power to sovereign states. Each level of government is dominant within its own sphere. The Supreme Court serves as the umpire between the national government and the states in case of a dispute over which government is in charge of a particular activity. During our first hundred years, dual federalism was the favored interpretation most of the time by the Supreme Court.

Cooperative Federalism stresses federalism as a system to deliver governmental goods and services to the people and calls for cooperation among various levels of governments in "getting the job done."

Marble Cake Federalism, coined by political scientist Morton Grodzins in 1960, conceives of federalism as a marble cake in which all levels of government are involved in a variety of issues and programs, rather than a layer cake with uniform divisions between layers or levels of government.*

Competitive Federalism, a term created by political scientist Thomas R. Dye, brings to the fore the fact that federalism provides us with a national government, 50 states, and thousands of other units, each competing with the others in the

---

TABLE 3–1
Number of Governments

U.S. government	1
States	50
Counties	3,043
Municipalities	19,279
Townships or towns	16,656
School districts	14,422
Special districts	31,555
Total	85,006

SOURCE: U.S. Bureau of the Census, *Statistical Abstract of the United States, 1996* (Government Printing Office, 1996), p. 295.

---

enormous range of subjects is clearly established, whether it concerns civil rights, highway speed limits, or the sale of holiday lights. Nonetheless, we can still argue about the proper division of responsibilities between the national and state governments: whether Congress should regulate welfare, Medicare, Medicaid, and the environment, or leave regulation to state discretion.

Such arguments, although couched in terms of national-state relations, almost always reflect differences among various interests about public policy. National and state governments are the arenas in which and through which battles take place between consumers and producers, workers and employers, airlines and railroads, pro-choice and right-to-life advocates, pro-growth and anti-growth forces, and all the other contending groups that make up our political system. People who think they can get more of what they want from the national government are likely to advocate national action; those who see state governments as more sympathetic are likely to argue for decentralization. Advocates of environmental protection, for instance, have generally found a more receptive audience in Washington than in their state capitals, especially in the West. They are likely to complain about "special interests" at the state house. Opponents of such regulation are likely to denounce the Washington bureaucrats.

In this chapter we begin by defining federalism and discussing its advantages. Next we look at the constitutional basis of our federal system. Then we see how the Supreme Court and political developments have shaped, and continue to shape, our modern system of federalism.

DEFINING FEDERALISM

Scholars have argued and wars have been fought about what federalism really means. One scholar counted 267 definitions.[8] **Federalism**, as we define it, is a form of government in which a constitution distributes powers between a central government and subdivisional governments—usually called states or provinces or republics—giving to both the national government and the regional governments substantial responsibilities and powers, including the power to collect taxes and to pass and enforce laws regulating the conduct of individuals.

The mere existence of both national and state governments does not make a system federal. What is important is that a *constitution divides governmental powers between the national government and the constituent governments* (called *states* in the United States), giving substantial functions to each. Neither the central nor the constituent government receives its powers from the other; both derive them from a common source—a constitution. This constitutional distribution of powers cannot be changed by the ordinary processes of legislation—by, for example, an act of either a national or a state legislature. Both levels of government operate through their own agents and exercise power directly over individuals. Other countries with federal systems include Canada, Switzerland, Mexico, and Australia. "Nearly 40 percent of the people of the world now live in nations with a federal form of government. Another third live in countries that use some elements of federalism."[9]

Constitutionally, the federal system of the United States consists of only the national government and the 50 states. "Cities are not," the Supreme Court reminded us, "sovereign entities." But in a practical sense, we are a nation of about 85,000 governmental units—from the national government to the school board district (see Table 3–1). This does not make for a tidy, efficient, easy-to-understand system; yet, as we shall see, it does have its virtues.

Alternatives to Federalism

Among the alternatives to federalism are **unitary systems** of government in which a constitution vests all governmental power in the central government. The central government, if it so chooses, may delegate authority to constituent units, but what it delegates it may take away. Britain, France, Israel, and the Philippines have unitary governments. In the United States, state constitutions usually create this kind of relationship between the state and its local governments.

At the other extreme are **confederations** in which sovereign nations by a constitutional compact create a central government but carefully limit the power of the central government and do not give it the power to regulate the conduct of individuals directly. The central government makes regulations for the constituent governments, but it exists and operates only at their direction. The 13 states under the Articles of Confederation operated in this manner, as did the southern Confederacy during the Civil War (see Figure 3–1).

To complicate this matter, the framers of our Constitution used the term "federal" to describe what we would now call a confederate form of government. Moreover, today the term "federal" is frequently used as a synonym for national; people often refer to the government in Washington as "the federal government." But it is the states and the national government *together* that make up our federal system.

Why Federalism?

In 1787, federalism was an obvious choice. Confederation had been tried and found wanting, but a unitary system was out of the question. Most of the people were too deeply attached to their state governments to permit subordination to central rule. Federalism was, and still is, thought to be ideally suited to the needs of a heterogeneous people spread over a large continent, suspicious of concentrated power, and desiring unity but not uniformity. Federalism offered, and still offers, many advantages for such a people.[10]

FEDERALISM CHECKS THE GROWTH OF TYRANNY Although in the rest of the world federal forms have not been notably successful in preventing tyranny and many unitary governments are democratic, Americans tend to associate freedom with federalism.[11] As James Madison pointed out in *The Federalist*, No. 10: If "factious leaders . . . kindle a flame within their particular states," national leaders can check the spread of the "conflagration through the other states" (*The Federalist*, No. 10, appears in the Appendix of this book). Moreover, when one political party loses control of the national government, it is still likely to hold office in a number of states. It can then regroup, develop new policies and new leaders, and continue to challenge the party in power at the national level.

Such diffusion of power creates its own problems. It makes it difficult for a national majority to carry out a program of action, and it permits those who control a state government to frustrate the consensus expressed through Congress and national agencies. To some of our Constitution's framers, these obstacles were an advantage. They were more fearful that a single-interest national majority might capture the national government and attempt to suppress the interests of others than that minority interests might frustrate the national will. Of course the size of the nation and the many interests within it are the greatest obstacles to the formation of a single-interest majority, a point often overlooked today but emphasized by Madison in *The Federalist*, No. 10. If such a majority were to occur, having to work through a federal system would act to check its power.

FEDERALISM ALLOWS UNITY WITHOUT UNIFORMITY National politicians and parties do not have to iron out every difference on every issue that divides us, whether it be abortion, divorce, gun control, gambling, capital punishment, education financing, or comparable worth. (**Comparable worth**, which mandates comparable pay for jobs requiring comparable skills, has been advanced as one way to correct pay inequities between higher-paying, male-dominated fields, such as plumbing, and lower-paying, female-dominated fields, such as teaching.) Instead,

Government under the Articles of Confederation: 1781–1788

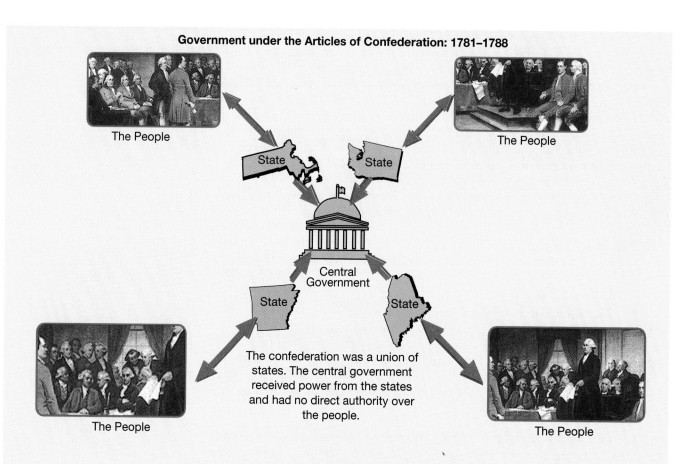

The People

The People

State State

Central Government

State State

The confederation was a union of states. The central government received power from the states and had no direct authority over the people.

The People

The People

Government under U.S.Constitution (Federation): 1789-

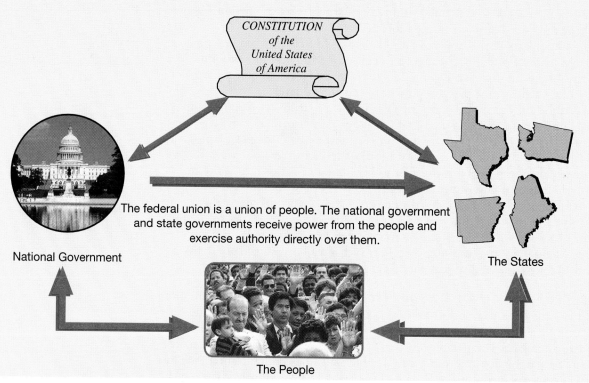

CONSTITUTION
of the
United States
of America

The federal union is a union of people. The national government and state governments receive power from the people and exercise authority directly over them.

National Government

The States

The People

FIGURE 3–1   A Comparison of Federalism and Confederation

these issues are debated in state legislatures, county courthouses, and city halls. This advantage of federalism is becoming less significant as more local issues become national and as events and outcomes in one state immediately affect policy debates at the national level.

FEDERALISM ENCOURAGES EXPERIMENTATION   Supreme Court Justice Louis Brandeis pointed out that state governments provide great "laboratories" for public policy experimentation, with states serving as proving grounds. If they adopt programs that fail, the negative effects are limited; if programs succeed, they can be adopted by other states and by the national government. Georgia, for example, was the first state to permit 18-year-olds to vote; Oregon is holding elections by mail; New York has been vigorous in its assault on water pollution; California has pioneered air pollution control programs, especially automobile emission standards. After federal leadership on environmental matters waned in the 1970s, New Jersey initiated programs to handle toxic wastes, radon gas testing, and mandatory recycling. Many states legalized abortion under certain conditions before the Supreme Court acted. (Whether these laws and regulations are good or bad depends, of course, on one's values, as do so many questions of politics.) "Sunset laws" (requiring periodic reauthorization for programs), equal housing, no-fault insurance, and "lemon laws" (providing consumer protection for faulty automobiles) are other examples of programs that originated in the states. Oregon and Hawaii are pioneers in creating new systems for the delivery of health care. Nevada is the only state, so far, to legalize statewide gambling, but some aspects of legalized casino gambling are now found in more than half the states. Not all innovations, even those considered successful, are widely adopted. Nebraska is the only state to have a unicameral legislature, although in recent years it has been discussed, not too seriously, in both Minnesota and California.

FEDERALISM KEEPS GOVERNMENT CLOSER TO THE PEOPLE   By providing numerous arenas for decision making, federalism involves many people and helps keep government closer to the people. Every day thousands of Americans are busy serving on city councils, school boards, neighborhood associations, and planning commissions. And since they are close to the issues and have firsthand knowledge of what needs to be done, they may be more responsive to the problem than the experts in Washington.

We should be cautious, however, about generalizing that state and local governments are necessarily "closer to the people" than is the national government. True, more people are involved in local and state politics than in national affairs, and in recent years confidence in the ability of state governments has gone up while respect for national agencies has diminished (see Figure 3–2). Yet national and international affairs are more often on people's minds than are state or even local politics. Fewer voters participate in state and local elections than in congressional and presidential elections. Some caution against "the romantic notion of power to the people" by pointing out, "The only thing worse than the U.S. Postal Service is the local motor vehicle department. . . . There is no efficiency magic in devolution."[12]

THE CONSTITUTIONAL STRUCTURE OF AMERICAN FEDERALISM

Dividing powers and responsibilities between the national and state governments requires thousands of court decisions, hundreds of books, and endless speeches to explain—and even then the division lacks precise definition. Nonetheless it is helpful to get a basic understanding of how the Constitution divides these powers and responsibilities among the national and state governments and what obligations it imposes on each level of government in its relations to the other.

Town meetings, like this one in Sandwich, New Hampshire, bring government closer to the people and provide firsthand knowledge of local needs and issues.

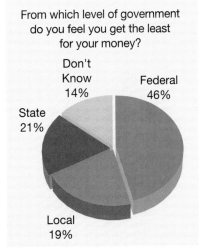

From which level of government do you feel you get the least for your money?

Don't Know 14%

Federal 46%

State 21%

Local 19%

FIGURE 3–2   The Least Popular Level of Government

SOURCE: Advisory Commission on Intergovernmental Relations, *Public Attitudes on Governments and Taxes, 1994* (Government Printing Office, 1994), p. 29.

Constitutional Division of Power

The formal constitutional framework of our federal system may be stated relatively simply:

1. The national government has only those powers delegated to it by the Constitution (with the important exception of the inherent power over foreign affairs).
2. Within the scope of its operations, the national government is supreme.
3. The state governments have the powers not delegated to the central government, except those denied to them by the Constitution and their state constitutions.
4. Some powers are specifically denied to both the national and state governments; others are specifically denied only to the states; still others are denied only to the national government.

Powers of the National Government

The Constitution, chiefly in the first three articles, delegates legislative, executive, and judicial powers to the national government. In addition to these **express powers**, such as the power to appropriate funds, the Constitution delegates to Congress **implied powers**, such as the power to create banks, which may be inferred from express powers. (We will see an example when we discuss the landmark case of *McCulloch v Maryland*.) The constitutional basis for the implied powers of Congress is the **necessary and proper clause** (Article I, Section 8, Clause 18). This clause gives Congress the right "to make all Laws which shall be necessary and proper for carrying into Execution the foregoing Powers, and all other Powers vested . . . in the Government of the United States."

In the field of foreign affairs the Constitution gives the national government **inherent powers**, so that the national government has the same authority to deal with other nations as if it were the central government in a unitary system. These inherent powers do not depend on specific constitutional grants. For example, the government of the United States may acquire territory by discovery and occupation, though no specific clause in the Constitution allows such acquisition. Even if the Constitution were silent about foreign affairs—which it is not—the national government would have the right to declare war, make treaties, and appoint and receive ambassadors.

Together, these express, implied, and inherent powers create a flexible system that has allowed the Supreme Court, Congress, the president, and the people to expand the central government's powers to meet the needs of a modern industrial nation operating in a global economy. This expansion of central government functions has rested on four constitutional pillars.

NATIONAL SUPREMACY ARTICLE One of the most important pillars is found in Article VI of the Constitution: "This Constitution, and the Laws of the United States which shall be made in Pursuance thereof; and all Treaties made . . . under the Authority of the United States, shall be the supreme Law of the Land; and the Judges in every State shall be bound thereby; any Thing in the Constitution or Laws of any State to the Contrary notwithstanding." All officials, state as well as national, are bound by constitutional oath to support the Constitution of the United States. States may not use their reserved powers to override national policies; this restriction also applies to local units of government since they are agents of the states. National laws and regulations of federal agencies preempt the field, so that conflicting state and local rules and regulations are unenforceable.

THE WAR POWER The national government is responsible for protecting the nation from external aggression and, when necessary, for waging war. In today's world, military strength depends not only on troops in the field but also on the ability to mobilize the nation's industrial might and to apply scientific knowledge to the tasks of defense. The national government has the power to wage war and to do what is necessary and proper to do so successfully. Thus the national government has the power to do almost anything not in direct conflict with constitutional guarantees.

THE POWER TO REGULATE INTERSTATE AND FOREIGN COMMERCE Congressional authority extends to all commerce that affects more than one state and to all those activities, wherever they exist or whatever their nature, whose control Congress decides is necessary and proper to regulate interstate and foreign commerce. Commerce includes the production, buying, selling, renting, and transporting of goods, services, and properties.[13] The **commerce clause** (Article 1, Section 8,

Clause 3) packs a tremendous constitutional punch; it gives Congress the power "to regulate Commerce with foreign Nations, and among the several States, and with the Indian Tribes." In these few words the national government has been able to find constitutional justification for regulating a wide range of human activity, including agriculture, transportation, finance, product safety, labor relations, and the workplace. Few, if any, aspects of our economy today affect commerce in only one state and are thus outside the scope of the national government's constitutional authority.

The commerce clause can also be used to sustain legislation that goes beyond commercial matters. When the Supreme Court upheld the 1964 Civil Rights Act forbidding discrimination because of race, religion, or national origin in places of public accommodation, it said: "Congress's action in removing the disruptive effect which it found racial discrimination has on interstate travel is not invalidated because Congress was also legislating against what it considers to be moral wrongs." Discrimination restricts the flow of interstate commerce; therefore, Congress could legislate against the discrimination. Moreover, the law could be applied even to local places of public accommodation because local incidents of discrimination have a substantial and harmful impact on interstate commerce. "If it is interstate commerce that feels the pinch, it does not matter how local the operation that applies the squeeze."[14]

After 60 years of almost unquestioned authority to regulate interstate commerce, in the Gun-Free School Zones Act of 1990 banning the possession of a firearm inside school zones, Congress did not even bother to specify how the presence of guns in schools affects interstate commerce. In 1995 the Supreme Court, in the case of *United States v Lopez*, declared that law unconstitutional by a vote of 5 to 4.[15] Chief Justice William H. Rehnquist stated for the majority that not only must Congress show that the possession of guns in schools affects interstate commerce, but it must show that it *substantially affects* interstate commerce. Some commentators call the *Lopez* case "the opening cannonades of a constitutional revolution"; others were doubtful.[16] Most likely it is just a judicial reminder to Congress that it has no general police power to regulate whatever it thinks is in the public interest. As the dissenting justices pointed out, if Congress wants to make it a federal crime to possess a gun in a school, it must make the case, which should not be difficult, that "gun-related violence near the classroom poses a serious economic threat" to interstate commerce.

THE POWER TO TAX AND SPEND Congress lacks constitutional authority to pass laws solely on the ground that they will promote the general welfare, but it may raise taxes and spend money for this purpose. This distinction between legislating and appropriating makes little difference most of the time. Congress, for example, lacks constitutional power to regulate education or agriculture directly, yet it does have the power to appropriate money to support education or to pay farm subsidies. By attaching conditions to its grants of money, Congress may thus regulate what it cannot directly control by law.

When Congress puts up the money, it determines how the money will be spent. By withholding or threatening to withhold funds, the national government can influence or control state operations and regulate individual conduct. For example, Congress has stipulated that federal funds should be withdrawn from any program in which any person is denied benefits because of race, color, or national origin; subsequently the categories of sex and physical handicap were added. Congress has also used its power of the purse to force states to raise the drinking age to 21 by tying such a condition to federal dollars for highways. (Louisiana is the only state to refuse to do so.)

Congress frequently requires states to do certain things—for example, provide services to indigent mothers and take action to clean up the air and water—or else

The power to regulate interstate commerce allowed Congress to forbid discrimination in places of public accommodation in the 1964 Civil Rights Act.

An Expanding Nation

A great advantage of federalism—and part of the genius and flexibility of our constitutional system—has been the way in which we acquired territory and extended rights and guarantees by means of statehood, commonwealth, or territorial status, and thus grew from 13 to 50 states.

Louisiana Purchase	1803
Florida	1819
Texas	1845
Oregon	1846
Mexican Cession	1848
Gadsden Purchase	1853
Alaska	1867
Hawaii	1898
Philippines	1898–1946
Puerto Rico	1899
Guam	1899
American Samoa	1900
Canal Zone	1904
U.S. Virgin Islands	1917
Pacific Islands Trust Territory	1947

Congress will impose even more stringent federal regulations. These requirements are called **federal mandates**. Often, Congress does not supply the funds required to carry out these mandates, and its failure to do so has become an important issue in states facing growing expenditures with limited resources.

These four constitutional pillars—*the national supremacy clause, the war power, the interstate commerce clause,* and, most especially, *the power to tax and spend for the general welfare*—have permitted a tremendous expansion of the functions of the national government, so much so that the national government has in effect almost full power to enact any legislation that Congress thinks will promote the general welfare, so long as it does not conflict with those provisions of the Constitution designed to protect individual rights.

Powers of the States

The Constitution *reserves for the states all powers not granted to the national government,* subject only to the limitations of the Constitution. Powers not given exclusively to the national government, by provision of the Constitution or by judicial interpretation, may be concurrently exercised by the states, as long as there is no conflict with national law. Each state has **concurrent powers** with the national government, such as the power to levy taxes and regulate commerce internal to each state (see Table 3–2).

Precisely how federalism limits the states' taxing powers is not simple to explain or understand. In general, a state may levy a tax on the same item as the national government, but a state cannot, by a tax, "unduly burden" commerce among the states, interfere with a function of the national government, complicate the operation of a national law, or abridge the terms of a treaty of the United States.

Federalism issues become even more complicated when states use their so-called "police powers" to protect the public well-being. Where Congress has not preempted the field, states may even regulate interstate businesses, provided these regulations do not cover matters requiring uniform national treatment or unduly burden interstate commerce. Who decides what matters require uniform national treatment or what actions might place an undue burden on interstate commerce? Congress does, subject to final review by the Supreme Court. When Congress is silent or does not clearly state its intentions, the courts—ultimately the Supreme Court—decide if there is a conflict with the national Constitution or if there has been federal preemption by law or regulation.

TABLE 3–2
The Federal Division of Powers

Types of Powers Delegated to the National Government	Some Powers Reserved for the States	Some Concurrent Powers Shared by the National and State Governments
• Express powers stated in Constitution • Implied powers that may be inferred from express powers • Inherent powers that allow nation to present a united front to foreign powers	• To create a republican form of government • To charter local governments • To conduct elections • To exercise all powers not delegated to the national government or denied to the states by the Constitution	• To tax citizens and businesses • To borrow and spend money • To establish courts • To pass and enforce laws • To protect civil rights

Constitutional Limits and Obligations

To make federalism work, the Constitution imposes certain restraints on both the national and the state governments. States are prohibited from:

1. Making treaties with foreign governments
2. Authorizing private persons to prey on the shipping and commerce of other nations—what the Constitution refers to as "granting letters of marque and reprisal," a practice common during times of war in the eighteenth century
3. Coining money, issuing bills of credit, or making anything but gold and silver coin a tender in payment of debts.

Nor may states without the consent of Congress:

1. Tax imports or exports
2. Tax foreign ships
3. Keep troops or ships in time of peace (except the state militia, now called the National Guard)
4. Enter into compacts with other states or foreign nations that "tend to increase the political power in the States, which may encroach upon or interfere"[17] with the supremacy of the national government
5. Engage in war, unless invaded (an invasion of one state would be an invasion of the United States itself) or in such imminent danger as will not admit of delay.

The national government, in turn, is required by the Constitution to refrain from exercising its powers, especially its powers to tax and to regulate interstate commerce, in such a way as to interfere substantially with the states' abilities to perform their responsibilities. Today, whatever protection states have comes primarily from the political process—in restraints that our system provides because individuals elected from the states participate in the decisions of Congress—rather than from judicially enforced limitations.

The Constitution also requires the national government to *guarantee to each state a "Republican Form of Government."* The framers used this term to distinguish a republic from a monarchy, on the one side, and from a pure, direct democracy, on the other. Congress, not the courts, enforces this guarantee and determines what is or is not a republican form of government. By permitting the congressional delegation of a state to take its seat in Congress, Congress in effect acknowledges that the state has the republican form of government guaranteed by the Constitution.

In addition, the national government is obliged by the Constitution to protect states against *domestic insurrection.* Congress has delegated to the president the authority to dispatch troops to put down such insurrections when so requested by the proper state authorities. If there are contesting state authorities, the president decides which are the proper ones.[18] The president does not have to wait, however, for a request from state authorities to send federal troops into a state to enforce federal laws. Today it is hard to imagine a situation of domestic insurrection against a state that would not also involve federal laws.

Horizontal Federalism: Interstate Relations

Three clauses in the Constitution, taken from the Articles of Confederation, require states to give full faith and credit to each other's public acts, records, and judicial proceedings; to extend to each other's citizens the privileges and immunities of their own citizens; and to return persons who are fleeing from justice.

Secessionism Lives On

Secession—an effort by a local region to break away from the parent state—recurs periodically in American and world history. England fought an unsuccessful war to prevent the 13 colonies from forming an independent nation. The United States waged the Civil War to prevent secession by the southern states. The Soviet Union dissolved after failing to hold its member republics together. And Yugoslavia has been violently torn apart by ethnic hatreds.

In 1992 the citizens of southwestern Kansas called for a constitutional convention to withdraw from Kansas and form the fifty-first state. The citizens of Staten Island recently voted to secede from New York City; the New York legislature is now considering the issue. In past years, citizens of Alaska, Nantucket, Virginia, Nebraska, Colorado, and California have also made unsuccessful attempts to secede. A northern California legislator is pushing for a statewide referendum to break California into three separate states. Texas, when admitted into the Union, received congressional consent to break into five states if it ever should wish to do so.

FULL FAITH AND CREDIT The **full faith and credit clause** (Article IV, Section 1), one of the more technical provisions of the Constitution, requires state courts to enforce the civil judgments of the courts of other states and accept their public records and acts as valid. (It does not require states to enforce the criminal laws of other states; in most cases, for one state to enforce the criminal laws of another would raise constitutional issues.) The clause applies especially to noncriminal judicial proceedings, such as enforcement of judicial settlements and court awards. The clause gives Congress the power by general law to "prescribe the Manner in which such Acts, Records and Proceedings" shall be given full faith and credit.

INTERSTATE PRIVILEGES AND IMMUNITIES Under Article IV, Section 2, states must extend to citizens of other states the privileges and immunities granted to their own citizens, including the protection of the laws, the right to engage in peaceful occupations, access to the courts, and freedom from discriminatory taxes. Further, because of this clause, states may not impose unreasonable residency requirements, that is, withhold rights to American citizens who have recently moved to the state and thereby have become citizens of that state. For example, a state may not set unreasonable time limits to withhold state-funded medical benefits from new citizens or to keep them from voting. How long a residency requirement may a state impose? A day seems about as long as the Court will tolerate to withhold welfare payments or medical care, 50 days or so for voting privileges, and one year for eligibility for in-state tuition for state-supported colleges and universities.

EXTRADITION In Article IV, Section 2, the Constitution asserts that when individuals charged with crimes have fled from one state to another, the state to which they have fled is to deliver them to the proper officials upon the demand of the executive authority of the state from which they fled. This process is called **extradition**. "The obvious objective of the Extradition Clause," the courts have claimed, "is that no State should become a safe haven for the fugitives from a sister State's criminal justice system."[19] Congress has supplemented this constitutional provision by making the governor of the state to which fugitives have fled the agent responsible for returning them.

Despite their constitutional obligation, governors of asylum states have on occasion refused to honor a request for extradition. So far in modern times no federal judge has had to try to enforce an extradition request. A few years ago, when the governor of Indiana refused to extradite Bobby Knight, the celebrated Indiana University basketball coach who had been convicted in absentia by a Puerto Rican court of assaulting a police officer during the Pan-American Games in Puerto Rico, the governor of Puerto Rico decided to drop the matter.

INTERSTATE COMPACTS The Constitution also requires states to settle disputes with one another without the use of force. States may carry their legal disputes to the Supreme Court, or they may negotiate **interstate compacts**. More often, interstate compacts are used to establish interstate agencies to handle interstate problems. Before most interstate compacts become effective, congressional approval is required. After a compact has been signed and approved by Congress, it becomes binding on all signatory states and its terms are enforceable by the Supreme Court. A typical state belongs to 20 compacts dealing with such subjects as environmental protection, crime control, water rights, and higher education exchanges.[20]

THE ROLE OF THE FEDERAL COURTS: UMPIRES OF FEDERALISM

The constitutional division of powers between the national and state governments is relatively easy to describe, but it is subject to constant definition and redefinition. The political process ultimately decides how power will be divided between the national and the state governments. Still, the federal courts—and especially the Supreme Court—have often been called on to umpire the ongoing debate about which level of government should do what, for whom, and to whom. This role for the Courts was claimed in the celebrated case of *McCulloch v Maryland*.

McCulloch versus Maryland

In *McCulloch v Maryland* (1819), the Supreme Court had the first of many chances to define the division of power between the national and state governments.[21] Maryland had levied a tax against the Baltimore branch of the Bank of the United States, a semipublic agency established by Congress. James William McCulloch, the cashier of the bank, refused to pay on the grounds that a state could not tax an instrument of the national government. Maryland's attorneys responded that, in the first place, the national government did not have the power to incorporate a bank, but even if it did, the state had the power to tax it.

Maryland was represented before the Court by some of the country's most distinguished lawyers, including Luther Martin, who had been a delegate to the Constitutional Convention. Martin had left the convention early when it became apparent that a strong national government was in the making. Basing his argument on the states' rights view of federalism, Martin said the power to incorporate a bank is not expressly delegated to the national government. He maintained that the necessary and proper clause gives Congress only the power to choose those means and to pass those laws absolutely essential to the execution of its expressly granted powers. Because a bank is not absolutely necessary to the exercise of any of its delegated powers, Congress has no authority to establish it. As for Maryland's right to tax the bank, Martin's position was clear: The power to tax is one of the powers reserved to the states; they may use it as they see fit.

The national government was represented by equally distinguished counsel, chief among whom was Daniel Webster. Webster conceded the power to create a bank is not one of the express powers of the national government. However, the power to pass laws necessary and proper to carry out Congress's express powers is specifically delegated to Congress. This delegation of implied powers should be interpreted to mean Congress has authority to enact any legislation convenient and useful for carrying out its delegated national powers. Therefore Congress may incorporate a bank as an appropriate, convenient, and useful means of exercising the granted powers of collecting taxes, borrowing money, and caring for the property of the United States.

Although the power to tax is reserved to the states, Webster argued that states cannot use their reserved powers to interfere with the operations of the national government. The Constitution leaves no room for doubt; in cases of conflict between the national and state governments, the national government is supreme.

Speaking for a unanimous Court, Chief Justice John Marshall rejected every one of Maryland's contentions. He wrote:

> We must never forget that it is a constitution we are expounding . . . a constitution intended to endure for ages to come, and consequently, to be adapted to the various crises of human affairs. . . . The government of the Union, then, . . . is, emphatically, and truly, a government of the people. In form and substance it emanates from them. Its powers are granted by them, and are to be exercised directly on them, and for their benefit. . . . It can never be to their

Qualifying for In-State Tuition

Financially independent adults who move into a state just before enrolling in a state-supported university or college may be required to prove that they have become citizens of that state and intend to remain after finishing their schooling by supplying such evidence of citizenship as tax payments, a driver's license, car registration, voter registration, and a continuous, year-round off-campus residence. Students who are financially dependent on their parents remain citizens of the state of their parents.

From 1937 until 1995 the Supreme Court
took most of the constitutional issues arising from federalism out of play. The
Court gave an expansive interpretation of
the commerce clause, allowing Congress
to exercise whatever powers it thought
necessary to promote the common good.
In 1985, by a 5 to 4 vote, in *Garcia v San
Antonio Metro*, the Supreme Court in
essence told federal courts to get out of
the business of protecting the states from
congressional interference. Congress, not
the courts, said the Court majority,
decides which actions of the states should
be regulated by the national government.*

In 1995 the Supreme Court dealt with
two major federalism issues in a way that
called into question whether future federal
courts will remain passive in resolving
state's rights issues. In the first of these two
important cases the Supreme Court, for
the first time in 60 years, declared an act
of Congress unconstitutional because Congress lacked authority under the commerce
clause. In this case, the Gun-Free School
Zones Act of 1990, Congress had made it
a federal offense "for any individual knowingly to possess a firearm at a place that
the individual knows, or has reasonable
cause to believe, is a school zone."**

The second case was *U.S. Term Limits,
Inc. v Thornton*, which challenged a state's
right to add qualifications for serving in
the Congress.† The Court again returned
to first principles of federalism. Justice
John Paul Stevens, writing for the five-
person majority, built his argument on the
concept of the federal union as espoused
by the great Chief Justice John Marshall,
as a compact among the people with the
national government serving as their
agent. What was unusual was that Justice
Clarence Thomas, writing for the minority
of four, espoused a view of federalism not

interest, and cannot be presumed to have been their intention, to clog and embarrass its execution, by withholding the most appropriate means.

Marshall summarized his views on the powers of the national government in
these now-famous words: "Let the end be legitimate, let it be within the scope of
the Constitution, and all means which are appropriate, which are plainly adapted
to that end, which are not prohibited, but consist with the letter and spirit of the
constitution, are constitutional."

Having thus established the doctrine of *implied national powers*, Marshall set
forth the doctrine of **national supremacy**. No state, he said, can use its reserved
taxing powers to tax a national instrument. "The power to tax involves the power
to destroy. . . . If the right of the States to tax the means employed by the general
government be conceded, the declaration that the Constitution, and the laws made
in pursuance thereof, shall be the supreme law of the land, is empty and unmean-
ing declamation."

The long-range significance of *McCulloch v Maryland* in providing support for
the developing forces of nationalism cannot be overstated. The arguments of the
states' righters, if accepted, would have strapped the national government in a constitutional straitjacket and denied it powers needed to handle the problems of an
expanding nation.

An Expanding Role for the Federal Courts

The authority of federal judges to review the activities of state and local governments has expanded dramatically in recent decades because of modern judicial interpretations of the Thirteenth, Fourteenth, and Fifteenth Amendments
(especially the Fourteenth) and congressional legislation enacted to implement
these amendments. Today almost every action by state and local officials is subject to challenge before a federal judge as a violation of the Constitution or of
federal law.

In carrying out their judgments, federal judges sometimes have taken over the
supervision of state prison systems, public hospitals, public schools, and other public
facilities. Although a more recent decision called the validity of this holding in doubt,
the Supreme Court has gone so far as to sustain a federal judge's right to order a local
school board in Missouri to ignore the state's constitutional constraints and to raise
taxes and sell bonds to fund the operation of a racially integrated magnet school.[22]

One of the major instruments for opening these issues for federal court review
is the Supreme Court's revitalization—some would say rewriting—during recent
decades of an 1871 civil rights act originally written to combat the Ku Klux Klan.
This act (now called Section 1983 after its designation in Title 42 of the United
States Code) permits individuals to go into federal court to sue cities and counties for damages or seek injunctions against any person acting "under the color of
law"—that is, in an official capacity—who they believe has deprived them of any
right secured by the Constitution or by any one of the several thousands of federal laws.[23] Although federal judges can order states to stop acting in a manner
that violates the federal Constitution or laws or treaties, the Eleventh Amendment
constrains federal courts from hearing damage suits against the states but not
against local government officials.

Federal judges have also become agencies to enforce federal mandates. Any citizen can now sue a state to make it carry out these duties. For example, doctors
and hospitals may sue a state to force it to provide "reasonable" reimbursement as
required by federal Medicare law. Parents may sue a state for allegedly failing to
provide their disabled children with a "free appropriate public education" or otherwise reimburse such parents for tuition in a private school.[24]

Federal judges spend a considerable portion of their time deciding cases in which the central issue is whether some provisions of federal laws have preempted state and local action. **Preemption** occurs when a federal law or regulation takes over and precludes enforcement of a state or local law or regulation. State and local laws are preempted not only when they conflict directly with federal laws and regulations but also if they touch a field in which the "federal interest is so dominant that the federal system will be assumed to preclude enforcement of state laws on the same subject."[25] Examples of federal preemption include the Coast Guard Authorization Act directing the secretary of transportation to develop standards for determining when people are considered intoxicated while operating a marine recreational vessel; dozens of laws regulating hazardous substances, water quality, and clean air standards; and many civil rights acts, most especially the Civil Rights Act of 1964 and the Voting Rights Act of 1965.

Over the years federal judges, under the leadership of the Supreme Court, have favored national powers (including their own). However, recently the Supreme Court has returned to the states several explosive political issues. Perhaps most notably in 1989 in *Webster v Reproductive Health Services* and in 1992 in *Planned Parenthood of Southeastern Pennsylvania v Casey*, the Court gave states considerable latitude to regulate abortion, setting off intense clashes between pro-choice and right-to-life groups in the state legislatures.[26]

Despite the Supreme Court's bias in favor of national over state authority, few would deny the Supreme Court the power to review and set aside state actions. As Justice Oliver Wendell Holmes once remarked: "I do not think the United States would come to an end if we lost our power to declare an Act of Congress void. I do think the Union would be imperiled if we could not make that declaration as to the laws of the several States."[27]

The Great Debate—Centralists versus Decentralists

From the beginning of the Republic there has been an ongoing debate about the "proper" distribution of powers, functions, and responsibilities between the national government and the states. The constitutional arguments revolving around federalism grow out of specific political issues: Did the national government have the authority to outlaw slavery in the territories? Did the states have the authority to operate racially segregated schools? Could Congress regulate labor relations? Does Congress have the power to regulate the sale and use of firearms around school yards? Does Congress have the right to tell states how to regulate air and water pollution? The debates in the past and those today are frequently phrased in constitutional language, with appeals to the great principles of federalism. But they are also arguments over who gets what, where, and how.

During the Great Depression of the 1930s, the nation debated whether Congress had the constitutional authority to enact legislation on agriculture, labor, education, housing, and welfare. Only 40 years ago some questioned the constitutional authority of Congress to legislate against racial discrimination. The debate continues, although no longer couched primarily in constitutional terms, between **centralists**, those who favor national action (or as we used to call them, *nationalists*) and **decentralists**, those who favor action at the state and local levels (or by the old-fashioned name, *states' righters*).

THE DECENTRALIST POSITION Among those favoring the decentralist or states' rights interpretation, with varying emphasis, were Thomas Jefferson, John C. Calhoun, the Supreme Court from the 1920s to 1937, and more recently, Ronald Reagan, George Bush, Bob Dole, the Republican leaders of Congress, Chief Justice William H. Rehnquist, and Justices Antonin Scalia, Clarence Thomas, and

Sandra Day O'Connor. Most decentralists contend that the Constitution is a treaty among sovereign states that created the central government and gave it carefully limited authority. As Justice Thomas, a modern-day ardent decentralist, wrote in a dissenting opinion supporting the argument that a state has the power to impose term limits on members of Congress, "The ultimate source of the Constitution's authority is the consent of the people of each individual State, not the consent of the undifferentiated people of the Nation as a whole."[28] Thus the national government is nothing more than an agent of the states, and every one of its powers should be narrowly defined. Any question about whether the states have given a particular function to the central government or have reserved it for themselves should be resolved in favor of the states.

Decentralists hold that the national government should not be permitted to exercise its delegated powers in a way that interferes with activities reserved for the states. The Tenth Amendment, they claim, makes this clear: "The powers not delegated to the United States by the Constitution, nor prohibited by it to the States, are reserved to the States respectively, or to the people." Decentralists insist state governments are closer to the people and reflect the people's wishes more accurately than does the national government. The national government, they add, is inherently heavy-handed and bureaucratic; to preserve our federal system and our liberties, central authority must be kept under control.

THE CENTRALIST POSITION   The centralist position has been supported by Chief Justice John Marshall, Abraham Lincoln, Theodore Roosevelt, Franklin Roosevelt, and throughout most of our history by the Supreme Court. Centralists reject the whole idea of the Constitution as an interstate compact. Rather, they view the Constitution as a supreme law established by the people. The national government is an agent of the people, not of the states, because it was the people who drew up the Constitution and created the national government. The sovereign people gave the national government sufficient power to accomplish the great objectives listed in the Preamble to the Constitution. They intended that the central government's powers should be liberally defined and that the central government should be denied authority only when the Constitution clearly prohibits it from acting.

Centralists argue that the national government is a government of all the people, and that each state speaks for only some of the people. Although the Tenth Amendment clearly reserves powers for the states, as Chief Justice Harlan Stone said, "The Tenth Amendment states but a truism that all is retained which has not been surrendered."[29] The amendment does not deny the national government the right to exercise to the fullest extent all the powers given to it by the Constitution. On the other hand, the supremacy of the national government, it is argued, restricts the states, because governments representing part of the people cannot be allowed to interfere with a government representing all of them.

As noted, the centralist position throughout most of our history has had the support of the dominant political forces of our political system. It has also had the Supreme Court's constitutional endorsement. But currently there are powerful political pressures and champions of a decentralist constitutional interpretation on the Supreme Court. Chief Justice Rehnquist, joined by Justices Scalia, Thomas, O'Connor, and frequently Justice Kennedy, have veered the court back to a more decentralist position. President Clinton's two appointees, Justices Ruth Bader Ginsburg and Stephen Breyer, joined by Justices David Souter and John Paul Stevens, are resisting this movement back to a states' rights interpretation of our federal system. The court is so narrowly divided on federalism issues that the next constitutional debate will very likely turn on the views of the next appointees.

FEDERALISM AND THE USE OF FEDERAL GRANTS

Congress authorizes programs, establishes general rules for how the programs will operate, and decides whether and how much room should be left for state or local discretion. Most important, Congress appropriates the funds for these programs and, until recently, has had deeper pockets than even the richest states. One of Congress's most potent tools for influencing policy at the state and local levels has been the federal grant (see Table 3–3).

Types of Federal Grants

There are three types of federal grants presently being administered: categorical-formula grants, project grants, and block grants (or, as the Clinton administration calls them, flexible grants). From 1972 to 1982 there was **revenue sharing**—federal grants to state and local governments to be used at their discretion and subject only to very general conditions. But when, in the second Reagan administration (1985–1989), federal budget deficits soared and there was no revenue to share, revenue sharing was terminated—to the states in 1986 and to local governments in 1987.

CATEGORICAL-FORMULA GRANTS Congress appropriates funds for specific purposes, such as school lunches or the building of airports and highways. These funds are allocated by formula and are subject to detailed federal conditions, often on a matching basis; that is, the government receiving the federal funds must put up some of its own dollars. Categorical grants, in addition, provide federal supervision to ensure that the federal dollars are spent as Congress wants. There are hundreds of grant programs, but two dozen, including Medicaid, account for more than half of total spending for categoricals.

Goals of Federal Grants

Federal grants serve four purposes, the most important of which is the fourth:

1. To supply state and local governments with revenue.
2. To establish minimum national standards for such things as highways and clean air.
3. To equalize resources among the states by taking money from people with high incomes through federal taxes and spending it in states where the poor live through grants.
4. To attack national problems yet minimize the growth of federal agencies.

TABLE 3-3
Federal Grants, 1970 to 1996

Year	Total grants (billions)	Annual percent change	Grants as a Percentage of		
			State-local govt. outlays	Federal outlays	Gross domestic product
1970	$ 24,065	19.3	19.0	12.3	2.4
1975	49,791	14.8	23.5	15.0	3.3
1980	91,451	9.7	26.3	15.5	3.5
1985	105,852	8.5	21.3	11.2	2.7
1988	115,342	6.4	18.6	10.8	2.4
1989	121,928	5.7	18.6	10.7	2.4
1990	135,325	11.0	18.7	10.8	2.5
1991	154,519	14.2	19.5	11.7	2.7
1992	178,065	15.2	20.8	12.9	3.0
1993	193,612	8.7	21.2	13.7	3.1
1994	210,596	8.8	21.8	14.4	3.2
1995	224,992	6.8	22.2	14.8	3.2
1996 (estimated)	236,730	5.2	(NA)	15.1	3.2

SOURCE: Office of Management and Budget, based on *Budget of the United States Government, Fiscal Year 97*.

PROJECT GRANTS Congress appropriates a certain sum, which is allocated to state and local units and sometimes to nongovernmental agencies, based on applications from those who wish to participate. Examples are grants by the National Science Foundation to universities and research institutes to support the work of scientists or grants to states and localities to support training and employment programs.

BLOCK GRANTS Categorical grants provide whatever federal funds are needed to support persons who qualify for the funds; block grants, on the other hand, are usually *capped*. Block grants are broad grants to states for prescribed activities—welfare, child care, education, social services, preventive health, and health services—with only a few specific strings attached. States have great flexibility in deciding how to spend block-grant dollars, but when the federal funds for any fiscal year are gone, there are no more matching federal dollars.

The Politics of Federal Grants

Republicans "have consistently favored fewer strings, less federal supervision, and the delegation of spending discretion to the state and local governments."[30] Democrats have generally been less supportive of broad discretionary block grants, favoring instead more detailed, federally supervised spending. The Republican-controlled 104th Congress (1995–1997) gave a high priority to the creation of block grants. However, Republicans ran into trouble when they tried to lump together welfare, school lunch and breakfast programs, prenatal nutrition programs, and child protection programs in one block grant.

The Republicans did make one major change in federal-state relations with the passage of the Personal Responsibility and Work Opportunity Reconciliation Act of 1996. This act, while retaining Medicaid as a federally funded entitlement program, gives states the option to deny Medicaid to immigrants, even those legally here. But the most important feature of the act was to end Aid to Families with Dependent Children (AFDC), the 61-year-old federally backed guarantee of welfare checks to all eligible mothers and children. The act substituted for it a block grant to each state, with caps on the amount of federal dollars that the state will receive. This act put the main cash welfare program, AFDC, into one welfare block grant and the major federal child-care program into another block grant (Child Care and Development Block Grant, CCDBG). But despite their avowed support for local discretion, Republican conservatives insisted upon some restrictions—for example preventing states from providing additional assistance for children born to welfare mothers and making illegal and legal immigrants ineligible for many welfare programs or food stamps until they become citizens or have worked in the United States for ten years.

The new welfare block grants give states considerable flexibility in how they provide for welfare, but there are federal strings. Most important, no federal funds can be used to cover recipients who do not go to work within two years, and no person can receive federally supported benefits for more than five years. And in order to slow down "the race to the bottom" in which states may try to make themselves "the least attractive state in which to be poor,"[31] Congress also stipulated that in order for states to receive their full share of federal dollars, they must continue to spend at least 75 percent of what they have been spending on welfare.[32]

The battle over the appropriate level of government to control the funds tends to be cyclical. A scholar of federalism explains, "Complaints about excessive federal control tend to be followed by proposals to shift more power to state and local governments. Then, when problems arise in state and local administration—and problems inevitably arise when any organization tries to administer anything—demands for closer federal supervision and tighter federal controls follow."[33]

REGULATORY FEDERALISM AND FEDERAL MANDATES

Fewer federal dollars do not necessarily mean fewer federal controls. On the contrary, the federal government has imposed mandates on states and local governments, often without any offsetting federal funds. State and local officials complain that new federal regulatory devices are far more intrusive than the old-fashioned conditions they used to complain about.[34] One observer concluded, "The role of Congress has changed since 1965 from a generous supplier of funds to a preemptor imposing costs that have the potential for bankrupting many small rural local governments and fiscally strained cities by the year 2000."[35] Nobody knows for sure how much unfunded federal mandates cost, but one study concludes that they may impose a cost on states and cities of $90 billion over the next five years.[36]

Protests from state and local officials against unfunded federal mandates were effective. In 1995 Congress, with President Clinton's support, passed the Unfunded Mandates Reform Act of 1995.[37] The act calls on the Congressional Budget Office and federal agencies to issue reports about the impact of unfunded mandates and to provide judicially enforceable cost-benefit analyses of mandates and regulations as well as to consult state and local officials prior to the issuance of regulations. In addition, the act imposes constraints on Congress itself. A congressional committee that approves any legislation containing a federal mandate must draw attention to the mandate in its report and describe its cost to state and local governments as well as to private companies. If the committee intends any mandate to be partially unfunded, it must explain why it is appropriate for the cost to be borne by the state and local government. With many significant exceptions—such as laws or regulations enforcing constitutional rights, prohibiting discrimination, requiring compliance with accounting and auditing procedures—any member of Congress may raise a point of order against proposals for unfunded mandates.

Whether the Unfunded Mandates Reform Act significantly slows downs federal mandates remains to be seen. The Americans with Disabilities Act, for example, calls on state and local governments to build ramps and alter curbs—renovations that are costing millions. Environmental Protection Agency regulations require states to build automobile pollution-testing stations and take other actions to reduce pollution, but without corresponding federal dollars. "Still, state officials praise the law for increasing congressional awareness of unfunded mandates."[38] One official of the National Conference of State Legislatures said, "We never expected it to be a single-shot deal where we were going to solve all of the unfunded mandates problems. . . . We view it as more of a tool to help us with unfunded mandates and get us sitting at the table more with federal decision-makers."[39]

New Techniques of Federal Control

DIRECT ORDERS   In a few instances, federal regulation takes the form of direct orders that must be complied with under threat of criminal or civil sanction. Examples are the Equal Employment Opportunity Act of 1982, barring job discrimination by state and local governments because of race, color, religion, sex, and national origin, and the Marine Protection Amendments of 1977, prohibiting cities from dumping sewage into the ocean. Because such direct orders raise mild constitutional concerns and more serious political ones, Congress favors other techniques for imposing the federal will on the states.

CROSS-CUTTING REQUIREMENTS   The first and most famous of these requirements (so-called because a condition on one federal grant is extended to all activities supported by federal funds regardless of their source) is Title VI of the 1964 Civil Rights Act, which holds that no person may be discriminated against in the

It is easier to answer questions about unfunded mandates in the abstract; it is hard when faced with specific problems. We need to get behind the abstraction. When we ask, "Should the federal government?" or when we talk about "the state," remember, we are talking about our own pocketbook, not somebody else's. The "national government" is just a shorthand way to ask, "Should we as federal citizens and taxpayers set standards for drinking water, or could we do it better and cheaper at the state level?" The answers to such questions are political in the best sense of the word; that is, they are policy choices, preferences among competing but legitimate values. Nonetheless, when called on to make these policy choices as citizens, we need to be informed so as to increase the probability that we will choose people and policies that will be responsive to our concerns.

use of federal funds because of race, color, or national origin; other laws extend these protections to persons because of gender or handicapped status. More than 60 cross-cutting requirements concern the environment, historic preservation, contract wage rates, access to governmental information, the care of experimental animals, the treatment of human subjects in research projects, and so on.

CROSS-OVER SANCTIONS These sanctions permit the use of federal dollars in one program to influence state and local policy in another. One example is a 1984 act that threatened to reduce federal highway aid by up to 15 percent for any state that failed to adopt a minimum drinking age of 21 by 1987.

TOTAL PREEMPTION This kind of control rests not on the national government's power to spend but on its powers under the supremacy and commerce clauses to preempt conflicting state and local activities. Building on this constitutional authority, federal law in certain areas just preempts state and local governments from the field. "There are fourteen types of total preemption laws, ranging from ones removing all regulatory powers from the states to ones authorizing states to cooperate in enforcing a statute."[40]

PARTIAL PREEMPTION In these instances federal law establishes basic policies but requires states to administer them. Some programs give states an option to participate, but if a state chooses not to do so, the national government then steps in and directly runs the programs. Even worse from the state's point of view is *mandatory partial preemption*, in which the national government requires the state to act on peril of losing other funds but provides no funds to support the state action. The Clean Air Act of 1990 is an example of mandatory partial preemption; the federal government sets national air quality standards and requires states to devise plans and pay for their implementation and enforcement.[41] If a state fails to adopt air pollution plans that are deemed to be adequate, so-called hammer provisions require federal implementation plans to be imposed on the state.[42] State violations of the clean air requirements can be "punished" by a variety of sanctions, including withholding of federal funds for a variety of purposes. Medicaid is another example of the national government providing some dollars but mandating states to provide services that cost more than the federal funds cover.

THE POLITICS OF FEDERALISM

The formal structures of our federal system have not changed much since 1787, but the political realities, especially during the last half-century, have greatly altered how federalism works. To understand these changes, we need to look at some of the trends that continue to fuel the debate about the meaning of federalism.

The Growth of Big Government

Over the past two hundred years there has been a drift of power from other institutions—families, churches and synagogues, the marketplace—to governments, and especially to the national government. "No one planned the growth, but everyone played a part in it."[43] How did this shift come about? For a variety of reasons. One is that many of our problems have become national in scope. Much that was local in 1789, in 1860, or in 1930 is now national—even global. State governments could supervise the relations between small merchants and their few employees, but only the national government can supervise relations between a multinational corporation and its thousands of employees, many organized in national unions.

As industrialization proceeded, powerful interests made demands on the national government. Business groups called on the government for aid in the form of tariffs, a national banking system, subsidies to railroads and the merchant marine, and uniform rules relating to the environment. Farmers learned that the national government could give more aid than the states, and they too began to demand help. By the beginning of this century, urban groups in general, and organized labor in particular, pressed their claims. Big business, big agriculture, and big labor all added up to big government.

The growth of the national economy and the creation of a national transportation and communications network altered people's attitudes toward the national government (see Figure 3–3). Before the Civil War, the national government was viewed as a distant, even foreign, government. Today, in part because of television, most people identify as closely with Washington as with their state capitals. We are apt to know more about our president than about our governor, more about our national senators and representatives than about our state legislators or even about the local officials who run our cities and schools.

The Great Depression of the 1930s stimulated extensive national action on such issues as welfare, unemployment, and farm surpluses. World War II brought federal regulation of wages, prices, and employment, as well as national efforts to allocate resources, train personnel, and support engineering and inventions. After the war the national government helped veterans obtain college degrees and inaugurated a vast system of support for university research. The United States became the most powerful leader of the free world, maintaining substantial military forces even in times of peace. The Great Society programs of the 1960s poured out grants-in-aid to states and localities. City dwellers who had migrated from the rural South to northern cities began to seek federal funds for—at the very least—housing, education, and mass transportation.

Although economic and social conditions created many of the pressures for expansion of the national government, so did political claims. Members of Congress, presidents, federal judges, and federal administrators actively promoted federal initiatives. And until the recent years of overwhelming budget deficits, Congress encouraged this trend. True, when there is widespread conflict about what to do—how to reduce the federal deficit, adopt a national energy policy, reform Social Security, provide health care for the indigent—Congress waits for a national consensus. But when an organized constituency wants something and there is no counterpressure, Congress "responds often to everyone, and with great vigor."[44] Once established, federal programs generate groups with vested interests in promoting, defending, and expanding them. Associations are formed, alliances are made. "In a word, the growth of government has created a constituency of, by, and for government."[45]

The politics of federalism are changing, however, and Congress is pressured to reduce the size and scope of national programs. Tax laws no longer permit automatic increases to compensate for inflation, so Congress faces reduced federal revenues. Second, the cost of entitlement programs such as Social Security and Medicare are going up because there are more older people and they live longer. These programs have widespread public support, and to cut them is politically risky. "With all other options disappearing, it is politically tempting to finance tax cuts by turning over to the states many of the social programs . . . that have become the responsibility of the national government."[46] Thus it is increasingly tempting for Congress to turn over the problems to the states by using block grants.

The Devolution Revolution—A Revolution or Just Rhetoric?

The Republican sweep of the Congress in the 1994 elections carried with it a pledge to return many functions, most especially welfare, back to the states. President Clinton appeared to agree with the general tone of his Republican opponents. In his

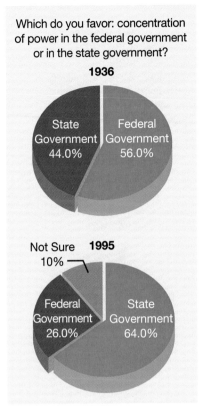

FIGURE 3–3   A Changing View of the Federal Government

SOURCE: Richard P. Nathan, "The Devolution Revolution: An Overview," *The Devolution Revolution* (Rockefeller Institute of Government, 1996).

State of the Union Address before the 104th Congress in 1996, he proclaimed, "The era of big government is over." However, he tempered his comments by saying, "But we cannot go back to the time when our citizens were left to fend for themselves."

In the 104th Congress (1995–1997), Republicans in the House of Representatives passed many bills that would have returned many functions to the states. Yet most proposals did not get through the Senate, and President Clinton vetoed most of those that did. Clinton repeatedly insisted that the federal government continue to guarantee funds to take care of Medicare, Medicaid, the environment, and education.

Then in the summer of 1996, as the elections approached, Congress and the president finally came together for a major overhaul of welfare. Congress also freed the states to set their own highway speed limits, changed the Safe Drinking Water Act to allow states to operate certain programs, and gave states a greater role over how federal rural development funds can be used.

Yet despite this dramatic shift in responsibilities from the national government back to the states, the 104th Congress, like its predecessors, increased the authority of the national government in many areas. "Legislation cleared by the first Republican majority in four decades established national criteria for state-issued driver's licenses, ended state registration of mutual funds, created national food safety standards, nullified state laws that had restricted telecommunications competition and extended federal criminal penalties to cover certain violent crimes."[47] Legislators made a whole host of crimes, including carjacking and stalking, federal crimes and federalized the crime of rape committed while carjacking. The appropriation bills pressured states to keep criminals behind bars by threatening to take grants away from states that failed to meet federal standards. And President Clinton, despite his statement that the era of big government is over, also pushed for an expanded federal role in many areas, calling for restrictions on guns, for changes in the 911 system, and for school uniforms.

In short, although pressure to balance the federal budget continues to constrain the expansion of the federal role and prevent the inauguration of costly new federal programs, and despite growing criticism of the national government, Americans continue to be pragmatic and to prefer whatever level of government seems to be best able to provide needed services, rather than to act because of an emotional or rational commitment to one level of government over another.

THE DEBATE CONTINUES

Until the civil rights revolution of the 1960s, segregationists feared that national officials—responding to different political majorities—would work for racial integration. Thus they praised local government, emphasized the dangers of overcentralization, and argued that the protection of civil rights was not a proper function of the national government. As one political scientist observed, "Federalism has a dark history to overcome. For nearly two hundred years, states' rights have been asserted to protect slavery, segregation, and discrimination."[48]

Today the politics of federalism, even with respect to civil rights, is more complicated than in the past.[49] With changing political power distributions, the national government is not necessarily more favorable to the claims of minorities than state or city governments. With the Supreme Court's not extending marital privacy rights to gays and lesbians, some state constitutions and state courts now provide more protection for these rights than does the U.S. Constitution. State and local governments also "have become the principal agents for advancing the cause of comparable worth. This role challenges the conventional

In recent years citizens have resisted taxes at all levels of government, making it more difficult to fund programs.

From Coast to Coast

Fiscal Capacity to Raise Revenue Through Taxes

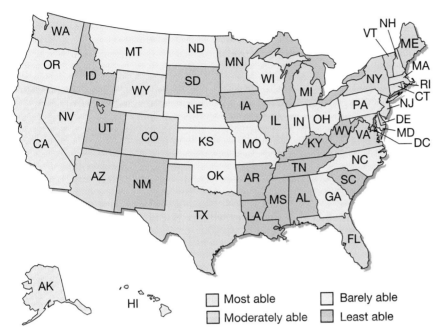

SOURCE: Advisory Commission on Intergovernmental Relations, *Significant Features of Fiscal Federalism*, vol. 2, (Government Printing Office, 1992), p. 268.

wisdom that only centrist alternatives can advance equal opportunity and civil rights for all citizens."[50]

As states more actively regulate the economy, some business interests have been arguing that conflicting state regulations are unduly burdening interstate commerce and are asking for preemptive federal regulation to save them, not only from stringent state regulations but from having to adjust to 50 different state laws.[51] "One national dumb rule is better than 50 inconsistent rules of any kind," says a lawyer who represents trade groups in the food industries and medical devices.[52]

The Reemergence of the States

When the national government slowed the rate of growth of its domestic spending, the states took over some of its responsibilities.[53] "Instead of getting government off the backs of the American people," Ronald Reagan "presided over a huge growth of big government at the state level."[54] Not only were programs shifted to the states, so were the costs of running them. For example, in 1970 Medicaid cost the states about 4 percent of their budgets; now it is in excess of 20 percent.[55] If given still more responsibility for Medicare and Medicaid, "states will have to go through an unbelievable transformation. The states will have to write laws to define disability and benefits . . . design new application forms . . . redo computer programs, cope with new political pressures."[56]

Abandoned by the national government, cities and counties have turned again to their own state capitals. States responded to this plea with mixed

Two Voices on Federalism

President Bill Clinton

Improved cooperation between the federal government and state and local government is critical to the success of our nation in the years ahead. First of all, we must reestablish the federal-state partnership. For too long, Washington has passed on mandates and requirements to the states without supplying the resources to pay for them. As a result, state and local governments have had to substantially increase taxes to provide the required services. In a Clinton administration, we will ensure that the federal government resumes its responsibilities, instead of just passing the buck on to others.

Second, I think we need to reassess the ways in which the federal government can help state and local governments carry out tasks that are traditionally state and local responsibilities. For instance, I believe the federal government can play a greater and more effective role in education, by passing federal standards and requiring national examinations of every American student.

Speaker Newt Gingrich

. . . We have to decentralize power out of Washington, D.C., and disperse power. Let me make this very clear, because they are two very different words. . . . [Decentralize] means we get out of Washington. Governors hear that and they love it because they think it goes to Albany or Atlanta or Sacramento. But we also want to disperse power. That means it actually goes back to the people from whom it comes. . . . So I keep reminding our governors, we're against unfunded mandates in Washington. They might talk to the mayors and county commissioners about unfunded mandates in the states.

SOURCE: *Civic Action* (March/April 1992); Newt Gingrich, "Inauguration Speech," January 4, 1995, from an archive of *The Washington Weekly,* 1996.

results. Some states—Florida, Massachusetts, New Jersey, New York, and Oklahoma—tried with some success to replace the withdrawn federal funds for their cities and schools until they, too, fell upon hard times in the early 1990s. Other states—California, for example—made little effort to replace the federal dollars.[57] These fiscal realities and the economic recession of the early 1990s stalled the states' resurgence. But later in the 1990s the states had reestablished their balanced budgets and had a combined surplus of $18 billion, while the federal government had a deficit in excess of $160 billion.[58]

Block grants give large sums to the states—and also major obligations. Some are concerned that this shift of responsibility back to the states may in fact create 50 budget crises. The coming years will be a severe test for the states, especially for their legislatures, many of which consist of citizen lawmakers. "State legislatures are much more competent than they were 25 years ago. They do have much more ability to make the important decisions, but that doesn't mean they are magicians."[59]

The Future of Federalism

In 1933, seeing state governments helpless during the Great Depression, one writer stated, "I do not predict that the states will go, but affirm that they have gone."[60] Those prophets of doom were wrong. States are stronger than ever. During recent decades state governments have undergone a major transformation. Most have improved their governmental structures, taken on greater roles in funding education, launched programs to help distressed cities, and—despite new constitutional limitations—expanded their tax bases. Able men and women have been attracted to many governorships. "Today, states, in formal representational, policymaking, and implementation terms at least, are more representative, more responsive, more activist, and more professional in their operations than they ever have been. They face their expanded roles better equipped to assume and fulfill them."[61]

The national government, however, is not likely to retreat to a pre-1930 posture or even a pre-1960 one. The underlying economic and social conditions that generated the demand for federal action have not been altered substantially. On

Steve Benson, Arizona Republic.

the contrary, in addition to such traditional issues as helping people find jobs and preventing inflation and depressions, which still require national action, countless new issues have been added to the national agenda by the growth of a global economy based on high technology, service, and information. It is worth remembering that in terms of gross domestic product, many American states are larger than many nations—California, for example, has an economy larger than that of Great Britain—yet most states still lack the jurisdiction by themselves to clean up the air, modernize the air traffic control system, regulate the economy, prevent pollution of rivers, deal with drug abuse, or prevent the spread of AIDS and find its cure. And there are issues such as the lack of decent housing and access to health care for inner-city African Americans and Hispanics and the sky-rocketing costs of health care for all Americans that are beyond the capacity of the states to solve alone.

One prominent student of federalism has written: "On the whole, the problems of American federalism have been greatly exaggerated. The state and local fiscal crises caused by the 1991 recession now seem to be temporary phenomena, not a harbinger of a torturous future. The national government is at least for the moment concentrating more on what it does best: caring for the sick, the poor, and the needy. State and local governments continue to foster the country's economic development."[62] Whether this division of responsibility continues depends in large part on the outcome of our elections.

Most Americans have strong attachments to our federal system—in the abstract. They remain loyal to their states and show a growing and healthy skepticism about the national government (see Figure 3–4). In the 30 years since 1964, distrust of the federal government has grown from 22 percent of the people to 78 percent of the people. Yet most of the time for most of the people, the concerns are about more immediate problems—clean air, safety in the streets, relations between men and women, jobs, the cost of medical care, heating fuel for their homes, and gasoline for their cars. They are not much concerned about the nature

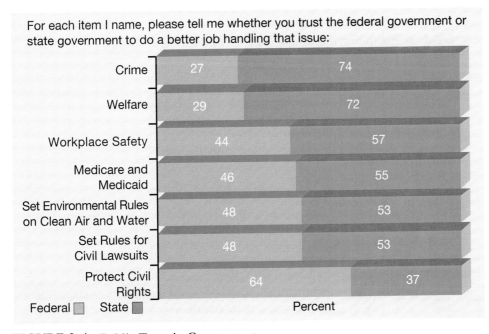

FIGURE 3–4   Public Trust in Government
SOURCE: Surveys by ABC News/Washington Post, March 16–19, 1995.

of federal grants or arguments about the virtues of national versus state action. "Some evidence suggests that the anti-government, anti-Washington consensus is 3,000 miles wide but only a few miles deep."[63] Most Americans are willing to use whatever governmental agencies or combinations of agencies they feel can best serve their needs and represent their interests.

American federalism has modified, and been modified by, the political and social issues facing us during the last two hundred years. It will continue to shape our society. Our federal system remains firmly rooted in our political system as well as our constitutional democracy. We are not about to abolish it or modify it drastically. But just as the federalism of today is as different from that of 1787 as a jet airplane is from a stagecoach, so federalism will continue to evolve as we move into the twenty-first century.

POLITICS ONLINE

Using the Net to Track Welfare Reform

Welfare reforms enacted in 1996 will have important ramifications for federalism for years to come. Under the Family Assistance Act, states are experimenting with a variety of different programs. What are these programs? How are they working?

Because many of the alternatives being tried in the states are new and decentralized, the media may not pay much attention to them. But an alternative source of current information is the Internet, and one of the best places to go is the Health and Human Services Web site:

> http://www.acf.dhhs.gov/ACFNews/press/index.html

Welfare reform is such an important issue for all levels of government that several think tanks are also following the issue. One of these think tanks, the Urban Institute, has prepared an in-depth report on current welfare issues:

> www.urban.org/welfare/overview.html

The Urban Institute also has references to several articles on federalism:

> http:///www.urban.org/index/html

Additional information on welfare reform can be obtained in many states by clicking on the home page for that state or the governor of that state.

Other more general Internet resources on federalism include the Advisory Commission on Intergovernmental Relations, which was abolished by Congress in 1997 but continues to provide material relevant to intergovernmental relations:

> gpo.gov/acir/anrept.html

Other places to check include the Council of State Governments:

> http://204.215.3.21

and the Nelson A. Rockefeller Institute of Government:

> http://rockinst.org

SUMMARY

1. Our federal constitutional system has evolved into something only slightly different in form, yet significantly different in operation, from the 1789 version.

2. It is not possible to divide functions between the national and state governments neatly and without controversy.

3. The national government has the constitutional authority, stemming primarily from its powers to tax and spend, to regulate commerce among the states, and from its war powers, to do what Congress thinks is necessary and proper to promote the general welfare and to provide for the common defense.

4. Although the Supreme Court has put forward some cautionary warnings, there are few if any judicially enforced limits to restrain Congress from interfering with the actions of the states.

5. Today we spend less time than we did in the past debating the constitutional structure of federalism; we have moved on to the politics of federalism. As now interpreted, the Constitution gives voters the option to decide through the political process what to do, who is going to pay, and who is going to get it done.

6. The centralization of constitutional power at the national level over the last two centuries does not mean that federalism is dead. Political power remains dispersed, and states remain active and significant political realities.

7. An individual's ideological bias in favor of either national or state action is likely to reflect concrete political objectives. However, conservative support for states' rights and liberal preference for national action are no longer predictable, as shifting political issues lead to shifting allegiances among the various levels of government.

8. The drive toward a greater role for the national government has been fueled more by underlying economic and social changes than by concerns about federalism, but we detect a vigorous trend toward the view that federalism as a political principle is worthy of being preserved.

9. The major instruments of federal intervention have been various kinds of financial grants-in-aid, of which the most prominent are categorical-formula grants, project grants, and block grants.

10. The national government controls the activities of state and local governments and creates national programs by direct orders, cross-cutting requirements, cross-over sanctions in the use of federal funds, total preemption, and partial preemption.

11. In the 1990s the underlying political struggles between Republicans and Democrats, combined with a tight federal budget, have kept Congress from inaugurating new federal programs and put pressure on it to shift some existing programs back to the states.

12. These political realities have accelerated trends that started in the 1970s. As we enter the twenty-first century, we may be in the midst of a "devolution revolution," but how many functions will be turned over to the states and for how long awaits further political and economic developments.

FURTHER READING

SAMUEL H. BEER, *To Make a Nation: The Rediscovery of American Federalism* (Harvard University Press, Belknap Press, 1993).

CENTER FOR THE STUDY OF FEDERALISM, *Publius: The Journal of Federalism* (Temple University, published quarterly; one issue each year is an "Annual Review of the State of American Federalism").

THOMAS R. DYE, *American Federalism: Competition Among Governments* (Lexington Books, 1990).

DANIEL J. ELAZAR, *The American Mosaic: The Impact of Space, Time, and Culture on American Politics* (Westview Press, 1994).

DANIEL J. ELAZAR, *Exploring Federalism* (University of Alabama Press, 1987).

MICHAEL FIX AND DAPHNE A. KENYON, *Coping with Mandates* (Urban Institute Press, 1990).

AL GORE, *From Red Tape to Results—Creating a Government That Works Better and Costs Less: Report of the National Performance Review* (U.S. Government Printing Office, 1993).

CHRISTOPHER HAMILTON AND DONALD T. WELLS, *Federalism, Power and Political Economy* (Prentice Hall, 1990).

JOHN KINCAID, ED., "American Federalism: The Third Century," *Annals of the American Academy of Political and Social Science* 509 (May 1990).

SUE O'BRIEN AND MARSHALL KAPLAN, *The Governors and the New Federalism* (Westview Press, 1991).

VINCENT OSTROM, *The Meaning of American Federalism* (ICS Press, 1991).

PAUL E. PETERSON, *The Price of Federalism* (Brookings Institution, 1995).

MARTIN REDISH, *The Constitution as Political Structure* (Oxford University Press, 1995).

WILLIAM H. RIKER, *The Development of American Federalism* (Academic Publishers, 1987).

HARRY N. SCHEIBER, *Federalism and the Judicial Mind: Essays on American Constitutional Law and Politics* (Institute of Governmental Studies, University of California at Berkeley, 1992).

THOMAS R. SCHWARTZ AND JOHN E. PECK, *The Changing Face of Fiscal Federalism* (M. E. Sharpe, 1990).

DAVID B. WALKER, *The Rebirth of Federalism: Slouching Toward Washington* (M. E. Sharpe, 1990).

JOSEPH F. ZIMMERMAN, *Contemporary American Federalism: The Growth of National Power* (Praeger, 1992).

4

First Amendment Rights

*C*ongress shall make no law," declares the First Amendment, "respecting an establishment of religion, or prohibiting the free exercise thereof; or abridging the freedom of speech, or of the press, or the right of the people peaceably to assemble, and to petition the Government for a redress of grievances." In this one sentence our Constitution lays down the fundamental principles of a free society: freedom of conscience and freedom of expression.

Although it was the framers who wrote the Constitution, in a sense it was the people who drafted our basic charter of liberties. As we have seen, the Constitution drawn up in Philadelphia included guarantees of a few basic rights, but it lacked a specific bill of rights similar to that found in most state constitutions. This omission aroused widespread suspicion among the people. In order to persuade delegates to the state ratification conventions to vote for the Constitution, the Federalists had to promise to correct this deficiency. In its first session, the new Congress proposed twelve amendments, ten of which were ratified by the end of 1791 and became part of the Constitution. These ten amendments are known as the Bill of Rights.[1] (As we saw in Chapter 1, another of those proposed amendments was ratified 202 years later to become the Twenty-seventh Amendment.)

Note that the Bill of Rights literally applies *only to the national government*. As John Marshall held in *Barron v Baltimore* (1833), the Bill of Rights limits the national government, not the state governments.[2] Why not the states? The people were confident they could control their own state officials, and most of the state constitutions already had bills of rights. It was the new and distant central government they feared. As it turned out, those fears were largely misdirected. The national government, responsive to tens of millions of voters from a variety of races, creeds, religions, and economic interests, has shown less tendency to curtail civil liberties than have state and local governments. Until recently, for the most part, state judges have not used the bills of rights in their respective state constitutions to protect civil liberties.

When the Fourteenth Amendment, which *does* apply to the states, was adopted in 1868, some contended that its **due process clause**—which states that no person shall be deprived of life, liberty, or property without due process of law—limits states in precisely the same way the Bill of Rights limits the national government. At least, they argued, freedom of speech should be protected by the Fourteenth Amendment. For decades the Supreme Court refused to interpret the Fourteenth Amendment in this way. Then in 1925, in *Gitlow v New York*, the Court announced: "For present purposes we may and do assume that freedom of speech and of the press—which are protected by the First Amendment from abridgment by Congress—are among the fundamental personal rights and 'liberties' protected by the due process clause of the Fourteenth Amendment from impairment by the States."[3]

THE NATIONALIZATION OF THE BILL OF RIGHTS

Gitlow v New York was a revolutionary decision. For the first time, the U.S. Constitution protected freedom of speech and of the press from abridgment by state and local governments. By the 1940s the other provisions of the First Amendment—religion, assembly, petition—had been brought within the scope of the Fourteenth Amendment. Today the First Amendment's restraints are applied to all who exercise governmental authority, at national, state, or local levels.

The Nationalization of the Bill of Rights

1890 No taking of property without just compensation (*Chicago, Milwaukee and St. Paul Ry v Minnesota*, 134 US 418, 1890)

1925 Freedom of speech (*Gitlow v New York*)

1931 Freedom of press (*Near v Minnesota*)

1932 Fair trial (*Powell v Alabama*)

1934 Free exercise of religion (*Hamilton v Regents of California*, confirmed in 1940 by *Cantwell v Connecticut*)

1937 Freedom of assembly (*De Jonge v Oregon*)

1942 Right to counsel in capital cases (*Betts v Brady*)

1947 Separation of church and state; establishment of religion (*Everson v Board of Education*)

1948 Right to a public trial (*In re Oliver*)

1949 Right against unreasonable searches and seizure (*Wolf v Colorado*)

1958 Freedom of association (*NAACP v Alabama*)

1961 Exclusionary rule (*Mapp v Ohio*)

1962 Right against cruel and unusual punishments (*Robinson v California*)

1963 Right to counsel in felony cases (*Gideon v Wainwright*)

1964 Right against self-incrimination (*Mallory v Hogan*)

1965 Right to confront witnesses (*Pointer v Texas*)

1965 Right of privacy (*Griswold v Connecticut*)

1966 Right to an impartial jury (*Parker v Gladden*)

1967 Right to a speedy trial (*Klopfer v North Carolina*)

1967 Right to compulsory process for obtaining witnesses (*Washington v Texas*)

1968 Right to a jury trial for all serious crimes (*Duncan v Louisiana*)

1969 Right against double jeopardy (*Benton v Maryland*)

1972 Right to counsel for all crimes involving a jail term (*Argersinger v Hamlin*)

If the First Amendment applies to the states, why not the other parts of the Bill of Rights, most of which have to do with the rights of persons accused of crimes and with restraints on police procedures? Beginning in the 1930s, and continuing at an accelerated pace during the 1960s, the Supreme Court **selectively incorporated** provision after provision of the Bill of Rights into the due process clause.[4] Today the Fourteenth Amendment imposes on the states all the provisions of the Bill of Rights except those of the Second, Third, Seventh, and Tenth Amendments and the grand jury requirements of the Fifth Amendment. When we talk about the Bill of Rights today, we are really talking about limits on the power of all who govern, whether they do so on behalf of the national government, the states, or local units of government.

How are we to distinguish between those provisions of the Bill of Rights that are incorporated into the Fourteenth Amendment—that is, made to limit state and local governments—from those that are not? The rights *not* incorporated are those the Supreme Court has concluded could be replaced by other procedures without necessarily resulting in a denial of justice or liberty. Whereas no nation could be considered free without freedom of speech, for example—which is why it is incorporated as part of the due process clause of the Fourteenth Amendment—justice could be done without necessarily requiring a grand jury indictment before bringing people to trial. That is why this provision in the Fifth Amendment has not been incorporated.

In addition to the rights specifically protected by the Constitution, the Supreme Court has found constitutional protection for other fundamental rights. For example, the rights of association and of privacy, as well as the right to travel, are not mentioned anywhere in the Constitution. Yet these important but unexpressed rights have nonetheless been found to share constitutional protection in common with explicit guarantees.[5]

After the Supreme Court incorporated most of the national Bill of Rights into the Fourteenth Amendment, little attention was paid by state judges—or anybody else—to the bills of rights in their respective state constitutions. "The Supreme Court took such complete control of the field that state judges could sit back in the conviction that their part was simply to await the next landmark decision."[6] Recently, however, stimulated in part by the U.S. Supreme Court's more limited interpretation of some provisions of the national Bill of Rights, there has been a renewal of interest in state constitutions as independent sources of additional protection for civil liberties and civil rights.[7]

Advocates of what has come to be called **new judicial federalism** contend that the U.S. Constitution should set minimum but not maximum standards to protect our rights. There is nothing, they argue, to keep state courts from using similar provisions of the bill of rights in their own state constitutions to provide more protection for rights than is to be found in the U.S. Constitution. Moreover, state bills of rights sometimes have language that encourages a more expansive protection of rights than does the national Bill of Rights. For example, a dozen states have an equal rights amendment in their constitutions, and eleven explicitly protect the right of privacy.[8] The Louisiana state constitution prohibits age discrimination; 35 state constitutions affirm the right of free speech; 36 state constitutions have clauses that could easily be construed as going beyond the Second Amendment in protecting the right to bear arms.[9] It should be noted that some state constitutions retain provisions that are in conflict with the national Bill of Rights, but they are inoperative because of the supremacy clause in the national constitution. For example, the Tennessee constitution, Article IX, Section 2, stipulates: "No person who denies the being of God, or a future state of rewards and punishments, shall hold any office in the civil department of this state." This conflicts with the establishment and freedom of religion clauses of the U.S. Constitution.[10]

Thirty-two state supreme courts have found some rights protected to a greater extent than the Supreme Court of the United States has found to be secured by the national Bill of Rights.[11] Nevertheless, state court decisions extending rights beyond the limits secured by the U.S. Constitution are exceptions and are to be found in a substantial manner in relatively few states, such as California, Alaska, Florida, and Massachusetts.

If a state supreme court goes too far beyond public sentiment in its own state, its decisions run the risk of being overturned by an amendment to the state constitution. In 1990, for example, in California and Alaska, after their respective state courts extended to criminal defendants some rights beyond those provided by the U.S. Constitution, "victims' rights" amendments were added to these state constitutions to reverse the effect of those decisions and to forbid state judges from so extending the rights of criminal defendants beyond those provided by the U.S. Constitution. And since most state judges lack lifetime tenure and are subject to electoral contests, state judges "who stray too far from most of the people of their state's understanding of their state constitutions are likely to get chucked out of office,"[12] as happened in California in 1988 with the defeat of Chief Justice Rose Bird and two other liberal justices. Thus, despite the revival of interest in state bills of rights, the U.S. Supreme Court and the national Bill of Rights remain the dominant protectors of civil liberties and civil rights.

CONGRESS SHALL MAKE NO LAW RESPECTING AN ESTABLISHMENT OF RELIGION

The first words of the First Amendment are emphatic and brief: "Congress shall make no law respecting an establishment of religion." The framers were reacting to the English system, wherein the Crown was the head not only of the government but also of the established church—the Church of England—and public officials were required to take an oath of support for the established church as a condition of holding office.

The **establishment clause** goes beyond merely forbidding the establishment of a religion. "A given law might not establish a state religion but nevertheless be one 'respecting' that end in the sense of being a step that could lead to such establishment and hence offend the First Amendment."[13] On the other hand, the clause does not prevent governments from accommodating to religious needs. To what extent and under which conditions governments may accommodate to these needs is at the heart of much of the debate among the justices in interpreting the clause.

Establishment clause cases are not easy. They stir deep feelings, and the justices, reflecting differences in the nation, are often divided among themselves. As Justice Clarence Thomas put it bluntly, "Our Establishment Clause jurisprudence is in hopeless disarray."[14] The prevailing doctrine, though under attack inside the Supreme Court and within the country, stems from a 1947 decision of the Supreme Court, *Everson v Board of Education*, that the establishment clause created a wall of separation between church and state, and that it prohibits any law or governmental action designed to confer any benefit on religion, even if all sects are treated the same.[15] This strict separation of church and state doctrine was further elaborated in *Lemon v Kurtzman* (1971), and despite considerable criticism of the so-called *Lemon test*, it has never been specifically overruled. Under this three-part test, (1) a law must have a secular legislative purpose; (2) its primary effect must neither advance nor inhibit religion; and (3) it must avoid "excessive government entanglement with religion." The establishment clause is designed to prevent three evils: "sponsorship, financial support, and active involvement of the sovereign in religious activity."[16] The *Lemon* test of what violates the establishment

Forms of Citation

In this and the next several chapters, we discuss constitutional rules at length, and to talk about the Constitution is to talk about Supreme Court decisions. Many of these decisions are cited in the notes at the back of the book so that you can look them up if you wish. Two forms of citation are used:

1. Official Supreme Court reports are cited as: *Gitlow v New York*, 268 US 652 (1925). This means that this case can be found in the 268th volume of the *United States Supreme Court Reports* on page 652, and it was decided in 1925. These reports are published by the U.S. Government Printing Office.

2. For more recent cases, see the advance sheets of *United States Supreme Court Reports*, published by the Lawyers' Cooperative Publishing Company of Rochester, New York. An example is a case involving First Amendment issues, *Denver Area Educational Television v FCC*, in which the Supreme Court upheld two provisions of a federal law permitting cable TV operators to prohibit indecent programming on leased access channels, but not two other provisions. It is cited as: 135 L Ed 2d 888 (1996). This means that it can be found in volume 135 of the Lawyers' Edition, second series, starting on page 888, and it was decided in 1996.

clause apparently still retains the support of Justices John Paul Stevens, Ruth Bader Ginsburg, and Stephen Breyer.[17]

A rival test championed by Justice Sandra Day O'Connor is the *endorsement test*: O'Connor believes that the clause forbids governmental practices that a reasonable observer would view as endorsing religion, even if there is no coercion.[18] The endorsement test has been honed in a series of decisions as the Court has struggled with the question of what governments may or may not allow religious symbols to be displayed on, in, or near public properties and in public places. For example, the Court concluded that when a city displayed a crèche (Nativity scene) in a shopping district along with Santa's house and other secular and religious symbols of the Christmas season, there was little danger that a reasonable person could conclude that the city was endorsing religion.[19] On the other hand, the Constitution does not permit a county to display the Nativity scene in a courthouse because, in this context, the county gives the impression that it is endorsing the display's religious message.[20]

Justice Anthony Kennedy has put forward a *coercion test*, under which he interprets the establishment clause not to prevent governmental actions that may accommodate to religious activities but to forbid governments from imposing any pressure on persons to participate in religious activities, even if such pressure falls short of legal compulsion, such as prayer at high school graduations.[21]

There is also a *neutrality test* emerging. As Justice David Souter recently restated for the Court, "The heart of the Establishment Clause [is] that government should not prefer one religion to another, or religion to irreligion."[22] The clause does not require or even allow a government to provide a religious exemption "from neutral laws of general applicability, even if religion is incidentally benefited."[23] Justice Antonin Scalia, speaking for a plurality of the Court, after going out of his way to repudiate an endorsement test, applied the neutrality test and announced: "Religious expression cannot violate the Establishment Clause where (1) it is purely private and (2) occurs in a traditional or designated public forum, publicly announced and open to all on equal terms, even if a reasonable observer would see the expression as indicating state endorsement."[24]

Chief Justice William Rehnquist and Justices Scalia and Thomas are edging toward a *nonpreferentialist test*.[25] They appear to believe that the Constitution simply prohibits favoritism toward a particular religion, but does not prohibit governmental accommodation of religious activities or even some nonpreferential support for religious organizations, so long as individuals are not legally coerced into participating in religious activities, and religious activities are not singled out for favorable treatment.

Applying these generalities, we find that the establishment clause forbids states, including state universities, colleges, and school districts, to introduce any kind of devotional exercises into the public school curriculum. However, the Supreme Court has not, as it is sometimes said, prohibited prayer in public schools. It is not unconstitutional for people to pray in a school building. What is unconstitutional is sponsorship or encouragement of prayer by public school authorities.[26] In 1992 the Court extended the ban against school-endorsed prayer in public schools to forbid the use of a nondenominational prayer at primary and secondary school graduations. The Court concluded that such a practice coerces students into participating in religious ceremonies.[27]

Devotional reading of the Bible, recitation of the Lord's Prayer, and posting of the Ten Commandments on the walls of classrooms in public schools are also prohibited by the Constitution. A state may not forbid the teaching of evolution or require the simultaneous teaching of "creation science"—that is, the belief that human life did not evolve but rather was created by a single act of God.[28]

Tax exemptions for church property, along with that of other nonprofit institutions, are constitutional. State legislatures and Congress may hire chaplains to open each day's legislative session—a practice that has continued without interruption since the first session of Congress. But if done in a public school, this practice would be unconstitutional. Apparently, the difference is that legislators, as adults, are not "susceptible to religious indoctrination or peer pressure."[29] Also, as the joke goes, legislators need the prayer more.

Parochial School Aid

A troublesome area involves attempts by many states to provide financial assistance to parochial schools. The Supreme Court has tried to draw a line between permissible public aid to students, including those in sectarian schools, and impermissible public aid to religion.

At the college level the problems are relatively simple. Tax funds may be used to construct buildings and operate educational programs at church-related schools, as long as the money is not spent directly on buildings used for religious purposes or on teaching religious subjects. Even if students choose to attend religious schools and become ministers, governmental aid to these students is permissible. Such aid has a secular purpose; its effect on religion is the result of individual choice, "and it does not confer any message of state endorsement of religion."[30]

At the elementary and secondary levels, however, the constitutional problems become more complicated, and "the current law on government aid to religious schools is a quagmire."[31] Here the secular and religious parts of institutions and instruction are much more closely interwoven. Students are younger and more susceptible to indoctrination, and the chances are greater that aid given to church-operated schools might seep into aid for religion.

Despite the constitutional obstacles, some states have attempted to provide tax credits or deductions for those who send their children to private, largely church-affiliated schools. Deductions or credits available only to parents of children attending nonpublic schools are unconstitutional, but allowing taxpaying parents to deduct or take a credit from their state income taxes for what they paid for tuition and other costs to send their children to school—public or private—is constitutionally permissible, even if most of the benefit goes to those who send their children to private religious schools.[32]

The Supreme Court has also approved using tax funds to provide students who attend primary and secondary church-operated schools (except those that deny admission because of race or religion) with textbooks, standardized tests, lunches, transportation to and from school, diagnostic services for speech and hearing problems, and other kinds of remedial help—provided such services take place outside of the school building and away from the "pervasively sectarian atmosphere of the church-related schools."[33]

Tax funds may not be used in religious schools to pay teachers' salaries, purchase equipment, provide counseling for students, produce teacher-prepared tests, repair facilities, or transport students on field trips. School authorities may not permit religious instructors to come into public school buildings during the school day to provide religious instruction on a voluntary basis.

However, in 1993, the Court upheld the assignment of a sign-language interpreter, paid for by public funds, to accompany a deaf child to a parochial school. The Court held that this was aid to a student, not to a religion. In the context of a state program that made such services generally available, there could be no danger that such a practice could be construed as an endorsement of religion. The minority contended that since the interpreter would be obliged to follow the deaf student throughout his day, including attendance at Mass, "the interpreter's every gesture would be infused with religious significance."[34]

Children may pray in public schools, provided that the prayer is not authorized, organized, or endorsed by the school authorities.

The board decided not to allow the Klan to put up the cross because to do so might be construed as state support for a religion contrary to the establishment clause. But the courts, ultimately the U.S. Supreme Court, concluded that under these circumstances the board had violated the Klan's free speech rights. Justice Antonin Scalia, speaking for three other justices, wrote: "Religious expression cannot violate The Establishment Clause where (1) it is purely private and (2) occurs in a traditional or designated public forum, publicly announced and open to all on equal terms." Justice Sandra Day O'Connor concurred to create a majority because she concluded that in these circumstances there was no endorsement of religion.*

*Capitol Square Review Board v Pinette, 132 L Ed 650 (1995).

Brookins, *Richmond Times Dispatch.*
© 1982 Field Enterprises, Inc.

Why is it constitutional for state governments to pay for books but not for maps? For bus trips but not for field trips? For standardized tests but not for tests prepared by teachers? For a sign-language interpreter, but not for teachers? Those on the "approved" side meet the three-part *Lemon* test, but those on the "forbidden" side fail one of the requirements. Thus, transportation to and from school, which is permitted, involves a routine trip that every student makes every day; it is unrelated to any aspect of the curriculum. Field trips, which cannot be paid for by tax funds, are controlled by teachers and are aids to instruction. Books and standardized tests, which can be bought by tax funds, can be easily evaluated to ensure that they are not designed to promote religion, whereas maps or teacher-prepared tests cannot be so readily checked. And in cases involving teaching by public teachers in parochial schools, the supervision to ensure avoidance of religious influences creates excessive entanglement of church and state, whereas a sign-language interpreter does no more than accurately interpret whatever material is presented to the class as a whole.

Right to Worship as One Chooses

The Constitution not only forbids the establishment of religion, but it also contains a **free exercise clause** that forbids Congress and the states from passing any law "prohibiting the free exercise thereof." "The Court has struggled to find a neutral course between the two religion clauses, both of which are cast in absolute terms, and either of which, if expanded to a logical extreme, would tend to clash with the other."[35] In addition, religious speech is protected by the Constitution. As the Court has pointed out: "There is a crucial difference between *government* speech endorsing religion, which the Establishment Clause forbids, and *private* speech endorsing religion, which the Free Speech and Free Exercise Clauses protect."[36]

The tension between the two religion clauses became evident when the University of Virginia denied a student group student fee funds to pay a printer for their religious newspaper. The university felt that because of the establishment clause it could not give public moneys to support a newspaper that "primarily promotes a belief in or about a deity." The students alleged that this action deprived them of their right to freedom of speech, including religious speech. The Supreme Court agreed with the students that the establishment clause did not justify a state agency making this kind of "viewpoint discrimination." As long as the state's action was neutral there was no violation of the establishment clause. On the contrary, "the neutrality commanded of the State by the separate Clauses of the First Amendment was compromised by the University's course of action."[37]

Unconventional religions are entitled to the same constitutional protection as are the more traditional ones. The Constitution provides no definition of a church or religion, and the Supreme Court has been reluctant, understandably, to get into these questions. The free exercise clause extends to those who act on sincerely held religious beliefs, not just to those who respond to a specific command of a particular church. But, although the Court does not "underestimate the difficulty of distinguishing between religious and secular convictions and determining whether a professed belief is sincerely held,"[38] only beliefs rooted in a religion are protected by the free exercise clause.

The right to hold any or no religious *belief* is one of our few absolute rights. No government has authority to compel the acceptance of any creed or to censor it. A state may not compel a religious belief or deny persons any right because of their beliefs or lack of them. Requiring religious oaths as a condition of public employment or as a prerequisite to running for public office is unconstitutional. In fact, the only time the Constitution mentions the word religion is to state: "No religious Test shall ever be required as a Qualification to any Office or public Trust under the United States" (Article VI).

Compulsory education laws cannot force Amish children to attend public schools beyond eighth grade.

Although carefully protected, the right to *practice* a religion has had less protection than the right to hold particular beliefs. Religious convictions do not ordinarily exempt one from obeying an otherwise valid and nondiscriminatory law or government regulation. Prior to 1990 the Supreme Court applied what is known as the *compelling interest test* and carefully scrutinized laws alleged to infringe on religious practices. The Court insisted that the government provide some compelling public purpose to justify the infringement: "Only those interests of the highest order and those not otherwise served can overbalance legitimate claims to the free exercise of religion."[39] In other words, the Constitution was thought to throw "a mantle of protection" around religious practices, and the burden was on the government to justify interfering with them.

Then, in 1990, the Rehnquist Court significantly altered the interpretation of the free exercise clause. In *Employment Division v Smith*, the Court discarded the compelling interest test, except as it applied to laws denying people unemployment compensation. Outside of this narrow field, so far as the Constitution is concerned, a government no longer has to show a compelling interest in order to apply its general laws to religious practices. As long as a law does not single out and ban religious practices because "they are engaged in for religious reasons, or only because of the religious belief they display," a general law may be applied to conduct even if it is religiously inspired. In this particular instance, Oregon was allowed to deny unemployment benefits to two Native Americans who were fired because they used peyote as part of their religious rituals.[40]

Three years later, however, the city of Hialeah, Florida, was told that it could not apply its ordinances forbidding the slaughtering of animals as part of religious rituals to the Santeria religious services since other forms of animal slaughtering are allowed, and it was clear that these ordinances had been designed specifically to forbid the slaughter of animals as part of religious rituals in the Santeria religion.[41] Similarly, in 1993, the Court declared unconstitutional a public school practice that made its facilities available after school hours to any organization except religious ones. The Court struck down this practice more as a content-based restriction on speech than as an interference with religious freedom, but it also held that to allow religious groups the same right to use school facilities outside of school hours as any other group did not violate the establishment clause.[42]

Even prior to *Employment Division v Smith*, when the Supreme Court was using the compelling interest test, it nonetheless upheld laws and regulations outlawing business activities on Sunday, as applied to Orthodox Jews, and forbidding military officers to wear headgear while indoors, as applied to an Orthodox Jew's wearing of a yarmulke (skullcap). Congress subsequently intervened to make such practices permissible. The Court has also sustained an Internal Revenue Service regulation denying tax exemption to religious schools that admit members of only one race.[43] The Forest Service was allowed to construct a road through a portion of national forest held sacred by Native Americans and used by them for religious ceremonies.[44]

On the other hand, a state may not require Jehovah's Witnesses (or anyone else, for that matter) to participate in public school flag-salute ceremonies. Although a state may compel parents to send their children to some kind of accredited school, parents have a constitutional right to send their children to a church-sponsored rather than to a public school. Similarly, a state's compulsory school laws cannot compel the Amish to send their children to school beyond the eighth grade. Through the eighth grade the interests of the state in ensuring that all children learn basic skills overbalance religious convictions; after the eighth grade, religious convictions are given priority.

The Religious Freedom Restoration Act of 1993

The Supreme Court's decision in *Employment Division v Smith* promoted "an unprecedented coalition of political forces and an extraordinary congressional reaction."[45] In 1993 Congress passed and President Bill Clinton signed the Religious Freedom Restoration Act, which was explicitly designed to reverse that decision and restore the use of the compelling interest test. The Religious Freedom Restoration Act exempts people from laws and governmental actions that burden their religious freedom, even if the burden results from "a rule of general applicability," except where the government can demonstrate that the burden is "the least restrictive means of furthering a compelling interest." By the terms of this law, "A person whose religious exercise" has been violated by a law or regulation may "assert that violation as a claim or defense in a judicial proceeding and obtain appropriate relief against [the] government."[46] It is not clear precisely how in practice one asserts this right.

In signing the bill, President Clinton said that reversing a decision of the Supreme Court "is a power that is rightly hesitantly and infrequently exercised by the United States Congress. But this is an issue in which that extraordinary measure was clearly called for."[47] That Congress can confer such a defense for persons who refuse to comply with federal laws and regulations is one thing; but that it can confer such a right on persons who do not comply with their own state and local laws and regulations raises interesting questions of federalism. It is not clear by what authority Congress can so diminish the power of state governments and restrict their power to legislate. If a religion permits individuals, under some circumstances, to avoid laws applied to others, it is predictable that people will claim this status, even though they may not be acting because of religious convictions or because of the commands of a church.

FREE SPEECH AND FREE PEOPLE

Government by the people is based on every person's right to speak freely, to organize in groups, to question the decisions of the government, and to campaign openly against it. Only through free and uncensored expression of opinion can government be kept responsive to the electorate and political power be transferred peacefully. Elections, separation of powers, and constitutional guarantees are meaningless unless all persons have the right to speak frankly and to hear and judge for themselves the worth of what others have to say.

Despite the fundamental importance of free speech to a democracy, some people seem to believe speech should be free only for those who agree with them. Americans overwhelmingly support principles of tolerance when such principles are presented in general, abstract fashion—for example, "Do you believe in freedom of speech?" They are less tolerant, however, when the speech is directed at them or is critical of their race, religion, or ethnic origin.

Free speech is not simply the personal right of individuals to have their say; it is also the right of the rest of us to hear them. John Stuart Mill, whose *Essay on Liberty* (1859) is the classic defense of free speech, put it this way: "The peculiar evil of silencing the expression of opinion, is that it is robbing the human race. . . . If the opinion is right, they are deprived of the opportunity of exchanging error for truth; if wrong, they lose what is almost as great a benefit, the clearer perception and livelier impression of truth, produced by its collision with error."[48]

Freedom of speech is, as Justice Robert H. Jackson said, "freedom to differ as to things that touch the heart of the existing order."[49] Yet some who say they believe in free speech draw the line at ideas they consider dangerous. What is a dangerous idea? Who decides? In the realm of political ideas, who can find an objective, eternally valid standard of right? Or as Chief Justice William H. Rehnquist put it for the Supreme Court, "The First Amendment recognizes no such thing as a 'false' idea."[50] The search for truth involves the possibility—even the inevitability—of error. The search cannot go on unless it proceeds freely in the minds and speech of all. This means, in the words of Justice Oliver Wendell Holmes, Jr., "not free thought for those who agree with us but freedom for the thought that we hate."[51]

Justice Hugo Black, a former U.S. senator from Alabama and a member of the Supreme Court from 1937 to 1971, was a noted champion of First Amendment Rights.

Even though the First Amendment explicitly denies Congress the power to pass any law abridging freedom of speech, the amendment has never been interpreted in such absolute terms. Like almost all rights, the freedoms of speech and of the press are limited. In discussing the constitutional power of government to regulate speech, it is useful to distinguish among *belief*, *speech*, and *action*.

At one extreme is the right to *believe* as we wish, a right as absolute as any can be for people living in an organized society. Despite occasional deviations in practice, the traditional American view is that thoughts are inviolable. No government has the right to punish a person for beliefs or to interfere in any way with freedom of conscience.

At the other extreme is *action*, which is usually restrained. The Constitution protects from governmental regulation our right to believe we should drive our automobile through red lights, but we have no constitutional right to ignore traffic signals. As has been said, "The right to swing your arm ends where the other person's nose begins."

Speech stands somewhere between belief and action. It is not an absolute right as is belief, but neither is it as exposed to governmental restraint as is action. Some kinds of speech—obscenity, child pornography, libel, sedition, or speech that constitutes fighting words—although not "entirely invisible to the Constitution"[52] are not entitled, in most circumstances, to any constitutional protection. Many problems arise in distinguishing between what does and does not fit into these categories of "unprotected speech." All other speech is constitutionally protected from governmental regulation—but how much protection?

Historic Constitutional Tests

It is useful to start with the three constitutional tests developed earlier in this century, for they continue to reflect basic judicial and public attitudes toward governmental regulation of speech. These are the *bad tendency doctrine*, the *clear and present danger doctrine*, and the *preferred position doctrine*.

THE BAD TENDENCY DOCTRINE According to the adherents of the **bad tendency doctrine**, the Constitution authorizes legislative bodies to forbid speech that has a tendency to lead to illegal action. Moreover, "the legislature cannot reasonably be required to measure the danger from every . . . utterance in the nice balance of a jeweler's scale. . . . It may, in the exercise of its judgment, suppress the threatened danger in its incipiency."[53]

This doctrine, which stems from the common law, has not had the support of the Supreme Court since *Gitlow v New York* in 1925. Nonetheless, many legislators, city council members, and others (including some state courts as late as 1982) appear to hold this position.[54] It also seems to be the view of many college students who want to see their institution punish student colleagues or faculty who express "hateful" or "offensive" ideas.

Does the Constitution permit a city council or the trustees of a public university to ban public utterances of abusive racial remarks or insulting sexual taunts because they might lead to violence, or because they are so demeaning to some that such speech would interfere with their rights to an education or to a positive workplace? Those who hold to the bad tendency test contend that such a law or regulation would be constitutional because abusive racial or insulting sexual remarks can in fact provoke violence, do inflict injury on individuals, and create damaging racial divisions. These laws and regulations, they contend, are reasonable means to preserve the public order to protect the rights of persons not to be abused because of their race or sex. Empowering public officials to make such judgments, however, runs the risk that they may restrict speech merely because they dislike it.

THE CLEAR AND PRESENT DANGER DOCTRINE Justice Oliver Wendell Holmes, Jr., announced this celebrated doctrine in *Schneck v United States*: "The question in every case is whether the words are used in circumstances and are of such a nature as to create a clear and present danger that they will bring about substantive evils that Congress has a right to prevent."[55] Justice Louis D. Brandeis further elaborated in a later case, "No danger flowing from speech can be deemed clear and present, and unless the incidence of the evil" that will result from a speech "is so imminent that it may befall before there is opportunity for full discussion."[56]

Supporters of the **clear and present danger doctrine** concede that speech is not an absolute right. Yet they believe free speech to be so fundamental to the operations of a constitutional democracy that no government should be allowed to restrict any particular speech unless it can demonstrate that there is such a close connection between the speech and an illegal action that the speech itself takes on the character of the action. To shout "Fire" *falsely* in a crowded theater is Justice Holmes's famous example. A government should not be allowed to interfere with speech unless it can prove, ultimately to a skeptical judiciary, that the particular speech in question presented an immediate danger of a major evil—for example, speech leading to a riot, destruction of property, corruption of an election, or direct interference with recruitment of soldiers.

Consider our earlier example of public university hate-speech codes and city ordinances against abusive or insulting language. Advocates of the clear and present danger doctrine would argue that, even though a legislature had made it illegal to make abusive racial or insulting sexual remarks in public or the public university had made it grounds for disciplining a student, the regulation could not be applied constitutionally to any person for anything he or she said or wrote, unless the government or university presents convincing evidence that the particular remarks made by the particular individual might clearly and presently have led to a riot or to direct injury to specific individuals or be the direct cause of some other serious activity the government has a right to make illegal or the university to punish.

THE PREFERRED POSITION DOCTRINE Those who hold to the **preferred position doctrine**, such as the late Justice Hugo L. Black, come close to the position that freedom of expression, that is, the use of words and pictures, may never be curtailed. This does not mean that there is nothing left for judges to decide, for a line must still be drawn between speech and nonspeech.

The preferred position interpretation of the First Amendment gives these freedoms a preferred position in our constitutional hierarchy. Judges have a special duty to protect these freedoms and should be most skeptical about laws trespassing on them. Legislative majorities are free to experiment with and to adopt various schemes regulating our lives in general, but when they tamper with freedom of speech, they interfere with the channels of the political process. Only if the government can show that limitations on speech are absolutely necessary to avoid imminent and serious substantive evils are such limitations to be allowed.

If we apply the preferred position doctrine to our example of a law against abusive racial or insulting sexual remarks, the law itself would be declared unconstitutional. Restraints on such abusive speech are not absolutely necessary to prevent riots or other social disturbances. Whatever danger may come from such remarks does not justify restricting free comment. Moreover, supporters of the preferred position doctrine contend that the law itself, by imposing a *chilling effect* on speech and not merely its application, violates the Constitution.

Current Constitutional Tests

The three historic doctrines just discussed continue to provide the background for debates on freedom of speech. Today, however, the Supreme Court is more apt to use the following doctrines to measure the limits of governmental power.

Prior Restraint Of all the forms of governmental interference with expression, judges are most suspicious of those that impose **prior restraint**—restraints prior to publication. Prior restraints include licensing requirements before a speech can be made, a motion picture shown, or a newspaper published. The Supreme Court has refused to declare all forms of prior censorship unconstitutional, but a "prior restraint on expression comes to this court with a 'heavy presumption' against its constitutionality. . . . The Government thus carries a heavy burden of showing justification for the enforcement of such a restraint."[57] Except as applied to motion pictures, most of the few examples of the Court's actual approval of prior restraints relate to military and security matters. The Court has also upheld the right of high school authorities to exercise "editorial control over the style and content of student speech" in school newspapers and other "school-sponsored expressive activities so long as their actions are reasonably related to legitimate pedagogical concerns."[58]

Vagueness Any law is unconstitutional if it "either forbids or requires the doing of an act in terms so vague that men of common intelligence must necessarily guess at its meaning and differ as to its application."[59] Laws touching First Amendment freedoms are required to pass even more rigid standards regarding vagueness. These laws must not allow those who administer them so much discretion that they could discriminate against those whose views they dislike. The law must also not be so vague that people are afraid to exercise protected freedoms. Such vague and overboard laws have a *chilling effect* on freedom of speech. The Supreme Court has struck down laws that condemn "sacrilegious" movies or publications of "criminal deeds of bloodshed or lust . . . so massed as to become vehicles for inciting violent and depraved crimes."[60]

Overbreadth Closely related to the vagueness doctrine is the overbreadth doctrine, the requirement that a statute relating to First Amendment freedoms cannot be so broad that it sweeps within its prohibitions protected speech as well as nonprotected activities; for example, a loyalty oath that endangers protected forms of association along with illegal activities. Because the very existence of overbroad

statutes tends to repress protected speech, such statutes may be declared unconstitutional on their face, that is, entirely and not in some particular application of the law.

LEAST DRASTIC MEANS   Even for an important purpose, a legislature may not choose a law that impinges on First Amendment freedoms if there are other ways to handle the problem. To illustrate, a state may protect the public from unscrupulous lawyers, but it may not do so by forbidding organizations to make legal services available to their members or by forbidding attorneys from advertising their fees for simple services. The state could adopt other ways to protect the public from such lawyers that do not impinge on freedom of association or speech; for example, providing for the disbarment of lawyers who misled their clients.

CONTENT NEUTRAL   Content-neutral laws are much less likely to be struck down than those that restrict speech because of its content. As the Court wrote, "Regulations which permit the Government to discriminate on the basis of the content of the message cannot be tolerated under the First Amendment."[61] For example, a law forbidding posting of handbills on telephone poles has been sustained. Yet a law prohibiting posting of handbills advocating racism or sexism would, in all probability, be declared unconstitutional because it would relate to what is being said rather than where and how it is being said.

The lack of content neutrality was the grounds for the Court striking down a St. Paul, Minnesota, ordinance that forbade burning crosses or displaying Nazi swastikas or other "fighting words" to arouse anger, alarm, or resentment on the basis of race, color, creed, religion, or gender because St. Paul did not forbid such displays to arouse anger on the basis of other matters, for example, political affiliation, union membership, or homosexuality. Said Justice Antonin Scalia for the Court, "Aspersions upon a person's mother . . . would seemingly be usable . . . in the placards of those arguing *in favor* of racial, color, etc., tolerance and equality, but could not be used by that speaker's opponents."[62]

CENTRALITY OF POLITICAL SPEECH   "Not all speech is of equal First Amendment importance. It is speech on 'matters of public concern that is at the heart of the First Amendment's protection.' "[63] There is some contradiction between content neutrality and centrality of political speech. Legislatures and city councils are supposed to pass laws that are content neutral, but in determining whether or not those laws violate the Constitution, judges may take into account what kind of speech is involved.

COMMERCIAL SPEECH   Commercial speech is speech that "proposes a commercial transaction."[64] The mere fact that it is uttered for a profit, for example, charitable solicitations, does not make it commercial speech. Even though commercial speech is constitutionally protected, common-sense differences exist between commercial and other kinds of speech. Commercial speech is, therefore, subject to much more regulation than other speech. For example, advertising the sale of anything illegal may be forbidden, as can false and misleading commercial advertising. However, a law forbidding false and misleading political speech or political advertising is clearly unconstitutional because government does not have the right to forbid anyone from expressing ideas because they are thought to be false or misleading.

Who Decides?

Plainly, neither doctrines nor constitutional tests decide cases; judges do. Doctrines are judges' starting points; each case requires a judge to weigh a variety of factors: What was said? Where was it said? How was it said? What was the intent of the person who said it? Which government is attempting to regulate the speech—a city council speaking for a few people, or the Congress speaking for many? Few acts of Congress have ever been struck down because of conflict with the First Amendment. How is the government attempting to regulate the speech? By prior censorship? By punishment after the speech? Why is the government acting? To preserve the public peace? To prevent criticism of those in power? These and scores of other considerations are involved in the never-ending process of determining what the Constitution permits and what it forbids.

FREEDOM OF THE PRESS

Freedom of the press is the same as freedom of speech, except that the clause relating to speech protects oral communications and the phrase relating to the press embraces written ones. When we speak of "the press," most people, including most journalists, think only of the print media.[65] Yet "the liberty of the press is not confined to newspapers and periodicals. . . . The press in its historic connotation comprehends every sort of publication which affords a vehicle of information and opinion."[66]

Although we still utilize street corner meetings and public rallies to communicate ideas and influence public policies, today most of us rely on television, newspapers, radio, movies—the mass media—to tell us what is happening in the world. The press thus includes electronic media—radio, television, E-mail, the World Wide Web. Differing constitutional rules apply, however, to each kind of media. Print media are largely unregulated; the electronic media are subject to limited regulation.

Some newspeople contend that the press, especially the written press, should have more freedom of speech than do nonjournalists. Former Chief Justice Warren Burger acknowledged that media representatives have a valid claim to function as "surrogates for the public and thus may be provided special seating and priority of entry [at trials] so that they may report what people in attendance have seen and heard."[67] "Media defendants" have more protection against libel suits than "nonmedia defendants."[68] The Supreme Court has been careful to protect the press from some kinds of tax burdens even when there is no evidence of any evil intent on the part of the taxing authorities.[69] And news corporations are not subject to the same kinds of limitations as other corporations on how they may spend corporate dollars to influence elections.

Still, the prevailing view is: "The First Amendment does not 'belong' to any definable category of persons or entities; it belongs to all who exercise its freedoms."[70] Representatives of the press continue to argue otherwise. They also claim not merely the constitutional right to publish but also a right of access, a right to protect their sources, and a right to secure their files against search warrants.

The Student Press

The First Amendment does not provide the same protection for the student press as it does for nonschool papers. The Supreme Court, although agreeing that the First Amendment was involved, nonetheless sustained the right of a St. Louis area high school principal to impose prior censorship upon a school newspaper written and edited by a journalism class. The paper was not a public forum, open by policy or practice "for indiscriminate use by the general public" or by student organizations. Rather, it was a school-sponsored paper and part of the school's educational program, and thus could be regulated by school authorities.[71] It is likely that the court would have a different view of the college press and would conclude that they are entitled to much the same protections as other newspapers, especially those university newspapers that have their own independent sources of funds and are operated by a corporation separate from the university.

Thinking It Through

The Supreme Court has declared that reporters, and presumably scholars, have no constitutional right to ignore legal requests and withhold information from judicial authorities.[*] If any privilege is to be given to newspeople, said the Court, it should be done by act of Congress and of the states. Congress has not yet responded to this suggestion, but many states have passed so-called "shield laws" that provide some protection from state court subpoenas.

A North Carolina jury has awarded Food Lion, a supermarket chain, $5.5 million in punitive damages because ABC's *Primetime Live* reporters lied to get jobs at the supermarket to show bad food handling. The reporters maintained that they had to get inside the stores by trespassing with hidden cameras to expose how unsafe and outdated food was relabeled and passed off to customers.[**]

The jury verdict is being appealed, and the appellate courts will be faced with determining whether the press's First Amendment claims that these kinds of tort action, which avoid the rigorous standards of traditional libel law, will discourage news organizations from aggressive reporting.

[*]*Branzburg v Hayes*, 408 US 665 (1972).

[**]See Frank Reuven, "Don't Hide the News from Hidden Cameras: The Ethics of Undercover Reporting in Light of Food Lion-ABC News," *Los Angeles Times*, February 17, 1997, p. B5; and Terry Tange, "Revisiting the Food Lion Case: Can Deception Serve a Useful Purpose?" *New York Times*, February 17, 1997 p. 22.

The issue of whether the press has the right to withhold information came into play when Public Radio commentator Nina Totenberg refused to reveal her sources for allegations of sexual harrassment against Justice Clarence Thomas at the time of his confirmation hearings.

Richard Jewell, cleared of suspicion for the Olympic Park bombing during the 1996 Olympics, sued the *Atlanta Chronicle* and NBC News for engaging in "a mad rush to judgment" that nearly destroyed his life. Jewell's mother broke into tears as he recalled his ordeal.

Does the Press Have the Right to Know?

Courts have carefully protected the press's right to publish information, no matter how the journalists got it. But reporters, editors, and others argue that this is not enough. If reporters are excluded from places where public business is being conducted or denied access to information in government files, they are not able to perform their historic function of keeping the public informed. The Supreme Court has refused to acknowledge a right to know, although it did concede that there is a First Amendment right for the press, along with the public, to be present at criminal trials.[72]

Although they have no constitutional obligation to do so, many states have adopted *sunshine laws* requiring public agencies to open their meetings to the public and the press. Congress requires most federal executive agencies to open hearings and meetings of advisory groups to the public, and most congressional committee meetings are open to the public. Federal and state courtroom trials are also open, but judicial conferences, when the judges discuss how to decide the cases, are not.

Congress has authorized the president to establish a classification system to keep some public documents and governmental files secret, and it is a crime for any person to divulge such classified information. So far, however, although they have been threatened, no newspapers have been prosecuted for doing so.

Executive Privilege Most presidents have claimed a constitutional right to withhold information not only from the press but from Congress and the courts if, in the president's judgment, its release would jeopardize national security or interfere with the confidentiality of advice. This claim is referred to as **executive privilege**. In the celebrated case of *United States v Nixon* (1974), the Supreme Court ruled that executive privilege does not shield a president from a judicial subpoena for material relevant to a criminal prosecution.[73] This historic decision, which marked the second time the Supreme Court decided a matter directly involving the president as a party to a case, rejected a claim of absolute executive privilege. The Court did, however, recognize that a president's "singularly unique role" gives the office a limited executive privilege to which judges should show the "utmost deference."

President Clinton, claiming lawyer-client confidentiality, at first refused to respond to a Senate subpoena to turn over to a Senate committee notes from a meeting he had had with his lawyers. The committee was investigating allegations about possible financial misconduct of the president when he was governor of Arkansas—what came to be known as the Whitewater investigation. President Clinton contended that the president, along with every other person, is entitled to have confidential conversations with his lawyers. The issue was complicated by the fact that at the meeting not only were the president's own private lawyers present but also lawyers from government agencies. When the Senate voted to go to court to try to enforce the subpoena, the president avoided a constitutional showdown and agreed to turn over the documents after investigators agreed not to use their release as a precedent to preclude the president from claiming lawyer-client privilege.[74]

Free Press versus Fair Trials

When newspapers and television report in vivid detail the facts of a crime, interview prosecutors and police, question witnesses, and hold press conferences for defendants and their attorneys, as in the O. J. Simpson and Timothy McVeigh cases, they may so inflame the public that finding a panel of impartial jurors and conducting a fair trial is difficult. In England, strict rules determine what the media may report, and judges do not hesitate to punish newspapers that comment on pending criminal proceedings. In the United States, in contrast, free comment is emphasized. Yet the Supreme Court has not been indifferent to protecting persons on trial from inflammatory publicity. Its remedies have been to order new trials or to instruct judges to impose sanctions on prosecutors and police, not on reporters. "Lawyers representing clients in pending cases may be regulated under a less demanding standard than that established for regulation of the press."[75] They may be disciplined for their comments prior to or during a trial even if the comments do not present a clear and present danger but merely if they are "substantially likely to have a materially prejudicial effect."

Federal rules of criminal procedure forbid radio or photographic coverage of criminal cases in federal courts, but most states permit televising of courtroom proceedings. Such TV programs have become popular. People around the world followed the O. J. Simpson criminal case, and it became one of the most publicized trials ever. Dissatisfaction with the results in some so-called "high profile" cases has led judges in some states to exclude television coverage. Defendants always have the right to present evidence that television interfered with their trial, prevented fair hearings, and deprived them of due process.[76]

OTHER MEDIA AND OTHER MESSAGES

When the Constitution was written, freedom of "the press" referred to leaflets, newspapers, and books. Today the Constitution also protects other media, such as the mails, motion pictures, billboards, radio, television, cable, telephones, fax machines, other electronic media, as well as expressive conduct. Because each form of communication entails special problems, each needs a different degree of protection.

The Mails

More than 75 years ago, Justice Oliver Wendell Holmes, Jr., wrote in dissent: "The United States may give up the Post Office when it sees fit, but while it carries it on, the use of the mails is almost as much a part of free speech as is the right to use our tongues."[77] In 1965, the Court adopted Holmes's views by striking down the first congressional act ever held to conflict with the First Amendment. That act had directed the postmaster general to detain foreign mailings of "communist political propaganda" and to deliver these materials only upon the addressee's request.[78] The Court has also set aside federal laws authorizing postal authorities to exclude from the mails materials they consider obscene.

Although government censorship of mail is unconstitutional, household censorship is not. The Court has sustained a law giving any householder the absolute right to ask the postmaster to order mailers to delete names in the household from all mailing lists and to refrain from sending any advertisements that householders, in their sole discretion, believe to be "erotically arousing or sexually provocative."[79] It makes no constitutional difference if a householder includes a mail order catalog in such a category. Moreover, Congress may forbid—and has forbidden—the use of mailboxes for any materials except those sent through the United States mails.

Motion Pictures and Plays

Films may be treated differently from books or newspapers, and prior censorship of films to prevent the showing of obscenity is not necessarily unconstitutional. However, laws calling for submission of films to a government review board are constitutional only if there is a prompt judicial hearing. The burden is on the government to prove to the court that the particular film in question is in fact obscene.

The 1966 Freedom of Information Act

The Freedom of Information Act (FOIA) of 1966, as amended, liberalized access to nonclassified government records. This act makes the records of federal executive agencies available subject to certain exceptions, such as private financial transactions, personnel records, criminal investigation files, interoffice memoranda, and letters used in internal decision making. If federal agencies fail to move promptly on requests for information, persons are entitled to speedy judicial hearings. The burden is on an agency to explain its refusal to supply material, and if the judge decides the government has improperly withheld information, the government has to pay the legal fees. Since the inception of FOIA, more than 250,000 people have requested information, and more than 90 percent of these requests have been granted.

Some critics are concerned that FOIA has had an adverse effect on our ability to carry out confidential investigations and that its implementation costs too much. Others are concerned that FOIA may be used by businesses to obtain competitors' secrets. But most observers, especially newspaper reporters and scholars, believe that FOIA gives real meaning to the citizen's right to know.

SOURCE: Page Putnam Miller, "Status Report on the Freedom of Information Act," *PS: Political Science and Politics* (Winter 1988), pp. 87–90. See also Michael Moss, "Federal Service Gets Wider Use by Sleuths, Snoops— and Senators: Freedom of Information Act Offers Surprise Benefits for Business, Investors," *Wall Street Journal*, January 3, 1996, p. A1.

You Decide!

Prior censorship of films by review boards used to be rather common in some places—for example, Massachusetts and Maryland and in some cities.

Live performances, such as plays and revues, are also entitled to constitutional protection.[80] Yet live theater is subject to greater regulation than either the printed page or the motion picture. The First Amendment does not protect liquor licensees from state regulations forbidding sexually suggestive performances in places where liquor is sold.[81]

Handbills, Sound Trucks, and Billboards

Religious and political pamphlets, leaflets, and handbills have been historic weapons in the defense of liberty, and their distribution is constitutionally protected. So, too, is the use of their more contemporary counterparts—sound trucks and billboards. A state, for example, cannot restrain the distribution of leaflets merely to keep its streets clean.[82] And the Supreme Court recently struck down an Ohio statue, similar to that found in all other states except California, that prohibited the distribution of campaign literature that did not contain the name and address of the persons or campaign official issuing the literature.[83] (The Court left open whether a state's interest in protecting the election process "might justify a more limited identification requirement.")

On the other side, the Supreme Court sustained a Tennessee statute prohibiting solicitation of votes and distribution of campaign literature within 100 feet of the entrance to a polling place. Even though this regulation applied to political speech, in a public forum, and was not content-neutral, and thus was subject to strict judicial scrutiny, nonetheless the Court concluded that the 100-foot limit was narrowly drawn means to accomplish the state's compelling interest in protecting the integrity of the vote and the secrecy of the ballot.[84]

As for sound trucks, those that emit loud and raucous noises may be banned. Further, content-neutral regulations detailing the time, place, and manner in which amplification devices may be used for musical performances such as rock concerts are also acceptable. Billboards, too, are entitled to constitutional protection, especially those used for noncommercial purposes.

Radio and Television

Television today is the most important means of distributing news, as well as the primary forum for appealing for votes. Yet of all the mass media, broadcasting has received the least First Amendment protection. Congress established a system of commercial broadcasting, supplemented by the Corporation for Public Broadcasting, which provides funds for public radio and television. The entire system is regulated by the Federal Communications Commission (FCC). The FCC grants licenses for limited periods and makes regulations for their use. Broadcasters, using publicly owned airwaves, have no constitutional right to use these facilities without licenses.

The First Amendment would prevent censorship if the FCC tried to impose it. Yet the First Amendment does not prevent the FCC from imposing sanctions on stations that broadcast *filthy words*, as the FCC did in 1993 when it fined Infinity Broadcasting for allegedly indecent remarks by "shock jock" Howard Stern, even though such indecencies are not legally obscene. Nor does the First Amendment prevent the FCC from refusing to renew a license if in its opinion a broadcaster has not served the public interest.

The First Amendment did not prevent the FCC from adopting what came to be known as the **fairness doctrine**, requiring broadcasters to cover issues of public significance and to reflect differing viewpoints, as was done from 1949 to 1987. Thus, if licensees made editorial statements or endorsed candidates, they had to give persons representing a different point of view an opportunity to respond.

Congress has imposed an additional **equal-time requirement**, requiring licensees to be sure that all candidates for public office had equal air time. Later Congress modified this requirement to make possible presidential debates between candidates of only the two major parties.[85]

The major argument in favor of allowing more government regulation of broadcasters than of newspaper and magazine publishers is that the public owns the limited number of airwaves, and those who have access to these airwaves have control over a limited resource. In a footnote to a 1984 decision, the Court noted, "The prevailing rationale for broadcast regulation has come under increasing criticism in recent years" because such technological changes as cable, direct-beam broadcast, and videotapes may be undermining the assumption that the scarcity of channels justifies government regulation. "We are not prepared, however," wrote Justice William J. Brennan, Jr., for the majority, "to reconsider our long-standing approach without some signal from Congress or the FCC that technological developments have advanced so far that some revision of the system of broadcast regulation may be required."[86]

In 1996, after years of debate, Congress gave that signal. Acknowledging that technological changes produced competition, Congress passed and the president signed the Telecommunications Act of 1996, which will allow phone companies, broadcasters, and cable TV to compete with one another. It will be years before the full impact of this law is realized, as many details are worked out by federal and state regulators and as the courts respond to Congress, making it clear that there is no longer the assumption of scarcity of channels to justify government regulation. However, adoption of the act did not mean that Congress abandoned all government regulation of the airways. On the contrary, the bill calls for many new regulations. It outlaws the transmission of "indecent material" over computer networks and requires that all new television sets sold in the United States be equipped with so-called "v-chips" that allow viewers to block programs containing violent and/or sexual material.

Telephones, Fax, E-Mail, Internet, and Cyberspace

Now that fax machines are in widespread use, states are beginning to pass "junk fax laws," making it illegal to fax unsolicited advertisements. Similar legislation is proposed to restrict autodialers, which send computerized telephone messages into homes. A dozen states and Congress have either banned or restricted the use of autodialers, and these regulations are being challenged in the courts on First Amendment grounds.[87] Although federal laws protect against eavesdropping on telephone conversations, including those conveyed by cellular phones, these laws do not as yet extend to walk-around phones that transmit messages via radio waves. Moreover, enforcing laws against electronic eavesdropping on cordless phones is difficult, if not impossible.[88]

As Congress and the states begin to deal with these problems, they and the judges who will be reviewing subsequent lawsuits that are filed will have to apply traditional constitutional principles to new situations. For example, what about pornography and obscenity over telephones and E-mail? Congress, reflecting concern about "dial-a-porn," especially as directed to persons under age 18, imposed a total ban on obscene and indecent interstate commercial telephone messages to any person, whatever their age. The Supreme Court found no constitutional obstacles to the law as it relates to "obscene" messages but declared unconstitutional the provision relating to "indecent" messages. Justice Byron R. White wrote for the Court:

> It may well be that there is no fail-safe method of guaranteeing that never will a minor be able to access the dial-a-porn system, . . . but from all we know . . . the FCC's technological

Thinking It Through

The courts are beginning to supply answers by applying traditional doctrines, moving slowly, watching actual experiences, and taking their cue from the Federal Communications Commission. The Supreme Court has held that any regulations of cable television are subject to more rigorous scrutiny than are those that apply to broadcast television but less rigorous than those that apply to the print media.

In 1996 the Court upheld provisions of a 1992 act of Congress permitting cable operators to refuse to permit programs over leased channels that the operators believe are patently offensive, but struck down provisions requiring that if the cable operator allows such programming, it must be blocked and unscrambled through special devices.[*] In 1997 the Court, by a 5 to 4 vote, upheld a congressional requirement that cable television systems must carry signals of local broadcast television stations.[**]

As David Kaplan pointed out: "It is an exquisitely vexing debate over cable television and the First Amendment. Trouble is, the First Amendment seems to be on both sides."[†]

[*]*Denver Area Educational Television v FCC*, 135 L Ed 2nd 888 (1996).
[**]*The New York Times*, April 1, 1997, p. A1.
[†]David A. Kaplan, "Is the Klan Entitled to Public Access?" *The New York Times*, July 31, 1988, p. A24.

New technologies like the Internet have opened up the question of whether the government can constitutionally control or censor material aimed at children.

approach to restricting dial-a-porn messages to adults who seek them would be extremely effective, and only a few of the most enterprising and disobedient young people will manage to secure access to such messages.[89]

The Court also distinguished between the limited ban on indecent messages over the airwaves that it had previously sustained[90] and the ban on such messages over telephones. Because of the unique attributes of broadcasting, its messages are readily available to children and can intrude into the privacy of the home without prior warning. Telephone messages, on the other hand, are available only to people who want to hear them. It also may be possible, as the Court suggested, to deny minors access to indecent telephone messages more readily than to indecent broadcasting, excepting, of course, "enterprising and disobedient young people."

Following the Court's decision against allowing Congress to ban indecent telephone calls, Congress passed a law narrowly tailored to protect minors from exposure to such materials. Based on that law, the FCC adopted regulations requiring that telephone companies that bill customers for calls to a 900 number block pornographic services to all households except those that specifically request access. The Supreme Court, by refusing to review a decision of a court of appeals upholding the constitutionality of this law and implementing regulations, cleared the way for its enforcement.[91]

What of the thousands of electronic bulletin boards, news groups, and the World Wide Web on which people from all over the world communicate with each other by computer? May those who provide these services be held responsible for obscene and indecent messages, and do they have a right to exclude hate messages or racially or sexually offensive matter? And if government agencies are involved, to what extent do the First and Fourteenth Amendments limit the ability of the agencies to control the content of the messages?[92] These are some of the unanswered constitutional questions raised by the information superhighway.

Congress is struggling with issues of pornography and hate messages in cyberspace. In a provision known as the Communications Decency Act of 1996 in the 1996 Telecommunications Act, Congress made it a federal crime to use the Internet to knowingly transmit indecent material to minors. The act also imposes criminal penalties for transmitting or receiving certain *abortion-related information.* "Indecency" is defined in the law as communication that depicts patently offensive materials about sexual or excretory activities as measured by contemporary community standards. A three-judge panel has unanimously ruled that this provision violates the First Amendment. The judges wrote that the Internet "as the most participatory form of mass speech yet developed deserves the highest protection from governmental intrusion." Cyberspace, the court concluded, should be treated like books and magazines and thus subject to their broad constitutional protection.[93] This decision was appealed directly to the Supreme Court, as the law provided. The Court's decision, *Janet Reno v The American Civil Liberties Union,* was handed down before the end of the 1996–1997 term. It merits your close attention. Appropriately, the decision and the oral argument can be found on the World Wide Web.[94]

Picketing

Picketing of employers is a normal trade union practice, and such picketing is constitutionally protected, as is picketing and protesting for various causes. A law forbidding all picketing would be an unconstitutional invasion of speech. However, "picketing involves elements of both speech and conduct, i.e., patrolling," and "because of this intermingling of protected and unprotected elements, picketing can be subject to controls that would not be constitutionally permissible in the case of pure speech."[95]

When picketing becomes coercive and interferes with the rights of customers to go into or out of a place of work, or keeps employees from going through a picket line, or interferes with people going into and out of places to which they are entitled to go, such as an abortion clinic, it may be regulated. Since First Amendment questions are involved, such regulations are subject to close judicial scrutiny. While indicating that it might not sustain a ban on all residential picketing, the Court upheld an ordinance that forbids picketing "before or about a single residence."[96] The Court also declined to adopt prior restraint analyses in reviewing the constitutionality of a state court injunction which restricted activities of antiabortion protesters where the protesters were simply prohibited from expressing their views within a 36-foot buffer zone around the property line of an abortion clinic and where the injunction was issued because of the prior unlawful conduct by the protesters.[97] On the other hand, while upholding a congressional prohibition on "hostile congregating" within 500 feet of a foreign embassy, the Court struck down a prohibition on "hostile picketing" in front of such embassies.[98]

Expressive Conduct

People express their views by many other means than just talking or writing. They raise flags, wave banners, march in parades, wear political buttons, carry signs. These various forms of expression, this symbolic speech (or, as it is coming to be called, expressive conduct), is constitutionally protected. This does not mean that people can claim exemption from otherwise valid laws merely by claiming that they are exercising their First Amendment rights. "We cannot accept the view," Chief Justice Earl Warren wrote, "that an apparently limitless variety of conduct can be labeled speech whenever the person engaged in the conduct intends thereby to express an idea."[99] Similarly, Chief Justice Warren Burger wrote:

> Conduct that the State police power can prohibit on a public street does not become automatically protected by the Constitution merely because the conduct is moved to . . . a "live theatre" stage, any more than a "live" performance of a man and woman locked in a sexual embrace at high noon in Times Square is protected by the Constitution merely because they simultaneously engaged in a political dialogue.[100]

Except when the government interest is directly aimed at the symbolic character of the conduct, such as laws forbidding flag burning, the burden is on those who engage in expressive conduct to show that the First Amendment applies. In reviewing laws that regulate expressive conduct, the Court uses a four-part test, first announced in *United States v O'Brien*.[101] The government may forbid or regulate expressive conduct if (1) the regulation is within the constitutional power of the government; (2) it furthers an important governmental interest; (3) the governmental interest is unrelated to the suppression of expression; and (4) the incidental restriction on alleged First Amendment freedom is no greater than is essential to the furtherance of the interest.[102]

Applying these tests, the Supreme Court has concluded that the government cannot forbid the burning of the American flag as a form of political protest, for the interest of the government is directly aimed at the suppression of expressive conduct. Nor can a city make it a crime to burn a cross or display a Nazi swastika even if such displays create anger, alarm, or resentment based on racial, ethnic, gender, or religious bias. However, the Court has strongly hinted that a carefully drawn, content-neutral ordinance might be sustained.[103]

On the other side, burning a draft card in violation of a congressional regulation is not a constitutionally protected form of expressive conduct because Congress, when it made the protection and presentation of such cards a requirement was doing so for purely administrative reasons. It was not trying to prohibit con-

Thinking It Through

Scientific inventions have confronted judges with new problems in applying the Fourth Amendment. Obviously, the writers of the Fourth Amendment intended such physical objects as books, papers, letters, and other kinds of documents to be protected from seizure by the government except in cases in which magistrates had issued search warrants. But what of overhearing phone conversations by tapping phone wires, or using electronic devices to eavesdrop, or using secret video cameras to make videotapes? In *Olmstead v United States* (1928) a bare majority of the Supreme Court held there was no unconstitutional search unless seizure of physical objects or actual physical entry into a premise was involved. Justices Oliver Wendell Holmes and Louis D. Brandeis, in dissent, argued that the Constitution should keep up with the times; the "dirty business" of wiretapping produced the same evil invasion of privacy the framers had in mind when they wrote the Fourth Amendment.* Forty years later, in *Katz v United States* (1967), the Supreme Court adopted the Holmes-Brandeis position:

> The Fourth Amendment protects people—and not simply "areas"—against unreasonable searches and seizures. Wherever a man may be [subsequently modified and limited to those places where a person has a legitimate expectation of privacy that society is prepared to recognize as reasonable],** he is entitled to know that he will remain free from unreasonable searches and seizures.†

Olmstead v United States, 227 US 438 (1928).

**Florida v Riley*, 488 US 445 (1989).

†*Katz v United States*, 389 US 347 (1967).

Should the Bill of Rights
be amended to prohibit flag
burning?

The American flag arouses patriotic
emotions in Americans, many of
whom have fought or seen friends die
under that banner. It is understandable that they will be angry to see that
flag burned by protesters. Do you
think flag burning should be prohibited by law, with appropriate punishments stipulated? Or do you think it
is one of the aspects of free speech
guaranteed by the Bill of Rights?

You Decide!

The Supreme Court ruled that
freedom of speech even covers
"symbolic speech" like burning the
U.S. flag.

duct because of its communicative attributes. In the same fashion, the National
Park Service was allowed to forbid persons from sleeping overnight in Lafayette Park
across from the White House as a way to protest the government failure to protect the rights of the homeless.[104] And although acrobatic and ballroom dancing are
not entitled to First Amendment protection, when nude dancing is performed as
entertainment in order to express erotic thoughts, such dancing is "within the outer
perimeters of the First Amendment." Said Chief Justice Rehnquist for the Court,
"We view such dancing as only marginally so." (At least he did not say "barely so.")
Nonetheless, the Court upheld the application of a state's public indecency statute
to such dancing, requiring dancers to wear pasties and a G-string.[105]

NONPROTECTED SPEECH

As we have noted, some kinds of speech are not entitled to constitutional protection. This does not mean that the constitutional issues relating to these kinds of
speech are simple. On the contrary, how we prove *libel*, how we define *obscenity*,
and how we determine which words are *fighting words* are hotly contested issues.

Libel

At one time newspaper publishers and editors had to take considerable care about
what they wrote, for fear they might be prosecuted for **libel**—written defamation—by the government or sued for money damages by individuals. Today,
through a progressive raising of constitutional standards, it has become more
difficult to win a libel suit against a newspaper or magazine.

In *The New York Times v Sullivan* and subsequent cases, the Supreme Court
established the guidelines for libel cases. The Constitution severely limits a state's
power to award damages in a libel action brought by a public official against critics of official conduct. Neither *public officials* nor *public figures* can collect damages for any comments made about them, unless they can prove with "convincing clarity" the comments were made with "actual malice."[106] *Actual malice* means
not merely that the defendant had bad motives, but that the "statements were
made with a reckless disregard for the truth," which in turn means that the defendant must have made the false publication with a "high degree of awareness of
probable falsity."[107]

Public figures cannot collect damages even when subject to outrageous, clearly
inaccurate, and false cartoons. Such was the case when *Hustler* magazine printed
a cartoon parodying the Reverend Jerry Falwell; the Court held such cartoons
cannot reasonably be understood as describing actual facts or actual events.[108] Nor
does the mere fact that a public figure is quoted as saying something that he or
she did *not* say amount to a libel. "Unless the alteration" in what the person has
said "results in material change," the mere fact that the words were deliberately
altered does not equate with the constitutionally required knowledge of falsity.[109]

Constitutional standards for libel charges brought by *private* persons are not so
rigid. State laws may permit private persons to collect damages without having to
prove actual malice if they can prove the statements made about them are false and
negligently published.

Obscenity

Today, fears about obscenity and pornography have replaced seventeenth-century
fears about heresy and 1950s fears about communism.[110] Obscene publications are
not entitled to constitutional protection, but members of the Supreme Court, like
everybody else, have great difficulty in defining obscenity. Almost 100 separate
opinions have been written on the matter.

In *Miller v California* (1973), the Court was finally able to assemble a majority opinion. Speaking for five members of the Court, Chief Justice Warren Burger once again tried to clarify a constitutional definition of **obscenity**. A work may be considered legally obscene provided: (1) the average person, applying contemporary standards of the particular community, would find that the work, taken as a whole, appeals to a prurient interest in sex (that is, patently offensive interests "over and beyond those that would be characterized as normal"[111]); (2) the work depicts or describes in a patently offensive way sexual conduct specifically defined by the applicable law or authoritatively construed; and (3) the work, taken as a whole, lacks serious literary, artistic, political, or scientific value.[112] Chief Justice Burger specifically rejected part of the previous test—the so-called *Memoirs v Massachusetts* (1966) formula: No work should be judged obscene unless it is "utterly without redeeming social value."[113] He argued such a test would make it impossible for a state to outlaw hard-core pornography.

Does the *Miller* decision mean that local communities can ban whatever a prosecutor could persuade a jury is obscene? Many hoped they could; many others feared they would. But how far could a jury go? Could it decide to ban "Little Red Riding Hood"? After all, who really knows what went on in that bedroom? A year after the *Miller* decision, the Supreme Court warned: "It would be a serious misreading of *Miller* to conclude that juries have unbridled discretion in determining what is patently offensive." Appellate courts, said Justice Rehnquist speaking for the Court, should review jury determinations to ensure compliance with constitutional standards. And the Supreme Court itself, after such review, ruled that the movie *Carnal Knowledge* was not obscene, contrary to the conclusion of a jury in Albany, Georgia.[114]

Obscenity, then, is not entitled to constitutional protection. But governments must proceed under laws that specifically define the kinds of sexual conduct forbidden in word or picture. Moreover, it is not a crime for booksellers to offer obscene books for sale; they must be shown to have done so *knowingly*. Otherwise, booksellers would tend to avoid placing on their shelves materials that some authorities might consider objectionable, and the public would be deprived of an opportunity to purchase anything except some person's determination of the "safe and sanitary." The mere private possession of obscene materials is not a crime either.

What about X-rated movies that fall short of the constitutional definition of obscenity? They are entitled to some constitutional protection, but less protection than political speech, and they are subject to greater government regulation. "The state may legitimately use the content of these materials as the basis for placing them in a different classification from other motion pictures."[115] Cities may also regulate, by zoning laws, where so-called adult motion picture theaters may be located.

Sexually explicit materials either about minors or aimed at them are *not* protected by the First Amendment. Provided they act under narrowly drawn statutes, state and local governments can, for example, ban the knowing sale of "adult" magazines to minors, even if such materials would not be considered legally obscene if sold to adults. And governments can make it a crime to depict sexual conduct by children, even if the depicted behavior would not be considered obscene if performed by adults.

Pornography

Pornography used to be merely a synonym for *obscenity*. Pressure for regulating pornography came primarily from political conservatives and religious fundamentalists concerned that it undermines moral standards. More recently, many feminists have joined them, arguing that "pornography is central in creating and main-

Thinking It Through

On June 21, 1989 the Supreme Court, in *Texas v Johnson*, decided by a 5 to 4 vote that the First Amendment protects the expressive act of burning the flag. President George Bush denounced the decision and called for a constitutional amendment that would nullify it. Congress responded by passing a federal law that would make it a crime to burn or to deface the flag—whatever one's purposes or intent. In June 1990, nine months after the first decision, the Supreme Court declared that law unconstitutional also in *United States v Eichman*, 496 U.S. 310 (1990).

The flag burning issue came up again in 1995, largely as a result of the 1994 elections that left Republicans in control of both the House and the Senate. In the summer of 1995 the House of Representatives readily approved such an amendment by a vote of 312 to 120. In the Senate the amendment was modified to take out the provision allowing states to act to avoid what Senator Joseph R. Biden, Jr. called "a potential patchwork of 50 idiosyncratic laws." In December 1995 the Senate came within three votes—63 to 36—of the required two-thirds. With public opinion polls showing strong support for the amendment, the issue is clearly not dead. "This amendment is not going to go away," sponsor Orrin G. Hatch (R-Utah) said minutes after the final vote. "We will debate it in the next Congress."

Before you decide, you might want to read the opinions of the Supreme Court justices: *Texas v Johnson*, 491 U.S. 397 (1989).

RAP LYRICS AND FREE SPEECH

The inflammatory and degrading messages in some popular records and on music television have aroused many groups to action. Starting several years ago with the wife of Vice-President Al Gore, Tipper Gore's campaign for ratings on sexually explicit records to keep them out of the hands of children, protests were also heard from parent groups who asked television networks to monitor the violence in programs targeted for young children. "Gangsta rap," and in particular a recording by Ice T calling for attacks on the police, brought out protests from police organizations and parents throughout the country and boycotts of the recording company. Women's groups voiced resentment of the portrayal of women as willing victims of brutal sex acts and the insulting language used to describe them in music videos.

Carol Moseley Braun, Illinois senator, presided over a hearing of the Juvenile Justice Subcommittee of the Judiciary Committee on the violent and vulgar lyrics of rap music. In their defense, music stations, recording companies, and rap singers cited the guarantees of free speech and maintained that they were speaking the truth as people in the ghettos saw it.

The rap group Ice T's records glorified killing cops and abusing women.

Senator Carol Moseley Braun looks on as young rappers prepare to testify before the Senate Judiciary Committee.

taining sex as a basis for discrimination."[116] They contend that pornography promotes sexual abuse of individual women and perpetuates social subordination of women as a class. Feminists define pornographic materials as sexually explicit pictures or words that depict women as sexual objects enjoying pain and humiliation or that present abuse of women as a sexual stimulus for men. Some have argued that the line should be drawn to permit regulation of "depictions of sexuality that involve rape and violence against women."[117]

Advocates of regulation of pornography argue that just as sexually explicit materials about minors are not entitled to First Amendment protection, so should there be no such protection for pornographic materials. They propose that civil penalties be imposed on pornographers, and that women—and others who have had pornography forced upon them—be given the right to file complaints and sue for damages. The Senate Judiciary Committee has proposed the Pornography Victim's Compensation Act allowing crime victims to sue producers, distributors, and exhibitors of a book, magazine, movie, or lyric "that the victim believes triggered the crime."[118]

Women and men have differed significantly in their attitudes about pornography (see Table 4–1). Men are less likely than women to think pornography damages adults who read it, and women are twice as likely to favor laws banning the sale of pornography, regardless of the age of the buyer, while men tend to favor restricting the sale of pornography to minors.[119]

Not all feminists favor antipornography ordinances, yet those who do have been joined by social conservatives, and thus a new era in the battle over pornography has begun. For this new antipornography coalition to be successful, a substantial alteration in constitutional doctrine will be required.[120] The Canadian Supreme Court has redefined obscenity to include materials that degrade women, and several cities in the United States have been considering the adoption of antipornography ordinances.[121] Only Indianapolis has passed such a law, which was declared unconstitutional in a decision affirmed by the Supreme Court without opinion.[122]

Censorship of films and books may be imposed by a variety of means other than formal action. In some cities, such local groups as the Legion of Decency may pressure authorities. Feminists, by threats of boycott, have pressured some stores to stop selling magazines they believe depict women in a demeaning and pornographic manner. Local police have been known to threaten booksellers with criminal prosecution if they persist in showing films or selling books of which some local people disapprove.

Fighting Words

Governments may punish certain well-defined and narrowly limited classes of speech that "by their very utterance inflict injury or tend to incite an immediate breach of peace."[123] These so-called **fighting words** "have a direct tendency to cause acts of violence by the person to whom, individually, the remarks are addressed."[124] That the words are abusive, harsh, or insulting, or that they create anger, alarm, or resentment based on racial, ethnic, gender, or religious basis is not sufficient. Thus, a four-letter word worn on a sweatshirt was not judged to be a fighting word in the constitutional sense, at least when it is not directed to any specific person.[125]

The "fighting words" category has taken on additional significance in recent years in view of the attempts by many state universities and colleges to regulate insulting racial, ethnic, and sexual slurs. The Constitution limits how public universities and colleges may punish students for what they say, and cases challenging these so called "hate codes" are working their way through the courts. That speech may be insulting or racially offensive or sexist does not mean that it lacks constitutional protection. As the Court has said, "If there is a bedrock principle underlying the First Amendment, it is that the Government may not prohibit the expression of an idea simply because society finds the idea offensive or disagreeable."[126]

The Supreme Court has gone out of its way to warn governments and public universities against moving to punish fighting words by codes designed to protect people against insults solely because of their race, sex, or religion. "The First Amendment does not," wrote Justice Antonin Scalia for the Court, "permit [governments] to impose special prohibitions on those speakers who express views on disfavored subjects."[127] But in the role of landlord for residence halls, universities and colleges may have greater authority to impose reasonable time, place, and manner regulations against insulting racial, sexual, or religious slurs directed toward fellow residents.

The speech of faculty and staff at universities and colleges, public or private, is also protected by the Constitution from governmental regulation. What of the power of the university or college itself to regulate the speech of its employees, including faculty, and its students? As state agencies, public universities and colleges are subject to the restrictions of the Constitution. Nonetheless, a public university as an employer has some leeway in regulating the speech of its employees, more

TABLE 4-1

Men and Women's Attitudes Toward Pornography

	Yes	No	DK/NA*
Sexual materials lead to a breakdown of morals.			
Men	50%	43%	7%
Women	67	26	7
Sexual materials lead people to commit rape.			
Men	39%	50%	11%
Women	61	27	11

	Men	Women
There should be laws against the distribution of pornography, whatever the age.	26%	49%
There should be laws against the distribution of pornography to persons under 18.	66%	4%7
There should be no laws forbidding the distribution of pornography	6%	3%
Don't know or No answer	2%	1%

SOURCE: National Opinion Research Center, University of Chicago, *General Social Surveys, 1972–1994.*

*Don't Know or No Answer.

Armed riot police stand guard during a White Supremacist rally in Georgia. Our Constitution defends the right of Ku Klux Klan members, neo-Nazis, and other controversial groups to express unpopular opinions.

leeway than it has in regulating the speech of its students, especially student speech outside of the classroom or outside of residence halls. A university, for example, has some discretion—in fact, under federal laws, some obligation—to control racially or sexually harassing speech by faculty and staff.

Private universities and colleges are not subject to these constitutional limitations on how they may regulate the speech of their students. However, state governments may protect the speech of students against undue regulation by these institutions, and colleges and universities that receive federal funds may find that their freedom to regulate the use of offensive speech by students is limited by federal laws and regulations. Federal and state laws regulating the responsibilities of employers to provide a workplace free from sexual harassment apply to universities, private and public.

RIGHT TO ASSEMBLE AND TO PETITION THE GOVERNMENT

Freedom of Assembly

In the winter of 1977, Frank Collins, "a self-avowed Nazi," threatened to lead his small band, dressed in brown shirts and carrying swastikas, in a jack-booted march through the streets of Skokie, Illinois, a Chicago suburb with a large Jewish population.[128] Skokie's citizens included survivors of Hitler's extermination camps; many of them had relatives who lost their lives in the Holocaust. Many people, including the officials of Skokie and a local judge, argued that Collins and his followers should not be allowed to march. They argued that this would be like shouting "Fire!" in a crowded theater, and that to permit such a use of the streets presented a clear and present danger of inciting people to violence. These same arguments were put forward to contend that Iranian followers of the late Ayatollah Khomeini should not be allowed to protest publicly in Washington, D.C., at a time when most Americans were angry about Khomeini's illegal and brutal treatment of innocent American hostages in Tehran. The right to assemble peaceably, they said, should not be extended to Iranian aliens who were abusing this right to provoke Americans to violence.

In both cases judicial authorities defended the rights of these unpopular minorities to demonstrate. (Collins never actually marched in Skokie, but he did march in another part of the Chicago area.[129]) But it is not always the "bad guys" whose rights have to be protected by the courts. It also took occasional judicial intervention in the 1960s to preserve for Martin Luther King, Jr., and for those who marched with him, the right to demonstrate in the streets of southern cities on behalf of civil rights for African Americans.

Such incidents present the classic free speech problem of the "heckler's veto," when the audience becomes so abusive that it is impossible for the speaker to be heard. It is almost always easier, and certainly politically more prudent, to maintain order by curbing public demonstrations of unpopular groups than by moving against those who are threatening them. On the other hand, if police did not have the right to order groups to disperse, public order would be at the mercy of those who resort to street demonstrations just to create tensions and provoke street battles.

Public Forums and Time, Place, and Manner Regulations

The Constitution protects the right to speak, but it does not give persons the right to communicate their views to everyone, every place, at any time they wish. No one has the right deliberately to incite others to violence, to block traffic, or to hold parades or make speeches in public streets or on public sidewalks whenever he or she wishes. Governments may not specify what can or cannot be said, but they can make reasonable *time, place, and manner* regulations for the holding of assemblies or protests or gatherings. The extent of government regulation varies with where the assembly takes place.

The Supreme Court has divided public property into three categories: public forums, limited public forums, and nonpublic forums. The extent to which governments may limit access depends on the kind of forums involved. *Public forums* are those public places historically associated with the free exercise of expressive activities, such as streets, sidewalks, and parks. Courts look closely at time, place, and manner regulations as they apply to these traditional public forums to ensure that they are being applied evenhandedly and that action is not taken because of what is being said rather than how and where or by whom it is being said.[130] Further, in these traditional public forums, no restrictive laws are permitted unless they are viewpoint neutral and the government in question can prove that they are necessary to serve a compelling government interest.

Other kinds of public property, such as designated rooms in a city hall or after-hour use of school buildings, may be designated as *limited public forums*, available for assembly and speech for limited purposes, a limited amount of time, and even for a limited class of speakers (such as only students, only teachers, or only employees), provided the distinctions between those allowed access and those not allowed access are viewpoint neutral.

Nonpublic forums include public facilities such as libraries, courthouses, schools, swimming pools, and government offices that are open to the public but are not public forums. As long as persons use such facilities within the normal bounds of conduct, they may not be constitutionally restrained from doing so. However, persons may be excluded from such places as a government office or a school if they engage in activities for which the facilities were not created. They have no right to interfere with programs or try to appropriate facilities—especially facilities such as a university president's office—in order to stage a political protest.

Does the right of peaceful assembly and petition include the right to violate a law nonviolently but deliberately? We have no precise answer. But in general, *civil disobedience*, even if peaceful, is not a protected right. When Dr. Martin Luther King, Jr., and his followers refused to comply with a state court's injunction forbidding them to parade in Birmingham without first securing a permit, the Supreme Court sustained their conviction, even though there was serious doubt about the constitutionality of the injunction and the ordinance on which it was based. Justice Potter Stewart, speaking for the five-member majority, said: "No man can be judge in his own case, however exalted his station, however righteous his motive, and irrespective of his race, color, politics, or religion." Persons are not "constitutionally free to ignore all the procedures of the law and carry their battles to the streets."[131] The four dissenting justices insisted that one does have a right to defy peacefully an obviously unconstitutional statute or injunction.

As a result of a campaign by anti-abortion protesters to shut down abortion clinics, the First Amendment rights of anti-abortion protesters to picket in front of abortion clinics came into conflict with some women's rights of access to abortion clinics. The protesters often massed in front of clinics shouting at employees and patrons and sometimes blocked the entrance to the clinic. Congress responded with the Freedom of Access to Clinic Entrances Act of 1994, which makes it a federal crime and imposes severe fines, including prison terms, on persons who use force, threats, or physical obstruction to interfere with anyone providing or receiving abortions and other reproductive health services. It allows abortion clinic employees and clients or the Department of Justice to sue for damages and seek federal injunctions against violators. Although the act explicitly exempts conduct protected by the free speech and assembly clauses, such as peaceful picketing and passing out leaflets, opponents of the legislation contend that this act interferes with the anti-abortion movement's right to engage in picketing and protesting. They maintain that the act imposes punishment far more severe than state laws and city ordinances for blocking sidewalks and sit-ins.[132]

The Supreme Court has confirmed the right of groups like Operation Rescue to conduct anti-abortion protests outside abortion clinics but has upheld restrictions that keep them from getting any closer than 15 feet from the buildings.

States too have tried to protect the patrons and employees of abortion clinics against coercive protesting, primarily via the issuance of injunctions. The Supreme Court, in trying to balance the legitimate speech rights of abortion protesters against the equally legitimate rights of access on the part of the patrons and employees of these clinics, upheld some provisions of a state court injunction and struck down others. The Court upheld those provisions which prohibited protesters from congregating, picketing, patrolling, and demonstrating within a 36-foot buffer zone around the property line of an abortion clinic. The Court concluded this prohibition was a narrowly drawn limit on the protesters that was necessary to accomplish the legitimate governmental interest in protecting entrance and exit from the clinic. The Court also upheld those provisions prohibiting singing, yelling, and using bullhorns within earshot of patients inside the clinic during specific hours as means to protect the health and well-being of the patients. On the other hand, the Court struck down provisions preventing protesters from picketing at the back of the clinic, the use of "images observable" to the patients, or prohibiting them from approaching within 300 feet of the clinic or of any person seeking services, and from using amplification devices within 300 feet. These provisions, the Court concluded, were too broad and therefore interfered with the protesters' First Amendment rights.[133]

Assembly on Private Property

The right to assemble does not include the right to trespass on private property. A state may protect property owners against those who attempt to convert property to their own uses, even if they are doing so to express ideas.

The profusion of large, privately owned shopping malls that cover many acres and are larger than some towns presents some difficult constitutional issues. The Supreme Court has set the following guidelines: Privately owned shopping malls are neither public streets nor places of public assembly; no one has a constitutional right to use such a mall to hand out political leaflets, to picket for political purposes, or otherwise to exercise First Amendment freedoms. On the other hand, states and cities may legally obligate the owners of such centers to permit their use for peaceful political purposes such as distributing handbills or getting people to sign petitions. In other words, although people have no constitutional right to engage in political action in a nonpublic shopping center, neither do the owners of such centers have a constitutional right to close them to political action in the face of reasonable state or local regulations providing for access that does not interfere with their primary commercial purposes.[134]

Freedom of Association

The right to petition the government for redress of grievances is specifically guaranteed by the Constitution. The right to organize to promote political and other causes is not expressly mentioned in the Constitution, but "it is beyond debate that freedom to engage in association for the advancement of beliefs and ideas is an inseparable aspect of the 'liberty' assured by the Due Process clause of the Fourteenth Amendment which embraces freedom of speech."[135]

The Supreme Court has written of freedom to associate in two distinct senses. In one line of decisions it has protected people's right to enter into and maintain "certain intimate human relationships" against "undue intrusion by the State. . . . In this respect, freedom of association receives protection as a fundamental element of personal liberty."[136] The other aspect relates to activities protected by the First Amendment: speech, assembly, petition, the redress of grievances, and the free exercise of religion.

Some troublesome constitutional questions arise from congressional and state regulation of the amount of money that candidates, political parties, and interest groups can raise and spend for political purposes. Is money speech? If so, then is government regulation of its use constitutionally suspect? Or is money more like action, and therefore open to governmental regulation?[137] In *Buckley v Valeo*, the Court sustained limits on the amount of money people may *contribute to candidates* and their campaign committees on the grounds that such limits only marginally restrict contributors' abilities to express political views.[138] But it struck down limits on the amounts that may be contributed to *associations* formed to support or oppose ballot measures submitted to popular vote.

Limits on what people can *spend*, in contrast to what they can contribute, have fared even less well. Governments may not set limits on the amounts that people (including candidates) can spend on political matters. Presidential candidates, such as Ross Perot in 1992 and Steve Forbes in 1996, who have access to their own wealth and who choose not to take federal funds for their campaigns, may not be limited in what they spend. Limits on what presidential candidates can spend apply only to expenditures by the candidate's party organizations and "coordinated groups," not to "independent groups or committees," who have a constitutional right to spend as much as they wish to further the candidate's election.[139]

SUBVERSIVE CONDUCT AND SEDITIOUS SPEECH

"If there is any fixed star in our constitutional constellation," Justice Robert Jackson said, "it is that no official, high or petty, can prescribe what shall be orthodox in politics, nationalism, religion, or other matters of opinion."[140] Any group can champion whatever position it wishes: vegetarianism, feminism, sexism, communism, fascism, black nationalism, white supremacy, Zionism, anti-Semitism, Americanism.

It is one thing to punish persons for what they *do*; it is another to punish them for what they *say*. The story of the development of constitutional democracy is in large measure the story of making this distinction clear.

The Sedition Act of 1798

The adoption of the Constitution and the Bill of Rights did not result in a quick, easy victory for those who wished to establish free speech in the United States.[141] In 1798, only seven years after the First Amendment had been ratified, Congress passed the first national law aimed against **sedition**—attempting to overthrow the government by force or to interrupt its activities by violence. Those were perilous times for the young Republic, for war with France seemed imminent. The Federalists, in control of both Congress and the presidency, persuaded themselves that national safety required some suppression of speech.

The Sedition Act marked a considerable advance over English common law in that it made truth a defense and allowed the jury, not a judge, to decide the fact of sedition as well as the fact of publication. It did, however, make it a crime to utter false, scandalous, or malicious statements intended to bring the government or any of its officers into disrepute or "to incite against them the hatred of the good people of the United States."[142]

Popular reaction to the Sedition Act helped defeat the Federalists in the elections of 1800. They had failed to grasp the democratic idea that a person may criticize the government of the day, oppose its policies, and work for its downfall, but still be loyal to the nation.

The Smith Act of 1940

The first peacetime sedition law since the Sedition Act of 1798 was the Smith Act of 1940. The Smith Act forbids persons to advocate overthrow of the government with the intent to bring it about; to distribute, with disloyal intent, matter teaching or advising the overthrow of government by violence; and to organize knowingly or to help organize any group having such purposes.

In *Dennis v United States* (1950), the Court agreed that the Smith Act could be applied to the leaders of the Communist party, who had been charged with conspiring to advocate the violent overthrow of the government.[143] Since then the Court has substantially modified its holding. Congress may not outlaw the mere advocacy of the abstract doctrine of violent overthrow: "The essential distinction is that those to whom the advocacy is addressed must be urged to do something now or in the future, rather than merely to believe in something."[144] Moreover, advocacy of the use of force may not be forbidden "except where such advocacy is directed to inciting or producing imminent lawless action and is likely to incite or produce such action."[145]

In short, seditious speech, if narrowly defined to cover only the advocacy of immediate and concrete acts of violence, is not constitutionally protected. Such narrow interpretation of the sedition laws means people are free to work for their political objectives as long as they abandon the use of force—or its specific and immediate advocacy—as a means of bringing it about.

POLITICS ONLINE

Surf Watch: Pornography on the Internet

Should government regulate the content of Internet communications that include indecent words or pictures children can access with the click of a mouse? In 1996, Congress passed the Communications Decency Act, which made it illegal to send "indecent" or "patently offensive" words or pictures online where they can be found by children. In defending the act before the Supreme Court, the Justice Department contended: "The Internet threatens to give every child a free pass into the equivalent of every adult bookstore and every adult video store in the country." But the American Civil Liberties Union countered that "The government cannot reduce the adult population to reading or viewing only what is appropriate for children." During oral arguments it appeared that the justices were uncertain whether Internet speech is most like speech on a street corner or in a park, communication over the telephone, or some type of publication. Even if the court upholds the 1996 law, it would not limit access to indecent online material from overseas. An alternative to the legislation would be the use of computer-blocking devices such as NetNanny, which allows parents to limit their children's access.

To learn more about this case and its implications, pull up the home page of your favorite newspaper and search for articles on the case, *Reno v American Civil Liberties Union*. For information on First Amendment issues more generally, go to:

http://www.fac.org/default.htm

Also see the home page of the Reporters Committee for Freedom of the Press:

http://www.rcfp.org/rcfp

For a liberal perspective on the First Amendment, check out the American Civil Liberties Union at:

http://www.ACLj.org

For a conservative perspective, check out the American Center for Law and Justice:

http://www.aclj.org

SUMMARY

1. First Amendment freedoms—freedom of religion, freedom from the establishment of religion, freedom of speech, freedom of the press, freedom of assembly and petition, and freedom of association—are at the heart of a healthy constitutional democracy.

2. Since World War I, the Supreme Court has become the primary branch of government for giving meaning to these constitutional restraints. And since 1925 these constitutional limits have been applied not only to Congress but to all governmental agencies—national, state, and local.

3. Clashes about First Amendment freedoms are not usefully thought of as battles between the "good guys" and the "bad guys" or as dramas in which judges rush to the rescue of liberty. Rather, these are arguments over conflicting notions of what is in the public interest.

4. Over the years, the Supreme Court has taken a practical approach to First Amendment freedoms. It has refused to make them absolute rights above any kind of governmental regulation, direct or indirect, or to say that they must be preserved at whatever price. But the justices have recognized that a constitutional democracy tampers with these freedoms at great peril. They have insisted upon compelling justification before permitting these rights to be limited. How compelling the justification is, in a free society, will always remain an open question.

FURTHER READING

STEPHEN BATES, *Battleground* (Poseidon, 1993).

LEE C. BOLLINGER, *Images of a Free Press* (University of Chicago Press, 1991).

JAMES MACGREGOR BURNS AND STEWART BURNS, *A People's Charter: The Pursuit of Rights in America* (Knopf, 1991).

T. BARTON CARTER, MARC A. FRANKLIN, AND JAY B. WRIGHT, *The First Amendment and the Fourth Estate*, 5th ed. (Foundation Press, 1991).

ZECHARIAH CHAFEE, JR., *Free Speech in the United States* (Harvard University Press, 1941).

JESSE CHOPER, *Securing Religious Liberty: Principles for Judicial Interpretation of Religion Clauses* (University of Chicago Press, 1995).

DONALD L. DRAKEMAN, *Church-State Constitutional Issues: Making Sense of the Establishment Clause* (Greenwood, 1991).

TERRY EASTLAND, ED., *Religious Liberty in the Supreme Court: The Cases That Define the Debate over Church and State* (Ethics and Policy Center, 1993).

IRA GLASSER, *Visions of Liberty: The Bill of Rights for All Americans* (Arcade, 1991).

MARK A. GRABER, *Transforming Free Speech: The Ambiguous Legacy of Civil Libertarianism* (University of California Press, 1991).

KENT GREENAWALT, *Fighting Words: Individuals, Communities, and Liberties of Speech* (Princeton University Press, 1995).

MARJORIE HEINS, *Sex, Sin and Blasphemy: A Guide to America's Censorship Wars* (New Press, 1993).

NAT HENTOFF, *The First Freedom: The Tumultuous History of Free Speech in America*, 2d ed. (Delacorte, 1988).

EUGENE W. HICKOK, JR., ED., *The Bill of Rights: Original Meaning and Current Understanding* (University Press of Virginia, 1991).

JAMES E. LEAHY, *The First Amendment, 1791–1991: Two Hundred Years of Freedom* (McFarland, 1991).

LEONARD W. LEVY, *The Establishment Clause: Religion and the First Amendment* (Macmillan, 1986).

ANTHONY LEWIS, *Make No Law: The Sullivan Case and the First Amendment* (Random House, 1991).

CATHARINE A. MACKINNON, *Only Words* (Harvard University Press, 1993).

JOHN STUART MILL, *Essay on Liberty* (1859), in *The English Philosophers from Bacon to Mill*, ed. Arthur Burtt (Random House, 1939), pp. 949–1041.

WILLIAM LEE MILLER, *The First Liberty: Religion and the American Republic* (Knopf, 1986).

MELVILLE B. NIMMER, *Nimmer on Freedom of Speech: A Treatise on the Theory of the First Amendment* (Mathew Binder, 1987).

J. W. PELTASON, *Understanding the Constitution*, 14th ed. (Harcourt Brace, 1997).

LUCAS A. POWE, JR., *The Fourth Estate and the Constitution: Freedom of the Press in America* (University of California Press, 1991).

JONATHAN RAUCH, *Kindly Inquisitors: The New Attacks on Free Thought* (University of Chicago Press, 1993).

GEOFFREY R. STONE, RICHARD A. EPSTEIN, AND CASS R. SUNSTEIN, EDS., *The Bill of Rights in the Modern State* (University of Chicago Press, 1992).

NADINE STROSSEN, *Defending Pornography: Free Speech, Sex, and the Fight for Women's Rights* (Scribner's, 1995).

CASS R. SUNSTEIN, *Democracy and the Problems of Free Speech* (Free Press, 1993).

ROBERT J. WAGMAN, *The First Amendment Book* (World Almanac, 1991).

RONALD C. WHITE, JR., AND ALBRIGHT G. ZIMMERAN, EDS., *An Unsettled Arena: Religions and the Bill of Rights* (Eerdmans, 1990).

5

Equal Rights
Under the Law

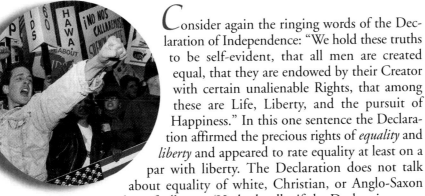

Consider again the ringing words of the Declaration of Independence: "We hold these truths to be self-evident, that all men are created equal, that they are endowed by their Creator with certain unalienable Rights, that among these are Life, Liberty, and the pursuit of Happiness." In this one sentence the Declaration affirmed the precious rights of *equality* and *liberty* and appeared to rate equality at least on a par with liberty. The Declaration does not talk about equality of white, Christian, or Anglo-Saxon men, but of *all* men. (Undoubtedly, if the Declaration were to be written today, the framers would speak of "persons" rather than "men.") This creed of individual dignity and equality is older than our Declaration of Independence; its roots go back into the teachings of Judaism and Christianity.

What about the Constitution? What was the framers' attitude toward liberty and equality? We know that the builders of our constitutional system cherished liberty as their highest ideal. And although you will not find any reference to the idea of equality (not even the word itself is in the Constitution or in the array of liberties that form the Bill of Rights), we know the framers believed that all men—at least all white men—were equally entitled to life, liberty, and the pursuit of happiness (the framers changed "pursuit of happiness" to "property" in the Bill of Rights). They felt strongly that there should be no noble or privileged class under the law. Like the Declaration, the Constitution refers to "men" or "him," not to women, and none of its lofty sentiments applied to slaves, who enjoyed neither liberty nor equality.

The framers resolved their ambiguity about what kind of equality and for whom by creating a system of government designed to protect what they called **natural rights**. Today we speak of **human rights**, but the idea is the same: All citizens are entitled to their dignity and worth. By equal rights the framers meant that every person has an equal right to protection against arbitrary treatment, an equal right to the liberties guaranteed by the Bill of Rights, and an equal right to protection by any laws passed by the new national government.

The Constitution itself provides two ways of protecting civil rights. First, it ensures that government imposes no discriminatory barriers; and second, it grants national and state governments authority to protect civil rights against interference by private individuals. This chapter is concerned with both the protection of our rights *from abuse by government* and the *protection through government* of our rights, to be free from abuse by our fellow citizens. In this chapter we focus on the struggles of women, African Americans, Native Americans, Hispanics, and Asian Americans to secure the basic civil rights to vote, to an education, to a job, and to a place to live on equal terms with their fellow citizens.

EQUALITY AND EQUAL RIGHTS

Americans are committed to equality. "Equality," however, is an elusive term, and "few issues have sparked more controversy or held more sway over the course of history."[1] Part of the difficulty is that "equality" lacks precise meaning. The concept for which there is the greatest consensus, and that is most clearly written into the Constitution, is that everybody should have *equality of opportunity* regardless of race, ethnic origin, religion, and, in recent years, sex. Ensuring this equality of opportunity is what we mean by the struggle for civil rights.

We The People

Women's History Is Half of History

Lucretia Mott,
Elizabeth Cady Stanton
barred from this
convention

Sewing machine
invented

Declaration of
Sentiments,
Seneca Falls

Harriet Beecher Stowe,
Uncle Tom's Cabin

Women's Rights
Convention

Sojourner Truth

Clara Barton,
Mother Bickerdyke,
nurses

Women's
Loyal
League

Harriet
Tubman
leads raid

1840

1860

World
Antislavery
Convention

Irish imigration
begins

Texas admitted
to the Union

Dred Scott
decision

Harper's
Ferry

Lincoln
elected

Fort Sumter

Emancipation
Proclamation

International
Council of
Women

*Ladies' Home
Journal*

General
Federation of
Women's Clubs

National
American Women
Suffrage
Association

Susan B.
Anthony

Jane Addams,
Hull House

Florence Kelley.
reformer

Charlotte Perkins
Gilman, *Women and
Economics*

Women's
Trade
Union
League

Comstock
laws

Brandeis brief,
protective
legislation

National
Woman's
Party

1900

Samuel Gompers,
American
Federation of
Labor

Populists

Immigration from
Southern Europe

Battle of
Wounded
Knee

Progressive
Era

Theodore
Roosevelt

Panama canal
begun

Woodrow
Wilson

WACS,
WAVES,
WASPS.
women's
service
corps

Rosie the
Riveter

800,000 women
fired by aircraft
companies

Suburbia

Dr. Spock

Mary McCarthy,
The Group

Betty Friedan,
*The Feminine
Mystique*

Title VII
prohibits sex
discrimination
in employment

Executive
Order
mandates
affirmative
action

The "Pill"

1940

1960

Pearl
Harbor

Atomic
bomb

World War II
ends

Television

Korea

Eisenhower

The New
Frontier

March one
Washington,
Martin Luther King Jr.

Kennedy
assassinated

Civil
Rights
Act

The
Great
Society

Vietnam

Peace
movement

Sandra Day O'Connor,
first woman Supreme
Court justice
appointed

ERA deadline
passed
without
ratification

ERA
reintroduced
in Congress

Geraldine Ferraro,
first woman
nominated as vice-
presidential
candidate of a major
political party (the
Democratic party)

State of Washington
adopts comparable
worth for some
State employees

Congress reverses
impact of *Grove*
decision that had
limited federal civil
rights laws

Supreme Court
restricts
Roe v Wade

Reagan

Challenger
explodes

Reagan-Gorbachev
talks, INF Treaty

Bush

"Battle Hymn of the Republic,"
Julia Ward Howe

Equal Rights Association

Frances Willard Woman's Christian Temperance Union

Clara Barton, Red Cross

Evaporated milk available

Radcliffe, Bryn Mawr founded

Emily Dickinson died 1886

Mother Mary Jones, labor organizer

1880

Lee surrenders to Grant

14th Amendment makes blacks citizens and adds the word "male" to the Constitution

15th Amendment provides for black male suffrage

Reconstruction

Custer, Little Big Horn, 1876

Transcontinental railroad completed, 1869

Civil service reform

Women's Joint Congressional Committee National Council of Defense

Margaret Sanger birth control

Alice Paul introduces Equal Rights Amendment (ERA)

Margaret Mead, *Coming of Age in Samoa*

Frances Perkins, secretary of labor

Claire Booth Luce, *The Women*

Suffragists jailed for White House demonstration

Women get the vote

League of Women Voters

The flapper

Frozen foods introduced

1920

U.S. enters World War I

Treaty of Versailles

19th Amendment secures Women's suffrage

Prohibition

Herbert Hoover

Depression

Stock market crash

FDR, New Deal

Eleanor Roosevelt

National Women's Strike

International Women's Year

Women's Educational Equity Act passed

National Women's Conference, Houston

Nancy Kassebaum elected to Senate

National Organization or Women (NOW)

Gloria Steinem, *Ms. Magazine*

ERA passed by Congress

Title IX prohibits sex discrimination in education

Supreme Court legalizes abortion in *Roe v Wade*

Episcopalians or dain women

ERA ratification deadline extended

1980

Student unrest

Resurrection City

Cambodia

Watergate

Carter

Nixon

Moon landing

Janet Reno named Attorney General

Clarence Thomas Supreme Court confirmation hearings

54 women elected members of Congress in "The Year of the Woman"

Supreme Court reaffirms core holding of *Roe v Wade*

Ruth Bader Ginsburg appointed to the Supreme Court

Madeleine Albright named Secretary of State

1992

Middle East Peace talks

1993

1997

no longer concerned themselves with the enforcement of civil rights laws, and Congress enacted no new ones. The Supreme Court either declared old laws unconstitutional or interpreted them so narrowly that they were ineffective. The Court also gave such a limited construction to the Thirteenth, Fourteenth, and Fifteenth Amendments that they failed to accomplish their intended purpose of protecting the rights of African Americans.

By 1900 white supremacy was unchallenged in the South, where most blacks lived. Blacks were kept from voting; they were forced to accept menial jobs; and they were denied educational opportunities. In 1896, in *Plessy v Ferguson*, the Supreme Court gave constitutional sanction to government-imposed racial segregation.[6] Even if the Court had declared segregation unconstitutional, a decision so contrary to popular feeling and political realities would have had little impact. In 1896, blacks were lynched an average of one every four days, and few whites raised a voice in protest.

During World War I, African Americans began to migrate to northern cities to seek educational opportunities and jobs in war factories. These trends were accelerated by the New Deal and World War II, and the South, through urbanization and industrialization, became more like the rest of the nation. As migration of African Americans out of the rural South into southern and northern cities shifted the racial composition of cities, the African American vote became important in national elections. Although discrimination continued, there were more jobs and more social gains. Above all, these changes created an African American middle class opposed to segregation as a symbol of servitude and a cause of inequality. By the middle of the twentieth century, urban blacks were active and politically powerful citizens. There was a growing, persistent, and insistent demand for the abolition of color barriers.

THE NATIONAL GOVERNMENT RESPONDS   Because of the special nature of the Electoral College and the dynamics of our political system, by the 1930s it became more difficult for the president—or anyone hoping to be president—to ignore the aspirations of African Americans. The commitment of our presidents, and in more recent decades of our senators, to the cause of equal protection became translated into the appointment of federal judges more sympathetic to an interpretation of the Thirteenth, Fourteenth, and Fifteenth Amendments that would carry

During World War I, African American flyers fighting in a segregated unit established a record for bravery and effectiveness.

out the amendments' original purpose of securing the civil and voting rights of African Americans.

In the 1930s, African Americans began resorting to lawsuits to secure their rights and to challenge the doctrine of segregation. They emphasized litigation because they had no alternative; they lacked sufficient political power to make their demands effective before either state legislatures or Congress. After World War II, civil rights litigation began to have an impact. Under the leadership of the Supreme Court, federal judges started to use the Fourteenth Amendment to reverse earlier decisions that rendered it and federal legislation ineffective. In 1954, in *Brown v Board of Education*, the Supreme Court reversed a half-century-old precedent and declared public school segregation unconstitutional. In the years that followed, the Court outlawed all forms of government-imposed segregation and struck down most of the devices that had been used by state and local authorities to keep African Americans from voting. Presidents used their executive authority to fight segregation in the armed services and the federal bureaucracy, and they directed the Department of Justice to enforce whatever civil rights laws were available.

As the 1950s came to a close, the emerging national consensus in favor of governmental action to protect civil rights and the growing political voice of African Americans in the northern states began to have some influence on Congress. In 1957 Congress overrode a southern filibuster in the Senate and enacted the first federal civil rights laws since Reconstruction. During the 1950s the conflict was primarily an attempt by the national government to compel southern state governments to stop segregating African Americans into inferior schools, parks, libraries, houses, and jobs. Then came the momentous 1960s.

A TURNING POINT A decade after the Supreme Court declared public school segregation unconstitutional, most black children in the South still attended segregated schools. In northern cities segregation in housing and education remained the established pattern as well. In the South most African Americans still were kept from voting, despite the fact that such action clearly violated the Constitution of the United States. Most legal barriers in the path of equal rights had fallen, yet most African Americans still could not buy houses where they wanted, secure the jobs they needed, or find educational opportunities for their children. In the South they could not eat in a restaurant or walk on the streets of so-called "white neighborhoods" without being insulted.

But times were changing. What had once been thought of as a "southern problem" was finally being recognized as a national challenge. By 1963 the struggles in the courtrooms were being supplemented by a massive social, economic, and political movement.

The "revolt" in 1963 was not unexpected. In one sense it began when the first black slave was educated three hundred years earlier. Its more recent origin was in Montgomery, Alabama, on December 1, 1955, when Rosa Parks refused to give up a seat in the front of a bus and was removed from the bus. The black community of Montgomery responded by boycotting city buses. The boycott worked.[7]

Montgomery produced a charismatic national civil rights leader: the Reverend Martin Luther King, Jr. Through his Southern Christian Leadership Conference and his doctrine of nonviolent resistance, Dr. King gave a new dimension to the struggle. By the early 1960s, new organizational resources came into existence in almost every city to support and sponsor sit-ins, freedom rides, live-ins, and nonviolent demonstrations.[8] These measures were sometimes met with violence, and at times state and local governments failed either to protect the victims or to prosecute those responsible for the violence.[9]

The forces of social discontent exploded in the summer of 1963. The explosion started with a demonstration in Birmingham, Alabama, which was countered by

I Have a Dream . . .

"Five score years ago, a great American in whose symbolic shadow we stand, signed the Emancipation Proclamation. This momentous decree came as a great beacon light of hope to millions of Negro slaves who had been seared in the flames of withering injustice. It came as a joyous daybreak to end the long night of captivity. But one hundred years later, we must face the tragic fact that the Negro is still not free. One hundred years later, the life of the Negro is still sadly crippled by the manacles of segregation and the chains of discrimination. One hundred years later, the Negro lives on a lonely island of poverty in the midst of a vast ocean of material prosperity. One hundred years later, the Negro is still languishing in the corners of American society and finds himself an exile in his own land. So we have come here today to dramatize an appalling condition. . . .

I have a dream that one day this nation will rise up and live out the true meaning of its creed: "We hold these truths to be self-evident, that all men are created equal."

I have a dream that one day on the red hills of Georgia the sons of former slaves and the sons of former slave owners will be able to sit down together at the table of brotherhood.

I have a dream that one day even the state of Mississippi, a desert state sweltering with the heat of injustice and oppression, will be transformed into an oasis of freedom and justice.

I have a dream that my four little children will one day live in a nation where they will not be judged by the color of their skin but by the content of their character."

SOURCE: Martin Luther King, Jr., address at the Lincoln Memorial, August 28, 1963.

the use of fire hoses, police dogs, and mass arrests. It ended in a march in Washington, D.C., where at least 250,000 people heard Dr. King and other civil rights leaders speak, and countless millions listened and watched them on television. By the time the summer was over, there was hardly a city, North or South, that had not had demonstrations, protests, or sit-ins. Some also had violence.

This direct action had some effect. Civil rights ordinances were enacted in many cities, and more schools were desegregated that fall than in any year since 1956. At the national level, President John Kennedy urged Congress to enact a comprehensive civil rights bill. Late in 1963, the nation's grief over the assassination of President Kennedy, who had become identified with civil rights goals, added political fuel to the drive for federal action.[10] President Lyndon Johnson gave civil rights legislation his highest priority. On July 2, 1964, after months of debate, he signed into law the Civil Rights Act of 1964.[11]

Two Societies? At the close of the 1960s the legal phase of the civil rights movement had come to a close, but as "things got better," discontent grew. When African Americans had been completely subjugated, they had lacked resources to defend themselves. Then, as is true of almost all social revolutions, as conditions began to improve, their demands became more insistent. Millions of impoverished African Americans demonstrated growing impatience with the discrimination that remained. This volatile situation gave way to racial violence and disorders. By 1965, the year of a brutal riot in Watts, a section of Los Angeles, racial disorders were clearly becoming part of the American scene. In 1966 and 1967 the disorders increased in scope and intensity. The Detroit riot in July 1967, the worst such disturbance up to that time in modern American history,[12] made clear the deep divisions between the races and the urgency of taking corrective action.

The Kerner Commission After the racial disturbances in 1967, President Lyndon Johnson appointed a special Advisory Commission on Civil Disorders to investigate the origins of the riots and to recommend measures to prevent or contain such disasters in the future. When the commission (called the Kerner Commission after its chair, Governor Otto Kerner of Illinois) issued its report, it said in stark, clear language: "What white Americans have never fully understood—but what the Negro can never forget—is that white society is deeply implicated in the ghetto. White institutions created it, white institutions maintain it, and white society condones it." The basic conclusion of the commission was that "our nation is moving toward two societies, one black, one white—separate and unequal" and that "only a commitment to national action on an unprecedented scale" could change this trend.[13]

The commission made sweeping recommendations on jobs, education, housing, and the welfare system. But other events diverted attention from these recommendations: the Vietnam War; the partial calming of racial tensions; Watergate; the election of Ronald Reagan and George Bush (especially the former), who were skeptical of governmental actions designed to enforce civil rights; and a growing skepticism about the effectiveness of governmental action generally. As one commentator summarized the central themes of the Reagan and Bush administrations: (1) change is very complex; (2) there are often negative and unanticipated consequences of well-intended reforms; (3) things will get better if the government stops trying to intervene; (4) inequality arises not from prejudice but from cultural deficiencies that are made worse by governmental paternalism.[14] The Clinton administration was much more sympathetic toward the use of governmental power to deal with issues of inequality, but because of budgetary constraints, it was unable or unwilling to promote any major initiatives directly aimed at the problems of our inner cities.

Native Americans

Of all the minorities in the United States, the nearly 2 million people who designate themselves as Native Americans in the census may encompass some of the greatest diversity. Almost half live on or near a reservation—a tract of land given to the tribal nations by treaty—and are enrolled as members of one of the 308 tribes within the continental United States or one of the 200 Native Alaskan communities served by the Bureau of Indian Affairs.[15] Native Americans speak 200 languages.

Native Americans speak of their tribes as "nations," yet they are not states, nor are they nations possessed of the full attributes of sovereignty. Rather, they are a separate people with power to regulate their own internal affairs, subject to congressional supervision. Congress has special responsibilities to Native Americans. States are precluded from regulating or taxing the tribes or extending the jurisdiction of their courts over the tribes unless authorized to do so by Congress.[16] Native Americans living off reservations and working in the general community pay taxes the same as everybody else.

By act of Congress, Indians are American citizens, and by acts of Congress and of the states in which they live, they have the right to vote. Off reservations they have the same rights as any other Americans. If they are enrolled members of a recognized tribe, they are entitled to certain benefits created by law and by treaty. These benefits are administered by the Bureau of Indian Affairs of the Department of the Interior. Moreover, Native Americans who belong to these federally recognized tribes have preference in employment within the bureau, a preference the Supreme Court upheld as a grant not to a "discrete racial group, but, rather, as members of quasi-sovereign tribal entities."[17]

As a result of the growing militancy of Native Americans and a greater national consciousness of the concerns of minorities, most Americans are now aware that most Native Americans live in poverty. Native Americans "are in far worse health than the rest of the population, dying earlier and suffering disproportionately from alcoholism, accidents, diabetes, and pneumonia."[18] Some reservations lack adequate health care facilities, educational opportunities, decent housing, and jobs. Congress has started to compensate Native Americans for past injustices and provide more opportunities for the development of tribal

Hundreds of Sioux Indians took part in a 220-mile March of Memory to mark the 100th anniversary of the Wounded Knee massacre.

economic independence. Judges are also showing a greater vigilance in the enforcement of Indian treaty rights.

Under Article I, Section 8, Congress has full power under the commerce clause to regulate commerce with Indian tribes. Although Congress abolished treaty making with the Indians in 1871, there has been a revived interest in interpreting earlier treaties in a way to protect the independence and authority of the Indian tribes. During the period of assimilation that began in 1887 and lasted until 1934, tribal governments were weak, some reservations were dissolved, and more than 100 tribes had their relationship with the federal government severed.[19] The civil rights movement of the 1960s created a more favorable climate for the concerns of Native Americans, and their goals are to reassert treaty rights and secure greater autonomy for the tribes. Under the leadership of the Native American Rights Fund (NARF), funded in part by the Ford Foundation, there have been more Indian law cases brought in the last several decades than at any time in our history.[20] In 1992 Ben Nighthorse Campbell, elected as a Democrat from Colorado but later changed to become a Republican, became the first Native American to be elected to Congress.

Hispanics

The struggle for civil rights has by no means been limited to women, African Americans, and Native Americans. Each new wave of immigrants has been considered suspect by those who arrived earlier—all the more so if its members were not white or English speaking. Formal barriers of law and informal barriers of custom have combined to deny equal rights. But as groups have established themselves—first economically, then politically—most of these barriers have been swept away, and constitutionally guaranteed rights have been asserted.

There are approximately 27 million Hispanics (or Latinos, as some prefer to be called), about 10 percent of the U.S. population. The largest group consists of 14 million Mexican Americans, sometimes called Chicanos. Most Mexican Americans live in California, Texas, Arizona, and New Mexico, but many now live in other parts of the country as well.[21]

The second largest group of Hispanics consists of the 2.7 million Puerto Ricans who reside on the mainland, often in the "barrios" of New York, Chicago, and other northern cities. They retain close ties with Puerto Rico and move back and forth from the island to the mainland.

The third subgroup of Hispanics consists of more than a million who fled from Castro's Cuba early in the 1960s and a second wave of refugees, called the Mariel refugees, who fled in the 1980s. These Cubans, many of whom live in south Florida, include a substantial number of well-educated, successful businesspeople and professionals. The fourth group includes a rapidly growing number of refugees from other nations in Central and South America who presently number about 5 million.[22]

To black power has been added "brown power"—sometimes as an ally, sometimes as a rival.[23] Yet many Hispanics lack the ties with the white power structure that provided some help for blacks before the civil rights movement—ties that, for example, helped create the historically black colleges and universities. Hispanics have also been handicapped because English, the primary language of the mainstream, is not their native tongue. Until recent decades "no provision whatsoever was made for the education of Mexican-American children" in the Southwest. "When eventually they were allowed into the schools, they were segregated from Anglo children because of their language handicap. Considered by school authorities to be children of an inferior race, they were often punished for speaking Spanish, heard their names involuntarily Anglicized, and saw their cultural background systematically ignored in textbooks."[24]

Hispanic Americans maintain many of their cultural traditions but are mainstream in their love of baseball.

Taking their cue from African Americans, Hispanics are becoming increasingly active in politics, although they do not yet register or vote in significant numbers as compared to blacks. There are only an estimated 5 to 6 million registered Latino voters. Immigrant Hispanics live in the United States for 18 years, on average, before becoming U.S. citizens, compared with the five-year average for Asian immigrants.[25] However, a million more Hispanics voted in 1996 than in 1992, with big increases in California and Texas.

Although Hispanics total about 10 percent of the United States population, there were only 18 Hispanic members in the 435-member U.S. House of Representatives in the 105th Congress (1997–99).[26] We have had only two Hispanic United States senators, and in 1996 there was a Hispanic nominee, Victor Morales, a Democrat in Texas. Less than 1 percent of elected local officials are Hispanic. However, this situation is beginning to change.

The political clout of the Latino electorate is growing "by an average of 19 percent across the country from one presidential election to the next."[27] In the state legislatures, 131 Latinos serve in the lower houses and 48 serve in the upper houses. New Mexico leads the nation in electing Latinos to its legislature. In 1996 Cruz Bustamente became Speaker of the state assembly in California with Latino Speakers also serving in New Mexico and Florida.[28] It is important to note that although there are 14 Hispanic members in California's 80-member assembly, only one has a constituency that includes more than 50 percent Hispanic registered voters.[29]

In Washington, some Hispanic members of Congress have gained seniority and occupy key roles, such as Henry B. Gonzalez (D.-Tex.), chair of the House Banking Committee. Two members of President Clinton's first-term cabinet—Secretary of Housing and Urban Development Henry Cisneros and Secretary of Transportation Federico Peña—were Hispanic. Peña became secretary of energy in Clinton's second term.

The number of Hispanics in local leadership positions is growing. There are more than 5,000 Hispanics serving on elective bodies nationwide, and almost 2,000 Hispanics hold elective office in Texas.[30] Hispanic mayors preside in cities like Miami and Tampa; Florida and New Mexico recently had Hispanic governors. The Mexican-American Legal Defense and Education Fund (MALDEF), the Puerto Rican Legal Defense and Education Fund, the Southwest Voter Registration and

Education Project, the League of United Latin American Citizens (LULAC, an umbrella organization hoping to coordinate the Hispanic community), and the National Hispanic Leadership Agenda (NHLA) are increasingly active politically.

Asian Americans

The term "Asian American" describes individuals from many different countries and many different ethnic backgrounds. Most people from Asian backgrounds do not think of themselves as "Asians" but as Americans of Chinese, Japanese, Vietnamese, Cambodian, Korean, or another specific ancestry. About 40 percent of our immigrants now are from Asia, with almost 11 million Asians projected by the Census Bureau for the year 2000. They live chiefly in the western states, but there has been a rapid increase in Asian Americans in New York and Texas.

Although Asian Americans are often considered a "model minority" because of their general success in education and business, the U.S. Civil Rights Commission (a federal fact-finding body of eight commissioners, half appointed by the president and half by Congress) found that "Asian-Americans do face widespread prejudice, discrimination and barriers to equal opportunity," and that racially motivated violence against them "occurs with disturbing frequency."[31]

The Chinese were the first Asians to come to the United States. Beginning in 1847, when young male peasants came here to get away from poverty and to work in mines, on railroads, and on farms, the Chinese encountered economic and cultural fears of the white majority, who did not understand them or their culture. In response, the Chinese seldom tried to assimilate but instead gravitated to "Chinatowns." Discriminatory immigration and naturalization restrictions, imposed beginning in 1882, were strengthened in the following years and were not removed until the end of World War II. Since that time, the Chinese have moved into the mainstream of American society, and they are beginning to run for and win local political offices. In 1996 Gary Locke, a Democrat and a graduate of Yale and Boston University, was elected governor of Washington, the first Chinese American to become a U.S. governor and the first Asian American to become governor of a continental state.

The Japanese first migrated to Hawaii in the 1860s and then to California in the 1880s. Most Japanese immigrants remained in the West Coast states. By the beginning of the twentieth century, they faced overt hostility. In 1905 labor leaders organized the Japanese and Korean Exclusion League, and in 1906 the San Francisco Board of Education excluded all Chinese, Japanese, and Korean children from neighborhood schools. Some western states passed laws denying the right to own land to aliens who were ineligible to become citizens—meaning, aliens of Asian ancestry. During World War II, anti-Japanese hysteria provoked the internment of West Coast Japanese, most of whom were American citizens guilty of no crimes, in prison camps at Manzanar and Tule Lake, California. During this time Japanese property was often sold at confiscatory rates. Following the war, the exclusionary acts were repealed, and by congressional, presidential, and court action, laws designed to keep Japanese Americans from participating fully in American economic and political life were set aside. In 1988, President Ronald Reagan signed a law providing $20,000 restitution to each of the approximately 60,000 surviving World War II internees.

Koreans—more than 800,000 of them—are concentrated in southern California, Colorado, Honolulu, and New York City. Until recently, like other Asian Americans, they faced overt discrimination in jobs and housing. A Korean middle class has been growing, with many becoming teachers, doctors, and lawyers. Many others continue to operate small family businesses such as dry cleaners, florist shops, service stations, and small grocery stores, often in inner cities.[32] As prosperous small businesspeople, they are often the target of the anger of the poor people whose neighborhoods they serve. Many Korean stores were destroyed in the 1992 Los Angeles riots.

When Filipinos first came to the United States in the early part of this century, they were considered American nationals because the United States then owned their native country. Nonetheless, they were denied their rights to full citizenship and faced discrimination and even violence, including anti-Filipino riots in the state of Washington in 1928 and later in California, where nearly one-third of the approximately 1.5 million Filipinos live.[33] Their economic status has improved, but their influence in politics remains as small as their numbers.

The newest Asian arrivals consist of more than a million Indo-Chinese refugees from Vietnam, Laos, and Cambodia, who first came to the United States in 1975 and settled in Los Angeles and California's Orange and San Diego counties. Although this group includes middle-class people who left during the fall of Saigon following the end of the Vietnam War, it also consists of large numbers of "boat people," mostly peasants in their homelands, who came to our shores without any financial resources. In a relatively short time most have established themselves economically. Although they are starting to have political influence (most apparently registered as Republicans), they remain socially and economically segregated and have not been in the United States long enough to become an effective part of the political process.

EQUAL PROTECTION OF THE LAWS: WHAT DOES IT MEAN?

The **equal protection clause** of the Fourteenth Amendment declares no state (including any subdivision thereof) shall "deny to any person within its jurisdiction the equal protection of the laws." Although there is no parallel clause limiting the national government, the Fifth Amendment's **due process clause**, which states that no person shall "be deprived of life, liberty, or property, without due process of law," has been interpreted to impose the same restraints on the national government. Note the restraints of equal protection apply only to the actions of governments, not to those of private individuals. Thus important questions are raised: Is the action being challenged that of a government, that is, is it state action? Or is the challenged discriminatory action that of private persons, unsupported and detached from the actions of a government?

The equal protection clause does not prevent governments from making distinctions among people. Governments could not legislate without doing so. What the Constitution forbids is *unreasonable* classifications. In general, a classification is unreasonable when there is no relation between the classes it creates and permissible governmental goals. A law prohibiting redheads from voting, for example, would be unreasonable. On the other hand, laws denying persons under 18 the right to vote, to marry without the permission of their parents, or to apply for a license to drive a car appear to be reasonable (at least to most persons over 18).

One of our most troublesome issues is how to distinguish between constitutional and unconstitutional classifications. The Supreme Court uses three tests for this purpose: (1) the traditional *rational basis* test for most laws; (2) the most stringent test of all, a *strict scrutiny* test for laws dealing with suspect classes and fundamental rights; and (3) the *heightened scrutiny* test, a middle-tier or intermediate test for laws dealing with quasi-suspect classifications.

The Equal Protection Clause

THE RATIONAL BASIS TEST The traditional test to determine whether a law complies with the equal protection requirement places the burden of proof on those attacking it. If the facts justify a classification, the law will be sustained, even if it

---

The Equal Protection Clause: Three Tiers of Tests

1. *Rational basis:* The burden is on those attacking the law, and the courts are likely to sustain the law so long as there are some facts and plausible reasons to justify the classification.

2. *Strict scrutiny:* The government has the heavy burden of persuading a court that there is a "compelling public interest" calling for such a classification, and that there is no other, less restrictive way to accomplish this compelling public purpose.

3. *Heightened scrutiny:* The burden shifts to the government to show that the classification serves important governmental objectives and is substantially related to those objectives.

results in some inequality. If the Supreme Court chooses to apply this rational basis test, the law in question will usually be upheld. For example, the Supreme Court concluded that there is a rational basis to support Minnesota's decision to ban the sale of milk in plastic nonreturnable bottles while allowing its sale in biodegradable paperboard nonreturnable cartons.[34]

SUSPECT CLASSIFICATIONS AND STRICT SCRUTINY The most stringent test, the strict scrutiny test, is used when a *suspect class* or a *fundamental right* is involved. The normal presumption of constitutionality is reversed. When a law is subject to strict scrutiny, it is not sufficient that the law be a reasonable means to handle a particular problem. Rather, the courts must be persuaded that there is both a "compelling public interest" to justify such a classification and no other less restrictive way to accomplish this compelling public purpose.

A suspect class is a class of people deliberately subjected to unequal treatment in the past, or relegated by society to a position of such political powerlessness as to require extraordinary judicial protection.[35] Classifications based on race or national origin are always suspect.

Laws that treat people differently because of their race or national origin are subject to strict scrutiny. It does not make any difference if the laws are designed for so-called "benign purposes"—that is, to help persons of a particular race or national origin—rather than invidious purposes—that is, to injure or denigrate them. Laws that classify people by their religion would also create a suspect class, although there is no specific Supreme Court decision to this effect, probably because governments seldom classify people according to religion. State or local laws that impose political limitations on aliens also create suspect classifications and thus are subject to strict scrutiny.

What of *national* laws classifying people by alien status? Federal laws and regulations dealing with aliens are subject, not to the strict scrutiny test, but to the slightly less stringent heightened scrutiny test. When it comes to race and national origin, however, national laws, like those of states and local governments, are subject to strict scrutiny even if adopted for benign or remedial purposes.[36]

QUASI-SUSPECT CLASSIFICATIONS AND HEIGHTENED SCRUTINY The intermediate test—more difficult than the rational basis test and slightly less burdensome than the strict scrutiny test—is called the heightened scrutiny test. It applies to what the court has called "quasi-suspect" classes. To sustain a law under this test, the burden is on the government to show that its classification serves "important governmental objectives" and is substantially related to these objectives.

An example of a quasi-suspect class is illegitimate children. Although some contend that state laws dealing with illegitimate children should be subject to the same strict scrutiny test as state laws based on race, the Supreme Court has been unwilling to go that far. However, in view of the long history of treating illegitimate children less favorably than legitimate ones, the Court has subjected laws dealing with illegitimate children to a heightened scrutiny test. Using this test, the Court has struck down as unconstitutional state laws imposing a one- or two-year time limit in which illegitimate children must sue to establish paternity and seek support by their fathers.[37]

Classifications based on gender are also subject to heightened scrutiny. Not until 1971 was any classification based on gender declared unconstitutional. Prior to that time, many laws that purported to provide special protection for women—such as a Michigan law forbidding any woman other than the wife or daughter of a tavern owner to serve as barmaid—were upheld. As Justice William J. Brennan, Jr., wrote for the Court in 1973: "There can be no doubt that our nation has had a long and unfortunate history of sex discrimination. Traditionally such discrimination was rationalized by an attitude of 'romantic paternalism' which in practical effect put women, not on a pedestal, but in a cage."[38]

Today the Court's view is that gender classifications, although not as suspect as those based on race, are subject to the heightened scrutiny test; that is, to sustain a classification based on gender, the burden is on the government to show that it serves "important governmental objectives" and is substantially related to these objectives. Treating women differently from men (or vice versa) is forbidden when supported by no more substantial justification than "archaic and overbroad generalizations," "old notions," and "the role-typing society has long imposed upon women."[39] If the government's objective is "to protect members of one sex because they are presumed to suffer from an inherent handicap or to be innately inferior," that objective itself is illegitimate.[40]

The Supreme Court has struck down most, but not all, laws brought before it that were alleged to discriminate against women. Those the Court has refused to strike down include the males-only draft and veterans' preference in civil service jobs.[41]

POVERTY AND AGE   The Supreme Court is being urged to designate additional categories of people as suspect or quasi-suspect classes in order to provide greater judicial protection for them. It is argued that just as racial minorities and women are entitled to special constitutional protection, so should be the poor and the elderly. The Supreme Court, however, "has never held that financial need alone identifies a suspect class for purposes of equal protection analysis."[42] Thus, a state may rely on property taxes for funds for schools, even if this means that schools in "rich" districts spend more per pupil than those in "poor" districts.

Age is neither a suspect nor a quasi-suspect class. Our laws and practices commonly make distinctions based on age: to obtain a driver's license, to marry without parental consent, to attend schools, to buy alcohol, and so on. Many governmental institutions have age-specific programs: for senior citizens, for adult students, for midcareer persons. Although the Supreme Court has refused to make age a suspect classification requiring extra judicial protection, Congress, responding to "gray power," is frequently treating age as a protected category. Congress has made it illegal for most employers to discriminate in their employment practices on the basis of old age. And except for a few exempt occupations, Congress prohibits employers from imposing mandatory age retirement requirements. About one-fourth of the court actions filed by the Equal Employment Opportunity Commission relate to claims of age discrimination.[43]

FUNDAMENTAL RIGHTS AND STRICT SCRUTINY   The Court also strictly scrutinizes laws impinging on **fundamental rights**. What makes a right fundamental in the constitutional sense? It is not the importance or the significance of the right that makes it fundamental, but whether it is explicitly or implicitly *guaranteed by the Constitution*.[44] Under this test, the rights to travel and to vote have been held to be fundamental, as well as such First Amendment rights as the right to associate for the advancement of political beliefs. Rights to an education, to housing, or to welfare benefits have not been held to be fundamental. Important as these rights may be, they are not guaranteed by the Constitution, meaning that there are no constitutional provisions specifically protecting these rights from governmental regulation.

Proving Discrimination

Does the fact that a law or a regulation has a differential effect—what has come to be known as *disparate impact*—on persons of different race or sex by itself establish that it is unconstitutional? In one of its most important decisions, *Washington v Davis* (1976), the Supreme Court said no. "The invidious quality of a law claimed

to be racially discriminatory must ultimately be traced to a racially discriminatory purpose."[45] "An unwavering line of cases" from the Supreme Court "hold that a violation of the Equal Protection Clause requires state action motivated by discriminatory intent; the disproportionate effects of state action are not sufficient to establish such a violation."[46] Or, as the Court said in another case: "The Fourteenth Amendment guarantees equal laws, not equal results."[47]

What do these rulings on disparate impact mean in practical terms? They mean, for example, that city ordinances that permit only single-family residences and thus make low-cost housing projects impossible are not unconstitutional—even if their effect is to keep minorities from moving into the city—unless it can be shown that they were adopted with the *intent to discriminate* against minorities. The rulings also mean that a preference for veterans in public employment does not violate the equal protection clause, even though its effect is to keep many women from getting jobs; the distinction between veterans and nonveterans was not adopted deliberately to create a sex barrier.

Still, the disparate impact that a law or governmental practice has is not irrelevant in determining its constitutionality. In a community with a large number of African Americans or Hispanics, it would be constitutionally suspicious if only a few of them were called for jury duty. Under such circumstances, the burden of proof shifts to the state or city to demonstrate that it has not engaged in unconstitutional discriminatory conduct.

What is constitutional can nonetheless be made illegal. Things that are unconstitutional are always illegal, but what is illegal may not be unconstitutional. One of the most hotly contested issues of recent years has been how to interpret the various civil rights acts, especially Title VII of the Civil Rights Act of 1964, which forbids discrimination in employment on the basis of race, color, sex, religion, or national origin. Congress has also intervened to make illegal some voting practices that are not necessarily unconstitutional. The Voting Rights Act of 1965 tests the legality of state voting laws and practices by their effects rather than by the intentions of those who passed them.

EDUCATION RIGHTS

Until the Supreme Court struck down such laws in the 1950s, southern states had made it illegal for whites and blacks to ride in the same train cars, attend the same theaters, go to the same schools, be born in the same hospitals, or be buried in the same cemeteries. **Jim Crow laws**, as they came to be called, blanketed southern life.[48] Southern states and some places in the North enforced segregation in transportation, places of public accommodation, educational facilities, swimming pools, and parks. How could these laws stand in the face of the equal protection clause? This was the question raised in *Plessy v Ferguson*.

Segregation, Discrimination, and *Plessy v Ferguson*

In 1896, in *Plessy v Ferguson*, the Supreme Court endorsed the view that racial segregation did not constitute discrimination if "equal" accommodations were provided for the members of both races.[49] Equal accommodations were required only for public facilities such as schools and colleges and for a limited category of public utilities such as trains and buses. Although the *Plessy* decision required equality as the price for compulsory segregation, the "equal" part of the formula was meaningless. States segregated blacks into unequal facilities, and blacks lacked the political power to protest.

The passage of time did not lessen the inequalities. Beginning in the late 1930s, blacks started to file lawsuits challenging the doctrine. They cited facts to show that in practice, separate but equal always resulted in discrimination against blacks. At

Thurgood Marshall (center), George E. C. Hayes (left), and James Nabrit, Jr., (right) argued and won *Brown v Board of Education of Topeka* before the Supreme Court in 1954.

first the Supreme Court was not willing to upset the separate but equal doctrine, but started to undermine it.

The End of Separate But Equal: *Brown v Board of Education*

In the spring of 1954, in *Brown v Board of Education*, the Supreme Court finally reversed its 1896 holding as it applied to public schools. It ruled that "separate but equal" is a contradiction in terms. Segregation is itself discrimination.[50] A year later the Court ordered school boards to proceed with "all deliberate speed to desegregate public schools at the earliest practical date."[51] In the years following the *Brown* decision, federal judges struck down a whole battery of schemes designed to evade the Court's ruling. Beginning in 1963, the Supreme Court gradually reversed its decision that granted school districts time to prepare for desegregation. In 1969 the Court completed that reversal, stating: "Continued operation of racially segregated schools under the standard of 'all deliberate speed' is no longer constitutionally permissible. School districts must immediately terminate dual school systems based on race and operate only unitary school systems."[52]

In the 1960s Congress and the president joined even more directly in the battle against school segregation. Title VI of the Civil Rights Act of 1964 stipulates that federal dollars under any grant program or project must be withdrawn from an entire school or institution of higher education that discriminates "on the ground of race, color, or national origin" in "any program or activity receiving federal financial assistance." Congress in 1972 added sex discrimination to this list; other acts have added the handicapped, the aged, Vietnam veterans, and disabled veterans. Title VI also imposes a responsibility on schools to take affirmative action to ensure that persons in the protected categories are not denied access to any federally supported program or activity.

From Segregation to Desegregation But Not to Integration

School districts which prior to *Brown v Board of Education* operated two kinds of schools, one for whites and one for blacks, have a positive constitutional obligation to develop plans and programs to move from segregation to integration. Desegregation is not enough; they have a duty to bring about integration. If they fail to do so on their own initiative, federal judges, when petitioned either by plaintiffs who have suffered from school segregation or by the Department of Justice, are to supervise school districts to ensure that they are doing what is necessary and proper to overcome the evils of segregation. In 1995 Justice Clarence Thomas, in *Missouri v Jenkins*, argued that "racial isolation itself is not a harm: only state-enforced segregation is."[53] His view is picking up support among some African American leaders and scholars.[54]

Since most neighborhoods are racially homogeneous, merely removing legal barriers to integration will not integrate the schools. To overcome this residential clustering by race, federal courts have mandated school busing across neighborhoods, moving white students to once predominantly black schools and vice versa. Busing students is not popular and has fostered widespread protest in many cities. The Supreme Court sustained the right of judges to order school districts to bus students to overcome racial imbalance *if and only if* it is to remedy the consequences of officially sanctioned or required segregation, that is, *de jure* segregation. The Court has refused to permit federal judges to order busing to overcome the effects of *de facto* segregation, segregation that arises from social customs or personal choice or as the result of residential segregation.[55] In other words, if judges find that authorities had operated segregated schools in the past or had caused segregation by systematic and purposeful actions, then they may order a school district to bus pupils.[56] But judges may not, said the Supreme Court in a

Thinking It Through

In 1971, in *Griggs v Duke Power*, concerning the requirement of a high school diploma for becoming a janitor, the Supreme Court held that showing the disparate impact of an employment practice was sufficient to shift the burden of proof to the employer to show that this practice or test was job related.[*] Eighteen years later, in *Wards Cove Packing Co. v Antonio*, the Supreme Court placed the burden on those charging discrimination to show that a challenged practice—say, a test—had a significantly disparate impact and was not connected with a business goal.[**] Then, in the Civil Rights Act of 1991, Congress stepped in to provide that once those charging discrimination show that a test or a physical requirement for a job results in reducing the number of women, or minorities, or handicapped, or persons of a particular religion eligible for that job, then the employer must "demonstrate that the challenged practice is job related for the position in question and consistent with business necessity."

SOURCE: This discussion is based on a summary of the Civil Rights Act of 1991 prepared by David S. Tatel of Hogan & Hartson, December 18, 1991.

[*] *Griggs v Duke Power*, 401 US 424 (1971).

[**] *Wards Cove Packing Co. v Antonio*, 490 US 642 (1989).

TABLE 5–1

Segregation Moves North and West

States with the largest percentage of Hispanic and African American students attending schools that have 90 to 100 percent minority populations.

African Americans

1.	Illinois	61.9%
2.	Michigan	59.6
3.	New York	57.1
4.	New Jersey	53.7
5.	Pennsylvania	47.0
6.	Maryland	46.0
7.	Alabama	38.2
8.	Tennessee	38.0
9.	Mississippi	36.9

Hispanics

1.	New York	57.3%
2.	New Jersey	43.4
3.	Texas	43.0
4.	California	38.7
5.	Illinois	34.9
6.	Connecticut	32.4
7.	Florida	27.6
8.	Pennsylvania	27.4
9.	New Mexico	20.0
10.	Arizona	18.9

SOURCE: Gary Orfield, Mark Bachmeier, David R. James, and Tamela Eitle, "Deepening Segregation in American Public Schools," Harvard Project on Desegregation, April 5, 1997.

case involving the Detroit metropolitan area, order busing between suburbs and cities or any other interdistrict lines to overcome racial imbalances in schools where such segregation was not caused by official actions.[57] But in metropolitan areas where there is residential segregation, it is difficult to integrate schools by judicial decree without busing. In fact, since the Supreme Court's decision in the Detroit case, there has been little progress in school desegregation.[58]

After a period of authorizing federal judges to use a wide range of desegregation remedies, even including requiring school districts to raise taxes,[59] the Supreme Court started to limit these mandates to those directly related to violations of the Constitution. For example, the Supreme Court denied a district judge the right to order school districts to create "magnet schools" (that is, schools for gifted and talented students in particular subject areas such as science or performing arts that are provided with good facilities, outstanding teachers, and comprehensive programs) to try to reverse white flight.[60] Federal judges have been instructed to restore control of a school system to the state and local authorities "once the judge concludes that the authorities have done everything practicable to overcome the past consequences of segregation."[61] As a result, in many cities that used to operate legally mandated dual schools systems, federal courts are ending their supervision of school boards' desegregation plans and releasing districts of any busing obligations.[62]

Although the federal government has intervened in more than 500 school desegregation cases in southern districts that once had governmentally mandated segregation, there has been no such judicial action for northern schools that have had *de facto* segregation. As a result, southern cities now have more integrated schools than do large northern cities (see Table 5–1). In large metropolitan areas in the North and South, many school districts in central cities are predominantly African American and/or Hispanic, partly as the result of "white flight" to the suburbs and private schools to escape court-ordered busing but in more recent years also due to higher birth rates and immigration among African Americans and Hispanics. By the 1991–1992 school year, "after decades of progress, schools in the South had rising concentrations of black students and those in the West had rising concentrations of Hispanic students," and two out of every three African American public school students attend schools where the enrollment is more than 50 percent black or Latino.[63]

The political support behind efforts to integrate the schools by busing is fading.[64] School districts are beginning to eliminate mandatory busing, which according to one expert is "threatening to get us to a level of segregation we haven't seen since before the civil rights movement."[65] Some African American leaders, while still supporting desegregation efforts, are paying more attention to improving the quality of inner-city schools than to desegregating them. As Dr. Beverly P. Cole, director of education and housing for the National Association for the Advancement of Colored People (NAACP), has said, "At the present time, we are more concerned with the quality of education and this has to take precedence over whether schools are integrated."[66]

VOTING RIGHTS

Under our Constitution, states determine voting qualifications, but they do so subject to a variety of constitutional restraints. Article I, Section 4, gives Congress the power to supersede state regulations as to the "Times, Places and Manner" of elections for representatives, senators, and presidential electors. Congress has used this authority to set age qualifications and residency requirements to vote in national elections, to establish a uniform day for all states to hold elections for members of Congress and presidential electors, and to give American citizens who reside outside the United States the right to vote for members of Congress and presidential electors in the states in which they previously lived.

The major limitations on the states' power to set voting qualifications are contained in the Fourteenth Amendment (forbidding qualifications that have no reasonable relation to the ability to vote), the Fifteenth Amendment (forbidding qualifications based on race), the Nineteenth Amendment (forbidding qualifications based on sex), and the Twenty-sixth Amendment (forbidding states to deny citizens 18 years of age or older the right to vote on account of age). These amendments also empower Congress to enact the laws necessary to enforce their provisions.

Getting Around the Fourteenth and Fifteenth Amendments

Despite fierce opposition to the Nineteenth Amendment, no organized resistance surfaced after its ratification gave women the right to vote. This was not so following ratification of the Fourteenth and Fifteenth Amendments. African American men were allowed to participate in the political life of southern states only when the federal government insisted upon it. As soon as federal troops were withdrawn from the South in 1877, southern Democrats regained control of state governments and set out to keep blacks from voting. They used social pressure and violence. Organized secret societies like the Ku Klux Klan engaged in terrorist activities such as midnight shootings, burnings, whippings, and lynchings.

These measures worked. But toward the end of the nineteenth century, and for the first time since the Civil War, parts of the South had two strong political parties: the Democrats and the Populists. White supremacists were fearful the parties might compete for the black vote, and blacks might come to hold the balance of power. White supremacists also feared that continued use of excessive force and fraud to disenfranchise blacks might cause the president and Congress to intervene.

Southern leaders reasoned that if they could pass laws depriving blacks of the vote on grounds other than race, blacks would find it difficult to challenge such laws in the courts. Some whites protested that such laws could be used against whites as well as blacks, but keeping poor whites from voting did not disturb the conservative leaders of the Democratic party, for they were often just as anxious to undermine white support for the Populist party as they were to disenfranchise blacks. "The disenfranchisement movement of the 1890s gave the Southern states the most impressive system of obstacles between the voter and the ballot box known to the democratic world."[67]

In the 1940s the Supreme Court began to strike down one after another of the devices used to keep blacks from voting. In 1944 (*Smith v Allwright*) the Court declared the **white primary** unconstitutional.[68] In 1960 it held that **racial gerrymandering**—the drawing of election districts so as to ensure that blacks are a minority in all districts—is contrary to the Fifteenth Amendment.[69] In 1964 the Twenty-fourth Amendment eliminated the **poll tax**—payment required as a condition for voting—in elections for members of Congress and presidential electors, and in 1966 the Court held that the Fourteenth Amendment forbade the poll tax as a condition in any election.[70]

Those wishing to deny African Americans the right to vote now were forced to rely on registration requirements. On the surface these requirements appeared to be perfectly proper, but it was the way they were administered that kept blacks from the polls. They were often applied by white election officers while white police stood guard, or with white judges hearing appeals from decisions of registration officials. Officials often seized on the smallest error in an application blank as an excuse to disqualify a black voter. In one parish in Louisiana, after four white voters filed affidavits in which they challenged the legality of the registration of black voters on the grounds that these voters had made an "error in spilling" (*sic*) in their applications, registration officials struck 1,300 out of approximately 1,500 black voters from the rolls.[71]

In many southern areas, **literacy tests** were used to discriminate against blacks. Some states required applicants to demonstrate that they understood the national and state constitutions and, furthermore, that they were persons of good character. Although poor whites often avoided registration out of fear of embarrassment from failing a literacy test, the tests were more often used to discriminate against blacks.[72] Whites were often asked simple questions; blacks were asked questions that would baffle a Supreme Court justice. "In the 1960s southern registrars were observed testing black applicants on such matters as the number of bubbles in a soap bar, the news contained in a copy of the *Peking Daily*, the meaning of obscure passages in state constitutions, and the definition of terms such as *habeas corpus*."[73] In Louisiana, 49,603 illiterate white voters were able to persuade election officials they could understand the Constitution, but only two illiterate black voters were able to do so.

The Voting Rights Act of 1965

For two decades after World War II, under the leadership of the Supreme Court, federal judges carefully scrutinized voting laws and procedures in cases brought before them. Yet this approach did not open the voting booth to African Americans, especially those living in rural areas of the Deep South. Finally Congress began to act. The Civil Rights Act of 1964 set aside, for elections for members of Congress and the president, literacy tests for persons who had completed the equivalent of the sixth grade and prohibited denial of the right to vote because of minor errors on application forms.

The Civil Rights Act of 1964 had hardly been enacted when events in Selma, Alabama, dramatized the inadequacy of depending on the courts to prevent racial barriers in polling places. A voter-registration drive in that city, led by Martin Luther King, Jr., produced arrests, marches on the state capital, and the murder of two civil rights workers. Still there was no dent in the color bar at the polls. Responding to events in Selma, President Lyndon Johnson made a dramatic address to Congress and the nation calling for federal action to ensure that no person would be deprived of the right to vote in any election for any office because of color or race. Congress responded with the Voting Rights Act of 1965.[74]

Section 2 of the Voting Rights Act prohibits any voting qualifications or standards that result in a denial of the right of any citizen to vote on account of race and color. Section 5 requires that states that had a history of denying African Americans the right to vote must clear any changes in any voting practice or laws that might result in dilution of voting power with the Department of Justice.[75] What precisely constitutes "dilution" and how it is to be measured are the subject of much litigation. Examples include changes in the location of polling places; changes in candidacy requirements and qualifications, such as changes in filing deadlines; changes in the composition of the electorate, such as changes from ward to at-large elections; changes in boundary lines of voting districts; and changes that affect the creation or abolition of an elective office and imposition by state political parties of fees to become delegates to nominating conventions.[76] The Court refused, however, to extend the act to cover changes in the distribution of power among officials after two Alabama counties altered the power of county commissioners in such a way as to reduce the authority of recently elected black commissioners.[77] It has also ruled that there is no prohibition in the act against operating a single commissioner form of county government, even if the consequence is to make it practically impossible for an African American to ever become the county commissioner.[78]

Following the 1990 Census, the Department of Justice refused to certify redistricting plans of southern state legislatures that failed to draw as many districts as

THE NEW AFRICAN AMERICAN ELECTORATE

Millions of African Americans now participate in our political life. More than 8,000 hold national, state, or local office. More than 300 are mayors in such key cities as Seattle, San Francisco, Atlanta, Birmingham, Denver, Baltimore, Oakland, Detroit, and Washington, D.C. There are African Americans in all southern legislatures, and there are more African Americans in the U.S. House of Representatives than at any time since Reconstruction. We have an African American United States senator, and Virginia recently had an African American governor.

Has all this made any difference? "A significant disillusionment with the franchise is said to be evident among many blacks today."[*] For example, Katherine Tate concludes, "At most, the new black political representation has benefited middle-class blacks, providing new economic opportunities through government employment and minority contracting in city governments."[**] The precise influence of black voting is a subject of much study, but the results are not clear and the patterns are changing.[#] Most scholars are coming to the conclusion that "if blacks (and Hispanics) organize, compete in the electoral arena, and elect one or more of their number to city council, they can lay claim to a larger slice of the public pie."[##] In effect, minorities can convert their voting potential into public policy if they mobilize their members.

Yet despite the fact that many of our largest cities have black mayors, black police chiefs, and black superintendents of schools, they have been unable to bring about major improvements in the social, economic, and educational conditions for large numbers of inner-city blacks, in large part because cities lack resources and powers to deal with the root causes.

The consequences of greater participation by blacks in the political process need to be measured by other means in addition to the number of black officeholders. When the influence of black voters is distributed over a larger number of districts, black voters may provide the margin of victory to a white candidate, even if they are unable to elect a black officeholder. As long as candidates of any race believe they have a chance of getting enough black votes to win, they will probably find it politically profitable to be concerned about the interests of black constituents. In fact, there is evidence that representatives in some districts with a majority of whites are as "strongly supportive of black interests as are representatives of majority black districts."[†]

Since the passage of the Voting Rights Act of 1965, governors and senators, especially in areas with large numbers of black voters, have become much more sympathetic to the concerns of black voters. The views of black constituents have become a fact of political life and have to be taken into account by policy makers, including presidents who appoint and senators who confirm federal judges.

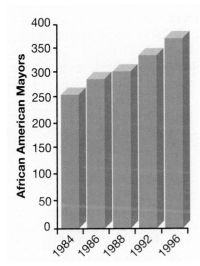

African American Mayors, 1984–1996

SOURCE: National Conference of Black Mayors.

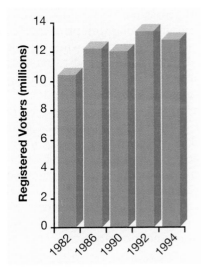

African American Registered Voters, 1982–1994

Statistical Abstract of the United States, 1996 (Government Printing Office, 1996), p. 286.

* Richard L. Engstrom, "Racial Voter Dilution: The Concept and the Court," in Lorn S. Foster, ed., *The Voting Rights Act: Consequences and Implications* (Praeger, 1985), p. 13.
** Katherine Tate, *From Protest to Politics* (Harvard University Press, 1993), p. 2.
# Huey L. Perry, ed., "Recent Advances in Black Electoral Politics," symposium in *PS: Political Science and Politics* 23 (June 1990), pp. 133–60.
Kenneth R. Mladenka, "Blacks and Hispanics in Urban Politics," *American Political Science Review* 83 (March 1989), p. 188.
† J. Phillip Thompson III, reporting on findings of Carol M. Swaing, *Black Faces, Black Interests: The Representation of African Americans in Congress* (Harvard University Press, 1993), in *Political Science Quarterly* (Winter 1993–94), p. 743.

possible in which minorities constitute a majority. Most of these districts tended to be Democratic, leaving the other congressional districts in these states heavily white and Republican. The lower federal courts sustained the Department of Justice's interpretation. As a result, there was a considerable increase in congressional districts represented by minorities and Republicans.[79]

The Supreme Court, however, in a series of cases beginning with *Shaw v Reno*, announced that although states may take race into account, they may not make race the *sole* reason for drawing district lines. The Department of Justice, said the Supreme Court, was wrong in forcing states to create as many **majority-minority districts** as possible. North Carolina's legislature created a majority-minority district 160 miles long and in some places only an interstate highway wide. "If you drove down the interstate," said one legislator about this district, "with both car doors open, you'd kill most of the people in the district." The Supreme Court ruled that North Carolina's reapportionment scheme was so "irrational on its face that it can be understood only as an effort to segregate voters into separate voting districts because of their race." All states have to do in order to comply with the Voting Rights Act, the Supreme Court explained, is provide for districts roughly proportional to the minority voters' respective shares in the voting-age population.[80]

Two years later, the Court expanded *Shaw* by clarifying that it "was not meant to suggest that a district must be bizarre on its face before there is a constitutional violation." Legislatures may be aware of racial considerations when they draw district lines, but when race becomes the overriding motive, the state violates the equal protection clause. The Court held that Section 5 of the Voting Rights Act only ensures that changes in voting procedures must not reduce the ability of racial minorities "to meaningfully exercise the electoral franchise."[81] As a result of these decisions, the reapportionment plans of several southern state legislatures are being challenged before the federal courts, with the result that there is likely to be a reduction in the number of majority-minority congressional districts.

RIGHTS TO PUBLIC ACCOMMODATIONS, JOBS, AND HOMES

As we have noted, the Fifth and Fourteenth Amendments apply only to governmental action, not to private discriminatory conduct. Moreover, our Constitution creates "a zone of privacy which precludes government from interfering with private clubs or groups. The associational rights which our system honors permit all-white, all-black, all-brown, and all-yellow clubs to be established. They also permit all-Catholic, all-Jewish, or all-agnostic clubs. . . . Government may not tell a man or a woman who his or her associates must be. The individual may be as selective as he desires."[82]

Families, churches, or private groups organized for political, religious, cultural, social, or expressive purposes are constitutionally different from large associations organized along other lines, such as the United States Jaycees (the Junior Chamber of Commerce) or a large law partnership. The Supreme Court, for example, has upheld the application of state and local human relations and public accommodations laws forbidding sex or racial discrimination to organizations such as the Jaycees, the Rotary Club, and large (in this case more than 400 members) private eating clubs. Such associations and clubs are not small intimate groups. Nor were they able to demonstrate that allowing women or minorities to become members would change the content or impact of their purposes.[83]

Until recent decades the fact that the Fourteenth Amendment is inapplicable to private conduct hindered Congress's ability to regulate against non-state-sanctioned discriminatory conduct. In 1883 the Supreme Court declared unconstitutional an act of Congress that made it a federal offense for any operator of a public conveyance, hotel, or theater to deny accommodations to any person because of race or color on the grounds that the Fourteenth Amendment does not give Congress authority to legislate against discrimination by private individuals.[84]

Since the 1960s, however, the constitutional authority of Congress to legislate against discrimination by private individuals is no longer an issue. The Court has so broadly construed the commerce clause, which gives Congress the power to regulate interstate and foreign commerce, that it alone justifies almost any action that Congress might want to take against discriminatory conduct by individuals.

The Court has also reinterpreted the Thirteenth Amendment, at least as far as racial discrimination is concerned, to sustain congressional legislation against discrimination. In addition to the Thirteenth and the Fourteenth Amendments, Congress has used the power to tax and spend to prevent not only racial discrimination but also discrimination based on ethnic origin, sex, disability, and age. It may also use the power to regulate interstate commerce, as it did in the most important and sweeping Civil Rights Act—that of 1964.

The Civil Rights Act of 1964

With this law, for the first time since Reconstruction, Congress authorized the massive use of federal authority to combat privately imposed racial discrimination.

TITLE II: PLACES OF PUBLIC ACCOMMODATION Title II makes it a federal offense to discriminate against any customer or patron in a place of public accommodation because of race, color, religion, or national origin. It applies to any inn, hotel, motel, or lodging establishment (except establishments with fewer than five rooms and occupied by the proprietor—in other words, small boardinghouses); to any restaurant or gasoline station that serves interstate travelers or serves food or products, a substantial portion of which have moved in interstate commerce; and to any movie house, theater, concert hall, sports arena, or other place of entertainment that customarily presents films, performances, athletic teams, or other sources of entertainment that are moved in interstate commerce.

Title II has been vigorously enforced, and African Americans have organized programs to test it. The Department of Justice filed more than 400 lawsuits. Within a few months after its adoption, the Supreme Court, in *Heart of Atlanta Motel v United States*, unanimously sustained its constitutionality.[85] As a result, public establishments, including those in the South, opened their doors to all customers.

TITLE VII: EMPLOYMENT The Constitution and numerous congressional laws forbid governments to deny persons employment because of race, color, religion, or sex. By Title VII of the Civil Rights Act, Congress has made it illegal for any employer or trade union in any industry affecting interstate commerce and employing 15 or more people (and, since 1972, any state or local agency such as a school or university) to discriminate in employment practices against any person because of race, color, national origin, religion, or sex.[86] Title VII forbids discrimination with respect to compensation, terms, conditions, or privileges of employment. The intent is to "strike at the entire spectrum of disparate treatment," which includes requiring people to work in a discriminatorily hostile or abusive environment.[87] Employers have an obligation to create workplaces that avoid such abusive environments. Other legislation makes it illegal to engage in discriminatory activities that affect those with physical handicaps, veterans, or persons over 40.

There are a few exceptions. Religious institutions such as parochial schools may use religious standards. Age, sex, or handicap may be considered where occupational qualifications are absolutely necessary to the normal operation of a particular business or enterprise.

In 1991, Congress amended Title VII to set aside several Supreme Court decisions and to make it easier to challenge employment practices—tests, qualifications,

Major Civil Rights Laws (continued)

cation Act Amendments applied only to the specific program or activity receiving federal aid and not to the entire institution. Congress also specified that antibias provisions applied to entire institutions if any segment received federal funding.

FAIR HOUSING ACT AMENDMENTS, 1988: PL 100–430 gives the Department of Housing and Urban Development greater authority to enforce the 1968 law and prohibits housing bias against the handicapped and families with children.

AMERICANS WITH DISABILITIES ACT, 1991: PL 102–119 prohibits discrimination based on disability in employment, places of public accommodations, and public services. It requires that facilities be made accessible to those with disabilities.

THE CIVIL RIGHTS ACT OF 1991: PL 102–166 counters the effects of nine Supreme Court decisions. It places a greater burden on employers to justify practices that negatively affect women and minorities by requiring employers to justify such practices as being job-related or showing that there are no alternative practices that would have a less negative impact on the protected group. It authorizes limited compensatory damages for intentional discrimination and punitive damages if the defendant acted with malice or reckless indifference to the rights of the individual based on sex, religion, or disability. It prohibits "race norming" of tests used for employment or promotion—that is, setting different cut-off scores on the basis of race or ethnic origin. The act also establishes a commission, appointed by the president and Congress, to examine the "glass ceiling" that seems to keep women from becoming executives and to make recommendations on how to increase promotion of women and minorities to management positions.

SOURCE: Adapted from *Social Policy*, May 13, 1989, p. 1122.

PL means Public Law, and the number following is the number of the Congress; thus PL 85-315 means it was enacted by the 85th Congress.

"Thanks for coming in. It's such a relief to be able to deny someone a loan when there's no possibility of being charged with sex, race, age, or ethnic bias."

Drawing by Ed Fisher. ©1976 The New Yorker Magazine, Inc.

conditions—that, whatever the intent, have a disparate adverse impact on women and minorities.

Title VII was passed to protect minorities and women; nonetheless, employers who discriminate against white males also violate its provisions. Moreover, when Congress adopted Title VII, it stated that the act should not be used to require any employer to grant preferential treatment to any individual or to any group on account of racial or sexual imbalance that might exist in the employer's work force. Title VII, however, does not preclude employers, public or private, from adopting race-sensitive affirmative action programs designed to overcome past discrimination against minorities and women.

Title VII has several special features. Not only do aggrieved persons have a right of private action to sue for damages for themselves, but they can do so for other persons similarly situated in a **class action suit**. In addition, Congress created the Equal Employment Opportunity Commission (EEOC) to enforce its provisions. The commission, which consists of five members appointed by the president with the consent of the Senate, works together with state authorities to try to bring about compliance with the act and may seek judicial enforcement of complaints against private employers. The attorney general prosecutes Title VII violations by public agencies. The vigor with which the EEOC and the attorney general have acted has varied over the years, depending on the commitment of the president in office.[88] Race-based cases make up about a third of the EEOC's case load, followed by claims based on gender discrimination and disabilities. Sexual harassment cases are also increasing.[89]

Title VII is supplemented, indeed in some instances even supplanted, by a 1965 presidential executive order requiring all contractors of the federal government, including universities, to adopt and implement affirmative action programs to correct for "underutilization" of women and minorities. Such programs may not establish racial or ethnic quotas for minorities or women, but they do call on contractors to establish timetables and goals; to follow open recruitment procedures; to keep records of applicants by race, sex, and national origin; and to explain why their labor force does not reflect the same proportion of persons in the covered categories that exist within the appropriate labor market pools. Failure of contractors to file and implement an approved affirmative action plan may lead to loss of federal contracts or grants.

The Fair Housing Act and Amendments, 1968 and 1988

Housing is the last frontier of the civil rights crusade, the area in which progress is slowest and genuine change most remote. "Blacks at every economic level are significantly segregated from whites of similar economic status."[90] "Housing segregation is serious because it is at the root of many other forms of segregation and inequality."[91] "Segregated housing contributes mightily to a vicious circle that also includes educational and employment discrimination. . . . Because of poor schools for many minorities, they cannot find well-paying jobs. Without such jobs they often cannot afford to live in nicer neighborhoods with decent housing. And because of their location in less desirable communities, good educational systems are less likely to be available."[92]

In 1948, in *Shelley v Kraemer*, the Supreme Court held that judges could no longer enforce racially **restrictive covenants** (a provision in a deed to real property restricting its sale).[93] In 1968 Congress passed the Fair Housing Act. This act, amended in 1988, excludes housing owned by private individuals who own no more than three houses, who sell or rent these houses without the services of an agent, and who do not indicate any preference or discrimination in their advertising; dwellings that have no more than four separate living units in which the owner maintains a residence (so-called Mrs. Murphy boardinghouses); and religious organizations and private clubs housing their own members on a non-commercial basis. For all other housing, the act forbids owners to refuse to sell or rent to any person because of race, color, religion, national origin, sex (since 1974), and handicap or because a person has children (since 1988). Housing for older persons is exempted from this family provision. No discriminatory advertising is permitted.

The Department of Justice has filed hundreds of cases, especially those involving large apartment complexes. Yet African Americans and Hispanics continue to be discriminated against when they attempt to rent apartments or buy houses. Realtors continue to steer blacks and Hispanics toward neighborhoods that are not predominantly white, to require larger rental deposits for minorities than for whites, and even to refuse outright to sell or rent to minorities.[94]

Less than 1 percent of these discriminatory actions are complained about because they are often so subtle that victims are often unaware that they are being discriminated against. Yet the number of discrimination complaints received by the Department of Housing and Urban Development and local and state agencies has been increasing as the result of more aggressive enforcement. Complaints about discrimination in housing also center around lending discrimination where the discrimination may often be subtle, but the results are to deny loans to minorities.

Voluntary segregation obviously also exists. "It's a fact of life that blacks like to live in black neighborhoods and whites like to live in white neighborhoods. . . . And real estate agents generally like to bring customers to places they will like and where the agent can make a sale."[95] Whatever the reasons, housing segregation persists. "While blacks and other minorities have made strides in voting rights, education and jobs, the homes they return to each night are in communities still largely defined by race."[96]

AFFIRMATIVE ACTION: IS IT CONSTITUTIONAL?

Prior to 1954, when white majorities were using state power to segregate blacks and discriminate against them, civil rights advocates cited with approval the words of Justice John Marshall Harlan: "Our Constitution is color-blind and neither knows nor tolerates class among citizens."[97] It was not until 1954 that Justice Harlan's views triumphed. In *Brown v Board of Education*, the Court called racial classifications "odious to our system" and made race a suspect class. In the years immediately following, the Court also established that, although the Fourteenth Amendment was adopted to protect blacks, its provisions extend to other minorities, to women, and to white males. The Court emphasized that the rights protected belong to each and every individual, not to the group to which he or she may belong.

By the 1960s there was a new set of constitutional and national policy debates. People began to assert that government neutrality was not enough. If governments and universities and employers merely stop discriminating against blacks, Hispanics, and women, yet change nothing else, those previously discriminated against are still kept from equal participation in American life. They have been so handicapped by past discrimination that in the competition for openings in medical schools or for skilled jobs or for their share of government grants and contracts, they suffer disabilities not shared by white males.

Governments started to respond to these arguments. Presidents issued executive orders, Congress adopted programs, state legislatures created requirements, cities adopted ordinances, and university trustees issued policies. Although the details

Alan Bakke, who won a historic affirmative action suit, is surrounded by reporters as he leaves class after his first day at the University of California medical school.

vary (and the details are constitutionally significant), these programs called on governments, governmental contractors, and in some instances private employers to take affirmative action to redress imbalances in work forces and governmental contracts to reflect more accurately the racial, sexual, and ethnic diversity of employment pools and to give opportunities to minority and women contractors. These remedies to overcome the consequences of past discrimination against blacks, Hispanics, Native Americans, and women may be known as *affirmative action* by those who support them, but they are regarded as *reverse discrimination* by those who oppose them.

What of the constitutionality of affirmative action programs? In 1974 the Supreme Court stalled on dealing with the constitutionality of affirmative action in college admissions by holding that since the petitioner challenging the University of Washington law school admissions programs had been admitted the issue was moot.[98] The first major statement of the Court came in a celebrated case relating to university admissions. Allan Bakke, a white male and a top student at Minnesota and Stanford universities as well as a Vietnam War veteran, applied both in 1973 and 1974 to the medical school of the University of California at Davis. In each of those years the school admitted 100 new students, 84 in a general admissions program and 16 in a special admissions program created for African Americans, Chicanos, Asian Americans, and Native Americans—groups who had been underrepresented until the special admissions program was established. Bakke's application was rejected each year, but students with lower grade-point averages, test scores, and interview ratings were admitted under the special admissions program. After his second rejection, Bakke brought a suit in federal court claiming he had been excluded because of his race, contrary to requirements of the Constitution and Title VI of the Civil Rights Act of 1964.

In *University of California Regents v Bakke* (1978), the Supreme Court ruled the Davis plan unconstitutional.[99] But in an opinion by Justice Lewis Powell, which no other member of the Court completely shared, the Court also declared that affirmative action programs are not necessarily unconstitutional. In order to achieve a diversified student body, a state university may properly take race and ethnic background into account as one of several factors in choosing students. However, the university's goal may not be to redress past misconduct by the society or to ensure that more minority members become doctors. The problem with the California plan was it created a category of admissions from which whites were excluded solely because of their race.

Following *Bakke*, the Court dealt with a variety of affirmative action programs, sustaining most but not all of them. Yet as Justice Byron White said, "Agreement upon a means for applying the Equal Protection Clause to an affirmative-action program has eluded this Court every time the issue has come before us."[100] In *Richmond v Croson* in 1989, a Court majority struck down a plan of the city of Richmond requiring nonminority city contractors to subcontract at least 30 percent of the dollar amount of their contracts to one or more minority business enterprises. Said Justice Sandra Day O'Connor for the Court, in language that called into question the validity of most state and local government affirmative action plans, "Race-sensitive remedial measures are to be justified only after a strong basis in evidence has established that remedial action is necessary to overcome the consequences of past discriminatory action." Justice Thurgood Marshall in dissent contended that there is "a profound difference separating governmental actions that themselves are racist, and governmental actions seeking to remedy the effects of prior racism." The proper test, he wrote, for race-conscious classifications designed to further remedial goals is merely that they have to be justified as serving important governmental objectives and must be substantially related to the achievement of those objectives. The majority, he said, "sounds a full-scale retreat from the effort to deliver on the century-old promise of equality and scuttled the efforts of a city to surmount its discriminatory past."[101]

Although *Richmond v Croson* was interpreted to signal a hardened attitude by the Court toward affirmative action, on the last day of the 1989–90 term, to the surprise of most, Justice William J. Brennan, Jr., speaking for four other justices in *Metro Broadcasting v Federal Communications Commission*, rejected the strict scrutiny test in favor of the less rigid heightened scrutiny test for governmental laws and regulations creating race classifications so far as the national government is concerned. The national government is not, said the Court, limited to using race-sensitive measures to overcome past discrimination but may use them for other legitimate governmental objectives. The Court upheld the right of the Federal Communications Commission, in response to congressional mandates, under certain conditions to limit the transfer of certain existing radio and television broadcast stations only to minority-controlled firms. Justice O'Connor, the author of the *Croson* opinion, wrote in dissent, "'Benign' racial classification is a contradiction in terms. Governmental distinctions among citizens based on race or ethnicity, even in the rare circumstances permitted by our cases, exact costs and carry with them substantial dangers. To the person denied an opportunity or right based on race, the classification is hardly benign. The right to equal protection of the laws is a personal right."[102]

Two years later Justice O'Connor, speaking for the Court in *Adarand Constructors, Inc. v. Peña*, overruled *Metro Broadcasting*. The Court rejected the view that racial classifications, whatever their purpose, benign or hostile, should ever be subject to less than strict scrutiny by either the national or state and local governments and could be justified only if such a classification is precisely tailored to serve a compelling governmental interest. Although Justice O'Connor went out of her way "to dispel the notion that strict scrutiny is strict in theory, but fatal in fact," the *Adarand* decision calls into question the constitutionality of many affirmative action programs.[103] It is worth noting that Justice Antonin Scalia, in concurring with Justice O'Connor, made clear that in his view "government can never have a 'compelling interest' in discrimination on the base of race in order to 'make up' for past racial discrimination in the opposite direction." Justice Clarence Thomas expressed a similar view. And as we have noted, the Court is opposed to the use of race as the sole criteria, even for remedial purposes, in cases relating to the drawing of electoral district lines where the injury to nonprotected groups is much less a concern.[104]

In the spring of 1996, the Court of Appeals for the Fifth Circuit, in *Hopwood v Texas*, set aside the University of Texas law school's affirmative action plan for the admission of students.[105] The judges concluded that Justice Powell's decision in the *Bakke* case no longer had the support of the Supreme Court and that the use of race as one factor in the admission process violated the equal protection clause. Following that decision, Texas University modified its plan and petitioned the Supreme Court to review the Court of Appeals decision. On the last day of the 1995–96 term, the Supreme Court announced that it would not do so. Justices Ruth Bader Ginsburg and David Souter took the unusual step of explaining that the Supreme Court's refusal to review the *Hopwood* decision should not be construed as indicating that the Court agreed with the Court of Appeals. Rather, since the law school had modified its plan, the issue of its constitutionality was no longer before the courts. Justice Ginsburg noted, "Whether it is constitutional for a public college or graduate school to use race or national origin as a factor in its admission processes is an issue of great national importance." But, she concluded, "this Court reviews judgments, not opinions."[106] Thus, until matters are clarified by the Supreme Court, as far as the United States Constitution is concerned, race—and presumably gender—

may no longer be considered as a factor for admission to public universities and colleges in the Fifth Circuit (Texas, Louisiana, and Mississippi), but may be considered in the rest of the nation.

Proposition 209

In July 1995, the Regents of the University of California, who in 1978 had carried the *Bakke* case to the Supreme Court, at the urging of Governor Pete Wilson voted to eliminate race or gender as factors in employment, purchasing, contracting or admissions at the University of California except where federal law or regulations required contrary action. Then in November 1996, Californians voted overwhelmingly for Proposition 209 to amend the state constitution to forbid state agencies—including schools, colleges, and universities—to discriminate against or grant preferential treatment to any individual or group of the basis of race, sex, color, ethnicity, or national origin in the operation of public employment, public education, or public contracting, except where necessary to comply with a federal requirement.

There are a variety of constitutional issues flowing from California's Proposition 209. Did California, by amending its state constitution to forbid legislative bodies and university trustees from granting preferences based on race and gender but not on other factors, deprive women and minorities of the equal protection of the laws guaranteed by the Fourteenth Amendment of the U.S. Constitution? To what extent do *federal* affirmative action requirements preempt the commands of California's Proposition 209? Although Proposition 209 clearly forbids universities and other state agencies from taking race and gender into account, does it also make unconstitutional state-supported outreach programs designed to recruit and encourage more women and minorities to become scientists and engineers? Does it prevent state universities from outreach programs aimed at schools with large minority enrollments?

Clearly the debate over the merits and constitutionality of affirmative action is not over. There are more decisions to come as the courts—and the nation—debate in elections and legislative halls as well as in courtrooms whether, as President Clinton has urged, affirmative action is a vital tool to overcome decades of discrimination that needs to be "amended not ended." Or, as the proponents of Proposition 209 contend, has affirmative action served its purpose, so that government-mandated preference for any person based on race or gender is always unfair and unjust to those not given the preference and demeaning to those to whom it is offered?

EQUAL RIGHTS TODAY

Today legal barriers have been lowered, if not removed, by civil rights legislation, executive orders, and judicial decisions. African Americans and other minorities can vote, get a meal where they want, and stay at hotels. Hundreds of thousands have entered the middle class. Although some people still find ways to circumvent or obstruct the force of civil rights laws, especially those that apply to housing, by and large the government's action in the 1960s opened the legal system and provided African Americans with equal rights under the law. Important as these victories are, "They were victories largely for the middle class—those who could travel, entertain in restaurants and stay in hotels. Those victories did not change life conditions for the mass of blacks who are still poor."[107]

However, more than a generation after the Kerner Commission issued its report, life for inner-city blacks is worse. As middle-class blacks have moved out of the inner city, the remaining *underclass*, as they are coming to be called, has become even more isolated from the rest of the nation.[108] Children are growing up on streets where drug abuse and crime are everyday events. These Americans live in "separate and deteriorating societies, with separate economies, diverging family structures and basic institutions, and even growing linguistic separation within the core ghettos. The scale of their isolation by race, class, and economic situation is much greater than it was in the 1960s, impoverishment, joblessness, educational inequality, and housing insufficiency even more severe."[109]

In November 1991, the entire world watched four white Los Angeles police officers beat Rodney King, an African American, as other members of the Los Angeles Police Department stood by and made no attempt to interfere. In April 1992, an all-white jury, after a long trial, failed to convict those officers for what appeared to almost all who saw the videotape as excessive use of force and police brutality. The three days of rioting in Los Angeles and other cities that followed the announcement of these acquittals resulted in more than 50 deaths and millions of dollars lost from looting and destruction. This outburst brought home the fact that the problems highlighted by the Kerner Commission three decades ago are still with us, and the sense of hopelessness and anger felt by many inner-city African Americans and Hispanics is as great today as ever.

Despite the lack of improvement in social conditions, the push for integration has lessened. "In fact, power on both sides of the color line is based to some extent on acceptance of segregation. On the black side of the color line, it is advantageous to keep blacks within black electoral areas and keep black-controlled resources within black institutions: integrationist policies are often viewed as posing larger threats than they actually do. On the white side of the line . . . some residents in outlying suburbs see critical advantages in their almost all-white and all middle-class status."[110]

Some contend attention should be paid to the plight of the underclass and that instead of focusing on issues of race, what is needed is a policy of increasing jobs.[111] Others say there has to be a revival of the civil rights crusade, a restoration of vigorous civil rights enforcement, job training, and above all, an attack on residential segregation.[112] As we approach the twenty-first century, the issue of race is still one of our dominant domestic issues. "The issue, more specifically, is the yet unsettled matter of the role of the black man in a white society."[113]

POLITICS ONLINE

Using the Internet to Reduce Sexual Harassment

Sexual harassment and other workplace abuses have become major issues. While not a problem exclusively for women, most victims are female. The National Organization for Women (NOW) uses its home page to advocate a "Women-Friendly Workplace Campaign." This campaign encourages employers to pledge to observe standards such as providing a discrimination-free workplace and refusing to tolerate sexual or racial harassment. NOW also advocates getting consumers to sign a pledge that they will support businesses that are women-friendly. The document also goes on to encourage local NOW chapters to set up a "Speak-Out-Line" where women can call in and report harassment and discrimination. These calls can then be counted and used to identify examples of problems in the community. The document also provides a sample press release, camera-ready copies of the consumer and employer pledges, and a list of suggested Women-Friendly Workplace actions, such as asking consumers and politicians to sign the pledge, targeting businesses that refuse to sign, holding a forum on workplace issues, and planning a "Women-Friendly Workplace" May Day rally.

It is hard to predict how much impact this particular NOW campaign will have, but it is clear that the Internet provides an effective means of getting extensive organizational information out to a lot of people quickly. One of the problems with the Internet for disseminating such information is that it is public. Critics of NOW and the media have the same access to the document as local NOW leaders have. For campaigns where mobilization strategy needs to be less public, the Internet poses problems.

If you want to read about this particular issue, go to:

http://www.now.org/issues/wfw/wfwlet.html

Several civil rights organizations maintain active home pages. See, for instance, the NAACP at:

http://www.naacp.org

or the United States Commission on Civil Rights at:

http://www.usccr.gov

SUMMARY

1. Americans are committed to equality, an elusive term, with most support for equality of opportunity, some for equality of starting conditions, and some for equality of results.

2. The crusade for women's rights was born partly out of the struggle to abolish slavery. Similarly, the modern women's movement learned and gained power from the civil rights movements of the 1950s and early 1960s. The fate of these two social movements has long been intertwined. Recently, concern for equal rights under the law has been expanded to include the rights of Native Americans, Hispanics, and Asians.

3. Progress in securing civil rights for blacks was a long time in coming. After the Civil War the national government briefly tried to secure some measure of protection for the freed slaves and to enforce the Thirteenth, Fourteenth, and Fifteenth Amendments and the civil rights laws passed to implement them. But when federal troops withdrew from the South in 1877, the national government withdrew from the field and blacks were left to their own resources. The rights granted by the Constitution became meaningless.

4. Not until 1954, in *Brown v Board of Education*, did the Supreme Court reverse an 1896 decision upholding racial segregation and announce that enforced racial segregation in public education was unconstitutional. Eventually Congress and the president threw their weight behind a major effort to prevent racial segregation and discrimination against blacks.

5. The Supreme Court uses a three-tiered approach to evaluate the constitutionality of laws challenged as violating the equal protection clause. Laws touching economic concerns are sustained if they are rationally related to the accomplishment of a legitimate government goal. Laws that classify people because of sex or illegitimacy are subject by the courts to heightened scrutiny and are sustained only if they serve important governmental objectives. Strict scrutiny is used to review laws that touch fundamental rights or classify people because of race or ethnic origin. Such laws will be sustained only if the government can show a compelling public interest.

6. In the 1960s federal courts began for the first time to interpret constitutional provisions to protect women against sex discrimination, and to secure legislative protection for African Americans, Hispanics, Native Americans, and Asian Americans.

7. The desirability and constitutionality of affirmative action programs that provide special benefits to those who have been subjected to past discrimination divide the nation and the Supreme Court. Remedial programs tailored to overcome specific instances of past discrimination are likely to pass the Supreme Court's suspicion of race, national origin, and sex classifications. However, the courts must still clarify constitutional issues concerning affirmative action in school admission and hiring practices.

Barbara R. Bergman, *In Defense of Affirmative Action* (Basic Books, 1996).

Janet K. Boles, ed., "American Feminism: New Issues for a Mature Movement," *Annals of the American Academy of Political and Social Science* (May 1991).

Taylor Branch, *Parting the Waters: America in the King Years, 1954–1963* (Simon & Schuster, 1988).

Stephen L. Carter, *Reflections of an Affirmative Action Baby* (Basic Books, 1991).

Laura L. Crites and Winifred L. Hepperle, *Women, the Courts, and Equality* (Sage Publications, 1987).

Chandler Davidson and Bernard Grofman, eds., *Quiet Revolution in the South* (Princeton University Press, 1994).

Janet Dewart, ed., *The State of Black America* (National Urban League, published annually).

Gertrude Ezorsky, *Racism and Justice: The Case for Affirmative Action* (Cornell University Press, 1991).

Ronald J. Fiscus, *The Constitutional Logic of Affirmative Action* (Duke University Press, 1992).

Bernard Grofman and Chandler Davidson, eds., *Controversies in Minority Voting: The Votings Rights Act in Perspective* (Brookings Institution, 1992).

Andrew Hacker, *Two Nations: Black and White, Separate, Hostile, Unequal* (Charles Scribner's Sons, 1992).

Fred R. Harris and Roger W. Wilkins, eds., *Quiet Riots: Race and Poverty in the United States—The Kerner Report Twenty Years Later* (Pantheon Books, 1988).

Richard Kluger, *Simple Justice* (Knopf, 1976).

Oren Lyons et al., *Exiled in the Land of the Free: Democracy, Indian Nations, and the U.S. Constitution* (Clear Light Publishers, 1992).

Susan Gluck Mezey, *In Pursuit of Equality: Women, Public Policy, and the Federal Courts* (St. Martin's Press, 1992).

Gary Orfield and Carole Ashkinaze, *The Closing Door: Conservative Policy and Black Opportunity* (University of Chicago Press, 1991).

Gary Orfield, Susan E. Eaton, and the Harvard Project on School Desegregation, *Dismantling Desegregation: The Quiet Reversal of Brown v Board of Education* (New Press, 1996).

J. W. Peltason, *Fifty-eight Lonely Men: Southern Federal Judges and School Desegregation* (University of Illinois Press, 1971).

Peter Skerry, *Mexican Americans: The Ambivalent Minority* (Free Press, 1993).

Shelby Steele, *The Content of Our Character: A New Vision of Race in America* (St. Martin's Press, 1990).

Maurilio E. Vigil, *Hispanics in American Politics: The Search for Political Power* (University Press of America, 1987).

Bob Zelnick, *Backfire: A Reporter's Look at Affirmative Action* (Regenery, 1996).

6

Rights to Life, Liberty, and Property

*T*hroughout much of the world men and women are rebelling against the police states under which they live, against governments in which the police are unrestrained in how they go about finding, capturing, and punishing so-called enemies of the people. When we in the United States get impatient about the time-consuming steps that must be followed before criminals are taken off the streets, or about the endless rounds of appeals and reviews available to those charged with crimes, we need to remember how fortunate we are to live in a society that values **due process**—established rules and regulations that restrain those who exercise governmental power. Such procedures are not available to citizens in Serbia, China, Rwanda, Liberia, and many other parts of the world.

Public officials in the United States do have great power. Under certain conditions they can seize our property, throw us into jail, and—in extreme circumstances—even take our lives. The framers of our Constitution recognized that it is necessary to give power to those who govern. It is also dangerous. It is so dangerous that to keep our officials from becoming tyrants we do not depend on the ballot box alone. We know political controls mean little when an elected majority uses its power to deprive unpopular minorities of their rights. Because political power can be dangerous, we parcel it out in small chunks and surround it with restraints. No single official can decide to take our lives, liberty, or property. Officials must act according to the rules. If they act outside the scope of their authority or contrary to the law, they have no claim to our obedience. These are the precious rights of all who live under the American flag—rich or poor, young or old, black or white, man or woman, alien or citizen. In this chapter, we look at the safeguards that protect our rights to life, liberty, and property.

RIGHTS IN THE ORIGINAL CONSTITUTION

Even though most of the framers did not think a Bill of Rights was necessary, they considered certain rights important enough to be included in the original Constitution. These include the right of a writ of *habeas corpus* and protection against *ex post facto* laws and bills of attainder.

The Writ of Habeas Corpus

Foremost among constitutional rights is the guarantee that the **writ of habeas corpus** will be available unless suspended in time of rebellion or invasion. Literally meaning "produce the body," this writ is a court order directing any official having a person in custody to produce the prisoner in court and to explain to the judge why the prisoner is being held. Permission to suspend the writ is found in the article setting forth the powers of Congress so, presumably, only Congress has the right to suspend it.

As originally used, the writ was merely a court inquiry to determine whether a person was being held in custody as the result of action by a court with proper jurisdiction. But over the years it has developed into a remedy "available to effect discharge from any confinement contrary to the Constitution or fundamental law."[1] Persons being held apply, usually through an attorney, for release and state why they believe they are being held unlawfully. The judge then orders the jailer to show cause why the writ should not be issued. If a judge finds a petitioner is being detained unlawfully, the judge may order the prisoner's immediate release. Although state judges lack jurisdiction to issue writs of *habeas corpus* to find out why national authorities are holding persons, federal district judges may do so to find out if state and local officials are holding people "in violation of the Constitution or laws or treaties of the United States."[2]

In recent years a controversy has erupted between those who believe federal judges should be given wide discretion to issue writs of *habeas corpus* to protect constitutional rights and those who believe the writ has been abused by state prisoners to touch off an endless and unessential round of reviews, which sometimes lead to convictions being set aside by a federal judge after the matter has been carefully reviewed by at least two state courts. As evidence, critics point to the many prisoners on death row who have successfully used *habeas corpus* to raise objection after objection, delaying the execution of their sentence for years.

Partly because of this criticism, partly from concern for maintaining the principles of federalism, and partly in response to a growing overload on federal courts, the Supreme Court has severely restricted the use of *habeas corpus* by federal judges.[3] In 1996 Congress, in the Antiterrorism and Effective Death Penalty Act, restricted state prison inmates' access to federal courts even further, especially those on death row. Congress placed time limits for the filing of petitions for *habeas corpus*, restricted the number of requests for such petitions, stopped appeals for most *habeas* petitions at the level of the U.S. courts of appeals, and called for deference by federal judges to the decisions of state judges on matters of fact and law unless those decisions are clearly "unreasonable." The Supreme Court took the unusual step of expediting review of the antiterrorism law, especially against the challenge that (1) the law violates the constitutional guarantee of Article I, Section 9, that the privilege of the writ of *habeas corpus* shall not be suspended unless in cases of rebellion or invasion, and (2) the challenge that the law unconstitutionally restricts the Supreme Court's jurisdiction by stopping most appeals at the courts of appeals.

At the end of the 1995–96 term the Court, by unanimous vote, held: (1) the added restrictions on second *habeas* petitions do not amount to a suspension of the writ contrary to Article I, Section 9; (2) although Congress had limited the Supreme Court's authority to review appeals from decisions of the courts of appeals denying such *habeas* petitions, the act, perhaps inadvertently, did not repeal an earlier law giving the Supreme Court jurisdiction to entertain *habeas* petitions brought directly to it. Thus, under these circumstances, there can be no plausible argument that the act deprived the Supreme Court of its appellate jurisdiction in violation of Article III.

Ex Post Facto Laws and Bills of Attainder

The Constitution forbids both the national and the state governments from passing *ex post facto* laws and enacting *bills of attainder* (Article I, Sections 9 and 10). An **ex post facto** law is a retroactive criminal law that works to the disadvantage of an individual. Examples would include a law making a particular act a crime that was not a crime when committed, increasing punishment for a crime after the crime was committed, or lessening proof necessary to convict for a crime after it was committed. The prohibition does not prevent the passage of retroactive penal laws that work to the benefit of an accused—a law decreasing punishment, for example. Nor does the prohibition prevent passage of retroactive civil laws. Income tax rates as applied to income already earned, for example, may be increased, as was done in 1993.

A **bill of attainder** is a legislative act inflicting punishment, including deprivation of property, without judicial trial on named individuals or members of a specified group. For example, Congress enacted a bill of attainder in conflict with this prohibition when it named three federal employees in an appropriations bill and declared they should receive no compensation from the federal treasury, other than for military or jury services, unless reappointed to office by the president with the consent of the Senate.

CITIZENSHIP RIGHTS

Every nation has rules that determine nationality and define who is a member of, owes allegiance to, and is a subject of the nation-state. But in a democracy, citizenship is more than nationality, more than being merely a subject.[4] Citizenship is an *office*, and, like other offices, it carries with it certain powers and responsibilities. How citizenship is acquired and retained should therefore be a matter of considerable importance to everyone.

How Citizenship Is Acquired and Lost

The basic right of citizenship was not given constitutional protection until 1868, when the Fourteenth Amendment was adopted. The Fourteenth Amendment states: "All persons born or naturalized in the United States, and subject to the jurisdiction thereof, are citizens of the United States and of the State wherein they reside." This means that all persons born in the United States, except children born to foreign ambassadors and ministers, are citizens of this country regardless of the citizenship of their parents. (Congress has defined the United States for this purpose to include Puerto Rico, Guam, the Northern Marianas, and the Virgin Islands.) Although the Fourteenth Amendment does not make Native Americans citizens of the United States and of the states in which they live, Congress has done so.

The Fourteenth Amendment confers citizenship according to the principle of *jus soli*—by place of birth. In addition, Congress has granted, under certain conditions, citizenship at birth according to the principle of *jus sanguinis*—by blood. A child born to an American citizen living abroad is an American citizen if the American parent has lived in the United States for ten years, including two years after age 14.

NATURALIZATION Citizenship may also be acquired by either collective or individual naturalization, a legal action conferring citizenship upon an alien. The granting of citizenship to the people of the Northern Marianas in 1977 by an act of Congress is an example of collective naturalization. Individual naturalization requirements are determined by Congress. Today, with minor exceptions, nonenemy aliens over age 18 who have been lawfully admitted for permanent residence and who have resided in the United States for at least five years and in the state in which they are residing for at least six months are eligible for naturalization, which is conferred by a court. Any state or federal court of record in the United States or the Immigration and Naturalization Service (INS) can grant citizenship. The INS, with the help of the Federal Bureau of Investigation (FBI), makes the necessary investigations. Any person denied citizenship after a hearing before an immigration officer may seek a *de novo* (completely new) hearing before a federal district judge.

Citizenship is granted if the judge or hearing officer is satisfied that the applicant has met all the requirements, renounces allegiance to his or her former country, swears to support and defend the Constitution and laws of the United States against all enemies, and promises to bear arms on behalf of the United States when required to do so by law. Those whose religious beliefs prevent them from

Rights in the Original Constitution

1. Writ of *habeas corpus*
2. No bills of attainder
3. No *ex post facto* laws
4. No titles of nobility
5. Trial by jury in national courts
6. Protection for citizens as they move from one state to another, including the right to travel
7. Protection against using crime of treason to restrict other activities and limitation on punishment for treason
8. Guarantee that each state has a republican form of government
9. No religious test oaths as a condition for holding a federal office.

COMING TO AMERICA

Although natural-born Americans tend to take citizenship for granted, most naturalized citizens cherish it, for it represents hard work and a sincere commitment on their part. Would natural-born Americans appreciate citizenship more if they had to meet the same standards as foreign-born applicants?

Naturalization Requirements

An applicant for naturalization must:

1. Be over age 18.
2. Be lawfully admitted to the United States for permanent residence and have resided in the United States for at least five years and in the state in which they are residing for at least six months.
3. File a petition of naturalization with a clerk of a court of record (federal or state) verified by two witnesses.
4. Be able to read, write, and speak English.
5. Possess a good moral character.
6. Understand and demonstrate an attachment to the history, principles, and form of government of the United States.
7. Demonstrate that he or she is well disposed toward the good order and happiness of the country.
8. Demonstrate that he or she does not now believe in, nor within the last ten years has ever believed in, advocated, or belonged to an organization that supports opposition to organized government, overthrow of government by violence, or the doctrines of world communism or any other form of totalitarianism.

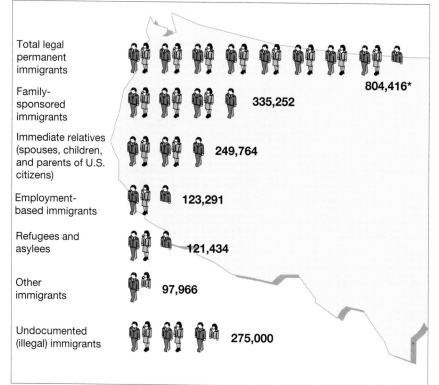

FIGURE 6–1   Coming to America, 1994

SOURCE: For legal immigrants, U.S. Bureau of the Census, *Statistical Abstract of the United States 1996* (Government Printing Office, 1996); for illegal immigrants, Eric Schmitt, "Illegal Immigrants Rose 5 Million in '96," *The New York Times National Edition*, February 8, 1997, p. Y7.

*Includes persons allowed to enter under amnesty and refuge provisions in addition to the 675,000 other aliens allowed to come in each year.

bearing arms are allowed to take an oath swearing that, if called to duty, they will serve in the armed forces as noncombatants or will perform work of national importance under civilian direction. The court or INS then grants a certificate of naturalization.

In 1995, when Congress stripped aliens of certain important welfare benefits, the number of applications for citizenship increased. The INS accelerated the process of handling petitions for citizenship in order to eliminate a growing backlog of applications. As the 1996 elections approached, some Republicans in Congress charged that the reason the INS was moving so quickly was to produce more Democratic voters, and in fact some persons were granted citizenship prior to the FBI's being able to complete a check of their records. As a result, the INS changed its procedures so that no person will be naturalized without confirmation from the FBI that a fingerprint check has been completed and no disqualifying felony conviction has been found.

Naturalized citizenship may be revoked by court order if the government can prove citizenship was secured by deception. In addition, citizenship, however acquired, may be renounced voluntarily. But citizenship cannot be taken from people because of what they have done—for committing certain crimes, for example, voting in foreign elections, or serving in foreign armies. Some actions, however, such as taking out citizenship in another country or swearing allegiance to another nation, may be taken into account as "highly persuasive evidence of a purpose to abandon citizenship." Even so, the government must prove that the citizen "not only voluntarily committed the expatriating act prescribed in the statute, but also intended to relinquish his citizenship."[5]

DUAL CITIZENSHIP Because each nation has complete authority to decide for itself the question of nationality, it is possible for a person to be considered a citizen by two or more nations. Dual citizenship is not unusual, especially for persons from nations that do not recognize the right of the individual to choose his or her own nationality, called the **right of expatriation**. (One of the issues of the War of 1812 was that England did not recognize sailors born in England as having abandoned their English citizenship on becoming naturalized American citizens.) Children born abroad to American citizens may also be citizens of the nation in which they were born. Children born in the United States of parents from a foreign nation may also be citizens of their parents' country. Dual citizenship carries negative as well as positive consequences; for example, a person with dual citizenship may be subject to national service obligations and taxes in both countries.

Rights of American Citizens

An American citizen becomes a citizen of one of our states merely by residing in that state. "Residence," as used in the Fourteenth Amendment, means the place one calls home. The legal status of residence should not be confused with the fact of physical presence. A person may be living in Washington, D.C., but be a citizen of California—that is, consider California home and vote in that state. Residence is primarily a question of *intent*.

Most of our most important rights flow from state citizenship rather than from United States citizenship. In the *Slaughter House Cases* (1873), the Supreme Court carefully distinguished between the privileges of United States citizens and those of state citizens. It held that the only privileges attaching to national citizenship are those that "owe their existence to the Federal Government, its National Character, its Constitution, or its laws."[6]

These privileges have never been completely specified, but they include the right to use the navigable waters of the United States, to assemble peacefully, to petition the national government for redress of grievances, to be protected by the national government on the high seas, to vote if qualified to do so under state laws, to have one's vote counted properly, and to travel throughout the United States.

THE RIGHT TO LIVE IN THE UNITED STATES This right, which is not subject to any congressional limitation, is perhaps the most precious aspect of

The United States has always drawn immigrants seeking opportunity and freedom. Here men, women, and children crowd the deck of a ship as it approaches New York in December 1906.

- Never have so many immigrants lived in this country, although the foreign-born proportion of the population was larger earlier in this century, when the U.S. population was smaller.

- The place of birth of most immigrants has shifted from Europe to Asia and Latin America.

- 19.7 million, or just under 8 percent of the U.S. population, are foreign-born.

- Nearly 32 million persons speak a language other than English at home, and more than 40 percent of them say they do not speak English very well.

- The number of immigrants from Mexico and from Asia has more than doubled in the last decade.

- Projected population percentages for Los Angeles County for the year 2000 are 40 percent Hispanic, 34 percent white, 16 percent Asian, and 10 percent black.

- The Los Angeles Unified School District (the second largest in the nation) serves more than 625,000 students speaking 80 different languages, more than 83,000 of them foreign-born.

SOURCES: U.S. Bureau of the Census; Barbara Vobejda, "A Nation in Transition: Census Reveals Striking Stratification of U.S. Society," *The Washington Post*, May 29, 1992, pp. A1, A18–A19.

American citizenship. Aliens have no such right. They may be stopped on the high seas or at the borders and turned away if they fail to meet the terms and conditions stipulated by the Congress for admission into the United States. Today millions of people around the world are yearning to come and live in the United States, but only American citizens have a constitutionally guaranteed right to do so.

THE RIGHT TO TRAVEL ABROAD Although the right of interstate travel is virtually unqualified, the right to international travel can be regulated within the bounds of due process. Under current law it is unlawful for citizens to leave or enter the United States without a valid passport (except as otherwise provided by the president, as has been done for travel to Mexico, Canada, and parts of the Caribbean). The president, acting through the secretary of state, may refuse to grant or may revoke a passport if the government concludes that a holder's activities in foreign countries are causing, or are likely to cause, serious damage to our national security or foreign policy.

Rights of Aliens

We are in a period of growing hostility toward aliens, so the protections of American citizenship and those of state citizenship that flow from it become even more precious, especially the right to live here. True, the Constitution protects many rights of all *persons*, not just of American citizens; for example, neither Congress nor the states can deny to aliens any more than to citizens the right of free exercise of religion or the right of freedom of speech. Nor can any government deprive any person, alien or citizen, the due process of the law or equal protection under the laws. However, Congress can, and has, denied many welfare and other kinds of benefits to aliens.

The Welfare Act of 1996 denied to aliens, both legal and illegal, the right to apply for food stamps or for most welfare benefits under almost all circumstances. In addition, Congress in 1996 required the deportation of any *legal* immigrant who falsifies an application for the few means-tested programs still available to them, such as the federally funded student loan programs. President Bill Clinton called for the Welfare Act of 1996 to be amended to restore welfare benefits to legal aliens, and this recommendation was supported by the governors of California, New York, Florida, and Texas, states where most legal aliens reside. At their meeting in February 1997, the National Governors' Association urged Congress to amend the law to protect legal immigrants in the United States who cannot become citizens because of age or disability.[7]

The 1996 Immigration Act added to the Welfare Act by denying, and permitting states to deny, most other benefits to illegal aliens, making an exception only for emergency medical care, disaster relief, and some nutrition programs. Congress debated a proposal allowing states to prohibit illegal immigrant children from attending public schools, but backed down under threat of presidential veto. This legislation would have challenged the Supreme Court's 1982 decision that states cannot constitutionally exclude children of undocumented aliens from the public schools or charge their parents tuition.[8]

Admission to the United States

President Franklin Roosevelt, reminding us of our heritage as a haven for people fleeing religious and political persecution, opened his address to a convention of the Daughters of the American Revolution with the salutation, "Fellow immigrants and revolutionaries." Some Americans, however, are concerned that admitting so many people from abroad will dilute American traditions and values.

Throughout our history debates have flared among those wishing to open our borders and those wishing to close them.

Aliens do not have a constitutional right to enter the United States. Congress has wide discretion in setting the numbers, terms, and conditions under which aliens can come and stay in the United States. By 1882 Congress began to restrict the entry of persons alleged to be "undesirable," such as prostitutes and revolutionaries. During World War I, Congress, for the first time, set limits on the number of aliens who could be admitted each year. The Immigration Act of 1924 created a system that discriminated against immigrants from Southern Europe and Southeast Asia on the basis of national origin.

In 1965, after years of debate, a new immigration law was adopted. It remains our basic legislation, although it has often been amended and was thoroughly revised in 1990 and modified again in 1996. It continues to be under congressional review, and new basic legislation is likely in the near future.

The 1965 law as amended sets an annual ceiling of 675,000 for nonamnesty, nonrefugee aliens allowed to come here as permanent residents. The law also sets an annual limit on immigrants from any single country. Preference is given for *family reunification*, allowing a minimum of 226,000 immediate relatives of United States citizens or permanent residents to enter the country each year. Families that petition for a visa for a close relative must show they have an income of 200 percent of the poverty level or 140 percent for spouses and minor children. Second preference is provided for granting 140,000 visas a year to people who have special job skills or who are needed to fill jobs for which U.S. workers are not available. Included in this category are professionals holding advanced degrees, persons of exceptional ability, and skilled workers. The law also provides special treatment for Hong Kong nationals, especially executives and managers of U.S. companies in Hong Kong. Another provision allows for the admission of "millionaire immigrants" who are willing and able to invest a substantial sum in the United States to create or support a business that will provide jobs for Americans. There have been few takers for admission under this provision. The 1990 act also created a "diversity" category to provide visas for 55,000 immigrants from 34 countries, chiefly but not exclusively European, whether or not they have relatives living in the United States. However, about 70 percent of all permanently admitted aliens in the United States still come under the family-reunification preference.

In addition to regularly admitted permanent resident aliens, more than 100,000 political refugees have been admitted in recent years. *Political refugees* are defined by law as persons who have well-founded fears of persecution in their own countries based on their race, religion, nationality, social class, or political opinion. Although the number of political refugees allowed is 50,000 annually, after consultation with Congress the president may set, and has been setting, a higher number. Persons who are admitted as political refugees can apply to become permanent residents after one year.

The attorney general, acting through the U.S. Immigration and Naturalization Service, may also grant *asylum* to persons already in the United States, at ports of entry, or in countries other than their own, if the attorney general agrees with the applicants that they, like political refugees, have well-founded fears of persecution in the country to which they would otherwise be returned, based on their race, religion, nationality, membership in a particular social group, or political opinion. It is not enough, however, that applicants face the same terrible conditions that all other citizens of their country face, or that they wish to escape from bad economic or political conditions. They must show individual danger of persecution. Where political conditions are extremely fluid, the Department of Justice can grant an individual "temporary protected status" while it tries to determine the peril the applicant actually faces at home.

The love of freedom is so strong that these Cuban "balseros" (boat people) were willing to risk death to get to the United States in this flimsy raft.

The Immigration Reform and Control Act of 1986 as Modified by the Illegal Immigration Reform and Immigrant Responsibility Act of 1996

- Undocumented aliens who had lived continuously in the United States since January 1, 1982, were permitted to apply for amnesty for a limited time.
- Employers who knowingly hire illegal aliens may be fined from $250 to $5,000 per alien, and repeat offenders may be given a prison term of up to six months.
- Employers are subject to penalty if they discriminate against legal residents because they are foreign born. However, in 1996 Congress made it harder for the federal government to act against employers by requiring the government to show intent to discriminate.
- A certain number of aliens are allowed to come into the United States to serve as temporary farm workers.
- A nationwide data base will track illegal immigrants convicted of crimes and provide for expedited deportation procedures for these immigrants.
- Pilot programs, including telephonic verification, will determine the eligibility of people applying for jobs or public benefits.

Of the estimated 2 to 3 million aliens eligible for amnesty under the 1986 act, about 1.8 million applied by the May 4, 1987, deadline. Others did not apply because of costs, inability to document their status, or fear that they might expose family members to deportation. Although passage of the act was followed by a brief decrease in the number of undocumented aliens coming across our borders, it did not accomplish its objective of stemming the flow. Large numbers of undocumented aliens continue to live and work here, and the number continues to increase.

SOURCES: Dan Carney, "As White House Calls Shorts, Illegal Alien Bill Clears," *Congressional Quarterly Weekly Report*, October 5, 1996, pp. 2864–66; Carney, "Law Restricts Illegal Immigration," *Congressional Quarterly Weekly Report*, November 16, 1996, pp. 3287–88.

Congress tightened these requirements in 1996 and called for: (1) screening at the ports of entry for those who appeared with fraudulent or no documents; (2) the immediate return of those who cannot prove a "credible fear" of returning; and (3) no asylum for those arriving from a country other than that from which they are seeking asylum. The 1996 act also streamlines the deportation procedures, provides for a one-year limit for filing asylum applications, and refuses any appeal if an application is denied.

The 1996 Act also tightened the restrictions on illegal immigrants and strengthened the hand of the attorney general, the INS, and other enforcement agencies in finding and deporting illegal aliens. It added the following grounds for deportation not only of illegal immigrants but for legal ones: incitement of terrorist activity, illegal voting in elections, and conviction of domestic violence. It also stipulated that persons who violate the terms of a student visa are inadmissible to the United States for five years.[9]

The Immigration and Naturalization Service may turn back at the border persons seeking asylum when it considers their requests insubstantial, or it may even hold them in detention camps.[10] The president may order the Coast Guard—as both George Bush and Bill Clinton did with respect to Haitian refugees—to stop persons on the high seas before they enter the territorial waters of the United States and return them to the country from which they have fled without determining whether they qualify as refugees.[11] Nonetheless, many people are still willing to risk great danger to get here and suffer detention once they arrive, just for the chance of being granted asylum.

Once in the United States, aliens are "subject to the full range of obligations, including the payment of taxes, imposed by the states' civil and criminal laws."[12] Aliens are counted in the census for the purpose of apportioning seats in the United States House of Representatives.

Undocumented Aliens

How should the United States government deal with the estimated 5 million undocumented aliens, mostly from Mexico and other nations in Central and South America and a few from Canada and Poland, who illegally cross our borders not because they fear political persecution but because they see greater economic opportunity in the United States?[13] It should be noted, however, that most undocumented immigrants from Mexico return to Mexico after only two years. "By 10 years, almost 70 percent of those who came to the United States have returned," according to one study.[14]

Inability to keep illegal aliens out of the country is not a question of constitutional power, for "over no conceivable subject is the legislative power of Congress more complete than it is over the admission of aliens."[15] Rather, the problems are political and practical. Although Congress in 1996 authorized an increase in the number of border patrol guards by 1,000 each year, for a total by 2001 of 10,000, and funded additional fencing of the California-Mexican border, there are thousands of miles of southern and northern borders. Moreover, it is difficult to track down undocumented aliens inside the United States, round them up, and expel them in a fashion consistent with the practices and policies of a free society.

Once here, undocumented aliens do not find it hard to become invisible, especially in our larger cities, or to find jobs. Some employers prefer to hire them because they work for less money than those who are here lawfully, and they are unprotected. One of the sponsors of the Immigration Reform and Control Act of 1986 described the vulnerability of this "subculture of human beings who are afraid to go to the cops, afraid to go to a hospital, afraid to go to their employer who says, 'One peep out of you, buster, and you are down the road.'"[16]

Congress has been faced with conflicting pressures: from Hispanic groups concerned that making it illegal to hire undocumented workers will make employers hesitate to hire any Hispanics; from employers who do not want to keep costly records and investigate the legal status of everybody they hire; from employers of farm workers who want to be sure they will have enough farm laborers to pick seasonal crops; from American workers who do not want undocumented workers being used to keep wages low; and from city and local governmental officials who have to find the funds to provide social services for undocumented aliens.

We tend to consider U.S. immigration policy a purely internal matter, yet it clearly affects our relations with other nations, most especially with Mexico, as the lengthy negotiations over the North American Free Trade Agreement (NAFTA) demonstrated. Whereas officials of the United States view immigration policy as a matter of sovereignty, "Mexicans see it as a bilateral process that requires a bilateral policy."[17]

PROPERTY RIGHTS

Constitutional Protection of Property

Property does not have rights. People do. **Property rights** are the rights of an individual to own, use, rent, invest in, buy, and sell property. Historically, the close connection between liberty and ownership of property, between property and power, has been emphasized in American political thinking and American political institutions.

A major purpose of the framers of the Constitution was to establish a government strong enough to protect people's rights to use and enjoy their own property. At the same time, the framers wanted to limit government so it could not endanger that right. As a result, the framers included in the Constitution a variety of clauses regarding property.

THE LEGAL TENDER AND CONTRACT CLAUSES Of special concern to the framers were the efforts of some state legislatures to protect debtors at the expense of their creditors by a variety of means, including issuing paper currency and setting aside private contracts. To prevent these practices, the Constitution forbids states from making anything except gold or silver legal tender for the payment of debts and from passing any "Law impairing the Obligation of Contracts."

The **contract clause**, Article I, Section 10, was designed to prevent states from extending the period during which debtors could meet their payments or otherwise get out of contractual obligations. The framers had in mind an ordinary contract between private persons. However, beginning with Chief Justice John Marshall, the Supreme Court expanded the coverage of the clause to prevent states from altering privileges previously conferred on corporations. In effect, the contract clause was used to protect property and to maintain the status quo at the expense of the power of the states to guard the public welfare.

In the 1880s, however, the Court gradually began to restrict the coverage of the contract clause and to subject contracts to what in constitutional law is known as **police powers**—the power to protect the public health, safety, welfare, and morals. By 1934 the Supreme Court actually held that even contracts between individuals—the very ones the contract clause was intended to protect—could be modified by state law in order to avert social and economic catastrophe.[18] Although the contract clause is still invoked occasionally to challenge a state regulation of property, it is no longer a significant limitation on governmental power.

What Happens When the Government Takes Our Property?

Both the national and state governments have the power of **eminent domain**—the power to take private property for public use—but the owner must be fairly compensated. This limitation, contained in the Fifth Amendment, was the first provision of the Bill of Rights to be incorporated within the Fourteenth Amendment—to be enforced as a limitation on state governments as well as on the national government.[19]

What constitutes a "taking" for purposes of eminent domain?[20] The clause does not require compensation merely because governmental action may result in property loss. For example, if a zoning regulation restricts an area to single-family residential use and thus lowers the value of a particular property, no compensation is due. Ordinarily, but not always, the taking must be direct, and a person must lose title and control over the property. Sometimes, especially in recent years, the courts have found that a governmental regulation has gone "too far" and must be deemed a "taking" for which the government must pay compensation to its owners, even when title is left in the hands of the owners.[21] These are called **regulatory takings**. Thus, if a government creates landing and takeoff paths for airplanes over property adjacent to an airport, making the land no longer suitable for its prior use (say, raising chickens), compensation is warranted.

Nor is "just compensation" always easy to define. In case of a dispute, the final resolution is made by the courts. By and large, "the owner is entitled to receive what a willing buyer would pay in cash to a willing seller at the time of the taking."[22] An owner is not entitled to compensation for the personal value of an old, broken-down house that is loved dearly. It will still bring compensation only for an old, broken-down house.

The *taking clause* has received renewed judicial attention in the last several years as many state and local units strive to protect the environment and quality of life by regulating the terms and conditions under which land may be developed. In the late 1980s the Supreme Court began using the taking clause to review these governmental regulations. For example, the Supreme Court held that if a government has prevented a property owner from developing property by regulations that turned out to be unconstitutional, the owner is entitled to just compensation

The Coast Guard confiscates cocaine off the coast of South Florida. The ship that smuggled the drug was also confiscated, and the money derived from its sale was applied toward drug prevention programs.

for the temporary taking, even if the government finally withdraws the regulation.[23] The Court also ruled that a government has engaged in a taking if it imposes an unrelated condition before issuing a building permit—requiring, for example, that the owner of a beach-front home allow the public to walk across the property to the beach as a condition for receiving a permit to enlarge the house.[24]

Due Process: New and Old

Perhaps the most difficult parts of the Constitution to understand are the clauses in the Fifth and Fourteenth Amendments that forbid national and state governments to deny any person life, liberty, or property without due process of law. These due process clauses have resulted in hundreds of Supreme Court decisions. Even so, it is impossible to explain due process precisely. In fact, the Supreme Court has refused to give *due process* a precise definition and has emphasized that "due process, unlike some legal rules, is not a technical conception with a fixed content unrelated to time, place and circumstances."[25]

PROCEDURAL DUE PROCESS   There are two kinds of due process: procedural and substantive. **Procedural due process** generally refers to the methods by which a law is enforced. But a law itself, as enacted, may violate the procedural due process requirement if it is too vague or if it creates an improper presumption of guilt. A vague statute fails to provide adequate warning and does not contain sufficient guidelines for law enforcement officials, juries, and courts.

A statute that creates an improper presumption of guilt denies due process by shifting the burden of proof from the government to the accused person. Laws presuming, for example, that all marijuana or cocaine in a person's possession must have been obtained illegally have been declared unconstitutional. But the Court did uphold a presumption with respect to heroin; as virtually all heroin is illegally imported, it is therefore not unreasonable to presume that a person who possesses heroin obtained it illegally.[26]

Traditionally, however, procedural due process refers not to the law itself but to the *way in which a law is applied*. To paraphrase Daniel Webster's famous definition, it requires a procedure that hears before it condemns, proceeds upon inquiry, and renders judgment only after a trial or some kind of hearing. Originally, procedural due process was limited to criminal prosecutions, but it now applies to most kinds of governmental proceedings. It is required, for instance, in juvenile hearings, disbarment proceedings, proceedings to determine eligibility for welfare payments, revocation of drivers' licenses, and disciplinary proceedings in state universities and public schools.

Procedural due process has taken on new importance with the expanded interpretation of the words "liberty" and "property." The liberty that is protected is more than freedom from being thrown into jail, and the property that is secured goes beyond the mere ownership of real estate, things, or money. Rather, liberty includes "the right of the individual to contract, to engage in any of the common occupations of life, to acquire useful knowledge, to marry, to establish a home and bring up children, to worship God according to the dictates of his own conscience, and generally to enjoy those common law privileges long recognized as essential to the orderly pursuit of happiness by free men."[27] The property protected by due process includes a variety of rights that may be conferred by state law, such as certain kinds of licenses, protection from being fired from some jobs except for just cause (for example, incompetence) and according to certain procedures, protection from deprivation of certain pension rights, and so on.

This expansion of the meanings of liberty and property has blurred the distinctions between liberty rights and property rights. Moreover, it has lessened the difference between a right and a privilege. Today public welfare, housing, educa-

The Pitfalls of Lawmaking

When faced with vexing social problems, we often mutter, "There ought to be a law." But devising clear laws and procedures in accordance with the Constitution and its guarantees of due process is easier said than done, as these examples show.

Some Statutes Declared Void Because of Vagueness

- A statute making it a crime to treat "contemptuously" the American flag.

- A vagrancy ordinance classifying vagrants as "rogues and vagabonds," "dissolute persons who go about begging," "common night walkers," and so on.

- An ordinance requiring persons who loiter or wander the streets to provide "credible and reliable" identification and to account for their presence when required by a police officer.

A Statute Not Considered Vague

- An ordinance requiring a license for businesses selling any items "designed or marketed for use with illegal cannabis or drugs"—what are commonly known as "headshops."

Some Laws Declared to Deny Substantive Due Process

- A school board regulation requiring teachers to cease teaching past the fourth month of pregnancy and barring them from returning to the classroom until three months after the birth of a child.

- A state law permitting confinement of nondangerous mentally ill persons against their wishes.

tion, employment, professional licenses, and so on, are increasingly becoming mat-
ters of entitlement, that is, a legal right. Their denial thus may raise some due
process questions.

Nevertheless, "the range of interests protected by procedural due process is not infinite." Not every "grievous loss visited upon a person by the State is sufficient to
invoke the procedural protections of the due process clause."[28] Whether or not an
interest is protected by due process depends on the nature of the interest, not its
importance to the individual. Faculty members in public institutions, for instance,
are not entitled to procedural due process before being denied tenure because they
have no constitutional right to teaching jobs. However, if public employees, including teachers, are given tenure rights by law or institutional policies, they are entitled
to due process before they may be deprived of property rights or jobs.[29] Since the due
process clause applies only to the action of governments, faculty members at private
institutions are not entitled to due process, but they, along with other employees,
public and private, are protected by provisions of federal and state civil rights laws.

"Once it is determined that due process applies, the question remains what process
is due." What is due varies with the kind of interest involved, the reliability of the
procedures used, and the governmental purposes to be served.[30] In a federal courtroom, due process requires the careful observance of the provision of the Bill of Rights
as outlined in Amendments Four through Eight. In a state courtroom, due process
requires the careful observance of all provisions of the Bill of Rights except indictment by grand jury and jury trials in civil cases. The question of what is due in other
kinds of proceedings is what must be done to ensure fundamental fairness. It is hard
to generalize because many kinds of proceedings are involved, but at a minimum the
person involved must have adequate notice and an opportunity to be heard.

SUBSTANTIVE DUE PROCESS   Procedural due process places limits on how governmental power may be exercised; **substantive due process** places limits on what
a government may do. Procedural due process pertains to the procedures of the
law, substantive due process to the content of the law. Procedural due process
mainly limits the executive and judicial branches; substantive due process mainly
limits the legislative branch. Substantive due process means that an "unreasonable" law, even if properly passed and properly applied, is unconstitutional. It
means that there are certain things governments *should not be allowed to do*, no
matter how they do it.

Before 1937, substantive due process was used primarily to protect liberty of
contract—that is, business liberty, or the right of employers to make contracts
with employees freely, without government interference. Indeed, the adoption of
the doctrine of substantive due process and the simultaneous expansion of the
meaning of liberty and property made the Supreme Court, for a time, the final
judge of our economic and industrial life. During this period the Supreme Court
was dominated by conservative jurists who considered almost all social welfare legislation unreasonable. They used the due process clause to strike down laws setting maximum hours of labor, establishing minimum wages, regulating prices, and
forbidding employers to fire workers for union membership.

The trouble with the substantive interpretation of due process is that what a
person, including a judge, thinks is a "reasonable" law depends on economic, social,
and political views rather than on legal doctrine. In democracies, elected officials
are supposed to accommodate opposing notions of reasonableness and to decide
what regulations of liberty and property are needed. When the Supreme Court substitutes its own ideas of reasonableness for those of Congress or state legislatures,
it acts like a superlegislature.

In response to this criticism, the Supreme Court since 1937 has largely refused
to apply the doctrine of substantive due process in reviewing laws regulating the

economy. The court now believes that deciding what constitutes reasonable regulations of business and commercial life is a legislative, not a judicial, responsibility. As long as the justices find a conceivable connection between a law regulating business and the promotion of the public welfare, the Supreme Court will not interfere. This does not mean, however, that the Court has abandoned substantive due process. On the contrary, substantive due process has taken on new life as a protector of civil liberties, most especially the right of privacy.

Substantive due process, resting on the notion that laws must be reasonable, has deep roots in concepts of natural law and a long history in the American constitutional tradition. For most Americans most of the time, it is not enough merely to say that a law reflects the wishes of the popular or legislative majority. We also want our laws to be just, and we continue to rely heavily on judges to decide what is just. In Chapter 16 we look again at the tensions between democratic procedures and judicial uses of substantive due process to review the constitutionality of the acts of elected officials.

PRIVACY RIGHTS

The most important extension of substantive due process in recent decades has been its expansion to protect the right of privacy, especially marital privacy. Although there is no mention of the right of privacy in the Constitution, the Supreme Court has put together some elements from the First, Fourth, Fifth, Ninth, and Fourteenth Amendments to recognize that personal privacy is one of the rights protected by the Constitution.

There are three aspects of this right: (1) the right to be free from governmental surveillance and intrusion, especially in marital matters; (2) the right not to have private affairs made public by the government; and (3) the right to be free in thought and belief from governmental compulsion.[31]

Congress showed concern about the first kind of privacy in the Family Educational Rights Act of 1974 and the Privacy Act of 1974. These laws limit record-keeping and record-disclosing activities of schools and universities that receive federal funds, place restraints on files kept by federal agencies, and, under certain conditions, give individuals access to government files in order to correct information about themselves. But privacy, although highly valued in the abstract, has often run afoul of other rights, such as freedom of the press. When in conflict with these other rights, it has not fared well before either Congress or the courts.

Abortion Rights

The most controversial aspect of constitutional protection for privacy relates to the extent of state power to regulate abortions. In *Roe v Wade*, decided in 1973, the Supreme Court ruled: (1) during the first trimester of a woman's pregnancy, it is an unreasonable and therefore unconstitutional interference with her liberty and privacy rights for a state to set any limits on her choice to have an abortion or on her doctor's medical judgments about how to carry it out; (2) during the second trimester, the state's interest in protecting the health of women becomes compelling, and a state may make a reasonable regulation about how, where, and when abortions may be performed; and (3) during the third trimester, when the life of the fetus outside the womb becomes viable, the state's interest in protecting the unborn child is so important that the state can proscribe abortions altogether, except when necessary to preserve the life or health of the mother.[32]

After two decades of heated public debate and attempts by both Presidents Reagan and Bush to select Supreme Court justices who could be expected to vote to reverse *Roe v Wade*, on the final day of the 1991–92 court term, *Roe v Wade* was reaffirmed. A bitterly divided Rehnquist Court, by a five-person majority

Eight members of the U.S. Supreme Court said that even if it is assumed that Ewing had such a right, the responsibility for determining academic matters belongs to the faculty, and judges should interfere only if there is "a substantial departure from accepted academic norms as to demonstrate that the faculty did not exercise professional judgment and acted clearly in an arbitrary and capricious manner."

Justice Lewis F. Powell, Jr., concurred, but would not even concede that Ewing might, for purposes of the decision, have a substantive due process property right not to be dismissed by a state university in an arbitrary manner. You might want to read this short opinion. You can find it in many libraries. Give this citation to the librarian: *Regents of the University of Michigan v Ewing*, 474 US 214 (1985).

(O'Connor, Kennedy, Souter, Blackmun, and Stevens), upheld the view that the due process clauses of the Constitution protect a woman's liberty to choose an abortion prior to viability. The Court, however, held that the right to have an abortion prior to viability is subject to state regulation that does not "unduly burden" it. In other words, states may make reasonable regulations on how a woman exercises her right to an abortion so long as "the State does not prohibit any woman from making the ultimate decision to terminate her pregnancy before viability."[33]

Applying the undue burden test, the Court held, for instance, that states can prohibit the use of state funds and facilities for performing abortions, that a state may make a minor's right to an abortion conditional on her first notifying at least one parent or a judge, that a state may condition an abortion on a 24-hour waiting period during which a doctor must inform the woman about alternatives in a state-prescribed talk. On the other hand, a state may not condition a woman's right to an abortion on her first notifying her husband.[34]

Sexual Orientation Rights

Although there is debate as to how much constitutional protection is provided for marital privacy, in 1986 the Supreme Court refused to extend any such protection to relations between homosexuals. By a 5 to 4 vote, the Court refused to declare unconstitutional a Georgia law that criminalized consensual sodomy as practiced by homosexuals. That homosexual conduct occurs in the privacy of the home, said the majority, does not affect the result. Justice Harry A. Blackmun, in dissent, wrote that "the Constitution embodies a promise that a certain private sphere of individual liberty will be kept largely beyond the reach of government," that the Court has long recognized that certain "decisions are properly for the individual to make," and that there are certain places, such as the home, where the government should intrude only in extreme circumstances.[35]

Without mentioning the 1986 decision, the Court in 1996, by a 6 to 3 vote, struck down a provision of the Colorado constitution that prohibited all legislative, executive, or judicial action at any level of state or local government designed to protect homosexuals. This provision, declared the court majority, violates the equal protection clause because it identifies persons by a single trait and then denies them protection across the board. Justice Antonin Scalia in dissent accused the

One controversial aspect of constitutional protection of privacy relates to sexual orientation. Support for gays is demonstrated in this march.

Court of taking sides in "the cultural wars through an act not of judicial judgment but of political will."[36]

Because of the strong emotions on both sides of this issue, the right of privacy as an element of substantive due process is one of the developing edges of constitutional law, one about which people both on and off the Court have strong feelings. How the Supreme Court handles privacy issues has become front page news.

RIGHTS OF PERSONS ACCUSED OF CRIMES

Freedom from Unreasonable Searches and Seizures

According to the Fourth Amendment "The right of the people to be secure in their persons, houses, papers, and effects, against unreasonable searches and seizures, shall not be violated, and no Warrants shall issue, but upon probable cause, supported by Oath or affirmation, and particularly describing the place to be searched, and the persons or things to be seized." Despite what we sometimes see in television police dramas and read in the press, law enforcement officers have no general right to break down doors and invade homes. They are not supposed to search people except under certain conditions, and they have no right to arrest them except under certain circumstances.[37]

Seizures, or what we now call police detentions and arrests, are in fact given less protection than searches of our property. Police may arrest people without warrants in *public places*, provided there is *probable cause*—a fair probability that the persons in question have committed or are about to commit crimes. No later than two days after making an arrest, the police must take the arrested person to a magistrate so that the latter—not just the police—can decide whether probable cause existed to justify the warrantless arrest.[38] Probable cause, however, does not, except in extreme emergencies, justify a warrantless arrest of people in their own homes.

Not every time the police stop a person to ask questions or to seek that person's consent to a search is there a seizure or detention requiring probable cause or a warrant. If all that happens is that the police ask questions or even seek consent to search that individual's person or possessions in a noncoercive atmosphere, there is no detention. "So long as a reasonable person would feel free 'to disregard the police and go about his business,' the encounter is consensual and no reasonable suspicion is required. The encounter will not trigger Fourth Amendment scrutiny unless it loses its consensual nature." But if the person refuses to answer questions or consent to a search, and the police, by either physical force or a show of authority, restrain the movement of the person, even though there is no arrest, the Fourth Amendment comes into play.[39] For example, if police approach people in airports and request identification, this act by itself does not constitute a detention. The same is true if police ask bus passengers for consent to search their luggage for drugs. But if the police do more, especially after consent is refused, then their actions create an "in-custody detention" that requires them to have some objective justification for the search beyond mere suspicion.

The Constitution does not forbid searches, only "unreasonable" ones. "It is a cardinal principle that searches conducted outside the judicial process, without prior approval by a judge or a magistrate, are unreasonable under the Fourth Amendment—subject only to a few specially established and well-delineated exceptions."[40] In fact, however, the number of exceptions keeps growing, and they are not well delineated. And there are various administrative searches by nonpolice government agents, such as teachers and health officials, not designed to uncover crimes. Rules governing the conduct of such administrative searches are more lenient than are those for searches by police investigating crimes.

Deadly Force

Under the common law, police officers apprehending a fleeing, suspected felon can use weapons that might result in such a felon's serious injury, even death. But the Fourth Amendment places substantial limits on the use of what is called "deadly force." It is unconstitutional to shoot at an apparently unarmed, fleeing, suspected felon unless the officer has probable cause to believe that the suspect poses a significant threat of death or serious injury to the officer or others. Also, when feasible, the officer must first warn the suspect: "Halt or I'll shoot."

1. Makes it a crime for any unauthorized person to tap telephone wires or to use or sell, in interstate commerce, electronic bugging devices.
2. Empowers the United States attorney general to secure a warrant from a federal judge authorizing federal agents to engage in bugging in order to track down persons suspected of certain federal crimes.
3. Permits wiretaps without prior court approval for 48 hours in emergency situations involving certain crimes, such as child pornography, illegal currency transactions, offenses against witnesses of crimes, or immediate danger of death or serious injury.
4. Authorizes the principal prosecuting attorney of any state or political subdivision to apply to a state judge for a warrant approving wiretapping or other oral intercepts for felonies. (Most state and local jurisdictions allow such intercepts.)
5. Permits judges to issue warrants only if they decide probable cause exists that a crime is being, has been, or is about to be committed, and that information relating to that crime may be obtained only by wiretapping.

"The court finds itself on the horns of a dilemma. On the one hand, wiretap evidence is inadmissible, and on the other hand, I'm dying to hear it."

Drawing by Handelsman. © 1972 The New Yorker Magazine, Inc.

Where the Fourth Amendment applies, the exceptions to the general rule against warrantless searches and seizures of what is found by police and customs officials are as follows:

1. *The Automobile Exception:* The exception is justified in part because of the mobility of automobiles and in part because persons are not entitled to the same expectations of privacy in their automobiles as in their homes or other places. If officers have probable cause to believe that an automobile is being used to commit a crime, even a traffic offense, or that it contains persons who have committed crimes, or that it contains evidence of crimes or contraband, they may stop the automobile, detain the persons found therein, and search them and any containers or packages found inside the car.[41]

2. *The Terry Exception:* First discussed in *Terry v Ohio*, these brief investigatory stops and searches were originally justified only when officers had reason to believe they were dealing with armed and dangerous persons, but they have subsequently been expanded to cover stops when the police have reason to believe that a person has committed or is about to commit a criminal offense. The intrusion permitted under a *Terry* search is limited to a quick pat-down to check for weapons that might be used to assault the arresting officer, to check for contraband, to determine identity, or to maintain briefly the status quo while obtaining more information.[42] If an officer stops and frisks a suspect to look for weapons and finds criminal evidence that might justify an arrest, then the officer can make a full search.[43] To illustrate: An officer, acting on an informer's tip, approached a man sitting in a car. The officer ordered the suspect to get out of the car, but the suspect merely rolled down the window. The officer saw a bulge on the suspect's waistband. He reached over into the car and removed a gun from the suspect's waistband. The officer arrested the suspect, although the mere possession of a weapon is not a crime, made a search, and found heroin.[44]

3. *Searches Subsequent to Valid Arrest:* When making a lawful arrest, either with an arrest warrant or because of probable cause, police may make a warrantless search of persons involved, the areas under their immediate control, and all the possessions they take with them to the place of detention. And police may make a protective sweep of the immediate area to be sure it does not harbor other dangerous persons.[45]

4. *Searches for Evidence:* When there is probable cause to make an arrest, even if one is not made, limited searches are permitted if necessary to preserve easily disposed of evidence, such as scrapings under fingernails.[46]

5. *Inventory Searches:* Searches that are part of the routine procedures of an arrest are permissible, provided there are established rules for inventory searches so that such a search does not become "a ruse for a general rummaging in order to discover incriminating evidence."[47]

6. *Consent:* Searches based on voluntary consent are allowed, even if the persons who give the consent are not told they have a right to refuse to grant permission.[48]

7. *Border Searches:* Searches of persons and the goods they bring with them are permissible at border crossings.[49] The border search exception also permits officials to open mail entering the country if they have "reasonable cause" to suspect it contains merchandise imported contrary to the law.[50] (The border search exception does not extend to searches by Puerto Rican authorities of persons coming from the continental United States; such persons are not making an international crossing.)[51]

8. *Plain-View Exception:* The plain-view exception permits officers to seize evidence without a warrant if: (1) they are lawfully in a position from which the evidence can be viewed; (2) it is immediately apparent to them that the items they observe are evidence of a crime or are contraband; and (3) they have probable cause—a reasonable suspicion will not do—that the evidence uncovered is contraband or evidence of a crime.[52]

9. *Exigent Circumstances:* Searches are permissible under "exigent circumstances," that is, when officers do not have time to secure a warrant before evidence is destroyed, or a criminal escapes capture, or when there is need "to protect or preserve life or avoid serious injury." An example of exigent circumstances is that fire fighters and police may enter a burning building without a warrant and may remain there for a reasonable time to investigate the cause of the blaze after the fire has been extinguished. However, after the fire has been put out, the emergency is not to be used as an excuse to make an exhaustive, warrantless search for evidence not in plain sight.[53] Films, books, and other materials that might be protected by the First Amendment may be seized under the exigent-circumstances exception only if there are multiple copies of the seized materials, most of which are left undisturbed.

10. *Foreign Agents:* Although never directly sustained by the Supreme Court, Congress has endorsed a presidential claim that the president can authorize warrantless wiretaps and physical searches of agents of foreign countries. Congress has created a special Foreign Intelligence Surveillance Court to approve such requests. This court, consisting of seven federal district judges, meets in secret. The attorney general submits an annual report to Congress consisting of a perfunctory one-paragraph letter.[54]

Police may detain and search cars and their passengers if they have probable cause to believe that the cars are involved in criminal activity, including even minor traffic offenses.

Outside of these exceptions, a police search without consent is constitutionally unreasonable unless it has been authorized by a valid **search warrant**, issued by a magistrate after the police indicate under oath that they have probable cause to justify its issuance. Magistrates must perform this function in a neutral and detached manner and not serve merely as rubber stamps for the police.

The Constitution not only ordinarily requires a search warrant, but it also requires a specific one because *general* search warrants—warrants that authorize police to search a particular place or person without limitation—are unconstitutional. When a magistrate issues a warrant, the warrant must describe: (1) what places are to be searched, and (2) what things are to be seized. And a warrant is needed to search a person in any place he or she has an "expectation of privacy that society is prepared to recognize as reasonable," for example, in a hotel room, in a rented home, in a friend's apartment.[55] In short, the Fourth Amendment protects people, not places, from unreasonable governmental intrusions.

The Exclusionary Rule

Combining the Fourth Amendment prohibition against unreasonable searches with the Fifth Amendment injunction that persons shall not be compelled to be witnesses against themselves, the Supreme Court ruled, in *Mapp v Ohio* (1961), that evidence obtained unconstitutionally cannot be used in a criminal trial as part of the government's main case against persons from whom it was seized.[56] This is the **exclusionary rule**. It was adopted in large part to prevent police misconduct. Because police are seldom prosecuted for making illegal searches and often can't afford to pay civil damages, the justices believed the exclusionary rule was the best—and maybe the only—sanction.

Critics of the exclusionary rule, including Chief Justice William H. Rehnquist, question why criminals should go free just because of police misconduct or ineptness. So far the Supreme Court has refused to abandon the rule. It has started making some exceptions to it, however, such as in cases in which police have relied in good faith on a search warrant that subsequently turned out to be improperly granted.[57]

The exclusionary rule covers only trials of those from whom the evidence was unconstitutionally seized, as one citizen, Jack Payner, found out. Internal Revenue Service agents, aided by a private investigator and operating in the best tradition of television police dramas, broke into Payner's banker's hotel room after a female undercover agent had lured the banker out to dinner. The agents "borrowed" the banker's briefcase, photographed documents, put the original documents back, and returned the briefcase. This "caper" was clearly a deliberate intrusion into the banker's privacy and a violation of his Fourth Amendment rights. Nonetheless, the evidence was allowed to be used to convict Payner, one of the banker's customers, of income tax evasion. Payner could expect neither privacy in his banker's briefcase nor any ownership of the documents taken from it.[58]

The Right to Remain Silent

During the seventeenth century, certain special courts in England forced confessions of heresy and sedition from religious dissenters. The British privilege against self-incrimination developed in response to these practices. Because they were familiar with this history, the framers of our Bill of Rights included in the Fifth Amendment the provision that persons shall not be compelled to testify against themselves in criminal prosecutions. This protection against self-incrimination is designed to strengthen a fundamental principle of Anglo-American justice: No person has an obligation to prove innocence. Rather, the burden is on the government to prove guilt.

The privilege against self-incrimination applies literally only in criminal prosecutions, but it has always been interpreted to protect any person subject to questioning by any agency of government, such as a congressional committee. It is not enough, however, to contend that answers might be embarrassing or might lead to loss of a job or even to civil suits; persons must have a reasonable fear that the answers might support a criminal prosecution or "furnish a link in the chain of evidence needed to prosecute" a crime.[59]

Sometimes authorities would rather have information from witnesses than prosecute them. Congress has established procedures so that prosecutors and congressional committees may secure a *grant of immunity* for such a witness. After immunity has been granted, a witness no longer has a constitutional right to refuse to testify. A person granted immunity can still be prosecuted for crimes subject to such investigations, but the government cannot use the information derived directly from the compelled testimony in any subsequent prosecution. This grant of immunity can be a formidable bar to successful prosecution, as was indicated by the government's inability to successfully prosecute Oliver North and others involved in the Iran-Contra affair.

The Miranda Warning

Police questioning of suspects is a key procedure in solving crimes. It can, however, be easily abused. Police officers sometimes forget or ignore the constitutional rights of suspects, especially those who are frightened and ignorant. Unauthorized detention and lengthy interrogation to wring confessions from suspects, common practice in police states, until recently were not unknown in the United States.

What good is the presumption of innocence if, long before the accused are brought before the court, they are detained and forced to prove their innocence to the police? Judges have done much to stamp out such police brutality. The

Supreme Court has ruled that admission into evidence of a coerced confession violates the self-incrimination clause, deprives a person of the assistance of counsel guaranteed by the Sixth and Fourteenth Amendments, deprives a person of due process, and undermines the entire proceeding.[60]

Federal and state laws require police officers to take those whom they have arrested before magistrates right away so that the magistrates may inform them of their constitutional rights and allow them to get in touch with friends and seek legal advice. Despite these requirements, in the past police were often tempted to quiz suspects first, trying to get them to confess before a magistrate informed them of their constitutional right to remain silent.

To put an end to such practices, the Supreme Court, in *Miranda v Arizona* (1966), announced that no conviction—federal or state—could stand if evidence introduced at the trial had been obtained by the police during "custodial interrogation" unless suspects have been: (1) notified that they are free to remain silent; (2) warned that what they say may be used against them in court; (3) told that they have a right to have attorneys present during questioning; (4) informed that if they cannot afford to hire their own lawyers, attorneys will be provided for them; and (5) permitted to terminate any stage of the police interrogation. If suspects answer questions in the absence of an attorney, the burden is on the prosecution to demonstrate that suspects knowingly and intelligently gave up their rights to remain silent and to have their own lawyers present. Failure to comply with these requirements leads to reversal of a conviction, even if other evidence is sufficient to establish guilt.[61]

Critics of the *Miranda* decision believe the Court has unnecessarily and severely limited the ability of the police to bring criminals to justice. The importance of pretrial interrogations is underscored by the fact that roughly 90 percent of all criminal convictions result from guilty pleas and never reach a full trial. Nevertheless, despite sustained attack, the Supreme Court has refused to reverse *Miranda*, although it has modified its original ruling to some extent. In order to deter perjury (lying under oath), evidence obtained contrary to the *Miranda* guidelines can be used to attack the credibility of defendants who offer contradictory testimony at their trials.

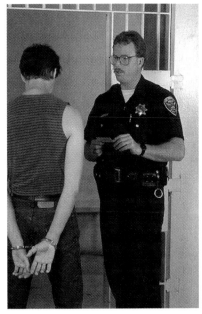

The *Miranda* warning is read to a suspect by a police officer before questioning him to inform him of his rights, such as the right to remain silent and the right to have an attorney present.

THE SHORT AND NOT TOO HAPPY LIFE OF JOHN CROOK

Many people consider the rights of persons accused of crime to be less important than other civil liberties. But, as Justice Felix Frankfurter observed, "The history of liberty has largely been the history of observance of procedural safeguards." Further, these safeguards have frequently "been forged in controversies involving not very nice people."[62]

The rights of persons accused of crime by the national government can be found in the Constitution and in the Fourth, Fifth, Sixth, and Eighth Amendments. To gain some idea of how these constitutional safeguards are applied, let us follow the fortunes and misfortunes of a fictitious character, John Crook, as he is prosecuted for a federal crime.

John Crook sent circulars through the mail selling shares in a nonexistent gold mine—an action contrary to dozens of federal laws. When postal offices uncovered these activities, they went to the district court and secured from a United States magistrate a warrant to arrest Crook and another warrant to search his home for copies of the circulars. They found Crook at home and read the *Miranda* warning to him, emphasizing especially his right to remain silent and to have the assistance of counsel. They showed him the warrant, arrested him for using the mails to defraud, and found and seized some of the circulars mentioned in the search warrant.

The Preliminary Hearing and Right to Counsel

Crook was promptly brought before a federal magistrate, who again emphasized that Crook had a constitutional right to assistance of counsel. Judges have a positive obligation to ensure that all persons subject to any kind of custodial interrogation are represented by lawyers.[63] Unless the record clearly shows that the accused were fully aware of what they were doing and gave up the right to counsel, or intelligently exercised the right to represent themselves, the absence of counsel will render criminal proceedings unconstitutional. The right extends to all hearings for all offenses for which an accused could be deprived of liberty, whether or not a jury trial is required. Trials in which fines are the only penalty are exempt from the assistance-of-counsel requirement. This assistance is required at every stage of a criminal proceeding after the initiation of formal charges—preliminary hearings, bail hearings, trial, sentence, and first appeal. When Crook told the judge he could not afford to hire his own counsel, the judge appointed an attorney paid for by the federal government to represent him.

At this point Crook had not been convicted of anything. In fact, he had not even been formally charged with any crime, and he was entitled to be free without having to pay excessive *bail*. (Note that the Eighth Amendment does not require that bail be set, but forbids imposition of excessive bail.) Suspects are entitled to a hearing within five days, and, when bail is imposed, judges or magistrates must explain in writing why they believe there is clear and convincing evidence that pretrial release might endanger the safety of other persons and the community.[64] The judge set Crook's bail at $5,000, and Crook was held over until the convening of the next federal grand jury. After hiring a professional *bondsman*, who posted the bail and collected a 10 percent fee, Crook was free as long as he remained within the judicial district.

The Indictment

Except for members of the armed forces, the national government cannot require anyone to stand trial for a serious crime except on a grand jury indictment. Grand jurors are concerned not with a person's guilt or innocence but merely with whether there is enough evidence to warrant a trial. The **grand jury** has wide-ranging investigatory powers and "is to inquire into all information that might bear on its investigations until it is satisfied that it has identified an offense or satisfied itself that none has occurred."[65] The strict rules that govern jury proceedings do not apply. The grand jury may admit hearsay evidence, and the exclusionary rule to enforce the Fourth Amendment does not apply. If a majority of the grand jurors agree that a trial is justified, they return what is known as a *true bill*, or *indictment*.

When the next grand jury was convened, the United States district attorney brought evidence before the 23 jurors to indicate that Crook had committed a federal crime. In Crook's case the grand jury was in agreement with the United States district attorney and returned a true bill against Crook.

After a copy of the indictment was served on Crook, he was again ordered to appear before a federal district judge. The Constitution guarantees the accused *the right to be informed of the nature and cause of the accusation* so that he or she can prepare a defense. Consequently, the federal prosecutor took care that the indictment clearly stated the nature of the offense, and she saw to it that copies were properly served on Crook and his lawyer.

Actually, prior to his hearing, Crook's attorney discussed with the United States attorney's office the possibility of Crook's pleading guilty to the lesser offense of false representation in return for which he would not have to stand trial for the more serious charge of using the mails to defraud. Prosecutors, faced with more cases than they can handle, like this kind of **plea bargaining**. Likewise, defendants are often willing to "cop a plea" for a lesser offense to avoid the risk of more serious punishment.

When defendants plead guilty, they are usually forever prevented from raising objections to their convictions. That is why, before accepting guilty pleas, judges question defendants to be sure their attorneys have explained the alternatives and they know what they are doing. It never came to this in Crook's case, however. After discussing the matter with his attorney, Crook elected to stand trial on the charge and entered a plea of not guilty.

The Trial

After indictment, Crook's bail was raised to $20,000. Now the federal government was obligated to give him a *speedy and public trial*. Do not, however, take the word "speedy" too literally. Crook had to be given time to prepare his defense. Defendants, in fact, often ask for delays, because delay often works to their advantage. If, in contrast, the government denies the accused a speedy trial in a constitutional sense, the remedy is drastic. Not only is the conviction reversed, but the case must be dismissed outright.

Crook's lawyer pointed out that under the Sixth Amendment, Crook had a right to trial before a **petit jury** selected from the state and district in which the alleged crime was committed because he was being tried for a serious crime, that is, one punishable by more than six months in prison or a $500 fine.[66] Although federal law requires juries of 12 members, the Constitution requires only that juries consist of at least six persons. Conviction in federal courts must be by unanimous vote. (The Constitution permits state courts to render guilty verdicts by nonunanimous juries, provided such juries consist of six or more persons.)

An *impartial* jury, one that meets the requirements of due process and equal protection, consists of persons who represent a fair cross-section of the community. Although defendants are not entitled to juries on which there are necessarily members of their own race, sex, religion, or national origin, they are entitled to be tried by juries from which jurors have not been *excluded* because of these categories.

"I'm not crazy about the way the judge said he would try to scrounge up a jury of my peers."

Dave Carpenter, *The Wall Street Journal*, June 1, 1994.

Marcia Clark, prosecuting attorney in the O.J. Simpson criminal trial, shows the bloody glove that was supposed to prove Simpson's guilt. The trial was followed on TV all over the world.

JURIES ON TRIAL

Public cynicism about the role of juries has increased in recent years as people learned the intimate details of some notorious trials because of around-the-clock television coverage and front-page newspaper attention. Resentment and bewilderment followed when juries failed to convict persons for what appeared to be obvious crimes. Examples included the 1992 acquittal of Los Angeles police officers whose extended beating of Rodney King had been videotaped and then witnessed by the entire nation (two officers were subsequently convicted of federal crimes); the 1993 trial of Damian Williams, whose brutal beating of truck driver Reginald Denny in the riots following the acquittal verdict in the King case was also captured on video, but who also received a relatively light sentence; the repeated trials of the Menendez brothers, who confessed to killing both their parents but whose first trials resulted in hung juries that could not agree on the precise nature of their crime and who were ultimately found guilty in a retrial.

The 1995 acquittal of O. J. Simpson after the criminal "trial of the century," whose televised details dominated the news not only in the United States but throughout much of the world, divided the nation. A year later, in a civil trial that was also closely covered by the media, Simpson was held responsible for the deaths of his ex-wife and her friend and subject to total damages of $33 million.

A majority of whites believed that the jury in the first trial—nine African Americans, two Hispanics, and one white—had ignored the evidence and had voted to acquit Simpson because of their resentment of the unfair treatment of African Americans at the hands of the Los Angeles Police Department. Most African Americans believed that the jury had done its duty. In the second trial, a jury consisting mostly of whites, plus one Hispanic and two Asian Americans, held that Simpson was responsible for the wrongful death of the friend and the battery of his wife. Opinions about fairness of the jury system again divided along racial lines and added to demands to revise the rules for jury trials.[*]

[*]Abigail Goldman and Mary Curtius, "For Many, It's as Simple as Black and White," *Los Angeles Times*, February 5, 1997, p. A16.

O.J. Simpson

Rodney King

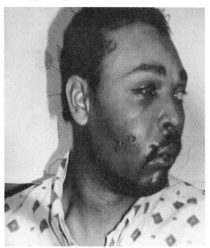

Lyle and Eric Menendez

Such discriminatory action also violates the civil rights secured by the equal protection clause of those denied the opportunity to serve on juries. Government prosecutors cannot strike persons from juries because of race or gender, and neither can defense attorneys use what are called *peremptory challenges* to keep people off juries because of race, ethnic origin, or sex.[67]

Crook told his lawyer he had had dinner with George Witness on the night on which he was charged with sending the damaging circulars. The attorney took advantage of Crook's constitutional *right to obtain witnesses in his favor* and had the judge subpoena Witness to appear at the trial and testify. Although Witness could have refused to testify on the grounds that his testimony would tend to incriminate him, he agreed to appear. Crook himself, however, chose to use his constitutional right not to be a witness against himself and refused to take the stand. He knew that if he did so, the prosecution would have a right to *cross-examination*, and he was fearful of what might be uncovered. To protect Crook's right against self-incrimination, the judge conducting the trial was required to caution the jury against drawing any conclusions from Crook's decision not to testify. All prosecution witnesses appeared in court and were available for defense cross-examination; the Constitution also insists that accused persons have the *right to be confronted with the witnesses against them.*

The Sentencing

At the conclusion of the trial, the jury brought in a verdict of guilty. The judge then raised Crook's bail to $50,000 and announced that she would hand down a sentence on the following Monday. The Eighth Amendment forbids the levying of excessive fines and the inflicting of cruel and unusual punishments.

The ban against cruel and unusual punishments limits government in three ways:

1. It limits the kinds and methods of punishment that may be imposed, prohibiting, for example, torture, intentional denial of medical care, inhumane conditions, unnecessary or wanton inflicting of pain, and deliberate indifference to medical and other needs of prisoners.[68]

2. It prohibits punishments grossly disproportionate to the severity of the crime. However, outside the context of capital punishment—where the Court has limited the death penalty to crimes in which a life has been taken—the Court has been "reluctant to review legislatively mandated terms of imprisonment,"[69] and "successful challenges to the proportionality of particular sentences will be exceedingly rare."[70]

3. It limits the power of the government to decide what can be made a criminal offense. For example, the mere act of being a chronic alcoholic may not be made a crime because alcoholism is an illness. However, being drunk in public may be a criminal offense.

Back to Mr. Crook. The judge, following the guidelines set down by the United States Sentencing Commission, gave Crook the maximum punishment of a $25,000 fine and three years in the penitentiary. Such a sentence could not be considered cruel and unusual. Crook could have appealed both his sentence and his conviction to the court of appeals, but he chose not to do so.

John Crook and the State Government

While still in the federal penitentiary, Crook was taken by federal authorities before the state courts to answer charges that when he solicited shares in his nonexistent gold mine, he had also violated several state laws. Through his state-appointed attorney, Crook protested he had already been tried by the federal government for

Three Strikes and You're Out

Although the crime rate is actually going down, public concern about crime is going up. At both the national and state level, presidents, governors, and legislators are vying with one another to show their toughness about crime. Laws have been proposed to require judges to impose lifetime sentences upon persons convicted of three felonies. In some states, the felonies have to be for violent crimes; in others any three felonies will do.

Scholars are skeptical that "three strikes and you're out" laws will reduce the crime rate; it will certainly require great expenditures of public funds to construct more jails and take care of aging felons.

Capital Punishment

After much soul searching, and many cases, the Supreme Court has ruled that the death penalty is not necessarily cruel and unusual punishment if it is imposed for conviction of crimes that have resulted in a victim's death, if the procedures used by the courts limit and channel "the discretion of judges and juries to ensure that death sentences are not meted out wantonly or freakishly," and if these processes "confer on the sentencer sufficient discretion to take account of the character and record of the individual offender and the circumstances of the particular offense to ensure that death is the appropriate punishment in a specific case."*

For a while the Supreme Court halted capital punishment until states could administer it in a fashion consistent with these guidelines. As more and more states have added the death penalty (there are now 38), and the national government has increased the number of crimes for which the death penalty may be imposed, the number of persons on death row has dramatically increased. Since capital punishment was reinstated in 1972, 350 people have been executed nationwide, with 3,000 still facing the death sentence.** California alone has almost 400 inmates on death row. California trial judges are imposing roughly 50 new death sentences per year, more than the California Supreme Court has been able to process in a year. At this rate, it will take ten years to process the existing cases.

Although the death penalty appears to have widespread public support, the American Bar Association has called for a halt to executions. The Bar Association's report criticized the Antiterrorism Act and charged that it and other federal and state laws have resulted in the administration of the death penalty in such a way that fundamental due process is now systematically lacking, and "decisions about who will die and who will live turn not on the nature of the offense . . . but rather the nature of the legal representation the defendant receives." The report has been opposed by many attorney generals, including Dan Lungren of California, who called the ABA report "irrelevant and outrageous."†

*Graham v Collins, 506 US 461 (1993).

**Henry Weinstein, "Execution Halt Sought by American Bar Assn.," Los Angeles Times, February 4, 1997, p. A13.

†Ibid.

using the mails to defraud. He pointed to the Fifth Amendment provision that no person shall be "subject for the same offense to be twice put in jeopardy of life or limb."[71] The judge answered: "The Supreme Court has said that *double jeopardy* prevents two criminal trials by the *same* government for the *same* criminal offense." **Double jeopardy** does not prevent punishment by the national and the state governments for the same offense or for successive prosecutions for the same crime by two states. Nor does the double jeopardy clause forbid civil prosecutions even after acquittal in a criminal trial for the same conduct, as most people remember from watching the 1996–1997 *civil* suit against O. J. Simpson for the battery of his ex wife and for causing the wrongful death of her friend after he had been acquitted in a 1995 *criminal* trial for their murder.

What constitutional rights can Crook claim in the state courts? First, every state constitution contains a bill of rights listing practically the same guarantees found in the national Bill of Rights. Until recently, most state judges were less inclined than federal judges to interpret the constitutional guarantees of their own state constitutions liberally in favor of those accused of crime. Although, as we noted in Chapter 4, some state judges now are more liberal in using the bills of rights in their own state constitutions to protect the rights of persons accused of crimes, most cases still turn on the application of the provisions of the Bill of Rights of the U.S. Constitution.

To what extent does the U.S. Constitution protect courtroom procedures from state actions? As noted, the Bill of Rights does not directly apply to the states, but the Fourteenth Amendment does. As the result of a series of Supreme Court decisions interpreting the Fourteenth Amendment, it now imposes on the states all the provisions of the Bill of Rights except those of the Second, Third, Seventh, and the Tenth Amendments and the grand jury requirements of the Fifth Amendment. No specific Supreme Court decision applies the excessive bail and fine limitation to the states. However, almost by definition, if a bail or fine is excessive, its imposition is likely to be considered a denial of due process.

The Supreme Court will probably not incorporate additional provisions of the Bill of Rights into the Fourteenth Amendment. Most lawyers, political scientists, and other observers believe states should be allowed to continue to conduct civil trials before judges without juries and to indict persons for serious crimes by means other than grand juries. Many states provide for some civil trials without juries. A number no longer require grand juries for any crimes; even more require them only for felonies; and less than a dozen require them for all except minor offenses. Other provisions in the Second, Third, and Tenth Amendments not incorporated are really not applicable to the states.

HOW JUST IS OUR SYSTEM OF JUSTICE?

What are the major criticisms of the American system of justice? How have they been answered?

Too Many Loopholes?

Some observers argue that by overprotecting the innocent and placing too much of a burden on the government not to make any mistakes, we delay justice, encourage disrespect for the law, and allow guilty persons to go unpunished. Justice should be swift and certain without being arbitrary. But under our procedures criminals may go unpunished because: (1) the police decide not to arrest them; (2) the judge decides not to hold them for a trial; (3) the prosecutor decides not to prosecute them; (4) the grand jury decides not to indict them; (5) the jury decides not to convict them; (6) the judge decides not to sentence them; (7) an appeals court decides to reverse the conviction; (8) a judge decides to release them on a *habeas corpus* writ; or (9) if retried and convicted, the executive decides to pardon, reprieve, or parole them. As a result, the public never knows whom to hold responsible when laws are not enforced. The police can blame the prosecutor, the prosecutor can blame the police, and they can all blame the juries and judges.

Others take a different view and point out that there is more to justice than simply securing convictions. All the steps in the administration of criminal laws have been developed over centuries of trial and error, and each step has been constructed to protect against particular abuses. History warns against entrusting the instruments of criminal law enforcement to a single officer. For this reason, responsibility is vested in many officials.

Too Unreliable?

Critics who say that our system of justice is unreliable often point to trial by jury as the chief source of trouble. No other country relies as heavily on trial by jury as does the United States. Jury trials are also time consuming and costly. Trial by jury, critics argue, leads to a theatrical combat between lawyers who base their appeals on the prejudices and sentiments of the jurors. "Mr. Prejudice and Miss Sympathy are the names of witnesses whose testimony is never recorded, but must nevertheless be reckoned with in trials by jury."[72]

The jury system allows for what has come to be called *jury nullification*, in which jurors ignore their instructions to consider only the evidence presented in court, and by voting for acquittal express their displeasure with the law or the actions of prosecutors or police. There were many who accused the jury in the O. J. Simpson criminal trial of voting to acquit him in order to express their displeasure with the Los Angeles Police Department and their belief that African Americans were routinely subject to police harassment. Jury nullification has a long history. In colonial times juries refused to convict colonists of political crimes against the king as a way to protest British rule. Prior to the Civil War, northern juries refused to convict persons for helping runaway slaves. Before the 1970s, white southern juries sometimes refused to convict police for actions of brutality against blacks.

Responding to growing public disenchantment with juries after a raft of unpopular verdicts, "State legislatures and court systems across the nation are starting to rewrite the rules of the jury system."[73] These changes include making it more difficult for people to be excused from jury service, allowing for more nonunanimous decisions, limiting the sequestration of jurors, and exerting more control over lawyer's statements to jurors.

Defenders of the jury system reply that trial by jury provides a check by nonprofessionals on the actions of judges and prosecutors.[74] There is no evidence that juries are unreliable; on the contrary, decisions of juries do not systematically differ from those of judges.[75] Moreover, the jury system helps to educate citizens and enables them to participate in the application of their own laws.

The grand jury system has also come under attack. In theory, the grand jury has two functions: (1) to protect the innocent from having to stand trial by requiring prosecutors to demonstrate behind closed doors that they have enough evidence to justify trial; and (2) to provide an independent agency, not controlled by those in power, to investigate wrongdoing. Critics charge, however, that the grand jury has become a tool of the prosecutor. Said Justice William O. Douglas, "It is, indeed, common knowledge that the grand jury, having been conceived as a bulwark between the citizen and the Government, is now a tool of the Executive."[76]

During the 1960s critics on the left of the political spectrum charged that grand juries had become instruments to intimidate radicals, blacks, and antiwar militants. However, by the 1970s grand juries were being used to investigate the exec-

Community policing, a program to improve relations between the police and the public, includes friendly contacts such as this.

utive branch. In the Watergate investigation of the Nixon administration, it was through the use of the grand jury that the special prosecutor was able to present to the courts his contention that the president had no constitutional right to withhold information about wrongdoing.

In 1996 a grand jury called upon President and Mrs. Clinton and their business partners, James and Susan Macdougal, to answer questions about their involvement in the Whitewater real estate venture. President and Mrs. Clinton responded, as did James Macdougal, who was waiting sentencing on other charges. Susan Macdougal went to jail rather than answer questions she claimed were designed by an independent prosecutor to force her to testify falsely against President and Mrs. Clinton.

In recent years, there have been calls to reform the federal grand jury system and remove some of the limitations on the right of federal jurors to make public comments, so that such juries might more effectively investigate allegations of wrongdoing by federal officials and look into social problems. As one advocate of such a reform has written, "Federal grand juries with broad investigatory powers would give citizens a new tool and a new platform. The public would be far more likely to listen to what the grand jurors said than to what the experts said."[77]

Too Discriminatory?

During the last several decades, the Supreme Court has worked particularly hard to enforce the ideal of equal justice under the law. Persons accused of a crime who cannot afford attorneys must be furnished them at government expense. If transcripts are required for appeals, such transcripts must be made available to those who cannot afford to purchase them. If appeals are permitted, the government must provide attorneys for at least one appeal of the decision of the trial court. Poor people cannot be imprisoned because of inability to pay a fine. Nor, once sentenced, can poor persons be kept in jail beyond the term of the sentence because they cannot afford to pay a fine. Even for civil proceedings—divorce proceedings, for example—fees cannot be imposed that deny poor persons their fundamental rights, such as the right to obtain a divorce. A state has no obligation, however, to waive fees for those seeking to be declared bankrupt. The Court apparently believes that people have a constitutional right to be absolved of the ties that bind but not of their debts.

Despite all these protections, it remains true that racial and ethnic discrimination in the criminal justice system, especially outside the courtroom, persists. How much it persists is hard to measure. The editors of the *Harvard Law Review* believe it is significant. "Racism still pervades the United States criminal justice system," they charge, and can be seen in the conduct of police, the actions of prosecutors, the decisions of jurors, and the sentences of judges. The editors blame the persistence of racism in the criminal justice system in part on the Supreme Court's requirement that litigants believing they are victims of racism in the criminal justice system cannot legally prove racism through general evidence about racism in the system except in cases involving juror selection. They must show through direct evidence relating to their particular cases the discriminatory intent of the decision maker and the adverse consequence flowing from this intent to their case.[78]

One expert close to the subject comes to a different conclusion. He reports that about 80 percent of the black overrepresentation in prison can be explained by differential involvement in crime, and about 20 percent by racially discriminatory processes.[79] "That is not at all to say that racial discrimination within the criminal justice system is unimportant; it certainly is important. What is suggested is only that it is relatively less important than other discriminatory pressures" in society in general outside of the criminal justice system.[80]

An American Dilemma

While the reforms envisioned by Gunnar Myrdal, a Nobel Prize–winning Swedish social scientist,[81] may have eliminated the more obvious examples of racial discrimination in the criminal justice system, they have not produced an equitable, or color blind, system of justice. Fifty years after the publication of Myrdal's book, *An American Dilemma*, African Americans still suffer discrimination at the hands of the criminal justice officials in the United States."[82]

One of the more acute problems of our society is the tension between the police and the African American and Hispanic communities congregated in the ghettos and barrios of our large cities. Such tensions were evident in the Rodney King beating and the 1992 Los Angeles riots. Many members of minorities do not believe they have equal protection under the law. The revelations of ex-detective Mark Furhman's racist remarks during the O. J. Simpson trial confirmed the view of many—especially African Americans—that the police are instruments of white intolerance. "Even before the Simpson trial, 83 percent of blacks said in a poll . . . that they didn't trust the criminal justice system."[83] "Whether the stated belief is well founded or not is at least partly beside the point. The existence of the belief is damaging enough."[84]

Blacks consider the police to be enforcers of white law. Studies proving prejudice on the part of some white police officers and examples of rough, if not brutal, police treatment of blacks are ample evidence to support this viewpoint. The general pattern, however, is that minorities are shot by the police at rates approximately proportional to rates of minorities engaged in street crime, but "there is a slight added increment and all you can conclude is the data support what common observation and folk tales make very clear—there is an element of racial prejudice in police shooting at minorities."[85]

In recent decades action has been taken to recruit more African Americans, Hispanics, and women as police officers, including appointment to command posts. In most larger cities there are now oversight boards including civilians to which complaints about police misconduct can be brought. Community relations programs have been established, and considerable progress has been made. Relations between police and minority communities in some cities appear to be improving.[86]

THE SUPREME COURT AND CIVIL LIBERTIES

Clearly, judges—especially those on the Supreme Court—play a major role in enforcing constitutional guarantees. This combination of judicial enforcement and written guarantees of enumerated liberties is one of the basic features of the American system of government. As Justice Robert H. Jackson wrote:

> The very purpose of a Bill of Rights was to withdraw certain subjects from the vicissitudes of political controversy, to place them beyond the reach of majorities and officials and to establish them as legal principles to be applied by the courts. One's right to life, liberty, and property, to free speech, a free press, freedom of worship and assembly, and other fundamental rights may not be submitted to vote: they depend on the outcome of no elections.[87]

This emphasis on constitutional limitations and judicial enforcement is an example of the "auxiliary precautions" James Madison believed were necessary to prevent arbitrary governmental action. In other free nations citizens rely more on elections and political checks to protect their rights; in the United States we appeal to judges when we fear our freedoms are in danger.

Such reliance on judicial protection of our civil liberties focuses attention on the Supreme Court. Yet only a small number of controversies are actually carried to the Supreme Court, and a Supreme Court decision is not the end of the policy-making process. Lower-court judges as well as police, superintendents of schools, local prosecutors, school boards, state legislatures, and thousands of others clarify the Court's doctrines.

The Supreme Court can do little unless its decisions over time reflect a national consensus. Judges by themselves cannot guarantee anything; neither can the First Amendment. As Justice Jackson asked:

> Must we first maintain a system of free political government to assure a free judiciary to guarantee free government? It is my belief that the attitude of a society and of its organized political forces, rather than its legal machinery, is the controlling force in the character of free institutions. Any court which undertakes by its legal processes to enforce civil liberties needs the support of an enlightened and vigorous public opinion.[88]

Thus, the Bill of Rights—and the other procedural and substantive liberties of our Constitution—cannot rest on a foundation merely of tradition. The preservation of these rights depends on wide, continuing, and knowledgeable public support. Inevitably that public support will be tested—sometimes sorely tested—in the years to come.

 POLITICS ONLINE

Are Your E-Mail Messages Private?

In an experiment designed to prove to Fortune 500 companies that none of their computer systems are invulnerable to break-ins, *Fortune* magazine commissioned a Texas security firm to break into a major corporation's presumably secure computer system. Over a long Christmas weekend, the hackers were able to gain "root access" (access available only to the corporation's computer system administrators) to five computers at corporate headquarters, including the one used to do taxes. They also invaded the "electronic heart" of the corporation, the computer used exclusively by the corporation's technology department.

Once hackers gain access to a computer, they can "steal trade secrets, destroy data, sabotage operations, even subvert a particular deal or career." One study found that 40 percent of companies and institutions reported recent break-ins, and break-ins have not been limited to the private sector. In one publicized case, a 16-year-old British youth and his associate broke into the Rome Laboratory, the U.S. Air Force top research and development facility, and used its computer to gain access to the South Korea Atomic Research Institute.*

What about the privacy of your e-mail? If you are sending or receiving e-mail at work or school, you may not have much privacy. Even messages that you have deleted may be backed up on the company's main-frame computer. One alternative is to send personal messages on your own account.

For information on criminal justice, consult an annotated bibliography maintained by the Emery University Law School:

http://www.law.emor.edu/CRIMPRO/scholarlit/bibindex.html

The home page for the U.S. Department of Justice provides information on federal law enforcement:

http://www.usdoj.gov

For the perspective of trial lawyers on our criminal justice system:

http://www.nacdl.org

*Richard Behar, "Who's Reading Your E-mail? *Fortune*, February 3, 1997, pp. 56–70.

SUMMARY

1. One of the basic distinctions between a free society and a police state is that in a free society there are effective restraints on the way public officials, especially law enforcement officials, perform their duties. In the United States these constitutional restraints are enforced by the courts.

2. The Constitution protects the acquisition and retention of citizenship. It protects the basic liberties of citizens as well as aliens.

3. The Constitution protects our property from arbitrary governmental interference, although debates about which interferences are reasonable and which are arbitrary are not easily settled.

4. The Constitution imposes limits not only on the procedures government must follow but also on the ends it may pursue. Some actions are out of bounds no matter wht procedures are followed. Legislatures have the primary role in determining what is reasonable and what is unreasonable. However, the Supreme Court continues to exercise its own independent and final review of legislative determinations of reasonableness, especially on matters affecting civil liberties and civil rights.

5. The framers knew from their own experiences that in their zeal to maintain power and to enforce the laws, public officials are often tempted to infringe on the rights of those accused of crimes. To prevent such abuse, the Constitution requires federal officials to follow detailed procedures in making searches and arrests and in bringing people to trial.

6. The Supreme Court interprets the Constitution, especially the Fourteenth Amendment, to impose on state and local governments almost the same restraints in the administration of justice as it imposes on the national government.

7. The Supreme Court continues to play a prominent role in developing public policy to protect the rights of the accused, to ensure that the innocent are not punished, and to guarantee that the public is protected against those who break the laws. The Court's decisions influence what the public believes and how police officers and others involved in the administration of justice behave. But the Court alone cannot guarantee fairness in the administration of justice.

FURTHER READING

GEORGE F. COLE, *Criminal Justice: Law and Politics*, 6th ed. (Wadsworth, 1993).

ROGER H. DAVIDSON AND WALTER J. OLESZEK, *Governing: Readings and Cases in American Politics*, 2d ed. (Congressional Quarterly Press, 1992).

RICHARD EPSTEIN, *Bargaining with the State* (Princeton University Press, 1993).

MACKLIN FLEMING, *The Price of Perfect Justice* (Basic Books, 1974).

NATHAN GLAZER, ED., *Clamor at the Gates: The New American Immigration* (ICS Press, 1985).

JOHN GUINTHER, *The Jury in America* (Facts-on-File Publications, 1988).

MARY M. KRITZ, ED., *U.S. Immigration and Refugee Policy* (Heath, 1982).

WAYNE R. LAFAVE, *Search and Seizure: A Treatise on the Fourth Amendment*, 2d ed. (West Publishing Co., 1987).

LEONARD W. LEVY, KENNETH L. KARST, AND DENNIS J. MAHONE, *Criminal Justice and the Supreme Court* (Macmillan, 1990).

ROBERT E. LITAN, ED., *Verdict: Assessing the Civil Jury System* (Brookings Institution, 1993).

J. W. PELTASON, *Corwin and Peltason's Understanding the Constitution*, 14th ed. (Harcourt Brace 1997).

GERALD D. ROBIN, *Introduction to the Criminal Justice System*, 4th ed. (Harper and Row, 1990).

JUDITH N. SHKLAR, *American Citizenship: The Quest for Inclusion* (Harvard University Press, 1991).

SPECIAL COMMISSION ON CRIMINAL JUSTICE IN A FREE SOCIETY, *Criminal Justice in Crisis* (American Bar Association, 1988).

ROBERT W. TUCKER, CHARLES B. KEELEY, AND LINDA W. RIGLEY, EDS., *Immigration and U.S. Foreign Policy* (Westview Press, 1990).

NORMAN L. ZUCKER AND NAOMI FLINK ZUCKER, *The Guarded Gate: The Reality of American Refugee Policy* (Harcourt Brace Jovanovich, 1987).

7

Political Culture and Ideology

*W*ith the fall of communism in Eastern Europe, what was once a unified nation—Yugoslavia—exploded into civil war. Muslims, Serbs, and Croats each demanded territory, autonomy, and independence from one another. The war in Bosnia was especially brutal, with more than 300 mass graves and an estimated quarter of a million people believed dead. The conflict between Serbs and Muslims in Bosnia continued for four years (1992–1995) until, under international pressure, Muslim, Serb, and Croat leaders signed the Dayton Peace Accord on December 14, 1995.

Before the collapse of Yugoslavia, the ethnic and religious populations of Bosnia had lived peacefully with one another; 16 percent of Bosnian children came from mixed marriages, a proportion higher than in any other part of Yugoslavia.[1] Before the war, Sarajevo, the capital of Bosnia, was a cosmopolitan city with a diverse ethnic population that had hosted the 1984 Winter Olympics. After the war, Sarajevo was largely reduced to rubble.

Why did Bosnia change from a peaceful society to one torn by civil war and atrocities? Part of the explanation is that these ethnic and religious groups had been held together by force under Yugoslav dictator Marshall Tito, who died in 1980. Another part of the explanation is the deeply rooted animosity the ethnic groups held for one another, an animosity so great that the competing factions practiced "ethnic cleansing" to eradicate the other ethnic groups from areas under their military control.

The conflict in Bosnia-Herzegovina became such an international issue that the North Atlantic Treaty Organization (NATO) carried out air strikes during the fall of 1995 in an effort to minimize territorial seizures by both groups. The air strikes reduced Serb-held territory from 70 percent to 50 percent and set the stage for the peace process. In November 1995, leaders of Bosnia, Croatia, and Serbia met with leaders of the NATO countries in Dayton, Ohio. There they established a plan under which Bosnia would be a single state consisting of two parts, a Muslim-Croat Federation (51 percent of territory), and a Serbian Republic (49 percent of territory). Sarajevo would be a multi-ethnic city under Muslim-Croat control and would house the central government.

A major step toward democracy and integration was taken on September 14, 1996, when Bosnian Muslims, Serbs, and Croats voted in national and regional elections. Though this progress was significant, Flavio Cotti, the Swiss foreign minister and chairman of the European organizations that administered the vote, put it in perspective: "What four years of war created cannot be eliminated in a few months or by elections. You need generations now for fear to disappear from the souls of the people."[2] The next few years will be a proving ground for the experiment in democracy for the people of Bosnia. Can they establish a democratic political culture?

We Americans also have many differences—religious, ethnic, and regional. So why did the people of Bosnia resort to warfare to decide their political future and we resorted to debating and voting? The people of Bosnia lacked a political system or common political culture that would give them confidence in the democratic process as a way to resolve differences and disputes. Regardless of our differences, we Americans share a political culture that underlies our political system. This commitment to democratic values and processes permits us to avoid the kind of strife experienced in Bosnia and other countries.

How Americans resolve conflicts tells us a lot about our political culture. How we propose to reconcile conflicts and similar problems depends on our *ideology*—

171

Values We Share

Americans distrust government: 50 percent think "government regulation of business usually does more harm than good," and 69 percent think that "when something is run by the government, it is usually inefficient and wasteful." Americans are more distrustful of the federal government than of local government; 78 percent think "the federal government should run only those things that cannot be run at the local level."

Americans are patriotic and share a sense of civic responsibility: 91 percent say they are "very patriotic," 93 percent feel it is their "duty to always vote," and 66 percent think that voting gives them some say in how the government runs things.

Most Americans believe in providing equal opportunity: 91 percent of Americans believe that "our society should do what is necessary to make sure that everyone has an equal opportunity to succeed."

Americans believe that government should help those in need: 63 percent of Americans believe that "it is the responsibility of government to take care of people who can't take care of themselves," and 59 percent think "the government should guarantee every citizen enough to eat and a place to sleep."

Americans are religious: 88 percent of Americans believe in the existence of God, and 78 percent see prayer as an important part of their daily life.

Americans see family and marriage as important: 84 percent of Americans say they have "old-fashioned values about family and marriage," and 75 percent think "too many children are being raised in day-care centers these days."

Americans distrust large corporations: 77 percent of Americans think "too much power is concentrated in the hands of a few big companies," and 53 percent think "business corporations make too much profit."

Americans are optimistic: 68 percent think that the United States "can always find a way to solve our problems and get what we want."

SOURCES: Times Mirror Center for the People and the Press, *The People, the Press, and Politics 1994: The New Political Landscape* (October 1994), pp. 132–165; Times Mirror Center for the People and the Press, *Voter Anxiety Dividing GOP: Energized Democrats Backing Clinton* (November 1995), pp. 84, 86; CBS News/New York Times Poll, October 25, 1995.

our ideas and beliefs about the proper role of government and political power. In this chapter, we look at the political culture that unites us as well as the ideologies that sometimes divide us.

THE AMERICAN POLITICAL CULTURE

Political scientists use the term **political culture** to refer to the widely shared beliefs, values, and norms concerning the relationship of citizens to government and to one another. The American political culture is the sum of our most cherished shared values. American democratic values include liberty, equality, individualism, democracy, justice, the rule of law, and economic freedom. There is, however, no definitive listing of American political values, and, as we noted in Chapter 1, these widely shared democratic values overlap and sometimes conflict.

Shared Values

The values and beliefs described here as part of the American political culture are grounded in a philosophical tradition called classical liberalism. This tradition influenced the founders of our Republic and continues to be important to democratic movements around the world today. **Classical liberalism**, which is not the same as modern-day liberalism, stresses the importance of the individual and of freedom, equality, private property, limited government, and popular consent. All these elements, you will remember, are part of what we have described as the political culture of the United States.

Before the American and French Revolutions, these were radically new and different ideas. Europe had been dominated by aristocracies, had experienced centuries of political and social inequality, and had been ruled by governments that were often arbitrary in the exercise of power. Liberal political philosophers rebelled against these traditions and instead postulated the principles of classical liberalism. They claimed individuals have certain **natural rights**, and that the state (or government), as a primary threat to these rights, must be limited and controlled. At the same time, the economic system was changing from mercantilism to capitalism. People began to think they could improve their lot in life. The principles of a free market system were accepted and adopted, and these ideas clearly influenced the thinking of the founders of our nation.

The American Revolution, based on values like individual liberty and popular consent, has often served as a focal point of the American political culture. The Fourth of July celebrations held in every corner of the country salute freedom and liberty. The Constitution, like the Revolution, also defines our nation and its values.

LIBERTY   Americans have always been united by a commitment to liberty or freedom. No value in the American political culture is more revered. "We have always been a nation obsessed with liberty. Liberty over authority, freedom over responsibility, rights over duties—these are our historic preferences," wrote the late Clinton Rossiter, a noted political scientist. "Not the good man, but the free man has been the measure of all things in this sweet 'land of liberty'; not national glory but individual liberty has been the object of political authority and the test of its worth."[3]

EQUALITY   Jefferson's famous words in the Declaration of Independence express the primacy of our views of equality: "We hold these truths to be self-evident, that all men are created equal, that they are endowed by their Creator with certain unalienable rights, that among these are life, liberty, and the pursuit of happiness." We have always believed in social equality. In contrast to the Europeans, our nation shunned aristocracy. For example, we explicitly banned titles of nobility in our

Constitution. Instead of having sharp distinctions between an upper and a lower class, our nation is characterized by its large middle class.

Equality also refers to *political equality*, the idea that every individual has a right to equal protection under the law and equal voting power. While political equality is a goal, it has not always been a reality. African Americans, Native Americans, and women have been denied political equality in the past.

Equality encompasses the idea of equal opportunity, especially with regard to improving economic status. Americans believe that social background should not limit our opportunity to achieve to the best of our ability, nor should race, gender, or religion. The nation's commitment to public education—programs like Head Start for underprivileged preschool children, state support for public colleges and universities, and federal financial aid for higher education—reflects our belief in equality.

INDIVIDUALISM   The United States is characterized by a persistent commitment to the individual. Under our system of government, individuals have both rights and responsibilities. The individual's importance and dignity are enhanced by our views of political equality.

Concern for preserving individual freedom of choice and what limits, if any, to place on individual choice generate intense political conflict. The debate over legalized abortion is often framed in terms of individual choice versus limits on that choice prescribed by law. While Americans agree with the idea of individual rights and freedoms, we also understand that rights often come into conflict with other rights or with the government's need to maintain order.

As Americans, we have faith in the common sense of the ordinary person. The tradition of Abraham Lincoln and Harry Truman, that anyone can become president, has been a bold one. We prefer action to reflection; we are often anti-expert and sometimes anti-intellectual. The emphasis on practicality and common sense has become part of our image. Poets like Walt Whitman, Stephen Vincent Benét, and Carl Sandburg, and storytellers like Mark Twain, Will Rogers, Eudora Welty, and Garrison Keillor have helped shape this tradition. This reverence for the common man and woman helps to explain our ambivalence toward power, politics,

The "ethnic cleansing" in Bosnia was contrary to the protection of minorities—a fundamental principle of our political heritage. These Muslim prisoners were torn from their home villages and moved to distant areas by the majority Serbs during the recent civil war.

Should the government confer titles of nobility?

In England, famous or noteworthy people are given titles of nobility. Originally, titles were inherited and had land and political authority attached to them. Today such titles do not have political influence, but they still convey prestige and honor. Some titles remain hereditary, but the more common pattern is for them to be awarded on the basis of national service or distinction in the arts or sciences. The awarding of titles can be controversial, and some people have even attempted to "buy" a title by offering money to the political parties or to conspicuous charities in hopes of gaining the recognition of Parliament and the Crown.

Here are some titles still in use in England, listed in order of prestige:

Duke (just below Prince)   Duchess
Marquess   Marquessa
Earl (Count in other   Countess
  countries)
Viscount   Viscountess
Baron   Baroness

Should our state and national governments honor people in the arts and sciences as is done in Great Britain? Think of the possibilities: Elvis could be the Duke of Memphis, Michael Jordan and Bill Gates could both be Earls. If people are willing to pay for titles, we might be able to raise money for a worthy cause or to reduce the budget deficit. What do you think? Should the United States adopt titles of nobility?

You Decide!

and government authority. In the United States, government is often viewed as a necessary evil.

DEMOCRACY, GOVERNMENT, AND THE CONSTITUTION The American political culture includes attitudes and beliefs about principles of government, procedures, documents, and institutions. A *democratic consensus*—a fairly widespread agreement on fundamental principles of governance and the values that undergird them—is essential to the maintenance of democracy and the other values we discuss here. We Americans have deeply rooted ideas about who has power to do what, how people acquire power, and how they are removed from power. These are fundamental "rules of the game" in which widespread consensus is important.

We believe in *majority rule*, yet we also believe that people in the minority should be free to try to win majority support for their opinions. We also strongly favor a two-party system and regular elections. Our institutions are based on the principle of representation and consent of the governed. We believe in *popular sovereignty*— that the ultimate power resides in the people. Government, from our perspective, should exist to serve the people rather than the other way around. The means by which the government learns the will of the people is through elections, perhaps the most important expression of popular consent. One of the most important jobs of government is to maintain order, something many of us take for granted.

Many of the limits on government are specified in the Constitution and the Bill of Rights. The Constitution is revered as a national symbol. Yet we often differ over what certain constitutional provisions require or over the precise meaning of the framers' original intentions. We Americans honor many of these rights more in the abstract than in particular situations (see Table 7–1). Almost half of us, for instance, think that books with dangerous ideas should be banned from public school libraries. Intolerance of dissenting or offensive views is amply demonstrated in

TABLE 7–1

It Depends on What You Mean by Rights and Freedoms

	Agree	Disagree	Don't Know
Gay marriages should be allowed.	28%	65%	7%
Welfare benefits should be denied to unwed teenagers.	36	56	8
Books with dangerous ideas should be banned from public school libraries.	45	52	3
Affirmative action programs to help blacks, women, and other minorities get better jobs and education should be continued.	58	36	4
The government should be able to censor news stories that it feels threaten national security.	62	34	4
The police should be allowed to search the houses of known drug dealers without a court order.	51	48	1
School boards should have the right to fire teachers who are known homosexuals.	39	58	3

SOURCES: The Pew Research Center for the People and the Press, *Republicans: A Demographic and Attitudinal Profile*, August 7, 1996, pp. 15–16; Times Mirror Center for the People and the Press, *The People, The Press, and Politics: A Times Mirror Political Typology*, October 11, 1990, pp. 126–27; and Times Mirror Center for the People and the Press, *The People, The Press, and Politics: The New Political Landscape*, October 1994, pp. 162–63.

many public opinion polls and is observed clearly on college and university campuses as well. Still, Americans can ordinarily be characterized as affirming support for democratic and constitutional values.

JUSTICE AND THE RULE OF LAW   Inscribed over the entrance to the U.S. Supreme Court are the words "Equal Justice under Law." The rule of law means that government is based on a body of law applied equally and by just procedures, as opposed to rule by an elite in which the whims of those in power decide policy or resolve disputes. Chief Justice John Marshall succinctly summarized this principle: "The government of the United States has been emphatically termed a government of laws, not of men."[4] We Americans believe strongly in the principle of fairness: All individuals are entitled to the same legal rights and protections.

NATIONALISM, OPTIMISM, AND IDEALISM   Americans are also highly nationalistic. We are proud of our past and tend to de-emphasize, or even forget, our nation's intolerance, diplomatic and military setbacks, the shame of slavery, and the denial of suffrage to women for more than a century. We are optimistic—about people, but not about government. We are also optimistic about opportunity, choice, options, individualism, and most of all, about freedom to improve ourselves and to achieve success with as little interference as possible from others or from government. As Table 7–2 indicates, U.S. citizens are more satisfied with their democratic government than are citizens of other countries, but the greater optimism among Americans may be based on their views of their country's future as well as the future of the world.

We know our system is not perfect. We often grumble that our elected officials have lost touch with the common people. We are disgusted by scandals and impatient with the slowness of the system to solve problems like health care, crime, and drug abuse. Yet we have an abiding faith in government by the people and in its ability to solve problems. Despite our dissatisfactions, a remarkable belief persists that our nation is better, stronger, and more virtuous than other nations. Doubtless this sense of *mission* is a source of discipline, a builder of morale, and a fortifier of nationalism. But an excessive or wrongheaded sense of mission can also cause problems. Like every country, the United States has interests and motives that are selfish as well as generous, squalid as well as idealistic. We, too, are part of human history. Still, our idealism persists, and our efforts in support of human needs and rights throughout the world are evidence of this idealism.

Political and Economic Change

Our political values are clearly affected by historical developments and by economic and technological growth. The Declaration of Independence and our Constitution identify such important political values as individual liberty, property rights, and limited government.[5] In the early years we emphasized separation of powers, checks and balances, states' rights, and the Bill of Rights. It took an additional generation or two before we also began to take seriously the ideal of democratic governance, the expansion of suffrage, and competitive nominations and elections. Notions of political equality and effective participation emerged during the presidency of Andrew Jackson and matured in the course of the nineteenth century. By the end of the nineteenth century, populists and suffragists turned ideals into action and formed large-scale movements to achieve more democratic forms of participation and more responsive forms of governance.

THE INDUSTRIAL TRANSFORMATION   By 1900, the agrarian society the framers knew was largely replaced by industrial capitalism and the growth of large corporations. With these changes, American ideology was irreversibly transformed. We committed ourselves to encourage economic growth by fostering privately owned corporations.

TABLE 7–2
Satisfaction with Democracy

	Satisfied	Dissatisfied
United States	64%	27%
Germany	55	27
Japan	35	32
United Kingdom	40	43
India	32	43
Venezuela	23	59
Hungary	17	50

SOURCE: Gallup Organization, "People's Satisfaction with Their Lives and Government Poll," April 1995.

Note: "Neither" responses were omitted, so totals do not equal 100%.

Thinking It Through

Our founding fathers resisted titles of nobility because they opposed the political and economic power wielded by the privileged few and their heirs. Instead, they attempted to foster a political culture without inherited position where individuals could rise to the level of their potential.

If titles of nobility do not have political or economic consequences, they are little different from being named a beauty queen or an all-star. Many organizations capitalize on people's desire for recognition, but most Americans would find the bestowal of titles of nobility unacceptable.

For government to adhere to the rule of law, its polices and laws should follow these five rules:

- *Generality*: Laws should be stated generally—not singling out any group or individual.
- *Prospectivity*: Laws apply to the future, not to punish something someone did in the past.
- *Publicity*: Laws cannot be kept secret and then enforced.
- *Authority*: Valid laws are made by those with legitimate power, and the people legitimate that power through some form of popular consent.
- *Due Process*: Laws must be enforced impartially with fair processes.

The use of child labor in factories is one aspect of the industrial transformation that still exists in parts of the world today.

The changed economic order had profound consequences for our political values—for how we viewed the role of government and how we related to one another. No one captures the implications of this shift better than political scientist Robert A. Dahl:

> One of the consequences of the new order has been a high degree of inequality in the distribution of wealth and income—a far greater inequality than had ever been thought likely or desirable under an agrarian order by Democratic Republicans like Jefferson and Madison, or had ever been thought consistent with democratic or republican government in the historic writings on the subject from Aristotle to Locke, Montesquieu, and Rousseau. Previous theorists and advocates had, like many of the framers of our own Constitution, insisted that a republic could exist only if the citizen body continued neither rich nor poor. Citizens, it was argued, must enjoy a rough equality of conditions.[6]

The success of the American industrial economy led to the accumulation of great wealth in the hands of a few—the robber barons or tycoons. Many had taken great risks and earned their fortunes through inventions and efficient production practices. As disparities of income grew, so did disparities in political resources. Economic resources can be converted into political resources, like time to spend on politics and money to contribute to parties and candidates.[7]

The rise of the large corporation and the concentration of individual wealth in the United States created divisions and bolstered resentment. The growth of **monopolies** prompted passage of antitrust legislation, and unsafe work conditions led to regulation of the workplace. More important, at the turn of the century, muckraking journalists charged that the robber barons behind the huge corporations were using their power to exploit workers and limit competition. Only the national government, it seemed, had the power to ensure fair treatment in the marketplace. This sentiment not only gave rise to the nation's first **antitrust legislation** but also sowed the idea that government could—and should—as the Constitution asserts, "promote the general welfare" by doing more to regulate the workings of business.

THE GREAT DEPRESSION AND NEW DEAL Then came the Great Depression and the near-collapse of the capitalistic system. Unrestrained capitalism and the unregulated market were faulted by many as a cause of the Depression. In any event, when it came, it brought the nation to the brink of disaster. There was no unemployment compensation, no guarantee on bank savings, no federal regulation of the securities exchanges, no Social Security. Americans turned to government to improve the lot of the millions of jobless and homeless citizens. With Franklin D. Roosevelt's New Deal, the idea gradually gained widespread acceptance that government should use its powers and resources to ensure some measure of equal opportunity and social justice.

Today free enterprise is no longer unbridled; government regulations, antitrust laws, job safety regulations, environmental standards, and minimum wage rates all balance the freedom of enterprise against the rights of individuals. Most people today support a semiregulated or mixed free enterprise system that checks the worst tendencies of capitalism while rejecting too much government intervention (see Table 7–3). Much of our politics centers on how to achieve this balance.

President Franklin Roosevelt's State of the Union Address in 1944 articulated an expanded "Second Bill of Rights" for all citizens. Roosevelt declared that this nation must make a firm commitment to "economic security and independence." Included in his Second Bill of Rights were:

- The right to a useful and remunerative job in the industries, shops, farms, or mines of the nation
- The right to earn enough to provide adequate food and clothing and recreation

TABLE 7–3

Attitudes on Business and Welfare, 1996

	Agree	Disagree	Don't Know
There is too much power concentrated in the hands of a few big companies.	76%	19%	5%
Business corporations make too much profit.	52	43	5
The government should do more to help poor and needy people.	48	46	6
Poor people have it easy.	52	39	9

SOURCE: The Pew Research Center for the People and the Press, *Republicans: A Demographic and Attitudinal Profile*, August 7, 1996, pp. 15–16.

- The right of every farmer to raise and sell his products at a return which will give him and his family a decent living
- The right of every businessman, large and small, to trade in an atmosphere of freedom from unfair competition and domination by monopolies at home or abroad
- The right of every family to a decent home
- The right to adequate medical care and the opportunity to achieve and enjoy good health
- The right to adequate protection from the economic fears of old age, sickness, accident, and unemployment
- The right to a good education.[8]

Roosevelt's policies and later efforts by John F. Kennedy and Lyndon Johnson in the 1960s to pass civil and voting rights legislation and launch a War on Poverty defined the ideological and political fights of the last half of the twentieth century.

Breadlines like this provided handouts of food to thousands of unemployed and destitute people during the Great Depression.

Modern-day liberalism and conservatism turn, in large measure, on how much one believes in Roosevelt's Second Bill of Rights and how much government assistance one thinks is owed to minorities, women, and others who have suffered discrimination or have been left behind by the industrial or technological revolutions of the twentieth century.

Today's party divisions are still based in large part on differing perspectives on the role of government in pursuit of social and economic policies. Passage of Johnson's Great Society programs of the 1960s gave renewed emphasis to an expanded view of rights and a larger role for the federal government. President Bill Clinton's efforts to provide health care to all Americans can be seen as an application of this approach to expanded rights. In calling for health care reform, Clinton referred to Roosevelt's Second Bill of Rights, asserting that "health care is a basic right all should have."[9]

THE BUDGET BATTLES OF THE '90S The agenda of American politics took an abrupt turn with the election of a Republican majority to both houses of Congress in 1994. Republicans, especially freshman House Republicans, took seriously their Contract with America, which promised to reverse the "welfare state" by balancing the budget, cutting taxes, passing procedural reforms, and reforming welfare. In the area of social welfare, Republicans proposed cutting spending for welfare programs, denying welfare benefits for additional illegitimate children born to women already on welfare, and enacting a two-years-and-out provision for welfare assistance in many cases. Newt Gingrich summarized their agenda:

> The greatest moral imperative we face is replacing the welfare state with an opportunity society. For every day that we allow the current conditions to continue, we are condemning the poor—and particularly poor children—to being deprived of their basic rights as Americans. The welfare state reduces the poor from citizens to clients. It breaks up families, minimizes work incentives, blocks people from saving and acquiring property, and overshadows dreams of a promised future with a present despair born of poverty, violence and hopelessness.[10]

As the 1996 campaign began in earnest, the Republican Congress and President Clinton reached a compromise on a major overhaul of the nation's welfare system. The new law abolished Aid to Families with Dependent Children (AFDC), the decades-old program for assistance to the poor, and delegated the primary administration of most welfare programs to the states through federal funds given to them in block grants. The new welfare law also had mandatory work requirements and imposed a five-year lifetime limit on many services. Legal aliens would be excluded from 19 programs and illegal aliens from 23 programs. Both Bill Clinton and the Republicans in Congress had promised welfare reform, and this legislation gave them something for which they could claim credit in the general election campaign.

The American Dream

Many of our political values come together in the **American Dream**, a complex set of ideas about the economy and its relation to individuals. Whether we realize it or not, this American Dream speaks to our most deeply held hopes and goals. The essence of the American Dream can be found in our endorsement of **capitalism**, an economic system characterized by private property, competitive markets, economic incentives, and limited government involvement in the production and pricing of goods and services.

The concept of private property enjoys extraordinary popularity in our political culture. In many European democracies, the state owns and operates transportation systems, the media, and other businesses that are privately owned and operated in the United States, although there is increasing privatization of state-

Colin Powell personifies the American Dream. Born of immigrant parents from Jamaica, Powell became a four-star general, National Security Adviser, and Chairman of the Joint Chiefs of Staff. He was urged to run for president in 1996 but declined for personal reasons.

owned businesses like telephone companies and broadcast media in Europe. Americans cherish the dream of acquiring property. Moreover, most of us believe that those who own property have the right to decide how it is to be used.

The right to private property is just one of the economic incentives that cement our support for capitalism and fuel the American Dream. We believe that this is the land of opportunity for the enterprising. Here the competitive, practical go-getter can build a dream home and make a fortune. People who have more ability or work extremely hard, we hold, should get ahead, should earn more, and should enjoy economic rewards. We also believe that those who earn a lot of money should be able to pass most of what they have accumulated along to their children and relatives. Even the poorest Americans oppose high inheritance taxes or limits on how much someone can earn. In fact, the widespread support of the American Dream is clearly more important than the number of people who actually achieve it.

We Americans believe our mixed free enterprise system gives almost everyone a fair chance, that this system is necessary for free government to survive, and that our freedom depends on it. We reject communism and socialism. Our faith in capitalism was fortified in the past decade when most communist nations shifted toward free enterprise systems.

In the United States, both individuals and corporations have acquired wealth and, at the same time, exercised political clout. Their power has, in turn, bred a certain amount of resentment. An increasing number of people believe the political system too often favors the rich over the poor. It is widely believed that when it comes to taxes, corporations and wealthy people do not pay their fair share. As tax reform is debated, a recurring issue is tax fairness. President Clinton argued that his 1993 tax package, by taxing the rich at higher rates, would achieve greater fairness. Dick Armey, who became House Majority Leader with the Republican sweep to power in 1994, criticized what Clinton did as "fake right, and run left." Armey contended that a flat tax would be fairer than the current system because "everybody pays a flat 17 percent rate on all income . . . and best of all, no tax attorneys, no lobbyists to plead your special case, no IRS to harass you."[11]

The flat tax was the centerpiece of Steve Forbes's bid for the Republican nomination in 1996. Although his campaign later fizzled, he did succeed in making the flat tax a frequent topic of conversation in Republican primaries and the mass media. Republican nominee Bob Dole promised a 15 percent cut in individual income tax rates as well as a $500 per child tax credit on the eve of his party's convention, but the idea did not generate much enthusiasm among voters. Democratic incumbent Bill Clinton questioned the wisdom of an across-the-board tax cut like Dole's. He proposed tax cuts targeted at the middle class, like a $10,000 tax deduction for college tuition.

The conflict in values between a *competitive economy*, in which individuals should be free to reap large rewards for their initiative and hard work, and *an egalitarian society*, in which everyone should be able to earn a decent living, carries over into our politics. How the public resolves this tension can change over time. For instance, social programs that sought to extend equality of opportunity enjoyed broad support in the 1960s. During the 1980s they were attacked and partially dismantled as Ronald Reagan sought to implement a more conservative, procapitalist policy.

As important as the American Dream is to our national consciousness, we must admit to certain realities. Many millions in this country are still denied equality of opportunity because of race, ethnic background, or gender. An underclass persists in the form of impoverished families, ill-nourished and ill-educated children, and people living in the streets.[12] Many cities are actually two cities, in which some live in luxury while others live in squalor. The gap between rich and poor has

The Family

One of the important sources of political culture in the United States and in other nations as well is the family. Children are taught from an early age what it means to be an American. They are curious about why people vote, what the president does, and whether Grandpa fought in World War II. The questions may vary somewhat from family to family, but the themes of authority, freedom, equality, liberty, and partisanship are common.* Families are the most important reference groups, and compared to families in other cultures, American families are much more egalitarian.

The Schools

Public schools are another source of the American political culture. Children and teachers often begin the school day by saluting the flag, reciting the Pledge of Allegiance, or singing the national anthem. Teaching American political and economic values is part of the curriculum. Not only are values taught in American history classes, but they are put into practice in school elections and newspapers and in encouraging students to participate in small-scale economic ventures.

Colleges and universities also play a role in fostering the American political culture. Students who attend college are often more confident than other persons in dealing with bureaucracy and politics generally, more likely to participate in politics and vote, and more knowledgeable about government. Many states require college students to take courses in American government or state government, in part to instill a sense of civic duty while imparting knowledge about state and national governments.

Religious and Civic Organizations

Religious freedom and diversity have played a part in the formation and maintenance of the American political

grown in recent years.[13] The gap between rich farms and marginal farms has deepened. And a sharp difference between white and black income persists tenaciously. Far more than we want to admit, people's chances for success still depend on the neighborhood they grow up in or the college they attend.

IDEOLOGY AND PUBLIC POLICY

Ideology refers to the structure of a person's ideas or beliefs about political values and the role of government. It includes the views people develop as they mature about how government should work and how it actually works. Ideology links our basic values to the day-to-day operations or policies of government.

Two major, yet rather broad, schools of political thinking dominate American politics today: *liberalism* and *conservatism*. Two lesser, but more defined, schools of thought, *socialism* and *libertarianism*, also help define the spectrum of ideology in the United States.

Liberalism

In the seventeenth and eighteenth centuries, classical liberals fought to minimize the role of government. They stressed individual rights and perceived of government as the primary threat to those rights and liberties. Thus they favored a limited government and sought ample guarantees of protection from governmental harassment. Over time the emphasis on individualism has remained constant, but the perception of the need for government has changed. Today liberals view government as protecting individuals from being abused by a variety of governmental and nongovernmental forces, such as market vagaries, business decisions, and discriminatory practices.

In its modern American usage, **liberalism** refers to a belief in the positive uses of government to bring about justice and equality of opportunity. Modern-day liberals wish to preserve the rights of the individual and the right to own private property, yet they are willing to have the government intervene in the economy to remedy the defects of capitalism. Contemporary American liberalism has its roots in Franklin D. Roosevelt's New Deal programs, designed to aid the poor and to protect people against unemployment and bank failures. Today liberals seek protection against inadequate or deficient medical assistance and inadequate or deficient housing and education. They generally believe in affirmative action programs, regulations that protect workers' health and safety, tax rates that rise with income, and the right of unions to organize as well as to strike.

On a more philosophical level, liberals generally believe in the possibility of progress. They believe things can be made to work, that the future will be better, that obstacles can be overcome. This positive set of beliefs may explain their willingness to believe in the potential benefits of governmental action, a willingness to alter or even negate the old Jeffersonian notion that "government governs best when it governs least." Liberals contend that the character of modern technology and the side effects of industrialization cry out for some limited governmental programs to offset the loss of liberties suffered by the less well-to-do and the weak. Liberals of the Mario Cuomo, Hillary Clinton, and Jesse Jackson stripe frequently stress the need for a compassionate and affirmative government. Hillary Rodham Clinton's *It Takes a Village and Other Lessons Children Teach Us* and Mario Cuomo's *Reason to Believe* defend a positive role for government.

Liberals contend that conservatives usually rule in their own interest and are motivated by the maxim, "Let the government take care of the rich, and the rich in turn will take care of the poor." Liberals, on the other hand, prefer that gov-

We the People

Differences in Political Ideology

	Conservative	Moderate	Liberal
Sex			
Male	42%	30%	27%
Female	43	32	25
Race			
White	43	31	25
Black	45	25	30
Age			
18–34	45	28	27
35–45	43	34	23
46–55	43	31	26
56–64	43	29	27
65+	40	36	24
Religion			
Protestant	57	25	18
Catholic	40	34	26
Jewish	16	21	63
Education			
Less than high school	36	47	17
High school diploma	36	42	21
Some college	46	30	24
Bachelor's degree	49	22	29
Advanced degree	44	15	40
Party			
Democrat	20	35	45
Independent	32	55	13
Republican	72	23	5

SOURCE: Center for Political Studies, University of Michigan, *1996 National Election Study.*

Note: We have combined with the moderates persons who do not know their ideology or had not thought much about it. For party identification, we have combined Independent leaners with their respective parties. Rows may not add up to 100 percent due to rounding.

Where We Learn the American Political Culture (continued)

culture. American churches, synagogues, and mosques have long fostered "a common set of moral understandings about good and bad, right and wrong, in the realm of individual and social action."[†] Freedom, including freedom of religion, individualism, pluralism, and civic duty, have all been fostered by churches. As churches do not all take the same positions on political issues, their impact is sometimes mitigated, but they have been important to such major social and political movements as abolition of slavery, expansion of civil rights, and opposition to war. Civic organizations like the Boy Scouts, 4-H, League of Women Voters, Rotary Club, and Chamber of Commerce encourage citizen participation and pride in community and nation.

The Mass Media
In modern times the mass media have taken over some functions previously performed by the family. By the time they are adults, children will probably have spent more time watching television than in conversation with their parents. They may have had more political instruction from MTV than from their parents or their schools.

Political Activities
Finally, Americans educate each other about political values in the workplace, at the PTA meeting, or in more expressly political activities.

[*]Fred I. Greenstein, *Children and Politics* (Yale University Press, 1965), p. 44.

[†]Robert N. Bellah, *The Broken Covenant: American Civil Religion in Time of Trial* (Seabury Press, 1975), p. ix. See also Charles W. Dunn, ed., *Religion in American Politics* (Congressional Quarterly Press, 1989) and Kenneth D. Wald, *Religion and Politics in the United States* (Congressional Quarterly Press, 1992).

ernment take care of the weak, for the strong can nearly always take care of themselves. "We have rejected the discredited theory that the fortunes of the nation should be in the hands of a privileged few," said President Harry Truman. "Instead, we believe that our economic system should rest on a democratic foundation and that wealth should be created for the benefit of all. . . . Every segment of our population and every individual has a right to expect from his government a fair deal."[14]

In the liberal view, all people are equal. Equality of opportunity is essential, and, toward that end, discriminatory practices must be eliminated. Some liberals

"He's trustworthy, loyal, obedient, cheerful, and all that, but he leans to the left."

Drawing by Dedini. ©1988 The New Yorker Magazine Inc.

favor the reduction of great inequalities of wealth that make equality of opportunity impossible. Most favor a certain minimum level of income. Rather than placing a cap on wealth, they want a floor placed beneath the poor. In short, liberals have sought "to lessen the harsh impact of oligarchical rule in economic life, to introduce a measure of democracy within or democratic controls over the industrial-technological process, to assure freedom from arbitrary command within the economic no less than within the political sphere."[15] They ask: How can citizens be equal and free if they are dependent on and necessarily servile to the powers that be?

TYPES OF LIBERALS   Liberals, it should be emphasized, come in many varieties. Some stress civil rights or women's rights or high-quality public education. Others urge government to adopt a more progressive tax system and do more to help the homeless, the handicapped, and society's "have-nots." Still others decry militarism and crusade for treaties and alliances that might bring about a world without terrorism and war. And yet other liberals are preoccupied with environmental or consumer issues. Some liberals embrace all these issues, placing them on an equal plane.

In a sense, liberals who emphasize economic issues may be called *New Deal liberals*; others are *social liberals* or *peace liberals*. If this is not confusing enough, there are those who call themselves neoliberals. **Neoliberals** believe in liberty, justice, and a fair chance for everyone, and they argue that the truly down-and-out must have government assistance. Yet they do not automatically favor unions and big government, nor do they automatically criticize big business and the military. Neoliberals are best characterized as liberals who have lost faith in many welfare programs and are skeptical about the efficiency and responsiveness of large, Washington-based bureaucracies. They are better at diagnosing some of the deficiencies of old liberalism than they are at pointing out what should be done. A sample of neoliberal thinking appears in *The Washington Monthly*.[16]

CRITICISMS OF LIBERALISM   Not everyone, by a long shot, is convinced that liberals, in whatever form, have the answers for the policy challenges of the twenty-first century. Critics of liberalism, old and new, say liberals place too much reliance on governmental solutions, higher taxes, and bureaucrats. Opponents of liberalism say that somewhere along the line liberals forgot that government, to serve our best interests, has to be limited. Power tends to corrupt, they add, and too much reliance or dependence on government can corrupt the spirit, undermine self-reliance, and make us forget about those cherished personal freedoms and property rights our Republic was founded to secure and protect. When government grows too big, it tends to start dictating to us, and then our rights and liberties are at risk. Further, too many governmental controls or regulations and too much taxation undermine the self-help ethic that has "made America great." In short, critics of liberalism contend that the welfare and regulatory state pushed by liberals will ultimately destroy individual initiative, the entrepreneurial spirit, and the very engine of economic growth that might lead to true equality of economic opportunities.

Some liberals admit that Ronald Reagan, Bob Dole, and Jack Kemp redefined the issues in the 1980s and 1990s in such a way that liberalism sounded unnecessary and dated, if not wholly harmful. These themes were emphasized by Republicans in the 1992 and 1996 election campaigns—arguing for less government. Wrapping themselves in the symbols of nationalism and patriotism, conservatives took a strong stand in favor of business, the death penalty, and prayer in schools—issues popular with most voters. Liberals, on the other hand, wrapped themselves in the symbols of compassion, fairness, equality, and social justice, also popular issues.

The 1992 election contest between Bill Clinton and George Bush centered on the economy. Clinton and the Democrats successfully focused the campaign on the need for economic growth, jobs, and a lower federal budget deficit. Once elected, Clinton's major preoccupation was health care reform; the resulting proposal was comprehensive, complex, and costly, and it offended many entrenched interests. Republicans in Congress were able to defeat health care reform and claim in the 1994 election that they could do a better job of governing. The Republican Contract with America argued for less government and lower taxes. As Dick Armey, one of the primary architects of the Contract, stated: "The sheer mass of our federal government is simply inconsistent with a free society. If nearly half of what you make is spent by someone else, that means that half your work time is spent working for someone else . . . The obvious solution frankly is to end many of these government programs and allow people to keep their own money, the better to provide for these benefits themselves."[17] This perspective reflected the laissez-faire economics advocated by many Republicans for decades and raises anew old questions about the role of the government in the economy and society.

President Clinton in his 1996 State of the Union message embraced some of this conservative thinking when he declared, "The era of big government is over." Later in 1996, to reinforce his shift to the right, Clinton signed into law a welfare reform bill that many liberals saw as a departure from a Democratic core commitment to the people. Clinton's efforts to end welfare, his inability to enact health care reform, and the weakened position of Democrats in Congress during 1995 and 1996 left liberals in the Democratic party without much of a voice.

Some liberals or progressives suggested a new agenda for the Democrats in response to the events of the 1990s and the success of conservative thinkers. E. J. Dionne, Jr.'s book on how progressives can regain power is aptly titled *They Only Look Dead*, referring to the conventional wisdom that liberal or progressive ideas are in decline. Dionne contends that "the current political upheaval can thus be defined less as a revolt against *big* government than as a rebellion against *bad* government—government that has proven ineffectual in grappling with the political, economic, and moral crises that have shaken the country."[18] Dionne challenges the claims of Clinton and Gingrich that big government is bad or even over. Pointing to past progressive or liberal successes, Dionne contends Americans want a government that eases economic transitions, helps "preserve a broad middle class," and "*expands* the choices available to individuals."[19]

James Carville, one of the political consultants credited with Clinton's 1992 election victory, has written "a handbook for spirited progressives," in which he counters conservative claims. He writes that the conservative Republican attack on big government in 1994 was deliberately vague. According to Carville, Republican legislative actions of 1995 and 1996 demonstrated that "big government is actually a code for Medicare, school loans, scientific research, and nutrition programs for pregnant mothers."[20]

Theodore Sorensen, a noted Democrat, agrees with Carville and Dionne that the best way to regain Democratic support is by sticking to key liberal principles. In his book, *Why I Am a Democrat*, Sorensen writes, "I believe that the Democratic Party, more moderate than the new Republican extremists, more concerned with the economic security issues that underlie the electorate's anxiety, and less divided on matters of race, peace, and philosophy than at any time in modern Democratic Party history, has every opportunity to become the majority party once again."[21]

As the agenda of American politics changes, so does the popularity of liberal or conservative positions. With the demise of communism, many Americans are now less concerned about defense spending and want less government generally. Yet the fiscal constraints imposed by the crushing budget deficit changed the debate about government solutions because politicians of both parties would rather promise tax cuts than raise taxes to fund new programs. Moreover, as our expanded trade with other countries demonstrates, we live in a global economy in which our jobs and economic progress are linked to our neighbors and to other countries around the world. The net effect of these changes is that our national government, while focusing on domestic issues like health care, crime, and welfare, does so in a context much more aware of the constraints of the budget deficit and the unpopularity of tax increases.

Conservatism

American **conservatism** has its roots in the political thinking of John Adams, Alexander Hamilton, and many of their contemporaries. They believed in limited government and encouraged individual excellence and personal achievement. Private property rights and belief in free enterprise are cardinal attributes of contemporary conservatism. In contrast to liberals, conservatives want to keep government small, except in the area of national defense. However, because conservatives take a more pessimistic view of human nature than liberals do, they maintain that people need strong leadership institutions, firm laws, and strict moral codes to keep their appetites under control. Government, they think, needs to ensure order. Conservatives are also inclined to believe that those who fail in life are in some way the architects of their own misfortune and thus must bear the main responsibility for solving their own problems. Conservatives have a preference for the status quo and desire change only in moderation. A sample of conservative thinking can be found in *The Weekly Standard* or *The National Review*, both weekly magazines.

Most conservatives opposed the New Deal programs of the 1930s and the War on Poverty in the 1960s, and they seldom favored aggressive civil rights and affirmative action programs. Human needs, they say, can and should be taken care of by families and charities. Equal treatment can be achieved by encouraging citizens to be more tolerant. Conservatives place their faith in the private sector, and they consider social justice to be essentially an economic question. They dislike the tendency to turn to government, especially the national government, for solutions to societal problems. Government social activism, they say, has been expensive for taxpayers and counterproductive. Conservatives also prize stability of the dollar relative to other currencies, and stability in international and economic affairs. They prefer private giving and individual voluntary efforts targeted at social and economic problems rather than government programs.

TRADITIONAL CONSERVATIVES Traditional conservatives recognize that government must exist, yet insist it should be limited in what it does, and that within its proper sphere of action, it should be strong and resolute. "The purpose of government is to maintain the framework of order within which other private institutions can operate effectively."[22] The traditional conservative applauds the heartfelt compassion implicit in Franklin Roosevelt's Second Bill of Rights but believes that to turn to the federal government to solve problems is to guarantee a too powerful, intrusive, and expensive government.

Liberals favor national action and a strong central government. Conservatives, however, contend that centralization means higher taxes, that the freedom of the majority would greatly diminish, and that the initiative and risk-taking entrepreneurial impulses of inventors, capital investors, and ingenious business leaders would be irreversibly discouraged.[23] "With the end of the Cold War, the case for a strong central government has been dramatically weakened," says Newt Gingrich. "The time has come for a reversion to first principles. In America, one of those first principles is that power resides first and foremost with the individual citizen. In America, individual citizens earn their bread, and the government had better have an overwhelming reason for taking it away from them."[24]

Traditional conservatives, in the name of freedom, are emphatically pro-business. Thus they oppose higher taxes and resist all but the most necessary antitrust, trade, and environmental regulations on corporations. The functions of government should be, say conservatives, to encourage family values, protect us against foreign enemies and criminals, preserve law and order, enforce private contracts, foster competitive markets, and encourage free and fair trade.

Traditional conservatives have customarily favored dispersing power broadly throughout the political and social systems to avoid concentration of power at the national level. They favor having the market, rather than the government, provide services. Traditional conservatives subordinate economic and social equality to liberty and freedom. Yet some conservatives, like 1996 vice presidential candidate Jack Kemp, advocate a role for government in helping the worst-off climb out of poverty. Kemp believes that government should create "enterprise zones" in impoverished urban areas by giving the private sector incentives to invest in poverty-stricken inner-city neighborhoods and create jobs for the urban poor.

THE NEW RIGHT Another brand of conservatism—sometimes called the New Right, ultra-conservatism, or even the Radical Right—emerged in the 1980s. The New Right shared the love of freedom shown by the traditional conservatives and backed an aggressive effort to combat international communism, especially in Central America. It also developed an activist public policy agenda that it would like implemented by conservatives in Congress and in the White House. The New Right favored the return of organized prayer in the public schools and the renewal of covert operations by the Central Intelligence Agency. It wanted strict limits on abortion; it opposed policies like job quotas, busing, and any tolerance of pornography and homosexuality. In short, a defining characteristic of the New Right was a strong desire to impose various social controls.

The New Right of the 1980s is embodied in the Christian Coalition of the 1990s. This group was founded by Pat Robertson after his candidacy for the presidency in 1988. Ralph Reed, former director of the College Republican National Committee and Students for America, took over as executive director in the mid-1990s. The Christian Coalition concentrates on such issues as abortion, pornography, gay rights, and education. The Christian Coalition lobbies for what they consider pro-family legislation, including a Religious Freedom Amendment to the U.S. Constitution, which is designed to guarantee free religious expression in public settings, including prayer in public schools. The Coalition publishes voter guides and score cards to help members decide which candidates best represent their values. Adherents of the Christian Coalition have been especially active at the state and local levels, in political parties and initiative campaigns, and on school boards. A 1992 initiative in Colorado to overturn ordinances protecting gays and lesbians from discrimination was placed on the ballot largely through their efforts.[25] The Colorado law was later declared unconstitutional by the state supreme court, a decision upheld by the U.S. Supreme Court.[26] An example of Christian Coalition views can be found in *Christian American*, a Coalition publication.

Some conservatives question the moralistic tone of the Christian Coalition. For example, Barry Goldwater, a former senator and Republican presidential candidate in 1964, worries that too much prominence and influence have been granted to the New Right, especially the Moral Majority and those he calls the "checkbook clergy." Our Constitution, Goldwater says, seeks to allow freedom for everyone, not merely those professing certain moral or religious views. Goldwater points to the bloody divisions in Northern Ireland, the holy wars in Lebanon, and the

The 1996 presidential primaries came down to a battle between moderate and conservative candidates "for the soul of the Republican party." Bob Dole won the support of party moderates; Pat Buchanan was seen as too extreme in his views.

pernicious religious righteousness in Iran as examples of the politicalization of churches. "The Moral Majority has no more right to dictate its moral and political beliefs to the country than does any other group, political or religious," says Goldwater. "The same is true of pro-choice, abortion, or other groups. They are free to persuade us because this land is blessed with liberty, but not to assign religious or political absolutes—complete right or wrong."[27] Goldwater fears that the great danger of the Christian Coalition is that it will tear his beloved Republican party apart.

NEOCONSERVATIVES   The past generation has also witnessed the emergence of people who call themselves **neoconservatives**. Many are former Democrats who admired FDR and Harry Truman but left the Democratic party over Vietnam, busing, and the decisions of the liberal (overly liberal in their view) Earl Warren Supreme Court. They want to continue programs that work and are truly necessary, but reject the rest. An example of a successful program they would be inclined to keep is Head Start, the federally funded program for disadvantaged preschool children. Neoconservatives believe that too many government programs will lead to a paternalistic state. Though willing to interfere with the market for overriding social purposes, neoconservatives prefer finding market solutions to social problems. An example of neoconservative writing can be found in *Commentary*, a monthly magazine.

Neoconservatives favor larger military expenditures than do liberals. They remain skeptical of the intentions of some other nations or terrorist groups. Conservatives favor sufficient military spending to permit the United States to play a role in mediating conflicts around the world, especially in settings where U. S. interests are involved. But conservatives are not always united in their support for the use of military force, as indicated by the opposition of some conservatives to the use of American troops in Somalia, Bosnia, and Haiti in the 1990s. They also favor the death penalty and are more worried about crime than about the homeless. They say the courts have gone too far in protecting the rights of the criminal and are too little concerned about the rights of the victims of crime.

Neoconservatives are credited with various original writings on social policy, supply-side economics, education, and the role of "national interest" in foreign affairs. The United States, in the neoconservative view, should use its power to shape events; it cannot retreat into isolationism. Thus neoconservatives heartily approved the use of military force in Panama and Kuwait, but were divided over the deployment of U.S. forces to Serbia and Bosnia. Some also supported **supply-side economics** (which during the 1980s was often called "Reaganomics"), the belief that lower taxes will encourage economic growth, new jobs, and ultimately new tax revenues. Bob Dole reactivated supply-side economics in his 1996 presidential campaign with a call for a 15 percent reduction in income taxes.

CRITICISMS OF CONSERVATISM   Not everyone agreed with Ronald Reagan's statement, repeated by candidates Dole and Kemp, that "government is the problem."[28] Indeed, critics of conservatism before and during the Reagan-Bush era saw hostility to government as counterproductive and inconsistent. Conservatives, they argued, have a selective opposition to government. They want more government when it serves their needs—regulating pornography and abortion, for example—but are opposed to it when it serves somebody else's. Critics point out that government spending, especially for defense, grew during the 1980s when the conservatives were in control. Conservatives are often criticized for insensitivity to the social needs of the homeless and mentally ill.

Conservatives place great faith in our market economy—critics would say too much faith. This posture often puts them at odds with labor unions and consumer activists and in close alliance with businesspeople, particularly large corporations. Hostility to regulation and a belief in competition led them to push for deregulation in the 1980s. The resulting changes did not always have the intended positive effects, as the collapse of many savings and loans revealed.[29] During the same decade, according to some critics, the Reagan administration's decision not to pursue antitrust actions encouraged a flurry of mergers and acquisitions that diverted our economy from more productive economic activity.[30] Conservatives counter that relying on "market solutions" and encouraging the free market are still the best course of action in most policy areas.[31]

The policy of the Reagan years of lowering taxes was consistent with the conservative hostility to government. In his 1981 address to the nation on the state of the economy, Reagan likened government to children who spend more than their parents can afford. He mentioned that such extravagance could be cured by "simply reducing their allowance," implying that government spending could be controlled by reducing the amount government was allowed to spend.[32] Many conservatives embraced the idea that if we lower taxes on the rich, their economic activity will "trickle down" to the poor. This view was criticized by many Democrats, who pointed out that the growth in income and wealth in the 1980s was largely concentrated among the well-to-do.[33]

Conservatives are also criticized for their failure to acknowledge and endorse policies that deal with racism and sexism in the United States. Their opposition to the civil rights laws in the 1960s and their opposition to affirmative action in the 1990s are examples of this perspective. Not only have conservatives opposed new laws in these areas, they have hampered the activity of the executive branch when in power, and have sought to limit the activity of the courts in these matters as well.

Bernard Sanders, former mayor of Burlington, Vermont, and a self-described Socialist, was elected to the House of Representatives by Vermont voters as an Independent.

Socialism

Socialism is an economic and governmental system based on public ownership of the means of production and exchange. Karl Marx once described socialism as a transitional stage of society between capitalism and communism. In a capitalist system, the means of production and most of the property are privately owned, whereas in a communist or socialist system, property is "owned" by the state in common for all the people. In the ultimate socialist country, justice is achieved by having participants determine their own needs and take what is appropriate from the common product of society. Marx's dictum was, "From each according to his ability, to each according to his needs."[34]

In one of the most dramatic transformations in recent times, Russia, its sister republics, and its former European satellites abandoned their version of socialism—communism—and are now attempting to establish free markets. These countries had previously rejected capitalism, preferring state ownership and centralized government planning of the economy. But by the 1990s the disparities in economic well-being between capitalist and communist nations produced a tide of political and economic reform that left communism intact in only a few countries, such as Cuba.

American socialists—of whom there are few prominent examples—favor a greatly expanded role for the government. They would nationalize certain industries, institute a public jobs program so that all who want work would be put to work, and place a much steeper tax burden on the wealthy. In short, American socialists favor policies to help the underdog by means of income redistribution programs. They also favor stepped-up efforts toward greater equality in property rights. American socialists would drastically cut defense spending as well.[35] Most of the democracies of Western Europe are far more influenced by socialist ideas than we are in the United States, but they remain, like the United States, largely market economies.

Libertarianism

Libertarianism is an ideology that cherishes individual liberty and insists on a sharply limited government. It carries some overtones of anarchism, of the classical English liberalism of the past, and of a 1930s-style conservatism. The Libertarian party has gained a modest following among people who believe that both liberals and conservatives lack consistency in their attitude toward the power of the national government.

Libertarians preach opposition to government and just about all its programs. They favor massive cuts in government spending, an end to the Federal Bureau of Investigation, the Central Intelligence Agency, and most regulatory commissions, and a defense establishment that would defend the United States only if directly attacked. They oppose *all* government regulation, including, for example, mandatory seat-belt and helmet laws. A poster at one of their recent national conventions read, "U.S. out of Latin America; U.S. out of North America!" Libertarians favor eliminating not only welfare programs but also programs that subsidize business, farmers, and the rich. They argue that the federal government has vastly overstepped its constitutional powers, and most current government functions should be eliminated entirely. Unlike conservatives, libertarians would repeal laws that regulate personal morality, including abortion, pornography, prostitution, and recreational drugs.

A Libertarian party candidate for president has been on the ballot in all 50 states in recent presidential elections, although never obtaining more than 1 percent of the vote. The Libertarian candidate for president in 1996, Harry Browne, ran on a platform that emphasized freedom from government. The 1996 Libertarian platform proposed immediate and complete removal of the federal government from education, energy, regulation, crime control, welfare, housing, transportation, health care, and agriculture; repeal of the income tax and all other direct taxes; decriminalization of drugs and pardons for prisoners convicted of nonviolent drug offenses; withdrawal of overseas military forces; and overall commitment to a smaller government, limited by the Constitution's specifications. Libertarian positions are rarely timid; at the very least, they prompt intriguing political debates.

A Word of Caution

Political labels have different meanings across national boundaries as well as over time. To be a liberal in certain European nations is to be on the right; to be a liberal in the 1990s in the United States is to be on the left. In recent elections, "liberal," which back in FDR's day had been popular, became "the L-word," a label most politicians sought to avoid. Even liberals have largely abandoned the term, now referring to themselves as progressives.

During the 1992 election, Bill Clinton defined himself as a "new Democrat," someone more in the country's political mainstream than some past Democratic candidates had been. In 1992 and 1996 Republicans accused Clinton of masquerading as a moderate, espousing Republican concerns like ending welfare. They pointed to Clinton's economic stimulus and health care reform proposals and his 1993 tax increase as evidence that he is a "tax and spend liberal." The varying ideological interpretations of Bill Clinton teach us that labels are rarely static, and that much of politics seeks to define the opposing party as extremists and one's own party as sensible moderates.

Ideological terms or labels can also be confusing on the conservative side of the spectrum. As discussed earlier, some conservatives are called neoconservatives, others New Right, and some have even adopted the term *paleoconservatives*—the prefix *paleo* meaning ancient or old. With so many terms in use to describe how

Harry Browne, Libertarian candidate for president in 1996, was on the ballot in all 50 states but got only 1 percent of the total vote.

people see politics and government, it is not surprising that political labels are in flux and often confusing. Yet on big questions—such as the role of government in the economy, in promoting equality of opportunity, in regulating the behavior of individuals or businesses, and on such issues as abortion—real differences separate conservative and liberal groups. This does not mean that persons who are conservative in one area are necessarily conservative in another.

It is also important to appreciate that ideology both causes events and is affected by them. Just as the Great Depression resulted in a tidal wave of ideological change, so did our involvement in World War II, Korea, and Vietnam, each in its own way. World War II, with its positive example of how government can work to defend freedom, strengthened positive views about the role of the national government. The Vietnam War probably had the opposite effect—disillusionment with government. The anti-government sentiment in recent presidential elections is undoubtedly related to Vietnam, the Watergate scandal, and the Iran-Contra affair.

Debates about communist expansionism are increasingly dated and irrelevant in American politics. There is little fear today that the United States will become communist, and the communist threat around the world is greatly diminished. But people of varying ideologies do indeed worry about whether the United States is becoming too soft and losing ground in the global economy. Today we are more likely to debate what will make us beat, or at least compete with, "those capitalists from Japan" and other Pacific Rim nations.

Ideological controversy today centers on how we can improve our schools, encourage a stronger work ethic, and stop the flow of drugs into the country; whether to permit openly gay people into the military or sanction gay marriages; and the best ways to instill religious values, build character, and encourage cohesive and lasting families.

Do social programs and job-training programs make things better or worse? Is reliance on the marketplace or on government planners a better way to make long-term policy decisions for the nation? What is the best way to balance the budget and curb inflation? Are foreign investors and international conglomerates shaping our lives as well as our economic policy decisions? Ideological debate and differences are always with us, but the nature of the issues changes, and there are likely to be even more changes as we approach the start of a new millennium.

IDEOLOGY AND THE AMERICAN PEOPLE

Despite the twists and turns of American politics, the distribution of ideology in our nation has been remarkably consistent in the past 20 years (see Closer Look box). There are more conservatives than liberals, but the proportion of conservatives did not increase substantially with the decisive Republican presidential victories of the 1980s.

One other important fact about ideology in the United States is that very few people see themselves as extreme conservatives or extreme liberals. In 1994, only 3 percent of the population saw themselves as extreme conservatives, and an even smaller percentage, 1 percent, saw themselves as extreme liberals. These percentages have changed very little over time. When given the option to describe themselves as "conservative" or "slightly conservative," 15 percent say "slightly conservative" and 18 percent say "conservative."[36] The same tendency is true of liberals. (We analyze party identification in Chapter 10, but it is important to note here that there are liberal and conservative wings in both parties.)

For those who have a liberal or conservative preference, ideology provides a lens through which to view politics. It helps simplify the complexities of politics, policies, personalities, and programs. An ideology may be an accurate or an inaccurate description of reality, yet it is still the way a person thinks about people, power, and society. For these reasons, it is important to understand how people view candidates, issues, and public policy. Ideology is even more important among

A Closer Look

HOW AMERICANS DEFINE THEIR IDEOLOGY

The most common measure of ideology is simply to ask people where they would place themselves on a liberal/conservative scale. Survey questions used to ascertain ideology permit respondents not only to answer "moderate" but also to indicate that they "don't know" their ideology or "have not thought much about it." The combined "moderate" and "don't know" categories are consistently much larger than either the conservative or liberal group and constitute a cluster more interested in pragmatism than ideology. In sum, most Americans are unconstrained by a consistent ideology.

What the Public Thinks It Means to Be a Liberal or a Conservative

Question: What sort of things do you have in mind when you say someone's political views are Liberal? (top five responses)

Accept change	38%
Favor social programs	20
Favor government spending/spend freely	17
Favor abortion	14
Favor freedom to do as one chooses/not interested in setting moral standards	11

Question: What sort of things do you have in mind when you say someone's political views are Conservative? (top five responses)

Resist change or new ideas	44%
Spend less freely/tight economic policy	18
Are slow or cautious in response to problems/do nothing	14
Oppose abortion	11
Support free enterprise/capitalism	13

SOURCE: Center for Political Studies, University of Michigan, *1992 National Election Study*.

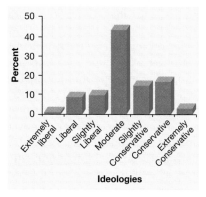

Ideology Curve

SOURCE: Center for Political Studies, University of Michigan, *1996 National Election Study*.

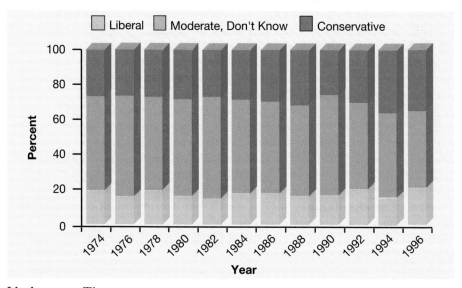

Ideology over Time

SOURCE: Center for Political Studies, University of Michigan, National Election Study Cumulative Data file, 1952–1992, *1994 National Election Study*, and *1996 National Election Study*.

Note: Those responding "don't know" or "haven't thought much about it" were included with the moderates.

legislators, lobbyists, and party activists. Their ideologies shape our social and political institutions and help determine public policies and constitutional change.

An alternative to the liberal/conservative self-identification measure of ideology is to ask people about their attitudes toward politicians and public policies. Most Americans do not organize their attitudes systematically. A voter may want increased spending for defense but vote for the party that is for reducing defense spending because he or she has always voted for that party or prefers its stand on the environment. Or a person may favor tax cuts and balancing the budget while not cutting spending substantially.

Consistency among various attitudes and opinions is often relatively low. Much of the time people view political issues as isolated matters and do not apply a general standard of performance in evaluating parties or candidates. Indeed, many citizens find it difficult to relate what happens in one policy situation to what happens in another. This problem becomes worse as government gets into more and more policy areas. Hence, many people, not surprisingly, have difficulty finding candidates who reflect their ideological preferences across a range of issues.

The absence of widespread and solidified liberal and conservative positions in the United States makes for politics and policy-making processes that are markedly different from those in many European and other nations. Our policy making is characterized more by coalitions of the moment than by fixed alignments that pit one set of ideologies against another. And our politics is marked more by moderation, pragmatism, and accommodation than by a prolonged battle between two, three, or more competing philosophies of government. Elsewhere, especially in countries where a strong Socialist or Christian Democratic party exists, things are different.

By no means, however, does this mean that policies or ideas are not elements in our politics. Such issues as affirmative action, the budget deficit, how to fund welfare, the Supreme Court's abortion rulings, health care reform, gun control, and environmental protection have aroused people who previously were passive about politics and political ideas.

"There's no justice in the world, Kirby, but I'm not convinced that this is an entirely bad thing."

Drawing by Handelsman. ©1986 The New Yorker Magazine, Inc.

IDEOLOGY AND TOLERANCE

Is there a connection between support for civil liberties and tolerance for racial minorities and the ideologies of liberalism and conservatism? Some political scientists assert that conservatives are generally less tolerant than liberals. This view is stoutly contested by conservatives, who have charged liberals with trying to impose a "politically correct" position on universities and the media. "Conservatives," observe Herbert McClosky and Alida Brill, "have repeatedly shown their fear of political and social instability. With rare exceptions, the conservatives have been the party of tradition, stability, duty, respect for authority, and the primacy of 'law and order' over all competing values."[37]

Liberals share many of these views but place a different emphasis on the interpretation. They have more faith in government and readily turn to government to help achieve greater equality of opportunity. Liberals are usually more tolerant of dissent and the expression of unorthodox opinions. However, liberals, too, can be intolerant—of anti-abortion forces, for example, or the National Rifle Association, or the views of Rush Limbaugh.

Most liberals are strongly opposed to crime and lawbreaking, yet they are as concerned about the roots or causes of crime as they are about the punishment of criminals. Perhaps for this reason, liberals exhibit somewhat greater concern than conservatives for the rights of the accused and are more willing to expand the rights of due process. Conservatives usually take a harder line and, in recent years, have won widespread popular support for their greater concern for the victims of crime than for the rights of the accused.

Such differences are most evident in the responses of liberals and conservatives to questions of civil rights and civil liberties. Research in the early 1980s found

Tolerance for the homosexual lifestyle is often a litmus test of liberal or conservative ideology. Although many religious groups view them as ungodly, these gay men and women do not see a conflict between their sexual orientation and their religion.

that, despite our common political culture and despite our widespread allegiance to constitutionalism and the Bill of Rights, many Americans sharply disagree on some basic political matters. Liberals are ordinarily more willing than conservatives to defend the rights of those who are in the minority, who may be wrong, or who take unorthodox or unpleasing stands.

In the area of free speech, conservatives are usually seen as less willing to permit speech that is out of the political or cultural mainstream. Perhaps conservatives are less tolerant because those who claimed to be exercising the right of free speech often attack established values. But the argument that liberalism is correlated with tolerance is more complicated and the evidence less persuasive, as some liberals want to suppress the speech of people they disagree with.

Conservatives believe that the United States has become too permissive. Many conservatives, especially in the New or Religious Right, are highly critical of homosexuals, drug users, prostitutes, unwed mothers, and pornographers. They worry about what they claim has been a decline in moral standards and, interestingly, call on government to help reverse these trends. Liberals, on the other hand, generally accept nonconformity in conduct and opinion as an inescapable by-product of freedom.[38] In this regard, liberals are like libertarians.

It is these sharp cleavages in political thinking that stir opposing interest groups into action. Groups such as the Christian Coalition, the American Civil Liberties Union, Amnesty International, Mothers Against Drunk Driving, Queer Nation, and countless others promote their views of what is politically desirable. It is also these differences in ideological perspectives that reinforce party loyalties and divide us at election time. Policy fights in Congress, between Congress and the White House, and during judicial confirmation hearings also have their roots in our uneasily coexisting ideological values.

Ideologies have consequences. Although Americans share many ideas in common, we as a people also hold many contradictory ideas. Our hard-earned rights and liberties are never entirely safeguarded; they are fragile and are shaped by the political, economic, and social climate of the day. In the next chapters we examine the interest groups and political parties that are ever-present to advance their values and compete in the always-evolving American political culture. Before turning to those topics, we will examine the social and economic diversity of the American political landscape in Chapter 8 and see why agreement on shared democratic values is all the more remarkable.

POLITICS ONLINE

In this chapter we discussed the idea that Americans are increasingly detached from each other—the so-called "bowling alone" idea. If people use the Internet as a mode of entertainment through which to look for information, shop, or pass their recreational time, this new technology will do little to reverse the trend of social disengagement. The stereotypical Internet "surfer" is antisocial, more interested in technology than people. Computer games, played in isolation from other people, would seem to reinforce this sense that Web users are isolated from one another.

But the Internet is also used by people to talk to each other through "chat rooms" that provide important organizing information, bring people together, and help mobilize voters. Examples of such "electronic communities" include environmental activists (ourworld.compuserve.com/homepages/stephen_south), libertarians (www.lp.org), the Christian Coalition (www.cc.org), women's groups (www.now.org), and many others.

Even with these "electronic communities," the question remains whether people learn the essential political skills of listening, compromise, accomodation, and mobilization through such a process. Face-to-face interactions may develop different interpersonal skills than chat lines do. To explore this idea, listen in or participate in one of these electronic conversations yourself.

SUMMARY

1. The United States, like every other nation or society, has a distinctive political culture. It consists of a widely held set of fundamental political values and accepted processes and institutions that help us manage conflict and resolve problems. In the United States, there is, at least in the abstract, respect for the Constitution, the Bill of Rights, a two-party system, and the right to elect officials on the basis of majority rule. Our belief in social equality has fostered acceptance of the notion that government should guarantee equality of opportunity through programs like education and job training.

2. Americans share a widespread commitment to classical liberalism, which embraces the importance of the individual and of freedom, equality, private property, limited government, and popular consent.

3. Perhaps the most notable tension in the American political culture is that we simultaneously believe in free market economics and a democratic society based on political equality. We want our economy to be relatively free from government controls and want major economic decisions to be shaped by the marketplace; yet we also want every American to enjoy the possibility of an equal voice in shaping our laws and policies, an ideal that may require government intervention.

4. American political values have been affected by the industrial transformation, the development of large corporations and other large institutions, the Great Depression, the rights revolution, and a global economy.

5. The sources of the American political culture include the family, the schools, religious and civic organizations, the mass media, and political activities.

6. Although many Americans are nonideological and are guided primarily by moderate pragmatism, a significant segment of Americans are conservatives or liberals.

7. There are at least four dimensions that shape a person's conservative or liberal views: the economy, civil rights and civil liberties, foreign and defense policy, and lifestyle.

8. The terms in use for conservative and liberal are numerous and often confusing. On the conservative side they include conservative, neoconservatives, religious right, and New Right. On the liberal side there are progressives, neoconservative-liberals, and old-fashioned liberals. Ideological terms change because they come in and out of favor and because some groups want to differentiate themselves from others in their ideological tradition and therefore invent a new name. The wide variety of terms is often more confusing than it is enlightening.

9. Our ideological orientation has a bearing on how tolerant we are of the views and conduct of others. Liberals tend to be more permissive, whereas conservatives generally favor tradition, stability, and greater levels of "law and order." These differences have consequences for electoral contests, judicial interpretation, and policy development in our political system.

FURTHER READING

DICK ARMEY, *The Freedom Revolution: The New Republican House Majority Leader Tells Why Big Government Failed, Why Freedom Works, and How We Rebuild America* (Regnery, 1995).

LEON P. BARADAT, *Political Ideologies: Their Origins and Impact*, 5th ed. (Prentice Hall, 1993).

WILLIAM F. BUCKLEY AND CHARLES R. KESLER, *Keeping the Tablets: Modern American Conservative Thought* (Harper & Row, 1988).

JAMES MACGREGOR BURNS, *Uncommon Sense* (Harper & Row, 1972).

JAMES CARVILLE, *We're Right, They're Wrong: A Handbook for Spirited Progressives* (Random House, 1996).

E.J. DIONNE, JR., *They Only Look Dead* (Simon & Schuster, 1996).

JOHN EHRMAN, *The Rise of Neoconservatism: Intellectuals and Foreign Affairs, 1945–1994* (Yale University Press, 1995).

DAVID FRUM, *What's Right* (HarperCollins, 1996).

NEWT GINGRICH, *To Renew America* (New York, HarperCollins, 1995).

LOUIS HARTZ, *The Liberal Tradition in America* (Harcourt Brace, 1955).

IRVING KRISTOL, *Neoconservatism: The Autobiography of an Idea* (Free Press, 1995).

IRVING KRISTOL, *Reflections of a Neoconservative: Looking Back, Looking Ahead* (Basic Books, 1983).

ROBERT KUTTNER, *The End of Laissez-Faire: National Purpose and the Global Economy after the Cold War* (Knopf, 1991).

HERBERT MCCLOSKY AND JOHN ZALLER, *The American Ethos: Public Attitudes Toward Capitalism and Democracy* (Harvard University Press, 1984).

KEVIN PHILLIPS, *Boiling Point: Democrats, Republicans, and the Decline of Middle-Class Prosperity* (Random House, 1993).

COLIN POWELL WITH JOSEPH E. PERSICO, *My American Journey* (Random House, 1995).

THEODORE SORENSEN, *Why I Am a Democrat* (Henry Holt, 1996).

8

The American
Political Landscape

A recent state court decision in Texas is a good example of the continuing national debate over issues of language and culture in the United States. During a child custody hearing in the summer of 1995, State District Judge Samuel C. Kiser, who is bilingual and minored in Spanish as a college student, ordered Marta Laureano to speak only English to her daughter at home. Until the hearing, Ms. Laureano spoke Spanish to her daughter, who is enrolled in her school's bilingual education program. During the hearing Judge Kiser accused Ms. Laureano of abusing her daughter because the family spoke only Spanish at home. He said, "There's lots of abuse and in my opinion, Ms. Laureano, you're abusing your child. If she starts first grade with the other children and cannot even speak the language that the teachers and the other children speak and she's a full-blood American citizen, you're abusing that child and you're relegating her to the position of a housemaid."

Texas Attorney General Dan Morales said Kiser's remarks were "way off base" and criticized him for "trivializing legitimate child abuse." Other critics went so far as to label Kiser a racist. Ms. Laureano, who has five children, defended her practice of speaking only Spanish at home because she wants her children to be bilingual so that they can communicate with Mexican relatives and have a competitive edge in two cultures. Judge Kiser defended his statement saying, "This is not a race issue. If you don't give your child as much help to get along in society as you possibly can, it is a form of abuse or neglect, one or the other." Ms. Laureano countered by saying, "This is a free country, and everybody who comes here brings something with them—their memories, their language, their culture. Nobody can take that away from us."[1]

This controversy is part of the continuing debate in the United States over language, culture, and politics. In recent decades, voters in Arizona, Colorado, California, and Florida voted overwhelmingly to make English—or as some insist, "American"—the official language. Nearly three out of four Californians and more than eight out of ten Floridians voted for English as the official language. Most states have considered similar measures.

What can we learn from these debates over language? Whatever side we choose in this debate, we have to be careful not to overgeneralize from our own experiences. Most of us do not stop to consider how people from other backgrounds might see things differently. This **ethnocentrism**—selective perception based on individual background, attitudes, and biases—is not uncommon among college students, who often assume that others share their economic opportunities, social attitudes, sense of civic responsibility, and self-confidence.

Albert Einstein once said few people are capable of expressing opinions that differ much from the prejudices of their social upbringing.[2] In this chapter we consider to what extent our social environment explains, or at least shapes, our opinions and prejudices. We also look at our diversity as Americans and the implications of geographic, social, and economic divisions for politics and government. Specifically, this chapter explores the effects of regional or state identity on political perspectives; the implications of differences in race, ethnicity, gender, sexual orientation, religion, wealth and income, occupation, and social class for opinions and voting choices; and the relationship between age and education and political participation.

A LAND OF DIVERSITY

Most nations consist of groups of people who have lived together for hundreds of years and who speak the same language, share the same concept of deity, and share a common history. Although Japan, for example, has some people from other nations, most of its citizens are Japanese in the fullest sense of the word, and it is the same in Germany, Sweden, Saudi Arabia, China, and France. The United States is different. We are largely a land of immigrants. We have attracted the poor and oppressed, as well as many talented newcomers, from all over the world, and we have been more open to accepting these people than have other nations.

One reason so many people want to come to the United States is that it is a land that holds a promise of religious, political, and economic freedom. It is also a place of opportunity for the enterprising. Our economic system has provided widespread (but not universal) opportunity for individuals to improve their economic standing. The American Dream—that everyone can "make it"—is widely shared.

Some elements of our diversity have become traditions that have political significance. Sectional differences persist between the South and the rest of the country, in part because of tradition. Third- or fourth-generation Americans may retain an identity with the native land of their ancestors even though their spouses and neighbors do not share that identity. Holding onto our differences is often the result of socialization in our families, churches, and other closely knit groups. **Political socialization** is the process by which parents and others teach children about the values, beliefs, and attitudes of a political culture. This teaching occurs during interactions in the family, on the playground, in the neighborhood.

Because where we live and who we are in terms of our religion and occupation affect how we vote, many who study voting and make predictions about it do so in terms of these factors, referred to as **demographics**. A political predisposition is a characteristic of individuals that is predictive of political behavior. Although demographics can be important, as this chapter and those that follow demonstrate, there are large individual differences within socioeconomic and demographic categories.

When social and economic differences coincide, they reinforce each other and make the differences more important. Social scientists call these differences **reinforcing cleavages**, and experience predicts that when this occurs, political conflict becomes more intense and there is greater polarization in society. Nations can also have **cross-cutting cleavages**, instances where differences do not reinforce each other. To illustrate, let's look at religion and income. If all the better-off individuals in a society were of one religion and the poor another, we would have reinforcing cleavages, and political conflict would be intensified. But if there were both rich and poor in all religions, and if people sometimes voted on the basis of their religion and sometimes on the basis of their wealth, then we would say the divisions are cross-cutting. American diversity has generally been more of the cross-cutting type than the cleavage type, lessening political conflict because individuals have multiple allegiances.

In some societies, politics centers largely around passions over economic and religious differences. In Northern Ireland, for instance, the religious differences between Catholics and Protestants produced a violent division. Although socioeconomic differences are important to understanding American government and politics, they are not as central to the form and structure of politics as religion is in Bosnia or tribal identity in Rwanda.

Americans, in the past as well as today, are not always tolerant of people from a different religion, class, or race. We often associate only with people "like us" and are suspicious of people "like them." From hostility toward German-speaking immigrants in the early colonies, to the anti-immigration movements of the late 1800s and early 1900s, to the anti-immigration and anti-civil rights ballot initiatives of the 1990s, Americans have sometimes exhibited ethnocentrism. For much of our history, minorities have been excluded from full participation in American political and economic life. Recently, Americans have begun to take greater pride in their racial, ethnic, and religious traditions and cultures. As discussed at the beginning of this chapter, language is increasingly seen as part of a group's identity, an identity that minorities want to protect legally. Whether groups seek to assimilate or maintain a strong group identity is much debated within such groups and in the society at large.

WHERE WE ARE FROM

You may have often been asked, "Where are you from?" In certain settings you answer the United States; in others, you may say Illinois, California, or Idaho; and in still others, Dallas, Brooklyn, or North Las Vegas. Where you are from can be important to your personal political identity, attached at the levels of town, city, state, and nation. Where you are from is also important to politics, because the history, economy, and social makeup of cities, states, and regions differ.

Geography and National Identity

The United States is a geographically large and historically isolated country. As Alexis de Tocqueville observed in 1835, the country has no major political or economic powers on its borders "and consequently [has] no great wars, financial crises, invasions, or conquests to fear."[3] Geographic isolation from the major powers of the world during our government's formative period helps explain American politics. The Atlantic Ocean served as a barrier to foreign meddling, giving us time to establish our political tradition and develop our economy. It also reinforced our sense of isolation from Europe and foreign alliances.

In our entire history we have fought only one foreign enemy on our own soil—England in the War of 1812. (The war with Mexico of 1846–48 was fought on Mexican land, some of which later became American land as a result of the war. The only other war fought on our soil was, of course, the Civil War.) In contrast, during the same period, Poland was invaded and eventually partitioned by Austria, Prussia, and Russia. The difference is largely explained by location: Poland was surrounded by Europe's great powers. Had the United States been closer to Europe, it may have been overrun like Poland, and our Constitution and institutions

Part of our national identity is bound up with the physical isolation many families endured as pioneers. This family was seeking a new home in Nebraska in 1886.

repeatedly changed to suit the invaders. Having powerful and aggressive neighbors makes it difficult for relatively weak nations to nurture democracy.

The United States is a large country. Its land mass exceeds that of all but three nations in the world. In contrast, India has a population more than three times larger than the United States on a land mass one-third the size. Geographic space gave the expanding population of the United States room to spread out. This meant that some of the political conflicts arising from religion, social class, and national origin were diffused because groups could isolate themselves from one another. (See James Madison, *The Federalist*, No. 10, in the Appendix, for a development of the large republic idea.) Moreover, the large and accessible land mass helped foster the perspective that the United States had a **manifest destiny** to be a continental nation reaching from the Atlantic to the Pacific oceans. This notion that the United States was "destined" to expand across the continent was used to justify taking land occupied by Native Americans and Mexicans, especially the land acquired following victory in the Mexican-American War.

The United States is a land of abundant natural resources. We have rich farmland, which not only feeds our population but makes us one of the three major exporters of food in the world. We are rich in such natural resources as coal, iron, uranium, and many precious metals. All these resources enhance economic growth, provide jobs, and stabilize government. "The physical causes, unconnected with laws, which can lead to prosperity are more numerous in America than in any other country at any other time in history," observed Alexis de Tocqueville. "In the United States not legislation alone is democratic, for Nature herself seems to work for the people."[4]

Geography also helps explain our diversity. Parts of the United States are wonderfully suited to agriculture, others to mining or ranching, and still others to shipping. These differences produce different regional economic concerns, which in turn influence politics. For instance, a person from the agricultural heartland may have a different perception of foreign trade than an automobile worker in Detroit. In addition, that automobile worker may be African American, a fact that may be more important than what she does or where she lives. To understand American politics, we must appreciate these differences.

In the United States—unlike Canada, Eastern Europe, and India—geography does not define an ethnic division. All the Serbs do not live in one place, all French-speaking Catholics in another, and all German immigrants in another. Sectional differences in the United States are primarily geographic, not ethnic or religious.

Sectional Differences

The most distinct section of the United States remains the South, although the South's differences are diminishing. From the beginning of the Republic, the agricultural South differed from the industrial North, but the most important difference between the regions was the southern institution of slavery. Northern opposition to slavery, which grew increasingly intense in the middle of the nineteenth century, reinforced the sectional economic interests that divided the nation. The 11 Confederate states, by virtue of their decision to secede from the Union, reinforced a common political identity that persists more than a century after the Civil War.

Sectional differences were strengthened by the policy of Reconstruction, the region's common economic interests, and especially the problems of race relations. The Civil War was fought over the issue of state self-determination in such matters as slavery. When the North won the war, African Americans were emancipated, but they were not politically, socially, or economically integrated. They did not, for example, have equal voting rights; as recently as 1960, only 5 percent of African Americans in Mississippi were registered to vote.[5]

Things have changed in the last few decades, and as a result the South is becoming less distinct today. The large migration of persons from outside the region who have moved to the former Confederate states has somewhat diminished the sense of regional identity. But the South has also undergone tremendous change. The civil rights revolution gave African Americans the right to vote, opened up new educational opportunities, and helped to integrate the South into the national economy. African Americans still lag behind whites in voter registration, but the gap is now no wider in the South than elsewhere and is explained more by differences in education than by race.[6] In economic terms, the South still falls below the rest of the country in per capita income and education, but much less so than 50 years ago. The religious and moral conservatism of the South remains notable.

Until recently, political observers spoke of the "solid South," a region that voted for Democrats at all levels. The reason for the connection between the South and Democrats is simple: "The Civil War made the Democratic party the party of the South, and the Republican party, the party of the North."[7] The Democratic "solid South" was to remain a fixture of American politics for more than a century. Since 1968 that has changed dramatically, first at the presidential level and increasingly at the state and local levels. As two respected observers of the region comment, "The fall of the South as an assured stronghold of the Democratic party in presidential elections is one of the most significant developments in modern American politics."[8] In 1984 and 1988, for instance, no southern state supported the Democratic ticket. The 1992 election was the first ever won by the Democrats in which they did not carry a majority of southern states. Even Bill Clinton and his fellow southern running mate, Al Gore, could win only four southern states in 1992. In 1996 Clinton and Gore again carried four of the formerly Confederate states—Arkansas, Louisiana, and Tennessee, which they had won in 1992, plus Florida.

What explains this dramatic reversal? Part of the explanation is that the Democrats' advocacy of aggressive action on civil rights in the 1960s alienated some southern whites. In addition, the debate within the Democratic party over Vietnam policy in the 1970s was "perceived by many southern voters as unpatriotic."[9] Republican presidential candidates have more recently exploited social and law-and-order issues that appeal to conservative southern voters.

Republican success at the presidential level was slow to reach contests for Congress and was less evident in state legislative races. The 1994 Republican landslide saw Republicans win 58 percent of southern votes for the U.S. House of Representatives (see Table 8–1) and swept them to governorships in 6 of the 11 former Confederate states. Republicans picked up another southern governorship in 1995 in Louisiana, while Democrats continued to hold the North Carolina governorship in 1996. The Republican share of U.S. House votes dropped to 53 percent in 1996. At the state legislative level in several southern states, the remnants of the old "solid South" remain but Republicans have made major inroads, and politics in the region is now much more competitive. Republicans continued the steady climb in state legislatures, reaching 44 percent of state house and senate members following the 1996 elections.

Other sectional differences have political importance. Alexis de Tocqueville saw the New England Puritan spirit as significant.[10] More recently, the West has developed an identity of individualism, hostility to government intervention, and belief in self-sufficiency. It was especially fertile ground for Ronald Reagan, who seemed to personify western values and swept the Rocky Mountain and Pacific Coast states in both 1980 and 1984.

Another common sectional division is the sun belt/frost belt (see map). Sun belt states have been growing in population much more rapidly than the rest of the country, in part because they are attractive places for retirees. As a result of population shifts revealed by the 1990 census, the sun belt states gained 17 seats in

TABLE 8–1

Voting Patterns in the Eleven Former Confederate States

Republican Vote for President

1980	50%
1984	62
1988	59
1992	43
1996	46

Republican Vote for U.S. Representatives

1980	40%
1982	39
1984	42
1986	41
1988	42
1990	43
1992	48
1994	58
1996	53*

Republican Share of State Legislators

	House	Senate
1980	18%	17%
1982	22	14
1984	23	17
1986	24	20
1988	27	24
1990	28	26
1992	31	31
1994	37	37
1996	44	44

SOURCES: U.S. Bureau of the Census, *Statistical Abstract of the United States, 1995* (Government Printing Office, 1995), pp. 273, 275; *Statistical Abstract of the United States, 1993*, p. 279; *Statistical Abstract of the United States, 1989*, p. 254; *Statistical Abstract of the United States, 1987*, p. 239; *Congressional Quarterly Report*, November 9, 1996, pp. 3250–3257.

*The 1996 Texas runoff elections are not included.

From Coast to Coast

Sun Belt/Frost Belt States

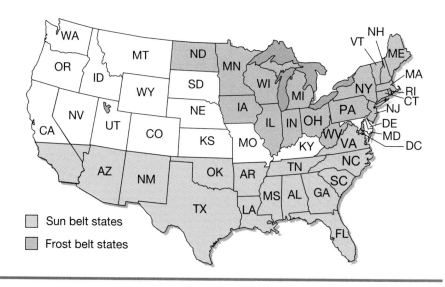

the U.S. Congress, while frost belt states lost 15 seats. However, this population growth in the South and West is occurring in different age groups. In the South, population growth is largest among those over 65; in the West, it is younger persons who provide the growth. Sun belt states have also experienced greater economic growth as industries headed south and southwest, where land is cheaper and more abundant, and where labor is cheaper as well (see Figure 8–1).

State and Local Identity

Americans move often, and they quickly become identified with the politics of the state in which they now live. Mention Wyoming, Mississippi, Oregon, New York, or Kansas, and it brings to mind a certain type of politics. The same is true for many other states. Like most stereotypes, these images are often misleading, but they reflect the fact that there is a sense of identity to states as political units that is supported by recent empirical evidence. States have distinctive political cultures that go beyond demographic characteristics, and each unique culture affects public opinion and policy outcomes in each state.[11] These state identities are reinforced by our electoral rules and other laws.

In American politics today, one state—California—stands out. More than one out of eight Americans is a Californian.[12] In terms of economic and political importance, California is in a league by itself; its 52 members of the House of Representatives exceed the total number of representatives from the smallest 20 states. No presidential candidate can afford to lose California's 54 electoral votes.[13] Californians like Richard Nixon and Ronald Reagan helped deliver these electoral votes to the Republicans in several elections since 1952. Hard hit by the recession, California went solidly for Clinton in 1992, helping to push him to victory. Clinton visited California often during his first term and claimed credit for "the golden state's" recovery. Despite some last-minute campaigning by Dole, Clinton carried California easily in 1996, getting 51 percent of the vote, compared to Dole's 38 percent.

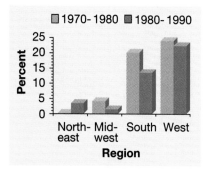

FIGURE 8–1 Population Gains by Region, 1970–1990

SOURCE: U.S. Bureau of the Census, *Statistical Abstract of the United States, 1992* (Government Printing Office, 1993), p. 48.

The Kinds of Places in Which We Live

Americans live in four kinds of places—central cities, suburbs, small communities, and rural areas. Most Americans, 80 percent of them, now live in central cities and their suburbs—what the Census Bureau calls *metropolitan areas*. During the early twentieth century, the movement of population was from rural areas to central cities, but the movement since the 1950s has been to the suburbs. During the 1970s and 1980s, Americans kept moving farther and farther out from the central cities to new suburbs. Today the most urban state is California (92.6 percent); Vermont is the least urban, with only 32 percent living in cities or suburbs. Regionally, the West and Northeast are the most urban, the South and Midwest the most rural. The four-fifths of the population that now lives in cities and suburbs occupies only 2.5 percent of the nation's land (see Figure 8–2). Nine of the largest 25 cities have lost population over the previous decade,[14] a continuation of a trend since World War II.

There are many reasons people leave the cities to move to the suburbs—better housing, new transportation systems that make it easier to get to work, the desire for cleaner air and safer streets, and *white flight*, the movement of whites away from the central cities so that their children can attend predominantly white schools and avoid being bused for racial integration. White, middle-class migration to the suburbs means that American cities have become increasingly poor, increasingly African American, and increasingly Democratic. Half of all African Americans now live in central cities, as opposed to only about one-quarter of whites. The proportions are very nearly reversed for suburbs, where more than half of all white Americans reside. Almost one-third of American suburbanites are now African American, up from one-fifth in 1980.[15]

In such large cities as Washington, D.C., Detroit, Baltimore, Atlanta, and New Orleans, the city population is now more than 50 percent African American (see Table 8–2). Hispanics constitute nearly two-thirds of the population of El Paso, Texas, and Santa Anna, California, and more than half of the population of Miami

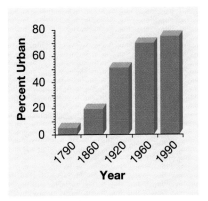

FIGURE 8–2   A Changing Landscape as America Becomes Urban

SOURCE: U.S. Bureau of the Census, *Population Profile of the United States, 1993* (Government Printing Office, 1993), p. 8.

TABLE 8–2

Cities with Populations of 100,000 or More That Are at Least 50 Percent African American, 1996

	Population	Percent African American
Atlanta, Ga.	394,000	67%
Baltimore, Md.	736,000	59
Birmingham, Ala.	265,000	63
Detroit, Mich.	1,028,000	76
Gary, Ind.	117,000	81
Inglewood, Calif.	110,000	52
Jackson, Miss.	197,000	56
Macon, Ga.	107,000	52
Memphis, Tenn.	619,000	55
Newark, N.J.	275,000	59
New Orleans, La.	497,000	62
Richmond, Va.	203,000	55
Savannah, Ga.	138,000	51
Washington, D.C.	607,000	66

SOURCE: U.S. Bureau of the Census, *Statistical Abstract of the United States, 1996* (Government Printing Office, 1996), pp. 44–46.

Urban areas are attracting ever-increasing numbers of people, who like the job opportunities, tempo, diversity, cultural attractions, and sophistication they find there.

and San Antonio.[16] As population shifts occur, the tax base of cities declines because the richer people have gone to the suburbs, where they now pay local sales and property taxes. At the same time, service needs in the cities increase as the remaining less affluent population must pay for education, police protection, and health care.

Metropolitan areas are much larger than central cities. More than four times as many people live in the metropolitan area of Los Angeles as actually live in the city.[17] Half the nation's population live in the 32 largest metropolitan areas of more than 1 million in population.[18] While people from the Chicago metropolitan area have some things in common—like an affinity for the Chicago Bulls basketball team—the characteristics of metropolitan areas as a whole can be quite different from the characteristics of the city.

Suburbs vary in relative affluence. Many older ones now face the same problems as the inner cities, but their populations typically have higher per capita income, fewer minorities, and more Republicans. Companies employing professionals or engaging in high-tech or service activities frequently relocate to the suburbs to avoid city congestion and to be closer to the bedroom communities of their workers. Political boundaries, which define local governments and delineate responsibility for services, create understandable tensions among cities, suburbs, and rural areas. Tax revenues, legislative representation, zoning laws, and governmental priorities are hotly contested issues on the local level.

WHO WE ARE

Race and Ethnicity

Among the most important distinctions in American politics are race and ethnicity. Our history as a nation of immigrants and our struggle with race relations have reinforced the importance of these differences, and they have become part of our political debate. **Race** can be defined as a grouping of human beings with common characteristics presumed to be transmitted genetically. **Ethnicity** is a social division based on national origin, religion, and language, often within the same race, and includes a sense of attachment to that group. In the United States, race issues focus on African Americans, Asians, and Hispanics, although Hispanics can be of any race.

About three out of four Americans are white, according to census estimates. The largest nonwhite racial group is African Americans. There are more than 33 million African Americans in the United States, roughly 13 percent of the population. Asian Americans constitute just under 4 percent of the population, and Native Americans just under 1 percent. Most American Hispanics are classified as white by the Census Bureau. The Census Bureau estimates that there are 27 million American Hispanics, constituting over 10 percent of the population.[19]

The racial and ethnic diversity of the American polity will only increase over time, due to different birth rates across different groups as well as different immigration patterns. Between 1981 and 1991, the white population experienced a natural increase (births minus deaths) of just under 5 percent, while American Indians, Asians and Pacific Islanders, and Hispanics all had natural increase rates of around 20 percent. African Americans were in between, at 14 percent.[20] The Census Bureau has projected that by the year 2050, whites will decline from over 75 percent of the total population today to just over half. The political system will have to accommodate this transformation.

AFRICAN AMERICANS Folklore tells us that people came to this country because it was a land of freedom and opportunity. For many it was, but for most African Americans it was the opposite. They came as slaves. African Americans were freed

We the People

Percentage of the Population by Race and Origin

	1990	1995	2000	2025	2050
White	83.9%	83.0%	82.1%	78.3%	74.8%
African American	12.3	12.6	12.9	14.2	15.4
American Indian, Eskimo, Aleut	0.8	0.9	0.9	1.0	1.1
Asian and Pacific Islander	3.0	3.5	4.1	6.6	8.7
Hispanic	9.0	10.3	11.4	17.6	24.5

SOURCE: U.S. Bureau of the Census, *Statistical Abstract of the United States, 1996* (Government Printing Office, 1996), p. 14.

Percentages do not equal 100 percent because Hispanics can be of any race. Figures for 2000, 2025, and 2050 are projections.

as a result of the Civil War, but race relations and racial divisions have been enduring issues of American politics.[21] (Many of the important civil rights cases and controversies are described in Chapter 5.)

Until 1900, more than 90 percent of all African Americans lived in the South.[22] In 1995 the figure was 52 percent.[23] Put another way, about 20 percent of the people in the South are African American. South Carolina, Alabama, Mississippi, and Louisiana are more than 30 percent African American. Two-thirds of the citizens of the District of Columbia are African American.

Many African Americans left the South after the turn of the century, hoping to improve their lives by settling in the large cities of the Northeast, Midwest, and West. The migration from the South was substantial: 4.5 million more African Americans left the South than migrated to it between the mid-1940s and late 1960s.[24] By the 1960s, many African Americans were living in poverty in large cities, without the economic and social resources to take advantage of recently won legal opportunities. More recently, some African Americans have been returning to the South, especially to its urban areas.

In economic terms, African Americans are much worse off than whites in the United States. African American median family income in 1995 was $24,698, compared to $40,884 for whites. About one-third of African Americans are below the poverty level, compared to 11 percent of whites.[25] Another way to measure economic well-being is in terms of assets or wealth. African Americans' net wealth is only one-tenth that of whites, and Hispanics have only slightly more wealth than African Americans (see Figure 8–3). As a result, African Americans and Hispanics have fewer resources to fall back on in hard times, and they are less likely to have the savings to help a child pay for college.[26] Some African Americans have become relatively prosperous: 17.1 percent of African American households had earnings in 1994 of over $50,000, a proportion still only half of the number for whites.[27] Some African Americans have risen to the top in earnings in their fields of endeavor. Athletes like Michael Jordan and Ken Griffey, Jr., and entertainers like Bill Cosby, Whitney Houston, and Oprah Winfrey are examples.

Middle-class African Americans provide role models and leadership to the civil rights movement, yet their comparatively small number in the past serves as a

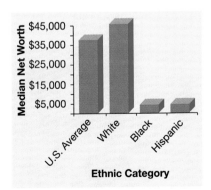

FIGURE 8–3   Wealth Distribution in the United States by Race

SOURCE: U.S. Bureau of the Census Home Page (http://www.census.gov/ftp/pub/hhes/wealth/wlth93f.html).

reminder that most African Americans remain behind whites in an economy that relies more and more on education and job skills. About 24 percent of whites graduate from college, whereas only about 13 percent of African Americans do.[28] Among 18-to-21-year-old high school graduates, 46 percent of whites go on to college but only 32 percent of African Americans.[29] Finally, the African American population is much younger than the white population; the 1994 median age for whites was 35.3, compared to 29.2 for African Americans.[30] The combination of the younger African American population, the lower level of education among African Americans, and the concentration of African Americans in economically hard-pressed urban areas has resulted in a much higher unemployment rate for young African Americans. Unemployment, in turn, leads to social problems like crime and drug abuse.

African Americans have had limited rights and little political power for most of the period since emancipation. Owing their freedom to the "party of Lincoln," most African Americans initially identified with the Republicans.[31] This loyalty started to change with Franklin Roosevelt, who insisted on equal treatment for African Americans in his New Deal programs.[32] In the period after World War II, African Americans came to see the Democrats as the party of civil rights. This perception was reinforced by the 1964 presidential campaign, in which the Democratic nominee, Lyndon Johnson, took credit for the Civil Rights Act of 1964, which his Republican opponent, Barry Goldwater, had voted against. The 1964 Republican platform position on civil rights espoused states' rights—then the creed of southern segregationists—in what appeared to be an effort to win the support of southern white voters. Virtually all African Americans voted for Johnson in 1964; and in presidential elections between 1964 and 1996, their Democratic vote has averaged 85 percent.[33]

Recently, African Americans have become much more important politically because of their increased level of voter participation and their concentrated population. African Americans constitute only .2 percent of Montana and .4 percent of Idaho, Maine, and South Dakota, but 36 percent of Mississippi, 31 percent of Louisiana, and 30 percent of South Carolina.[34] Southern senators and representatives can no longer afford to ignore the African American vote.[35] Evidence of growing African American political power is the dramatic increase in the number of African American state legislators, a number that rose from 168 in 1970 to 575 in 1996.[36]

ASIAN AMERICANS Asian Americans are a heterogeneous group of persons classified together by the census for statistical purposes but with significant differences in culture, language, and political experience in the United States. The group includes persons of Chinese, Japanese, Korean, Vietnamese, and Filipino origin, as well as persons from the Pacific Islands (see Table 8–3). In 1994, the United States was home to more than 9 million Asian Americans and Pacific Islanders, residing primarily in the western states, especially Hawaii, California, and Washington.[37] Asian Americans are the most successful racial group economically and educationally. More than two out of every five Asian Americans have graduated from college, compared to just over one of every five white Americans.[38]

The numbers of Asian Americans grew during the 1970s and 1980s, largely as a result of Southeast Asian immigration. In the 1990 census, persons from Asia had climbed to one of four of all foreign-born persons living in the United States, and the Philippines was surpassed only by Mexico as the country of birth for foreign-born persons living in this country. Immigration from the Pacific Islands more than doubled during the 1980s. Most persons in this group reside in three states: California, New York, and Hawaii. Pacific Islanders are also a diverse group in terms of language and culture. In states with heavy concentrations of Asian immi-

Gary Locke, newly elected Democratic governor of Washington State, is the first Asian American to be elected governor in the continental United States.

grants, these groups are now becoming more politically important and visible in politics. In Washington in 1996, for example, Gary Locke was the first Chinese American to be elected governor of a state in the continental United States.

NATIVE AMERICANS Centuries ago, explorers sailed west looking for another passage to India. Colonists followed, often holding grants of land from their own government—grants they believed gave them a right to land in the New World. However, by virtue of prior usage, the land belonged to "Indians," the tribal peoples who had long inhabited the land. As settlers moved west, colonial leaders dealt with Indian representatives to obtain land for colonists and to reserve certain lands for Native Americans.

The Native American population today is more than 2 million.[39] Native Americans have incomes well below those of other Americans, and Native American families are generally twice as likely to be below the poverty level as are African Americans or whites.[40] Native Americans are below the rest of the nation in the proportion of persons completing high school; the proportion completing college is roughly half that of the rest of the population.[41] In western States like Colorado and Idaho, Native Americans have won statewide elections. Colorado's Senator Ben Nighthorse Campbell is an example at the national level.

HISPANICS/LATINOS Hispanics (persons of Spanish-speaking descent) are defined by the U.S. Census Bureau as an ethnic group, and they can be of any race. For example, the president of Peru, Alberto Fujimori, is Hispanic of Japanese ancestry. Even if the Spanish-speaking descent is one or more generations removed (grandparents or great-grandparents), that person is still considered Hispanic.

The terms "Latino" and "Chicano" are preferred by some persons of Spanish-speaking descent, in part because they lack association with Spain, a colonial power against which many fought wars of independence, and "the term 'Hispanic' emphasizes the white European culture of Spain."[42] "Hispanic" is the term most widely used by government agencies and the media, while "Latino" appears more popular among leaders of the group. "Chicano" is often associated with the politically active Mexican American movement of the 1960s and 1970s. Most Mexican Americans, Puerto Rican Americans, and Cuban Americans prefer to be called American rather than Latino or Hispanic.[43]

Latinos are not a monolithic group, and while they share a common linguistic heritage, they often differ from one another, depending on which country they emigrated from (see Table 8–4). Cuban Americans, for instance, tend to be Republicans, while Mexican Americans and Puerto Ricans are disproportionately Democrats.[44] Socioeconomically, Cuban Americans approximate the white population, while Puerto Rican Americans and Mexican Americans are generally at the lower end of the scale.[45] Socially, Latinos divide up along these lines as well, and there can be intense rivalry among Hispanic groups. Politically, Latinos can differ on their levels of support, depending on whether the candidate is from Puerto Rico, Cuba, or Mexico.

A recent study of Latinos found differences among Latinos of Mexican, Puerto Rican, and Cuban descent in partisanship, ideology, and rates of participation but widespread support for a liberal domestic agenda, including increased spending on health care, crime and drug control, education, the environment, child services, and bilingual education.[46] Given the overall growth of the Latino population, it is not surprising that both major parties have aggressively sought to cultivate Hispanic candidates. Two Hispanics have won elections to the U.S. Senate, both from New Mexico, and President Clinton has had several Hispanics in his cabinet.

The divisions among Latinos are politically important because of the tendency of the groups to settle in different areas. Nearly two-thirds of Cuban immigrants live in Florida, especially greater Miami; Puerto Rican immigrants are concen-

TABLE 8–3

Ethnic Asian Population in the United States (in thousands)

	1980	1990
Japanese	701	848
Chinese	806	1,645
Indian	362	815
Korean	355	799
Filipino	755	1,407
Total	**226,546**	**248,710**

SOURCE: U.S. Bureau of the Census, *Statistical Abstract of the United States, 1993* (Government Printing Office, 1993), Table 18, p. 18.

Anger Against Immigrants Overflows

In his greasy auto mechanic's clothing and beat-up Datsun pickup truck, Eddie Cortez hardly looks like the mayor of a large American city. So when Immigration and Naturalization Service agents pulled him over, little did they suspect that the brown-skinned man they were threatening to deport was not only a citizen but the first Latino mayor of Pomona, California.

"I actually got pulled over and harassed, rousted, questioned, and threatened," said Cortez, a Mexican American and a conservative Republican, "If I hadn't identified myself, I was going to get thrown in the van with—as they put it—'the rest of them.' "

Cortez's story is echoing through immigrant and civil rights organizations in California and sounding a chord with many citizens and immigrants, legal and illegal. Up and down the coast, people are talking about the insults and indignities they are suffering as the anti-immigration movement explodes.

- Heriberio Camargo, a 16-year-old San Diego resident, was stopped by border officials as he was walking out of a corner store. When he failed to show them his birth certificate, they handcuffed him and placed him in a van. Neighbors alerted his mother, who came running down the street with his birth certificate. He was then released.

- Irma Munoz, a 20-year-old engineering student at the University of California at Davis, was reportedly attacked by two white males. "They insulted me. They beat me, and they wrote things on my arms and leg [that] they said I should always remember, [such as] 'Go home illegal wetback,'" Munoz said.

SOURCE: Suzanne Espinosa, Benjamin Pimentel, Susan Yoachim, and Nanette Asimov, *San Francisco Chronicle*, August 27, 1993, pp. 1, 6; also *San Francisco Chronicle*, October 22, 1993, pp. 1, 4.

TABLE 8–4
Persons of Hispanic Origin in the United States (in thousands)

	1980	1990	1995
Mexican	8,740	13,496	17,982
Puerto Rican	2,014	2,728	2,730
Cuban	803	1,044	1,156
Central/South American	N/A	N/A	3,686
Other*	3,051	5,086	1,967
Total	**226,546**	**248,710**	**262,755**

SOURCE: U.S. Bureau of the Census, *Statistical Abstract of the United States, 1993* (Government Printing Office, 1993), Table 16, p. 17; U.S. Bureau of the Census, *Statistical Abstract of the United States, 1996* (Government Printing Office, 1996), Table 53, p. 51.

*Includes Central and South America in 1980 and 1990 figures.

---

trated in or around New York City, and Mexican American immigrants in the southwest and California. The Census Bureau estimated in 1995 that more than 9.1 million Hispanics live in California alone.[47]

The issue of illegal aliens became the focus of a much publicized ballot initiative in California in 1994—Proposition 187. California voters, by a margin of 59 percent to 41 percent, adopted a measure that would deny most state spending on illegal immigrants. The constitutionality of the initiative was immediately challenged in court.

THE TIES OF ETHNICITY Except for Native Americans, all Americans are immigrants or are descended from immigrants. The largest number of immigrants came between 1900 and 1924, when 17.3 million people relocated to the United States—by far the largest immigration to one country in any quarter-century in human history. From 1991 to 1994, there were more than 4.5 million immigrants.[48] This new wave of immigrants comes primarily from Latin America, especially the Caribbean and Mexico, and from Asian countries such as the Philippines, Vietnam, and China. The foreign-born proportion of the U.S. population increased during the 1980s, rising from 14 million in 1980 to 20 million in 1990, the largest number of foreign-born in U.S. history. Table 8–5 shows the origin of foreign-born population in 1980 and 1990. Note that among U.S. foreign-born, the proportion of Asian and Mexican immigrants has pulled even with or surpassed the number of Europeans. Having large numbers of immigrants can pose challenges to any political and social system. They are often the source of social conflict as they compete with more established groups for jobs, rights, political power, and influence.

Politically important ethnic groups in the United States include Irish Americans, Italian Americans, German Americans, Polish Americans, Hispanic Americans, and Greek Americans. The country's early settlers were generally English-speaking Protestants; even today, people of English, Scottish, and Welsh background make up the largest ethnic group in the United States. Irish immigrants, largely Catholics, started coming before the potato famine in the 1840s and came in larger numbers after it. They experienced economic exploitation and religious bigotry. The Irish American response was often to retreat among themselves, forming a strong ethnic group consciousness. Other ethnic groups that followed—Italians, Greeks, Chinese—each experienced a similar cycle: flight from their homeland and happy arrival here, then discrimination, exploitation, residential clustering, and the formation of a strong group identity.

Ethnic group identity is often persistent. In certain ethnic sections of large cities, people still converse in their native languages and shop in ethnic specialty stores. Ethnic groups gain in political importance as they become more affluent; eventually they support candidates "of their own kind," ultimately electing mayors, governors, or even presidents.

Gender

For most of U.S. history, politics and government were men's business. As discussed in Chapter 5, women gained the right to vote primarily in the western territories, beginning with Wyoming in 1869 and Utah in 1870, and then in Colorado and Idaho before the turn of the century.[49] The right was extended nationally with passage of the Nineteenth Amendment in 1920. The fears of some opponents of women's suffrage—that women would form their own party and vote largely for women or fundamentally alter our political system—have not been realized. During Susan B. Anthony's suffrage campaign, Jonas H. Upton, editor of the *Democratic Salem Monitor* in Salem, Oregon, contended that women, if given the right to vote, would combine to vote for war because they were exempt from the draft.[50] Others said women would unite to vote for prohibition.[51]

Instead of voting as a bloc, women have typically divided their vote between the two major political parties. However, in 1992 and 1996 women were more likely than men to vote for Clinton and less likely to vote for Perot (see Figure 8–4). For most of the period after gaining the right to vote, they voted at a lower rate than women in other Western democracies, but this trend appears to be changing.[52] For the past twenty years, women have voted at nearly the same rate as men, with the result that in recent elections, because females in the population outnumber males, the female vote has outnumbered the male vote.[53] Women have chosen to work within the existing political parties and do not overwhelmingly support female candidates, especially if they must cross parties to do so.

The numbers of women elected to public office have been low; since 1917, less than 6 percent of representatives in the U.S. House have been women. A high point came after the 1992 election, when the number of women elected to the House of Representatives reached 47 and the number of women in the Senate rose to 6. The number of women in the House remained at its all time high after the 1994 elections, and the number of women serving in the Senate rose to 8. Following the 1996 election, the number of women in the U.S. House rose to 52 and the number in the Senate reached 9. There were 2 female governors—Christine Whitman in New Jersey and Jeanne Shaheen in New Hampshire. Barbara Burrell argues that women win office as often as men when they run under similar circumstances, and the rising number of women holding office is due to more women running for office, especially for *open seats*—contests with no incumbent running.[54]

Abortion has been a significant issue for decades, but the women's movement in American politics encompasses a comprehensive agenda, including voting and political rights as well as extending the basic liberties of the Bill of Rights and Fourteenth Amendment. In addition to rights and liberties, women seek equal opportunity, education, jobs, skills, respect, and self-esteem in what has been a male-dominated system.[55]

There are serious inequalities between men and women in income. About 73 percent more women than men work at or below the minimum wage.[56] In 1993, 45 percent of women earned less than $10,000 compared to only 25 percent of men.[57] While women now earn on average only about 70 cents for every dollar earned by men, this figure has improved from the 60 cents for every dollar in 1980.[58] Because an increasing number of women today are the sole breadwinners for their families, the implications of this low income level are even more significant. The problem

TABLE 8–5
Origin of Foreign-Born Population, 1980 and 1990 (in thousands)

	1980	1990
European	4,743	4,812
Asian	2,540	5,412
Mexican	2,199	4,447
Caribbean	1,258	1,987
Central American*	354	1,103
South American	561	1,107
African	200	401
Total	**14,080**	**21,632**

SOURCE: U.S. Bureau of the Census, *Statistical Abstract of the United States* (Government Printing Office, 1992), Table 46, p. 42.
*Excluding Mexican.

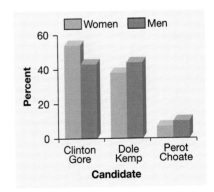

FIGURE 8–4 Gender and the Vote for President, 1996
SOURCE: Voter News Service Exit Poll, *New York Times*, November 10, 1996, p. 16.

of lower pay for women is not restricted to working mothers. Among college graduates ages 25 to 34, women earn an average of 80 cents for every dollar earned by men of the same age and education. As age increases, the earnings gap widens, so that 55-to-64-year-old college educated women earn only 51 cents for every dollar earned by men of the same age and education.[59] Increasing women's income is an important issue to the women's movement.

There is a **gender gap**—significant differences between men and women—in public opinion and voting. Women are more likely to oppose violence in any form—death penalty, new weapons systems, or the possession of handguns. Evidence suggests that women as a group are more compassionate than men and so are more likely to favor government that provides health insurance and family services. Women are more concerned than men about women's rights, enforcement of child support, sexual abuse and rape, unequal treatment of women in the legal system, the environment, peace, and pornography. These so-called "gender issues" are becoming increasingly important. American women identify work and family issues such as day-care, prenatal and postnatal leave, and equality of treatment on the job as important.[60] Other gender issues, some of them focal points in recent elections, include reproductive rights and sexual harassment.[61]

Providing a workplace in which people are not subject to sexual harassment came to the top of the political agenda after being raised during the confirmation of Supreme Court Justice Clarence Thomas (see Chapter 16) and again because of charges raised against U.S. Senator Bob Packwood. Former staff workers had accused Packwood of sexual harassment after his reelection in 1992. Following a protracted dispute with the Senate Ethics Committee, including a dispute over Packwood's refusal to turn over his personal diaries, the committee unanimously recommended that Packwood be expelled from the Senate. Packwood resigned rather than face a vote by the full Senate on his expulsion, and he was replaced by Democrat Ron Wyden in a special election in early 1996. The Supreme Court and Congress, as we noted in Chapter 5, have provided legal protections against sexual harassment, and the number of lawsuits filed is on the increase (see Table 8–6).

Sexual Orientation

The 1990s have seen a growing visibility and increased awareness of diversity in sexual orientation. Gays and lesbians have more aggressively pursued their political agenda of antidiscrimination laws, access to legally sanctioned homosexual mar-

---

TABLE 8–6

Sexual Harassment in the Workplace

	1990	1991	1992	1993	1994	1995	1996
Cases Filed	6,127	6,883	10,532	11,908	14,420	15,549	15,342
Cases Resolved	5,671	6,718	7,484	9,971	11,478	13,802	15,861**
Compensation*	$7.7	$7.1	$12.7	$25.1	$22.5	$24.3	$27.8

SOURCE: U.S. Equal Employment Opportunity Commission, Office of Communications and Legislative Affairs, *Sexual Harassment Statistics, FY 1990–FY 1995*; personal communication. EEOC headquarters preliminary data.

*Dollar amounts in millions.

**Cases resolved may be higher than cases filed due to cases from past years.

riages, rights to the custody and adoption of children, and access to employee benefits for homosexual partners. Groups like Queer Nation, Act Up, and the National Gay and Lesbian Task Force have organized marches and otherwise sought to heighten gay awareness.

During the 1992 election, the question of gays in the military became an issue. Candidate Bill Clinton promised to drop the ban on homosexuals, and early in his administration he set out to fulfill this campaign promise. However, military leaders, including the Joint Chiefs of Staff, opposed the idea, as did key members of the congressional committees dealing with the armed forces. A slight majority of the public did not approve of Bill Clinton's decision to ease the ban on homosexuals in the armed forces.[62] In the face of intense and well-organized opposition and a possible defeat in Congress, the Clinton administration abandoned its original proposal and settled for a compromise policy of "Don't ask, don't tell"—meaning that the military will no longer ask recruits if they are homosexual, and military personnel are under no obligation to divulge their sexual orientation. Some remnants of the old policy remain, however, including an understanding that practicing homosexuals will be discharged from the military if their homosexuality is discovered.

One focal point of the politics of sexual orientation has been AIDS. Acquired immune deficiency syndrome, or AIDS, has disproportionately affected the homosexual community and motivated gays and lesbians to become more politically active, visible, and well organized. Public fear of AIDS was behind a 1986 California ballot initiative to quarantine all persons with the disease, a measure that was defeated.

Controversy has also developed around the issue of legalizing gay marriages. The Hawaii Supreme Court has ruled that to deny gays and lesbians the right to marry may violate the state constitution. A circuit court judge ruled in December 1996 that the state had shown no compelling reason to retain the state's ban on same-sex marriages. An appeal to the state supreme court is already underway, but it is expected that they will uphold the lower court's ruling. Hawaii would then be required to issue marriage licenses to same-sex couples. Because states typically honor each others' laws relating to matters like marriage, the Hawaii decision has national ramifications. In 1996 Congress passed and President Clinton signed into law the Defense of Marriage Act, which bars federal recognition of gay marriages and allows states not to honor same-sex marriages performed legally in other states. Even if Hawaii does allow same-sex marriages, this act will deny federal tax, pension, and other benefits for gay spouses.

As the homosexual rights movement grew in visibility and power, an opposition movement also became part of American politics. During the 1970s, voters in some cities and states voted on measures targeted at homosexual rights. One unsuccessful measure in California, for instance, would have removed suspected homosexuals from the public school classroom until a hearing could be held. In 1992, 1993, and 1994, voters in several states and cities voted on ballot measures to remove special protections previously granted to homosexuals. These plebiscites reflect a backlash against what their sponsors see as laws legitimizing homosexuality. Not surprisingly, the campaigns and debates over these votes are heated. The consequence of these votes has been to put gays and lesbians on the defensive, fighting to hold onto the advances they had made in the 1980s. The most publicized of these votes took place in Colorado in 1992. Voters by a 53 percent majority approved the repeal of special protections granted gays and lesbians in some localities. The Colorado initiative was later declared unconstitutional by the U.S. Supreme Court in *Romer v Evans*, 94–1039 (1996).

Religious observances in this country are as diverse as the population: African Americans celebrate Kwanza, Jewish Americans observe the Sabbath, and Muslim Americans obey the call to prayer during Ramadan.

Religion

In some parts of the world, religious differences can be a source of violent conflict. In Iraq and Turkey the Kurdish people have been subjected to expulsion and even to genocide. The war in Bosnia-Herzegovina was a religious and ethnic battle among Muslims, Serbs, and Catholics. Countries like Afghanistan, Israel, Lebanon, India, and Sri Lanka have also experienced intense religious conflict. Jews have often been the target of religious discrimination and persecution (anti-Semitism), including the Holocaust, during which an estimated 6 million Jews were murdered.[63] The United States has not been immune, despite its principle of religious freedom. In 1838, Governor Lilburn W. Boggs of Missouri issued an extermination order against the Mormons.[64]

Although the intensity of religious conflict varies, it can become especially strong if there is one predominant or official faith, which is why the framers of our Constitution did not sanction a national church in the United States. In fact, James Madison wrote in *The Federalist*, No. 51, "In a free government the security for civil rights must be the same as that for religious rights. It consists in the one case in the multiplicity of interests, and in the other in the multiplicity of sects."

The absence of an official American church does not mean that religion is unimportant in American politics; indeed, there were established state churches until the 1830s. Politicians frequently refer to God in their speeches or demonstrate their piety in other ways. And many share John Conway's view that "at the root of American political and social values . . . is the distinctive Puritanism of the early New England settlers."[65] Many Americans take their religious beliefs seriously, more so than peoples of other industrial democracies.[66] Nearly two-thirds of Americans attend houses of worship several times a year, more than half attend a church or synagogue at least once a month, and more than one-third attend nearly every week.[67] Religion, like ethnicity, is a *shared identity*—people identify themselves as Baptist, Catholic, or Buddhist. Sometimes church attendance or nonattendance is more important than differences between religions in explaining attitudes. "Among both Catholics and Protestants, frequent church-goers are less likely to support abortion than those who rarely or never attend."[68]

Religion can be an important catalyst for social change, as it was in the overthrow of communism in Central Europe[69] and in the leadership of the black church in the American civil rights movement. As writer Taylor Branch explains, the black church "served not only as a place of worship but also as a bulletin board to a people who owned no organs of communication, a credit union to those without banks, and even a kind of people's court."[70] African American ministers, like the Reverend Martin Luther King, Jr., became leaders of the civil rights movement; others, like the Reverend Jesse Jackson, have run for office. Hence religion can be important not only as a source of personal values and attitudes but as a means of political activity and organization.

In recent years there has been an increase in political activity among fundamentalist Christians. Led by ministers like Jerry Falwell and Pat Robertson, they have supported political organizations like the Moral Majority and Christian Coalition. Throughout the 1980s and 1990s, they sought to influence the national agenda, and Robertson ran for president in the Republican party in 1988. More recently, they have focused their attention at the local level—school boards, city councils, mayorships, and local GOP leadership.[71] Their agenda includes the return of school prayer, the outlawing of abortion, restrictions on homosexuals, and opposition to gun control. They achieved some successes in the elections of 1994 and 1996 and are seen as an important political force in some parts of the country.

One defining characteristic of religion in the United States is the tremendous variety of denominations. About half the people in the United States describe

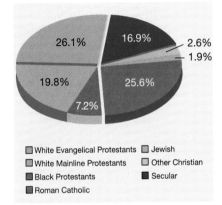

RELIGION AND POLITICS

At one time we thought a Catholic could not be elected president. With the election of 1960 that issue was resolved. John F. Kennedy directly confronted the question of whether a Catholic would put aside religious teachings if they conflicted with constitutional obligations. He said, "I am not the Catholic candidate for President. I am the Democratic party's candidate for President who happens also to be Catholic. I do not speak for my church on public matters, and the church does not speak for me." A candidate's religion may still become an issue if religious convictions on sensitive issues such as abortion threaten to conflict with public obligations.

26.1%   16.9%   2.6%
1.9%
19.8%   25.6%
7.2%

☐ White Evangelical Protestants ☐ Jewish
☐ White Mainline Protestants   ☐ Other Christian
☐ Black Protestants   ☐ Secular
☐ Roman Catholic

**Religious Denominations
of Americans**

Source: Lyman A. Kellstedt and John C. Green, "Knowing God's Many People: Denominational Preferences and Political Behavior," in *Rediscovering the Religious Factor in American Politics*, eds. David C. Leege and Lyman A. Kellstedt (M. E. Sharpe, 1993), p. 70. Religious divisions based on Kellstedt/Green index.

---

themselves as Protestant. The largest Protestant denomination is Baptist, followed by Methodists, Lutherans, Presbyterians, and Episcopalians. Because there are so many different Protestant churches, Catholics have the largest single membership in the United States, constituting more than one-quarter of the population. Jews constitute less than 2 percent of the population. Protestants came to the United States first; most Catholics and Jews immigrated after the 1840s. It was not until 1960, however, that Americans elected a Catholic president.

In recent presidential elections, a majority of Protestants voted Republican, while majorities of Catholics and Jews voted Democratic.[72] The perception among many Catholics and Jews that the Democratic party is more open to them partly explains the strength of their Democratic identification. The Democrats won the loyalty of many Catholics by their willingness to nominate Al Smith for the presidency in 1928 and John Kennedy in 1960. Southern Protestants are Democrats for different reasons, largely having to do with the sectional issues discussed earlier. Religious groups vary in their rates of participation. Jews have the highest rate of reported voter turnout, 79 percent in 1992, while those who claim no religious affiliation have the lowest, 62 percent. Catholics voted at a slightly higher rate than Protestants.[73]

"To the rich, the very rich, and the super rich! Have I left anybody out?"

Drawing by Mirachi. © 1988 The New Yorker Magazine, Inc.

Religion is especially important in American politics because of the clustering of populations. Hence Catholics make up about one-quarter of the U.S. population, yet they are more than 50 percent of the population of Rhode Island, Massachusetts, and Connecticut. Baptists represent 19 percent of the U.S. population, yet they are more than 50 percent of the population of Mississippi, Alabama, and Georgia. Mormons are only 2 percent of the U.S. population, yet they are more than 70 percent of the population of Utah. The South is the most Protestant—61 percent. The state of New York has the highest percentage of Jews, 7 percent; New York City is 14 percent Jewish.

Religious differences can be related to other politically important characteristics. For instance, Jews are the most prosperous and best educated of any ethnic or religious group. More than 46 percent of Jewish adults graduated from college, compared to 22 percent of Protestants and 20 percent of Catholics. In this example, as in others, religion is a cross-cutting cleavage in American politics; the differences do not reinforce one another. On the basis of income and education, Jews predictably would be Republicans, but 43 percent of American Jews are Democrats, while only 22 percent are Republicans.[74] Similarly, southern Protestants would predictably be heavily Republican, but many of them are Democrats.

Wealth and Income

The United States is a wealthy nation in a world of scarcity and intense economic conflict over the distribution of wealth. Indeed, to some knowledgeable observers, "the most striking thing about the United States has been its phenomenal wealth."[75] A large proportion of the people in the United States lead comfortable lives in terms of housing, nutrition, and medical care, and they enjoy a standard of living beyond the reach of many who live in other countries. But even in affluent societies, the distribution of wealth and income can result in important political divisions and conflicts.

Wealth encompasses the things of economic value (savings, stocks, property) you possess; *income* is how much money you make from your job or investments. Wealth is more concentrated than income. The wealthiest families hold most of the property and other forms of wealth like stocks and savings. Traditionally, one of the problems with concentrated wealth has been that it fosters an aristocracy. Jefferson sought to break up the "aristocracy of wealth" by changing from laws based on *primogeniture* (the eldest son's exclusive right to inherit his father's estate) to laws that encouraged people to divide their estates equally among all their children, the result being smaller landholding. He sought to foster an "aristocracy of virtue and talent" through a public school system open to all for primary grades and for the best students through the university level.[76] Education has been one of the most important means for Americans to achieve economic and social mobility. Those with an education are wealthier, and those with wealth are more inclined to get an education.

"The most common and durable source of factions has been the various and unequal distribution of property," wrote James Madison in *The Federalist*, No. 10. He continued, "Those who hold, and those who are without property, have ever formed distinct interests in society" (see Appendix). Madison was right. Economic differences often lead to conflict, and Americans remain divided politically along economic lines. Aside from race, income may be the single most important factor in explaining views on issues, partisanship, and ideology. Most rich people are Republicans, and most poor people are Democrats, and this has been true since at least the Great Depression of the 1930s.

The distribution of income within a society can have important consequences for democratic stability. If there is a perception that only the few at the top of the economic ladder can hope to earn enough for an adequate standard of living, then domestic unrest and revolution may follow. Income is related to participation in politics. Poor people who need the most help from government are the least likely to participate. They are also the most likely to favor social welfare programs.

Income has been rising in the United States. Even after adjusting for inflation, income doubled in the period between the early 1950s and early 1970s. Since the early 1970s, inflation-adjusted income has gone up and down, but the steady rise seen earlier has not occurred (see Figure 8–5).[77] Economists debate the causes for this change; some cite higher energy costs, low levels of personal savings, and the worldwide slowdown in productivity growth.[78] In terms of income, the Northeast is the most prosperous region and the South the least prosperous. Compared to other nations, our purchasing power is higher than that of any other advanced democracy, including Japan.[79]

Most college students come from the top quarter of American families in income—those earning $50,000 a year or more. In fact, students from these families graduate from college at nearly twice the rate as those from the bottom 75 percent of the socioeconomic ladder.[80]

At the other end of the economic continuum are the poor. In the last quarter-century, roughly one in every ten Americans has come from a family whose income is below the poverty line. In 1997 the official poverty level for a family of four was income below $16,029.[81] Most persons classified as below the poverty line are in families in which adults of working age either do not have jobs or work in jobs with low pay. Families headed by a female have three times the chance of falling below the poverty line, and nearly 39 percent of all households headed by females fall below the poverty line.[82] In an average month, both African Americans and Hispanics are nearly three times as likely to be poor than whites.[83] Close to 22 percent of the poor are children under 18 years of age, and many appear to be trapped in a cycle of poverty (see Figure 8–6).[84]

The definition of poverty is itself political. The poverty-level figure of $16,029 identifies persons who cannot meet a minimum standard in such basics as housing, food, and medical care. Regardless of how one defines poverty, however, the poor are a minority who lack political power. While there are fewer persons over the age of 65 than there are poor people, older Americans are a much more potent force in American politics.[85] The poor vote less and are less confident and organized in dealing with politics and government. During the Reagan years of the 1980s, there was increasing inequality between rich and poor, a trend quite different from the 1960s, when the gap between rich and poor narrowed.[86] Although the gap did begin to decrease under the Bush administration, since 1992 the inequality between rich and poor has again been on the rise.[87]

Following the 1994 elections, one of the priorities that President Clinton and the Republican Congress agreed upon was welfare reform. Welfare as a broad public policy has long been unpopular with the American people, but specific welfare programs like aid to the blind and disabled, support for mentally retarded, and unemployment compensation have been widely supported. Unlike other public policy programs, the beneficiaries of welfare are not well organized politically. This lack of political muscle was evident in 1996, as Congress passed and Bill Clinton signed into law a welfare reform bill that imposes lifetime limits and work requirements and gives states much greater leeway in administering welfare programs.

Occupation

Americans at the time of Thomas Jefferson and for several generations after worked primarily in agriculture. In 1800, 83 percent of the entire U.S. labor force was engaged in farming.[88] The agrarian period was characterized by a large number of independent, landowning farmers with little formal schooling.

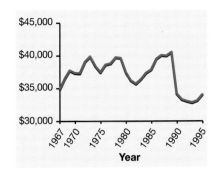

FIGURE 8–5 Annual Inflation-Adjusted Median Family Income, 1967–1995 (In constant 1995 dollars, using Consumer Price Index)

SOURCES: U.S. Bureau of the Census, *Money Income and Poverty Status in the United States*, Current Population Reports, Series P-60, no. 168 (Government Printing Office, 1989), p. 14; U.S. Bureau of the Census, *Statistical Abstract of the United States, 1996* (Government Printing Office, 1996), Tables 727, 745, pp. 471, 483; U.S. Department of Commerce, *Money Income in the United States, 1995*, Series P60, no. 193 (Government Printing Office, 1995), Table 1, p. 1.

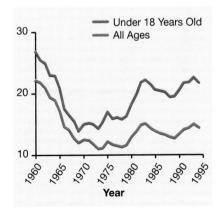

FIGURE 8–6 Percentage of Americans Living in Poverty, by Age, 1960–1995

SOURCE: U.S. Bureau of the Census, *Poverty in the United States* and *Income, Poverty, and Valuation of Noncash Benefits*, Current Population Reports, Series P-60, nos. 185, 189 (Government Printing Office, 1992, 1994).

INCOME DISTRIBUTION IN THE UNITED STATES

The bar chart on the left demonstrates that most of the population is what we might call "middle class," with 65 percent of American families having incomes ranging from $15,000 to $75,000 and with the median income at $30,786. Political scientists term such a distribution "normal" because it peaks in the middle. In some societies, notably developing countries, most people are either in the high- or low-income ranges, giving two peaks to the distribution. Though the bar chart shows a large middle class, the pie chart on the right indicates that the richest 20 percent earn twelve times more than the poorest 20 percent, or nearly half of all income.

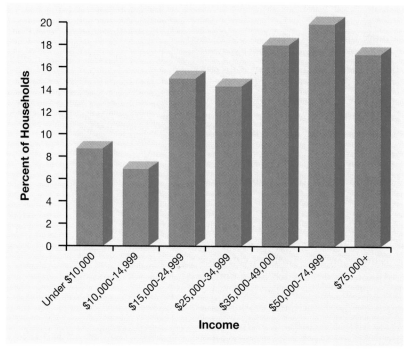

Total Money Income of Households, 1994

SOURCE: U.S. Bureau of the Census, *Statistical Abstract of the United States, 1996* (Government Printing Office, 1996), p. 466.

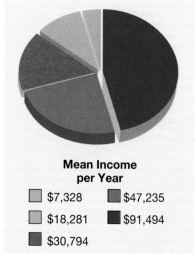

Mean Income per Year

$7,328	$47,235
$18,281	$91,494
$30,794	

Share of Aggregate Income Received by Fifths of Households, 1992

SOURCE: U.S. Bureau of the Census, *Money Income of Households, Families, and Persons in the United States, 1992*, Current Population Reports P 60, no. 184 (Government Printing Office, 1993), p. B-6.

By 1920, the United States had become the world's leading industrial nation. This dramatic transformation also resulted in the expansion of American cities as large numbers of workers moved there to find jobs. Labor conditions, including child-labor practices, became important political issues. The invention and application of technology, such as Henry Ford's assembly line, when combined with abundant natural and human resources, meant that the U.S. gross domestic product (GDP) rose by more than 550 percent in real terms over the 66-year period from 1929 to 1995.[89]

The United States has now entered what Daniel Bell, a noted sociologist, has labeled the "post-industrial phase of our development." "A post-industrial society, being primarily a technical society, awards less on the basis of inheritance or property . . . than on education and skill."[90] Knowledge is the organizing device of the

post-industrial era. Post-industrial societies have greater affluence and a class structure less defined along traditional labor versus management lines.

The changing dynamics of the American labor force can be seen in Figure 8–7, which shows the percentage of the U.S. labor force in various occupations since 1900. As the figure demonstrates, there has been tremendous growth in the white-collar sector of our economy, rising from under 20 percent of the work force at the turn of the century to more than half by 1980. The white-collar sector includes managers, accountants, and lawyers as well as professionals and technicians in such rapid growth areas as communications, finance, insurance, and research. This shift has been accompanied by a dramatic decline in the number of people engaged in agriculture and a more modest decline in the number of people in manufacturing. Today less than one in three working Americans produces goods, and only 3 percent work on farms.

Governments are among the biggest employers in this country. Slightly more than one-sixth of our Gross Domestic Product (GDP) is produced by federal, state, and local governments.[91] Education is one of our largest industries, with approximately 3.8 million teachers.[92] The Department of Defense employs nearly 2.5 million civilian and military personnel.[93]

Women and racial minorities have distinct occupational patterns (see Figure 8–8). Women are much less likely than men to work in blue-collar jobs and more likely to work as professionals and technicians in white-collar jobs. More than one in four working women are employed as clerical workers, and another 18 percent are in service occupations. As noted earlier, women generally earn less than men of the same age and education. Occupations in which women predominate, like teaching and clerical work, are generally lower paying than industrial or management jobs. And as women advance in their careers, especially in management, they encounter the "glass ceiling" as a barrier to advancement.

Like women, African Americans and Hispanics tend to have occupations different from those of white males. African Americans are more likely than whites or Hispanics to be engaged in clerical work or service sector jobs. Large numbers of Latinos work as operators and laborers, in service jobs, and on farms.

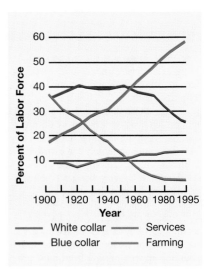

FIGURE 8–7   Occupational Distribution in the United States, 1900–1995

SOURCE: U.S. Department of Labor, *Employment and Earnings*, vol. 43, no. 1 (Government Printing Office, 1996), p. 30.

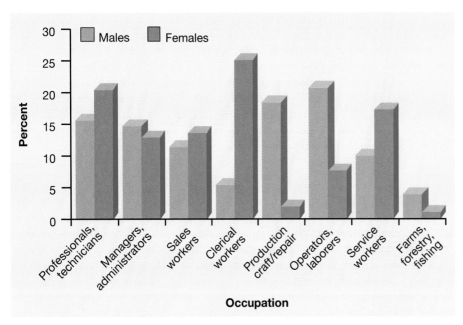

FIGURE 8–8   Occupational Distribution by Gender, 1995

SOURCE: U.S. Department of Labor, *Employment and Earnings*, vol. 43, no. 1 (Government Printing Office, 1996), p. 31.

Even in occupations in which African Americans or Hispanics have done better at finding jobs, they run into barriers. The courts and Congress have confronted some of these barriers.[94] The 1991 Civil Rights Act gave workers more protection against discrimination and greater monetary damages and the reimbursement of legal costs for those who could convince the courts of employment bias.[95] (See Chapter 5 for a discussion of employment discrimination and affirmative action issues.)

Social Class

Many commentators have questioned why Americans do not divide themselves into social classes as many Europeans do. American workers have not formed their own political parties, nor does class help to explain much about our political life. Marxist categories of *proletariat* (those who sell their labor) and *bourgeoisie* (those who own or control the means of production) are not as important here as they are in Europe. But we do have social classes and what social scientists call **socioeconomic status (SES)**—a division of the population based on occupation, income, and education. Such measures help explain some citizen behavior in American politics, but these categories have some obvious inconsistencies. For instance, some individuals perform working-class tasks (such as plumbing), but their income is middle class or even upper middle class. A schoolteacher's income is below that of many working-class jobs, but in terms of status, the job ranks at least with middle-class fields.

Most Americans, when asked what class they belong to, say "middle class." The second most frequently mentioned category is "working class." Very few Americans see themselves as lower class or upper class. But what constitutes "middle class" is highly subjective. George Bush once defined "middle class" as persons making over $50,000.[96] Actually, only 5.7 percent of Americans had that much income.[97] In many other industrial democracies, large proportions of the population think of themselves as working class instead of middle class.[98] In England, nearly three out of five persons see themselves as working class.[99] But to many Americans there is something undesirable about the label "working class."

One explanation for Americans' responses may be the elements of the American Dream that involve upward mobility. Or their responses may reflect the hostility many feel toward organized labor, which gives workers solidarity. European labor unions are stronger than American labor unions. In any case, compared to many countries, class divisions in the United States are less defined and less important to politics. As political scientist Seymour Martin Lipset has written, "The American social structure and values foster an emphasis on competitive individualism, an orientation that is not congruent with class consciousness, support for socialist or social democratic parties, or a strong union movement."[100]

Age

Americans are living longer, a phenomenon that has been called the "graying of America" (Figure 8–9). Not only are we living longer, but fewer babies are being born proportionate to the population. This demographic change is already having important consequences; it has increased the demand for medical care, retirement benefits, and a host of other age-related services. Persons over the age of 65 constitute 13 percent of the population yet account for 43 percent of the total medical expenditures.[101] The growing population of older persons was most pronounced in the West during the 1980s, but Florida remains the state with the largest proportion of persons over age 65.

As a group, older Americans have a political agenda, and they vote. Figure 8–10, which plots voter turnout rate by age, shows a clear relationship: As age increases,

so does the propensity to vote. In recent presidential elections, less than half of all 18- and 19-year-olds voted. In contrast, four out of every five 68- and 69-year-olds turned out to vote.[102] As a group, they fight to ensure that Social Security is protected; they value Medicare and favor catastrophic health insurance. Despite their desire for services that benefit themselves, they are also in favor of tax cuts. Past legislative victories have changed the lives of older citizens. For instance, the poverty rate among this age group dropped from 35 percent in 1959 to 12 percent in 1994, a change partly due to improved medical benefits passed during the 1960s.[103]

The "gray lobby" not only votes in large numbers but also has four other political assets that make it politically powerful—disposable income, discretionary time, a clear focus on issues, and effective organization—factors not found in any other age group. When older Americans compete for their share of the budget pie, the young, minorities, and the poor often lose out. During the prolonged budget fight between Congress and the president in 1995 and 1996, President Clinton twice vetoed Republican budget proposals, in part, he said, because they cut too deeply into Medicare, the health care program for the elderly. The popularity of this program and the political importance of this group bolstered Clinton's standing in the polls and forced the Republicans to back down, helping reelect Clinton in 1996.

In 1993 President Clinton sought the support of older Americans for his health care reform package by promising no reduction in benefits for older Americans and reduced overall costs.[104] The American Association of Retired Persons (AARP), the largest and most powerful arm of the "gray lobby," disappointed President Clinton by refusing to endorse his health care reform bill. Instead, it, like other interest groups, sought to make its own case before the Congress.

Age is important to politics in two additional ways: life cycle and generation. *Life-cycle effects* have shown that as people become middle-aged, they become more politically conservative, less mobile, and more likely to participate in politics. As they age further and rely more on the government for services, they tend to grow more liberal.[105]

There are also *generational effects* in politics that arise when a particular generation has had experiences that make it politically distinct. An example is the experience of the Great Depression, which, for those who lived through it, shaped lifelong views of parties, issues, and political leaders. Some members of this generation saw Franklin Roosevelt as the leader who saved the country by pulling it out of the Depression; others felt he sold the country down the river by launching too many government programs. A more recent generation that shared a common and distinctive political experience is the Vietnam generation. Americans who came of age politically during the Vietnam War experienced not only an unpopular war but also the civil rights movement. As with the Great Depression, not everybody saw the Vietnam War and civil rights battles in the same way. Such differences do not diminish the importance of the experience in shaping a generation's perspective on politics and government.

Education

Education has long been linked to citizenship and civic virtue. Thomas Jefferson wrote of education, "Enlighten the people generally, and tyranny and oppressions of body and mind will vanish like evil spirits at the dawn of day."[106] The vast majority of people in the United States are educated in public schools. Nine out of every ten students in kindergarten through high school attend public schools, and four out of five students in college are in public institutions.[107]

The number of years of school completed varies greatly in the United States. Only recently did the number of college graduates in America surpass the number of persons who had not graduated from high school.[108] High school dropout rates have declined in the last decade, yet African Americans, Hispanics, and individuals from low income families still have higher than average dropout rates. Roughly

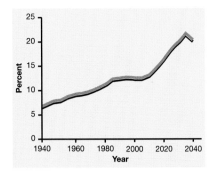

FIGURE 8–9   Percent of Population over Age 65, 1940–2040

Source: U.S. Bureau of the Census, *Current Population Reports, Series P-25*, nos. 98, 310, 519, 917, 1018, 1130 (Government Printing Office, 1950, 1960, 1973, 1995).

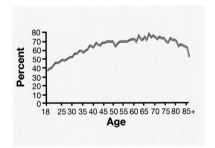

FIGURE 8–10   Percent Voting in the 1992 Presidential Election by Age

Source: U.S. Bureau of the Census, *Voting and Registration in the Election of November 1992* (Government Printing Office, 1993).

We the People

Distribution of Education in the United States (in percent)

	4 Years of High School	1–3 Years of College	4+ Years of College	Total
Total	33.9%	24.7%	23.0%	81.6%
Male	31.9	23.9	25.9	81.7
Female	35.7	24.7	20.2	80.6
White	34.0	25.0	24.0	83.0
African American	36.2	24.3	13.3	73.8
Hispanic	26.3	17.8	9.2	53.3
Non-Hispanic	34.6	25.4	24.2	84.2
Other	25.9	21.0	28.5	75.4
Age				
25–34	34.0	28.2	25.0	87.2
35–44	33.3	28.4	26.6	88.3
45–54	32.5	25.7	28.0	86.2
55–64	37.3	20.8	19.0	77.1
65–74	36.4	18.3	14.2	68.9
75+	30.2	15.3	11.2	56.7

SOURCE: U.S. Bureau of the Census, *Statistical Abstract of the United States, 1996* (Government Printing Office, 1996), p. 160.

two-thirds of Americans have not gone to college, though many college students assume that the college experience is widely shared.

Americans are becoming more educated. In a 50-year period, the number of Americans 25 years and older with four or more years of college has gone from only 5 percent in 1940 to more than 22 percent in the mid 1990s.[109] Impressive gains have been made by all groups in the proportion graduating from high school, yet racial and ethnic minorities still lag behind whites in completing four or more years of college. African Americans have increased their rate of completion of four or more years of college tenfold since 1940, and Hispanics have almost doubled their college attendance since 1974, when data were first collected. To compete for jobs in a post-industrial society, more education, especially technical education, is necessary.

Compared to persons in other industrial democracies, Americans and Canadians are more likely to go to college.[110] Yet the experience of higher education has not been uniformly shared. The proportion of whites who are college graduates is nearly double that for African Americans and more than double that for Hispanics; roughly 26 percent of African Americans and nearly half of all Hispanics stopped their schooling before completing high school.[111]

Part of the difference among whites, African Americans, and Hispanics in years of school completed is a function of age. Older African Americans and Hispanics are much less likely to have completed high school. Just over one in ten African Americans and 26 percent of Hispanics over the age of 65 stopped school before the fifth

grade.[112] In contrast, younger African Americans (those under the age of 29) are more likely than whites to have stayed in school through the eighth grade, but they then have a higher dropout rate than whites in high school. Hispanics, on the other hand, have high rates of dropout, even in the lower grades; 3 percent did not go beyond the fourth grade, and one in five did not go to high school, as opposed to 0.3 percent and 6 percent of African Americans, respectively.[113] These differences in education affect not only economic well-being but political participation and involvement.

Education is one of the most important variables in predicting political participation, confidence in dealing with government, and awareness of issues. Education is also related to the acquisition of democratic values. Those who have failed to learn the prevailing norms of American society are far more likely to express opposition to democratic and capitalist ideals than those who are well educated and politically knowledgeable.[114] Education is, in short, a factor we will return to again and again in subsequent chapters as we study government by the people.

"It's like this. If the rich have money, they invest. If the poor have money, they eat."

Drawing by Dana Fradon. © 1992 The New Yorker Magazine.

UNITY IN A LAND OF DIVERSITY

As remarkable as American diversity is, the existence of a strong and widely shared sense of national unity and identity may be even more remarkable. Writing about the United States some years ago, a famous reporter, John Gunther, summarized his insights from extensive travels:

> Whoever invented the motto E Pluribus Unum [one out of many] has given the best three-word description of the United States ever written. The triumph of America is the triumph of a coalescing federal system. Complex as the nation is almost to the point of insufferability, it interlocks. Homogeneity and diversity these are the stupendous rival magnets. . . . Think of the United States as an immense blanket or patchwork quilt solid with different designs and highlights. But, no matter what colors burn and flash in what corners, the warp and woof, the basic texture and fabric is the same from corner to corner, from end to end.[115]

Americans have always been united by their commitment to liberty. Equally important has been the belief that government should exist to serve the people, rather than the reverse. What shapes our political culture is the persistent commitment to the individual. One author recently concluded that "equality, individualism and openness are the crucial values of American politics in the 1990s."[116]

Part of the explanation for our unity is the unifying effect of the American Dream—the belief that this is the land of opportunity for enterprising individuals. Unity in the midst of diversity has also been enhanced by a sense of a common fate, often highlighted by a crisis. Social and economic differences become less important, for example, when we fight wars. World War II enabled many Americans to experience life in different parts of the country and confirmed the patriotism of diverse groups. One question for the late 1990s will be: Can we maintain the same degree of unity in a world with fewer foreign enemies and only one military superpower? Finally, the United States has achieved a measure of unity through residential mobility, intermarriage, the mass media, and a common culture.

Social scientists sometimes speak of the *melting pot*, meaning that as minorities, especially ethnic groups, associate with other groups, they are assimilated into the rest of American society and come to share democratic values like majority rule, individualism, and the notion that America is the land of opportunity. Recently the melting pot idea has been criticized as assuming that differences between groups are to be discouraged. In its place, critics propose the notion of the *salad bowl*, in which "though the salad is an entity, the lettuce can still be distinguished from the chicory, the tomatoes from the cabbage."[117]

As we have seen, important differences persist among groups, and in that sense the salad bowl analogy is accurate. Divisive issues like immigration, affirmative action,

and programs for the poor have reinforced our differences. But in another way, our society has achieved a unity of commitment to democratic values and processes—a political culture—that is, at least in part, a consequence of such elements of the melting pot theory as public schools, a common language, and hope for a better life for one's children. While ethnic divisions in the United States have posed challenges to the institutions and processes of government, the public has generally accepted diversity in political appointments, government jobs and contracts, and other aspects of policy. This is in sharp contrast to the problems of ethnicity in Canada, India, and the former Yugoslavia and Soviet Union. But what is the appropriate balance among recognition, preservation, and representation of ethnic groups and the needs for assimilation, common commitments, and a shared identity?

POLITICS ONLINE

Surfing the Political Landscape

If you assume that opinions expressed on your favorite chat box are representative of people generally, or even of young people, you are mistaken. A study by the Pew Research Center for the People and the Press found that online users tend to be young, affluent suburbanites who are better educated than the general public. Fifty-eight percent of online users are men, but there is little difference between Internet users and the public in terms of political ideology.

The Web ia an excellent place to learn about different racial, ethnic, economic, religious, and other groups in the United States. Our social and economic diversity is evident in the wide range of home pages devoted to these differences. Latinos, for instance, have a Web page at:

http://www.catalog.com/favision/latnoweb.htm

If you want to learn about the Catholic or Mormon Churches, you can go to:

http://www.catholic.net or http://www.lds.org

The Christian Coalition can be found at:

http://cc.org

Voices United for Israel is at:

http://knowledge1.knowledge-tree.com/israel/voices

Labor unions, trade associations, and small business groups also use the Internet and provide a sense of our economic diversity.

The most useful place to go for information on demography is the U.S. Census Bureau at:

http://www.census.gov

There you can find data on the population, current economic indicators, income, poverty, labor force, households, GDP, wages, prices, and jobs. For example, the Census Bureau provides results of surveys regarding home-based businesses; there are 422,373 home-based businesses owned by Hispanics, 424,165 owned by African Americans, 376,711 by other minorities, 4,114,787 by women, and 8,755,252 by nonminority males:

http://www.census.gov/epcd/econ/www/answers.html#q9.

SUMMARY

1. The character of a political society, its social and economic divisions, its traditions, and its sectional and local identifications are important to understanding public opinion, participation,

voting, interest groups, political parties, and the communications process. It is often a mistake to generalize solely from one's own experience, background, beliefs, and values.

2. Geography, room to grow, abundant natural resources, wealth, and relative isolation from "foreign entanglements" help to explain American politics and traditions, including the notions of manifest destiny, ethnocentrism, and isolationism.

3. The South has been the most distinct region in the United States, in large part because of the issue of slavery and race relations. Other important sections include the frost belt/sun belt division.

4. Americans moved from farms to cities and more recently from cities to suburbs. Population movements were largely responses to economic opportunities, including the large migration of African Americans from the South. Today, large cities are increasingly poor, African American, and Democratic, surrounded by suburbs that are primarily middle class, white, and Republican.

5. The United States is a land of tremendous diversity in race, ethnicity, religion, wealth and income, occupation, social class, age, and education. Divisions by gender and sexual orientation have recently become more important. This diversity is often significant in our politics.

6. Race has been among the most important of the differences in our political landscape. Although we fought a civil war on the issue of freedom for African Americans, the issue of racial equality was largely postponed until the latter half of this century. Race remains an important issue in our politics and government. Ethnicity, including the rising numbers of Hispanics, continues to be a factor in politics, as demonstrated by the controversy over English as the offi-cial language. Religion is a difference that helps explain political behavior both in terms of persons from different religions behaving differently and in terms of differences between those who are religious and those who are not.

7. Gender is important in American politics. Women have gradually acquired political rights. They now play important roles in our government, and they differ from men in their attitudes on some issues. Sexual orientation is also becoming increasingly important to politics and policy.

8. While the United States is a land of wealth and is known for its large middle class, not everyone has an adequate share in the American economic success. Poverty has grown over the past decade, and it is most concentrated among African Americans, Native Americans, Hispanics, and single-parent households. Women as a group continue to earn less than men, even in the same occupations. Differences in income and wealth remain important.

9. Age and education are important to understanding American politics. Our aging population poses important challenges to public policy. Because they participate so much more than young voters, older Americans are a potent political force. Education not only opens up economic opportunities in America but also explains many important aspects of political participation.

10. Despite our diversity, Americans share an important unity. We are united by our shared commitment to democratic values, economic opportunity, the work ethic, and the American Dream. National experiences like wars and global economic competition have also unified us.

FURTHER READING

DOUGLAS L. ANDERTON, RICHARD BARNETT, AND DONALD BOGUE, *The Population of the United States*, 3d edition (Free Press, 1996).

DAVID H. BENNETT, *The Party of Fear* (University of North Carolina Press, 1990).

EARL BLACK AND MERLE BLACK, *The Vital South: How Presidents Are Elected* (Harvard University Press, 1992).

URIE BRONTENBRENNER ET AL., *The State of Americans: The Disturbing Facts and Figures on Changing Values, Crime, the Economy, Poverty, Family, Education, the Aging Population, and What They Mean for Our Future* (Free Press, 1996).

LOIS LOVELACE DUKE, ED., *Women in Politics: Outsiders or Insiders?* (Prentice Hall, 1993).

RODOLFO O. DE LA GARZA, LOUIS DESIPIO, F. CHRIS GARCIA, JOHN GARCIA, AND ANGELO FALCON, *Latino Voices: Mexican, Puerto Rican, and Cuban Perspectives on American Politics* (Westview Press, 1992).

SARAH H. EVANS, *Born for Liberty: A History of Women in America* (Free Press, 1989).

ANDREW HACKER, *Two Nations: Black and White, Separate, Hostile, Unequal* (Charles Scribner's Sons, 1992).

SEYMOUR MARTIN LIPSET, *Continental Divide: The Values and Institutions of the United States and Canada* (Routledge, 1990).

NANCY E. MCGLEN AND KAREN O'CONNOR, *Women, Politics, and American Society* (Prentice Hall, 1995).

PETER NABOKOV, ED., *Native American Testimony: A Chronicle of Indian-White Relations from Prophecy to the Present, 1492–1992* (Viking, 1991).

KEVIN PHILLIPS, *The Politics of Rich and Poor: Wealth and the American Electorate in the Reagan Aftermath* (Random House, 1990).

STEVEN J. ROSE, *Social Stratification in the United States: The American Profile Poster Revised and Expanded* (New Press, 1992).

ARTHUR M. SCHLESINGER, JR., *The Disuniting of America* (W.W. Norton, 1992).

STUDS TERKEL, *Race: How Blacks and Whites Think and Feel About the American Obsession* (W.W. Norton, 1992).

ALEXIS DE TOCQUEVILLE, *Democracy in America*, ed. J. P. Mayer, trans. George Lawrence (Doubleday and Company, 1969).

KENNETH D. WALD, *Religion and Politics in the United States*, 3d ed. (CQ Press, 1996).

9

Interest Groups: The Politics of Influence

$\mathcal{A}$fter losing their battle to block the North American Free Trade Agreement (NAFTA) and facing a Republican majority in the U.S. House of Representatives for the first time in 40 years, labor unions mounted a targeted campaign in 1996 to defeat 30 House Republican incumbents. Their tactic was to direct large amounts of money against these incumbents in the form of *issue advertising*. Under a Supreme Court ruling handed down in 1995, parties and interest groups can spend unlimited and undisclosed amounts of money on ads for or against candidates, so long as the commercials do not expressly call for the election or defeat of a specific candidate.[1] Interest groups of all types regularly contribute to candidates through their political action committees (PACs), but these contributions are limited to $5,000 in the primary and $5,000 in the general election.

Business groups had long outspent labor unions in congressional campaigns. In the 1996 campaign, they donated more than $242 million through PACs, compared to $35 million contributed by labor PACs. About 72 percent of business money went to Republicans, with the remainder going to Democrats; 93 percent of labor money went to Democrats.[2] The AFL-CIO advertising campaign in 1996 spent about $20 million, but that is only an estimate as there is no disclosure requirement.

Labor leaders were outspoken about their desire to influence the composition of Congress through these ads. John Sweeney, president of the AFL-CIO executive council, said, "We expect that the people who will be elected to Congress will want to address the issues we've raised in this campaign."[3] Labor was not the only group to mount issue advertisements during the 1996 campaign. The Chamber of Commerce also targeted an estimated $5 to $7 million for ads in selected districts, often in response to the labor union ads.

One of the House Republicans targeted by organized labor for defeat in 1996 was J. D. Hayworth of Arizona. Hayworth was first elected in the Republican tidal wave of 1994, and once elected, he was an unabashed supporter of Speaker Newt Gingrich. Before running for Congress in 1994, Hayworth had been a sportscaster for the CBS television affiliate in Phoenix. In 1996 Hayworth's Democratic opponent, Steve Owens, mounted a visible and well-funded campaign, spending $801,552 compared to Hayworth's $1,511,069.[4]

In Arizona's Sixth District race between Hayworth and Owens, labor spent more money on its issue ads critical of Hayworth than was spent by the campaigns of both candidates.[5] The Chamber of Commerce responded before election day by running issue ads supportive of Hayworth.

Owens came very close to defeating Hayworth on election day, losing by less than 1 percent of the vote. Seventeen Republicans who were also targets of AFL-CIO issues advertising were defeated, but that was not enough for Democrats to reclaim the majority in the House. However, labor still claimed a victory, asserting that, as a result of the 1996 campaign, "the Gingrich Revolution is over."[6]

The Hayworth-Owens congressional campaign in Arizona in 1996 is only one example of competing interest groups seeking to elect officials who they hope will support their policy proposals. Interest groups also compete in other ways as well. In this chapter we examine the tremendous variety of such interest groups. We begin by discussing their roles and types, then turn to one of their most important activities—lobbying government. Finally, we examine the problems interest groups pose and ways to regulate them.

223

Some Facts About Interest Groups

In the United States there are:

- 68,490,000 million families
- 77 religions with at least 50,000 adherents
- 257,648 religious congregations
- 2,000 trade associations
- 3,000 organizations with offices in Washington, D.C.; one-quarter of them founded since 1970
- 4,016 political action committees (PACs)

In Washington, D.C., there are:

- 29 percent of all national nonprofit associations
- representatives of more than 4,000 individual corporations
- more than 37,000 lawyers
- 15,000 individual representatives of groups working to influence government policies
- 5,000 representatives of 2,200 trade and professional associations and labor unions
- 2,500 advocates for public interest groups, representing interests from the environment to abortion to gun control
- 2,500 public and government relations consultants and professional managers of interest groups
- 200 officers of political parties or political action committees
- 300 advocates for policy think tanks
- 30 religious lobbies
- 40 groups dedicated to preserving Alaska's environment

SOURCES: U.S. Bureau of the Census, *Statistical Abstract of the United States, 1995* (Government Printing Office, 1995), pp. 57, 69; *World Almanac and Book of Facts, 1996* (Funk & Wagnalls, 1995). Federal Election Commission Home Page: http://www.fec.gov/press/012396.htm

INTEREST GROUPS PAST AND PRESENT

One of the enduring features of democracy is the interplay of interests. Freedom and democracy seem to go hand in hand, with individuals acting politically on their perceived interests. But concern about how to limit the tendency of self-interested persons to seek more political power is also enduring. From the founding of our Republic to the present time, students of government have debated how to limit zealous political interests without damaging essential freedoms.

The Mischiefs of Faction

What we call "interest groups" today, James Madison called **factions**.[7] (Madison also thought of political parties as factions.) For Madison and the other framers of the Constitution, the daunting problem was how to establish a stable and orderly constitutional system that at the same time would respect the liberty of free citizens. Madison warned of the tendency of popular government toward the "vice" of faction, toward "instability, injustice, and confusion." Still, he would not sacrifice the liberty that led to the formation of factions. How could this dilemma be resolved?

Madison, a good practical politician and a brilliant theorist, offered both a diagnosis and a solution. The solution had already taken concrete form in the new Constitution that Madison firmly believed would control the effects of factionalism; Madison summarized this solution in *The Federalist*, No. 10 (reprinted in the Appendix).

The genius of *The Federalist*, No. 10, lies in the manner in which Madison describes the factions of the day. He begins with a basic proposition: "The latent causes of faction are thus sown in the nature of man." Madison does not take a simplistic approach to faction. Factions are not merely religious, economic, or political but a combination of these, and factions can be further divided into subfactions. Thus property owners can be divided into landed, manufacturing, mercantile, and moneyed subfactions. Madison demonstrated that Americans live in a maze of group interests. Yet he went on to argue that the "most common and durable source of factions, has been the various and unequal distribution of property."

In the late eighteenth century, Madison was concerned about religious, political, and economic factions. What are the key interest groups and issues today? What are the sources of the groups' strengths and weaknesses? How do these interests seek to influence government? Are they as dangerous to the public interest now as Madison feared they were in his time? If so, what has been done about it, and what else may be done?

A Nation of Interests

The United States has been described as a nation of joiners. Europeans sometimes make fun of us for setting up all sorts of organizations, and we ourselves are often amused by the behavior of our groups—the noisy conventions of veterans' associations, the solemn rites of great fraternal organizations, and the oratory of patriotic societies. Yet most of these groups have serious goals and play an important role in politics. Some scholars have recently questioned the extent to which Americans engage in groups and build up *social capital*—features of social organization that foster social interaction.[8] Political scientist Robert Putnam theorizes that the decline in membership in organizations in America negatively influences democracy (see Chapter 1). As an illustration, Putnam explains that more and more Americans are bowling alone. The significance of this observation lies in the "social interaction and even occasionally civic conversations over beer and pizza that solo bowlers forgo."[9] Some dispute Putnam's theory, and Americans continue to join and be active in movements and associate with other people who share common interests in rather large numbers.

How many groups are there in the United States? There is no way to give an accurate count. The family is the most basic and important group, and there are more than 68 million families in the United States. There are also one-quarter million religious congregations, diverse farm groups and labor unions, and more than two thousand trade associations. As we noted in Chapter 8, Americans naturally form groups according to their race, gender, ethnic background, age, occupation, and so forth. All these are groups in the broadest sense of the term; that is, their members share some common outlook or attitude, and they interact with one another in some way.

Interest groups are groups of people who share a common concern. Interest groups usually work within the framework of government and employ tactics such as lobbying to achieve their goals. They are increasing in number. Sometimes referred to as "special interests," they are viewed by many as selfish, concerned only with promoting their own well-being. Indeed, for many people, the discussion of interest groups conjures up images of powerful moneyed interests pressuring legislators to retain tax loopholes, or groups such as the National Rifle Association lobbying against gun control. Yet even these special interests would claim that their actions promote common national interests. Frequently the power of special interests angers Americans. In the 1930s and 1940s, labor unions were often seen as greedy and power hungry. Today the image of labor unions may be even worse, although corporate conglomerates more often come under attack. Occasionally—perhaps when a powerful corporation squares off against a strong union—the public may utter a "curse on both your houses."

Interest groups seek to work inside the existing political channels. They try to influence elections and then to influence public officials. This is the ordinary and continuing way we do business in the United States.

Social Movements

Interest groups sometimes have their beginnings as movements. A **movement** is a large body of people who are interested in a common issue, idea, or concern that is of continuing significance and who are willing to take action on that issue. Examples of movements include civil rights, environmental, antitax, and women's rights. Each of these movements represents groups who feel "left out" of government. They often arise at the grass-roots level and evolve into national groups. Movements tend to see their causes as morally right and the positions of the opposition as morally wrong. To illustrate the dynamics of movements, we will briefly examine the women's movement.

THE WOMEN'S MOVEMENT American women in the 1770s, like their sisters in Western Europe, were dependents of their fathers or husbands. Women could not make legal arrangements or contracts, earn wages separate from those of their husbands, or vote. By marrying, they forfeited to their husbands legal custody of themselves as well as custody of all property and children.[10] Lacking the right to vote, women could not turn to electoral politics to overcome discrimination. Rather, they "determined to ferment a rebellion," in Abigail Adams's words, for "we would not hold ourselves bound by any laws in which we have no voice or representation."[11] Formal education for women was restricted to female academies in which the daughters of the wealthy were taught social graces and other "female arts." Women began to gain a sense of group consciousness when they worked so their husbands could fight in the Revolutionary War and the War of 1812 and when they worked in New England textile mills.[12]

The women's movement began in response to this sense of powerlessness as well as in response to social problems that concerned women, such as illiteracy, slavery, and liquor. An 1848 convention in Seneca Falls, New York, called for equal rights

Straightening Out the Terms

Factions: A term used by James Madison and other founders of this country to refer to political parties as well as what we now call special interests or interest groups.

Interest groups: People who share common goals, interact with one another, and are organized to press claims on government: veterans, soybean growers, bankers.

Movements: People united but loosely organized around a central idea whose goal is to change attitudes or institutions, not just policy: the civil rights movement, women's movement, anti-abortion movement.

Associations: Formal organizations created by interest groups: the National Association for the Advancement of Colored People (NAACP), National Organization for Women (NOW), National Rifle Association (NRA).

Political action committees (PACs): The political arms of interest groups, which are legally entitled to raise and spend campaign contributions.

Groups: People who share common goals and who interact with one another: union leaders, your family, the senior class of your college.

Women in the United States have been involved in a long struggle for their rights, from these suffragettes who campaigned for the right to vote, to today's legal battles to achieve equal pay, equal opportunities for advancement, and workplaces free of sexual harassment.

MOVEMENTS IN THE UNITED STATES

- Abolitionist
- Suffragist
- Temperance
- Peace
- Single tax
- Populist
- Civil rights
- Anti-Vietnam War

- Gay rights
- Moral Majority
- Nuclear freeze
- Animal rights
- Earth First
- Antitax
- Term limits

Individuals who share a common identity or concern form movements to advance their rights or issues. The agenda and success of these movements vary widely. Some accomplish their goals and go away, others evolve into concern for other issues, and some become established interest groups that persist over time.

Movements in the United States today run the gamut from the Christian Coalition and other religious groups to paramilitary groups like the Michigan Militia.

in marriage, property, contracts, trades, professions, and universities; the convention also called for the adoption of *women's suffrage*, the right to vote. Suffrage was gradually extended to women and was finally included in the Constitution with the passage of the Nineteenth Amendment in 1920. (See the time line in Chapter 5 showing women's role in history.)

Having achieved one of its most important goals, the women's movement shifted its attention to other issues: the welfare of children, voter education, prison reform, antilynching measures, and peace. One continuing issue of importance has been women's rights. But the women's movement, like all movements, has competing concerns and interests. Should it focus on women's rights only, or on the needs of other disadvantaged groups like African Americans, children, and low-paid workers? Which right should be most aggressively pursued: the right to an education, to legal protection, to equal pay, to a decent job? The answer is that the women's movement is not just one movement but several movements that share some, yet not all, concerns.

One of the most important women's issues in the 1970s and 1980s was the Equal Rights Amendment. This proposed amendment sought to guarantee "equality of rights under the law" regardless of gender. While most women's groups, most women, and the Democratic party remain committed to the ERA, the amendment has not been the driving concern it once was. In its place have come issues like abortion, affirmative action for women, and the changing of particular laws that discriminate against women.

Abortion has been seen as a women's issue because it is women more than men whose bodies and lives are affected. As Justice Harry A. Blackmun said in *Roe v Wade*, "Freedom of personal choice in matters of marriage and family life is one of the liberties protected by the due process clause of the Fourteenth Amendment. . . . That right necessarily includes the right of a woman to decide whether or not to terminate her pregnancy."[13] But both women and men are divided on the issue of abortion, and there are women's groups on both sides of the issue.

The story of women's movements in the United States is the story of groups whose members originally lacked political power, developed a sense of group consciousness, entered politics despite countless frustrations and setbacks, and, after long struggles, achieved some of their major political goals. The story continues, as the movement still faces important unresolved issues.

Movements and Democracy

New movements constantly form as people discover new needs and the old ones become satisfied. A movement that has recently become increasingly vocal and militant, for example, is the animal rights movement.

Movements polarize opinion, but they can also persuade people to change their attitudes, and they often raise public consciousness about social issues that government might otherwise ignore.[14] In many countries movements are viewed as a threat to government—as indeed they may be, as the governments of South Africa, China, and others have learned.

To a marked degree, our Constitution continues to protect the liberties and independence of movements. The Bill of Rights guarantees movements—whether popular or unpopular—free assembly, free speech, and due process. Hence militants do not have to engage in terrorism or other extreme activities in the United States, as they do in some countries, and they need not fear persecution for demonstrating. In a democratic system that restricts the power of those in authority, movements have considerable room to operate *inside* the constitutional system.

We the People

EQUAL RIGHTS AMENDMENT (ERA)

Proposed March 22, 1972. Died June 30, 1982, three state legislatures shy of the thirty-eight needed for ratification.

Section 1. Equality of rights under the law shall not be denied or abridged by the United States or by any State on account of sex.

Section 2. The Congress shall have power to enforce, by appropriate legislation, the provisions of this article.

Section 3. This amendment shall take effect two years after the date of ratification.

TYPES OF INTEREST GROUPS

Interest groups vary widely: some are formal associations or organizations; others have no formal organization; some are organized primarily to lobby; some have other goals, such as securing wage increases, conducting research, or broadly influencing public opinion by publishing reports and mass mailings.

Interest groups can be categorized into several broad types: (1) economic, including both business and labor; (2) ideological; (3) public interest; (4) foreign policy; and (5) government itself. Obviously these categories are not mutually exclusive; some business groups are both ideological and economic. The variety and overlapping nature of interest groups in the United States have been described as *interest group pluralism*, meaning that competition among open, responsive, and diverse groups helps preserve democratic values and limits the concentration of power in any single group.

As Alexis de Tocqueville observed long ago, Americans form associations for every conceivable purpose and function. And as government has become more central to Americans' lives, these groups have turned their attention to government. In Washington today, interest groups rival the federal bureaucracy in number and complexity.

Economic Interest Groups

Madison pointed out that some of the most common and durable factions derive from property interests, or how we make our living and manage what we own. There are thousands, even tens of thousands, of economic interests: agriculture, skilled laborers, plumbers, northern businesses, southern businesses, labor unions, the airplane industry, landlords, developers, bond holders, savings and loan investors, and so on.

BUSINESS The most familiar business institution is probably the large corporation. Corporations range from small, one-person enterprises to large multinational entities. Large corporations—General Motors, AT&T, and Fortune 500 companies—exercise considerable political influence, as do hundreds of smaller corporations.

In the last century, both the national and state governments began to regulate business practices. Antitrust legislation was adopted to limit monopolies; labor laws were enacted to protect workers. The 1980s brought the need to regulate business and financial institutions back to the forefront as a result of leveraged buyouts and savings and loan scandals. In the mid-1990s, questions about such corporate practices as work force reductions ("downsizing"), government subsidies of big business ("corporate welfare"), and disproportionately high salaries for top management became political issues. As we move into the next century, corporate power and the implications of a changing domestic and global economy will make corporations and their practices important political issues.

TRADE AND OTHER ASSOCIATIONS Businesses with similar interests in government regulations and other issues join together as trade associations. They are as diverse as the products and services they provide. In addition, businesses of all types are organized into large, nationwide associations such as the Conference Board, the Business Roundtable, the Business Higher-Education Forum, and the Chamber of Commerce.

The broadest business trade association is the Chamber of Commerce of the United States. Organized in 1912, the Chamber is a federation of several thousand local Chambers of Commerce representing tens of thousands of business firms. Loosely allied with the Chamber on most issues is the National Association of Manufacturers, which, since its founding in the wake of the depression of 1893, has tended to speak for the more conservative elements of American business. Large nationwide business associations often take up issues that involve many industries. One such group is the 120,000 Independent Insurance Agents of America, which launched an intensive lobbying campaign to combat banking reform that would permit banks to sell insurance across state lines.[15] In the endless battle of factions, however, even the influence of well-funded and politically focused interests is limited when strong competing interests exist.

LABOR   The American work force is the least unionized of almost any industrial democracy (Table 9–1). Workers' associations have a range of interests, from professional standards to wages and working conditions. Labor unions are one of the most important groups representing workers.

Probably the oldest "unions" in the United States were farm organizations. The largest farm group now is the American Farm Bureau Federation, which is especially strong in the corn belt. Originally organized around government agents who helped farmers in rural counties, the federation today is almost a semigovernmental agency, but it retains full freedom to fight for such goals as price supports and expanded credit. A number of other farm organizations are based on the interests of producers of specific commodities, such as the American Soybean Association.

Other workers, too, have long been organized. Throughout the nineteenth century, workers organized political parties and local unions. Their most ambitious effort at national organization, the Knights of Labor, claimed 700,000 members. By the beginning of this century, the American Federation of Labor (AFL), a confederation of strong and independent-minded national unions mainly representing craftworkers, was the dominant organization. During the ferment of the 1930s, unions more responsive to industrial workers broke away from the AFL, which was seen as more responsive to workers long organized by trade, and formed a rival

A three-week strike in 1996 at General Motors shut down most of the company's plants. Workers were protesting against "outsourcing"—the use of nonunion labor to produce parts more cheaply.

TABLE 9–1

Union Membership in the United States Compared to Other Countries

	Union Membership as a Percentage of		
	Nonagricultural Employment	Full-Time Workers	Full-Time Manual Workers
Sweden	96%	—	—
Austria	61	52	57
Australia	56	70	69
Ireland	51	48	49
United Kingdom	50	47	53
Italy	45	33	37
Germany	43	34	39
Canada	36	—	—
Netherlands	35	42	47
Switzerland	33	37	37
France	28	—	—
Japan	28	—	—
United States	**17**	**19**	**27**

SOURCE: David G. Blanchflower and Richard B. Freeman, "Unionism in the United States and Other Advanced OECD Countries," *Industrial Relations* 31 (Winter 1992), pp. 56–79.

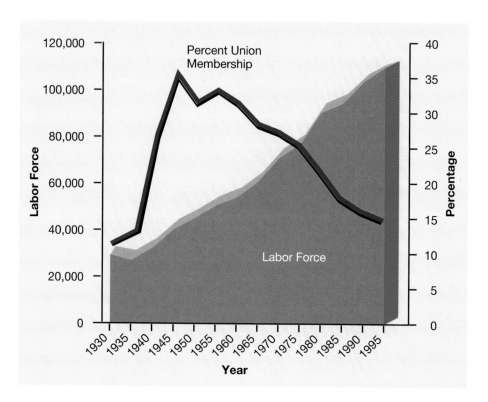

FIGURE 9–1 Labor Force and Union Membership, 1930–1995

SOURCE: *The World Almanac and Book of Facts, 1997.* (K-III Communications Company, 1996.)

national organization for workers organized by industry, the Congress of Industrial Organizations (CIO). Later the AFL and CIO reunited in the organization that exists today.

For some years the Committee on Political Education (COPE) of the AFL-CIO was one of the most respected—and most feared—political organizations in the country. In the Kennedy-Johnson years it won a reputation for political effectiveness. It encouraged and supervised grass-roots political activity, and at the national level it prepared and adopted a detailed platform that spelled out labor's position on issues. Labor contributed money to candidates, ran registration and get-out-the-vote campaigns, and otherwise supported its favorites. In recent elections COPE has had a fair, but not spectacular, record of wins for its endorsed House and Senate candidates.[16] Labor unions invested heavily in the 1992 fight against NAFTA, claiming it would cost jobs. Labor's defeat in this battle was compounded by the 1994 and 1996 elections, which put Republicans in charge of Congress. As we discussed at the beginning of this chapter, the AFL-CIO mounted a major campaign to elect a Democratic majority in Congress in 1996 by spending roughly $20 million in issue advertising targeted against Republican incumbents.[17]

Because the AFL-CIO is a federation of powerful and independent national unions, state and local groups or federations of unions have sometimes been politically divided. Leadership of the AFL-CIO had been in the hands of only a few men who, once elected, held office for a long time. Moreover, the AFL-CIO by no means speaks for all workers; union labor represents only about 16 percent of the nation's work force, and AFL-CIO membership amounts to about 80 percent of the total number of those organized.[18]

Organized labor's political and lobbying muscle is obviously limited, and the prospects for increasing influence in the future are dim. Figure 9–1 demonstrates that organized labor's membership is dwindling relative to the increase in the national work force. Union membership is optional in states whose laws permit the **open shop**. In states with the **closed shop**, union membership may be required as a condition of employment. In both cases, the unions conduct negotiations with management, and the benefits the unions gain will be shared with all workers. It is understandable in open shop states that many workers choose not to affiliate with the union when they can secure the same pay without incurring the costs associated with union membership.

The decline in the proportion of union membership is explained in part by the shift from an industrial to a service economy. There has been growth in public sector unions, however. Closely identified with the Democratic party, unions have not enjoyed the same relationship with Republican administrations. Given its limited resources, one option for labor is to form temporary coalitions with consumer, public interest, liberal, and sometimes—especially when faced with the issue of foreign imports—even with industry groups. But labor pays a price for such collaboration. It must water down or give up some of its own goals. Few of labor's recent legislative initiatives have been successful, and with Reagan and Bush appointees still serving, labor faces a much less sympathetic Supreme Court.

PROFESSIONAL ASSOCIATIONS Professional people have organized some of the strongest "unions" in the nation. Some are well known, such as the American Medical Association and the American Bar Association. Others are divided into many subgroups. Teachers, for example, are organized into large groups such as the National Education Association, the American Federation of Teachers, the American Association of University Professors, and also into subgroups based on specialties, such as the Modern Language Association and the American Political Science Association.

Many professions are regulated by government, especially on the state level. Lawyers, for example, are licensed by states, which, often as a result of pressure from lawyers themselves, have set up certain standards of admission to the state bar. Professional associations also use the courts to pursue their agenda. In the area of medical malpractice, for example, doctors lobby hard for limited liability laws, while the trial lawyers association resists such efforts. Teachers, hair stylists, and marriage therapists work for legislation or regulations of concern to them. It is not surprising, then, that among the largest donors to political campaigns through political action committees are those representing professional associations such as the American Medical Association and the American Realtors Association (see Table 9–2).

Ideological Interest Groups

Virtually all interest groups convince themselves that they are devoted to the public welfare and not merely to their own self-interests; their cases are usually presented in terms of their value to the "public interest." Countless groups have organized around specific issues, such as civil liberties, birth control, abortion, environmental protection, nuclear energy, and nuclear disarmament.[19] One of the best-known ideological groups is the American Civil Liberties Union (ACLU), with roughly one-quarter million members committed to the protection of civil liberties.[20] Some highly ideological religious groups are thriving in the otherwise pragmatic, pluralistic politics of the 1990s.[21]

Public Interest Groups

So-called "public interest" groups arose out of the political ferment of the 1960s. Common Cause, founded in 1970 by independent Republican John W. Gardner and later led by noted Watergate prosecutor Archibald Cox, campaigns for electoral reform and for making the political process more open. Its Washington staff

TABLE 9–2

PACs That Gave the Most to Federal Candidates in 1995–1996 (contributions in millions)

Democratic Republican Independent Voter Education Committee	$2.61
American Federation of State, County, and Municipal Employees	2.51
United Auto Workers Voluntary Community Action Program	2.47
Association of Trial Lawyers of America Political Action Committee	2.36
Dealers Election Action Committee of the National Automobile Dealers Association	2.35
National Education Association Political Action Committee	2.33
American Medical Association Political Action Committee	2.32
Realtors Political Action Committee	2.10
International Brotherhood of Electrical Workers Committee on Political Education	2.08
Active Ballot Club, A Department of United Food & Commercial Workers International Union	2.03

SOURCE: Federal Elections Commission, *PAC Activity Increases in 1995-96 Election Cycle*, Press Release, April 22, 1997, p. 19.

"There's getting to be a lot of dangerous talk, about the public interest."

The Herblock Gallery (Simon & Schuster, 1968).

raises money through direct mail campaigns, oversees state chapters, issues a flood of research reports and press releases on current issues, and lobbies on Capitol Hill and in major government departments. Ralph Nader started a conglomerate of consumer organizations that investigates and reports on governmental and corporate action—or inaction—relating to consumer interests. Public Interest Research Groups (PIRGs), founded by Ralph Nader, today number among the largest interest groups in the country. PIRGs have become important players on Capitol Hill and in several state legislatures, promoting environmental issues, safe energy, consumer protection, and good government.

Ideological and public interest groups behave very much like economic interest groups although they may not be motivated by a desire to make money. Some of these groups are single-issue groups, often highly motivated and seeing politics primarily as a means to pursue their one issue. Such groups are often adamant about their position and unwilling to negotiate compromises.

A specific type of public interest group is the *tax-exempt public charity*, organized under section 501(c)(3) of the Internal Revenue Code. Examples include the American Heart Association, the Girl Scouts, and the American Cancer Society. Organizations must meet certain conditions, such as educational or philanthropic objectives, to qualify for this preferred status. Not only are public charities tax exempt, but donations to these organizations are tax deductible, and the organizations are not required to disclose information about their donors publicly. These organizations cannot participate in elections or support candidates, nor benefit an individual or small group. Despite these limitations, tax-exempt charitable organizations have been very active in voter registration efforts and in advertising campaigns designed to influence public opinion. Two notable foundations are the Dole Foundation, founded some years earlier by 1996 Republican presidential candidate Robert Dole, to promote the employment of the disabled,[22] and House Speaker Newt Gingrich's tax-exempt organization, the Progress and Freedom Foundation, established in 1993, to support a college course, "Renewing American Civilization." Gingrich was later reprimanded by Congress for having spent hundreds of thousands of dollars of tax-deductible contributions on a course whose purpose was expressly partisan and was run by Gingrich's own political action committee—GOPAC.[23]

Foreign Policy Interest Groups

Issues of domestic policy are not the only matters of concern to interest groups. More and more, groups are organizing to promote or oppose certain foreign policies. Among the most prestigious (although not uncontroversial) foreign affairs group is the Council on Foreign Relations in New York City. Other groups, devoted to narrower areas of American foreign policy, exert pressure on legislators or the executive to enact specific policies. Among these are interest groups concerned with the Arab-Israeli conflict and the contending factions in Bosnia. Formal lobbies for both Israel and the Arab nations—the American Israel Public Affairs Committee and the National Association of Arab-Americans, respectively—have competed to influence policy makers in Washington. Interest group pressure also influenced U.S. policy toward South Africa and played a role in South Africa's decision to abandon apartheid. Groups ranging from student organizations to national lobbies like the American Committee on Africa urged divestment, sanctions, or other policy measures that ultimately promoted change in South Africa from the outside.

Government Interest Groups

Government itself is the source of important interest groups. Some may think that odd, but as the size of government has grown and the scope of its activity has expanded, so has governmental lobbying. Many cities and most states retain

Washington lobbyists, and cities also hire lobbyists to represent them at the state legislature. Governors are organized through the National Governors Association, cities through the National League of Cities, and counties through the National Association of Counties.

Government is an important source of interest groups in other ways as well. Public employees form a large and well-organized group. The National Education Association (NEA), for example, claims more than 2.75 million members. Public employees are also important to organized labor. The fastest growing unions in the AFL-CIO are public employee unions.[24]

Other Interest Groups

Americans are often emotionally and financially involved in a variety of groups: veterans groups such as American Legion or Veterans of Foreign Wars; nationality groups such as the multitude of German, Irish, Hispanic, and Korean organizations; or religious organizations such as the Knights of Columbus or B'nai B'rith. More than 150 nationwide organizations are based on national origin alone.

In recent years there has been a virtual explosion in the number and variety of interests and associations.[25] This is especially true for single-issue interest groups. These groups crusade tirelessly for or against politically "hot" issues, such as abortion or the sale of firearms. Numerous environmental groups press for legislation at all levels of government; Table 9–3 offers a sample of environmental groups. Such associations are not new. The Anti-Saloon League of the 1890s was single-mindedly devoted to barring the sale and manufacture of alcoholic beverages, and it did not care whether legislators were drunk or sober, as long as they voted dry.

CHARACTERISTICS AND POWER OF INTEREST GROUPS

The United States has long been known for the number and diversity of its interest groups. Most Americans' interests are represented by a number of interest groups, some of which they are aware of and others of which they may not be. For instance, older citizens may not be aware that their interests are represented by the American Association of Retired Persons (AARP). Others may not know that when they join the American Automobile Association (AAA), they not only purchase travel assistance and automobile towing when needed but also join a group that lobbies Congress and the Federal Highway Administration on behalf of motorists. Groups vary in their goals, methods, and power. Among the most important group characteristics are size, resources, cohesiveness, leadership, the political and social system in which they operate, and how they activate members. Interest groups also differ in the ways they attempt to influence government.

Size and Resources

Obviously size is important to political power; an organization representing 5 million voters has more influence than one speaking for 5 thousand. Perhaps even more important than size is the extent to which members are actively involved and focus on the attainment of policy objectives. Often people join an organization for reasons that have little to do with its political objectives. They may want to secure group insurance, take advantage of travel benefits, participate in professional meetings, or get a job. If organizational leaders can depend on the political backing of their followers, the organization is able to put its full strength into pursuing its aims and will have an enormous advantage in the political arena. If the leaders cannot motivate the members, the organization will not be effective.

While the size of an interest group is often important, so, too, is its *spread*—the extent to which membership is concentrated or dispersed. Automobile

We the People

Some Associations with an Ethnic, Religious, Racial, or Gender Interest

- American-Arab Relations Committee
- American Gay/Lesbian Atheists
- American Jewish Congress
- Anti-Defamation League of B'nai B'rith
- Black Women Organized for Educational Development
- Buddhist Peace Fellowship
- Catholic War Veterans of the U.S.A.
- Chinese Alliance for Democracy
- Committee on South Asian Women
- Confederation of Independent Aryan Organizations
- Cowboys for Christ
- Dutch Family Heritage Society
- Episcopal Peace Fellowship
- Gray Panthers
- Greek Orthodox Young Adult League
- Men's Rights Association
- National Conference of Christians and Jews
- National Council of Churches
- National Organization for Women
- Pacific Islands Association

TABLE 9–3
Some Environmental Groups and How They Do Business

Group	Membership	Issues	Style
Greenpeace USA	2.3 million (worldwide)	Whales, oceans, toxics	Media events; mass mailings; door-to-door canvassing; does not lobby government
Natural Resources Defense Council	168,000	Energy, air and water pollution, nuclear waste	Lobbies; litigates; employs lawyers and scientists to compete with experts from agencies and industry
Sierra Club	650,000 (one-third in California)	Wildlands, pollution, endangered species	Grass-roots action; liberal, Democratic politics; hierarchy of 382 local groups making up 55 U.S. and 2 Canadian chapters; fierce internal debates
Wilderness Society	370,000	Strictly public lands	No local chapters; once a backpacker advocacy group, now has a more general, Washington-insider focus

SOURCE: *Governing*, April 1992, p. 35.

manufacturing is concentrated in Michigan and a few other states, and as a result its influence does not have the same spread as that of the American Medical Association, which has an active chapter in virtually every congressional district. An association consisting of 3 million supporters concentrated in a few states will usually have less influence than another group consisting of 3 million supporters spread out in a large number of states. A group whose goals are contrary to widely accepted values will have a more difficult time than a group that can present its demands as advancing the public interest. Most interest groups cultivate specific and recognizable identities.[26]

Interest groups also differ in the extent to which they preempt a policy area or share it with other groups. Doctors and the AMA have effectively preempted the health care policy area because they play such an important role in the delivery of health care. In the transportation policy area, railroads must compete with interstate trucking and even air-freight companies.

Groups also differ in their *resources*, which include money, volunteers, expertise, and reputation. Some groups can influence many centers of power—both houses of Congress, the White House, federal agencies, the courts, and state and local governments—while others cannot.

Although members of a group all have a common interest in obtaining the collective benefit of group action, they do not all share a common interest in paying the cost of securing that benefit, whether it be a sacrifice of time or a membership fee to finance the group's activities. People will not usually participate unless the benefits outweigh the costs. This observation helps explain the relative success of small groups compared to large groups. Members of large groups might rationally choose not to contribute to an organization that represents them because their individual contribution is so small and would probably "not make a difference anyway." However, in a small group, in which each member gets a substantial proportion of the total gain, a common interest must be achieved through the voluntary, self-interested action of the group's members.[27] An individual who does not join an interest group representing his or her interests, yet naturally receives the benefit of the influence the group achieves, is known as a *free rider*.

How do associations motivate potential members to join them? Individuals will not always join an organization for the benefits of collective action. Organizations must provide selective incentives, material or otherwise, that are compelling enough to attract the potential free rider.[28] Unions are organized not just for lobbying but also to perform other important services for their members. They derive much of their strength from their negotiating position with corporations, which they use to obtain wage increases or improved safety standards. Similarly, the AARP, in addition to lobbying against Social Security cuts and speaking out on other issues of concern to older citizens, offers incentives such as a free subscription to its magazine, *Modern Maturity*, and member discounts at certain hotels. This combination of size and strength sets these groups apart from other large organizations in their effectiveness, as members derive numerous benefits from joining.

Large groups often become organized only when an important issue excites the public or when effective leadership can guide the organization. The mobilization of business interests has been successful in recent years in large part because of the interest of the nation's corporations and trade associations in the outcome of the legislative and elective process.[29]

The Gray Panthers exert their influence on legislation affecting senior citizens. One of the most powerful interest groups is the American Association of Retired Persons (AARP).

Cohesiveness

Because many Americans are members of many associations, their loyalties are divided. This overlapping membership largely determines the cohesiveness of an association and can create problems for organizational leaders. For example, suppose a union official asks a dozen members to come to a meeting. Several may say they will come, but two belong to a club that bowls that night, two others may have to stay home with their families, and another may have to attend a church supper. Even those who attend the meeting may not be 100 percent supporters. Suppose they are asked to vote for a particular candidate in a coming election. Some will, but one may decide to vote for the other candidate because she is a neighbor, and another will vote for her because they are both Italian Americans. Political party loyalties or American Legion membership may also interfere with a union request. Or perhaps one union member will not know what to do and will not vote at all. Obviously, the unity of the membership is a key element, as is the ability to act quickly and decisively. Unity, however, is easier to achieve in a small group that focuses on a relatively specific and concrete concern.

Usually a mass-membership organization is made up of three types of members.[30] The first type comprises a relatively small number of formal leaders who may hold full-time, paid positions or at least devote much of their extra time, effort, and money to the group's activities. The second includes persons intensely involved in the group, organizationally and psychologically. They identify with the group's aims, attend meetings, faithfully pay dues, and do a lot of the legwork. The third type consists of people who are members in name only. They do not participate actively, they do not look on themselves as Teamsters or Rotarians or Legionnaires, and they cannot be depended on to vote in elections or otherwise act as the leadership wants. In a typical large organization, for every top leader there might be a few hundred hard-core activists and thousands of essentially inactive members.

Another factor in group cohesiveness is its organizational structure. Some associations have no formal organization; others are local organizations that have joined together in some sort of loose state or national federation in which they retain a measure of separate power and independence, just as the states did when they entered the Union. Separation of powers may be found as well: the national assembly of an organization establishes, or at least ratifies, policy; an executive committee meets more frequently; a president or director is elected to head and speak for the group; and permanent paid officials form the organization's bureaucracy. Power may be further divided between the organization's main headquarters and its Washington office. An organization of this sort tends to be far less cohesive than a centralized, disciplined group such as the army or some trade unions.

Leadership

Closely related to cohesion is the nature of the leadership. In a group that embraces many attitudes and interests, leaders may either weld the various elements together or sharpen their disunity. The leader of a national business association, for example, must tread cautiously between big business and little business, between exporters and importers, between chain stores and corner grocery stores, and between the producers and the sellers of competing products. Yet leaders must not be at the mercy of different interests, for above all they must lead. They must show how to achieve organizational goals. The group leader is in the same position as a president or a member of Congress; he or she must know when to lead followers and when to follow them.

Techniques of Interest Groups

Interest groups seeking to wield influence choose from a variety of political weapons and targets. They carefully monitor federal agencies and departments, both houses of Congress, the White House staff, and state and local governments. They also become involved in litigation. Other techniques include persuasion, rule making, election activities, and lobbying.

PUBLICITY AND MASS MEDIA APPEALS Interest groups exploit the communications media—television, radio, newspapers, leaflets, signs, direct mail, and word of mouth—to influence voters during elections and to motivate constituents to contact their representatives between elections. Business enjoys a special advantage in this arena, and businesspeople have the money to use propaganda machinery. As large-scale advertisers, they know how to deliver their message effectively or to find an advertising agency to do it for them. Most important, they generally have easy access to the means of disseminating propaganda, such as the press. Business groups for and against NAFTA and Medicare reform launched major media campaigns on these issues to mobilize public opinion to their point of view.

MASS MAILING New technologies have increased the reach and effectiveness of interest groups. One of these new technologies is computerized and targeted mass mailing.[31] For many decades, interest groups have been sending out huge mailings to people whose names are on lists culled from telephone directories and other sources. Most of these mailings are sent out indiscriminately. Mass mailing is used by all kinds of interest groups, but it has been especially refined by public interest groups, who are sometimes accused of being a small headquarters with a good mailing list. Today's technology can produce personalized letters targeted to specific groups. Speaking of the National Rifle Association, Congressman William J. Hughes (D.-N.J.) said, "It's a lobby that can put 15,000 letters in your district overnight and have people in your town hall meeting interrupting you."[32] Such targeted direct mail can also appeal to people who share a common concern, such as environmental groups.

LITIGATION When groups find the usual political channels closed to them, they may turn to the courts.[33] The Legal Aid and Defense Fund of the National

The latest in available weaponry is demonstrated at a National Rifle Association annual convention.

Association for the Advancement of Colored People (NAACP), for example, initiated and won numerous court cases in its efforts to improve legal protection for African Americans. In recent decades, urban interests and environmental groups, feeling underrepresented in state and national legislatures, have turned to the courts to influence the political agenda.[34] Women's groups—such as the National Organization for Women and the American Civil Liberties Union's Women's Rights Project—have also used the courts to pursue their objectives.[35]

Despite the general impression that association litigants achieve great success in the courts, groups are no more likely than individuals to win their cases at the district court level.[36] In addition to initiating lawsuits, associations can gain a forum for their views in the courts by filing **amicus curiae** (literally "friend of the court") **briefs** in cases in which they are not direct parties.

INFLUENCE ON RULE MAKING   Organized groups have ready access to the rule-making process by which executive and regulatory agencies write the rules that implement laws passed by Congress. Agencies publish proposed regulations in the ***Federal Register*** and invite responses and reactions from all interested persons before the rules are finalized. (The *Federal Register* is published every weekday. You can find it in your school or public library.) Well-staffed associations and corporations peruse the *Register*, ever alert for actions that will affect their interests. Lobbyists, who are often lawyers, prepare written responses to the proposed rules, draft alternative rules, and appear at the hearings to make their case. These lobbyists seek to be on good terms with the staff of the agencies so that they can learn what rules are being considered long before they are released publicly and thus have input in the early stages. Administrative rules are defined over time through legal cases and agency modifications, so even if an interest group fails to get what it wants, it can fight the rules in court or press for a reinterpretation when the agency leadership changes hands.

Finally, an interest group can seek to modify rules it does not like by going back to Congress to change the legal mandate for the agency or have the agency's budget reduced, making enforcement of existing rules difficult. In short, interest groups and lobbyists never really quit fighting for their point of view.

An example of lobbyists using U.S. senators to alter administrative regulations was the case of Charles Keating and the failed Lincoln Savings and Loan. Five U.S. senators were accused of taking campaign money from Keating, owner of the Lincoln Savings and Loan, including nearly $1 million given to California Senator Alan Cranston for his nonprofit voter registration efforts. These senators in turn lobbied savings and loan regulators.[37] Despite extensive investigation and televised hearings, the Senate did not seriously punish any of the five senators, but the negative publicity may have been a factor in the decision of three of the five not to seek reelection. In another example, media mogul Rupert Murdoch was accused of trying to buy favor with Speaker Newt Gingrich by offering him a $4.5 million advance on a book in 1995.[38]

ELECTION ACTIVITIES   Although nearly all large organizations say they are non-political, almost all are politically involved in some way. What group leaders usually mean when they say they are nonpolitical is that they are *nonpartisan*. A distinguishing feature of organized interest groups is that they often try to work through *both* parties; usually this means working for individual candidates.

Labor usually favors Democrats. The AFL-CIO supported Democrats Hubert Humphrey, Jimmy Carter, Walter Mondale, Michael Dukakis, and Bill Clinton. The Teamsters Union during this period endorsed Richard Nixon, Gerald Ford, Ronald Reagan, and George Bush. But in 1992 the Teamsters reversed this pattern and endorsed Democrat Bill Clinton. In 1996 the union did not endorse a candidate for president. Clinton also benefited from the endorsement and support of the National Education Association, a group with more than 2 million members, most of them teachers. Bob Dole's attack on teachers unions in his acceptance speech served to further activate the group in support of Clinton in 1996.

Business groups generally endorse the incumbent but favor Republicans when no incumbent is running. Some organizations are prevented from taking a firm position by the diversity of their members. A local retailers' group, for example, might be composed equally of Republicans and Democrats, and many of its members might refuse to take an open position on a candidate for fear of losing business. In such cases more subtle means may be equally effective. At meetings, word may be passed around that Candidate X is sound from the organization's point of view, and Candidate X may also receive a campaign contribution from the organization's political action committee.

Ideological groups "target" certain candidates, seeking to change the candidates' positions, or failing that, to influence voters to vote against that candidate. Americans for Democratic Action and the American Conservative Union publish ratings of incumbents' voting record on liberal and conservative issues, as do the U.S. Chamber of Commerce and the AFL-CIO, among others.

How effective is electioneering by interest groups? Everything depends on the factors we have been discussing: group size, cohesiveness, objectives, political resources, leadership, and the political context. In general, though, the mass-membership organizations' power to mobilize their full strength in elections has been exaggerated in the press. Too many cross-pressures are operating in the pluralistic politics of the United States for any one group to assume a commanding role. Some groups reach their maximum influence only by allying themselves closely with one of the two major parties. They may place their members on local, state, and national party committees and help send them to party conventions as delegates, but such alliances mean losing some independence and singleness of purpose.

FORMING A POLITICAL PARTY   Another interest group strategy is to form a political party. These third parties are organized less with the intent to *win elections* than to *publicize a cause*. The Free Soil party was formed in 1848 to propagandize against the spread of slavery, and the Prohibition party was organized 20 years later to ban the sale of liquor. Farmers have formed a variety of such parties. In 1991 the National Organization for Women (NOW) announced it was forming a political party to call attention to issues of concern to its membership, but NOW ended up without candidates or votes in the 1992 election. More often, however, interest groups prefer to work through existing parties.

In 1992 and in 1996, we witnessed a partly authentic and partly self-engineered movement to put H. Ross Perot in the White House. And there are scores of movements that have formed to fight for better schools, a cleaner environment, and lower taxes. Will our more than two-hundred-year-old constitutional democracy be able to cope with a future tide of larger, more activist movements, each proclaiming some essential cause? Or will the movements engulf and endanger our slow-moving, often deadlocked governmental system?

COOPERATIVE LOBBYING   Interest groups often form alliances. An example is the Food Group, a 30-year-old informal conference group in Washington that has represented more than 60 business and trade associations. In addition, it spawned an Information Committee on Federal Food Regulations to fight "truth-in-packaging" legislation. Although the Food Group has been fairly effective, it does run into the predictable problem of differences among its constituents over goals and priorities and has found it difficult to put strong and unified pressure on Congress and government agencies.

Other like-minded groups have also joined together as cooperative groups. In 1987 the Leadership Conference on Civil Rights brought together many groups in the battle to defeat the nomination of outspoken federal judge Robert Bork to the U.S. Supreme Court.[39] Different types of environmentalists work together, as do consumer and ideological groups on the right and on the left. Women continue to be represented by a large variety of groups that reflect diverse interests, but the larger the coalition, the greater the chance that members may divide over such issues as abortion.

THE INFLUENCE OF LOBBYISTS

Despite their negative public image, lobbyists perform useful functions for government. They provide information for the decision makers of all three branches of government, they help educate and mobilize public opinion, they help prepare legislation and testify before legislative hearings, and they contribute a large share of the costs of campaigns. Yet many people are concerned that lobbyists have too much influence on government and add to legislative gridlock by being able to stop action on pressing problems.

Who Are the Lobbyists?

The typical image of interest groups in action is that of powerful, hard-nosed lobbyists who skillfully employ a combination of knowledge, persuasiveness, personal influence, charm, and money to influence legislators and bureaucrats. **Lobbyists** are the employees of associations who try to influence policy decisions and positions in the executive and especially in the legislative branches of our government. They are experienced in the ways of government, often having been public servants before going to work for an organized interest group or association or corporation. They might start as staff in Congress, perhaps on a congressional committee. Later, when their party wins the White House, they gain an administration post, often in the same policy area as their congressional committee work. After a few years in the administration, they are ready to make the move to lobbying, either by going to work for one of the interests they dealt with while in the government or by obtaining a position with a lobbying firm.

This employment cycle from government to interest group is known as the **revolving door**. Contacts made during government service are crucial to effective lobbying, and many former members of Congress make good use of their congressional experience as full-time lobbyists. Immediately upon leaving the White House staff, Michael Deaver, one of Ronald Reagan's principal advisers, became a lobbyist representing corporations like CBS and TWA as well as the governments of South Korea, Singapore, and Canada. The Republic of South Korea paid him $1.2 million over three years to protect its interests.[40] About a year into Bill Clinton's first term Roy Neel, his deputy chief of staff and a longtime aide to Vice-president Al Gore, left the administration to become the president and chief executive officer of the United States Telephone Association. This trade association was heavily involved in pushing for the telecommunications bill that passed Congress with the support of the Clinton administration. Neel was not involved in Clinton's 1996 reelection campaign.[41]

The revolving-door tendency between government and interest groups produces networks of people who care about certain issues. These networks have been called **iron triangles**—meaning mutually supporting relationships among interest groups, congressional committees and subcommittees, and the government agencies that share a common policy concern. Sometimes these relationships become so strong and mutually beneficial that the issue network becomes very powerful. Retired military officers, for example, can go to work for defense contractors after leaving

Why Are They Called Lobbyists?

The terms "lobbying" and "lobbyist" were not generally used until around the middle of the nineteenth century in the United States. The root in these words refers to the lobby or hallway outside House and Senate chambers in the U.S. Capitol. It was also used to refer to hotel lobbies in Washington, where the petitioners and agents of influence congregated. Thus a senator coming out of the Senate chamber might be accosted politely by several lobbyists seeking to influence his vote on some measure. Or a president might be dining at the Old Willard Hotel, a few blocks from the White House, and make reference to the number of "lobbyists" hanging around in the hotel lobby.

The noun "lobby" has been turned into a verb in this political context. Thus "to lobby" is to seek to influence legislators and government officials, and we call this lobbying even if there is no lobby in sight.

"Please understand. I don't sell access to the government. I merely sell access to the guys who <u>do</u> sell access to the government."

Drawing by Ed Licber. ©1986 The New Yorker Magazine, Inc.

the military, although they are banned for life from selling Department of Defense contracts. This restriction does not preclude them from providing advice to corporations on how best to compete for defense projects.

What Do Lobbyists Do?

Lobbying, one of the best-known weapons of group influence, is probably also the oldest; it is certainly one of the most criticized. Generations of Americans have been angered by exposés of an "invisible government," accusations that unelected interest groups are the ones really making the decisions. From the time of the Yazoo land frauds two hundred years ago, when a whole state legislature was bribed and the postmaster general was put on a private payroll as a lobbyist, to the latest interest-peddling scandals in Congress, Americans have denounced lobbyists.

Lobbying today is far more extensive and sophisticated, though not necessarily more effective. Thousands of lobbyists are active in Washington, but few of them are as glamorous or as unscrupulous as the media suggest, nor are they necessarily influential. One limit on their power is the competition among interest groups. Rarely does any one group have a policy area all to itself. For example, transportation policy involves airplanes, trucks, cars, railroads, consumers, suppliers, state and local governments—the list goes on and on.

To members of Congress, the single most important thing lobbyists provide is money for their next reelection campaign. "Reelection underlies everything else," writes political scientist David Mayhew.[42] Money from interest groups has become instrumental in this driving need of incumbents. Interest groups also provide volunteers for campaign activity. Also their failure to support the opposition can enhance an incumbent's chances of being reelected.

Some people defend lobbyists as a kind of "third house" of Congress. Whereas the Senate and House are set up on a geographical basis, lobbyists represent people on the basis of interests: jobs or other economic interests, issue positions, and ideological leanings. Small but important groups can sometimes get representation in the "third house" when they cannot get it in the other two. In a nation of vast and important interests, this kind of functional representation, if it is not abused, can be a useful supplement to geographical representation. Should the former kind of representation supplant the latter? Most analysts say no, because legislative institutions are important for representing people in the totality of their lives and needs.

Beyond their central role in campaigns and elections, interest groups provide another essential commodity to legislators: information of two important types,

Lobbyists during the administration of President Grant operated in much the same way as today's lobbyists do.

political and substantive. The political information provided by lobbyists includes such matters as who supports or opposes legislation and how strongly they feel.[43] Substantive information such as the impact of proposed laws might not be available from any other source. Lobbyists often provide technical assistance on the drafting of bills and amendments, identify persons to testify at legislative hearings, and formulate questions to ask of administration officials at oversight hearings.

Legal and political skills, along with specialized knowledge, have become so crucial in executive and legislative policy making as to become a form of power in themselves. Elected representatives increasingly depend on their staffs for guidance, and these staffs in turn are linked to the staffs of executive departments and of lobbyists. Issue specialists know more about Section 504 or Title IX or the amendment of 1972—and who wrote that amendment and why—than most political and administrative leaders, who are usually generalists. It is in this gray area of policy making that many interest groups and lobbyists play a vital role, as people move freely from congressional or agency staff to association staff and perhaps back again.

MONEY AND POLITICS

A **political action committee (PAC)** is the political arm of a business, labor, trade association, or other interest group that is legally entitled to raise funds on a voluntary basis from members, stockholders, or employees in order to contribute funds to favored candidates or political parties.[44] PACs link two vital techniques of influence—giving money and other political aid to politicians, and persuading officeholders to act or vote "the right way" on issues. Thus PACs are the means by which interest groups seek to influence who the legislators are and what they do once they take office.[45]

PACs can be categorized according to the type of interest they represent: corporations; trade, and health organizations; labor unions; ideological organizations (called nonconnected by the FEC); cooperative organizations; and corporations without stock. Figure 9–2 represents the total of campaign contributions to congressional candidates for each type of PAC since 1978. In 1978 there was little difference in the level of campaign activity of PACs representing corporations, labor unions, or trade associations.[46] But that has changed, with corporate PACs spending more than the others, and ideological PACs at roughly half the level of spending of trade and labor PACs. In the 1993–94 election cycle, corporate PACs spent $78.2 million dollars, nearly $30 million more than labor PACs and $18 million more than trade PACs.[47]

Let's look at some specific cases. In the 1995-1996 election cycle, Congressman Daniel Schaefer raised a war chest of $742,000, with nearly three-quarters of it coming from PACs; Congressman Gerald Solomon raised $570,000, with nearly 90 percent coming from PACs. Both congressmen won with minimal opposition. In the Senate, Republican Thad Cochran raised over 70 percent of his campaign funds from PACs in an unopposed race in Mississippi. Republican Pat Roberts raised more than half of his campaign funds from PACs in a successful campaign for the open seat in Kansas. PACs in 1996 made a total donation of $217.8 million to House and Senate candidates, an all-time record.

The Growth of PACs

Ironically, considering that the explosion of PACs has occurred mainly in the business world, it was organized labor that invented this device. In the 1930s, John L. Lewis, president of the United Mine Workers, set up the Non-Partisan Political League as the political arm of the newly formed Congress of Industrial Organizations. When the CIO merged with the American Federation of Labor, the new labor group established the Committee on Political Education (COPE), whose

Suggested Steps to Successful Lobbying

• Anticipate and analyze the political situation and the key players.
• Define a realistic objective.
• Understand the timing.
• Target your audience.
• Always tell the truth, the whole truth.
• Always work with the professional staff.
• Know when to play offense and when to play defense.
• Support your political friends.
• Be sensitive to outside strategy needs.
• Be aware of the special opportunities presented by presidential campaigns.

SOURCE: Terrence D. Straub, "Changing Faces," Speech to the Graduate School of Political Management, New York University, April 11, 1988.

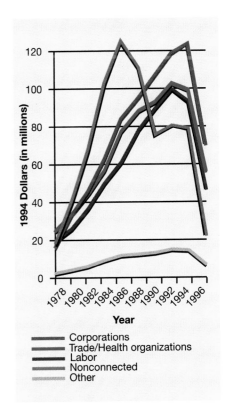

FIGURE 9–2 PAC Contributions to Congressional Candidates (1994 dollars, in millions)

SOURCE: Howard W. Stanley and Richard G. Niemi, *Vital Statistics on American Politics*, 5th ed. (Congressional Quarterly Press, 1995), p. 164.

activities we have already described. This unit came to be the model for most political action committees: "From the outset, national, state, and local units of COPE have not only raised and distributed funds, but have also served as the mechanism for organized and widespread union activity in the electoral process, for example, in voter registration, political education, and get-out-the-vote drives."[48] Some years later, manufacturers formed the Business-Industry Political Action Committee, but this committee, and the few other PACs in the 1960s, played a limited role.

The 1970s brought a near-revolution in the role and influence of PACs, ironically as the result of the post-Watergate reforms. The number of PACs increased dramatically, from about 150 to more than 4,000 today. Corporations and trade associations contributed most to this growth; today their PACs constitute the majority of all PACs. Labor PACs, on the other hand, increased only slightly in number, representing less than 10 percent of all PACs. But the increase in the number of PACs is less important than the intensity of recent PAC participation in elections and in lobbying.

How PACs Invest Their Money

In response to reporters' questions concerning the influence of money in politics, controversial banker Charles Keating once said, "One question, among the many raised in recent weeks, [has] to do with whether my financial support in any way influenced several political figures to take up my cause. I want to say in the most forceful way I can: I certainly hope so."[49] PACs take part in the entire election process, but their main influence lies in their capacity to contribute money to candidates. Candidates today need big money to wage their election or reelection campaigns. It is no longer uncommon for House candidates to spend more than a million dollars, and for many senators or would-be senators to spend ten times that amount.[50]

As corporate, industry, and labor PACs increase in number and dollars contributed, their influence grows accordingly. What counts is not only the amounts they give but also to whom they give: the more influential incumbents. All ten of the top PAC recipients in 1990 were Democrats, and only five of the top 50 were Republicans; Newt Gingrich, at the time Republican party whip, was among the top five House PAC recipients. In 1994, top PAC recipients in the House included Newt Gingrich, as well as former House Democratic leaders Tom Foley (former Speaker), Richard Gephardt (former majority leader), and Dan Rostenkowski (former chair of the Ways and Means Committee).[51] When Republicans won control of the House in 1994, they won all chairmanships and the opportunity to cash in with PACs. Committee chairs have a powerful say over the agenda for their committee. PACs with an interest in that agenda seek to curry favor with the chair. In 1996, for the first time, most PAC money went to Republicans, up from 33 percent in 1994. Some Democrats continue to do very well with PACs, as eight of the ten top PAC recipients in 1996 were Democrats. The leader in PAC receipts was Democrat Vic Fazio of California, who raised nearly $1.4 million in PAC money for his 1996 election.

Despite reports of freewheeling spending by big corporations, most business PACs proceed cautiously.[52] In deciding which candidates to help and with how much, PACs first consider the candidate's record and the likelihood of his or her voting as the PAC wishes. But other factors are also important: the likelihood that the candidate will win; the difference money will make in the campaign; whether the candidate is an incumbent (and hence would reasonably have more chance of winning); and the PAC's access to the candidate if he or she is elected. Party is not a major criterion for corporate-related PACs, although they do contribute slightly more to Republican candidates than to Democratic ones. Labor PACs, on the other hand, give overwhelmingly to Democrats.

PACs, like individuals, are limited by law in the amount of money they can contribute to any single candidate in an election cycle. The Federal Election Campaign Act of 1971 limits PACs to $5,000 per election or $10,000 per election cycle (primary and general elections). Individuals have a limit of $2,000 per candidate per election cycle. PACs have found some creative ways around this limit. They can host fund-raisers attended by other PACs to boost their reputation with the candidate, or they can "bundle" contributions. In 1986, ALIGNPAC, the political action committee of independent insurance agents, "collected contributions of more than $250,000 from individual insurance agents and presented them in a bundle to Senator Robert Packwood, who was chairman of the Senate Finance Committee."[53] Through bundling, PACs and interested individuals can increase their clout with elected officials.

The role of foreign lobbyists and PACs for companies owned by foreigners have received recent attention as the result of campaign contributions from various foreign countries, allegedly to influence American policy. Both parties have accepted money from foreign nationals in the past, but the 1996 Clinton campaign had one fund-raiser, John Huang, a former Department of Commerce aid who was then a staff member of the Democratic National Committee, who raised $2.5 million, some of it from Indonesian businessman James Riady, a friend of Clinton's from Arkansas. Once before entering government as a Commerce Department official and then twice while in government, Huang arranged for Riady to meet President Clinton in the White House. Republicans accuse Huang of allowing "Riady to lobby Clinton on trade policy in exchange for political contributions."[54] The Democratic party later returned almost half the money Huang raised for the 1996 campaign.

The role of foreign money in our election process was placed on the agenda of campaign finance reform following the 1996 election. Under current law, foreign-owned corporations can engage in election activities as long as the individuals making the allocation decisions are U.S. citizens and the foreign corporations or foreign citizens do not provide funds for the PAC.[55]

The Effectiveness of PACs

How much does PAC money influence election outcomes, legislation, and representation? One critic has written, "When politicians start to see a dollar sign behind every vote, every phone call, every solicitation, those other factors sometimes weighed during governance, like the public good and equal access to government, become less and less important."[56] An organization called Citizens Against PACs publishes attacks on members of Congress who, in their opinion, accept too many out-of-state PAC contributions. In this area, as in others, money obviously talks. But it is easy to exaggerate that influence. While a candidate may receive a great amount of PAC money, only a fraction of that total comes from any single interest. In addition, it is debatable how much campaign contributions affect election outcomes and uncertain that winning candidates will be willing and able to "remember" their financial angels or that the money in the end produces a real payoff in legislation. So even big PACs have learned to be patient. Bernadette A. Budde, political education director of the Business-Industry PAC, declared, "You know you're not going to make 10 yards on the first down, so you try to make 2 or 3 or 4 yards at a time."[57]

Much depends, however, on the context in which money is given and received. Many campaigns—especially congressional and state and local campaigns—are small-scale undertakings in which a big contribution makes a difference. Amid all the murk of campaigning, a candidate may feel grateful for so tangible and convertible a contribution as money. Studies demonstrate a

Thinking It Through

Some evidence indicates the increase in PAC corporate spending is not as great as it appears; in fact, much of the PAC money may be "old wine in new bottles"—that is, money given publicly that used to be given in legal or illegal personal campaign contributions by business chiefs.* One argument against reform is that it is impossible in a free society to restrict the flow of money. Laws can be passed to limit or regulate the flow of money in politics, but money will find an alternative way to accomplish its purpose of influencing elections. Finally, in the spirit of the Bill of Rights, whatever the evils, no action should be taken that may remotely threaten the liberties and autonomy of corporations or interest groups in general.

Those who favor banning PACs contend that, unlike individuals, PACs do not have a constitutional right to spend money to influence an election. Because PAC money is so frequently given to incumbents, critics contend that it alters the competitive environment of elections and makes it much harder for challengers to compete. Moreover, PACs often represent interests beyond the boundaries of the state or congressional district, creating a constituency that is different from the voters in the district. Efforts to ban PACs encounter strong First Amendment arguments relating to freedom of speech and association.

*Michael J. Malbin, "Campaign Financing and the 'Special Interest,'" *The Public Interest* 56 (Summer 1979), pp. 21–42. But for a somewhat different view, see David Cohen and Wendy Wolff, "Freeing Congress from the Special Interest State: A Public Interest Agenda for the 1980s," *Harvard Journal of Legislation* 17 (1980), pp. 253–93.

TABLE 9-4

Top Ten PAC Recipients in the House of Representatives, 1995–96

Victor Fazio (D-CA)	$1.348 million
Richard Gephardt (D-MO)	$1.169 million
Jonas Frost (D-TX)	$1.113 million
Newt Gingrich (R-GA)	$1.099 million
Thomas Delay (R-TX)	$1.067 million
Kenneth Bentsen (D-TX)	$911 thousand
John Dingell (D-MI)	$879 thousand
David Bonior (D-MI)	$862 thousand
Barton Gordon (D-TN)	$743 thousand
Charles Rangel (D-NY)	$711 thousand

SOURCE: Federal Elections Commission, *Congressional Fundraising and Spending Up Again in 1996*, Press Release, April 14, 1997, pp. 32–51, 54.

significant relationship between PACs giving money and receiving favorable treatment in congressional committees.[58]

PACs are pragmatic. They give mostly to incumbents, and in so doing win friends (see Table 9-4). Politicians, from local officials to the president of the United States, all want to be reelected, but Congress, perhaps more than any other institution, has come to epitomize the "career politician." Incumbents need money to ensure their reelection, and PACs, sensing this opportunity, have been happy to assist.[59] By giving two out of three dollars to incumbents in the 1996 elections, and 15 percent or less to challengers, PACs have not only helped incumbents but severely damaged the chances of challengers.[60]

PACs, like individuals, influence the outcome of elections through **independent expenditures**—money spent for or against a candidate that is not connected to the campaign chest of the candidate or his or her opponent. Independent expenditures can be made by individuals or PACs and can be spent in any way the spender wishes: TV spots, billboards, newspaper advertisements. In 1996, nearly $21 million was spent as independent expenditures in federal elections.[61] The largest such independent expenditure was $1.22 million spent in an unsuccessful effort against Mary Landrieu in the 1996 Louisiana open seat race. In 1984, the largest such independent individual expenditure was over $1 million in a successful effort to defeat Illinois Senator Charles Percy.[62] This was unusual, however, since independent expenditures are most often used to help someone win an election rather than defeat an opponent. This kind of spending does not preclude the group also giving the maximum permitted contribution to the candidate they wish to help. Independent expenditures are different from **soft money**, which is money given to a state or local party and often not disclosed because of lax disclosure laws at that level. But soft money and independent expenditures are alike in the sense that they are unlimited by federal election law.

CURING THE MISCHIEFS OF FACTION— TWO HUNDRED YEARS LATER

If James Madison were to return today, more than two hundred years after writing *The Federalist*, No. 10, he would not be surprised by the existence of interest groups. Nor would he be surprised by the variety of interest groups. He *might* be surprised, however, by the intense expression of *factionalism*—the varied weapons of group influence, the deep involvement of interest groups in the electoral process, and the vast number of lobbyists in Washington and the state capitals. And doubtless Madison, were he alive today, would be concerned about the power of faction, especially its tendency toward instability and injustice.

Concern about the evils of interest groups has been a recurrent theme throughout U.S. history. President Ronald Reagan in his farewell address warned of the power of "special interests."[63] Reagan, however, defined iron triangles to include the news media rather than executive agencies. This is an unusual change because, as Reagan himself pointed out, special interests prefer their "cozy relationship" to be kept as far from the public eye—the news media—as possible.[64] President Reagan was not alone in warning about the problems of cozy relationships between special interests and policy makers. President Dwight Eisenhower used his farewell address to warn against the military-industrial complex.

Single-interest groups organized for or against particular policies—abortion, handgun control, tobacco subsidies, animal rights—have aroused much concern in recent years. "It is said that citizen groups organizing in ever greater numbers to push single issues ruin the careers of otherwise fine politicians who disagree with them on one emotional issue, paralyze the traditional process of governmental compromise, and ignore the common good in their selfish insistence on getting their own way."[65] But which single issues reflect narrow interests? Women's rights—

even a specific issue such as the Equal Rights Amendment—are hardly "narrow," women's rights leaders contend, because they would help over half the population. Peace groups, too, claim that they represent the whole population, as do those who support prayer in schools. These issues may seem quite different from those related to subsidies to dairy farmers, for example. But some doubt the feasibility of distinguishing between narrower and broader issues or between "special" and "general" interests.

Americans today are worried about the power of faction; specifically, they fear that:

1. The struggle among factions is not a fair fight; narrower, more highly organized, and better-financed single-issue groups hold a decided advantage over more general groups.

2. The interest-group battle leads to great inequities, because lower-income people are grossly underrepresented among interest groups as compared to richer, more highly organized people, many of whom are represented by well-financed organizations and lobbyists.

3. Even though the organization of hundreds of single-issue groups has diffused power in government, as the Constitution's framers desired, it has led to incoherent policies, waste and inefficiency, endless delays, and the inability to plan ahead and anticipate crises.

4. The role of interest groups in elections has made incumbents more secure (diminished electoral competition) and enhanced the power of interest groups in relation to Congress and state and local governments.

What should be done, if anything? For decades Americans have tried to find ways to keep interest groups in check. They have agreed with James Madison that the "remedy" of suppressing factions would be worse than the disease. It would be absurd to abolish liberty simply because it nourished faction. And the existence and activity of interest groups and lobbies are solidly protected by the Constitution. But by safeguarding the value of *liberty*, have Americans allowed interest groups to threaten *equality*, the second great value in our national heritage? The question remains: How can interest groups be regulated in a way that does not threaten their constitutional liberties?

Federal and State Regulation

Americans have generally responded to this question by seeking to regulate lobbying in general and political money in particular. Concern over the use of money—especially corporate funds—to influence politicians goes back well over a century, to the Credit Mobilier scandals during the administration of Ulysses S. Grant. During the "progressive" first two decades of this century, Congress legislated against corporate contributions in federal elections and required disclosure of the use of the money.

In 1925, responding to the Teapot Dome scandal during Warren G. Harding's administration, Congress passed the Federal Corrupt Practices Act. It required disclosure reports, both before and after elections, of receipts and expenditures by Senate and House candidates and by political committees that sought to influence federal elections in more than one state. Note that these were federal laws applying to *federal* elections; regulation of state lobbying and elections was left to the states.

Federal legislation, including the 1925 Federal Corrupt Practices Act and the 1946 Federal Regulation of Lobbying Act, was not very effective. It was, in fact, largely unenforced. Many candidates filed incomplete reports or none at all. The reform mood of the 1960s brought basic changes, "nurtured by the ever-increasing costs of campaigning, the incidence of millionaire candidates, the large disparities

Lobbying Disclosure Act of 1995

After a long battle, a new law restricting lobbying took effect January 1, 1996. The major provisions of the bill make the following changes in existing law:

1. *Covered Officials.* While the 1971 Federal Election Campaign Act covered only those who lobby members of Congress, the new bill covers lobbyists who seek to influence congressional staff members and policymaking officials of the executive branch, including the president, top White House officials, cabinet secretaries and their deputies, and independent agency administrators and their assistants.

2. *Disclosure Requirements.* Lobbyists have to register within 45 days of being hired or within 45 days of making their first contact, either oral or written, to a covered official, whichever came first. Lobbyists who expected to receive $5,000 or less in a six-month period, or organizations that expected to spend $20,000 or less in a six-month period on lobbying with their own employees, do not have to disclose their activities. After registering, lobbyists are required to file semiannual reports detailing their activities during each six-month period.

3. *Information Requirements.* The registration forms have to include the

in campaign spending between various candidates and political parties, some clear cases of unique influence on the decision-making process by large contributors and special interests, and the apparent disadvantages of incumbency in an age of mass communications with a constant focus on the lives and activities of office-holders."[66] The upshot was the Federal Election Campaign Act (FECA) of 1971, which supplanted the earlier legislation.

FECA, which has been amended three times, establishes reporting or disclosure requirements for all candidates for the U.S. House of Representatives, the Senate, and the presidency, as well as their political parties and campaign committees. It also requires disclosure of the amounts spent to influence federal elections by others, including individuals and political action committees. The act established partial public financing for presidential candidates, financed by a voluntary check-off on federal income tax forms. *Spending by candidates* for Congress is not limited, but *contributions to these candidates* and to presidential candidates is limited.

There have been notable problems with the act, including the soft money loophole and an ineffective Federal Election Commission. The act has had its critics, and Congress has frequently debated reforming campaign financing. (We discuss these reform proposals in greater detail in Chapter 12.) There have also been significant attempts to regulate interest-group activity in elections at the state level. Some states, like Wisconsin, Minnesota, and Hawaii, provide for public financing of state offices and state legislative races; others, like Michigan, New Jersey, and Massachusetts, provide partial public financing of gubernatorial elections; a dozen more help underwrite parties with public funds.[67]

Recently, there has been renewed interest in regulating not only lobbyists but those who may someday become lobbyists. Bill Clinton required top appointees to his administration to agree "not to lobby their former agencies for five years after leaving the government . . . [and] never to become lobbyists for foreign governments or foreign political parties." The White House staff "pledge[d] not to lobby any agency for which they have had 'substantial personal responsibility' for five years after leaving office."[68]

In his 1995 State of the Union Address, President Clinton challenged the new Republican majority in Congress to send him bills on campaign finance and lobby reform—two elements Republicans had been criticized for leaving out of their Contract with America. The 104th Congress did not address campaign finance reform, but it did produce the first major overhaul of lobbying laws since 1946. Under the Lobbying Disclosure Act of 1995, the definition of lobbyist was significantly expanded to include part-time lobbyists and those who deal with congressional staff or executive branch agencies. This act is expected to increase the number of registered lobbyists anywhere from three to ten times its current level.[69] Clinton has continued to press for campaign finance reform in his second term, while at the same time continuing to raise large amounts of money for his party.

The Effects of Regulation

What have been the effects of campaign-finance reforms on interest groups? Ironically, one has been to increase the number and importance of such groups. The strategy of the 1971 law was to authorize direct and open participation by both labor and corporate organizations in elections and lobbying in the hopes that a visible or proper role for interest-group activity, backed by effective enforcement, would be constitutional under the First Amendment and effective in the world of practical politics. The 1971 act allowed unions and corporations to communicate on political matters to members or stockholders, to conduct registration and get-out-the-vote drives, and to spend union and company funds to set up "separated segregated funds" (PACs) to use for political purposes.

The 1971 act opened the door to corporations and trade associations to form PACs, and they made the most of it. The growth in numbers and contributions from corporate and trade association PACs like doctors and realtors was great.[70] But what changed the rules of the game even more for corporate interests was passage in 1974 of limits on individual contributions, something not part of the 1971 act. An explosion of corporate PACs followed this 1974 amendment.[71] But as organized labor had less need of the act, except to legitimize what it was already doing, there was little increase in the number of labor PACs. The result, labor leaders contend, was a greater imbalance than ever between the political action and spending by a relatively small number of corporation executives and stockholders, on the one hand, and the large membership of labor unions on the other.

An important result of recent efforts at regulation of interest-group activity was disclosure of how politicians fund their campaigns. With the important exception of soft money, we now have a much better idea of how much money candidates raise and how they spend it. Without disclosure, much of what we have written here about PACs, for instance, would not be public knowledge. Disclosure permits the press and the public to assess the implications of how candidates finance their campaigns. Candidates and some appointed officials must also disclose their personal finances, permitting voters and the press to see what investments and resources candidates have that may affect their ability to be impartial. Such public disclosure of personal worth, the value of property owned, and outstanding debts no doubt discourages some persons from entering public life, but it also makes officeholders accountable for certain obligations and actions once they enter office.

Is Reform Possible?

Will Congress reform the PACs and campaign finance in general? Not only is reform itself complex and difficult, but it is doubtful that most members of Congress really *want* reform. Many members of Congress thrive on the present arrangements, and the leaders and members of both parties actually compete for PAC dollars. When the National Association of Home Builders, a richly funded lobby, began to give more and more money to Republican candidates, Democratic leaders of the House warned the lobby that it had better help Democrats too, or its "good relationship" with the Democrats might be "damaged." One reason members of Congress become entrenched in their seats is that they become increasingly funded by PACs. Some of them are reluctant to give up such a cozy relationship. Thus the real question may be not whether Congress can reform the interest-group lobbies, but whether Congress can reform itself.[72]

In recent Congresses, campaign finance reform legislation has been passed by one and sometimes both houses, but because both houses have not agreed to the same bill, no changes have been enacted. During the 1980s and early 1990s, Presidents Ronald Reagan and George Bush pledged to veto campaign finance reform bills passed by a Democratic Congress. Bill Clinton promised during his 1992 and 1996 campaigns to push for campaign finance and lobbying reform, and Ross Perot was an even more outspoken proponent of change. But in his first term, Clinton chose to defer to congressional leaders from his party and did not press hard on the issue.

With Republicans retaining a majority in both houses of Congress in 1996, attention focused on the fund-raising activities of the Clinton administration, but actual campaign finance reform legislation continues to encounter the problem that incumbents benefit from the status quo. Republicans can now reap the same benefits Democrats enjoyed from PACs interested in enhancing their legislative contacts with committee chairs and the majority party leadership. Speaker Newt Gingrich has been a successful PAC fund-raiser and has not supported campaign

Lobbying Disclosure Act of 1995 (continued)

name, address, principal place of business, and phone number of the registrant, plus a general description of the registrant's business or activities, as well as the same information about any client. The semiannual reports have to list the special issues lobbied on, the chambers of Congress and the executive agencies contacted, the lobbyists involved, and the involvement, if any, of a foreign entity. The lobbyist does not have to disclose the names of the law-makers, staff members, executive branch officials, or congressional committees contacted. The semiannual reports also have to include an estimate of the cost of the lobbying campaign.

4. *Foreign Agents.* The bill requires representatives of a U.S. subsidiary of a foreign-owned company and lawyer-lobbyists for foreign entities to register. Both groups were previously exempt from registration requirements.

5. *Exceptions.* The bill exempts all grass-roots lobbying and that of all tax-exempt religious organizations, such as churches, from disclosure requirements.

SOURCE: Adapted from Jonathan D. Salant, "Highlights of Lobby Bill," *Congressional Quarterly Weekly Report*, December 2, 1995, p. 3632.

Money from Outsiders

U.S. Senate elections in some sparsely populated states like North and South Dakota are examples of the role of interested money from out of state. In total spending, nearly $25 was spent per voter in South Dakota in 1986, a figure well in excess of the national average of $2.81. PACs provided much of this money, but large individual contributions were also important. In his successful 1988 reelection campaign, North Dakota Senator Quentin Burdick raised 99 percent of his large individual contributions from persons outside his state.* This level of campaign underwriting from individuals and groups outside a state raises important issues of representation.

*David B. Magleby, "More Bang for the Buck: Campaign Spending in Small-State U.S. Senate Elections," paper presented to the Western Political Science Association Annual Meeting, Salt Lake City, Utah, 1989.

finance reform, and such reforms were not part of the Republicans' Contract with America. Democrats missed their opportunity to reform campaign finance when they controlled both houses of Congress and the White House, and they now face a Republican party that has always been better at raising money. As the 1996 elections demonstrated, business-related PACs gave to Republican incumbents in record-setting amounts. Republicans, who only a few years earlier had been calling for the abolition of PACs, were now the beneficiaries of the same system that had long benefited Democratic incumbents. But the controversy surrounding the role of foreign money in the 1996 Clinton campaign and the widespread public concern about the role of money in elections may revive reform efforts.

As the efforts of the 1970s should teach us, reforming interest groups and regulating campaign money often lead to unintended consequences. The provisions of laws written to protect labor unions in effect helped promote nonunion PACs. Efforts to limit the cost of campaigns often served to protect incumbents, because the "return on campaign expenditures is much greater for challengers than incumbents."[73] But the consequences of doing nothing at all about our current system will mean continued dependence by candidates on PACs and other forms of interested money, uncontested races, and challengers who are often grossly underfunded.

Some observers favor tougher regulation of political money and publicly financed congressional elections. Others call for removal of regulation of the political arms of interest groups, hoping that the groups will find a natural and proper balance. Still others believe the balance must be righted between the present wide and intense activity of corporate PACs and the far less influential role of PACs for consumer groups, women's groups, environmental groups, and civil rights groups.[74]

A different school of thought holds that none of these "solutions" will work. The problem lies outside interest groups and PACs rather than within them. This school cites James Madison, who concluded that while the *causes* of faction could not be removed, the *effects* could be controlled only by fundamental changes in the whole political system. His solutions were to extend the sphere of government to take in "a greater variety of parties and interests," create federal-state-local tiers of government, and fragment the power of government so no majority or minority could control it.

Finally, some believe the main problem lies not in interest groups but in the way public opinion is formed, managed, and manipulated—above all, by the barons of the electronic media in a new "age of communications" politics. These observers urge Congress to limit what commercial television stations can charge for political advertising and to discourage so-called "negative targeting" of candidates in political advertising.

Strengthening the political parties might be one way to reduce the power of special interests. If campaign contributions were directed more to parties than to candidates, then candidates would be more accountable to the parties and less tied to any particular interest. Parties are also more likely to invest in challengers than are PACs. Finally, because parties must seek to broaden their appeal, they cannot risk becoming captive of a particular narrow interest.

POLITICS ONLINE

The Christian Coalition

One interest group that has effectively used the new media of computers, fax machines, and talk radio is the Christian Coalition. Ralph Reed, the young and energetic former leader of the group, makes no secret of the importance of these media. In his book, *Politically Incorrect*, Reed makes clear that "people of faith are enthusiastically embracing the emerging technologies of computers and interactive television that will make up the information superhighway of the future." The Christian Coalition has a well-developed home page at:

http://www.cc.org

The Coalition's home page also includes its Congressional Scorecard of how members of Congress voted on matters important to the Coalition, announcements of upcoming events, and statements about the goals and purposes of the organization.

Other interest groups also make extensive use of the Web. Labor unions like the AFL-CIO (http://www.aflcio.org), animal rights advocates (http://www.peta-online.org), and proponents of term limits (http://www.termlimits.org/homepage.shtml) all use this technology. Pick your favorite issue or interest group, and check out what they have to say on the Internet.

SUMMARY

1. Interest groups exist to make demands on government. The dominant interest groups in the United States are economic or occupational, but a variety of other groups—religious, racial, ideological, ethnic—have memberships that cut across the big economic groupings; thus their influence is both reduced and stabilized.

2. Movements of large numbers of people who are frustrated with government policies have always been with us in the United States. Blacks, women, Native Americans, and the economic underdogs have at various times organized themselves into movements.

3. The long-standing women's movement has been important in the expansion of suffrage and the framing of social issues, and it continues to press for equal rights.

4. Elements in interest-group power include size, resources, cohesiveness, leadership, and the ability to contribute to candidates and political parties as well as the ability to fund lobbyists. But the actual power of an interest group stems from the manner in which these elements relate to the political and governmental environment in which the interest group operates.

5. For many decades, interest groups have engaged in lobbying, but these efforts have become far more significant as groups become more deeply involved in the electoral process, especially through the expanded use of political action committees (PACs). Interest groups also take their messages directly to the public through mass mailings, advertising campaigns, and cooperative lobbying.

6. Concern for PACs centers on their ability to raise money and spend it on elections on behalf of endorsed candidates, typically incumbents. This concern has led to proposals to ban PACs or to more strictly limit their authority. Yet their existence and rights are protected by our First Amendment.

7. Reforms of interest-group excess often include strengthened political parties or regulations that seek fairness, disclosure, and balance between interest groups. All reform efforts must operate in such a way as not to take away basic constitutional rights of individuals. The key issue today in "controlling factions" is whether to allow groups to proliferate and so balance each other, to try to regulate groups, or to seek reforms outside the groups by fostering balanced power in political parties or elsewhere.

FURTHER READING

JEFFREY M. BERRY, *The Interest Group Society,* 3d ed. (Longman, 1997).

JEFFERY H. BIRNBAUM, *The Lobbyists: How Influence Peddlers Get Their Way in Washington* (Times Books, 1992).

WILLIAM P. BROWNE, *Groups, Interests, and Public Policy* (Georgetown University Press, 1998).

ALLAN J. CIGLER AND BURDETT A. LOOMIS, EDS., *Interest Group Politics,* 4th ed. (Congressional Quarterly Press, 1994).

ALLEN D. HERTZKE, *Representing God in Washington: The Role of Religious Lobbies in the American Polity* (University of Tennessee Press, 1988).

RONALD J. HREBENAR, *Interest Group Politics in America* (M.E. Sharpe, 1997).

MANCUR OLSON, *The Logic of Collective Action* (Harvard University Press, 1965).

MARK P. PETRACCA, ED., *The Politics of Interests: Interest Groups Transformed* (Westview Press, 1992).

DAVID VOGEL, *Kindred Strangers: The Uneasy Relationship Between Politics and Business in America* (Princeton University Press, 1996).

JACK L. WALKER, JR., *Mobilizing Interest Groups in America: Patrons, Professions, and Social Movements* (University of Michigan Press, 1991).

CLYDE WILCOX, *Risky Business?: PAC Decisionmaking in Congressional Elections* (M.E. Sharpe, 1994).

JOHN R. WRIGHT, *Interest Groups and Congress: Lobbying Contributions and Influence* (Allyn and Bacon, 1996).

10

Political Parties: Essential to Democracy

*I*magine you are voting in an election for the junior college board of trustees for your area. The board has seven members, all to be selected in the election. The election is nonpartisan, and each voter has seven votes. Any registered voter can run if he or she pays the $50 filing fee and gathers 500 valid signatures on a petition supporting the candidacy; 133 candidates have qualified for the ballot. On what basis would you determine how to cast your votes? Such an election actually happened in Los Angeles in April 1969. It offers a useful case study of what politics would be like without political parties, which generally narrow the field of candidates and thereby simplify the voting choice.

What explained how people voted in this unusual context? Primarily, ballot order. Candidates were listed alphabetically, and those whose names began with the letters *A* to *F* did better than those who come later in the alphabet. Being well known helped. Endorsements by *The Los Angeles Times* also influenced the outcome, as did the activity of a conservative campaign group or a Mexican-American surname.[1] In this election an important voting cue was absent: incumbency. Because the board of trustees was newly created, none of the candidates were incumbents.

Rarely are American voters asked to choose from among 133 candidates. This is because political parties facilitate voting by organizing elections and simplifying choices. E. E. Schattschneider, a noted political scientist, once said, "The political parties created democracy, and modern democracy is unthinkable save in terms of the parties."[2] This provocative statement is true. The view that parties are essential to democracy runs counter to a long-standing and deep-seated American fear and distrust of parties. Yet few of us would prefer a democracy in which we were asked to choose from among a large number of candidates for each office on the ballot. To most Americans, then, parties are a "necessary evil."

This chapter begins by examining the purposes parties serve that make them so vital to the functioning of democracy. We then examine the evolution of American political parties in our democratic experience. Although American political parties have changed over time, they remain important in three quite different settings: as institutions, in government, and in the electorate. It is important to understand how parties facilitate democracy in all three settings. Finally, we will turn to a discussion of the strength of parties today and the prospects for party reform and renewal.

WHAT PARTIES DO FOR DEMOCRACY

Political parties are essential to make democracy work, as the new democracies in Europe are quickly learning. Parties need not be strong and cohesive like those in Western Europe and Britain, but without some kind of party system, these democracies are not likely to survive.

Party Functions

American political parties serve a variety of political and social functions, some obvious and some not so obvious. They perform some of them well and others not so well, and how they perform them differs from place to place and time to time.

ORGANIZE THE COMPETITION One of the most important functions of parties is to organize the competition by choosing candidates to run under their label—an important task we often take for granted. To organize the competition, parties do

Functions of Political Parties

- Organize the competition by registering and activating voters and by providing resources to candidates
- Simplify the choices facing the electorate
- Recruit and nominate candidates for office
- Unify the electorate and moderate conflicts
- Translate public preferences into policy
- Help organize government
- Bridge the separation of powers and foster coordination and cooperation in our system of checks and balances
- Provide a loyal opposition to elected officials at the national, state, and local levels

many things: they recruit and nominate candidates for office; they register and activate voters; they help candidates by training them, raising money for them, providing them with research and voter lists, and enlisting volunteers to work for them. Recently parties have been replaced in some of these functions by campaign consultants and professionals.

A party's ability to organize the competition is influenced by how states organize their ballots. In many states, candidates are listed in party columns, called the **party column ballot**, or Indiana ballot, which makes it somewhat easier for voters to vote a *straight ticket*—for all party candidates. Some states permit straight-ticket voting by flipping one switch in the voting machine. Other states organize the ballot by office—the so-called **office block ballot** or Massachusetts ballot—which makes it somewhat harder to cast a vote for all the candidates of a single party. Even though many voters are *split-ticket voters*, casting votes for candidates in more than one party, the party label of the candidates means something to most voters and is important in their voting decision. Parties simplify the choices for the electorate.

Getting the party's name on the ballot reduces but does not eliminate the need for parties to help candidates during an election. In some states for some elections, there are no party labels. Many elections for judges use a nonpartisan ballot, as do many local government elections.

UNIFY THE ELECTORATE   Parties help unify the electorate and bring together voters from different ethnic backgrounds, parts of the country, and political ideologies. Thus they also help moderate conflicts within the body politic. When the Democratic party fell apart over the issue of slavery in 1860 and could no longer hold together its northern and southern wings, the very fabric of this nation was torn apart by the vehemence of the North-South rupture. For more than a century since the Civil War, however, Republicans and Democrats have held domestic conflict within acceptable bounds. Party leaders and candidates for public office appeal to diverse groups and sections, if only because these groups represent a large number of votes. Groups such as women, gays, African Americans, and Jews have seen parties as allies in their fights for social justice and equality.

Even when the differences between the parties over controversial social issues are intense—such as over civil rights, abortion, and the Equal Rights Amendment—there have nonetheless been sufficient differences *within* each of the two parties so that the conflict *between* the two parties has stayed within the limits of tolerance. For example, the Democratic party platform in recent years has endorsed the right of women to choose to have an abortion, whereas the Republican party platform has opposed abortion. But within each party, there are many who differ on this issue, and party candidates often do their best to conceal rather than intensify the differences.

DETERMINE WHO HOLDS OFFICE   Elections have important consequences. They determine who shall hold office and have political power. Parties are an integral part of making elections work, and elections serve the vital task of deciding who can legitimately exercise political power. We take for granted the peaceful transfer of power from one elected official to another, from one party to another, yet in new democracies the transfer of power following an election is often problematic. Bill Clinton is powerful and important because he won the presidential election; Bob Dole and Ross Perot have much less influence because they lost the election.

TRANSLATE PREFERENCE INTO POLICY   Winning parties have the opportunity to translate public preferences into policy. The elections of Republican majorities in both houses of Congress in 1994 and 1996 transformed the agenda of American politics from one dominated by Bill Clinton and the Democrats to one dominated by the Republican Contract with America and welfare reform. While our parties are not as cohesive as those in Britain, for example, in which after an election the party that wins takes over the entire government and all party members are expected to support the party and enact its promises into law, the consequences of winning our elections do change the broad orientation of government.

HELP ORGANIZE GOVERNMENT   Parties help organize the machinery of government and influence the men and women they have helped put into office. The president serves as party leader; Congress is organized on party lines; even bureaucrats are supposed to respond to new party leadership. Governors and legislative majorities serve in the same way in the states. Thus parties may help to bridge the separation of powers and foster coordination and cooperation in our system of constitutional checks and balances.

Another way in which parties organize government is that the winning party gets the **patronage**. Presidents, governors, mayors, and legislators all make party a primary consideration in the appointment of staff and key decision makers. They are limited only by civil service regulations that restrict patronage typically to the top posts, but these posts number in the thousands in the federal government, including most people who work for Congress, and they are numerous at the state and local levels. Party considerations are also important in the appointment of judges at all levels.

American parties have had only limited success in setting the course of national policy, however, especially when compared with traditionally strong European parties.[3] The European model of party government, which has been called a *responsible party system*, assumes that parties discipline their members through their control over nominations and campaigns. Politicians in such party-centered systems are expected to act according to party wishes or they will not be allowed to run again under the party label. Moreover, candidates run on fairly specific party platforms and are expected to implement those policies if they win control in the election.

Because American parties do not tightly control nominations, they are unable to discipline members with views contrary to those of the party. The American system is *candidate centered*; politicians are nominated largely on the basis of their qualifications and personal appeal, not party loyalty. In fact, it is more correct to say that we have candidate or officeholder politics rather than party politics. As a consequence, party leaders cannot guarantee passage of their program, even if they are in the majority.

On important issues most, but not all, Democrats vote together, as do most, but not all, Republicans. And then there are times, rather unusual but not unprecedented, when a president of one party receives more votes from the opposing party than from his own, as President Clinton did on the 1992 North American Free Trade Agreement (NAFTA) vote in the House.

PROVIDE LOYAL OPPOSITION   Parties provide a loyal opposition. This role was first played by the Jeffersonians during the Washington administration. After a polite interval following an election—the **honeymoon**—the opposition party begins to criticize the party that controls the White House, especially when the opposition party controls one or both houses of Congress.[4] In his first term Bill Clinton's honeymoon with the Republicans and even some Democrats was unusually brief as he faced early opposition on permitting gays in the military and had to abandon most of his economic stimulus package.

The Nomination of Candidates

From the beginning, parties have been the mechanism by which candidates for public office are chosen. The earliest method, the **caucus**—a closed meeting of local leaders—was used in Massachusetts only a few years after the *Mayflower* landed, and it played an important part in pre-Revolutionary politics. For several decades after the United States was established, party groups in the national and state legislatures served as the caucus. The legislators in each party simply met separately to nominate candidates. Our first presidential candidates were chosen by senators and representatives who met as party delegates.

As early as the 1820s, the legislative caucus brought charges of "secret deals" and "smoke-filled rooms." Moreover, it could not be representative of the people from an area where a party was in a minority or nonexistent, as only officeholders were members. Efforts were made to make the caucus more representative. The *mixed caucus* brought in delegates from districts in which the party had no elected legislators.

Then, during the 1830s and 1840s, a system of **party conventions** was instituted. Delegates, usually chosen directly by party members in towns and cities, selected the party standard-bearers, debated and adopted a platform, and built party spirit by celebrating a bit. But the convention method soon came under criticism that it was subject to control by the party bosses and their machines.

To involve more voters and reduce the power of the bosses to pick party nominees, states adopted the **direct primary** election in which people could vote for the party's nominees for office. Primaries spread rapidly after their introduction in Wisconsin—in the North as a Progressive era reform and in the South as a way to bring democracy to a region that had seen no meaningful general elections due to one-party rule by the Democrats since the end of Reconstruction. By the end of Woodrow Wilson's second administration in 1920, direct primaries were used for at least some offices in almost all states.

Today the direct primary is the typical method of picking party candidates. However, primaries vary significantly from state to state. They differ in terms of: (1) who may run in a primary and how one qualifies for the ballot; (2) whether the party organization can or does endorse candidates before the primary; (3) who may vote in a party's primary—that is, whether a voter must register with a party in order to vote; and (4) how many votes are needed for nomination—a plurality, a majority, or some other number determined by party rule or state law. The differences among primaries are not trivial; they have an important impact on the role played by party organization and on the strategy used by competing candidates.[5]

In states with **open primaries**, any voter, regardless of party, can participate in whichever primary he or she may choose. This kind of primary permits **crossover voting**—Republicans and Independents helping to determine who the Democratic nominee will be, and vice versa, for example. Some states use **closed primaries**, in which only persons already registered in a party may participate.

In 1996, California voters approved an initiative (Proposition 198) establishing an open primary system patterned after those in Washington and Alaska. Under the new system, all candidates from all parties are randomly listed by office, and voters have one vote per office. Proponents of the change contend it will benefit moderates in both parties. It will also give Independents a say in who the nominees will be in the general election. Opponents fear that some voters will vote for the weakest candidate in the other party as a way of helping their own party in the general election.

Direct primaries were introduced in large part to reduce the influence of party leaders, which they have done, but many believe that this change has had more undesirable than desirable consequences. Leaders now have less influence over who gets to be the party's candidate, and candidates are less accountable to the party for what they do, both during the election and after it. Along with modern communications and fund-raising techniques, direct primaries have really cut out most of the influence of leaders of political parties.

The rise of direct primaries has not meant the death of caucuses or conventions. In fact, caucuses have reappeared in a number of states as a step in nominating pres-identical and other candidates. But they have returned in a much more participatory form, open to *all* party members. Local party caucuses choose delegates to attend the regional meetings, which in turn select delegates to state and national conventions, where they nominate party candidates for offices. The Iowa caucuses, in which hundreds of thousands of Iowans participate, are highly publicized as the first important test of potential presidential nominees.[6]

In a few states, conventions still play a role in the nominating process. In Connecticut, for example, convention choices become the party nominees unless they are challenged. Candidates who attain at least 15 percent of the vote in the convention have an automatic right to challenge, but they do not always exercise this right.[7] In other states, convention nominees are designated as such on the primary ballot; they may or may not receive help from the party organization. Conventions are also used to invigorate the party faithful by enabling them to meet with their leaders.

Nominees for president and vice-president are formally chosen at **national party conventions**. Although they once played decisive roles in selecting the nominees, presidential conventions today almost always ratify the results of earlier primaries and caucuses. National conventions are still important as gatherings of the party, as occasions for uniting divided factions, as forums for emerging party leaders to be tested before a national audience, and as a place at which future courses are charted.[8]

Nomination by petition without party designation is available in all but a few states, but it is seldom used. The campaign of Ross Perot in 1992 demonstrated, however, that candidates with sufficient volunteers or resources can get on the ballot without a party. Perot used his own millions to build an organization of volunteers who got his name on the ballot as a candidate, not of a political party but of his own organization—United We Stand, America. In 1992 Perot received 19 percent of the vote—the most for a minor party candidate since 1912. In 1996 Perot garnered only 9 percent of the total, running this time as the Reform party nominee. Colin Powell was urged to run as an Independent in 1996 but announced he was a Republican and would not be a candidate. Should Independent candidates who get on the ballot by petition increase in number, the trend could produce a longer ballot and a crowded general election field.

Party Systems

What would a different party system look like? We have an electoral system in which two parties dominate; most other democracies have a *multiparty system*. These systems usually arise in countries with strong parliamentary systems, where the legislature is the most important branch of government, and the head of government (often called the prime minister or premier) is the leader of one of the major parties in the legislature. Because of the profusion of small parties, the head of government often assembles a *coalition* of parties to gain sufficient votes to govern with a majority in the legislature. Such coalition governments are common in countries like Israel and Italy. Minor parties can gain concessions—positions in a cabinet or support of policies they want implemented—in return for their participation in a coalition. Major parties need the minor parties and are therefore willing to bargain. Thus the multiparty system favors the existence of minor parties by giving them incentives to persevere. Britain, however, has a strong two-party system even though it is a parliamentary system. Most democracies with multiparty legislatures also have somebody who serves as president or chief of state, often only in ceremonial functions.

In multiparty parliamentary systems, individual districts frequently elect more than one member of the legislature. Parties run slates of candidates for those positions, and winners are determined by **proportional representation**. The parties

Functions of National Party Conventions

• Nominate the national ticket
• Attempt to unify the party's diverse factions
• Adopt the party platform
• Showcase past and future party leaders
• Attack the opposition party
• Use the free television time to appeal for mass support
• Inspire party activists to organize and get out the vote
• Raise money for state and national candidates
• Decide upon party rules

Thinking It Through

The answer to the question of whether we need more political parties depends a lot on what you want out of our democracy. More parties would foster greater diversity in issue positions, more candidates to choose from, and, some might argue, higher voter turnout. If we were to abandon our winner-takes-all system and adopt proportional representation, more parties would probably lead to coalition governments in Congress and perhaps the instability that some democracies face because of coalitions that fall apart.

Our current party system encourages democracy not only between the parties but within them as well. Issue activists and candidates seek to move our two major parties to their preferred position. Our two major parties have demonstrated an ability to adapt to the competitive situation they face in an effort to secure a majority.

Too many parties and too many choices can overwhelm some voters. As the example at the beginning of this chapter illustrated, when asked to choose from among 133 candidates, voters resorted to such things as ballot order and ethnicity as substitutes for party.

receive the proportion of the legislators corresponding to their proportion of the vote. In our **winner-take-all** system, only the candidate with the most votes in a district or state takes office. Because a party does not gain anything by finishing second, minor parties in a two-party system can rarely overcome the assumption that a vote for them is a wasted vote.[9] Even if a third-party candidate can keep either major party candidate from receiving more than 50 percent (a *majority*) of the vote, the candidate with the most votes (a *plurality*) wins. The winner-take-all system pertains in all states except Maine, which uses a district system.

In multiparty systems, parties at the extremes are apt to have more influence than in our two-party system, and their legislatures more accurately reflect the full range of the views of the electorate. Political parties in multiparty systems can be more doctrinaire than ours because they do not have to appeal to masses of people. Even though parties that do not become part of the governing coalition of parties may have little to say in setting government policy, they survive because they appeal to some voters. In contrast, our two-party system tends to create centrist parties that appeal to moderate elements and suppress the views of extremists in the electorate. Moreover, once elected, our parties do not form as cohesive a voting block as do the ideological parties. Under such a system, an incentive exists for third, fourth, or additional parties to run because they may win some seats.

Another consequence of multiparty parliamentary systems is that they make governments unstable, as coalitions form and collapse. In addition, the swings in policy when party control changes can be quite dramatic. Two-party systems lead to majority governments that tend to be stable and centrist, and as a result, policy shifts occur incrementally.

Minor Parties: Persistence and Frustration

Two-party politics is the American norm, but **minor parties**—sometimes called **third parties**—have also played a role. Minor parties are of two basic types: those that arise around a *candidate* and usually disappear when the charismatic personality does, and those that are organized around an *ideology* that persists over time. Communist, Prohibition, or Libertarian parties are of the ideological type. Minor parties of both types come and go, but there are usually several minor parties running in any given presidential election, and some in state and local elections as well.

Some parties arise around a single issue, like the States' Rights party that split with the Democratic party in 1948 over President Harry Truman's civil rights policies. To be sure, third and minor parties have had indirect influence by drawing attention to controversial issues and by organizing groups such as the antislavery and the civil rights movements. However, they have never won the presidency or more than a handful of congressional seats.[10] They have never shaped national policy from inside the government, and their influence on national policy in general, and on the platforms of the two major parties, has been limited.[11]

Third parties often revolve around a particular political personality. The Bull Moose party of Theodore Roosevelt and George Wallace's American Independent party (AIP) exemplify this type of third party. AIP polled more than 13 million votes and won 46 electoral votes in 1968 after Wallace broke with the Democratic party over desegregation and conservative social issues.

A minor party currently somewhat active on the national scene is the Libertarian party. Founded in 1972, this party wants to turn all, or almost all, government services over to the private sector. It would end the welfare state, reduce the military to a bare minimum, terminate foreign commitments (including membership in the United Nations), and abolish laws legislating morality, such as laws dealing with prostitution, drugs, gambling, abortion, and gay rights. In 1980 the party

MINOR PARTIES IN AMERICAN POLITICS

Minor parties have succeeded in calling attention to controversial issues by organizing groups such as the antislavery and anti-civil rights movements. They boast, sometimes correctly, that they are champions not of lost causes but of causes yet to be won. But they have never won the presidency or more than a handful of congressional seats. They have never shaped national policy from inside the government. And their influence on national policy in general and on the platforms of the two major parties has been limited.

Theodore Roosevelt.

George Wallace.

Ross Perot.

Year	Party	Candidate	Percent of Vote	Electoral Vote
1832	Anti-Masonic	William Wirt	8	7
1856	American (Know-Nothing)	Millard Fillmore	22	8
1860	Democratic (Secessionist)	J.C. Breckinridge	18	72
1860	Constitutional Union	John Bell	13	39
1892	People's (Populist)	James B. Weaver	9	22
1912	Bull Moose	Theodore Roosevelt	27	88
1912	Socialist	Eugene V. Debs	6	0
1924	Progressive	Robert M. La Follette	17	13
1948	States' Rights	Strom Thurmond	2	39
1948	Progressive	Henry A. Wallace	2	0
1968	American Independent	George C. Wallace	14	46
1980	National Unity	John Anderson	7	0
1992	United We Stand, America	Ross Perot	19	0
1996	Reform	Ross Perot	9	0

- Parties began in this country as soon as people started taking sides in the debate over ratifying the U.S. Constitution, although it took a few years for them to organize into formal bodies.
- Political parties, and especially our two-party system, have persisted over the course of our history.
- Ours has almost always been a two-party system, differentiating us from most nations, which have a one-party or multiparty system.
- Since 1830 we have witnessed reasonably effective competition in our national party system.
- Our parties have historically been decentralized and fragmented. Parties are organized around units of competition (states, congressional districts, countries, cities), which in our governmental structure make state parties the most important units.
- Winning office and power have been more important to party leaders than specific issues or platforms; political parties in the United States are primarily organized to win or obtain political power.
- Our parties can be characterized as moderate, centrist, and pragmatic, with only modest ideological cohesion and voting discipline, especially when compared to European political parties.

polled more than 1 million votes, but its strength slipped later in the 1980s, leading some to think that Ronald Reagan had partially stolen some of its support and agenda. The Libertarian presidential candidate in 1996, Harry Browne, got less than 1 percent of the vote.

Ross Perot and the Reform Party

Before the primary elections had run their course in 1992, Ross Perot, a wealthy Texas businessman, made known his interest in running for president. Perot was initially "interested" but "not committed" to running and indicated that if citizens were successful in getting his name on the ballots of all 50 states, then he would run.

Perot's defeat in the election did not remove him from the stage of national politics. In 1993 he lobbied hard against NAFTA and even debated Vice-President Al Gore on CNN's *Larry King Live*. Perot continued to call for campaign finance and lobbying reform, putting pressure on Clinton and Congress to take action on this issue before the 1994 elections. After losing on NAFTA, Perot again injected himself into the national political process with his outspoken opposition to the Clinton health care proposal.

In October 1995, Ross Perot formed a new third party, called the Reform party, in time for the 1996 elections. Originally Perot said the Reform party would find its own presidential candidate, but when Richard Lamm, former governor of Colorado, stepped forward, Perot declared his own candidacy and won the nomination. The novelty of a Perot candidacy was no longer present in 1996, and his low standing in the polls meant he was excluded from the 1996 presidential debates. Voters and the media did not pay nearly as much attention to him in 1996 as they had in 1992. Perot accepted $29 million in federal matching funds, much of which he used to buy television time. Despite these expenditures, his vote total dropped by half from 1992, and he again did not carry a single state. Whether the Reform party survives as a factor in the years ahead remains to be seen. Most third parties do not survive beyond their charismatic founder but there are signs that the Reform party may persist beyond Perot.

A BRIEF HISTORY OF AMERICAN POLITICAL PARTIES

Our First Parties

To the leaders of the young Republic, parties usually meant bigger, better organized, and more fierce factions, and they did not want that. Benjamin Franklin worried about the "infinite mutual abuse of parties, tearing to pieces the best of characters." In his farewell address, George Washington warned against the "baneful effects of the Spirit of Party." And Thomas Jefferson said, "If I could not go to heaven but with a party, I would not go there at all."[12]

How, then, did parties get started? Largely out of practical necessity. The same early leaders who so frequently stated their opposition to political parties also recognized the need to organize officeholders who shared their views so that government could act. To get its measures passed through Congress, the Washington administration had to fashion a coalition among factions. This job fell to Treasury Secretary Alexander Hamilton, who built an informal Federalist party, while Washington stayed "above politics."

Secretary of State Jefferson and other officials, many of whom despised Hamilton and his aristocratic ways as much as they opposed the policies he favored, were uncertain about how to deal with these political differences. The overriding concern was the success of the new government; personal loyalty to Washington was a close second. Thus Jefferson stayed in the cabinet, despite his opposition to administration policies, during most of Washington's first term. When he left the cabinet at the end of 1793, many who joined him in opposition to the administration's economic policies remained in Congress, forming a group of legislators opposed to Federalist fiscal policies and eventually to Federalist foreign policy, which appeared "soft on Britain." This party was later known as Republicans, then as Democratic-Republicans, then as Democrats.

Realigning Elections

American political parties have evolved and changed over time, but some underlying characteristics have been constant. We have historically had a two-party system with minor parties. Our parties are moderate and accommodative—meaning that they are open to people with diverse outlooks. Political scientist V. O. Key and others argue that our party system has been shaped in large part by *realigning elections*, turning points that define the agenda of politics and the alignment of voters within parties during periods of historic change in the economy and society.[13] Realigning elections are characterized by intense electoral involvement by the voters, disruptions of traditional voting patterns, changes in the relations of power within the community, and the formation of new and durable electoral groupings. They have occurred cyclically, not randomly.[14] These elections tend to coincide with expansions of the suffrage or changes in the rate of voting.[15] We focus here on four realigning elections: 1824, 1860, 1896, and 1932.

President Andrew Jackson, organizer of a people's coalition of voters, celebrated his arrival at the White House with an inaugural party open to all that nearly tore the place down.

1824: ANDREW JACKSON AND THE DEMOCRATS Party politics was invigorated following the election of 1824, in which the leader in the popular vote—the hero of the battle of New Orleans, Democrat Andrew Jackson—failed to achieve the necessary majority of the electoral college and was defeated by John Quincy Adams in the runoff election in the House of Representatives. Jackson, brilliantly aided by Martin Van Buren, a veteran party builder in New York State, later knit together a winning combination of regions, interest groups, and political doctrines to win the presidency in 1828. The Whigs succeeded the Federalists as the opposition party. By the time Van Buren followed Jackson in the White House in 1837, the Democrats had become a large, nationwide movement with national and state leadership, a clear party doctrine, and grass-roots organization. The Whigs were almost as strong; in 1840 they put their own man, General William Henry Harrison ("Old Tippecanoe") into the White House. A two-party system had been born. We have had that two-party system ever since—one of few such systems worldwide.

1860: THE CIVIL WAR AND THE RISE OF THE REPUBLICANS Out of the crisis over slavery evolved a new party: the second Republican party—ultimately the "Grand Old Party" (GOP).[16] Abraham Lincoln was elected in 1860 with the support not only of financiers, industrialists, and merchants, but also of large numbers of workers and farmers. For 50 years after 1860, the Republican coalition won every presidential race except for Grover Cleveland's victories in 1884 and 1892. The Democratic party survived with its durable white male base in the South.

1896: A PARTY IN TRANSITION The Republican party's response to industrialization and hard times for farmers transformed it in the late 1800s. A combination of western and southern farmers and western mining interests sought an alliance with workers in the East and Midwest to "recapture America from the foreign moneyed interests responsible for industrialization. The crisis of industrialization squarely placed an agrarian-fundamentalist view of life against an industrial-progress view."[17] This realignment of 1896 differs from the others, however, in that the party in power did not change hands. In that sense it was a converting realignment because it reinforced the Republican majority status that had been in place since 1860.[18]

The Progressive era, the first two decades of this century, was a period of political reform led by the Progressive wing of the Republican party. Much of the agenda of the Progressives focused on the corrupt political parties. Civil service reforms shifted some of the patronage out of the hands of party officials. The direct primary election took control of nominations from party leaders and gave it to the rank-and-file. And in a number of cities, nonpartisan governments were instituted, totally eliminating the role of a party. With the ratification of the Seventeenth Amendment to the Constitution in 1913, United States senators came to be popularly elected. Women obtained the right to vote when the Nineteenth Amendment was ratified in 1920. Thus within a short time, the electorate changed, the rules changed, and even the stakes of the game changed. Democrats were unable to build a durable winning coalition during this time. In fact, they remained the minority party until the early 1930s, when the Hoover administration was overwhelmed by the Great Depression.

1932: FRANKLIN ROOSEVELT AND THE NEW DEAL ALIGNMENT The 1932 election, like critical elections before it, was a turning point in American politics. In the 1930s the United States faced a devastating economic collapse. After a century of sporadic government action, the New Dealers stepped in and fundamentally altered the relationship between government and society. Between 1929 and 1932, the gross national product fell over 10 percent per year and unemployment rose from 1.5 million to more than 15 million, with millions more working only part-time. Herbert Hoover and the Republican majority in Congress had responded to the Depression by arguing that the problems with the economy were largely self-correcting and that their long-standing policy of *laissez-faire*, a hands-off approach to the economy, was appropriate. Voters wanted more. Franklin D. Roosevelt and the Democrats were swept into office in 1932 by a tide of anti-Hoover and anti-Republican sentiment. Roosevelt rode this wave and labeled his response to the Depression as the New Deal. He rejected *laissez-faire* economics and instead relied on Keynesian economics, which asserted that government could influence the direction of the economy through fiscal and monetary policy.

The central issue on which the Republicans and Democrats disagreed in this New Deal period was the role of government regarding the economy. Roosevelt Democrats argued that the government had to do something to pull the country out of the Depression. Republicans disagreed with the scope of government activity and of its intrusion into the economy. This central division about whether the national government should play an active role in regulating and promoting our economy remains one of the most important divisions between the Democratic and Republican parties today, although, with time, the country and both parties accepted many of the New Deal programs. For the two decades following the 1932 election, the Republican party was relegated to watching the majority Democrats—a new coalition of union households, immigrant workers, and those hurt most by the Great Depression—implement their domestic policies. During the Second World War, both parties cooperated in embracing a bipartisan foreign policy.

Divided Government

During the period since 1952, voters have shown a willingness to place one party in charge of the executive branch and the other in charge of one or both houses of the legislative branch. Since 1953, we have had this type of **divided government** twice as often as we have had one party in control of both legislative and executive branches. Until the 1994 election, the strength of the Republicans had been in presidential elections, where they often won with landslide margins. Part

of the explanation was their ability to attract popular candidates like Dwight Eisenhower and Ronald Reagan. Republicans also reaped the rewards of Democratic party divisiveness and generally weaker Democratic presidential candidates. Republicans benefited from the breakup of the once solidly Democratic South in presidential voting when the Democratic party decided in the 1950s and 1960s to take a strong stand on civil rights that offended many white southern Democrats. Yet many of these "presidential Republicans" did not give up their Democratic allegiance when voting for candidates for the Senate, the House, or for governor and other state and local officials.

Republican victories in presidential elections between 1952 and 1992 had been achieved with the support of elements of Roosevelt's New Deal coalition. New Deal programs that benefited these very groups and expanded the middle class made possible the conservative "hold onto what we've got" thinking of voters in the 1980s and 1990s. The deviation from this pattern that occurred in the 1980 election, when Ronald Reagan's coattails helped secure victories, created a Republican majority in the U.S. Senate for the first time since 1954. But in 1986 the Democrats regained their majority in the U.S. Senate and held it until 1994. Although Bill Clinton won back many so-called Reagan Democrats in 1992, the Republican victory in 1994 was far reaching, securing a majority for their party in both houses of Congress, winning control of seven of the eight largest states, and making substantial inroads in state governorships and legislatures as well.

More than most elections, 1994 was an election with a partisan agenda. During the campaign, at the instigation of Newt Gingrich and other House Republican leaders, the Republicans had issued a Contract with America that described a legislative agenda the Republicans would carry out if they took control of Congress. Republicans also benefited from a well-funded and talented group of candidates who put the Democrats on the defensive.

In the months before the 1994 election, Republicans chose to use the filibuster in the Senate to block passage of the Clinton legislative agenda. Their astounding success in 1994 left Clinton and the Democratic minority in Congress with a dilemma. Should they compromise and help enact some of the Republican legislative agenda? Or should they adopt the same strategy the Republicans used in 1993 and 1994 of trying to block or veto the actions of the opposing party? In either event, American politics entered a period of intensified partisanship in Congress.

Bill Clinton's substantial 1996 victory deflated Republican claims that their 1994 victories were a harbinger of a long-term Republican trend. However, Clinton's coattails were ineffective, and the Republicans retained control of both congressional chambers, giving some credence to Republican claims that the country had moved to the right. Neither party could make a claim for a strong mandate from the voters. Clearly, the electorate had no qualms about divided government. In fact, they seemed to prefer it.

AMERICAN PARTIES TODAY

What is the current state of political parties in the United States? American parties are weak as organizations. As we pointed out earlier, party leaders no longer make the most crucial decision in national party politics—the choice of the presidential nominee. This choice is made by voters in primary elections and precinct caucuses. Parties have also been weakened by the loss of patronage. American political scientists have been worrying about weak and undisciplined parties for decades. Since the founding of the Republic, parties have operated within our constitutional system of separation of powers and checks and balances, which limits their ability to dominate our government.[19]

Ronald Reagan's presidency initiated a period of Republican control of the White House along with Democratic control of one or both houses of Congress. With the support of disgruntled Democrats and Independents, he was able to reverse many of the social welfare programs dating back to the New Deal.

Thinking It Through

It is naive to believe that the removal of parties will negate conflict, self-interest, or ambition. A political system without parties would be a society without the means to deal with disagreements over policies, economics, or social values. Americans expect legislatures to be partisan, to be contentious, and to make the most of partisan opportunities. Divided government may be less efficient, but it clearly has not bothered voters, who routinely have elected legislators from one party and governors or presidents from another. Finally, people with judicial or administrative ambitions understand the role that parties play in appointments, giving them an incentive to get involved in a party. This is not all bad because, as we have seen, it is possible for idealistic individuals to redefine and reshape a party.

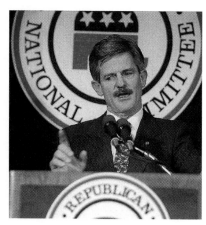

Jim Nicholson, a small businessman from Colorado, is the Republican National Committee Chair.

Most Americans are largely indifferent about political parties. If anything, most people are critical or even fearful of the major parties. Parties are, in a word, distrusted. Some see parties as corrupt institutions, interested in the spoils of politics. Critics charge that the parties evade the issues; that they fail to deliver on their promises; that they have no new ideas; that they follow public opinion rather than lead it; or that they are just one more special interest.

Still, many Americans understand that parties are necessary. Most Americans want party labels kept on the ballot, think of themselves as Democrats or Republicans, and typically vote for candidates from their party. They even contribute millions of dollars to the two major parties. More individual contributions go to the Republicans than to the Democrats.[20] Thus, Americans appreciate, at least vaguely, that you cannot run a big democracy without parties, or something like them.

Both the Democratic and Republican parties are moderate in their policies and leadership.[21] Each party usually takes its extremist supporters more or less for granted and seeks out the voters in the middle. Successful party leaders must be diplomatic; to win presidential elections and congressional majorities, they must find a middle ground among more or less hostile groups so that they can reach agreement on general principles.

Parties as Institutions

Writing more than two centuries ago, Edmund Burke, the frequently cited English political philosopher, defined a political party as "a body of men united, for promulgating by their joint endeavors the national interest, upon some particular principle in which they are all agreed."[22] A theorist has expressed a much less idealistic view of parties as "a group whose members propose to act in concert in the competitive struggle for political power."[23] In the United States, parties have demonstrated both tendencies—the pursuit of principle and power. **Political parties**, then, are organizations that seek political power by electing people to office so that their positions and philosophy become public policy. Like other institutions of American government—Congress, the presidency, the courts—parties have rules, procedures, and organizational structure, and they make policy. What are the institutional characteristics of political parties?

NATIONAL PARTY LEADERSHIP The supreme authority in both major parties is the national party convention, which meets every four years to nominate candidates for president and vice-president, to ratify the party platform, and to adopt rules. The delegates have only four days in which to accomplish their business, although many key decisions have been made ahead of time.

More directly in charge of the national party is the *national committee*. In recent years both parties have strengthened the role of the national committee and enhanced the influence of individual committee members. The committees are now more representative of the party rank-and-file. But in neither party is the national committee the center of party leadership.

The *national party chair* is the top official of each of the two major parties. The chair is formally elected by the national committee but in reality is the choice of the presidential nominee. Although they are the heads of their national party apparatus, they remain largely unknown to the voters. The chair may play a major role in running the national campaign. After the election, the power of the national chair of the victorious party tends to dwindle. Even though he or she serves as a liaison between the party and the White House, the chair actually serves at the pleasure of the president and does the president's bidding with the national party. The chair of the party without an incumbent president has considerable independence, yet works closely with the party's congressional leadership. The national committee usually elects a new head after electoral defeats.

In the past the national committee gave large states only a little more representation than small ones. Committee members were usually influential in their states but had little national standing, and the committees rarely met. In recent years, both parties have made their national committees more representative. The Democrats, for instance, enlarged their national committee to make it more responsive to areas that tended to be more populous and more Democratic and to groups that have traditionally supported Democratic candidates. But such changes in both national committees have not necessarily brought stronger leadership.

Winning the White House is the major focus of the national party committees; winning congressional elections is the concern of the congressional and senatorial campaign committees. Republican and Democratic senatorial campaign committees are composed of senators chosen for two-year terms by their fellow party members in the Senate; congressional campaign committees are chosen in the same manner by the House. The chairs of these committees, appointed by their party leadership, have much more to say about which candidates get campaign funds.

These committees once offered only token contributions to selected candidates, but today they play an important role in recruiting candidates, training them, and assisting with campaign finance. Republicans saw the potential for these committees earlier than did Democrats. In the late 1970s, in coordination with the Republican National Committee, they developed extensive fund-raising lists and raised enough money to help fund most Republican candidates for the House or the Senate.[24] Democrats in the House and Senate copied the tactic and closed fund-raising gaps and made their campaign committees more effective.

National party organizations are often agents of an incumbent president in securing his renomination; in other instances they try to influence party nominations. Politicians invest in personal organizations and expect the party to remain neutral during the primary campaign. Although heated primary contests often preclude having a united party in the general election, national parties are helpless to prevent them.[25]

Colorado Governor Roy Romer, Democratic Committee National Chair.

Businessman Steven Grossman assists Roy Romer with the day-to-day operations of the Democratic National Committee.

PARTIES AT THE GRASS ROOTS The major parties are decentralized, organized around elections in states, cities, or congressional districts. Like the government itself, they have national, state, and local organizations. Party organization at the state and local levels is structured much like the national level. Each state has a *state committee*, headed by a *state chair*. State law determines the composition of the state committees and sets rules regulating them. Members of the state committees are usually elected from local areas, but party auxiliaries such as the Young Democrats or the Federation of Republican Women are sometimes represented as well. In many states these committees are dominated by governors, senators, or coalitions of local elected business and ethnic leaders. State chairs are normally elected by the state committees, although approximately one-quarter are chosen at state conventions. When the party controls the governorship, chairs are often agents of the governor, but some can be quite independent.[26]

Some powerful state parties have developed in recent years. Despite much state-to-state variation, the trend is toward stronger state organizations, with Republicans typically much better funded.[27] In some states, third and fourth parties play a role in local elections. New York, for instance, has both a Liberal and a Conservative party in addition to Democratic and Republican parties. The role these parties play in statewide elections can be important, even though they rarely win office themselves.

Below state committees are *county committees*, which vary widely in function and power. The key role of these committees is recruiting candidates for such offices as county commissioner, sheriff, and treasurer; but the recruiting job often involves finding a candidate for the office, not deciding among competing contenders. For a party that rarely wins an election, the county committee has to struggle to find someone willing to run. When the job is valued by those seeking it, however, primaries, not the party leaders, usually decide the winner.[28] Many county organizations maintain a significant level of activity, distributing campaign literature, organizing telephone campaigns, putting up posters and lawn signs, and canvassing door-to-door. In other areas, county committees do not function at all, and many party leaders are just figureheads.

In recent years the efforts of state and county organizations have been aided by financial assistance from the party's national committee, which has distributed millions of dollars in **soft money**—money that does not have to be reported under the Federal Election Campaign Act (1971 and amendments). This money must be spent for the benefit of the party rather than for a particular congressional, senatorial, or presidential candidate.

At the base of the party pyramid—at the city, town, ward, and precinct level—we find the grass roots of the party, if we find any party activity at all. In a few places, local ward and precinct leaders still do favors for constituents, from fixing parking tickets, to organizing clambakes, to obtaining horse-racing passes in a state like Arkansas. But strong local party organization is rare. Most local committees are poorly financed and inactive except during the few weeks before election day.[29]

Despite this organizational structure, party politics tends to be organized around candidates. Party organizations and leaders play some role in winning elections, but the fact is their role is becoming less significant, especially at the state and local levels, where candidate's organizations are superseding party organizations. Candidates for office—a mayor of a large city, a governor, a member of the House or Senate—rely less on the party structure and more on the personal organizations they themselves put together.

Party Platforms and Party Differences

The typical **party platform**—the official statement of party policy—is often a vague and ponderous document that hardly anyone reads. Platforms are ambiguous by design, giving voters few substantive reasons to vote *against* the party. This generalization could be overstated. Many voters see their own party as well as the opposition party as standing for something. Thus most business and professional people believe that the Republican party best serves their interests, while workers tend to look to the Democrats to speak for them. The proportion of voters discerning important differences between the parties increased sharply during the Reagan years, when parties seemed to become more polarized.[30] Intense partisanship continued with policy pronouncements like the Contract with America issued by House Republicans in the 1994 election.

Many politicians contend platforms rarely help elect anybody, but platform positions can hurt a presidential candidate. Because the platform-writing process is not always controlled by the nominee, it is possible for presidential candidates to disagree with their own party platform. Jimmy Carter ended up with a platform in 1980 that was more liberal than his administration had been.[31] But the platform-drafting process gives partisans, especially issue activists, an opportunity to express their views, and it serves to identify the most important values and principles upon which the two parties are based.

Once elected, politicians are rarely reminded of what their platform position was on a given issue. One major exception to this was President Bush's promise not to raise taxes if elected in 1988 with his memorable "Read my lips—no new taxes." Clinton and Perot repeatedly raised this broken promise in the 1992 campaign. Clinton had to backpeddle on his 1992 promise that if elected he would lower taxes on the middle class; his budget and tax recommendations raised taxes on wealthy Americans but did not lower taxes on the middle class.

Differences at the national level between the two major parties were very sharp just before the Civil War and again during the New Deal, when voters were loyal to either political party because of how they felt about Franklin Roosevelt's response to the Depression. Those who approved of his programs or were helped by them favored the Democrats and thought Roosevelt a hero; those who did not like Roosevelt and saw his programs as "social engineering" favored Republicans. Later, as much of the New Deal philosophy came to be accepted by both parties, the lines between the parties became blurred again.

Party platforms in 1996 were carefully controlled by the Dole and Clinton campaigns and were largely designed to minimize problems for the candidates in their general election campaigns. The Democratic platform, for example, stressed opportunity, responsibility, security, freedom, peace, and community. Like apple pie and motherhood, these were not issues delegates or voters were likely to oppose. The platform spelled out the Democrats' commitment to improving education, guaranteeing economic security for families, fighting crime, and strengthening national security. In part because Bill Clinton so thoroughly dominated his party's nomination process, the document provided no targets for Republican attacks.

Many parts of the Republican platform were also intended to reinforce broad areas of political consensus, but the Republican platform of 1996 was more explicit in its discussion of social issues. The GOP platform opposed same-sex marriages, supported California's Proposition 209 to eliminate affirmative action programs in the public sector, and called for the abolition of the Department of Education. The most contentious issue in the 1996 Republican platform deliberations was abortion. Republican platforms between 1976 and 1992 had endorsed a human-life constitutional amendment making abortion illegal. Yet prominent Republican governors like William Weld of Massachusetts, Pete Wilson of California, and Christine Todd Whitman of New Jersey pushed the party to moderate this language in 1996. GOP nominee Bob Dole wanted to come part way to meeting the concerns of these influential Republican moderates. Rather than modify the language of the platform, the Republicans added a clause in the appendix to the platform that expressed "tolerance" for differing views on abortion. Differences between 1996 Democratic and Republican platforms are highlighted in Table 10–1.

Typically, both major parties have been moderate, expressing support for a strong defense, a stable Social Security system, and economic growth. As a rule, Democrats are ideologically more diverse than Republicans. The Democratic umbrella encompasses the conservative Coalition for a Democratic Majority, the moderate Democratic Leadership Council (dominated by an array of southern governors and senators), and the liberal Americans for Democratic Action. The Democratic coalition embraces activists in the civil rights and other liberal-left movements.

Parties in Government

Despite the organizational weakness of political parties, they remain central to the operation of government in the United States. Parties as organizations play a more important role after the election in the operation of government than they play in the elections.

IN THE LEGISLATIVE BRANCH   Members of Congress take their partisanship seriously, at least while they are in Washington. Their power and influence are determined in part by whether their party is in control of the House or Senate. They also have a stake in which party controls the White House. The chairs of all standing committees in Congress come from the majority party. The presiding officials of both chambers come from the majority party, except when the vice-president

TABLE 10–1

Key Party Differences: Excerpts from Republican and Democratic Party Platforms, 1996

Democratic	Republican
Taxes	
America cannot afford to return to the era of "something-for-nothing tax cuts." Supports a "$500 tax cut for children" and additional reductions for college tuition payments, small businesses, and the self-employed. Allows money in individual retirement accounts to be used to buy a first home and to pay education and medical expenses.	Supports a 15 percent reduction in tax rates, a $500-per-child tax credit, a 50 percent cut in the capital gains rate, expansion of Individual Retirement Accounts (IRAs), and lower taxes on Social Security benefits. These are "interim steps toward comprehensive tax reform." The Internal Revenue Service "must be dramatically downsized."
Balanced budget	
Promises to balance the budget by 2002.	Supports a constitutional amendment requiring a balanced budget.
Economy	
"Today, America is moving forward. The economy is stronger, the deficit is lower, and the government is smaller."	"We cannot go on like this. For millions of families, the American dream is fading."
Education	
Supports strengthening public schools.	Favors using federal money to help parents pay private-school tuition.
Environment	
Emphasizes government regulation to protect the environment.	Emphasizes consideration of private property rights and economic development in conjunction with environmental protection.
Foreign affairs	
Opposes revival of the land-based missile defense system known as Star Wars (Strategic Defense Initiative). In the area of trade, insists that international trade agreements include standards to protect children, workers, and the environment.	Favors development of the Strategic Defense Initiative missile defense system. In the area of trade, opposes using trade policy to pursue "social agenda items."
Gun control	
Supports a waiting period for buying handguns and a ban on the sale of certain assault weapons.	Defends "the constitutional right to keep and bear arms" and favors mandatory penalties for crimes committed with guns.
Homosexuality	
Supports attempts "to end discrimination against gay men and lesbians, and further their full inclusion in the life of the nation."	Rejects the "distortion" of civil rights laws that would "cover sexual preference."
Immigration	
Would permit the children of illegal immigrants to attend public schools, allow legal immigrants to receive welfare and other benefits, and make it easier for eligible immigrants to become United States citizens.	Would prohibit the children of illegal immigrants from attending public schools and restrict welfare to legal immigrants. Supports a constitutional amendment denying automatic citizenship to children born in the United States to illegal immigrants and legal immigrants who are in this country for a short time.
Abortion	
Supports a woman's right to choose to have an abortion in all circumstances currently legal. "Respect the individual conscience of each American on this difficult issue."	Supports a constitutional amendment that would outlaw abortion in all circumstances. Only mention of tolerance for other views on abortion is in an appendix at the end of the platform.
Affirmative action	
"We should mend it, not end it."	"We will attain our nation's goal of equal rights without quotas or other forms of preferential treatment."

SOURCE: Based on "Party Platforms: How They Compare," *The New York Times*, August 27, 1996, p. A11.

is in attendance at the Senate. Members of both houses sit together with fellow partisans on the floor and in committee, leading to the expression often heard in floor debate, "the other side of the aisle."

Members of the congressional staff are also partisan. From the volunteer intern to the senior staffer, members of Congress expect their staff to be loyal first to them and then to their party. Should you decide to go to work for a representative or senator, you would be expected to identify yourself with that person's party and would have some difficulty working for the other party later. Employees of the House and Senate—from elevator operators to the Capitol Hill police and even including the chaplain—hold patronage jobs. With few exceptions, such jobs go to persons from the party that has a majority in the House or the Senate.

IN THE EXECUTIVE BRANCH   The presidency is no less partisan. Rarely will a senior White House official be selected from the opposing party. However, partway through President Clinton's first year in office, he named a prominent Republican, David Gergen, to a White House position to work on press relations. He began his second term by promising a bipartisan foreign policy, and backed up the promise by selecting a Republican, former Maine Senator William Cohen, as his secretary of defense. Presidents, however, typically surround themselves with advisers who have campaigned with them and proven their loyalty. President Clinton's first-term advisers and cabinet officers who fit this description included George Stephanopoulos (managed media relations in the campaign and went on to be a senior White House adviser), Ron Brown (national chair of the Democratic party who became secretary of commerce), and Mickey Kantor (worked on the campaign and was then appointed Clinton's trade negotiator).

Partisanship is also important in presidential appointments to the highest levels of the federal bureaucracy. The party that wins the White House has more than 4,000 noncareer positions to fill.[32] Included in these positions are cabinet-level appointments and ambassadorships around the world. Party commitment, including making campaign contributions, is expected of persons who seek these positions.

Sometimes it is not enough for presidents to find fellow partisans; they must also be acceptable to certain power centers in the party. For example, Republicans in the Reagan and Bush administrations insisted on conservative as well as Republican judges. Clinton, while picking almost all Democrats, gave more emphasis to gender and race than to ideology in selecting judges.

IN THE JUDICIAL BRANCH   The judicial branch of the national government, with its lifetime tenure and political independence, is designed to operate in an expressly nonpartisan manner. Judges, unlike Congress, do not sit together by political party. But the appointment process for judges has been partisan from the very beginning. The landmark case establishing the principle of judicial review, *Marbury v Madison* (1803), concerned the efforts of one party to stack the judiciary with fellow partisans before leaving office. Today party remains an important consideration in the naming of federal judges. While the party of the nominee is not called for on any form, those responsible for the screening and evaluating of candidates certainly take party and ideology into account.

STATE AND LOCAL LEVELS   The importance of party in the operation of local government varies somewhat among states and localities. In some states, such as New York and Illinois, local parties play an even stronger role than at the national level. In others, such as Nebraska, parties play almost no role at all. In Nebraska, the state legislature is expressly nonpartisan, though factions perform like parties and still play a role. Parties are likewise unimportant in the government of Minneapolis. But in most states and many cities, parties are important to the operation of the legislature, governor, or mayor. Judicial selection in most states is a partisan matter.

We the People

Portrait of the Electorate

Sex	Rep.	Dem.	Ind.
Male	40%	53%	7%
Female	39	53	8
Race			
White	38%	54%	8%
Black	43	51	6
Hispanic	41	48	11
Age			
18–34	43%	50%	7%
35–45	37	54	9
46–55	39	51	10
56–64	40	53	7
65+	39	57	4
Income			
Less than $10,000	29%	60%	11%
$10,000–$19,999	35	57	8
$20,000–$29,999	33	59	8
$30,000–$39,999	46	46	8
$40,000–$59,999	49	46	5
$60,000+	57	35	8
Religion			
Jewish	14%	77%	9%
Catholic	39	54	7
Protestant	46	47	7
Ideology			
Liberal	8%	89%	3%
Moderate/ Don't Know	32	56	12
Conservative	72	23	5
Region			
Northeast	36%	54%	1%
Northcentral	41	49	10
South	38	53	9
West	39	56	5
Total	39	53	8

SOURCE: 1996 American National Election Study, Center for Political Studies, University of Michigan.

Note: We have classified Independents who lean toward a party with that party.

In short, political parties are important to the operation of American government. They play an important role in filling senior executive branch and judicial positions. They are the organizing device in legislatures. And for the party of the president or governor, they provide a bridge that spans the separation of powers between the executive branch and legislative branches.

Parties in the Electorate

Political parties would be of little significance if they did not have meaning to the electorate. Parties remain important to voters for all of the reasons described earlier in this chapter: they organize the competition, simplify the voting choices, and provide a link between the people and their government. Adherents of the two parties are drawn to them by a combination of factors: stand on particular issues; personal or party history; religious, racial, or social peer grouping; attractiveness of candidates. The emphases among these factors change over time, but they are remarkably consistent with those identified by political scientists more than 35 years ago.[33]

PARTY REGISTRATION   For citizens in many states, "party" has a particular legal meaning—**party registration**. At the time voters register to vote in these states, they are asked to state their party preference. They then become *registered* Democrats, Republicans, Libertarians, or whatever. Voters can subsequently change their party registration. Why do some states have party registration? One reason is to limit the participants in primary elections to persons from that party; hence, in states like California, only registered Democrats can vote in the Democratic primary.

PARTY ACTIVISTS   This group tends to fall into three broad categories: party regulars, candidate activists, and issue activists. *Party regulars* place the party first. They value winning elections and understand that compromise and moderation may be necessary to reach that objective. They also realize that in our system it is important to keep the party together as much as possible, because a fractured party only helps the opposition.

Candidate activists are followers of a particular candidate who see the party as the means to place their candidate in power. Politicians who generate a devoted following often see the political party as the means to achieve their electoral objectives. Candidate activists are often not concerned with the other operations of the party—with nominees for other offices, for example, or with raising money for the party.

People who supported David Duke in his Louisiana contest for governor and his unsuccessful run for the presidency in 1992 would be classified as candidate activists. Duke, a former Ku Klux Klan leader with an antiblack and anti-Semitic record, disavowed his past and tried to win support as a Republican from enough voters to become governor of Louisiana. While ultimately losing the gubernatorial election, he generated national attention and made himself visible and well known. Candidate activists like those who supported Duke fade in interest and involvement when their candidate loses and leaves the political scene.

Issue activists see politics from a focused perspective. They wish to push the parties in a particular direction on a single issue or narrow range of issues: abortion, taxes, school prayer, the environment, or civil rights. To issue activists, the party platform is an important battleground because they seek the party endorsement for their position. Issue activists are also often candidate activists if they can find a candidate willing to embrace their position.

Both issue activists and candidate activists have been called purists because they see politics and the party as a battle over their issue, and they insist on making their "statement" on that issue or for their candidate, regardless of the electoral consequences. Such purists do not want to compromise. They prefer to lose the election rather than accept less than what they want.

Party activists thus include a diverse group of people who come to the political party with different objectives. It is not surprising then, that some of the most interesting politics you will observe are over candidate selection and issue positions within the political parties. Fights over strategy and party position are conducted in open meetings and under democratic procedures. Political parties foster democracy not only by competition *between* the parties but *within* the parties as well.

Party Identification

Unfortunately, the vast majority of Americans are mere spectators of party activity. They lack the partisan commitment and interest needed for this level of involvement. This is not to say that parties are irrelevant or unimportant to them. For them, partisanship is what political scientists call **party identification**—an informal and subjective affiliation with a political party that most people acquire in childhood, a standing preference for one party over another.[34] This type of voter will sometimes vote for a candidate from the other party, yet in the absence of a compelling reason to do otherwise, most will vote according to their party identification.

Party identification is measured by the answers to the following question:

> Generally speaking, in politics do you usually think of yourself as a Republican, a Democrat, an Independent, or what?

Persons who answer Republican or Democrat to this question are then asked:

> Would you call yourself a strong or a not very strong Republican/Democrat?

Persons who answered Independent to the first question are asked this follow-up question:

> Do you think of yourself as closer to the Republican or the Democratic party?

Persons who did not indicate Democrat, Republican, or Independent to the first question rarely exceed 2 percent of the electorate and include persons who are apolitical or who identify with one of the minor political parties. Because of their consistently small numbers, they are typically not very important to election outcomes.

The party identification question thus produces seven categories of persons: Strong Democrats, Weak Democrats, Independent-leaning Democrats, Pure Independents, Independent-leaning Republicans, Weak Republicans, and Strong Republicans. Over the 40-year period during which political scientists have been asking these questions, the partisan preferences of the American public have been remarkably stable. Table 10–2 presents the party identification breakdown for the period from 1952 to 1996.

Party identification is the single best predictor of how people will vote. Unlike candidates and issues, which come and go, party identification is a long-term element in voting choice. The strength of party identification is also important in predicting participation and political interest. Strong Republicans and Strong Democrats participate more actively in politics than any other groups and are generally more knowledgeable and informed. Pure Independents, on the other hand, are just the opposite; they vote at the lowest rates and have the lowest levels of interest and awareness of any of the categories of party identification. This evidence runs counter to the notion that persons who are strong partisans are unthinking party adherents.[35] Party identification, generally acquired from parents, is reinforced by peers and early political experiences. It is part of the *political socialization* process described in Chapter 7.

To say that most persons have the same partisanship as their parents is not to say that some do not identify with the other party. There are lots of Democratic children of Republican parents and vice versa, but that is not typical. People do not change parties as often as they change their attitudes on issues or enthusiasm for candidates or politicians. To define party identification as a stable, long-term force in voting does not preclude change in the underlying support for the parties or a major realignment.

TABLE 10–2
Party Identification, 1952–1996

	Strong Democrat	Weak Democrat	Independent-leaning Democrat	Pure Independent	Independent-Leaning Republican	Weak Republican	Strong Republican	Apolitical
1952	22%	25%	10%	6%	7%	14%	14%	3%
1956	21	23	6	9	8	14	15	4
1958	27	22	7	7	5	17	11	4
1960	20	25	6	10	7	14	16	3
1962	23	23	7	8	6	16	12	4
1964	27	25	9	8	6	14	11	1
1966	18	28	9	12	7	15	10	1
1968	20	25	10	11	9	15	10	1
1970	20	24	10	13	8	15	9	1
1972	15	26	11	13	11	13	10	1
1974	18	21	13	15	9	14	8	3
1976	15	25	12	15	10	14	9	1
1978	15	24	14	14	10	14	8	2
1980	18	23	11	13	10	14	9	3
1982	20	24	11	11	8	14	10	2
1984	17	20	11	11	12	15	12	2
1986	18	22	10	12	11	15	11	2
1988	18	18	12	11	13	14	14	2
1990	17	19	12	11	13	17	11	2
1992	18	18	12	11	13	14	14	2
1994	15	19	13	10	12	14	16	1
1996	19	20	14	8	11	15	13	0.1

SOURCE: American National Election Studies, Center for Political Studies, University of Michigan.

PARTISAN CHANGE, REFORM, AND RENEWAL

Partisan Realignment and Dealignment

The current system of party identification is built upon a foundation of the New Deal and the critical election of 1932, events that took place more than 60 years ago. How can events so removed from the present still be important in shaping our party system? When will there be another **realignment**—an election that dramatically changes the voters' partisan identification? Whether a realignment has occurred is frequently debated in the literature of political science, but most political science researchers believe we have not experienced any major realignment since 1932.[36] Partisan identification for the past four decades has been stable, and while new voters have been added to the electorate—minorities and 18-to-21-year-olds—the basic character of the party system has not changed dramatically.

In presidential voting, Republicans have done well, winning five of the last eight presidential elections. Bill Clinton's victories in 1992 and 1996 demonstrated, however, that Democrats still have the ability to assemble a winning coalition. Many so-called "Reagan Democrats" returned to the Democratic party to vote for Bill Clinton, especially in heavily populated states. While people may not be changing their underlying party preference, they seem willing to vote for candidates from the other party: Democrats have supported Republicans, and persons from both parties

PARTY DIFFERENCES

American parties are sometimes criticized for being too similar, too mainstream, and nonideological. Our parties are moderate, centrist parties, but there are important differences, both in the positions the parties take on some issues and in how the public perceives the two parties. Americans differentiate the parties in substantial ways, as represented by public opinion polls on which one party is perceived as doing better on certain issues. The parties do have different racial, religious, or regional makeups. A final piece of evidence that Americans see the parties as different is the tendency for there to be national tides that benefit one party over the other.

Public Confidence in the Parties

Question: Which political party, Republican or Democratic, do you think would do a better job with each of the following?

	Republican	Democratic
Reforming the welfare system	35%	39%
Handling the problem of pollution and environment	12	45
Making health care more affordable	17	52
Handling foreign affairs	36	28
Handling the nation's economy	31	32
Handling the problem of poverty	18	47
Handling the budget deficit	33	27
Dealing with the crime problem	29	26

Question: Which party is more likely to cut Social Security benefits?

	Republican	Democratic
	50%	11%

Question: Which party is more likely to improve race relations?

	Republican	Democratic
	8%	37%

Question: Which party is more likely to raise taxes?

	Republican	Democratic
	30%	34%

SOURCE: The Gallup Poll.

How to Tell 'em Apart

- Republicans usually wear hats. Democrats usually don't.
- Democrats buy banned books. Republicans form censorship committees and read them.
- Democrats eat the fish they catch. Republicans hang them on the wall.
- Republicans study the financial pages of the newspaper. Democrats put them on the bottom of the bird cage.
- On Saturday, Republicans head for the golf course, the yacht club, or the hunting lodge. Democrats get a haircut, wash the car, or go bowling.
- Republicans have guest rooms. Democrats have spare rooms filled with old baby furniture.
- Republicans hire exterminators. Democrats step on the bugs.
- Republicans sleep in twin beds—some even in separate rooms. That is why there are more Democrats.

SOURCE: The National Republican Congressional Committee Newsletter.

"Very Republican. I love it."

Drawing by Tobey. ©1986 The New Yorker Magazine, Inc

defected to vote for Ross Perot in 1992. Perot's support waned in 1996, and many voters returned to their underlying partisan preferences in presidential voting.

Further evidence of a voting realignment came in the early 1980s, when Republicans won several close Senate elections and gained a majority in that body. Democrats, however, won back the Senate in 1986, and until 1994 they appeared to have a permanent majority in the House. All of that seemed to change with the 1994 election, as Republicans were swept into office with a tidal wave of victories. Republicans made major inroads in the South and strengthened their share of the vote among white males.

The 1996 election does little to resolve the debate over realignment. Republicans could claim that their congressional victories and their continued strong showing in the South are evidence of a gradual shift to their party. Clinton's ability to bounce back from the 1994 Democratic defeat and his skill in redefining himself and his party might be a sign of a revitalized Democratic party. Theories of realignment often assume important differences between the parties on major issues. Clinton's move to the center muted issue differences in 1996. The voters' choice of divided government means a realignment has not yet happened.

What, then, should we make of recent voting behavior and a possible realignment? One argument, often espoused by Democrats, is that Republican success in presidential elections is the result of their stronger candidates and better campaigns. Republican presidential candidates have generally been seen in more positive terms than Democratic candidates. Voters have just liked them more. Republican presidential campaigns have also done a better job of focusing the campaign on issues and themes that benefit their candidates and hurt Democrats. An exception to this was Clinton's keeping the focus of the 1992 election on the economy ("It's the economy, stupid!)," which helped him and hurt Bush. Clinton may not have been able to sustain this focus had it not been for Perot also stressing the deficit and economic issues.

Some think that, instead of a realignment, we are experiencing the rejection of partisanship in favor of becoming Independents, and there has indeed been an increase in the number of persons who characterize themselves as Independents. Hedrick Smith, formerly of *The New York Times*, expresses a widespread view: "The most important phenomenon of American politics in the past quarter century has been the rise of independent voters who have at times outnumbered Republicans."[37] The implications of this contention have been speculated about by many political scientists.[38]

The **dealignment** argument—that people have abandoned both parties to become Independents—would be more persuasive were it not that two-thirds of all Independents are really partisans in their voting behavior and attitudes. One-third of those who claim to be Independents lean toward the Democratic party and vote Democratic election after election. Another one-third of Independents lean toward Republicans and just as predictably vote Republican. The remaining one-third, who appear to be genuine Independents and who do not vote predictably for one party, turn out to be people with little interest in politics.

Despite the reported growth in Independents, there were proportionately about the same number of Pure Independents in 1992 as there were in 1956.[39] There are, in short, at least three types of Independents, and most of them are predictably partisan. Table 10–3 summarizes voting behavior in contests for president in 1992 and 1996 and for U.S. House of Representatives in 1994 and 1996.

Strong partisans are loyal to their party. Since 1952, Strong Republicans have voted Republican on average over 95 percent of the time, and Strong Democrats have voted Democratic more than 85 percent of the time. Weak and Independent-leaning Democrats have voted Democratic roughly two-thirds of the time over the past 40 years. Weak and Independent-leaning Republicans are even more predictably partisan, with more than 85 percent voting Republican on average since 1952. Weak and Independent-leaning Republicans defect from their party more when voting for the U.S. House; about 1 in

TABLE 10-3

Voting Behavior of Partisans and Independents, 1992–1996

| | Percent of Democratic Vote | | | |
| | President | | U.S. House | |
	(1992)	(1996)	(1994)	(1996)
Strong Democrats	93%	96%	88%	87%
Weak Democrats	68	82	73	70
Independent-leaning Democrats	70	76	68	69
Pure Independents	41	35	55	41
Independent-leaning Republicans	11	20	25	21
Weak Republicans	14	20	21	21
Strong Republicans	3	5	7	3

SOURCE: American National Election Studies, Center for Political Studies, University of Michigan.

3 votes Democratic. Pure Independents are volatile, voting heavily Republican for president in 1988 yet giving a plurality of their vote to Clinton (41 percent) in 1992.

In 1996, Pure Independents voted for Dole slightly more than for Clinton, with Perot a distant third. More than nine out of ten strong partisans voted for their party for president, and roughly 80 percent of the weak and Independent-leaning partisans voted for their party. Democrats of all types were somewhat less loyal in voting for the House in 1996 than in voting for President Clinton, while Republicans voted more consistently Republican.

Because most Independents are really closet partisans in their voting behavior and have been so for a long time, much of the case for the dealignment theory fails. Something about the parties inhibits most Independents from labeling themselves as partisans. However, it is a mistake to assume that all Independents see the political world in similar terms and constitute a monolithic force. There are instead at least three groups, and most of them are predictably partisan.

Why has realignment moved so slowly? Why aren't all conservatives now happily ensconced in the Republican party and all liberals gladly lodged in the Democratic party? Americans do not casually cross party lines. If you grew up in a conservative New Hampshire family whose forebearers voted Republican for a century, you are pretty much conditioned to stay with the GOP. Even if that party took a direction you disliked, you might continue to register as a Republican but quietly vote Democratic to avoid friction in the family. Or if you come from a "yellow dog" Democratic family in Texas (meaning your family would vote for a "yellow dog" before it would vote for a Republican), you might continue to vote for Democrats locally even though you disliked various Democratic candidates for president or senator. Evidence indicates that this pattern is common throughout the South.

The other reason for slow realignment is the local nature of the parties. For decades, conservative Democrats in the South have been voting for Republican candidates for president—not only Bush and Reagan but for Nixon and even Eisenhower—without changing their identification from the Democratic party to the Republican. Why? Partly because they still see themselves as Democrats, but partly because the Democratic party remains much stronger at the state and local level in the South. So if candidates and voters want to have an impact on local politics, in which the only meaningful elections may be in the Democratic primaries, they retain their Democratic affiliation.

Are the Political Parties Dying?

The American party system faces three main charges: (1) parties do not take meaningful and contrasting positions on issues, especially the issues of the 1990s; (2) party membership is essentially meaningless, so that parties neither define issues critically nor are able to prosper organizationally; and (3) parties are so concerned with accommodating those on the middle of the ideological spectrum that they are incapable of serving as an avenue for social progress. Are these statements true, and if true are they important?

Some experts fear parties are so weak they may be mortally ill, or at least in a severe decline. They point first to the long-run impact of the Progressive reforms early in this century, reforms that robbed party organizations of their control of the nomination process by allowing masses of independent and "uninformed" voters to enter the primaries and vote for candidates who might not be acceptable to party leaders. They also point to nonpartisan elections in cities and towns and the staggering of national, state, and local elections that made it harder for parties to influence the election process. Legislation limiting the viability and functions of parties was bad enough, say the party pessimists, but parties suffer from further ills today.

The rise of television and electronic technology and the parallel rise in campaign, media, and direct-mail consultants may have made parties irrelevant in educating, mobilizing, and organizing the electorate. These new media have reinforced the role of candidates and lessened the role of parties. (See Chapter 13 for more on the media in this role.) In addition, partly as a result of media influence, the most powerful electoral forces today are candidate organizations, not party organizations. Office seekers, supported by money and media, organize their personal following to win nominations (while the party leaders are supposed to stand by neutrally). If they win office, they are far more responsive to their personal following than to the party leadership, which means that the party lacks clout over politicians and policy.[40]

Advocates of strong parties concede parts of this diagnosis may be correct: the demise of political machines at the local level, the decline in strong partisan affiliations, the weakness of grass-roots party membership. Yet they also see signs of party revival. The national party organizations—the national committees and the congressional and senatorial campaign committees—are significantly better funded than they were in earlier days; they even own permanent, modern headquarters in Washington, D.C. Moreover, the parties are more capable of providing assistance to candidates and to state and local party organizations because of their strong financial base from soft money contributions and because they have defined their role as providing expertise to those who need it but cannot otherwise obtain it. Optimists hope these advances will give the national parties some leverage over the positions that candidates and officeholders take on party issues.[41]

How can the "spin doctors" differ so widely in diagnosing the condition of the ailing parties? Pessimists concentrate mostly on the Democratic party, which has been much weaker nationally than the Republican party, and on presidential elections, where the Democrats are weakest, rather than on congressional or gubernatorial results. With Clinton in the White House, Democrats show signs of rebirth as a viable national organization. Optimists, seeing what Republicans have been able to do for some years, have predicted correctly that Democrats would follow suit.

During the first years of the Reagan administration, the Republican party in Congress demonstrated a remarkable cohesiveness on issues of importance to the president's program. This trend can be measured by the *party unity score*, defined as the percentage of members of a party who vote together on roll call votes in Congress on which a majority of the members of one party vote against a majority of the members of the other party. Clinton had the highest party unity scores from his party in 1993 than any party gave its president in the past 40 years—88 percent of the Democrats voted together, while 87 percent of the Republicans voted together.[42] Clinton needed the strong support from his party in key votes on the budget and tax proposals but benefited also from strong Republican support on the NAFTA vote. During the Republican-controlled 105th Congress, House and Senate Republicans voted together 89 percent of the time—a new all-time high. Democrats in both houses were less unified than they had been in Clinton's first two years in office, dropping to 80 percent in the House and 83 percent in the Senate.[43] Thus, while rank-and-file voters do not seem to be returning to strong partisan ties, party organizations and the party in government do show distinct and significant signs of strength.

One other measure of party unity is a president's ability not to have to use the veto power, something Clinton was able to avoid in his first 23 months in office—only the second time a president has done so in more than 60 years. Clinton's ability to avoid vetoes ended when Republicans took over Congress in early 1995. In 1995 alone, he vetoed 11 bills, the bulk of them being appropriations bills.[44] In 1996 Clinton exercised the veto more sparingly, in part because he and the Republicans had decided that cooperation was more in their interest than confrontation.

Party Reform and Renewal

As we have seen, by the dawn of the twentieth century, middle-class reformers took the nominating process "back to the people" by means of the party primary, the direct election of U.S. senators, nonpartisan local elections, and civil service reforms. But the primary helped bring about the downfall not only of party bosses but also of parties themselves, at least in terms of deciding who could run under the party label. Conventions had not been just a way to pick candidates; they had also organized the grass-roots leadership of the party. Now in most cities and some states, the convention—and with it much of the leadership—simply disappeared.

REFORM AMONG THE DEMOCRATS A second wave of party reform occurred after the 1968 election, when the Democrats, responding to the disarray during their Chicago convention and disputes about the fairness of delegate selection procedures, agreed to a process that led to greater use of direct primaries and greater representation of younger voters, women, and minorities as elected delegates. Another reform was the abolition of the rule that a winner of a state's convention or primaries got all the state's delegates (the *unit rule*). This rule was replaced by a system of *proportionality*, in which candidates received delegates in rough proportion to the votes they received in the primary election.

Chicago's mayor Richard Daley, father of the current mayor of Chicago, and many other party stalwarts argued that these reforms would make the party reflective of the views of college professors and intellectuals, and not working-class people, unionists, the elderly, and elected officials. Responding to this criticism, the party created "superdelegate" positions for elected officials and party leaders.

REFORM AMONG THE REPUBLICANS Republicans were not immune to criticism that their party conventions and party procedures were keeping out the rank-and-file. During this period they did not make changes as drastic as those made by the Democrats, but they did give the national committee more control over presidential campaigns in an effort to avoid Watergate-type excesses, and state parties were urged to encourage broader participation by all groups, including women, minorities, youth, and the poor. While making these concessions to reformers within their own party, Republicans put more of their emphasis on improving the party structure to win elections.

The Republican party entered the 1980s with a party organization far superior to that of the Democrats. The GOP emphasized grass-roots organization and membership recruitment. Seminars were held to teach Republican candidates how to make speeches and hold press conferences, and weekend conferences were organized for training young professionals. Both parties now conduct training sessions with candidates on campaign planning, advertising, fund raising, using phone banks, recruiting volunteers, and campaign scheduling.[45]

PARTY RENEWAL Some politicians and scholars are more interested in party renewal than party reform. Those pushing for renewal focus on the need to change the parties into better structured, more active, more effective, and more policy-oriented organizations.

The outcry over President Clinton and Vice-President Gore's shaking of the soft-money tree in 1995 and 1996 and the ensuing congressional investigations reinforced public cynicism over the role of money in politics, but because the system so clearly benefits incumbents of both parties, there is little incentive to change. Soft money is simply a loophole that permits federal candidates to avoid spending and contribution limitations. There may be some enhancement of party staffing, databases, and expertise that comes with the soft money, and this may help revitalize the parties. But most soft money is spent to help elect candidates and has little bearing on the next election.

Political parties, as we have seen, have enjoyed something of a resurgence during the past decade. Moreover, the claim that Americans do not consider partisanship when voting is largely false, and the reported growing role of Independents is a myth. Parties remain important in government. They are in all these respects vital to our democracy.

POLITICS ONLINE

Parties Online

Our major and minor parties now have Web sites where you can learn about the party, its platform, and its issue positions. The sites are interactive in the sense that you can volunteer for a host of party activities. A constant of party home pages is fund raising—both directly through contributions and indirectly by purchasing party paraphernalia.

Democratic party activists use the Internet as a means of mobilizing people to party causes. Calling themselves "Digital Democrats," they provide an online newsletter and make available a software package called Precinct Walker, which helps manage a precinct, ward, or neighborhood, and provides information on recruiting volunteers, raising funds, identifying voters, processing absentee ballot requests, and managing get-out-the-vote efforts. You can also register to vote through their site:

http://www.digitals.org/digitals/

Republicans ask visitors to their Web site to sign the official Petition for Balancing the Budget and Real Tax Cuts. Republicans provide a frequently updated survey to get feedback from the party faithful on policy issues.

If you would like to volunteer for a party, you can do so through their home page:

http://www.rnc.org/ or www.republicanweb.com

http://www.democrats.org/

http://www.reformparty.org

http://www.libertarian.org

SUMMARY

1. Political parties are essential to democracy— simplifying voting choices, organizing the competition, unifying the electorate, determining who holds office, translating public preferences into policy, helping to organize government by bridging the separation of powers and fostering cooperation among branches of government, and providing loyal opposition.

2. Political parties help structure voting choice by nominating candidates to run for office. Before the advent of direct primaries where voters determine the party nominees, the parties had more control of who ran under their label. States determine the nomination rules. While most states employ the direct primary, some use a caucus or mixed caucus system where more committed partisans have a larger role in the decision of who gets nominated.

3. American parties are moderate. They bring factions and interests together in coalitions broad enough to win the presidency and other elections. Third parties have not been notably successful. One reason for this is our single-member district, winner-takes-all election rules. In systems with proportional representation or multi-member districts, there is a greater tendency for more parties and the need to assemble governing coalitions across parties.

4. American parties have experienced critical elections and realignments. Most political scientists agree the last realignment occurred in 1932. In the period since the 1970s, there has been an increase in the number of persons who call themselves Independents. This is sometimes called "dealignment," but most Independents are closet partisans who vote for the party toward which they lean.

5. Parties are vital in the operation of government. They are organized around elected offices at the state and local levels. Congress is also organized around parties, and judicial and many executive branch appointments are based in large part on partisanship.

6. Parties are governed by their national and state committees, and the focal point of party organization is the national and state party chairs. When the party controls the executive branch of government, the executive (governor or president) usually has a determining say in selecting the party chair. Parties out of power in the executive branch usually have less effect on the aims of the party. With the rise of soft money in recent elections, parties now have more resources to spend on politics.

7. Frequent efforts have been made to reform our parties. The Progressive movement saw parties, as then organized, as an impediment to democracy and pushed direct primaries as a means to reform them. Following the 1968 election, the Democratic party took the lead in pushing primaries and stressing greater diversity in those elected as delegates. Republicans have also moved more toward primaries.

8. Compared to some European parties, ours remain organizationally weak. There has been some party renewal in recent years as party competition has grown in the South and soft money has flowed to state parties.

FURTHER READING

JOHN H. ALDRICH, *Why Parties? The Origin and Transformation of Party Politics in America* (University of Chicago Press, 1995).

DAN BALZ AND RONALD BROWNSTEIN, *Storming the Gates: Protest Politics and the Republican Revival* (Little, Brown and Company, 1996).

MICHAEL BARONE, *Our Country: The Shaping of America from Roosevelt to Reagan* (Free Press, 1990).

JOHN F. BIBBY, *Politics, Parties, and Elections in America*, 3d ed. (Nelson-Hall, 1996).

MARY C. BRENNAN, *Turning Right in the Sixties: The Conservative Capture of the GOP* (University of North Carolina Press, 1995).

STEPHEN C. CRAIG, ed., *Broken Contract: Changing Relationships Between Americans and Their Government* (Westview Press, 1996).

LEON EPSTEIN, *Political Parties in the American Mold* (University of Wisconsin Press, 1986).

JEFF FAUX, *The Party's Not Over: A New Vision for Democrats* (Basic Books, 1996).

PAUL S. HERRNSON, *Party Campaigning in the 1980s: Have the National Parties Made a Comeback as Key Players in Congressional Elections?* (Harvard University Press, 1988).

WILLIAM J. KEEFE, *Parties, Politics, and Public Policy in America*, 7th ed. (Congressional Quarterly Press, 1994).

BRUCE E. KEITH, DAVID B. MAGLEBY, CANDICE J. NELSON, ELIZABETH ORR, MARK WESTLYE, AND RAYMOND E. WOLFINGER, *The Myth of the Independent Voter* (University of California Press, 1992).

WILLIAM G. MAYER, *The Divided Democrats: Ideological Unity, Party Reform, and Presidential Elections* (Westview, 1996).

SIDNEY M. MILKIS, *The President and the Parties: The Transformation of the American Party System Since the New Deal* (Oxford University Press, 1993).

KELLY D. PATTERSON, *Political Parties and the Maintenance of Liberal Democracy* (Columbia University Press, 1996).

STEVEN J. ROSENSTONE, ROY L. BEHR, AND EDWARD H. LAZARUS, *Third Parties in America: Citizen Response to Major Party Failure*, 2d ed. (Princeton University Press, 1996).

JAMES SUNDQUIST, *Dynamics of the Party System: Alignment and Realignment of Political Parties in the United States*, rev. ed. (Brookings, 1983).

MARTIN P. WATTENBERG, *The Decline of American Political Parties, 1952–1992* (Harvard University Press, 1994).

HERBERT F. WEISBERG, ED., *Democracy's Feast: Elections in America* (Chatham House, 1995).

11

Public Opinion, Participation, and Voting

*A*t the end of a nationally televised presidential debate in 1980, ABC News conducted a "call-in-your-vote" poll to determine the winner of the debate. Ted Koppel introduced the poll at 11:30 p.m. (Eastern Time) by saying:

> Good evening. The great presidential debate of 1980 is now history. For the past half-hour, and continuing throughout this broadcast, . . . ABC News is conducting a massive computerized telephone poll, nationwide. There will be no scientifically selected sample; only the votes of those who call in will be counted. . . . The telephone company is charging 50 cents a call, which will be added to your bill. . . . A few of you are calling in and complaining that although you are calling for one candidate, you are receiving a recorded message confirming your vote for another candidate. We have checked that out with the telephone company; they assure us that the system is in fact working. It's the telephone company's system; we have to take their word for it.
>
> If you haven't called yet and would like to, here's how you can register your opinion as to who gained the most from tonight's debate: If you think President Carter gained the most, simply dial 1-900-590-1800. If you believe Governor Reagan gained more, dial 1-900-590-7400.[1]

Koppel stated that multiple calls from one telephone would not be recorded. At the end of the program Ronald Reagan had won. He had received 67 percent of the "vote," compared to Jimmy Carter's 33 percent. The ABC-News Poll was cited by newspapers the next day as the first poll that declared Reagan the winner.[2]

Was this a valid poll? Did it correctly measure public opinion on the presidential debate? The answer is clearly no. The poll was flawed in a number of ways. First, the sample was self-selecting and not likely to be representative of the public or even of people who watched the debate on television. Despite ABC's claim, multiple voting may well have taken place. The timing of the poll also may have skewed the results. Many of Carter's supporters in his home region would have gone to bed before the poll began at 11:30 p.m., while in Reagan's home base of California it was only 8:30 p.m. Given the costs involved, poor people and those with less interest would have been discouraged from calling. It is also difficult to know whether the reports of switched recordings indicate that votes were miscounted. Finally, Koppel changed the wording of the question during the program from "Who won tonight's debate?" to "Who gained the most in tonight's debate?" This slight change could have brought different responses from some viewers.

This ABC call-in-your-vote poll is not the only example of how *not* to measure public opinion. Many local television news programs interview people on the street to assess local public opinion. Some major daily newspapers conduct weekly call-in polls that ask intentionally provocative questions. Even a straw poll of a meeting of Iowa hog farmers can generate national news.

In this chapter we look at the nature of public opinion and how to measure it, how we formulate our political beliefs, the factors that affect the formation of our opinions, the nature and level of political participation in the United States, and why people vote as they do.

PUBLIC OPINION

All governments in all nations must be concerned with public opinion, for unrest and protest can topple them. But in a constitutional democracy like ours, public opinion plays an even larger role. As we discussed in Chapters 1 and 7, our widely

Measuring public opinion has become very important in American elections. Here a *Los Angeles Times* pollster tabulates voter responses to an exit poll.

shared values include a belief in popular sovereignty, political equality, and majority rule. Individuals have opinions and express those opinions in a variety of ways, including protest demonstrations, letters to newspaper editors, and voting in free and regularly scheduled elections. Elected officials refer often to public opinion as a basis for their actions. In short, democracy and public opinion go hand in hand.

What Is Public Opinion?

We define **public opinion** as the distribution of individual preferences or evaluations of a given issue, candidate, or institution within a population. *Distribution* means the proportion of the population that holds one opinion or viewpoint as compared to those with opposing opinions or those with no opinion at all. For instance, had ABC pollsters conducted a scientific poll in 1980, they might have found 47 percent who felt Ronald Reagan had won the debate, 37 percent who felt Jimmy Carter had won, and 16 percent who did not know who won. This would be the distribution. The distribution of voting intentions in the last pre-election poll done by Gallup in 1996 was Clinton 52 percent, Dole 41 percent, Perot 7 percent, and undecided 0 percent. The actual outcome was Clinton 49 percent, Dole 41 percent, and Perot 8 percent.

Individual preference means that when we measure public opinion, we are asking *individuals*—not groups, elected officials, or journalists—about their opinions. The *universe* or *population* is the relevant group of people for the question. When a substantial percentage of a sample agree on an issue—for example, that we should honor the American flag—there is a *consensus*. But on most issues, opinions are divided in various proportions. When a large portion of opposing sides feels intensely about an issue, voters are said to be *polarized*. Vietnam in the 1960s and abortion in the 1990s are polarizing issues (see Table 11–1).

INTENSITY This factor produces the brightest and deepest hues in the fabric of public opinion. The fervor of people's beliefs varies greatly. For example, some individuals mildly favor gun control legislation, while others mildly oppose it; still others are emphatically for or against it. Some people may have no interest in the

TABLE 11–1

How Opinions Differ on Abortion

	Percent Saying Abortion Should Be			
	Legal Under Any Circumstances	Legal Under Certain Circumstances	Illegal in All Circumstances	Don't Know
Total Adults	24%	52%	17%	7%
Age				
18–29	34	48	15	2
30–49	33	55	12	1
50–64	26	53	15	5
65 +	22	53	18	7
Sex				
Men	23	53	18	6
Women	26	50	17	7
Education				
Less than high school	12	56	26	7
High school graduate	29	57	11	3
Some college	39	45	14	2
College graduate	42	47	10	1
Race				
White	31	53	13	3
Nonwhite	27	50	22	2
Black	21	52	26	1
Religion				
Protestant	29	54	15	3
Catholic	28	59	13	2
Political Philosophy				
Liberal	47	40	13	—
Moderate	29	57	11	4
Conservative	27	55	17	2
Party Identification				
Republican	27	56	13	5
Independent Republican	34	48	18	—
Independent	35	51	13	2
Independent Democrat	40	48	11	1
Democrat	31	52	16	1
Income				
Less than $20,000	26	54	17	4
$20,000–$29,999	26	61	10	4
$30,000–$49,999	33	51	15	—
More than $50,000	43	45	12	—

SOURCE: Data for "Total Adults," and for gender are from a national survey by the Gallup Organization, September 1996. Other data are from a national survey by the Gallup Organization, January 1992. Figures may not add up to 100 percent due to rounding.

"It should be 'yes' or 'no' or 'undecided'—we don't accept a 'don't give a damn' answer!"

The Wall Street Journal

matter at all; still others may not even have heard of it. Intensity is typically measured by asking people to indicate how strongly they feel on an issue or about a politician. Such a question is often called a *scale*.

Taking the Pulse of the People

Public opinion polls have been part of American politics for a long time. The advent of computers, widespread access to telephones, and modern social science techniques enormously expanded the use of survey research. The hallmarks of scientific polls are proper sampling, unambiguous and fair questions, professional interviewing, and thorough analysis and reporting of the results.

Proper sampling is based on random choices of the appropriate set of people. Random choice means that every individual has an equal chance of being selected. The sample of randomly selected respondents should be appropriate for the questions being asked. For instance, a survey of 18-to-24-year-olds should not be done solely among college students since roughly three-quarters of this age group is not attending college.

The art of asking questions is also important to scientific polling. The wording of questions can influence the answers given. Good questions have been pretested and are delivered by trained and professional interviewers who read the questions exactly as written and without any intonation in their voices. Questions are worded in different ways to measure factual knowledge, opinions, the intensity of opinion, or views on hypothetical situations. Sometimes open-ended questions are asked that permit the respondents to answer in their own words. The order of questions can also alter the responses.

Thorough analysis and reporting of the results are expected of scientific polls. In the computer era, when most polls are conducted on the telephone, polls can be released once the accuracy of the sample is validated and any possible misunderstanding of the questions is considered. Scientific polls inform the public of the sample size, the margin of expected statistical error for a standard question, and when the poll was conducted.

It is important to remember that public opinion can change and that most polls are really snapshots of opinion at a point in time rather than moving pictures of opinions over time.

LATENCY Latency refers to political opinions that exist merely as a potential; they may not have crystallized, yet they are still important, for they can be evoked by leaders and converted into action. Latent opinions set rough boundaries for leaders who know that if they take certain actions they will trigger either opposition or support from millions of people. If leaders have some understanding of latent opinions—people's real wants, needs, and hopes—they will know how to mobilize them and draw them to the polls on election day. Many who lived in communist Poland, East Germany, Czechoslovakia, or Yugoslavia must have had latent opinions favorable to democracy—opinions supporting majority rule, freedom, meaningful elections. The speed with which the public embraced democratic reforms in those countries was possible when leaders encouraged widespread expression of such ideas.

SALIENCE What causes opinions to be stable or fluid, intense or latent? A major factor is salience. By salience we mean the extent to which people feel that issues are relevant to them. Your next-door neighbor may feel intensely about abortion or gun control or school prayer, whereas you may get excited about health care or welfare reform. Most people are more concerned about personal issues like paying the bills and keeping their jobs than about national issues, but if their personal concerns are connected with national issues, salience rises sharply.

Salience may change over time. During the Great Depression of the 1930s, Americans were mainly concerned about jobs, wages, and economic security. By the 1940s, foreign affairs issues came to the fore. In the 1960s, problems of race and poverty aroused intense feeling. Vietnam and then Watergate riveted people's attention in the 1970s. By the 1990s, concern about jobs, drugs, street crime, welfare, health care, and the state of the environment had become salient issues.

How Do We Get Our Political Opinions and Values?

No one is born with political views. We learn them from many teachers. The process by which we develop our political attitudes, values, and beliefs is called **political socialization**. This process starts in childhood, and the family and the schools are probably the two most important political teachers. Children learn the content of our culture in childhood and adolescence but reshape it as they live their lives.[3] Socialization also lays the foundation for political beliefs, values, ideology, and partisanship.

A common element of political socialization in all cultures is *nationalism*, a consciousness of the nation-state and of belonging to that entity. Robert Coles describes it this way:

> As soon as we are born, in most places on this earth, we acquire a nationality, a membership in a community. . . . A royal doll, a flag to wave in a parade, coins with their engraved messages—these are sources of instruction and connect a young person to a country. The attachment can be strong, indeed even among children yet to attend school, wherever the flag is saluted, the national anthem sung. The attachment is as parental as the words imply—homeland, motherland, fatherland. . . . Nationalism works its way into just about every corner of the mind's life.[4]

The sources of our views are immensely varied in the pluralistic political culture of the United States. Political attitudes may stem from religious, racial, gender, ethnic, or economic beliefs and values. But we can make at least one generalization safely: We form our attitudes in *groups*, not only in groups such as schools and social organizations, but especially in close-knit groups like the family. When we identify closely with the attitudes and interests of a particular group, we tend to see politics through the "eyes" of that group.[5]

Group affiliation does not necessarily mean that individual members of the group do not think for themselves. Each member brings his or her own emotions, feelings, memories, and resistances to groups. The extent to which people are captive to groups is indeed a running argument among scholars from different disciplines. Sociologists tend to emphasize the pervasive influence of groups over their members. Certain schools of psychology focus more on the developmental stages within individuals that alternately prompt them to be joiners or loners. Political scientists have traditionally tended to agree more with the sociological approach.[6] Political psychologists seek to combine both approaches.

The considerable variation in the factors that influence our political beliefs produces a wide array of attitudes in society. However, children in the United States at an early age adopt common values that provide continuity with the past and legitimize the American political system. Young children know what country they live in, and their loyalty to the nation develops early. Although the details of our political system may still elude them, most young Americans acquire a respect for the Constitution and for the concept of participatory democracy, as well as an initially positive view of the most visible figure in our democracy—the president.

FAMILY American children typically show political interest by the age of ten or even earlier, and by the early teens their interest may be fairly high. Learning experiences gradually shape the values and beliefs people acquire in childhood. Consider your own political learning process. You probably formed your picture of the world by listening to a parent at dinner or by absorbing the tales your older brothers and sisters brought home from school. Perhaps you heard about politics from grandparents, aunts, and uncles. You, in turn, influenced your family, if only by bringing some of your own hopes and problems home from school. What we first learn in the family is not so much specific political opinions as basic *attitudes* that shape our opinions—attitudes toward our neighbors, political parties, other classes or types of people, particular leaders (especially presidents), and society in general.

Studies of high school students indicate a high correlation between the political party of the parents and the partisan choice of the child. And this relatively high degree of correspondence continues throughout life. Such a finding raises some interesting questions: Does the direct influence of parents create the correspondence? Or are parents and children equally influenced by living in the same social environment—neighborhood, church, socioeconomic group? The answer is *both*, and one influence often strengthens the other. A daughter of Democratic parents growing up in a small southern town with strong Democratic leanings will be affected by friends, by other adults, and perhaps by youngsters in a church group, all of whom may reinforce the attitudes of her parents.[7]

SCHOOLS Schools also mold young citizens' values and attitudes. American schools see part of their purpose as preparing students to be citizens and active participants in governing their communities and nation. At an early age, schoolchildren begin to pick up specific political values and acquire basic attitudes toward our system of government. Education, like the family, prepares Americans to live in society. It is a massive enterprise.

From kindergarten through college, children generally develop political values that will enhance their citizenship and legitimize the American political system. In their study of American history, schoolchildren are introduced to our nation's heroes and heroines, the important events in our history, and the ideals of our society. Other aspects of the student's experience, such as the daily Pledge of Allegiance, usually reinforce respect of country. Children also gain practical experience in the workings of democracy through elections for class or school officers and student government. In some colleges, the state legislature or college

How You Ask It Shapes How You Answer It

How you ask a polling question makes a lot of difference in the responses people give, as demonstrated by the way three different polls asked about special interests and campaign finance. The first question was written by Ross Perot's organization, not by a survey researcher. It was published in *TV Guide* and asked individuals to send in their answers. Perot's survey was criticized widely by survey organizations for its skewed sample and biased questions. The second and third questions were part of national surveys conducted by professional polling firms using random samples.

1. Should laws be passed to eliminate all possibilities of special interests giving huge sums of money to candidates?

   Yes   99%

2. Should laws be passed to prohibit interest groups from contributing to campaigns, or do groups have a right to contribute to the candidate they support?

   Prohibit contribution   40%
   Groups have right   55%

3. Please tell me whether you favor or oppose this proposal: The passage of new laws that would eliminate all possibility of special interests giving large sums of money to candidates.

   Favor   70%
   Oppose   28%

SOURCE: Daniel Goleman, "Pollsters Enlist Psychologists in Quest for Unbiased Results," *The New York Times*, September 7, 1993, pp. C1, C11.

trustees have made courses in U.S. history or American government a graduation requirement.

Do school influences give young people greater faith in political institutions? Yes and no. A classic study examined relationships among community leaders' attitudes, civics texts, and students' attitudes in three Boston communities—one upper-middle class, one lower-middle class, and one working class. The school texts in all three communities stressed the right of citizens to try to influence government, but only the texts used in the upper-middle-class community stressed politics as conflict and as a process for adjusting differing group demands. And only the upper-middle-class community had leaders who underscored politics as a conflict process, thus reinforcing the lessons in the texts. Edgar Litt, a political scientist, concluded that the lower-middle-class students were learning that government was a process carried out by institutions on their behalf, while the upper-middle-class students were learning that the political process was something they could influence.[8]

How does college influence political opinions? One study suggests that students planning to attend college are more likely to be knowledgeable about politics, more in favor of free speech, and more likely to talk and read about politics.[9] Reflecting national trends, conservatism and Republicanism on college campuses increased in the 1980s, but there are indications from the same study that college students in the 1990s are again more liberal.[10] Is this the influence of the professors, the curriculum, or the students? It is difficult to generalize. Parents sometimes fear professors have too much influence on their college-age children; however, most professors doubt they have significant influence over students. The debate about whether there is peer pressure on college campuses to conform to certain acceptable ideas—so-called *political correctness* (PC)—highlights the role higher education can play in shaping attitudes and values.

MASS MEDIA   Family and school are not the only influences on children and adolescents. The mass media also serve as agents of socialization by providing a link between individuals and the values and behavior of others. The mass media present information about our society, and when we watch, listen, and read, we discover which values and role models are considered important. News broadcasts present information about our society; events that get intensive media coverage often focus our attention on certain issues. For example, the televised trial of O. J. Simpson directed widespread attention to the criminal justice system.

OTHER INFLUENCES   Religious and ethnic attitudes also serve to shape opinions, both within and outside the family. Historically, Protestant families are more likely to be more conservative than Catholics on economic and welfare issues, whereas Jewish families are more likely to be more liberal on both economic and noneconomic issues than either Catholics or Protestants. Protestants express varying opinions ranging from conservative to liberal on certain social issues. Evangelicals—whose numbers include a small percentage of Catholics but are mainly made up of Protestants from the more fundamentalist sects—are generally much more socially conservative than nonevangelicals.[11]

Generalizations about how people vote are useful, but we have to be careful about stereotyping people. True, Jewish families tend to be more liberal on both economic and noneconomic issues than either Catholics or Protestants, but there are lots of conservative Jewish families and lots of liberal Catholic and Protestant ones. It is dangerous to assume that because we know a person's religious affiliation or ethnic background we can know his or her political opinions. Moreover, all persons are subject to **cross-pressures**—racial, religious, ethnic, or other group pressures that pull an individual in different directions.

What happens when a young person's parents and friends disagree? One study revealed that when high school students were cross-pressured in this way, they tended to go along with parents rather than friends on party affiliation, with friends rather than parents on issues like the death penalty or gun control, and somewhere in between on their actual votes in presidential elections.[12]

Stability and Change in Public Opinion

Most of us do not change our opinions very often. Even if the world changes rapidly around us, we are slow to change our minds about things that matter to us or to shift our loyalties. In general, people who remain in the same place, in the same occupation, and in the same income group throughout their lives tend to have stable opinions. But people carry attitudes with them, and families who move from cities to suburbs often retain their big-city attitudes long after they have moved.

Adults are not simply the sum of all their early experiences, however. Political analysts are becoming more interested in the ways in which adults modify their views after completing school or college. A major factor may be a harsh experience, such as a war, economic depression, or loss of a job, that shocks people out of their existing attitudes.

Some of our opinions change very little because they are part of our basic values. Thus our views on abortion, the death penalty, and doctor-assisted suicide remain basically stable over time. On issues that are less central to our values, such as our view of how a president is performing his job, opinions can show substantial change over time.

Public Opinion and Public Policy

For much of human history it has been difficult to measure public opinion. "What I want," Abraham Lincoln once said, "is to get done what the people desire to be done, and the question for me is how to find that out exactly." Another president, Woodrow Wilson, once complained to the newspapers that they had no business saying what people thought: "You do not know, and the worst of it, since the responsibility is mine, I do not know, what they are thinking about. I have the most imperfect means of finding out, and yet I have got to act as if I knew."

Politicians in our day do not face the uncertainty about public opinion faced by Lincoln and Wilson. They can and do know what public opinion is on all major policy issues. But public opinion is not always stable and consistent. On many issues, public opinion can change once the public learns more about the issue or perceives there is another side to the question. It is on these issues that politicians can help shape attitudes.

A clear example of how public opinion change can lead to policy change occurred during the Vietnam War: "Public opinion had a substantial impact on the rate of troop withdrawals."[13] In the Persian Gulf War, opposition to the use of U.S. forces was greatly reduced after a few days of success in the air and ground war. When American forces were dispatched to Somalia in Operation Restore Hope in January 1993, 79 percent approved of the use of troops to ensure the delivery of humanitarian aid, food, and medical provisions. But when U.S. soldiers were killed and dragged through the streets of Mogidishu, support fell to only 17 percent in October of the same year.[14]

An important issue regarding polling is the question of leadership. Walter Lippmann's classic book *Public Opinion* raises the concern that political leaders could defer too much to public opinion rather than informing and leading it.[15] Edmund Burke, a political philosopher and member of Parliament writing in the 1770s, distinguished between officials who saw their job as following public opinion (a group he called *delegates*) and officials who believed they had been elected to lead (a group Burke called *trustees*).

ELECTION FORECASTING

The use of polls to predict how an election will turn out has not always been accurate. On the whole, the record of leading forecasters in "day before" polling has been good, but the most sensational slip occurred in the 1948 presidential battle between President Harry Truman and New York Governor Thomas E. Dewey. Most polls indicated that Truman was running far behind, and most pollsters held to that prediction to the very end. Gallup gave the president only 45 percent of the popular vote in its final forecast, and Roper predicted 37 percent. *The Chicago Tribune* even ran its early edition with a headline to that effect. When all votes were tallied, Truman had won the election with 48 percent of the popular vote, and the pollsters were subjected to much ridicule.

So sure was the *Chicago Herald Tribune* that Thomas Dewey would win the 1948 election, they printed the headline before the results were final.

Presidential Winners Forecast by the Pollsters

Year	Actual Vote	Roper Poll	Gallup Poll	Harris Poll
1944	54%	54%	53%	—
1948	49	37	45	—
1952	45	43	46	—
1956	42	40	40	—
1960	49	47	49	—
1964	61	—	61	—
1968	43	—	40	43
1972	38	—	35	35
1976	51	51	46*	46*
1980	41	—	44	41
1984	41	45	41	44
1988	46	—	45	48
1992**	43	—	44	44
1996***	49	—	52	48

*In 1976 both Gallup and Harris said it was a "toss-up" and refused to make a prediction. They also reported that more people than usual had not made up their minds.

**In 1992, CBS/*New York Times*, *The Washington Post*, *USA Today*/CNN, and *The Wall Street Journal*/NBC all predicted Bill Clinton would win with 44 percent of the vote; ABC predicted his vote as 43 percent.

***Roper did not make an estimate in 1996. In 1996, CNN/*USA Today* and ABC/*Washington Post* predicted Clinton would win with 51 percent of the vote; NBC/*Wall Street Journal* predicted his vote as 52 percent; CBS/*New York Times* predicted his vote as 53 percent.

More typically, elected officials seek to follow public opinion. Gaining reelection has been found to be a driving motive for most members of Congress.[16] There is evidence that "legislators show greater attention to public opinion as election day looms," and the closeness of fit between constituent opinion and roll call voting reflects that connection.[17] Candidates use polls to determine where to campaign, how to campaign, and even whether to campaign. In the years and months preceding a national convention, politicians watch the polls to determine who among the hopefuls has political appeal. Have polls become more important than voters in influencing who can mount a viable campaign?

The accuracy of some political polls is suspect. More than 80 percent of newspapers and half of television stations conduct or commission their own polls.[18] These media polls are often not conducted as carefully as the academic polls conducted at major universities, but they play a major role in shaping public opinion.[19]

Surely polls are no substitute for elections. Faced with a ballot, voters must translate opinions into concrete decisions. They must decide what is important and what is not. Democracy is more than the expression of views, more than a simple mirror of opinion. It also involves choosing among leaders, taking sides on certain issues, and selecting the governmental actions that may follow. Democracy is the thoughtful participation of people in the political process. It means using heads as well as counting them. Elections, with all their failings, still establish the link between the many voices of "We the People" and the decisions of their leaders.

Awareness and Interest

For most people, politics is of secondary importance to earning a living, raising a family, and having a good time, and some Americans are more concerned about which team wins the Super Bowl than they are about who wins the school board elections, who gets to be mayor, or even who gets to be president of the United States. Most people find politics complicated and difficult to understand. And they should, for democracy *is* complicated and difficult to understand. But it helps to understand the mechanics and structures of our government: how the government operates, how the Electoral College works, how many chambers there are in Congress, the length of terms for the president and for members of the Senate and House of Representatives, for example.

These aspects of government are typically best known by younger persons, who remember learning them in school. The general adult public, however, fares poorly when quizzed about their elected officials (see Table 11–2). Just over a quarter of Americans are able to recall the name of their member of Congress, and only 60 percent can name even one of their U.S. senators.[20] With so many voters not knowing who represents them in Congress, it is not surprising that "on even hotly debated congressional issues, few people know where their Congress member stands."[21]

Although the public's knowledge of institutional and candidate issues is poor, its knowledge of important public policy issues is worse. In 1982, after years of debate over ratification of the Equal Rights Amendment, nearly one-third of the adults in the United States indicated they had never heard of it. In late August 1993, several weeks before the vote in Congress on the North American Free Trade Agreement (NAFTA), six out of ten Americans reported they were not following the NAFTA story at all.[22]

Fortunately, not all Americans are uninformed or uninterested. Figure 11–1 presents varying levels of interest in politics. Since 1960, about 25 percent of the public have been interested in politics most of the time. They are the **attentive public**, people who know and understand how the government works, vote in

TABLE 11–2

Political Participation and Awareness in the United States

Vote in presidential elections	50%
Vote in congressional elections	36
Know name of U.S. representative	28
Sign a petition	48
Write congressman or state representative	30
Vote in local elections	10–30
Try to persuade vote of others	23
Display campaign button, sticker, or sign	7
Attend dinner, meeting, or rally for candidate	6
Contribute to candidate	5
Contribute to party	4

SOURCE: U.S. Bureau of the Census, *Statistical Abstract of the United States, 1995* (Government Printing Office, 1995), p. 290; 1994 American National Election Study Center for Political Studies, University of Michigan, Ann Arbor; CBS News/*New York Times* Poll, October 29–November 1, 1994, of 1,429 adults nationwide; Institute for Social Inquiry, Roper Center Poll, August 22–29, 1994, of 1,053 adults nationwide.

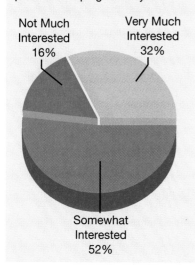

Question: Would you say that you were very much interested, somewhat interested, or not much interested in following the political campaigns this year?

Not Much Interested 16%

Very Much Interested 32%

Somewhat Interested 52%

FIGURE 11–1 **Level of Interest in Politics, 1996**

SOURCE: 1996 American National Election Study, Center for Political Studies, University of Michigan, Ann Arbor.

most elections, read a daily newspaper, and "talk politics" with their families and friends. They tend to be better educated and more committed to democratic values than are other Americans.

At the opposite end of the spectrum are *nonvoters*, people who are rarely interested in politics or public affairs and rarely vote. Since 1960, about 35 percent of Americans have indicated that they have little interest in politics or are only occasionally interested.[23] A subset of this group might be called chronic political know-nothings. These individuals not only avoid political activity but have little interest in government and limited knowledge about it.

Between the attentive public and the nonvoters are the *part-time citizens*, roughly 40 percent of the American public. These individuals participate selectively in elections, voting in presidential elections but usually not in others. Politics and government do not greatly interest them; they pay only minimal attention to the news, and they rarely discuss candidates or elections with others.

Our democracy can exist even with a large number of citizens who are passive and uninformed, as long as there is a substantial number of people who serve as opinion leaders and who are interested and informed about public affairs. But obviously, opinion leaders will have much greater influence than their less active fellow citizens.

PARTICIPATION: TRANSLATING OPINIONS INTO ACTION

Americans can influence their government's actions in several different ways, many of which are protected by the Constitution. They may vote in elections, join interest groups, go to political party meetings, ring doorbells, place calls to friends urging them to vote for issues or candidates, sign petitions, write letters to the editors of newspapers, and make calls to radio talk shows.

Destruction of property and physical violence fall into a category of *unlawful participation*. Our political system is remarkably tolerant of protest that is not destructive or violent; boycotts, picketing, sit-ins, and marches are all legally protected. Rosa Parks and Martin Luther King, Jr., used the peaceful breaking of the law to protest what they saw to be problems with the law. The number of Americans who participate in protests is small, but the impact of their actions in shaping public opinion can be substantial.

A distinguishing characteristic of a democracy is that citizens can influence government decisions by participating in politics. In totalitarian societies, participation is very limited, forcing people who want to influence government to violence or revolution. When the citizens of Belgrade turned out night after night to protest the nullification of their elections, they forced Slobodan Milosevic to recognize the opposition victories. But protests and responses are not always peaceful or successful. The protest of Chinese students in Tiananmen Square failed to stop the onslaught of tanks and the repression that followed. Americans sometimes forget that our democracy was born of revolution, but that maintaining a constitutional democracy is also difficult and demands public participation. The people of Haiti, Zaire, Liberia, Rwanda, and Serbia are experiencing these difficulties firsthand during the 1990s.

Even in an established democracy, people may feel so strongly about an issue that they would rather fight than accept the verdict of an election. Our most classic example is the Civil War. Following the election of 1860 the South took up arms, sensing a popular tide against slavery. War marked the breakdown of democracy. Examples in our own time include antiabortion groups that use violence to press their political agenda and militia groups that arm themselves for battle against government restrictions.

Large numbers of Americans routinely participate in such rituals of democracy as singing the National Anthem or reciting the Pledge of Allegiance. They communicate their views about government and politics to their representatives in Washington and the state capital. They serve as jurors in courtrooms and enlist in the military. They express concern about the involvement of American military forces in foreign hostilities. They complain about taxes and government regulations. And each year millions of Americans visit Washington, D.C., and other historic sights.

For most people, politics is a private activity. Some books on manners still consider it impolite to discuss politics at dinner parties. To say that politics is private does not mean people do not have opinions or will not discuss them when asked by others, including pollsters. But often politics is avoided in discussions with neighbors, work associates, even friends and family, as too divisive or upsetting. Typically, less than one person in five attempts to influence how another person votes in an election. An even smaller number actually work for a candidate or party. Only one in twenty people make a contribution to a candidate, and only one in four designate one dollar of their taxes to the fund that pays for presidential general elections.

Few individuals attempt to influence others by writing letters to elected officials or to editors of newspapers for publication. Even smaller numbers participate in protest groups or activities. Despite the small number of persons who engage in these activities, it would be a mistake to assume that small numbers of individuals cannot make a difference to politics and government. Often an individual or small group can generate media interest in an issue and expand the impact. Peaceful protests for civil rights, environmental issues, and abortion have generated public attention and may perhaps even change public opinion.

Voting

Voting is the type of political activity most often engaged in by Americans. The United States is a constitutional democracy with many decades of free and open elections and a tradition of the peaceful transfer of power between competing groups and parties.

Originally the Constitution left the individual states free to determine the crucial question of who could vote, and the qualifications for voting differed considerably from state to state. All states except New Jersey barred women from voting, many did not permit African Americans to vote, and property ownership was sometimes a requirement. By the time of the Civil War, the franchise had been extended to all white male citizens in every state. Since that time, eligibility standards for voting have been expanded by legislation and constitutional amendments.

1870 Fifteenth Amendment forbade states from denying the right to vote because of "race, color, or previous condition of servitude."

1920 Nineteenth Amendment gave women the right to vote.

1924 Congress granted Native Americans citizenship and voting rights.

1964 Twenty-fourth Amendment prohibited the use of poll taxes.

1965 Voting Rights Act removed restrictions that kept blacks from voting.

1971 Twenty-sixth Amendment extended the vote to citizens age 18 and older.

The civil rights movement in the 1960s, which made voting rights a central issue, secured adoption of the Twenty-fourth Amendment and passage of the 1965 Voting Rights Act. The Voting Rights Act banned literacy tests, eased registration requirements, and provided for the replacement of local election officials with federal registrars in areas where the denial of the right to vote had been most blatant. Its passage resulted in a dramatic expansion of African American registration and voting. Once African Americans were permitted to register to vote, "the focus of voting

The State of the Union or the O.J. Simpson Verdict: What Is a News Director to Do?

Early in each new session of Congress, the president delivers his State of the Union Address. Once submitted in writing, it is now a television event complete with both houses of Congress, the cabinet, the Supreme Court, and guests hand-picked by the president to sit in the gallery near the First Lady who, by their presence, reinforce some of the central messages of the speech. The address is broadcast live on all major networks.

Much to everyone's surprise, towards the end of President Cinton's 1997 State of the Union speech, the jury in the O.J. Simpson civil trial decided to announce its verdict. Although the civil trial generated less publicity than the criminal trial, in part because it was not televised, there was still great public interest in how a different jury would decide what humorist Art Buchwald called "The Trial of the Century, Part II." What was a news editor to do—continue televising the speech or shift to Los Angeles for the verdict?

Some news directors resolved the issue by going to a split screen with the president on the one side and the courtroom on the other; others ran script across the screen while the president was speaking, telling viewers of the verdict. Perhaps because of the O.J. verdict, the 1997 State of the Union Address received the highest ratings ever.

Viewers apparently paid closer attention to the O.J. verdict than to the president's speech. One poll found that 75 percent of people could correctly identify the amount of compensatory damages ($9 million) that the jury ordered Simpson to pay, as opposed to only 52 percent who knew that Clinton had made education the top priority for his second term.[**]

*Art Buchwald, "We Interrupt This Nation to Bring You . . . OJ," *Newsday*, February 12, 1997, p. A42.

**"OJ Fate Tops State of the Union." Poll conducted by the Pew Research Center for the People and the Press, Press Release, February 28, 1997, p. 4.

In an effort to make voter registration easier, states have made registration forms available at motor vehicle stations, schools, public buildings, and even at highway toll booths.

discrimination shifted . . . to preventing them from winning elections."[24] In southern legislative districts where African Americans are in the majority, however, there has been a "dramatic increase in the proportion of African American legislators elected."[25]

Registration

One peculiarly American legal requirement—**voter registration**—discourages voting. Most other democracies have automatic voter registration. Average turnout in the United States is more than 30 percentage points lower than in countries like Australia, Austria, Belgium, Denmark, Germany, and Italy; only Switzerland has lower average turnout[26] (see Table 11–3). This was not always the case. In fact, in the 1800s, turnout in the United States was much like that of Europe today. Turnout began to drop significantly around the turn of the century, in part as a result of election reform (see Figure 11–2).

American elections in the 1800s were quite different from those of today. Ballots were prepared by the parties, often using different colors of paper that allowed them to monitor how people had voted. In some areas charges of multiple voting gener-

TABLE 11–3

Registration and Voting in the World's Democracies, 1980s and 1990s

	Turnout as Percent of Eligible Vote	Compulsion Penalties*	Automatic Registration**
Australia	94%	Yes	No
Austria	91	No	Yes
Belgium	93	Yes	Yes
Canada	76	No	Yes
Denmark	86	No	Yes
Finland	78	No	Yes
France	66	No	No
Germany	84	No	Yes
Greece	85	Yes	Yes
Ireland	69	No	Yes
Israel	80	No	Yes
Italy	91	Yes	Yes
Japan	71	No	Yes
Netherlands	86	No	Yes
New Zealand	87	No	No
Norway	84	No	Yes
Spain	71	No	Yes
Sweden	86	No	Yes
Switzerland	46	No	Yes
United Kingdom	75	No	Yes
United States	53	No	No

Source: Thomas T. Mackie and Richard Rose, *The International Almanac of Electoral History*, 3d ed. (Congressional Quarterly Press, 1991); G. Bingham Powell, Jr., "American Voter Turnout in Comparative Perspective," *American Political Science Review* 80 (March 1986), p. 38. Iceland, Luxembourg, Malta, and Portugal were not included in the Powell study and were therefore omitted from this table.

*Compulsion penalties are fines or other possible state actions against nonvoters.

**Automatic registration utilizes other forms of citizen identification like a driver's license.

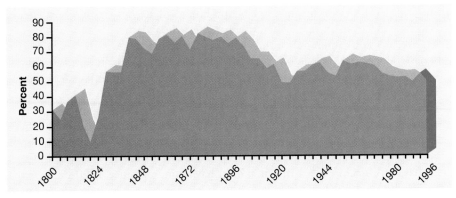

FIGURE 11–2 Voter Turnout in Presidential Elections, 1800–1996

SOURCE: For 1800 to 1992, Walter Dean Burnham, "The Turnout Problem," in *Elections American Style*, ed. A. James Reichley (Brookings Institution, 1987), pp. 113–14; for 1960 to 1992, U.S. Bureau of the Census, *Statistical Abstract of the United States, 1993* (Government Printing Office, 1993), p. 284; for 1996, Committee for the Study of the American Electorate.

ated a reform movement that substituted the **Australian ballot**, a secret ballot printed by the state, for the party ballots and initiated voter registration to reduce multiple voting and limit voting to those who had previously established their eligibility.

Registration laws vary by state, but in every state except North Dakota registration is required in order to vote. Three states permit election-day voter registration. The most important provision regarding voter registration may be the closing date. A few years ago it was not uncommon for closing dates to be six months before the election; now, by federal law, no state can stop registration more than 30 days before an election.[27] Voter registration places a responsibility on voters to take an extra step—usually filling out a form at the county courthouse, when renewing a driver's license, or with a roving registrar—some days or weeks before the election. Other important provisions include places and hours of registration, and the closing date for registration.[28]

Turnout

Americans hold more elections for more offices than do citizens of any other democracy. In most states citizens can vote in a general election, one or more primary elections, and special elections on local matters. For example, in a two-year period, voters in Pasadena, California, had the option of voting in as many as five elections.

In part because there are so many elections, American voters tend to pick and choose which elections to vote in. Americans elect officeholders in general elections, determine party nominees in primary elections, and replace senators who have died or left office in special elections. Elections held in years when the president is on the ballot are called *presidential elections*, elections held midway between presidential elections are called *midterm elections*, and elections held in odd-numbered calendar years are called *off-year elections*. Midterm elections (like the one in 1994) elect about one-third of the U.S. Senate, all members of the House of Representatives, and most governors and other statewide officeholders as well as large numbers of state legislators. Many local elections are held in the spring of odd-numbered years to elect city councils and mayors.

Turnout—the proportion of the voting-age public that votes—is highest in presidential general elections (see Figure 11–3). Turnout is higher in general elections than in primary elections and higher in primary elections than in special elections. Turnout is higher in presidential general elections than in midterm general elections and higher in presidential primary elections than in midterm primary elections.[29] Turnout is higher in elections in which candidates for federal office are

Motor-Voter

After many years of debates, voter registration was eased a bit when, on May 20, 1993, President Clinton signed the National Voter Registration Act, the "Motor-Voter" bill, so called because it allows people to register to vote while applying for or renewing a driver's license. It also requires states to designate offices that provide welfare and disabled assistance to facilitate voter registration. States have the option to include public schools, libraries, and city and county clerks' offices as registration sites. The law also requires states to allow registration by mail using a standardized form.

Motor-Voter requires a questionnaire be mailed to registered voters every four years in order to purge for death and change of residence, but forbids purging for any other reasons, such as nonvoting.

Proponents of the law say it will reach the 49 million Americans of voting age with driver's licenses or identification cards who have not registered to vote. Opponents claim the new law is another federal mandate that does not provide money to pay for the costs involved. They also assert it will increase election fraud because of the difficulty in removing names from voting rolls.

It appears that the law has been successful, at least in terms of numbers of new voters registered. One source estimates that Motor-Voter meant that "for the 1996 election there were 12 million new registered voters and an estimated 3 million more by the start of 1997,"* Early data on the impact of Motor-Voter suggest that neither Democrats nor Republicans are the primary beneficiaries because most who have registered claim to be Independent.

*Human SERVE, "The Impact of the National Voter Registration Act (NVRA), January 1995–June 1996: The First Eighteen Months" (October 1996). See also: http://www.esential.org/human_serve.html.

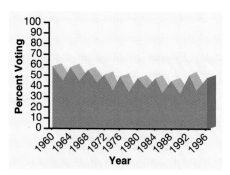

FIGURE 11-3 Voter Turnout in Presidential and Midterm Elections, 1990–1996

SOURCE: U.S. Bureau of the Census, *Statistical Abstract of the United States, 1995* (Government Printing Office, 1995), p. 284. For 1996, Committee for the Study of the American Electorate.

on the ballot (U.S. senator, member of the House of Representatives, president) than in state elections in years when there are no federal contests. Some states elect their governor and other state officials in odd-numbered years to separate state from national politics. The result is generally lower turnout. Finally, local or municipal elections have lower turnout than state elections, and municipal primaries have even lower rates of participation. For example, in Pasadena, the 1992 general election saw a 45 percent turnout, while the 1996 general election fell to 35 percent, and fewer than one in ten residents of Pasadena of voting age voted in several recent school board elections (see Table 11–4).

In 1960, turnout peaked at almost 63 percent of persons over 21 years of age, but it has since declined.[30] Turnout should have gone up since 1960 because the Voting Rights Act of 1965 added large numbers of African Americans to the pool of registered voters. Women, another historically underrepresented group, have also increased their voting levels.[31] Finally, our electorate has grown richer and more educated since the 1960s, and since wealth and education are related to voting, we should have seen an increase instead of a decrease in voting. However, 85 million Americans failed to vote in recent presidential elections; the nonvoting figures are even higher for congressional, state, county, and local elections.[32] Voting did increase in 1992, rising by 5 percent over 1988—a result of the high level of interest in that particular election—but it fell again to 49 percent in 1996, just under the percentage that voted in 1988 (50 percent) and well below the 55 percent who voted in 1992. Minnesota led the country with more than two-thirds voting, while turnout was lowest in Georgia and South Carolina (41 percent).

TABLE 11–4
Voter Participation in Pasadena, California, 1990–1996

	Number	Percent
1990 statewide primary election	24,692	24%
1990 statewide general election	34,909*	34
1991 March, school board primary election	8,112**	8
1991 April, school board general election	6,397**	6
1992 statewide primary election	23,193	22
1992 statewide general election	47,346	45
1993 March, school board primary election	9,064**	9
1993 April, school board general election	6,588*	6
1993 statewide special election	18,303	17
1994 statewide primary election	17,236	16
1994 statewide general election	31,225	30
1995 March, school board primary election	10,735**	10
1995 April, school board general election	8,692**	8
1996 statewide primary election	20,842	19
1996 statewide general election	36,943	35
1997 March, city election	13,486	13

SOURCE: Los Angeles County Registrar, Election Information Office; Pasadena City Clerk Department; census data from Department of Finance, California State Data Center.

Note: All percentages were calculated using an estimated voting-age population for each year; 1996 voting age population: 106,911.

*Absentee ballots not counted at city level; county-wide average of 14 percent added for estimate of in-person and absentee voting.

**Pasadena turnout on the basis of 62 percent of registered voters in school district residing in Pasadena.

Why Is Turnout So Low?

Although Americans can hardly avoid reading or hearing about political campaigns, roughly 85 million Americans fail to vote in presidential elections. Who are they? Why do they not vote? Is the fact that so many Americans choose not to vote a cause for alarm? If so, what can we do about it?

The simplest explanation for low turnout is that people are lazy. But the problem is not that simple. Of course, some people are apathetic, but the vast majority of Americans are not. Paradoxically, we compare favorably with other nations in political interest and awareness,[33] but for a variety of institutional and political reasons, we fail to convert these qualities into votes (see Table 11–5).

The cost of voting is higher in the United States than in other industrial democracies, while the perceived benefits are lower.[34] By "cost" we mean the expenditure of time and effort required to vote. In our system, individuals are required to register to vote, and they must make sense of a range of political alternatives that do not necessarily meet their interests. Voter registration, already examined, appears to be the major block to voting.[35]

Another factor in the decline of voter turnout since the 1960s is the Twenty-sixth Amendment, which lowered the voting age to 18. It increased the number of eligible voters, but that group is least likely to vote. With ratification of the amendment in 1971, turnout fell from 61 percent in 1968 to 55 percent in 1972.[36] The effect of adding this low turnout group to the electorate has been to lower the overall turnout rate. Efforts to activate younger voters through programs like "Rock the Vote" fostered increases in voter registration in 1996, but turnout in 1996 declined to 49 percent.

In other large industrialized democracies, the political parties shoulder much of the burden of persuading people to vote, but American parties are too weak to take on this task. In particular, the Democratic party, which has an enormous stake in a heavy voter turnout from lower-income Americans, seldom achieves the voting participation it wants.

Another factor in low turnout is the absence of real competition in many election contests. Many cities and regions have a "one-and-a-half party" system—as in Chicago, Boston, Washington, Rhode Island, Utah, Hawaii, and Kansas. In such cities or states one party dominates while the other party competes only occasionally.

Other critics say the reason people do not vote is that our political leaders do not appeal to the voters. Candidates, it is argued, do not offer "real" choices. They are not exciting, or they avoid taking positions on important issues. Yet in several recent elections there have been important differences between the candidates, including stands on such salient issues as abortion, welfare, jobs, and how to achieve a balanced budget.

Who Votes?

The extent of voting varies widely among different groups. The level of education especially helps predict whether people will vote; as education increases, so does the propensity to vote. "Education increases one's capacity for understanding complex and intangible subjects such as politics," according to one study, "as well as encouraging the ethic of civil responsibility. Moreover, schools provide experience dealing with a variety of bureaucratic problems, such as coping with requirements, filling out forms, and meeting deadlines."[37] Race and ethnic background are linked with different levels of voting in large part because they correlate with education. Blacks in general turn out at lower rates than whites. However, women, another historically underrepresented group, increased their voting levels to the point where, in 1988, 1992, and again in 1996, turnout among women actually exceeded that of men.[38]

We the People

Voter Turnout by Demographic Factors

	1992	1994
Sex		
Men	60.2%	44.4%
Women	62.3	44.9
Age		
18–20	38.5	16.5
21–24	45.7	22.3
25–34	53.2	32.2
35–44	63.6	46.0
45–64	70.0	56.0
65+	70.1	60.7
Education		
8 years or less	35.1	23.2
Some high school	41.2	27.0
High school graduate	57.5	40.5
Some college	68.7	49.1
College graduate	81.0	63.1
Race		
White	63.6	46.9
Black	54.0	37.0
Hispanic	28.9	19.1

SOURCE: U.S. Bureau of the Census, *Statistical Abstract of the United States, 1995* (Government Printing Office, 1995), p. 289.

TABLE 11–5
Why People Don't Vote

Satisfied with government as it is	2%
Fed up with government and choices offered	25
Think their vote doesn't count	35
Don't know enough about candidates or issues to vote	35
Don't know/refused to answer	3

SOURCE: Provided by Public Opinion Online, Roper Center at University of Connecticut.

We the People

Who Voted in 1996?

Race
White	79%
Black	13
Hispanic	5

Sex
Men	49%
Women	51

Education
Some high school	5%
High school graduate	22
Some college	32
College graduate	22
Postgraduate	19

Voted in 1992 for
Clinton	45%
Bush	37
Perot	12

This country is
Going in the right direction	37%
Off on the wrong track	59

SOURCE: Marjorie Connelly, "Portrait of the Electorate," *The New York Times*, November 10, 1996, p. B4.

Data collected by Voter News Service (VNS) based on a national sample of 16,627 voters at 300 polling places. Data for the "right direction/wrong track" question was obtained directly from VNS, and the sample for that question was 4,185.

From Coast to Coast

Turnout in Presidential Elections by State, 1980–1996

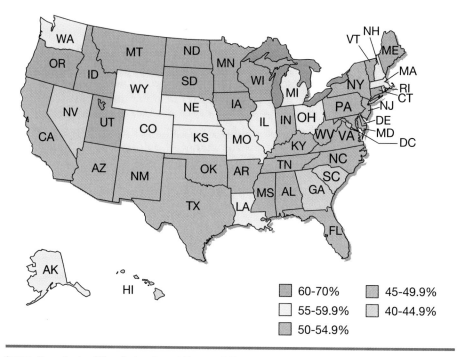

Legend: 60-70% | 45-49.9% | 55-59.9% | 40-44.9% | 50-54.9%

SOURCE: Royce Crocker, "Voter Registration and Turnout: 1948–1990," *Congressional Research Service*, August 11, 1992, pp. 20–31; Royce Crocker, "Voter Turnout in the Presidential Election of 1992: The States," *Congressional Research Service*, January 26, 1993.

Income and age are also important factors. Those with higher family incomes are more likely to vote than those with lower incomes. Income, of course, corresponds to occupation, and those with higher-status careers are more likely to vote than those with lower-status jobs. Poor people are less likely to feel politically involved and confident, and their social norms tend to de-emphasize politics.[39] Older people, unless they are very old and perhaps infirm, are more likely to vote than younger people. Persons 18 to 24 years of age have a poor voting record; so do persons over 70. Women's recent higher turnout is generally attributed to increasing levels of education and employment; black women in particular are influenced by their party identification and by attitudes on gender issues.[40]

How Serious Is Nonvoting?

Some political scientists argue that nonvoting is not a critical problem. "Nonvoting is not a social disease," contends Austin Ranney, a noted student of politics. He points out that legal and extralegal denial of the vote to African Americans, women, Hispanics, persons over 18, and other groups has now been outlawed, so nonvoting is voluntary. He quotes the late Senator Sam Ervin: "I don't believe in making it easy for apathetic, lazy people to vote."[41]

Those who say that nonvoting is a critical problem cite the "class bias" of those who do vote. The social makeup and attitudes of nonvoters are significantly different from those of voters and hence greatly distort the representative system. "The very poor . . . have about two-thirds the representation among voters than their numbers would suggest." Thus the people who need help the most from the government lack their fair share of electoral power to obtain it. And, it is argued, this situation is growing worse.[42]

Those who see a class bias defend their observations. Low voting, they say, reflects "the underdevelopment of political attitudes resulting from the historic exclusion of low-income groups from active electoral participation." In short, part of the problem of low-income, less-educated people is their failure to be conscious of their real interests. Dynamic leadership or strong party organization, or both, would not only attract the poor to the polls but make clear their "class grievances and aspirations."[43]

Others reject this class-bias argument. They admit nonvoters are demographically different, yet they cite polls showing that nonvoters' attitudes are not much different from voters' attitudes. One study, comparing the party identification of voters with that of all Americans, found the proportion of Democrats was nearly identical (51.4 percent of all citizens and 51.3 percent of voters), while Republicans as voters were slightly overrepresented (36 percent of citizens and 39.7 percent of voters). All other political differences are considered to be much smaller than this 3.7 percent gap. Further, voters are not "disproportionately hostile" to social welfare policies.[44]

Another study asserts that the typical nonvoter is no longer just a poor high school dropout but is dispersed among other socioeconomic categories. In 1960, 72 percent of nonvoters had less than a high school education, and 60 percent were poor. In 1992, the figures dropped; only half of those who did not vote had not attended school beyond the eighth grade, and of those with incomes in the bottom third, 55 percent did not vote.[45]

What effect might increased voter turnout have in national elections? It might make a difference, since there are partisan differences between different demographic groups, and candidates would have to adjust to the demands of an expanded electorate. A noted political scientist, while acknowledging that no political system could achieve 100 percent participation, pointed out that the entire balance of power in the political system could be overturned if the large nonvoter population decided to vote.[46] However, others argue that the difference may not be as pronounced. Nonvoters are not more in favor of government ownership or control of industry, and they are not more egalitarian. Nonvoters are, however, more inclined to favor additional spending on welfare programs.[47]

Another way to think of low voter turnout is to see it as a sign of approval with things as they are, whereas high voter turnout would signify disapproval and widespread desire for change. Even on the subject of how to interpret low turnout there is disagreement.

VOTING CHOICES

Why do people vote as they do? Political scientists have identified three main elements of the voting choice: party identification, candidate appeal, and issues. These elements often overlap.

Voting on the Basis of Party

Party identification is the subjective sense of identification or affiliation that a person has with a political party, a long-standing preference for one party over the other (see Chapter 10). Party identification has a lot to do with one's evaluation of the candidates and often predicts a person's stand on issues. It is part of our national mythology that Americans vote for the person and not the party because, as we will see, the person we vote for is most often from our party. Partisanship is typically acquired in childhood or adolescence as a result of the socialization process in the family, then reinforced by peer groups in adolescence. In the absence of reasons to vote otherwise, people depend on party identification to simplify their voting choices. Party identification is not party registration; it is not party

Party identification is sometimes obvious, as in the case of this delegate to the Republican National Convention.

Young people generally vote less than older voters do. But these young volunteers traveled across the country in 1996 registering voters on the MTV "Choose or Loose" bus tour.

membership in the sense of being a dues-paying, card-carrying member, as in some European parties. Rather, it is a psychological sense of attachment to one party or another. See Chapter 10 for a discussion of how we measure party identification and the way people answer these questions.

There has been a dramatic increase in the number of Independents beginning in the mid-1970s. Nominally there are more Independents in the electorate today than Republicans. But two-thirds of all Independents are, in fact, partisans in their voting behavior. Independent Democrats are predictably Democratic in their voting behavior, and Independent Republicans vote heavily Republican. Independent-leaners are thus very different from each other and from the Pure Independents. Pure Independents have the lowest rate of turnout but generally do side with the eventual winner in presidential elections. These data on Independents only reinforce the importance of partisanship as an explanation of voting choice, because when we consider Independent Democrats and Independent Republicans as Democrats and Republicans respectively, there were only 8 percent Pure Independents or others without a party in 1996, and the average for the period 1952–96 was only 11 percent.[48]

Although party identification has fluctuated somewhat in the past 40 years, it remains more stable than attitudes about issues or political ideology. Fluctuations in party identification appear to come in response to economic conditions and political performance, especially of the president.[49] The more information voters have about their choices, the more likely they are to defect from their party and vote for a candidate from the other party.

Voting on the Basis of Candidates

While long-term party identification is important, it clearly is not the only factor in voting choices; otherwise the Democrats would have won every presidential election since the last realignment in 1932. In fact, since 1952, Republicans have been more successful in winning the White House than Democrats. The answer to this puzzle is largely found in a second major explanation of voting choice—candidate appeal.

The elections of the 1980s mark a critical threshold in the emergence of the candidate-centered era in American electoral politics. The change in focus from parties to candidates is an important historical trend, which has been gradually taking place over the last several decades.[50] Clinton's election victories in 1992 and 1996 reinforce the importance of candidates. He was especially popular among younger voters, women, and African Americans, but he also persuaded many "Reagan Democrats"—those who had defected to the Republicans in the 1980s—to return to their party. Evidence that his 1996 victory was largely candidate-centered is the Democrats' inability to regain a majority in the House or Senate.

The focus on candidates and their strengths or weaknesses is not new, but the greater weight given to these candidate evaluations is an important development in American politics.[51] Candidate appeal or the lack of it—in terms of leadership, experience, good judgment, integrity, competence, strength, and energy—is often more important than party or issues. Dwight Eisenhower had great candidate appeal. He was a legendary five-star hero of the Allied effort in World War II. Yet not all generals are successful in politics. Rather, it was Ike's unmilitary manner, his moderation, his personal charm, and his lack of a strong party position that made him appealing across the ideological spectrum. Ronald Reagan generated positive candidate appeal, in part by asserting mainstream values the public found lacking in Jimmy Carter—leadership and strength. Reagan also attempted to broaden his appeal in his acceptance speech in 1980 by conspicuously quoting Franklin D. Roosevelt, the leader of the modern Democratic party.

Candidate appeal often involves an assessment of a candidate's character. Is the candidate honest? Is the candidate consistent? Is the candidate dedicated to "family values"? Does the candidate have religious or spiritual commitments? The American press in recent elections has sometimes played the role of "character cop," often asking, as candidates Gary Hart and Bill Clinton learned, questions about private lives and lifestyles. The press asks these questions because voters are interested in a presidential candidate's background—perhaps even more interested in a candidate's character than in his position on hard-to-understand health care or regulatory policy issues.

Reagan's effort to generate positive candidate appeal was successful. Carter had hoped that Reagan would behave more like Barry Goldwater, who in his acceptance speech in 1964 had said, "Extremism in the defense of liberty is no vice. . . . Moderation in the pursuit of justice is no virtue."[52] Lyndon Johnson, Goldwater's opponent, benefited from public perception that Goldwater and those who nominated him were out of the mainstream of American politics. This perception was confirmed when Goldwater's supporters at the convention refused for several minutes to let Governor Nelson Rockefeller speak.

George McGovern, like Barry Goldwater in 1964, was a candidate with negative appeal. Many of his supporters, by their dress and manner, appeared out of the mainstream of American politics. McGovern raised doubts about his judgment and leadership by how he handled his choice of a vice-president. McGovern named Missouri Senator Tom Eagleton as his running mate, only to discover that Eagleton had been hospitalized previously for treatment of emotional exhaustion and depression. McGovern initially stood behind Eagleton, but as press coverage and criticism of McGovern's lack of investigation into Eagleton's past grew, McGovern dropped Eagleton and named a new running mate. In the end, "only about one-third of the public thought McGovern could be trusted as president."[53]

Increasingly, campaigns today focus on the negative elements of candidates. Opponents and the media are quick to point out the limitations or problems of any given candidate. Many saw the 1988 election as a very negative presidential campaign, in which the Bush-Quayle ticket called attention to the alleged errors of Governor Michael Dukakis—furloughing criminals like Willie Horton and not stopping pollution in Boston harbor. The Dukakis campaign did not reciprocate, thereby permitting George Bush both to define Dukakis in negative terms and to define himself positively.

The 1992 election was somewhat more positive. Bush did his best to attack Bill Clinton's unwillingness to serve in the Vietnam War, and Ross Perot and Clinton attacked Bush's economic record. Both Bush and Clinton, however, were gentle toward Perot, as they both hoped to get his endorsement or his supporters' votes.

The 1996 primary campaigns in the Republican party were often negative in tone, with candidates claiming that Bob Dole had been in Washington too long and was too old, that Pat Buchanan had never held public office and was an extremist, or that Steve Forbes lacked experience and was attempting to buy the election.

In the 1996 presidential campaign, Bob Dole and Bill Clinton displayed very different styles. Clinton's skill in thinking on his feet, establishing rapport with his audience, and articulating his position were important parts of his candidate appeal. Dole emphasized his war record and his having overcome serious injuries as evidence of his strength of character. For most of the general election campaign, Dole was unwilling to attack Clinton's character: his rumored extramarital affairs, disputed honesty, the ethical problems associated with the Whitewater scandal, and Federal Bureau of Investigation (FBI) records of Republicans requested by his White House staff.

What did Americans make of the character issue in 1996? On dimensions of candidate character like "has high personal and moral standards" and "honest and trustworthy," people found Dole more appealing. On other elements of candidate character like "has new ideas" or "understands the problems of people like me," pollsters found that voters preferred Clinton to Dole. Polls taken soon after Clinton's reelection show that more than half the voters did not see him as honest and forthcoming regarding Whitewater.[54] But to most voters in 1996, issues like the economy and jobs mattered more than a candidate's character.

Voting on the Basis of Issues

Analysts of voting behavior heatedly debate the role of issues in voters' choices. Most scholars agree that issues, while important, are not as central to the decision process as partisanship and candidate appeal.[55] Part of the reason is that candidates often intentionally obscure their positions on issues, an understandable strategy.[56] Richard Nixon said he had a plan to end the Vietnam War in 1968, clearly the most important issue in that year, but he would not reveal the specifics of that plan. By not detailing his plan, he stood to gain votes from those who wanted a more aggressive war effort as well as those who wanted a cease-fire.

Voting on the basis of issues presumes a level of interest in issues that only a few voters have. For issue voting to occur, the issue must be important to voters, opposing candidates must take opposing stands on the issues, and voters must know these positions and vote accordingly. Rarely do candidates focus on only one issue. Voters often will agree with one candidate on one issue and with the opposing candidate on another. In such an instance, issues will likely not be the determining factor. But lack of interest by voters in issues does not mean candidates can take any issue position they wish.[57]

Voting a certain way because of candidate positions on specific policy questions, such as how to lower health care costs or whether to lower the capital gains tax, is an unrealistic expectation. More likely than *prospective issue voting* (voting based on what a candidate pledges to do about an issue if elected) is *retrospective issue voting* (holding incumbents, usually the president's party, responsible for performance on issues such as the economy or foreign policy).[58] In times of peace and prosperity, voters will reward the incumbent; if the nation falls short on either, voters will elect the opposition.

Scholars have found that voter approval or disapproval of the performance of an outgoing president like Ronald Reagan in 1988 can have an impact on the vote for a presidentially endorsed successor. For example, 92 percent of those who strongly approved of Reagan's handling of the economy voted for George Bush in 1988.[59] But by 1992, Bush's handling of the economy came to be the most important issue in his defeat by Bill Clinton. More than two-thirds of Americans responding to exit polls described the economy in negative terms.

Bush attempted to divert attention away from the economy to issues of character, experience, and trust, but voters were more concerned about change than about these generalized qualities. Nearly half of Americans thought Clinton was lying about his draft record, but they did not consequently vote for Bush; in fact more than half of all veterans voted for Clinton. Bush's vice-presidential running mate, Dan Quayle, sought to make "family values" an issue, but only one in six voters thought the issue important in deciding their vote. In fact, Republican attacks on nontraditional families may have alienated more voters than they attracted. Abortion, another issue many thought would be important to the election outcome, was cited by only 12 percent of voters as important in their voting decisions in 1992.[60]

The state of the economy is often the central issue in midterm elections as well as presidential ones. Several studies have found a positive relationship between the state of the economy and "out" party gains (and "in" party losses) in congressional seats.[61] Political scientists have also been able to locate the sources of this effect in individual voter's decision making. Voters tend to vote against candidates of the "in" party, including incumbents, if the voters perceive a decline or standstill in their personal financial situations.[62] Voters see responsibility for the economy resting more with the president and Congress than with governors or local officials.[63] Socioeconomic status is also important. Less-educated and low-income voters tend to judge a candidate on the basis of their personal financial condition. Upper-status voters, who personally tend to suffer less when economic conditions decline, are more likely to watch the overall performance of the economy and to judge candidates on that basis.[64]

Despite generally good economic news and success in lowering the federal budget deficit, Democrats suffered a substantial defeat in 1994. Why? Part of the explanation lies in Bill Clinton's low approval ratings. In spite of his efforts to improve his popularity by trips to the Middle East shortly before the election, the public continued to have doubts about his leadership. Clinton, who had won election two years earlier on the theme of change, found that he and Democrats in Congress were targets of the same voter frustrations they had directed at George Bush. Republicans in Congress had used the filibuster and other tactics to defeat much of the Clinton and Democratic legislative agenda and then succeeded in arguing that Congress was in need of wholesale change. Republicans captured the "change" theme in 1994 by presenting their Contract with America, which included a commitment to a Balanced Budget Amendment, term limits for members of Congress, and other reforms. This strategy kept Democrats off balance and enabled Republicans to take advantage of voter anger.

The Clinton campaign won the battle of issues in 1996. Clinton made the economy and job creation a centerpiece of his reelection bid, and voters rewarded him with a second term in office. Exit polls indicated that voters, by a margin of three to two, saw the condition of the nation's economy as excellent or good, compared to those who saw it as poor or not so good. The Dole campaign countered that the economy was not growing fast enough and tried to revive one of the themes of the Republican presidential primaries that there was uncertainty about the stability of employment and the economy. Dole, Clinton, and Perot all stressed deficit reduction. Voters, however, by a margin greater than two to one, rejected Dole's supply-side argument that he could lower taxes by 15 percent and still reduce the federal budget deficit.

Thinking It Through

This table shows which issues mattered most to voters in the 1996 presidential election.

Balancing the budget/ budget deficit	6%
Crime	13
The economy	5
Unemployment	6
Welfare	3
Ethics/morality	10
Homelessness	2
Health care	4
Medicare/Social Security	3
Drugs	9
Clinton administration	3
Race relations	2
Education	6
Taxes	1
Poverty	2
Political corruption	2
Foreign policy	2
Other	11
Don't Know/No Answer	4

SOURCE: Roper Center at University of Connecticut, Public Opinion Online, CBS/*New York Times* Poll, January 19, 1997.

Foreign and defense policy were rarely mentioned by voters as important problems. Although Clinton and Dole disagreed occasionally over how much money to spend on defense or when to commit U.S. forces as peacekeepers, the issue did not matter to many voters. Both Bob Dole and Ross Perot attempted to make Bill Clinton's character an issue in the general election campaign. His first term had been plagued with controversy surrounding the dismissal of the White House travel staff, whether confidential FBI reports had been improperly obtained, whether the president or first lady had broken any laws in their failed Whitewater business venture, and whether the campaign contributions on behalf of foreign business interests had been proper. Both of Clinton's opponents raised the issue of multiple investigations against the president should he be reelected, but most voters saw issues affecting their lives—like the economy, jobs, and medical leave—as more important.

POLITICS ONLINE

Cyber Voting

In January 1996, voters in Oregon cast their ballots for U.S. Senator in the first federal election conducted through the mail. Proponents of the mail-in system argued that it would increase turnout, foster more deliberative voting, and be less expensive. Critics warned that voters might be subject to manipulation without the scrutiny of election judges, and that such a system might encourage voter fraud.

Many of the same arguments would apply to voting by the Internet. As more and more citizens gain access to the new technology and become comfortable using it, the same tool could be used for voting and various other political purposes. Some communities, such as Columbus, Ohio, have already experimented with encouraging citizens to watch city council meetings on television and then telephone in their vote.

The equivalent of electronic town meetings is already taking place on the Internet as people participate in political chat groups. You might observe one of these political discussions to get an idea of the range of public opinion and breadth of policy concerns:

> http://www.4-lane.com/politicalchat

You can also access current public opinion information gathered by respected polling organizations at:

> http://www.gallup.com   or   http://www.people-press.org

By accessing these sites, you can often participate in polls as well.

SUMMARY

1. Public opinion is a complex combination of views and attitudes individuals acquire through various influences from childhood on. Public opinion takes on qualities of stability, fluidity, intensity, latency, consensus, or polarization—each of which is affected by people's feelings about the salience of issues.

2. Political socialization, the process by which we develop our political attitudes, values, and beliefs, is influenced from early childhood by family, schools, the mass media, and groups to which one belongs.

3. The American public has a generally low level of interest in politics, and most people do not follow politics and government closely. The vast majority of Americans do not engage in such forms of participation as working in campaigns, writing letters to newspaper editors or elected officials, or even attempting to influence how another person will vote.

4. Better educated, older, and party- and group-involved people tend to vote more; the young tend to vote the least. Voter turnout tends to be higher in national than in state and local elections, and higher in presidential than in midterm elections.

5. Party identification remains an important element in the voting choice of most Americans. It represents a long-term attachment and is a "lens" through which voters view candidates and issues as they make their voting choices. Candidate character and record are another key factor in voter choice. Voters decide their vote less frequently on the basis of issues.

FURTHER READING

JOSEPH A. AISTRIP, *The Southern Strategy Revisited: Republican Top-Down Advancement in the South* (University of Kentucky Press, 1996).

HERBERT ASHER, *Polling and the Public: What Every Citizen Should Know*, 3d ed. (Congressional Quarterly Press, 1995).

EARL BLACK AND MERLE BLACK, *The Vital South: How Presidents Are Elected* (Harvard University Press, 1992).

M. MARGARET CONWAY, *Political Participation in the United States*, 2d ed. (Congressional Quarterly Press, 1991).

ROBERT S. ERIKSON AND KENT L. TEDIN, *American Public Opinion: Its Origins, Content and Impact*, 5th ed. (Allyn and Bacon, 1995).

WILLIAM H. FLANIGAN AND NANCY H. ZINGALE, *Political Behavior of the American Electorate*, 8th ed. (Congressional Quarterly Press, 1994).

JOHN G. GEER, *From Tea Leaves to Opinion Polls: A Theory of Democratic Leadership* (Columbia University Press, 1996).

ROBERT HUCKFELDT AND JOHN SPRAGUE, *Citizens, Politics, and Social Communication: Information and Influence in an Election Campaign* (Cambridge University Press, 1995).

BRYAN D. JONES, *Reconceiving Decision-Making in Democratic Politics: Attention, Choice and Public Policy* (University of Chicago Press, 1994).

BRUCE E. KEITH, DAVID B. MAGLEBY, CANDICE J. NELSON, ELIZABETH ORR, MARK C. WESTLYE, AND RAYMOND E. WOLFINGER, *The Myth of the Independent Voter* (University of California Press, 1992).

V. O. KEY, JR., *Public Opinion and American Democracy* (Alfred A. Knopf, 1961).

ANTHONY KING, *Running Scared: Why America's Politicians Campaign Too Much and Govern Too Little* (Free Press, 1997).

PHILIP A. KLINKNER, ED., *Midterm: The Elections of 1994 in Context* (Westview Press, 1996).

WARREN E. MILLER AND J. MERRILL SHANKS, *The New American Voter* (Harvard University Press, 1996).

MICHAEL NELSON, ED., *The Elections of 1996* (Congressional Quarterly Press, 1997).

RICHARD G. NIEMI AND HERBERT F. WEISBERG, *Classics in Voting Behavior* (Congressional Quarterly Press, 1993).

RICHARD G. NIEMI AND HERBERT F. WEISBERG, *Controversies in Voting Behavior*, 3d ed. (Congressional Quarterly Press, 1993).

BENJAMIN I. PAGE AND ROBERT Y. SHAPIRO, *The Rational Public: Fifty Years of Trends in Americans' Policy Preferences* (University of Chicago Press, 1992).

FRANK R. PARKER, *Black Votes Count: Political Empowerment in Mississippi After 1965* (University of North Carolina Press, 1990).

GERALD M. POMPER, ED., *The Election of 1996: Reports and Interpretations* (Chatham House, 1997).

SAMUEL L. POPKIN, *The Reasoning Voter: Communication and Persuasion in Presidential Campaigns* (University of Chicago Press, 1991).

SUSAN J. TOLCHIN, *The Angry Citizen: How Voter Rage Is Changing the Nation* (Westview Press, 1996).

JOHN ZALLER, *The Origins and Nature of Mass Opinion* (Cambridge University Press, 1992).

See also *Public Opinion Quarterly, American Journal of Political Science,* and *American Political Science Review.*

12

Campaigns and Elections: Democracy in Action

*H*ow did Bill Clinton reverse his political fortunes from his party's stunning defeat in 1994 to his reelection victory in 1996? An essential part of this turnaround was Clinton's ability to frame the issues in the 1996 election in terms of preserving Medicare, Medicaid, education, and the environment. The strategy behind Clinton's move to the center on a wide range of issues was well known, and the chief architect of the strategy, political consultant Dick Morris, even became front-page news himself with his sudden departure from the campaign on the day of Clinton's acceptance speech at the Democratic National Convention due to a personal scandal.

Clinton used paid advertising and the news-making opportunities of the presidency to define himself and his opponent in 1996. Clinton established the battle lines with the Republicans on balancing the budget, reducing crime, and reforming welfare. As early as June 1995, he pushed a proposal for a balanced budget in ten years, later agreeing to seven years. He reinforced his "tough on crime" image by pressing Congress to provide funding for his 1994 Crime Control Act, which would put 100,000 more police officers on city streets. When the House voted to overturn the Brady Bill's ban on assault rifles, Clinton said Congress was siding with "the Washington gun lobby over the interests of the law-enforcement people of this country and the law abiding citizens of this country."[1] Clinton even laid claim to welfare reform by agreeing to a compromise with Republicans in Congress and then using the issue to publicly disagree with the liberal elements in his own party. Later in the campaign, when Bob Dole unsuccessfully tried to define Bill Clinton as a liberal, Dole's argument rang hollow because of Clinton's moderate policy initiatives in 1995 and 1996.

Dole had been advised to attack Clinton's character, something Clinton's own polls had shown to be his major weakness. In a memorandum written early in the campaign, Mark Penn, Clinton's pollster, summarized the extent of Clinton's character problem by saying, "We lose the family vote." Penn argued that the way to get around the problem was to distinguish public from private morality.[2] Clinton followed this advice and began speaking about how Republicans had "violated," "ignored," "trampled," and "dishonored" American values, which Clinton pledged to "cherish," "protect," and "defend."

Such rhetoric is often meaningless in campaigns, but in 1996 it became important because of a strategic blunder committed by House Speaker Newt Gingrich. Speaking with reporters on what his plans were for entitlement programs such as Medicare, Gingrich said the bureaucracy running the program would one day "wither on the vine."[3] The distinction between the Medicare bureaucracy and the program itself was not one most observers noticed, and Democrats skillfully used this sound bite in advertisements aimed at defining the Republicans as extremists and Clinton as a moderate. The Republican position on Medicare gave the Clinton media team a concrete example of their "values" message.

In a 1996 ad named "Moral," schoolchildren were seen raising an American flag. The voice of the announcer said, "As Americans, some things we do simply and solely because they are moral, right, and good." Visually, the commercial then shifted to black and white photos of Newt Gingrich and Bob Dole with the Capitol between them. In red letters, the words CUT MEDICARE appeared. The image then shifted to Bill Clinton in the Oval Office as the announcer said, "President Clinton: doing what's moral, good, and right by our elderly." Other

Alaska	1994
Arizona	1992
Arkansas	1992
California	1992
Colorado	1990*
Florida	1992
Idaho	1994
Maine	1994
Massachusetts	1994
Michigan	1992
Missouri	1992
Montana	1992
Nebraska	1994
Nevada	1994
North Dakota	1992
Ohio	1992
Oklahoma	1994
Oregon	1992
South Dakota	1992
Utah	1994**
Washington	1992
Wyoming	1992

Voters rejected term limits in:

Washington	1991
Utah	1994
Mississippi	1995

*Colorado voters modified their 1990 term limits initiative in 1994 to shorten the possible terms for U.S. House of Representatives from six terms (12 years) to three terms (6 years).

**The Utah State Legislature approved term limits contingent upon 25 other states also enacting them. A 1994 ballot initiative to have term limits take effect immediately failed.

pro-Clinton ads later in the campaign built on this theme as well. *Newsweek*'s interpretation was: "These strategically targeted ads reached millions of viewers in the fall of '95. Morris watched happily as Clinton's favorable rating inched up with each ad, from 47 percent in August to the mid-50s by December. It was arguably the turning point in Clinton's campaign for re-election."[4] Clinton also skillfully used news briefings and press conferences to depict his concerns about education, the environment, and the elderly in the protracted budget battle that resulted in government shutdowns.

Bob Dole had a chance to define the issues and candidates, but his campaign was poorly focused. Dole fired his media consultants soon after his first set of fall campaign ads appeared. Politicians and candidates typically use the media to communicate their messages to the public, but Clinton's 1996 presidential campaign skillfully used paid advertising and media events to drive home the Democratic agenda.

The amount of media attention focused on the presidential race far exceeds any other contest, but elections at any level generate media coverage. Americans vote more often and for more offices than do the citizens of any other democracy. In 1996 we elected not only a president and vice-president but governors in 12 states, 35 U.S. senators, and all 435 members of the U.S. House of Representatives. At the state level, we elected insurance commissioners, secretaries of state, and, in most states, judges.

We hold thousands of elections for everything from community college directors to county sheriffs. About half a million persons hold elected state and local offices.[5] In addition to electing people, voters can place laws or constitutional amendments on the ballot by petition in 27 states. In all states except Delaware, voters must approve all changes in the state constitution. Voters decide directly on issues such as limiting automobile insurance rates, lowering taxes, and setting term limits for elected officials.

In this chapter we begin by explaining the implications of our election rules. We note four important problems that deserve attention: lack of competition for some offices, problems associated with nominating presidential candidates, complexities and distorting consequences of the Electoral College, and the influence of money in our elections. We also discuss proposed reforms in each of these areas.

ELECTIONS: THE RULES OF THE GAME

The rules of the game—the electoral game—make a difference. Although the Constitution sets certain conditions and requirements, and Congress has been exercising this power with greater frequency, most electoral rules remain matters of state law.

Regularly Scheduled Elections

In our system, elections are set in advance and at fixed intervals that cannot be changed by the party in power. It does not make any difference if the nation is at war or in the midst of a crisis; when the calendar calls for an election, the election is held. In many parliamentary democracies, such as Great Britain and Canada, elections are called by the existing government at a time of its choosing, as long as the election is held within five years of the previous election. Elections for members of Congress occur the first Tuesday after the first Monday in November of even-numbered years. Although there are some exceptions (special elections or peculiar state provisions), participants know *in advance* just when the next election will be.

Fixed, Staggered, and Sometimes Limited Terms

Our electoral system is based on *fixed terms*, meaning that the length of a term in office is set, not indefinite. The Constitution has set the term of office for the U.S. House of Representatives at two years, the Senate at six years, and the presidency at four years. Fixed terms of office mean that politicians can anticipate the next election for a given office and plan for it.

Our system also has *staggered terms* for some offices; not all offices are up for election at the same time. All House members are up for election every two years, but only one-third of the senators are up for election at the same time. Because House members are perpetually campaigning, many have expressed support for lengthening their terms to four years. Also, House members must now give up their seats to run for the Senate; with a four-year term, they could run for the Senate at the middle of their term and, if they lost, still retain their House seat. Senators strongly oppose this change, even though the same concern affects those senators who think of running for the presidency. If the presidential election occurs two or four years into their six-year term, senators can run for the presidency without fear of losing their seat. But if their Senate term expires the same year as the presidential election, the laws of all states except Texas require them to give up their Senate seat to run for president or vice-president or any other position. Texas is an exception because Lyndon Johnson had state law changed to permit him to run for both vice-president and the Senate in 1960. This same rule permitted Lloyd Bentsen to run for both offices in 1988.

Limits on the number of terms a person can hold a particular office are another feature of our electoral system with important consequences. The Twenty-second Amendment to the Constitution, adopted in 1951, limits presidents to two terms. Knowing that a president cannot run again changes the way Congress, the opposing party, and the press regard the president. A politician who cannot, or has announced he or she will not, run again is called a **lame duck**. Efforts to limit the terms of other politicians have become a major issue in several American states. The most frequent targets have been state legislators.

Term limits are popular. Proposals to impose constitutional limits on terms have been defeated in only three states (Washington, Utah, and Mississippi); 22 states have enacted them on their own.[6] Three-fourths of all voters favor term limits, as do nine out of ten Strong Republicans and seven out of ten Strong Democrats.[7] Still, despite their popularity, proposals for term limits have repeatedly lost when they have come to a vote in recent sessions of Congress. In the 1996 elections, voters in 14 states encountered a new variant of term limits—initiatives on state ballots that would inform voters whether incumbents had voted for or against term limits and whether nonincumbents were pledged to support term limits if elected. These so-called "informed voter" initiatives passed in nine states and were defeated in five.

The Supreme Court, by a vote of 5 to 4, declared that a state has no power to impose limits on the number of terms for which its members of the U.S. Congress are eligible either by amending its own constitution or state law.[8] Thus, if term limits are to be imposed on Congress, it will have to be done either by an amendment to the U.S. Constitution or a change in the decisions of the Supreme Court.

Winner-Takes-All

One of the most important features of our electoral system is the **winner-takes-all** rule.[9] In most American electoral settings, the candidate with the most votes wins. The winner does not necessarily need to have a *majority* (more than half the votes cast); in a multicandidate race the winner may have only a *plurality* (the largest number of votes), as Bill Clinton did in 1992 (43%) and in 1996 (49.5%).

Most American election districts are **single-member districts**, meaning that in any district for any given election—senator, governor, U.S. House, state legislative seat—the voters choose one representative or official.[10] When a single-member

Support for Term Limits

Question: A law has been proposed that would limit the members of Congress to no more than 12 consecutive years of service in that office. Do you favor or oppose such a law?

	Favor	Oppose
Gender		
Male	79%	21%
Female	81	19
Age		
18–34	85	15
35–45	78	22
46–55	78	22
56–64	83	17
65+	83	17
Race		
White	81	19
Black	76	24
Income		
0–$10,000	82	18
$10,000–$19,999	79	21
$20,000–$29,999	82	18
$30,000–$39,999	82	18
$40,000–$59,999	81	19
$60,000+	78	22

Source: University of Michigan, Center for Political Studies, 1996 National Election Study.

district system is combined with the winner-takes-all rule, there is a powerful push to sustain a two-party system. Third and fourth parties, under these systems, may get a large number of votes but very few, if any, seats. For example, even if a third party gets 25 percent of the vote in many districts, it will get no seats. Under our electoral rules, the best way for either party to win an election is to assemble a large coalition that leads to a majority or at least a plurality.

The single-member district winner-takes-all system is different from **proportional representation** systems, in which political parties secure legislative seats and power in proportion to the number of votes they receive in the election. Let's assume a hypothetical state has three representatives up for election. In each of the three contests, the Republican defeats the Democrat, but in one district by only a narrow margin. If you add up the statewide vote, the Republicans get 67 percent and the Democrats 33 percent. Under our winner-takes-all and single-member district system, the Republicans get all three seats. But under a system of proportional representation, in which the three seats represent the whole state, the Democrats would receive one seat because they got roughly one-third of the vote in the entire state. Proportional representation thus rewards minor parties and permits them to participate in government. Countries that practice some form of proportional representation include Germany, Israel, and Japan.

Other examples of election practices that are significant are nominating party candidates by direct primaries rather than by party elites and electing U.S. senators by a vote of the people rather than by the state legislature (prohibited by the Seventeenth Amendment). The form of the ballot adopted by the state can also affect the outcome.

The Electoral College

We elect our president and vice-president by an indirect device known as the **Electoral College**. The framers of the U.S. Constitution devised this system to remove the choice of president from a simple majority vote by the people. Under this system each state has as many electors as it has representatives and senators. Thus California, for instance, has 54 electoral votes, and Vermont has 3. Each state is free to determine how its electors are selected. Electors are often longtime party workers who are appointed by the state parties. They are expected, if elected, to cast their electoral votes for the party's candidates for president and vice-president.

The Twelfth Amendment requires electors to vote separately for president and vice-president. To demonstrate how this works, if you voted for Bill Clinton for president in 1996, you were actually voting for electors pledged to vote for Clinton for president and Al Gore for vice-president. If you voted for Bob Dole and Jack Kemp, you were in fact voting for electors pledged to them. Who the electors are does not make a difference in the outcome, and few people pay any attention to who the electors are.

The U.S. Constitution does not prescribe voting rules for electors but states generally have said candidates who win a plurality of the popular vote in a state secure all that state's electoral vote. The exceptions are Nebraska and Maine, which allocate electoral votes to the winner in each congressional district plus two electoral votes for whoever carried the state as a whole. The winning electors go to their state capital on the first Monday after the second Wednesday in December to cast their ballots. These ballots are then sent to Congress, and early in January, Congress formally counts the ballots and declares to the world what everybody already knows—who won the election for president and vice-president.

It takes a majority of the electoral votes to win. If no candidate gets a majority of the electoral votes for president, the House chooses among the top three candidates, with each state delegation having one vote. If no candidate gets a majority of the electoral votes for vice-president, the Senate chooses among the top two candidates, with each senator casting one vote.

Concern about the Electoral College is renewed every time there is a serious third-party candidate for the presidency, as was the case in 1992 and 1996 when Ross Perot ran for president. People began to ask questions like: Which Congress casts the vote, the one now serving or the new one just elected? The answer is the new one, the one elected in November and taking office the first week in January. But what happens if a state's delegation cannot agree on a candidate? Then its vote does not count. Would it be possible to have a president of one party and a vice-president of another? Yes, if the election were thrown into the House and Senate.

The operation of the Electoral College—with its statewide winner-takes-all rule by which a candidate wins either all of a state's electoral votes or none—sharply influences presidential politics. To win a presidential election, a candidate must appeal successfully to urban and suburban groups in the big states of California, Texas, Ohio, and Illinois.[11] California's electoral vote of 54 currently exceeds the combined electoral votes of the 14 least populated states plus the District of Columbia. Figure 12–1 provides a visual comparison of state size according to electoral votes.

Presidential candidates do not ordinarily waste time campaigning in a state unless they have at least a fighting chance of carrying that state; nor do they waste time in a state in which their party is a sure winner. Richard Nixon in 1960 was the last candidate to promise to campaign in all 50 states. He did so, but lost valuable time traveling to and from Alaska, while John Kennedy focused on the more populous states. The contest usually narrows down to the medium-sized and big states, where the balance between the parties tends to be fairly even.

Our Electoral College system makes it possible for a person to receive the most popular votes and not get enough electoral votes. This happened in 1824, when

Vice-President Al Gore reacts gleefully as Speaker Newt Gingrich and members of Congress carry out their constitutional duty to tally the Electoral College votes. No one was surprised when they opened the envelopes and discovered that Bill Clinton was reelected.

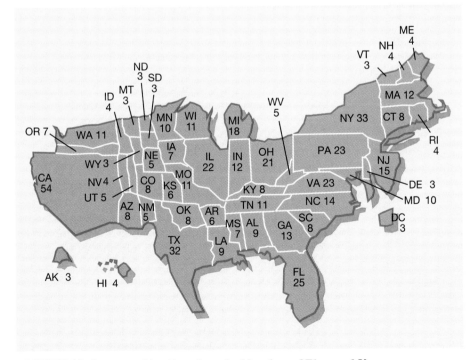

FIGURE 12–1   State Size Based on the Number of Electoral Votes

SOURCE: Holly Idelson, "Count Adds Seats in Eight States," *Congressional Quarterly Weekly Report,* December 29, 1990, p. 4220.

The House Decides

When there are only two major candidates for the presidency, the chances of an election being "thrown into the House" are remote. But twice in our history the House has had to act: in 1800, before the Twelfth Amendment was written, the House had to choose in a tie vote between Thomas Jefferson and Aaron Burr; in 1824 the House picked John Quincy Adams over Andrew Jackson and William Crawford. Henry Clay, who was forced out of the race when he came in fourth in the Electoral College, threw his support behind Adams. When Adams was elected, he made Clay his secretary of state.

The 1824 vote in the House was especially contentious. Jackson, winner of the popular vote, was passed over when the vote went to the House. This outcome infuriated Jackson, who won the Electoral College vote by a wide margin four years later.

Andrew Jackson won 12 percent more of the vote than John Quincy Adams; in 1876, when Samuel Tilden received more popular votes than Rutherford B. Hayes; and again in 1888, when Benjamin Harrison won in the Electoral College although Grover Cleveland received more popular votes. It almost happened in close elections in 1960 and 1976, when the shift of a few votes in a few key states could have resulted in the election of a president without a popular majority. In a year with a serious minor party candidate, the result could be the election of a president without a plurality of the vote.

In two of the three elections in which popular vote winners did not become president, the Electoral College did not decide the winner. The 1824 election was decided by the U.S. House of Representatives. In 1876 the electoral vote in three southern states was disputed, resulting in the Hayes-Tilden Commission deciding how those votes should be counted. Only in 1888 did the Electoral College award the presidency to the candidate with fewer popular votes. But the Electoral College system—including the tradition of states awarding electoral votes in winner-takes-all blocks and states determining the means of selection and voting for electors—meant no winner could be declared in 1824 or 1876 by the Electoral College.[12]

RUNNING FOR CONGRESS

How candidates run for Congress depends on the nature of their district or state, on whether candidates are incumbents or challengers, on the strength of their personal organization, on how well known they are, and on how much money they have to spend on their campaign. We can, however, note several similarities in House and Senate elections.

First, most congressional elections are not close. In districts where most people belong to one party or where incumbents are popular and enjoy fund-raising and other campaign advantages, there is often little competition.[13] Defenders of constitutional democracy are concerned that so many officeholders have **safe seats**. When officeholders do not have to fight to retain their seat, elections are not performing their proper role.[14]

Congressional elections tend to be more competitive than state legislature elections, and mayoral elections are often hotly contested also. Competition is also more likely when funding is adequate for both candidates, which is not often the case in U.S. House elections. Elections for governor and for the U.S. Senate are more seriously contested and adequately financed than those for the U.S. House of Representatives.

Second, the extent of presidential popularity affects both House and Senate elections during presidential election years as well as midterm elections. The impact of presidential popularity in a presidential election is the **coattail effect**, the boost candidates from the president's party get from a popular presidential candidate running in the same election. Winning presidential candidates do not always provide such a boost. The Republicans suffered a net loss of six seats when George Bush won the presidency in 1988, and the Democrats suffered a net loss of ten seats when Bill Clinton won the 1992 presidential election. Democrats fared better in 1996, picking up a net gain of nine seats in the House, but this was not enough to permit them to regain control of the chamber. Overall, "measurable coattail effects continue to appear," according to congressional elections scholar Gary Jacobson, but they are "erratic and usually modest" in their impact.[15]

In midterm elections, presidential popularity and economic conditions have long been associated with the number of House seats a president's party loses.[16] These same factors are associated with how well the president's party does in Senate races, but the association is not as strong.[17] Figure 12–2 shows the number of seats in the House of Representatives and U.S. Senate gained or lost by the party con-

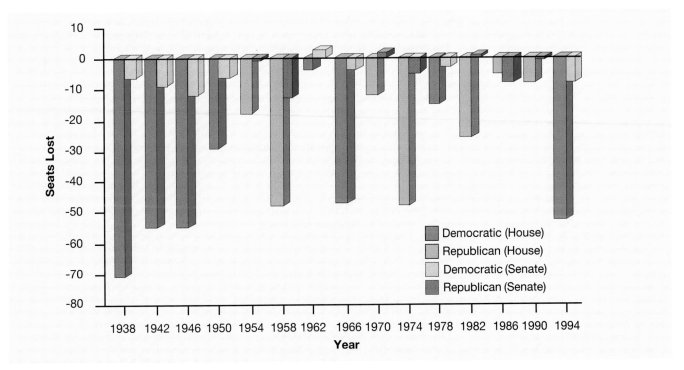

FIGURE 12–2 **Seats Lost by the President's Party in Midterm Elections for the House of Representatives and U.S. Senate, 1938–1994**

trolling the White House in midterm elections since 1938. In each of these elections, the party controlling the White House lost seats in the House. The range of losses, however, is quite wide, from a low of 4 seats for the Democrats in 1962 to a high of 71 seats for the Democrats in 1938.

Republicans did better in 1994 than in any midterm election since 1946, picking up 53 seats. The Republican sweep included the defeat of House Speaker Tom Foley, the first sitting Speaker to be defeated since 1860, and other senior Democrats, such as Dan Rostenkowski and Jack Brooks. The Republican tide was not limited to the House but included a net gain of nine seats in the Senate, counting the postelection switch of Alabama Senator Richard Shelby to the Republican party. Republicans also won major victories that same year in governors' races.

The number of seats lost is partly a function of how well the president's party did in the preceding presidential election. Lyndon Johnson's landslide victory in 1964 may have helped produce a net gain of 47 Democratic seats that year, the exact number of seats that the Democrats lost back to Republicans two years later. Other presidential elections do not result in large gains for the president's party.

Third, technology is increasingly influential in all campaigns. Congressional candidates need campaign managers, opinion pollsters, direct-mail fund raisers, computer experts, media specialists, and many other consultants. Much effort is centered on television, especially television advertising. Because television time is so expensive, the cost of campaigns has soared and the importance of money has increased. Television advertising is less efficient for House candidates whose districts are in large cities where their ads reach more people outside their district than in it. In these districts, House candidates use direct mail or other forms of advertising instead of television.

A fourth characteristic is the use of *negative campaigning*—focusing on an opponent's alleged failings. Negative campaigning has been with us since the beginning, but in recent years it has become more the norm than the exception, not only in congressional campaigns but in campaigns for president and governor. In 1996,

Novice Democrat Loretta Sanchez defeated conservative Republican incumbent Robert Dornan of California in a close vote for the House of Representatives in 1996. Dornan called for a recount, but the final total showed her to be the winner.

Uncontrollable Factors
- Incumbent running
- Strength of party organization
- National tides or landslide possibility
- Socioeconomic makeup of district

Organizational Factors
- Registration drives
- Fund-raising machinery
- Campaign organization
- Volunteers
- Media campaign
- Direct-mail campaign efforts
- Get-out-the-vote efforts

Candidate's Personal Leadership Factors
- Personal appeal
- Knowledge of issues
- Speaking and debating ability
- Commitment and determination
- Ability to earn free, positive media coverage

Republicans ran ads in which Democratic congressional candidates in California were transformed (morphed) into Richard Allen Davis, the man who brutally murdered Polly Klaas, a 12-year-old girl kidnapped from her bedroom at a slumber party. The much-publicized trial and conviction of Davis called attention to the latitude given judges in imposing the death penalty. The argument for linking the candidates to Davis was that the Democrats at some point had expressed opposition to the death penalty.[18] Both parties have used the "morph" technique to link local candidates to unpopular figures. Democrats in 1996 ran commercials in which local Republicans were transformed into the image of Newt Gingrich.[19]

And finally, politics in the 1990s is more *candidate-centered*, as opposed to *issue- or party-oriented*, and increasingly dependent on the mass media rather than on party leaders determining who runs under their label. Politicians essentially nominate themselves for office by winning votes in the primary election. To do this, candidates must rely on name identification and campaign funds spent on advertising.[20] Concern with governing becomes less important than winning reelection or positioning oneself for a run at a higher office.[21] In 1994, Democrats sought to downplay their partisanship and distance themselves from Clinton, while Republicans sought to link the Democrats with Bill and Hillary Clinton. In 1996, some Republicans tried to distance themselves from Bob Dole, whom they perceived as a loser.

The House of Representatives

Every two years, as many as 1,000 candidates—including approximately 400 incumbents—campaign for Congress. After deciding to take the plunge, candidates must first plan a primary race unless they face no opponents for the party's nomination. Incumbents are rarely challenged for renomination from within their own party, and when they are, the challenges are seldom serious. In 1988 and 1990, for example, only one House incumbent was defeated in a primary election. In 1994 only four incumbents seeking reelection were not renominated, and in 1996 only two. Challengers running against entrenched incumbents rarely encounter opposition in their own party.[22]

Mounting a Primary Campaign The first step for would-be challengers in contested primaries or for those seeking open seats is to build a *personal organization*. The party organization usually stays neutral until the nomination is decided. A candidate can build an organization while holding another office, such as a seat in the state legislature, or by deliberately getting to know people, serving in civic causes, helping other candidates, and being conspicuous without being controversial.

The next steps are to hire campaign managers and technicians, buy television and other advertising, conduct polls, and pay for a variety of activities. All these things depend on raising funds, which most candidates find difficult before they have secured the nomination.

A candidate's main hurdle is gaining visibility. Candidates work hard to be mentioned by the media. As the old cliché goes, "It doesn't matter what they say about you as long as they spell your name right." In large cities with many simultaneous campaigns, congressional candidates are frequently lost in media "noise," and in rural areas the press often plays down political news. Candidates rely on personal contacts, on hand shaking and door-to-door campaigning, and on identifying likely supporters and courting their favor—the same techniques used in campaigns for lesser offices. The turnout in primaries tends to be low, except in campaigns in which large sums of money are expended on advertising.

Campaigning for the General Election General election campaigns can usefully be divided into four types: incumbent campaigns, weak challenger campaigns, serious challenger campaigns, and open seat campaigns.

As we have mentioned several times, most members of Congress win reelection.[23] Since 1970, over 95 percent of incumbent House members seeking reelection have won. Even in 1994, which is often seen as a year of major change in the U.S. House, over 90 percent of incumbents seeking reelection were returned to office, and in 1996, 94 percent of incumbent House members running for reelection were successful.[24] Knowing the advantage of incumbency, potential challengers often choose not to run, thereby helping the incumbent further.[25] In recent House elections, incumbents outspent their challengers roughly 3 to 1; in the Senate the difference was closer to 2 to 1.[26] Most challengers spend little money, run campaigns that are not significantly more visible than primary campaigns, contact few voters, and lose badly.

A few challengers in each election mount serious challenges because of the incumbent's perceived vulnerability, the challenger's own wealth, party, or political action committee efforts, or a combination of factors. Often their campaign expenditures rival those of the incumbents, yet most of them lose. In 1988, only 6 challengers defeated incumbents; only 40 others polled more than 40 percent of the votes in the November election. The number of challengers defeating incumbents rose to 15 in 1990, when just under 4 percent of incumbents seeking reelection were defeated. In 1992, however, many incumbents chose to retire or run for other offices, and others were denied reelection. The Republican sweep of 1994 removed as many as 30 House and 2 Senate Democratic incumbents from office, and other incumbents won by very close margins. Republican incumbents fared much better, as no Republican House or Senate incumbents were defeated in 1994. They did not do so well in 1996, as 11 freshmen were defeated as well as 4 members who had served more than one term.[27]

Why is keeping a House seat so much easier than gaining it? Incumbents have a host of advantages that help them gain reelection. These "perks" include free mailings to constituents (the *franking* privilege), the free use of broadcast studios to record radio and television tapes to be sent to local media outlets, and perhaps most important of all, a large staff to perform countless favors and send a stream of press reports and mail, in the member's name, back to the district. All these advantages help a House member build not only name recognition but also a positive image.[28] Representatives also try to win committee posts, even on minor committees, that relate to the needs of their districts and build connections with constituents.[29] Congressional careers are built on a variety of personal contacts: shaking hands, canvassing homes, emphasizing local problems, remembering people's names, doing favors.[30] If an incumbent is successful at building "constituent trust," he or she will win reelection again and again.[31]

If incumbents win so often, how do we get significant turnover in the House of Representatives at all? Turnover comes when incumbents die, decide to retire, or seek some other office. Redistricting, which happens once each decade, often promotes some turnover, as it did in 1992 when incumbents were forced to run in new districts. More than one-third of the U.S. House has retired in the last three elections: 65 retired in 1992, 48 in 1994, and 36 in 1996. Reasons for retirement vary, but the effect has been to reinforce the partisan and ideological shift in the House to greater conservatism and Republicanism.

Retirements and redistricting create open seats, which often result in more competitive elections. Potential candidates, as well as political action committees and political party committees, all watch open seat races closely. But as noted, most races have incumbents and most incumbents win, lending credibility to the charge that we have a "permanent Congress." One solution to the problem of the permanent Congress is to limit the number of terms a person can serve. Typically, the proposed limit is 12 years: 6 two-year House terms, 2 six-year U.S. Senate terms, and 3 four-year state Senate terms. The Supreme Court ruled in 1995 that a

"Please, Senator Fairchild, you have to leave. You lost."

Drawing by Sauers. © 1983 The New Yorker Magazine, Inc.

MONEY AND CONGRESSIONAL CAMPAIGNS

The costs of congressional elections have risen dramatically over the past 15 years, while the rates of reelection have risen. Part of the explanation for the success incumbents have enjoyed is their "special" relationship with political action committees (PACs). Since 1980 over 90 percent of House incumbents seeking reelection have been returned to office, leading critics to charge that what we have in Washington is "the permanent Congress."

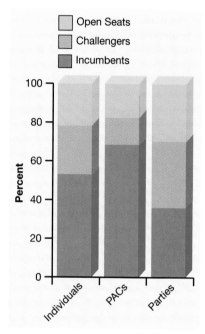

Incumbents' Dependence on PAC Money, 1996

SOURCE: Federal Elections Commission, press release, April 14, 1997, p. 10.

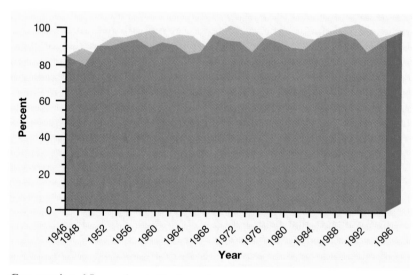

Congressional Incumbents Reelected

SOURCE: Federal Elections Commission, press release, April 14, 1997, pp. 32–51.

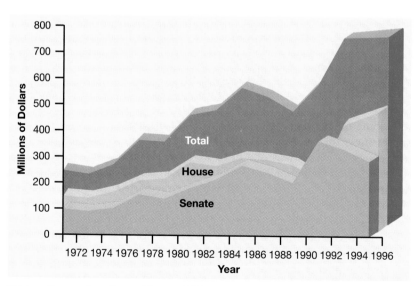

Rising Campaign Costs (General Elections)

SOURCE: Federal Elections Commission, press release, April 14, 1997, p. 1.

constitutional amendment would be required to specify term limits for members of Congress.[32]

The Senate

Running for the Senate is big-time politics. The six-year term and the national exposure make a Senate seat a glittering prize, so competition is usually intense. Senate campaigns generally feature state-of-the-art campaign technology; a race normally costs millions of dollars.[33] Still, Senate races tend to be much like those for the House. The essential tactics are to raise lots of money, get good people involved, make as many personal contacts as possible (especially in the states with smaller populations), avoid giving the opposition any positive publicity, and have a simple campaign theme.

Incumbency is an advantage for senators, although not as much as for representatives.[34] Incumbent senators are more widely known through the media, but so are many of their opponents. Many House members run against little-known opponents. Because senators and Senate candidates are far more visible than House candidates, they cannot easily duck tough issues. Much of what citizens hear about House members, in contrast, is generated from the members' own offices. Further, senators normally face tougher competition—challengers who frequently are already well known or who raise and spend significant amounts of money.[35]

When there is a chance to switch party control of the Senate, as was the case twice in the 1980s and again in 1994, more good candidates run, and the number of competitive elections increases. But the cost of Senate campaigns can vary greatly. California has 69 times the number of potential voters as Wyoming, and the political culture and nature of their media markets differ dramatically. A seat from Wyoming is much cheaper than a seat from California. As a result, disproportionately large amounts of money are spent in many small states when the stakes of controlling the Senate are high. It is not surprising that Senate elections in less-populated states have become battlegrounds.[36]

RUNNING FOR PRESIDENT

Presidential elections are major media events, with candidates seeking as much television as possible and trying, at the same time, to avoid negative news coverage. The formal election process involves seeking the nomination of a major party and then amassing enough votes on the first Tuesday after the first Monday in November to win a majority in the Electoral College. The formal campaign has three stages: winning the nomination, campaigning at the convention, and mobilizing support in the general election.

Stage 1: The Nomination

Presidential hopefuls must make a series of critical tactical decisions. The first is when to start campaigning. Some candidates begin almost as soon as the last presidential election is over. Early decisions are increasingly necessary for candidates to be able to raise the money and assemble the organization to be competitive. The problem with having to decide on a race for the presidency years before the next election is that circumstances change. A president who is popular can suffer a dramatic loss of popularity, and a front runner who appears invincible may stumble. Campaigning begins well before any actual declaration of candidacy, as candidates try to line up supporters to win caucuses or primaries in key states and to raise money for their nomination effort.

One of the hardest jobs for candidates and their strategists is calculating how to deal with the complex maze of presidential primaries and caucuses that constitutes

Michael Huffington spent over $25 million of his own money in an unsuccessful bid to represent California in the U.S. Senate in 1994. Incumbent Dianne Feinstein also spent heavily and defeated him by a slim margin in the most expensive Senate campaign in U.S. history.

From Coast to Coast

Voter Turnout in the 1996 Presidential Primaries

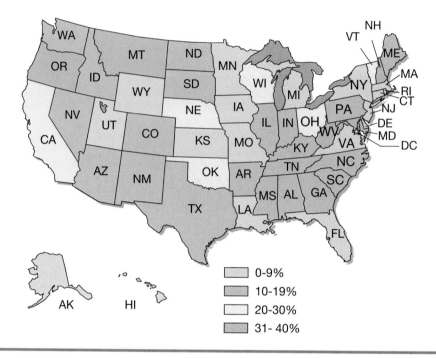

▨	0-9%
▨	10-19%
▨	20-30%
▨	31- 40%

SOURCE: Federal Election Commission home page: http://www.fec.gov

the delegate selection system. This complex system varies from state to state and often from one party to the other in the same state. Although the process is influenced somewhat by federal regulation of campaign financing and national party rules, within broad limits states can set up the systems they prefer. The result is a complex maze that critics call flawed.[37]

PRESIDENTIAL PRIMARIES State presidential primaries, unknown before this century, have become the main method of choosing delegates. Today more than three-fourths of the states use presidential primaries. In 1996 primaries selected 78 percent of the Democratic delegates and 88 percent of the Republican delegates.[38] The rest of the states use caucuses or conventions.

Voters in states like Iowa and New Hampshire bask in media attention for weeks and even months before they cast the first ballots in the presidential sweepstakes. Because these early contests have had the effect of limiting the choices of voters in states that come later in the process, there has been a tendency for states to move their primaries up. California, which traditionally held its primary in June, moved it to March in 1996 so that its voters would play a more important role in selecting the nominee. Other states did the same thing. As a result, the 1996 primary season was compressed into several weeks of intense activity. Yet even with the change, Bob Dole emerged as the Republican winner before Californians voted.

Presidential primaries have two main features: a "beauty contest," in which voters indicate which candidate for president running in the primary they prefer, but do not actually elect delegates to the convention, and actual voting for delegates pledged to a candidate. Candidates may win the beauty contest or popularity vote and find their opponents doing better in actual delegates elected because they failed to put a full slate of delegates on the ballot or because local notables were running for a delegate pledged to another candidate. Different combinations of these two features have produced the following systems:

1. *Proportional representation*: Delegates to the national convention are allocated on the basis of the votes candidates win in the "beauty contest." This system has been used in most of the states, including several of the largest ones. The Democrats now mandate a proportional representation rule for all their primaries.[39] In some states Republicans use this same system, but Republicans are much more varied in their delegate selection processes.[40]

2. *Winner-takes-all*: In some states there is a winner-takes-all rule that whoever gets the most votes wins all that state's delegates, as Bob Dole did in the California Republican primary in 1996. To win all the delegates of a state like California is an enormous bonus to a candidate. Only the Republicans still use the winner-takes-all system at the state level, and in 1996 about half of all states used this rule at either the state or congressional district levels.

3. *Delegate selection*: In several states, large and small, voters choose delegates who may or may not have pledged how they will vote in the national party convention. The names of the presidential hopefuls do not appear separately on the ballot, and there is no declared presidential preference. Under this arrangement, delegates are free to exercise their independent judgment at the convention. This system is used only by the Republicans; in 1996 it was used most prominently in New York and Illinois.

4. *Delegate selection and separate presidential poll*: In several states, including New Hampshire (where for many years the first presidential primary has been held), voters decide twice: once to state their choice for president, and once to choose delegates pledged, or at least favorable, to a presidential candidate. This system is one of the oldest kinds of presidential primary.[41]

CAUCUSES AND CONVENTIONS A **caucus** is a meeting of party members and supporters of various candidates. About a dozen states use a caucus and/or convention system for choosing delegates.[42] There are many variations of the caucus and convention system because they are regulated by each state's parties and legislature. The best known example of a caucus is in Iowa, because Iowa has held the earliest caucuses in most recent presidential nominating contests. The caucus or convention is the oldest method of choosing delegates and is fundamentally different from the primary system because it centers on the *party organization*. In principle, the caucus and convention system is far simpler than the primary method.

Delegates who will attend the national party conventions are chosen by delegates to state or district conventions, who themselves are chosen earlier in county, precinct, or town caucuses. The process starts at local meetings open to all party members, who discuss and take positions on candidates and issues and elect delegates to represent their views at the next level. This process repeats until national nominating convention delegates are chosen by conventions of delegates throughout a district or state.

Whoever the candidates may be in 2000, on a Monday evening in early February of that year, Iowans will hold hundreds of Democratic and Republican precinct meetings. Large numbers of voters will attend these small town meetings. Although an even larger number of Iowans would doubtless vote in a primary if one were held, the thousands attending these caucuses will have a chance to meet and exchange views on issues and candidates, rather than merely pulling a lever in a voting booth or placing an *X* on a ballot. A special feature of the Iowa meetings is that college students can attend local caucuses in their college towns or hometowns, as they prefer, with a minimum of hassle.

To Thy Candidate Be True?

How tightly should convention delegates be bound to the presidential candidates to whom they were pledged in the primaries? This question dominated the first day of proceedings at the 1980 Democratic convention. Delegates supporting President Jimmy Carter, who had won most of the primaries, argued that if delegates could violate their "pledges," primaries would be a farce and conventions undemocratic and unrepresentative. Delegates backing Senator Edward Kennedy contended that such a rule would make delegates into "pawns" and conventions into "rubber stamps." Why have a convention at all, they asked, if delegates could not act in a deliberative—rather than merely a representative—capacity, especially because months had gone by since many delegates had been selected and conditions had changed?

A majority of the convention supported Carter's position, and party rules appeared to require that "delegates elected to the national convention pledged to a presidential candidate shall in all good conscience reflect the sentiments of those who elected them."*

*Delegate Selection Rules for the 1984 Democratic National Convention (Democratic National Committee, 1982), p. 13.

STRATEGIES   Strategies for gaining delegates to the national convention have changed over the years. Some candidates think it wise to skip some of the earlier contests and enter first in states where their strength lies. This strategy was challenged by the "go everywhere" plan Jimmy Carter pursued in winning the 1976 Democratic nomination. Most candidates choose to run hard in Iowa and New Hampshire, hoping that early showings in these states, which receive a great deal of media attention, will move them into the spotlight for later efforts.

During this early phase, candidates win or lose by their ability to adapt their own strengths to changing circumstances: the number of candidates running, the ideological splits among the candidates, the calendar of events, the amount of money available for the campaign, the ways in which the media cover a particular state, and the events that disrupt planning. Especially important is the ability of candidates to manage the media's expectation of their performance. Lyndon Johnson actually won the New Hampshire primary in 1968, but because Eugene McCarthy did better than the press had expected, McCarthy was interpreted as the "winner." Winning in the primaries thus becomes a game of expectations, and candidates may intentionally downplay their expectations so that "doing better than expected" might generate momentum for their campaign. Pat Buchanan made the most of his early victories in Alaska, Louisiana, and New Hampshire in 1996 and generated a lot of free publicity. As the field of candidates narrowed, however, Bob Dole picked up supporters and handily defeated Buchanan. Steve Forbes spent approximately $37 million of his own money in a few selected states early in the process, and as a result he won in Arizona and Delaware. Forbes, however, was unable to sustain his strong showing and dropped out of the race soon after the New York primary.

Stage 2: The Convention

National party conventions are the national meeting of the delegates elected in primaries, caucuses, or state conventions who assemble to pick the party's presidential and vice-presidential candidates. Historically, delegates arrived at national nominating conventions with differing degrees of commitment to presidential candidates. Some delegates were pledged to no candidate at all, others to a specific candidate for one or two ballots, and others firmly to one candidate only. Recent conventions have merely ratified decisions already made in the primaries and caucuses, in part because delegates were required to pledge themselves to a specific presidential hopeful (in the Democratic party) or because one candidate has been able to amass the necessary number of delegates in advance. And because of "reforms" encouraging delegates to stick with the person to whom they are pledged, there has been less room to maneuver at conventions. National party conventions used to be events of high excitement because they determined who would be the party nominees, but in every election since the Republican convention of 1948 and the Democratic convention of 1952, the nominee has been chosen on the first ballot.

Despite being a foregone conclusion, conventions attract national attention. It is a chance to focus attention on the nominee, party luminaries, and the spectacle of the convention, not to mention the excitement generated by the selection of a vice-presidential running mate. In 1988, Democrats averaged 27.1 million viewers and Republicans 24.5 million. In 1992 the parties had nearly identical average viewership, although Democratic viewership in 1992 may have been reduced because CBS broadcast baseball's All-Star Game on the second night of the convention. Network television news coverage of major party conventions in 1996 was reduced to a few hours in prime time each night on the major networks, and viewership was down compared to previous years. In 1996 Democrats averaged 18 million viewers on the major networks, compared to the Republicans' average 1996 audience of 16.6 million viewers.[43]

The long-term trend of declining viewership and reduced hours of coverage has altered the parties' strategies for evening prime time. In 1996, even more than in previous years, the parties placed their most important speakers and highlighted their most important messages in the limited time given them by the networks. Because conventions no longer are the place where the real decisions about who will be the presidential candidates are made, it is likely that in 2000 the major networks will leave gavel-to-gavel coverage to CSPAN and CNN.

Conventions follow standard rules, routines, and rituals. Usually the first day is devoted to a keynote address and other speeches touting the party and denouncing the opposition; the second day to committee reports, including party and convention rules and the party platform; the third day to presidential balloting; and the fourth to choosing the vice-presidential nominee and winding up with the presidential candidate's acceptance speech.[44] Balloting for president used to be the highlight of the proceedings, but now dramatic struggles occur over the adoption of the rules and the platform. Not long ago sharp encounters occurred over credentials—that is, over which delegates should be seated. The matter was most often in dispute when southern states sent all-white delegations to the Democratic convention. Credential fights have decreased since standard procedures for choosing delegates have been enforced and African Americans have secured the right to vote.

THE PARTY PLATFORM   Delegates to the national party conventions decide upon the platform, which sometimes involves a divisive fight. Why? Critics have long pointed out that the party platform is binding on no one and is more likely to hurt than help a candidate. But presidential candidates as well as delegates take the platform seriously because it gives an indication of the general direction a party wants to take. Also, despite the charge that the platform is ignored, most presidents make an effort to implement it.[45] In recent years the parties have been successful in working out their platform before the convention so that delegates seldom debate and vote on more than a couple of controversial issues.

THE VICE-PRESIDENTIAL NOMINEE   The choice of the vice-presidential nominee generates widespread attention. The presidential nominee generally dictates the choice of a running mate, although this practice is not taken for granted. Rarely does a person actually "run" for the vice-presidential nomination because only the presidential nominee's "vote" counts, but there is a good deal of maneuvering to capture that one vote. Sometimes the choice of a running mate is made by the presidential nominee at the convention—not a time conducive to careful and deliberate thought. More often the choice is made before the convention, and the announcement is timed to enhance media coverage and momentum going into the convention. Bob Dole's choice of Jack Kemp helped energize the Republicans at their convention and reinforced Dole's promise of a 15 percent tax cut, but it also meant that Kemp needed to reverse his stand on such issues as immigration and affirmative action.

Traditionally the presidential nominee chooses a running mate who will "balance the ticket." Democratic presidential nominee Walter Mondale raised this tradition to a dramatic new height in 1984 by selecting a woman, Representative Geraldine A. Ferraro, to run with him. Mondale's bold decision was an effort to strengthen his appeal to women voters. Presidential candidates sometimes ignore the idea of a balanced ticket, as Bill Clinton did when he chose another southern white male, Al Gore, to be his running mate.

THE VALUE OF CONVENTIONS   Why do the parties continue to have conventions if the nominee is known in advance and the vice-presidential nominee is the choice

Hugging babies and waving to crowds at whistle stops are all part of the campaign hoopla that candidates must go through in the seemingly endless lead-in to Election Day.

of one person? What role do conventions play in our system? For the parties, they are a time of "coming together" to endorse a party program and to build unity and enthusiasm for the fall campaign. For future candidates, they are a chance to capture the national spotlight and further their political ambitions. Speeches in conventions by Mario Cuomo, Pat Buchanan, Bill Clinton, and Jack Kemp have generated interest in them as future presidential candidates. For nominees, they are an opportunity to define themselves in positive ways. The potential is there to heal wounds festering from the primary campaign and move into the general election united. Of course, the potential is not always achieved. Many campaign managers in recent elections have seen conventions as potentially dangerous to their candidate and coalition. As a result, they work at damage control as well as celebration.

NOMINATION BY PETITION There is a way to run for president of the United States that avoids the grueling process of primary elections and conventions—if you are rich enough or well known enough. H. Ross Perot in 1992 and John Anderson in 1980 met the various state petition requirements or paid the $500 filing fee in Louisiana and made it onto the ballot in all 50 states. In 1996, the petition process was as simple as submitting the signatures of 200 registered voters in Washington State, or as difficult as getting the signatures of 3 percent of registered voters (72,784 signatures) in Maryland. Perot and Anderson demonstrated that you do not need a political party to run for president, although in 1996 Perot was nominated at the Reform party convention.

These contenders also demonstrated that you do not need a political party to run a visible campaign that is taken seriously by your opponents and the American people. In 1992, Perot and his running mate, James Stockdale, got nearly one-fifth of the popular vote. Perot was not nominated by any political party, did not run in any primaries, and had not sought any office before. How did he do it? He spent about $65 million of his own money to promote himself as a candidate. Perot's candidacy was unusual because it generated so much media attention; he skillfully used free media, like the television program *Larry King Live* on which he opened his campaign and appeared many times during its course. Perot's antipolitician, anti-Washington, and antideficit message struck a responsive chord in the American public. His folksy and often humorous manner of communicating reinforced his appeal.

Despite some early mistakes and difficulties with his staff, Perot ran a respectable campaign in 1992 and played an important role in defining the issues. In fact, there was the possibility that he might come in second in the race or win enough electoral votes to throw the election into the House of Representatives. Perot did come in second in two states—Utah and Maine—and he garnered almost 20 million votes. However, he won no electoral votes.

Following the election, Perot continued to be courted by both Republicans and Democrats, who hoped to win back his supporters for the 1994 and 1996 elections. His influence fell after the televised debate over the North American Free Trade Agreement (NAFTA) with Vice-President Al Gore, in which Perot was widely seen as testy, whiney, and a "bossy, old billionaire bully."[46] Perot's 1996 campaign, run under the banner of his Reform party, never generated the kind of media attention or popular support that his 1992 campaign did. In 1992 he was important in keeping the focus of the campaign on issues like the budget deficit, but in 1996 the issue agenda of the campaign was set by the two major parties. Perot's 1996 popular vote dropped substantially, and again he won no electoral votes.

Stage 3: The General Election

The national party convention adjourns immediately after the presidential and vice-presidential candidates deliver their acceptance speeches to the delegates and the national television audience. The time between the conventions and Labor

Day was traditionally a time for resting, binding up convention wounds, gearing the party for action, and planning campaign strategy. In recent elections, however, the campaigns have hardly paused after the convention.[47]

Strategy differs from one election to another, but politicians, pollsters, and political scientists have collected enough information to agree broadly that a number of basic factors affect election outcomes. Whether the nation is prosperous probably has the most to do with who wins a presidential election, but, as we have noted, most voters vote on the basis of party and candidate appeal.[48] Much depends on voter turnout as well. The Democrats' advantage in number of people who identify themselves as Democrats is mitigated by the higher voter turnout among Republicans. Republicans also usually have better access to money.

THE MEDIA AND THE IMAGE Candidates and their campaign staff devote considerable attention to defining themselves positively and the opposition negatively. In 1968, Richard Nixon struggled to shed his old image of divisiveness and failure.[49] In 1992, Clinton succeeded in keeping the focus of the campaign on the economy rather than on foreign policy or elements of Clinton's background like his Vietnam era draft status or his involvement with the Whitewater failed real estate development in Arkansas. Clinton used the media to highlight his moderate positions on welfare reform, gun control, and the government shutdown in his 1996 race. He used campaign ads that linked Bob Dole to the unpopular House Speaker Newt Gingrich and labeled the Republican positions on guns, the budget, and tobacco as extreme.

PRESIDENTIAL DEBATES Televised presidential debates are now a major feature of presidential elections. The 1960 debate between John Kennedy and Richard Nixon boosted Kennedy's campaign and elevated the role of television in our politics.[50] In 1964 and 1972, incumbents Lyndon Johnson and Nixon refused to debate their challengers. In 1976, President Gerald Ford debated Jimmy Carter and mistakenly said, while defending his record of negotiating with the Soviet Union, that each country in Eastern Europe "is independent, autonomous, it has its own territorial integrity, and none was under Soviet domination." That mistake damaged his credibility. Ronald Reagan's performance in the 1980 debate was dignified, as he highlighted his concerns about leadership and the economy.

In 1980 the question arose whether to include third-party candidate John Anderson in the televised debates, as it did again in 1992 with Ross Perot. Perot and his running mate, James Stockdale, were included in all presidential and vice-presidential debates. The 1992 debates generated large viewing audiences, averaging over 80 million for each debate (around 110 million people watched football's 1994 Super Bowl). Each debate used a different format, one of which had undecided voters asking the presidential candidates questions. The debates did not result in large numbers of voters changing their minds about the candidates; rather, they reinforced voters' prior choices and brought additional attention to Ross Perot.

Fewer viewers watched the 1996 debates than in the past. Perot was excluded because he failed to meet one of the criteria, a plausible chance of winning any electoral votes. The two presidential and one vice-presidential debates were informative and helped clarify differences between the candidates. None of the candidates made any major mistakes. Still, the debates changed few voters' minds, and most viewers had their opinions about the candidates reinforced.

Although some journalists are quick to express their dissatisfaction with presidential candidates for being so concerned with makeup and rehearsed answers, and although the debates have not significantly affected the election outcomes, they have provided important opportunities for candidates to distinguish themselves and for the public to weigh their qualifications. Candidates who do well in

"My former opponent is supporting me in the general election. Please disregard all the things I said about him in the primary."

Dunagin's People by Ralph Dunagin. Reprinted with special permission of NAS, Inc.

No one has captured the spirit of presidential campaigning better than Adlai E. Stevenson, the unsuccessful Democratic candidate in 1952 and 1956:

You must emerge, bright and bubbling with wisdom and well-being, every morning at 8 o'clock, just in time for a charming and profound breakfast talk, shake hands with hundreds, often literally thousands, of people, make several inspiring, "newsworthy" speeches during the day, confer with political leaders along the way and with your staff all the time, write at every chance, think if possible, read mail and newspapers, talk on the telephone, talk to everybody, dictate, receive delegations, eat, with decorum—and discretion!—and ride through city after city on the back of an open car, smiling until your mouth is dehydrated by the wind, waving until the blood runs out of your arm, and then bounce gaily, confidently, masterfully into great howling halls, shaved and all made up for television with the right color shirt and tie—I always forgot—and a manuscript so defaced with chicken tracks and last-minute jottings that you couldn't follow it, even if the spotlights weren't blinding and even if the still photographers didn't shoot you in the eye every time you looked at them. (I've often wondered what happened to all those pictures!) Then all you have to do is make a great, imperishable speech, get out through the pressing crowds with a few score autographs, your clothes intact, your hands bruised, and back to the hotel—in time to see a few important people.

But the real work has just commenced—two or three, sometimes four hours of frenzied writing and editing of the next day's immortal mouthings so you can get something to the stenographers, so they can get something to the mimeograph machines, so they can get something to the reporters, so they can get something to their papers by deadline time. (And I quickly concluded that all deadlines were yesterday!) Finally sleep, sweet sleep, steals you away, unless you worry—which I do.

SOURCE: Adlai E. Stevenson, *Major Campaign Speeches*, 1952 (Random House, 1953), pp. xi–xii. Copyright © 1953 by Random House, Inc.

these debates are at a great advantage. They have to be quick on their feet, well rehearsed, and project a positive image. But these are not necessarily the qualities that make for a successful presidency.

IMPROVING ELECTIONS

Concern over how we choose presidents now centers on two issues: (1) the number, timing, and representativeness of presidential primaries, and (2) the role of the Electoral College, including the possibility that a presidential election might be thrown into the House of Representatives, with possibly controversial results.[51] Electoral reform focuses on encouraging greater turnout and changing the way we finance elections.

Reforming Presidential Primaries

The main argument in favor of presidential primaries is that they open the nominating process to more voters than do caucus or convention methods. Today the media play up the primary in every important state, and voters follow the races in other states as well as their own. In so doing, they can judge the candidates' political qualities: their abilities to organize campaigns, communicate through the media, stand up under pressure, avoid making mistakes (or recover if they do make them), adjust their appeals to shifting events and to different regions of the country, control their staffs as well as utilize them, and be decisive, articulate, resilient, humorous, informed, and ultimately successful in winning votes. In short, supporters claim, primaries test candidates on the very qualities they must exhibit in the presidency.[52]

Primaries are not only the most participatory but also the most representative way to choose our presidents. With millions of voters participating in more than 30 state primaries, more people take part than was the case before the use of primaries expanded in the 1970s.[53] As primaries take place, some aspirants drop out. With the number of entrants thus narrowed, the public focuses its attention on the remaining candidates. Despite Bob Dole's poor showing in the early primaries of 1996—losing New Hampshire to Buchanan and Arizona to Forbes—he rallied in March to win the nomination and the last 25 primaries without a loss. Only Pat Buchanan remained a candidate through the entire race.

Critics of primaries grant that more voters take part in primaries than in the caucus and convention methods of choosing delegates, but they question the quality of the participation. For one thing, supporters of the different candidates have no opportunity to deliberate together in public. Voters in primaries must depend largely on the news media and advertising for their information and basis for judgment. Voters in presidential primaries tend to be more influenced by candidates' personalities and media skills than their positions on vital issues.[54] Participation has been low in recent years. In the 1996 primaries, turnout was generally under 20 percent of the voting age population, and it declined as the primary season progressed and the field of candidates narrowed.[55]

Low levels of turnout in primaries open the possibility that extreme groups will have a disproportionate say; the "selectorate" replaces the electorate. In addition, candidates are forced to appeal to highly motivated voters, usually from the conservative wing of the Republican party and the liberal wing of the Democratic party. As a result, candidates often take ideologically extreme positions during the primaries.

The primary voting mechanism—each citizen casting one vote for one candidate, often in a multicandidate field—does not allow voters to express relative preferences. In 1976, for instance, a number of liberal Democratic candidates ran in the New Hampshire primary. Jimmy Carter was the only one seen as moderate or conservative. Liberal candidates split the liberal vote; Carter received the moderate and conservative vote. Thus, liberal voters had no opportunity to say they preferred any of the liberal candidates over Carter. Such an electoral system does not allow for rank ordering that may reflect voter preferences.[56]

Another criticism is that the primaries are badly scheduled and the primary season lasts too long.[57] Twenty states, including most southern states, usually hold their primaries on the same day—Super Tuesday—in March. The intention of this schedule is to enhance the position of the South in the nominating process, helping moderate candidates or candidates from the region.[58] Super Tuesday gave Bill Clinton's campaign a boost in 1992. Bob Dole's 1996 strategy was to capture the nomination early and deny his opponents any momentum. Dole had spent 70 percent of his primary spending limit by January. As political scientist Anthony Corrado said of Dole, "He was the only candidate who had developed campaign operations in every state and had made the ballot in every state with full slates of delegates in every district. He was best positioned to win a war of attrition."[59] Dole's strategy to capture the nomination early was enhanced by states moving their primary dates up. The most notable example of this was California, which moved its presidential primary from June to March in 1996. Dole carried California and won 25 straight primaries in the month of March.

Moreover, the length of the nominating campaign exhausts the candidates and tries the patience of the voters. Even with the compressed 1996 schedule, the "primary season" lasts roughly three months, and during that period primaries are held at least twice a month, and at times weekly. But the nomination campaign begins months and sometimes years in advance of the Iowa caucus and New Hampshire primary as candidates raise money, assemble their staff, position themselves, and make frequent visits to key primary states. In this grueling battle, victory might go to the candidate with the greatest stamina.[60]

Finally, some critics directly contradict those who say that primaries test the qualities needed to be president. Instead, candidates have only to win "the media game" in which they must be witty, resourceful, attractive, and articulate. These may not be the most important qualities to be a good president. Thomas Jefferson, Abraham Lincoln, and Harry Truman were able presidents, but they did not have great "media appeal." Critics are disturbed by the gap between the qualities required to carry primary contests and the qualities needed to govern: to organize an administration, get support on issues, make hard decisions, and deal with congressional leaders, governors, and mayors. Yet no system guarantees that the candidate who would make the best president will win.

Reforming the Nominating Process

What would the critics substitute for state presidential primaries? Some argue in favor of a *national presidential primary*. This would take the form of a single nationwide election, probably held in May or September, or separate state primaries held in all the states on the same day. Supporters contend that a one-shot national presidential primary (though a runoff might be necessary) would be simple, direct, and representative. It would cut down the wear and tear on candidates, and it would attract a large turnout because of intensive media coverage. Opponents argue that such a reform would make the present system even worse. It would enhance the role of showmanship and gamesmanship; and, being enormously expensive, it would hurt the chances of candidates who lack strong financial backing.[61] Generally, voting mechanisms that promote candidates who have won strong support and eliminate those with less support more accurately reflect voter preferences than mechanisms that give all candidates, no matter how poor their showing, a proportionate share of the delegates.

A more modest proposal is to hold *regional primaries*, possibly at two or three week intervals across the country—in other words, expand on the South's Super

Dan Wasserman. © 1996 Boston Globe. Distributed by Los Angeles Times Syndicate.

Tuesday idea. Regional primaries might bring more coherence to the process, encourage more emphasis on issues of regional concern, and also cut down on wear and tear. But such primaries would retain most of the disadvantages of the present system—especially the emphasis on money and media. Clearly, they would give an advantage to candidates from whatever region held the first primary, and this advantage would encourage regional candidates and might increase polarization among sections of the country.

A different proposal is to cut down drastically on the number of presidential primaries and make more use of the caucus system. The turnout of voters in the Iowa caucuses in recent elections shows that participation can be high, and the time participants spent discussing candidates and issues shows that such participation can be thoughtful and informed. In caucus states, candidates are less dependent on the media and more dependent on convincing political activists. By centering delegate selection in party meetings, the caucus system would also, some say, enhance the role of the party.[62]

Still another idea—used by Colorado for nominations to state officers and by Utah for nominations to federal and state office—would turn the process around. Beginning in May, local caucuses and then state conventions would be held in every state. They would then send delegates—a certain percentage of whom would be unpledged to any presidential candidate—to the national party conventions, which would be held in the summer. The national conventions would select two or three candidates to compete in a national primary to be held in September. In this Colorado plan, or national preprimary caucus and convention plan, voters registered by party would be allowed to vote for their party nominee in the September primaries.[63]

How we choose nominees for president is determined by a combination of party rules and state laws. Reformers agree that the current process is flawed but disagree over which aspects of it require change. Democrats have been most unhappy with the current system because, until 1992, it had produced nominees who did not fare well in the general election. Some blamed the rules for these defeats, but others expressed doubt that a change of rules would result in more successful Democratic candidates. The debate now will probably shift to the Republican party, where the race for the 2000 election may include a fight over nominating rules and procedures.

Reforming the Electoral College

The possibility of three viable presidential candidates in 1992 once again put reform of the Electoral College on the national agenda. Defenders say that opponents exaggerate the possible dangers; the system has not broken down so far, and it probably never will. This is the "if it ain't broke, don't fix it" school of thought. If the Electoral College is antipopular or antimajoritarian, so what? "The Electoral College avoids uncertainty when the popular vote is extremely close (as in 1960, 1968, and 1976) and prevents candidates with narrow appeal from making it to the White House."[64]

The most frequently proposed reform of the Electoral College system is *direct popular election* of the president. Presidents would be elected directly by the voters, just as governors are, and the Electoral College and individual electors would be abolished. Such proposals usually provide that, if no candidate receives at least 40 percent of the total popular vote, a *runoff election* would be held between the two contenders with the most votes. Supporters argue that direct election would give every voter the same weight in the presidential balloting in accordance with the one-person, one-vote doctrine. Winners would take on more legitimacy because their victories would reflect the will of the voters. The dangers and complications of the present electoral system would be replaced by a simple, visible, and decisive method.

Opponents contend that the plan would further undermine federalism, that it would encourage unrestrained majority rule and hence political extremism, and that it would hurt the smaller states, which would lose some of their present influence. Some also fear that the plan would make presidential campaigns more remote from the voters; candidates might stress television and give up their forays into shopping centers and city malls.[65] Some also fear that the plan would increase the reliance of presidential campaigns on television.

From time to time, Congress considers proposals for a constitutional amendment to elect presidents directly. Such proposals, however, seldom get far because of the strong opposition of various interests that believe they may be disadvantaged by such a change. Groups such as African Americans and farmers, for example, fear they might lose their swing vote power—their ability to make a difference in key states that may tip the Electoral College balance.

The failure of attempts to change the system of elections—like the failure of the attempt to change the nominating process—points to an important conclusion about procedural reform: Americans normally do not focus on procedures. Only after a major Electoral College crisis is any significant change likely. Then citizens will focus on problems of the electoral system, not on hypothetical problems discussed by political scientists and democratic theorists, but on the real problems facing them.

MONEY IN AMERICAN ELECTIONS

Election campaigns cost money, and the methods of obtaining the money have long been controversial. Campaign money can come from a variety of sources: a candidate's own wealth, political parties, interested individuals, or interest groups. Money is contributed to candidates for a variety of reasons, ranging from altruism to self-interest. **Interested money** is given by persons or groups in hopes of influencing the outcome of an election and subsequently influencing policy. Concern about campaign finance stems from the possibility that candidates, in their pursuit of campaign funds, will decide it is more important to represent their contributors rather than their conscience or the voters. The potential corruption that results from politicians' dependence on interested money concerns many observers of American politics.

Scandals about money influencing policy are not new. In 1925, responding to the Teapot Dome scandal in which a cabinet member was convicted of accepting bribes, Congress passed the Corrupt Practices Act, which required disclosure of campaign funds but was "written in such a way as to exempt virtually all of them [members of Congress] from its provisions."[66]

The 1972 Watergate scandal, the illegal break-in of Democratic party headquarters by persons associated with the Nixon campaign to steal campaign documents and plant listening devices, led to discoveries by news reporters and congressional investigators that large amounts of money from corporations and individuals were "laundered" in secret bank accounts outside the country for political and campaign purposes. Nixon's 1972 campaign spent more than $60 million, more than twice what it had expended in 1968. Investigators discovered that wealthy individuals made large contributions to influence the outcome of the election or secure ambassadorships and administrative appointments.

In the early 1990s, Charles Keating and his failed Lincoln Savings and Loan spotlighted the possibility that undue influence comes with large contributions. Keating asked five U.S. senators, all of whom had received substantial campaign contributions or other "perks" from him, to intervene on his behalf with federal bank regulators looking into his savings and loan business. These senators came to be called the Keating Five. The reelection campaign of California Senator Alan Cranston, in

What's Wrong with the Electoral College?

1. Critics contend that small states and large "swing" states are overrepresented.

2. The winner-takes-all aspect distorts equal representation of all voters, so that a candidate who receives fewer popular votes than an opponent can still be elected.

3. Electors can (and do) vote for a person other than the candidate for whom they were pledged to vote.

4. If no candidate wins a majority of the electoral vote, the issue is thrown into the House of Representatives, where each state delegation, no matter how large or small, has one vote, thus distorting the representative process even more.

THE CHINESE CONNECTION

The issue of foreign contributions in our electoral process came to a head in 1996 with the infusion of foreign money into the Democratic party's campaign treasury. The most visible source of the money was John Huang, a former Commerce Department official and fund-raiser for the Democratic National Committee. Huang had long been associated with the Lippo Group, a multi-billion-dollar empire run by the Riady family in Indonesia. The connections went back to international trade operations in Arkansas. The Riadys, who also have Chinese dealings, consistently contributed large sums of money to Bill Clinton and the Democrats. Following their contributions to his 1992 campaign, Clinton reversed his campaign stance and renewed the most-favored-nation trading status for China.

Huang devised a strategy, the National Asian Pacific American Campaign Plan, to raise $7 million from Asian Americans by offering rewards to the largest donors, including meetings with President Clinton. This strategy led to at least $1.2 million in improper donations, which were later returned by the Democratic National Committee. Huang illegally took donations from foreign corporations and from people who were neither American citizens or foreign citizens living legally in the United States.[*]

A second source was Charlie Trie, owner of a Chinese restaurant in Arkansas that Bill Clinton frequented as governor. Trie had links with the Chinese government and John Huang. Together Huang and Trie raised hundreds of thousands of dollars during the 1996 campaign, including $639,000 returned by Clinton's legal defense fund. Whether due to his longtime association with President Clinton or his fund raising, Trie had frequent access to Mr. Clinton, visiting the White House 23 times in Clinton's first term.[**]

Republicans in Congress urged Attorney General Janet Reno to assign an independent counsel to investigate these contributions, but she maintained that nothing illegal had taken place. A Senate investigating committee pursued the investigation.

Republican party officals also admitted accepting contributions from questionable foreign sources during the 1996 campaign. They returned $122,000 contributed by a Hong Kong company through its American subsidiary. This same firm was reported to have loaned over $2 million to the National Policy Forum, a think tank associated with the 1994 Republican campaign.[†]

John Huang.

[*]Tim Weiner and David E. Sanger. "Democrats Hoped to Raise $7 Million from Asians in U.S.," *The New York Times*, December 28, 1996, p. A1.

[**]Tim Weiner, "FBI Looks at Whether China Funneled Money to Democrats," *The New York Times*, February 14, 1997, p. A21.

[†]Leslie Wayne, "Hong Kong Money Returned by GOP," *The New York Times*, May 9, 1997.

particular, had clearly benefited from the more than $1 million Keating had contributed to a voter registration and get-out-the-vote effort run by the senator's son.

The high costs of television advertising diminish the ability of challengers to mount visible campaigns. Declining competition in our democracy is explained in part by the difficulty challengers have in raising money. Incumbents have a substantial advantage in raising interested money from wealthy individuals and **political action committees (PACs)**, the political arms of interest groups that are allowed to make political contributions. Hence it is not only the source of campaign money that is a problem but the pattern of unequal distribution as well.

Efforts to Reform

Long campaigns—especially presidential campaigns—have required big money for some time. Neil O. Staebler, who observed politics for more than half a century as a state committee member, a state chair, a national committee member, a member of Congress, and eventually a member of the Federal Election Commission, commented, "Money corruption has been present in politics for 170 or 180 years. We've been actively working at it since Teddy Roosevelt started back in 1907. But for sixty years practically nothing useful was done. . . . Politics was very much the art of figuring out what you could get away with."[67]

In the past, reformers have tried three basic strategies to prevent abuse in political contributions: (1) imposing limitations on giving, receiving, and spending political money; (2) requiring public disclosure of the sources and uses of political money; and (3) giving governmental subsidies to presidential candidates, campaigns, and parties, including incentive arrangements. Recent campaign finance laws have tended to use all three strategies for dealing with a problem that sometimes seems unsolvable.

THE FEDERAL ELECTION CAMPAIGN ACT   In 1971 Congress passed two significant laws dealing with campaign funding. The Federal Election Campaign Act (FECA) limits amounts that candidates for federal office can spend on media advertising, requires the disclosure of the sources of campaign funds as well as how they were spent, and requires political action committees active in federal campaigns to register with the government and report all major contributions and expenditures. This 1971 law also provided a tax checkoff that allows taxpayers, by checking a box on their income tax form, to direct $1 of general revenue to a fund to subsidize presidential campaigns.

POST-WATERGATE REFORMS   Further campaign funding reform was prompted by Watergate and widespread public concern about money in elections. In 1974 Congress passed and President Gerald Ford signed the most sweeping campaign reform measure in U.S. history. These amendments to the Federal Election Campaign Act established realistic limits on contributions and spending, tightened disclosure, and provided for public financing of presidential campaigns. The amount of the public subsidy rises with inflation.

The law had to be extensively amended after the 1976 *Buckley v Valeo* decision, which overturned several of its provisions on grounds that they violated the First Amendment.[68] However, the basic outline of the act, emphasizing limitations on contributions and full and open disclosure of all fund-raising activities by candidates for federal office, remained unchanged.[69] Later amendments sought to encourage volunteer activities and party building by permitting national political parties, corporations, labor unions, and individuals to give unlimited amounts to state parties in so-called "soft money." These funds circumvent the more limited and disclosed "hard money" sources in federal campaigns.

The public subsidy of candidates has worked rather well. All presidential candidates except wealthy self-financed candidates have accepted the voluntary limitations on "hard money" spending that come with partial public financing of presidential campaigns. The three exceptions are John Connally, who sought the Republican nomination in 1980, independent H. Ross Perot in his 1992 race, and Steve Forbes, who sought the Republican nomination in 1996. Even Ronald Reagan, who opposed public financing, accepted public subsidies in all three of his major presidential campaigns. But the system is not without problems. The number of taxpayers checking off on their income tax forms that they want $1 of their taxes to be directed to the presidential campaign fund has been declining,

The Federal Election Campaign Act, 1971, and Amendments, 1974

- Establishes a Federal Election Commission appointed by the president with the advice and consent of the Senate to regulate the campaign financing of candidates for president, senator, and representative.

- Requires all candidates to designate one principal campaign committee to report all contributions and expenditures.

- Provides for public financing of presidential general election campaigns (with funds from the tax checkoff) and for partial public financing (on a matching basis) of presidential nominating campaigns.

- Provides for subsidies to the two national parties for their convention expenses and to any minor party that polled 5 percent of the total vote in the previous presidential election.

- Limits spending by candidates for presidential nominations (on a state-by-state basis and in total) and in the presidential general elections for those candidates who accept public funding.

- Limits the amounts that national parties may spend on presidential campaigns and on individual congressional and senatorial campaigns.

- Sets a limit of $1,000 on the amount that any individual can give to a candidate for the U.S. Senate or for the U.S. House of Representatives in the primary election, a limit of $1,000 per candidate in the general election, and a limit of $5,000 per candidate per election ($5,000 in primary and $5,000 in general election) for multicandidate organizations (political action committees).

- Sets an overall limitation of $25,000 on the amount that any individual can donate to all candidates for federal office in an election cycle (no similar limitation applicable to political action committees).

- Sets no limit on the amount of their own money candidates can spend on their campaign.

- Sets no limit on the amount that individuals or groups can spend independently (that is, on activities not coordinated with a candidate's campaign).

although enough did so to cover all the costs of the 1996 elections.[70] The Federal Election Commission, designed to oversee the process, is prone to unending partisan deadlock, and in recent years the commission has not been given sufficient funds to maintain its full disclosure activity.

THE UNSOLVED PROBLEM OF SOFT MONEY The most serious problem with the presidential campaign finance system is **soft money**—funds given to state and local parties by political parties, individuals, or PACs for voter registration drives and party mailings. No limits are set on the amount of such contributions. The money is called "soft" because federal law does not require disclosure of its source or use. Although soft money is supposed to benefit only state and local parties, it influences federal elections. Presidential candidates in both parties have made raising soft money a high priority. In 1988 at least 375 people contributed $100,000 each in soft money to the Democratic and Republican parties.[71] Soft money has risen in presidential campaigns from roughly $19 million in 1980 and 1984, to $45 million in 1988, to $66 million in 1992.[72] In 1996 as much as $250 million in soft money was spent in roughly equal amounts by the two major parties.[73]

One reason for the dramatic rise in soft money expenditure resulted from a case involving the Colorado Republican party that was decided by the Supreme Court in 1995. The decision was interpreted to mean that parties could spend an unlimited amount of money on advertisements as long as the advertisements did not explicitly call for a vote for or against a specific candidate.[74]

Another part of the explanation for the surge in soft money spending is that there are individuals and groups willing to make large contributions to the parties. Bill Clinton's 1996 campaign raised serious questions about the role of foreign contributors and opportunities to meet with the president at the White House as inducements for giving large soft money donations to the party. If the soft money loophole is not closed, it is likely to undermine most other FECA provisions, including disclosure requirements, spending limitations, and contribution limitations.

Consequences of Current Campaign Financing

Complicated as it is to regulate how presidential campaigns are financed, it is more difficult to get consensus about what, if anything, should be done about congressional campaigns. The problem is easy to identify. Dramatically escalating costs, a growing dependence on PAC money, decreasing visibility and competitiveness of challengers (especially in the House), the ability of wealthy individuals to fund their own campaigns, and the danger of large contributions altering election outcomes are all related to current campaign financing practices.

RISING COSTS OF CAMPAIGNS Since the FECA became law in 1972, total expenditures by candidates for the House have more than doubled after controlling for inflation, and they have risen even more in Senate elections (see Table 12–1). Television advertising is expensive, limiting the field of challengers to those who have sufficient time or desire to spend more than a year raising money. The American ideal that anyone—a person from humble beginnings or of modest wealth—can seek and hold high public office is no longer true. And rising costs mean incumbents spend more time raising funds and therefore less time legislating and representing their districts.

Candidates for federal office and related party activity spent an estimated $2.7 billion in 1996, of which $765 million was spent on congressional campaigns. These are big sums, but they must be put into perspective. The $2.7 billion spent on national elections is but a fraction of a percent of the total cost of government. One Trident submarine, for example, costs hundreds of millions of dollars. In the 1988

Hard and Soft Money, 1984–1996

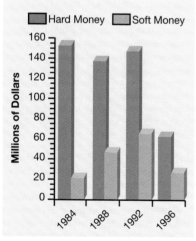

SOURCE: Federal Elections Commission, "FEC Reports Major Increase in Party Activity for 1995–1996," Press Release, March 19, 1997, pp. 1–2.

TABLE 12–1

Average Campaign Expenditures of Candidates for the House of Representatives, 1988–1996

| | Amount Spent (rounded in thousands) | | |
	Incumbent	Challenger	Open Seat
Republican			
1988	441.8	65.5	175.3
1990	437.7	70.5	185.4
1992	532.2	94.3	162.8
1994	512.5	140.7	229.4
1996	805.0	111.1	216.3
Democrat			
1988	413.4	80.0	216.7
1990	449.2	64.0	226.5
1992	558.6	68.0	176.9
1994	606.8	78.3	207.3
1996	625.1	171.1	230.1

SOURCE: Federal Elections Commission, "Congressional Fundraising and Spending Up Again in 1996," Press Release, April 14, 1997, p. 9.

presidential campaign, the candidates collectively spent around $500 million. Spending was down in the nomination phase of the 1992 election, but during the general election phase it increased largely due to the lavish media campaign waged by Ross Perot, who spent roughly $65 million from his own vast fortune,[75] but in 1996 Perot financed his campaign with the $29 million given him in public funding.

DECLINING COMPETITION Unless something is done to help finance challengers, incumbents will continue to have the advantage in seeking reelection. Challengers in both parties are typically underfunded. House Republican challengers averaged $111,100 in spending in 1996. In today's world of expensive campaigns, candidates are invisible if they can only spend $100,000 to $150,000. Democratic challengers did somewhat better (see Table 12–1). Incumbents in both parties can and do spend much more, and if they feel seriously challenged, they can raise even more money.

The high cost of campaigns dampens competition by discouraging individuals from running for office. Potential challengers look at the fund-raising advantages enjoyed by incumbents—at incumbents' campaign chests, which sometimes have $1 million before the campaign even starts, and at the time it will take for them to raise enough money just to launch a minimal campaign—and then decide to direct their energies elsewhere. Moreover, unlike incumbents, who are being paid while campaigning and fund raising, most challengers have to support themselves and their families for the duration of the campaign, which for the House and Senate now is roughly two years.

INCREASING DEPENDENCE ON PACS AND WEALTHY DONORS Where does the money come from to finance these expensive election campaigns? For most House incumbents the answer is political action committees (PACs). In 1996, for instance, 174 of the 387 incumbents seeking reelection raised more money from PACs than from individuals.[76] Senators are somewhat less dependent on PACs in the percentage of their total fund raising, but because they spend so much more, they raise even more money from PACs than House incumbents do. Challengers for seats in either chamber receive little from PACs because PACs do not want to offend politicians in power, and politicians in power want to stay in office. This marriage of interests has meant that congressional incumbents court PAC contributions, and PACs are happy to oblige.

Politicians also turn to individual donors who can contribute $500 or $1,000 to their campaigns. Persons who make such contributions expect that legislators they have helped win will respond to their concerns. Given congressional incumbents' preoccupation with reelection, contributions from PACs or large individual contributions are likely to be remembered.

To be sure, PACs and individuals give political money for many reasons. But the American Medical Association's PAC, the realtors' PAC, the foreign auto dealers' PAC, the public employees' PAC, and hundreds of other interest groups share something in common: They want certain laws to be passed or repealed, certain funds appropriated, or certain administrative decisions rendered. At a minimum, they want access to officeholders, a chance to talk with members before key votes.

Defenders of PACs point out that there is no demonstrable relationship between contributions and roll call votes. But influence in the legislative process depends on *access* to staff and members of Congress, and most agree that campaign contributions give the donors unusual access. PACs influence the legislative process in other ways as well. Their access helps them structure the legislative agenda with friendly legislators and influence the drafting of legislation or amendments to existing bills. These are all advantages that others do not have.

Candidates' Personal Wealth Campaign finance legislation cannot constitutionally restrict rich candidates—the Rockefellers, the Kennedys, the Perots—from giving heavily to their own campaigns. Big money makes a big difference, and wealthy candidates can afford to spend big money. In presidential politics this advantage can be most meaningful in the period before the primaries begin. There may be no constitutional way to limit how much money people can spend on their own campaigns.

Independent Expenditures Similarly, current finance laws do not constrain independent expenditures by groups or individuals who are separate from political candidates. This loophole has been permitted by the Supreme Court on free speech grounds. Groups sympathetic to, but independent of, candidates are allowed to raise and spend funds to help elect them or to defeat their opponents. For example, in 1984 Michael Goland, a Californian, spent $1,100,740 as an independent expenditure to defeat Illinois Senator Charles Percy.[77] As long as there is no collusion between the independent spender and the candidate, an individual or PAC can spend an unlimited amount of money for or against a candidate. Independent expenditures are not soft money; they are fully disclosed. Soft money is given to state parties for "party building." It is not limited, and if state law does not require disclosure, it is not disclosed.

Issue Advertising The 1996 election saw a surge in a new form of campaign activity called **issue advertising**. Labor unions and business organizations spent large but undisclosed amounts of money similar to independent expenditures in that it is not limited. In a case involving the Colorado Republican party, the Supreme Court decided that as long as the ads do not explicitly call for the election or defeat of a specific candidate, interest groups and political parties may spend what they wish on them.[78] The advent of issue advertising in the late 1990s means that campaign finance reform will be of little consequence if it does not take into account this new way for parties and interest groups to influence elections.

Some also contend the Federal Election Campaign Act (FECA) fails because it provides vast sums for presidential campaigns and relatively little—mainly for convention costs—to the national parties. Helping candidates at the expense of parties, it is said, intensifies the growing trend toward more personalized, fragmented, and individualized politics. Some favor greater subsidies to parties until they can be self-supporting. It was in response to the needs of parties that the soft money exemption was created.

Prospects for Reform

In his first few months in office, President Clinton proposed comprehensive campaign finance reform—including partial public financing of congressional elections, limitations on the amount of money congressional candidates could accept from PACs, and virtual elimination of soft money in presidential elections. Not surprisingly, Democrats and Republicans in Congress objected and quickly embarked on their own campaign finance reform agendas. House Democrats were less eager for change than Clinton was, and the president was forced to downplay his campaign promise for change.

Clinton also had to worry about Ross Perot's frequent charge that "running up and down the halls of Congress all day, everyday, are the organized special interests who have the money that makes it possible to buy the television time to campaign to get reelected next year."[79] Clinton thus found himself in a crossfire, with his campaign promises and Perot's rhetoric coming at him from one side and Democratic party leaders in Congress from the other.

Public disgust with the excesses of the 1996 elections, including foreign money, letting wealthy contributors spend a night in the Lincoln Bedroom of the White House, unlimited and unchecked use of issue advertising, and the willingness of both parties to raise and spend large amounts of soft money, may provide enough pressure for Congress to pass campaign finance legislation. The same disincentives that stopped legislative action in the past remain. For the 535 members of Congress, the current system works rather well. They won under the "rules" now in place, and they know that they have tremendous advantages under the present campaign finance system. Winning reelection is one of the most central motives of incumbents, so it will take a major public outcry for them to change a campaign finance system that benefits them in a significant way.

INTERPRETING THE 1992, 1994, AND 1996 ELECTIONS

Even though he won election in 1992 by a margin of only 5 percent of the total popular vote, Bill Clinton swept to a landslide victory in the Electoral College. Clinton ran as a "different kind of Democrat" in 1992, arguing that he was different and more moderate politically than Walter Mondale and Michael Dukakis. Part of his strategy was to avoid the "liberal Democrat" label that Bush and Reagan had pinned on Democratic nominees. Exit polls demonstrated that Clinton succeeded in recapturing more than half the Democrats who had voted for George Bush in 1988.[80]

In 1994 Republicans won stunning victories in contests for Congress, governor, and state legislatures across most of the country. Democrats lost control of both houses of Congress for the first time since 1954; several prominent Democrats, including Speaker Tom Foley, were defeated. Republicans won control of governorships that had been Democratic in New York, Texas, Pennsylvania, Tennessee, Alabama, and Idaho. Republicans gained an additional 450 seats in state legislatures and achieved control of 15 state legislative chambers. Part of the explanation for the Republican success was a very good set of candidates, often well financed.

Republicans also capitalized on the strong antigovernment sentiment in the country. Much of this anger was directed at Congress because of the check-cashing

Millionaire Steve Forbes demonstrated the easy way to finance a presidential campaign—just reach into your own pocket.

Current law permits contributions from subsidiaries of foreign corporations as long as they are directed by American employees and the money does not come from the foreign corporate parent. In the 1996 campaign, American subsidiaries of foreign concerns gave millions of dollars to both political parties. Republicans received the most, but Democrats were not far behind. Charges about the role of foreign contributions led to congressional hearings and mobilized campaign finance reformers.

SOURCE: Robert Hershey, Jr., "Panel Chairman Says Inquiry into Fund Raising Is Expanding," *The New York Times*, February 17, 1997, p. A12.

scandal, corruption in the House Post Office, and a sense that the institution was not working. Republicans were successful in arguing that change was needed because of the 40-year period of Democratic dominance in Congress.

The shift to Republicans was especially pronounced in the South, which had tended to vote Republican for president in recent elections but remained Democratic in Congress. Republicans changed that in 1994, picking up a net gain of 2 Republican senators and 16 House members in the 11 former confederate states. Republicans also enjoyed a net gain of 3 governors in this once solidly Democratic region.

In a remarkable turnaround, Bill Clinton came from a notable rejection of his party in the 1994 election to a landslide victory in 1996. Clinton seized the middle of the political spectrum and linked Bob Dole to the unpopular Speaker Gingrich. The issue that helped him most in this objective was the protracted budget battle in which the government was shut down twice for several days. The Republicans also committed the error of proposing Medicare cuts that were deeper than any proposed by Clinton, an issue used by Clinton in the general election campaign to mobilize senior citizens to vote for him. Clinton also used such issues as gun control, welfare reform, and environmental deregulation to demonstrate the "extreme" position of Gingrich's House majority.

Dole's general election campaign failed to generate much momentum, even after he resigned his Senate seat and reversed his long-held view that deficit reduction was more important than tax cuts, promising an across-the-board 15 percent tax cut. None of these moves changed the polling numbers much.

Clinton started his media blitz in the summer, linking Dole to the Gingrich Congress. Dole was unable to run counter ads because he had spent his preconvention money in the primaries. Both parties spent large amounts of soft money in 1996, raising questions about whether the post-Watergate campaign finance reforms were of any consequence. Clinton's fund raising was more controversial than Dole's because of charges that he had raised large sums from foreign nationals and had granted access to White House sleepovers and coffees to large contributors.

POLITICS ONLINE

Rock The Vote

In 1990 people from the recording industry organized Rock the Vote to fight "a wave of political attacks on freedom of speech and artistic expresssion":

www.rockthevote.org/INSIDERTV/155/15_5.html

Millions watched their commercials that encouraged young people to vote. What is less known is that Rock the Vote has become involved in legislation on issues like health care reform and in support of Americorps, the national service program for young adults. Rock the Vote uses its home page not only to provide information on public issues but to register voters as well. Perhaps some of the readers of this book registered to vote through Rock the Vote home page:

http://www.rockthevote.org

The Internet is a wonderful resource for current information on campaigns and elections, polling information, and even political jokes:

http://www.abc.com/pi

More good places to go are:

www.newpolitics.com

www.agora.stm.it/politic

members.aol.com/govtdc/pol.html

SUMMARY

1. Our electoral system is based on winner-takes-all rules, with typically single-member district or single-officeholder arrangements. These rules encourage a moderate, two-party system. That we have fixed and staggered terms of office adds predictability to our electoral system.

2. The Electoral College is the means by which presidents are actually elected. To win a state's electoral votes, a candidate must have a plurality of votes in that state. Except in two states, the winner takes all. Thus candidates cannot afford to lose the popular vote in the most populous states. The Electoral College also gives disproportionate power to the smallest states and has the potential for defeat of the popular vote winner. Reform efforts have been unsuccessful because the system has worked in the past.

3. Many congressional, state, and local races are not seriously contested. The extent to which a campaign is likely to be hotly contested varies with the importance of the office and the chance a challenger has of winning. Senate races are more likely to be contested, though most incumbents win.

4. The race for the presidency actually takes place in three stages: winning enough delegate support in presidential primaries and caucuses to secure the nomination, campaigning at the national party convention, and mobilizing voters for a win in the Electoral College.

5. Even though presidential nominations today are usually decided weeks or months before the national party conventions, these conventions still have an important role in setting the parties' direction, unifying their ranks, and firing up enthusiasm. Speakers who are highlighted are positioned to pursue nominations in future years.

6. The present presidential selection system is under criticism because of its length and expense and because it seems to test candidates for media skills less needed in the White House than the ability to govern, including the capacity to form coalitions and make hard decisions.

7. Because large campaign contributors are suspected of improperly influencing public officials, Congress has long sought to regulate political contributions. The main approaches of reform have been: (1) imposing limitations on giving, receiving, and spending money; (2) requiring public disclosure of the sources and uses of political money; and (3) giving governmental subsidies to presidential candidates, campaigns, and parties, including incentive arrangements. Present regulation includes all three approaches.

FURTHER READING

LARRY M. BARTELS, *Presidential Primaries and the Dynamics of Public Choice* (Princeton University Press, 1988).

JUDITH A. BEST, *The Choice of the People: Debating the Electoral College* (Rowman and Littlefield, 1996).

EARL BLACK AND MERLE BLACK, *The Vital South: How Presidents Are Elected* (Harvard University Press, 1992).

ALAN EHRENHALT, *The United States of Ambition: Politicians, Power, and the Pursuit of Office* (Times Books, 1991).

THOMAS FERGUSON, *Golden Rule: The Investment Theory of Party Competition and the Logic of Money-Driven Political Systems* (University of Chicago Press, 1995).

LINDA L. FOWLER AND ROBERT D. MCCLURE, *Political Ambition: Who Decides to Run for Congress* (Yale University Press, 1989).

THOMAS GAIS, *Improper Influence: Campaign Finance Law, Political Interest Groups, and the Problem of Equality* (University of Michigan Press, 1996).

PAUL S. HERRNSON, *Congressional Elections: Campaigning at Home and in Washington* (Congressional Quarterly Press, 1995).

GARY C. JACOBSON, *The Politics of Congressional Elections*, 4th ed. (Longman, 1997).

MARION R. JUST, ANN N. CRIGLER, DEAN E. ALGER, TIMOTHY E. COOK, MONTAGUE KERN, AND DARREL M. WEST, *Crosstalk: Citizens, Candidates and the Media in a Presidential Campaign* (University of Chicago Press, 1996).

JOHN KESSEL, *Presidential Campaign Politics*, 4th ed. (Brooks Cole, 1992).

JONATHAN S. KRASNO, *Challengers, Competition, and Reelection: Comparing Senate and House Elections* (Yale University Press, 1994).

ROBERT D. LOEVY, *The Flawed Path to the Presidency, 1992: Unfairness and Inequality in the Presidential Selection Process* (State University of New York Press, 1994).

DAVID B. MAGLEBY AND CANDICE J. NELSON, *The Money Chase: Congressional Campaign Finance Reform* (Brookings Institution, 1990).

NELSON W. POLSBY AND AARON B. WILDAVSKY, *Presidential Elections: Contemporary Strategies of American Politics*, 9th ed. (Chatham House, 1995).

GERALD M. POMPER ET AL., *The Election of 1992* (Chatham House, 1993).

SAMUEL L. POPKIN, *The Reasoning Voter: Communication and Persuasion in Presidential Campaigns* (University of Chicago Press, 1991).

FRANK J. SORAUF, *Inside Campaign Finance: Myths and Realities* (Yale University Press, 1992).

JAMES A. THURBER AND CANDICE J. NELSON, EDS., *Campaigns and Elections American Style* (Westview Press, 1995).

STEPHEN J. WAYNE, *The Road to the White House, 1996: The Politics of Presidential Elections*, 5th ed. (St. Martin's Press, 1996).

See also *Public Opinion Quarterly, American Journal of Politics,* and *American Political Science Review.*

13

The Media
and American Politics

*A*mericans have more ways to find out what is going on in the world than do citizens of any other democracy. We have widespread access to television. We get constant around-the-clock news. The Internet provides millions with a wide range of news options and even permits individuals to interact with journalists and news makers. Our magazines reflect all kinds of opinions and perspectives and promote every conceivable cause. We have some of the world's greatest newspapers. Although we have experienced some censorship of the news during wartime, with very few exceptions people in this country are free to say or write whatever they wish.

The 1996 presidential election presents an example of the importance of the media as a source of information. Nearly three out of four voters report getting news about the campaign from television (down from 82 percent in 1992); nearly 20 percent got news about the presidential election from radio; and 10 percent went online to learn about the campaign.[1] As these numbers suggest, voters were using more than one source to learn about Bill Clinton, Bob Dole, Ross Perot, and the hundreds of state and local candidates and ballot propositions.

When interviewed after the campaign, 75 percent of voters reported that they felt they had learned enough about the candidates to make an "informed choice" on election day. Despite the large amounts spent by Dole, Clinton, and Perot on advertising and airtime, voters found news coverage a much better way to get information about the candidates than paid advertising; 77 percent found news reports more informative, while 16 percent favored commercials; roughly two-thirds or more of all voters thought the press had been fair to Bob Dole and Bill Clinton.[2]

Despite the ready access to our media and its wide variety, Americans are quick to criticize the media. James Fallows, a journalist himself, begins his book on the media by saying:

> Americans have never been truly fond of their press. Through the last decade, however, their disdain for the media establishment has reached new levels. Americans believe that the news media have become too arrogant, cynical, scandal-minded, and destructive.[3]

How often have you or your friends blamed the media for the limited information on issues during elections, criticized the frenzy that surrounded the O. J. Simpson trial, or denounced the "if it bleeds it leads" mentality of local television news? Polling data reveal that people criticize the press for being biased, negative, critical, prone to sensationalism, and for focusing too much on private matters. The public gave press coverage of the 1996 election an average grade of C, with only 29 percent giving As or Bs; 47 percent felt that the press had too much influence on the election, though clear majorities said that the press was "fair" to both candidates.[4] People even proposed regulating the free press because of excesses in some television shows and other media outlets.

Our free press is perhaps our most important guarantee that our government is not only democratic but honest. This is not to say that press coverage of politics and government in the United States is without problems. Our Constitution guarantees a free press, not a responsible one. People often blame the media for many of our ills—for increasing tension between the races, for biased attacks upon public officials, for sleaze and sensationalism, and for being more interested in making money than in conveying unbiased information. Media bashing has become something of a national pastime, and there is considerable merit to all of these charges.

Some Key Terms

When we refer to "the media," what do we mean? Years ago the only means of communication to large numbers of people was through the press. With the advent of radio and television, we adopted the term "mass media," a general term that refers to television, newspapers, and magazines.

- *Media*—a general term that refers to all forms of communication. The term "the media" is an abstraction that often lacks precision.
- *Mass media*—communication by the media on a large scale.
- *Media event*—activity undertaken to generate news coverage and publicity that would not be done if news reporters or cameras were not present.
- *The press*—the news media, in popular language often limited to print media.
- *News media*—print and broadcast coverage of the news.
- *Journalist*—a news reporter who writes news for the press or broadcasts news via electronic media.
- *Fourth estate*—the press and news media in general. In medieval Europe the three estates were the nobility, clergy, and commons; news reporters have been called the fourth estate because of their influence on government.
- *Fourth branch of government*—again the press and news media in general. The news media are sometimes referred to as supplementing the three traditional branches of government—executive, judicial, and legislative.

Many in the media even agree with some of them.[5] But the media may simply be an abstraction for those who prefer criticizing the messenger to avoid dealing with the message. Comments like, "It is the media's fault that we have lost our social values," or "The media's preoccupation with negative traits of candidates turns Americans off to politics," are overly broad assertions. The media do have certain tendencies that affect American politics and public policy, but, as we shall see, far more problems are blamed on the media than they deserve.

No discussion of American politics today is complete without assessing the role of the media. The media provide the major source of information, even for policy makers. A free press is also essential for the maintenance of democracy. This chapter examines the media's role in American politics, beginning with the factors promoting the rise of the media as an independent force, continuing with a discussion of the media's influence on each of us as citizens and on election campaigns, and culminating in an appraisal of the media's role in the governance of our nation.

THE INFLUENCE OF THE MEDIA

Is the influence of the media in politics real or a myth? The media, in particular the print media, have been called "the other government," "the fourth estate," and "the fourth branch of government."[6] Evidence that the mass media influence our culture and politics is plentiful. Before we can examine that influence, however, we must define some terms. The **mass media** are means of communication that reach the mass public; they include newspapers and magazines, radio, television (broadcast, cable, and satellite), films, recordings, and books.[7] The news media emphasize news, but the distinctions are not clear-cut. Some media critics contend there is now a combination of the two—a medium called "infotainment" that uses entertainment techniques to present the news. As evidence, they point to evening news programs featuring "happy talk" between news anchors, to prime-time news-magazine programs such as *60 Minutes, Primetime, 20/20*, and talk shows with hosts like Rush Limbaugh, Larry King, and Oprah Winfrey.

By definition, the mass media disseminate their message to a large and often heterogeneous audience at the same moment. Because they must have broad appeal, their messages are often simplified, stereotyped, and formulaic. Certainly the mass media are big business. They live off high audience ratings and substantial advertising revenues, which are essential to their "bottom line" of big profits. But does profit spell political clout? Two factors are important here: the media's pervasiveness and their role as a linking mechanism.

The Pervasiveness of Television

Almost all Americans see television every day, and most homes have at least two sets, each turned on for an average of seven hours per day. While television is primarily an entertainment medium, most Americans use it for news as well. Three out of four Americans watch television news regularly.[8]

Television, perhaps more than any single other innovation, has changed the character of American politics. It provides instant news from around the globe, permitting citizens and leaders alike to observe, firsthand, a hostage crisis in Peru or a bombing in Hebron. Television has elevated the role played by the president in both domestic and international politics. Our electoral campaigns now focus much more on image and appearance. Successful candidates must be able to communicate with voters through this medium. Campaign managers must deal with the implications of television and even worry about the strength of railings at presidential campaign stops or the visual backdrop for a videoclip intended for the evening news. Politicians increasingly communicate with citizens through what are

Television brought the pain of war in Bosnia into American living rooms with scenes of the carnage in a Sarajevo marketplace following a Serbian mortar attack. As a result of the public outcry, President Clinton ordered the bombing of Serbian gun emplacements around the city, which forced the withdrawal of all heavy weapons outside a safety zone.

called "sound bites," 15-to-45-second segments for the television or radio news. Politicians who are skilled in short and direct communication do well with this type of news coverage. Increasingly, our politics and our elections are influenced by 30-second commercials. Groups advocating one position or another—on health care reform, trade agreements, affirmative action—use paid advertising on television to influence the public, who may in turn influence decision makers.

For several decades the three network evening news programs captured more than 90 percent of the audience for television news, and national news was available only at set times in the morning and early evening hours. Today many options exist for broadcast news information, and Americans rely more and more on these alternative sources. One-quarter of Americans say they are regular viewers of CNN, while two out of five say they regularly watch network prime-time news-magazine shows.[9]

The Rise of Talk Radio

Television has not displaced radio. On the contrary, radio continues to reach more American households than does television. Only one household in a hundred does not have a radio. Nine out of ten Americans listen to the radio every day.[10] Cars and radios seem to go together.

Americans get more than "the facts" from radio. They also get analysis of the news. Many people will not decide "what to think" before they have heard from their favorite commentators. Radio commentators and talk show hosts like Rush Limbaugh, Michael Reagan, Oliver North, and G. Gordon Liddy have committed followers. Talk show hosts have their own home pages on the World Wide Web and provide around-the-clock conversation. Some hosts are noted for their extreme views and conspiracy theories. In 1996 they were the source of personal attacks on presidential candidates, notably President Bill Clinton.[11] Some commentators themselves become important political figures, as Patrick J. Buchanan did in 1992 and 1996; his regular participation on CNN's *Crossfire* increased his public visibility before he ran for the presidency.

The debate between Vice-President Al Gore and Ross Perot on the merits of the North American Free Trade Agreement (NAFTA) on *Larry King Live* was watched by 11.2 million people and played a big part in winning public approval of NAFTA.

Talk Shows: The Newest Forum

Every day, around the clock, in homes all over the United States, talk shows provide a kind of 1990s American town meeting. With an audience of millions, hosts, hostesses, and their guests analyze the day's news events and vent their feelings from all political perspectives. Radio and television are today's major political arenas.

Presidential candidates appeared frequently on television and radio talk shows during the 1992 and 1996 campaigns, and televised talk shows continued to be major media events after the election. In the 1996 tug-of-war between Congress and the president over balancing the budget, leaders of both sides appeared frequently on the *News Hour with Jim Lehrer* and the Sunday morning news panels. Throughout the primary and the election campaigns that year, the airwaves were filled with talk, talk, talk. Phone-in radio and TV shows give ordinary citizens a way to react to events and offer advice to the candidates, providing a give-and-take of political opinion reminiscent of the direct democracy of the town meeting.

Talk radio has been a major growth medium in the last decade and is now the most listened-to AM radio format in most major media markets.[12] Conservatives and Republicans have made widespread use of talk radio, with the exception of Bob Dole, who largely shunned it during his unsuccessful 1996 campaign. In contrast, Newt Gingrich and others active in the Republican resurgence in the U.S. House of Representatives made widespread use of talk radio. The television talk format is perhaps most closely identified with Larry King, who provided the announcement of Ross Perot's candidacy for the presidency in 1992 and the debate between Vice-President Al Gore and Ross Perot over the North American Free Trade Agreement in November 1993.

The Continuing Importance of Newspapers

Recent technological advances have created intense competition for advertising revenues and have contributed to sweeping changes in the manner in which news is transmitted and received. Satellites, cable television, computers, the Internet, and videocassette recorders (VCRs) make vast amounts of political information available 24 hours a day; satellites eliminate the obstacles of time and distance; computers increase the volume of information that can be stored and retrieved; and cable channels and VCRs increase viewing options.

Despite vigorous competition from the broadcast media, many Americans still read newspapers. Newspaper circulation has held steady at about 63 million nationwide—or about one copy for every four people—for the past 20 years. Another indication of the media's pervasiveness is the rise of national newspapers. *The Wall Street Journal*, with a circulation of nearly 1.8 million, has long acted as a national newspaper with a specialization in business and finance. Other national newspapers with more general interests have also emerged. *USA Today*, created in 1982 by the Gannett Corporation, now has a circulation of nearly 1.5 million. In addition, *The New York Times* has a national edition that is read by more than 1 million people (see Table 13–1).

The World Wide Web

Yet another example of the multiplicity of media available to many Americans is the Internet or World Wide Web. Humble beginnings as a Pentagon research project in the 1970s blossomed in the 1990s into an international phenomenon. By

1996 there were more than 30 million home pages, including one for this book, which you can find at the following address: http://www.prenhall.com/burns.

Evidence of the widespread use of the Web is that on one Web directory alone in 1996 there were 641 candidates for Congress listed, with others listed on other directories. Users of the Web increased from around 11 million in 1994 to nearly 40 million in 1996. "Over one in five Americans now go online—either at home, work, or school. Nearly three-fourths of this group sometimes get news from the World Wide Web or from a commercial service."[13] Users of the Internet can read news from a variety of sources and obtain direct links to politicians and candidates. They can also interact with other people or politicians about politics through electronic mail or "chat rooms."

A Linking Mechanism

The pervasiveness of the media alone does not prove their political influence. But it does place the media in a position to be influential because they can reach so much of the American public so quickly. With a large population scattered over a continent, both the reach and speed of the modern media elevate their importance.

The media have become the primary linking mechanism in American politics—a way of connecting policy makers, candidates, and the public in a national, largely electronic, communication network. Candidates talk to voters. Voters respond to candidates. Policy makers and constituents interact. And policy makers and other elite groups—such as interest groups and policy experts—communicate with each other through the media. The media do more than pass along information. The information transmitted can change voters' perceptions of social reality and affect their responses to those perceptions. Candidates also tap voter sentiment from media polls. Policy makers assess policy effectiveness in part through media coverage. And people rely on the media to evaluate governmental performance and policy.

The Rise of an Autonomous Press

Back in the eighteenth century, not only was there no television or radio, there were only a few newspapers, and those that did exist were run by political parties. Their purpose was not to distribute the news but to defend their own party and attack

TABLE 13–1

Top Ten Newspapers in Circulation, 1997

The Wall Street Journal	1,837,194
USA Today	1,662,060
The New York Times	1,107,168
The Los Angeles Times	1,068,812
The Washington Post	818,231
The Daily News (New York)	728,107
The Chicago Tribune	664,586
Newsday	559,233
The Houston Chronicle	549,856
The San Francisco Chronicle	494,093

SOURCE: *The New York Times*, May 6, 1997, p. C8.

Average Monday-through-Friday circulation of the 10 largest American daily newspapers for reporting periods ended March 31, 1997.

Before the advent of television and radio, people relied primarily on newspapers for information. Here a group of newsboys in 1909 prepare to deliver the day's papers.

the other party. The framers relied heavily upon pamphlets and essays to get their messages to the public.

POLITICAL MOUTHPIECE At the time of the ratification of the Constitution, newspapers consisted of a single sheet, often printed irregularly by store owners to hawk their services or goods. Newspapers rarely lasted more than a year, due to delinquent subscribers and high costs.[14] But the framers understood the important role the press should play as a watchdog of politicians and government.

The new nation's political leaders, such as Alexander Hamilton and Thomas Jefferson, recognized the need to reach the people. Political party organizations as we know them did not exist, but the active role of the press in supporting the Revolution had fostered a growing awareness of the political potential of newspapers. Hamilton recruited staunch Boston Federalist John Fenno to edit and publish a newspaper in the new national capital of Philadelphia. Jefferson responded by attracting Philip Freneau, a talented writer and editor and a loyal Republican, to do the same for the Republicans. (Jefferson's Republicans later became the Democratic party.)

Although the two newspapers competed in Philadelphia only several years, their lasting significance was as a model for future partisan newspapers. They became the nucleus of competing partisan newspaper networks throughout the nation. Federalist and Republican editors relied on each other for government news and editorials. The free mailing of newspapers among editors allowed by the U.S. Post Office encouraged this usage.

The linkage between newspaper editors and politicians was maintained through several methods. Politicians loaned or gave money to partisan editors to set up newspapers. Hamilton and other prominent Federalists gave $1,000 each for the start-up of the *New York Evening Post* and helped solicit subscriptions from party supporters.[15] Government patronage appointments were extended to favorite editors. John C. Calhoun, for example, while serving as secretary of war, hired his favorite editor as federal superintendent of Indian trade. Another form of patronage was designation as a government newspaper duly authorized to print the text of laws, reports, speeches, and treaties.[16]

The early American press served as a political mouthpiece for political leaders. Its close connection with politicians and political parties offered the opportunity for financial stability, but at the cost of journalistic independence.

FINANCIAL INDEPENDENCE The Jacksonian era of the 1820s and 1830s was characterized by increased participation in American politics through the elimination of property qualifications for voting and by opportunities to join in rallies, bonfires, and local political clubs. As the vehicle for communication with the public, the press began to shift its appeal away from elite readers and toward large masses of less well educated and less politically interested readers. This movement was reinforced by rising literacy rates that supported greater circulation for newspapers. These two forces—increased political participation by the common people and the rise of literacy among Americans—began to alter the relationship between politicians and the press.

Some newspaper publishers began to experiment with a new financing structure. They charged a penny a paper, paid on delivery, instead of the traditional annual subscription fee of $8 to $10, which was beyond the ability of most readers to pay. Through expanded circulation and more emphasis on advertising, newspapers could become financially independent. The plan for a new "penny press" not only worked; it became a common model for the press thereafter.

The effect of this new independence on the political role of the press was not immediate; in keeping with the strong partisanship of the nineteenth century, many publishers continued to promote partisan causes and candidates anyway. However, some began to criticize their own party. Republican Horace Greeley, editor of the *New York Tribune*, felt at liberty to criticize Abraham Lincoln during the Civil War. Several Republican newspapers abandoned their party's candidate for president in 1884.[17]

The changing finances of newspapers also affected the definition of what constituted news. Before the "penny press," all news was political—speeches, documents, editorials—directed at a politically interested readership. The "penny press" reshaped the definition of news as it sought to appeal to the less politically aware with human interest stories, sports, crime and public trials, and social activities.

As news about politics began to constitute a smaller proportion of the newspaper, politicians searched for alternative ways to communicate with the public. In the 1850s, members of Congress used their mail privileges—the *franking privilege*—to distribute copies of their speeches. During the first half of 1858, for example, members of Congress mailed 800,000 copies of their speeches without charge.[18]

President Franklin Roosevelt was the first president to recognize the effectiveness of radio to reach the public. His fireside chats were the model for today's Saturday morning talks on radio by Bill Clinton.

"OBJECTIVE JOURNALISM" The death knell of the partisan press sounded with the rise of "objective journalism." Many journalists began to argue that the press should be independent of the political parties. *New York Tribune* editor Whitelaw Reid eloquently expressed this sentiment:

> Independent journalism! That is the watchword of the future in the profession. An end of concealments because it would hurt the party; an end of one-sided expositions . . . ; an end of assaults that are not believed fully just but must be made because the exigency of party warfare demands them . . . that is the end which to every perplexed, conscientious journalist a new and beneficent Declaration of Independence affords.[19]

Journalists also began to view their work as a profession and established professional associations with codes of ethics and publication of journals. This professionalization of journalism reinforced the notion that journalists should be independent of partisan politics—a notion that still pertains today. The rise of the wire services as the primary source for national news (they were politically neutral in order to attract more customers) further strengthened the trend toward objectivity.

THE IMPACT OF BROADCASTING Radio and television changed the media's role in politics by nationalizing and personalizing the news. Radio did it first, beginning with the creation of networks in the 1920s. Radio dominated national politics until the rise of television after World War II.

Political speeches, campaign advertising, and coverage of political events such as national party conventions were carried on radio. Members of Congress used radio extensively. During the 1930s, more than one thousand speeches were made by members of Congress on one network alone.[20] Radio provided a means to bypass the editorial screening of the press, since politicians could speak directly to listeners without editing. It also contributed to increased interest in national and international news, since activities outside a listener's local area could be heard as if one were actually there.

President Franklin Roosevelt used radio with a new effectiveness. Before 1933 most radio addresses were formal orations, but Roosevelt spoke to his audience on a personal level that showed how radio could be used as a one-to-one conversation. Roosevelt's "fireside chats" established a standard for presidential use of the broadcast media still followed today. Frances Perkins, secretary of labor, recalled that when Roosevelt began speaking over the microphone, he would visualize the average citizen in front of him. "His face would smile and light up as though he were actually sitting on the front porch or in the parlor with them."[21]

Television added a visual dimension, which greatly contributed to rising audience interest in national events. Audience interest grew to the point that by 1963, two major networks doubled the length of their evening news broadcast from 15 to 30 minutes. Today the amount of time devoted to news broadcasts by most stations has grown again, with many providing as much as 90 minutes in the evening and a half hour at noon. With the advent of cable television, the coverage of news has expanded as well as the range of possible programs. Viewers can now watch news programs 24 hours a day. Specialized cable stations give substantial coverage to Congress and the courts, and some local cable stations provide live coverage of city councils and other public meetings. As we learned during the Persian Gulf War and later in Bosnia, American cable news is watched around the world for instantaneous coverage of news stories. Coverage of news-related issues in the prime evening hours is provided in programs like *60 Minutes*, *20/20*, and *Crossfire*.

MOST IMPORTANT NEWS SOURCE What is the most important source of news for most Americans? In 1959, when this question was first asked, the proportion for newspapers was 6 percent higher than for television; the remaining group said they used both television and newspapers. Television is now the most frequently used source of the news. Generally, about two-thirds of Americans indicate that television is their most important news source. This number climbed to over 80 percent in early 1991, when television coverage of the Persian Gulf War kept the nation glued to their TV sets night after night. Newspapers have dropped in influence and are most trusted by about 1 in 4 Americans. In 1996 about 10 percent of American voters listed the Internet as their primary source of news.[22]

THE NEW JOURNALISM By the 1960s, a new sense of professionalism among news reporters for both print and broadcast media had given the press greater autonomy. Schools of journalism were attracting students who wanted to contribute to social change.[23] Press autonomy was enhanced by a press corps self-confident enough to feel equal to politicians. One consequence of objective journalism was the creation of a press that acted as a "common carrier" of information between government and the public. Some journalists, however, challenged this role by arguing they should be more than mere conduits of official information; they should provide their own analysis and interpretation of events to balance the government's position. Others went so far as to advocate that journalists should side with those who are less powerful in society and unable to speak for themselves—a practice termed *advocacy journalism*.[24] A related trend was toward *adversarial journalism*—the practice of challenging government and serving as the opposition to public officials, particularly the president.[25] Notable examples include the reporting of Seymour Hersh of *The New York Times*, who exposed secret documents that came to be known as the Pentagon Papers on how the United States became involved in the Vietnam War; Robert Woodward and Carl Bernstein of *The Washington Post*, who played an important role in uncovering the Watergate conspiracy; and Nina Totenberg of National Public Radio, whose reporting on sexual harassment charges helped force the Senate Judiciary Committee to extend the hearings on the confirmation of Clarence Thomas to the U.S. Supreme Court. This type of reporting was a consequence of how the people choosing journalism as a profession defined their role.

MEDIA CONGLOMERATES But can journalists maintain independence in the face of news monopolies? Television can be profitable. One reason is that governmental limitations on competition permit monopoly ownership of broadcast licenses. Radio networks and newspapers were the first to purchase the new medium and establish cross-ownership patterns that persist today. For example, in 1996 the Gannett Corporation owned 92 daily newspapers, 15 television stations, 11 radio stations, and cable television systems in 5 states. Media conglomerates with large financial resources now dominate the media business and have contributed to the centralization of news. The Federal Communications Commission in 1992 relaxed ownership rules permitting one owner to control up to 30 AM and 30 FM radio stations.

Are a few media conglomerates likely to provide sufficient competition of ideas to support a democratic system?[26] And without them, can local populations scattered around the country, depending only on local media, find out what is happening in the nation's capital? Why not have government-owned media carry out educational and information functions as well as entertainment functions, as they do in Great Britain and France?[27] The answer is that Americans continue to put great stock in an independent press and news media and find centralized government-owned media unacceptable.

Another concern has been the gobbling up of American communication assets by large corporations and by foreign interests. Local newspapers, radio, and television stations used to be owned primarily by local firms; today large firms, many of them foreign, have acquired ownership of many newspapers and broadcasting stations. The merger of the Disney organization with ABC/Capital Cities, approved early in 1996, cost Disney $19 billion but gave Disney control not only of the ABC television network but also ESPN, the cable television sports station. Months later the Westinghouse Company bought the CBS television network for $7.5 billion.[28] Time Warner purchased Turner Broadcasting System in late 1996 for reportedly just under $7 billion.[29] In this instance, an industrial corporation expanded to include a communications and entertainment company.

A national press—*USA Today*, *The Wall Street Journal*, and *The New York Times*—has also developed. Local outlets depend heavily on news that is gathered, edited, and distributed by national organizations like United Press International and Associated Press. As a result, some people contend that information these days is more diluted, homogenized, and moderated than it would be if the newspapers and broadcast stations were locally owned and the news was gathered and edited locally.[30]

A New Mediator in American Politics

Political parties and interest groups were long seen as political mediators between private individuals and the government—mediators who help organize the world of politics for the average citizen. This role is less important today because the media now serve that function, and political parties have lost their exclusive control over the nominating process. Moreover, there is much greater attention given today to judging candidates not so much in terms of party affiliation and platform but in terms of character and competence. The press, not the parties, is performing this evaluative function.

Journalists now contend they have a proper function of screening candidates and looking into their characters—a function that once belonged to party leaders. Thus in recent presidential elections, candidates have been subjected to investigative reporters looking into their sex and drug practices as well as going through their records all the way back to college to see if there is anything that might be considered "improper."

News media have also taken over the role of "speaking for the people." Journalists tell politicians what "the people" want and think, and then they tell the people what politicians and policy makers are doing about it. Politicians understand this, and they know how dependent they are on the media in getting their message out to voters. They know a hostile press can hurt them. Clearly, today's politicians have to spend much of their time cultivating the press. President Clinton, after a

---

Rupert Murdoch and His Media Empire

There's a new player in the high stakes game of television networks and media companies—Rupert Murdoch. Murdoch is the owner of the Fox empire, including Fox network, Fox movie studios, Fox television production company, *TV Guide* magazine (which has the largest circulation in America), HarperCollins publishing, British Sky Television, Star Television in Asia (which has an estimated viewing audience of 220 million alone), and News Corp (an Australian-based company). Murdoch has established an international media empire that spans the globe and took in $9 billion in revenue in 1994. Some of his recent actions have included adding at least 12 stations to Fox early in 1995, outbidding CBS for television rights to the National Football League, and creating a global news team that could rival Ted Turner's CNN.

In fact, there is no love lost between Murdoch and Turner. Murdoch recently launched his all-news cable channel to compete with CNN. The focal point of their battle quickly became New York City, where Turner, a member of the board of Time Warner Corporation, fought to keep Murdoch's new channel from airing on local cable stations. Mayor Rudy Giuliani tried to defend Murdoch but ended up getting dragged down in the conflict when *The New York Times* editorialized against Giuliani, describing him as "servile" in working for Murdoch. For his part, Ted Turner called Murdoch "slimy" and compared him to Hitler.

Murdoch has been accused of seeking to buy access to Congress by offering House Speaker Newt Gingrich a $4.5 million advance on his book through Murdoch's publishing house, HarperCollins. Shortly after HarperCollins extended the advance, Murdoch and a group of other broadcasters attended a closed meeting with House Republican leaders and the Commerce Committee staff. After word of the $4.5 million book deal became public, Gingrich was forced to reject the offer. Some media observers claimed the private meetings concerned turning over public broadcasting channels to private broadcasters.

SOURCE: Walt Belcher, "Murdoch's Moves Make Many Shake," *Tampa Tribune*, December 11, 1994, p. 1; Nat Hentoff, "Cable Television vs. Viewer Rights," *Rocky Mountain News*, November 4, 1996; "Who's Afraid of Rupert Murdoch?" *Frontline*, November 7, 1995.

rocky start with the White House press corps, hired David Gergen to help him improve his press relations and coverage. Gergen had previously worked for Republican presidents, most notably Ronald Reagan. In addition, Clinton counted on the services of George Stephanopoulos, James Carville, and Dick Morris.

Presidents experience both positive and negative news coverage. When the news is good, they are happy to spend time with the media; when it is bad, they limit their contact as much as possible. Bill Clinton experienced positive news coverage when he helped orchestrate the Middle East and Bosnian peace processes, but he became testy with the media over their coverage of Whitewater and the role of Hillary Rodham Clinton in the firing of the White House travel office employees. Press coverage of Mrs. Clinton also went through highs and lows. She received positive coverage for her mastery of the complexities of health care reform in 1993, but in 1996 her statements about Whitewater prompted *New York Times* columnist William Safire to call her a "congenital liar."[31] President Clinton's response was that he wished he could "deliver a more forceful response . . . on the bridge of Mr. Safire's nose."[32] Safire and other columnists continued to attack the Clintons throughout the 1996 election by raising questions about Whitewater allegations and the money the Clinton campaign had accepted from Indonesian and Chinese sources.

THE MEDIA AND PUBLIC OPINION

Scholars, journalists, politicians, and political pundits have long debated the power of the media over public opinion. Do the media shape opinions? Do they alter people's behavior? Can they even affect our core values? For a long time, analysts tended to play down the influence wielded in American politics as compared with the influence wielded by political leaders. The impact of Franklin D. Roosevelt's "fireside chats" symbolized the power of the politician against that of the news editor. Roosevelt spoke directly to his listeners over the radio in a way and at a time of his own choosing, and no network official was able to block or influence that direct connection. President John Kennedy's use of the televised press conference represented a similar direct contact with the public. President Ronald Reagan was nicknamed the "Great Communicator" because of his ability to talk persuasively and often passionately about public policy issues with the people through television. Ross Perot emerged on the national scene because of his skill in using television talk shows and "infomercials."

The news media are now so important that elected officials and politicians spend considerable time trying to learn how to use them. Presidential events and "photo opportunities" are planned with the evening news and its format in mind.[33] Members of Congress use Capitol Hill recording studios to tape messages for local television and radio stations. The media often respond positively to these activities by politicians. White House press briefings are frequently included in the evening news, and Congress has excellent access to local media. How government officials use the press, how the press uses government officials, and to what extent the press and television can and should be regulated are critical questions for study.

In recent years many entertainment shows have broken the stereotypes about women and minorities and shown them as major figures in their own persona. In the past such shows tended to show African Americans, Hispanics, and gays and lesbians in stereotypical gender and race roles that subtly reinforced cultural values of sexual and racial inequality. Subtle political messages are found in all types of programming; for example, every sports event begins with the National Anthem, which encourages people to be proud of their country. Many entertainers feature jokes about political figures and institutions like the Congress. Clearly the media play an important role in reinforcing norms and attitudes.

"Would you say Attila is doing an excellent job, a good job, a fair job, or a poor job?"

Drawing by Charles Adams. © 1982 The New Yorker Magazine, Inc.

Audience

People are not just empty vessels into which politicians pour information and ideas. How they interpret political messages depends on a variety of factors: political socialization, selectivity, needs, and the individual's ability to recall and comprehend the message.

POLITICAL SOCIALIZATION   Although we would like to believe we consume the news with an open mind, the reality is that we employ a set of filters or screens to help us interpret and integrate information. When we watch television or read newspapers, magazines, and books, we bring with us values and attitudes that have been shaped by family, peers, school, and the groups to which we belong.[34] We develop our political attitudes, values, and behavior through an education process that social scientists call **political socialization**. (See Chapters 7 and 11 for more detail on this process.) The media, particularly television, may influence our values and attitudes, but they are not as important in the formation of our political attitudes as is our family.[35] Face-to-face contacts often have far more impact on us than the more impersonal television or newspaper. Strong identification with a party also acts as a powerful filter.[36] A conservative Republican from Arizona might watch the "liberal Eastern networks" night after night and year after year and complain about the biased news coverage while sticking to his or her own opinions.

SELECTIVITY   People practice **selective exposure**—screening out those messages that do not conform to their own biases. They subscribe to newspapers or magazines that already support their views. People also practice **selective perception**—perceiving what they want to in media messages and disregarding the rest.[37] One dramatic example is viewers' varying responses to Professor Anita Hill and Judge Clarence Thomas in the 1991 Senate hearings on Thomas's nomination to the Supreme Court. Those who believed Anita Hill's testimony on sexual harassment perceived Thomas as untruthful, while those who believed Thomas's denials discounted Hill's testimony. A similar example of selective perception was the differing views of whites and blacks on the guilt or innocence of O. J. Simpson in his much-followed criminal and civil trials.

NEEDS   Another mitigating factor in how the media influence opinions is the use to which people put media messages. People read newspapers, listen to the radio, or watch television for very different reasons—sometimes because they are bored, tired, or have nothing better to do, sometimes to get information.[38] People who want to gain information and cultivate an interest in politics are affected differently from those who use media primarily for entertainment.[39] For those who are most interested in entertainment, gossip about President Clinton's alleged affairs or Senator Phil Gramm's financing of an X-rated movie is more important than Clinton's or Gramm's political opinions or deeds. Thus events like rape trials are likely to draw more attention than foreign policy speeches by presidential candidates. Members of the broader audience are also more likely to follow news that directly affects their lives, such as interest rate changes.[40]

RECALL AND COMPREHENSION   Still another limitation of media influence on public opinion is the extent to which the audience can recall the stories or comprehend their importance. Candidates and officials send out tons of information designed to influence what people think and do, especially how they vote. But people forget or fail to comprehend much of it.[41] The fragmentary and rapid mode of presentation of television news contributes to the problem.

Given all the information available to people about politics and government, it is not surprising most people pick and choose which media source—television,

We the People

Who Watches the Nightly Network News?

	Regularly	Sometimes	Hardly Ever/ Never
Sex			
Male	41%	27%	32%
Female	42	32	26
Age			
18–29	22	39	39
30–49	35	34	31
50–64	60	19	21
65+	64	17	18
Race			
White	42	29	29
Nonwhite	40	35	25
Black	42	34	24
Other	34	37	29
Education			
College graduate	43	28	29
Some college	37	33	29
High school graduate	40	31	29
Less than high school graduate	47	24	29
Income			
$75,000+	44	28	28
$50,000–$74,999	39	31	30
$30,000–$49,999	41	31	28
$20,000–$29,999	45	29	26
Less than $20,000	41	26	33

SOURCE: Pew Research Center for the People and the Press, *TV News Viewership Declines*, Press Release, May 13, 1996, p. 29.

"VALUES" AND THE MEDIA

For decades conservatives have claimed that the mass media in this country are too liberal—advancing a liberal agenda and attacking traditional values. The issue surfaced again in the 1996 presidential campaign when all the Republican candidates stressed the need for a return to "family values." President Clinton picked up on the theme in his State of the Union Address and in his campaign speeches. Hearings in Congress proposed the use of a V-chip to allow parents to screen out violent or sexually explicit programs they did not want their children to see.

Studies show that moviemakers are more liberal than the general public. A survey of 104 top television writers and executives found that many of their attitudes toward moral and religious questions are not shared by their audience.

Jack Valenti, president of the Motion Picture Association of America, flanked by Representative Sonny Bono (R.-Calif.) and House Speaker Newt Gingrich, presented a ratings system for television shows that was similar to the age categories used in movie ratings. Parent groups and many members of Congress were not satisfied and held out for a system more descriptive of content in terms of violence, sexual activity, and language.

Believe adultery is wrong
Hollywood	49%
Everyone else	85

Have no religious affiliation
Hollywood	45%
Everyone else	4

Believe homosexual acts are wrong
Hollywood	20%
Everyone else	76

Believe in a woman's right to an abortion
Hollywood	97%
Everyone else	59

SOURCE: Center for Media and Public Affairs, reported in *Newsweek*, July 20, 1992.

radio, newspapers—to pay attention to and which news stories they consider important. One scholar who studied the process of selecting which news people pay attention to and remember found that comprehension varied widely, "depending on the nature of stories, the use of visuals, and the concerns and lifestyles of the audience."[42] The best predictor of retention of news stories is political interest. People tend to fit today's news stories into their general assumptions or beliefs about government, politicians, or the media itself.

Bias

There is continuous debate over whether newspapers, radio commentators, television reporters, magazine writers, and especially the mass media are biased. Americans believe they are.[43] Conservatives complain the media are too liberal; liberals claim the media represent the interests of the establishment; politicians complain the media do not get their messages across. Although people blame many things either on politicians or on the media, the public does not always give the media a failing grade. As we have seen, most felt press treatment of the candidates during the 1996 election had been fair. In contrast, voters were more critical of campaign advertising, believing that advertisements "rarely" or "almost never" could be trusted.[44]

How can we assess the political bias of the news media? Some contend that television networks are large corporations whose first and foremost concern is profit.[45] For many critics of the media, this observation defines the peculiar nature of the news media. They are dedicated, on the one hand, to the impartial reporting of "fact" and, on the other, to boosting ratings and pleasing circulation managers, advertisers, sponsors, and stockholders. Somewhere along the line, the search for truth may get lost, although news organizations pride themselves on their objectivity.[46]

In addition, it is becoming increasingly difficult to distinguish news from entertainment. Political jokes abound on late-night comedy shows, and we get pungent political messages from the cartoon pages and prime-time network shows. Hollywood actors have become politicians, and politicians have become actors. Political analysis creeps onto the front pages of most papers, and many fear that the politics of the editorial page influences coverage of the news.

David Broder of *The Washington Post* voices similar concerns about the confusion of roles by journalists who have served in government. According to Broder, a line should divide objective journalism from partisan politics, but many in the print and television media have crossed this line. Broder opposes the idea of journalists becoming government officials and vice versa.[47] Others argue that, because of their government service, journalists with close working relationships with politicians can give us a valuable perspective on government without losing their professional neutrality.

Equally disturbing to some observers is the media's alleged political bias, whether liberal or conservative. But to whom are these critics referring? To reporters, writers, editors, producers, or owners of TV and newspapers? Do they assume a journalist's personal politics will be translated into biased reporting? And does the public think so?

Conservatives say the press is too liberal. They criticize the press for advocating liberal social causes and ignoring the conservative viewpoint.[48] Rush Limbaugh, an influential conservative talk show host, speaking of the media argues, "They all just happen to believe the same way. . . . They are part of the same culture as Bill Clinton."[49] Journalists usually are more liberal than the population as a whole, while editors tend to be a bit more conservative than their reporters, and media owners are more conservative still. Twenty-three percent of the public describe themselves as liberal, compared to 38 percent of college-educated professionals, from whose ranks most journalists are drawn. But even among the professionals, journalists' liberalism stands out: 55 percent describe themselves as liberals.[50]

The far left also accuses the media of bias. Leftist critics contend the mainstream press is purely a propaganda device of the ruling class, creating the boundaries of acceptable thinking and thereby shutting out left-wing viewpoints. Leftist critics see the mass media as capitalist enterprises that dislike airing anticapitalist sentiments. As well as being a tool of the business class, according to these critics, the

Reporter Sam Donaldson is a moderator on ABC's Sunday morning news magazine, in which he expresses his personal opinions of events. He is also a member of the Washington press corps and covers presidential news conferences and other Washington activities. Do his views on politics bias his reporting of the news?

media are also a tool of government propaganda that seeks to distort the facts. Others see this "conspiracy theory" as merely a rationalization by leftists who are disgruntled over the failure of their views to take hold with the American people.[51]

Another theory of bias has to do with the possible cultural bias of journalists. Elite journalists—those who work for national news media organizations—tend to share a similar culture: cosmopolitan, urban, upper class. Their approach to the events and issues they cover is governed by their common worldview. Part of this bias may be derived from their professional training.[52] The result is an almost unconscious perspective that produces bias because elite journalists give greater weight to the side of issues that corresponds to their own version of reality.[53] Newspapers and television news often set a tone of dissatisfaction with the performance of the national government and cynicism about politics and politicians.

A critical tone may be an inevitable element in the mind set of the press. But to whose benefit does that critical tone work? Conservatives and the far left are not the only ones who perceive bias. Liberals point to newspaper endorsements of Republican presidential candidates to support their claim that newspapers are biased toward conservative policies and candidates. Daily newspapers tend to endorse Republicans over Democrats for president by a ratio greater than 2 to 1.

The critical question is not whether the press is biased but whether the press bias, whatever the direction, seeps into the content of the news. The answer to that question is still not settled. Some empirical studies of news content have failed to find the expected bias.[54]

Public Opinion

The media can make a big difference in what Americans believe. Television, because of its visual dimension, is especially important in shaping opinion, and television news exposure cuts across age groups, educational levels, social classes, and races. Television, with all its concreteness and drama, has an emotional impact that print cannot hope to match.[55] Newspapers, on the other hand, provide more detail about the news and often contain contrasting points of view, at least on the editorial pages, that help inform the public more substantially. Both print and broadcast media are a potent influence in agenda setting and issue framing.

AGENDA SETTING The power to set the public agenda is significant, and by calling public attention to certain issues, the media help to determine what topics will become the subject of public debate.[56] However, the agenda-setting function of the media is not uniformly pervasive. It is limited by the audience and the nature of the issue.[57]

One politician who effectively used the media for agenda setting was Ronald Reagan. More than any other president before him, Reagan and his advisers carefully crafted the images and scenes of his presidency to fit the role of television. Thus television became an "electronic throne." According to former Vice-President Walter Mondale, "If I had to give up . . . the opportunity to get on the evening news or the veto power, . . . I'd throw the veto power away. [Television news] is the President's most indispensable power."[58]

Agenda setting has significant political consequences. It focuses public attention on certain aspects of American politics and ignores others.[59] In assessing governmental or candidate performance, the media can affect the ultimate choice of a policy or a candidate.[60] Politicians often attempt to use the media to promote their candidacy. For example, Indiana Senator Richard Lugar carefully timed the announcement of his 1996 presidential candidacy for a Monday, typically a slow news day on which he was likely to get greater coverage. However, on that Monday the bombing of the Oklahoma City federal building occurred, and Lugar's announcement was barely noticed.

ISSUE FRAMING The context given an issue or event in a news story can affect public perceptions.[61] For example, when United States involvement in Bosnia was framed in news stories as a repetition of Vietnam, Clinton administration officials were understandably anxious about vanishing public support. When George Bush sought support for the Persian Gulf War, he compared Suddam Hussein to Adolf Hitler so as to frame the conflict in stark terms. The same kind of framing has been part of the abortion debate, with those favoring abortion defining their position in terms of freedom of choice and those opposing abortion defining it as murder. Similarly, when voters decide ballot questions, the side that most effectively defines the issue generally wins.[62] Bill Clinton framed the protracted battle with Republicans in Congress on balancing the budget by broadening the issue to include the need to protect Medicare, Medicaid, education, and the environment from severe budget cuts.

Regulation

Charges of media bias and the importance of agenda setting and issue framing are only some of the reasons why some urge government to regulate the media. Traditionally, newspapers have not been regulated because of our First Amendment guarantee of freedom of the press and because competition among newspapers has been seen as a way to limit bias. Critics of the growth of media conglomerates propose that newspaper chains be broken up through antimonopoly legislation that restores competition.

Regulation of the broadcast media has existed in some form since its inception. Because of the limited number of television and radio frequencies, government has overseen matters like licensing, financing, and even content. One such regulation required "fairness" in news programming.[63] As written into law and interpreted by the Federal Communications Commission, the "fairness doctrine" imposed on radio and television license holders an obligation to ensure that differing viewpoints were presented about controversial issues or persons. With the advent of cable television and the Reagan administration's antiregulatory perspective, the doctrine was repealed in 1987.

The media are criticized for sensationalism, overemphasis on "theater" and spectacles, obsession with violence, lack of self-criticism, lack of objectivity, and superficial reporting. They have been urged to provide more explanation, interpretation, and analysis; to look more closely at the activities of the government and depend less on "packaged" news handed out by government bureaucracies; to be more aggressive in covering the White House; and to become better educated themselves about what really goes on in Congress.[64]

Critics hesitate to propose harsh or sweeping remedies lest controls threaten First Amendment liberties. But critics are also uncertain about how serious and widespread the problem of media influence really is and how improvement can best be accomplished.[65] For example, in closely balanced election races in which media influence or bias might be strong enough to tilt the outcome one way or the other, the opinions put forth by major press and networks may be crucial. But in our pluralistic nation, which comprises an enormous variety of groups and movements, Americans have so many "filters" through which to observe events that it is extremely difficult to influence public opinion.

THE MEDIA AND ELECTIONS

Do news stories determine who wins or loses elections, who gets nominated for office, or which referenda get passed? News stories probably have more influence today because of the shift to greater direct democracy in our political system. Primaries nominate candidates, with little role left for parties, and voters decide many

---

Thinking It Through

The movement to have a ratings system for television programs has gained enough support that the television and movie industries have proposed their own rating system similar to that used for movies, in part to avoid one legislated by Congress.

Jack Valenti, president of the Motion Picture Association of America, argues that these ratings will help parents make decisions. Valenti and others in the television industry say that to go further than their proposal would violate First Amendment rights.

The opposition, led by Representative Ed Markey (D-Mass.), says these ratings are insufficient because they do not give content-specific information about the programs, such as the degree of violence or the type of sexual material. Markey and most parent and family groups want a more detailed system of ratings and description of program content.

Those who oppose such ratings systems contend that, once started, they can become a type of censorship. Moreover, they assert there is a lot of subjectivity in evaluating programs. What some may see as too violent or sexually explicit, others may not find objectionable. Then there is the added cost to equip televisions with V-chips and to employ people to rate the programs. Ultimately it will be advertisers who pay the costs of the ratings and consumers who pay for the V-chip.

The counterargument is that children learn what is acceptable behavior from the media, especially television. Critics point to an increasing incidence of violent and sexually explicit actions and language on TV. They contend, the industry will not regulate itself. The V-chip, when combined with content disclosure and a detailed ratings system, would give parents control over this powerful socializing force.

SOURCE: Hillary Rodham Clinton, remarks to the 1996 National Media Literacy Conference, October 4, 1996; "TV Industry Unveils Ratings System to Mixed Reviews," December 19, 1996, www.allpolitics.com.

important issues directly through initiatives and referenda. While the influence of the media may be greater due to these changes, there is little evidence such influence controls elections. Generally, the more visible the campaign, the less likely voters are to be swayed by any one source. Hence, news coverage is more likely to be important in a city referendum than in an election for president or the Senate.

Diversification of the news media also lessens the ability of any one medium to dominate politics. Newspaper publishers who were once seen as very important in state and local politics know that today politicians and their media advisers can communicate their message through television, radio, direct mail, videocassettes, the Internet, and cable television. Hence, while the news media remain an important means of communication, there is now more competition among the various media, and politicians and candidates can get their message out regardless of what the editor of the state's largest newspaper may think.

The Electoral Campaign

Campaigns today are run differently from the way they were run a generation ago. During the 1960 election, John Kennedy's effort to attract media attention by winning the early primaries was considered novel; today it is standard operating procedure.

CHOICE OF CANDIDATES The role of the media begins with the decision of who will run. Television greatly affects the preferred traits for presidential candidates. A hundred years ago, successful candidates needed a strong pair of lungs; today it is a "telegenic" appearance, a pleasing voice, and no obvious physical impairments. Back in the 1930s, the press chose not to show Franklin Roosevelt in his wheelchair or using braces, whereas today the country knows every intimate detail of the president's health. The importance of the public's perception of these traits is evident in the ridicule often directed at candidates. In 1996, Bob Dole was criticized for his boring speaking style, and even candidates who are good on television, like Bill Clinton, were derided as "slick."

If the news media pay no attention to a candidate, he or she is not likely to win any elections. Although the media insist they pay attention to all who have a chance to win, they also influence who has such a chance. Some candidates have come up with creative ways to generate media attention. Lawton Chiles, running for the U.S. Senate from Florida, captured media attention by walking across the state. The novelty of the idea meant that reporters gave Chiles lots of free media coverage. Sometimes candidates can make their advertisements generate news coverage. Paul Wellstone used creative advertisements in his 1990 Minnesota Senate campaign in which he said that he did not have much money to pay for ads, so he would have to talk fast to cram what he had to say into fewer commercials. The witty way he did this became a news event itself—and got Wellstone additional coverage.

CAMPAIGN EVENTS Because of the importance of media attention for communicating with voters, candidates schedule media events—talk shows, press conferences, interviews, and "photo opportunities"—with various groups and in visual settings that reinforce the verbal message. Even the national party conventions have become less focused on actually choosing the nominee than on serving as the first media event of the general election campaign.[66] In the wake of declining viewership of the conventions, the political parties have sought to regain audience interest by reliance on "movie stars, entertainment routines, and professionally produced documentaries in their convention proceedings."[67] Coverage of national political conventions in 1996 was scaled back to key personalities a few hours each night on the major networks, and only C-SPAN broadcast the entire proceedings of both conventions.

"Hey, do you want to be on the news tonight or not? This is a sound bite, not the Gettysburg Address. Just say what you have to say, Senator, and get the hell off."

Drawing by Zeller. © 1989 The New Yorker Magazine, Inc.

The 1996 presidential debates pitted a somewhat somber and uncomfortable Bob Dole against a relaxed master of the medium, Bill Clinton. The debates drew smaller audiences than in previous campaigns and did not seem to affect people's voting preferences.

MEDIA TECHNOLOGY   Thanks to new media technology, candidates finally can be in more than one place at a time. Satellites allow candidates to conduct local television interviews without actually traveling to the area and to communicate with party workers across the country. Specific voter groups can be targeted through cable television systems or low-power television stations that reach homogeneous neighborhoods or small towns. Videocassettes with messages from the candidates further extend the campaign's reach.[68] Many candidates for Congress and president in 1996 made themselves and their positions available through a home page on the World Wide Web.

The expense associated with media technology has contributed to the skyrocketing costs of campaigning (discussed in Chapter 12). Candidates wonder if they are really getting "the bang for their buck." Political scientist Michael J. Robinson concludes that paid advertising has little effect on voters in primary contests. It is most useful as a means to respond to other candidates' advertisements and as a measure of candidate viability to the press.[69]

Technology permits campaign staffers to cover their own candidate, following the candidate around with cassette recorders and minicams and taping anything he or she does that resembles news. These tapes are then delivered to radio and television stations and cable systems. This low-cost technology permits campaign staffs to make these sound bites available to the media, which often broadcast them intact without much editorial comment.[70]

Image Making

Do the media tend to prefer image over issues? Actually, image has always been an important part of presidential campaigns.[71] Presidential campaign sloganeering such as "Tippecanoe and Tyler Too" in 1840 and "Abe the Rail Splitter" in 1860 were not issue oriented. The new kinds of media have expanded this "defining" role, which in turn has affected candidates' vote-getting strategies and their ability to communicate messages. Television is especially important here because of the power of the visual image. Edmund Muskie crying while defending his wife's reputation in 1972, Ronald Reagan taking charge of a debate against George Bush in 1980, and Ross Perot speaking in down-home language in 1992 are all examples.

Candidates recognize that their messages about issues are often ignored or given little attention. The press tends to emphasize goofs and gossip or tensions within the campaign or among party leaders. In the 1996 election, for instance, the press reported on a $1,000 campaign contribution given to Bob Dole by the Log Cabin Republicans, a gay and lesbian group, that was initially returned by the Dole campaign. Dole later reversed the decision of his campaign staff and said they had not consulted him in the decision.[72] Bill Clinton's campaign also returned campaign contributions in 1996, but here the amounts were much larger, and the money was only returned after the contributions became known in the national news.

Media Consultants

Image making has contributed to the rise of new players in campaign politics—media consultants, campaign professionals who provide candidates with advice and services such as media relations, advertising strategy, and opinion polling.[73] In the 1992 election, for instance, consultants attempted to counter the impression that Hillary Clinton was too assertive by having her discuss her cookie-making skills, drop her maiden name in campaign references, and play the role of the supportive spouse.[74]

Some media consultants have been credited with propelling candidates to success. Dick Morris was seen as important to Clinton's resurgence until he had to resign from the campaign following a personal scandal. Republican consultants like Roger Ailes and Don Sipple, and Democratic consultants like James Carville and Robert Squire, have acquired powerful reputations among political activists. But media consultants have also been blamed for the negative themes of recent presidential campaigns. The classic example was a 1988 ad linking Michael Dukakis to Willie Horton, a convicted murderer who murdered again while on a prison furlough program. Candidates whose campaigns are struggling sometimes replace their media consultants, as Bob Dole did in 1996.

Media consultants have taken over the role formerly played by party politicians. Before World War II, candidates for office at all levels from president to dog catcher were advised by party professionals. Such leaders made their judgments about possible candidates on the basis of long observation of the candidates' performances under fire, decisiveness, conviction, political skill, and other "presidential" qualities (in addition to their chances of victory). Party professionals told candidates which party and interest-group leaders to placate, which issues to stress, and which topics to avoid. Today candidates are more interested in the advice of a media consultant. Consultants think more in terms of the candidates' image, television technique, flexibility, "salability," and the like. Consultants report the results of *focus groups* (small sample groups of people who are asked questions about candidates and issues in a discussion setting) and public opinion polls, which in turn determine what the candidate says and does. Some critics allege that political consultants have become a new "political elite" who can virtually choose candidates by determining in advance which men and women have the right images, or at least images that can be restyled for the widest popularity.[75] But political consultants who specialize in media advertising and image making realize their own limitations in packaging candidates. As one media consultant put it, "It is a very hard job to turn a turkey into a movie star; you try instead to make people like the turkey."[76]

Voter Choice

The media play an especially important role during political campaigns because they are seen as the most important source of news by the public. Candidates accordingly court the media and develop a media strategy. The media in turn provide information about candidates, help set the agenda of important issues, and provide cues on how to vote.

TABLE 13–2
Election News Coverage, 1988–1996*

	1988	1992	1996
Amount of Coverage			
Number of Stories	589	728	483
Minutes per Day	17	25	12
Average Sound Bite (seconds)	9.8	8.4	8.2
Focus of Coverage (percent of stories)			
Horse Race	58%	58%	48%
Policy Issues	39%	32%	37%
Tone of Coverage (percent of good press)			
Democratic Nominee	31%	52%	50%
Republican Nominee	38%	29%	33%

SOURCE: *Media Monitor*, November/December, 1996.

*Based on evaluation by nonpartisan sources in election stories on ABC, CBS, and NBC evening newscasts.

INFORMATION ABOUT CANDIDATES   What voters know about candidates is based largely on media coverage. If the media have not covered a candidate, the voters generally know little about him or her. The images voters receive from the media tend to be more stylistic than issue oriented. Journalists are more likely to comment on a candidate's personal background, style of campaigning, or standing in the polls compared to other candidates—in what is sometimes called the "horse race"[77] (see Table 13–2). "Many stories focus on who is ahead, who is behind, who is going to win, and who is going to lose, rather than examining how and why the race is as it is."[78] Reporters focus on the tactics and strategy of campaigns because they perceive that the public is interested and influenced by such coverage.[79] The media also seem to alternate between a kind of "gee whiz" attitude toward their current hero and a tendency to pounce on a candidate's ill-chosen remarks (Table 13–3).

INFORMATION ABOUT ISSUES   The media's propensity to focus on the "game" of campaigns displaces coverage of issues. When there is a scarcity of issue information on television news, voters may learn more about issue positions from televised political advertisements or newspapers.[80] But advertising is becoming increasingly negative in tone. A rule of thumb in the "old politics" was to ignore the charges of the opposition, thus according one's rival no importance or standing. That practice seems to be changing, however, as candidates trade charges and countercharges increasing in viciousness and character assassination.

Political advertising may be even more important to campaign workers, contributors, and the reporters and analysts who cover the election.[81] Recent evidence suggests that expensive media campaigns fostering negative impressions of the candidates contribute to lower turnout.[82] In referendum elections, advertising is the most important source of information in voter decision making.[83]

THE DECISION   Newspapers and television seem to have more influence in determining the outcome of primaries than of general elections.[84] This is probably because voters are less likely to know about the candidates and have fewer clues about how they stand in a primary. By the time of the November general election, however, party affiliation, incumbency, and other factors moderate the impact of

TABLE 13–3
Themes of Election News Coverage, 1996

	Number of Stories	Percent of Stories
Dole Strategy	103	26%
Clinton Strategy	68	17
Tone of Dole Campaign	29	7
Taxes	26	7
State of Economy	26	7
Clinton Character—General	24	6
Perot Exclusion from Debates	23	6
Foreign Contributions to Democrats	22	6
Iraq	21	5
Education	19	5
Drugs	19	5
Voter Interest/Involvement	19	5

SOURCE: *Media Monitor*, November/December 1996.

Note: Stories may have more than one topic.

media messages. The mass media are more likely to influence undecided voters, voters who in a close election can determine who wins and who loses.

ELECTION NIGHT REPORTING Does election night reporting affect the outcome of elections? Election returns from the East come in three hours before the polls close on the West Coast. As major networks often project the presidential winner well ahead of poll closings in western states, some western voters have been discouraged from voting. As a result, voter turnout in congressional and local elections has been affected. In a close presidential election, however, such early reporting may well stimulate turnout because voters will know their vote could determine the outcome. In short, it is only in elections in which one candidate appears to be winning by a large margin that television reporting makes voters believe their vote is meaningless.[85]

THE MEDIA AND GOVERNANCE

Walter Lippmann termed the media's influence on public affairs the "beam of a searchlight that moves restlessly about, bringing one episode and then another out of darkness into vision."[86] The searchlight lands on a policy issue because of a combination of factors, including "the efforts of political actors who seek to illuminate the process for their own purposes, as well as the particular news values of the media."[87]

The press serves as both observer and participant.[88] As observer, it records and transmits information to and from actors in policy making. But as participant, it acts as watchdog or critic and functions as the "eyes and ears" of the general public. It helps set the agenda of policy issues and serves as a check on the abuse of power.

But the press's role as participant is limited by its own news values. The policy stage at which the press is most powerful is that of agenda setting. The press brings problems to the fore and challenges policy makers to address them but rarely follows the policy process to its conclusion. Rather, it leaves the issue at the doorstep of public officials. By the time the issue reaches the stages of policy formulation and implementation, the press has moved on to another issue. While policies are being formulated and implemented, decision makers are at their most impressionable, yet the press has little impact at this stage.[89]

Lack of media interest in policy implementation explains the lack of coverage of the bureaucracy. Bureaucratic activities rarely constitute news. Only in the case of a scandal, such as the savings and loan debacle in the early 1990s or the Housing and Urban Development disclosures of abuse in 1989, does the press take notice. Some agencies, however, prefer bureaucratic anonymity. After his study of government press offices, Stephen Hess of the Brookings Institution wrote, "Most executives would be satisfied with a press strategy of no surprises. All their press officers need do to be doing their job is provide a rudimentary early warning system [for crises] and issue routine announcements."[90] But the assumption of most policy makers, even those handling classified national security information, is that their actions will leak out sooner or later.

Some media critics contend a negative consequence of the media's searchlight approach to policy coverage is the media's pressure on policy makers to resolve a problem immediately once the searchlight focuses on it. Foreign policy may be in particular danger from such quick responses due to media attention. Presidential adviser Lloyd Cutler asserts the press's pressure on a president can be difficult to resist:

> If an ominous foreign event is featured on TV news, the president and his advisers feel bound to make a response in time for the next evening news broadcast. . . . If he does not have a

response ready by the late afternoon deadline, the evening news may report that the president's advisers are divided, that the president cannot make up his mind, or that while the president hesitates, his political opponents know exactly what to do.[91]

Political Institutions and the Press

The president has become a star of media coverage, particularly television, and has made the media his forum for setting the public agenda and achieving his legislative aims. Presidential news conferences command attention (see Table 13–4). Every public activity, both professional and personal, is potentially newsworthy; a presidential cold or sickness can become front page news, as can presidential vacations and family pets.

A president attempts to manipulate news coverage to his benefit. Speeches are used to set the national agenda or spur congressional action. Travel to foreign countries usually boosts popular support at home, thanks to the largely favorable news coverage. Better yet for the president, most coverage of the president—either at home or abroad—is favorable or at worst neutral.[92]

Congress, on the other hand, has suffered at the hands of the media. News coverage of Congress is typically negative and portrays a badly fragmented body unable to act quickly on much of anything.[93] Congress's problem is that it does not meet news imperatives. Unlike the presidency, it lacks an ultimate spokesperson—a single individual who can speak for the whole institution.[94] A good example of the disadvantage Congress faces in a political battle with the White House is the budget deadlock of 1995 and 1996, which resulted in much of the federal government being shut down for several weeks. The most visible spokesperson for Congress during this political battle was Speaker Newt Gingrich, but at times Bob Dole broke away from Gingrich, once again demonstrating the inability of Congress to speak with one voice. Polls showed that the public blamed Congress more than the president for the shutdown.

Congress does not organize its work to make it easy for the press. While the White House engages in the "care and feeding" of the press corps, Congress does not arrange its schedule to suit the media; floor debates, for example, often compete with committee hearings and press conferences.[95] By its nature, Congress does not act quickly. Singularly dramatic actions are nearly impossible for Congress, but such actions constitute news for the press. The press, therefore, turns to the president to describe federal government activity on a day-to-day basis and treats Congress largely as a foil to the president. Most coverage of Congress is of its reaction to the initiatives of the president,[96] except when Republicans in the 104th Congress grabbed the spotlight by implementing much of their Contract with America.

The federal institution least dependent on the press is the Supreme Court, which relies little on public communication for political support. Rather, it relies indirectly on public opinion for continued deference and compliance with its decisions.[97] The Court has strong incentives to avoid the perception of direct manipulation of the press, so it retains an image of aloofness from politics and public opinion. Thus, manipulation of press coverage of the Court is far more subtle and complex than for the other two institutions.[98]

The news media's greatest role as a participant in the governing process may be at the local level. Most of us have multiple sources for finding out what is happening in Washington that act as a check on the biases and limitations of reporters who cover national government and policy. But when it comes to finding out about the city council, the school board, or the local water district, most of us are dependent on the work of a single reporter. Consequently the media's influence is much greater when there are fewer news sources.

TABLE 13–4
Presidential News Conferences with White House Correspondents

President	Average per Month	Total Number
Herbert Hoover (1929–33)	5.6	268
Franklin D. Roosevelt (1933–45)	6.9	998
Harry Truman (1945–53)	3.4	334
Dwight Eisenhower (1953–61)	2.0	193
John Kennedy (1961–63)	1.9	64
Lyndon Johnson (1963–69)	2.2	135
Richard Nixon (1969–74)	0.5	37
Gerald Ford (1974–77)	1.3	39
Jimmy Carter (1977–81)	0.8	59
Ronald Reagan (1981–89)	0.5	44
George Bush (1989–93)	3	142
Bill Clinton (1993–97)	2.7	129

SOURCE: Samuel Kernell, *Going Public* (Congressional Quarterly Press, 1986), p. 69; *Public Papers of the Presidents, Ronald Reagan, Book II, 1988–89* (Government Printing Office, 1991), p. C8; *Public Papers of the Presidents, George Bush, Book II, 1992–93* (Government Printing Office, 1993), p. C7; *Weekly Compilation of Presidential Documents*, vol. 31, Annual Index, p. C12.

Presidents use the news conference to get certain information out to the public but run the risk of having to respond to criticism and challenges by reporters.

The Media and Constitutional Democracy

Critics have chided the press for failure to fulfill certain roles in a democratic society. There is no shortage of critics with suggestions on how newspeople might do better, such as greater specialization by policy area and more stringent separation between the entertainment and news functions of a network, newspaper, or magazine. Others, chiefly political scientists, have suggested that journalists should show less interest in the "game" aspect of campaigns. However, Thomas Patterson, a political scientist, does not think these reforms will work or make any significant difference. The problem, according to Patterson, is that the news business cannot, no matter how hard it tries, perform the functions once carried out by our political parties. It is not that the journalists are not doing their job, but that political parties no longer function as the chief connection between candidates and voters.[99] Newspeople now play that role and have made parties less necessary.

Other critics believe that the influence of the press has been vastly overstated. They claim that parties, interest groups, and the personalities of politicians are more important influences. City, state, and federal governments, they assert, have far more impact on a person's politics than does television or the press. Religion, friends, family, teachers, wars, depressions, and assassinations are all more important than the media.

Not all those who think the media are powerful agree that their power is harmful. After all, they argue, the media perform a vital educative function. Further, they continue, almost 70 percent of the public think the press is a watchdog that keeps government leaders from doing bad things.[100] At the very least, the media have the power to mold the agenda of the day; at most, in the words of the late Theodore White, they have the power to "determine what people will talk and think about—an authority that in other nations is reserved for tyrants, priests, parties, and mandarins."[101]

POLITICS ONLINE

Computer Users Watching TV Less

During the last few years, there has been a general decline in viewing television news programs. This decline may be related to the use of personal computers, which has increased markedly among young people. National television networks and major newspapers all have extensive Web sites with the day's news as well as archived past editions, and many local newspapers are also available on the Internet.

Watched TV News Yesterday			
	June 1995	April 1996	Difference
Computer User	63%	56%	-7
On-line User	63	56	-9
Non-User	66	63	-3

SOURCE: Pew Research Center, *TV News Viewership Declines*, May 13, 1996

News consumption over the Internet allows flexibility. Instead of sitting through an entire news program waiting for your topic of interest, you can use a search engine to find a specific news item immediately. Are you among those who still consume their news the old-fashioned way, through the newspaper or nightly news? If so, check out these Web sites:

www.nbc.com   www.abc.com   www.nytimes.com   www.cnn.com

SUMMARY

1. The news media include newspapers, television, radio, electronic communication, magazines, and books in all of their forms. These means of communication have been called "the fourth branch of government."

2. The news media are a pervasive feature of American politics and generally help to define our culture. Moreover, the rise of new communications technologies has made the media more influential throughout American society. The news media provide a "linking" function between politicians and government officials and the public.

3. Our modern news media emerged from a more partisan and less professionalized past. The autonomy of the media from political parties is one of the important changes. Now, journalists strive for objectivity and see themselves as important to the political process. Broadcasting on radio and television has changed the news media, and most Americans use television and radio as primary news sources. The role of corporations, especially media conglomerates, has emerged in the past few years and raises questions about media competition and orientation.

4. The influence of the mass media over public opinion is significant yet not overwhelming. People may not pay much attention to the media or believe all they read or see or hear. They may be critical or suspicious of the media and hence resistant to it. People tend to "filter" the news in part through their political socialization, selectivity,

needs, and ability to recall or comprehend the content of the news.

5. The media are criticized as biased both by conservatives (who charge that the media are too liberal) and by liberals (who claim that the media are captive of corporate interests and major advertisers). The mass media are big business, but their product is information, which is protected under the First Amendment. Little evidence exists of actual, deliberate bias in news reporting.

6. A major effect of mass media news is agenda setting, that is, determining what problems will become salient issues for people to form opinions about and to discuss. The media are also influential in defining issues.

7. The media are under attack for sensationalism, superficial reporting, biased coverage, and overemphasis on the "theatrical." Any efforts at comprehensive reform will be frustrated, however, by at least two factors: reformers do not agree on what course to follow, and virtually all Americans fear taking any action that might threaten the freedom of the press.

8. Presidential campaigns are dominated by media coverage during both the pre- and post-convention stages. One effect of media influence is that most people seem more interested in the contest as a "game" or "horse race" than as an occasion for serious discussion of issues and candidates.

FURTHER READING

STEPHEN ANSOLABEHERE AND SHANTO IYENGAR, *Going Negative: How Attack Ads Shrink and Polarize the Electorate* (Free Press, 1996).

LANCE W. BENNETT, *Governing Crisis: Media, Money, and Marketing in American Elections* (St. Martin's Press, 1992).

TIMOTHY COOK, *Making Laws and Making News: Press Strategies in the U.S. House of Representatives* (Brookings Institution, 1990).

RICHARD DAVIS, *The Press and American Politics: The New Mediator* (Prentice Hall, 1996).

RICHARD DAVIS, ED., *Politics and the Media* (Prentice Hall, 1994).

JAMES FALLOWS, *Breaking the News: How the Media Undermine American Democracy* (Pantheon Books, 1996).

CAROL FELSENTHAL, *Power, Privilege and "The Post": The Catherine Graham Story* (Putnam, 1993).

SUZANNE GARMENT, *Scandal: The Culture of Mistrust in American Politics* (Times Books, 1991).

DORIS A. GRABER, *Mass Media and American Politics*, 5th ed. (Congressional Quarterly Press, 1997).

LAWRENCE K. GROSSMAN, *The Electronic Republic: Reshaping Democracy in the Information Age* (Viking, 1995).

ROD HART, *Seducing America: How Television Charms the Modern Voter* (Oxford University Press, 1994).

STEPHEN HESS, *Live from Capitol Hill: Studies of Congress and the Media* (Brookings Institution, 1991).

KATHLEEN HALL JAMIESON, *Dirty Politics: Deception, Distraction, and Democracy* (Oxford University Press, 1992).

PHYLISS KANISS, *Making Local News* (University of Chicago Press, 1991).

HOWARD KURTZ, *Hot Air: All Talk All the Time* (New York Times Books, 1996).

S. ROBERT LICHTER AND RICHARD E. NOYES, *Good Intentions Make Bad News: Why Americans Hate Campaign Journalism* (Rowman and Littlefield, 1995).

S. ROBERT LICHTER, STANLEY ROTHMAN, AND LINDA S. LICHTER, *The Media Elite* (Adler and Adler, 1986).

JOHN ANTHONY MALTESE, *Spin Control: The White House Office of Communications and the Management of Presidential News* (University of North Carolina Press, 1992).

RUSSELL W. NEWMAN, *Common Knowledge: News and the Construction of Political Meaning* (University of Chicago Press, 1991).

THOMAS E. PATTERSON, *Out of Order* (Knopf, 1993).

TOM ROSENSTEIL, *Strange Bedfellows: How Television and the Presidential Candidates Changed American Politics, 1992* (Hyperion, 1993).

SIMON SEFATY, *The Media and Foreign Policy* (St. Martin's Press, 1990).

KENNETH T. WALSH, *Feeding the Beast: The White House versus the Press* (Random House, 1996).

DARRELL M. WEST, *Air Wars: Television Advertising in Election Campaigns, 1952–1992* (Congressional Quarterly Press, 1993).

14

Congress: The People's Branch

$\mathcal{F}$ormer President Woodrow Wilson, as a young writer, called our political system "Congressional Government." The framers of our Constitution considered Congress so central to our system that they devoted the lengthy and detailed First Article of the Constitution to it. Congress plays a crucial role in a government by the people. Indeed, genuine constitutional democracy is impossible without a strong, effective national legislature.

"Representative democracy is a grand experiment," writes legislative scholar Richard F. Fenno, Jr. "The idea that ordinary citizens freely elect other ordinary citizens to make certain decisions on their behalf and then hold them electorally accountable is not foreordained. It cannot be taken for granted; it is not simple to maintain; and it is not readily appreciated."[1]

The United States Congress is one of the most praised yet most criticized political institutions in America. It is praised because it is a representative and democratic institution. It is praised, too, because it is one of the most deliberative and open legislative bodies in the world. It is revered, finally, because it has nurtured many outstanding legislators who have contributed greatly to the success of the American political experiment.

Yet Americans relentlessly criticize both Congress and its members. Most Americans don't think members of Congress understand their needs, and most citizens also think members of Congress put the concerns of special interests ahead of those of the average person.

Complicating matters, however, is the fact that although most Americans profess a devotion to democracy, many have little or no appreciation of what a practicing democracy requires. Political scientists John Hibbing and Elizabeth Theiss-Morse note, "People do not wish to see uncertainty, conflicting options, long debate, competing interests, confusion, bargaining, and compromised, imperfect solutions." Instead, they would like their government to perform its job quietly, efficiently, and without public bickering and gridlock. "In short," Hibbing and Theiss-Morse conclude, the American people "often seek a patently unrealistic form of democracy."[2]

Congress may be widely criticized, but it plays an absolutely crucial role in the American political system. Presidents cannot lead if they do not have a working relationship with both chambers of Congress. Congress controls key decisions on budgets, taxes, trade policy, the shape of the federal bureaucracy, and appointments to the cabinet, to our embassies, and to our courts. A president has a certain amount of freedom in initiating key foreign policy decisions, yet even here a president's policy will rarely be successful or properly implemented without support from Congress.

Ours is a system of shared powers. Consequently, Congress and the president are inevitably engaged in a collaborative process. Part of the reason why it is difficult to appreciate or understand Congress is that much of what it does depends on its relationships with the other branches of government as well as with state and local governments.

In this chapter we examine the politics of representation and how Congress organizes itself to do the work of law making and representation. We also look at how this highly public, open, and genuinely political institution cannot avoid provoking conflicts over policy that lead to sometimes bitter clashes with the White House and other rivals for influence in the shaping of American public policies.

Members of Congress are politicians, and they get their jobs by winning an election. Ironically, it is often good politics for them to deny they are politicians and to lead the charge against the institution they serve in. The outcome of any congressional election depends on many factors. By far the most important is the nature of the state or district in which the candidate runs. Is it a **safe seat**—one that is predictably won by one party or the other—or is it a highly competitive one? Other factors affecting winning elections are personal appeal of the candidate, whether the opponent is an incumbent or a newcomer, local issues, campaign strategies, the fund-raising abilities of the candidate, and, occasionally, national political tides, such as in the 1964, 1974, and 1994 elections.

Incumbents have traditionally enjoyed a great advantage over challengers, but incumbency isn't always an advantage. Critics like Ross Perot, Ralph Nader, Steve Forbes, and Rush Limbaugh have targeted the "Washington insiders" and helped create a climate of antagonism toward Congress as an institution. Because of this, there have been repeated unsuccessful efforts in recent years in Congress to pass constitutional term limits on congressional terms. But more than 90 percent of incumbents who run for reelection to Congress continue to beat their challengers; 94 percent did so, for example, in 1996.

Districting and Apportionment

The Constitution gives Congress the right to apportion representatives among the states according to population, and Congress, in turn, has given state legislatures control over the drawing of their respective congressional districts. Senators, of course, represent entire states, but House seats are distributed among the states according to population; each state receives at least one seat. Subject to a gubernatorial veto, state legislatures draw the district lines for the House of Representatives. The party in control of the state legislature traditionally draws the lines to enhance its own political fortunes.[3] This is known as **gerrymandering**, after Governor Elbridge Gerry of Massachusetts, who, in 1811, reluctantly signed a redistricting bill that created a distinctly partisan district shaped like a salamander.

State legislatures are free to draw congressional districts pretty much as they wish, subject to some constitutional limitations. First, each district must be equal in population, or as equal as possible.[4] To accommodate population shifts, **redistricting** occurs once a decade, after each national census. Because population shifts also occur between states, it is necessary after each census to reapportion seats for

Why Do Incumbent Members of Congress Usually Win?

- They enjoy better name recognition, and to be known at all is generally to be known favorably. Challengers are almost always less well known.
- They enjoy free mailings (called the franking privilege) to every household in the state or district. These mailings—which often resemble campaign brochures—portray members as hardworking and influential.
- They have greater access to the media.
- They raise campaign money more easily than challengers, because lobbyists and political action committees (PACs) seek their ears and their favors. Also, many campaign contributors know that incumbents are more likely than challengers to get reelected, so they give to those they know will win.
- They usually have had more campaign experience, and they can claim to have had more experience in Congress and in Washington.
- They have staffs to help with casework and constituency services for the folks back home.
- They take credit for federal money that gets allocated to their region.
- They are in a better position than challengers to take advantage of government research staffs, new government studies, and even classified information.

No one of these factors can guarantee a member's reelection, yet skillful use of them makes it difficult to unseat a healthy incumbent.

The word *gerrymander* comes from the name of a governor of Massachusetts, Elbridge Gerry, and the salamander-shaped district that was created to favor his party.

the U.S. House of Representatives. Thus, in 1990, 13 states lost representatives and 8 gained new seats in the House. After the census in 2000, Congress will have to again reapportion representatives among the states, and it is anticipated again that some eastern and northern states will lose House seats, and some sun belt and western states will gain seats. A state legislature must not be overzealous in favoring one party at the expense of another. The Supreme Court has held that grossly partisan gerrymandering is, under certain circumstances, unconstitutional.[5] Finally, although a state legislature can design congressional districts to virtually guarantee the election of a member of a particular minority, it must be careful not to do so in a fashion that focuses only on racial considerations and ignores such matters as county lines and city boundaries.[6] Indeed, the Supreme Court has ruled that making race "the predominant factor," while ignoring traditional redistricting principles such as compactness is unconstitutional.[7]

A Profile of Members of Congress

The entire membership of the House of Representatives (435) is elected to two-year terms in even-numbered years. Elections for the six-year Senate terms are staggered, so that one-third of the Senate's 100 members are chosen every two years. Members of the House of Representatives must be 25 years old and have been citizens for seven years. Senators must be at least 30 and have been citizens for nine years.

In the 105th Congress (1997–99) 91 percent of U.S. senators and 88 percent of U.S. representatives were male. Most are well-educated and middle-aged and come from upper-middle or upper income backgrounds. Two-thirds have advanced degrees. Eighty-five percent are married, and about 43 percent, not surprisingly, are lawyers, or at least have gone to law school. Until recently, they were also mainly white Anglo-Saxon Protestants (WASPs). Larger numbers of Roman Catholics and many Jews now bring Congress's religious makeup closer in line with that of the general population.[8] But there are still fewer Hispanics and African Americans in Congress than in the general public, and only a handful of Asian Americans, as well as just one Native American. Women remain especially underrepresented, indeed "much more underrepresented, in relation to their proportion of the U.S. population, than are black and Hispanic Americans."[9] There are also some farmers,

Senator Ben Nighthorse Campbell (R.-Colo.) and Senator Carol Moseley Braun (D.-Ill.), elected in 1992, were, respectively, the first Native American and the first African American woman to win seats in the U.S. Senate.

The new members of the 105th Congress reflect the increasing diversity of the membership: more women, African Americans, Hispanics, and members of other ethnic groups than served in Washington in the past.

We the People

A Profile of the 105th Congress, 1997–1999

House

Republicans	52%
Democrats	48%
Independent	1
Sex:	
Women	12%
Men	88%
Race:	
African American	8%
Hispanic	4%
Asian American	1%
White	87%
Average Age:	52 years
Religion:	
Catholic	29%
Jewish	6%
Protestant	60%
Other/none	5%
Lawyers:	40%

Senate

Republicans	55%
Democrats	45%
Sex:	
Women	9%
Men	91%
Race:	
African American	1
Asian American	2
Hispanic	0
Native American	1
White	96
Average Age:	58 years
Religion:	
Catholic	24%
Jewish	10%
Protestant	57%
Other/none	9%

Lawyers: 56%

SOURCE: *The New York Times*, January 19, 1997, p. E5.

teachers, clergy, a lot of businesspeople, three former professional athletes, and even two former actors. But few members come from blue-collar occupations. That most members are the products of middle- and upper-middle-class families does not necessarily mean they are interested only in improving the position of that portion of the population. Senators like Edward Kennedy (D.-Mass.) and Jay Rockefeller (D.-W.Va.), for instance, are affluent white males, yet they are strong advocates of legislation to protect women, minorities, and poor people.

Issues of special interest to women have received increased attention in Congress lately, no doubt due in part to the doubling of the number of women in Congress in the 1990s. Thus, Congress has enacted laws to combat violence against women and to improve medical research on diseases that affect women. Congress has also made it a crime to block access to abortion clinics by force.

THE STRUCTURE AND POWERS OF CONGRESS

The most important fact about Congress is it is *bicameral*—that is, made up of two houses. Few other national legislatures are genuinely bicameral. Many have two houses, but one is usually largely ceremonial. In the United States, the Senate and the House each have an absolute veto over the other's law making. Each chamber runs its own affairs, sets its own rules, and conducts its own investigations. The law-making role, however, is shared. Each must be seen as a separate institution, even though both houses reflect similar political forces and share common organizational patterns.

As James Madison explained in *The Federalist*, No. 51, the protection against giving too much power to the legislature "is to divide the legislature into different branches; and to render them, by different modes of election and different principles of action, as little connected with each other as the nature of their common functions, and their common dependence on the society will admit." (*The Federalist*, No. 51, is reprinted in the Appendix.) The House of Representatives was expected to reflect the popular will of the average citizen, whereas the Senate was to provide for stability, continuity, and in-depth deliberation. Many of the framers hoped the Senate would stem any rash populist impulses of the other chamber.

In Article I, the Constitution outlined the structure, powers, and responsibilities of Congress, giving it "All legislative Powers herein granted": the power to spend and tax in order to "provide for the common Defense and general Welfare of the United States"; the power to borrow money; the power to regulate commerce with foreign nations and among the states; the power to declare war, raise and support armies, and provide and maintain a navy; the power to establish post offices; and the power to set up the federal courts under the Supreme Court. As a final catchall, the Constitution gave Congress the right "to make all Laws which shall be necessary and proper for carrying into Execution" the powers set out. Several nonlegislative functions were also granted, such as participating in the process of constitutional amendment and impeachment (given to the House) and trying an impeached federal officer (given to the Senate).

The Constitution confers additional responsibilities on the Senate. The Senate has the power to confirm many presidential nominations—sometimes as many as 500 key executive and judicial nominees a year. In a two-year Congress there may be more than 5,000 civilian nominations and 90,000 military nominations needing senatorial approval. The Senate must also give its consent, by a two-thirds vote of the senators present, for presidential ratification of treaties.

Although the Seventeenth Amendment to the Constitution (1913), which provides for direct election of U.S. senators, altered the character of the Senate's membership, the two chambers still have many differences (see Table 14–1). However,

TABLE 14-1

Differences Between the House of Representatives and the Senate

House of Representatives	Senate
Two-year term	Six-year term
435 members	100 members
Smaller constituencies	Larger constituencies
Fewer personal staff	More personal staff
Equal populations represented	States represented
Less flexible rules	More flexible rules
Limited debate	Unlimited debate
More policy specialists	Policy generalists
Less media coverage	More media coverage
Less prestige	More prestige
Less reliance on staff	More reliance on staff
More powerful committee leaders	More equal distribution of power
Very important committees	Less important committees
20 major committees	20 major committees
Nongermane amendments (riders) not allowed	Nongermane amendments (riders) allowed
Important Rules Committee	Special treaty ratification power
Some bills permit no floor amendments (closed rule)	Special confirmation power
	Filibuster is allowed

the two houses are more similar today in their membership and operations than they were two hundred or even one hundred years ago.

The House has some distinctive responsibilities, but they are not as important as those given to the Senate. For example, although all revenue bills must originate in the House, this practice does not give the House much advantage, as the Senate has freely amended spending bills, sometimes changing everything except the title.

The framers did not intend Congress to be all-powerful. They reserved certain authority for the states and for the people and gave other powers to the executive and judicial branches of the national government. As time passed, Congress gained power in some respects and lost it in others. The power of Congress also changed with the times and the president. For example, Clinton was more effective in getting legislation passed in his first two years in office than after the Republican takeover in 1995.

As the role and authority of the national government have expanded, so have the policy-making and oversight responsibilities of Congress. Still, Congress has difficulty keeping pace with its great rival, the presidency. The president's national security responsibilities, preparation of the budget, media visibility, and agenda-setting influence have all enhanced the position of the presidency. The growth of executive authority may be part of a worldwide trend. Legislative bodies almost everywhere have become subordinate to the executive at all levels of government.

Despite its sometimes secondary role in recent decades, however, Congress still performs seven important functions:

1. *Representation* involves expressing the diversity and conflicting views of the regional, economic, social, racial, religious, and other interests in the United States.

2. *Law making* is enacting measures to help solve substantive problems.

3. *Consensus building* is the bargaining process by which these interests are reconciled.

4. *Overseeing the bureaucracy* means ensuring that laws and policies approved by Congress are faithfully carried out by the executive branch and that they accomplish what was intended.

5. *Policy clarification* (or policy incubation, as it is sometimes called) is the identification and publicizing of issues.

6. For the Senate, *confirming by a majority vote presidential appointees* and by two-thirds vote presidential ratification of treaties.

7. *Investigating the operation of government* agencies, including the White House.

The House of Representatives

The organization and procedures in the House are different from those in the Senate, if only because the House is more than four times as large as the Senate. *How* things are done affects *what* is done. The House assigns different types of bills to different calendars. For instance, finance measures—tax or appropriations bills—are put on a special calendar for quicker action. The House has other ways to speed up law making, including electronic voting. Ordinary rules may be suspended by a two-thirds vote, or immediate action may be taken by unanimous consent of the members on the floor. By sitting as the *committee of the whole*, the House is able to operate more informally and more quickly than under its regular rules. A quorum in the committee of the whole is composed of only 100 members, rather than a majority of the whole chamber, and voting is quicker and simpler. Members are limited in how long they can speak, and debate may be cut off simply by majority vote.

THE SPEAKER AND OTHER LEADERS The **Speaker** is the presiding officer in the House of Representatives.[10] The Constitution mandates that the House of Representatives shall choose its Speaker, yet it does not say anything about duties or powers of the office. This officer is formally elected by the House yet is actually selected by the majority party; it is usually someone with broad appeal in the party. Revolts in 1910 by rank-and-file Progressives stripped Speakers of much of their power, including control over who served on which congressional committees. As the highest-ranking officer in Congress, the Speaker represents it on ceremonial occasions. Third in line of succession to the presidency (in case of death, resignation, or impeachment), the Speaker must keep the White House informed about his whereabouts.

The routine powers of the Speaker include recognizing members who wish to speak, ruling on questions of parliamentary procedure, and appointing members to select and conference committees—that is, temporary committees, not standing committees. In general, the Speaker directs business on the floor of the House. More significant, of course, is a Speaker's political and behind-the-scenes influence. When the Republicans won control of the House in 1994, they elected Newt Gingrich as Speaker. As the first Republican Speaker in 40 years, he was a novelty in Washington. "I had set out to do a very unusual job," said Gingrich, "which was part revolutionary, part national political figure, part Speaker, part intellectual."[11]

Gingrich immediately established his authority—naming committee chairs, bypassing the seniority rule, reorganizing House committees, and reducing perks and committee staffs. He delegated considerable power to his fellow Republican leaders, yet claimed for himself the main role as spokesperson for major policy initiatives. He published a book detailing his ideas about government, and he cheerfully took on the White House and the national press.[12]

Gingrich won attention for his positions and eventually for himself. He sometimes seemed to be performing the role of an American prime minister, but he admitted that he found it demanding to perform the many roles of the speakership. He soon found it difficult to control the ideologically oriented Republicans, especially the 73 Republican first-term members elected in 1994. He sometimes lost his temper with the press, and after a while, he became as much of a lightning rod for the public's discontent with Congress as many of his Democratic predecessors had been in the 1980s and early 1990s.

Following a spate of charges against Gingrich and a two-year investigation, the House Ethics Committee found Gingrich had showed disregard and lack of respect for standards of conduct that applied to the use of tax-exempt funds. For at least three years he had insisted there was little overlap between his partisan political activities and his supposedly nonpartisan educational endeavors. But the committee recommended, and the House of Representatives quickly passed, a reprimand of Gingrich and imposed a stern fine of $300,000 on him for misusing the charitable deduction for political purposes and for misleading the House Ethics Committee. This was an unprecedented rebuke for a Speaker, indeed, the only such reprimand of a Speaker in the 208-year history of the House.[13]

Still, in January of 1997 Newt Gingrich was reelected Speaker, but with nine members of his own party refusing to vote for him. "To the degree I was too brash, too self-confident or too pushy, I apologize" said Gingrich. "To whatever degree in any way that I brought controversy or inappropriate attention to the House, I apologize."[14]

The Speaker is assisted by a **majority leader** who helps plan party strategy, confers with other party leaders, and tries to keep members of the party in line. The minority party elects a **minority leader**, who usually steps into the speakership when his or her party gains a majority in the House. These positions are also sometimes called majority and minority floor leader. Assisting each floor leader are the party **whips**. (The term comes from the "whipper-in," who in fox hunts keeps the hounds bunched in a pack.) The whips serve as liaison between the House leadership of each party and the rank-and-file. They inform members when important bills will come up for a vote, prepare summaries of the bills, do nose counts for the leadership, exert mild pressure on members to support the leadership, and try to ensure maximum attendance on the floor for critical votes.

At the beginning of the session and occasionally afterward, each party holds a **caucus** of all its members (called a **conference** by Republicans) to elect party officers, approve committee assignments, elect committee leaders, discuss important legislation, and perhaps try to agree on party policy.

THE HOUSE RULES COMMITTEE   The House, unlike the Senate, has a Rules Committee that helps regulate the time of floor debate for each bill as well as limitations on floor amendments. In the normal course of events, a bill does not come up for action on the floor without a rule from the Rules Committee; the rule sets the length of debate and specifies whether the bill can or cannot be amended. By failing to act or refusing to grant a rule, the committee can delay consideration of a bill. A **closed rule** prohibits amendments altogether or provides that only members of the committee reporting the bill may offer amendments; closed rules are usually reserved for tax and spending bills. An **open rule** permits debate within the overall time allocated to the bill.

From the New Deal era until the mid-1960s, the Rules Committee was dominated by a coalition of Republicans and conservative Democrats. Liberals denounced it as unrepresentative, unfair, and dictatorial. More recently, the Rules

Committee membership has come to reflect the views of the total membership of the majority party. The Rules Committee today is an arm of the leadership, and rather than block legislation, it offers a "dress rehearsal" on procedural issues like time allotted for debate to those trying to press for new measures.

The Senate

The Senate has the same basic committee structure, elected party leadership, and decentralized power as the House, but because the Senate is a smaller body, its procedures are more informal, and it permits more time for debate. Television has made the Senate an even more visible and key political forum. It has become more open and outward looking, and its members today share influence more equitably than in the past. The Senate now addresses a wider range of issues than ever before.

The president of the Senate (the vice-president of the United States) has little influence over Senate proceedings. A vice-president can vote only in case of a tie and is seldom consulted when important decisions are made. The Senate also elects from among the majority party a **president pro tempore**, usually the most senior member, who is official chair in the absence of the vice-president. Presiding over the Senate on most occasions is a thankless chore, so the president pro tempore regularly delegates this responsibility to junior members of the chamber's majority party.

Party machinery in the Senate is somewhat similar to that of the House. There are party caucuses (conferences), majority and minority floor leaders, and party whips. Each party has a *policy committee*, composed of the leaders of the party, which is theoretically responsible for the party's overall legislative program. In the Senate the party steering committees handle only committee assignments. Unlike the House party steering committees, the Senate's party policy committees are formally provided for by law, and each has a regular staff and a budget. Although the Senate party policy committees have some influence on legislation, they have not asserted strong legislative leadership or managed to coordinate policy.

The Senate *majority leader*—the elected leader of the majority party in the Senate—is an influential person within the Senate and sometimes nationally. This is certainly true of the current majority leader, Senator Trent Lott (R.-Miss.). He took over from Senator Bob Dole in mid-1996 and has become a major spokesperson for the Republican party. As the Senate's major power broker, the majority leader has the right to be the first senator heard on the floor. In consultation with the *minority leader*, the majority leader determines the Senate's agenda and has much to say about committee assignments for members of the majority party. The position confers somewhat less authority than the speakership in the House, and its influence depends on the person's political and parliamentary skills and on the national political situation.[15]

POLITICAL ENVIRONMENT Senators have more diverse policy interests than do members of the House, serve on more committees, and are more likely to wield power in their state parties. For these reasons, the character of the Senate is different from that of the House. Even first-term senators can become visible and politically significant. This possibility for prominence is due to the smaller size of the Senate, its greater access to the media, and the larger staffs that senators enjoy.

The contemporary Senate is individualistic. With the expanding role of subcommittee chairs and enlarged staff, the influence of committee chairs has declined, and key decisions are often made on the Senate floor. The Senate is a more open, fluid, and decentralized body now than it was a generation or two ago. Indeed, it is often said that the Senate has one hundred separate power centers and is so splintered that the party leaders have difficulty arranging the day-to-day schedule.[16]

Senator Trent Lott of Mississippi was selected by his fellow Republicans to take over as Senate majority leader in 1996 when Bob Dole resigned to campaign for the presidency. He was reelected majority leader in 1997.

THE FILIBUSTER A major difference between the Senate and the House is that debate is much less limited in the Senate. A senator who gains the floor may go on talking until he or she relinquishes the right to talk voluntarily or through exhaustion. This right to unlimited debate may be used by a small group of senators to **filibuster**—delay Senate proceedings in order to delay or prevent a vote. At one time the filibuster was a favorite weapon of southern senators intent on blocking civil rights legislation. More recently the filibuster has been used for a wider range of issues. The Senate in 1987 had, for instance, a week-long filibuster opposing a congressional campaign finance reform bill. And in 1993, Republicans used a filibuster to kill President Bill Clinton's economic stimulus package. A filibuster, or the threat of a filibuster, is typically most potent at the end of a congressional session, when there is a fixed date for adjournment, because it could mean that many bills that have made it to the end of the legislation process will die for lack of a floor vote. The knowledge that a bill might be subject to a filibuster is often enough to force a compromise satisfactory to its opponents. Sometimes the leaders, knowing that a filibuster will tie up the Senate and keep it from enacting other needed legislation, do not bring a controversial bill to the floor.

"Listen pal, I didn't spend seven million bucks to get here so I could yield the floor to you."

Drawing by Dana Fradon. 1987 The New Yorker Magazine, Inc.

A filibuster can be defeated. Until 1917 the Senate could terminate a filibuster only if every member agreed. That year, however, the Senate adopted its first debate-ending, or **cloture**, rule. Now, as long as the senators who are doing the talking stay on their feet, debate can be stopped only by a cloture vote. The rule of cloture specifies that two days after 16 members sign a petition, the question of curtailing debate must be put to a vote. If three-fifths of the total number of senators (60 of the 100 members) vote for cloture, no senator may speak for more than one hour. A final vote must be taken after no more than 30 hours of debate, including all delaying tactics, such as quorum calls and roll call votes on procedure. After the 30 hours of debate, the motion before the Senate must be brought to a vote.

The filibuster is frequently used for partisan and parochial purposes. Indeed, senators usually anticipate a filibuster on contested controversial measures.[17] The tactic or the threat of a filibuster is available to Senate minorities to force the majority to compromise and modify its position, and both parties have learned to use it well when they are in the minority. Cloture votes are more common today than in earlier years, in part because the Senate reduced the number of votes needed from 67 to 60.

THE POWER TO CONFIRM The Senate has the constitutional power to confirm presidential appointments to such positions as the cabinet, the U.S. Supreme Court and other federal courts, all ambassadorial positions, and many executive-branch positions. As with other legislative business, the confirmation process starts in committees, with the relevant standing committee having jurisdiction. The Judiciary Committee considers judges and Supreme Court nominees; the Foreign Relations Committee considers all ambassadorial appointments. Nominees appear before the committee to answer questions, and they typically have met individually with key senators well before the hearing.

The framers of the Constitution regarded the confirmation process and its advice and consent by the Senate as an important check on executive power. Alexander Hamilton viewed it as a way for Congress to prevent the appointment of "unfit characters." Today the U.S. Senate and the president often struggle over control of top personnel in the executive and judicial branches.

The Constitution leaves the question somewhat ambiguous: "The President . . . shall nominate, and by and with the Advice and Consent of the Senate, shall appoint Ambassadors, other public Ministers and Consuls, Judges of the Supreme Court, all other officers of the United States." Presidents, however, have never enjoyed exclusive control over hiring and firing in the executive branch. The Senate jealously guards its right to confirm or reject major appointments; during the period of strong Congresses after the Civil War, presidents had to struggle to keep their power to appoint and dismiss. But for most of the twentieth century, presidents gained a reasonable amount of control over top appointments, in part, because a growing number of people in and out of Congress believe that chief executives without compatible cabinet-level appointees of their choice cannot be held accountable.

In recent years the Senate has taken a somewhat tougher stand on presidential appointments, and time spent evaluating and screening presidential nominations has increased. The Senate rejected several nominees of Presidents George Bush and Ronald Reagan, and President Clinton has had to withdraw nominees for attorney general and several other posts because of Senate opposition. In 1997, for example, Anthony Lake, Clinton's nominee for director of the Central Intelligence Agency, withdrew his name after a particularly grueling week of confirmation hearings indicated he might not win confirmation in a Senate vote.

The Senate's role in the confirmation process was never intended to eliminate politics but rather to use politics as a safeguard. When the Senate was Democratic and the White House Republican, conservatives complained that the Senate was interfering with the executive power of the president by rejecting nominees because of their political beliefs. Yet when the Republicans controlled the Senate and the Democrats the White House, it was the liberals who made the same complaint.

By a tradition called **senatorial courtesy**, a president confers with the senator or senators from the state where an appointee is to work. A nomination is less likely to secure Senate approval against the objection of these senators, especially if these senators are members of the president's party, even if his party does not control the Senate. Thus, for nearly all district court judgeships and a variety of other positions, senators can exercise what is, in fact, a veto that can be overridden only with difficulty. Further, it is usually exercised in secret and subject to little accountability. But this form of patronage is sufficiently important to senators that senatorial courtesy is likely to continue.

It is useful to note a distinction between judicial appointments, especially those to the Supreme Court, and administration appointments. The Senate plays a greater role in judicial appointments because judges serve for life and constitute an independent and, as we discuss in Chapter 16, vital branch of the government.[18] When it comes to cabinet-level positions in the executive branch, it is assumed that a president ought to be able to choose those who will carry out the general views of the White House; in contrast, a president is not expected to enjoy partisan loyalty from those nominated to the bench.

The confirmation provisions in the Constitution have fulfilled most of the intentions of the framers. The Senate has been able to use its power to reject unqualified nominees, and it has also been able to prevent those with serious conflicts of interest from taking office. In addition, senators have been able to use the confirmation process to make their views known to prospective executive officials. Indeed, the very existence of the confirmation process generally deters presidents from appointing weak, questionable, or "unfit characters."

The Consequences of Bicameralism

Defenders of **bicameralism**—having a two-chamber legislature—say it serves as a moderating influence on the partisanship or possible errors of either of the chambers. This constitutionally mandated process also guarantees that many votes will be taken before a policy is finally approved. It provides more opportunities, too, for bargaining, and it allows legislators with different policy goals a role in the shaping of national laws.

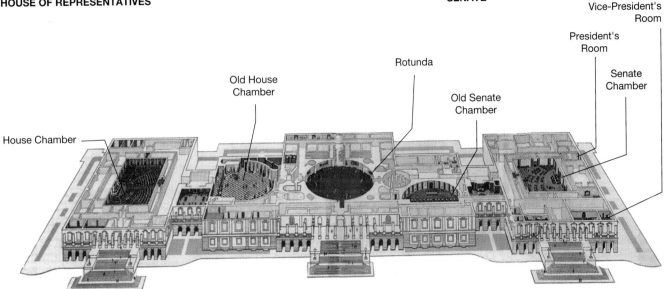

James Madison and the framers of the Constitution hailed this feature of our system as a beneficial and, indeed, a highly desirable protection of our liberties. Yet not everyone views it this way. Critics point out that the U.S. Senate is the only legislature in the country where the principle of equal representation does not apply. Further, because each state has two senators regardless of population, the Senate represents constituencies that are more rural, white, Republican, and conservative than would be the case if the one-person, one-vote norm applied to Senate elections.

Political scientist Patrick Fisher contends smaller states get more than their "fair share." "Bicameralism," he writes, "is biased in favor of certain demographic and political groups who have much greater political clout than their raw numbers would indicate. . . . When it comes to making laws . . . we may have too much of checks and balances and not enough tough decisions being made for the well-being of the nation as a whole." Fisher concludes that having both a House and a Senate "works in favor of narrow interests to the detriment of broad interests."[19]

Most political scientists and constitutional scholars prefer to emphasize the positive benefits of bicameralism. And, as a practical reality, our legislative system is not going to change. Still, it is worth trying to assess the merits of our constitutional arrangements.

THE JOB OF THE LEGISLATOR

Congress as a Place to Work

The elegant U.S. Capitol building is the working center of our nation's legislative process. It is flanked by half a dozen House and Senate office buildings, the sprawling Library of Congress, and a number of other office buildings that help Congress do its work. Although staff size has been cut in recent years, members of Congress still employ over 16,000 staff aides who work in Washington, D.C. or in local district offices. Another 5,000 work for the General Accounting Office, the Congressional Research Office, the Congressional Budget Office, the Architect of the Capitol, and other agencies under the direct control of Congress. (We exclude for this count the Library of Congress and the U.S. Government Printing

Office, which technically report to Congress, yet in fact serve the entire government as well as the general public.)

Congressional staffs grew enormously in the 1960s and 1970s. But in more recent years, critics as well as elected officials have called for major reductions in the number of both staffs and committees. Bill Clinton, Newt Gingrich, Ross Perot, and Ralph Nader differ on many things, yet all of them favored cutting committee staffs and shrinking the size of the legislative branch.[20] These staffs are now at least 10 percent smaller than they were in the early 1990s.

Legislators as Representatives

Congress has a split personality. One Congress is a *law-making institution* that writes laws and makes policy for the entire nation. In this capacity, all the members are expected to set aside their personal ambitions and perhaps even the concerns of their own constituencies. Yet Congress is also a *representative assembly*, made up of 535 elected officials who serve as links between their constituents and the national government. The dual roles of making laws and responding to constituents' demands force members to balance national concerns against the specific interests of their states or districts.

For whom does a representative speak? The geographical district and its immediate interests? The party? The nation? Some special interest? His or her conscience? Congress was intended to serve as a forum for registering the interests and values of the nation. It was never intended that the legislative branch represent views identical to those of the executive. But to whom does the individual representative listen?

Members of Congress perceive their roles differently. Some believe they should serve as **delegates** from their districts. These legislators believe it is their duty to find out what "the folks back home" want and act accordingly. This orientation is often assumed by Republicans, nonleaders, nonsoutherners, or members with low seniority.

Other members see their role as that of **trustee**. Their constituents, they contend, did not send them to Congress to serve as mere robots or "errand-runners." They act and vote according to their own view of what is best for their district or state as well as the nation. As one member explained, "I have a responsibility not only to follow [my constituents], but to inform them and lead them. I'm not going to betray my responsibility to my constituents. I owe them not only my industry but my judgment. That's why they sent me here."[21] In this view a legislature is a place for deliberation and learning, not a mere gathering of ambassadors from localities. The trustee focus is more common among Democrats, House leaders, southerners, and high-seniority members.

Although the question of delegate versus trustee is an old one, it poses a false dichotomy. Representatives cannot follow detailed instructions from their constituents because such instructions seldom exist. On many important policy questions, members hear nothing from their constituents or they hear only from those who agree with them. Still, a legislator should be able to define, or help define, the national interest, and this means trying to understand the needs and aspirations of millions of people. Most legislators shift back and forth between the delegate and trustee role, depending on their perception of the public interest, their standing in the last and next elections, and the pressures of the moment. Most also view themselves more as free agents than as instructed delegates for their districts. Still, nearly everyone in Congress spends a lot of time building constituency connections, mending political fences, and worrying about how a vote on a controversial issue will "play" back home.[22]

Legislators as Lawmakers

Members of Congress cast hundreds of votes each year. In the 104th Congress (1995–97), House members cast a yea or nay vote on 1,321 occasions.[23] When they vote, members of Congress are influenced by their own philosophy and values, their understanding of the problem addressed by the legislation, their perceptions of their constituents' interests, and the views of their trusted colleagues, staff, party leaders, lobbyists, and the president.

POLICY AND PHILOSOPHICAL CONVICTIONS Most of the time, members vote their ideological beliefs, knowing that constituents tend to grant them considerable leeway. A liberal on social issues is also likely to be a liberal on tax and national security issues. Thus, on controversial issues such as national health insurance, taxes, or defense spending, knowing the general philosophical leanings of individual members provides a helpful guide both to how they make up their minds and how they will vote.

One voting pattern, described as the **conservative coalition**, cuts across party lines. It consists of southern Democrats and Republicans who vote together against other Democrats. In the 1950s and 1960s, the coalition formed on about one-quarter of the important roll call votes. From the mid-1980s to the mid-1990s, the coalition came together on roughly a dozen votes a year, and when it did, it won more than 80 percent of the time in the House and did even better in the Senate.[24] The conservative coalition generally forms around domestic issues, especially social welfare legislation.

The conservative coalition has been less of a factor since Republicans gained control of Congress in 1994. Some southern Democrats switched and became Republicans; others were replaced by Republicans at the polls. But more important, the conservatives would have won most of the major votes anyway, because Republicans enjoyed majorities in both chambers.

VOTERS Legislators pay attention to the views of their constituents on issues as well as their "potential views" as issues become more important. Party and executive branch pressures also play a role, but when all is said and done, the members' political futures depend on how most voters in their district feel about their performance. Rarely does a legislator consistently and deliberately vote against the wishes of the people back home. Legislators might pay more attention to voter attitudes on controversial or heavily publicized matters than on lesser-known issues.

A paradox is evident here. Members of Congress sometimes think what they do and how they vote makes a lot of difference to voters back home. Yet the fact is most voters don't have the slightest idea of how their member of Congress votes. In practice, most voters don't think much about most issues that come before Congress. Most legislators overestimate their visibility. Most citizens in fact don't even know the names of their senators and representatives.[25] Aside from periodic polls, members hear most often from the **attentive public**—those who follow public affairs carefully—rather than the general public. Still, members of Congress are generally concerned about how they will explain their votes, especially around election day. Even if only a few voters are aware of their stand on a given issue, this group might make the difference between victory and defeat.

COLLEAGUES Legislators are often influenced by the advice of their close friends in Congress. Their busy schedules and the great number of votes force them to depend on the advice of like-minded colleagues. In particular, they look to respected members of the committee who worked on a bill, especially the committee chair or ranking member of the minority party.[26]

The Many Meanings of Representation

Representation is one of the most challenging concepts in political science, yet one of the most important. These definitions may be helpful.

- *Formal representation* is the authority to act in another's behalf, gained through an institutional process or arrangement such as free and open elections. The formal arrangement of selection, not the behavior of the representative, defines representation in this usage.

- *Descriptive or demographic representation* is the extent to which a representative mirrors the characteristics of the people he or she formally represents. According to this usage of the term, a representative legislature should be an exact portrait, in miniature, of the people.

- *Symbolic representation* is the extent to which a legislator is accepted as believable and as "one of their own" by the folks back home. This usage has a lot to do with a legislator's style and nonverbal signals.

- *Substantive representation* is a legislator's responsiveness to constituents. Do the policy and voting views of a legislator match those of constituents, or does the legislator rely primarily on his or her own judgment? This approach is that of a guardian or trustee, as opposed to a direct delegate of the citizens.

The introduction of television cameras on the floor of Congress opened a window on the daily activities and decisions of our representatives, which could enable citizens to participate more directly in influencing their political positions.

Unlike voters back home, other members usually have detailed knowledge about issues before Congress. Their views are often public; they may have voted on the matter in previous sessions or in committee, and their public statements have been entered in the *Congressional Record*. On occasion, members say they have been impressed by watching another member's speech on C-SPAN while working in their office. More often, legislators find out how their friends stand on an issue, listen to the party leadership's advice, and take into account the various committee reports. If they are still in doubt, they consult other friends and staff. The members most often consulted are those who represent similar districts or the same region or state, like-minded members of the same party or faction, and those on the committee from which the legislation has come. Sometimes, members are influenced to vote one way merely because they know a colleague is on the other side of the issue.

For some legislators, the **state delegation**—senators and representatives from the same state—reinforces a common identity. Texas Democrats have long been a strong and cohesive delegation; other states, like California, have less cohesive state delegations.

A member may also vote with a colleague in the expectation that the colleague will later vote for a measure about which the member is concerned—called **log rolling**. Some vote trading takes place to build coalitions so that members can "bring home the bacon" to their constituents. Other vote trading reflects reciprocity in congressional relations or deference to colleagues' superior information or expertise.

Many forces—regional, local, ties of friendship—can override party influence. Members are sometimes influenced by informal groups (ideological groups, ethnic caucuses, regional groupings, and even the class of colleagues with whom they were elected—for example, "the class of 1994"). Ideological groups in Congress ranging from the Congressional Progressive Caucus to the more conservative Family Concerns or New Federalists groups also can provide voting cues.

CONGRESSIONAL STAFF For years, political scientists urged Congress to strengthen and expand its staff. Without additional help, they said, representatives and senators were at a disadvantage in dealing with the executive branch and were overly dependent on information supplied by the White House or lobbyists. Complexity of the issues and increasingly demanding schedules, too, created pressures for additional staff. Congress responded, and greatly expanded their staffs, and this indeed helped to strengthen the role of Congress in the public policy process. Yet, as noted earlier, these staffs have been reduced in recent years.

Every congressional committee, however, and every subcommittee is now at least minimally staffed. In addition, all members of Congress have increased the number of personal staff members working for them both in their Washington and home-district offices. About one-third of the House of Representatives staff and one-fourth of the Senate staff are based back home. Local staff members help members of Congress communicate with the voters and provide constituency services and casework. Much of the work done in district offices is akin to a continuous campaign effort: generating favorable publicity, arranging for local appearances and newspaper interviews, scheduling, and contacting important civic and business leaders in the region.

Because of the complexity of their responsibilities, members of Congress delegate all kinds of tasks to their staffs. As a result, some members occasionally wonder whether they or their staffs are in charge. This is especially true of senators, who tend to have a wider range of subject matter specialties than do representatives. At congressional hearings, it is often a staff member who suggests to the legislator what questions to ask. Congressional staffers become knowledgeable about special policy areas and deal on a day-to-day basis with their counterparts in the executive departments and interest groups. Indeed, some observers say that some of the most powerful people in Washington are congressional staffers. Staffers draft bills, conduct research, and often do much of the legislative negotiating and coalition building. Professional staffers often have the opportunity to influence legislative decisions. And certainly there is some truth to the notion that the more staffers there are, the more they look for things to do, such as preparing more legislation, suggesting more investigations, and in general making more work for themselves.

But we should not exaggerate the independent power base of staffers, who can be summarily fired at the whim of those they serve. They are not civil servants. Although they cannot be dismissed because of their race, sex, or national origin, they know that if they wander too far from the views of the one person who can fire them, they will quickly be called back into line.

PARTY Most members of Congress are influenced in how they vote by their political party ties. Naturally, there is a fair amount of agreement among party colleagues, and friendships tend to develop within the party. On some issues, the pressure to conform to a party position is immediate and direct, even when a member does not believe in the party position. Members most often vote with their party. Whether as a result of party pressure or natural affinity, on major bills there is a tendency for most Democrats to be arrayed against most Republicans.

Partisan voting has been increasing in the House since the early 1970s and has intensified since the 1994 elections. Party differences are stronger over domestic, regulatory, and welfare reform measures than over foreign policy or civil liberty issues.

Party leaders in both chambers do their best to get their members to vote together. Speaker Gingrich in the mid 1990s claimed cohesive voting was the only way Republicans could implement their party platform and satisfy the majorities who elected them. Senators are usually more independent, so party leaders in the Senate generally have a harder time encouraging party discipline than do leaders in the House.

On the Party Connection

Party cohesion and control in the House of Representatives falls short of what is to be found in parliamentary systems or even in many state legislatures. . . . But the parties retain a central role in both the present functioning of the Congress and in periodic efforts to improve its performance.

The party structure is the most important mechanism we have to contain those excesses and impose a measure of collective responsibility on ourselves. The precise rewards and costs of party loyalty will differ for members who are differently situated, but for all, I believe, there ought to be a presumption that enables a House of disparate parts to function.

SOURCE: David E. Price, *The Congressional Experience: A View from the Hill* (Westview Press, 1993), pp. 73, 90.

In 1995, Republicans managed "to hold an average of 91 percent of their caucus in line in the House and 89 percent in the Senate." Democrats stuck together in the House and Senate only about 80 percent of the time.[27] Still, this level of party cohesion is the highest in recent times. Much of it may be due to the decline of the liberal wing of the Republican party and a similar decline of the conservative wing in the Democratic party.

INTEREST GROUPS Lobbyists represent interest groups in the legislative process. Interest groups, acting through their political action committees (PACs), make substantial contributions to congressional elections, giving largely to incumbents. In addition to their role as financiers of elections, interest groups (through their lobbyists) are important participants in the legislative process because they provide information.

THE PRESIDENT Through effective use of their constitutional and political powers, presidents have become full-time partners in the legislative process.[28] Members of Congress are reluctant to admit that they are influenced by pressure from the White House. On key domestic issues, legislators generally say they are more likely to be influenced by their constituents and by their own policy convictions than by what the White House wants. But the White House works hard to influence public opinion and to win members over to the president's point of view. Presidents, on key votes, usually win needed majority support more than half the time. Indeed, Bill Clinton, in his first term, according to the *Congressional Quarterly*, won an impressive 64 percent support from Congress on roll call votes on which he had taken a clear position.[29]

Presidents and executive branch officials also influence how legislators vote, particularly on foreign policy or national security issues.[30] President Bush benefited from a bipartisan coalition that passed the resolution authorizing the use of military force in the Persian Gulf. President Clinton benefited from strong Republican support in Congress to help win approval for the North American Free Trade Agreement, even when large numbers in his own party opposed this measure. Congress is sometimes overwhelmed by the greater public relations and persuasive abilities of a president.

THE LEGISLATIVE OBSTACLE COURSE

Congress operates under a system of multiple vetoes. The framers dispersed powers so they could not be accumulated by any would-be tyrant. In addition to the checks of bicameralism, Congress has also developed an elaborate set of customs to accompany these constitutional features that serve to distribute power. Follow a bill through the legislative process, and you clearly see this dispersion of power (see Figure 14–1). The procedures and rules of the Senate differ somewhat from those of the House, but in each chamber power is fragmented and influence is decentralized.

Every bill, including those drawn up in the executive branch, must be *introduced* in the House and the Senate by a member of that body. Bills are then *referred* by the leadership to the appropriate standing committee. Roughly 90 percent of the bills introduced every two years die in a subcommittee for lack of support. For bills that have significant backing, a committee or subcommittee holds *hearings* to receive opinions. It then meets to *mark up* (discuss and amend) and vote on the bill. If the subcommittee and then the parent committee vote in favor of the bill, it is *reported*—that is, sent—to the full chamber, where it is debated and *voted* on. In the House the bill must go first to the Rules Committee for a *rule* that sets the time limit for debate and indicates whether floor amendments are allowed.

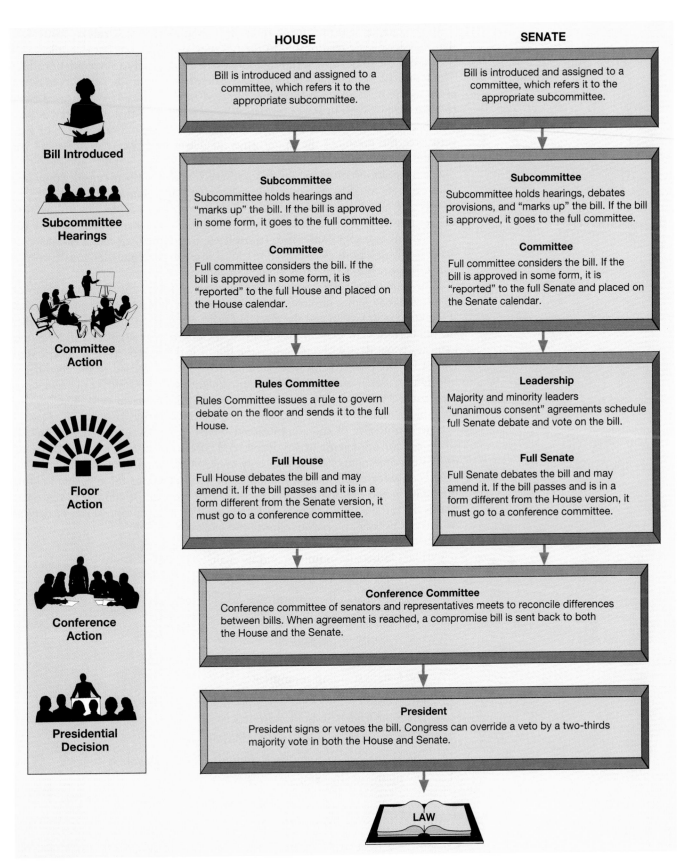

HOUSE

Bill is introduced and assigned to a committee, which refers it to the appropriate subcommittee.

Subcommittee

Subcommittee holds hearings and "marks up" the bill. If the bill is approved in some form, it goes to the full committee.

Committee

Full committee considers the bill. If the bill is approved in some form, it is "reported" to the full House and placed on the House calendar.

Rules Committee

Rules Committee issues a rule to govern debate on the floor and sends it to the full House.

Full House

Full House debates the bill and may amend it. If the bill passes and it is in a form different from the Senate version, it must go to a conference committee.

SENATE

Bill is introduced and assigned to a committee, which refers it to the appropriate subcommittee.

Subcommittee

Subcommittee holds hearings, debates provisions, and "marks up" the bill. If the bill is approved, it goes to the full committee.

Committee

Full committee considers the bill. If the bill is approved in some form, it is "reported" to the full Senate and placed on the Senate calendar.

Leadership

Majority and minority leaders "unanimous consent" agreements schedule full Senate debate and vote on the bill.

Full Senate

Full Senate debates the bill and may amend it. If the bill passes and is in a form different from the House version, it must go to a conference committee.

Conference Committee

Conference committee of senators and representatives meets to reconcile differences between bills. When agreement is reached, a compromise bill is sent back to both the House and the Senate.

President

President signs or vetoes the bill. Congress can override a veto by a two-thirds majority vote in both the House and Senate.

LAW

Bill Introduced

Subcommittee Hearings

Committee Action

Floor Action

Conference Action

Presidential Decision

FIGURE 14–1   How a Bill Becomes a Law

In the Senate, it is not uncommon for legislators to attach **riders**—provisions that may have little relationship to the bill they are riding on. For example, riders that have little to do with spending money can be attached to appropriations bills. The House of Representatives has stricter rules that require amendments to be relevant to the bill, but no such rule is enforced in the Senate. Senators used riders to force the president to accept legislation attached to a bill that was otherwise popular, because the president had to either accept the entire bill or veto it. The **item veto** gave the president the opportunity to delete offending parts of a bill (see Chapter 15).

On most important topics (aside from taxes), both chambers consider their own bills, often at roughly the same time. There is no requirement that one act first. If only one chamber passes the bill, it dies. If both houses pass bills on the same subject but there are differences between the bills—and there often are—the two versions must go to a **conference committee** for reconciliation. If a bill does not make it through both chambers in identical form in the same Congress (two-year term), it must begin the entire process in the next Congress.

When a bill has passed both houses in identical form, it then goes to the president, who may sign it into law, veto it, or veto parts of it with the item veto power. If Congress is in session and the president waits ten days (excluding Sundays), then the bill becomes law *without* his signature. If Congress has adjourned and the president waits ten days without signing the bill, it is then defeated by a **pocket veto**. Except for the pocket veto, when a bill is vetoed it is returned to the chamber of its origin by the president with a message explaining the reasons for the veto. Congress can vote to **override** the veto with a two-thirds vote in each chamber, but assembling such an extraordinary majority is often difficult.

The complexity of the congressional system provides a tremendous built-in advantage for opponents of any measure. Those who sponsor a bill must win at every step; opponents need to win only once. Multiple opportunities to kill a bill exist because of the dispersion of influence. At a dozen or more points in committee or in the House or Senate a bill may be stopped or allowed to die (inaction is the same as killing a bill). Whether good or bad, a proposal can be delayed or rejected by any one of the following:

1. The House subcommittee and its chair
2. The chair of the House standing committee
3. The House standing committee and its leaders
4. The House Rules Committee
5. The majority of the House
6. The Senate subcommittee and its chair
7. The Senate standing committee
8. The majority of the Senate
9. The floor leaders in both chambers
10. A few senators, in the case of a filibuster
11. The House-Senate conference committee, if the chambers disagree
12. The president (by veto)

Authorization and Appropriation

Congress acts by a two-step process; it *authorizes* and it *appropriates*. After Congress and the president authorize a program, Congress, with the president's concurrence, has to appropriate the funds to implement it. Appropriations are processed by the House and Senate Appropriations Committees and their sub-committees. For example, the 1992 Education Act and its several titles reauthorize a variety of programs for a five-year period, including those for federal loans and grants for college students. The authorization act sets the limits on the amount that students may borrow and the conditions under which they must pay back the loan. But the authorization is useless until Congress appropriates funds and the president signs the appropriations bill into law each year. Congress is often likely to appropriate less money for student loans and grants than it has authorized.

The Importance of Compromise

Clearly, a bill does not become law unless its sponsors are willing to compromise to get the votes necessary for its passage. One tactical decision at the start is whether to push for action in the Senate first, in the House first, or in both simultaneously. For example, if a bill is expected to be opposed in the Senate, its sponsors may seek passage in the House and hope that a sizable victory there will spur the Senate into action. Another decision concerns the committee to which the bill is assigned. Normally, referral to a committee is automatic. Sometimes, however, a bill involves more than one jurisdiction and can be written in such a way that it may go to a committee that will look more kindly on it.

Getting a bill through Congress requires that majorities be mobilized over and over again—in subcommittee, in committee, in chamber, and possibly again in chamber to override a presidential veto. These majorities shift and change, and they involve different legislators in different situations at different points in time. New coalitions must be built again and again.[31]

Effective legislators are good at building coalitions, overcoming the objections of legislators who are undecided or only slightly opposed to the bill, and reciprocating when colleagues' bills are put forward. The job of a legislator, in sum, requires the ability to compromise and to work well with others.

COMMITTEES: THE LITTLE LEGISLATURES

It is sometimes said that Congress is a collection of committees that come together in a chamber every once in a while to approve one another's actions. There is much truth in this. Congress has long relied on committees to get its work done. Woodrow Wilson, a teacher of political science before he became president, expressed a similar thought: "Congress in session is Congress on display. Congress in committee is Congress at work."[32] Today we would say that Congress in subcommittee is Congress at work. The initial struggle over legislation takes place in subcommittees.[33]

Congress also utilizes **joint committees** whose members are selected from both houses to oversee such institutions as the Library of Congress or to investigate issues like the Iran-Contra affair in the Reagan administration. Committees organized to conduct investigations are called **select or special committees**.

The House Democratic caucus divides standing committees into three categories. The first category is *exclusive committees* and includes Appropriations, Ways and Means, and Rules. Members who serve on one of these committees may not serve on any other standing committee. The second category is *major committees*, which include committees like National Security; members can serve on only one of these but can add assignments to two nonmajor committees, such as Small Business. House members rarely serve on more than three standing committees.

Standing committees and their subcommittees are where most of the legislative work is done. **Standing committees** are permanently established legislative committees that review proposed legislation and report bills and resolutions to their parent chamber. Bills can be pigeonholed for weeks, amended beyond recogni-

COMMITTEES: CONGRESS AT WORK

Major committees of the Senate each have 12 to 29 members. Major committees of the House of Representatives, with a couple of exceptions, have an average membership of about 46 representatives. These committees have a total of about 85 subcommittees. Committees are "the eye, the ear, the hand, and very often the brain of the House."

What Senate and House Committees Do

- Study legislative proposals
- Consider communications from the executive branch
- Confirm or reject federal appointees
- Conduct hearings and investigations
- Review ongoing executive operations
- Prepare reports and surveys
- Make recommendations about corrective legislation
- Review reports, documents, and research related to committee policy
- Meet informally with public and private-sector leaders about their committee domain
- Conduct on-site visits and inspections

Major Committees of the House of Representatives:

- Agriculture
- Appropriations
- Banking and Financial Services
- Budget
- Commerce
- Economic and Educational Opportunities
- Government Reform and Oversight
- House Oversight
- International Relations
- Judiciary
- National Security
- Resources
- Rules
- Science
- Select Intelligence
- Small Business
- Standards of Official Conduct (Ethics)
- Transportation and Infrastructure
- Veterans' Affairs
- Ways and Means

Major Committees of the Senate:

- Agriculture, Nutrition, and Forestry
- Appropriations
- Armed Services
- Banking, Housing, and Urban Affairs
- Budget
- Commerce, Science, and Transportation
- Energy and Natural Resources
- Environment and Public Works
- Finance
- Foreign Relations
- Governmental Affairs
- Indian Affairs
- Judiciary
- Labor and Human Resources
- Rules
- Select Ethics
- Select Intelligence
- Small Business
- Special Aging
- Veterans' Affairs

tion, or kept in committee forever. Or a bill can fly through a committee in a hurry. A committee reports out favorably only a small fraction of all the bills that come to it. Although a bill can be forced to the floor of the House through a **discharge petition** signed by a majority of the membership, legislators are reluctant to bypass committees. They regard committee members as experts in their fields. Sometimes, too, they are reluctant to risk the anger of committee leaders. And there is a strong sense of *reciprocity*: "You respect my committee's jurisdiction, and I will respect yours." Not surprisingly, few discharge petitions gain the necessary number of signatures.

While members of the House hold relatively few committee assignments, each senator normally serves on three standing committees and at least seven subcommittees. Senators are more likely to serve on choice committees (committees that have clout). Among the most important Senate committees are Foreign Relations, Budget, Finance, and Appropriations. Senate committees have the same powers over the framing of legislation as do those of the House, but they have somewhat less power to keep bills from reaching the floor.

Choosing Committee Members

Control and staffing of standing committees are partisan matters. The chair and a majority of each standing committee come from the majority party. The minority party is represented on each committee roughly in proportion to its membership in the entire chamber, except on some powerful committees on which the majority may want to enhance its position. Getting on a politically advantageous committee is important to members of Congress. A representative from Kansas, for example, would much rather serve on the Agriculture Committee than on the Banking and Financial Services Committee. Members usually stay on the same committees from one Congress to the next, although less senior members who have had less desirable assignments often seek better committees when places become available.

How are committee members chosen? In the House of Representatives, a Committee on Committees of the Republican membership allots places to Republican members. This committee is composed of one member from each state having Republican representation in the House; the member is generally the senior member of the state's delegation. Because each member has as many votes in the committee as there are Republicans in the delegation, the group is dominated by senior members from the large state delegations. On the Democratic side, assignment to committees is handled by the Steering and Policy Committee of the Democratic caucus in negotiation with senior Democrats from the state delegations.

In the Senate, veterans also dominate the assignment process; each party has a small Steering Committee that makes committee assignments. In making assignments, leaders are guided by various considerations: how talented and cooperative a member is, whether his or her region is already well represented on a committee, and whether the assignment will aid in reelecting the member.

Senator Bill Bradley, who retired in 1997, said "there were fierce battles" within the Democratic Steering Committee which is charged with assigning members to committees. "The battles are generally drawn along classic lines—liberal/conservative, environment/industry, rural/urban, East/West."[34]

One reason Congress can cope with its huge workload is that its committees and subcommittees are organized around subject matter specialties. This specialization allows members to develop technical expertise in specific areas and to recruit skilled staffs. Thus Congress is often able to challenge experts from the bureaucracy. Interest groups and lobbyists realize the great power a specific committee has in certain

The Public Is Still Unhappy About Congress

The American public continues to look unfavorably on Congress, according to a series of polls by the Pew Research Center for the People and the Press. Poll respondents were asked: "Would you say your overall opinion of Congress is very favorable, mostly favorable, mostly unfavorable or very unfavorable?" The chart below combines the two favorable and the two unfavorable categories.

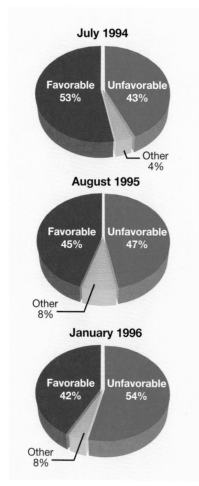

July 1994

Favorable 53%
Unfavorable 43%
Other 4%

August 1995

Favorable 45%
Unfavorable 47%
Other 8%

January 1996

Favorable 42%
Unfavorable 54%
Other 8%

SOURCE: "Congressional Facts and Figures," *National Journal*, February 3, 1996, p. 268.

areas and focus their attention on its members. Similarly, members of executive departments are careful to cultivate the committee and subcommittee chairs and members of "their" committees. One powerful Senate committee chair reminded his constituents of the amount of federal tax money being spent in their state: "This does not happen by accident," the senator's campaign pamphlet said. "It takes power and influence in Congress."

Committees are not all alike. Some are powerful, others are less important. Because of the Senate's special role in foreign policy, for example, the Senate Foreign Relations Committee is usually more influential than the House Committee on National Security. For the two Appropriations Committees, however, the reverse is true; the House Appropriations Committee plays a more significant role than the Senate Appropriations Committee, although these differences are less than they used to be. We should also note that committees differ not only for institutional reasons but also according to the goals and abilities of their members.[35]

How Congress uses committees is critical in its role as a partner in policy making. In recent years progress has been made in opening hearings to the public and improving the quality of committee staffs, but it is difficult to restructure committee jurisdictions so that they do not overlap. Thus, a dozen different committees deal with energy, education, and the war on drugs. Efforts to make the committee system more efficient are often considered threats to the delicate balance of power within the chamber.

Seniority Rule

Forty years ago committee chairs determined the total workload of committees, hired and fired staff, and formed subcommittees and assigned them jurisdictions, members, and aides. Chairs also managed the most important bills assigned to their committees. Since the mid-1970s, however, less senior members have insisted they be given more authority. Subcommittee chairs have also become more independent. It is not uncommon these days for a member of Congress to become chair of an important subcommittee after only one or two terms, and indeed such placement is the tradition in the Senate. In recent years there have also been moves to strengthen the powers of the party leaders and caucuses at the expense of the committee chairs.

Until recently, most chairs were selected on the basis of the **seniority rule**; the member of the majority party with the longest continuous service on the committee becomes chair upon the retirement of the current chair or a change in the party in control of Congress. The seniority rule gives power to representatives who come from safe districts where one party is dominant and a member can build up years of continuous service. Conversely, the seniority rule lessens the influence of states or districts where the two parties are more evenly matched and where there is more turnover.

Both Democrats and Republicans have occasionally passed over the most senior committee member in order to place someone with more energy or with a more compatible policy perspective in a committee chair position. In 1975 Democrats removed a few aging committee chairs and generally appointed the next ranking members to chair several committees. In 1995 Speaker Gingrich and his allies appointed several committee chairs who did not have the most seniority on the committee. Thus Republicans Bob Livingston, Tom Bliley, and Henry Hyde became chairs of Appropriations, Commerce, and Judiciary, respectively, even though they did not have seniority. "In each case," said Gingrich, "I thought they would bring a level of aggressiveness and risk taking that we would need in these very important positions."[36]

Still, the practice of elevating the senior member of a committee to serve as committee chair remains the general rule. It has long been respected in Congress for several reasons: it encourages members to stay on a committee; it encourages specialization and expertise; it also reduces the interpersonal politics that would arise if several members of a committee "ran" for election to become chair.

Investigations and Oversight

The power to investigate is one of Congress's most important functions; some think it even more important than its power to legislate. Congress conducts investigations to determine if legislation is needed, to gather facts relevant to legislation, to assess the efficiency of executive agencies, to build public support, to expose corruption, and to enhance the image or reputation of its members.[37] Hearings by standing committees, their subcommittees, or special select committees are an important source of information and opinion. They provide an arena in which experts can submit their views, and statements and statistics can be entered into the record.

Among the more important functions of congressional hearings is the *oversight* function—the responsibility to question executive branch officials to see whether their agencies are complying with the wishes of the Congress and conducting their programs efficiently. Authorization committees regularly hold oversight hearings, and appropriations committees, exercising "the congressional power of the purse," often use appropriations hearings to communicate committee members' views about how agency officials should carry out their business. Cabinet members and agency heads have been known to dread the loaded questions of hostile members of Congress and to hate having to watch themselves on the evening news trying to explain why their agency made some mistakes.

Some of Congress's investigations are controversial, especially such well-publicized open hearings as those of the Senate Foreign Relations Committee during the Vietnam War and more recently the Whitewater hearings examining the Clinton family investments and hearings on campaign finance irregularities in the 1996 presidential election. The Senate Watergate Committee's televised investigation into election practices and campaign-finance abuses in 1973 was intended less to obtain new information than to arouse citizens and promote support for electoral reforms.

Conference Committees

When the framers created a two-house national legislature, they anticipated the two chambers would represent sharply different interests. The Senate was to be a small chamber of persons elected indirectly by the state legislatures to hold long, overlapping terms. It was to be a chamber of scrutiny, a gathering of wise leaders who would counsel and sanction a president—whether that president liked it or not. The House of Representatives, elected anew every two years, was to be a more direct reflection of the people.

The Senate did serve as a conservative check on the House, especially in the late nineteenth and early twentieth centuries, when it was extremely conservative and something of a rich man's club. But some factors—chiefly political—have altered the character of both the House and the Senate. Today the House tends to be more conservative than the Senate. Executive departments and agencies, for instance, occasionally consider the Senate to be a court of appeals for appropriations that have been shot down by the House.

Given the differences between the House and the Senate, it is not surprising that the version of a bill passed by one chamber may differ substantially from the version passed by the other. Only if both houses pass an absolutely identical measure can it become law. Most of the time one house accepts the language of the other, but at least 15 percent of all bills passed (usually major ones) must be referred to

Public Views About Congress

Question: "Do you think most members of Congress are more interested in helping the people they represent, or more interested in helping special interest groups?"

Special Interests	65%
People	23%
Don't Know/NA	12%

Question: "Do you think most members of Congress understand the needs and problems of people like you, or not?"

Doesn't Understand	64%
Understands	29%
Don't Know/NA	8%

SOURCE: *The New York Times/CBS News Poll,* October 17–20, 1996, pp. 13–14.

Note: This poll tabulated responses from 1,148 registered voters.

Congressional committee hearings perform the investigative and oversight functions of Congress.

How would you "reform" Congress?

Which of these proposed reforms do you think should be adopted to improve Congress?

- Move to a European-style parliamentary system
- Extend House terms to four years
- Limit House and Senate tenure to 12 years
- Provide for public financing of campaigns and ban campaign contributions
- Permit only people who live in a district or state to contribute to candidates for Congress
- Radically reduce the number of committees and subcommittees
- Strengthen the power and resources of the party leaders
- Reduce the size of congressional staffs
- Set and abide by an agenda agreed to at the beginning of each session
- Have shorter sessions for Congress, so members can spend more time in their districts

You Decide!

a **conference committee**—a special committee of members from each chamber—that settles the differences between versions. Both parties are represented, but the majority party has more members.

The proceedings of a conference committee are usually an elaborate bargaining process. When the proposed bill is brought back to the two chambers, the conference report can be accepted or rejected (often with further negotiations ordered), but it cannot be amended. Conference members of each chamber must convince their colleagues that any concessions made to the other chamber were on unimportant points and that nothing basic to the original version of the bill was surrendered.

How much leeway does a conference committee have? Ordinarily members are expected to stay somewhere between the different versions. On matters for which there is no clear middle ground, members are sometimes accused of exceeding their instructions and producing a new bill. The conference committee has even been called a "third house" of Congress, one that arbitrarily revises policy. Conference committees are also criticized on the ground that they are not representative, even of the committees approving the bill, and that they disproportionately represent senior committee leaders. Critics also complain that little can be done about the subtle new features slipped into a bill by a conference committee. Despite such criticism, some kind of conference committee is needed for a two-house legislature to work. Conference committees integrate a bill as it comes from the two chambers.

Which chamber, House or Senate, wins more often in conference committees? On the surface it appears that the Senate's version wins more often, but this is partly because the Senate more often than not acts on its legislation after the House. Political scientist David J. Vogler concludes that "by creating the original bill and setting the agenda for debate on the issue, the House is judged to have the more real impact on the final shape of legislation as it passes through conference than does the Senate."[38] In effect, the House plays a dominant law-making role, while the Senate plays a key representational role through amendments.

CONGRESS: AN ASSESSMENT AND A VIEW ON REFORM

More than two hundred years after its creation, Congress is a much larger, more vital, and very different kind of institution from the one envisioned by the framers. Yet most of its major functions remain the same, and their effective exercise is crucial to the health of our constitutional democracy. Even as we prepare to enter the twenty-first century, we still look to Congress to make laws, raise revenues, represent citizens, investigate abuses of power, and oversee the executive branch, and the Senate still confirms top administrative and judicial appointees. Congress remains a bicameral organization, and its chambers still check one another as together they check and balance the executive and judicial branches of government. The interests of states and regions are still represented, debated, and brokered.

Today most members engage in continual electioneering to stay in office. So many members appear driven by their desire to win reelection that much of what takes place in Congress seems mainly designed to promote reelection. These efforts usually pay off for members of Congress. Most of them get reelected. At the same time, these efforts also pay off for our democracy. The concern of members with reelection fosters *accountability*; the desire to please the voters.

Congress is also characterized by internal fragmentation and diffusion of power. More and more of the work these days is done in committees or subcommittees. Multiple, successive decision points make it much easier to prevent than to pass legislation.

William Cohen, a popular Republican Senator from Maine (now Secretary of Defense in the Clinton Cabinet), observed as he was leaving the Senate that he admired

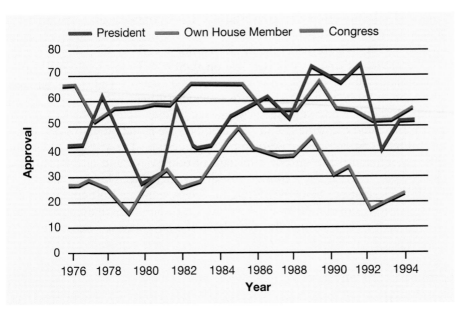

FIGURE 14–2 **Presidential, Congressional, and Own House Member Approval Ratings, 1975–1996**

SOURCES: The Gallup Poll, CBS News/New York Times Poll, ABC/Washington Post Poll, NBC News/Wall Street Journal Poll.

Congress's deliberative process, yet he worried that too many checks and too much partisanship have made it hard for Congress as an institution to get needed results:

> Our republic, we know, was designed to be slow-moving and deliberative. Our founding fathers were convinced that power had to be entrusted to someone, but that no one could be entirely trusted with power. They devised a brilliant system of checks and balances to prevent the tyranny of the many by the few. They constructed a perfect triangle of allocated and checked power. . . . There could be no rash action, no rush to judgment, no legislative mob rule, no unrestrained chief executive.
>
> The difficulty with this diffusion of power in today's cyberspace age is that everyone is in check, but no one is in charge. . . .
>
> But more than the constitutional separation of powers is leading to the unprecedented stalemate that exists today. There has been a breakdown in civil debates and discourse. Enmity at times has become so intense that members of Congress have resorted to shoving matches outside the legislative chambers.[39]

How does such a Congress make any progress? In an institution where most members act as individual entrepreneurs and consider themselves leaders, the task of providing institutional leadership is increasingly difficult. This is particularly true in the Senate, which prides itself on extended debate and deliberation. With limited resources, and only sometimes aided by the president, congressional leaders are asked to bring together a diverse, fragmented, and independent institution. The congressional system acts only when majorities can be achieved. That the framers accomplished their original objective—creating a Congress that would not move with imprudent haste—has been generally well realized.

Americans often characterize Congress as a bickering, timid, ignorant, selfish, or narrow-minded body. Yet we also admire the stamina and civic responsibility of the members of Congress we know. Individual members of Congress are invariably more popular than the institution, perhaps because we expect Congress to solve most of our national ills, yet we judge individual members primarily on how well they serve the interests of their states and districts and on their personal appeal (see Figure 14–2).

Thinking It Through

No "reform" is neutral in terms of effects. Some groups will benefit more than others from the passage of each reform proposal. Most reforms also have unanticipated consequences that may create more problems. Some would require amendments to our Constitution. Still, the search goes on for practical ways to improve Congress's ability to do the people's work.

Congress spent a lot of time in the mid-1990s trying to come up with procedural and fund-raising reforms, but despite great public pressure to reform, Congress did little to alter its traditional ways. New legislation did, however, require lobbyists to register and limited the kind and amount of gifts members could receive from lobbyists. And the 105th Congress is considering various campaign finance reforms.

Fed up with bickering and gridlock, an unusually large number of key Democratic members of Congress decided not to run for reelection in 1996. Among them were Senator Bill Bradley, Representative Pat Schroeder, and Senator Sam Nunn.

Some of the criticism of Congress is justified. Yet critics usually forget that our national legislature is particularly exposed, and some of our expectations of it are unrealistic. First, Congress does nearly all its work directly in the public eye, even more public now that it is televised live on C-SPAN. Unfortunate incidents—quarrels, name calling, evasive actions, inaccurate statements, and ethical lapses—that might be hushed up in the executive or judicial branches are almost always observed and duly reported by the news media. Second, Congress by its nature is controversial and argumentative. Its 535 members are found on both sides, sometimes on half a dozen sides, of every important question. The average citizen who holds one opinion is likely to be intolerant of other views and of the legislators holding them. There is also a considerable difference between holding an opinion and writing legislation. Moreover, during the 1990s Congress has both raised taxes and cut services, closed military bases, reduced spending for welfare, the arts, and many research programs, and also shut down the government—not a recipe for popularity!

Criticisms of Congress

CONGRESS IS INEFFICIENT   House and Senate procedures are, some charge, simply not suited to the needs of a modern information-age nation. Too much time is required to get bills through the complicated legislative process, and bills are often buried or defeated by procedural devices. Members are not as well informed as they should be. The dispersion of power guarantees slowness.

Some of this criticism is exaggerated. Evaluating procedure and structure is difficult to separate from evaluating policy, about which everyone has an individual preference. From the White House's vantage point, for example, Congress is inefficient when it does not process the president's bills quickly.

Congress deals with an enormous number of complex measures. Many procedures in both houses expedite handling of bills, and the committee and subcommittee system is a reasonable device for hearing arguments and compiling information.

Still, the question of efficiency remains. Many members feel defeated by the system. Study groups inside and outside Congress have urged the chambers to reduce the number of committee assignments, establish better information systems, centralize more power in their leadership positions, and strengthen majority rule. Congress has done many of these things recently, yet the pace of legislation has not improved.

Some of the paralysis in Congress is caused by the proliferation of subcommittees, the overlapping jurisdictions of these committees, and a congressional staff seeking to advance the agenda of individual members or subcommittees. A complicated budget process also adds to the paralysis.[40] Better-educated and more independent-minded people are being elected to Congress. These younger and more independent members sometimes make it difficult for party leaders to build coalitions and to maintain an efficient agenda for Congress.

CONGRESS IS UNREPRESENTATIVE   The complaint is often made that Congress represents regional or constituents' interests over the national interest. Defenders of Congress respond that representing their districts is precisely what Congress was designed to do. Legislators are described as being obsessed with staying in office—indeed, as concentrating solely on winning reelection—often at the expense of critical national issues such as the deficit, drug abuse, foreign policy, and trade. Former House Republican leader John Rhodes was perhaps too harsh when he said "the majority of congressional actions are not aimed at producing results for the American people as much as perpetuating the longevity and comfort of the men who run Congress."[41]

Can the members of Congress, who are so much the products of upper- or upper-middle-class backgrounds, really speak for the needs of low-income groups? Can a Congress that has only 11 percent women and 6 percent African American membership truly represent our female and minority populations? Moreover, the seniority system, even with its modifications, biases both houses toward conservatism. Defenders of Congress respond that there should be a strong institution to guarantee minority rights and to act as a check on mindless majority rule. Critics answer by arguing that minorities should have a right to publicize and delay what the majority proposes to do but not to defeat it.

In fact, we have a system of dual representation in which both Congress and the president can and do claim to speak for the people. But because "the people" seldom, if ever, speak with a single voice, the structure and character of the two systems tend to give us a Congress that speaks for one majority and a president who often speaks for another. Between the two, sometimes we get a balance—and sometimes gridlock.

CONGRESS IS UNETHICAL Some critics claim we have "the best Congress money can buy." Many people allege that special interests and single-issue groups are stronger than ever and that they are able to fragment and often delay or block proceedings in Congress. The current system of financing congressional elections has been called a scandal. It forces members of Congress to beg for money from wealthy individuals and political action committees representing interest groups whose primary purpose is to seek support for pet legislation. The elections of 1996 made this clear.

Critics complain that some members of Congress are tied to the economic interests they are asked to regulate and are beholden to the political action committees that increasingly fund their campaigns. Others charge that members of Congress get too many personal privileges and that there have been too many abuses, such as the check-cashing privileges for members.

In response to occasional scandals, both houses have passed ethics codes and have created ethics subcommittees. These codes require public disclosure of income and property holdings by legislators, key aides, and spouses. They also ban most gifts of over $50 to a legislator, a staff member, or a legislator's family from a registered lobbyist, an organization with a political action committee, a foreign government, or a business with an interest in legislation before Congress. In 1995 the House made it impossible for a lobbyist to take a member out to dinner and pay for it. But even these actions have apparently not improved the image of Congress.

CONGRESS LACKS COLLECTIVE RESPONSIBILITY Others wonder if the problems of Congress arise because each branch can blame the other for inaction or mistakes in policy. Some suggest, for example, that we might be better served by having four-year terms for members of the House and permitting members of Congress to serve simultaneously in the president's cabinet, on the model of the British parliamentary system. A few scholars even propose that we elect presidents and members of Congress on a "team ticket," that is, send a partisan team to Washington and prevent split-ticket voting. These reformers also seek means to strengthen partisan ties and efforts to link Congress and the president.[42]

Some critics see the main problem in Congress as the dispersion of power among committee and subcommittee leaders, elected party officials, factional leaders, informal caucus leaders, and other legislators. It is a "nobody's-in-charge" system. This dispersion of power means that to get things done, congressional leaders must bargain and negotiate. The result of this "brokerage" system is that laws may be watered down, defeated, delayed, or written in vague language. According to some critics, too much leeway is given to unelected bureaucrats to develop the regula-

"When my distinguished colleague refers to the will of the 'people,' does he mean his 'people' or my 'people'?"

Drawing by Richter. © 1976 The New Yorker Magazine, Inc.

tions that will enforce the legislation. Accountability is confused, responsibility is eroded, and well-organized special interests that know how to work the system have an unfair advantage.

Critics also worry that if Congress responds to powerful interest groups, it cannot speak for the great majority or for the nation as a whole.[43] It cannot anticipate problems, plan ahead, and put together political coalitions to deal with critical problems. Some of those concerned about congressional irresponsibility do not blame the special interests alone. They argue that brokerage is mainly the result of a constitutional system that divides authority, checks power with power, and disperses political leadership. Yet other factors making it difficult for Congress to act as a unified branch arise from the fact that each chamber may be controlled by a different political party.

CONGRESS DELEGATES TOO MUCH TO THE EXECUTIVE BRANCH Because of the complexity of modern problems and the inability to work out coalitions and compromises, there is a tendency for Congress to say to the executive branch: "Do something" about drugs; or "Do something" about AIDS and acid rain. If Congress turns a matter over to an administrative agency, the result may be that the rules and regulations issued by the administrators effectively become the law.

CONGRESS IS TOO RESPONSIVE TO ORGANIZED INTERESTS It is also charged that the committee system is too responsive to organized special interests. Both houses, critics hold, overrepresent well-organized economic power structures at the expense of the average citizen. This final charge suggests that even though members of Congress are rarely bought by campaign contributions, the way Congress conducts its business—and who gets heard at its hearings and in its corridors—is influenced to a great extent by those who can raise and disburse large sums of money as campaign contributions through political action committees.[44]

Defenders of Congress insist these charges are overstated. They say money would hardly influence the three dozen or more millionaires who are members of the Senate and the one hundred or so members of the House who are well-off financially. Defenders of Congress also point out that some members of Congress regularly turn down certain types of campaign contributions. Because of various campaign reform laws, candidates for Congress must now report all major campaign contributions to the Federal Election Commission. Thus, who gives what to whom is at least part of the public record. Still, the criticism is valid, and a large number of Americans are perplexed or disturbed about the degree of influence seemingly associated with campaign contributions from political action committees and wealthy individuals.

A Defense of Congress

Some criticize Congress for being both imperial and lazy—criticisms that contradict one another yet are nonetheless widespread. For example, the Bush and Reagan administrations often said Congress interfered with the president's conduct of foreign policy, was tied to parochial interests, and was too slow, too unwieldy, and too captured by sectional and special interests. Unlike the presidency, they added, Congress was more like a lawyer representing special clients than like a judge weighing the larger picture and the longer-term interests of the entire nation.

Supporters of Congress say that a president and Congress are given co-equal responsibility for shaping both foreign and domestic policy. The challenge that confronted the framers—how to reconcile the need for executive energy with republican liberty—is still with us. The history of constitutional democracy has always been the search for limitations on absolute power and for techniques of sharing power. Our American style of constitutionalism and separation of powers, espe-

Why One Senator Left

There was no one moment when I decided to leave the Senate. As I worked through my decision, I remembered 14-hour days: running from one room to another and one office building to another because four of my committees were meeting at the same time; lunching just off the Senate floor while waiting for my amendment to come up; dashing to the Capitol steps for photos with three groups from home and back to my offices for five appointments on pending legislation or projects—all followed by three or four hours of returning new phone calls, answering dozens of new letters, and reading a pile of urgent action memos from staff members asking directions on issues or constituent problems. Those days usually ended at 10 P.M. with dinner at my desk.

There was no time for reflection, no time to exchange ideas with fellow senators. . . . My family life and personal friendships paid a stiff price. There were only three weekends last year when I was not airborne. . . . One month it took 27 days before my wife and I could have dinner together and an unscheduled evening at home. At the end of certain days, I sometimes asked myself what I had really done to help solve the major problems facing our country. My honest answer was: not much.

SOURCE: Adapted from David L. Boren, "Why I Am Leaving the Senate," *The New York Times*, May 13, 1994, p. A15.

cially in the absence of a major crisis, often means a slow-moving and sometimes inefficient decision-making system. It means a system that often hinders rather than facilitates leadership. It is a system that invites contention, division, debate, delay, and political conflict. Critics often call this gridlock or deadlock or even paralysis. Defenders of the Congress prefer to call it the world's greatest deliberative body.

Plainly, however, members of Congress are rarely lazy. A typical day for a senator might begin with an early morning breakfast with constituents or a visiting group of businesspeople, students, or foreign dignitaries. This meeting is followed by subcommittee and committee meetings, a working lunch, several trips to the Senate floor to vote, and interviews with journalists, professors, and prospective staff in the afternoon. Then there is a dinner with other committee members to work out the details of a bill, interrupted by votes on the Senate floor. Often a senator will finish the day around 10 P.M. or later.

Some members are criticized for taking so-called "junkets," that is, trips abroad in connection with the work of their committee assignments. But most of the travel of members of Congress is hard work. They travel back home generally once a month, where they speak from morning to night and meet with students, public officials, and constituents, including a few irate ones. Then they get back on the plane and head for Washington, D.C. It is a demanding schedule.

Although scandals in the 1990s brought attacks on Congress to the forefront of American politics, attacking or poking fun at Congress has been a national pastime for generations. Will Rogers told some of his best jokes at the expense of Congress, as Jay Leno and David Letterman do today. Cartoonists love Congress for its unfailing ability to put its worst foot forward. Even members of Congress often "run" against Congress when they are at home in their districts.

Criticism of Congress—its alleged incompetence, its overresponsiveness to organized interests, its inefficiencies—are difficult to separate from the context of policy preferences and democratic procedures. Sometimes criticism tells us more about the critic than it does about the effectiveness of Congress. Constitutional democracy is not the most efficient form of government. Congress was never intended to act swiftly; it was not created to be a rubber stamp or even a cooperative partner for presidents. Its greatest strengths—its diversity and deliberative character—also weaken its position in dealing with the more centralized executive branch. Its members will rarely be fast on their feet. The 535 members, divided into two houses, two parties, dozens of committees, and nearly two hundred subcommittees, will often have a difficult time arriving at a common strategy to combat a president determined to use executive powers to the fullest.

Let's not forget that Congress is supposed to reflect geographical and narrow interests, to register the diversity of the United States. In *The Federalist*, No. 57, James Madison wrote: "Who are to be the electors of the Federal Representatives? Not the rich more than the poor; not the learned more than the ignorant; not the haughty heirs of distinguished names more than the humble sons of obscure and unpropitious fortune."[45] Yet as the costs of campaigning increase, and as the body of elected officials continues to come from the upper or upper-middle classes, we do have to ask whether ours is the open, representative, responsive, and responsible legislative system we can point to with pride as a model for those in other parts of the world who yearn for constitutional democracy.

As Congress prepares for the twenty-first century, the following questions need to be debated: Can Congress overcome partisan bickering and agree on legislation that will solve problems? Can Congress keep the president, the cabinet, and the bureaucracy accountable to the voters? Can Congress reform itself to ensure that campaign money or narrow interests do not have undue influence in shaping national policies? And can Congress deal with crime, welfare, health, economic development, the creation of jobs, and other issues that require immediate action?

POLITICS ONLINE

Thomas

For political science students, the legislative process and consideration of actual bills hold great interest. What hot bills are coming up this week? Has the House already voted on a matter of concern to you? How many times has the Senate voted to stop a filibuster on the Balanced Budget Amendment? The Legislative Reference Service of the Library of Congress provides just this kind of information on its World Wide Web cite named after Thomas Jefferson—Thomas. Some of the options it offers are bill tracking, congressional records, committee information, historical documents, and what's going on in Congress this week. Just for fun, you might click on Congressional Record Text, where you will find summaries and even complete texts of what Congress has passed into law during this session. You can also use Thomas to search for bills on specific issues like welfare reform:

http://thomas.loc.gov

Most members of Congress also maintain their own home page. Why not check out your representative or senator, either from your home district or where you are attending college. What kinds of resources does your member of Congress make available to constituents? What kind of image is portrayed? How are votes explained? You might contrast your member with one from another state or party and see what differences emerge. Political scientists have long believed that members use different home styles to relate to constituents. To what extent does their home style permeate their electronic style?

SUMMARY

1. Members of Congress are largely driven by the desire to win reelection. Much of what Congress does is in response to this motive. Members work hard to get favors for their districts, to serve the needs of constituents, and to maintain a high visibility in their districts or states.

2. Incumbents have advantages that help explain their success at reelection: they have greater name recognition; they have large staffs; they are better able to raise campaign money; and they have greater access to the media.

3. Partisanship, candidate appeal, and important issues contribute to the voters' choice for Congress.

4. Senators and representatives come primarily from middle- and upper-middle-class backgrounds. They are better educated than Americans as a whole. The typical member of Congress is still a middle-aged, white, male lawyer. Redistricting and reapportionment have shaped a Congress that somewhat more accurately reflects the population.

5. Congress performs these functions: representation, law making, consensus building, overseeing, policy clarification, and investigating. The Senate also confirms presidential appointments and ratifies treaties. As a collective body, Congress must attempt to accomplish its tasks even

as most of its members serve as delegates for their constituents.

6. Most of the work in Congress is done in committees and subcommittees. Congress has attempted in recent years to streamline its committee system and modify its methods of selecting committee chairs. Seniority practices are still generally followed, yet the threat of removal forces committee chairs to consult with younger members of the majority party.

7. Subcommittees are important. They can prevent or delay legislation from being enacted. But there are numerous other stages where bills can be killed, making it easier to stop legislation than to enact it.

8. The workload for Congress is exhausting. Much could be done to make our national legislature perform its functions more effectively. To this end the roles of the Speaker and of party Steering Committees have been enhanced. Congress has made itself subject to the same laws it passes for corporations, universities, and other organizations. Congress has also passed measures that require lobbyists to register and to disclose how they spend their money, and it has limited gifts and entertainment by lobbyists.

JOEL D. ABERBACH, *Keeping a Watchful Eye: The Politics of Congressional Oversight* (Brookings Institution, 1990).

DICK ARMEY, *The Freedom Revolution* (Regnery, 1995).

SARAH A. BINDER AND STEVEN S. SMITH, *Politics or Principles? Filibustering in the United States Senate* (Brookings Institution, 1997).

BARBARA BOXER, *Strangers in the Senate* (National Press, 1993).

BILL BRADLEY, *Time Present, Time Past: A Memoir* (Knopf, 1996).

STEPHEN L. CARTER, *The Confirmation Mess: Cleaning Up the Federal Appointments Process* (Basic Books, 1994).

GARY COX AND MATTHEW MCCUBBINS, *Legislative Leviathan: Party Government in the House* (University of California Press, 1993).

ROGER H. DAVIDSON AND WALTER J. OLESZEK, *Congress and Its Members*, 5th ed. (Congressional Quarterly Press, 1996).

CHRISTOPHER J. DEERING AND STEVEN S. SMITH, *Committees in Congress*, 3d ed. (Congressional Quarterly Press, 1997).

LAWRENCE C. DODD AND BRUCE J. OPPENHEIMER, EDS., *Congress Reconsidered*, 5th ed. (Congressional Quarterly Books, 1993).

RICHARD F. FENNO, JR., *Home Style: House Members in Their Districts* (Little, Brown, 1978).

RICHARD F. FENNO, JR., *Senators on the Campaign Trail: The Politics of Representation* (University of Oklahoma Press, 1996).

MORRIS FIORINA, *Congress: Keystone of the Washington Establishment*, 2d ed. (Yale University Press, 1989).

LAVERNE MCCAIN GILL, *African American Women in Congress* (Rutgers University Press, 1997).

NEWT GINGRICH, *To Renew America* (HarperCollins, 1995).

RICHARD L. HALL, *Participation in Congress* (Yale University Press, 1996).

FRED HARRIS, *Deadlock or Decision: The U.S. Senate and the Rise of National Politics* (Oxford University Press, 1992).

JOHN R. HIBBING AND ELIZABETH THEISS-MORSE, *Congress as Public Enemy: Public Attitudes Toward American Political Institutions* (Cambridge University Press, 1995).

GARY C. JACOBSON, *The Electoral Origins of Divided Government: Competition in U.S. House Elections, 1946–1988* (Westview Press, 1990).

GARY C. JACOBSON, *The Politics of Congressional Elections*, 3d ed. (HarperCollins, 1992).

VICTOR KAMBER, *Giving Up on Democracy: Why Term Limits Are Bad for America* (Regnery, 1995).

MARCY KAPTUR, *Women in Congress* (Congressional Quarterly Press, 1996).

JOHN W. KINGDON, *Congressional Voting Decisions*, 3d ed. (University of Michigan Press, 1989).

BURDETTE A. LOOMIS, *The Contemporary Congress* (St. Martin's Press, 1996).

THOMAS MANN AND NORMAN ORNSTEIN, EDS., *Renewing Congress: A Second Report* (American Enterprise Institute and Brookings Institution, 1993).

JANET M. MARTIN, *Lessons from the Hill: The Legislative Journey of an Education Program* (St. Martin's Press, 1993).

DAVID R. MAYHEW, *Congress: The Electoral Connection* (Yale University Press, 1974).

WALTER J. OLESZEK, *Congressional Procedures and the Policy Process*, 4th ed. (Congressional Quarterly Press, 1995).

NORMAN J. ORNSTEIN, THOMAS E. MANN, AND MICHAEL J. MALBIN, *Vital Statistics on Congress, 1995–1996* (Congressional Quarterly Press, 1996).

TIMOTHY PENNY AND MAJOR GARRETT, *Common Cents* (Little, Brown, 1995).

RONALD M. PETERS, JR., ED. *The Speaker: Leadership in the U.S. House of Representatives* (Congressional Quarterly Press, 1995).

DAVID E. PRICE, *The Congressional Experience: A View from the Hill* (Westview Press, 1993).

WARREN B. RUDMAN, *Combat: Twelve Years in the U.S. Senate* (Random House, 1996).

DAVID SCHOENBROD, *Power Without Responsibility: How Congress Abuses the People Through Delegation* (Yale University Press, 1994).

PAUL SIMON, *Advice and Consent: Clarence Thomas, Robert Bork and the Intriguing History of the Supreme Court's Nominating Battles* (National Press Books, 1992).

ALAN K. SIMPSON, *Right in the Old Kazoo: A Lifetime of Scrapping with the Press* (Morrow, 1997).

BARBARA SINCLAIR, *The Transformation of the U.S. Senate* (Johns Hopkins University Press, 1989).

STEVEN S. SMITH, *Call to Order: Floor Politics in the House and Senate* (Brookings Institution, 1989).

CAROL M. SWAIN, *Black Faces, Black Interests: The Representation of African-Americans in Congress* (Harvard University Press, 1993).

STEVEN WALDMAN, *The Bill: How Legislation Really Becomes Law: A Case Study of the National Service Bill* (Penguin, 1996).

Students of Congress also should consult *Congressional Quarterly Weekly Report, National Journal, Role Call,* and *The Hill.*

15

The Presidency:
The Leadership Branch

$\mathcal{A}$s he traveled slowly up the east coast from Mount Vernon to New York (the temporary seat of government) in 1789, newly elected President George Washington was showered with parades and fireworks. His whole trip was one long ovation, a celebration of the people's yearning for a strong individual who could provide continuity and leadership for the nation.

Yet Washington and his compatriots were of two minds about the power of the presidency. The framers both admired and feared leadership. They realized the country needed a more effective, centralized government, yet they were suspicious of the potential abuses of power, especially power vested in a single individual. Given what they had lived through in the preceding decades, they had every right to these fears. Moreover, they hardly wanted to jeopardize the rights and liberties they had fought so hard to win in the recent revolution.

Americans still have not resolved their ambivalence toward the presidency. Should a president be "above politics" and wait for a consensus to emerge from the people and Congress? Or should presidents be clearly political, leading the people and leading Congress? Should presidential powers be narrowly defined, or should the presidency be granted broad authority to respond to national and international emergencies? Is an office created more than two hundred years ago in an agrarian society adequate for the twenty-first century, when the United States must play a leading role in global trade, diplomacy, peacekeeping, and environmental conservation? Can any person meet such high expectations of the presidency? And does the greatly enlarged role of the presidency under today's circumstances alter and perhaps undermine some of the fundamental checks and balances in our constitutional democracy? We try to answer these questions as we take a closer look at the central role of the American presidency.

WHAT WE LOOK FOR IN PRESIDENTS

The framers conceived their president in the image of George Washington, the man they expected would first occupy the office. Like Washington, the American executive was to be a wise, moderate, dignified, nonpartisan leader of all the people. Washington had served his country in a variety of ways, most notably as commander in chief of the Continental Army for eight years and as an instigator of, and later presiding officer at, the Constitutional Convention of 1787. No one commanded the trust and respect that Washington did, and he was unanimously elected as the first president of the new republic in 1789. George Washington knew the people needed to have confidence in their fledgling government, a sense of continuity with the past, a time of calmness and stability, free of emergencies and crises. He knew, too, that the new nation faced many foreign dangers.

Article II of the Constitution outlined the nature and scope of presidential power. It responded to George Washington's calls for vigorous executive leadership. Washington's misgivings about his qualifications and about the scope of presidential power faded as he set precedents and fulfilled the hopes of the people.[1] He was sensitive to the fine line between providing strong leadership and infringing on individual rights and liberties. He knew then, as every president after him has either known or learned, that Americans have a strong streak of anti-government and even anti-authority sentiment. We want strong presidential leadership when the times demand it or when it serves our favorite causes,

George Washington was inaugurated as first President of the United States at Federal Hall in New York City on April 30, 1789.

The One Quality Voters Say They Want Most in a President

Honesty/integrity	43%
Leadership/ability to make decisions	11
Sense of responsibility to people	6
Believes United States rates first	5
Understanding of the poor	4
Sound economic program	4
Intelligence	2
Good judgment	2
Self-confidence	2
Experience	2
High moral standards	2
Accessibility	1
Other	3
No answer/don't know	12

SOURCE: CBS News-*New York Times* Poll, April 1996.

yet we insist that no elected official or governmental agency dare infringe on our rights.

We are not at all clear about how much power we want to vest in the president. When presidents take charge and try to run the country, they are often criticized for trying to impose their will on the nation. If they are not activist leaders, however, they are criticized because they do nothing and, even more likely, are blamed for whatever happens to the country—for an inadequate health policy, for an unfair tax system, for a recession, for inflation, for the homeless, for corporate downsizing and loss of jobs, or for ethnic warfare in remote nations. People who like what the president is doing are champions of presidential leadership, but people who disapprove of what the president is doing point to the dangers of dictatorship.

What kind of person does it take to perform this delicate balancing act? Our Constitution establishes only three qualifications for the office: a president must be at least 35 years of age, have lived in the United States for 14 years, and be a natural-born citizen. Our "unwritten presidential job description"—the one we carry around in our heads—says a president has to be many things to many people. Every four years Americans search the national landscape for a potential heroic leader who is blessed with the judgment of a Washington, the mind of a Jefferson, the steadfastness of a Lincoln, the calm of an Eisenhower, and the grace of a Kennedy.

Americans want leadership, but what kind of leadership? We want someone who can provide a sense of purpose, someone who can remind us of our shared aspirations as a constitutional democracy and a pragmatic, hardworking, generous nation. Yet we also want someone who can pay close attention to our immediate needs—jobs, peace, prosperity.

Voters sometimes place as much emphasis on a presidential candidate's character and integrity as they do on a candidate's political philosophy and specific policy views. Such emphasis is not misguided. Presidents have enormous power, especially in times of crisis. They also select the people who run the executive departments and serve on our courts, and thus they have much to do with the standards of governmental performance and ethics. Hence it is important to weigh their character and their allegiance to democratic values and to the spirit of the Constitution.[2]

We also pick our candidates in terms of their personalities. Can they get along with members of Congress, the press, fellow party leaders, and leaders of other nations? We also ask whether the would-be president displays vision, judgment, moral character, a grasp of history, a sense of proportion, and a sense of humor. To be sure, people prefer candidates whose views on issues accord with their own; if they like a person's personality, they trust that individual's policy proposals. A candidate's character and policy preferences sometimes get blurred—if not reversed—in the voter's mind.

In addition, even in a democracy the public wants a president to be tough, decisive, and competent. Voters recognize the need for strong leadership. They yearn for a leader with foresight and personal strength. Moreover, people want someone who will simplify politics, symbolize the protective role of the state, and yet be concerned with them. We want effectiveness but also fairness. Do we ask too much? The novelist John Steinbeck thought so: "We give the President more work than a man can do, more responsibility than a man should take, more pressure than a man can bear. We abuse him often and rarely praise him. We wear him out, use him up, eat him up. . . . He is ours and we exercise the right to destroy him."[3]

Americans applaud presidents when things go well and blame them when things go wrong. Disasters as well as triumphs are credited to presidents—Wilson's League of Nations, Hoover's Depression, Roosevelt's New Deal, Johnson's Vietnam War, Nixon's Watergate, Bush's Persian Gulf War, Clinton's Bosnia. An exaggerated sense of presidential wisdom and power sometimes causes us to forget there are limits to what presidents can accomplish. Although the tragedies of American involvement in Vietnam and of presidential involvement in the Watergate scandal deglamorized the presidency, the vitality of our constitutional democracy still depends in large measure on creative presidential leadership.[4]

Original Intent

The framers of the Constitution created a presidency of limited powers. They wanted a presidential office that would steer clear of parties and factions, enforce the laws passed by Congress, handle relations with foreign governments, and help states put down disorders. They wanted a presidency strong enough to match Congress, yet not so strong it would overpower Congress. They seemed to have in mind that a president should be an elected and highly responsible king with substantial personal authority, who would serve the common good and minimize the negative influence of the worst factions. They combined the ceremonial head of government with the actual head of government. The term of office would be four years, and presidents would be indefinitely eligible to succeed themselves. (The two-term limit would be added to the Constitution much later, in 1951.)

Although independent from the legislature, presidents would still share considerable power with Congress. The essence of the arrangement would be in intermingling powers with Congress. To enact government business, the separate branches would have to cooperate and consult with one another. A president's major appointments would have to be approved by the Senate; Congress could override the chief executive's veto by a two-thirds vote of each chamber; and the president could make treaties only with the advice and consent of two-thirds of the senators. All appropriations (the power of the purse) would be legislated by Congress, not the president. But even a presidency with such limited powers, hemmed in by the system of checks and balances, worried many Americans in 1787. The framers deliberately outlined the powers of the president broadly. The president, they thought, should have discretionary power to act when other governmental branches failed to meet their responsibilities or to respond to the urgencies of the day.

The Politics of Shared Power

Our constitutional democracy was designed to be one of both shared powers and division. The framers wanted disagreement as well as cooperation because they assumed that the checks and balances within the government would prevent the

"If George Washington never told a lie, how did he get to be president?"
Edgar Argo

Presidential integrity was called into question when investigation of Democratic party fund raising revealed that President and Mrs. Clinton had entertained Chinese business executives. Large donations from Chinese and Indonesian business interests were later returned by the Democrats.

president and Congress from "ganging up" against the people's liberties. The framers actually made disagreements inevitable by providing that the president, Senate, and House of Representatives would be elected by different constituencies and for different lengths of service.

The United States is unique among major world powers because it is neither a parliamentary democracy nor a wholly executive-dominated government. Our Constitution plainly invites both Congress and the president to set policy and govern the nation. Leadership and policy change are encouraged only when two, and sometimes all three, branches of government concur on the desirability of new directions.

A president and members of Congress are legitimate participants in a whole range of policy activities. Triumphs for a president acting alone in a system of separated powers are rare. "Whenever powers are shared, attention must be devoted to the other decision makers," writes political scientist Charles O. Jones. "How do they view the problem? What are their present commitments? On what basis will they compromise? The test in a separated system is not simply one of presidential success. It is rather one of achievement by the system, with presidents and members of Congress inextricably bonded and similarly judged."[5]

The politics of shared power has often been stormy, as the balanced budget battles, welfare reform, the Whitewater and campaign finance investigations illustrate. The politics of shared power is characterized by changing patterns of cooperation and conflict depending on the partisan and ideological makeup of Congress, the popularity and skills of the president, and various events that shape the politics of the times.

The Roots of Divided Government

We can point to numerous roots of divided government in the United States: constitutional ambiguities, different constituencies, varying terms of office, divided party control of the branches (most of the time in recent years), weak political parties, and fluctuating public support.

CONSTITUTIONAL AMBIGUITIES   Article I of the Constitution grants to Congress "all legislative Powers" but limits them to those "herein granted." It then sets forth in some detail the powers vested in Congress. In contrast, Article II vests in the president "the executive Power" without limiting it to such powers as are "herein granted" and then proceeds to describe those powers in very general terms. Is this difference in language between Articles I and II significant? Some scholars and most presidents have argued that a president is granted by Article II a general and undefined power to act to promote the well-being of the United States, subject only to precise constitutional limits. Therefore, they contend, a president is *not* limited to the specific powers spelled out in the Constitution, as is Congress, but has all the executive powers of the United States.[6] Other scholars and many members of Congress say the president either has no such inherent power or has it only in extraordinary circumstances.[7]

Whatever the language of the Constitution, the president has often exercised powers not expressly defined in it. These powers have been given a variety of names: *implied*, *inherent*, or *emergency powers*. For example, George Bush sent troops into Panama to help overthrow its government and capture General Manuel Noriega, and he did so without asking for a declaration of war and largely without consulting Congress. Bush was criticized by Congress for acting without congressional approval. Yet even the most faithful defenders of congressional prerogatives recognize that in extraordinary emergencies a president "may have to act promptly without clear constitutional or statutory support."[8] And Bill Clinton figured out a way to lend Mexico billions of dollars to overcome a financial crisis even though Congress essentially refused to do so. Differences between Capitol Hill and the White House over a president's emergency powers are merely one of several ambiguities in our constitutional arrangements.

DIFFERENT CONSTITUENCIES Another root of divided government comes from the different constituencies Congress and the president represent. Members of Congress represent state and local districts, and hence reflect specific geographic, ethnic, and economic interests. James Madison and other framers of the Constitution anticipated legislators would often be pressured by local and state interests, and presidents and their aides often think Madison was right. Members of Congress, of course, see sensitivity to state and local concerns as essential to their job as representatives. As a result, members of Congress—even those from a president's own party and own region—may look at problems and solutions somewhat differently from the way a president does, as a president represents a national perspective.

There is an old saying in Washington that "where you stand depends on where you sit." President Lyndon Johnson, for example, viewed the importance of civil rights legislation differently when he was in the White House from the way he viewed it when he represented Texas in the U.S. House and Senate. And President Gerald Ford quipped, "When I was in the House for 25 years, I almost always looked down Pennsylvania Avenue at the White House, regardless of whether Democrats or Republicans were there, and wondered why they were so arrogant. Then, when I was in the White House myself, I looked up at the Congress and wondered how there could be 535 irresponsible members of Congress."[9]

VARYING TERMS OF OFFICE Presidents serve for four years with a chance of reelection to a second term; senators have the luxury of six-year terms; members of the House of Representatives are elected for two-year terms. Different constituencies and lengths of service make these national offices responsive to different moods and points of view. Different electoral forces are at work in different election years. A majority of the voters can win control over only part of the national government at a time—and this arrangement, too, was by design.

Presidents often act quickly to shape national priorities in their first year following the flush of their electoral victories. They act to win support for their agendas before the almost inevitable decline in public approval. Congress, on the other hand, moves more slowly. As President Bush once joked, "The way to slow down old age is to move it through Congress." Congress is inefficient in part "because it represents a vast array of local interests. Congress passes new laws slowly and reviews old ones carefully."[10] The decision-making pace of Congress and of the president is not the same because of their different terms of office. The result is often conflict and deadlock.

Moreover, members of Congress may have been in office for 10 or 15 years and perhaps look forward to serving more terms. Some members of Congress are, in effect, career politicians who stay in office a long time. Hence they assume they will outlast the president, who has a limited term of service and is a lame duck in the second term. Presidents, however, think mainly about today and tomorrow.

DIVIDED PARTY CONTROL OF THE BRANCHES As we have noted already, since 1952 there has been a split in partisan control of the presidency and Congress for most of the time. Republican Presidents George Bush, Gerald Ford, and Richard Nixon had to deal with a Congress that was entirely under the control of Democrats. Bill Clinton has had a Congress controlled by the Republicans except in his first two years. And Republican Presidents Ronald Reagan and Dwight Eisenhower had to deal with Congresses that most of the time were under the control of Democrats. Only Presidents John Kennedy, Lyndon Johnson, and Jimmy Carter enjoyed majority control by their own party in Congress, and even then they had considerable trouble getting support for their legislative programs.

We the People

How Representative Are Our Presidents?

Sex: All male

Race: All white

Ethnic background: All but five were of Anglo ancestry, which includes English, Irish, Scots, and Welsh. Presidents whose ancestors were not from the British Isles were: Martin Van Buren (Dutch), Theodore Roosevelt (Dutch, Scots-Irish, and French Huguenot), Franklin D. Roosevelt (Dutch, French-Dutch), Herbert Hoover (Swiss-German), and Dwight D. Eisenhower (Swiss-German).

Age:

Oldest when elected: Ronald Reagan, 69 (first term), 73 (second term)

Youngest when elected: John F. Kennedy, 43

Average age at inauguration: 55

Religion:

Baptist: Warren G. Harding, Harry Truman, Jimmy Carter, Bill Clinton

Congregationalist: Calvin Coolidge

Disciples of Christ: James A. Garfield, Lyndon B. Johnson, Ronald Reagan

Dutch Reformed: Martin Van Buren, Theodore Roosevelt

Episcopalian: George Washington, James Madison, James Monroe, William Henry Harrison, John Tyler, Zachary Taylor, Franklin Pierce, Chester A. Arthur, Franklin D. Roosevelt, Gerald R. Ford, George Bush

Methodist: James K. Polk, Ulysses S. Grant, Rutherford B. Hayes, William McKinley

Presbyterian: Andrew Jackson, James Buchanan, Grover Cleveland, Benjamin Harrison, Woodrow Wilson, Dwight D. Eisenhower

Roman Catholic: John F. Kennedy

Society of Friends: Herbert Hoover, Richard M. Nixon

Unitarian: John Adams, John Quincy Adams, Millard Fillmore, William Howard Taft

No specific denomination: Thomas Jefferson, Abraham Lincoln, Andrew Johnson

SOURCE: Adapted from Tim Taylor, *The Book of Presidents* (Arno Press, 1972), pp. 663, 667.

In the days, weeks, and sometimes months following their inauguration, presidents usually enjoy what has been called the **honeymoon**, a period of generally positive relations with the press and Congress. Franklin Roosevelt, Lyndon Johnson, Ronald Reagan, and Bill Clinton all enjoyed legislative success in their first year in office.

The opposition party in Congress regularly mounts its own programs. It will, when possible, defeat a president's policy initiatives and substitute its own. This effort becomes all the more troublesome for a president when Congress is controlled by the opposition party—as Bill Clinton clearly learned when the Republicans swept into power in Congress following the 1994 elections.

WEAK POLITICAL PARTIES   Political parties in the United States, as we have noted in earlier chapters, are organizationally weak and highly decentralized when it comes to managing elections. Moreover, they are also weak in giving the president and the national party leaders power to discipline party members.

Most members of Congress finance their elections with only minimal assistance from their national party. They customarily respond to local conditions and run their campaigns independently of their party's presidential candidate or national platform. Thus they feel few obligations to go along with the president of their own party, unless a measure is in the interest of their home district or state. And although parties have recently become somewhat stronger inside Congress, there are always a few independent thinkers who will at times—sometimes crucial times for the White House—go their own way rather than cooperate with the White House even when the president is a member of the same party.[11]

FLUCTUATING PUBLIC SUPPORT   The American public's waxing and waning support for Congress complicates the problems of divided government. We often like our own members of Congress while being highly critical of Congress as a whole.[12] In recent years Americans have generally held presidents in higher esteem

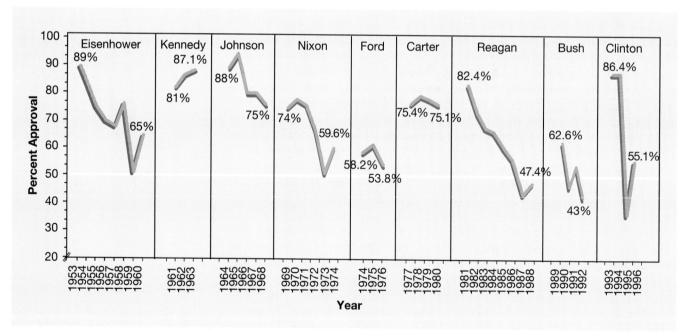

FIGURE 15–1   Presidential Support from Congress, 1953–1996

SOURCE: *Congressional Quarterly*, December 21, 1996, p. 3455.

Note: Percentages represent average scores for both chambers of Congress.

than Congress as an institution, and this fluctuating prestige has had consequences. Greater prestige for the presidency can give the incumbent in the White House a slight edge in battles with Congress.[13]

Congress is viewed by most people as inefficient, in part because it has to represent local interests and respond (some think too much) to narrow-minded constituencies. Yet when presidents decline in popularity, such as after the Watergate scandal, Americans turn to Congress to hold the president and the presidency accountable. At such times the public insists Congress be strengthened and asks it to play a more equal role in governing the nation. Americans often remind themselves that they do not want presidents unilaterally dictating policies and laws. They want a Congress that does more than just rubber-stamp presidential decisions.

Although separation of powers and divided government are obstacles, they are not insurmountable barriers to good public policy making. Presidents and Congress can legislate when the leaders of both institutions bargain and compromise in ways that overcome the roots of division discussed here. In fact, although the Constitution disperses power and invites a continual struggle between these two branches, it also requires the two branches to integrate the fragmented parts of the system into a workable government. And usually these two branches of government do work together. Even when the relationship is regarded as hostile, "bills get passed and signed into law. Presidential appointments are approved by the Senate. Budgets are enacted and the government is kept afloat. This necessary cooperation goes on even when control of the White House and the Capitol is divided between the two major parties."[14]

The presidential record of dealing with Congress in recent decades is mixed (see Figure 15–1). Presidents enjoy considerable success in getting most of their nominations confirmed by the Senate, and relatively few presidential vetoes are overturned by Congress. Also, most presidential budget requests eventually win approval, although Congress jealously guards its right to modify them, especially in certain areas such as defense and agriculture. On the other hand, Congress approves only about 50 percent of the president's major policy recommendations. Congress itself is, in fact, the source of many laws offered as part of the president's program.

The battle between the president and Congress over the 1996 budget illustrates the power struggle between the legislative and executive branches. Republicans in Congress hoped to force acceptance of their proposed spending cuts and tax relief by threatening a government shutdown when the federal spending authorization expired. To keep the government running, Congress had to pass and the president had to sign a **continuing resolution**, which allows the federal government to continue paying its bills until a new budget is passed. Because the resolution Congress sent to the president contained terms that President Clinton would not accept, he vetoed the resolution and thousands of federal workers were sent home without pay. A second shutdown in January was into its third week before Congress, smarting under the negative publicity generated by its actions, finally passed a continuing resolution that allowed time for negotiations to settle the impasse for that fiscal year.

A relatively unified Congress can make life pretty miserable for a president. It can, for example, refuse to confirm a president's vital nominations, reduce funds for key programs, and reject treaties. It can also override the chief executive's vetoes. Bill Clinton certainly learned what an opposition Congress was all about when he had to face Speaker Newt Gingrich's relatively cohesive House Republicans in 1995. Yet the historical record suggests most presidents have enjoyed greater cooperation from Congress than Clinton's difficulties might imply, and modern-day presidents are more powerful than those of the last century, even though their constitutional powers have not changed.

Thinking It Through

Favor a Six-Year Term

- It might help take politics out of the presidency and thereby lessen the likelihood of scandals like Watergate.
- Four years is too short a time to get the job done.
- Budgets are already cast for about two years ahead when a president gets into office.
- Presidents could concentrate on the job rather than on reelection.
- During wartime a president would not waste time campaigning.
- Six years is enough even for the healthiest of presidents.
- Few second terms have been successful (for example, Wilson, Nixon, and Reagan).

Against a Six-Year Term

- A six-year term would give us two more years of the "clunkers" and two fewer years of the great ones.
- Four years is long enough to tell whether a president is doing the job.
- The best way to be reelected is to do the job well, maintain majority support, and be an effective leader.
- The four-year term forces presidents to be accountable for their promises and platforms.
- Some of our great presidents served ably for more than six years (for example, Washington, Jefferson, FDR, and Eisenhower).
- A healthy, democratic country needs a politician in the White House, one who can bargain, persuade, build crucial political coalitions, and get diverse political factions to work together.
- We should not surrender a hard-won democratic right: to kick a leader *out* of office.

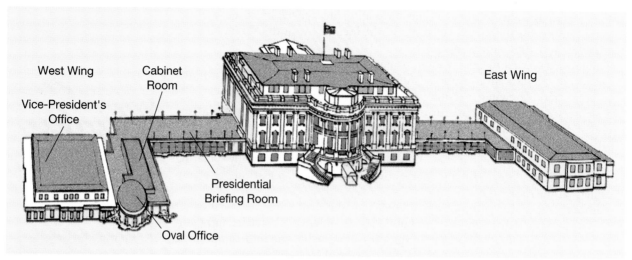

West Wing
Vice-President's Office
Cabinet Room
East Wing
Presidential Briefing Room
Oval Office

The White House is an executive office, a ceremonial mansion, and a home. Some presidents have viewed it almost as a jail, preferring to spend as much time as possible at other retreats outside Washington, but most Americans view the rather elegant White House as the center of political and social activity in the nation's capital. It is also something of a national shrine and draws millions of people from the United States and around the world to visit it each year.

The Extension of Executive Power

After two centuries, the presidential track record is good. Perhaps in no other nation have leaders with so much power at their command so carefully complied with the restraints imposed on them by a written Constitution. The exact dimensions of executive power at any given moment are partly the consequence of the incumbent's character and energy, combined with the needs of the time, the party balance in Congress, the values of the citizenry, and the challenges to our nation's survival. By and large, the history of presidential power is one of steady, if uneven, growth. Of the individuals who have filled the office, about one-third have enlarged its powers. Andrew Jackson, Abraham Lincoln, and both Roosevelts, for example, redefined both the institution and many of its powers by the way they set priorities and responded to crises.

In this extension of the executive power, Congress and the courts have sometimes been willing partners. In emergencies Congress often delegates discretion to the executive branch, and the legislature sometimes seems incapable of dealing with matters that are highly technical or that require immediate response and constant management. Some people think what Congress lacks most is the will to use the powers it already has. But this explanation is hardly satisfactory, as the weakness of Congress is not unique among legislative bodies. During the last two centuries in all democracies, and at all levels, power has drifted from legislators to executives. The English prime minister, the French president, governors of our states, and mayors of our cities all play more dominant roles than they did, generally speaking, one hundred years ago.

In the history of presidential–Supreme Court relations, the nation's highest court has generally aided and abetted an expansive interpretation of presidential power. The Court has on occasion halted a presidential action or ruled a presidential decision unconstitutional, but it has more frequently labored to approve and give legitimacy to the growth of presidential power. Political historian Clinton Rossiter once lamented that the Court was "clearly one of the least reliable restraints on presidential activity."[15]

Roots of Presidential-Congressional Conflict

- Varying terms of office
- Diverse geographical constituencies
- Conflicting responsibilities and constitutional ambiguities
- Different partisan ties
- Constitutional provisions requiring extensive sharing of power
- Congress seen as disorganized and inefficient by the president and by the public
- The White House viewed as arbitrary and insensitive by Congress
- Each wants the credit for successes, and each seeks to blame the other when things go wrong

Several factors have strengthened the presidency. The danger of war plainly increases a president's influence on the nation's affairs. The cold war—with its enormous standing armies, nuclear weapons, and widespread intelligence and alliance operations—invited presidential leadership in national security matters. Television doubtless also contributed to the growth of presidential influence. With access to prime time, presidents can take their case directly to the people, and this invitation to bypass and sometimes ignore Congress, the Washington press, and even party leaders weakens the checks once imposed on the presidency.

Growth of the federal role in domestic and economic matters has also increased presidential responsibility and contributed to an enlarged presidential establishment. Problems not easily delegated to any one department often get pulled into the White House. When new programs involve several federal agencies, someone near the president is often asked to set a consistent policy and reconcile conflicts. White House aides, with some justification, claim the presidency is the only place in government where it is possible to establish and coordinate national priorities. And presidents constantly set up central review and coordination units that help formulate new policies, settle jurisdictional disputes among departments, and provide access for the well-organized interest groups who want their views to be given weight in decision making.

The growth of the presidency is also encouraged by public expectations. Although we may dislike or condemn individual presidents, popular attitudes toward the institution of the presidency remain positive. We want very much to believe in our presidents, perhaps because we have no royal family, no established religion, and no common ceremonial leadership. Sometimes, in an effort to live up to exaggerated expectations, presidents overextend themselves. Wanting to maintain popularity encourages them to make frequent appeals to the general public. These television appeals become bargaining chips that may help presidents temporarily improve their public image and even win occasional fights in Congress. But if used too often, these appeals can undermine a president's relations with Congress and render the parties less important in supplying policy ideas and in keeping presidents accountable. Also a president risks wearing out his or her welcome with the public.

THE JOB OF PRESIDENT

Today a president is asked to play several roles that are not carefully spelled out in the Constitution. We want the chief executive to be an international peacemaker as well as a national morale builder, a politician in chief as well as a commander in chief, and a unifying representative of all the people. We want the president to be the architect of "a new world order" who negotiates favorable trade pacts with major trading partners. We want every new president to be virtually everything all our great presidents have been, and then some. In addition to the obvious leadership responsibilities a president has in foreign policy, economics, and domestic policy, six broad functional kinds of leadership are expected of a president. These policy areas and functions permit us to develop a job profile of an American president (see Table 15–1).

Presidents as Crisis Managers

"The President shall be Commander in Chief of the Army and Navy of the United States," reads Section 2 of Article II of the Constitution. Even though this is the first of the president's powers listed in the Constitution, the framers intended the military role to be a limited one—far less than a king's. Congress would declare war and call up the army and navy. Congress would also control the power of the

---

Factors That Influence a President's Success in Congress

- Same party in control of Congress
- Similar ideological interests in control of Congress
- National emergencies
- The "honeymoon" effect experienced during the early months in office
- High public approval ratings for the president
- Effective presidential lobbying of the Congress
- Threat of presidential veto
- Presidential bargaining with use of patronage powers
- Clear presidential priorities that win consensus in the nation
- President's "bully pulpit" publicity efforts, including addresses and news conferences

---

"Bully Pulpit"

This term was made popular by President Theodore Roosevelt (TR), who believed the office of president provided an enormous opportunity to inspire and even preach to a national constituency as if it were a national congregation. "Bully" is a term of approval and affirmation. TR used it as in "Bully for you," meaning terrific, great, or well done! Presidents like Woodrow Wilson, Franklin Roosevelt, John Kennedy, and Ronald Reagan have been noted for their use of the presidential "bully pulpit."

Should presidents be limited to two terms in office?

Before he left office, former President Ronald Reagan called for the repeal of the Twenty-second Amendment to the Constitution, the one that limits a president to two terms. Why do you think he opposed the amendment? What additional reasons could be put forth to persuade people to repeal this relatively new (1951) provision in the Constitution? What are the best reasons for retaining the Twenty-second?

purse and hence the funding of wars. Yet it was important, the framers insisted, that the people's elected representative—the president—be in charge of the military. This principle of *civilian control over the military* is a central element in our constitutional democracy.

This principle has meant that in the United States today we do not worry, as people do in many nations around the world, whether the military establishment will accept the outcome of elections. General Douglas MacArthur tested this principle of American constitutionalism during the Korean War when he challenged President Harry Truman. Truman, an unpopular president at the time, had to tell the popular general to leave his command—and the general left. Many people consider civilian supremacy over the military one of our most significant contributions to the survival of constitutional democracy. We put the president, a civilian, on top.

When crises and national emergencies occur, Americans instinctively turn to the chief executive, who is expected to provide not only executive and political leadership but also the appearance of a confident, "take-charge" executive who has a steady hand at the helm. Public necessity forces presidents to do what Lincoln and Franklin Roosevelt did during the national emergencies of their day: provide the stability and continuity needed to protect the union and safeguard vital American interests.

Two centuries of national expansion and recurrent crises have increased the powers of the president beyond those specified by the Constitution. The complexity of Congress's decision-making procedures, its unwieldy numbers, and its constitutional tasks make Congress a more public, deliberative, and divided organization than the presidency. When crises occur, Congress traditionally holds debates and, almost as predictably, delegates authority to the president, charging that official to take whatever actions are deemed necessary. This is essentially what Congress in the 1990s has done in response to presidential calls for U.S. involvement in Kuwait, Haiti, and Bosnia.

TABLE 15–1

A Presidential Job Description

| Functional Leadership | Examples of Policy Responsibilities | | |
	Foreign Policy	Economics	Domestic Policy
Crisis management	Liberating Kuwait (Persian Gulf War)	FDR's handling of the Depression, 1930s	Response to urban riots
Symbolic and morale-building leadership	Clinton's trip to Helsinki to meet Yeltzin	Being bullish on American productivity	Visiting flood and disaster victims; helping Alaska clean up oil spill
Recruitment of top officials	Selecting Joint Chiefs of Staff chair	Hiring wise economic advisers	Nominating a chief justice
Priority setting and problem clarification	Working with United Nations on peacekeeping priorities	Outlining tax-cut or revenue-producing programs	Setting priorities in environmental protection and health care
Legislative and political coalition building	Negotiating with Congress on aid to Eastern European nations	Clinton's efforts to pass welfare reform	Fighting for domestic spending programs
Program implementation, administration, and oversight	Making Middle East peace accords work	Monitoring Internal Revenue Service performance	Appraising the impact of federal social programs

President Clinton took a leadership role in bringing an end to the civil war in Bosnia. At the signing of the peace treaty on December 14, 1995, Serbian President Slobodan Milosevic shakes hands with his former enemy, Croatian President Franjo Tudjman, as Bosnian President Alija Izetbegovic and other heads of government look on.

The primary factor underlying this transformation in the president's function as commander in chief has been the changed role of the United States in the world, especially since World War II. In the postwar years every president from Truman to the present argued for and won support for the use of U.S. troops overseas as part of the North Atlantic Treaty Organization (NATO) or various United Nations peacekeeping forces. Nations grew dependent on our assistance, which often became translated into treaties, pacts, and diplomatic agreements. These commitments, plus the fear of nuclear war and the importance of deterrence, prompted Congress to give presidents flexibility in the foreign policy area. This does not mean Congress will always agree with a president. Congress may set detailed limits of time and scope for the use of U.S. troops, as when Congress specified in 1995 that U.S. participation in Bosnia was for one year and only under U.S. command. Congress later accepted the extension of the role in Bosnia to support the development of civilian institutions there.

Presidents are expected to be crisis managers in the domestic sphere as well. Whenever things go wrong, we demand presidential-level planning and problem solving. When terrorists attack U.S. citizens, people assume their president will retaliate. When a disastrous oil spill occurs, or a hurricane, or a flood, or a drought, people expect the head of state to step in and assist. When riots occur in our cities, we ask what the president is going to do about it. In many crises, however, presidents are little more than victims of fast-breaking events and forces outside of their control. They are sometimes surprised, overtaken by developments, and placed on the defensive.

Presidents as Morale Builders

Presidents are the nation's number-one celebrities; almost anything they do is news. Presidents command attention merely by jogging, fishing, or going to church. By their actions they can arouse a sense of hope or despair, honor or dishonor.

The framers of the Constitution did not fully anticipate the symbolic and morale-building functions a president must perform. Certain magisterial functions, such as receiving ambassadors and granting pardons, were conferred. But over time the pres-

Thinking It Through

Reagan said the people should be able to reelect a president as many times as they want, just as they now reelect House and Senate members. He also hinted that the Twenty-second Amendment might weaken a president late in his second term by making him a lame duck, less powerful because everyone knows he will not be around in a year or so. Advocates of repeal also say we may sometimes need to keep a veteran president in office during a crisis period, much as we retained Franklin Roosevelt in 1940. Others say eight years may not be enough time to resolve certain major problems.

The Twenty-second Amendment is not only a limit on the incumbent but also on the electorate, the first since the ratification of the Constitution to restrict the power of the electorate rather than expand it. It is based, advocates of repeal suggest, on the assumption that the voters cannot be trusted.

Those who favor keeping the Twenty-second Amendment cite these reasons: First, the presidency is so powerful today that we need the Twenty-second Amendment as an additional check and balance against abuse of this power. Second, the amendment encourages both parties to seek out quality candidates to succeed to office and discourages dependence on a single ruler. Third, few leaders are likely to have the health, the intellectual energy, and the new ideas needed to perform the demanding responsibilities of the presidency beyond eight years in office. Finally, Americans have always believed in citizen-leaders rather than career politicians, and this amendment encourages this ideal.

President Clinton's visit to the troops in Bosnia generated good will and good publicity. Although public opinion was divided on the Bosnia action, most people wanted to show support of our men and women in service.

idency has acquired enormous symbolic significance. People turn to national leaders just as tribespeople turn to shamans—for meaning, healing, empowerment, assurance, and a sense of purpose. Many people find comfort in an oversimplified image of the president as a warrior-captain at the helm of the great ship of state—liberator, prophet, defender of liberty and democracy, and spokesperson for the American Dream.

Presidential head-of-state duties often seem trivial and unimportant; for example, throwing out the ceremonial first baseball of the season, promoting Easter seals, or pressing buttons that start big power projects. Yet a president is continually asked to champion our common heritage, unify the nation, and create an improved climate within which the diverse interests of the nation can work together.

The morale-building job of the president involves much more than just ceremonial, cheerleading, or quasi-chaplain duties. Presidential leadership, at its finest, radiates confidence and empowers people to give their best, to unlock the possibility for good that exists in the nation. Our best leaders have been able to provide this special and often intangible element.

Some expectations for presidents are inconsistent with one another. On the one hand, the president is a representative of a segment of the population loosely identified with a particular party. As such, the president not only directs the national party organization but, as chief legislator, also takes specific positions on issues for or against some groups. On the other hand, as ceremonial leader and chief of state, the president attempts to act in a nonpartisan way for all the people. A chief executive must faithfully administer the laws, whether passed by Democratic or Republican majorities in Congress. Yet in making appointments and in applying the law, presidents often understandably think first of the interests of those who elected them.

Presidents as Recruiters

Often a single appointment may have a lasting impact, more so than scores of presidential policy initiatives. President Eisenhower's nomination of Earl Warren to be chief justice of the United States may have been the single most significant decision of his administration in the area of domestic policy. Warren served for more than 15 years and presided over vast changes in civil rights and civil liberties. President Clinton's Supreme Court nominees, Ruth Bader Ginsburg and Stephen Breyer, are also likely to have long-term effects. In a similar way, the selection of a secretary of state, a top economic adviser, a secretary of the interior, or top White House aides can have an enormous impact on long-term national policy.

President Clinton has won both praise and criticism for his performance as a recruiter. He won praise for appointing cabinet members like Interior Secretary Bruce Babbitt, Treasury Secretary Bob Rubin, and Defense Secretary William Cohen. Yet he was faulted for his appointments at Agriculture, Energy, and the Central Intelligence Agency (CIA). His first surgeon general, Jocelyn Elders, was forced out of office for her statements on birth control education that offended many Americans.

Although his management style has been criticized, Clinton succeeded in making the cabinet and his administration "more like America." More women and minorities have served in his administration than under previous presidents, including Madeleine Albright, the first woman secretary of state.

Presidents control more than 4,000 appointments, including hundreds of federal judgeships and top positions in the military and diplomatic service. (Note, however, that many appointments require the approval of the Senate.) Effective presidents shrewdly use their appointment powers not only to reward campaign supporters and enhance ties to Congress but also to communicate priorities and policy directions. The chief executive needs the best possible managers and motivators in crucial positions because the top appointees are a link between the White House and the millions of people who serve in the federal and military career services.

Besides identifying and recruiting them, the president must also try to keep the most talented of these officials in government as long as possible. The turnover problem is acute. Many able people come to top positions in the cabinet or subcabinet and stay for just two years; less than one-third stay for more than three years. These top federal posts do not pay as much as similar positions in the private sector, and living in Washington is expensive. Moreover, the White House in recent decades has often placed loyal campaign aides in key deputy positions to ensure cabinet member loyalty to the White House.[16]

Various financial disclosure and conflict-of-interest requirements, imposed on presidential appointees as a result of the Ethics in Government Act of 1978, discourage some potential appointees from accepting government jobs. They must fill out many forms, and they must testify at sometimes complicated, time-consuming, confusing, and embarrassing congressional hearings. Media scrutiny of citizen-leaders called to government service has also become more intensive. Recruiters for recent presidents report they often go to their second or third choice before they find someone willing to accept an appointment. "No other nation relies so heavily on noncareer personnel for the management of its government. . . . If talented Americans decline the opportunity for public service, if they endure it only for brief periods, or if they are ill-prepared for the challenges they will face in the public sector, the system will not deliver on its promise."[17]

A president must strengthen the hand of the ablest people working in the bureaucracy and promote them to higher positions at the senior reaches of the executive branch. In short, the personnel responsibilities of a president are great and require much time.[18]

Presidents as Priority Setters

Presidents, by custom, have become responsible for proposing initiatives in the areas of foreign policy, economic growth and stability, and the quality of life in the United States. This was not always the case. But beginning with Woodrow Wilson,

---

The Job of President

Constitutional Responsibilities

Act as commander in chief

Negotiate treaties

Receive foreign ambassadors

Nominate top federal officials, including federal judges

Veto bills

Faithfully administer federal laws

Pardon persons convicted of federal offenses

Address Congress and the nation

Informal Roles

Crisis manager

World leader

Legislative leader

Party leader

Morale builder

Personnel recruiter

Priority setter

Budget setter

Conflict resolver

Coalition builder

Bargainer and persuader

and especially since the New Deal, a president is expected not only to promote peace but also to prevent depressions and propose reforms to ensure domestic progress. New ideas to improve national policies are seized upon by a president searching for campaign issues or legislative program material, and they are refined by the executive office staff, by special presidential task forces, and by Congress.

NATIONAL SECURITY POLICY   The framers foresaw a special need for speed and unity in our dealings with other nations. As a result, presidents generally have more leeway in foreign policy and military affairs than they have in domestic matters. For example, President Clinton sent troops to Haiti and Bosnia despite widespread public opposition and grudging acceptance in Congress. The Constitution vests in a president command of the two major instruments of foreign policy—the diplomatic corps and the armed services. It also gives the chief executive responsibility for negotiating treaties and commitments with other nations, although Congress usually gets to vote on these matters.

Congress has granted presidents discretion in initiating foreign policies, for diplomacy frequently requires quick action, and the Supreme Court has upheld strong presidential authority in this area. In *United States v Curtiss-Wright* (1936), the Court referred to the "exclusive power of the president as the sole organ of the federal government in the field of international relations—a power which does not require as a basis for its exercise an act of Congress, but which, of course, like every other governmental power, must be exercised in subordination to the applicable provisions of the Constitution."[19] These are sweeping words.[20] Yet a determined Congress that knows what it wants and can agree on action does not lack power in foreign relations. Congress must authorize and appropriate the funds that back up our policies abroad.

ECONOMIC POLICY   Ever since the New Deal, presidents have been expected to keep unemployment low, fight inflation, keep taxes down, and promote economic growth and prosperity. The Constitution did not specify these duties for the executive, yet presidents know that when the nation is not prosperous and jobs are scarce, they may suffer the fate of Herbert Hoover, who was denounced for his alleged inaction at the beginning of the Great Depression. The growth and complexity of economic problems since the depression of the 1930s have placed even more initiatives in the president's hands. The delicate balancing required to keep a modern economy operating means that presidents must regularly make key fiscal and budgetary policy decisions.[21] The presidential elections in 1980, 1992, and 1996, in particular, turned largely on economics.

Although presidents sometimes get their economic advice elsewhere, their chief advisers on economic policy are the secretary of the treasury, the three members of the Council of Economic Advisers, and the director of the Office of Management and Budget. The chair of the Federal Reserve Board of Governors is also an influential, if independent, adviser on the economy.

DOMESTIC POLICY   A leader is one who knows where the followers are. Lincoln did not invent the antislavery movement. Kennedy and Johnson did not begin the civil rights movement. Clinton was hardly the first leader to notice the unfairness of health care and welfare policies. But they all, in their respective times, became embroiled in these controversies, for a president cannot long ignore what divides or inspires a nation.

The essence of the modern presidency lies in its potential to resolve societal conflicts. To be sure, much of the time a president will try to avoid conflict, seeking instead to defer, delegate, or otherwise delay controversial decisions. An effective president, however, will clarify the major issues of the day, define what is

THE PRESIDENTIAL WAR POWER

The Constitution delegates to Congress the authority to declare the legal state of war (with the consent of the president), but in practice the commander in chief often starts the fighting or initiates actions that lead to war. This power has often been used by our presidents. From George Washington's time until Clinton's, the president, by ordering troops into battle, has often decided when Americans will fight and when they will not. When the cause has had political support, the president's use of this authority has been approved. In 1846, James K. Polk ordered American forces to advance into disputed territory; when Mexico resisted, Polk informed Congress that war existed by act of Mexico, and a formal declaration of war was soon forthcoming. Abraham Lincoln called up troops, spent money, set up a blockade, and fought the first few months of the Civil War without even calling Congress into session. William McKinley's dispatch of a battleship to Havana harbor, where it blew up, helped precipitate war with Spain in 1898. The United States was not formally at war with Germany until late 1941, but prior to the Japanese attack on Pearl Harbor, Franklin Roosevelt ordered the navy to guard convoys to Great Britain and to open fire on submarines threatening the convoys. Since World War II, presidents have sent forces without specific congressional authorization to Korea, Berlin, Vietnam, Lebanon, Grenada, Cuba, Libya, Panama, Kuwait, Somalia, and Rwanda—in short, around the world.

In 1973, Congress overrode Richard Nixon's presidential veto and enacted the War Powers Resolution, which declared that henceforth the president can commit the armed forces of the United States only: (1) after a declaration of war by Congress; (2) by specific statutory authorization; or (3) in a national emergency created by an attack on the United States or its armed forces. After committing the armed forces under the third circumstance, the president is required to report to Congress within 48 hours. Unless Congress has declared war, the troop commitment must be ended within 60 days. The president is allowed another 30 days if the chief executive claims the safety of the United States forces requires their continued use. A president is also obligated by this resolution to consult Congress "in every possible instance" before committing troops to battle. Moreover, at any time, by concurrent resolution not subject to presidential veto, Congress may direct the president to disengage such troops.

Not everyone was pleased by the passage of the War Powers Resolution of 1973. Nixon vetoed it because he said it encroached on presidential powers. Others said it gave away a constitutional power plainly belonging to Congress—namely, the war-making or war-declaring power—for up to 90 days. Still other observers, however much they may have thought this resolution was defective, believed nonetheless that war powers legislation was of symbolic and institutional significance because it reflected a new determination in Congress at the time. Presidents from Nixon to Clinton have not changed their behavior much, yet they have been put on notice that the commitment of American troops is subject to congressional approval. According to the resolution, presidents have to persuade Congress and the nation that their actions are justified by the gravest of national emergencies. Presidents in the future will, at least occasionally, hold back from conflict until they get what, in effect, might be a congressional declaration of war.

President Franklin D. Roosevelt signed the declaration of war against Japan on December 8, 1941, as leaders of Congress looked on. It was the last time a president of the United States signed a formal declaration of war.

possible, and organize the governmental structure to realize important goals. A president has the opportunity to focus the legislative agenda on administration priorities, whatever their origins.

A president—with the cooperation of Congress—can set national goals and propose legislation. Close inspection indicates, however, that in many if not most instances, "new initiatives" in domestic policy are measures that have been under consideration in previous sessions of Congress. Just as the celebrated New Deal legislation had a fairly well-defined history extending back several years before its embrace by Franklin Roosevelt, many of Bill Clinton's initiatives—health care and "the end of welfare as we know it"—are the fruits of long campaigns by congressional activists and certain interest groups.

Presidents as Legislative and Political Coalition Builders

The Constitution provides that the president "shall from time to time give to the Congress information on the State of the Union, and recommend to their Consideration such Measures as he shall judge necessary and expedient." From the start, strong presidents have exploited this power. George Washington and John Adams went in person to Congress to deliver information and recommendations. Thomas Jefferson and many presidents after him sent written messages, but Woodrow Wilson restored the practice of delivering a personal, and often dramatic, message. Franklin Roosevelt used radio talks and personal appearances to draw the attention of the whole nation to his program, as have most subsequent presidents. Bill Clinton visited Congress soon after he was elected and went back on several occasions to mingle with members of Congress or to give major reports to the nation. Clinton also held numerous television forums in attempts to win public support for his legislative programs.

Less public, yet equally important, are the frequent written policy messages dispatched from the White House to the members of Congress on a range of public problems. These messages are important in defining the administration's position and in giving assistance to friendly legislators. Moreover, these messages are often accompanied by detailed drafts of legislation, which members of Congress often sponsor with little or no change. These White House proposals, the products of bill-drafting experts on the president's staff or in the executive departments and agencies, may be strengthened or diluted by Congress, but many of the original provisions survive.

An effective president is an effective politician—the most visible and potentially the strongest mobilizer of influence in the American system of power. "Politician" is a nasty word to many Americans; it often connotes a scheming, evasive, self-interested person. Little wonder many politicians claim they are "above politics." There is, however, a more constructive definition of "politician": one who helps manage conflict; one who knows how to negotiate, bargain, and help reconcile different views in order to make the difficult and desirable become reality.[22]

Presidents cannot escape political coalition-building tasks. As candidates, they have made promises to the people. To get things done and to get reelected, they must work with interest groups and people who have differing loyalties and responsibilities. Inevitably, presidents become embroiled in legislative, bureaucratic, and lobbying politics, and their approval ratings suffer as a consequence (see Figure 15–2).

Presidents make good on more of their promises than the general public appreciates. Most presidents enjoy at least partial success on most of the initiatives they favored during their campaigns or soon after they came to the White House. Although presidents control much of what they recommend to Congress, other institutions and realities—especially the leaders in Congress, the health of the econ-

An effective president must be an effective politician who both leads and follows his supporters. Here President Lyndon Johnson celebrates with Martin Luther King, Jr., the passage of the Civil Rights Act of 1964.

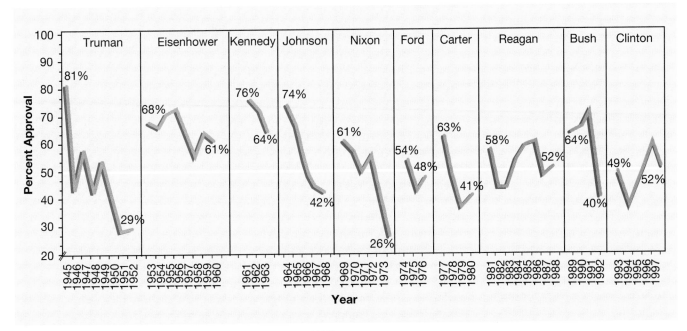

FIGURE 15–2 Presidential Approval Ratings, 1945–1997

SOURCE: The Gallup Organization.

omy and budget deficits—shape what presidents can achieve. President Clinton enjoyed considerable success with his program in Congress in his first two years, but his success rate with Congress in 1995 dropped to 36 percent, the lowest point since *Congressional Quarterly* began measuring presidential success.[23] Yet his success improved to a respectable 55 percent in 1996.[24]

Despite their formal powers, presidents can rarely command; they spend most of their time *persuading* people. Potentially, presidents have enormous persuasive power, but in a government of separated institutions that share powers, some congressional, bureaucratic, and military leaders are beyond the president's political reach. They have their own constituencies—a House committee, for example, or a powerful interest group. Presidents cannot simply give orders like a first sergeant.

Many students of the presidency think the power to persuade is the president's chief resource and that such power comes through bargaining. Bargaining, in turn, comes primarily through getting others to believe it is in their self-interest to cooperate. Hence the skill of a president in communicating and winning others over is the necessary energizing factor in moving the institutions of the national government to action. This school of thought also holds that a president cannot be above the battle or above politics. Rather, a president must enjoy the give-and-take of congressional-presidential relations as well as between the parties and between the White House and the press. Classic examples of effective presidential coalition building are Franklin Roosevelt's winning public support for his New Deal programs, Lyndon Johnson's getting his Great Society legislation passed, and Bill Clinton's mobilizing public and congressional support to win approval for the North American Free Trade Agreement (NAFTA) in 1993.

From a president's vantage point, it is seldom helpful to punish legislators from one's own party who, for whatever reason, decide not to support part of the president's legislative program. With power dispersed and decentralized in Congress, it is just too risky for a president to single out a few party "disloyalists" for retribution. White House congressional relations aides abide by the motto of "No

Why Presidential Approval (in Polls) Usually Declines the Longer Presidents Are in Office

Political scientists are not exactly sure of the precise relationships among the following factors; different studies produce different findings. These factors are, however, plainly some of the more important ones, and some of them are doubtless interrelated.

- Expectations that are raised in campaigns are dashed as time forecloses resources and options.

- Things that go wrong get blamed, rightly or wrongly, on presidents, whether or not presidents have the power to deal with these matters.

- Rising disapproval of incumbent presidents is often influenced by inflation and unemployment.

- Major negative events, such as the Vietnam War, Watergate scandal, Iranian hostage crisis, or Paula Jones allegations, influence how people evaluate presidents.

- Press and media criticism accumulates over time and sharpens the public's dissatisfaction with a president. Perhaps, too, time in office simply wears out our welcome for a president.

How the White House Won a Reluctant Senator's Vote

Former U.S. Senator Warren Rudman (R-N.H.) did not especially respect President Bush's nomination of Clarence Thomas for the Supreme Court, yet he went along with the White House request for at least two reasons.

I don't know what inspired George Bush to nominate Thomas. Perhaps his political staff convinced him it would be clever to challenge liberals to vote against a black conservative. Bush had the audacity to call Thomas the best-qualified candidate for the job, but he wasn't even close to being that.

Yet I voted for him. Why? Essentially, because he was going to be confirmed regardless of what I did. The final tally was 52–48 but that was misleading, because the White House had several votes held in reserve, mainly Democrats who would have supported Thomas if their vote was needed. If my vote had been the deciding one, I would have voted against Thomas, no matter what the consequence, but once it was clear that he would be confirmed I made a political decision.

The struggle to confirm Thomas had been exceedingly bitter, one of those legislative conflicts that damage everyone involved. I had no doubt that if I voted against Thomas, my ability to go to the White House and obtain federal funds and projects for New Hampshire would be at least temporarily crippled, along with my hopes of gaining the president's support for several lawyers who I believe would make outstanding federal judges.

SOURCE: Warren B. Rudman, *Combat: Twelve Years in the U.S. Senate* (Random House, 1996), p. 251.

permanent allies, no permanent enemies." Someone whose vote is lost today may cast the crucial supportive vote on some other measure next week.

This is also true of a president's dealings with interest groups. Thus Clinton and the leaders of organized labor were on opposite sides of the NAFTA vote, yet they were able to patch things up and work together on several issues thereafter, especially the presidential and congressional elections of 1996.

Presidents are sometimes in a better position to bargain and trade for votes with members of Congress than are the members themselves. In addition to receiving presidential help in their reelection campaigns, members of Congress also want federal projects for their districts, patronage for their supporters, help with their own pet legislative measures, and defense contracts and benefits for major industries in their districts or states. "The White House political staff controls a great deal of patronage and becomes expert at wielding it," writes former U.S. Senator Warren Rudman. "Typically, senators traded their votes on foreign policy issues . . . for a new highway for their state or a new science center for their state university."[25]

The White House has a number of resources with which to influence most members of Congress. Presidents can make stirring appeals for party unity—especially if their party enjoys a majority in Congress. They can also try to educate and rally the public around their programs. Much of the time, however, a president must deal with a Congress that moves according to its own pace and that responds to a variety of constituent and organized interests above and beyond the requests and appeals coming from the White House.

THE PRESIDENTIAL VETO A president can veto a bill by returning it, together with specific objections, to the house in which it originated. Congress, by a two-thirds vote in each chamber, may **override** the president's veto. Another variation of the veto is known as the **pocket veto**. In the ordinary course of events, if the president does not sign or veto a bill within ten weekdays after receiving it, it becomes law without the chief executive's signature. But if Congress adjourns within the ten days, the president—by taking no action—can kill the bill.

The veto's strength lies in the difficulty Congress has in getting a two-thirds majority of both houses. From 1789 through mid-1997, presidents have exercised their regular veto power 1,437 times; only 105 of these vetoes have been overridden by Congress. However, when scholars separate out the vetoes of private bills (bills dealing with individual claims against the government, or land titles, or matters such as immigration and naturalization) from public bills, they find that about 19 percent of the public bill vetoes have been overridden by Congress. Still, writes Robert Spitzer, "a presidential success rate of more than 80 percent for important legislation poses a daunting challenge to anyone seeking to overturn a veto."[26]

In short, there is little Congress can do when confronted with a veto. It must either get enough votes to override the veto or modify the legislation and try again (see Table 15–2). Presidents are able to make the vast majority of their regular vetoes stick.

Presidents can also use the veto power in a positive way. They can announce that bills under consideration by Congress will be turned back unless certain changes are made. They can use the threat of a veto against a bill Congress wants badly in exchange for other bills that they want. A presidential veto can also protect a national minority from hasty, unfair legislation passed in the heat of the moment. But the veto is essentially a negative weapon of limited use to a president who is pressing for action.

THE POLITICS OF THE ITEM VETO President Clinton in 1996 signed into law a bill passed by Congress authorizing the **item veto**, which, he said, would allow future presidents to fight "special interest boondoggles, tax loopholes, and pure pork."[27] ("Pork," or **pork-barrel** legislation, refers to government benefits or programs that may help the economy of a member's district—as in "bring home the bacon.") Clinton was only the most recent in a list of modern-day presidents to call for the right to veto subsections or items within major appropriation bills passed by Congress. To fight deficit spending and to cut expenditures whose main purpose was to help members of Congress win reelection, he sought the authority to remove "pork" and **riders**—unrelated items added to appropriations bills, often at the last minute, because their proponents knew they lacked widespread support but also knew there was little chance a president would veto an entire bill, especially an appropriations bill, because of them. Supporters of the item veto also noted that 43 state governors had the item veto authority, and it has worked reasonably well in the states.[28]

The item veto applies to discretionary spending, new direct spending, and items of limited tax benefit. The president has 5 calendar days following Congress's passing of a bill to notify Congress of his decision to "rescind" an item. Congress has 30 days to respond by passing the item again by a majority vote, not a two-thirds vote, of each house. Or Congress may choose not to act. Item veto authority was granted to presidents for eight years, from after which Congress would decide whether to extend it.

Adoption of the item veto was a victory for both Bill Clinton and for the Republicans, who had listed it as a key provision of their Contract with America. But the item veto has been challenged as unconstitutional. Senator Robert C. Byrd of West Virginia had long campaigned against the item veto, saying it was a colossal mistake that upsets the balance of powers laid out in the Constitution. He and other critics charged it gave away too much congressional control over the purse strings. In April 1997, U.S. District Court Judge Thomas P. Jackson sided with Senator Byrd and other members of Congress who had challeneged the constitutionality of the item veto law. Jackson wrote that the power to make the laws of the nation "is the exclusive, nondelegable power of Congress."[29] In declaring the president's item veto authority unconstitutional, Judge Jackson said it violates the doctrine of separation of powers. It is now up to the Supreme Court to settle the controversy.

PRESIDENTS AND PUBLIC OPINION The press conference is an example of how a president can employ the machinery of communication to build legislative and political coalitions. Years ago press conferences were rather casual affairs. Franklin Roosevelt ran his get-togethers informally and was a master at withholding information as well as giving it. Under Harry Truman the conference became an institutionalized part of the presidential communications apparatus. John Kennedy authorized regular live telecasts of press conferences and used them frequently for direct communication with the people. Ronald Reagan effectively used five-minute Saturday afternoon radio chats to communicate his views, ask for support, and win Sunday morning media coverage. Clinton occasionally uses the press conference, which has aided him in his efforts to deal with Congress and the media, and he, too, speaks directly to the public on his Saturday morning radio broadcasts.

Press conferences influence public opinion, and presidents regularly commission private polls to find out how they are doing. They want to learn about the public's whims, estimate the strength and direction of its thinking, and respond to its impatience. Presidents must know not only *what* to do but *when* to do it. Public opinion can be unstable and unpredictable. Lyndon Johnson recognized that his wide popular support of the mid-1960s had melted away by 1968, when he decided not to run again. Nixon's dramatic drop of nearly 40 percentage points in public opinion polls, a result of the Watergate scandal, helped force his resignation. Bush won unusual public approval during and after the successful military efforts in the Persian Gulf in early 1991, but his popular approval sharply diminished during the

TABLE 15–2
Presidential Vetoes, 1933–1997

President	Vetoes
Franklin D. Roosevelt	635
Harry S. Truman	250
Dwight D. Eisenhower	181
John F. Kennedy	21
Lyndon B. Johnson	30
Richard M. Nixon	43
Gerald R. Ford	66
Jimmy Carter	31
Ronald Reagan	78
George Bush	46
Bill Clinton (first term)	17

SOURCE: Congressional Quarterly and Office of Executive Clerk, The White House.

The president's chief of staff carries a large part of the administrative burden. Here Bill Clinton's second-term chief, Eskine Bowles *(left)*, and former chief, Leon Panetta *(right)*, attend swearing-in ceremonies for members of the new cabinet.

The Cabinet

Vice-President
Secretary of State
Secretary of Treasury
Secretary of Defense
Attorney General
Secretary of Interior
Secretary of Agriculture
Secretary of Commerce
Secretary of Labor
Secretary of Health and Human Services
Secretary of Housing and Urban Development
Secretary of Transportation
Secretary of Energy
Secretary of Education
Secretary of Veterans Affairs
Chief of Staff at the White House
Director of the Office of Management and Budget
U.S. Trade Representative
U.S. Representative to the United Nations
Chair, Council of Economic Advisers
Administrator, Environmental Protection Agency
Director, Drug Control Office

economic downturn that followed. Most presidents lose support the longer they are in office. Dissatisfaction sets in; interest groups grow impatient; unkept promises must be accounted for; and the president gets blamed for many of the things that go wrong.

Both as a candidate and in the White House, Bill Clinton has had especially testy relations with the press and has complained a lot about the media.[30] Clinton used every available means to get his message out to the American public. He was the first president to appear on MTV, and he turned up on town meetings and talk shows with regularity. Both he and Hillary Clinton have had to deal with the press in an era of "in your face journalism," where many of the old rules and courtesies about the separation of public and private life have disappeared, especially those having to do with marital and extramarital relations. We have to remember, however, that Thomas Jefferson, Abraham Lincoln, and Franklin Roosevelt were all vilified by the press and rarely shown much reverence in their lifetimes. Presidents, along with members of Congress, are always fair game for media critics.[31]

PARTY LEADERSHIP Another potential source of influence for the president is the political party. Most presidents since Jefferson have been party leaders, and generally the more effective the president, the more use he has made of party support. Wilson, the two Roosevelts, and Reagan fortified their executive and legislative influence by mobilizing support within their party. Yet presidents are often led by their party, or at least constrained by it, as much as they lead it; no president has ever wholly dominated his party.[32]

Presidents as Administrators

The Constitution charges the president to "take Care that the Laws be faithfully executed." Presidents, however, must delegate much of their administrative authority. Because their other responsibilities demand most of their attention, presidents are very often dependent on their subordinates. Theoretically, at least, orders flow down an administrative line: from president, to cabinet members, to bureau chiefs, to smaller offices. Like all top executives, a president is assisted by a staff who advise the chief executive. This *line and staff organization* is typical of every large administrative entity, whether it be the army, General Motors, or the United Nations.

Presidents have come to rely heavily on their personal staffs. Nowhere else—not in Congress, not in the cabinet, not in the party—can presidents find the loyalty and single-mindedness that often develop among their closest White House aides. Cabinet heads, on the other hand, are often perceived as staunch advocates of their departments and the constituencies their departments serve. Presidents assume, however, that their aides will provide them with neutral and objective advice, but there are substantial costs to listening only to one's closest aides. The White House can usually be thought of as a palace court in which strong presidents create an environment that weeds out any assistant who persists in presenting irritating or opposing views.

The number of employees in the presidential entourage grew steadily from the early 1900s through the early 1990s. Today a White House staff of about 400 operates at a slight reduction from previous years. This staff makes up just one part of the Executive Office of the President.

THE INSTITUTIONALIZED EXECUTIVE OFFICE Approved by Congress in 1939, the **Executive Office of the President** was the recommendation of Franklin Roosevelt's Committee on Administrative Management. The intention was to provide presidents with the help they obviously needed to carry out the growing responsibilities imposed by the Great Depression and by the enlarged role of government. The Executive Office of the President consists of the Office of Management and Budget, the Council of Economic Advisers, and several other staff units (see Figure 15–3).

The staff of the White House office can be categorized by their primary functions: (1) domestic policy; (2) economic policy; (3) national security or foreign policy; (4) administration and personnel matters (as well as personal paperwork and scheduling for the president); (5) congressional relations; and (6) public relations.

Presidential aides sometimes insist they are simply the eyes and ears of the president, that they make few important decisions, and that they never intrude between the chief executive and the heads of departments. But the White House staff and the inevitable emergence of a few strong White House advisers have made this traditional picture nearly obsolete. Some White House aides, impatient with bureaucratic and congressional bottlenecks or even political sabotage, come to view the presidency as if it alone were the whole government.

The **Office of Management and Budget (OMB)** continues to be the central presidential staff agency. Its director advises the president in detail about the hundreds of government agencies—how much money they should be allotted in the budget and what kind of job they are doing. OMB seeks to improve the planning, management, and statistical work of the agencies. It makes a special effort to see that each agency conforms to presidential policies in its dealings with Congress; each agency has to clear its policy recommendations to Congress through OMB first.

A budget is more than just a financial plan, because it reflects power struggles and indicates national priorities (and wishful thinking). To the president, the budget is a means of control over administrators who may be trying to join ranks with politicians or interest groups to thwart presidential priorities. Through the long budget preparation process, presidents use OMB as a way of conserving and centralizing their own influence.

THE CABINET It is hard to find a more unusual institution than the president's cabinet. The cabinet is not specifically mentioned by name in the Constitution (but see the Twenty-fifth Amendment). Yet since George Washington's administration, every president has had one. Washington's consisted of his secretaries of state, treasury, and war, plus his attorney general.

Today the selection of cabinet members is the first major job for the president-elect. The cabinet consists of the president, the vice-president, the officers who head the 14 executive departments, and a few others a president considers cabinet-level officials. The cabinet has always been a loosely designated body, and it is not always

Line of Succession to the Presidency

The Constitution leaves succession after the vice-president up to Congress. Thus this is the line of succession according to law passed by Congress. However, the constitutional qualifications still apply. For example, if the secretary of state was born in a foreign country of parents who were not U.S. citizens, he or she would be bypassed in this line.

1. Vice-President
2. Speaker of the House of Representatives
3. Senate President Pro Tempore
4. Secretary of State
5. Secretary of the Treasury
6. Secretary of Defense
7. Attorney General
8. Secretary of the Interior
9. Secretary of Agriculture
10. Secretary of Commerce
11. Secretary of Labor
12. Secretary of Health and Human Services
13. Secretary of Housing and Urban Development
14. Secretary of Transportation
15. Secretary of Energy
16. Secretary of Education
17. Secretary of Veterans Affairs

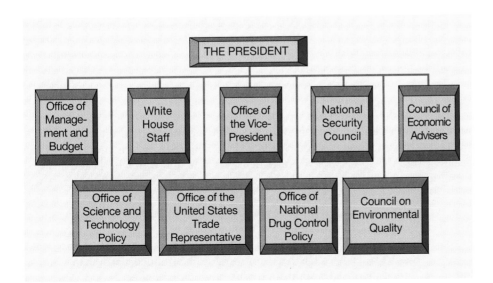

FIGURE 15–3 Executive Office of the President

First Lady: A Search for the Appropriate Role

A president cannot by law appoint a spouse to a federal job. Yet Hillary Rodham Clinton became an influential and important adviser to President Bill Clinton. In his first term she headed the planning for national health care; however, her proposals failed to win majority support in Congress. She also took an active role in the selection of various nominees for cabinet and judicial posts.

Political spouses have often influenced their husbands or wives. Earlier presidential spouses—including Eleanor Roosevelt, Edith Wilson, and Dolley Madison—counseled and lobbied their presidential husbands. Every "first spouse" defines her responsibilities differently. Bess Truman and Pat Nixon chose to remain in the background.

Hillary Clinton was as controversial as she was influential. Her role as an advocate of health care initiatives and women's rights attracted criticism as well as praise. Her role in the Whitewater real estate development and her alleged failure to answer specific questions about it caused additional concerns. She became the first First Lady to be subpoenaed to testify before a grand jury, and she, along with her husband, was questioned by a federal independent counsel.

Hillary Clinton has been hailed as a first lady for our times and a model for contemporary women who choose to have both a career and a family, but she has also been seen as a political liability. She was criticized in the press, satirized in the novel *Primary Colors*, and ridiculed by opposition politicians and pundits—especially William Safire, Alfonse D'Amato, Rush Limbaugh, and Pat Buchanan.

According to a CBS poll in early 1996, nearly a majority of Americans disapproved of the way Hillary Clinton was handling her job as First Lady. Later that year CBS found 41 percent of those surveyed in their poll believed Hillary Clinton had too much influence on the decisions her husband made as president. Another poll indicated 47 percent thought she should "focus on being a more traditional First Lady," while only 29 percent felt she should "be actively involved in setting White House policy."*

Future presidential partners doubtless will carefully weigh the Hillary Clinton experience. The question also arises of whether the husband of our first woman president will continue with his career, be active in policy planning, or play a passive, ceremonial role.

National Journal, December 21, 1996, p. 276.

clear who belongs in it. In recent years, certain executive branch administrators and White House counselors have been accorded cabinet rank.

Presidents need strong and creative aides to sift through the competing advice that comes to the White House and a staff to help them monitor the implementation of policies in the sprawling federal executive departments. But presidents also need a strong cabinet and allies in Congress and elsewhere to provide alternative views to help ensure that they do not become isolated by an overly protective entourage.

Cabinet government as practiced in parliamentary systems—where the voice and the vote of the cabinet members count for a lot—simply does not exist in the United States. In fact, an American president is not required by the Constitution to form a cabinet or to hold regular meetings. Kennedy, Johnson, and Nixon all preferred small conferences with individuals specifically involved in a problem. Kennedy saw no reason to discuss defense department matters with his secretaries of agriculture and labor, and he thought cabinet meetings wasted valuable time for too many already busy people. Both Carter and Reagan tried to revive the cabinet, and both met often with their cabinets during their first two years. But the longer they remained in office, the less frequently they met with their cabinets as a whole. Clinton, like those he followed, prefers smaller meetings with key staff and crucial cabinet leaders rather than frequent full cabinet meetings. Clinton held just 18 full cabinet meetings in his first term in office.[33]

Presidential advisers and the heads of various White House-based cabinet-level councils or review units, such as the National Security Council and the Office of Management and Budget, have gained equal or even superior status to many of the department and cabinet secretaries. This shift has occurred in part because these people are physically located in or next door to the White House. Further, presidents are aware that some cabinet members adopt narrow "advocate" views: the agriculture cabinet secretary as a strident advocate for the farmers; the Housing and Urban Development cabinet secretary as an ambassador for the housing industry and, to some extent, also for big city mayors; and so on through much of the cabinet, especially those preoccupied with domestic policy matters. As good relations between presidents and cabinet members weaken, presidents, in frustration, turn to trusted senior White House staff aides to settle conflicts and coordinate policy. Tension almost always builds between senior White House aides and their counterparts in the cabinet. Personal staff members remain close to the president's ear and are more influential as a result.

Recent presidents have formed various committees of certain cabinet or sub-cabinet members, such as Clinton's National Economic Council, in an attempt to integrate key departmental and White House advisers around major policy matters. Such committees or councils are patterned after the National Security Council, established in 1947 to confer with the president on matters relating to national security. These initiatives are aimed at decentralizing policy discussions while giving cabinet members a genuine feeling that they are being consulted and involved in important policy developments.

THE VICE-PRESIDENT

Although the vice-presidency is now a part of the presidential establishment, it has not been so for long. Most vice-presidents served mainly as president of the Senate. Up to the 1950s, the vice-president was at best a "fifth wheel" and at worst a political rival who sometimes connived against the president. The office was often dismissed as a joke. One reason for the vice-president's posture as an outsider was that presidential nominees prior to Clinton usually chose running mates who were geographically, ideologically, demographically, and in other ways likely to "balance the ticket." Clinton ignored tradition and picked another white, male, progressive southerner who has been not only a like-minded partner to Clinton but has assumed increased responsibility for presidential policy.

Today the vice-presidency brings both advantages and liabilities to a person who aspires to the presidency. The job surely provides exposure to the issues and of the office, but it is sometimes hard to appear "presidential" while at the same time avoiding the appearance of being disloyal to or upstaging the president.

Ideally, a vice-president serves several roles in addition to the ceremonial function of acting as president of the Senate. A vice-president gets to cast the tie-breaking vote if the Senate has a tie vote, but this situation usually occurs less than once a year. The vice-president is also a member of the National Security Council. Vice-president Al Gore headed a national review of the federal bureaucracy for President Clinton, a temporary yet highly visible presidential assignment.[34] He effectively debated Ross Perot in a widely viewed TV debate on the North American Free Trade Agreement. Gore also spearheaded various "information superhighway" initiatives for Clinton. And Gore readily outdebated and outcampaigned Bob Dole's running mate, Jack Kemp, in the 1996 presidential election campaign.

The real test of the role of vice-president is whether he or she is fully integrated into the decision-making process in the White House. All vice-presidents are "back-up equipment" in case something happens to the president. They can head up any number of councils, visit any number of countries, and still not be much involved in the day-to-day operations of the presidency. President Carter included Walter Mondale in the daily processes of decision making in the White House; President Reagan sometimes included George Bush in a similar way; President Clinton has used Al Gore as an important adviser and confidant on domestic as well as foreign policy matters and key appointments.

Tensions sometimes develop between presidential aides and vice-presidents and their staffs. Part of the problem arises because few presidents wish to give up any ceremonial duties for which they themselves can win credit. Neither do cabinet members like to share their responsibilities with vice-presidents, making it hard for vice-presidents to gain administrative experience. Presidents often delegate unpleasant political chores to their vice-presidents.

The importance of the vice-presidency is underscored, however, by the fact that nine presidents have not been able to finish their terms. Four presidents have been assassinated, four have died naturally, and one has resigned. One-third of our presidents were once vice-presidents, including Truman, Lyndon Johnson, Nixon, Ford, and Bush.

The vice-presidency has been significantly affected by two constitutional amendments. The Twenty-second Amendment, ratified in 1951, imposes a two-term limit on presidents; consequently, vice-presidents have a better chance of moving up to the Oval Office. The Twenty-fifth Amendment, ratified in 1967, confirms the prior practice of making the vice-president not an acting president, but president, in the event of the death of a president. Also of significance, this amendment outlines a procedure to determine whether an incumbent president is unable to discharge the powers and duties of the office and establishes procedures to fill a vacancy in the vice-presidency.[35] For a few hours in 1985, George Bush became the first "acting president" when President Reagan underwent a minor cancer operation.

The amendment also provides that in the event of a vacancy in the office of vice-president, the president nominates a vice-president, who takes office upon confirmation by a majority vote of both houses of Congress. This procedure generally ensures the appointment of a vice-president in whom the president has confidence. Thus vice-presidents who have to take over the presidency can be expected to reflect most of their predecessor's policies.

Although the sort of tensions between president and vice-president that existed in the past do not plague Clinton and Gore, common tension between a president and a vice-president is natural. After all, except for the vice-president, everybody

In some ways, the 1996 presidential campaign turned into a battle of the first ladies. At the nominating conventions of their respective parties, Hillary Rodham Clinton and Elizabeth Dole were featured on prime-time TV and were influential in winning the support of delegates for their husbands.

The 1996 vice-presidential debate had Jack Kemp and Al Gore fielding questions from moderator Jim Lehrer.

who works closely with a president can be fired. It is almost certain that vice-presidents will continue to have an undefined ad hoc set of assignments, subject more to the good will and mood of the president than to any fixed description.[36]

CONSTRAINTS ON THE PRESIDENT

Presidential power may be greater today than ever before; it is misleading, however, to infer from a president's capacity to begin a nuclear war that the chief executive has similar power in most policy-making areas. Seldom are presidents free agents in bringing about significant social change. As priority setter, politician, and executive, a president shares power with members of Congress, bureaucrats, and interest-group elites. But the ability to set priorities is not the same as the ability to enact new laws or to enforce laws and administer them properly. Presidents who want to be effective in implementing policy changes know they face a number of constraints. Besides the formal system of checks and balances, effective presidents learn to deal with media criticism, cultural challenges, and international pressures. Presidents are also shaped by their times, by the ideological leanings of the people, and by the successes and failures of their immediate predecessors.[37]

Media Criticism

Ronald Reagan once walked away from one of his news conferences and, turning to an aide, blasted the reporters, not realizing a microphone was picking up his every word. John F. Kennedy once canceled more than 50 White House subscriptions to the *New York Herald Tribune* because he was furious about the way the paper treated his decisions. Lyndon Johnson regularly planted "softball questions" (questions he could easily answer) among friendly reporters at presidential press conferences. Bill Clinton complained about "gotcha journalism" and was especially upset at the media's rough treatment of his wife. All recent presidents have complained that the modern media misrepresent them and disproportionately report bad news.

Enjoying enormous First Amendment rights in this country, reporters usually go about their business of analyzing and criticizing presidents with gusto. Scores of media representatives are regularly stationed at the White House, and they travel everywhere the president goes, reporting on every move. Reporters from all the

Factors that Constrain Presidents

The Constitution
Federalism
Separation of powers
Congress
Federal courts
News media
Public opinion
Opposing party
Opposing factions in president's party
Interest groups
Editorial opinion (and cartoonists)
Bureaucratic resistance
Opposing world powers and the international economy
World public opinion and UN policies
World leaders
Presidential advisers
Regularly scheduled elections
Unrealistic expectations
Party platforms
Independent counsels
The shape of the economy and the imperatives of economic development
Fear of losing next election for self or party

major networks and newspapers are assigned to be with the president 24 hours a day; they call this "the death watch." Presidential statements—even on trivial matters—are sent back to the newsrooms and immediately printed or aired. Major statements and policy initiatives are reported and subjected to analysis. The media, at the White House and elsewhere, call attention to subjects that might never have been discussed publicly in earlier times and that seldom are discussed in other countries.

Presidents, of course, want all their initiatives publicized and praised as much as possible. But media people believe they should provide a context in which presidential statements can be understood; hence they not only tell people what a president says but often try to explain what the statement means. This type of interpretation is offered primarily by columnists, editorial writers, and commentators. Those who manage newspapers and radio and television stations also want to balance their coverage of what presidents say—especially in presidential speeches—with an equal amount of time for spokespersons of the opposition party or persons who hold different points of view.

In recent years this kind of *adversarial* media coverage has often left the impression that a president's influence is more divisive than unifying. Except when a president attends a baseball game or welcomes some noted sports or arts hero to the White House, media coverage involves interpretation. No reporter has ever won a Pulitzer Prize for writing a story favorable to an administration; the journalism profession invariably honors those who uncover wrongdoing.

What have presidents done about this? Typically, they have been patient and respected the critical dialogue as essential in a democracy. However, presidents and their aides have also engaged in extensive public relations efforts aimed at winning admiration and support for the president and White House policies.[38] Out-of-town editors are invited in for special briefings, and extra effort is made to get the president out of Washington for meetings with local and regional media representatives, who are generally viewed as less critical than Washington-based media. White House media experts devise ways to get the president's point of view out to the public, to get the president on prime-time television, or to arrange for flattering action photos.

The modern media are indeed a formidable adversary of the modern presidency. But the presidency is not being brutally wounded, and its capacity for leadership is seldom sapped because of aggressive media coverage. Defenders of the press like to quote Thomas Jefferson, who, although angered by the press when he was president, said: "Were it left to me to decide whether we should have a government without newspapers or newspapers without a government, I should not hesitate to prefer the latter."

Defenders of the media say presidents have often lied or manipulated the public's understanding of the issues. The media, they contend, are obligated to cover opposition views, especially when they think a president is wrong. Even though journalists may have political sympathies, they prize their objectivity and seldom play the role of cheerleader. "Their fault may be the opposite: seeing politicians and their handlers up close, they have no faith in any of them and are carriers, as well as recorders, of the prevailing disenchantment."[39]

No matter who is in the White House, presidents and the media will be in conflict. This ongoing struggle is inherent in a constitutional democracy. Exposés of the Watergate, Whitewater, and campaign-contribution scandals fortified the media through their important role in bringing the scandals to public attention. Further, because the media—especially television—are viewed as more trustworthy and believable than some other national institutions, most Americans, most of the time, believe what they hear and see on television. But the resources of the White House and the amount of free media coverage given presidents—especially communicators like Franklin Roosevelt, John Kennedy, and Ronald Reagan—provide an effective counterpoint to the media.

Unrealistic Expectations?

The presidency is laden with the cumulative weight of contradictory expectations. Thus, we want our presidents to be:

- Gentle and kind, but also forceful, cunning, and decisive
- A common person who can give an uncommon performance
- Above politics, yet a skilled political coalition builder
- An inspirational leader who never promises more than he or she can deliver
- Ahead of the times, yet always responsive to popular majorities
- A moral leader, yet not too preachy or moralizing
- A bipartisan leader of all the people but also a leader of one political party
- A "take charge" leader yet someone who listens a lot

Cultural Challenges

Because all presidents face cultural dilemmas (for example, attitudes and values toward gay rights or abortion), they need to understand the cultural contexts and cultural values of those they would lead. Political scientists Richard Ellis and Aaron Wildavsky contend presidents can be evaluated in terms of dilemmas confronted, evaded, created, or overcome. The "great" presidents, like Washington, Jefferson, Jackson, and Lincoln, provided solutions to the cultural and societal dilemmas of their day. Borrowing from the work and theories of anthropologists, Ellis and Wildavsky suggest there are at least three contrasting political cultures: *hierarchical*, *egalitarian*, and *individualistic*. "The type of leadership preferred and feared, and the kinds of support given to and demands made upon leaders, we hypothesize, vary by political culture."[40]

In a hierarchical culture, characterized by respect for authority and acceptance of formal hierarchical relations (as for example, in the marines or on a college basketball team), leadership is relatively easy to exercise. On the other hand, those who try to provide leadership in a society that yearns for equality are invariably frustrated, for egalitarians (lovers of equality) are dedicated to diminishing differences among people. "Would-be egalitarian leaders are thus in trouble before they start," for authority and leadership inherently create inequalities.[41]

In the individualist culture, Ellis and Wildavsky see governance organized to maximize individual freedom and thus minimize the need for governmental authority. Citizens in such a culture perform a delicate balancing act between permitting leaders to arise when they are needed and getting rid of them whenever possible.

These authors note that the United States is rightly characterized by its strong individualism, weak hierarchies, and only occasional bursts of egalitarianism. Thus, "with egalitarians rejecting authority, individualists desiring to escape it, and hierarchical forces too weak to impose it, presidents seeking to rely on formal authority alone are in a precarious position."[42]

One of the contributions of George Washington's leadership was his commitment to central government yet wise appreciation for the limits of authority in the United States. Abraham Lincoln is credited with skillfully exercising executive leadership in a notably antileadership system, but doing so in a way that showed a government could provide emergency leadership in times of total war without allowing this power to lead inexorably to permanent dictatorship in peacetime. Lincoln delicately balanced the need for leadership with the need for assurances that the circumstances were extraordinary.

At their best, presidential leaders are individuals who perceive what is needed and understand how to mobilize people and resources to accomplish mutual goals. Effective presidents build on strengths—their own as well as those of their followers and colleagues—and on the opportunities afforded by their culture and situation.

Effective presidents sense a deep connection with the needs, dreams, and anxieties of the people. The political culture may in large measure shape presidents and what we expect of them, yet the great presidents understand the character of their times and are tenacious in promoting a right course. Historian Arthur Schlesinger, Jr., insists presidents matter:

> To succeed, presidents must have a port to seek and must convince Congress and the electorate of the rightness of their course. Politics in a democracy is ultimately an educational process, an exercise in persuasion and consent. Every president stands in Theodore Roosevelt's "bully pulpit." National crisis widens his range of options but does not automatically make the man. The crisis of rebellion did not spur Buchanan to greatness, nor did the Depression turn Hoover into a bold and imaginative leader. Their inadequacies in face of crisis allowed Lincoln and the second Roosevelt to show the difference that individuals can make in history.[43]

International Pressures

Nearly all scholars call attention to the growing number of international pressures facing any president. Historian Paul Kennedy bluntly observed that the task facing American leaders as the nation enters the twenty-first century is to recognize that broad trends are under way on a global scale and that "there is a need to 'manage' affairs so that relative erosion of the United States' position takes place slowly and smoothly."[44] Our presidents and leaders, he and others are saying, have to learn to cooperate with and persuade allies, and they must have the ability to win the support of leaders elsewhere as well.

Presidents today are forced to deal with a much stronger European Union and with the increasingly powerful economic force of several Pacific Rim nations. Multilateral action usually makes far more sense than unilateral action. Presidents have to secure not only the support of Congress and the American people; they must also win the cooperation of foreign nations. It is increasingly clear, as Bill Clinton has surely learned, that the international system, especially the international economy, is stronger than any president or prime minister.

Most other nations long ago learned that to succeed in an international system requires understanding other nations as well as one's own. Current and future presidents will have to be even better prepared than in the past to take global needs, aspirations, and politics into account.

LEADERSHIP IN A CONSTITUTIONAL DEMOCRACY

Some people worry about "imperial presidents" and about the possible alienation of the people from their leaders, especially as complex issues continue to centralize responsibilities in the hands of the national government and the executive. Those who are concerned about these matters will not content themselves—nor should they—with the existing safeguards against misuse of presidential powers. It is not easy, however, to contrive devices that will check a president who would misuse powers without hamstringing a president who would use those same powers for appropriate purposes and democratically acceptable ends.

James Madison warned that our country could never trust "parchment barriers" to halt the encroaching abuse of power. In the end, constitutions live only if they embody the spirit, values, and deeply held civic beliefs of the people. As the poet Walt Whitman reminded us, tyranny is always a possibility—if the people lose their supreme confidence in themselves and their spirit of defiance. Tyranny may always enter; there is no bar or charm against it. The only bar against it is a large, resolute breed of citizens.

Too much has been made by too many presidents and too many scholars of the view that only the president is the representative of all the people. Members of Congress do not represent the people exactly as a president does, but the two houses collectively represent the people in ways a president cannot and does not.

In the end, the issue is not so much whether the presidency should be stronger than Congress or vice versa. The real issue is that Congress and the presidency must *both* be strengthened to do the pressing work required for the well-being of the American people.

The most compelling restraint on presidential power is the opinion of the American people. Citizens have more power than they realize. Presidents listen when citizens are "sending a message." Citizens can also "vote" between elections in innumerable ways—by changing parties, by organizing protests, by voting for the opposition party in off-year elections, by voting in state referenda, and by protests.

Americans have a healthy skepticism about presidential decisions. The lesson of Watergate is not that the powers of the presidency should be lessened but that other institutions—parties, Congress, the courts—need constantly to be revitalized. Unless we can find ways to renew and reinvigorate our political parties and to

People who believe a president should be immune from civil suits contend a president's responsibilities are unique and therefore a president should be protected from distractions such as civil lawsuits until he or she leaves the White House. If a president were subject to such suits, Clinton's lawyer held, it could lead to a flood of frivolous lawsuits that would distract the president from effectively conducting the nation's business. In effect, he maintained, a president should be treated as special, at least while in office, because otherwise his ability to serve the public could be seriously compromised.

The Supreme Court ruled in 1982 that presidents are immune from lawsuits for their official acts, yet the court never granted immunity to a public official for unofficial acts.

In 1997, the Supreme Court, in a unanimous 9 to 0 vote, decisively ruled that a sitting president can indeed be sued for actions that fall outside the scope of presidential duties. The Court rejected Clinton's and his lawyer's request to delay proceeding in the sexual harassment civil suit brought by Paula Jones. The Court ruled that neither the U.S. Constitution nor public policy justified delaying pretrial proceedings and a trial until after Clinton leaves office, but made no reference to the validity of the charges, leaving that to the trial judge and jury.*

*For excerpts from this decision, see *The New York Times*, May 28, 1997, pp. 1 and 13.

awaken the responsiveness of the electorate, we might develop an American version of General Charles de Gaulle's government in France in the 1960s—a highly personalized and centralized system totally dependent on a charismatic individual.

Ultimately, there is, of course, no foolproof way to guarantee our presidents will possess the leadership skills and moral character the job requires. America has had several great presidents, yet we have also had a good many flawed and ineffective presidents. The presidency is clearly a unique and necessary yet dangerous institution. Thus James Madison's advice remains useful: "A dependence on the people is, no doubt, the primary control of the government; but experience has taught mankind the necessity of auxiliary precautions" (see *The Federalist*, No. 51, in the Appendix). Americans must maintain the effectiveness of these "auxiliary precautions"—Congress, political parties, the courts, the press, the Bill of Rights, and concerned citizens' groups—to ensure a properly balanced and constitutional presidency.

 POLITICS ONLINE

Protesting Via the Internet

On February 8, 1996 President Clinton signed the Telecommunications Reform Bill, which was seen by many as imposing too many constraints on the Internet. Online protests were organized by the Center for Democracy and Technology (http://www.cdt.org), along with the Voters Telecommunications Watch (http://www.vtw.org), and the Citizens Internet Empowerment Coalition (http://www.ciec.org). To highlight their opposition, they organized an Internet blackout. The protest was supported by thousands of Web pages, including major sites like Yahoo, Netscape, Infoseek, Webcrawler, Surfwatch Software, and the home pages of Senator Patrick Leahy (D-VT) and Congressman Jerrold Nadler D-NY). Surfing the net today, you will find a blue ribbon to support free speech online, as promoted by the Libertarians' Blue Ribbon Campaign (http://www.eff.org/blueribbon.html).

Using the Internet to protest an action by President Clinton is somewhat ironic, because he has been an outspoken advocate of connecting schools to the Internet and has made use of the Web for White House communications. If you want to send a message to the White House, visit its home page at:

> http://www.whitehouse.gov

This Web site also provides the text of presidential speeches, copies of news releases, current events at the White House, information regarding the federal government, and White House tours. The vice-president and various departments of the executive branch also maintain home pages; if you need information relating to the State Department, Treasury Department, or the Bureau of Land Management, just search out their home pages.

SUMMARY

1. The office of the president encompasses a huge presidential establishment, a president's personality, the cultural dilemmas of the day, high popular expectations, and the heavy demands on the chief executive. It is still being reshaped as new presidents with ideas and styles of their own move into the White House.

2. Several factors can cause conflict in our system of divided government. Among them are constitutional ambiguities,

different constituencies, varying terms of office, divided party control of the different branches, weak party discipline, and fluctuating public support for Congress or the president.

3. The separation of powers and necessity of shared decision making, especially in foreign affairs, produce a creative tension between the White House and Congress. Both presidents and Congress have occasionally overstepped their roles in recent years; the process is never neat and tidy; complete accord is only sometimes achieved. Yet the two branches do cooperate, and somehow the business of government does get done.

4. The expansion of presidential powers has been a continual development during the past several decades. Crises, both foreign and economic, have enlarged these powers. When there is a need for decisive action, presidents are asked to supply it. Congress, of course, is traditionally expected to share in the formulation of national policy. Yet Congress is often so fragmented that it has been a willing partner in the growth of the presidency. At the same time, Congress is constantly setting boundaries on how far presidents can extend their influence. Every president must learn anew the need to work closely with the members of Congress.

5. Presidents must act as crisis-managing, morale-building, personnel-recruiting, priority-setting, coalition-building, and managerial leaders. No president can divide the job into tidy compartments. Ultimately, these responsibilities overlap.

6. Presidents generally exercise more leadership in foreign and national security policy than does Congress, and generally, though not always, Congress is more supportive of presidential requests in these areas. These tendencies have led to the notion that there are "two presidencies"—a stronger, more successful one in foreign affairs and a somewhat weaker, less influential one in domestic policy.

7. The overriding task of American citizens is to bind presidents to the majority's will without shackling them. To expect too much of our presidents may be to weaken them in the leadership tasks we need them to perform. To require immediate accountability might paralyze the presidency. Presidential leadership, properly defined, must be more than the power to persuade and less than the power to coerce. It must be the power to achieve by democratic and constitutional means results acceptable to the people.

FURTHER READING

DAVID GRAY ADLER AND LARRY N. GEORGE, EDS., *The Constitution and the Conduct of American Foreign Policy: Essays on Law and History* (University Press of Kansas, 1996).

JAMES DAVID BARBER, *The Presidential Character*, 4th ed. (Prentice Hall, 1992).

JON R. BOND AND RICHARD FLEISHER, *The Presidents in the Legislative Arena* (University of Chicago Press, 1990).

PAUL BRACE AND BARBARA HINCKLEY, *Follow the Leader: Opinion Polls and the Modern Presidents* (Basic Books, 1992).

THOMAS E. CRONIN, *The State of the Presidency*, 2d ed. (Little, Brown, 1980).

THOMAS E. CRONIN AND MICHAEL GENOVESE, *The Paradoxes of the American Presidency* (Oxford University Press, 1998).

TERRY EASTLAND, *Energy in the Executive* (Free Press, 1992).

LOUIS FISHER, *Constitutional Conflicts Between Congress and the President*, 3d ed. (University Press of Kansas, 1991).

LOUIS FISHER, *Presidential War Power* (University Press of Kansas, 1995).

MICHAEL GENOVESE, *The Dilemmas of Presidential Leadership* (HarperCollins, 1995).

CHARLES O. JONES, *The Presidency in a Separated System* (Brookings Institution, 1994).

SAMUEL KERNELL, *Going Public: New Strategies of Presidential Leadership* (Congressional Quarterly Press, 1986).

THOMAS S. LANGSTON, *With Reverence and Contempt: How Americans Think About Their President* (Johns Hopkins University Press, 1995).

LEONARD W. LEVY AND LOUIS FISHER, EDS., *Encyclopedia of the American Presidency* (Simon & Schuster, 1994).

JOHN A. MALTESE, *Spin Control: The White House Office of Communications and the Management of the Presidential News* (University of North Carolina Press, 1992).

SIDNEY M. MILKIS, *The President and the Parties: The Transformation of the American Party System Since the New Deal* (Oxford University Press, 1993).

MICHAEL NELSON, ED., *Guide to the American Presidency* (Congressional Quarterly Press, 1989).

RICHARD E. NEUSTADT, *Presidential Power and the Modern Presidents* (Free Press, 1991).

MARK A. PETERSON, *Legislating Together: The White House and Capitol Hill from Eisenhower to Reagan* (Harvard University Press, 1990).

JAMES P. PFIFFNER, *The Strategic Presidency: Hitting the Ground Running*, 2d ed. (University Press of Kansas, 1996).

GLENN A. PHELPS, *George Washington and American Constitutionalism* (University Press of Kansas, 1993).

GERALD M. POMPER, ED. *The Election of 1996* (Chatham House, 1997).

DAN QUAYLE, *Standing Firm* (Harper Paperbacks, 1995).

ROBERT B. REICH, *Locked in the Cabinet* (Knopf, 1997).

STANLEY A. RENSHON, *The Psychological Assessment of Presidential Candidates* (New York University Press, 1996).

ALLEN SCHICK, *The Federal Budget: Politics, Policy, Process* (Brookings Institution, 1995).

ARTHUR M. SCHLESINGER, JR., *The Imperial Presidency* (Houghton Mifflin, 1973).

ROBERT SPITZER, *The President and Congress: Executive Hegemony at the Crossroads of American Government* (McGraw-Hill, 1993).

GIL TROY, *Affairs of State: The Rise and Rejection of the Presidential Couple Since World War II* (Free Press, 1997).

KENNETH T. WALSH, *Feeding the Beast: The White House versus the Press* (Random House, 1996).

SHIRLEY ANNE WARSHAW, *Powersharing: White House-Cabinet Relations in the Modern Presidency* (State University of New York Press, 1996).

THOMAS J. WEKO, *The Politicizing Presidency: The White House Personnel Office, 1948–1994* (University Press of Kansas, 1995).

BOB WOODWARD, *The Agenda: Inside the Clinton White House* (Simon & Schuster, 1994).

16

The Judiciary: The Balancing Branch

*I*t was not an inspiring occasion. The few people present could hardly know they were witnessing the first meeting of what was to become the most important court in the world, the Supreme Court of the United States. It began on February 2, 1790. Chief Justice John Jay from New York, Justice James Wilson from Pennsylvania, and Justice William Cushing from Massachusetts were the only three of the original six appointees who made it through the snowy roads to New York City. They met in the Royal Exchange Building, an open-air market for butchers, which was the seat of the new federal government. The term lasted ten days, there were no cases to hear, and there was no quorum. The time was devoted to the admission of lawyers to practice before the Court.[1]

Four years later, Chief Justice John Jay resigned, in part because the federal court system lacked "energy, weight, and dignity," and in part to become governor of New York. But by the end of Chief Justice John Marshall's service (1801–35), the Supreme Court had taken its place as a coequal third branch of the federal government. In fact, foreign visitors are often amazed at the power Americans give their judges, especially their federal judges. In 1834, after his visit to the United States, French aristocrat Alexis de Tocqueville wrote: "If I were asked where I place the American aristocracy, I should reply without hesitation . . . that it occupies the judicial bench and bar. . . . Scarcely any political question arises in the United States that is not resolved, sooner or later, into a judicial question."[2] A century later the British political scientist Harold J. Laski observed, "The respect in which federal courts and, above all, the Supreme Court are held is hardly surpassed by the influence they exert on the life of the United States."[3]

Why do judges play such a central role in our political life? One reason, as we saw in Chapter 2, is that in *Marbury v Madison* (1803), Chief Justice John Marshall successfully claimed for judges the power of **judicial review**, that is, the power to interpret the Constitution authoritatively. Only a constitutional amendment or a later Supreme Court can modify the Court's doctrine. Justice Felix Frankfurter once put it tersely: "The Supreme Court is the Constitution."

Besides exercising the power of judicial review, judges—and not just those on the Supreme Court—resolve disputes involving millions of dollars, decide conflicts among interests, supervise the criminal justice system, and make rules that affect the lives of millions of people. They are not only resolvers of legal conflicts; through their equity powers they have, in effect, become managers of schools, prisons, mental hospitals, and complex businesses.[4] Sometimes, in fact, they decide the details of how these institutions should be run. Still, the role of our judges is limited by the scope and nature of judicial power.

THE SCOPE OF JUDICIAL POWER

The American judicial process rests on an *adversary system*. A court of law is a neutral arena in which two parties argue their differences and present their points of view before an impartial arbiter. The adversary system, or *fight theory*, may or may not be adequate to arrive at the truth, but it is the basis of our judicial system. The logic of the adversary system imposes formal restraints on the scope of judicial power, and its rhetoric leads us to conceive the role of the judge in a special way.

Types of Law

Statutory Law
Law that comes from authoritative and specific lawmaking sources, primarily legislatures but also including treaties and executive orders.

Common Law
Judge-made law that originated in England in the twelfth century, when royal judges traveled around the country settling disputes in each locality according to prevailing custom. The common law continues to develop according to the rule of *stare decisis*, which means "let the decision stand." This is the rule of precedent, which implies that a rule established by a court is to be followed in all similar cases.

Equity Law
Law used whenever common law remedies are inadequate. For example, if an injury done to property may do irreparable harm for which money damages cannot provide compensation, under equity a person may ask the judge to issue an injunction ordering the offending person not to take the threatened action. If the wrongdoer persists, he or she may be punished for contempt of court.

Constitutional Law
Statements interpreting the United States Constitution that have been given Supreme Court approval.

Admiralty and Maritime Law
Law applicable to cases concerning shipping and waterway commerce on the high seas and on the navigable waters of the United States.

Administrative Law
Law relating to the authority and procedures of administrative agencies as well as to the rules and regulations issued by those agencies.

Criminal Law
Law that defines crimes against the public order and provides for punishment. Government is responsible for enforcing criminal law, the great body of which is enacted by states and enforced by state officials in state courts. The criminal caseload of federal judges is growing.

Civil Law
Law that governs the relations between individuals and defines their legal rights. However, the government can also be a party to a civil action. Under the Sherman Antitrust Act, for example, the federal government may initiate civil as well as criminal action to prevent violations of the law.

Judicial power is essentially passive. Judges cannot reach out and instigate a case. Furthermore, not all disputes are within the scope of judicial power. Judges decide only **justiciable disputes**—those that grow out of actual cases and are capable of settlement by legal methods. Not all constitutional disputes are justiciable. Some raise **political questions**, which require knowledge of a nonlegal character, or the use of techniques not suitable for a court, or are explicitly assigned by the Constitution to Congress or the president. Which of two competing state governments is the proper one? What does the Constitution mean when it provides that the national government should guarantee to each state a republican form of state government? Which group of officials of a foreign nation should be recognized by the United States as the government of that nation?[5] These are all political questions.

Judges are not supposed to use their power unless there is a real case or controversy. "It was never thought that, by means of a friendly suit, a party beaten in the legislature could transfer to the courts an inquiry as to the constitutionality of a legislative act."[6] (This, of course, is exactly what is done in nonfriendly suits. In such cases, however, the two parties have an interest in getting the full facts before the court.) In addition, litigants must have *standing to sue*; that is, they must have sustained or be in immediate danger of sustaining a direct and substantial injury. It is not enough merely to have a general interest in a subject or to believe that a law is unconstitutional.[7]

Of increasing importance in recent years are **class action suits** in which a small number of persons are allowed to represent all other persons similarly situated—a suit on behalf of all students in a university, for example, or all patients in a hospital, or all persons who bought a particular model of an automobile. "Would-be class action litigants must show that they are proper representatives for the class of persons they seek to champion, that the types of issues they wish to raise are common to the class, and they must be able to demonstrate how a remedy can be formed that will meet the needs of the class."[8]

Do Judges Make Law?

"Do judges make law? Course they do. Made some myself," remarked Jeremiah Smith, judge of the New Hampshire Supreme Court.[9] Most judges, even today, are less candid. Judges obviously make law, but to admit it is somehow disturbing. Such statements do not conform to our notions of what a judge should do.

Why do we think judges should not make law? Many people equate a judge's role with that of a referee in a prizefight. We expect referees to be impartial and disinterested, to treat both parties as equals. We expect them to apply rules, not make them.

Laws are not made, however, in the same way as the rules of a sport, and herein lies the answer to our question. Not only do judges make law, but they *must*. Legislatures make law by enacting statutes, but judges apply statutes to concrete situations. In some cases, applicability is clear: "If anything is a vehicle, a motorcar is one."[10] But does the word "vehicle" in a statute include bicycles, airplanes, and roller skates? A judge is constantly faced with situations that possess some features of similar cases but lack others. Statutes are drawn in broad terms: drivers shall act with "reasonable care"; no one may make "excessive noise" in the vicinity of a hospital; employers must maintain "safe working conditions." Such broad terms must be used because legislators cannot know exactly what will happen in the future.

These problems are intensified when judges are asked—as American judges are—to apply the Constitution, which was written more than 200 years ago. The Constitution is full of generalizations: "due process of law," "equal protection of the laws," "unreasonable searches and seizures," "Commerce . . . among the several

States." Recourse to the intent of the framers or just to the words of the Constitution is not likely to help judges faced with cases involving electronic wiretaps, multinational corporations, or birth control pills.

Adherence to Precedent

Just because judges make policy, however, does not mean they are free to make it as they wish. They are subject to a variety of limits on what they decide—some imposed by the political system of which they are a part, some by their own professional obligations as lawyers. Among these constraints is the rule of **stare decisis**, the rule of precedent.

Stare decisis pervades our judicial system. Judges are expected to abide by all previous decisions of their own courts and all rulings of superior courts. Although adherence to precedent is normal, the doctrine of *stare decisis* is not nearly as restrictive as some people think.[11] Consider, for example, the father who, removing his hat as he enters a church, says to his son: "This is the way to behave on such occasions. Do as I do."[12] Like the judge trying to follow a precedent, the son has a wide range of possibilities open to him. How much of his father's behavior must he imitate? Does it matter if the hat is removed slowly or quickly? If the hat is put under the seat? If it is not replaced on the head inside the church? The judge can distinguish precedents by stating that a previous case does not control the immediate one because of differences in context. In addition, many areas of law have conflicting precedents, one of which can be chosen to support a decision for either party.

The doctrine of *stare decisis* is even less controlling in the field of constitutional law. Because the Constitution itself, rather than any one interpretation of it, is binding, the Court can *reverse* a previous decision it no longer wishes to follow, as it has done dozens of times. Supreme Court justices are, therefore, not seriously restricted by *stare decisis*. As the first Justice John Marshall Harlan told a group of law students, "I want to say to you young gentlemen that if we don't like an act of Congress, we don't have too much trouble to find grounds for declaring it unconstitutional."[13]

FEDERAL JUSTICE

"The judicial Power of the United States," says Article III of the Constitution, "shall be vested in one supreme Court, and in such inferior Courts as the Congress may from time to time ordain and establish." Courts created to carry out this judicial power are called *Article III* or *constitutional courts*. Congress may also establish *Article I* or *legislative courts* to carry out the legislative powers the Constitution has granted to it. The main difference between a legislative and a constitutional court is that the judges of the former need not be appointed to "hold their Offices during good Behavior" and may be assigned other than purely judicial duties.

The Constitution requires a Supreme Court. It is a necessity if the national government is to have the power to frame and enforce laws superior to those of the states. The lack of such an agency to maintain national supremacy, to ensure uniform interpretation of national legislation, and to resolve conflicts among the states was one of the glaring deficiencies of the central government under the Articles of Confederation.

Congress decides whether there will be national courts in addition to the one Supreme Court ordained by the Constitution. The Constitution also allows Congress to determine the size of the Supreme Court. The First Congress divided the nation into districts and created lower national courts for each district. That decision, though often supplemented, has never been seriously questioned.

Examples of Special Article III (Constitutional) Courts

In addition to courts of general jurisdiction, Congress has created constitutional courts with special jurisdiction:

United States Court of International Trade (formerly U.S. Customs Court)
Consists of nine judges who review rulings of customs collectors and conflicts arising under various tariff and trade laws.

United States Court of Appeals for the Federal Circuit
Consists of 12 judges who sit in panels of three to hear appeals of cases from all federal courts relating to patents as well as to review decisions of the Patent Office and of the Court of International Trade.

Foreign Intelligence Surveillance Court
Composed of seven district court judges appointed by the chief justice. They serve on a regular rotation and meet in secret to hear requests from the Department of Justice acting on behalf of the National Security Agency, the Federal Bureau of Investigation, and other intelligence agencies that engage in electronic surveillance and physical searches of the homes end offices of foreign agents. To get an FISC order, the government must show probable cause that the person in question is either acting for a foreign power or is an agent of a foreign power who knowingly engages in clandestine intelligence on behalf of a foreign power.

Federal Courts of General Jurisdiction

Today the hierarchy of national courts of general jurisdiction consists of district courts, courts of appeals, and one Supreme Court (see Figure 16–1). Although the Supreme Court and its justices receive most of the attention, the workhorses of the federal judiciary are the district courts within the states, in the District of Columbia, and in the territories. Each state has at least one district court. Larger states have as many as the demands of judicial business and the pressure of politics require, although no state has more than four.

There are 623 permanent district judges organized into 94 district courts in the 50 states and in the District of Columbia and the Commonwealth of Puerto Rico. There are also territorial district courts in Guam, the U.S. Virgin Islands, and the Northern Mariana Islands. Each has at least 2 judges but may have as many as 28. District judges normally sit separately and hold court by themselves. Except for the three territorial courts that are Article I courts, all district judges, like all Article III federal judges, hold office for life.

Although justices of the Supreme Court get considerable public attention, the workhorses of the federal judicial district are the district courts, the trial courts of **original jurisdiction**. They are the only federal courts that regularly employ **grand juries** (indicting) and **petit juries** (trial). Many cases tried before district judges involve citizens of different states, and the judges apply the appropriate state laws. Otherwise, district judges are concerned with federal laws. For example, they hear and decide cases involving crimes against the United States—suits under the national revenue, postal, patent, copyright, trademark, bankruptcy, and civil rights laws.[14]

District judges are assisted by clerks, bailiffs, stenographers, law clerks, court reporters, probation officers, and United States magistrate judges. All these officials are appointed by the judges. The 406 full-time and 85 part-time *federal magistrate judges* are becoming increasingly important.[15] After being screened by panels composed of residents of the judicial districts, full-time magistrates are appointed for eight-year renewable terms, part-time magistrates for four-year renewable terms.

Magistrates "look like a judge, act like a judge, and speak like a judge."[16] Magistrates, most of whom wear robes and since 1990 are called "Judge," issue war-

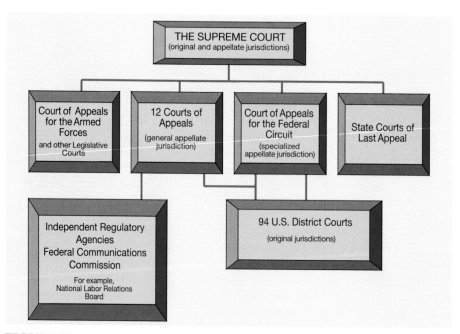

FIGURE 16–1   The Structure of the Federal Courts

rants for arrest, hold hearings to determine whether arrested persons should be held for action by the grand jury, and, if so, set bail. They hear motions subject to varying kinds of review by their district judges. They preside over civil trials—jury and nonjury—with the consent of both parties, and over nonjury trials for petty offenses with the consent of the defendants.[17] Under the supervision of the district judge, and with the consent of the accused, they may preside over the selection of a jury for a felony trial.[18]

District judges are bound by the precedents of the appellate courts that review their decisions, but these judges have considerable discretion in applying these precedents As a former Iowa federal district judge, Henry N. Graven, said to political scientists, "The people of this district either get justice here with me or they don't get it at all. I've had a number of cases appealed over the years, but I've never been overruled. And I've never had a case go to the Supreme Court. . . . Here at the trial court—that's where the action is."[19]

Except for the few cases that may be taken directly to the Supreme Court, a final decision of a district court is reviewable by a *court of appeals*. The United States is divided into 12 *judicial circuits*, one of which is the District of Columbia (see map). Each has a court of appeals consisting of 6 to 28 permanent judgeships (167 in all). The Court of Appeals for the Federal Circuit has national jurisdiction. Each court of appeals normally hears cases in panels of three, but for especially important and controversial cases, all judges may be present; that is, they may sit *en banc*.

From Coast to Coast

The U.S. Courts of Appeals

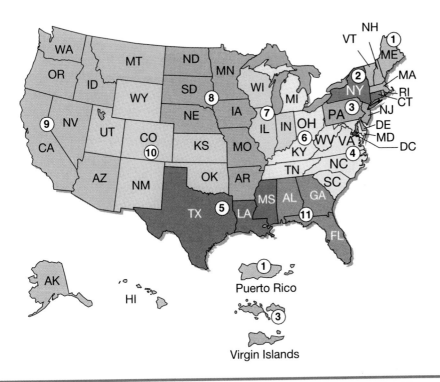

SOURCE: *The Federal Register.*

The Court of Appeals for the Ninth Circuit, the largest, has 28 circuit judges and 99 district judges who serve in California, Arizona, Nevada, Oregon, Washington, Idaho, Montana, Alaska, and Hawaii. The Ninth's liberalism often brings it into conflict with the more conservative United States and California supreme courts. Republicans are trying to split the Ninth, ostensibly because it is too large, but the battle is also over politics and public policy. The proposal currently before the U.S. Senate and House leaves only California, Hawaii, Guam, and the Northern Marianas in the Ninth. The northwestern states, along with Arizona and Nevada (Arizona and Nevada were added to the proposed new circuit in order to get the votes of the senators from those states) would become a new Twelfth Circuit.[20] Senators from those states would have more influence over future nominations in their circuit. Proponents of the change hope it would also "isolate and diminish the power of progressive judges" from California left in the Ninth.[21] Mining and oil interests from the Northwest hope to remove judges from California, who tend to be rigorous on environmental issues.

The last circuit to be divided was the old Fifth Circuit, which covered the Deep South. In 1981 it was split: Texas, Louisiana, and Mississippi remained in the Fifth; Georgia, Florida, and Alabama became the Eleventh Circuit. This split was opposed by some of the more liberal judges who had presided over the abolition of public school segregation.

Courts of appeals have only **appellate jurisdiction**, the authority to review decisions of the district courts within their circuits and also some of the actions of the independent regulatory agencies, such as the Federal Trade Commission. These courts are powerful policy makers.[22] Less than 1 percent of the cases from these courts are looked at carefully by the Supreme Court. As the policy role of federal courts has become a prominent political issue, more attention is being focused on these courts and the judges who serve on them.[23]

State and Federal Courts

In addition to federal courts, each state maintains a judicial system of its own, and many large municipalities have judicial systems as complex as those of the states. State courts have sole jurisdiction to try all cases not within the judicial power the Constitution grants to the United States.

The federal and state court systems are related, but they do not exist in a superior-inferior relationship. Except for the limited **habeas corpus** jurisdiction of the district courts (the power to release persons from custody if the judge is not satisfied that the person is being constitutionally detained), the Supreme Court is the only federal court that may review state court decisions. And it may do so only under special conditions.

Other than the original jurisdiction the Constitution vests directly in the Supreme Court, no federal court has any jurisdiction except that granted to it by act of Congress. Congress also determines whether this judicial power of the United States will be exercised exclusively by federal courts or concurrently by both federal and state courts.

PROSECUTION AND DEFENSE

Federal Lawyers

Judges decide cases; they do not prosecute persons. On the federal level, the job of prosecution falls to the Department of Justice: the attorney general, the solicitor general, the 94 United States attorneys, and some 1,200 assistant attorneys. The president, with the consent of the Senate, appoints a United States attorney for each district court. United States attorneys serve a four-year term but may be dismissed by the president at any time. These appointments are of great interest to senators, who exercise significant influence over the selection process through **senatorial courtesy**—the presidential custom of submitting the names of prospective appointees for approval to senators from the states in which the appointees reside. Because U.S. attorneys are almost always members of the president's political party, it is customary for them to resign if the opposition party wins the White House.

The attorney general, in consultation with the U.S. attorney in each district, appoints assistant attorneys. Some districts have only one; the largest, the Southern District of New York, has more than 65. These attorneys, working with the U.S. attorney and assisted by the Federal Bureau of Investigation and other federal law-enforcement agencies, begin proceedings against those alleged to have broken federal laws. They also represent the United States in civil suits.

Prosecutors and the Solicitor General

Prosecutors decide whether to charge an offense and which offense to charge. They have largely unreviewable discretion. "So long as the prosecutor has probable cause to believe that the accused committed an offense defined by statute, the decision whether or not to prosecute, and what charge to file or bring before a grand jury, generally rests entirely in his [or her] discretion."[24]

Prosecutors negotiate with the lawyers for **defendants** (those accused of an offense) and often work out a **plea bargain**, whereby defendants agree to plead guilty to one offense to avoid having to stand trial for a more serious offense. Prosecutors make recommendations to judges about what sentences to impose.

Attorneys from the Department of Justice and from other federal agencies participate in well over half the cases on the Supreme Court's docket. Of special importance is the *solicitor general* (SG), who represents the government before the Supreme Court. (When the SG appears before the Supreme Court, he wears a formal dark vest, tails, and striped pants.) When the solicitor general petitions the Supreme Court and asks it to review an opinion of a lower court, the Court is likely to do so. "Overall, the government is involved in about two-thirds of all cases heard during a term, and the solicitor general's record of wins has been fairly consistent in the past decade. About 75 percent of all rulings goes his way."[25] Moreover, no appeal may be taken by the United States to any appellate court without the approval of the solicitor general.[26]

Although the solicitor general reports to the attorney general and has always been responsive to the views of the president, the SG (sometimes called the "Tenth Justice") has traditionally been given some measure of independence from the White House. In recent decades that independence has been reduced. The Reagan administration used the SG to carry its social policy agenda to the Supreme Court—to try to persuade the justices, for example, to limit affirmative action and to restrict the right of women to have abortions.[27] The Clinton administration's first solicitor general, Drew S. Days, and the second, Walter Dellinger, with a staff of 23 lawyers continued in the activist manner of their immediate predecessors in the Reagan and Bush administrations, although on the opposite side on many issues. The office became embroiled with the Republican-controlled Senate Judiciary Committee over whether it had properly come to the aid of states in cases before the Supreme Court, contending that they had invaded the constitutional rights of prisoners.[28]

A Department of Justice office that is becoming increasingly important is the *assistant attorney general*, who heads up the Office of Legal Counsel. The OLC is "the principal legal guardian in the executive branch of the constitutional prerogatives and powers of the presidency"[29] and works closely with the Office of the Counsel to the President located in the White House.

Jurisdiction of the Federal Courts

Federal courts can hear and decide cases or controversies in law and equity if:

1. They arise under the Constitution, a federal law, or a treaty.
2. They arise under admiralty and maritime laws.
3. They arise because of a dispute involving land claimed under titles granted by two or more states.
4. The United States is a party to the case.
5. A state is a party to the case (but not if a suit was begun or prosecuted against a state by an individual or a foreign nation).
6. They are between citizens of different states.*
7. They affect the accredited representatives of a foreign nation.

*Congress has chosen to limit this *diversity jurisdiction* of federal courts, as it is called, to cases in which the amount in controversy exceeds $50,000.

The Liability Revolution: The Tort Law Explosion

In recent decades, there has been a huge increase in *tort law*, that part of civil law covering the liability of those whose conduct injures others and the compensation they must pay.

"Throughout most of American history, liability law has been an obscure legal byway . . . with little discernible effect on the wider society or economy."* Today liability has dramatically expanded, and the targets are mainly manufacturers, physicians, hospitals, towns and counties, and their insurance carriers.

Judges have played a leading role in this liability revolution, to the praise of some who believe judges have provided protection for the weak against the powerful, to the criticism of others who believe judges have usurped legislative responsibilities and impaired the effectiveness of our economy.

This is yet another example of the important role judges play. They not only resolve disputes between individuals, but in so doing they are central policy makers.

*Walter Olson, "The Liability Revolution: New Directions in Liability Law," *Proceedings of the Academy of Political Science* 37, no. 1 (1988), p. 1.

Federal Defense Lawyers

The federal government also provides lawyers for poor defendants in criminal trials. District courts have some discretion in how they provide this assistance. Most districts use the traditional system of assigning a private attorney. About half of the judicial districts, however, have opted to use the **public defender** system. These salaried public defenders operate under the general supervision of the Administrative Office of the United States Courts. The Judicial Conference of the United States has said the most important problem confronting the federal defender program is lack of money.[30] Congress is now reviewing the effectiveness of these procedures.

The Legal Services Corporation (LSC) provides financial assistance to 323 organizations that furnish legal help to the poor in noncriminal legal matters.[31] The corporation is the center of controversy. There are those, primarily Republicans, who would like to abolish it and who have been able to slash its funding by 25 percent and have barred it from filing class action suits; from representing prisoners, illegal aliens, and people being evicted from public housing for alleged drug activity; from litigating abortion or redistricting issues; and from challenging the legality of state or federal welfare laws. These restrictions extended not just to the use of federal funds, but also to the use by legal services organizations of nonfederal money raised from private or state sources. The Legal Services Corporation is thus restricted to suing landlords, employers, husbands, or wives in traditional legal battles.

On the other side are those, primarily Democrats, who would fund the Legal Services Corporation more adequately and would allow it to use class action suits to challenge the status quo. Some legal aid lawyers and organizations have challenged the restrictions against class action as being unconstitutional.[32] The LSC is governed by an 11-member board of directors appointed by the president with the advice and consent of the Senate. Hillary Rodham Clinton was chair of the Legal Services Corporation when her husband was governor of Arkansas.

THE POLITICS OF JUDICIAL SELECTION

The selection of federal judges has always been part of the political process. It makes a difference who serves on the federal courts—a difference in how the Constitution is interpreted and how goods and services and values are distributed. It has always been so, but as the courts have come to play an even more important role in the political process, and as more and more interests—African Americans and women, for example—have become empowered to participate in that process, judicial selection politics have come front and center on the political stage.

The president selects federal judges with the advice and consent of the Senate. Political reality imposes constraints on the president's discretion, and the selection of a federal judge is actually a complex bargaining process. The principal figures involved are the candidates, the president, and the "subpresidency for judicial selection"[33] consisting of key members of the Department of Justice, United States senators, the Standing Committee on the Federal Judiciary of the American Bar Association, party leaders, and, increasingly, interest groups.

Recent presidents have inserted the White House much more directly into the process than did their predecessors. Department of Justice officials and key White House staff meet often to review proposed names. President Bill Clinton, a former professor of constitutional law and a state attorney general, takes a special interest in judicial appointments. He takes an active role in finding and suggesting nominees to the Supreme Court and the courts of appeals, as does the First Lady Hillary Rodham Clinton, also a lawyer.[34]

Before the White House submits names of nominees for the federal district courts to the Senate, the president observes the practice of senatorial courtesy by consulting with appropriate senators. Even a senator from the opposition party is usually consulted. If negotiations are deadlocked between the senators or between the senators and the Department of Justice, a seat may stay vacant for years.[35] The custom of senatorial courtesy no longer applies to Supreme Court appointments and is not often applied to the selection of judges for the courts of appeals because these judges do not serve in any one senator's domain. This difference in selection politics means that district court judges often reflect values different from those of persons appointed to the courts of appeal or the Supreme Court.[36]

President Clinton has given Democratic senators "clear guidelines about the kind of judges he wants."[37] These senators, however, have frequently not waited for names to be cleared with them but have taken the initiative and sent recommendations to the Department of Justice. Most senators create screening panels of lawyers and citizens from their state to suggest names to them.

After the Republicans took control of the Senate in 1994, President Clinton, "using an approach that would have been unthinkable in recent administrations," instructed his "judge-pickers" to consult closely with Republican Senator Orrin Hatch, chair of the Senate Judiciary Committee, and with "hostile senators to assuage their fears." Clinton dropped from consideration any candidates that were likely to "engender serious opposition."[38]

By the end of his first term, Clinton had nominated and the Senate had confirmed 198 judges and 2 justices of the Supreme Court, more than half of whom were women or minorities.[39] Even so, because most federal judges had been chosen by Republican presidents, the federal judiciary still consisted well over half of Republican appointees.[40]

As he opened his second term, Clinton was faced with nearly 100 judicial vacancies because, during the second session of the 104th Congress, the Senate, hoping that a Republican would be in the White House by 1997, confirmed only 17 district judges and, for the first time in 40 years, failed to confirm any judges for the courts of appeals.[41] Some conservative senators argued that since the Republicans controlled the Senate, they should be allocated half the opening slots, indicating that they would give the president more discretion with the other half. President Clinton, however, insisted on exercising his power to appoint. Although his appointees will still have to be confirmed by the Senate and will face intense scrutiny by conservative groups—who formed a coalition of 260 conservative organizations and 35 talk show hosts, called the Judicial Selection Monitoring Project—it is highly likely that by the time Clinton leaves office, he will have picked 400 judges, half the entire federal judiciary, more federal judges than any other president.[42]

The American Bar Association's Standing Committee on the Federal Judiciary plays a special role in the appointment process. Presidents are hesitant to submit for Senate confirmation a candidate rated "not qualified" by the ABA. During an earlier period, the American Bar Association was thought to introduce a bias favoring the conservative "corporation lawyer." In recent years, however, conservative groups have mounted an attack on the ABA's role, contending it reflects a liberal bias and gives low ratings to "sandbag conservative nominees." In his 1996 campaign for the presidency, Bob Dole promised if elected to do as many conservatives had urged: "Strip the American Bar Association of its special role in the judicial selection process."[43] "In place of the narrowly partisan and ideologically liberal ABA," said Dole, "I will create a nonpartisan Judicial Integrity Panel, consisting of police, prosecutors, crime victims, legal scholars, and representatives of other legal and professional organizations."[44] Senator Orrin Hatch, chair of the Judiciary Committee, threatened to alter the ABA's role, saying, "I think the time has come, once and for all, to decide what role, if any, the ABA should play in the Senate's judicial confirmation process."[45] He can eliminate the ABA's role in advising the Senate but cannot stop the White House from continuing to rely on it.

Liberal interest groups, such as People for the American Way and Alliance for Justice, as well as conservative groups, such as the Heritage Foundation and the Free Congress Research and Education Foundation, have become active in the preliminaries, making known their views about nominees even before the names are released to the public or sent to the Senate Judiciary Committee for confirmation.[46]

The Senate: Advice and Consent

The normal presumption is that the president should be allowed considerable discretion in the selection of federal judges. Despite this presumption, the Senate takes seriously its responsibility to confirm presidential nominations, especially when the party controlling the Senate is different from that of the president, as has often been the case in recent years.

Most nominations, especially those for the lower federal courts, are processed without much controversy, especially when a president whose party controls the Senate nominates a highly qualified candidate. This action usually results "in a lopsided, consensual vote." When the president nominates a less well-qualified candidate, especially when the president and a majority of the Senate are from different political parties, "then a conflictual vote is likely."[47]

The major battle over judicial confirmations, if there is one, ordinarily takes place before the Senate Judiciary Committee. The Senate usually goes along with the recommendations of its Judiciary Committee without much debate. Yet floor debates are not all that rare. Overall, the Senate has refused to confirm 29 of the 138 presidential nominations for Supreme Court justices, including 7 in this century.[48]

Prior to 1955, only two nominees for the Supreme Court had made personal appearances before the Senate Judiciary Committee: Harlan F. Stone in 1925 and Felix Frankfurter in 1939. The common practice was for the Senate to look into candidates' qualifications and background, yet not examine them in person. More recently, the committee has felt free to ask judicial candidates a full range of questions in the glare of television cameras, since it is now crystal clear that a candidate's political orientation is the major factor in determining how he or she will vote on the cases that come before the Court. Except for Robert Bork, nominated by President Ronald Reagan in 1987, judicial nominees have steadfastly refused to answer questions when the answer might reveal how they would decide a case likely to come up to the Supreme Court. Judge Bork had written so many articles, made so many speeches, and decided so many cases that he thought he had to clarify his constitutional views. His candor may well have contributed to the Senate's rejection of him and is likely to scare off future nominees from responding to similar questions.

The Role of Party, Race, and Sex

Presidents so seldom nominate judges from the opposing party (around 90 percent of judicial appointments since the time of Franklin Roosevelt have gone to persons from the president's party) that partisan considerations are taken for granted, and partisan affiliation is rarely mentioned (see Table 16–1). Today journalists pay more attention to other characteristics, such as race and gender.

President Jimmy Carter, who had no opportunity to appoint anyone to the Supreme Court, selected more African Americans, Hispanics, and women for the lower federal courts than all other prior presidents combined—40 women, 38 African Americans, and 16 Hispanics. President Ronald Reagan, although the first to appoint a woman to the Supreme Court, appointed fewer minority members or women than did Carter, perhaps in part because fewer minorities and women could pass the

TABLE 16–1
Party Affiliation of District and Appeals Judges Appointed by Presidents

President	Party	Appointees from Same Party
Roosevelt	Democrat	97%
Truman	Democrat	92
Eisenhower	Republican	95
Kennedy	Democrat	92
Johnson	Democrat	96
Nixon	Republican	93
Ford	Republican	81
Carter	Democrat	90
Reagan	Republican	94
Bush	Republican	89
Clinton	Democrat	90*

SOURCE: Sheldon Goldman, "Judicial Selection Under Clinton: A Midterm Examination," *Judicature*, May/June 1995, p. 280. Updated by Sheldon Goldman, University of Massachusetts, Amherst, Mass.

*Figures for President Clinton are for nominations during his first term. Figures for other presidents are for confirmed appointments.

We the People

Female and Minority Appointments To Federal Judgeships

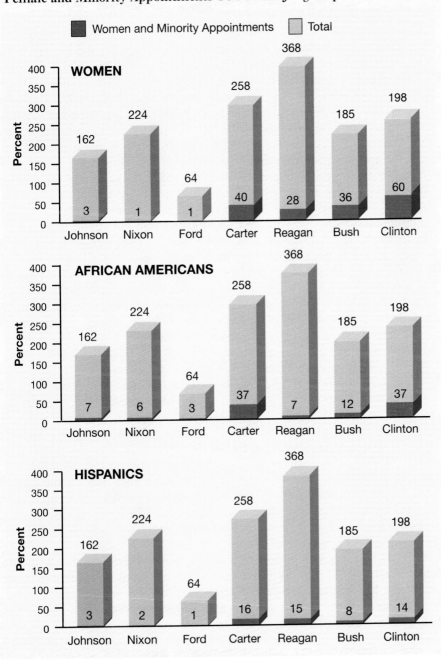

Legend: ■ Women and Minority Appointments □ Total

WOMEN

President	Total	Appointments
Johnson	162	3
Nixon	224	1
Ford	64	1
Carter	258	40
Reagan	368	28
Bush	185	36
Clinton	198	60

AFRICAN AMERICANS

President	Total	Appointments
Johnson	162	7
Nixon	224	6
Ford	64	3
Carter	258	37
Reagan	368	7
Bush	185	12
Clinton	198	37

HISPANICS

President	Total	Appointments
Johnson	162	3
Nixon	224	2
Ford	64	1
Carter	258	16
Reagan	368	15
Bush	185	8
Clinton	198	14

Reagan administration's ideological screening. Twenty percent of George Bush's appointees were women, 7 percent African Americans, and 4 percent Hispanics.[49]

Bill Clinton promised to appoint federal judges who would be more "representative" of the ethnic makeup of the United States. "There will not be an ideological blood test, like there was during the Reagan and Bush years, to see if the candidate is a moderate or liberal," said a prominent Democratic member of the Senate Judiciary Committee, "but there will be an insistence upon diversity."[50] Clinton lived up to his pledge; almost half of his appointees during his first term were women or minorities.

The Role of Ideology

Finding a party member is not enough; presidents want to pick the "right" kind of Republican or "our" kind of Democrat to serve as judge. By and large they have been able to achieve this goal. Republican judges picked by Republican presidents tend to be judicial conservatives (with the notable exception of President Dwight Eisenhower's nomination of Chief Justice Earl Warren), and most Democratic judges picked by Democratic presidents are more likely to be liberals. Both of these orientations were tempered by the fact that judges had to go through a senatorial confirmation screen that during the administrations of Reagan and Bush was of the opposite persuasion from that of the White House.[51]

In appointments to the Supreme Court, the policy orientation of the nominee is likely to be foremost among presidential concerns. As President Abraham Lincoln told Congressman George S. Boutewell when he appointed Salmon P. Chase to the Supreme Court: "We wish for a Chief Justice who will sustain what has been done in regard to emancipation and legal tender."[52] Theodore Roosevelt voiced the same concern about appointing the "correct" person in a letter to Senator Henry Cabot Lodge about Judge Oliver Wendell Holmes, Jr., of the Massachusetts Supreme Judicial Court, whom he was considering for the Supreme Court: "Now I should like to know that Judge Holmes was in entire sympathy with our views, that is with your views and mine. I should hold myself guilty of an irreparable wrong to the nation if I should appoint any man who was not absolutely sane and sound on the great national policies for which we stand in public life."[53]

President Ronald Reagan's two terms made it possible for him to join Presidents Franklin D. Roosevelt and Dwight D. Eisenhower as the only presidents in modern times to appoint a majority of the federal bench. All told, Reagan appointed 346 lifetime judges. Like his predecessors, he was concerned about the ideologies of those he nominated, and his administration acted carefully to nominate only those whose views about the role of the courts and constitutional issues were consistent with Reagan's own.[54] Not only were a large number of judicial conservatives appointed, but many of them—because they were comparatively young—will continue to have an effect on judicial policy making well into the next century. But despite the care given to their selection, there is some evidence that the new Reagan judges may not be that much more conservative than judges appointed by other presidents.[55]

As President Bush's commitment to conservatism was somewhat less well established than Reagan's, conservatives and their organizations—the Heritage Foundation, the Pacific Legal Foundation, and the Federalist Society—focused their attention on Bush's judicial appointments, "turning on the heat . . . so that the Bush administration doesn't squander any opportunity to tip the U.S. Supreme Court further to the right or turn its back on President Reagan's legacy of appointing conservatives to the federal bench."[56] Bush, looking to lower federal and state courts for candidates, appointed 148 district judges, 37 appellate judges, and 2 Supreme Court justices—David Souter and Clarence Thomas. His appointees were among the most conservative in recent history.[57] Their conservative constitutional views helped consolidate the Court's "turn to the right," a turn President Bill Clinton is trying to reverse.[58]

The Role of Judicial Philosophy

What about a candidate's judicial philosophy? Does a candidate believe that judges should try to interpret the Constitution to reflect what the framers intended and what its words literally say; that is, does the candidate believe in **judicial restraint**? Or does the candidate believe the Constitution cannot and should not be interpreted literally, but rather be adapted to reflect current conditions and philosophies; that is, does the candidate believe in **judicial activism**?

Judicial philosophy is closely related to political ideology. Throughout most of our history, federal courts have been more conservative than Congress, the White House, or state legislatures. Prior to 1937, judicial self-restraint was the battle cry of liberals who objected to judges interpreting the due process clauses of the Fifth and Fourteenth Amendments to strike down many laws passed to protect labor and women and to keep the national and state governments from regulating the economy. These judges broadly construed the words of the Constitution to prevent what they thought to be unreasonable regulations of property.

By the time of Richard Nixon, Ronald Reagan, and George Bush, however, the judicial shoe was on the other foot, and it was conservatives who were advocates of judicial self-restraint. What is wanted, they argued, are judges who will let Congress, the president, and the state legislatures do what they want, unless it clearly contravenes the precise words of the Constitution: regulate or forbid abortions, for example, adopt prayers for public schools, impose capital punishment, or authorize police to engage in wiretapping.

It would be wrong to assume that judicial philosophy is nothing more than another way to argue about political ideology. Some conservatives, for example, favor judicial activism because they want current judges to reverse the last half-century of precedents and actively seek to protect property rights from government regulation. Some liberals favor judicial restraint because they believe democracy will flourish when judges stay out of policy debates. Nonetheless, most of the country understands enough about the policy-making role of judges to recognize that debates about the proper role of the courts and the interpretation of the Constitution reflect differing convictions about the public interest. The debate over the Supreme Court's role today is less about activism and restraint than it is about competing conceptions of the proper balance between government authority and individual rights.

Judicial Longevity and Presidential Tenure

Ideology and judicial philosophy affect not only presidents' nominations for the federal courts but also when sitting judges choose to retire. Because federal judges serve for life, they may be able to schedule their retirement to allow a president whose views they approve to nominate their successors. Chief Justice Roger B. Taney stayed on the bench long after his health began to fail to prevent President Abraham Lincoln from nominating a Republican. In 1929 Chief Justice William Howard Taft wrote: "I am older and slower and less acute and more confused. However, as long as things continue as they are, and I am able to answer in my place, I must stay on the court in order to prevent the Bolsheviki [Herbert Hoover, a conservative Republican, was in the White House] from getting control."[59]

Although former Chief Justice Warren Burger denied that he retired in 1986 in order to permit President Ronald Reagan to replace him with a constitutional conservative, his retirement did give Reagan an opportunity to rejuvenate the conservative wing of the Court by promoting 61-year-old William H. Rehnquist, an articulate constitutional conservative, to replace 78-year-old Burger. Reagan then picked another constitutional conservative, 50-year-old Antonin Scalia, from the Court of Appeals for the District of Columbia, to take the seat vacated by Rehnquist.[60] Liberal Supreme Court justices William J. Brennan, Jr., and Thurgood Marshall held onto their seats well into their 80s, and many assumed that they were doing so in the hope that they might be able to stay on the Court until the time that a president more congenial to their views might be in the White House. They did not make it, and their successors were appointed by Republican President Bush rather than by a Democrat.

Reforming the Selection Process

The televised Bork and Thomas confirmation hearings aroused considerable criticism from both liberals and conservatives and created widespread complaints that "something is wrong with the process." Everybody appeared to be dissatisfied with it. Democratic senators were frustrated by their inability to get nominees to explain their judicial philosophies or to reveal their constitutional values. They argued that unless candidates respond about their constitutional philosophy, the Senate should refuse to confirm. Republican senators and the Bush White House accused Senate Democrats of improperly trying to force candidates to commit how they would decide cases and thus jeopardize the independence of the courts and compromise their ability to be impartial judges. Senators, they argued, should content themselves with checking into candidates' integrity and legal background and not ask about political and constitutional orientation or badger candidates to reveal how they might vote on cases that would come before them for decision.[61]

A group of experts agreed that judicial appointments could not and should not be free of political considerations but recommended that an attempt be made to constrain the partisan politics surrounding the confirmation process for Supreme Court justices. They recommended, among other things, that "Supreme Court nominees should no longer be expected to appear as witnesses during the Senate Judiciary Committee's hearings on their confirmation" and that the Senate return to the practice of judging nominees on their written record and on the testimony of legal experts.[62] It is unlikely, however, that there will be any fundamental alteration in the selection process. Presidents of all persuasions are not likely to want to limit their discretion in selecting judges, and their political opponents are not likely to abandon their concern about the judicial views of presidential nominees. As one scholar pointed out:

> The cries to depoliticize the process are not only naive, but perhaps too hastily considered. The apparent decorum of the past was achieved at the expense of participation and accountability. Few who viewed the agony and personal tragedies of the Clarence Thomas proceedings can avoid the almost instinctive desire to return to less visible and contentious proceedings, but the stakes are too high and involve the vital interests of too many forces to seek refuge in the ways of the past.[63]

The politics of judicial selection may shock those who like to think judges are picked strictly on the basis of legal merit and without regard for party, race, sex, or ideology. But as a former Justice Department official has said, "When courts cease being an instrument for political change, then maybe the judges will stop being politically selected."[64] Moreover, as another scholar put it, "Supreme Court Justices have always been appointed for political reasons by politicians, and their confirmation process has always been dictated by politicians for political purposes." He concludes, "In fact, however, not despite the politicization of the appointment and confirmation process, but because of it, the Supreme Court has endured as a flexible, viable force in the American democracy for over 200 years."[65]

"We all make mistakes, as Your Honor knows, having been twice reprimanded by the New York State Commission on Judicial Conduct."

Drawing by Stevenson. © 1981 by The New Yorker Magazine, Inc.

CHANGING THE NUMBERS   Partisan politics also affects decisions about the number of federal judges. One of the first actions of a political party after gaining control of the White House and Congress is to increase the number of federal judgeships. With divided government, however, when one party controls Congress and the other holds the White House, a stalemate is likely to occur, and relatively few new judicial positions will be created. During Andrew Johnson's administration, Congress went so far as to reduce the size of the Supreme Court to prevent the president from filling two vacancies. After Johnson left the White House, Congress returned the Court to its former size to permit Ulysses S. Grant to fill the vacancies. In 1937, President Franklin Roosevelt proposed an increase in the size of the Supreme Court by one additional justice for every member of the Court over the age of 70, up to a total of 15 members. Ostensibly, the proposal was aimed at making the Court more efficient. In fact, Roosevelt and his advisers were frustrated because the Court had declared much New Deal legislation unconstitutional. Despite Roosevelt's popularity, his "court-packing scheme" aroused intense opposition. Roosevelt's proposals to change the Court's size failed. He lost the battle but won the war, as the Court began to sustain some important New Deal legislation.

CHANGING THE JURISDICTION   Congressional control over the structure and jurisdiction of federal courts has been used to influence the course of judicial policy making. Although unable to get rid of Federalist judges by impeachment, the Jeffersonians abolished the circuit courts created by the Federalist Congress just prior to their losing control. In 1869 radical Republicans in Congress altered the Supreme Court's appellate jurisdiction in order to snatch from the Court a case it was about to review involving the constitutionality of some Reconstruction legislation.[66]

During the Reagan administration, a number of bills were introduced in Congress either to eliminate the jurisdiction of all federal courts over cases relating to abortion, school prayer, and school busing or to eliminate the appellate jurisdiction of the Supreme Court over such matters. These bills sparked debate about whether the Constitution gives Congress authority to take such actions. Congress has not yet decided to make what could amount to a fundamental shift in the nature of the relationship between Congress and the Supreme Court.

HOW THE SUPREME COURT OPERATES

Supreme Court justices are in session from the first Monday in October through the end of June. They listen to oral arguments for two weeks and then adjourn for two weeks to consider the cases and write their opinions. By agreement, six justices must participate in each decision. Cases are decided by a majority. In the event of a tie vote, the decision of the lower court is sustained, although, on rare occasions, the case may be reargued.

At 10:00 A.M. on the days when the Supreme Court sits, the eight associate justices and the chief justice, dressed in their robes (Chief Justice Rehnquist has four gold stripes on each sleeve of his robe)[67] file into the Court. As they take their seats—arranged according to seniority, with the chief justice in the center—the clerk of the Court introduces them as the "Honorable Chief Justice and Associate Justices of the Supreme Court of the United States." Those present in the courtroom, asked to stand when the justices enter, are seated, and counsel take their places along tables in front of the bench. The attorneys for the Department of Justice, dressed in formal morning clothes, are at the right. The other attorneys are dressed conservatively; sport coats are not considered proper. Dress and ceremony are all part of the high ritual of the Court:

The majesty of its courtroom; the black robes of the justices; the ritual of its proceedings at oral argument and on decision day; the secrecy and isolation of its decision-making

CONFIRMATION POLITICS

Examination of recent nomination battles highlights the interplay of party, race, sex, ideology, and judicial philosophy in the process of selecting and confirming a Supreme Court justice.

The Bork Battle

When Justice Lewis F. Powell, Jr., who had had the swing vote on such critical issues as affirmative action and abortion, announced his retirement as he neared 80 years of age at the end of the term in July 1987, he made it possible for Ronald Reagan to select a justice who could have a decisive vote on many issues. President Reagan quickly nominated Judge Robert Bork, a member of the Court of Appeals for the District of Columbia and a noted jurist and legal scholar. Despite Bork's controversial writings on many current constitutional issues, his scholarly and legal qualifications made it appear initially that he would be confirmed. However, his nomination so offended women's and black organizations that they organized a campaign to block the Bork nomination. After almost four months of national debate, 12 days of acrimonious questioning by the members of the Senate Judiciary Committee, and 23 hours of debate on the Senate floor, the Senate voted 58 to 42 against Bork's confirmation.

Robert Bork.

The Souter Solution

The political bruises resulting from the Bork confirmation proceedings were traumatic. Political pundits speculated that in the future, presidents would seek noncontroversial candidates for the Supreme Court. This prediction came true in 1990 with George Bush's nominee to replace William J. Brennan, Jr., leader of the liberal bloc on the Supreme Court, who had been able to blunt the conservative impact of Rehnquist, Scalia, and Kennedy. President Bush chose David Souter, who had been on the Court of Appeals for three months and had been a member of the New Hampshire Supreme Court. Educated at Harvard and Oxford, he had written no law articles, made practically no speeches, and lived the secluded life of a sitting judge. When he appeared before the Judiciary Committee, Souter steadfastly refused to answer any questions that might reveal his orientation on abortion and privacy issues, to the frustration of the Senate Democrats. He was confirmed by an overwhelming vote.

David Souter.

The Thomas Tangle

When Justice Thurgood Marshall retired in 1991, President Bush sent to the Senate the name of a controversial jurist, Judge Clarence Thomas, then sitting on the Court of Appeals for the District of Columbia. Thomas is a conservative African American. Prior to his brief service on the Court of Appeals, he had served as chair of the Equal Employment Opportunity Commission (EEOC) and in the

conferences; the formal opinions invoking the symbols of Constitution, precedent, and framers' intent; and all the other elements of setting and conduct distinguish the Supreme Court, a body of constitutional guardians, from all other government officials.[68]

Which Cases Reach the Supreme Court?

When citizens vow they will take their cases to the highest court of the land even if it costs their last penny, they underestimate the difficulty of securing Supreme Court review, overestimate the cost (although it costs plenty), and reveal a basic

Office of Civil Rights. During five days of grueling questions about his constitutional views, Judge Thomas, as had his predecessor, refused to respond. The Senate Judiciary Committee narrowly recommended his confirmation.

Two days before the Senate was due to vote on his confirmation, documents leaked to the press revealed that a former associate of Judge Thomas, Anita Hill, had accused him of sexually harassing her when she worked for him in the Department of Education and the EEOC. Women's and liberal groups exploded in outrage. There followed three days of dramatic and emotion-charged hearings telecast to the nation in which Judge Thomas categorically denied the charges presented persuasively by his accuser. Panels of witnesses pro and con came forward to testify. Judge Thomas was confirmed by the Senate 52 to 48, the closest Supreme Court confirmation vote in modern times.

Clarence Thomas.

The Clinton Choices

Almost as soon as President Clinton took office, Justice Byron White announced he would leave the Court at the end of its 1992–93 term. It was clear that with this appointment, Clinton could arrest the Court's conservative drift and fulfill his campaign pledge to appoint justices committed to protect the right of privacy—that is, to preserve a woman's freedom to choose an abortion.

After several months of deliberation, including the rather public consideration of other candidates, President Clinton nominated Ruth Bader Ginsburg. Judge Ginsburg was a 13-year veteran of the Court of Appeals for the District of Columbia, to which she had been appointed by President Carter. On the Court of Appeals she had earned a reputation for fairness and moderation. She was readily confirmed by the Senate and took her seat for the opening of the 1993–94 term.

Clinton had a second opportunity when Harry A. Blackmun, at age 85, announced his intention to leave the Court during the spring of 1994. Blackmun, best known for writing the opinion in *Roe v Wade*, was thought at first to be a judicial conservative, but by the time of his retirement, he had become the most liberal member of the Court.

Ruth Bader Ginsburg.

The leading candidates were all sitting judges except for Interior Secretary Bruce Babbitt and Senate Majority Leader George Mitchell. After Mitchell withdrew from consideration and Senate opposition developed against Babbitt, President Clinton nominated Stephen G. Breyer, chief judge of the First Circuit, a noncontroversial judicial moderate. Justice Breyer, a graduate of Stanford University, Oxford, and Harvard Law School, served as Supreme Court law clerk for Justice Arthur Goldberg and was a member of the faculty at Harvard Law School before being appointed by President Carter as a Federal Appeals Court judge. After a cordial hearing before the Senate Judiciary Committee in July 1994, Breyer was easily confirmed by the Senate.

Stephen G. Breyer.

misunderstanding of the Court's role. The rules for appealing a case to the Supreme Court are established by act of Congress. Today almost all appellate cases come before the Court by means of a discretionary **writ of certiorari**, a formal writ used to bring a case up to the Court. Until 1988 there were a few types of cases the Supreme Court was obliged by law to review. In addition, the Constitution stipulates the Supreme Court has original jurisdiction in a few specified situations. But the fact is the Supreme Court has control of its agenda and decides which cases it wants to consider. In recent years the justices have closely reviewed and issued signed opinions in less than 100 of the thousands of cases presented to them.[69]

It is not enough, for example, that Jones thinks he should have won his case against Smith. There probably has already been at least one appellate review of the trial, either in a federal court of appeals or in a state supreme court. The Supreme Court will review Jones's case only if his claim has broad public significance. For instance, the rulings among the courts of appeals may conflict; by deciding the Jones case, the Supreme Court can establish which rule is to be followed throughout the judicial system. Or Jones's case may raise a constitutional issue on which a state supreme court has presented an interpretation with which the Court disagrees. The crucial factor in determining whether the Supreme Court will hear a case is its importance not to Jones but to the operation of the governmental system as a whole.

The Court accepts cases under the *rule of four*. If four justices are sufficiently interested in a petition for a writ of *certiorari*, the petition will be granted and the case brought forward for review. Nowadays the law clerks (called the "cert pool") read the petitions and write a memorandum on each for circulation to all the justices in the pool. Only Justice John Paul Stevens stays out of the pool, and even he, it is rumored, divides up the cert petitions among his own clerks and reads only a few of them himself.[70]

Denial of a writ of *certiorari* does not mean that the justices agree with the decision of the lower court, nor does it establish precedents. Refusal to grant such a writ may indicate all kinds of possibilities. The justices may not wish to become involved in a political "hot potato," or the Court may be so divided on an issue that it is not yet prepared to take a stand.[71]

Briefs and Oral Arguments

Before a case is heard in open court, the justices receive printed *briefs* in which each side presents legal arguments, historical materials, and relevant precedents. In addition, the Supreme Court may receive briefs from **amici curiae** (literally, "friends

THE SUPREME COURT

1. Courtyards
2. Solicitor General's Office
3. Lawyers' Lounge
4. Marshall's Office
5. Main Hall
6. Court Hall
7. Conference and Reception Rooms

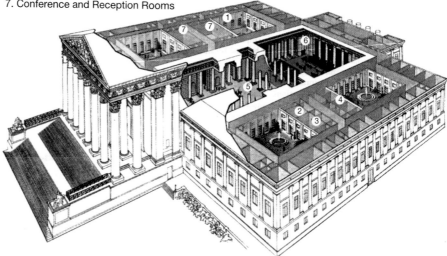

of the court"), who may be individuals, organizations, or government agencies that have an interest in the case and claim they have information of value to the Court. This procedure guarantees that the Department of Justice is represented if a suit between two private parties calls the constitutionality of an act of Congress into question. The *amicus curiae* brief is also used by presidents, through the Department of Justice, to see that the views of the current administration are brought to the Court's attention.[72]

Often organizations file *amicus curiae* briefs before the Supreme Court grants a writ of *certiorari* in order to lobby the Supreme Court to review the case. Their doing so enhances the probability that the court will take the case for review but has almost no influence on how the case is decided.[73] A brief brought by a private party or interest group may help the justices by presenting an argument or point of law that the parties to the case have not raised. Often the briefs are filed as a means of pressuring the Court to reach a particular decision. In the *Bakke* case, in which the Supreme Court dealt with affirmative action, 37 *amicus* briefs were filed for the University of California, 16 for Allan Bakke, and 5 that did not take sides. In *Webster v Reproductive Health Services*, dealing with a Missouri law regulating abortions and a request for the Court to reverse *Roe v Wade*, 78 *amicus* briefs were filed.[74]

In *United States v Lopez*, which challenged congressional authority to ban guns in and around schools, more than 40 parties filed a dozen *amicus* briefs. Ohio, New York, and the District of Columbia argued in favor of federal power, as did associations of police and school officials. On the other side were some conservative public interest firms, the National Governors' Association, and the National League of Cities.[75]

Formal oratory before the Supreme Court, perhaps lasting for several days, is a thing of the past. As a rule, counsel for each side is limited to 30 minutes. Lawyers use a lectern to which two lights are attached. A white light flashes five minutes before time is up; when the red light goes on, the lawyer must stop, even in the middle of an "if."

The entire procedure is formally informal. Sometimes, to the annoyance of attorneys, justices talk among themselves or consult briefs or legal volumes during the oral presentation. Sometimes, if justices find a presentation particularly bad, they ostentatiously consult their watches. Justices freely interrupt the lawyers to ask questions and request additional information. In recent years, "the justices seem barely able to contain themselves, often interrupting the answer to one question with another query."[76] The 30-minute limit is becoming a problem, especially when the solicitor general participates, since his ten minutes comes out of the time of the two parties before the Court.

If a lawyer seems to be having a difficult time, the justices may try to help him or her present a better case. Occasionally, justices bounce arguments off a hapless attorney and at one another. Justice Antonin Scalia is a harsh questioner. "When Scalia prepares to ask a question, he doesn't just adjust himself in his chair to get closer to the microphone like the others; he looks like a vulture, zooming in for the kill. He strains way forward, pinches his eyebrows, and poses the question, like '. . . do you want us to believe?' "[77] Justice Sandra Day O'Connor commented about him, "Some of our members are former law professors and haven't lost their technique of asking questions."[78] Justice Thurgood Marshall did "a terrible job of keeping his mouth away from the mike" when whispering.[79] Justice Ruth Bader Ginsburg is a particularly persistent questioner, frequently rivaling Justice Scalia in asking the most questions. Justice Clarence Thomas almost never asks a question. Justice David Souter has a thick New England accent. He once asked an attorney during oral arguments in an affirmative action case, "What's the floor?" The attorney hemmed and hawed until, with a smile, Souter explained he meant "flaw," not "floor."[80]

The Rise of the Law Clerks

Beginning in the 1930s, federal judges began the practice of hiring the best recent graduates of law schools to serve as clerks for a year or two. As the judicial work load increased, more law clerks have been appointed. Today each Supreme Court justice is entitled to four clerks (circuit judges have three, and each court of appeals has "staff attorneys"). Clerks draft opinions and screen writs of *certiorari*, which determine the cases the Court will review. Justices often talk through their cases with their law clerks.

Law clerks are young and energetic, and they know how to use computers to do research and prepare drafts of opinions. As the number of law clerks and computers has increased, so has the number of concurring and dissenting opinions. Further, today's opinions are longer and have more substantive footnotes and elaborate citations of cases and law review articles. As Justice Harry A. Blackmun said about his colleague, Justice John Paul Stevens, "He uses hundreds of footnotes. Sometimes I think what he does is to outline his opinion, give it to his clerks and say, 'You put the footnotes in,' and of course there's an ego trip for the clerks and they have all kinds of footnotes."*

*Harry A. Blackmun, quoted in Stuart Taylor, Jr., "When High Court's Away, Clerks' Work Begins," *The New York Times*, September 23, 1988, p. 22.

You Decide!

Can states refuse to provide free education for undocumented aliens?

A few years ago the Texas state legislature decided Texas taxpayers should no longer provide a free public education for the children of undocumented aliens.

Then, in 1994, Californians adopted Proposition 187, which forbids schools and colleges to admit undocumented aliens and public hospitals to provide any treatment other than emergency care to them.

Setting aside for a moment whether you think such a policy is desirable, in your judgment, is there anything in the United States Constitution, especially in the equal protection clause, that should prevent the Texas legislature or the California electorate from making such a choice? What dilemmas of democracy does this case illustrate?

Behind the Curtains: The Conference

Wednesday afternoons and all day Friday the justices meet in conference. They have heard the oral arguments, read and studied the briefs, and examined the petitions. Before every conference, each justice receives a list of the cases to be discussed. Each brings to the meeting a red leather book in which the cases and the votes of the justices are recorded. These conferences are secret affairs, although in recent years the secrecy has been penetrated. They are marked by informality and by vigorous give-and-take; they are both "collegial and substantive."[81] The chief justice presides, usually opening the discussion by stating the facts, summarizing the questions of law, and making suggestions for disposing of the case. Each member of the Court is then asked, in order of seniority, to give his or her views and conclusions. Recently the justices have not bothered with formal votes because they express their views when they discuss the case.[82]

In a case challenging the constitutionality of a Texas law making it a crime to desecrate the American flag, Chief Justice Rehnquist called his colleagues' attention to an earlier dissent of his in which he had stated, "Flag-burning and fighting words may be punished constitutionally." Justice Brennan disagreed. This was, he argued, a classic case of speech being punished solely because of objection to the message. Justice White was next. He supported Chief Justice Rehnquist. To affirm the decision of the Texas Criminal Court of Appeals declaring the Texas statute to be an unconstitutional abridgment of the First Amendment rights, he argued, would run "the First Amendment in the ground." Justice Marshall agreed with Brennan. Justice Stevens was "uncharacteristically tentative" and passed without giving his vote. Justice O'Connor appeared to support Justice Brennan: "This is core speech for political purposes," she declared. Nonetheless, she said that her decision to affirm the Texas Criminal Court of Appeals "was still tentative," and she would make a final decision after reading the circulated opinions. Justices Scalia and Kennedy said they agreed that this was a free-speech case and would affirm the Texas court ruling declaring the statute unconstitutional. Justice Brennan, as the senior justice in the majority, had the responsibility to prepare the opinion for the Court.[83]

Opinions

As a general rule, Supreme Court opinions state the facts, present the issues, announce the decision, and, most important, explain the reasoning of the Court. These opinions are the Court's principal method of expressing its views to the world. Perhaps the primary function of opinions is to instruct the judges of all other state and federal courts in the United States on how to decide similar cases in the future.

Judicial opinions may be directed at Congress or at the president. If the Court regrets that "in the absence of action by Congress, we have no choice but to . . ." or insists that "relief of the sort that petitioner demands can only come from the political branches of government," it is clearly asking Congress to act.[84] Justices also use opinions to communicate with the public. A well-handled opinion may increase support among specialized groups—especially lawyers and judges—and among the general population for a policy the Court favors. For this reason, the Court delayed declaring school segregation unconstitutional until unanimity could be secured. The justices understood that any sign of dissension on the bench on this major social issue would be an invitation to evade the Court's ruling.

ASSIGNING OPINIONS The justice to whom writing an opinion is assigned knows that he or she must influence the outcome, for no vote in conference is final. Justices are free to change their minds if persuaded by the draft opinion. When voting with the majority, the chief justice decides who drafts the opinion. When the chief justice is in the minority, the senior justice among the majority makes the assignment, often to himself or herself. Justices are free to write a **dissenting opinion** if they wish. Dissenting opinions are, in Chief Justice Charles Evans Hughes's words, "an appeal to the brooding spirit of the law, to the intelligence of a later day."[85] Dissenting opinions are quite common, as justices hope that someday these dissenting opinions will command a majority of the court. If a justice agrees with the majority on how the case should be decided but differs on the reasoning, that justice may write a **concurring opinion**.

CIRCULATING DRAFTS Writing an opinion for the Court is an exacting task. The document must win the support of at least four—even more, if possible—intelligent, strong-willed persons, all of whom may have voted the same way but for different reasons. Assisted by the law clerks, the assigned justice writes a draft and sends it to colleagues for comments. If the justice is lucky, the majority will accept the draft, perhaps with only minor changes. If the draft is not satisfactory to the other justices, it must be redrafted and recirculated until a majority can reach agreement.

If the initial version is not acceptable to a majority, an elaborate bargaining process occurs. The opinion ultimately published is not necessarily the opinion the author would have liked to write. Like a committee report, it represents the common denominator. Justice Oliver Wendell Holmes, Jr., bitterly complained to British political scientist Harold J. Laski that he had written an opinion in terms to suit the majority of the brethren, although it did not suit him.

> Years ago I did the same thing in the interest of getting a job done. I let the brethren put in a reason that I thought bad and cut out all that I thought good and I have squirmed ever since, and swore that never again—but again I yield and now comes a petition for rehearing pointing out all the horrors that will ensue from just what I didn't want to say.[86]

The two weapons justices can use against their colleagues are their votes and their willingness to write separate opinions attacking a doctrine the majority wishes to see adopted. Especially if the Court is closely divided, one justice may be in a position to demand that a given argument be included in, or removed from, the opinion as the price of his or her vote. Sometimes this bargaining occurs even though the Court is not closely divided. An opinion writer who anticipates that a decision will bring critical public reaction may wish to have it presented as the view of a unanimous Court and may be prepared to compromise to achieve unanimity. See Table 16–2 for a comparison of dissent rates in various Courts.

In the Texas flag desecration case mentioned earlier, Justice William J. Brennan, Jr., drafted a narrow opinion in an attempt to win the support of as many of his colleagues as possible. As James F. Simon wrote, "Justice Brennan approached his task of writing the majority opinion in *Texas v Johnson* cautiously. He could anticipate an unflinching opinion from the chief justice defending the government's right to protect the American flag. Justice White had made it clear that he would support the chief. Both O'Connor and Stevens had appeared to lean Brennan's way at the conference, but none too confidently; Brennan could not depend on their votes. And Justice Blackmun "a usually reliable liberal justice," voiced uneasiness about the case in a note to Brennan, three months after the conference. Ultimately, Brennan's draft was endorsed by Justices Kennedy, Blackmun, Marshall, and Scalia; Justices O'Connor and Stevens, who had kept their vote tentative in conference, dissented. Thus the decision came down 5 to 4 against the Texas law.[87]

The Powers of the Chief Justice

The chief justice of the United States is appointed by the president and confirmed by the Senate and holds tenure for life. This method of selecting the chief justice gives him (in our entire history they have all been men) greater visibility than if

Thinking It Through

Proposition 187 is currently being challenged in the courts, but in *Plyler v Doe* (1982), five members of the United States Supreme Court ruled that the Texas law violated the equal protection clause because Texas had failed to show its action would, as alleged, protect the state from an influx of illegal immigrants, improve the overall quality of education, or save substantial sums of money. "If the state," wrote Justice William J. Brennan, Jr., "is to deny a discrete group of innocent children the free public education it offers to other children residing within its borders, that denial must be justified by a showing that it furthers some substantial state interests. No such showing was made here."

Chief Justice Warren Burger, dissenting along with Justices Byron R. White, William H. Rehnquist, and Sandra Day O'Connor, wrote: "I agree without hesitation that it is senseless for an enlightened society to deprive any children—including illegal aliens—of an elementary education. However, the Constitution does not vest in this Court the authority to strike down laws because they do not meet our standards of desirable social policy, 'wisdom,' or 'common sense.'. . . Today's cases, I regret to say, present yet another example of unwarranted judicial action which in the long run tends to contribute to the weakening of our political process."

TABLE 16–2

Comparison of Dissent Rates

Justice	Number of Dissenting Opinions
"The Great Dissenters"	
William Johnson (1804–34)	30
John Catron (1837–65)	26
Nathan Clifford (1858–81)	60
John Marshall Harlan (1877–1911)	119
Oliver Wendell Holmes (1902–32)	72
Louis Brandeis (1916–39)	65
Harlan F. Stone (1925–46)	93
Felix Frankfurter (1939–62)	251
Justices Serving on the Burger and Rehnquist Courts, 1969–1994	
William O. Douglas (1969–1975)	231
John Paul Stevens (1975–1994)	400
William Brennan, Jr. (1969–1990)	402
Thurgood Marshall (1969–1991)	335
William Rehnquist (1971–1994)	269
Harry A. Blackmun (1970–1994)	245
Lewis F. Powell, Jr. (1971–1987)	159
Byron R. White (1969–1993)	233
Antonin Scalia (1986–1994)	61
Ruth Bader Ginsburg (1993–1994)	7
Sandra Day O'Connor (1981–1994)	89
Warren E. Burger (1969–1986)	111
Clarence Thomas (1993–1994)	19
Anthony M. Kennedy (1988–1994)	37
David Souter (1990–1994)	17

SOURCE: David M. O'Brien, *Storm Center: The Supreme Court in American Politics*, 4th ed. (Norton, 1996), p. 331.

selected by rotation of fellow justices, as is the practice in the state supreme courts, or by seniority, as is the practice in the federal courts of appeals. But as Chief Justice Rehnquist said when he was still an associate justice, the chief deals not with "eight subordinates whom he may direct or instruct, but eight associates who, like him, have tenure during good behavior, and who are as independent as hogs on ice."[88]

The ability of the chief justice to influence the Court has varied considerably.[89] Chief Justice Charles Evans Hughes ran the conferences like a stern schoolmaster, keeping the justices talking to the point, moving the discussion along, and doing his best to work out compromises. He tried to achieve unanimous votes in order to give decisions greater weight. Chief Justice Harlan F. Stone, on the other hand, encouraged justices to state their own points of view and let the discussions wander. Chief Justice Warren Burger devoted much of his time to judicial reform, speaking to bar and lay groups and trying to build political support for modernizing the judicial process.

Chief Justice William H. Rehnquist had 15 years of Court experience prior to his elevation to the post of chief justice. He had demonstrated his personal warmth and charm. He "has not utilized his position as Chief Justice to shape the decisions of the Court."[90] But as the Reagan-Bush justices are still a majority, his constitutional views, formerly expressed only in his dissenting opinions, are now the opinions of the Court.[91] "The Chief Justiceship does not guarantee leadership. It only offers its incumbent an opportunity to lead. Optimum leadership inheres in the combination of the office and an able, persuasive, personable judge."[92]

After the Lawsuit Is Over

Victory in the Supreme Court does not necessarily mean that winning parties get what they want. As a rule, the Court does not implement its own decision but *remands*, that is, sends back the case to the lower court with instructions to act in accordance with the Supreme Court's opinion. The lower court often has considerable leeway in interpreting the Court's mandate as it disposes of the case.

Although Congress or a president has occasionally "ignored" or "construed" a Supreme Court ruling to avoid its impact, decisions whose enforcement requires only the action of a central governmental agency usually become effective immediately. Thus, when the Supreme Court held that President Harry Truman lacked constitutional authority to seize steel companies temporarily to avoid a shutdown during the Korean War,[93] the president promptly complied. Of course, subsequent presidents have great discretion in determining how that particular precedent should be applied to them.

The impact of a particular ruling announced by the Supreme Court on the behavior of those who are not immediate parties to a lawsuit is even more uncertain. Many important decisions require further action by administrative and elected officials before they become the law of the land, yet sometimes Supreme Court decisions are simply ignored. For example, despite the Supreme Court's holding that it is unconstitutional for school boards to require prayers within schools, some school boards continue this practice.[94] And for years after the Supreme Court held public school segregation unconstitutional, many school districts remained segregated.[95]

The most difficult Supreme Court decisions to implement are those that require the cooperation of large numbers of officials. For example, a Supreme Court decision announcing a new standard for warrantless searches is not likely to have an impact on the way police make arrests for some time, since not many police officers subscribe to the *United States Supreme Court Reports*. The process is more complex. Local prosecutors, state attorneys general, chiefs of police, and state and federal trial court judges must all participate to give "meaning" to Supreme Court decisions. The Constitution may be what the Supreme Court says it is, but a Supreme Court opinion, for the moment at least, is what a trial judge or police officer or a prosecutor or a school board or a city council says it is.

JUDICIAL POWER IN A CONSTITUTIONAL DEMOCRACY

An independent judiciary is one of the hallmarks of a free society. As impartial dispensers of equal justice under the law, judges should not be dependent on the executive, the legislature, the parties to the case, the electorate, or a mob outside the courtroom. But this very independence, essential to protect judges in their roles as legal umpires, raises basic problems when a democratic society decides—as ours has—also to allow these same judges to make policy. Perhaps in no other society do the people resort to litigation as a means of making public policy as much as they do in the United States.

The involvement of our courts in politics exposes the judiciary to political criticism. Throughout our history, the Supreme Court has been attacked for engaging in "judicial legislation." This is nothing new. Yet the active role of the federal courts on behalf of liberal causes since 1937 and the Reagan, Bush, and Dole attacks on that role have returned these issues to the forefront of public debate.

Since the end of World War II, federal courts under the Supreme Court's leadership have removed most of the constitutional restraints on government regulation of business. At the same time, they have imposed many more restraints to protect civil liberties and civil rights, especially for the poor and minorities. Since 1789 the Supreme Court has reversed more than 160 of its own decisions as well as overturned more than 140 acts of Congress, more than 925 pieces of state legislation and state constitutional provisions, and more than 110 city ordinances (see Table 16–3). In one 1983 decision, *Immigration and Naturalization Service v Chadha*, it called into question 200 provisions of various federal laws.[96]

Whereas in earlier times judges occasionally told public officials what they could not do, today they often tell them what they *must* do. For example, federal judges, responding to class action complaints, have told Congress, state legislatures, and local officials that they must provide attorneys for the poor, ensure adequate care for mental patients, modernize prisons, and even break up the telephone system. (In this last case, the Department of Justice initiated the action.) Often judges retain jurisdiction for years as they preside over the implementation of the decrees they have issued.[97] Judges have always been policy makers; that role is not a matter of choice but flows from the roles they play in deciding cases. But today they also govern.[98]

The Great Debate over the Proper Role of the Courts

Some people contend that the courts have a duty to protect the long-range interests of the public as defined in the Constitution, even against the short-range wishes of the voters (but then what is and is not defined by the Constitution is the issue). Defenders of this *activist* judicial role argue that if Congress, the White House, and the state legislatures are unable to resolve pressing problems when people are being denied justice and their constitutional rights, then the courts should resolve those problems. The Supreme Court, they say, should be "a leader in a vital national seminar that leads to the formulation of values for the American people."[99]

Critics of judicial activism contend that for the last half a century the federal courts, in their zeal to protect people, became unhinged from their political moorings in the political and constitutional system. These critics argue that even if

Chief Justice William Hubbs Rehnquist was formerly an assistant attorney general and then an associate justice of the Supreme Court from 1971 to 1986.

Who Were the Great Justices?

Although this question is asked often, the answers are necessarily subjective and tell you as much about the values of the evaluators as they do about the merits of the justices. Nonetheless, two law professors surveyed about 65 law school deans and professors of law and political science. Respondents were asked to evaluate the performance of 96 justices who had served from 1789 to 1970. The 12 rated "best" or "great" were:

John Marshall*

Joseph Story

Roger B. Taney*

John Marshall Harlan

Oliver W. Holmes, Jr.

Charles Evans Hughes*

Louis D. Brandeis

Harlan F. Stone*

Benjamin Cardozo

Hugo Black

Felix Frankfurter

Earl Warren*

*Chief justices

SOURCE: Henry J. Abraham, *Justices and Presidents: A Political History of Appointments to the Supreme Court*, 3d ed. (Oxford University Press, 1992), p. 412. Copyright © 1992 by Henry J. Abraham. Reprinted by permission of Oxford University Press.

TABLE 16–3

Decisions of the Supreme Court Overruled and Acts of Congress Held Unconstitutional, 1789–1996

Year	Supreme Court Decisions Overruled	Acts of Congress Overturned	State Laws Overturned	Local Ordinances Overturned
1789–1800, Pre-Marshall				
1801–35, Marshall Court	3	1	18	
1836–64, Taney Court	6	1	21	
1865–73, Chase Court	3	10	33	
1874–88, Waite Court	11	9	7	
1889–1910, Fuller Court	4	14	73	15
1910–21, White Court	6	12	107	18
1921–30, Taft Court	5	12	131	12
1930–40, Hughes Court	14	14	78	5
1941–46, Stone Court	24	2	25	7
1947–52, Vinson Court	11	1	38	7
1953–69, Warren Court	46	25	150	16
1969–86, Burger Court	50	34	192	15
1986–, Rehnquist Court	26	13	64	16

SOURCE: David H. O'Brien, *Constitutional Law and Politics*, 3d ed. (W. W. Norton, 1997), p. 38.

courts make the "right" decisions, it is not right for courts to take over the legislative function of elected representatives.

Others claim the debate between those who favor judicial restraint and those who favor judicial activism oversimplifies the choices. Judges, they argue, should take a leadership role in some areas but a restrained role in others. They stand with Chief Justice Harlan F. Stone, who argued that courts have a special duty to intervene: (1) whenever legislation restricts the political process by which decisions are made, or (2) whenever legislation restricts the rights of "discrete and insular minorities." In all other areas, the political process should be allowed to work, and judges should not set aside legislation or interfere with administrative agencies merely because judges would prefer some other policy or even some other interpretation of the Constitution.[100]

For a brief time when the Reagan and Bush jurists dominated both the Supreme Court and the lower federal courts, conservatives supported an active judicial role, and liberals were skeptical about conservative judges using judicial power.[101] With President Clinton in a position to reverse the conservative makeup of the federal judiciary through future appointments, liberals may become less skeptical about an active judiciary, and conservatives may become more likely to prefer restrained judges.

The People and the Court

Whether judges are liberal or conservative, defer to legislatures or not, try to apply the Constitution as they think the framers intended, or interpret it to conform to current values, there are linkages between what the judges do and what the people want done. The linkages are not direct, and the people never speak with one mind, but these linkages are the heart of the matter.[102] In the first place, the president and the Senate are likely to appoint justices whose decisions reflect their values. When the people elected George Bush, they got judges who reflected his perspectives; when they elected Bill Clinton, they got judges who reflected his values and preferences.

Bush was able to pick two Supreme Court justices—David Souter and Clarence Thomas—who, as expected, joined the Reagan appointees to complete the Court's "turn to the right." Yet at the end of the 1991–92 term, that Court, by a 5 to 4 vote in *Planned Parenthood v Casey*, nonetheless refused to overturn *Roe v Wade* and upheld its core holding that the Constitution protects the right of a woman to an abortion, although subjecting that right to state regulations that do not "unduly burden" it.[103]

This close vote on abortion made it clear that the 1992 presidential election would determine whether that right would continue to be protected by the Constitution. At stake was whether it would be George Bush or Bill Clinton who would nominate new members of the Supreme Court. Clinton pledged to nominate only persons committed to the view that the Constitution protects a woman's right to choose. Bush continued to disavow that he had any "litmus test" for his nominees and insisted that it would be improper to inquire how they would vote on specific issues, but he made it clear that he would continue to appoint conservative jurists who could be expected to vote to reverse *Roe v Wade*.

Although in 1992 voters gave Democrats control over both the Senate and the White House, in 1994 they put Republicans in charge of the Senate, so that Clinton's judicial appointments had to be filtered through a conservatively dominated Senate Judiciary Committee. Clinton was able to substantially increase the number of African Americans and women on the federal bench, but some liberal critics accused him of working so closely with the Republicans that he was unable to reverse the conservative legacy of the Reagan-Bush years.[104] In a second term, conservatives worried, "Mr. Clinton might come a bolder judge-picker, selecting name liberals from law faculties and displaying a willingness to duke it out with Senate Republicans."[105] Bob Dole tried in vain to mobilize voters by describing the 1996 elections as a choice "between a candidate who will appoint conservative judges to the court and a candidate who appoints liberal judges who bend the laws to let drug dealers free."[106]

Also at stake in that election was the tone and direction of Supreme Court constitutional interpretation. By the 1996 elections, the conservative hold on the Supreme Court was clear yet tenuous. After decades of effort, the Nixon-Reagan-Bush attempts to alter the course of constitutional direction were having results. Chief Justice Rehnquist and Justices Thomas and Scalia were increasingly joined by Justices Kennedy and O'Connor to provide a five-person majority on issues relating to the establishment clause, affirmative action, and criminal justice. The future direction of constitutional interpretation was once again a campaign issue in 1996.

When the voters returned Clinton for a second term but left Republicans in control of the Senate, they increased the probability that centrists would be selected as federal judges, since only candidates who would please both President Clinton and the conservative Republicans who dominate the Senate Judiciary Committee would be likely to be nominated and confirmed. But they also enhanced the likelihood that constitutional conservatives would not be able to consolidate their control over the Supreme Court.

Scholars debate how public opinion influences what judges decide, whether it is direct or indirect through presidential appointments and Senate confirmations, but there is little question that there is a correlation between public opinion and judicial decisions.[107] Judicial opinions that reflect what the people want have the greatest survival value. When a new political coalition takes over the White House or Congress, the old regime stays on in the federal courts, or as one unknown wit put it: "The good a president does is oft interred with his bones, but his choice of Supreme Court Justices lives after him."[108] New electoral coalitions eventually take over the federal courts, and before long, new interpretations of the Constitution reflect the dominant political ideology.

Judges have neither armies nor police to execute their rulings. Although Congress cannot reverse Supreme Court decisions that relate to constitutional interpretations, and only three Supreme Court decisions have been reversed by formal constitutional amendment, the political system alters judicial policy in more subtle ways. Decisions are binding on the parties to a particular case, but the policies involved in judicial decisions are effective and durable only if they are supported by the electorate. To win a favorable Supreme Court decision is to win something of considerable political value, but the policies reflected by that decision may or may not alter the way people behave. "American courts are not all-powerful institutions."[109] If the Court's policies are too far out of step with the values of the country, the Court is likely to be reversed. As Chief Justice William H. Rehnquist has written, "No judge worthy of his salt would ever cast his vote in a particular case simply because he thought the majority of the public wanted him to vote that way, but that is quite a different thing from saying that no judge is ever influenced by the great tides of public opinion that run a country such as ours."[110]

"The people" speak in many ways and with many voices. The Supreme Court—and the other courts—represent and reflect the values of some of these people. Although the Court is not the defenseless institution portrayed by some commentators, and its decisions are as much shapers of public opinion as reflections of it, ultimately the power of the Court in our constitutional democracy rests on retaining the support of most of the people most of the time. No better standard for determining the legitimacy of a governmental institution has been discovered.

POLITICS ONLINE

Lexis/Nexis, Westlaw, and the Practice of Law

The legal profession was one of the first professions to go online, and the early pioneers in providing interactive computers service were Westlaw and Lexis/Nexis. Beginning in 1973, Lexis provided access to full texts of federal and state cases, statutes, regulations, and public records from several states. In 1979, the Nexis news and information service became a companion to Lexis, offering online information from newspapers, news wires, magazines, trade journals, and business publications. Nexis also provides stock and brokerage house information, information on corporations, and political analysis and information. Each week more than 9.5 million documents are added to the more than 1 billion documents online at Lexis/Nexis.

Lexis/Nexis and other online services like Westlaw are now part of most law school curricula, and students are instructed in their use in their first year of law school. The service is given to law schools at a discounted rate, but students must use it only for academic purposes. Lawyers in all types of practice, as well as judges, clerks, and legal academics, all use these tools extensively. Lawyers can search for similar cases and make sure there are no more recent cases with conflicting rulings.

Many college libraries make these services available. Talk to your librarian or check out home pages at:

http://www.westlaw.com   http://www.lexis-nexis.com

For a description of the federal courts and documents relating to them, go to:

http://www.uscourts.gov/

Supreme Court decisions can be found at:

http://supctlaw.cornell.edu/Supct/   http://www.usscplus.com/

SUMMARY

1. Judges in the United States play a more active role in the political process than they do in other democracies. Federal courts receive their jurisdiction directly from Congress, which must decide the constitutional division of responsibilities among federal and state courts.

2. Federal judges apply statutory law, common law, constitutional law, equity law, admiralty and maritime law, and administrative law. They apply federal, criminal, and civil law. Although bound by procedural requirements, including *stare decisis*, they can exercise discretion.

3. Partisanship and ideology are important factors in the selection of federal judges, and these factors ensure a linkage between the courts and the rest of the political system, so that the views of the people are reflected, even if indirectly, in the work of the courts.

4. The Supreme Court, which has almost complete control over the cases it chooses to review as they come up from the state courts, the courts of appeals, and district courts, is a revered but somewhat mysterious branch of our government. Annually its nine justices dispose of thousands of cases, but most of their time is concentrated on the 75 to 100 cases per year that establish guidelines for lower courts and the country.

5. A continuing concern of major importance is the reconciliation of the role of judges—especially those on the Supreme Court—as independent and fair dispensers of justice with their vital role as interpreters of the Constitution. This is an especially complex problem in our democracy because of the power of judicial review and the significant role courts play in making public policy.

6. The debate about how judges should interpret the Constitution is almost as old as the Republic. More than two hundred years after the Constitution was adopted, the argument between those who contend judges should interpret the document literally and those who believe they cannot, and should not, has returned to the headlines.

FURTHER READING

HENRY J. ABRAHAM, *Justices and Presidents: A Political History of Appointments to the Supreme Court*, 3d ed. (Oxford University Press, 1992).

HENRY J. ABRAHAM, *The Judiciary: The Supreme Court in the Governmental Process*, 10th ed. (New York University Press, 1996).

STEPHEN L. CARTER, *The Confirmation Mess: Cleaning Up the Federal Appointments Process* (Basic Books, 1994).

PHILLIP J. COOPER, *Battles on the Bench: Conflict Inside the Supreme Court* (University Press of Kansas, 1995).

PHILLIP COOPER AND HOWARD BALL, *The United States Supreme Court: From the Inside Out* (Prentice Hall, 1996).

CLARE CUSHMAN, *The Supreme Court Justices: Illustrated Biographies, 1789–1993* (Congressional Quarterly Press, 1993).

RICHARD DAVIS, *Decision and Images: The Supreme Court and the Press* (Prentice Hall, 1994).

LEE EPSTEIN AND JOSEPH F. KOBYLKA, *The Supreme Court and Legal Change: Abortion and the Death Penalty* (University of North Carolina Press, 1993).

KERMIT L. HALL, ED., *The Oxford Companion to the Supreme Court of the United States* (Oxford University Press, 1992).

PETER IRONS AND STEPHANIE GUITTON, EDS., *May It Please the Court: Transcripts of 23 Recordings of Landmark Cases as Argued Before the Supreme Court* (New Press, 1993).

THOMAS R. MARSHALL, *Public Opinion and the Supreme Court* (Unwin Hyman, 1989).

JOHN MASSARO, *Supremely Political: The Role of Ideology and Presidential Management in Unsuccessful Supreme Court Nominations* (State University of New York Press, 1990).

DANIEL JOHN MEADOR AND JORDANA SIMONE BERNSTEIN, *Appellate Courts in the United States* (West Publishing, 1994).

WALTER F. MURPHY AND C. HERMAN PRITCHETT, *Courts, Judges and Politics: An Introduction to the Judicial Process*, 4th ed. (Random House, 1986).

DAVID M. O'BRIEN, *Constitutional Law and Politics*, 3d ed. (W. W. Norton, 1997).

DAVID M. O'BRIEN, *Storm Center: The Supreme Court in American Politics*, 4th ed. (W. W. Norton, 1996).

J. W. PELTASON, *Federal Courts in the Political Process* (Doubleday, 1955).

BARBARA A. PERRY, *A "Representative" Supreme Court? The Impact of Race, Religion, and Gender on Appointments* (Greenwood Press, 1991).

GERALD N. ROSENBERG, *The Hollow Hope: Can Courts Bring About Social Change?* (University of Chicago Press, 1991).

C. K. ROWLAND AND ROBERT A. CARP, *Politics and Judgment in Federal District Courts* (University Press of Kansas, 1996).

DAVID G. SAVAGE, *Turning Right: The Making of the Rehnquist Supreme Court* (John Wiley & Sons, 1992).

BERNARD SCHWARTZ, *A History of the Supreme Court* (Oxford University Press, 1993).

JAMES F. SIMON, *The Center Holds: The Power Struggle Inside the Rehnquist Court* (Simon & Schuster, 1995).

PAUL SIMON, *Advice and Consent: Clarence Thomas, Robert Bork, and the Intriguing History of the Supreme Court Battles* (National Press Books, 1992).

ELLIOT E. SLOTNICK, *Judicial Politics: Readings from "Judicature"* (Nelson-Hall, 1992).

HARRY P. STUMPF, *American Judicial Politics* (Harcourt Brace Jovanovich, 1988).

STEPHEN L. WASBY, *The Supreme Court in the Federal Judicial System*, 4th ed. (Nelson-Hall, 1993).

17

The Bureaucracy:
The Real Power?

"*The* era of big government is over," said President Clinton as he kicked off his reelection campaign in 1996. A year later, in his Second Inaugural Address, Clinton told the American people he appreciated their yearnings for smaller and more efficient government. "Government is not the problem, and government is not the solution. We, the American people, we are the solution," Clinton declared. "We need a new government for a new century, a government humble enough not to try to solve all our problems for us."[1]

Clinton in his first term had seen his comprehensive health care program attacked and defeated. He had been lectured repeatedly by Ross Perot, Bob Dole, and Newt Gingrich about the arrogance and failings of entrenched federal bureaucracies.[2] He had watched as the Republicans, running an antigovernment campaign, took control of both houses of Congress.[3] And he and his strategists became increasingly aware of the public's lack of confidence in many, if not most, federal programs[4] (see Figure 17–1).

The government of the United States is big, complex, and confusing. "It employs millions of people and spends millions of dollars every year. It is heavily layered, with thousands of overlapping political jurisdictions and political institutions."[5] But there has been a major effort in recent years—at all levels of government, and in the public as well as private sector—to create customer-centered organizations and to make bureaucracies leaner and more responsive to the people they should be serving. Customer-service reforms took hold in business before they did in governments; now these reforms and significant downsizing are occurring in the federal government's bureaucracy as well.[6]

"REINVENTING GOVERNMENT" IN THE 1990S

Encouraged by most members of Congress, Bill Clinton worked hard to cut the size of the federal government's civilian and military work force. The end of the cold war obviously made it easier (though not all that easy) to close military bases and to downsize the post–cold war military ranks. The Clinton administration cut the civilian work force by about 250,000 positions in its first term. Indicating the importance he gave the subject, Clinton issued an executive order insisting that every federal agency that deals with the public should deliver service equal to the best in business.

At the start of his first term, President Clinton appointed Vice-President Al Gore to conduct a major review of the bureaucracy's performance. Both Clinton and Gore took this effort seriously, and they clearly wanted to change the way the government did business: how it bought goods and services, how it dealt with vendors, how it served citizens, how it listened to its citizen customers, and how it could do a better job with fewer employees and less red tape. That was a tall order. Al Gore's subsequent National Performance Review team made exhaustive studies, held numerous conferences, and then in 1993 issued hundreds of recommendations for encouraging efficiency, productivity, and responsiveness in government operations. Illustrative recommendations were:

- Close or consolidate 1,200 field offices of the Department of Agriculture.
- Allow the sale of the Alaska Power Administration.
- Reduce the number of Department of Education programs from 230 to 189.

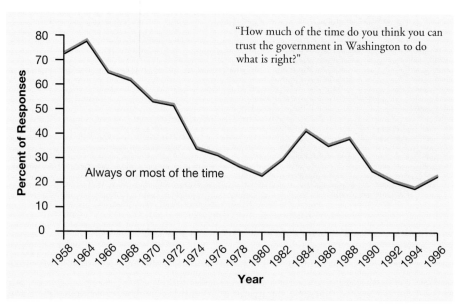

FIGURE 17–1   Level of Confidence in the National Government
SOURCE: Gallup Organization, University of Michigan National Election Study.

- Eliminate federal support payments (subsidies) for mohair, wool, and honey.
- Remove people who are no longer disabled from disability insurance rolls.
- Allow all federal agencies funds for creative innovation.
- Encourage market-based approaches to reducing pollution.
- Eliminate the Government Printing Office's monopoly on publishing government documents and reports.
- Reduce the time required to fire incompetent federal employees by half.
- Insist that all agencies survey customers, measure customer satisfaction, and establish service standards equal to the best in business.[7]

One of Bill Clinton's campaign promises was that his administration would "reinvent government" and get rid of bureaucratic waste and inefficiency. Vice-President Al Gore was assigned the job of working out a plan, which Clinton is shown here releasing to the public.

By 1996, the executive branch claimed considerable progress with "putting customers first, empowering employers to get results, cutting red tape, and cutting back to basics." The departments and agencies "established customer service standards and streamlined their operations," said Clinton. "They also are working with my Office of Management and Budget to focus more on 'performance'—what federal programs actually accomplish."[8] In his Second Inaugural Address, Clinton boasted that the federal bureaucracy was the smallest since the administration of John Kennedy.

Clinton and Gore were responding to the widespread popular perception that there was too much waste and inadequate responsiveness by federal bureaucrats. They borrowed ideas about privatization, competition, choices, and reliance on a market orientation.[9] And they usually, though not always, went along with Republican calls to shift responsibility to the states whenever possible. This last "solution" hardly solves the problem of bureaucracy; it merely shifts the problem from national to state bureaucracies.

Although the Clinton-Gore reforms of the federal bureaucracy have largely been ignored by the public and the media, they have had an impact on the way the national government operates. Several federal departments and agencies—though certainly not all—have improved their procedures to encourage common sense and accountability. There is growing recognition, both in and out of government circles, that "a reinvented civil service will have to invest more in people than in process. People will have to be more mobile and faster to learn; agencies will have to acquire more flexibility to attract the people they need."[10]

Most public administration experts believe that managers in government need greater freedom to hire, promote, and fire workers, based on merit performance and merit promotion, with systems in place to measure program effectiveness. Encrusted bureaucratic procedures of the past had so constrained executive discretion that managers could not apply common sense to making reasonable decisions.

Few of these innovations have been in effect long enough to change people's views about bureaucracy. And maybe they will never win much praise. But they may have won Clinton some political credit as he ran successfully for reelection in 1996. He at least was able to claim he had a strategy for improving government and for making the bureaucracy more accountable and more effective.

Government bureaucrats, however, will always be an inviting target or scapegoat. There is hardly a citizen who has not been offended, irritated, or at least regulated at one time or another in dealing with the Internal Revenue Service (IRS), the Federal Bureau of Investigation (FBI), the U.S. Army, the Environmental Protection Agency (EPA), or the Food and Drug Administration (FDA). And all of us have stood in lines at the post office or been kept waiting and gotten inept responses when we called government agencies. No matter that these agencies can also be a big help to us; we tend to remember the hassles and mistakes.

For most people, the government appears to have become increasingly distant and impersonal. Everything in life is regulated. Rules are numerous and inflexible. One critic writes that our government in the 1990s "acts like some extraterrestrial power, not an institution that exists to serve us. Its actions have an arbitrary quality. It almost never deals with real-life problems in a way that reflects our understanding of the situation." We have, he adds, constructed a system of regulatory laws and rules "that basically outlaws common sense. Modern law, in an effort to be 'self-executing,' has shut out our humanity."[11]

And whatever the Clinton-Gore administration may have achieved, it will never be enough for conservative Republicans. As the opposition party in Congress, they continue to press for more reform and less government. U.S. Senator Sam Brownback (R.-Kans.) insists:

We must continue our push for a smaller, more focused, more efficient federal government concerned with core principles and functions. We must also eliminate corporate welfare—those direct

Corporate Welfare: Public Good or Pork?

These are the 12 federal programs identified by Representative John R. Kasich (R.-Ohio) and his allies as corporate welfare programs that should be eliminated, with the estimated five-year savings.

- **Rural Utilities Services**
  Successor to the Rural Electrification Administration established during the New Deal to bring electricity to remote areas. Now provides subsidized loans to electric cooperatives. *$190 million.*

- **Market Access Program**
  Subsidizes advertising by exporters of food and wine. *$347 million.*

- **Animas-La Plata Project**
  A public works project in Colorado to divert water from the Animas and La Plata rivers to irrigate farmland. *$432 million over the life of the project.*

- **Pyroprocessing Program**
  Creates new fuel from the spent fuel of nuclear reactors. *$100 million.*

- **Appalachian Regional Commission Roads Program**
  Builds roads in 13 Appalachian states. *$500 million.*

- **Fossil Energy Research and Development**
  Energy Department program to develop new technology for oil, coal, and natural gas companies. *$1.37 billion.*

- **Timber Roads**
  Builds roads in national forests for timber companies and recreational users. *$100 million.*

- **Clean Coal Technology**
  Subsidizes companies that develop technology for lowering coal emissions. *$500 million.*

- **The Overseas Private Investment Corporation**
  Provides loans and insurance to American companies that invest in developing countries. *$281 million.*

- **General Agreements to Borrow**
  Part of the International Monetary Fund. Provides money in international economic emergencies (for example, when a country is on the verge of default). *$3.5 billion.*

- **Enhanced Structural Adjustment Facility**
  An I.M.F. low-interest loan program for developing countries. *$150 million.*

- **Highway Demonstration Projects**
  Road repair and construction projects specifically requested by individual lawmakers. *$4 billion.*

SOURCE: *The New York Times*, February 2, 1997, p. 6E.

spending subsidies that only benefit very narrow groups. We should start by eliminating the two cabinet-level agencies that contain the most corporate welfare of all: the departments of Energy and Commerce. Obviously we must maintain the vital core programs of these agencies, including Nuclear Weapons Development, the National Weather Service, the Patent and Trademark Office, and the Census Bureau. But many others can be eliminated, privatized, or devolved to state and local levels of government. . . . These savings should be used to reduce the deficit and cut taxes.[12]

Various estimates of what Senator Brownback calls "corporate welfare" weigh in at from $87 billion to $150 billion a year.[13] See the box for examples of "corporate welfare" programs that have attracted attention from federal budget cutters.

Bureaucracy is, however, a fact of modern life. Of course we have a lot of "red tape" and overlap in our public administration process—too much. It is important to ask, as we enter the twenty-first century, whether our bureaucracy and its methods are stifling innovation, productivity, and common sense.

In this chapter we explain who the bureaucrats are, examine the origins, functions, and realities of our national public bureaucracy, and explore how elected officials in both Congress and the executive branch are trying to make the bureaucracy leaner, more responsive, and more accountable to the American people.

THE FEDERAL BUREAUCRACY

Bureaucrats, or career government employees, work in the executive branch, in the 14 cabinet-level departments, and in the more than 50 independent agencies embracing about 2,000 bureaus, divisions, branches, offices, services, and other subunits of government. Five big agencies—the Departments of the Army, the Navy, and the Air Force (all three in the Department of Defense), the Department of Veterans Affairs, and the U.S. Postal Service—tower over the others in size. Most agencies are directly responsible to the president, yet some, like the Postal Service, are partly independent. Agencies exist by act of Congress; legislators can abolish them either by passing a new law or by withholding funds.[14]

The terms "bureaucrat" and "bureaucracy" are of recent origin. Initially referring to a cloth covering the desks of French government officials in the eighteenth century, the term "bureau" came to be linked with the suffix "ocracy" signifying rule of government (as in "democracy" or "aristocracy"). **Bureaucracy**, as it came to be used one hundred years ago, referred to a rational, efficient method of organization. "Bureaucracy" today can refer to a professional corps of officials organized in a pyramidal hierarchy and functioning under impersonal, uniform rules and procedures. The term "bureaucracy" typically refers to the whole body of non-elected and non–presidentially appointed government officials in the executive branch who work for presidents and their political appointees. In this chapter we use the terms "bureaucracy" and "bureaucrat" in their neutral sense, although popular usage of these terms is typically negative.

Bureaucracies are public or private organizations that are large and hierarchical in structure, with each employee accountable to a superior through a chain of command. They provide each employee with a defined role or responsibility, base their decisions on impersonal rules, and hire and promote employees according to skills related to their jobs.[15] Bureaucracies in the modern sense came into being in government to provide predictability and efficiency and to minimize the arbitrary practices that so often characterized rule under dictatorial monarchs.

Critics believe the federal bureaucracy is an overzealous guardian of the status quo and is too lazy or unimaginative to innovate or experiment. Others fear that a powerful national bureaucracy encourages a wasteful welfare state. Many people also think the federal bureaucracy is too large, too powerful, too unaccountable. Indeed, 60 percent of a national survey by the Gallup organization in 1995 complained that the federal government had too much power. And nearly everyone surveyed was suspicious that there was waste and "fat" in government, especially those who had heard about Defense Department procurement cost overruns, welfare fraud, Central Intelligence Agency (CIA) tragedies, and general inefficiencies. Such stereotypes are widespread, for bureaucracies have never been popular, but the skepticism and hostility toward public bureaucracies are greater today than in previous generations.[16]

Bureaucracy in a large, complex society is virtually inevitable. Most of us will work in some public or private bureaucracy for part, if not most, of our careers. Public bureaucracies pose special challenges because they report to competing political institutions and must function within our constitutional democracy of shared powers and multiple checks and balances.

How Did the Bureaucracy Evolve?

From 1789 until about 1829, the federal service was drawn from an upper-class, white male elite. In 1829, President Andrew Jackson called for greater participation by the middle and lower classes. He introduced what was labeled a **spoils system**, which his successors followed until well into the 1890s. This system, epitomized by the phrase "to the victor belong the spoils," operated on the theory that party loyalists should be rewarded and that government would be effective and responsive only if followers of the president held most key federal posts. Besides, it was thought that government should not be complicated; almost anybody should be able to do the job. With each new president came a full turnover in the federal service.

Red Tape

The term "red tape" comes from the ribbon English civil servants once used to tie up and bind legal documents. Today, along with taxes and death, we think of red tape as inevitable. We are annoyed when we have to wait in lines while officials check files or consult with their supervisors. We are furious when officials lose important documents. Red tape often takes the form of an official's punctilious adherence to rigid procedures. We may view it as a hopeless tangle of rules and regulations that keep public servants from doing anything but stamping and shuffling papers.

But these same rules and regulations help ensure that public servants act impartially. In other words, red tape stems from our desire not to give public servants too much discretion and to hold them accountable. After all, they are spending our money. Remember, too, that one person's red tape is another person's prudent system or proper cautiousness.

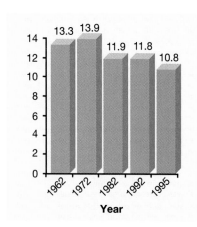

FIGURE 17–2 Federal Employment per 1,000 Americans

SOURCE: U.S. Census Bureau, Office of Personnel Management.

Later in the nineteenth century, however, a sharp reaction set in against this system. In response to the various abuses and most immediately to the assassination of President James Garfield in 1881 by a disappointed office seeker, Congress passed the Pendleton Act. It set up a limited **merit system** based on a testing program for evaluating candidates. Federal employees were to be selected and retained according to their "merit," not their party loyalty. Federal service was placed under the control of a three-person bipartisan board called the Civil Service Commission, which functioned from 1883 to 1978.[17]

By the 1950s, coverage under the merit system had grown from 10 percent of all federal employees when it was first established to about 90 percent. In 1978 the Civil Service Reform Act abolished the Civil Service Commission and split its functions between two new agencies. This split was necessary to avoid a conflict of interest inherent in the agency that recruits, hires, and promotes employees also being the same agency that passes judgment on employee grievances about fairness and discrimination.

Today the Office of Personnel Management (OPM) administers civil service laws, rules, and regulations. An independent Merit Systems Protection Board is charged with protecting the integrity of the federal merit system and the rights of federal employees. The board conducts studies of the merit system, hears and decides charges of wrongdoing, considers employee appeals against adverse agency actions, and orders corrective and disciplinary actions against an agency executive or employee when appropriate.

Who Are the Bureaucrats?

We are mainly interested here in the approximately 4 million people (2.7 million civilians and somewhat over 1.4 million in the military services) who make up the executive branch of the federal government. Certain facts about these people need to be emphasized:

1. Only about 10 percent of the career civilian employees work in the Washington area. The vast majority are scattered throughout the country and around the world. California alone has more federal employees than does the District of Columbia.

2. Nearly 30 percent of the civilian employees work for the army, the navy, the air force, or some other defense agency.

3. The welfare state may consume a sizable portion of the U.S. budget, yet the size of the federal bureaucracy that administers it is relatively small. Less than 15 percent of the bureaucrats work for welfare agencies such as the Social Security Administration or the Rural Electrification Administration. Almost half of those who do work for the Department of Veterans Affairs.

4. Federal employees are not all of one type. Indeed, in terms of social origin, education, religion, and other background factors, bureaucrats are more broadly representative of the nation than are legislators or politically appointed executives.

5. Federal employment per 1,000 people in the U.S. population has decreased steadily from over 14 percent in the early 1970s to little over 10 percent by the late 1990s (see Figure 17–2).

6. Bureaucrats work at an endless variety of jobs. More than 15,000 different personnel skills are represented in the federal government. Unlike Americans as a whole, however, most federal employees are white-collar workers: secretaries, clerks, lawyers, inspectors, engineers.

The vast number of senior bureaucrats are honest professionals and experts at their business. Presidents, Congress, and other elected officials ignore the bureau-

From Coast to Coast

Federal Employment Is Widely Dispersed

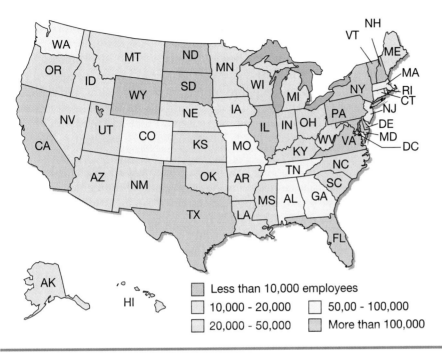

Less than 10,000 employees
10,000 - 20,000
20,000 - 50,000
50,00 - 100,000
More than 100,000

SOURCE: U.S. Census Bureau, Office of Personnel Management.

cracy's advice at their peril. A compelling example is provided by the CIA's perceptive memoranda (many of them later published in the celebrated *Pentagon Papers*) arguing that the Vietnam War as President Lyndon Johnson wanted to conduct it would be a failure. This was good advice from an expert bureaucracy, but Johnson paid it too little attention.

What Do Bureaucrats Do?

After the president has signed a bill into law, it must be implemented. Implementation of policy is the function of the executive branch, its bureaucracy, and in some instances, state, county, and local governments as well.

More is involved in policy implementation than the literal translation of goals into practice. Indeed, it is during this stage that many key decisions are made. The coalition that pushes a bill through Congress often does not stay together after the bill has been enacted. And the legislation itself is often deliberately vague to conceal serious policy differences. Because of policy differences among the supporters of a bill, Congress sets general goals and passes the responsibility for interpretation on to the bureaucrats. Legislators are frequently more concerned with the symbolic potency of legislation than with its substantive content. As a result, the bureaucracy is given some latitude to translate general guidelines into specific directives. Bureaucrats are sometimes blamed for the confusion, yet they are merely trying to carry out ambiguous policies in a political atmosphere characterized by conflict and competition.

Consider civil rights legislation. Often differences among women's groups, African American groups, Latino groups, employer groups, and trade unions are

*Executive Branch
Departments*

- Department of State (1789)
- Department of the Treasury (1789)
- Department of Defense (1947, originally War, 1789)
- Department of Justice (1789)
- Department of the Interior (1849)
- Department of Agriculture (1862)
- Department of Commerce (1913, originally Commerce and Labor, 1903)
- Department of Labor (1913, originally Commerce and Labor, 1903)
- Department of Health and Human Services (1979, originally Health, Education and Welfare, 1953)
- Department of Housing and Urban Development (1965)
- Department of Transportation (1966)
- Department of Energy (1977)
- Department of Education (1979)
- Department of Veterans Affairs (1989)

Dates indicate when the department was established.

momentarily resolved and a bill becomes law. But after the bill has been enacted, the coalition that supported the bill falls apart, and conflicting pressures are felt by the agencies trying to implement the policies. Employers claim that the agencies' regulations are unrealistic and interfere with their rights; women's groups contend agencies are failing to enforce the law vigorously enough; African American groups claim agencies favor the women's groups but ignore African Americans. The more controversial the issue, the greater the chance of delay, as powerful interest groups clash over a program and force bureaucrats to move cautiously.

The implementation process involves a long chain of decision points. At each decision point a public official or community leader can often advance or delay the program. The more decision points a program needs to clear, the greater the chance of failure or delay. Special problems result if the successful implementation of a national program depends on the cooperation of state and local officials. One state or community may be eager to help; another may be opposed to a program and try to stop it.

A number of federal programs have failed to accomplish their desired goals because of problems in administration. Sometimes these difficulties lead to the outright failure of a program, but more often they mean excessive delay, watered-down goals, or cost overruns. John Kennedy's economic reform programs in Latin America, Lyndon Johnson's Model Cities program, Richard Nixon's and Gerald Ford's crime control programs, the Reagan-Bush antidrug crusade, and Bill Clinton's national service program all faced problems of implementation.[18] When such failures occur, it is easier to blame the legislation than the implementation. Of course, poorly written legislation and badly conceived policy yield poor results, but even the best legislation can fail because of problems encountered after it is passed.

Like so much of politics, successful policy implementation cannot be guaranteed. It depends on the creation of stable routines for implementation, the ability to adjust to changing circumstances, the quality of the working relationship between implementers at various levels, the degree of conflict invoked by the policy, and its general level of public support.

How Is the Bureaucracy Organized?

FORMAL ORGANIZATION The executive branch departments are headed by cabinet members called *secretaries* (except Justice, which is headed by the attorney general). The secretaries are directly responsible to the president. Although departments vary greatly in size, they have certain features in common. A deputy or an undersecretary takes part of the administrative load off the secretary's shoulders, and several assistant secretaries direct major programs. The secretaries have assistants who help them in planning, budget, personnel, legal services, public relations, and other staff functions.

Departments are subdivided into bureaus and smaller units, and the basis for their division may differ. The most common basis is function. For example, the Commerce Department is divided into the Bureau of the Census, the Patent and Trademark Office, and so on. The basis may also be clientele (for example, the Bureau of Indian Affairs of the Interior Department), or work processes (for example, the Economic Research Service of the Agriculture Department), or geography (for example, the Alaskan Air Command of the Department of the Air Force).

Government corporations, such as the Corporation for Public Broadcasting and the Federal Deposit Insurance Corporation, are a cross between business corporations and regular government agencies. Government corporations were designed to make possible a freedom of action and flexibility not always found in the regular agencies. These corporations have been freed from certain regulations of the Office of Management and Budget and the comptroller general. They also have more leeway in using their own earnings. Still, because these corporations are a part of the government, the government retains control over their activities.

Government entities that are not corporations and do not fall within cabinet departments are called **independent agencies**. They consist of many types of organizations with differing degrees of independence. Many, however, are no more independent of the president and Congress than the departments. The huge General Services Administration (GSA), for example, the function of which is to operate and maintain federal properties, is not represented in the cabinet, but its director is responsible to the White House and its actions are closely watched by Congress.

Another type of agency is the **independent regulatory board or commission**. Examples are the Securities and Exchange Commission, the National Labor Relations Board, and the Federal Reserve Board. Congress deliberately set up these boards to keep them somewhat free from White House influence; the president nominates them and Congress confirms them, but the president can fire them. They exercise **quasi-legislative and quasi-judicial** functions. Congress has protected their independence in several ways: the boards are headed by three or more commissioners with overlapping terms; they often have to be bipartisan in membership (that is, they must have some Democrats as well as some Republicans); and members are appointed for fixed terms in office, some for only 3 years but others for up to 14 years.

Within each of the departments, corporations, and independent agencies and commissions are many subordinate units. The standard name for the largest subunit is the **bureau**, although it is sometimes called an office, administration, or service. Bureaus are the working units of the federal government. In contrast to the big departments, which often consist of a variety of agencies, bureaus usually have fairly definite and clear-cut duties, as their names show: the Bureau of the Census in the Commerce Department, the Forest Service in the Agriculture Department, the Social Security Administration in the Department of Health and Human Services, the Bureau of the Mint in the Treasury Department, the Bureau of Indian Affairs and the National Park Service in the Interior Department, and the Bureau of Prisons, Federal Bureau of Investigation, and Drug Enforcement Administration in the Justice Department.

Under lax supervision by government agencies, savings and loan associations were allowed to expand their operations and undertake risky investments during the 1980s. When they failed in record numbers, the government had to make good the losses of depositors.

By assigning specific functions to each unit, placing an official at the head, and holding that official responsible for performance, formal bureaucracy allows for both specialization and coordination, permits ready communication, and in general makes a large and complex organization more manageable.

INFORMAL ORGANIZATION To look at a formal organization chart is only to begin to understand how an agency works, for we also need to understand the informal organization (see Figure 17–3). Bureaucrats differ in attitudes, motives, abilities, experiences, and political clout, and these differences matter. Leadership in an organization is exercised in a variety of places; some officials may have considerably more influence than others with the same formal status. Further, loyalties of officials cut across the formal aims of the agency.

Informal organization can have a significant effect on administration. A subordinate official in an agency might be especially close to the chief because they went to the same college, or because they play racquetball together, or because the subordinate knows how to ingratiate himself with the chief. A staff official may have tremendous influence not because of formal authority but because of experience, fairness, common sense, and personality. In an agency headed by a chief who is

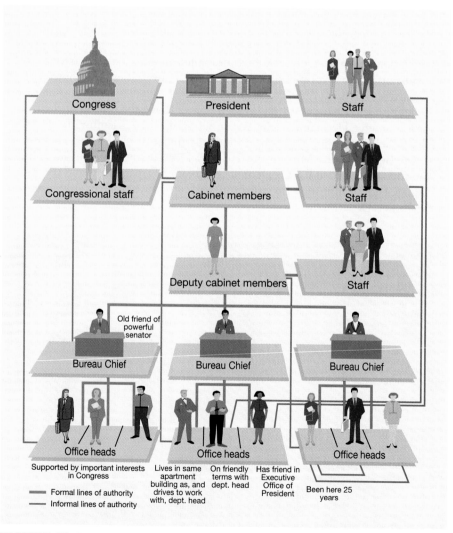

FIGURE 17–3 Hypothetical Relationships Within the Executive Branch

weak or unimaginative, a vacuum may develop that encourages others to take over. Such informal organization and communication, cutting across regular channels, are inevitable in any organization—public or private, civilian or military.

THE BUREAUCRACY IN ACTION

Hiring Practices and Employee Regulations

Senior government administrators work with the Office of Personnel Management in staffing their agencies. OPM acts as a policy maker for recruiting, examining, and appointing government workers. It advertises for new employees, prepares and administers oral and written examinations throughout the country, and compiles a register of names of those who pass the tests. OPM delegates to the individual agencies the responsibility for hiring new personnel, subject to its standards. Individual agencies may promote people from within or transfer a civil servant already in the government. If, however, they wish to consider an "outsider," they request OPM to certify possible candidates from its roster of applicants. OPM typically certifies the top three applicants who have applied for the departmental or agency opening, and the agency normally selects one of these. However, the agency can decide to make no appointment or to request other applicants if it thinks none of the three is qualified.

These procedures are intended to protect the merit principle and to meet agencies' needs for qualified personnel. In practice, the two objectives are not the same. Trade-offs have to be made, particularly between central control by OPM and delegation of discretionary authority to the agencies. Further, the pursuit of both objectives is enfeebled by the introduction of additional and often incompatible objectives—the veteran preference system, for example.

THE HATCH ACT, OLD AND NEW In 1939 Congress passed an Act to Prevent Pernicious Political Activities, usually called the **Hatch Act** after its chief sponsor, Senator Carl Hatch of New Mexico. The act was designed to neutralize the danger of a federal civil service being able to shape, if not dictate, the election of presidents and members of Congress. In essence, the Hatch Act permitted federal employees to vote, but not to take an active part in partisan politics. The Hatch Act also made it illegal to dismiss non-policy-making federal officials (those below cabinet and subcabinet rank) for partisan reasons.[19]

In 1993, Congress, with the encouragement of the Clinton administration, overhauled the Hatch Act and made many forms of participation in partisan politics permissible. The revised Hatch Act still bars federal officials from running as candidates in partisan elections, but it does permit most federal civil servants to hold party positions and involve themselves in party fund raising and campaigning. This new law, which took effect in 1994, was welcomed by those who believed the old Hatch Act discouraged political participation by more than 2 million individuals who might otherwise be vigorous political activists.[20]

The new Hatch Act spells out many restrictions on federal bureaucrats; they cannot raise campaign funds in their agencies, and those who work in such highly sensitive federal agencies as the CIA, FBI, Secret Service, and certain divisions of the Internal Revenue Service are specifically barred from nearly all partisan activity. Those who work in the U.S. military have stricter rules regulating their political involvement.

EMPLOYEE UNIONS Since 1962, federal civilian employees have had the right to form unions or associations that represent them in seeking to improve government personnel policies, and about one-third of them have joined such unions. Some

Hatch Act Rules:
What Federal Civilian
Employees May
and May Not Do

May register and vote as they choose

May assist in voter registration

May express opinions about candidates and issues

May participate in campaigns as off-duty activities

May contribute money to political organizations or attend political fund-raising functions

May wear or display political badges, buttons, or stickers

May attend political rallies and meetings

May join political clubs or parties

May seek and hold positions in political parties

May campaign for or against referendum questions, constitutional amendments, and municipal ordinances

May not be candidates for public office in partisan elections

May not use official authority to interfere with or affect the results of an election

May not collect contributions or sell tickets to political fund-raising functions from subordinate employees

May not solicit funds or discourage the political activity of any person who has business before the employee's office

May not solicit funds or discourage political activity by any person who is the subject of an ongoing audit, investigation, or enforcement action

These rules apply to nearly all federal civil servants. Rules are stricter for military personnel and certain agencies like the FBI, CIA, and Secret Service.

SOURCE: Adapted from the U.S. Merit Systems Protection Board publications and from *Congressional Quarterly*, November 13, 1993, p. 3146.

of the more important unions representing federal employees today are the American Federation of Government Employees, the National Treasury Employees Union, the National Association of Government Employees, and the National Federation of Federal Employees. Unlike unions in the private sector, these groups lack the right to strike and are not able to bargain over pay and benefits. What can they do? They attempt to negotiate better personnel policies and practices for federal workers, and they represent federal bureaucrats at grievance and disciplinary proceedings. They also lobby Congress on measures affecting personnel changes.

Principles of Bureaucratic Management

Early in this century, several scholars developed a formal model of administration from which they derived certain principles:

1. *Unity of command.* Every officer should have a superior to whom to report and from whom to take orders.
2. *Chain of command.* There should be a firm line of authority running from the top down and responsibility running from the bottom up.
3. *Line and staff.* The staff advises the executive but gives no commands, whereas the line has operating duties.
4. *Span of control.* A hierarchical structure should be established so that no individuals supervise more agencies directly than they can effectively handle.
5. *Decentralization.* When possible, administrators should delegate decisions and responsibilities to lower levels.

Woodrow Wilson, while still a Princeton University professor, adopted many of these views in his writings. Politics and public administration, he said, should be carefully separated. Leave politics to Congress and management to administrators who adhere to the laws passed by Congress. Followers of the noted German sociologist Max Weber contended that a properly run bureaucracy could be a model of efficiency based on rational and impartial management.[21]

According to the textbook model, bureaucrats should be closely controlled by established rules and regulations. Although this is not always true in practice, it is generally the case. Administrators are not free to make any rules they wish or to decide disputes any way they please. Several kinds of limitations exist:

1. The basic legislative power of Congress compels agencies to identify the will of Congress and to interpret and apply laws as Congress would wish. Congress can amend a law to make its intent clearer, conduct oversight hearings and investigations, or restrict appropriations.
2. Congress has closely regulated the procedures to be followed by regulatory agencies. Under the Administrative Procedures Act of 1946, agencies must publicize their procedures and organization, give advance information of proposed rules to interested persons, allow such persons to present written information and arguments, and allow parties appearing before the agency to be accompanied by counsel and to cross-examine witnesses.
3. Under certain conditions, final actions of agencies may be appealed to the courts.
4. Some federal agencies are created for the specific purpose of overseeing and limiting their fellow agencies. Examples are the Office of Management and Budget (OMB), which is supervised by the White House, and the General Accounting Office (GAO), which is supervised by Congress. In addition to

reviewing an agency's budget requests annually in the name of the president, OMB reviews management, organization, and administrative practices on a more or less continuous basis. GAO conducts audits of agency spending and investigates the effectiveness of alternative programs designed for similar ends.

5. Administrators are constrained by informal political checks. They must keep in mind the demands of professional ethics, the advice and criticism of experts, and the attitudes of Congress, the president, interest groups, political parties, private persons, and so on. In the long run, these informal safeguards may be the most important of all.

This classical or textbook model remains influential because it reflects reality. Laws of Congress, although not the whole story, are an important part of the story. Federal agencies and career servants are creatures of the enabling laws under which they work.

But many of the federal agencies are changing how they hire people and go about their work. Innovation and customer service have become priorities in the 1990s. Hierarchical pyramids have become flatter. Applicants can now use regular résumés instead of federal forms in applying for government jobs. A World Wide Web site lets people find out what jobs are available, and applicants can apply by phone or fax for many jobs. And workers are being evaluated and rewarded in terms of how well their teams achieve measurable results.

Reformers have junked all but a few sections of the 10,000-page *Federal Personnel Manual* that specified everything down to the color of personnel folders. "We actually hauled it out to a dumpster in a wheel barrow. The death of the manual gave agencies more freedom to tailor things to fit their own operations."[22]

The government is also trying to make the federal bureaucracy a more family-friendly workplace. The Clinton administration supported the Family Leave Act (1993) and has encouraged job sharing, part-time work, alternative work schedules, telecommuting from home, and child and elder services. Vice-president Gore, who championed many of these promising changes, says, "We are changing the systems so all our people can devote more of their time, intelligence, and energy to what they signed up for in the first place—serving the people of America."[23]

Bureaucratic Realities

Suppose Congress passes a law setting federal standards for automobile safety and designates the Department of Transportation to carry out a law that all automobiles must have side-impact air bags by 2002. Conflicts over this requirement do not stop with the adoption of the law. Or suppose a president announces that we must wage war on drug abuse, and Congress appropriates funds and designates the agencies to carry out programs. Politics—conflicts over who is to get what and who is to do what—continue to be important as the policy is applied to changing conditions.

Career administrators are in a good position to know when a program is not operating properly and what action is needed. But one of the major complaints about bureaucrats is that they do not go out of their way to make things better. The problem is that many bureaucrats often learn by hard experience that they are more likely to get into trouble by attempting to improve or change programs than if they just do nothing. Hardening of administrative arteries is more likely, some critics say, than administrative aggressiveness.

Often the fiercest battles in Washington are not over principles or programs but over jurisdictional boundaries, personnel cuts, and fringe benefits. Career employees come to believe the expansion of their organization is vital to the public interest. They sometimes become more skillful at building political alliances to

We the People

Problems Faced by Women Bureaucrats

Although women constitute about 50 percent of the federal career work force, they are severely underrepresented in top positions. And they often complain that male supervisors tend to give preference to other males in hiring and promotions. Some women bureaucrats suggest that men progress more rapidly because they have more opportunities to "network" than women do.

The journal *Government Executive* surveyed 156 women serving in the elite Senior Executive Service and found:

- 65 percent said they have the impression that their views were not respected as much as if they were male.
- 63 percent said they have been mistaken for a secretary at a business meeting.
- 54 percent said they have felt that a male subordinate resisted taking direction from them because they were female.
- 30 percent said they felt that their personal lives were scrutinized more closely than those of their male colleagues.
- 21 percent said they have felt sexually harassed.

SOURCE: Bobbi Nodel, "Women in Government," *Government Executive*, August 1988, p. 13.

Federal employees were caught in the middle of a battle between congressional Republicans and President Clinton over a balanced budget. After Clinton vetoed Republican demands, thousands of government workers were "furloughed" without pay during the 1995 Christmas season. Nightly broadcasts put a sympathetic face on the "faceless bureaucrats" who were deprived of money for gifts, rent, and food.

protect their own organization than at building political alliances to ensure their programs' effectiveness.

Organizations, both public and private, also tend to resist change and to resent "outside" direction, whether by a president or by other external supervisors or boards. A department head in the government, a large corporation, or a university is often likely to consider the president of the organization to be an outsider whose judgment in matters affecting his or her bureau is always suspect.

Career administrators often become involved in politics. Some of them have more bargaining and alliance-building skills than the elected and appointed officials to whom they report. In one sense, agency leaders are at the center of action in Washington. Over time, administrative agencies may come to resemble entrenched pressure groups in that they operate to advance their own interests. The FBI is a good example; it is always seeking more funds, new projects, and as much independence as possible from the Justice Department in which it is located.

Career bureaucrats develop a keen sensitivity to the political environment and get caught up in a network of issue experts and politicians who specialize in certain policy areas. The growth of federal programs from the 1930s through the 1970s brought an increase in the number of policy aides on Capitol Hill, of Washington law firms that specialize in assisting clients who are interested in policy developments, and of lobbyists (some say at least 40,000) who work with Congress and the federal bureaucracy to advance various economic and professional interests.

Groups that perceive real or potential harm to their interests cultivate the bureau chiefs and agency staffs of concern to their programs. They also work closely with the committees or subcommittees of Congress that authorize, appropriate, and oversee programs run by these key bureaucracies. One former cabinet member, testifying before a congressional committee, described the process this way:

> It is a fact, unknown to the general public, that some elements in Congress and some special interest lobbies have never really wanted the departmental Secretaries (cabinet members) to be strong. As everyone in this room knows but few people outside of Washington understand, questions of public policy nominally lodged with the Secretary are often decided far beyond the Secretary's reach by a trinity—not exactly a holy trinity—consisting of (1) representatives of an outside lobby, (2) middle-level bureaucrats, and (3) selected Members of Congress, particularly concerned with appropriations.
>
> In a given field these people may have collaborated for years. They may have formed deep personal and family friendships. They have traded innumerable favors. They have seen Secretaries come and go. . . . They have a durable alliance that cranks out legislation and appropriations in behalf of their special interest.[24]

Members of Congress cultivate bureau officials, just as special interests nurture close ties with both Congress and bureau heads. Congress controls agency budgets and has the power to approve or deny requests for relevant legislation. Bureau officials are especially careful to develop good relations with members of the congressional committees and subcommittees that handle their legislation and appropriations.

Some bureaucrats become more entangled than others with these external coalitions. Bureau chiefs are logical targets for the efforts of concerned interest groups. On the other hand, recognizing the power of interest groups, bureau chiefs frequently recruit them as allies in pursuing common goals. What these bureau officials have in common with interest groups and their allies in Congress is a shared view that more money should be spent on federal programs run by the bureau in question. These alliances among bureaucrats, interest groups, and subcommittee members and their staffs on Capitol Hill are sometimes described as **iron triangles**.

The executive branch is not the smooth operating hierarchy it is made to appear on an organization chart. The president, cabinet members, and their politically appointed undersecretaries and assistant secretaries have their work cut out for them as they try to impose their will on the permanent civil service. Bureaucrats, with their strong allies in Congress and the interest groups, often resist change and direction from their appointed or elected political "superiors." Some view these external relations as "administrative guerrilla warfare" and a serious roadblock to holding elected leaders accountable. Others anticipate a clash over values as inevitable in a system that provides ample opportunities for such clashes. After all, the bureaus themselves are merely one more forum for registering the many demands that make up the people's will.

The Case of Bureau Chief George Brown

The following case is fictional, yet based on actual experiences of a typical bureaucrat. (Note that not only is our main character, George Brown, fictitious, but so are the Bureau of Erosion and the Department of Conservation. Other agencies mentioned do exist.) This case illustrates some of the painful choices bureaucrats have to make.

George Brown is chief of the Bureau of Erosion in the Department of Conservation. A graduate of North Dakota State University, Brown is a career official in the federal service and a member of the Senior Executive Service. He is 47; his appointment to the post was a result of both ability and luck. When his old bureau chief retired, the president wanted to bring in an erosion expert from Illinois, but influential members of Congress pressed for the selection of a recently "retired" (actually he was defeated in the last election!) member of the House of Representatives from a farm state. After deadlock and delay, Brown, then a division head in the Bureau of Erosion, was promoted to bureau chief as a compromise.

Early in March of Brown's second year in his new post, his boss, the secretary of conservation, summoned him and the other bureau heads to an important conference and informed them that he had just attended a cabinet meeting in which the president had called on each department to make at least a 10 percent cut in spending in the coming fiscal year. The president, the secretary reported, was responding to popular demands for federal fiscal restraint.

Brown quickly calculated what this cutback would mean for his agency. For several years the Bureau of Erosion had been spending about $800 million a year to help farmers protect their farmland. Could it get along on about $700 million, and where could savings be made? Returning to his office, Brown called a meeting of his personnel, budget, and management officials. After hours of discussion, it was agreed that savings could be effected only by decreasing the scope of the program, a step that would involve terminating about 1,500 of the bureau's employees. Brown asked his subordinates to prepare a list of employees who were the least useful to the bureau. He would decide which to drop after checking with the affected members of Congress.

A few weeks later Brown presented a $710 million budget to Secretary Jones, who approved it and passed it along to the White House. The president then went over the figures in a conference with the director of the Office of Management and Budget, and a few weeks later the White House submitted the budget for the whole executive department, incorporating the Erosion Bureau's $710 million, to Congress.

Meanwhile Brown was running into trouble. News of the proposed budget cut had leaked immediately to the bureau's personnel in the field. Nobody knew who would be dropped if the cut went through, and some officials were already looking around for other positions. Morale fell. Hearing of the cut, farmers' representatives in Washington notified local farm organizations throughout the country. Soon Brown began to receive letters demanding certain services be maintained. Members of the farm bloc in Congress were also becoming restless.

Shortly after the president's budget went to Congress, Representative Jim Smith of Kansas asked Brown to meet with him. Smith was chair of the Subcommittee

J. Edgar Hoover, Consummate Bureaucrat

J. Edgar Hoover (1895–1972), chief of the Federal Bureau of Investigation for almost half a century, was in theory subject to direction from the attorney general and the president of the United States. In fact, he was so popular with Congress and the public that he was practically immune to control. Part of this "popularity," we now know, came from his investigatory power, which was feared as well as abused. That immunity served the country poorly at times, such as when Hoover was able to wiretap Dr. Martin Luther King, Jr., or others he disliked, but it served the country well when Hoover was able to thwart President Richard Nixon and his aides in certain of their illegal efforts to undermine political opponents.[*] But how safe is a democracy when the administrative head of a major agency can defy even the elected president?

[*]See Anthony Summers, *Official and Confidential: The Secret Life of J. Edgar Hoover* (Putnam, 1993).

on Agriculture of the influential House Appropriations Committee and thus a powerful factor in congressional treatment of the budget. Smith said he had consulted his fellow subcommittee members, both Democratic and Republican, and they all agreed the Erosion Bureau's cut must not go through. The farmers needed even more than the usual $800 million because of severe flood conditions in some sections of the country. He warned they would rise up in arms if the program were reduced. Members of Congress from agricultural areas, Smith went on, were under tremendous pressure. Leaders of farm groups in Washington were mobilizing farmers everywhere. Besides, Smith said, the president was unfair in cutting down on the farm program; he did not understand agricultural problems, and he failed to recognize that programs designed to increase agricultural output were the best way to reduce the trade imbalance. Let the cuts in federal programs be made elsewhere.

Smith then came to the point. Brown, he said, must vigorously oppose the budget cut. Hearings on appropriations would begin in a few days, and Brown as bureau chief would, of course, testify. At that time he must insist that the cuts would hurt the bureau and undermine its whole program. Brown would not have to volunteer this statement, Smith said. He could just respond to leading questions put by committee members. Brown's testimony, Smith thought, would help clinch the argument against the cut because the committee would respect the judgment of the administrator closest to the problem. Other bureaucrats were fighting to save their appropriations. Obviously, said Smith, they are counting on public reaction to get them exemptions from the 10 percent cutback, and Brown would be foolish not to do the same.

Brown was in an embarrassing position. He had submitted his estimates to the secretary of conservation and to the president, and it was his duty to back them up. The rules of the game demanded, moreover, that agency heads defend budget estimates submitted to Congress, whatever their personal feelings might be. The president had appointed Brown to his position and had a right to expect loyalty. On the other hand, Brown was on the spot with his own agency. The employees all expected their chief to look out for them. Brown had developed cordial relations with his staff, and he squirmed at the thought of having to let more than a thousand employees go. What would they think when they heard him defend the cut? More important, he wanted to maintain friendly relations with the farmers, the farm organizations, and the farm bloc in Congress. Finally, Brown was committed to his program. He grasped its true importance, whereas the president's budget advisers did not. And he knew that his pet project—aid to poverty-stricken areas in Appalachia—would probably be sacrificed because it was not supported by a powerful constituency.

Brown turned for advice to an old friend in the Office of Management and Budget. This friend urged him to defend the president's budget. He appealed to Brown's professional pride as an administrator and career public servant. He reminded him that the chief executive must have control of the budget and that agency heads must subordinate their interests to the executive program. He said the only way to balance the budget would be for all agencies to make program cuts. As for the employees to be dropped—well, that was part of the game. Some of them might be able to get jobs in other government agencies; civil service would protect their status. Anyway, they would understand Brown's position. In a parting shot he mentioned that the president had Brown in mind for bigger things.

The next day Brown had lunch with a North Dakota senator, wise and experienced in Washington ways, who had helped him get his start in government. The senator was sympathetic. But there was no doubt about what Brown should do, the senator said. He should follow Representative Smith's plan, of course, being as diplomatic as possible about it. That way he would protect his position with those who would be most important in the long run.

"After all," the senator said, "presidents come and go, parties rise and fall, but Smith and the other members of Congress will be here a long time, and so will the farm organizations. They can do a lot for you in future years. And remember one other thing," the senator concluded. "These people are the elected representatives of the people. Constitutionally, Congress has the power to spend money as it sees fit. Why should you object if they want to spend an extra $70 or $80 million?"

Leaving the Dirksen Senate Office Building, Brown realized his dilemma was worse than ever. The arguments on both sides were persuasive. He felt hopelessly divided in his loyalties and responsibilities. The president expected one thing of him; Congress expected another. As a professional administrator, he felt obliged to side with the president. As head of a bureau, however, he wanted to protect his team and his programs. His future? Whatever decision he made, he was bound to antagonize important people and interests.

After much soul searching, Brown decided the issue involved more than loyalties, ambitions, and programs. Ultimately it boiled down to two questions: First, to whom was he, Brown, legally and administratively responsible? Formally, of course, he was responsible to the chief executive who appointed him, who was accountable to the people. Brown knew, too, that he was accountable to Congress, which after all has the power over all fiscal matters. Second, which course of action did he think was better for the welfare of all the people? Looking at the question this way, he believed the president was right in asking for fiscal restraint. As a taxpayer and consumer himself, Brown recognized the need to reduce the federal budget deficit. To be sure, Congress must make the final decision. Yet to make the decision, Congress had to act on the advice of the administration, and the administration should speak with one voice for the majority of the people, or it should not be speaking out at all.

With mixed feelings Brown decided to support the president. Being a seasoned alliance builder, however, he hedged his bets. He came out strongly for the president's budget, yet at the same time he sent friendly members of Congress some questions to be asked of him in future hearings so he could explain the impact of the cutbacks. He also circulated to some of these same members of Congress an analysis of the impact of personnel and funding cuts in their states and districts.

Our fictional account of George Brown and similar case studies leads to three important generalizations about bureaucrats:

1. Bureaucrats are people, not robots, and are subject to many influences—the president, OMB, the cabinet, the House, the Senate, the courts, competing interest groups, public opinion, as well as their own sense of what is right.

2. Bureaucrats do not respond merely to orders from the top but to a variety of motives stemming from their own personalities, political attitudes, educational and professional backgrounds, formal and informal organization and communication, and the political context in which they operate.

3. Bureaucrats are important in government. Some of them have considerable discretion and make decisions of great significance. The cumulative effect of all their policies and actions on our daily lives is enormous.

WHAT THE PUBLIC THINKS OF BUREAUCRATS AND THE BUREAUCRACY

Big bureaucracy in the abstract is unpopular, especially when it is out of sight and what it does is little understood. It engages in so many activities that most people find something it does offensive (like taxing them, inspecting them, or regulating them). Big bureaucracy is sometimes defined as that part of the government people dislike.

Thinking It Through

Unannounced drug testing raises serious Fourth Amendment questions. The idea that a group of people should be subjected to random searches without reasonable individual cause has been resisted since the outset of our life as a nation. When Congress, or the president, or the head of a federal agency requires testing as a condition of employment, even if evidence of drug use would not be used to dismiss employees, skeptical judges must be persuaded that the testing is not an "unreasonable" search and seizure.

The Supreme Court ruled in two 1989 decisions involving railway workers and U.S. Customs Service employees that mandatory blood and urine tests may be required for certain workers without a showing of "individualized suspicion." Writing for the Court in the railway workers' case, Justice Anthony Kennedy said the government's interest in testing even without a showing of individual suspicion is compelling. Employees subject to the tests discharge duties fraught with such risks of injury to others that even a momentary lapse of attention can have disastrous results.

The two cases dealt with post-accident testing of railway personnel on duty at the time of a major accident and with customs officials who carry firearms, handle classified information, or intercept drugs.

Drug testing of all federal employees, or even only those in policy-making positions, presents difficult constitutional issues. Supporters of privacy rights and civil liberties are uncomfortable with carrying this policy too far. Drug testing, some concede, may be necessary for certain individuals where public safety is genuinely involved, but it is not needed and would be an unconstitutional deprivation of privacy rights under the Fourth Amendment as a general policy.

THE BUREAUCRATS: PAPER SHUFFLERS OR EMPIRE BUILDERS?

One of the paradoxes of public attitudes toward bureaucrats is that some of the time we criticize federal employees for working too little, for being lazy, or for lacking initiative—for failing to abide by the so-called "work ethic." Yet at the same time we view federal workers as too powerful and we accuse them of intervening in or regulating our lives far too much. Can bureaucrats in reality be both timid *and* empire builders? In fact, there are enough bureaucrats to fulfill all kinds of contrasting stereotypes, so despite the seeming contradiction, perhaps both views are valid.

Even federal employees gripe about the system. Although top federal employees say they like the challenge of their work, the opportunity to participate in forming and managing important policies, and the quality of people with whom they work, most workers dislike the rigidity, the red tape, and the frustrations of dealing with interest groups and politicians.

"Think of it. Presidents come and go, but WE go on forever!"

Berry's World. Reproduced by permission of Newspaper Enterprise Association, Inc.

Criticisms of Federal Workers

Bureaucrats as Paper-Shuffling Clerks Are:	Bureaucrats as the Real Power in Washington Are:
Timid and indecisive	A self-anointed elite in our nation's capital
Flabby, overpaid, and lazy	An oppressive foreign power
Ruled by inertia	The fourth branch of government
Unimaginative	Intolerably meddlesome
Devoted to rigid procedures	A demanding giant
Slow to accept new ideas	The permanent government
Slow to abandon unsuccessful policies	Superbureaucrats who wield vast power
Impersonal and lacking individuality	Influential enough to do great injury
Red tape artists	Intrusive, arrogant empire builders
On "one long coffee break"	

What Top Federal Career Employees Like Least and Most About Their Work

Like Least:	Like Most:
Inability to take personal actions that should be a manager's prerogative (hiring and discipline)	Challenging assignments
Inadequate resources (personnel, budget)	Opportunity to have an impact on policy programs
Personal financial sacrifice	Opportunity for public service
Red tape	Opportunity to use and expand knowledge and skills
Frustrations in dealing with interest groups and Congress	Caliber of colleagues

As individuals, civil servants are appreciated, but as a class they are not. Citizens who have dealings with federal employees on a face-to-face basis say they are pleased by employees' performance. In contrast to scorn for bureaucrats and bureaucracy in general, Americans seem to approve the conduct of individual federal employees—Postal Service delivery persons, forest rangers, Veterans Affairs Department officials, or the county field agents who help with the local 4-H programs. They also admire astronauts, marines, FBI agents, and Coast Guard officers, all of whom are also federal employees.

Still, bureaucrats as a group are a favorite punching bag—a convenient scapegoat—for reporters and politicians who want to place the blame on someone for things that go wrong in government. An irreverent journal in the nation's capital, *The Washington Monthly*, rails against clumsy bureaucracy in every issue. Most newspapers and magazines feature stories and cartoons critical of the federal bureaucracy. Some members of Congress like to joke that there is a parlor game played in the nation's capital: "It's called Bureaucracy," they say. "And there is only one rule. The first one to move loses."

Red Tape and Waste

We Americans are skeptical of, if not cynical about, big government. We equate bigness with remoteness, incompetence, and unresponsiveness. We also assume that the bigger government gets, the less efficient it is, and the more it wastes. Perhaps the most criticized aspect of the federal bureaucracy is that career public employees seem to enjoy the closest thing to job security; they are almost as secure in their jobs as if they were confirmed for life on the Supreme Court.

When Thomas Jefferson was president, the federal government employed 2,120 persons: Indian commissioners, postmasters, collectors of customs, tax collectors, marshals, lighthouse keepers, and clerks. Today the president heads an executive branch of, as noted earlier, 2.7 million civilians and 1.4 million military employees, who work in at least 2,000 units of federal administration (see Figure 17–4).

A central problem with the bureaucracy, critics say, is that we have failed to subject it to the control and discipline alleged to operate in the private sector. Despite the great federal government shutdowns in late 1995 and early 1996, and the talk about numerous federal programs facing the guillotine, most federal agencies survived.

The tests of efficiency and cost effectiveness that are the basic standards of business are much less important in decisions about which federal programs survive. A number of outdated and ineffective programs endure because both Republicans and Democrats forge coalitions of convenience based on a desire to deliver favors and protect programs that help their particular districts.

In the private sector, if you are displeased with the service provided by a company such as AT&T, you can switch to MCI or Sprint. This is now happening with respect to some government services. It used to be that you could use only the U.S. Postal Service to deliver your messages, whether you liked the service or not. Now numerous delivery services compete for your business, and e-mail adds to your options. (It should be noted that the postal service is getting better—blame it on the competition?)

One economics writer points to farm and maritime fleet subsidies, Amtrak, public broadcasting subsidies, the Small Business Administration, and government-owned power plants as wasteful and no longer needed. "Some of these programs qualify as corporate welfare; all are unneeded. . . . Other programs should revert to the states."[25]

Defining what is truly in the national interest is hard. And deciding what is no longer in the national interest is also equally hard for presidents and members of

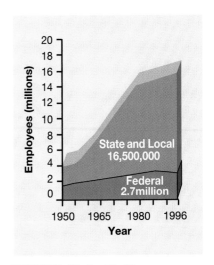

FIGURE 17–4 Civilian Government Employees

SOURCE: Bureau of Labor Statistics, U.S. Department of Labor.

In his second term, President Clinton named Andrew Cuomo as Secretary of Housing and Urban Development, a department that had seen considerable downsizing during the previous term.

Congress. Take, for example, the subsidies for public radio and public television. Many Republicans in the Newt Gingrich coalition in Congress wanted to end support for public broadcasting, saying that *Sesame Street*, *Car Talk*, and *Wall Street Week* would all be picked up by the networks and that today's diversity of cable television channels makes publicly subsidized broadcasting no longer necessary.[26]

Congress throughout the 1990s has taken steps to downsize federal agencies. It abolished the Interstate Commerce Commission; it called for the gradual privatization of Amtrak; and it scaled back the Environmental Protection Agency, the Bureau of Mines, the Bureau of Indian Affairs, and several scientific advisory boards and projects. Still, many Americans believe Congress has spared too many programs and agencies that do not serve us well.

In 1995 there was a major Republican crusade to dismantle the Departments of Energy, Commerce, Housing and Urban Development, and Education. "But even as they claimed a mandate to end 'big government,' these Republicans discovered that voter sentiment about closing down agencies typically ranged from apathy to uneasiness to outright opposition."[27]

Republicans showed less eagerness to cut cabinet departments in Clinton's second term, due in part to the downsizing of some of these departments, in part to many programs being made into block grants to states and localities, and in part because they knew President Clinton would wield his veto power to retain these departments. Moreover, various interest groups came to the defense of these departments. For example, a coalition of major corporations—including AT&T, IBM, Boeing, General Electric, and Motorola—came together to support the Commerce Department and its trade promotion and industrial research operations.[28]

Still another charge leveled against bureaucrats is that once a program is established, the people assigned to it become committed to "the cause." In the Office of Civil Rights in the Department of Education, for example, appointments generally go to those concerned about protecting the rights of women and minorities. The protection of rights is their assigned task, and in their zeal they strengthen their authority. Those assigned to the Drug Enforcement Administration are likely to be convinced that enforcement of the federal laws against narcotics is of supreme importance; in carrying out their duties, they sometimes go beyond their vested authority. Groups outside the government who want their programs carried forward pressure the agencies; women's groups and minority advocacy groups carefully watch the Office of Civil Rights, for instance.

A Positive Perspective

Bureaucracy is a function not only of governments but also of corporations, universities, and private associations. It is a reality of modern existence. The challenge as we enter the twenty-first century is not to wish away big bureaucracies, but to learn how to improve their performance and make them more efficient and accountable. Recent efforts at some state and local government levels have made their bureaucracies more entrepreneurial. The cities of St. Paul, Minnesota, and Indianapolis, Indiana, and the states of Florida under Governor Lawton Chiles and Massachusetts under Governor William Weld have introduced various market incentives, rewards, and public-private partnerships that encourage efficiency and responsiveness.[29] Competition and incentives can prudently be built into various government monopolies so that bureaucracies become more responsive to their customers.

A comparison of the performance of our bureaucracy with most bureaucracies in the world suggests we should be grateful for the service we get from our public employees. The U.S. Postal Service provides a good example. Although it is criticized as being a dinosaur, it is more efficient and less costly than comparable services around the world. And, as noted earlier, it is getting better. Another example is the United States tax system; although it is constantly cursed, it is the most effective such system in the world.

Compared to most other nations, U.S. government employment has not grown. Government employment grew by more than 20 percent in Sweden in the past generation and by over 11 percent in Italy and Germany during the same period. There has been a steady decline in U.S. government employment during the last ten years, especially lately. Moreover, government employment as a percentage of total employment in the United States is 30 to 50 percent lower than in most Western European democracies.

One study finds that American public bureaucracies respond well to effective political leadership. Under such conditions, federal bureaucracies are competitive, adaptable, and dynamic. "Agencies respond systematically to changes in political leadership, as manifested through appointments, changing budgets, reorganizations, and various other tools of administrative control."[30]

BUREAUCRATIC RESPONSIVENESS

One of the most complex questions concerning public bureaucracies is whether they are responsive enough to the citizens and the elected officials who represent them. Being responsive means being quick to react and treating those who need assistance sympathetically. Determining how responsive an agency is depends on the perceptions of the person involved. A person who has had to stand for hours in a long line, whether at the post office or at a welfare agency, will complain about unresponsive bureaucrats. Someone who feels that a federal bureaucrat treats him "by the book" rather than by common sense also develops a critical view.

Standard Operating Procedures

Bureaucracies develop routines and standard operating procedures to ensure efficiency and productivity. Unfortunately, reliance on routine reduces flexibility. Just about everyone has at one time or another been turned away from the local post office because a package to be mailed was too large, or too small, or in the wrong kind of container. It is hard on such occasions to hold back our anger: Why can't they be flexible? Why can't they be reasonable? Why can't they deal with me in a personal way?

Procedures that allow the post office, the army, or the Internal Revenue Service to perform efficiently sometimes also diminish their ability to respond to the personalized needs of individuals. Routines help to prevent chaos and allow government behavior to be consistent, uniform, and impartial. The inevitable and necessary result of big bureaucracy is often a trade-off; quick, personalized, and sympathetic service is sacrificed for order.

Privatization

Can certain problems be better handled by agencies other than government bureaucracies? For example, should the government run railways, prisons, and a public television channel, or should we encourage the private sector and free market mechanisms to handle these responsibilities?

Privatization is the process of contracting public services to private organizations. Examples of privatization include the contracting out by San Francisco of its budget analysis to a private firm, contracting out by Massachusetts of much of its tax collecting, and contracting out by the city of Chelsea, Massachusetts, of the operation of its schools to Boston University. The National Aeronautics and Space Administration (NASA) contracts out most of the manufacturing of its space vehicles.

Private or nonprofit firms handle a vast array of services, from repairing ships to delivering "meals-on-wheels" to the home-bound elderly. Some people suggest that our state and federal prisons might be more effectively operated by private firms. Advocates of privatization claim it would reduce costs and provide better service than reliance on the federal bureaucracy.[31]

Critics of privatization point to the cost overruns and waste in the procurement of weapons systems as failures of privatization. Those who advocate privatization on the ideological grounds that business is always superior to government are, according to David Osborne and Ted Gaebler, "selling the American people snake oil." Privatization is one answer, they say, yet not *the* answer:

> Services can be contracted out or turned over to the private sector. But governance cannot. We can privatize discrete [governmental programs], but not the overall process of governance. If we did, we would have no mechanism by which to make collective decisions, no way to set the rules of the marketplace, no means to enforce rules of behavior. We would lose all sense of equity and altruism: services that could not generate a profit, whether housing for the homeless or health care for the poor, would barely exist. . . .

> Business does some things better than government, but government does some things better than business. The public sector tends to be better, for instance, at policy management, regulation, ensuring equity, preventing discrimination or exploitation, ensuring continuity and stability of services, and ensuring social cohesion. . . . Business tends to do better at performing economic tasks, innovating, replicating successful experiments, adapting to rapid change, abandoning unsuccessful or obsolete activities, and performing complex or technical tasks.[32]

Would we be better off if the U.S. Postal Service were turned over to private firms? A business executive who recently served as postmaster general, Anthony Frank, says no. He praises the Postal Service for its high on-time delivery and points out that all Americans, no matter where they live, get essentially the same service at the same price. "If you privatize it," Frank pointed out, "the cost would go up for a lot of Americans. [Thirty-two] cents compared to anywhere else in the world is an incredible bargain," says Frank. "It's 67 cents in Germany, 47 cents in Japan, and 42 cents in Canada. And they don't have any overnight service."[33]

BUREAUCRATIC ACCOUNTABILITY

The question of bureaucratic *responsiveness* is extremely difficult to disentangle from the question of bureaucratic *accountability*. In determining the responsiveness of the U.S. Navy or the FBI or the Department of Transportation, we must also ask who should oversee and control them.

Should bureaucrats be accountable to the president's cabinet, the majority who elected the president, or the majority in Congress? Plainly, most Americans would like the bureaucracy to be responsive to them as taxpaying customers. In general terms they would say it should be responsive to the public interest. But defining the public interest is the crucial problem. The president and the House and the Senate and the committees of Congress all claim to speak on behalf of the public interest. Moreover, to whom bureaucrats should be accountable is an inherently political question. Certain forms of accountability favor some groups and interests over others. Accountability to the White House, for example, depends in large measure on the supporters' partisanship toward the president. Republicans, not surprisingly, favor strong presidential control over the bureaucracy when Republicans occupy the White House, as do Democrats when their party wins the White House.

To the President

Modern presidents invariably contend the president should be in charge, for the chief executive is responsive to the broadest constituency. A president, it is argued, must see that popular needs and expectations are converted into administrative action. When the nation elects a conservative president who favors cutbacks in federal programs and less governmental intervention in the economy, his policies must be carried out by the bureaucracy. The voters' wishes can be translated into action only if the bureaucrats support presidential policies.

Yet, as we have seen, under the American system of checks and balances the party winning a presidential election does not acquire total control of the national government or even of the executive branch itself. Under our Constitution, the president is not even the undisputed master of the executive structure. Congress sets up the agencies, broadly determines their organization, provides the money, and establishes the ground rules under which they operate. Congress constantly reviews the activities of the bureaucrats in appropriation hearings, special investigations, or informal inquiries. And, as we have also seen, the Senate confirms important cabinet-level leaders.

Presidents come into an ongoing system over which they have little control and within which they have little leeway to make the bureaucracy responsive. Still, some presidential control over the bureaucracy may be exercised through the powers of appointment, reorganization, and budgeting. More specifically, a president can attempt to control the bureaucracy by appointing or promoting sympathetic personnel, mobilizing public opinion and congressional pressure, changing the administrative apparatus, influencing budget decisions, using extensive personal persuasion, and if all else fails, shifting a bureaucracy's assignment to another department or agency (although this shift requires tacit if not explicit congressional approval).

Presidents appoint about 4,000 people to top positions within the executive branch; however, many of these are confidential assistants or special aides to cabinet officers, and many require Senate confirmation and are not exclusively a president's choice. Some suggest that a president's hand could be strengthened if the chief executive were able to make two or three times as many political appointments.

ASSISTANT SECRETARIES: A WEAK LINK   Although presidents can usually recruit to their cabinets people of prominence and influence, they find it much harder to hire outstanding people at the assistant secretary level. Assistant secretaries infuse the views and values of the White House into the federal bureaucracy. These citizen-leaders serve as links between the people who elect the presidents and the civil servants. Many people, however, are not willing to interrupt their professional or business careers to become assistant secretaries.

Over the last three decades the position has become one of relatively low pay, little prestige in Washington, short tenure (people stay, on average, barely two years in these posts), and high cost to one's family. As a result, presidents often fill these slots with relatively young people who, from the day they arrive in Washington, are looking for their next job. These assistant secretaries, or people in comparable appointed posts, are forced to wear "kid gloves" with those they are supposed to regulate because it is from them that their next job is often likely to come. Others have strong ideological convictions but little experience in administration and congressional politics. Still others use the position as a transition to retirement.

These presidential appointees have to deal with civil servants who know their "bosses" will not be there long. Most civil servants have virtually secure jobs, and sometimes all they have to do to ignore presidentially selected assistant secretaries is to wait them out for a year or two. Moreover, in and around Washington, government workers constitute a powerful political group. Assistant secretaries who try to significantly alter the policy directions of those who are supposedly under their supervision may do so at considerable political and legal peril.

THE SENIOR EXECUTIVE SERVICE   The Civil Service Reform Act of 1978 created a Senior Executive Service. This pool of about 8,000 career officials (which can include up to 10 percent political appointees by an administration) can be filled

Why Presidents Like to Reorganize the Bureaucracy

- Shake up an organization to increase managerial control
- Simplify or streamline the bureaucracy or a specific agency
- Reduce costs by lessening overlap, duplication, inefficiencies
- Symbolize priorities by signaling new responsibilities in new agencies
- Improve program effectiveness by bringing separate but logically related programs to the same agency
- Improve policy integration by placing competitive or conflicting interests within a single organization
- Downgrade the importance of a program to weaken it
- Increase power over an unresponsive agency by installing their own people.

without senatorial confirmation, and its individual members are subject to transfer from one program to another within a department according to an administration's wishes. The service was created to make senior career bureaucrats—especially those enmeshed in issue networks—more responsive to the goals and policy preferences of the White House. This new service gave presidents greater flexibility in selecting, promoting, and rewarding with financial bonuses those in the top career service who are productive and responsive.

The Civil Service Reform Act of 1978 was viewed with skepticism. Some feared an executive service would be put to political use. Others worried that without strong White House support, the noble intentions of the act would not be achieved. The Senior Executive Service has not lived up to expectations. It has had little impact on the federal workers it was supposed to help. Because of federal budgetary problems, the bonuses and related incentives have been less than was expected. Morale in the senior ranks of the federal bureaucracy is pretty much the same as it was before the service was created. The White House, however, has enjoyed an increase in the flexibility of assignments, and recent presidents have shrewdly used this flexibility to their advantage to influence and discipline the upper reaches of the executive branch.

THE OFFICE OF MANAGEMENT AND BUDGET Ever since Franklin Roosevelt strengthened the presidential staffs, the budget bureau (currently called the **Office of Management and Budget**) has been a key resource. OMB's primary task is to prepare the president's annual budget. The budget is a major vehicle for shaping a president's policy priorities. It is the place and the process that determines which programs will get more funds, which will be cut, and which will remain the same. Departments and agencies fight to win larger chunks of the president's budget projections. OMB supervises the preparation of the budget and hence assists very directly in the formulation of policy. It weighs and evaluates the merits of the countless proposals and pleas that constantly pour in upon the White House.

Ninety-six percent of OMB's staff are career officials trained to evaluate ongoing projects and new spending requests. OMB's top officials are presidential appointees, and they are often among a president's most important advisers. They help a president make critical decisions not only about the budget but also about management practices, collaborative efforts among government agencies, and legislative planning. OMB makes sure that both the departments and Congress are informed of the president's legislative preferences, and it plays an important role in expanding the policy and administrative options open to a president.

To Congress

Congress has a number of ways to exercise control over the bureaucracy: by establishing agencies, formulating budgets, appropriating funds, confirming personnel, authorizing new programs or new shifts in direction, conducting investigations and hearings, reorganizing authority, and rebuking officials.

The foundation of this bureaucratic power is legal authority. A bureaucrat's information and expertise augment this legal authority. Ordinarily, bureaucrats know more than anyone else about their programs and the consequences of what they are doing. Recognizing this, Congress may request agency heads to make initial proposals and provide cost and price estimates. To reduce bureaucratic deception, Congress has imposed stiff penalties for providing misleading information.

Still, Congress is under fire, at least in some quarters, for encouraging the growth of federal spending and for deliberately allowing the bureaucracy to remain too independent. Members of Congress, so this reasoning goes, profit from the growth and complexity of the federal government. Most constituents, especially businesspeople, turn to their members of Congress for help as they battle federal red tape.

Hence, as the federal bureaucracy and its funds grow, so does the influence of members of Congress. Members of Congress regularly earn political credit by interceding in federal agencies on behalf of their constituents.

> The brutal fact is that only a small minority of our 535 members of Congress would trade the present bureaucratic structure for one which was an efficient, effective agent of the general interest—the political payoffs of the latter are lower than those of the former. Congressional talk of inefficient, irresponsible, out-of-control bureaucracy is typically just that—talk—and when it is not, it usually refers to agencies under the jurisdiction of other legislators' committees. Why do reformers continually ignore the fact that Congress has all the power necessary to enforce the "people's will" on the bureaucracy? Congress can abolish or reorganize an agency. Congress can limit or expand an agency's jurisdiction, or allow its authority to lapse entirely. Congress can slash an agency's appropriations. Congress can investigate. Congress can do all these things, but individual congressmen generally find reasons not to do so.[34]

Congress, it is charged, anxious whenever possible to avoid conflict, adopts such sweeping legislation and delegates so much authority to the bureaucracy that bureaucrats, in effect, have become the nation's lawmakers. Congress could pass laws with precise wording, but it would get too bogged down in details to complete its work. Congress does not generally specify details. Instead, Congress declares policy in general terms and empowers appropriate agencies to make appropriate decisions to meet varying circumstances throughout the nation.

It is not Congress as a whole that shares the direction over the bureaucracy with the president. More accurately, individual members and committees specialize in the appropriations and oversight processes. They oversee policies of a particular cluster of agencies—often the agencies serving constituents in their own districts. Some legislators stake out a claim over more general policies. Members of Congress, who see presidents come and go, come to think they know more about particular agencies than the president does (and often they do). Some congressional leaders prefer to seal off "their" agencies from presidential direction to maintain influence over public policy. Sometimes their power is institutionalized; the army chief of engineers, for example, is given authority by law to plan public works and report to Congress without going through the president.

Another factor works in favor of congressional control. Every day thousands of bureaucrats are involved in making millions of decisions. A president has limited time, limited resources, and limited political influence over many of these agencies. Presidents and their staffs can become involved only in matters of significant political interest. Members of Congress, with an institutional staff of well over 20,000, however, can operate in areas far from the presidential spotlight.

So, whose bureaucracy is this anyway? Presidents and members of Congress both strive to exercise control over the bureaucracy, each in their own way. Interest groups and court rulings also influence the way the bureaucracy operates. For their part, career bureaucrats say they are responsive to the laws and statutes they work under and to their own standards of professionalism and responsibility. No one answer exists to the question of who or what controls the bureaucracy. And therefore the search for improved means of ensuring bureaucratic accountability is never-ending. Experiments with countless instruments—reorganization, deregulating the public service, sunset practices, selective privatization, budgetary planning, and oversight hearings—also continue.

It is increasingly clear, moreover, that virtually all national bureaucracies are more responsive nowadays than once was the case. Even organizations such as the FBI or the Corps of Engineers are now reasonably accountable to Congress and the White House, and ultimately to the American people. "Thanks to Freedom of Information statutes and other 'sunshine' legislation, [the bureaucracy] has become less selective, and the weakening of iron triangles has made it much more responsive to broad constituencies and much less the creature of its own clients."[35] Also,

Attorney General Janet Reno was pressured by congressional Republicans to name an independent counsel to investigate fund-raising irregularities by President Clinton and the Democrats, but she steadfastly maintained her accountability to the law and to the president.

Thinking It Through

From this list of possibilities, select one or more as your preferences:

The Constitution

Laws and statutes

Congress

The president

Their administrative superiors, including bureau chiefs and cabinet officers

Their own view of "the public interest"

Court rulings

Public opinion

Interest groups

The media

Their profession

Public-employee unions

Political parties and their platforms

Intellectual opinion

Their co-workers and colleagues

Taxpayers

new restrictions in the Clinton era prohibit those who leave government from working for the agency they recently left on any contractual basis.

REFORM AND REORGANIZATION

Some writers call for a radical overhaul of the civil service system. One observer, for example, calls for appointments for only 6 to 12 years—term limits for civil servants. Job security creates deadwood, he argues, so periodic reexamination of employee qualifications would greatly increase employee productivity and responsiveness. Another suggestion is to rotate professionals from outside the government or from other agencies to loosen up stiffened joints, bring new blood, and encourage breadth. Such rotation might also break up the iron triangles—alliances that get fixed among senior civil servants, members of Congress, and outside client interest groups.

More realistic are the efforts, some of which have been noted earlier, to give more discretion to civil service executives and provide greater flexibility in the way government personnel systems operate. But members of Congress remain jealous of their prerogatives and are reluctant to delegate additional powers to the executive branch.

From 1949 to 1983, Congress delegated considerable discretion to presidents in reorganizing the executive departments. Each president made major reorganizing proposals, most of which Congress approved. Today presidents' proposals for reorganization must be approved by a joint resolution of the two chambers, making reorganization more difficult.

Congress is always sensitive to the implications of any reorganization that may affect its committee structure. Congressional committee leaders are aware that if they restructure the executive branch, they may have to reorganize their own committee systems, possibly upsetting the balance of power in Congress. "A willingness to surrender turf is as rare among members of Congress as it is among cabinet secretaries."[36]

Presidents, however, still have reasonably broad powers to reorganize the bureaucracy within the various cabinet departments. Yet even here, congressional committees take an active interest in how and why these changes are implemented. Interest groups also watch proposed changes and try to calculate how they will affect pet programs. In short, changing the shape of an administration is more than a matter of efficiency and economy. It is also a matter of policy outcomes: who gets what, how, and why.

POLITICS ONLINE

Government Business on the Web

Bill Clinton and Al Gore have made information technology part of their agenda since they were first elected in 1992, forming the National Information Infrastructure Advisory Council. Headed by Ira Magaziner, President Clinton's senior adviser for policy development, their goal is to make a deliberate attempt to centralize Internet policy at the highest level, advocating a *laissez-faire*, market-driven approach to Internet regulation. They have encouraged all governmental units to make use of the Internet and have done so themselves through their home page:

www.whitehouse.gov

One interesting application of this new information technology is found in the Federal Acquisition Streamlining Act, which created a Federal Acquisition Network (FACNET). Under this act, all federal agencies were to use electronic means for routine purchasing. Previously, procurement of things government uses—from paper clips to paint—required purchase orders and supporting memos. Not surprisingly, implementing such a change ran into lots of problems involving computer hardware and software. FACNET, which was to have been fully implemented by January 1997, has fallen well behind schedule, and many agencies are instead using the Internet to purchase equipment, but no one doubts that this new technology will eventually become an integral part of the federal bureaucracy.

SUMMARY

1. We often condemn bureaucracy and bureaucrats, yet we continue to turn to them to solve our toughest problems and to render more and better services. Our bureaucratic agencies, then, reflect how our political system has tried to identify our most important national goals and how policies are implemented.

2. The 1990s have witnessed major efforts to overhaul and improve the workings of the federal bureaucracy. Vice-president Al Gore has recommended numerous initiatives to streamline the government, eliminate waste, and make, where possible, government more like an effective business. In its first term, the Clinton administration cut the civilian work force by about 250,000 positions.

3. The American bureaucracy does not adhere to the textbook model of management organization, as it is not fully subordinate to any branch of government. It has at least two immediate bosses: Congress and the president. It must pay considerable attention as well to the courts and their rulings and, of course, to well-organized interest groups and public opinion. In many ways the bureaucracy is a semi-independent force—a fourth branch of government—in American politics.

4. Debates and controversy over big government and big bureaucracy, and over how to reorganize and eliminate waste in them, continue. Compared with many other nations and their centralized bureaucracies, the hand of bureaucracy rests more gently and less oppressively on Americans than on citizens elsewhere. Efforts to make the bureaucracy more responsive are enduring struggles in a constitutional democracy.

5. Whom and how the government hires and what discretion or powers it grants its employees are controversial topics. To work in the career public service is to have the opportunity to serve people, solve problems, and try to bring about a better society.

FURTHER READING

JOEL D. ABERBACH, *Keeping a Watchful Eye: The Politics of Congressional Oversight* (Brookings Institution, 1990).

DAN BAUM, *Smoke and Mirrors: The War on Drugs and the Politics of Failure* (Little, Brown, 1996).

JOHN J. DIIULIO, JR., ED., *Deregulating the Public Service: Can Government Be Improved?* (Brookings Institution, 1994).

JOHN J. DIIULIO JR., GERALD GARVEY, AND DONALD F. KETTL, *Improving Government Performance: An Owner's Manual* (Brookings Institution, 1993).

ANTHONY DOWNS, *Inside Bureaucracy* (Little, Brown, 1967).

JAMES W. FESLER AND DONALD F. KETTL, *The Politics of the Administrative Process* (Chatham House, 1991).

CHARLES T. GOODSELL, *The Case for Bureaucracy*, 3d ed. (Chatham House, 1994).

AL GORE, *The Best Kept Secrets in Government: How the Clinton Administration Is Reinventing the Way Washington Works* (Random House, 1996).

AL GORE, *Creating a Government That Works Better and Costs Less: The Report of the National Performance Review* (Plume-Penguin, 1993).

LARRY HILL, ED., *The State of Public Bureaucracy* (M. E. Sharpe, 1992).

PHILIP K. HOWARD, *The Death of Common Sense: How Law Is Suffocating America* (Random House, 1994).

PATRICIA INGRAHAM AND DAVID ROSENBLOOM, EDS., *The Promise and Paradox of Civil Service Reform* (University of Pittsburgh Press, 1992).

HERBERT KAUFMAN, *The Administrative Behavior of Federal Bureau Chiefs* (Brookings Institution, 1981).

DONALD F. KETTL AND JOHN J. DIIULIO, JR., EDS., *Inside the Reinvention Machine: Appraising Governmental Reform* (Brookings Institution, 1995).

PAUL C. LIGHT, *Thickening Government: Federal Hierarchy and the Diffusion of Accountability* (Brookings Institution, 1995).

PAUL C. LIGHT, *Monitoring Government: Inspectors General and the Search for Accountability* (Brookings Institution, 1993).

DAVID OSBORNE AND TED GAEBLER, *Reinventing Government: How the Entrepreneurial Spirit Is Transforming the Public Sector* (Addison-Wesley, 1992).

DAVID OSBORNE AND PETER PLASTRIK, *Banishing Bureaucracy: The Five Strategies for Reinventing Government* (Addison-Wesley, 1997).

JAMES Q. WILSON, *Bureaucracy: What Government Agencies Do and Why They Do It* (Basic Books, 1989).

B. DON WOOD AND RICHARD W. WATERMAN, *Bureaucratic Dynamics: The Role of Bureaucracy in a Democracy* (Westview Press, 1994).

Four useful journals are *Journal of Policy Analysis and Management, National Journal, Public Administration Review,* and *Government Executive.*

18

Making Economic Policy

$\mathcal{T}$he majestic Preamble to the Constitution of the United States makes it clear that the Constitution was ordained and established in order "to form a more perfect Union, establish Justice, insure domestic Tranquility, provide for the common defence, promote the general Welfare, and secure the Blessings of Liberty to ourselves and our posterity."

In the preceding chapters we have concentrated on the *structure* of our federal system and how government institutions are organized and operate. In the next several chapters we will focus on what the national government *does*, how voters, interest groups, and institutions (Congress, the White House, the entire executive branch, the courts) all interact to provide for the common defense and promote the general welfare. We will be talking about making and implementing public policy. **Public policy** is what a government does; it can also be what a government decides not to do. Although in this chapter the focus will be upon making and implementing economic policy, these introductory comments are applicable as well to the three policy-making chapters that follow.

MAKING PUBLIC POLICY

Thousands of individuals work in Washington in the policy-making process. They have come to be known by the slang name of "policy wonks." One of the most fascinating aspects of Washington politics is the way these policy activists in different branches of government and nongovernmental organizations (research institutes, foundations, the media) join forces. These policy subsystems grow up around interrelated issues. Formal titles are less important to participation in the group than information, imagination, energy, and persistence. Activists learn how to capture support from members of Congress and senior White House aides who are often looking for new ideas.[1] Important players include White House staff and executive branch officials, senior congressional committee staff, lobbyists, professional political consultants, and unelected policy specialists who have served long periods within a given policy area and in a variety of governmental or nongovernmental positions. Also influential are journalists and TV pundits. "Policy wonks" help clarify issues, resolve conflicts, and facilitate cooperation across institutions. Only by understanding their backgrounds, values, and roles can we appreciate the intricacies of national policy making.

Much scholarly work on policy issues is performed at "think tanks" such as the Brookings Institution, the John F. Kennedy School of Government at Harvard University, and the Institute of Governmental Studies at the University of California at Berkeley. Conservative-oriented ones such as the Heritage Foundation, Cato Institute, American Enterprise Institution, and the Hoover Institution, and liberal-oriented ones such as the Institute for Policy Studies, Center for Responsive Politics, Center for Law and Social Policy also play a role. Scholars and analysts at these think tanks write books, prepare studies and reports, and make their findings available to decision makers and the general public.

Stages in the Policy-Making Process

There are numerous approaches to the study of public policy making. The choice of which approach is most appropriate depends on what policies are being considered, the particular stage of the process selected for analysis, and the analyst's

Approaches to the Study of Public Policy

Despite their limitations, policy models help us to understand some of the complexities of policy making. At least four approaches have been used to study policy making:

1. *Rational Person Model.* A policy is adopted if its benefits, broadly defined, outweigh its costs. "The rationalist model requires an awareness of alternative courses of action, knowledge of the likely consequences of each alternative, substantial theoretical understanding of causal mechanisms, and choice among the alternatives on the basis of well-defined criteria."* This model is often called the *rational choice model.*

2. *Power Elite Model.* Businesses and wealthy individuals have a "privileged position" since politicians and the wealthy are mutually dependent for success. This approach advises that we should study government inaction as much as action.**

3. *Incremental Model.* Struggles for power among competing groups mean policy answers will be arrived at gradually. Our system of checks and balances promotes such a piece-meal approach to policy.†

4. *Policy Systems Model.* Policy "inputs," or the stages of the process, translate into "outputs," or laws. "The way policies are made affects the content of public policy."††

*Davis B. Bobrow and John S. Dryzek, *Policy Analysis by Design* (University of Pittsburgh Press, 1987), p. 11. See also Frances Fox Piven and Richard Cloward, *Regulating the Poor: The Functions of Public Welfare* (Vintage Books, 1971).

**C. Wright Mills made the classic statement of this view in *The Power Elite* (Oxford University Press, 1956).

†Charles E. Lindblom, *The Intelligence of Democracy: Decision-Making through Mutual Adjustment* (Free Press, 1965).

††Thomas R. Dye, *Understanding Public Policy,* 8th ed. (Prentice Hall, 1995), p. 25.

assumptions and political values. Nevertheless, the following distinct stages in the policy-making process can be identified.

- *Problem Identification*: What is the problem? How and by whom is the problem defined? How does the problem fit with existing policy categories and rankings of goals? Does the government need to help out, intervene, regulate, or make some kind of decision? Should the issue or problem even be placed on the government's agenda? What forces determine whether the problem will reach the attention of government officials? A variety of factors and people are involved in problem identification: events, crises, changes in expert opinion, changes in mass opinion, interest-group agitation, and greater involvement by elected officials and their staffs.

- *Policy Formulation*: What should be done? What alternatives should analysts consider? How can we best assess the alternatives? Who should be involved in the planning and design of the policy?

- *Policy Adoption*: Who needs to act? What branch of government should get involved? What constitutional, legal, or political requirements must be met? How specific or how general must the decision be? Should Congress or some regulatory body be asked to hold hearings on the matter and come up with recommendations? Or should the matter be turned over to the president, who can issue executive orders and deliver major addresses urging the public to comply?

- *Policy Implementation*: Once adopted, how should the policy be carried out? At what level of government—federal, state, local, or all three—will the policy be most effectively implemented? How much money should be spent, where, and how? How can the policy be administered effectively? How and by whom will the implementation of the policy be defined? During this stage policy is translated into practice. Congress often passes ambiguous legislation that conceals serious policy differences. As a result, agencies responsible for implementing the policy are given considerable latitude to translate vague ideas into specific directives.[2]

- *Policy Evaluation*: Is the policy working? How is the effectiveness of the policy measured? Who evaluates the policy? What are the consequences of policy evaluation and congressional oversight? Program supporters and administrators tend to exaggerate the success of their favorite programs to justify the funds allocated to them. On the other hand, an agency may build in delays and deficiencies during evaluation to hide the real cost of its operations. Evaluation is never entirely nonpolitical; it is sometimes used by one party, branch of government, department, or agency against another.[3]

The Importance of Nondecisions

Some matters of great importance do not even get on the public agenda. Matters like the inadequacies of our educational system and the unresolved problems of our cities fail to get the attention that some people think they deserve.[4] Indeed, there are many ways in which issues fail to reach the national political agenda, and one of the advantages of our federal system is that some issues are dealt with at the state and local level. However, "nondecisions" can occur at numerous places throughout the process of policy making. The absence of government activity does not necessarily mean government is without a policy in that area, for inaction is itself a policy. Inattention to an issue can be as important as decisive action. Thus governmental indifference to racial or sexual discrimination is clearly policy—very important policy for those affected by it.

In sum, every policy has political consequences, including doing nothing. Inaction by some policy makers often forces an issue to another part of the political system. All branches of the national government—as well as the bureaucracy, media, and interest groups—seem to take turns initiating policy changes.

MAKING FISCAL POLICY

Our national government unquestionably has tremendous economic power. But both soaring government spending and deficits have raised a number of questions about how effectively the government is doing its job. Through two types of policy—**fiscal policy** (taxing and spending) and **monetary policy** (control of the money supply)—the government attempts to manage the economy's ups and downs, moderating both while encouraging steady economic growth. This management power emerged earlier this century through such developments as the Federal Reserve System, the income tax, deficit spending, and the growth of government spending.

Does the government have the same direct control over the national economy that it has, say, over the military or national forests? No. Only if we had a socialized economy administered from Washington would we have a managed economy in that sense. In our capitalist economy, a great deal of power is left to private individuals and enterprises. Yet the government keeps a firm hand on many of the gears and levers that control not only the economy's general direction but the rate at which it moves. These controls are taxes, spending, and borrowing.

The federal government has been involved from its start in setting policies that have social and economic consequences. The Constitution grants Congress power to regulate interstate and foreign commerce. This role was later broadened to include the power to provide internal improvements such as roads, dams, and harbors, which eventually led to the establishment of the Second Bank of the United States. With the Industrial Revolution came the need to deal with monopolies, child labor, and workplace safety. The government's involvement in the economy grew dramatically as a result of the Great Depression. The scale of social and economic dislocation prompted a governmental response well beyond anything seen before. In many ways it was those events more than a half century ago that today shape the way we approach the making of social and economic policy.

Treasury Secretary Robert Rubin, a former Wall Street executive, is one of the president's foremost advisers on economic policy.

The Budget: Policy Blueprint

Of the two great instruments used to manage the economy we begin with fiscal policy—federal taxing and spending. The implementation of public policies requires money. Nothing reflects the growth of federal programs and the rise of big government more clearly than the increased spending by the national government. In 1933, the national government spent only $4 billion, about $30 per capita. In 1997 the respective figures are $1,635 billion, about $6,100 per capita.

Today federal, state, and local governments spend sums of money equal to about one-third of the income of all Americans, and the national government is the biggest spender of all, more than all state and local governments combined. With revenues of $1.495 billion and a national budget of about $1.635 billion for 1997, our national government annually spends 22 percent of the gross domestic product (GDP), or nearly one dollar out of every four. The national debt reached about $5.5 trillion in 1997, and we pay $238 billion each year in interest payments on that debt.[5]

Where the Money Comes From

"In this world," Benjamin Franklin once said, "nothing is certain but death and taxes." Tax collecting is one of the oldest activities of government. The federal government gets most of its funds from taxes (see Figure 18-1). Other moneys

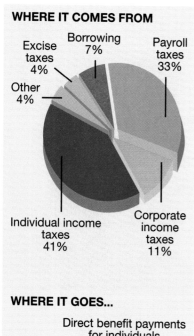

WHERE IT COMES FROM

Excise taxes 4%
Borrowing 7%
Payroll taxes 33%
Other 4%
Individual income taxes 41%
Corporate income taxes 11%

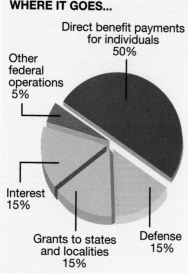

WHERE IT GOES...

Direct benefit payments for individuals 50%
Other federal operations 5%
Interest 15%
Grants to states and localities 15%
Defense 15%

FIGURE 18-1 **The Federal Government Dollar**

SOURCE: *Budget of the United States Government, Fiscal Year 1998* (Government Printing Office, 1997).

come from borrowing, special fees and fines, grants and gifts, and administrative and commercial revenues. Despite these other sources, most federal revenue is derived from personal and corporate income taxes and social insurance or payroll taxes (Social Security).

Putting power over taxation into the hands of the people was a major achievement in the development of self-government. "No taxation without representation" has been a battle cry the world over. The Constitution clearly provided that Congress "shall have Power To lay and collect Taxes, Duties, Imposts, and Excises." **Tariffs** (import duties) and **excise taxes** (consumer taxes on a specific kind of merchandise) have to be levied uniformly throughout the United States, while direct taxes other than income taxes have to be apportioned among the states according to population.

Raising money is only one objective of taxation. Regulation and, more recently, promoting economic growth are others. In a broad sense all taxation regulates human behavior. For example, a **progressive income tax**—by which people with high incomes generally pay larger fractions of their incomes than people with lower incomes—has a leveling tendency on incomes.

In the federal budget for fiscal year 1997, federal receipts include the following:

1. *Individual income taxes.* Taxes on individuals' incomes account for about 43 percent of the federal government's tax revenue, or 33 percent of the government's total revenue when you include borrowing. Over the years, the income tax has grown increasingly complex as Congress responded to claims for differing kinds of exemptions and rates, and simplification or even elimination of the income tax has been advocated by some politicians. The great advantage of the income tax is its flexibility.

2. *Corporate income taxes.* These account for just over 11 percent of the national government's tax revenues. As late as 1942, revenue from corporate income taxes exceeded that from individual income taxes.

3. *Social insurance receipts.* This is the second largest and most rapidly rising source of federal revenue, accounting for 33 percent of all federal revenue, not including borrowing. Most people pay more in Social Security taxes than in federal income taxes. These are highly **regressive taxes**, meaning that low-income people generally pay larger fractions of their income than do high-income people.

4. *Excise taxes.* These taxes account for roughly 4 percent of federal revenue. Federal taxes on liquor, tobacco, gasoline, telephones, air travel, and other so-called "luxury items" are projected to total about $60 billion in 1997.

5. *Customs duties and tariffs.* Although no longer the main source of federal income, in recent years these taxes provided an annual yield of almost $20 billion.

6. *Borrowing.* Since World War II, the government has regularly resorted to borrowing money to finance itself. Since 1969, the government has never had a surplus, and it has resorted to borrowing in 38 of the last 42 years. Roughly one in four dollars is raised by borrowing.[6]

The **deficit** is the difference between the revenues raised and the expenditures of government, including the interest on past borrowing in any one year. The deficit is not to be confused with the debt. The **debt** is the total of our deficits, minus our surpluses, over the years. Today, the total debt reaches into the trillions of dollars. Reducing the federal budget deficit has been a frequent refrain in presidential elections since 1992. In 1996 candidates Bill Clinton, Bob Dole, and Ross Perot each claimed he would be most effective at deficit reduction.

Where the Money Goes

Where does the money go? Much of it, of course, goes for benefit payments and national defense. In 1997, 16 percent went to national defense; 15 percent to interest on the national debt; 17 percent to grants for states and localities; 45 percent to direct benefit payments for individuals (such as Social Security, Medicare, Medicaid, and other major social programs), and 6 percent for all other federal operations (see Figure 18-1).

Another way of understanding how the money is spent is to consider federal outlays as a percentage of the nation's **gross domestic product (GDP)**, an estimate of the total output of all U.S. economic activity. **Gross national product (GNP)** was the standard measure of economic activity through the 1980s; gross domestic product is now preferred by economists because it more accurately gauges the American economic activity. In fiscal year 1997, our GDP was $7,819,900,000,000. Spending on domestic **entitlement programs**—programs such as Social Security, Medicare, and unemployment insurance to which qualified citizens are "entitled" by national legislation—now runs at about 11 percent of the GDP. Spending for defense is a little more than 3 percent of GDP; payments on the deficit make up another 3 percent of GDP, and nondefense discretionary spending is around 3.3 percent.

Years ago, federal revenues and outlays were so small that national taxing and spending had little impact on the overall economy. Today the federal government extracts billions of dollars from certain areas of the economy and pumps them back into others, with profound effects on the United States and world economies. Much of the federal budget is "uncontrollable" in the sense that "mandatory growth" in many programs is built into the law. These programs do not come up for annual review or decision by either the Congress or the president; they just keep on growing automatically. The most uncontrollable parts of the budget are Social Security, Medicare, unemployment benefits, outstanding contracts, and other fiscal obligations. The most controllable part of the budget is defense spending. With the collapse of the Soviet Union, real cuts in defense spending were anticipated, but military expenses for peacekeeping and humanitarian aid wiped out most of the expected "peace dividend."

The Budget Process

Before the Budget and Accounting Act of 1921, each executive agency dealt with Congress on its own, requesting that Congress appropriate funds for its activities with no presidential coordination. In 1921 the Bureau of the Budget (changed to the Office of Management and Budget in 1970) was created in the Treasury Department, and for the first time, the executive branch presented one budget to Congress.

THE EXECUTIVE BRANCH The federal government's fiscal year begins on October 1. The budget process begins nearly two years in advance, when the various departments and agencies estimate their needs and propose their budgets to the president.[7] While Congress is debating the budget for the coming fiscal year, the agencies are making estimates for the year after that (see Table 18-1). Agency officials take into account not only their needs as they see them but also the overall presidential program and the probable reactions of Congress. Departmental budgets are detailed; they include estimates on expected needs for personnel, supplies, office space, and the like.

The **Office of Management and Budget (OMB)**, a staff agency of the president, handles the next phase. Budget examiners in the OMB review each agency budget and bring it into line with the president's overall plans. Executive branch

GNP and GDP

National output is the total amount of goods and services produced by a country and is measured either by *gross national product* (GNP) or *gross domestic product* (GDP). GNP measures *all* output attributed to labor or property supplied by residents of the United States. A manufacturing plant in Singapore owned by the United States would increase GNP, but a Japanese-owned automobile plant located in the United States would not. On the other hand, GDP is the total amount of goods and services produced *domestically*—regardless of ownership. In this case, the automobile plant would count toward GDP; the manufacturing plant in Singapore would not. GDP is now the preferred measure of domestic economic activity.

TABLE 18-1
Major Steps in the Budget Process

February–December 1995	Formulation of the President's budget for Fiscal 1997.	Executive Branch agencies develop requests for funds and submit them to the Office of Management and Budget. The President reviews the requests and makes the fiscal decisions on what goes in his budget.
December 1995–February/March 1996*	Budget preparation and transmittal.	The budget documents are prepared and transmitted to the Congress.
March–September 1996	Congressional action on the budget.	The Congress reviews the President's proposed budget, develops its own budget, and approves spending and revenue bills.
October 1, 1996	The fiscal year begins.	
October 1, 1996–September 30, 1997	Agency program managers execute the budget provided in law.	
October–November 1997	Data on actual spending and receipts for the completed fiscal year become available.	

*Due to unusual circumstances the president submitted the 1997 budget in two steps—one in February, the other in March.

hearings are then held to give agency people a chance to clarify and defend their estimates. The OMB director and staff often prune the agencies' requests severely.

Finally, the OMB director goes to the president with a single, consolidated set of estimates of both revenue and expenditures—the product of perhaps a year's work. The president takes several days to review these figures and make adjustments. The budget director also helps the president prepare a budget message that will stress key aspects of the budget and tie it to broad national goals. The president must submit the budget recommendations and accompanying message to Congress between the first Monday in January and the first Monday in February. The president's budget covers thousands of pages.

THE LEGISLATIVE BRANCH   Presidential submission of a budget proposal is only the beginning. Under our Constitution, Congress must appropriate the funds and raise the taxes, but the president also plays a role, since all appropriation and tax proposals are subject to a presidential veto. Thus the White House is an active participant in the congressional budget battles. When Congress acts on the budget, it does so by first approving the overall budget resolution. The actual appropriation of funds for programs that are not permanently authorized goes through 13 different bills, each of which is presented to the president for his approval.

In 1974 Congress adopted the Budget Reform Act to give Congress a more effective role in the budget process. This act specifies that when submitting proposals, the president must include proposed changes in tax laws, estimates of amounts of revenue lost through existing preferential tax treatments, and five-year estimates of the costs of new and continuing federal programs. The act also calls on the president to seek authorizing legislation for a program a year before asking Congress to fund it.

13 Appropriations Bills Submitted by 13 Subcommittees

1. Agriculture, Rural Development, and Related Agencies
2. Commerce, Justice, State and the Judiciary
3. Defense
4. District of Columbia
5. Energy and Water Development
6. Foreign Operations
7. Interior
8. Labor, Health and Human Services, and Education
9. Legislative Branch
10. Military Construction
11. Transportation
12. Treasury, Postal Service, and General Government
13. Veterans Administration, Housing and Urban Development, and independent agencies

THE DEFICIT

When ordinary people are faced with emergency expenses, they borrow money. The same is true of governments. During past military and economic crises, our federal government went heavily into debt; it engaged in *deficit spending*. But recently, we have also incurred great debts during a period of peace with a relatively healthy economy. The federal government borrowed $23 billion during World War I, about $13 billion during the Great Depression of the 1930s, and $200 billion during World War II. As of 1998, the estimated total federal debt is about $5.75 trillion. Each individual's share of the national debt now exceeds $19,603.

Borrowing costs money. Although the federal government can borrow at a relatively low rate, the interest on the federal debt is more than $225 billion a year. The federal government borrows from investors who buy treasury notes, treasury bills, and U.S. savings bonds. These investors include individuals (foreign and domestic), U.S. government accounts, banks, and other investors.

The size of the debt and the interest payments alarm many Americans. How long can we allow the debt to grow at this rate? When dealing with this question, keep two considerations in mind. First, the government owes roughly 90 percent of the money to its own citizens rather than to foreign governments or investors, although the amount owed to foreigners is growing. Second, the economic strength and resources of the country are more significant than the size of the debt. Still, interest payments on the debt are a cause for concern.

Why do we have huge annual deficits? These deficits are not the result of a weak economy, and they apparently cannot be cured simply by economic growth. The fact is that the United States is committed to spending more for defense and domestic programs than current tax revenues can provide, even though the economy is running at relatively full capacity. By tolerating unprecedented deficits in the 1980s, the Reagan administration was able to "create an austere political climate in which proposed cuts, not expected increases, became the focus of discussions about federal domestic programs."* These budgetary limitations obviously carried over to the Bush and Clinton administrations.

*Paul E. Peterson, "The New Politics of Deficits," in *New Directions in American Politics*, eds. John Chubb and Paul E. Peterson (Brookings Institution, 1985), p. 365.

Presidents and Their Deficits (in billions)

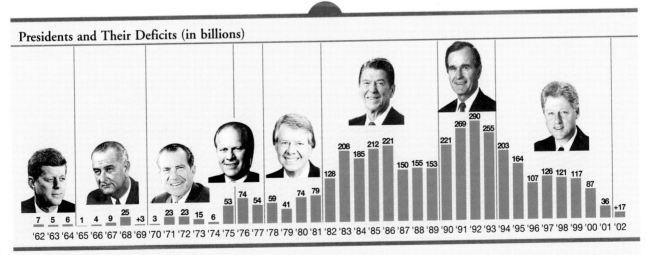

SOURCE: Greg Hester, *Los Angeles Times*, February 7, 1997, p. A20.

During the 1996 budget battles between the president and Congress, Speaker Gingrich and former Senate Majority Leader Bob Dole threatened to shut down the government to force President Clinton to agree to a balanced budget in seven years.

The 1974 Budget Reform Act also created the **Congressional Budget Office (CBO)**, which gave Congress its own independent agency to prepare budget data and analyze budgetary issues. By February 15 of each year, the CBO furnishes its analysis of the presidential recommendations to the House and Senate Budget Committees. The CBO also provides Congress with biannual forecasts of the economy, analyzes alternative fiscal policies, prepares five-year cost estimates for carrying out any bills proposed by congressional committees, and undertakes studies requested by committees. The CBO also keeps score for Congress by monitoring the results of congressional action on individual appropriations and revenues against the targets or ceilings specified by legislation.

The Gramm-Rudman-Hollings Act (1985), as modified by the 1990 Budget Enforcement Act, calls for Congress to adopt a **concurrent resolution** for the next fiscal year by April 15. This resolution sets levels of new budget authority and spending, which become the ceiling limits for the appropriations committees. Congress may adopt a budget resolution later that revises or reaffirms the earlier resolution.

In recent years Congress has been resorting to what is called **reconciliation**, in which Congress, by a budget resolution, sets ceilings on what the various appropriations subcommittees can appropriate and then leaves the discretion of deciding how to achieve the required limits to the committees.

In the 1985 Gramm-Rudman-Hollings Act, Congress also established a procedure designed to gradually reduce the federal deficit to zero. Under this procedure, if it appears that there will be a deficit beyond a stipulated level, then across-the-board cuts in discretionary spending are put into effect automatically and become the ceiling limits for the Appropriations Committees. It is important to note that the fastest growing part of the budget—entitlement spending—is exempt from the Gramm-Rudman caps. Hence no automatic cuts are permitted in Social Security, Medicare, interest on the national debt, veterans' compensation, veterans' pensions, unemployment assistance, and student loans.

THE GENERAL ACCOUNTING OFFICE   After Congress appropriates money, it checks on the way that money is being spent by two major methods: (1) congressional committees hold oversight hearings in which they call on agency heads to explain how they have spent the money; (2) Congress works through the **General Accounting Office (GAO)**, which uses spot sampling to check vouchers and make audits in the field.[8] The GAO is headed by the **comptroller general**, who is appointed by the president with the approval of the Senate for a 15-year term. Although the comptroller general has the authority to disallow expenditures, approval is no longer needed for the disbursement of funds. In the past 20 years, the GAO has taken on broader responsibilities in investigating and evaluating programs by checking on the adequacy and effectiveness, as well as the honesty, of a program's performance.[9]

The Politics of Taxing and Spending

One function of taxes is to decide who shall pay how much to finance the government. In practice, however, tax legislation has also sought to promote economic growth and to reward certain types of behavior, such as owning a home, contributing to charities, and investing in high-risk but desirable (from a national standpoint) energy or housing ventures. Cynics suggest, too, that from a member of Congress's point of view, tax legislation has the additional and important function of raising campaign funds. As long as tax legislation is under consideration in Congress, swarms of lobbyists are eager to attend expensive campaign dinners and contribute generously to campaign coffers.[10]

THE TAX BURDEN No one likes taxes. Most of us complain that our tax load is too heavy and that someone else is not paying a fair share. People with high incomes that put them in the highest tax brackets naturally grumble. People with low incomes complain that even a low tax may deprive them of the necessities of life. People with middle incomes consider their situation the worst of all. Their incomes are not high, but their taxes are.

What is the best type of tax? Some say a *progressive income tax*, also called a *graduated income tax*. It is relatively easy to collect, hits hardest those who are most able to pay, and hardly touches those at the bottom of the income ladder. Others argue that *excise taxes* are the fairest because they are paid by people who spend money for luxury goods and thus obviously have money to spare. Further, by discouraging people from buying expensive goods, excise taxes occasionally have a deflationary effect when prices are on the rise. On the other hand, excise taxes are more expensive to collect than income taxes. In some cases, such as the tax on tobacco, they may hit the poor the hardest. Excise taxes also face strong resistance from affected industries: tobacco, liquor, and airlines, for example. An excise tax on yachts passed by Congress in 1990 but repealed in 1993 had the unintended consequence of putting several thousand yacht builders out of business.[11]

The most controversial tax is a general **sales tax**, which is levied by almost all states on the sale of most goods, sometimes exempting food and drugs. Labor and liberal organizations see sales taxes as *regressive*, meaning that because a sales tax is the same for all persons, these taxes are not related to a taxpayer's ability to pay. Poor persons pay a higher percentage of their income in sales taxes for the goods and services they buy than do rich ones. Proponents of a national sales tax stress its potential anti-inflationary effect and point to its successful use in a number of states.

The sales tax is exclusively a state and local tax in the United States, but in Europe a similar tax, a **value-added tax (VAT)**, is used to raise revenues for national governments. The VAT differs from a sales tax in that it collects a tax on the increased value of a product *at each stage of production and distribution* rather than just at the point of sale, as with a sales tax. A loaf of bread would thus have value added at each stage of production: the farmer would pay a value-added tax on the grain before selling to the miller, who would be taxed before selling to the

Budgetary Language

- **Authorization:** Congress decides that the activity authorized is a necessary and desirable thing for the federal government to be doing. When it authorizes a program, usually for a fixed term of five years, it also sets limits on the amount that may be spent annually.

- **Appropriation:** Congress decides how much money will be spent each year for authorized programs.

- **Budget authority:** Congress's authorization legislation sets the amount that may be spent for certain programs; what the government actually spends is an *outlay*. For example, the law may authorize spending $3 billion for two aircraft carriers. Congress will then appropriate $1 billion in budgetary authority, which will take five years to spend. In the first year, Congress may make an outlay of $200 million.

- **Budget resolution:** Congress passes a budget resolution that sets ceilings for total spending and sets limits within budget categories.

- **Discretionary spending:** Roughly one-third of all federal spending, which the president and Congress deal with each year through 13 annual appropriations bills.

- **Mandatory spending:** Authorized by law, not by the 13 annual appropriations bills. This federal spending is *uncontrollable* unless the president and Congress act each year. Social Security, Medicare, and interest on the national debt are examples.

- **Continuing resolution (CR):** If Congress and the president are unable to agree on the budget by October 1, the beginning of the fiscal year, Congress must pass a continuing resolution to keep the money flowing so that the federal government can continue to operate.

- **Caps:** If the estimated deficit for a fiscal year exceeds specific maximum amounts for budget items, or caps, across-the-board cuts are supposed to go into effect, but Congress is free to lift these caps. In 1995 Congress established caps and set a target date for a zero deficit by 2002.

- **Off budget:** Some programs are not carried in the annual budget but are put into a separate trust account and then paid out from it, such as Social Security and the Postal Service.

- **Ways and Means Committee:** The House committee that has jurisdiction over raising revenues.

- **Senate Finance Committee:** The Senate committee that has jurisdiction over raising revenues.

- **Senate and House Budget Committees:** The committees that have jurisdiction over the concurrent resolutions setting caps in the annual budget.

- **Senate and House Appropriations Committees:** The committees that process the 13 appropriations bills.

The 1986 Tax Reform Bill

As finally passed, the tax reform package embraced the following principles:

- Simplify the tax process.
- Make it more fair.
- Lower the marginal tax rates for individuals.
- Slightly increase the tax burden on corporations.
- Encourage productive investments while discouraging wasteful investments in the economy.

In the end, Congress reduced the number of tax brackets from 15 to 2, raised personal and standard deductions slightly, repealed scores of previously existing deductions, and limited certain other tax breaks. For example, in the past, when a businessperson took a customer to lunch, the entire expense used to be deductible; after the tax reform, only 80 percent of the cost was deductible. Medical expenses and state and local sales taxes that were once deductible were only partially deductible after the 1986 tax reforms.

Many business groups fought vigorously to stop the reduction of business deductions, especially on investment credits, which they had enjoyed under the previous tax code. Although they were successful in fighting off some of the proposed changes, businesses were defeated on many of the tax expenditures granted under earlier tax laws.

baker, and so forth. The value-added tax is seen by some as a way to infuse a large amount of new revenue into the federal government. Opponents of the tax see it as regressive and increasing the tax burden. States see a federal VAT as invading their turf, since most states assess sales taxes. Since it taxes consumption and not savings, a VAT could have the effect of encouraging savings and investment, both of which are vital to economic growth. Obviously, the kinds of taxes a government imposes have policy implications.

THE ANTITAX MOVEMENT The United States has experienced many tax revolts, from the one that helped spark the American Revolution in the 1770s to those of the present day. The agenda of American politics was altered by the tax revolt of the 1970s, the supply-side experiment of Ronald Reagan in the early 1980s, and the partisan deadlock on taxes and spending issues in the 1990s. The political context of the fight over taxes and deficit spending may be even more important than the economic theories that are often given as reasons for one policy or another.

Voters in one state set the tax agenda for the entire nation when they passed a tax limitation in June 1978. That was Proposition 13, a citizen initiative to lower and permanently cap property taxes in California. Similar measures had been on the ballot before and were routinely defeated, but by approving Proposition 13, Californians made tax cuts a central issue in the 1978 and 1980 elections. Tax limitation measures like Proposition 13 were later approved in scores of states and localities, and the success of the issue at the local level gave antitax activists at the national level renewed energy.

The antitax sentiment became a central issue of Ronald Reagan's 1980 presidential campaign. He promised a 30 percent reduction in income taxes, phased in over a three-year period. Once elected, Reagan made cutting taxes his highest priority. In a stunning victory over the House Democratic leadership, he got almost all of what he wanted in 1981. He had promised the country that by cutting taxes and government spending in nondefense areas, he could stimulate the economy and fund his other priority—national defense. This policy, dubbed "Reaganomics," was based in part on the theory of *supply-side economics*, which holds that production can be stimulated by cutting taxes and reducing government regulation.

Reaganomics did not stimulate economic growth enough to work as promised, but few question that it worked politically. Since the tax cut in 1981, the agenda of American politics has largely been to reduce spending in hopes of reducing the high federal budget deficits. Hence the Democrats, who typically would want to propose new or expanded government programs, have been placed on the defensive; today, new programs or policies need to be either inexpensive or their costs shifted to state or local governments. As a result, the legislative and executive branches of government blame each other for the growing federal debt, with neither willing to risk the voters' wrath by proposing a tax increase. The easier political course is to accept higher and higher levels of debt—or deficit spending—while directing the blame at someone else.

Tax Reform

Talk of tax reform occurs every few years as people complain that our tax system is unfair and confusing and that it is not doing what it is supposed to do. In 1986, after a major political battle, Congress enacted and the president signed into law a new tax system that brought more changes to the tax code than any reform in the previous 70 years.

Even though overall tax rates came down, the taxable income base was increased by the elimination of many deductions, or what are technically called tax expenditures. **Tax expenditures** are government revenue losses due to provisions of federal tax laws that provide special tax incentives or benefits to individuals and businesses. These benefits, which now total more than $400 billion, come from special exclusions, exemptions, or reductions from gross income or from special credits, preferential tax rates, or deferrals of tax liability. Tax expenditures are one means by which the national government carries out public policy objectives. In most cases, they can be considered an alternative to a direct-spending program. For example, the government encourages investment in research and development by allowing such costs to be deducted from a company's taxes. A program of direct federal grants could also achieve this objective. One of the largest tax expenditures permits persons buying a home to deduct the mortgage interest from their taxes. In 1997, this deduction amounted to $57 billion in tax expenditures.[12]

Critics assert that the rich get their "welfare" through tax loopholes and tax expenditures. This form of "welfare" does not require a visible appropriation of money—one plainly identified as such in the budget. However meritorious the objective of tax expenditures are—encouraging home ownership, research and development, retirement savings—these tax benefits are a cost to government that does not benefit all levels of society. In many instances, they cause investors to waste their resources on low-yield investments that carry large tax benefits; meanwhile, high-yield investments without such benefits go unfunded. "The result is reduced national output, lower productivity, and sluggish economic growth."[13]

Did the new tax system make much of a difference? Most observers hailed the 1986 legislation as a notable improvement over the old system. But nothing prevented the political process that produced the previous system from starting over again. Shortly after the tax reform was passed, Milton Friedman, a well-known conservative economist, reminded us, "As lobbyists get back to action, and as members of Congress try to raise campaign funds, old loopholes will be reintroduced and new ones invented, and tax rates will start creeping up to offset the resulting loss of revenue."[14]

Tax reformers in Congress play upon concern about the constantly escalating national debt and the way that it is crowding social and environmental programs out of the budget.

The Clinton Tax Policy

Bill Clinton made the economy the centerpiece of his 1992 campaign. He promised a middle-class tax cut as well as major spending cuts, but Clinton and the Democrats in Congress raised taxes in 1993 by $357 billion. Perhaps the most unpopular part of Clinton's budget was the decision to raise additional revenue by making the tax increase on the rich retroactive to the beginning of 1993, more than seven months before it became law. The constitutionality of this action was challenged by several Republicans and some Democrats, although the Supreme Court had upheld similar retroactive tax increases in the past. The Senate needed the tie-breaking vote of Vice-President Al Gore for the package to pass. Clinton's budget plan passed strictly along party lines and by the slimmest possible margin. The House passed the package 218 to 216, with all Republicans and 40 Democrats voting against the plan. This was "the first time in postwar congressional history and possibly the first time ever that the majority party has passed major legislation with absolutely no support from the opposition."[15] The vote carried strong implications for Clinton's chances of reelection. If the economy went down, the Republicans could say, "I told you so." If the economy made a strong recovery, as it did, the Democrats could take the credit, as they did.

The Republicans made the economy a main issue in 1994, and many attributed the Republican victory in taking control of both houses of Congress in that year to the Clinton tax increases. Two years later the economy was strong, and Clinton and the Democrats argued in the 1996 election campaign that it was because of their tax program. The Republicans countered that the Democratic tax policies had stifled economic growth.

"Here, take this before Clinton gets his hands on it."

Drawing by Schoenbaum. © 1993 The New Yorker Magazine, Inc.

The 1996 Election and Tax Policy

During his 36 years in the Senate, Bob Dole made his reputation as a "budget hawk," openly skeptical of the Reagan supply-side wing of his party. Dole had been doubtful that a tax cut could produce enough economic growth to counterbalance the deficits caused by lost revenue. Still, as the Republican candidate for president in 1996, he proposed a tax cut that over six years was supposed to provide a $551 billion reduction in revenues. He proposed a 15 percent reduction in tax rates for all taxpayers, a 50 percent reduction in capital gains, and a $500 per child tax credit to lower- and middle-income families. Dole also promised spending cuts in many areas except defense. To strengthen his tax position, he selected as his vice-presidential running mate Jack Kemp, a longtime supply-side advocate within the Republican party.

Clinton not only criticized the Dole proposals as guaranteeing skyrocketing deficits and increasing interest rates and inflation, but he also reemphasized his early proposals to provide targeted tax cuts for families to support education, a deduction of up to $10,000 to cover tuition for college, and an actual tax credit of up to $1,500 to attend a community college.

The 1996 elections were thus essentially a referendum on tax policy. As a result of Clinton's reelection in 1996 and the increased number of Democrats serving in Congress, tax policy in the remaining years of this century is more likely to reflect the Clinton rather than the Dole proposals. However, the startling fact is that, sooner or later, the nation will have to face the increasing costs of major entitlement programs such as Social Security and Medicare, which will call for either more dramatic and drastic reductions in these programs or larger increases in taxes than has proved to be politically possible in recent decades.

The Balanced Budget Amendment

The apparent inability of the federal government to balance its budget has led many politicians and some economists to propose that a balanced budget be constitutionally mandated. A proposed Balanced Budget Amendment would require Congress to adopt a budget in which projected spending is no larger than projected tax receipts. In addition, such an amendment would limit the increase in taxes (or spending or both) in any fiscal year to the percentage increase in the GDP during the previous calendar year. The amendment would have two escape clauses: Congress could waive the requirements of the amendment by a vote of three-fifths of all members of both houses, and the provisions of the amendment would not apply in any year in which a war has been declared.

Advocates of a Balanced Budget Amendment claim that it is necessary to correct what they call the "spending bias" that currently exists in government decision making and to reduce the large budget deficit from past years. They argue that well-organized, powerful, and heavily financed interest groups overwhelm relatively weak taxpayer lobbies and regularly win on spending measures in Congress.

Opponents of a Balanced Budget Amendment say it would reduce the flexibility of economic policy makers and virtually eliminate fiscal policy as a tool for managing the economy. In times of economic downturn, government spending in excess of revenues should increase employment, generate investment, stimulate demand, prevent a recession from deepening into a depression, or respond to natural disasters. If a balanced budget were adopted, Congress might resort to subterfuges, "pretending" it would have balanced the books. Opponents also say it would be unwise to insert an economic theory into the Constitution, which should be, they contend, a broad charter of fundamental principles of governance, not a document with specific theories of economic management. The Balanced Budget Amendment would clearly change the "rules of the game" and make it easier for social and economic conservatives to win more legislative battles. More voting support would be required to adopt new programs, and some programs would require a three-fifths majority in Congress for the appropriation of money.

The Balanced Budget Amendment enjoys widespread public support in opinion polls. It came before Congress several times in the 1990s and came very close to getting the necessary two-thirds vote needed for a constitutional amendment to be presented to the states for ratification. The Republican party endorsed it in its 1996 platform, and Bob Dole made it a major item in his presidential campaign. Because of strong public support and because the Republicans picked up two additional Senate seats in the 1996 elections, Dole's defeat does not end the matter. In fact, it is likely that a Balanced Budget Amendment will be proposed by Congress. However, if Congress and the president achieve a balanced budget, that could take some of the steam out of the drive for a constitutional amendment.

The Item Veto

In 1996, after years of debate, Congress passed and President Clinton signed into law the **item veto**, which was to take effect starting in 1997. The bill permits the president to strike specific items from the budget passed by Congress. Governors in 43 states have this power, sometimes called the *line item veto*. Since the federal budget is not itemized by line like many state budgets, the new veto power given to the president is called the item veto. Congress granted the president the item veto power through a statute rather than a constitutional amendment, which means that Congress may at some future date decide it does not want the president to have this power and overturn the statute.

The president may not lower appropriations for specific items to his preferred amount; he must either keep or reject the appropriation for the specific item. Existing entitlement programs like Medicare and Social Security are exempt from the item veto, but the president could apply the item veto to new entitlement programs. The item veto could be used to eliminate tax breaks enacted by Congress that affect 100 or fewer individual taxpayers or ten or fewer businesses.

If the president strikes an item in the budget, such as a new entitlement program or a tax break for a small group, Congress can restore spending provisions or tax breaks by passing new legislation within 30 days. The president would be able to veto those measures, but his veto would be subject to the same override procedures as other vetoes—a two-thirds vote of both houses of Congress.[16]

Advocates of an item veto, including Bill Clinton and recent former presidents, contend that the reform will discourage "pork-barrel" spending since a president will not have to eliminate an entire appropriations bill to get rid of a few objectionable sections.[17] The idea is not new; Ulysses S. Grant advocated an item veto in 1873. The item veto is available to most governors, and proponents assert that the process must be working at the state level because no state that adopted it has abandoned it. Governors have also generally felt that it is an important bargaining tool with the legislature.[18]

Opponents of the change, like Senator Robert Byrd of West Virginia, term the law a "colossal mistake."[19] They argue that this measure muddies the waters of separation of powers too much, allowing a president excessive control over Congress. Congressional leadership has long tacked items the president may not want onto legislation that he does want to force him to accept them. The item veto enhances presidential power and diminishes Congress's constitutional control over spending. Some argue that the item veto will inevitably lead to more presidential vetoes. Instead of presidents bargaining with Congress over the content of legislation, they may wait until the legislation has been passed and simply veto provisions they don't like. It may also mean that legislators will lobby the president to veto parts of bills

Thinking It Through

Though it is easy to chastise the government for fiscal irresponsibility, it is difficult to pare down entrenched programs. Most people have a close family member who is dependent upon Social Security or a relative who is in the armed services. Real cuts are hard to make when they cause the loss of jobs or lower someone's standard of living. And with our crumbling infrastructure, crucial needs in public education, and demands to improve the environment, cuts in those areas are a political liability.

The deficit forces the United States to pay more than $230 billion a year in interest alone, and servicing the debt forces interest rates higher, thus stifling economic activity. In 1998, 35 cents of every dollar of personal income tax paid to Washington will go to pay interest on the national debt.

A BALANCING ACT

Republicans and Democrats alike have been concentrating on getting the federal budget into balance by the year 2002. In May 1997, President Clinton and congressional leaders agreed to a plan to achieve that goal and even produce a surplus of $17 billion by 2002. But the question remains: What about 2003 and beyond? The real problem comes when members of the baby-boom generation start to reach retirement age around 2008, and the costs of Medicare, Medicaid, and Social Security begin to explode.

Robert D. Reischauer, a Brooking Institution budget expert who headed the Congressional Budget Office (CBO) from 1989 to 1995, warned that unless lawmakers made far more sweeping changes than Clinton proposed, the deficit would come back after 2002 with a vengeance. CBO figures show that barring a major restructuring, the deficit would mushroom from zero in 2002 to 4.5 percent of the gross domestic product by 2010 and 9.5 percent by 2025.

Federal Reserve Chairman Alan Greenspan cautioned that while eliminating the deficit by 2002 would be laudable, "It is far more important that it be achieved in a manner which implies balance [in later] years as well." Frank Raines, the new director of the Office of Management and Budget, maintained that after 2020, the budget would run a small surplus through 2050 and beyond.

SOURCE: Steven Findlay, *USA Today*, February 7, 1997, p. 6A.

The Annual Federal Deficit (in billions)

Spending Projections under the Clinton Budget (in billions)

Category	1996	1997	1998
Social Security	$350	$368	$384
Defense	$266	$267	$259
Net interest	$241	$247	$250
Income security	$226	$239	$247
Medicare	$174	$194	$207
Health	$119	$128	$138
Education, training, employment and social services	$52	$51	$56
Veterans' benefits and services	$37	$40	$41
Transportation	$40	$39	$39
Administration of justice	$18	$21	$24
Natural resources/environment	$22	$23	$22
Science, space, technology	$17	$17	$16
International affairs	$13	$15	$15
General government	$12	$13	$13
Agriculture	$9	$10	$12
Community, regional development	$11	$13	$11
Commerce and housing credit	-$11	-$9	$3
Energy	$3	$2	$2
Offsetting receipts	-$38	-$46	-$56
Total	**$1,560**	**$1,631**	**$1,687**

SOURCE: Office of Management and Budget. Amounts may not jibe with totals because of rounding.

they don't like but could not persuade Congress to change. Finally, opponents contend that there is little data for evaluation of the item veto across the states,[20] and that "the transferability of this experience to the federal sector is limited."[21]

Senator Byrd, joined by others from Congress, has sought to have the courts declare the item veto an unconstitutional violation of the doctrine of separation of powers. A federal district judge has agreed with them, and the matter will be decided by the Supreme Court. Even if the Supreme Court upholds the measure—and it will be close—as the president and Congress test this new procedure and apply it to actual legislation, the federal courts will be called upon to be the arbiters of this new separation-of-powers battle.[22]

MAKING MONETARY POLICY

The other chief way the national government affects the economy is through monetary policy. The core element of **monetarism** is the idea that prices, income, and economic stability are primarily a function of growth in the money supply. Monetarists contend the money supply is the key factor affecting the economy's performance. They argue that there should be restrained yet steady growth in the money supply, enough to encourage solid economic growth but not inflation.

Tightening the money supply can slow inflation, but that in turn can lead to a recession. This is what happened in the early 1980s as the Federal Reserve Board, with encouragement from the Reagan administration, tried to slow inflation. The result was a long and deep recession that seemed to succeed, at least temporarily, in reducing inflationary pressures. As inflation went down, unemployment went up, reaching double-digit levels.

The Federal Reserve System

Monetary policy is not made by either Congress or the president but by the **Federal Reserve System**, most especially its Open Market Committee. The members of that committee, some of the most powerful people in the United States, have a lot to say about how much interest you pay on the car you are buying and whether you refinance your home because of lower interest rates. They can stimulate the economy so that it could be easier for you to find a job, or slow it down so that it could be harder. Who are these people with so much power, and how do they influence economic policy?

The Federal Reserve System, or "The Fed," as it is called, consists of a chair and six other members of the Board of Governors that sit in Washington and are appointed by the president with the consent of the Senate for 14-year terms, with one member's term expiring every two years. These long, staggered terms for members of the board are designed to insulate them from politics as much as possible. There are 12 Regional Federal Reserve Banks, each headed by a president, with a nine-member board of directors chosen from the private banking business in that district.

The Federal Open Market Committee, known as the FOMC, is made up of all 7 members of the Board of Governors plus the presidents of the Reserve Banks. At any point in time, only 5 of the 12 presidents serve as voting members, although all participate fully in each meeting. The president of the New York district serves as a permanent voting member, while the other presidents rotate annually.[23]

The 12 members of the Federal Open Market Committee are all professional economists or bankers, most of whose names are unfamiliar to most people. Yet this group, which meets about every six to eight weeks, decides how much money will be allowed to enter the economy, manages foreign currency operations, and regulates banks. It does this by buying and selling government securities, which can encourage either lower or higher interest rates. Other lenders closely watch the

The Federal Reserve System

The Board of Governors

Helps carry out policy for regulating the supply of money and credit

Conducts open market operations through the purchase and sale of government securities

Sets reserve requirements for the depository institutions

Sets the discount rate on its loans to banks

Makes margin rules for purchases of securities on credit

Oversees major banks by regulating the nation's 6,441 bank holding companies

Inspects and regulates 982 state banks that are members of the Federal Reserve System

Monitors the economy

Deals with international monetary problems

Enforces consumer credit laws

Supervises Federal Reserve Banks

Federal Reserve Banks

Have responsibility for the amount of credit that may be used for purchasing or carrying equity securities

Act as lender of last resort to banks, savings associations, and credit unions in trouble

Keep reserves deposited by depository institutions

Regulate the U.S. activities of foreign banks and foreign activities of U.S. banks

Supply currency and coins to banks

Destroy worn-out bills and coins

Operate clearinghouses for checks

Serve as fiscal agents for the U.S. Treasury

Conduct domestic and foreign monetary operations through the New York Federal Reserve Bank as agents for the Federal Open Market Committee

SOURCE: *Seventy-eighth Annual Report of the Board of Governors of the Federal Reserve System, 1991* (Federal Reserve, 1992).

How the Fed Controls Inflation

1. The board sets the *discount rate*, the rate the Fed charges to lend money to banks. Raising rates is deflationary by increasing costs for money and credit; lowering rates is inflationary by decreasing the cost for money and credit.

2. The Fed's *open market operations* are its most flexible and important monetary policy tool. The Fed buys or sells federal bonds. Buying is deflationary by taking money and credit out of circulation; selling is inflationary by increasing money and credit in circulation. For example, if the Fed purchases $1 billion of government securities, the Fed pays for it by adding $1 billion to the reserve account that the security dealer keeps at the Fed, and the bank in turn credits the security dealer's account for that amount. As these funds are spent and respent, the stock of money and credit will increase by much more than the original $1 billion. If the Fed sells $1 billion, the amount is deducted from the security dealer's account, with less money flowing through the economy.

3. The Fed sets *reserve requirements* for nationally charted banks. Raising reserves is deflationary by reducing the funds banks have available to lend; decreasing reserves is inflationary by increasing funds banks have available to lend. The Fed seldom changes reserve requirements because such changes can have a dramatic effect on institutions and the economy.

SOURCE: "The Fed: Our Central Bank," the Federal Reserve System on the Internet (http://www.frbkc.or/infofrs/ifrsmain.htm).

From Coast to Coast

The Twelve Federal Reserve Districts

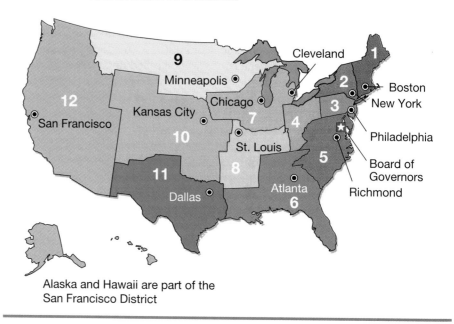

Alaska and Hawaii are part of the San Francisco District

decisions of the Fed and typically make their interest rates consistent with Fed decisions. As lenders make it either more or less expensive to borrow money, they influence a wide range of economic activity. The Fed is an independent central bank that controls how our economy operates.

The chair of the Board of Governors, by tradition an economist, is appointed by the president to a four-year term. The current chair, Alan Greenspan, is one of the most influential public policy officials. Greenspan was first appointed by President Bush and reappointed in 1996 by President Clinton. The reappointment of a chair, even one originally appointed by a president from another party, is not unusual. Because of the critical role played by the Fed, presidents understandably want someone sympathetic to their policies. The staff of the Federal Reserve System reports directly to the chair, not to the board, and the chair is the one who appears before the Congress and the country to explain the policies of the Federal Reserve System. The chair heads the Federal Open Market Committee and is credited or blamed for the decisions made by the Fed.

The role of the Fed is much debated. Some have blamed the Great Depression of the late 1920s and 1930s on the Fed because it did not reverse the sharp money supply decline that started in 1929.[24] Others point to the tight money policy of the Fed in the 1980s as effective in lowering inflation but deepening the recession.[25] Not surprisingly, the Fed often comes under pressure from Congress and the president to lower interest rates and stimulate the economy.

Note the map of the twelve federal reserve districts. At the time the system was established in 1913, these regional banks were located according to the population, economy, and politics of that time. As John R. Wilke has written, "Today, these locations make little sense. Missouri, once an economic and political power because of its riverboat economy, has two Fed Banks; booming Florida has none. California and its vast economy have only one Fed Bank—which also serves eight other states and covers 20 percent of the population."[26]

The twelve Fed Banks process one-third of the checks written in the United States, and the electronic network dollar volume of transfers is approaching $200 trillion annually.[27] Today there is no economic or technical need for so many banks, but since the Fed banks are even more independent from Congress than the Fed's Board of Governors in Washington, there is not likely to be any change in its basic structure. As its check-clearing business begins to be altered by competition from private clearinghouses, and as new technologies proliferate in the years ahead, Fed operations may come under closer scrutiny. But as one insider commented, "The market has changed, and the technology has changed . . . . [But] do we really want to fool around with the Fed's independence just to save a few hundred million dollars a year?"[28]

The Lessons of the Great Depression

Depression is a hard teacher, and the 1930s had a tremendous impact on American thinking about the role of government in the economy. Although we had experienced long, severe depressions before, for example in the 1870s and 1890s, the Great Depression that began in 1929 brought mass misery. "One vivid, gruesome moment of those dark days we shall never forget," wrote one observer. "We saw a crowd of some fifty men fighting over a barrel of garbage which had been set outside the back door of a restaurant. American citizens fighting for scraps of food like animals!"[29]

Despite the efforts of the Franklin Roosevelt administration to cope with the Depression, it hung on. Faint signs of recovery could be seen in the mid-1930s, but the recession of 1937–38 indicated that the country was by no means out of the woods. Between eight and nine million people were jobless in 1939. Then came World War II, and unemployment seemed cured. Millions of people had more income, more security, and higher standards of living. Lord Beveridge in England posed a question that bothered many thoughtful Americans: "Unemployment has been practically abolished twice in the lives of most of us—in the last war and in this war. Why does war solve the problem of unemployment which is so insoluble in peace?"[30] Worried that the economy might collapse after the war, thousands of people came up with plans to ensure jobs for all.

Although some people think the Great Depression resulted from mismanagement by the Federal Reserve System, others think the Depression lasted so long because the New Deal was hostile to business. Government intruded too long and too much into the economic life of the nation. Proponents of this theory urged the government to reduce spending, lower taxes, curb the power of labor, and generally leave business and the economy alone.

Another group said that the trouble with the New Deal was not that it had done too much, but that it had done too little. This group's thinking was deeply influenced by the work of English economist John Maynard Keynes.[31] In visits to the United States during the 1930s, Keynes warned that if people did not consume enough or invest enough, the national income would fall. The way to increase national income is to spend money on consumer goods (such as clothes or food or automobiles), on investment goods (education and dock facilities), or on both. Most important, in a recession government must do the spending and investing if private enterprise by itself will not or cannot.

Keynesian economics still influences government management of the economy; government takes responsibility for increasing aggregate demand by spending during business slumps and curbing spending during booms. Politically, Keynesian economics presents a problem. It is much easier to increase spending and government programs than it is to curb them. As a result, deficit spending has become the norm over the past 50 years. To stimulate demand, the government spends more money than it takes in. For many years, this policy was thought to be beneficial to the

Federal Reserve Chairman Alan Greenspan set the stock market fluctuating wildly with remarks about the "irrational enthusiasm" of investors.

economy. It was also convenient politically. However, the deficit has soared in recent years, and there have been no surpluses, even with economic growth.

Economists found that such policies, when accompanied by a loose-money policy by the Federal Reserve, resulted in a hidden cost: inflation. Because government programs introduced extra money into the economy without a corresponding increase in goods, each dollar became worth less, and prices rose to compensate. Although government spending is not responsible for all inflation, it has been a major contributor; as a result, new economic remedies have been sought.

Supply-Side Economics

Ronald Reagan preached an alternative to Keynesian economics, despite the fact that he, more than any other president, relied on deficit spending to encourage economic growth. He pledged to balance the budget by cutting both taxes and government spending—supply-side economics. In simple terms, **supply-side economics** holds that large cuts in taxes will inspire productive investment, so that the initial loss of federal revenues will be offset by the taxes generated from expanded private economic activity.

Once in office, President Reagan discovered it was easier to cut taxes than to cut spending, so in 1981 he pushed the largest tax cuts in our history through Congress. Critics of supply-side economics, including most economists, doubted tax cuts alone would result in the economic expansion necessary to generate more tax revenues. The extraordinary revenue growth forecast by supply-side economists in the early 1980s did not materialize.

Although it was never admitted publicly, the Reagan administration had become "born-again Keynesians, converted to easy money, large tax cuts, big increases in government spending, and huge deficits," writes economist Lester Thurow. "Midway through his first term of office President Reagan had adopted precisely the policies which he had spent a lifetime denouncing."[32]

Supply-side economics received a new lease on life when Bob Dole embraced it as a major theme in his 1996 presidential campaign. He reaffirmed it by picking its champion, Jack Kemp, as his vice-presidential running mate. Their defeat in 1996 may put supply-side economics on the back burner. Exit polls demonstrated that most voters did not believe that Dole could lower taxes by 15 percent and reduce the deficit at the same time. However, with Jack Kemp as a potential Republican presidential nominee in 2000, along with Steven Forbes, a billionaire who campaigned almost exclusively in the presidential primaries in 1996 on a 15 percent flat federal income tax, the issue is not dead yet.

Promoting Commerce

The national government promotes a prosperous economy through its monetary and fiscal policies. It also provides various services to business and industry. The Department of Commerce is sometimes known as the nation's "service center for business." Its cabinet secretary, nearly always a person with an extensive business background, is a spokesperson for business interests. Historically, the department has been at the center of the government's efforts to promote economic growth and encourage business research and development. Its National Institutes of Standards and Technology (NIST) provides highly valued technical assistance to corporations like General Electric, DuPont, and IBM. The NIST has helped companies study the structures of enzymes, look at submicroscopic flaws in jet-engine turbine blades, and probe the structure and properties of various materials used in biotechnology, electronics, fiber optics, and other fields.[33] The Department of Commerce also undertakes basic research in ocean science and engineering, meteorology, and weather forecasting. Its National Oceanic and Atmospheric Administration is currently performing research on hurricane predictions, acid rain, marine fisheries, and a wide assortment of undersea research activities.

Also part of the Department of Commerce, the Patent and Trademark Office (PTO) administers the patent system that Congress established to carry out its responsibilities "to promote the Progress of Science and useful Arts" under Article I of the Constitution. Each year the United States Patent and Trademark Office issues more than 100,000 patents to cover new and useful inventions that provide their owners certain exclusive rights for 17 years.[34]

The Republican platform of 1996 called for the elimination of the Department of Commerce, along with the Departments of Housing and Urban Development, Education, and Energy. Republicans claimed they could save $15 billion annually by cutting the Department of Commerce budget in half.[35] President Clinton, on the other hand, has given the Department of Commerce a leadership role in actively promoting American business abroad.

Promoting Agriculture

The impressive success and competitiveness of American agriculture owe much to the federal government and its subsidies—almost as much as to fertile soil, hard work, and the technology revolution. Agriculture and food-related businesses are our largest industry, bigger than computers and automobiles or the movie and recording industries. Agribusiness generates nearly one out of every five jobs in the private sector and accounts for almost 20 percent of the GDP and 15 percent of our exports. It is also an industry with a high rate of productivity. Thanks in part to federal support for research in land grant institutions, agricultural productivity has increased at a rate of about 3 percent a year in the past decades. Farmers in the United States produce nine times as much per work hour today as they did in 1947.[36]

Our great agricultural production reflects one of the most successful partnerships between government and private enterprise. The federal government has invested large sums in basic and applied agricultural research. Much of this work is done at land grant state universities and colleges. What is learned in the laboratories is tested on experimental farms, and new techniques and products are then brought to farmers, primarily through the Agricultural Extension Services of these schools. Local county agents, part of the Agricultural Extension Service, are supported by a combination of national, state, and local funds.

The Great Depression of the 1930s ravaged virtually every farmer. The New Deal helped to get farmers back on their feet by means of credit support, loans, and crop price supports. Federal initiatives in irrigation and rural electrification fostered significant strides in productivity. Loans and credit programs were established to help farmers purchase needed equipment. Some of these programs were eventually self-financing, even though they began with public money. Other federal initiatives stabilized income and output with price supports and acreage controls.

Although the farm subsidy programs include benefits for growing—or not growing—everything from tobacco to mohair, two-thirds of the money has been spent on grain. The government spends billions to buy up, at a guaranteed minimum price, any surplus grain that is produced. Most of the burden falls on consumers in the form of higher prices at the supermarket.

It took more than a century to move the United States from an agricultural to an industrial nation, from a nation where almost everybody was involved in producing food and fiber to a nation in which only a very small number of producers provide not only enough for all the people of the United States but for the world. Still, American farmers have fallen on difficult times in recent decades.

The Federal Agriculture Improvement and Reform Act of 1996

In 1996 Congress adopted a major new farm program, the Federal Agriculture Improvement and Reform Act (FAIR), with its Freedom to Farm payments. FAIR is a complex and massive piece of authorizing legislation. It calls for an end of subsidies to wheat, corn, feed grain, cotton, and rice farmers over seven years, to be replaced by fixed but declining Freedom to Farm payments. The act continues subsidies at a reduced rate for peanut, sugar, and dairy programs, continues conservation programs that pay farmers to leave idle 36.4 million acres of cropland, provides for crop insurance, and maintains food stamps and other nutrition programs for two years.

The assumption behind this act is that the farmers who receive these Freedom to Farm payments, while still being allowed to plant anything they want in any amount they want, will use these direct cash payments to cushion the loss of subsidies and payments by the government to maintain the price of farm commodities. At the end of the seven years, it is hoped that the marketplace will work and farmers will be able to make a living by producing what the nation needs at lower prices for consumers. However, if farm incomes substantially decline or food prices go way up, it is very likely that the Freedom to Farm plan will come under attack and be modified by Congress. And it should be noted that the 1996 act only *authorized* this program, which means that each year Congress must *appropriate* the funds to implement it. These yearly battles will provide ample opportunities for the many interests involved in farming to alter how the law is funded.

American automobile manufacturers encourage consumers to "buy American," but these same manufacturers often sell cars made abroad.

Hundreds of thousands simply closed their operations, either because of bankruptcy or mortgage foreclosure. The bleaker the farm situation becomes, the greater the cry by farmers for more help: extensions on loans, bailouts of the farm credit system, and more subsidies or direct aid.

Plainly, the array of subsidies, loans, credits, and related programs of research and investment has helped American farmers be successful in the past. Many economists point out, however, that not only do the big farmers gain the most from federal programs, but farm subsidies hurt poor people by driving up the price of food. Thus although helping farmers encourages productivity, it also increases poverty. Why do we do this? Although there are not large numbers of farmers, they are politically active. Moreover, by granting two senators to each state regardless of population, the federal system exaggerates the political clout of farmers. Farmers are well organized, and like senior citizens, unions, and the savings and loan industry, they know how to present their case to Congress.[37] Nonetheless, as the century comes to a close and the nation faces the need to cut federal expenditures, political support is eroding for the continuation of farm programs costing billions of dollars to subsidize farmers not to grow things.

FREE TRADE OR PROTECTIONISM?

The United States is the world's leading exporting nation, but our competitive edge eroded in the 1970s and 1980s. Today the United States must strive to be an equal among peers. Our biggest challenge comes from Pacific Rim nations such as Japan, Korea, Taiwan, and Singapore.

Two areas in which we had a large competitive trading edge have come under attack. Our leadership in research and technology and our vast agricultural industry are now both threatened by other nations, which are quickly moving up and doing what we do at lower costs and with a fresh assertiveness. The implications for U.S. workers are staggering. Thousands of plants have been closed. Hundreds of thousands of workers at steel mills, machine-tool factories, and textile and apparel-manufacturing plants and in the computer, electronics, and communications industries have been laid off. In what is now becoming a familiar refrain, both industry and the unions blame their problems on imports. In some clothing products, foreign competitors now enjoy more than half of our market.

Trade Deficits and GATT

In 1971 the United States experienced its first **trade deficit**—where the value of imports exceeded the value of exports—in more than a century. By 1987, our foreign trade imbalances, including services and investment income, temporarily peaked at $160 billion. (The figure would be over $200 billion if services and investment were excluded.) Since that time the trade deficit has declined, with some year-to-year fluctuation. In 1992, it dropped to $78 billion, but in 1993 it rose to $85 billion, and in 1996 it set an all-time record of $162 billion, surpassing the old mark set in 1987.[38]

Congress and the president are under continuing pressure from industry, unions, and regional political leaders to save American jobs, companies, and communities from foreign competition. These pressures come not only from the textile and auto industries but from glass, steel, shoe, lumber, electronics, book publishing, aluminum, farming, and domestic wine and spirit coalitions, to name just a few. They claim that the trade deficit justifies the imposition of tariffs and other trade sanctions.

The problem is not that we are importing too much but that we are exporting too little. German cars, Japanese radios, and Indonesian textiles are fine products; if other countries can produce better cars or shoes at a lower price, then free traders argue we should deploy our labor and capital to other areas where we can do better. Although many question whether we still have a competitive edge, economists maintain that the United States still has an absolute advantage in more products than any other country in the world.

The question is also whether our products are given fair treatment by other nations. American agricultural products are denied entry into some countries and subject to very high tariffs in others. American automobile manufacturers complain of unfair restrictions imposed by the Japanese on our cars. Finally, some countries attempt to exploit the U.S. advantage in technology by slavishly copying our products and then selling them back to us or to other countries at a profit.

In 1947 a group of countries formed a trade organization to negotiate free trade by lowering tariffs and quotas and any other disadvantages countries face when trading with other countries. Today this trade organization, known as the **General Agreement on Tariffs and Trade (GATT)**, includes 111 countries around the world, and its membership accounts for four-fifths of the world's trade. GATT has negotiated agreements through seven rounds of trade negotiations (the most recent was called the *Uruguay Round*, named after the site of the initial conference). The United States has tried to focus GATT negotiations on trade in agriculture items, foreign investment, and protection of technological innovations and intellectual property. Although many trade restrictions still face U.S. imports and those of other countries, GATT has done much to lower tariffs and quotas as well as to increase "fair" trade throughout the world. GATT has also incorporated several methods of retaliating against countries that practice unfair trade.

One unfair practice used by the United States as well as other countries is *dumping*—selling products in a country below the cost of manufacturing or below their domestic price with the obvious intention of driving other producers out of the market and then raising prices to profitable levels. Another practice is *subsidizing* certain industries. Some countries, for example, subsidize steel for export; others require lengthy inspection procedures for imported goods. Japan has protected several of its industries—producers of automobiles and baseball bats, for example—by specifying standards that are virtually impossible for us to meet.

The United States, of course, often reciprocates. In recent years, we have imposed "voluntary" limits on Japanese automobiles and European steel imports. Japan opened its markets to U.S. cellular phone companies in 1994 because of stiff trade sanction threats against Japanese electronics industries. And, as already indicated, our federal government has long subsidized our agricultural exports in the form of price supports and inexpensive credit.

Americans have usually favored free trade. More than two hundred years ago, Thomas Jefferson traveled to France to request that American whale oil, tobacco, and fish be allowed into that country without being subject to the intolerable tariff burdens the French had imposed. And over the years Americans have usually discovered that foreign trade is a two-way street; if we want people in a foreign market to buy our goods, we must be willing to buy theirs.

The North American Free Trade Agreement (NAFTA)

On December 17, 1992, leaders of the United States, Canada, and Mexico signed the **North American Free Trade Agreement (NAFTA)**, which formed the largest free-trade zone in the world, even surpassing the European Community's 13-country conglomerate. Although President Bush signed NAFTA near the end of his presidency, the agreement could not become law until ratified by Congress. President Clinton promoted NAFTA and played a critical part in supporting it, even though members of his party were the most vigorous opponents. Congress passed NAFTA by a thin margin in a bipartisan vote in which the Democrats were the minority.

Thinking It Through

What constitutes an "American" car? After finishing this short quiz, you know (if you did not know already) that company name has little relevance. Many foreign companies have plants in the United States that employ American workers and use a high percentage of American parts. General Motors, Ford, and Chrysler all have joint ventures with foreign-owned companies that place some of their models in the "import" category. Is a Toyota Camry an American car if it is built in Mexico in a plant partially owned by Ford? What defines an American product? Ownership of company? Nationality of employees? Location of physical plant? Domestic content of components?

The "Buy American" movement reached its apex in 1992. In January of that year, the president of Monsanto (an American chemicals manufacturer) offered each of its 12,000 employees $1,000 to buy or lease a new American car. Other countries charged discrimination, arguing that our government should have no role in promoting homegrown products over imports. Citizens, they maintained, should choose the best product available, not the one that says "Made in the U.S.A."

SOURCE: Jacqueline Mitchell, "Growing Movement to 'Buy American' Debates the Term," *The Wall Street Journal*, January 24, 1992, p. A1.

The vote on the North American Free Trade Agreement was preceded by battles between business owners and workers, between economists and environmentalists, and between free traders and protectionists.

Though trade among the United States, Canada, and Mexico will not be absolutely "free" or unimpeded, the agreement will have a tremendous impact on the economies of all three countries. After the United States and Canada ratified a free-trade agreement in 1991, the debate over NAFTA focused on Mexican-United States trade. Today Mexico is the United States' third most important trading partner, and the United States is Mexico's most important trading partner.

Critics of NAFTA are worried because Mexican antipollution laws are significantly less stringent than those in the United States, and Mexican workers are willing to work for lower wages. Both of these factors may make relocation to Mexico attractive to many U.S. companies seeking to lower labor and pollution-control costs.

Advocates of NAFTA, including Gerald Ford, Jimmy Carter, George Bush, and Bill Clinton, claim a free-trade zone will create jobs for Americans and increase profits for U.S.-owned companies. These proponents predict that our exports to Mexico will increase when tariff barriers are eliminated. In addition, Mexico has a responsibility to enforce health and environmental laws according to NAFTA's side agreements.

Some estimates had indicated that 112,000 U.S. jobs would be eliminated as U.S. firms expanded in Mexico, but as many as 130,000 new U.S. jobs would be created, many of them high-tech, high-wage jobs. Not all studies came to the same conclusion, however. Some studies estimated that 1.5 million U.S. jobs would be created by the end of the decade due to NAFTA, while others concluded the United States would lose up to 900,000 jobs.[39]

Three years after NAFTA had been in effect, a study by researchers at the University of California at Los Angeles concluded that the claims of both those who argued that it would dramatically increase jobs as well as those who predicted there would be great job losses were exaggerated. Despite the collapse of the Mexican economy during that period, NAFTA's impact on jobs had been slight. The increase in imports had killed an estimated 28,000 jobs. The increase in exports had created 31,000 jobs. Of course, it is too early to come to any firm conclusions about how NAFTA will work, but the recovery of the Mexican economy should have a positive effect on job creation.[40]

The Ups and Downs of Protectionism

Protectionism—erecting barriers to protect domestic industry—sounds easy and workable as a solution to trade deficits, but trade deficits are only symptomatic of more profound economic problems. Most economists favor free trade and strongly dislike protectionism because it prevents efficient use of resources and because consumers pay much more for protected products than they would otherwise. Tariffs merely divert attention away from real solutions like increased productivity and capital investments. Tariffs also inevitably invite retaliation from foreign countries.[41] Protectionism will only magnify most of the problems associated with U.S. trade.

In the 1930s many nations experienced high unemployment, low production, and general economic misery. The United States was no exception. In an effort to aid ailing American industries, Congress passed the Smoot-Hawley tariff, the highest general tariff the United States had ever had. Supporters hoped high tariffs on imported goods would increase the demand for goods produced in the United States and thus help get the country out of the Great Depression. The exact opposite occurred. Other nations retaliated with high tariffs on American goods. Demand fell, intensifying the Depression.

In 1934, Congress gave the president power to negotiate mutual tariff reductions with other nations, subject to certain restrictions. By the early 1970s, tariffs on industrial products had been substantially reduced. But restrictions on agricultural commodities remain, along with nontariff limitations such as quotas, minimum import prices, and prohibitions on the sale of certain products.

In the 1990s trade barriers are generally less imposing than they were during the Smoot-Hawley era, but substantial restrictions still exist. Some politicians and business leaders prefer the nebulous term "fair trade," and elected officials from Bill Clinton on down speak of the need to "level the playing field" against unfair competition. The policies of fair trade—tariffs, quotas, voluntary export restraints, and excessive import regulations—limit American consumption of foreign products. Developing countries struggling to restructure their weak economies especially suffer at the hands of American protection. For example, Mexico is allowed to sell Americans no more than 35,292 brassieres a year, thanks to Congress and a strong textile lobby.[42] Restrictions on clothing and textile imports cost American consumers $1 for each 1 cent of increased earnings of American textile and clothing workers.[43] All told, trade barriers cost American consumers $80 billion a year— equal to more than $1,200 per family.[44]

Others argue that fair trade and protection bestow benefits. Workers in unskilled or semiskilled occupations, who may find a job change difficult, can still keep their jobs. In addition, industries like steel and textiles that may be necessary for security reasons must be protected, even though the cost may be high.

Another side in this debate favors some sort of **industrial policy** by which government officials target specific industries they think can compete with foreign firms and help them with tax breaks and financial incentives.[45] Advocates of such a policy see the faults of protectionism but still want the government to become more involved in assisting domestic industry, as governments of many foreign nations do. Proponents cite Japan's sustained postwar economic recovery as an example of how government and industry can work together profitably. Opponents worry about creating another layer of bureaucracy and have doubts that the government could objectively pick industries that will be successful, especially given the strength of lobbyists who would no doubt try to persuade Congress to favor their special interest, regardless of merit. Critics of industrial policy also point out that other countries will retaliate with industrial policies of their own—like the effect of the Smoot-Hawley tariff in the 1930s—thus negating any gains.

In sum, our economic policy in the future will probably be some combination of free trade, selective protectionism, and industrial policy. Though protectionism shields highly visible industries from competition at home or abroad, such measures are often another kind of subsidy that protects one industry at the expense of another—and always at high cost to American consumers. Protectionism is more expensive than taxpayers realize and will rarely be a good long-term solution. Instead, the United States must continue, through hard negotiations with trading partners, to remove unfair trade practices; encourage greater investments in what we have traditionally done well (science, technology, and medical and agricultural research); educate workers with better skills and executives with greater leadership abilities; and encourage labor-management experiments that can maximize productivity with an eye toward higher-quality products that will be highly prized abroad.[46] As Cordell Hull, secretary of state under Franklin Roosevelt, concluded, "Unhampered trade dovetailed with peace; high tariffs, trade barriers, and unfair economic competition, with war."[47]

As the United States enters the new millennium, the economic needs of the nation take on greater importance. Any new or expanded social programs will be debated in the context of the large federal budget deficit. Further, the perception shared by many politicians that increased taxes are a political liability inhibits effective social and economic policy making in the United States. In our system, social and economic policy choices are becoming highly controversial. Americans see a limited role for their government in social spending and have never liked taxes. One of the challenges for a government by the people is to reconcile the costs of government with the burden of taxes.

POLITICS ONLINE

Using the Web to Learn about Securities

As a potential investor, you can now track a wide range of investments, purchase your own stocks, and even build your own investment portfolio using your personal computer (or you can pretend to do it). To begin your investment voyage, first choose an on-line brokerage firm with whom to open your account. A list of possible online brokers can be found at:

www.investorguide.com/Brokerages.htm#onlinetrading

After opening your account and depositing funds with your broker, you can then buy and sell stocks over the Internet whenever you desire. To assist you in making investment choices, extensive and updated stock information can be found at the Web site of your brokerage firm or at other popular sites like:

www.nasdaq.com

In the past, investors ran the risk of being unaware of a class-action suit or other claim pending against a company. However, by order of the Federal Courts for the Northern District of California, all securities class actions must now be posted on the Internet. This service is currently provided by the Stanford Law School at:

securities.stanford.edu

Whether this model of using the Internet for such legal postings will become commonplace is still uncertain. But it is clear that demand for information relating to possible investments does exist, and that people are increasingly using the Internet to access that information and to participate in online stock trading.

SUMMARY

1. There are five stages in the policy-making process: problem identification, policy formulation, policy adoption, policy implementation, and policy evaluation. When the process turns to implementation and evaluation, new problems are identified, and the process begins again. Many problems exist but do not result in policy or legislation, and similarly, many policies are proposed but never adopted. Inaction is also a policy. Every policy has political consequences.

2. The national government influences our economy and how wealth is produced and distributed primarily via fiscal policy (taxing and spending) and monetary policy (control of the money supply).

3. Fiscal policy is implemented by the federal budget, which is annually negotiated between the president and Congress. Since in recent decades the national government has spent more than it has taken in, primarily in the form of tax revenues, how to manage the federal deficit has become a major national issue.

4. During the past few years, efforts have been undertaken to reform the tax code (lowering tax rates and simplifying the tax system) and to devise economic policies (both fiscal and monetary) that will encourage economic growth but prevent inflation, high interest rates, and unemployment.

Few policies have succeeded completely, but economists and political leaders continue to grope for a mix of the right economic strategies. Meanwhile, virtually everyone agrees that annual budgetary deficits and the soaring national debt are monumental problems.

5. Monetary policy is primarily under the control of the Federal Reserve System, which has considerable independence from both Congress and the president as it works to supply sufficient amounts of money and credit so that the economy will grow, but not so much that it will lead to inflation.

6. The role of government as promoter of economic growth and jobs is not new. It is as old as the Republic itself. The federal government has long been involved in promoting agriculture and concerned about the health of producers and consumers of these commodities. Working through the Department of Commerce, it also promotes business.

7. The national government is also involved in promoting trade and commerce with other nations. Our ability to buy from other nations and sell them our goods and services has much to do with the health of our economy. In recent decades the national government has worked to reduce trade barriers through various treaties and agreements such as GATT and NAFTA.

FURTHER READING

JAGDISH BHAGWATI, *The World Trading System at Risk* (Princeton University Press, 1991).

JEFFERY H. BIRNBAUM AND ALAN S. MURRAY, *SHOWDOWN AT GUCCI GULCH: LAWMAKERS, LOBBYISTS, AND THE UNLIKELY TRIUMPH OF TAX REFORM* (Vintage, 1988).

DAVID P. CALLEO, *The Bankrupting of America: How the Federal Budget Is Impoverishing the Nation* (William Morrow, 1992).

DANIEL P. FRANKLIN, *Making Ends Meet: Congressional Budgeting in the Age of Deficits* (Congressional Quarterly Press, 1993).

OTIS GRAHAM, *Losing Time: The Industrial Policy Debate* (Harvard University Press, 1992).

WILLIAM GREIDER, *Secrets of the Temple: How the Federal Reserve Runs the Country* (Simon & Schuster, 1987).

ROBERT HEILBRONER AND PETER BERNSTEIN, *The Debt and the Deficit: False Alarms/Real Possibilities* (W. W. Norton, 1988).

CALVIN MACKENZIE AND SARANNA THORTON, *Bucking the Deficit: Economic Policymaking in America* (Westview Press, 1996).

B. GUY PETERS, *The Politics of Taxation: A Comparative Perspective* (Blackwell, 1991).

PETER G. PETERSON, *Facing Up: Paying Our Nation's Debt and Saving Our Children's Future* (Simon & Schuster, 1994).

ALICE M. RIVLIN, *Reviving the American Dream: The Economy, the States, and the Federal Government* (Brookings Institution, 1992).

LESTER THUROW, *Head to Head: The Coming Economic Battle among Japan, Europe, and America* (William Morrow, 1992).

AARON WILDAVSKY, *The New Politics of the Budgetary Process* (Scott, Foresman, 1988).

19

Making Regulatory Policy

*W*hat do lawn mowers, automobiles, telephones, smoke detectors, roller blades, cereal ads, fat substitutes, nicotine patches, pornography, banks, natural gas companies, nuclear power plants, breast implants, cable television, animal cloning, baby food, and workers' wages all have in common? They are all *regulated* in some way by the federal government. Because virtually every activity in the United States today is supervised by government in one form or another, regulation is a vast enterprise. And any activity as pervasive as this is bound to generate controversy.

Our regulatory arrangements were not created arbitrarily; the framers of the Constitution explicitly authorized Congress to regulate commerce among the states and with foreign nations. In our government's earliest years, Congress and the president used their regulatory power to impose or suspend tariffs on imports from other nations. In the nineteenth century, the federal government created a number of agencies that regulated the conduct of citizens and commercial enterprises with an eye toward promoting economic development. Among these were the Army Corps of Engineers (1824), the Patent and Trademark Office (1836), the Steamboat Inspecting Service (1837), and the Copyright Office of the Library of Congress (1870). In 1887 Congress created the Interstate Commerce Commission to deal with the widespread dissatisfaction over railroad service across the country.

Additional regulations came into existence to break up monopolies, to clean up meat-packing conditions such as those exposed in Upton Sinclair's *Jungle* (1906), to prevent the kind of pesticide contamination described in Rachel Carson's *Silent Spring* (1962), to correct the lack of auto safety documented in Ralph Nader's *Unsafe at Any Speed* (1965), and to respond to discrimination in employment on the basis of race, color, national origin, religion, sex, and age. More recently, regulations have been enacted to protect us from raw sewage in rivers, lead in paint and gasoline, toxins in the air, radon gas in our homes, and asbestos, cotton dust, and hazardous substances in toys and furniture. Regulations exist both to encourage competition and to achieve valued social objectives, like protecting us from unsafe and dangerous products and environments.

For most Americans the politics of regulation is a relatively obscure and confusing subject, not something you talk much about in civics courses or at cocktail parties. Regulation policies and procedures are also hard to understand. For example, few Americans follow highly technical and complex antitrust negotiations or grasp the importance of the novel provisions in the Telecommunications Act of 1996. Moreover, few Americans have ever heard of the hundreds of federal regulators who head up the dozens of federal regulatory agencies.

Yet the regulatory activities of the federal government have an enormous impact on how we live our lives and how businesses and organizations function in the United States. And this involvement is reflected in elections for federal office. Candidates for Congress and the White House do take sides and make promises about clean air and clean water, the minimum wage, nicotine, air safety policies, television violence, the cost of cable television service, job safety, and affirmative action. These and countless similar issues are ultimately settled by federal regulations that must be defined, implemented, and enforced.

President Bill Clinton and members of Congress have frequently been embroiled in the politics of making regulatory policy. There were partisan battles over legislation to enable cable TV, local phone companies, and long-distance carriers to work together. The Brady Bill antagonized many politicians by mandating a waiting period before handguns could be purchased, and battles have been waged over air bags and their protection or harm of children. Meat inspections have been overhauled by new government rules. The Food and Drug Administration and the Federal Aviation Administration are continually issuing new guidelines about the foods we eat and the planes we fly. Some members of Congress question whether the health benefits from cleaning up auto emissions are compelling enough to justify the enormous expense of stricter pollution control.[1]

Both Republicans and Democrats have promised to eliminate excessive regulations. They point out that in 1935 there were 4,000 pages of regulations in the ***Federal Register*** (a daily publication containing information about proposed and existing federal regulations), and by 1995 there were more than 65,000 pages of regulations. Both parties say regulatory overkill threatens to overwhelm entrepreneurs and divert them from building vital, innovative companies. Republican members of Congress say that while some regulations are needed, a great many are very costly, and these costs outweigh the benefits: "Regulations add as much as 33 percent to the cost of building an airplane engine and as much as 95 percent to the price of a new vaccine. Federal regulation also adds about $3,000 to the cost of a new car."[2]

Like the Reagan and Bush administrations, the Clinton administration has pursued a goal of downsizing regulatory staffs, reducing federal regulations, and working out partnerships with businesses to help them design more effective and efficient methods of achieving the goals of regulatory policy.[3]

Just what is regulation and regulatory policy? Do we need to regulate business enterprises more rigorously in order to protect the environment, ensure worker safety, and preserve the marketplace? Or is business already so closely regulated that it can no longer produce the goods and services the nation wants at reasonable prices? Do we need less regulation for certain private-sector activities and more regulation for others? This chapter will examine these questions as we look at what regulations exist and what impact they have. We shall also treat the now well-developed deregulation movement in the United States.

Tainted meat in hamburgers at a Jack in the Box restaurant caused the death of Michael Nole and the poisoning of his two sisters. Here the Nole family makes a strong plea to a congressional investigating committee for stronger government regulation of meat inspections.

WHAT IS REGULATION?

In a broad sense, **regulation** is any attempt of the government to control the behavior of corporations, other governments, or citizens. Regulation, as we use the term in this chapter, occurs when the government steps in and alters the natural workings of the open market to achieve some desired goal. The main regulatory role of government is economic: to improve or supplant markets when they do not or cannot function effectively. In this sense regulation is a middle ground between socialism (or government ownership) and a **laissez-faire** ("hands-off") policy. Left to itself, the free market is characterized by self-adjustment, or *natural regulation*. Regulation by government interjects political goals and values into the economy in the form of rules that direct behavior in the marketplace. These rules have the force of law and are backed by the government's police power.

All economies follow sets of rules and regulations; there simply are no unregulated economies. The United States operates with a competitive market economy in which wages, prices, the allocation of goods and services, and the employment of resources are generally regulated by the laws of supply and demand. We rely on private enterprise and market incentives to carry out most of our production and distribution. However, "perfect competition" is seldom perfect, so regulation is necessary to protect people from undesirable side effects of the market, such as pollution or discrimination or false advertising.

The presumption in the United States is against regulation. Most people feel that businesses should be allowed to buy and sell products and produce goods without government regulation. Our government and our courts have to justify regulations, and they do so only because people, through the representative process, have come to demand certain protections.

Types of Regulation

It is customary to talk of two general categories of regulation: economic and social regulation. *Economic regulation* generally refers to government controls on the behavior of business in the marketplace: the entry of individual firms into particular lines of business, the prices that firms may charge, the standards of service they must offer. Public utilities, transportation, and television are examples of regulated industries. As already noted, economic regulation began almost as early as the founding of the republic and expanded in earnest in 1887, when the Interstate Commerce Commission (ICC) was established; it has continued in the twentieth century with the Federal Communications Commission (FCC), Commodity Futures Trading Commission (CFTC), and a host of regulatory agencies, boards, or commissions responsible for enforcing statutes in particular industries (see Table 19–1). In the twentieth century, we moved from about five regulatory bodies to about 80 regulatory organizations at the federal level that employ more than 100,000 people who work to enforce thousands of federal regulations.

The second type of regulation, *social regulation*, refers to government corrections of a wide variety of side effects, usually unintended, brought about by economic activity. Concerns for worker health and safety and for hazards to the environment have brought about social regulation. Social regulation also includes the efforts made by government to ensure equal rights in employment, education, and housing. Whereas economic regulation is usually organized along industry lines, social regulation cuts across these lines.

The Environmental Protection Agency (EPA), the Consumer Product Safety Commission (CPSC), and the Occupational Safety and Health Administration (OSHA) are regulatory agencies engaged in social regulation. In economic terms, producers regulated by social regulation must now pay for external costs that once were free, such as using rivers, landfills, or the atmosphere for waste disposal. These

Regulation in the News

The politics of regulation and new regulatory rules seldom make front page news. Yet every week you read about new regulations or debates about regulatory policy, such as:

- "Congress Considers Regulations on Cable TV"
- "EPA to Require New Pollution Emissions Controls"
- "Nutrition Labeling on Products for Kids Proposed"
- "FDA Panel to Hold Hearings on Safety of Acne Medicines"
- "FAA to Tighten Rule on Takeoffs in Snow and Ice"
- "FCC Considers Rules to Spur Economic Growth"
- "Member of Transit Safety Board Leaves with Parting Shots"
- "Congress May Break Deadlock on Food Safety Laws"
- "FDA to Set Limits on Breast Implants"
- "FDA Approves Laser System for Angioplasty"
- "Panel Urges FDA to Approve Female Condom"
- "FDA Revises Labeling on Antacids"
- "A Decade's Acrimony Lifts in the Glory of Clean Air"
- "FAA Plans Close Look at Plane Braking Mechanism"
- "FCC Adopts Limits on TV Ads Aimed at Children"
- "EPA to Shame Industries into Reducing Pollution"
- "FDA Plans Cigarette Assault"
- "President Bans Federal Research on Cloning"

TABLE 19–1

Some Regulatory Agencies and Their Missions

	Year Established	Primary Functions
Federal Trade Commission (FTC)	1914	Administers certain antitrust laws concerning advertising, labeling, and packaging to protect consumers from unfair business practices
Food and Drug Administration (FDA)	1931	Establishes regulations concerning purity, safety, and labeling accuracy of certain foods and drugs; issues licenses for manufacturing and distribution.
Federal Communications Commission (FCC)	1934	Licenses civilian radio and television communication; licenses and sets rates for interstate and international communication
Animal and Plant Health Inspection Service	1953	Sets standards; inspects and enforces laws relating to meat, poultry, and plant safety
Environmental Protection Agency (EPA)	1970	Develops environmental quality standards; approves state environmental plans
Occupational Safety and Health Administration (OSHA)	1970	Develops and enforces worker safety and health regulations
Bureau of Alcohol, Tobacco and Firearms	1972	Enforces laws and regulates legal flow of these materials
Consumer Product Safety Commission (CPSC)	1972	Establishes mandatory product safety standards and bans sales of products that do not comply
Nuclear Regulatory Commission (NRC)	1974	Licenses the construction and operation of nuclear reactors and similar facilities and regulates nuclear materials; also licenses the export of nuclear reactors and the export and import of uranium and plutonium

Approaches to Regulation

Regulatory techniques can be classified into four approaches:

1. *Market approaches*, which rely on the economic incentives of the free market to nudge industry in the direction of the public interest
2. *Performance standards*, which replace regulations that spell out exactly how industry must meet a particular goal with broader statements that set standards yet allow industry to choose the means
3. *Informational approaches*, which, instead of banning products, require that manufacturers disclose complete information about their products, on the theory that consumers can then make intelligent choices
4. *Self-regulation*, whereby the government does little more than help industry set its own voluntary standards

SOURCE: Timothy Clark, "New Approaches to Regulatory Reform: Letting the Market Do the Job," *National Journal*, August 11, 1979, p. 1316. See also Don L. Boroughs with Betsy Carpenter, "Cleaning Up the Environment," *U.S. News and World Report*, March 25, 1991, pp. 45–55.

costs, however, are often passed along to the consumer, so the true cost of the product is more accurately reflected in its price. Some goods subsequently become too costly, and demand drops. Others become more popular (for instance, safe toys), and demand increases. The final goal of social regulation is socially beneficial allocation of resources.

Congress has created two types of regulatory agencies: those within the executive branch and **independent regulatory agencies** that deal with policy areas in which independence from Congress and the president is desired. Members of executive branch agencies serve at the pleasure of the president. Executive branch regulatory agencies include the Food and Drug Administration (FDA), the Office of Surface Mining, the National Highway Traffic Safety Administration, and the Comptroller of the Currency. Members of independent agencies are appointed by the president, confirmed by the Senate, and removable only for some specific cause. Independent agencies, usually headed by a board composed of seven members, include the Federal Communications Commission, the Equal Employment Opportunities Commission, the Nuclear Regulatory Commission, and the Federal Reserve Board.

The Regulation Debate

Arguments pro and con about what governments should regulate vary depending on what the target is; some regulations are designed to protect our health, others our pocketbooks. Another debate concerns whether to depend on the market system to self-regulate or whether to depend on government to establish controls and supervision. One of the historic rationales for regulation is to maintain a competitive market system and prevent monopolies and unfair economic competition.

To achieve many economic goals, including the best allocation of resources, government must encourage competition. When one company dominates an industry (a **monopoly**), everyone else suffers. In such a situation, when power is concentrated in the hands of only one or a few firms, the U.S. government was expected to "bust the trusts"—the monopolies—to restore competition. This is the aim of **antitrust regulation**.[4] Natural monopolies are allowed to exist when it would be grossly inefficient to permit competition in a particular industry. Electric utilities used to be the primary example. Because of the size of their operation and the vast capital investment needed, it was assumed that consumers were better served by allowing one utility company to supply electric power. Technology is changing even that. By the end of the 1990s, consumers will be able to choose which company they want to supply their electricity.

Regulation can also compensate for market imperfections. Even those who oppose regulation recognize the market does not always solve every problem. Consider pollution. For a long time no price was imposed on a business for using air and water to discharge toxic wastes. Therefore, market forces did not consider what it cost society to have its air and water polluted. When the market fails to set appropriate costs and benefits, pressures develop for the government to step in.[5] The government can, for example, pass regulations that impose costs on air pollution. Or consider commuters who use their cars to go to work; the more who do so, the more difficult it is for them to get to work. (Commuters frequently favor mass transportation so that other people will use it and thus open the roadways for them.) Still, market forces do not encourage taking a bus instead of a car to work. If we enacted higher taxes on gasoline, our fuel costs would be brought more in line with Europe's, and such a policy would also reduce our dependency on Middle East oil and promote domestic energy production.

Finally, the government has involved itself directly in the economy to protect those who lack economic power. It has, for instance, worked to establish a minimum wage and to prevent such abuses as child labor; it has also sought to control the conflict between labor and management and protect workers' right to organize. In its role as guardian of the weak, the government has sought to ensure equal opportunity and protect the investor or consumer from fraud and unsafe products. The landmark Civil Rights Act of 1964, for example, prohibited discrimination in employment on the basis of sex, race, color, religion, and national origin. The Equal Employment Opportunity Commission (EEOC) was created to enforce this legislative ban. The EEOC investigates complaints and can file a suit in individual job discrimination cases and in cases where a general pattern of discrimination exists throughout an industry or large corporation.

Opponents of government regulation say that it is generally not needed. The basic objectives are the same, opponents say—a clean, safe environment and an equitable and efficient economy—but the means are different. Critics of regulation say the best mechanisms for attaining both economic and social goals are the free market and the forces of competition. With meaningful competition, the consumer gets the most goods at the best price.

Critics say regulation is inefficient. The labyrinth of federal rules dampens productivity, fuels inflation, and blunts our competitive strength abroad. Further, they argue, public officials cannot know as much about the intricacies of any particular industry as do those engaged in the business on a daily basis. This lack of knowledge results in regulations that unduly hamper production and cost much more than the benefits they provide.

Farewell Reflections by a Former FDA Commissioner

David Kessler was appointed Food and Drug Administration commissioner by President George Bush in 1990 and stayed on until 1997, when he became dean of Yale Medical School. Many of his initiatives began during the Bush administration, but his role became even more controversial under President Bill Clinton. His efforts to change food labeling laws and tighten vitamin supplement regulations generated applause and criticism. Under his leadership, the FDA first studied and then concluded that nicotine should be a "controlled substance." Kessler looked back on his years at the Food and Drug Administration as "a good fight":

> My six years at the agency . . . have been a challenge. I have had to deal with the issues that the FDA faces as a public-health agency and learn to cope with the relentless pressures that are always part of the job. Both the agency and I have been vilified. I feel very strongly, however, that if you believe in what you're doing, all the name calling in the world won't stop you. . . .
>
> For a public-health agency to make a difference, there is no better strategy than prevention. The two chief causes of preventable death in the United States are poor diet and smoking. The new food labels that FDA developed are helping millions of Americans make healthier choices. . . .
>
> Then there's smoking. In August [1996], President Clinton took a historic and unprecedented action when he announced that the FDA was asserting its jurisdiction over cigarettes and smokeless tobacco. We issued a regulation that will make it more difficult for children and adolescents to obtain tobacco products and tougher for the industry to aim its advertising at young people. . . . Our goal over the next seven years is to cut in half the number of children who start to smoke. . . .
>
> Maybe the world in which our children live will be a little bit safer. . . . The things we have done at FDA can and will affect the public's health—and that means we've fought the good fight.

SOURCES: Jeffrey Goldberg, "Next Target: Nicotine," *The New York Times Magazine,* August 4, 1996, pp. 22–27, 36–44; also David Kessler, "We've Fought the Good Fight," *Newsweek,* December 9, 1996, p. 28.

Spraying crops increases yields to farmers but may be a health hazard to consumers.

Government regulation is often counterproductive, critics say, hurting the very people it is intended to help and actually working to protect monopolies and cartels. Some federal regulations penalize consumers, to whom the costs of regulations are usually passed along. For example, the extra costs of automobile safety and auto emission devices can add a few thousand dollars to the price of a new car. Another criticism of regulation, from a strictly economic standpoint, is that it diverts resources from potentially productive endeavors.

The debate about regulation is usually about more versus less rather than all or nothing. Few Americans call for unlimited government intervention in economic and social activity. And few advocate absolute removal of government participation from the marketplace. Indeed, most people call for more regulation in some areas and less in others. Sometimes those who call for more regulation are surprised by the results, as the effort to insist on air bags in passenger seats illustrates.

The deregulation of cable television offers yet another example of unintended or undesired results. Soon after the deregulation of television in the mid-1990s there was a dramatic growth in the cable television industry. The number of cable subscribers increased, as did the number of households that could have access to cable.[6] The dramatic growth in access to cable was accompanied by a dramatic increase in fees, something the Department of Justice attributed, at least in part, to the monopoly held by local cable companies. The Federal Communications Commission and Congress were pressured to address the rapid increases in the cost of cable television, so Congress passed legislation with the intention of regulating fees. Ironically, rates went up for about half of the country following regulation.[7] Defenders of Congress's law see the fee increases as part of an effort to establish a "benchmark" from which prices will not grow as rapidly in the future. Opponents point not only to the higher costs associated with regulation but to the fear that Congress may seek to regulate subscriber fees as well as the rates the companies pay for programs.[8] Others argue that with cable now able to compete with telephone and satellite companies, greater regulation is inevitable.

The Politics of Regulation

A critical task of modern constitutional democracies is to make wise, balanced choices among courses of action and competing objectives, and regulation is no exception. Often the social benefits of regulation conflict with the economic objectives. Critics say regulation contributes to higher inflation, lower productivity, and economic stagnation, while proponents point to improvements in environmental quality, worker safety, and consumer protection.[9]

How desirable is it to have cleaner air or safer workplaces? Although it is relatively inexpensive to remove a large percentage of air pollution, and therefore socially desirable, it becomes increasingly expensive to remove all or even almost all of it. To do so would require an allocation of resources that, from a taxpayer's point of view, might be better used for something else—perhaps more soccer fields or public schools. Is there a socially optimal point of pollution control or worker safety beyond which it is too costly to go? The challenge for policy makers is to determine what this point is. In our political system, with its many competing interest groups, there are always plenty of different views on this point.

Faced with this problem, Congress often legislates broad objectives for the regulatory agencies, which then set specific rules for meeting these goals. Agency regulations have been largely in the form of specific rules that a firm may not violate without being punished. They have been criticized as being arbitrary, costly, and inflexible. Under pressure from businesses and their allies in Congress, recent presidents and their administrations have cut back some of these regulations. For example, OSHA trimmed more than 1,000 "nitpicking" regulations that governed such things as the shape of toilet seats.

REGULATING BUSINESS

Business has never been free of regulation, but during most of the nineteenth century our national policy was to leave business pretty much alone. However, four major waves of regulatory legislation have occurred in our nation's history: at the turn of the century, in the 1910s, in the 1930s, and in the late 1960s through 1980 (see Figure 19–1). In each case, changing political circumstances and forces gave rise to the legislation. The primary reasons for regulation were controlling monopoly, compensating for market imperfections, and defending the economically weak.

Antitrust Policy

Social critics and populist reformers in the late nineteenth century believed consumers were being cheated, especially in the oil, sugar, whiskey, and steel industries, where large monopolies called **trusts** controlled goods and services, often in combinations that worked to reduce competition. At the same time, people began to have mixed feelings about big business. Americans, who have always been impressed by bigness—the tallest skyscraper, the largest football stadium, the biggest steel mill—and the efficiency that often goes with bigness, became skeptical about giant enterprises. These mixed views were reflected in attempts to prevent monopoly and the restraint of competition through antitrust policy.

In 1890 Congress responded to this new mood by passing the **Sherman Antitrust Act.** (Senator John Sherman [R.-Ohio] had run for the Republican nomination for president in 1888 and was upset by some of the predatory tactics of big businesses.) Designed to foster competition and stop the growth of private monopolies, the act made clear its intention "to protect trade and commerce against unlawful restraints and monopolies." Henceforth, persons making contracts, combinations, or conspiracies in restraint of trade in interstate and foreign commerce could be sued for damages, required to stop their illegal practices, and subjected to criminal penalties. The Sherman Antitrust Act had little immediate impact. Presidents made little attempt to enforce it, and the Supreme Court's early interpretation of the act limited its scope.[10]

In 1914, during the administration of Woodrow Wilson, Congress added the **Clayton Act** to the antitrust arsenal. This act outlawed such specific abuses as charging different prices to different buyers in order to destroy a weaker competitor, granting rebates, making false statements about competitors and their products, buying up supplies to stifle competition, and bribing competitors' employees. In addition, **interlocking directorates** (by which an officer or director in one corporation serves on the board of a competitor) were banned, and corporations were prohibited from acquiring stock (amended in 1950 to include assets) in competing concerns if such acquisitions substantially lessened interstate competition. In 1914, Congress established the Federal Trade Commission (FTC), run by a five-person board, to enforce the Clayton Act and prevent unfair competitive practices. The FTC was to be the "traffic cop" for competition.[11]

Although monopolies as such have generally disappeared from the economic arena, in their place are new threats to competition: the **oligopoly**, a situation in which a few firms dominate a market, such as in the automobile industry. Others are concerned about the **conglomerate**, a firm that owns businesses in many unrelated industries. Still others worry about firms such as Microsoft that have such a dominant position that it appears to be able to outresearch and outmarket its would-be competitors.

Regulating Today's Economy

Are the nation's antitrust laws, drawn up a century ago, still practical for today's economy? Some members of Congress and some former regulatory commissioners and Justice Department officials believe we need to design

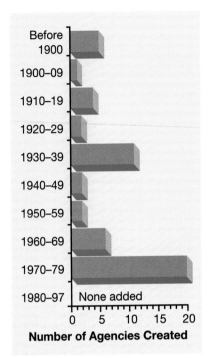

FIGURE 19–1 The Rise of Regulatory Agencies

SOURCE: Based on data from the Center for the Study of American Business.

"As far as I'm concerned, they can do what they want with the minimum wage, just as long as they keep their hands off the maximum wage."

Drawing by Mankoff. © 1989 The New Yorker Magazine, Inc.

tighter penalties, impose more regulatory guidelines, and expand antitrust enforcement.

During recent years there has been an enormous wave of *corporate mergers*; one company buys another out, or two companies pool assets to form a larger single company. Thousands of mergers took place in the 1980s and 1990s, many of them among competing companies: General Motors bought Hughes Aircraft; R. J. Reynolds absorbed Nabisco; GE and RCA merged; ABC became part of Capital Cities Communications; Philip Morris merged with General Foods; Warner Communications merged with Time; and McDonnell Douglas became part of Boeing. Several airlines have also merged. The effect of many of these mergers may have been to decrease competition, and many of them raise questions about whether consumers and stockholders suffered.

The Antitrust Division in the Justice Department investigates proposed corporate mergers and acquisitions to determine whether they will restrain competition and whether they will be detrimental to stockholders and consumers. With a staff of about 300 lawyers, it works on complaints initiated by competitors, customers, or suppliers.

The Antitrust Division investigates possible violations of antitrust laws by civil investigations, by conducting grand jury proceedings, by preparing and prosecuting antitrust cases, and by negotiating and enforcing final judgments. "Two major areas of enforcement activity are investigation, detection, and criminal prosecution of price fixing, and investigation and civil litigation to prevent anticompetitive mergers and bid rigging."[12]

The Reagan and Bush administrations generally adopted a permissive policy toward mergers, and few were prevented. These Republican administrations assumed that most mergers were inherently good for the consumer and the economy, not—as the common wisdom had it in the 1960s—that such mergers were suspect.[13] The Clinton administration has been somewhat more vigorous in enforcing antitrust laws and other regulations that affect mergers, yet both the Antitrust Division and the Federal Trade Commission have looked favorably on most large mergers and have been willing to endorse attempts by trade associations to enforce open competition.[14]

REGULATING LABOR AND MANAGEMENT

Government regulation of business is essentially restrictive. Most laws and rules curb business practices and steer private enterprise into socially useful channels. But regulation cuts two ways. In the case of American workers, most laws in recent decades have tended not to restrict labor but to confer rights and opportunities on it. Actually, many labor laws do not touch labor directly; instead, they regulate its relations with employers.

Among the more important federal regulations designed to protect workers are the following:

1. *Public contracts.* The Walsh-Healy Act of 1936, as amended, requires that no worker employed under contracts with the national government in excess of $10,000 be paid less than the prevailing wage, and that he or she be paid overtime for all work in excess of 8 hours per day or 40 hours per week. Two contested questions today are whether to retain this provision, and if so, how to determine what is the prevailing wage. Skilled craftsworkers and union officials insist that the Davis-Bacon provision, as it is known, is still necessary to protect their standard of living and to ensure quality work on government projects. Others argue that the prevailing wage requirement makes public work unreasonably expensive and that the pro-

vision merely gives craftsworkers a special privilege at the expense of the taxpayers.

2. *Wages and hours.* The Fair Labor Standards Act of 1938 set a maximum work week of 40 hours for all employees engaged in interstate commerce or in the production of goods for interstate commerce (with certain exemptions). Work beyond that amount must be paid for at one-and-one-half times the regular rate. Minimum wages, first set at 25 cents an hour, were progressively increased; in the early 1990s the minimum wage was $4.25; in the late 1990s the minimum wage was increased to $5.15 an hour (as a result of the Minimum Wage Increase Act of 1996).

3. *Child labor.* The Fair Labor Standards Act of 1938 prohibits child labor (under 16 years of age, or under 18 in hazardous occupations) in industries that engage in, or that produce goods for, interstate commerce.

4. *Industrial safety and occupational health.* The Occupational Safety and Health Act of 1970 created the first comprehensive federal industrial safety program. It gives the secretary of labor broad authority to set safety and health standards for companies engaged in interstate commerce.

During the first half of this century, labor's basic struggle was for the right to organize into unions. For many decades trade unions had been held lawful by acts of state legislatures, but the courts had chipped away at their status by legalizing anti-union devices. The most notorious was the **yellow-dog contract**, by which employers made new workers, as a condition of employment, promise not to join labor organizations. If labor organizers later tried to unionize the workers, the employers, on the basis of such contracts, could apply for court orders to stop the organizers. In 1932 the Norris–La Guardia Act made yellow-dog contracts unenforceable and granted labor the right to organize. With the New Deal, under President Franklin D. Roosevelt, Congress began to enact a series of laws to protect workers and their right to form trade unions.

The National Labor Relations Act

Do unions need federal laws to protect their right to organize? The history of union efforts before 1933 suggests that organizing without federal protection was extremely difficult. Indeed, union membership and strength were waning fast until New Deal measures granted workers the right to organize and bargain collectively. The **National Labor Relations Act (1935)** (usually called the Wagner Act) made these guarantees permanent and gave them federal backing. The preamble declares that workers in industries affecting interstate commerce (with certain exemptions) have the right to organize and bargain collectively and that inequality in bargaining power between employers and workers leads to industrial strife and economic instability.

The act makes five types of employer action unfair: (1) interfering with workers in their attempt to organize unions or bargain collectively; (2) supporting company unions (unions set up and dominated by the employer); (3) discriminating against members of unions; (4) firing or otherwise victimizing an employee for having taken action under the act; and (5) refusing to bargain with union representatives. The act prevents employers from using violence, espionage, propaganda, and community pressure to resist unionization.

A regulatory commission was established to administer the act. The National Labor Relations Board (NLRB) of five members, holding overlapping terms of five years each, has the ticklish job of determining the appropriate *bargaining unit;* that is, whether employees may organize by plant, by craft, or some other basis. The board operates largely through regional officers, who investigate charges of

Unemployment among young people is a serious problem. The youth unemployment rate is usually double that of the adult population; for black teenagers, it is several times that of all adults. A subminimum wage might encourage employers to put more young people to work. It would probably also create some jobs and provide training opportunities for unskilled workers.

But if there were a subminimum wage, young people would often displace older workers because they would be cheaper to hire. This debate over a subminimum wage for teenagers distracts attention from the more important issue of the substantial erosion in the minimum wage for all. Still, a case can be made that a two-tier minimum wage should be tried for a period.

unfair labor practices and issue formal complaints, and through trial examiners, who hold hearings and submit reports to the board in Washington.

The Taft-Hartley Act

Congress passed a major modification of the labor laws in 1947, the Labor-Management Relations Act, commonly called the **Taft-Hartley Act**. It remains the most important legislation regulating union activity in the United States. The act:

1. Outlaws the **closed shop** (a company that requires an employer to hire and retain only union members in good standing) and permits the **union shop** (a company in which new employees must join the union within a stated period of time) only under certain conditions.
2. Outlaws **jurisdictional strikes** (strikes arising from disputes between unions over whose members should perform a particular task); **secondary boycotts** (efforts by unions involved in disputes with employers to encourage other unions to boycott a third party—usually other employers—who, in response to such pressure, might put pressure on the original offending employers); excessive union dues or fees; and strikes by federal employees.
3. Makes it an unfair labor practice for unions to refuse to bargain with employers.
4. Permits employers and unions to sue each other in federal court for violation of contracts.
5. Allows limited use of the **labor injunction** (a court order forbidding specific individuals or groups to perform acts the court considers harmful to the rights or property of an employer or community).
6. Permits states to outlaw union shops. Right-to-work laws, which states could now adopt, typically make it illegal for **collective bargaining** agreements (terms and conditions of employment negotiated by representatives of the union and the employer) to contain closed shop, union shop, preferential hiring, or any other clauses calling for compulsory union membership.

The Taft-Hartley Act also set up machinery for handling disputes affecting an entire industry or a major part of it, if a work stoppage threatens national health or safety. The act has been invoked against strikes in vital sectors of the economy such as atomic energy, coal, shipping, steel, and telephone service. Sometimes a president and the secretary of labor attempt to mediate strikes without resorting to the act.

When a strike threatening national safety breaks out, the following steps are authorized:

1. The president appoints a special board to investigate and report the facts.
2. The president may then instruct the attorney general to seek, in a federal court, an 80-day injunction against the strike.
3. If the court agrees that national health or safety is endangered, it grants this injunction.
4. If the parties have not settled the strike within the 80 days, the board informs the president of the employer's last offer of settlement.
5. The NLRB takes a secret vote among the employees to see if they will accept the employer's last offer.
6. If no settlement is reached, the injunction expires, and the president reports to Congress with such recommendations as he may wish to make.

The Taft-Hartley Act can be used if a strike threatens national health or safety, for example, a strike by hospital or health care workers.

The effectiveness of this act is difficult to assess because legislation is only one of the many factors that affect industrial peace. Labor unions are now so weak that the federal government seldom has to invoke Taft-Hartley to prevent strikes in vital services. Still, one basic issue remains unresolved. Strikes are part of the price we pay for the system of collective bargaining. But under what conditions does the price become so high that the federal government should intervene, stop the strike, and force a settlement?

Labor Today

Organized labor is deeply concerned with the traditional conditions of work, such as hours, wages, and pensions. It must also deal with the issue of *job security*, which is increasingly threatened by various technological revolutions and the nationwide trend toward downsizing and moving operations to countries where labor is cheaper.

Some business owners insist that higher wages and benefits force businesses to charge more for their products in order to make a profit, and these higher costs may price American goods and services out of the global market. Less expensive labor has helped other countries compete successfully with American industries like automobiles, steel, clothing, and computer components.

Unions have been losing strength for some decades. In the late 1990s union membership had fallen below 15 percent of the total employed wage and salary workers in the United States.

In some areas labor is cooperating with management to raise productivity in exchange for lifetime jobs and institutional security for the union. The United Auto Workers (UAW) helped General Motors design work practices that use new technology in producing the much-talked-about Saturn car. In return, GM pledged to hire UAW members from other plants to staff new plants and ensured that the UAW will be the bargaining agent. In this particular instance, employees were given a greater voice in operations, and certain traditional work rules and job classifications were relaxed.

The major league baseball strike of the mid-1990s, while atypical of labor-management disputes, illustrates how labor (in this case well-paid ballplayers) preferred to resort to the NLRB and the courts, while management (the owners) preferred to hire replacement workers.

> The baseball owners threatened to replace striking players. The players, on the other hand, succeeded in April 1995 in obtaining a court injunction ordering the owners to restore certain provisions of the players' contracts, the unilateral cancellation of these provisions being ruled an unfair labor practice by the NLRB. The injunction in effect ended the walkout in the union's favor, because the court's declaration that the owners had engaged in an unfair labor practice would have barred them from using replacement players.[15]

Labor conflicts in professional sports provide high-profile cases of NLRB rule making. But 99 percent of its work, as it is for most federal regulatory agencies, is well outside of the glare of the publicity spotlights.

REGULATING ENVIRONMENTAL PROTECTION

The issue of pollution vividly illustrates the regulatory dilemma. Critics of strict controls on air, water, and noise pollution say the pursuit of a clean environment damages our economy and causes unemployment. They call attention, for example, to the disastrous economic consequences of the shutdown of one large company or even of an industry for pollution violations. Proponents of tough antipollution laws contend we must pay the price for decades of environmental abuse.

We the People

Union Membership (in thousands)

	1983	1995
Male	11,809	9,919
Female	5,908	6,441
White	14,844	13,172
Black	2,440	2,516
Hispanic	NA	1,352
Total	17,717	16,360

SOURCE: U.S. Bureaus of the Census, *Statistical Abstract of the United States, 1996* (Government Printing Office, 1996), pp. 436 and 438.

Government environmental protection efforts usually win praise from environmentalists and the general public, but the cost of cleanups must be borne by small and medium-sized companies, some of which may be driven out of business by costs they cannot afford.

For example, residents and business owners in Leadville, Colorado, have grown tired and resentful of the EPA's efforts to clean up their high-altitude mining community. Leadville's state representative and former mayor, Ken Chlouber, put it this way: "When the EPA came in to clean up a teensy little creek, that was OK. Anybody could see heavy metals were being dumped into the river. . . . However, since then, they [EPA] have grown like a cancer. Every square inch of Leadville, every person, every property, is under a cloud. We have this EPA we can't get rid of."

EPA folks typically shrug and merely say, "We're from the government, and we're here to help you—we'll protect you from past and future environmental disasters." EPA doubtless is helping, yet its efforts often meet resistance and make it hard for certain businesses to survive.

Quoted in Katie Kerwin, "Residents, EPA, Feud over Pollution Cleanup," Rocky Mountain News, August 7, 1994, p. 72A.

They say the longer we delay, the greater the costs to society, both in dollars and in lives. Today the immediate cost of pollution control tends to fall on the polluter, so we would expect opposition from industry. The benefits, on the other hand, go to everyone. Thus, the issue evokes concentrated opposition as well as widespread support.

Environmental issues used to be handled by local and state governments, although one political scientist found that inaction had been a regular response to the air pollution problem in communities throughout the nation: "The federal government has taken on new responsibilities in the field of pollution abatement not so much because these local officials demand it, but because these lower levels of government have often failed to take action themselves."[16]

The federal government finances research on control devices and assists states both in maintaining their own pollution-control programs and in building waste-treatment facilities. The primary federal agencies concerned with the environment are the Council on Environmental Quality in the Executive Office of the President, which develops and recommends policy options to the president and Congress, and the Environmental Protection Agency, which is responsible for enforcing federal environmental laws and regulations. Other federal agencies that regulate the environment include the Interior Department, the Food and Drug Administration, and the Departments of Energy and Transportation.

Arguments about pollution control rarely concern whether to act or not; rather, they ask what price we are willing and able to pay for a clean environment and how best to achieve it. Laws now on the books cost the average homeowner several dollars a month in electricity costs. Some private interests, including the automotive industry and the chemical industry, have been hard hit by pollution control laws, and the Clean Air Act of 1990 adds yet additional costs.[17]

The National Environmental Policy Act of 1969 set up the controversial requirement of **environmental impact statements** to assess the potential effects of new construction or development on the environment. Most projects utilizing federal funds must file such statements. Since 1970 thousands of statements have been filed. Supporters contend the statements have pointed out major flaws in projects and have led to cost saving along with greater environmental awareness. Critics claim environmental impact reviews simply represent more government interference, paperwork, and delays in the private sector.

Opponents of the North American Free Trade Agreement (NAFTA) charge that its implementation will hurt the environment. Because Mexico does not impose strict environmental restrictions on its manufacturers, they can produce goods more cheaply than we can in the United States. Opponents further contend that rather than comply with the environmental regulations dictated by NAFTA, Mexican manufacturers will choose to pay the fines and continue to pollute the air and water. Supporters of NAFTA respond that its adoption has already exerted effective pressure on the Mexican government and industry to improve their procedures. They maintain that even the modest improvements in environmental controls brought about by NAFTA will be welcome.

Clean Air

The 1970 amendment to the Air Quality Act of 1967 established national standards for states, pollution guidelines for automobiles, and regulations concerning stationary sources of pollution. Yet enforcement of the act greatly disappointed environmentalists, who noted that EPA had brought only about seven of some nearly 300 industrial air toxins under federal regulation. Amendments to the act passed in 1977 extended yet did not greatly strengthen the original legislation. Throughout the 1980s the potential in lost jobs and costs for industry and consumers stalled both more rigorous enforcement and tighter restrictions.

Los Angeles smog has often been the subject of jokes, but it is no laughing matter to local residents. However, strict automobile emissions standards have helped improve the situation.

But in 1989 George Bush, acting on his pledge to be an "environmentalist president," introduced a bold clean air bill. The 1990 Clean Air Act was designed to remedy the failings and lax enforcement of the 1970 and 1977 acts. It tightened controls on automobiles and the fuel they use. It required automakers to install pollution controls to reduce emissions of hydrocarbons and nitrogen oxides. Stiff standards for the kinds of gas that can be sold were set for the smoggiest cities. The 1990 act stipulated that plants that emit any of 189 toxic substances have to cut those emissions to the average level of the 12 cleanest similar facilities. Plants posing a 1 in 10,000 risk of cancer to nearby residents by the year 2003 may be shut down. The act also promoted the phasing out, more rapidly than earlier measures, of chlorofluorocarbons and other chemicals that harm the earth's protective ozone layer and may be a factor in global warming.[18]

The 1990 Clean Air Act has been called the most expensive piece of environmental legislation ever passed, with some estimates saying compliance will cost as much as $25 billion per year. But most people, including many leaders in our nation's basic industries, acknowledge we have made a mess of the environment, and the sooner we clean it up the better.

Some economists urge that the profit motive be harnessed in the pursuit of pollution control. With this in mind, EPA has pressed for new regulatory strategies that encourage market solutions for ecological problems. The principle works like this: "Government sets broad limits on the amount of pollution allowed for a region or industry and allots permits to firms for their share of that total. Polluters can buy or sell these allowances, so that firms that can reduce a pollutant inexpensively will benefit by selling their allowances to dirtier neighbors."[19] Initial efforts along these lines have been successful, saving billions.

Secretary of the Interior Bruce Babbitt is regarded as a strong advocate of environmental protection. A geologist, attorney, and former governor of Arizona, Babbitt also headed a conservation advocacy group before joining the Clinton cabinet.

Acid Rain

More than 50,000 synthetic chemicals now exist, and 1,000 new ones are created each year. Although most have beneficial effects, some are known to cause sickness and death to humans; others are suspected of such effects. For example, at least 60 licensed chemicals now widely used in processed food have been found in laboratory animal tests to cause cancer.[20] Until the 1990s, chemicals were generally used without much control, without regard for their effect on humans, and without

Factories that emit pollutants now have to install expensive air purification equipment, and the expense is usually passed on to consumers.

attention to the harm they might do in the future, as they accumulate in the atmosphere and rivers.

Until a few years ago the debate over *acid rain* (created when sulfur dioxide and nitrogen mix with rain, sleet, or snow and alter the acidity of the water and soil) focused on whether there really was a problem. Today the scientific consensus is that sulfur dioxide and other air pollutants belched from coal-burning utility boilers and industries in the Midwest are damaging northeastern and Canadian lakes and water supplies and are contributing to the damage of forests in the American South and elsewhere.

The challenge for national policy makers has been what to do and how to do it. The Clean Air Act of 1990 mandated that power plants install "scrubbers," complex equipment that removes sulfur dioxide from smokestacks. Industries and utilities have the option of switching to low-sulfur coal or cleaning the coal before using it. But purchasing the scrubbers is expensive, and switching to low-sulfur coal means eliminating thousands of mining jobs in the East. Each option thus involves considerable costs and political liabilities. Regional politics are also involved. Benefits accrue mainly to the Northeast, while costs are borne disproportionately by states in the Midwest or coal-producing states like West Virginia.

The political fights over the acid rain problem have divided mining unions, utilities, Democrats and Republicans, coal associations, and governors. Sharp differences of view also separate the United States and Canada. Solutions to this problem will be costly and long.

The Politics of Environmental Regulation

Protection of the environment was not a particularly partisan issue until the 1980s. Both Democrats and Republicans had previously responded to the intense concern about pollution, carcinogens, and hazardous wastes that cause sickness, injury, and death. President Ronald Reagan, however, appointed regulators who were generally hostile to the environmentalist agenda. Their different outlooks, combined with serious budgetary cutbacks, led to a marked change in how provisions of environmental laws were applied. The Reagan administration curbed the regulation of air pollutants and set a policy of proceeding slowly with the cleanup of hazardous wastes. Air and water quality programs were cut, and efforts to control acid rain were slow to evolve. "Under-staffed, under-funded and under-Reagan" became the lament of those concerned with environmental regulation.[21]

The Reagan administration was plainly skeptical that environmental regulation was justified by the facts and contended that the nation had been scared into adopting programs that would cost a lot but that brought little public benefit. Both Reagan and Bush administration economists emphasized that economic growth and environmental protection can be compatible only if regulation does not impose unnecessary costs and brings about genuine benefits. Although George Bush failed to win the support of politically active environmentalist groups, he did win praise for championing the Clean Air Act of 1990.

Bill Clinton won election in 1992 on a platform that promised aggressive leadership on environmental matters. His vice-president, Al Gore, had long been associated with environmental reform. Clinton's appointments to key environmental policy positions were praised, but he generally tried to strike a middle ground between the Reagan position on the one hand and vigorous environmentalists on the other. In both his first and second term, Clinton promised more leadership in environmental matters than he was able to exercise. His efforts to cut regulations, reduce staff, and balance the federal budget made it difficult to strengthen EPA and similar agencies to do their job effectively. Clinton raised expectations yet achieved relatively modest success in this policy area.

REGULATING OCCUPATIONAL SAFETY AND HEALTH

The Occupational Safety and Health Administration, a unit in the Department of Labor, is one of the most criticized federal regulatory agencies, although that criticism has decreased in recent years. You have no doubt come across reports of its endless rules or its allegedly patronizing warnings to business operators. OSHA has thousands of rules in the *Code of Federal Regulations*. Despite vigorous efforts by antiregulation groups to slash its budget and cut its staff, OSHA still employs over 2,000 persons, about half of whom are safety and health inspectors.

OSHA was created because interest groups effectively publicized that many people were becoming disabled or were dying from work-related accidents. By 1970, for example, more than 14,000 people were dying each year in industrial accidents, and an estimated 100,000 a year were being permanently disabled in workplace injuries.

The mandate of OSHA is to protect the health and safety of more than 60 million workers in about 5 million workplaces. It is also asked to issue compulsory safety and health standards and to monitor compliance. To achieve these objectives, OSHA is empowered to inspect businesses and to issue notices of violation and fines.

Criticism of OSHA

In business circles OSHA quickly became a "four-letter word." Many business executives criticized OSHA's standards as having only nuisance value. Inspectors, they said, were not familiar enough with their operations to offer helpful suggestions, and many OSHA regulations did not protect workers. Executives claimed that the costs of many OSHA requirements had an inflationary effect.

In the first years of OSHA, small businesses complained that OSHA rules were too numerous, too complex, and too technical. The costs of compliance were supposedly prohibitive for small business operators. Some businesses claimed they would be forced to close down because of governmental regulations. Yet a majority of industrial fatalities occur in businesses employing 25 or fewer workers.

Labor groups were OSHA's major source of support in its early years. But labor officials criticized OSHA in the 1980s and 1990s for being a "toothless watchdog"

Risky Businesses

**Annual Fatalities
per 100,000 Workers**

- Mining 43
- Construction 31
- Agriculture, forestry, and fishing 44
- Transportation, communications, and public utilities 22

**Annual Injuries and Illnesses
per 100 Full-Time Workers**

- Meat packing 46
- Shipbuilding and repairing 44
- Prefabricated wood building 24
- Structural wood manufacturing 23
- Mobile home manufacturing 23
- Motorcycles, bicycles, and parts 22
- Leather tanning and finishing 20

SOURCE: U.S. Bureau of the Census, *Statistical Abstract of the United States, 1993* (Government Printing Office, 1994), p. 433.

In May of 1996, Valujet Flight 592 crashed in the Florida Everglades, killing 110 people. Critics charged that the Federal Aviation Agency (FAA) should have inspected Valujet's planes more closely and warned about possible violations. Valujet had grown rapidly over a two and a half year period from two planes to a fleet of more than fifty planes, many of them refurbished older planes.

FAA Director David Hinsen told Congress in a 1996 hearing into the crash, "It is apparent now that the extraordinarily rapid growth [of Valujet] created problems that should have been more clearly recognized and dealt with sooner and more aggressively."*

Valujet Flight 592 crashed because it was carrying hazardous materials that were incorrectly labelled. But the crash highlighted lax inspection procedures and focused attention on the operations of a regulatory agency that had had its funds and personnel cut back as a result of federal downsizing.

The FAA has the unreachable goal of zero airplane accidents. Its officials are constantly searching for inspection systems and training programs that will make a zero accident record possible. Flying is still the safest way to travel, but it can never be accident-free.

*Quoted in Douglas B. Feaver, "A New Route to Safety," *The Washington Post Weekly Edition*, August 12–18, 1996, p. 22. See also Mary Schiavo with Sabra Chartrand, *Flying Blind, Flying Safe* (Avon, 1997).

and not strict enough. Nevertheless, the backlash from business interests was intense. Proposals sprang up in Congress to exempt small businesses from OSHA's provisions. Ronald Reagan campaigned for the White House in 1980 promising to curb OSHA—and he did. He wanted OSHA to be more conciliatory and concentrate on major industries and serious workplace hazards. The whole tone of OSHA changed in the Reagan years. It streamlined its restrictions, modified its enforcement policies, cut the number of its inspectors, and reduced penalties. Critics in the labor and environmental movements said the White House in the 1980s virtually dismantled the agency. Even the Supreme Court worked to modify OSHA; it held that OSHA's practices of making unannounced inspections of all businesses for violations, even though authorized by Congress, violated the Constitution.

OSHA will celebrate its thirtieth anniversary in 2000. It has not been as bad as its critics maintain, but neither has it been as effective as its proponents hoped would be the case. OSHA deserves credit for the decrease in work-related injuries and illnesses and for its action against polyvinyl chloride and other serious threats to workers' health. OSHA has tried to concentrate its limited energies on severe health hazards and make more use of its emergency power to restrict dangerous substances. It has dropped many trivial safety rules and focused on four major industries—construction, heavy manufacturing, transportation, and petrochemicals—that are considered hazardous. It also keeps pressure on a few industries it considers potentially dangerous, such as auto repair, dry cleaning, and building materials. Today it uses specific guidelines and simplified paperwork as well. Court decisions, union complaints, and congressional investigations have prodded OSHA to be more aggressive, and it has fined a number of industrial giants such as General Motors, Ford, Chrysler, General Dynamics, Caterpillar Tractor, and Campbell Soup. In the late 1990s OSHA is working with states to identify the most unsafe workplaces, "giving companies the option of adopting a voluntary safety partnership with OSHA or else facing stiffer penalties."[22]

The Continuing Controversy

Controversies in OSHA enforcement are inevitable. Workers are exposed to a host of substances and job hazards whose effects on human health are rarely fully understood. For example, even when something is known to be toxic, the precise degree of risk or an acceptable amount of exposure is hard to calculate, and the costs of total protection can run very high. The harmful effects of many substances, such as asbestos and cotton dust, do not appear until years later, making proof of causation more difficult and the establishment of regulations more tenuous.

OSHA's problems stem in part from the fact that it generally intervenes in the private sector by using *command-control devices*—dictating what must and must not be done—rather than through economic incentives. Many liberals as well as conservatives now suggest that regulatory administration might be more efficient if businesses were given a greater role in determining cost-effective means of achieving agreed-upon goals.

THE DEREGULATION DEBATE

One solution to the problems of government regulation has been **deregulation**—cutbacks in the amount of regulation attempted by the federal government, not the dismantling of all regulatory procedures.

Transportation

No industry has undergone more extensive deregulation than the transportation industry. Over the past generation, airlines, trucking, and railroads have been granted considerable freedom in conducting their operations.

Deregulation of the airlines may have reduced fares in some areas, but it also led to reductions in service and long lines at the counters in other areas.

AIRLINES   The Civil Aeronautics Board (CAB) was established by the federal government in 1938 to protect airlines from unreasonable competition by controlling rates and fares. Critics of CAB regulation charged that airlines were competing only in the frequency and convenience of flights and in the services they offered on flights. Because there was no competition over price, consumers were forced to pay high rates for services they may not have desired. Others claimed CAB regulation of fares kept them higher than they would have been under more competitive conditions. It was also charged that airlines were too slow to open new routes under CAB supervision.

In light of these and other considerations, Congress in 1978 passed the Airline Deregulation Act. The act phased out the CAB (which was legislated out of existence in 1985) and relaxed restrictions on airline fares and routes. Airlines, in effect, were free to set whatever fares their markets would bear, and free entry and free exit were allowed in all markets.

One of the first results of deregulation was that some medium-sized cities lost service as carriers found it more profitable to use their aircraft in busier markets. Critics charged that airlines were raising fares on routes over which they had monopolies in order to subsidize lower fares on more competitive routes. Critics also charged that safety precautions and maintenance suffered as a result of cutthroat competition and the ease with which new airlines could enter the market. Perhaps the most serious complaint about deregulation has been that since 1978 a dozen airline companies have merged or gone out of business, and others, like TWA, Continental, and America West, were forced into bankruptcy.

Although these problems have been associated with deregulation, it has resulted in generally lower fares (after controlling for inflation), greater choice of routes and fares in most markets, and more efficient use of assets by the industry.[23] Deregulation of the airlines has been judged a success by both the surviving airlines and most observers of the industry. If an airline is overcharging passengers on a route, a competitor will eventually steal those travelers away by offering better or lower-priced service—so long as there are real opportunities to compete. Southwestern Airlines and Western Pacific both are examples of discount airlines that took advantage of deregulation to take on larger airlines in the west. In the long run, deregulation is strengthening the industry by forcing companies to streamline operations in order to survive in a competitive market.

TRUCKING AND RAILROADS Deregulation of the trucking and railroad industries soon followed airline deregulation. By 1980 the railroad industry was in poor condition, as it had been for several decades, especially in the East. Many railroads were in serious financial trouble; two went bankrupt. In addition, many observers believed the Interstate Commerce Commission, which had regulated the railroads since 1887, was too rigid in interpreting and enforcing federal regulations. A growing body of economic evidence suggested that regulation was causing great inefficiencies, and that market forces could generate better service to shippers and travelers at lower prices.

The trucking industry was much healthier. ICC regulations had limited the entry of new competitors into trucking and kept rates high. Competition was generally low, allowing trucking companies to charge relatively high rates for hauling cargo. Both the trucking owners and the Teamsters Union opposed deregulation, fearing it would alter this mutually beneficial situation. Calls for deregulation came primarily from businesses that were forced to pay high rates to have their goods transported.

In 1980 Congress passed the Staggers Rail Act to deregulate railroads and the Motor Carrier Act to deregulate trucking. Both acts loosened restrictions on entry into their respective industries, made it easier for railroads and trucking companies to abandon unprofitable activities, and allowed each industry more freedom in setting rates.

The effects of deregulation on both industries have been broadly similar and positive. In the case of trucking, the primary benefit of deregulation has been to increase profitability. In addition, new firms are entering the industry. Railroad deregulation has led to discounted rates, more competition, and service innovations.

The deregulation of the transportation industry illustrates the practical application of economic theory. This form of deregulation signaled a return to reliance on market forces. Legislation enhanced competition and reduced prices by putting pressure on firms to operate more efficiently. And while the government may not have acted quickly enough in some instances to provide safety restrictions, deregulation has generally had positive effects. These results were sufficiently positive that the Interstate Commerce Commission was abolished as a result of the ICC Termination Act of 1995, although a Surface Transportation Board (STB) was created the following year within the Department of Transportation. The STB still monitors or reviews certain aspects of the railroad industry, water and motor carriers, and surface pipeline rates.

Banking and the S&Ls

The relatively successful deregulation of airlines, railroads, and trucking encouraged the relaxation of federal supervision over other industries as well. One such industry was banking. The banking industry had long been regulated by the federal government. The trauma caused by the numerous bank failures during the Great Depression of the 1930s led to controls and regulations designed to ensure that such a disaster would never recur. Many economists believed the banking industry performed a special role in the economy and therefore warranted special treatment. Because banks and other financial institutions control the flow of money, the lifeblood of the economy, observers believed the federal government must supervise the industry to guarantee the uninterrupted flow.

Regulation of the banking industry consisted mainly of protective devices. The federal government established the Federal Deposit Insurance Corporation (FDIC) to insure bank deposits up to a specified amount. In recent years the FDIC has had to assist many banks that failed or required support.

The Federal Savings and Loan Insurance Corporation (FSLIC), which performs a similar function for savings and loans institutions (S&Ls), had enormous problems, and its lax regulations produced the biggest failure of government regulation in American history. Savings and loan banks had a tough time in the 1970s and 1980s. High interest rates were a major factor in the emergence of money-market mutual funds, a rival to the S&Ls. Higher interest rates also produced widespread losses on mortgage portfolios. Then, during the 1980s the deregulation movement, which some thought would benefit the S&Ls, wound up costing American taxpayers hundreds of billions of dollars as hundreds of insolvent savings and loan institutions were liquidated or sold at enormous loss.

What went wrong? Congress, the Reagan administration, and the regulatory agencies created a flawed deposit insurance system and allowed deregulation to go too far. Under intense lobbying from the savings and loan industry, Washington policy makers allowed federally chartered S&Ls to engage in consumer, business, and commercial real estate lending and also permitted adjustable-rate home mortgages. Interest-rate ceilings were eliminated, and other rules were relaxed. Economic advisers at the White House later acknowledged this mistake of deregulating an already weak industry:

> These changes were designed to enhance the industry's health by permitting the S&Ls to compete more effectively for deposits, to diversify across a broader set of assets, and to reduce their exposure to interest rate risk. Though these changes were generally beneficial to S&Ls, subsequent events showed the danger in giving new, unfamiliar powers to weak or insolvent institutions. . . . Failing to provide appropriate supervision in the light of the S&Ls' enhanced opportunities to make risky investments proved to be a costly mistake.[24]

The federal government responded to the savings and loan mess with a massive bailout program and the imposition of new regulations to prevent this situation from happening again. Minimum capital requirements for federally insured savings institutions were raised to make capital requirements as stringent as those for national banks. Criminal and civil sanctions for illegal activities involving savings institutions were strengthened. The savings and loan debacle is a lesson in the perils of excessive deregulation. The net effect of the crisis has been to impose more regulations, not less—or what is called *reregulation*.

The Telecommunications Act of 1996

After years of debate, President Clinton signed into law the Telecommunications Act of 1996, the most sweeping regulatory reform of telecommunications since the Communications Act of 1934. The main objective of the new law was to increase competition among phone, cable, and other communications companies. Telephone companies that were once divided into seven local "mini-Bell companies" are now allowed to offer services outside their defined regions. Local telephone companies won the freedom to provide long distance service, manufacture communications equipment, and offer video service in competition with cable television. At the same time, local telephone companies must now open their network to competition for local telephone service from cable television and long distance companies. In short, a number of business restrictions were removed so that cable television and local and long distance telephone companies could effectively compete with one another. The bill thus opens up large areas of telecommunications to companies that once were regulated both in the services they could provide and the prices they could charge.

Advocates argue that this competition will not only lower prices but expand the range of service options. As in other deregulation efforts, there is some uncertainty about what will happen in areas where there is not much competition. Will prices soar? Will services even be available?

Two controversial aspects of the Telecommunications Act of 1996 are the regulation of the Internet content and the advent of the "V-chip" to allow parents to block out television shows with objectionable content. The act prohibits any person or company knowingly to make indecent material accessible to minors by a computer; selling or obtaining drugs are similarly prohibited. In reaction to President

Clinton's signing of the bill, Internet activists organized a 48-hour blackout of World Wide Web pages.

Congress has long been under pressure to regulate the increasingly violent content of television. The invention of the V-chip permits parents themselves to limit access. But the rating system based on age level that was proposed by industry has been criticized by parent groups. They prefer ratings for excessive violence, offensive language, or nudity. The constitutionality of these restrictions is being challenged and will be settled by the courts, but the debate continues on who will decide what is deemed violent or offensive.[25]

REGULATORY OUTCOMES AND ISSUES

While the need for regulation, especially in areas affecting health and safety, is widely accepted, there are concerns about the negative consequences of regulation as well. A marked decrease in lead paint poisonings, the use of childproof bottle tops, and the banning of many cancer-producing pesticides are all outcomes of federal regulatory activity. On the negative side, regulations have increased the cost of some products and may have hampered such industries as railroads and airlines.

Criticisms of Regulation

REGULATION DISTORTS AND DISRUPTS THE OPERATION OF THE MARKET Sometimes governmental intervention upsets the normal adjustment processes of the market and thus encourages higher prices, misallocation of resources, and inefficiency.

REGULATION CAN DISCOURAGE COMPETITION Some forms of regulation (often the kind desired by industry) actually have the reverse of their desired effect. This is especially true when the government grants operating licenses and charters to maintain a certain level of quality or stability in the market. Regulatory red tape has also been charged with discouraging entry into industries and driving small businesses out.

REGULATION MAY DISCOURAGE TECHNOLOGICAL DEVELOPMENT It is argued that if the reward for innovation is a new set of rules and a struggle for permission to use a new product, business may not find it worth the effort to innovate.

REGULATORY AGENCIES ARE OFTEN "CAPTURED" BY THE INDUSTRIES THEY REGULATE It is suggested, especially by those on the political left, that some regulatory bodies are controlled by the big businesses they are supposed to be regulating. There is evidence, too, that some people consider jobs in regulatory agencies as stepping-stones to lucrative careers in private industry, and the industries obviously benefit in several ways from hiring the more able regulators.

REGULATION INCREASES COSTS TO INDUSTRY AND TO THE CONSUMER Federal regulations, as noted earlier, are costly. One conservative think tank estimates that government regulations cost more than $8,000 annually for every household in the United States.[26] Such figures are disputed by many labor and consumer advocates, who say health and safety standards are the best investment we can make. Every life and every limb we save, and every disease we prevent, represents not only a valuable achievement but also a reduction in the nation's enormous hospital and medical bills. Plainly, the side you take in the debate over the cost of federal regulations depends in part on where you sit—that is, on whether you favor labor or management, producer or consumer, energy developer or ecologist, and in part on how much you are willing to spend to move toward a risk-free society.

REGULATION HAS OFTEN BEEN INTRODUCED WITHOUT COST-BENEFIT ANALYSIS
Critics say too little attention is given to whether the benefits of a particular piece of regulation are great enough to justify its cost. Is it worth it to delay approval of new drugs while some who would benefit may die? Is it worth it to clean up 95 percent of automobile emissions if the cost is many times that of an 85 percent cleanup? One report claims we're spending $1.75 million per cancer case arising from exposure to hazardous waste.[27] Is that worth it?

REGULATORY AGENCIES LACK QUALIFIED PERSONNEL Critics of regulation, and some heads of regulatory agencies themselves, say regulators lack the expertise to do their jobs properly. Regulatory agencies complain they need larger budgets to do their job properly and attract more qualified staff. Critics argue, too, that government should not meddle in complex chemical or technological industries about which it knows little.

Evaluating Deregulation

For more than 30 years every president has proposed a program for regulatory reform. Economists from a variety of ideological perspectives are all but unanimous in their view that certain kinds of regulation are unnecessary and that some of it uses the wrong strategy. Even if various parties agree that reform is needed, heated debate arises over what specific actions to take.

Although regulatory reform was not part of the 1994 Republican Contract with America, many Republicans wanted a moratorium on all new government agency regulations. Democrats contended that a moratorium would threaten the safety and health of the American people, because the Food and Drug Administration, Federal Aviation Administration, and other agencies need to be free to regulate as necessary. Republicans believe that their party's opposition to regulation is a popular position, while Democrats are just as sure that the public wants what they see as the benefits of regulation—safe airlines, clean water, and safe prescription drugs.

Deregulation appears to be working better in some areas than in others. In the area of drug deregulation, the results are mixed. The Food and Drug Administration, especially since 1981, relaxed the requirements for introducing new medicines. People in the drug industry applaud these efforts. They argue that as a result of deregulation the public gets better medicines faster and cheaper. Opponents contend, and with some evidence, that the accelerated approval process is endangering public health by prematurely allowing potentially hazardous drugs on the market.

Advocates of deregulation say consumers are capable of making intelligent choices and are profiting from the lower prices and expanded services brought about by deregulation. Opponents contend that deregulation results in such confusion in the marketplace that consumers cannot make sensible choices.

One other point: In our federal system the mere fact that the national government stops regulating an industry does not mean the particular industry will be unregulated. On the contrary, sometimes 50 different state regulators take over, making it even more difficult for that industry to operate on a large scale. California, for example, has much tougher automobile air-pollution rules than does the national government. Variations in state regulations are the reason businesspeople themselves sometimes call for more, not less, national regulation; they would prefer one set of national regulations to 50 different state ones.

The overall effects of deregulation trends, especially as they affect traditional economic regulation, appear to be positive. An exception, of course, was the deregulation of the savings and loan industry. Deregulation has forced some industries to become more efficient, and most consumers have had better service at less cost.

"I think we can agree, gentlemen, that one can respect Mother Nature without coddling her."

Drawing by Lorenz. © 1986 The New Yorker Magazine, Inc.

POLITICS ONLINE

Reaction to Corporate Mergers on the Internet

It is the responsibility of the Federal Trade Commission (FTC) to rule on proposed corporate mergers and seek public comment on these matters. In 1997, for the first time, the FTC invited public comment on the proposed merger between Office Depot and Staples, retail outlets that sell the same types of products. Before the merger, they were the two largest national office supply chains. The question before the FTC was whether such a merger would constitute a monopoly and therefore be bad for competition.

The FTC received thousands of comments via e-mail from people around the country. One group promoting the use of electronic communications in such policy matters is the Consumer Project on Technology, a site created by Ralph Nader to disseminate information on telecommunications, intellectual property, privacy, and antitrust legislation:

> http://www.cptech.org

For a sampling of home pages of agencies and interest groups involved in regulatory policy, go to:

> http://www.public-domain.org   or   http://www.essential.org/antitrust

One of the most important and least understood institutions in economic policy is the Federal Reserve Board. To learn more about it, go to:

> http://www.bog.frb.fed.us

Information on the federal budget can be found at:

> http://www/acces.gpo.gov

SUMMARY

1. Regulation in the United States is neither socialism nor *laissez-faire* policy but a set of government rules and laws issued to alter or control the operations of economic enterprises, yet based on a widely held commitment to a free market economy. Although we often think of politics as the pursuit of private power and private interests, it is plainly also an effort to define the public interest. The government sets up regulatory agencies to enforce federal rules and regulations in an effort to serve the public interest and to achieve various desired goals.

2. Even though the members of regulatory bodies are nominated by the president, their powers derive from legislative delegation, and their decisions are subject to review by the courts. Independent regulatory agencies have a scope of responsibility in the American economy that sometimes exceeds that of the three regular branches of government. They often have a major say in how our economy performs.

3. Regulation is a means of eliminating some of the abuses and problems generated by the private economy, while avoiding government ownership and the risks of too much centralization. Regulation is an inevitable by-product of a complex, industrialized, high-technology society.

4. A deregulation movement designed to get the government out of the regulation of certain businesses has taken place during the last 30 years. Liberals sometimes favor deregulation if they believe it will foster more competition. Conservatives generally favor deregulation that will get federal regulators off their backs in areas such as safety, health, and environmental and consumer-protection standards.

5. There are always winners and losers with deregulation. Businesses would like further deregulation of the Occupational Safety and Health Administration, Food and Drug Administration, and Environmental Protection Agency, but yet this move would be vigorously opposed by labor and environmental interests.

JAMES RING ADAMS, *The Big Fix: Inside the S&L Scandal* (Wiley, 1990).

PAUL ASCH, *Consumer Safety Regulation* (Oxford University Press, 1988).

JAMES BARTH, *The Great Savings and Loan Debacle* (American Enterprise Institute, 1991).

GARY BRYNER, *Blue Skies, Green Politics: The Clean Air Act of 1990*, 2d ed. (Congressional Quarterly Press, 1995).

BRYAN BURROUGH AND JOHN HELYAR, *Barbarians at the Gate: The Fall of RJR Nabisco* (Harper & Row, 1990).

THOMAS W. CHURCH AND ROBERT T. NAKAMURA, *Cleaning Up the Mess: Implementation Strategies in Superfund* (Brookings Institution, 1993).

ROBERT W. CRANDALL AND HAROLD FURCHTGOTT-ROTH, *Cable TV: Regulation or Competition?* (Brookings Institution, 1996).

MARTHA DERTHICK AND PAUL J. QUIRK, *The Politics of Deregulation* (Brookings Institution, 1985).

MARC ALLEN EISNER, *Regulatory Politics in Transition* (Johns Hopkins University Press, 1993).

AL GORE, *Earth in the Balance: Ecology and the Human Spirit* (Houghton Mifflin, 1992).

JAMES GRANT, *Money of the Mind: Borrowing and Lending in America* (Farrar, Straus and Giroux, 1992).

BLAINE HARDEN, *A River Lost: The Life and Death of the Columbia* (Norton, 1996).

PHILIP K. HOWARD, *The Death of Common Sense: How Law Is Suffocating America* (Random House, 1994).

ALFRED KAHN, *The Economics of Regulation* (MIT Press, 1988).

RICHARD KLINGLER, *The New Information Industry: Regulatory Challenges and the First Amendment* (Brookings Institution, 1996).

ROBERT KUTTNER, *Everything for Sale: The Virtues and Limits of Markets* (Knopf, 1997).

PAUL W. MACAVOY, *Industrial Regulation and Performance of the American Economy* (W. W. Norton, 1992).

JERRY L. MASHAW AND DAVID L. HARFST, *The Struggle for Auto Safety* (Harvard University Press, 1990).

PAUL McCLURE, ED., *Congressional Quarterly's Federal Regulatory Directory*, 8th ed. (Congressional Quarterly Press, 1997).

STEVEN A. MORRISON AND CLIFFORD WINSTON, *The Evolution of the Airline Industry* (Brookings Institution, 1995).

MARY SCHIAVO WITH SABRA CHARTRAND, *Flying Blind, Flying Safe* (Avon, 1997).

JAMES B. STEWART, *Den of Thieves* (Simon & Schuster, 1991).

JOHN WARGO, *Our Children's Toxic Legacy: How Science and Law Fail to Protect Us From Pesticides* (Yale University Press, 1997).

MARCIA LYNN WHICKER, *Controversial Issues in Economic Regulatory Policy* (Sage, 1993).

LAWRENCE J. WHITE, *The S&L Debacle: Public Policy Lessons for Bank and Thrift Regulation* (Oxford University Press, 1991).

20

Making Social Policy

$\mathcal{S}$tates such as Wisconsin and California for the last decade or so have been laboratories of welfare reform. They have experimented with establishing work incentives for those on welfare, discouraging births to teenagers and to mothers already on welfare, mandating time limits for welfare benefits, expanding eligibility for two-parent families to discourage divorce, and requiring minors with children who need assistance to reside with their parents and attend school. The federal government and many state governments copied these innovations.

One of the most important policy changes of the past decade occurred in 1996 when Bill Clinton and the Republican-controlled Congress abandoned the large welfare program called Aid to Families with Dependent Children (AFDC) and replaced it with Temporary Assistance for Needy Families (TANF). Dating back to the days of the New Deal, the AFDC program of financial assistance to poor people was largely federally funded but locally administered. Politicians in both parties had long criticized AFDC as creating a permanent underclass and providing incentives for husbands to abandon their families and for mothers to have illegitimate children.

Public opinion polls have shown little support for welfare expenditures and programs generally, but the public is much more supportive of specific welfare programs like Head Start, the preschool program for children from impoverished homes. Hence the debate at the state and national levels was not about abandoning welfare entirely, but replacing it with a different kind of public assistance. The new legislation is called the Personal Responsibility and Work Opportunity Reconciliation Act of 1996, a name that captures two themes of the new approach—individuals taking more responsibility for themselves and replacing welfare with work.

Congress and President Clinton shifted the administrative burden for the new program entirely to the states. The federal government now gives block grants of money to states and generally requires states to match those funds. Public assistance is limited to five years over a person's lifetime, recipients must engage in work activities within two months of receiving benefits, and states can exempt up to 20 percent of cases from the work requirements and lifetime limits—an exemption intended for blind and disabled persons. Consistent with the wave of anti-immigration sentiment, the new law excludes legal immigrants from 19 welfare programs and illegal immigrants from 23. To discourage persons on welfare from moving to states with more generous assistance payments, the law gives states the option of limiting welfare to newcomers from another state.

Reforming welfare illustrates the complexity of making social policy. What motivates people to take a job, to get married, to move to another state? What is the responsibility of government in assisting people who, for whatever reason, cannot provide for themselves? Where should the line be drawn in excluding certain groups from assistance or in limiting their benefits? The purpose of this chapter is to introduce the basic elements of social policy as an illustration of some broader themes and issues discussed earlier in this book. The development of social policy teaches us a lot about how the separation of powers, the overlapping roles of Congress and the presidency, the continuing importance of federalism, the role of ideology and public opinion in the making of domestic policy, and the ongoing debate about the appropriate scope of government power actually work in practice. As with other aspects of public policy, social policy is not static; the way government provides services changes constantly. As we shall see, there have been periods of fundamental reform in which dramatic changes were made.

The extremes of wealth and poverty in our country are epitomized by this photo of a homeless man bedded down in front of a billboard on the streets of New York.

THE ROLE OF GOVERNMENT IN SOCIAL POLICY

What is the proper role of government in education, health care, housing, job security, care for the elderly, and public safety? These questions encompass a large part of the agenda of our national government today, yet such functions were once thought to be mostly private matters or were left to local government. Debates over private versus public responsibilities in social policy and the role of different levels of government have shaped the partisan and ideological differences of this century, and they continue to be important as the nation initiates major changes in social policy.

Public versus Private

Those who favor primarily private approaches to social policy do so for a host of reasons, including a belief that individuals need to take responsibility for their own lives rather than relying on the government to care for them. These people doubt the efficiency and effectiveness of public solutions to social problems and are confident the free market will provide opportunities for those with ambition and a willingness to work hard. Opponents of government solutions say public assistance robs people of their ambition and work ethic.

A preference for private solutions to social problems is closely linked with conservatism in American politics and has long been a central precept of the Republican party. Some conservatives today advocate a purely private form of health insurance, with no government requirement or participation. Allowing parents to choose where to send their children to school by giving them vouchers that can be redeemed at any private or public school is another example of a conservative approach to a social policy issue.

Conservatives often point to the long-standing tradition in the United States that private charities, churches, and foundations should raise contributions from individuals and businesses to build hospitals and nursing homes, fund medical research, provide scholarships for students, feed and house the homeless, care for abandoned children, and perform many similar services. The private approach to social policy points to such activities as evidence that people can and will seek to remedy social problems on their own, without the higher taxes, bigger government, and wasteful bureaucracy they see connected to public remedies.

Advocates of public solutions to social problems believe it is the responsibility of government to provide some minimum standard of living—a job, an education, health care, housing, and basic nutrition—for all citizens. They argue that human dignity not only requires some minimum standard of living, but that such a policy is also pragmatic. Without it, our cities would have far more homeless and hungry people, desperate for survival. Advocates of government solutions say that private solutions to social problems do not work because there is simply not enough charitable giving to address the social needs of poor people, the elderly, and those without health insurance. Moreover, they argue, the United States is far behind other countries in social service programs and funding. Government support for public housing, welfare, health care, and education is simply a fact of life for the modern nation-state, they contend.

National versus State and Local

Social policy was long considered primarily a responsibility of state and local governments. Consequently, the ideological debate about social policy issues includes questions of which level of government should address the policy problems, the national government or the state and local governments? Conservatives advocate leaving most social policy matters to states and localities, where programs can be adapted to local needs. Liberals counter that history has taught that state and local governments are unable or unwilling to address problems like health care, homelessness, and crime on their own, so the national government needs to play a major role in funding programs and setting policy standards.

Governors have become increasingly vocal about the tendency of the national government to mandate social policy programs that the states must administer with little or no federal funding for implementation. Such *unfunded mandates* force state governments to raise taxes or reduce funding for various other state programs. With all the attention health care and welfare reform have received, the governors clearly want to make the point that whatever new programs are enacted, they need to be fully funded by the national government. The issue of federalism in social policy is this: Do Americans want a variety of social programs with some differences between the states? Or should the poor, the young, and those with disabilities be treated the same, regardless of which state they live in?

A BRIEF HISTORY OF SOCIAL POLICY IN THE UNITED STATES

Promoting "the general welfare"—which could include health care, welfare, public education, and crime control—is listed in the Preamble to the Constitution as one of the tasks of government. In order to "form a more perfect Union," the framers also stated that it was government's responsibility to "insure domestic Tranquility," "provide for the common defense," and "secure the Blessings of Liberty." How Americans view each of these elements has changed over time.

Long after other Western democracies had expanded their social services, welfare in the United States was left to private charities and to local governments. Why? Part of the answer is that this nation was seen as the land of opportunity. Our millions of acres of free land, our enormous natural resources, and our technical advances all helped absorb people who otherwise might not have made a go of it. Closely linked with this growth and opportunity was the widely held philosophy of *rugged individualism*: If people did not get ahead, it was their own fault. For others, the idea of equality of opportunity meant that government played only a limited role in people's lives. Government's primary function was to secure traditional individual rights and provide **public goods**, such as roads, harbors, postal services, and public order. Rather grudgingly, state governments in the early twentieth century extended relief to needy groups, especially the old, the blind, and the orphaned. But government aid was limited, and much reliance was placed on private charity.[1]

Most Americans today expect their governments to play a greater role in the delivery of social services than did their predecessors. These expectations have changed as a result of wave after wave of reformers who pushed their agenda of social services. Two social policy reform efforts deserve special attention: The New Deal and the Great Society.

The New Deal

The Great Depression of the 1930s drastically expanded the involvement of the national government in social programs. As the value of stocks and real estate fell after the 1929 stock market crash and unemployment, homelessness, and poverty rose to unprecedented heights, the inadequacy of state and local government programs and private charities became apparent. In 1933 the federal government began making loans to states and localities for public relief. When state and local funds dried up, the federal government assumed more responsibility.

Before long, people grew critical of so-called "make-work projects" and the cost and waste of relief programs. They wanted to go back to simple handouts of food or cash by the government. But there was growing support for a well-planned,

---

Major New Deal Programs

Franklin D. Roosevelt's administration established relief programs designed to stimulate the economy and put people back to work:

- The Works Progress Administration (WPA) spent billions of dollars on local projects such as public housing, courthouses, and parks.
- The Public Works Administration (PWA) built larger permanent projects, like dams and roads.
- The Agricultural Adjustment Act (AAA) raised farm prices.
- The Civilian Conservation Corps (CCC) put people to work protecting natural resources on federal land.
- The Tennessee Valley Authority (TVA) supervised the construction of dams and power plants on the Tennessee River to electrify and modernize the rural South.

The WPA program, part of President Roosevelt's New Deal, created jobs for thousands of unemployed during the Great Depression of the 1930s.

long-term program that would foster both the security and self-respect of the people needing assistance. However, the first federal attempt at an extensive security program—the Railroad Retirement Act of 1934—was declared unconstitutional by the Supreme Court.[2] The act permitted the establishment of a fund that all railroad workers would pay into, and then at their retirement or disability, they would receive payments from this fund. The Court declared the act unconstitutional because Congress had established the fund under the Constitution's commerce clause. When Congress passed the same act the next year referring to the Constitution's general welfare clause, the act was upheld.

Social Security

As a part of the New Deal, the United States inaugurated **Social Security** in 1935, perhaps the most significant social legislation in our history. At the time it was controversial; today it is politically untouchable. Social Security is actually many programs, the most important being a retirement program supported by a combination of employee and employer taxes, now covering more than 90 percent of the American work force. Other Social Security programs include financial support for disabled workers and for children of deceased or disabled workers. Health insurance for retired and disabled persons is also part of Social Security.

Social Security was based on the assumption that society must take care of the elderly and the unemployed. Before Social Security, when large families were common, much of the cost of caring for the elderly was borne by children and grandchildren. Families usually had the resources to provide the necessities of life for Grandma, Aunt Suzie, and Uncle George. But during the 1930s, "taking care of one's own" was no longer a practical solution, given the extensive economic dislocation and fractured families caused by the Depression.

Since Social Security began, the program has experienced steady growth and is now the world's largest insurance program for retirees, survivors, and people with disabilities. Combined with the cost of Medicare, its expenditures totaled about $529 billion by 1996.[3] Programs like Social Security are called **entitlement programs** because they provide a specified set of benefits as a matter of right to all who meet the criteria established by law.

Social Security pays over 43 million Americans every month, while 140 million working people contribute to it; the average retired person receives about $745 per month.[4] Full benefits are paid to those between the ages of 65 and 70 who are not currently earning wages of more than a certain amount; after age 70, people are entitled to retirement benefits regardless of wage earnings. The universal nature of Social Security is one reason it is politically so popular: everyone benefits, regardless of need.

Until the 1970s, growth in Social Security benefits was relatively noncontroversial, largely because "the costs were initially deceptively low," while the benefits increased steadily, making the system politically painless.[5] The liberalization and expansion of benefits to include medical insurance for the elderly and poor were made possible by the steady economic growth of the 1950s and 1960s. But increased life expectancy and a steadily declining birthrate placed the burden of supporting the Social Security system for more and more senior citizens on fewer and fewer workers. Today the system provides monthly benefits to 26.8 million retired Americans, as well as benefits to 5.4 million widows and widowers, 4.4 million disabled workers, 3.8 million children of deceased or disabled persons, and 3.2 million entitled wives and husbands.[6]

Social Security, unlike many other welfare programs, is financed not from general taxes but from a trust fund into which taxes on employees and employers are placed—the Federal Insurance Contribution Act, commonly known as FICA. In some ways, this fund is like a private pension plan in which an investor puts money into a pension account. Over the years, Congress has added benefits to the Social Security system without adding enough money to the trust fund to cover the added expense. In 1983, Congress was forced to put Social Security on a more sound financial foundation by passing reforms that raised the retirement age at which one qualifies for Social Security benefits, increasing Social Security taxes, and taxing half of the Social Security payments of upper-income individuals—a figure that has more recently been raised to 85 percent.[7]

The Social Security system is presently running a surplus, meaning that the amount that is brought in through Social Security taxes is greater than the amount of money going out in benefits. The surpluses are invested in Treasury bonds, with the promise that they will be repaid with interest later. Experts predict that the Social Security system will feel its next financial strain in about 2010, when baby boomers start to retire and the system has to start spending the interest on today's investments.[8]

Social Security taxes have increased over time until they are now the largest tax paid by roughly two-thirds of all Americans, exceeding the amount they pay in income tax. Both employers and employees are required to pay 7.65 percent, up

The CPI: A Technical or a Social Problem?

In December of 1996, a commission led by Michael J. Boskin of Stanford University reported that the Consumer Price Index (CPI) overstates inflation by 1.1 percent. The commission went on to recommend that Congress revise the CPI and that the Bureau of Labor Statistics redesign its methods of calculating it. If the CPI were simply one of the many obscure government statistics that is reported almost daily, there would be little to talk about. The CPI, however, is the government's measure of inflation, which is used to adjust government spending on programs such as Social Security, Medicare, and pensions for retired government workers.

While economists may view the CPI as a mere statistic to be examined technically, politicians are surrounded by recipients of entitlements arguing for more relief and by others demanding a balanced budget. The CPI is the political equivalent of a "silver bullet" because much of the entitlement spending in the budget could be reduced if the CPI were adjusted. Politicians in both parties have been reluctant to make this change in the CPI, fearing the wrath of those who benefit from the current CPI formula. But the widespread consensus among economists that the CPI is an overestimate of true inflation persists, as is the temptation not to lower entitlement spending.

SOURCE: Louis Uchitelle, "Measuring Inflation: Can't Do It, Can't Stop Trying," *The New York Times*, March 16, 1997, p. D4.

IT'S OUR MONTHLY PAYMENT FROM SOCIAL SECURITY WITH A LITTLE NOTE SAYING THERE'S NO NEED TO WORRY, THE GOVERNMENT HAS WORKED OUT A FUNDING SOLUTION FOR THE PROGRAM BUT STRONGLY IMPLYING IT WOULD BE A BIG HELP IF WE DROPPED DEAD A LITTLE EARLIER THAN USUAL.

Drawing by Wright for *The Miami News*.

to $4,085 per year, of their earnings into the Social Security fund. A single person with no dependents would have to earn $30,000 before paying more federal income tax than Social Security tax; families with two children would have to earn over $40,000 before their income tax would exceed their Social Security tax. Some experts believe that if Social Security expenditures are not controlled, more than half of every paycheck will be used to finance the program by 2040.[9]

Because people are living longer and demanding more benefits, concerns about the financial stability of Social Security over the long term have grown. When the baby boomers retire, there will be a major increase in the number of people receiving benefits in proportion to those contributing to the system. This increase would not be a problem if the money being contributed to Social Security by today's workers was being saved for their eventual retirement. But much of the money taken from today's workers goes to pay for today's retirees. Social Security is thus a transfer program in which today's young workers finance the retirement of today's elderly. At some point, this reality is likely to foster intergenerational tension between workers and retirees.

Some believe that Social Security will run out of money by the year 2030.[10] Former House Ways and Means Committee Chair Dan Rostenkowski suggested the following measures to fix the system: increase payroll taxes, reduce benefits, and make those born after 1949 wait until they are 67 to retire if they want full benefits.[11] Such proposals would generate widespread and intense opposition, and therefore Congress is likely to postpone any action until the problems are much more immediate.

Although the demographics of Social Security are a policy concern, the politics of Social Security are clear. Few politicians today would risk proposing changes that might be construed by the powerful constituency of elderly voters as cutting back on the program or its benefits. The 1993 budget, including an increase in taxes on Social Security earnings, passed on a party line vote in Congress. Democrats voted for the increase; Republicans voted against it. This action shows that retirement programs are not immune from change, but such votes are rare. The issue of Social Security came up again in 1997 when the Senate debated a Balanced Budget Amendment, and some politicians insisted that Social Security not be included in the formula when calculating a balanced budget. Protecting Social Security may have given some senators political cover for an unpopular vote on the Balanced Budget Amendment.

The Great Society

Another significant expansion of social services came in the 1960s. At a commencement speech at the University of Michigan in May 1964, President Lyndon Johnson described a vision of a "great society," one that would end poverty and racial prejudice, in which education would be available to every child, and in which people residing in cities would live "the good life." In his State of the Union Address to Congress a few months earlier, Johnson had called for a "declaration of war on poverty in America." Johnson's agenda was as broad as his rhetoric, and as with the New Deal, Congress enacted much of it in a fairly short period of time. Great Society programs dramatically increased the role of the federal government in education, extended voting and civil rights, expanded Social Security to include medical benefits for retired Americans, provided health care to poor Americans, financed housing programs to provide decent housing to the poor, offered job training through the Job Corps, and offered preschool education to poor children in a program called Head Start.[12] Congress followed Johnson's lead, appropriating funds for most of what he had asked for in his first year of the War on Poverty.

Changes in social policy typically are led by presidents who have made social policy a key part of their agenda. Many of the ideas of the Great Society, for instance, had been discussed during the Roosevelt and Truman administrations but had not been acted on. The combination of a changed mood in the country, a growing restlessness about racial injustice and poverty, and a commitment to government programs as a means to address social problems all came together in the 1960s and spawned a remarkable series of policy changes.

The leadership and political skill of President Lyndon Johnson were critical. His motivation stemmed from his own values but also reflected a response to pressures within his party and the country and, some might argue, a desire to deflect attention away from the Vietnam War. Johnson combined a passion for the agenda with great skill in working with Congress. During Johnson's five years as president, 1,902 proposals were submitted to Congress. Only 57 percent of them were approved, yet of Johnson's 115 Great Society proposals submitted to Congress, 78 percent were passed.[13] Johnson's effectiveness was enhanced by his party's large majority in Congress following his landslide victory in 1964, his ability to mobilize public opinion for his programs, and his skill in dealing with individual legislators, which came from his years of experience in Congress, including several years as Senate majority leader.

The central article of faith in the Great Society agenda was that social and economic problems could be solved, or at least reduced, by government action. In the period since 1968, there has been considerable debate over whether the Great Society was a success or failure.[14] Some Great Society programs were later disbanded during the Reagan and Bush administrations, while spending on other programs was reduced. The 1994 Republican Contract with America proposed further cuts in domestic social programs. Republicans, controlling the House of Representatives for the first time in 40 years, passed legislation to cut welfare spending and Medicare. Their push for change slowed in the Senate. The 1996 welfare reform legislation marked a reversal of Great Society thinking. Bill Clinton's declaration that the "era of big government is over"[15] and his willingness to "end welfare as we know it"[16] reflect a sense that government should do less, and that government services should be decentralized as much as possible.

Some Great Society ideas remain popular, and Clinton's 1996 reelection campaign proposed that individuals be able to take unpaid time off from work for a sick family member without fear of being fired. One way to track the expanded role of government is to look at the relative share of government spending by levels of government in different policy areas over time. Figure 20–1 compares federal with state and local spending by policy areas since 1927.

Reaganomics and Constraints on Social Policy

The departure from New Deal and Great Society approaches to social policy can trace its roots to Ronald Reagan's two terms as president. Reagan's policy of tax benefits to the rich that would "trickle down" to help the poor included a 25 percent reduction in marginal tax rates and a 20 percent increase in defense spending over five years. The result was historic budget deficits and no money to try out new social policy ideas or programs. When George Bush took office in 1989, he called for a "kinder and gentler" approach, but severe spending constraints meant that nothing new would be considered in the social policy area. The 1990 budget deal negotiated between Bush and Congress required that new social spending not be funded through additional deficit spending. Concern about the deficit continues to be a factor in the debate over welfare and health care reform during the 1990s.

Reducing entitlement programs such as Social Security, military pensions, and Medicare is not regarded as a politically viable possibility. Entitlements act as a constraint on social policy change precisely because people believe these programs are *guaranteed*. Entitlements constrain any new social policy initiatives because they take up such a large part of the budget. When added up, the portion of the federal

Major Legislation of the Great Society

1964

- *Civil Rights Act*—the most comprehensive civil rights legislation since Reconstruction
- *Food Stamp Act*—expansion of the New Deal program to improve the nutrition of the poor
- *Economic Opportunity Act*—job training, adult education, and loans to small businesses to attack the roots of unemployment and poverty
- *Nurses Training Act*—grants for training nurses and construction of nursing schools
- *Omnibus Housing Act*—addition of four federal housing programs to existing programs
- *Community Mental Health Centers Act*—federal grants for staffing mental health centers

1965

- *Medicare*—health care benefits for the elderly, linked to Social Security
- *Medicaid*—health care benefits for the poor, linked to Aid to Families with Dependent Children (AFDC)
- *Elementary and Secondary Education Act*—federal funding and programs in public education for disadvantaged children
- *Higher Education Act*—federal funding for colleges and college students
- *Department of Housing and Urban Development*—new department with responsibility for low-rent housing and urban renewal programs
- *Older Americans Act*—Administration on Aging and grants to the states
- *Voting Rights Act*—unparalleled federal enforcement of right to vote in federal elections within the state voting process

1968

- *Housing and Urban Development Act*—expansion of federal housing and urban development programs
- *Omnibus Crime Control and Safe Streets Act*—federal aid for local law enforcement, crime prevention, and corrections programs

SOURCES: *Congress and the Nation, 1945–1964: A Review of Government and Politics*, vol. 1 (Congressional Quarterly Press, 1965), vol. 1; *Congress and the Nation, 1965–1968: A Review of Government and Politics During the Johnson Years* (Congressional Quarterly Press, 1969), vol. 2.

Head Start: A Great Society Success Story

Many Great Society programs have been politically controversial, but one program has enjoyed strong bipartisan support—Head Start. This preschool program prepares impoverished three- and four-year-olds for elementary school by teaching them basic academic and social skills. The program also teaches good nutrition and personal hygiene and provides immunizations and medical and dental screening. Parents of children in the program receive instruction on parenting. Since 1965 nearly 15 million children have participated in Head Start, but the 784,000 students enrolled in 1996 still represent only about half of all eligible children. Head Start makes extensive use of volunteers, with a ratio of volunteers to paid staff of nearly 10 to 1. Even with this large volunteer effort, the program costs taxpayers $4,746 per student per year, with an annual overall budget of more than $3.6 billion.

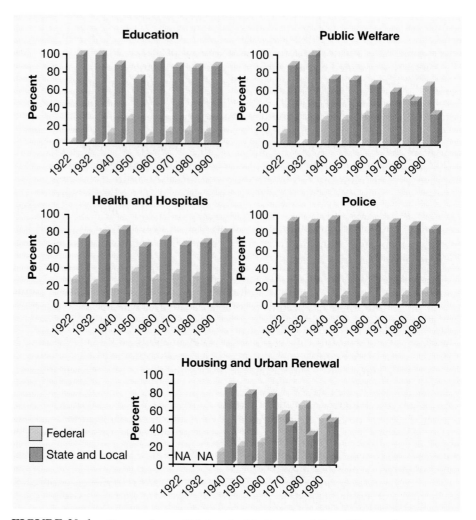

FIGURE 20–1   Comparison of Federal with State and Local Expenditures by Policy Area, 1922–1990

SOURCE: U.S. Bureau of the Census, *Statistical Abstract of the United States, 1992* (Government Printing Office, 1992), pp. 280, 299; *Statistical Abstract of the United States, 1982* (Government Printing Office, 1982), p. 275; *Historical Statistics, Colonial Times to 1970* (Government Printing Office, 1972), pp. 1123–28.

budget earmarked for defense spending, entitlements, and interest on the national debt equals 80 percent, with 53 percent going to entitlements alone,[17] leaving little money for policy innovation (see Table 20–1).

With the decreasing threat from the Soviet Union and the ability to convert at least some defense expenditures to domestic needs, the agenda of American politics shifted to domestic rather than foreign policy. Spending on defense dropped in 1992 and every year thereafter.[18] Reduced defense spending, except for long-term procurement and retirement benefits, offered one way to secure money to pay for a more expansive social policy, but the Clinton administration and the Republican-controlled Congress agreed instead to scale back welfare.

The election of Bill Clinton in 1992 and 1996 did not result in a shift back to some pre-Reagan agenda for social policy. As a "New Democrat," Clinton emphasized economic growth, policy reform, business and government partnerships, and improved efficiency. His program reflected the goals of the social policy liberals, especially his unsuccessful efforts to reform health care, but his willingness to compromise with Republicans on welfare reform alienated many liberals.

TABLE 20–1

Entitlement Spending, 1962–2002*

	Billions of Dollars (in constant 1992 dollars)	Percentage of Total Outlays
1962	144.5	31%
1970	242.1	36
1980	490.0	48
1990	655.0	48
1991	656.0	48
1992	687.1	50
1993	687.8	50
1994	715.7	51
1995	726.2	52
1996	748.4	53
2002	885.0	61

SOURCE: Office of Management and Budget, *Budget of the United States Government, Fiscal Year 1998*, p. 110. Online access: http://www.access.gpo.gov.

*Entitlement spending includes Social Security, deposit insurance, and means-tested entitlements (including Medicaid, food stamps, family support assistance, supplemental security income, child nutrition programs, earned income tax credits, welfare contingency fund, child care entitlement to states, temporary assistance to needy families, and veteran pensions).

WELFARE

Welfare programs in the United States are much more complex than merely handing out checks to poor people. They incorporate job training, transportation subsidies, housing subsidies, free school lunches, food stamps, food for pregnant mothers and babies, and tax credits for low-income people (see Table 20–2). The government also provides financial assistance to farmers and certain industries and underwrites the cost of such "middle-class welfare" as national parks (supported by taxpayers but rarely used by poor people) and loans to college students. But when we hear the term "welfare," we tend to think of public assistance for poor, handicapped, or disadvantaged people. Public assistance can take many forms.

TABLE 20–2

Social Insurance and Benefit Program Payments, 1980–2000 (in billions of 1996 dollars)

Program	1980	1985	1990	1995	2000 (estimated)
Social Security	$227.7	$275.3	$298.5	$345.6	$381.6
Medicaid	60.4	94.8	116.0	163.1	207.8
Medicare	27.2	33.43	49.8	92.4	107.9
Family support (AFDC and TANF)	14.2	13.5	14.8	17.8	20.4
Food stamps	17.3	18.2	19.1	26.4	28.4

SOURCE: Office of Management and Budget, *Budget of the United States Government, Fiscal Year 1998* (Government Printing Office, 1997), pp. 118–22, 193; and *Budget of the United States Government*: http://www.access.gpo.gov.

New Democrats

People who advocate government-sponsored solutions to social problems are considered liberals. Most often they are Democrats, but there are exceptions within both parties. Some Republicans favor universal health care, and some Democrats would vote to lower the minimum wage.

One prominent group of Democrats—calling themselves "New Democrats"—tried to establish an identity somewhere between the liberal and conservative positions. These New Democrats are usually affiliated with the Democratic Leadership Council (DLC), a group formed in 1985 to steer the Democratic party away from the more liberal elements and policy positions of the party. Bill Clinton served for a time as chair of the DLC, and seven members of his cabinet have been affiliated with it. Clinton has indicated that he is "proud to govern as a New Democrat."*

The DLC/New Democrat agenda includes support for the North American Free Trade Agreement, welfare and health care reform, deficit reduction, and the earned-income tax credit. New Democrats also advocate policies that encourage economic growth rather than redistribution, and they are willing to challenge popular government programs they believe are inefficient and ineffective. They emphasize the values of community and individual responsibility that conservatives long laid claim to. New Democrats emphasize reducing bureaucratic red tape, favor programs that are more decentralized, make use of market approaches, and place more reliance on individual responsibility.

*Quoted in David Corn, "Working with the New Democrats," *The Nation*, January 3–10, 1994, p. 16.

We the People

People in Poverty

	Number (millions)	Percent
Race		
White	28.4	10.2
Black	7.0	27.4
Hispanic*	3.2	22.6
Age		
Under 18	15.2	21.8
18–24	4.5	18.0
25–34	5.5	13.2
35–44	4.4	10.6
45–54	2.4	7.8
55–59	1.1	10.4
60–64	1.1	11.4
65+	3.7	11.7
Education		
No high school diploma	2.9	24.8
No college	2.3	10.9
Some college	1.3	7.8
College graduate	.4	2.6
All persons	8.0	11.6

*The U.S. Census Bureau defines persons of Hispanic origin to be of any race.

SOURCE: U.S. Bureau of the Census, *Statistical Abstract of the United States, 1996* (Government Printing Office, 1996), pp. 473, 476.

- Direct payments to single parents with young children, the unemployed, and the disabled
- Vouchers that can be exchanged for food
- Subsidies that reduce the cost of housing or the provision of public housing
- Reduced cost or free access to public transportation, higher education, or job training
- Subsidized medical care.

These programs are targeted to the more than 37 million people living under the official poverty line of just under $16,000 for a family of four in 1996, or roughly 15 percent of the population. One study has estimated that there has been a 39 percent decline in poverty due to social welfare programs.[19]

The poor tend to be disproportionately African American, Hispanic, young, and female. More than half of all poor families are headed by females. The fact that more women and children are impoverished has been called the "feminization of poverty."[20] Examples of the range of problems encountered by women include the male-female wage gap for men and women doing the same work, the concentration of women in low-paying jobs, the differential economic impact of divorce on men and women, the disproportionate responsibility women assume for child care, the abandonment of family by men who fail to pay child support, and illegitimate births. Traditional welfare programs are aimed at these problems, but they have largely failed to solve them.

The Current Welfare System

As with much of social policy, the welfare system traces its roots to the New Deal. In the face of widespread unemployment and poverty during the Great Depression, the government enacted social policies intended to provide a system of "social security" for the nation's elderly and disabled as well as jobs programs for the unemployed. In 1950, the federal government contributed just 44 percent of all public assistance, but by 1990, the federal government paid over 72 percent of all benefits.[21]

During his 1992 presidential campaign, Bill Clinton promised to "end welfare as we know it" by providing education, training, day-care, and health coverage during the first two years on welfare, and then helping welfare recipients find work in private-sector or community service jobs as a way to eliminate the "permanent dependence on welfare." Such rhetoric from the candidate was very popular on the campaign trail because it struck a responsive chord of the American ethic of individual responsibility and hard work. Soon after taking office, Clinton appointed a task force to prepare a reform package that incorporated his vision. The problem was that actually doing what he envisioned cost a lot of money, and he had to scale back his proposal substantially.[22]

1996 Welfare Legislation

Welfare reform was a major issue throughout the 104th Congress. House and Senate reformers appeared to be reacting to a growing sentiment that welfare recipients are not victims; they just need help to pull themselves up by their bootstraps. The "safety net" should be only a temporary aid, and more should be required of recipients.

In early 1995, as part of the vigorous campaign to reduce the federal deficit, Congress proposed a slash in eligibility, a cap on federal funding of welfare, and state responsibility to run a revamped welfare program. House proposals attempted to combine dozens of welfare programs into large block grants to the states. Each state was to set eligibility requirements and administer child-care programs, school meals, nutrition programs for pregnant women and young children, and possibly cash welfare,

The Republican Contract with America set forth plans to reduce welfare spending by cutting back many of the programs initiated under previous Democratic administrations.

child protection, and food stamps, through these block grants. With limited funds, the priority would be on American children; illegal immigrants would be excluded from 23 welfare programs and legal aliens from 19. These proposals required welfare recipients to find work after two years of benefits, and they set a lifetime cap for benefits at five years. House Republicans were criticized for these proposals because, in attempting to cut costs, they provided little help for getting and keeping jobs, and children were penalized if their parents did not move toward self-sufficiency.

President Clinton, who had advocated time limits for welfare, work requirements, tougher child support enforcement, and requiring teen-age mothers to live at home as a condition of assistance, vetoed the measure, saying the budget cuts were too deep. Congressional Republicans had attempted to implement welfare reform through the budget process, something Clinton also objected to. When they passed welfare reform legislation with essentially the same provisions, Clinton again vetoed it.

The National Governor's Association (NGA) then came forward with some compromise welfare reform proposals of their own. The NGA plan was based on the defeated welfare bill in that it embraced the block-grant approach and state discretion and responsibility. With bipartisan support, the governors agreed that more money for child care was needed than Congress offered, that states must spend funds to match federal block grants, and that school lunch programs should stay intact and not become a block grant. Funds for most welfare programs would be sent to the states in a block grant with few strings attached. The states would be relatively free of interference from Washington, but they would have access to a federal "rainy-day fund" during times of recession or when demand for welfare services exceeded state capacity. The governors' proposals later served as a basis for compromise.

Congress and the president did reach a compromise in August 1996 on a welfare reform bill that incorporated the NGA block-grant idea. House proposals such as a lifetime limit on benefits and decreasing aid to legal immigrants were included, as was Clinton's proposal that welfare be linked to work and that welfare benefits have a time limit. The federal government would continue to fund about three-quarters of welfare costs but that figure could change as the reforms are instituted. The compromise bill gave Clinton and the Republicans in Congress an important legislative accomplishment as they entered the general election phase of the 1996 presidential election.

". . . thanks to my welfare reforms, Larry started his own business and became so successful that he made a giant contribution to the Democratic Party and is now under investigation by the Justice Department . . ."

Walt Handelsman, Tribune Media Services.

An important participant in any welfare reform is Senator Daniel Patrick Moynihan (D.-N.Y.), a Harvard government professor before he entered the Johnson and Nixon administrations. While working for Nixon, Moynihan helped draft the Family Assistance Plan, which guaranteed a direct cash payment to families to push them above the poverty level in return for work. The plan was criticized by conservatives as too expensive and by liberals as insufficient. Now, nearly three decades later, Moynihan is senior Democrat on the Senate Finance Committee and remains a major figure in the welfare reform debate.

Senator Moynihan led the opposition to the 1996 welfare reform bill on Capitol Hill. He opposed both the additional burden on state and local governments and the decreased benefits to children and families in need, saying that the revisions would drive thousands of families into homelessness and create financial disasters for state and city governments. He conjured up visions of "children sleeping on grates." Moynihan charged that budget cuts and program changes were too severe, turning children into victims. The reform's "fearsome assumption is that the behavior of certain adults can be changed by making the lives of their children as wretched as possible." Moynihan favors some amendments to lessen the harsh effects of the welfare legislation, but is pessimistic that any will be passed.

SOURCE: Anthony Lewis, "Abroad at Home; Are There No Prisons?" *The New York Times*, August 5, 1996, p. A17.

Welfare Reform

Besides reflecting a fundamental American belief in self-help and individualism, the new welfare bill has significant ramifications for our federal system. This *devolution* of power to the states in the area of welfare is seen as a testing ground for the future. Based upon how well states perform their new responsibilities, the nature of American federalism may potentially be altered. If states are creative and successful in enacting welfare reform, other federal programs and powers may also be handed down to the states.

Welfare policies are often criticized because they fail to accomplish the purposes identified for them. But most of them have multiple goals that cannot all be achieved at the same time. Policies are bundles of compromises; they include contradictions that are responses to political demands, interests, and preferences. We try to help people who are poor as well as help prevent people from becoming poor. We try to eliminate the causes of poverty, so that welfare will eventually not be needed. But support payments may serve to reward the existing conditions and create disincentives for the changes necessary to become independent.

Welfare reform proponents have been fond of making ambitious promises, and the 1996 reformers are no exception. The 1988 Family Support Act, according to its leading sponsor, Senator Pat Moynihan, was going to "turn the welfare program upside down." But the act itself included only modest goals. It authorized states to pay for child care and to require that recipients be involved in some kind of preparation for employment, but it excused about half of recipients—primarily mothers with young children—from this requirement. Politicians regularly create high expectations and enact reforms, but then only fund them halfheartedly. In the end, for most welfare recipients, there is little change. Scholars no doubt will closely monitor the 1996 changes to assess their impact on poverty and those who need assistance.

HEALTH CARE

The federal government has three major approaches to health policy: research, access, and cost control. First, the government has adopted a wide range of programs to promote research, target particular diseases, regulate drugs, monitor health care providers, gather and disseminate information, and in general deal with health issues with a public dimension. States receive grants-in-aid to construct hospital and research facilities and maintain medical programs, including maternal and child welfare services. State and federal governments underwrite part of the costs of training doctors, dentists, nurses, and pharmacists. The government has gathered data on infant mortality, life spans, and diseases in an effort to monitor the success of its programs.

The chief agency of the national government for these kinds of programs is the Public Health Service (PHS), headed by the surgeon general. The service carries out its research through the National Institutes of Health. Researchers in these institutes, working closely with experts in private laboratories, study causes and seek cures for serious diseases. Fellowships for health research are granted to able scientists and physicians. The Public Health Service also administers grants to states and local communities to help them improve public health. As we discussed in Chapter 19, another agency promoting health is the Food and Drug Administration (FDA).

The second governmental concern with health care can be summed up in one word: access. Most people feel that the United States provides the best medical care money can buy. But that is precisely the problem: not everyone can afford our increasingly expensive medical care. What does the government do for sick people who cannot afford care? Efforts to improve access are related to the government's role as a major consumer. Although the national government provides direct medical care for 20 million people through veterans' hospitals and other clinics, covers the cost of health care for the 28 million poorest Americans through Medicaid, and helps provide health care for 35 million of the nation's elderly through Medicare, government involvement falls short of universal health care for all citizens—the stated goal of many other industrial democracies and a desired objective for most Americans.

Most Americans have private insurance, usually through their employers, which pays for health care and hospitalization. Private health insurance began in 1910 when the Montgomery Ward Company started the first health insurance plan for its employees. Limited access to health care and hospitals for those who could not afford private insurance resurfaced during the Great Depression, when large numbers of Americans were unemployed. President Franklin Roosevelt organized a Committee on Economic Security, which recommended compulsory national health insurance, but those recommendations did not go far. However, the committee's recommendations that the Social Security program provide money for maternal and child health care as well as aid for the disabled were adopted as part of the original Social Security legislation. Harry Truman was reelected in 1948 with universal health care as one of his stated policy goals. The idea was labeled as socialism, however, and was not seriously pursued.

In 1965, as part of Lyndon Johnson's Great Society legislation, Congress passed Medicare and Medicaid. **Medicare** is the national health insurance program for the elderly and disabled; it provides hospital and medical insurance for people 65 years of age and older. Disabled people under age 65 are also entitled to Medicare. **Medicaid** provides medical benefits for low-income persons; it is funded largely by the federal government but also requires state funding and administration. Eligibility for Medicaid is limited to persons who receive welfare cash payments—the visually impaired, the elderly, the disabled, and families with dependent children where one parent is absent, incapacitated, or unemployed. Both programs took effect in 1966.[23]

The Medicare program covers most charges for most illnesses, but some catastrophic and long-term conditions result in major costs to patients for which there is no Medicare coverage. Responding to pressure to add catastrophic coverage and prescription drugs to the plan, Congress enacted the Medicare Catastrophic Coverage Act of 1988. To cover the costs of this expanded coverage, many senior citizens had to pay higher Medicare premiums—something they disliked—and a year later, Congress repealed the law. The lesson from this reversal has not been lost on members of Congress: The public wants expanded health care benefits but does not want to pay more for them.

The third approach to health care policy is cost control. Government pays for approximately 44 percent of the health care costs through veterans' hospitals and programs for the poor, elderly, and disabled. Developments in health care thus have a profound impact on government. Take the 1995 budget, in which we allocated nearly $251 billion on health care. If that amount were reduced by 1 percent, it would fund the Head Start program for poor preschool children. If it could be reduced by 2 percent, it would fully fund the new National Service program in which college students receive financial assistance in return for public service, and if it could be reduced by 5 percent, it would pay for the entire food stamp program.

A Mostly Private Health Care System

Health care for most Americans has traditionally been provided by physicians of their choice whose bills were covered by insurance companies. This arrangement is known as **fee for service**. When these patients go to a hospital, their costs are covered by insurance—the **third-party payer**, meaning neither the doctor nor hospitals that provide the service nor the patient who gets the service covers the costs. Generally, big companies provide better benefits than do small businesses with fewer than 100 workers (see Figure 20–2). For instance, large companies are much more likely to provide extras like dental and eyeglass benefits to their employees.

What Welfare Reform Does

The changes made by the 1996 Welfare Reform legislation shifted responsibility from federal to state governments:

- States now administer all programs through federal block grants, which generally require state matching funds.
- This legislation replaces Aid to Families with Dependent Children (AFDC) with Temporary Assistance for Needy Families (TANF).
- Recipients must engage in work activities within two months of receiving benefits (Workfare).
- There is a five-year lifetime limit on receiving benefits.
- This law denies funds to unmarried parents under age 18 unless they attend school or other training and live with an adult.
- This law expands eligibility for two-parent families to discourage divorce.
- This law establishes stricter requirements for children to qualify as disabled to receive Supplemental Security Income (SSI).
- This law excludes legal immigrants from 19 programs and illegal immigrants from 23 programs.
- States have more leeway in determining who may receive benefits. They have the option to:

  exempt up to 20 percent of their caseload from work requirements and lifetime limits

  deny all benefits to illegal immigrants

  deny assistance to children born to welfare recipients

  deny benefits to parents under age 18

  limit welfare to newcomers from another state.

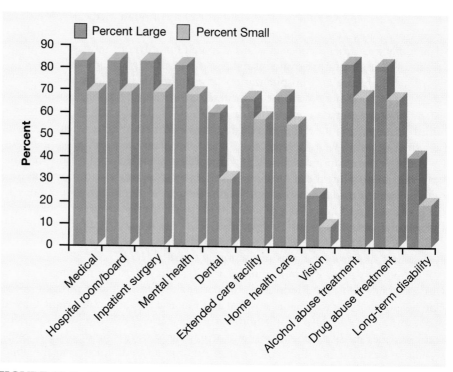

**FIGURE 20–2 Percentage of Large and Small Businesses That Provide
Employees with Certain Categories of Health Benefits**

SOURCE: U.S. Bureau of the Census, *Statistical Abstract of the United States, 1993* (Government Printing Office, 1994), p. 431.

The traditional ways of paying for health care are rapidly being challenged by other forms of coverage—especially health maintenance organizations (HMOs) in which people or their employers are charged a set amount, and the HMO provides them health care and covers hospital costs. However, 39.7 million Americans are uninsured and yet are not covered by Medicaid.[24] They often rely on government or charity to pay for their medical care.[25] More than 25 percent of all households in the United States donate an average of $139 a year to volunteer health organizations to help those in need, an amount second only to religious donations.[26]

Under current law, employers have a tax incentive to provide health insurance to employees. The government treats employers' costs of insurance as a deductible business expense, reducing their corporate tax obligations, and these benefits are not counted as taxable income for employees either. In addition, employees may deduct any medical expenses that exceed 7.5 percent of their gross adjusted income when they pay their income taxes.

Americans want the freedom to choose their own doctor, and this preference is often cited by those who oppose health care reform as one of the major reasons not to make a change. Opponents assert that many reforms will remove freedom of choice in medical care. In reality, many Americans already have limited choices in their medical care; for example, costs of care, type of care, insurance restrictions, and where a patient lives all restrict choices. In practice, patients rarely shop for cheaper care, rarely challenge the doctor's recommendations for procedures, and rarely protest their bills—primarily because their insurance companies are paying the bill. Thus, the belief in patient choice of doctors is deeply rooted but often limited.

Problems with Health Care

The problems with health care in the United States include rising costs, an increasing number of uninsured Americans, unnecessary procedures, endless paperwork, high costs of litigation, and avoidable illnesses. Generally speaking, the quality of health care in the United States is not a problem; as noted earlier, we have the best health care money can buy. But that is precisely the problem. Those who have insurance and money also have greater access to new and expensive procedures like organ transplants or new treatments. Those without insurance or money either forgo needed services or simply make do with minimum care.

RISING COST OF HEALTH CARE Health care costs in the United States have risen from $287.5 billion in 1970 to $988.5 billion in 1995 (in inflation-adjusted dollars), a 344 percent increase (see Table 20–3). Another measure of the rising cost of health care is the percentage of the gross domestic product (GDP) devoted to health care: in 1960, 5.1 percent of the GDP was devoted to health care; this figure rose to 13.6 percent in 1995;[27] some analysts predict it could reach 26 percent of GNP by 2030.[28] In specific areas like childhood vaccines, costs have risen 1,000 percent in one decade. The cost of pharmaceuticals has risen between 40 percent and 88 percent each year over the past six years.[29]

Who pays for the rapid rise in costs? Employers pay a large share of the costs of health insurance. The cost of employer-sponsored health plans increased 47 percent from 1988 to 1995. By 1995, employee benefits consumed 28 percent of employee compensation.[30] Individual consumers also pay more for health care, and the health care costs paid by government have risen twelvefold over the last 20 years; the government now pays for 46 percent of all health expenditures in the United States.[31]

One reason costs have risen is advances in medicine mean people live longer. Life expectancy increased by over five years between 1970 and 1995, and most experts believe it will continue to rise.[32] As people live longer, they place greater demands on our health care system. New and advanced medical technology—life-support systems, ultrasound, sophisticated x-ray equipment, and genetic counseling—have all increased the costs of health care. Americans also seek elective health care in comparatively high numbers. Examples of elective health care include cosmetic surgery that is not medically necessary, like liposuction, some dermatology, and some orthopedic surgery. Advances in medications are also expensive and have significantly added to the rising costs of health care. These factors in rising health care costs are not going to go away; instead, they are likely to continue to grow in importance and increase the demand for medical care.

Cost containment has been a frequent refrain of large corporations and consumer groups. In the 1970s and 1980s, business leaders reduced benefits, increased co-payments, and encouraged employees to join managed care plans, especially health maintenance organizations, hoping to contain costs. During the 1980s and 1990s, HMO enrollment increased fourfold, from just under 10 million in 1980 to almost 40 million patients in 1993.[33] This move to managed care benefited large insurance companies that had the resources to enter the HMO business. The alliance of big insurance companies with big employers became part of the politics of the health care reform debate in Bill Clinton's first administration. Not surprisingly, smaller insurance companies, feeling left out, resorted to direct appeals to voters.

THE UNINSURED As noted, approximately 39.7 million people, over 15 percent of the U.S. population, are not covered by any private health insurance or state or federal Medicaid benefits. A very large proportion of this number—84

TABLE 20–3
National Health Expenditures, 1970–1995 (in millions of 1995 dollars)*

Year	Total Amount Spent	
	Nominal	Real
1970	$73.2	$287.5
1975	130.7	370.2
1980	247.2	457.2
1985	428.2	606.4
1990	697.5	813.3
1991	761.3	851.9
1992	833.6	905.5
1993	892.3	941.1
1994	949.4	976.3
1995	988.5	988.5

SOURCE: For 1970–94, U.S. Bureau of the Census, *Statistical Abstract of the United States, 1996* (Government Printing Office, 1996), p. 111; for 1995, Health Care Financing Administration Web page: http://www.hcfa.gov/news/n970127.htm.

*Nominal dollars are the actual dollars spent per year. To compare spending over time, we need to take inflation into account. The *Real* column accounts for inflation by converting nominal dollars into inflation-adjusted dollars against the base year, which in this case is 1995.

"You boys sure your medical insurance is gonna cover this?"

From Coast to Coast

The Uninsured, 1994

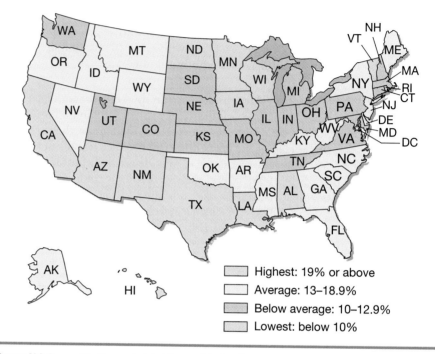

Highest: 19% or above

Average: 13–18.9%

Below average: 10–12.9%

Lowest: below 10%

SOURCE: U.S. Bureau of the Census, *Statistical Abstract of the United States, 1996* (Government Printing Office, 1996), p. 120.

After the failure of Bill and Hillary Clinton's massive health care proposal, smaller, incremental changes in health care were more successful. Here Senator Edward Kennedy (D.-Mass.) and Senator Nancy Kassebaum (R.-Kansas) discuss their bill to make health insurance coverage portable when changing jobs.

percent—are full-time employees but because their incomes fall just above the poverty line, they do not qualify for Medicaid. And because they work near the minimum wage in jobs that are part-time, seasonal, or menial, their employer does not provide health insurance benefits. Uninsured individuals have to hope they do not get sick, but if they do, they usually seek care in hospital emergency rooms only when their illness has reached a critical stage. Delay drives up costs because critical care is much more expensive than preventive medicine or early treatment.

It is not just the poor who may end up uninsured. Persons who change jobs may often go without coverage for several months until their new insurance takes effect. People who develop serious medical conditions may find the insurance company unwilling to cover their expenses, claiming that the illness is a "pre-existing condition." Some insurance companies set limits on their coverage, meaning that families faced with very expensive illnesses end up essentially uninsured.

UNNECESSARY PROCEDURES Doctors and insurance companies claim that they have to perform and pay for procedures that may be unnecessary medically but are needed to reduce the risk of being sued by patients. It is estimated that between 15 and 30 percent of all medical procedures in the United States are not necessary.[34] These procedures add up to billions in unnecessary costs, but they do not improve the quality of care provided to patients.[35] To avoid malpractice suits, obstetricians may perform as many as 500,000 unnecessary caesarean sections each year.[36] Critics also accuse hospitals of charging high prices for items that are not used or not needed. Since few patients are knowledgeable enough to audit their hospital bills, insurance companies must monitor these expenses.

The need to hold down rising hospital bills was one motivation for Medicare reform in 1983, and it remains a concern today. There are understandable reasons for the penchant for expensive new tests and procedures; people want to do everything possible to prolong life, and if a test or procedure has a chance, however limited, of doing so, they want it.

ENDLESS PAPERWORK   In medicine as in other activities, paperwork is necessary to document what services were provided and to prevent fraud. One avoidable expense that virtually all health care reformers agree on is the inefficient and uncoordinated system of paperwork in the present system. The large number of insurance companies—each of which has its own forms—combined with government forms mean that the task of filling out forms cost health consumers more than $58 billion in 1995, accounting for 6 percent of total health costs.[37] A standardized insurance form that could be submitted electronically could save billions of dollars.[38] Computerized patient records, electronically transmitted prescriptions, and hand-held computers that send doctors' orders and comments to a computer could also cut down on paperwork. Some estimate that computerization of the medical industry could save almost 15 percent on overall medical expenditures in the United States.[39]

LITIGATION EXPENSES   Physicians frequently complain about the high cost of malpractice insurance. Malpractice premiums in the United States are nine times higher than in Canada. Malpractice insurance for all physicians, on average, has climbed from an annual premium of $7,000 in 1983 to $14,500 in 1993 and is highest for doctors in specialties like anesthesia, obstetrics and gynecology, and heart and brain surgery.[40]

Huge malpractice awards are defended by trial lawyers who represent people whose health was damaged or families of those whose lives were lost due to medical malpractice. They argue that physicians, like all professionals, have a responsibility to exercise sound professional judgment in their jobs, and when they do not, they should provide restitution to victims. Trial lawyers contend the only fair solution to medical malpractice litigation is better medical practices.

PREVENTION: LIFESTYLE AND ENVIRONMENTAL CAUSES OF ILLNESS   Part of the health care "crisis" in the United States is avoidable. Medicare alone spent $16 billion in 1994 on treating cigarette-related diseases, and over the next 20 years the cost will be an estimated $800 billion. During 1994, Medicare spent an additional $4 billion on alcohol- and drug-related health problems.[41] Lung cancer—a prime example of a disease that is largely avoidable—caused some 150,000 deaths in 1993. The relationship between lung cancer and smoking has been clearly established; giving up smoking significantly reduces the chance of contracting lung cancer. Other illnesses at least partly related to lifestyle include heart disease, liver disease, and Acquired Immune Deficiency Syndrome (AIDS). Some states have recently sued tobacco companies to recover Medicaid expenses, and others use educational programs to discourage teenagers from beginning to smoke.

Health Care Reform

Bill Clinton made health care reform a major priority in his first administration, appointing Hillary Rodham Clinton to head the National Task Force on Health Care Reform. It concluded that our health care system is in need of reform in terms of cost and access, but its proposals, which were complicated and bureaucratic, were defeated by Congress in 1993.

Tobacco Regulation

Tobacco companies have long denied the addictive and harmful effects of smoking or chewing tobacco. They have also contended that since tobacco is technically not a food or drug, it should not be regulated by the Food and Drug Administration (FDA). As scientific evidence has mounted, however, this claim has become tenuous. The Liggett Company, one of the five big U.S. tobacco companies, recently admitted that nicotine is an addictive substance, or a drug. This places the tobacco industry under the jurisdiction of the FDA, making it subject to FDA health standards. The Liggett Company's admission opened the door for the FDA to restrict the production and sale of tobacco products to the public, giving it greater power to protect the public's health.

SOURCE: Lauran Neergaard, "North Carolina Ruling Favors Legal Efforts; Judge Boosts Tobacco Foes," *Chattanooga Free Press*, April 27, 1997, p. A4.

The spread of AIDS is being attacked by an educational campaign that includes posters such as this Norman Rockwell painting.

While there are many different proposals for health care reform, the essential approaches include single-payer, managed competition, employer-mandated coverage, spending caps, individual responsibility, and medical savings accounts.

SINGLE-PAYER Under a single-payer system the government, using broad-based taxes, covers the costs of health care and hospitalization and sets the rates. Like the system used in Canada, such a plan would provide universal coverage and benefits to all Americans. No longer would people need to worry about the costs of catastrophic illnesses or a change in jobs that would exclude them from coverage. Proponents claim that the single-payer system would save billions of dollars in administrative expenses by reducing the number of insurers from about 1,200 to 1. Opponents of the single-payer system claim it would lead to a bureaucratic mess, with little incentive for innovation, cost control, or diversity of coverage. They further claim that the government would be put in the position of deciding which procedures to pay for and how to ration access to these procedures. As a result, they contend, Americans would lose not only quality in their health care but their freedom of choice.

Business leaders generally oppose single-payer coverage out of concern for costs and what the program would do to taxes and the federal budget deficit. The American Medical Association, U.S. Chamber of Commerce, Health Insurance Association of America, and other interest groups representing health care providers oppose the single-payer system because they see it leading to lower wages for their employees and reduced profits for their stockholders. Labor unions, some senior citizens groups, and most consumer groups advocate this type of plan.

MANAGED COMPETITION In his first administration President Clinton proposed managed care as part of the health care reforms. Managed competition calls for greater use of health maintenance organizations (HMOs) and creation of large purchasing groups of employers (alliances) and other consumers powerful enough to bargain with the HMOs for lower costs. This plan would leave each person with some choices of the type of medical care he or she wants. Even though the Clinton health care reforms were defeated, HMOs have continued to grow. Between 1980 and 1995, HMO enrollment grew five-fold, and in the five years between 1990 and 1995, it grew 137 percent.[42]

EMPLOYER-MANDATED COVERAGE Most people get some form of medical insurance as a benefit that goes with their job. President Richard Nixon proposed in 1971 that employers be required to provide and pay all employees' health insurance.[43] President Clinton recommended that all employers be required to provide their employees with health insurance, suggesting that employers pay 80 percent of the costs. But many small businesses assert they cannot afford to provide their employees with this benefit and stay in business. Some have estimated that costs of health care benefits to small businesses may be 10 to 40 percent higher than for large businesses, so many do not now provide health care benefits. For instance, of those businesses with fewer than 25 employees, only about one-third of the workers receive coverage directly from their employer.[44] Mandating coverage does not solve this economic problem, nor does it take care of those who do not have jobs.

Proponents counter that these negative consequences can be mitigated through tax credits and higher levels of productivity. They also point out that if all small businesses provide health insurance, none of them will be put at a disadvantage compared to other small businesses. The federal government already allows businesses to deduct what they pay in health benefits to employees as a business expense and gives tax credits to low-income families to purchase coverage for their children. The cost of these tax deductions and credits under the current system has been estimated to be as high as $50 billion.[45]

SPENDING CAPS The cost of providing health care each year consumes a larger and larger share of our gross domestic product, and if we change the system, there is concern that the costs will go up even faster. Some have proposed an overall expenditure cap on health care that applies not only to public expenditures but to private ones as well. Supporters of a cap include the business-dominated National Leadership Coalition for Health Care Reform, some economists, and some prominent Democrats.

It is hard to know how such controls would really work, and this doubt understandably evokes fear among health care providers. The American Hospital Association, American Medical Association, and Pharmaceutical Manufacturers Association vigorously oppose the idea. They argue that spending caps would limit research and development in medicine and reduce the quality of people entering the medical profession.

INDIVIDUAL RESPONSIBILITY FOR COVERAGE Another proposal for health care reform seeks to apply a free-market approach to health care by abolishing *all* employer-provided benefits and encouraging individuals to buy health insurance on their own in much the same way that individuals are now responsible for purchasing their own automobile insurance. Those with low incomes, including people not now covered, would have tax credits or vouchers to assist in the purchase of insurance.

Those who advocate such a proposal say that if individuals purchased their own insurance, they might pay more attention to costs and more closely monitor doctor and hospital fees. When higher wages are combined with tax credits, some individuals could end up with improved benefits tailored to their individual needs. Such a plan would also eliminate the need to impose price controls or find a way to pay for federally mandated health insurance. It is unlikely, however, that employees would recover all they now spend on health care from their employers, so costs to individual consumers might increase. It is also unlikely that all currently uninsured persons who need government assistance would be able to obtain coverage without a tax increase to pay for it. Perhaps most important, such a proposal would run into so much political opposition that it presents an unlikely alternative.

MEDICAL SAVINGS ACCOUNTS A new item on the health care agenda is medical savings accounts, which Congress enacted as a viable alternative in 1996. Medical savings accounts allow individuals with high deductible insurance plans to make tax deductible contributions to a special medical savings account. These funds can be used to pay for any medical expenses and may be saved from year to year. Withdrawals for other purposes are taxable and subject to an early withdrawal penalty.

Supporters of medical savings accounts say that they will lower individuals' health care costs by giving them the incentive to spend their own money more carefully. They will also reduce the hassle by allowing people to go to a doctor of their own choosing without approval from their insurance company. Opponents of medical savings accounts, including President Clinton, say that they amount to nothing more than a tax break for the wealthy and the healthy. Because of high deductibles, people will be discouraged from getting needed services and preventive care. Opponents also argue that because healthier people are more likely to sign up for medical savings accounts, sicker people will pay higher premiums.

PROSPECT FOR REFORM Most proposals for health care reform would not reorganize the industry but would address some of the problems within the existing system. Proposals include greater government regulation of insurance companies; group purchasing agreements among small companies banding together when purchasing insurance; expanded Medicare and Medicaid coverage to include more of the presently uninsured; standardized insurance forms that would reduce paperwork and lower the cost of administration for doctors and hospitals; medical

Thinking It Through

Although we all have our own ideas about health care reform, the American people are split over what approach is best. More than half do not want restrictions on their choice of doctors and hospitals, and almost half do not think that the country spends enough on health care. A 1996 Pew poll found these results:

Do you think the nation spends too much, too little, or the right amount on health care?

Too much	33%
Too little	44
Right amount	20

Which of the following statements comes closest to expressing your overall view of the country's health care system?

1. On the whole, the health care system works pretty well and only minor changes are necessary to make it work better
2. There are some good things in our health care system, but fundamental changes are needed to make it work better.
3. Our health care system has so much wrong with it that we need to completely rebuild it.

Works pretty well, only minor changes necessary	11%
Fundamental changes needed	52
Need to completely rebuild it	35
Not sure	1

SOURCE: National adult poll conducted by Louis Harris and Associates on December 16, 1996, and printed in *Harris Poll*, January 6, 1997.

A Closer Look

HEALTH CARE IN ADVANCED INDUSTRIAL DEMOCRACIES

Advanced industrial democracies like Canada, Germany, Japan, the Netherlands, and the United Kingdom provide health care for their entire population either through national health insurance or a national health service. Although one-seventh of all U.S. citizens do not have health insurance and do not regularly receive health care, the United States outspends all these countries in terms of health expenditures as a percent of the gross domestic product (GDP).

Our high spending on health care does not mean we are a more healthy population. Our infant mortality rates, for instance, are among the worst in all industrialized countries, and we rank below average in male and female life expectancy at birth. However, the United States does rank first in the quality and access to first-rate medical technology, and for those Americans who can afford the best health care, our system is excellent.

The United States also differs from other countries in the extent to which health care costs are paid by public funds. Approximately three-quarters of the cost of health care in most advanced industrial democracies is funded by central or local governments. In 1992, for instance, the government paid 72 percent of the costs of health care in Japan and Germany, 84 percent in the United Kingdom and 86 percent in Sweden. In 1992, the U.S. government paid 46 percent of the costs.

Whether health care reform will actually lead to better or to poorer care is hotly debated, with those opposed to change heightening fears and those favoring reform seeking to reduce fears. Health care systems in other countries are often used by opponents of reform as examples of "socialized medicine." Proponents of reform point to high-quality health care in countries with greater government intervention.

SOURCE: Organization for Economic Cooperation and Development, *Health Care Reform: The Will to Change*, Health Policy Studies, No. 8. (1996).

Total Health Care Expenditures as a Share of Gross Domestic Product, 1996

United States	14.2%
Canada	9.8
France	9.7
Germany	8.6
Japan	7.3
United Kingdom	6.9

SOURCE: U.S. Bureau of the Census, *Statistical Abstract of the United States, 1996* (Government Printing Office, 1996), p. 834.

Infant Mortality and Life Expectancy Rates in Ten Industrialized Nations, 1996

Country	Infant Mortality Rate[*]	Life Expectancy
Japan	4.4	79.6
Sweden	4.5	78.1
Netherlands	4.9	77.7
Germany	6.0	76.0
France	6.2	78.4
Canada	6.1	79.1
Australia	5.5	79.4
United Kingdom	6.4	76.4
Italy	6.9	78.1
United States	6.7	76.0

SOURCE: U.S. Bureau of the Census, *Statistical Abstract of the United States, 1996* (Government Printing Office, 1996), pp. 831–32.

[*]Infant mortality rate is the number of deaths of children under one year of age per 1,000 live births in a calendar year.

malpractice reform; and regulation of the rates doctors and hospitals can charge for certain procedures.

Bill Clinton's health care proposals lost momentum and ultimately did not pass for several reasons. First, the various measures all fell under the jurisdiction of different committees and subcommittees in Congress, thus greatly complicating and lengthening the process of creating coherent legislation. Because of these difficulties, Congress ultimately ran out of time before the 1994 congressional elections. A major problem with the complex health care program Clinton envisioned was the expense. Although many Americans were in favor of reform, they were not willing to pay the costs associated with such large-scale changes. Perhaps the most troubling problems with Clinton's health care plan were ideological. With its goal of universal health care, the plan was labeled as a socialist program by its opponents. They maintained that America was built on foundations of individual hard work and achievement that are embodied in the American Dream, and these values seemed to conflict with the goals set forth in Clinton's plan.

The complexity of financing health care means that it will be a recurrent issue in American politics. It was central to the social policy agenda for the Clinton administration in his first term, but took less precedence in his second term. Clinton's strong commitment to the issue helped move it to center stage in American politics for a time. But interest groups, congressional committees, partisan politics, the bureaucracy, and even the media all play a role in the development of this national issue and policy controversy. Most Americans agree that there is a crisis in health care but are satisfied with their own coverage. They want universal coverage without significant tax increases and lower costs without additional restrictions. No wonder elected officials struggle to find a reform package that is both viable and meaningful.

EDUCATION

Americans have always given a high priority to educating their children. To our nation's founders, education was closely connected with the survival of democracy because it provided the citizenry with a moral sense, an ability to reason, and a general knowledge about history and government.[46] The founders believed education should not be limited to the rich, but rather should be widely shared. Public education, like much of social policy generally, was left to state and local governments to develop, and a strong tradition of private education existed as well. Today education is one of the areas still solidly under the control of state and local governments.

Education, especially in a competitive global economy, is essential for the economic well-being of society. For nations in a world of high technology and rapid change, a work force that has the necessary skills is crucial. For individuals, education is the route to a job and an adequate standard of living. Education can also have the effect of bridging the gaps between the races and between rich and poor, although it has not always done so.[47]

The United States is committed to a system of public education with local control. Most children go to public schools run by local school boards and funded, at least partly, by property taxes. Since local districts vary from areas with large homes to very poor neighborhoods, the funds for local schools vary. The effect is often that children from poor districts are not as likely to have as good public schools as those from rich districts. Other enduring problems in public schools are the uneven quality of teacher preparation and performance, high dropout rates, and inequality in the educational opportunities provided people of color.

Hope Scholarships

President Clinton made education the centerpiece of his 1997 State of the Union address. He said, "We must make the 13th and 14th years of education—at least two years of college—just as universal in America by the twenty-first century as a high school education is today, and we must open the doors of college to all Americans. To do that, I propose America's HOPE scholarship, based on Georgia's pioneering program: Two years of a $1,500 tax credit for college tuition, enough to pay for the typical community college. I also propose a tax deduction of up to $10,000 a year for all tuition after high school; an expanded IRA you can withdraw from tax-free for education; and the largest increases in Pell Grant scholarships in 20 years."

Clinton had raised these new programs in the 1996 presidential election and they seemed to engender little controversy. However, they do constitute a significant expansion of the education entitlement. States that pay most of the costs of education understandably will worry about how to pay for two more years of education, and the implications for the federal budget deficit of a new tax deduction will engender opposition as well. What Clinton has done is identify a policy area where public opinion is more supportive of an expanded government role—no small accomplishment in an era of limited government.

The Federal Role in Education

The federal government's first involvement in education policy came with the Northwest Ordinance of 1787, in which Congress set aside one lot in each township for support of public schools. In 1862, the Morrill Land Grant Act provided grants of land to state colleges if they specialized in mechanical or agricultural arts. As early as 1867, a U.S. Office of Education was established to oversee these programs, but the scope of federal involvement was modest by today's standards.

Following World War II, the federal government launched the G.I. Bill, which paid tuition at any college or university for veterans. The G.I. Bill helped provide college education to approximately 20 million veterans. During the cold war, the view that education, especially in the sciences, was closely linked to national defense became popular. When the Soviet Union launched *Sputnik*—the first successful satellite to orbit the earth—in 1957, efforts to expand the federal role in funding education grew. In 1958 Congress passed the National Defense Education Act to upgrade science, language, and mathematics courses.

The next expansion of federal government activity in education came with President Johnson's Great Society. In 1964 Congress created the Head Start program and college-level work-study programs. Then in 1965 Congress passed the Elementary and Secondary Education Act (ESEA), which focused on poverty-stricken schools, supplied educational materials for underprivileged public school students, and provided funding for educational research on how to assist children from underprivileged backgrounds. Even with this expanded role, the federal government today funds only 8.3 percent of the $386 billion spent on public education in the United States.[48]

The new federal programs left intact local control over school construction, curriculum, teacher salaries, teacher standards, and governance. The federal government took a keen interest, however, in school desegregation. The Supreme Court's landmark 1954 decision in *Brown v Board of Education of Topeka* held that the previous education policy of "separate but equal" was inherently unconstitutional. This decision gave the federal government an added incentive to improve schools for poor and underprivileged students of all races and put added pressure on local school officials and district courts to end segregation. School desegregation efforts also led to forced busing programs mandated by state and federal courts.

College and university students have also benefited from federal funding. Many college students today receive Pell Grants or Stafford Loans, present-day versions of federally insured student loans. Over half of all college students receive some federal financial aid. Pell Grants for low-income students and low-interest Guaranteed Student Loans continue to be the most available and most used payment for college expenses.

Goals 2000: Education for the Next Century

As governor of Arkansas, Bill Clinton led an effort to reform public education in his state, so it is not surprising that when he became president he proposed legislation that built on his earlier experience. The Goals 2000: Educate America Act had as its centerpiece a set of national standards for education by the year 2000. The project was actually started by President George Bush and the nation's governors at a meeting in 1990 during which they agreed on such goals as higher graduation rates, lower drug and crime rates, higher literacy, and improved curricula. The Clinton administration translated these goals into more precise objectives and standards that stressed the need for cooperation among local schools, school districts, states, and the federal government. The program is voluntary, and states may choose not to participate.

Educational policy has been the province of state and local governments since the first public school was opened in the United States. Therefore, any encroachment by the federal government in this area is scrutinized warily. To overcome concerns about excessive federal regulation with Goals 2000, the program identifies goals that virtually everyone can agree on and the federal role is minimal. There are no regulations, and no goals have been implemented for Goals 2000. All a state must do to apply for Goals 2000 funding is fill out a simple four-page document. The application process has been so streamlined that "review, approval and the obligation of funds generally take less than three weeks" after the application is approved.[49] All states are receiving or have applied for Goals 2000 monies. One of the last states, Virginia, finally accepted use of the funds "for the sole purpose of purchasing classroom computers and related technology."[50]

The Goals 2000 legislation has renewed the debate over how best to improve the quality of education in the United States. Proponents assert that real educational change requires the infusion of new resources from the federal government that are conditioned on real improvement at the state and especially local levels. The program is a way to help states and local school districts help themselves. Proponents also point to greater accountability based on measurable student achievement. They argue that local control will be maintained because the legislation does not contain any new federal mandates. Critics of the program counter that Goals 2000 is a first step toward a centralized administration of education and the loss of local autonomy. Few states or localities have the political will to turn down federal dollars; consequently, they will forsake local control, although education may be an exception, given the relatively small proportion of federal dollars in the overall education budget and the strong tradition of local control. They also argue that this program will remove incentives for local experimentation. As one opponent put it, "This debate is about one issue: Who can best determine what is right for the child? Is it the parent or is it the government?"[51]

The issue of parental control has surfaced in recent years in two other ways. One proposal would provide parents with a *voucher* or check towards their child's education. The voucher could be redeemed at a public or private school of the parents' choosing. Vouchers, proponents argue, introduce the element of competition into the educational system. Voucher plans have been tried in a few states and cities with some success. In Milwaukee one of the largest programs has been specifically targeted to help low-income students, covering the full cost of tuition and allowing them to go to private schools.[52] Bob Dole proposed vouchers in his 1996 presidential campaign, but they have been rejected by voters when they have been on the ballot in states like Oregon.

A second type of reform proposal calls for charter schools. A *charter school* receives public funds but has a contract or charter giving it greater autonomy and flexibility than public schools. Proponents of charter schools argue that this autonomy leads to greater accountability. Charter schools have only been in existence since 1991, but as of the fall of 1996 there were 480 charter schools in 17 states. The states with the greatest activity in this area are Arizona, California, and Michigan.[53]

Education Reform

The debate over education is rarely over what the goals or standards ought to be. It is more often a question of how much local control to permit, how much of a difference in local funding to tolerate, and who will ensure that the needs of the poor, those with learning disabilities, and minorities are considered and met. Conservatives have long seen these matters as primarily local. Liberals have argued for a strong national government role, especially in requiring localities to deal with the needs of groups that were otherwise ignored. The Goals 2000 proposals are really an extension of earlier national efforts to set standards for educational attainment, although these are more directly targeted to overall student and school district performance.

Thinking It Through

Arguments for abolishing the Department of Education center on the long-standing policy that education is primarily a state and local government responsibility. Local control of education policy—including teacher hiring and certification, curriculum content, and selection of books—has always been determined locally, and even with the Department of Education, these matters remain largely local functions. The debate also covers federal mandates that require schools to fund women's athletics programs more equitably, or requirements for special services for handicapped children.

The issue has important symbolic dimensions relating to the size and scope of the federal government. Eliminating one department, even if most of its functions and staff would be transferred to another department, can be perceived as reducing the size of the federal government.

Defenders of the need for a Department of Education understand the symbolism of a federal department charged with education policy. They argue that education policy is one of our most important national concerns, and that there needs to be a role for the national government. Supporters also argue that ensuring fair and equitable treatment of all students has been the federal government's role. Support for keeping the department appears to be winning the battle of public opinion, because despite Republican majorities in both houses of Congress, the department still stands.

The role of schools in our society has gone through a dramatic transformation. We ask a lot more of our schools than just to educate students. Schools are now a major means by which basic nutrition is provided to millions of poor children; schools screen at-risk children and attempt to get them psychological assistance; schools provide sex education and sometimes condoms; schools seek to socialize students into socially acceptable behaviors, often in the face of increasing violence in the surrounding neighborhoods. The presence of police officers in most American high schools is relatively new and speaks to the problems of maintaining some minimal control over violence, drugs, and gangs.

The importance of an educated work force, concerns over equality of educational opportunity, civil liberties, and individual freedoms, and the increasing mobility of Americans all create pressures for national policies and programs. But national intervention collides with strongly held views that schools are primarily a local matter. Satisfying demands for more effective programs and more accountability to parents may be beyond the reach of the federal government without the option of dramatic increases in federal funds. As a result, more attention is directed to innovative efforts by states and local communities to improve their schools.

CRIME

In recent years, crime control, once a state and local issue, has been forced onto the national political agenda. The issue of getting tough on crime surfaced in several recent presidential campaigns and has been a primary concern in many public opinion polls since then. President Clinton and Congress responded with legislation establishing a comprehensive federal program, including federal funds to help state and local governments hire more police officers.

More and more crimes are now defined as *federal crimes*—for instance, blocking entrance to abortion clinics—and federal laws are being interpreted more broadly by courts. Punishment for federal crimes is more severe, and spending on federal prisons is increasing (see Table 20–4 and Figure 20–3). The 1995 bombing of a federal government office building in Oklahoma City gave rise to proposals in Congress to enact antiterrorist legislation that would give the federal government more authority to investigate and prosecute terrorist actions.

As crime and violence in cities and small towns have increased, the federal government has been pressured to step in. But the fact remains that crime control is primarily a state and local matter. The national government usually acts as a banker,

---

TABLE 20–4

The Cost of Crime in the United States, 1993 (in billions)

Criminal justice system	$78
Private protection	64
Loss of life and work	202
Crimes against business	120
Stolen goods and fraud	60
Drug abuse	40
Driving while intoxicated	110
Total	$674

SOURCE: "Cost of Crime," *U.S. News and World Report*, January 17, 1994, pp. 40–41.

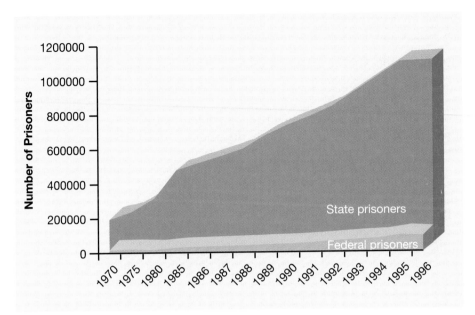

FIGURE 20–3   **Federal and State Prisoners, 1960–1996**

SOURCE: U.S. Bureau of the Census, *Statistical Abstract of the United States, 1996* (Government Printing Office, 1996), p. 219; 1995 numbers from: http://www.ojp.usdoj.gov/pub/bjs/press/pam95.pr; 1996 numbers from: http://www.ojp.usdoj.gov/pub/bjspress/pjimy96.pr.

providing grants to states and local governments to hire more police officers, improve the enforcement of drug laws, or deal with organized crime.

An exception to this decentralized criminal justice system is the Federal Bureau of Investigation (FBI), created in 1908 and charged with gathering and reporting evidence in matters relating to federal laws or to crimes that cross state boundaries. In addition, the FBI provides investigative services on a cooperative basis to local law enforcement in fingerprint identification and laboratory services. Other agencies of the federal government that take on law enforcement activities include the Drug Enforcement Agency (DEA), which is responsible for controlling the flow of illegal narcotics into the United States, patrols U.S. borders, and conducts joint operations with countries where drugs are produced, and the Bureau of Alcohol, Tobacco and Firearms (ATF), which monitors the sale of destructive weapons and guns inside the United States.

Lyndon Johnson's War on Crime

Just as Lyndon Johnson launched a "war on poverty" as part of his Great Society, he also launched a "war on crime." Johnson commissioned a blue-ribbon panel of experts to study the causes of crime and violence and propose remedies. These experts pointed out the relationship between poverty and crime and called attention to the understaffed and inefficient criminal justice system—police, prosecutors, judges, and prisons.[54]

Partly as a result of these studies, Congress in 1965 established the Law Enforcement Assistance Administration (LEAA), which over its 12 years of existence made grants exceeding $8 billion to state and local governments. These federal dollars were used to hire more police officers, purchase squad cars and radios, and provide for greater coordination within the criminal justice system. Part of the money was spent studying crime and identifying areas for future funding. Evaluations of the LEAA found that money was spent on what local governments could get grants for rather than on what the most pressing needs were. Other critics maintained that Washington

Thinking It Through

Proponents of the voucher system argue that choice empowers parents to demand better schools. Opponents argue that education is not as responsive to marketplace forces and competition as businesses are because schools are service institutions, not markets.

Injecting greater accountability into the education system would be a good thing. But shopping for schools will be challenging for many parents, and it may be very difficult to get children from inner-city schools accepted in better schools in outlying areas.

Vouchers would also permit parents to direct tax dollars to private schools, raising issues about public support for religious schools or for schools that may practice discrimination in the admission of students. Students most at risk in terms of finishing school, staying out of trouble with the law, and breaking the cycle of poverty may be the least skilled in how to use vouchers, and as a result may find themselves again left behind.

gave up too much control over how the money was spent. Much of the LEAA money was wasted, and the program was abolished during the Carter administration.[55]

Gun Controls, Crime Rates, and Domestic Terrorism

After years of debate, Congress passed and President Clinton signed into law the Brady Bill, which provides for a five-day waiting period and requires a background check when purchasing a handgun. Clinton was also successful in winning enough votes in 1994 to ban the sale of some semiautomatic assault weapons. Both of these votes were a test of strength for the National Rifle Association (NRA), long thought to be one of the most powerful lobbies in the country. President Clinton marshaled the support of police chiefs and victims of violent crime in a skillful campaign to pressure Congress to pass these two bills. The NRA, long an opponent of these bills, staged its own all-out campaign to defeat the legislation. The assault weapon ban passed by only two votes (216 to 214) in the House. Opponents of gun controls of any type, like the National Rifle Association, have stressed the importance of the constitutional right to keep and bear arms. Proponents of gun control believe that such prohibitions will reduce violent crime. The debate over gun controls at the local, state, and national levels remains intense.

In 1994, after an initial defeat in the House and an intense lobbying effort by President Clinton, Congress passed an omnibus anticrime bill that authorized $30.2 billion in spending on federal crime initiatives. The money will fund a long list of programs, including hiring up to 100,000 new police officers and constructing new prisons and "boot camps" for juvenile offenders. The bill also had new assault rifle restrictions, a long list of federal offenses punishable by the death penalty, federal penalties and programs aimed at curbing domestic violence, and the "three strikes and you're out" provision mandating life imprisonment upon conviction for a third violent felony. It is not

President Clinton signs the Brady Bill, which limited access to certain types of guns, as James Brady (seated) and (left to right) Vice President Al Gore, Attorney General Janet Reno, Sarah Brady, and the Brady children look on. Brady was wounded during an assassination attempt on President Reagan's life, after which he and his wife campaigned for gun control legislation.

surprising that Clinton and the Congress emphasized these actions in the 1996 elections.

The crime rate since 1991 has been declining. There is good evidence that there is a systematic underreporting of some crimes, but that is not a new phenomenon. The widespread perception, however, is that crime and violence are increasing and that the federal government needs to step in. President Clinton discovered that some of his most popular lines in speeches had to do with getting tough on crime, so his administration joined the ongoing efforts in Congress to fight crime.

Domestic terrorism, long a worry, became a reality with the bombing of the Federal Building in Oklahoma City in 1995 and with the Olympic Park bombing during the 1996 Atlanta Olympic Games. Concerns about armed militia movements also became part of the domestic terrorism debate. Finally, the serial bomber known as the "Unabomber" had an explicit political agenda. As with terrorist groups everywhere, domestic terrorism seeks to use fear and violence to achieve political goals. In 1996 President Clinton signed the Terrorism Act, which limits federal appeals by inmates sentenced to death, makes it easier to deport foreign terrorists, bans fund raising by Americans for foreign terrorist groups, and authorizes spending $1 billion to fight terrorism.

Fighting crime may be a major social policy challenge of the 1990s, but the goal of reducing crime must compete with other expectations we have for our government. Can we combat crime in ways that protect traditional civil liberties? Random drug tests, searches of private automobiles, curfews in urban areas, electronic eavesdropping, sting operations to catch criminals, and other steps law enforcement officials believe are necessary often conflict with the individual liberty and freedom from government restraint that Americans cherish. Must we give up some of those individual freedoms in order to fight crime? Should we build more prisons and impose harsher sentences on convicted criminals? Or should we focus more on remedying the poverty and lack of opportunity that lead to criminal behavior? Like other social policies, policies aimed at fighting crime must ultimately balance competing values, one of the most complex and difficult tasks we delegate to government.

THE POLITICS OF SOCIAL POLICY

Social policy issues now dominate the agenda of American politics. Crime, welfare, health care, and their costs concern people more than foreign policy does. Both Republicans and Democrats are attempting to address key domestic issues that win broad support. Recent elections demonstrate how unsettled public opinion is on these issues. The focus of the Reagan-Bush years had been on foreign policy and downsizing the federal government, giving the Clinton administration ample opportunity to propose widespread changes in health care, welfare, education, and crime. Although the proposed changes in some areas are not as sweeping as those enacted by the New Deal or Great Society, the changes in welfare are dramatic, and the widespread media coverage given to social policy questions has helped propel them to the forefront in the national debate.

The nation long ago answered questions about whether the government is responsible to provide decent housing, adequate health care, and a solid education to all of its citizens. The answer—to use Ronald Reagan's phrase—is that government provides a "safety net" for those who cannot provide for themselves. But how to provide that net and what programs or approaches to try are very much debated. And what we can afford and are willing to pay for expanded social services is the main issue. These decisions will remain central to American politics as we enter the twenty-first century.

Tracking Social Policy

One of the great resources of the Web is its ability to research current policy issues using primary sources. In many instances, you can get more current information than you will find in newspapers or journal articles. Take, for example, the Goals 2000 legislation discussed in this chapter. To find out about the program generally, you can go to the U.S. Department of Education Web site for this program. As with many Web sites, it opens up a set of additional resources:

> http://www.ed.bov/G2K/

What if you want to compare how states are implementing this legislation? One way to research this question is through any of the standard search engines using key words like Goals 2000, or Educate America Act, or National Education Standards. You might find that North Dakota has organized a planning panel to help meet national education standards. Similar updates will be posted as states implement this legislation.

To track other social policy questions like health care reform, smoking regulation, or crime policy, begin with the home page of the relevant agency or department of national government. Also check congressional resources like Thomas:

> http://thomas.loc.gov

or groups interested in the issue, like the American Medical Association for health policy:

> http://www.ama-assn.org

or the American Cancer Society for tobacco policy:

> http://forces.org/pages/p07-95-1.htm

SUMMARY

1. Conservatives advocate private solutions to most social problems, while liberals argue that it is the responsibility of government to provide a minimum standard of living—including a job, education, health care, housing, and nutrition—for all citizens. Since the New Deal, some government involvement in social programs has been widely accepted, although the extent of involvement has waxed (under Lyndon Johnson) and waned (under Ronald Reagan and George Bush).

2. Social Security, inaugurated in 1935 as part of the New Deal, is perhaps the most significant social legislation in U.S. history. Through a system of employee and employer taxes, retired workers and disabled individuals receive monthly payments. With the country's changing demographic profile, tensions in the system are likely to increase.

3. Welfare takes many forms, including direct payments to the poor, the unemployed, and the disabled; food stamps; job training; housing subsidies; free school lunches; tax credits; subsidized medical care; and others. Public assistance programs began with the New Deal and have grown ever since; the federal government pays about three-fourths of their costs.

4. Welfare has long been criticized as creating disincentives to work, and many proposals have been put forward to make programs more effective and efficient. The most recent welfare reform, which became law in August of 1996, transferred the administrative burden to the states, including giving them more discretion over recipients and their benefits, while helping to fund welfare programs through block grants of federal money.

5. The federal government supports medical research and has increased its role in health care cost control and access as the country's mostly private health care system is beset by rising costs, increasing numbers of uninsured Americans, unnecessary procedures, endless paperwork, high litigation costs, and limited access. A variety of proposals for reform are under consideration, including a single-payer system, managed competition, employer-mandated coverage, spending caps, individual responsibility for coverage, and medical savings accounts.

6. Crime control has been forced onto the national agenda by public perceptions of increases in crime and violence and by politicians eager to accuse opponents of being "soft on crime." Although crime rates since 1991 have actually declined during the Clinton administration, pressures for federal action resulted in passage of the Brady Bill, which imposes a five-day waiting period on the sale of handguns, a ban on some semiautomatic assault weapons, and other proposals that would add to the number of police officers and further restrict gun sales. Republican efforts to overturn part of this legislation demonstrate the contentious nature of the crime and gun control issue.

FURTHER READING

MARY JO BANE AND DAVID T. ELLWOOD, *Welfare Realities: From Rhetoric to Reform* (Harvard University Press, 1994).

FRANK FISCHER, *Evaluating Public Policy* (Nelson-Hall, 1995).

LAURENE A. GRAIG, *Health of Nations: An International Perspective on U.S. Health Care Reform* (Congressional Quarterly Press, 1993).

CHRISTOPHER JENCKS, *The Homeless* (Harvard University Press, 1994).

THOMAS E. MANN AND NORMAN J. ORNSTEIN, EDS., *Intensive Care: How Congress Shapes Health Policy* (Brookings Institution, 1995).

THEODORE R. MARMOR, JERRY L. MASHAW, AND PHILIP L. HARVEY, *America's Misunderstood Welfare State: Persistent Myths, Enduring Realities* (Basic Books, 1990).

DANIEL PATRICK MOYNIHAN, *Miles to Go: A Personal History of Social Policy* (Harvard University Press, 1996).

CHARLES MURRAY, *Losing Ground: American Social Policy, 1950–80* (Basic Books, 1984).

DAVID OSBOURNE AND TED GAEBLER, *Reinventing Government: How the Entrepreneurial Spirit Is Transforming the Public Sector* (Addison-Wesley, 1993).

B. GUY PETERS, *American Public Policy: Promise and Performance*, 4th ed. (Chatham House, 1996).

THEDA SKOCPOL, *Social Policy in the United States: Future Possibilities in Historical Perspective* (Princeton University Press, 1995).

BOB WOODWARD, *Agenda: Inside the Clinton White House* (Simon & Schuster, 1994).

21

Making Foreign and Defense Policy

$\mathcal{T}$he United States finds itself today in a wholly new age of world affairs. "It is an age which, for all its confusions and dangers," observed distinguished diplomat George F. Kennan, "is marked by one major blessing: for the first time in centuries, there are no great-power rivalries that threaten immediately the peace of the world."[1] We have a vested interest in keeping it this way. Yet Kennan and nearly every U.S. citizen understand that even if the cold war is over and even if the United States is the world's dominant and unrivaled military power, the world is still full of conflicts between and within nations. In addition, the population explosion, drugs, poverty, environmental problems, and nuclear weapons create a highly unsettled and unstable world.

In the absence of the cold war frame of reference, both American public opinion and congressional actions have swung, sometimes unpredictably, between support and opposition to the deployment of U.S. troops in places such as Somalia, Haiti, Bosnia, and Zaire. Our hopes and aspirations are often contradictory; that we want to promote democratic values abroad yet also secure our sources of energy sometimes forces us to strengthen nondemocratic governments such as Saudi Arabia. We want to protect the environment yet also support American business overseas; we want to encourage human rights in China yet want China to buy our airplanes and our wheat; we favor progressive trade and immigration policies yet are angry about the job losses that sometimes result from such policies.

There are major differences in Congress and among the American people about the nature of U.S. foreign policy and national security interests. The debate over the U.S. role in Bosnia revealed sharply contrasting conceptions of American interests. Foreign policy scholar Richard Ned Lebow observes:

> Former Cold Warriors, on the whole hostile to intervention [in Bosnia], maintained that nothing that happened in the former Yugoslavia directly threatened American security. Together with other opponents to intervention, they were prone to portray the civil war in Yugoslavia as the latest episode in an historical struggle between hostile ethnic groups that could not be resolved or significantly ameliorated by third parties.
>
> Many of the Americans who favored a more interventionist policy [by the United States] had been active in or generally sympathetic to the goals of the peace movement. They believed that it was imperative for the United States and its European allies to prevent "ethnic cleansing" and uphold the most basic principles of international justice. They maintained that Bosnia was the test case of the post–Cold War order, the same claim made by many former Cold Warriors to justify intervention in Kuwait.[2]

American officials and the American public want the United States to remain the premier global power, yet we balk at bearing the costs of this position. We question the need for foreign aid. We wonder whether the Central Intelligence Agency is as necessary now as it was during the cold war. We fret about the bloated and inefficient United Nations and ask whether it is worth saving. Moreover, we are puzzled about the future of warfare in this high-tech cyberspace era.

How should we restructure our foreign and defense policies to meet twenty-first century conditions? Have economic and trade competition replaced superpower military conflicts? What role do environmental and drug issues now play in foreign policy? Should we link trade agreements with human rights? How much should we aid former enemies? How much does domestic politics shape foreign and national security policy?

U.S. Foreign Policy Priorities

1. *Promoting democratic values.* Human rights, political choice, the rule of law, and self-determination are important humanitarian goals of U.S. foreign policy.

2. *Fostering global growth by promoting market principles.* The United States pursues an active economic agenda bilaterally with our major trading partners and multilaterally through the International Monetary Fund, the World Bank, and the General Agreement on Tariffs and Trade (GATT).

3. *Promoting a peaceful world.* The United States encourages coexistence, celebrating Western culture yet respecting Islamic, Chinese, Japanese, and various other non-Western cultures.

4. *Working with all allies.* New transnational threats, such as environmental degradation, narcotics, terrorism, and economic espionage, require international cooperation.

5. *Helping nations.* We want Mexico, China, Russia, Egypt, Turkey, Spain, South Africa, and other less-developed nations to make the transition to full-fledged members of the global economy.

And is it possible—or desirable—to fashion a single grand strategy of foreign policy to replace our longtime goal of containing and defeating the Soviet Union? As the once-clear lines between foreign and domestic policy become irretrievably blurred, how will the increased participation by Congress and the increased influence of public opinion affect the traditional primacy of the American president in the politics of foreign policy decision making? In short, what should our foreign policy be, and who should make it? In this chapter we explore possible answers to these difficult questions.

VITAL INTERESTS IN THE POST–COLD WAR WORLD

In the cold war years, the United States concentrated on containing and undermining the Soviet threat, and that became the guiding plan of foreign policy. Now, with the cold war in our past, and with the United States as the world's only military superpower, there are still considerable limits on what we *can* do, as well as hard decisions about what we *should* do.

Over the past several generations, the United States has become involved in world affairs to a degree unprecedented in our history. Much of this activity was due to the cold war, 1945 to 1990. Yet there are other reasons as well. U.S. interests, security, and economic prosperity are so closely tied to what happens in the rest of the world that, whether we like it or not, events far from home affect our life, liberty, and pursuit of happiness.

Defining Our Vital Interests

Our political values are a factor in defining our vital interests. We want peace. We favor human rights. We generally support United Nations peacekeeping missions. We have a commitment to protect weaker nations against aggression. We want to encourage democracy and market-oriented economies. We want, where possible, to improve the standard of living in less-developed nations. We are also committed to improving the global environment. Our vital interests have long been defined by our commitment to free trade. As a leading trader, the United States needs markets for its products, imports of raw materials, and adequate supplies of energy. Plainly, the task of defining our interests requires extensive balancing of sometimes competing or contradictory goals.

The United States' interest in maintaining peace in the Middle East prompted President Clinton to invite Palestinian leader Yasser Arafat, Jordan's King Hussein, and Israel's Prime Minister Benjamin Netanyahu to Washington to try to break the impasse in negotiations over the status of Jerusalem. However, the meeting was rather frosty and achieved very little progress.

New Foreign Policy Challenges

The end of the cold war surely has not meant that the United States no longer faces challenges to its security or economic well-being. The removal of communism as a constraint has led to the reemergence of old national hatreds throughout Eastern Europe. Some nations, such as Yugoslavia and Czechoslovakia, have broken apart. The Middle East remains unsettled. In Latin America, democracies have emerged, yet there have also been setbacks. China, Myanmar, North Korea, and Indonesia remain under military rule. The United States is especially concerned over the proliferation of nuclear weapons, the invasion of drugs into our country, and the persistence of brutal civil wars in several countries around the globe.

The United States may be militarily strong, yet we face stiff competition for influence in the world as the power base shifts from military might to economic strength. Our foreign policy has to address vital issues that have been simmering for many years, plus some concerns that are recent. Table 21-1 lists issues of major concern both to leaders and to the general public. Notice here again how what people think is important is often contradictory.

POPULATION GROWTH AND POVERTY Americans are alarmed at the world's population explosion in the face of widespread poverty. Still, our support for population control programs abroad is embroiled in controversy in Congress between anti-abortion and pro-choice interest groups. Most of the world's nearly 6 billion people are already virtually excluded from economic opportunity. In China alone, more than 300 million live below the international poverty level. Moreover, there

TABLE 21–1
Foreign Policy Goals: What Is Important?

	Percent Answering "Important" or "Very Important"	
	Leaders	The Public
Stopping flow of illegal drugs into the United States	57%	85%
Protecting jobs of American workers	50	83
Preventing the spread of nuclear weapons	90	82
Controlling and reducing illegal immigration	28	72
Securing adequate supplies of energy	67	62
Reducing our trade deficits with foreign countries	49	59
Improving global environment	49	58
Combating world hunger	41	56
Protecting interests of American business abroad	38	52
Strengthening the United Nations	33	51
Maintaining superior military power worldwide	54	50
Defending our allies' security	60	41
Promoting and defending human rights in other countries	26	34
Helping to bring a democratic form of government to other nations	21	25
Protecting weaker nations against foreign aggression	21	24
Helping to improve standards of living in less-developed nations	28	22

SOURCE: Adapted with permission from John E. Rielly, *American Public Opinion and U.S. Foreign Policy, 1995* (Chicago Council on Foreign Relations, 1995), p. 15.

Public sample was N=1,492. Leaders sample included 383 elected officials, business leaders, educators, editors, and union officers.

Some Key Foreign Policy Terms

- *Internationalism*: A foreign policy that recognizes that concern for trade, human rights, and international peace requires not only a strong military but also the willingness to intervene where U.S. vital interests are at stake. The goal is to create an international order consistent with American values.

- *Isolationism*: A foreign policy that curtails U.S. military aid and intervention abroad as much as possible. It was the dominant policy in this country during the nineteenth century and to some degree in the 1920s and 1930s. It was put forward again by Pat Buchanan during the 1996 presidential primaries.

- *Realism or Realpolitik*: A foreign policy based on practical and self-interest factors rather than on moral, idealistic, or theoretical considerations. Realists say the United States should intervene in world affairs only if its vital interests are in jeopardy or if a dispute involves overt outside aggression, not simply internal rebellion.

- *Containment*: A foreign policy aimed at halting the spread of communism, especially the influence of the former Soviet Union. This was the underlying foreign and national security policy of the United States between 1947 and 1990.

- *New World Order*: A vague and often confusing label pinned on the post–cold war period—one in which the United States presumably plays a vital role as the only remaining superpower in preserving peace and encouraging economic and human rights throughout the world.

Former U.S. Trade Representative Mickey Kantor met with Japanese Prime Minister Morihiro Hosakawa in an effort to ease Japan's trade restrictions on some American imports.

continues to be a significant transfer of wealth from poor countries to rich, and the information technology revolution accelerates this disparity.

TRADE WITH JAPAN AND CHINA A serious trade imbalance exists between the United States and both Japan and China. Some U.S. citizens believe we should force Japan to open its markets to imports of our products and impose restrictions on the manufacture of exported Japanese products, even if such restrictions would make those products cost more.

Trade with China poses additional concerns. China has one of the fastest growing economies in the world. U.S. exports to China have tripled in the last several years. Human rights advocates believe we should link trade and tariff agreements to China's human rights record. It is well known that China does not regard human rights in the same way that constitutional democracies do. President Bill Clinton has, from time to time, threatened to withhold most favored nation status from China unless there was a marked improvement in their treatment of dissidents. **Most favored nation** status is an international trade policy whereby we grant to a country the same favorable trade concessions and tariffs that our best trading partners receive.

Loss of trade with China would deal a serious blow to the American economy, especially on the West Coast, and especially to huge companies such as Boeing. This potential setback came into conflict with the desire to protect human rights, and when push came to shove, President Clinton "separated" the two issues and extended China's favored nation status. This issue persists as an obstacle in United States–Chinese diplomatic and economic relations.

NUCLEAR AND BIOLOGICAL ARMS CONTROL Probably the single greatest threat to the security of the United States and the rest of the world is the proliferation of weapons of mass destruction. At present, only a handful of nations have usable nuclear weapons. What happens if such weapons fall into the hands of nations like Libya, Iraq, and North Korea, which have no democratic controls on their governments and whose leaders may have dreams of world conquest?

Twenty-seven nations, including the United States and Russia, have agreed to curb the sale of materials that could be used in the manufacture of nuclear weapons. This agreement was a direct result of a close call in early 1990, when Iraq was detected trying to build nuclear weapons. Although the agreement established limits on the sale of materials or machinery that can be used either for peaceful purposes or for building nuclear bombs, experts still caution that "good intentions on export controls are often undermined by ignorance and greed."[3]

In the mid-1990s, the United States created an international coalition to deal with the threat of nuclear proliferation in North Korea, a move that many thought was unwise. For example, former Secretary of Defense Caspar Weinberger called it an "appeasement agreement" that gives North Korea two large plutonium reactors, years of free oil, and much else in return for a promise to stop making nuclear weapons.[4] Others think this agreement postpones or even avoids a military confrontation with North Korea. However, the severe food shortages plaguing North Korea have diverted their attention from military adventures and made them more amenable to negotiating with the United States and South Korea.

Some foreign policy experts suggest that the United States may some day have to resort to "preemptive intervention" in nations like North Korea, Iran, Iraq, Syria, Libya, or Algeria to prevent a rogue nation from acquiring menacing nuclear weapons.[5] This is hardly a strategy most Americans would like, and no government official has espoused it. Still, modern warfare writers note that "modern missiles and bombs are so powerful that each side will have a strong incentive to strike first and thus stop the enemy doing anything."[6]

THE CHEMICAL WEAPONS CONVENTION The United States has entered into a variety of agreements to restrict the use of biological or chemical materials. President Clinton and his supporters waged a major legislative battle in 1997 with Senator Jesse Helms, *The Wall Street Journal*, and many conservatives over whether the United States should ratify the Chemical Weapons Convention. Treaty supporters, such as Bill Clinton, George Bush, and Senator John McCain (R.-Ariz.), said the security of our soldiers and citizens was at stake. They noted we were already destroying our chemical weapons stockpile and argued that all treaty signers must do the same. Routine inspections would take place in all member nations, and this convention (or treaty) would punish nonmembers by restricting their ability to import or export restricted chemicals.

Critics called the Chemical Weapons Convention a dangerous treaty because cheaters could easily evade detection. They also opposed it because rogue nations such as Libya, Iraq, Syria, and North Korea were not going to join as members: "How can a treaty that professes to address the problem of chemical weapons be credible unless it addresses the threat from the very countries, such as Syria and Iraq, that have actually deployed these weapons?"[7]

In the spring of 1997, the Senate voted to ratify our participation in the Chemical Weapons Convention. Just before the vote was taken, President Clinton won the critically important support of Senate Majority Leader Trent Lott, enabling the convention to pass by more than the needed two-thirds majority.

THE FORMER SOVIET UNION AND EASTERN EUROPE Several of the countries that emerged from the former Soviet Union and its satellites are now torn by economic chaos and shortages. Americans want to be of assistance yet are weary of giving direct aid that will raise U.S. taxes and enlarge the U.S. national debt. Still, foreign policy experts contend such aid is essential to help with the transition to a market economy and to encourage the gradual development of healthy constitutional democracies in that region.

THE EUROPEAN ECONOMIC UNION AND THE FUTURE OF NATO The European Economic Union has adopted measures that bind European nations together for the purpose of economic growth. An economically powerful Europe poses challenges for U.S. companies and trade. With the end of the cold war, Europe, Canada, and the United States have redefined the mission and goals of the North Atlantic Treaty Organization (NATO). In Bosnia, NATO forces conducted the alliance's first "out of the area" military operation. NATO also expanded in 1997,

"Dad, what was the Soviet Union?"
The Wall Street Journal.

George Marshall (Truman)

John Foster Dulles (Eisenhower)

Dean Rusk
(Kennedy and Lyndon Johnson)

Henry Kissinger (Nixon and Ford)

welcoming former Warsaw Pact nations. However, NATO's expansion raised considerable fear in Russia and among some foreign policy experts.[8]

DRUG TRAFFIC United States' relations with Mexico, Colombia, and other Latin American nations are greatly affected by drug traffic issues. The drug epidemic in the United States is fed by drugs smuggled into this country from Western Hemisphere nations. Should the U.S. military be involved? Are drugs a domestic problem that needs to be solved at home, or should American addictions be perceived as a combined domestic, economic, and foreign policy problem? Few issues are as complicated and fraught with both foreign policy and civil liberty implications.

THE GLOBAL ENVIRONMENT The United States is at the same time one of the world's leading environmental forces and one of its major polluters. A 1992 U.N. conference in Rio de Janeiro on conserving and improving the world's natural resources pointed the way toward many new policies, but most nations, including the United States, have moved slowly on implementing policies to achieve these goals, despite grim warnings about global warming.

KEY PLAYERS IN FOREIGN POLICY

Although presidents share with Congress the responsibility for making overall foreign policy decisions, the operations of foreign policy are directly under the president. In practice, a president has the primary responsibility to shape foreign policy. Presidents can bargain, negotiate, persuade, apply economic pressures, threaten, or even use armed force.

The Constitution puts control of foreign policy in the hands of those who run the national government: the president, the Senate, and, in some cases, the Congress as a whole. In England, the king controlled foreign policy; the framers of our Constitution tried to redress the balance, and many of the powers given to Congress by the Constitution reflect the decision to limit the powers of the executive branch. Thus Congress has the power to declare war, to appropriate funds, and to make rules for the armed forces. But the president is commander in chief of the armed forces and is expected to negotiate treaties and receive and send ambassadors—that is, to recognize or refuse to recognize other governments. The Senate confirms ambassadors and gives consent to treaty ratification. The courts have the power to interpret treaties, but by and large they have ruled that relations with other nations are matters for the executive to negotiate.

The primacy of the executive in foreign policy is a fact of political life of all nations, including constitutional democracies. To appreciate this phenomenon, let us look at the people within the executive branch who make up the foreign policy establishment.

The President's Foreign Policy Advisers

Officially, the president's principal foreign policy adviser is the secretary of state, though today competing advisers are sometimes more influential. The secretary of state administers the State Department, receives visits from foreign diplomats, attends international conferences, and usually heads our delegation in the General Assembly of the United Nations. The secretary also serves as the administration's chief coordinator of all governmental actions that affect our relations with foreign nations. In practice, a secretary of state delegates the day-to-day responsibilities for running the State Department and spends most of his or her time negotiating with the leaders of other countries.[9]

Today, because of the interdependence of foreign, economic, and domestic policies, the president calls on an increasing number of civilian and economic advisers in addition to the secretary of state. The conduct of foreign affairs is now the business of several major departments and agencies: State, Defense, Treasury, Agriculture, Commerce, Labor, Energy, the Central Intelligence Agency (CIA), and others. The need for immediate reaction and preparedness has transferred more responsibilities directly to the president—and to a great extent, to the senior White House aides who assist in coordinating information and advice. Yet no matter what the system for advice and coordination, there is always overlap, redundancy, and competition to influence the president.

Secretaries, agency chiefs, and their senior subordinates are chosen by the president and are expected to support and carry out his decisions. At the same time, they retain a measure of independence; they naturally tend to reflect and defend the views of the departments and agencies they head. As a result, our presidents have found a need to appoint White House advisers whose loyalties lie solely with the chief executive.

The National Security Council

The key coordinating agency for the president is the National Security Council (NSC). Created by Congress in 1947, it is intended to help presidents integrate foreign, military, and economic policies that affect national security. The National Security Council serves directly under the president. By law, it consists of the president, vice-president, secretary of state, and secretary of defense. Recent presidents have sometimes included the director of the CIA, the White House chief of staff, the attorney general, and the national security adviser as ex-officio members of the NSC.

The national security adviser, appointed by the president, has gradually emerged as one of the most influential foreign policy makers, sometimes rivaling in influence the secretary of state. Presidents come to rely on these White House aides both because of their proximity (down the hall in the west wing of the White House) and because they owe their primary loyalties to the president, not to any department or program. Each president has shaped the NSC structure and adapted its staff procedures to suit his personal preferences, but over the years the NSC, as both a committee and a staff, has taken on a major role in making and implementing foreign policy.[10] President Clinton, for example, sees and talks with his NSC adviser on a daily basis but may chat with his secretary of state only twice a week.

The State Department

The primary duty of the State Department has always been the security of the nation. Although our armed forces remain our ultimate line of defense, the State Department is our first line. It is dedicated to an around-the-clock, worldwide effort to see that troops and weapons are not used except in genuine emergencies. It is also the central agency in the day-to-day management of foreign affairs. Among the State Department's main priorities are the following:

1. To promote peace and human rights
2. To negotiate with other nations and international organizations
3. To protect American citizens and interests abroad
4. To promote American commercial interests and enterprises
5. To collect and interpret intelligence
6. To represent an American "presence" abroad.

The State Department's budget of $5.5 billion in 1998 is the lowest of all the cabinet departments—less than 2 percent of the Department of Defense's approximately

Cyrus Vance (Carter)

George Shultz (Reagan)

James Baker (Bush)

Warren Christopher (Clinton)

Madeleine Albright is the first woman to become U.S. Secretary of State. In her years as our representative to the United Nations, Albright established a reputation as an outspoken advocate of human rights and international cooperation.

$260 billion budget. Considering the State Department's role and prestige, its staff of 24,000 worldwide is small, especially compared with the 2.2 million civilian and military personnel in the Department of Defense. Like most other federal agencies, State has had to eliminate nearly 10 percent of its staff in the 1990s. If Republican Senator Jesse Helms had his way, it would have cut at least twice that amount.

The Foreign Service

The American Foreign Service is the eyes and ears of the United States in other countries. Although part of the State Department, the service represents the entire government and performs jobs for many other agencies. Its main duties are: carry out foreign policy as expressed in the directives of the secretary of state; gather political, economic, and intelligence data for American policy makers; protect Americans and American interests in foreign countries; and cultivate friendly relations with host governments and foreign peoples.

The Foreign Service is composed of Foreign Service officers, reserve officers, and staff officers. At the core of the service are the Foreign Service officers, comparable to army officers in the military. They are a select, specially trained group expected to take assignments any place in the world on short notice. There are approximately 4,300 such officers; in recent years fewer than 250 junior officers won appointment each year. Approximately two-thirds of our U.S. ambassadors to nearly 150 nations come from the ranks of the Foreign Service. The others are usually political appointees, such as former Tennessee Senator James Sasser, the current ambassador to China, or large donors or friends of the president, such as Ambassador Swanee Hunt, a recent U.S. ambassador to Austria.

The Foreign Service is one of the most prestigious yet most criticized career services of the national government. Criticism sometimes comes as much from within as from outside. Critics claim the organizational culture of the Foreign Service stifles creativity; attracts officers who are, or at least become, more concerned about their status than their responsibilities; and requires new recruits to wait 15 years or more before being considered for positions of responsibility. These problems are recognized in Washington, and the task of improving the service continues. Outside critics point to a social homogeneity among the Foreign Service, but that is probably overstated. More women and minorities have been recruited in recent years.

Perhaps the greatest challenge for foreign service diplomats is how to function effectively in a high-tech world. Some have even suggested that diplomats be replaced altogether and most of their work be conducted by e-mail, fax, and videoconferencing from Washington.[11] Yet having a diplomat on the scene in Iran or Saudi Arabia who speaks Farsi and Arabic and who knows a country's major leaders is often a better method than relying on even the most advanced new technologies—especially when making subtle judgments about a nation's political and economic policies.

Intelligence and the CIA

What is the nuclear capability of the North Korean military? How strong are the rebel forces in Zaire? What are the internal political struggles in Bosnia and Haiti? How stable is the political situation in Colombia, Peru, or Venezuela? Before our foreign policy makers can act on important issues, they have to know as much as possible about other countries: their possible reactions to a particular policy, their strengths and weaknesses, the character of their leaders, and if possible, their strategic plans and intentions. Thus those who gather and analyze intelligence data are among the most important advisers to policy makers.[12]

The Central Intelligence Agency, an outgrowth of the World War II Office of Strategic Services, was created in 1947 to coordinate the gathering and analysis of information that flows into various parts of the U.S. government from all over the world. In recent years, the CIA has had nearly 20,000 employees and has helped direct and integrate the intelligence products of the State Department's Bureau of Intelligence and Research, the Defense Intelligence Agency (which combines the intelligence operations of the Army, Navy, Air Force, and Marine Corps), the National Security Agency (which specializes in electronic reconnaissance and code breaking), the supersecret National Reconnaissance Office (which runs the U.S. satellite surveillance programs), the Federal Bureau of Investigation (FBI), and a small intelligence operation run by the Departments of Energy and Treasury. In the late 1990s, these agencies were spending an estimated $30 billion a year on intelligence work.[13]

Although most of the information the CIA gathers comes from open sources, the term "intelligence" conjures up visions of spies and undercover agents. Secret intelligence occasionally does supply crucial data. But it is not all glamour; much is routine. Intelligence work involves three basic operations: reporting, research, and dissemination. *Reporting* is based on the close and rigorous observation of developments around the world; *research* is the attempt to detect meaningful patterns out of what was observed in the past and to understand what appears to be going on now; and *dissemination* means getting the right information to the right people at the right time.

CIA analysts detected the military buildup by Iraq's Saddam Hussein in 1990, but their warnings about an invasion of Kuwait were too cautious and too late, according to later analyses. Indeed, President George Bush, himself a former CIA director, is reported to have been misinformed that Iraq really was not adequately recovered from its war with Iran to mount another military invasion.

For 40 years the CIA and other intelligence agencies used their best personnel to understand and help undermine our primary enemy—the Soviet Union. Now that the Soviet Union is gone, the CIA has had to redefine its role, address new challenges, and reverse its long-term growth pattern. Among its new challenges are gathering intelligence on terrorism, drug trafficking, and the growing number of nations that have ballistic missiles with chemical, biological, and nuclear warheads. Our intelligence agencies are also asked to prevent espionage by other nations.

What about the need for *covert operations*—operations that deliberately try to destabilize governments or insurgent groups in other nations? The CIA has been credited with both successful and failed covert operations abroad. The ill-fated Bay of Pigs invasion of Cuba in 1961 was directed by the CIA. Later the CIA organized and trained anticommunist forces in Laos and supported the anti-Allende forces in Chile. Because of its past record and because it must act when our government cannot intervene officially, there is a tendency to credit (or blame) the CIA for many coups, purges, and revolts whether the agency was involved or not.

In the Reagan years the CIA played an important role in several Central American nations. For example, the U.S. supported the government in El Salvador but aided the antigovernment rebels in Nicaragua. Some observers believed these and related activities represented an integral part of U.S. diplomacy and preparedness and helped us achieve our goals in that region. Others denounced these activities as jeopardizing the values of freedom and liberty the United States is dedicated to defending.[14]

The CIA's influence, its information, its secrecy, its speed in communication, its ability to act, and its enormous budget make it a potent force. These same characteristics also make the CIA controversial. Congress has tried to see that this power is used only by publicly accountable decision makers. Committees have been set up in both the Senate and the House of Representatives to hold the CIA accountable to Congress, although earlier efforts by similar committees sometimes failed to do an adequate job.[15]

The Peace Corps

The Peace Corps, established by the Peace Corps Act of 1961 in the Kennedy administration, has a mission to encourage world peace and friendship, help other countries in meeting their social and development needs, and promote greater understanding between Americans and other peoples. Peace Corps volunteers are expected to serve in another nation for two years and become part of the community they are serving. Volunteers work on a variety of projects, such as teaching math and science, doing community development work, and improving water and sanitation systems.

What qualifications does one need to apply? Generally a college degree, experience, or a combination of both. There is no age limit. In fact, about 10 percent of the 7,000 current volunteers are over 50 years old. The Peace Corps picks up the expenses and typically trains each volunteer in language and job skills for about three months prior to service abroad.

The Peace Corps operates in about 95 nations and has had funding of about $230 million a year. More than 150,000 Americans have been Peace Corps volunteers. Eight Peace Corps alumni serve in Congress, evenly divided between Republicans and Democrats. The Peace Corps is wholly separate from the State and Defense Departments or the intelligence agencies.

The Peace Corps motto to would-be volunteers says, "The Peace Corps—the toughest job you'll ever love."

For more information, write Peace Corps, Volunteer Service Office, 1990 K Street, NW, Washington, D.C. 20526, or call 1-800-424-8580. For a useful history of the origins and early years of the Peace Corps, see Gerald T. Rice, *The Bold Experiment: JFK's Peace Corps* (University of Notre Dame Press, 1985).

Congress became especially outraged at the CIA's leadership in 1994, when it was discovered that a senior CIA agent, Aldrich Ames, had spied for the Soviets and the KGB for much of the 1980s. Ames confessed to what is considered the worst betrayal of U.S. intelligence in the history of the CIA. It will take years for the CIA to recover the credibility it lost from this tragic case.

While the U.S. intelligence agencies have made mistakes over the years, most experts believe these agencies are needed. Political scientist Loch Johnson writes that "the likelihood that they contributed significantly to warding off a third world war has been enough to earn their keep."[16] Their analysis of complicated political and military developments in the Middle East has also proved strategically important.

An extensive review of the CIA by a bipartisan commission in 1996 recommended strengthening the hand of the director of central intelligence, reducing the work force of these agencies, and "refocusing its efforts on global crime such as terrorism, narcotics trafficking, proliferation of weapons of mass destruction and international organized crime syndicates."[17] The commission recommended that the intelligence agencies strengthen their accountability to the executive and legislative branches, yet concluded that their missions of information gathering and analysis were vital to the security of the United States.[18]

THE POLITICS OF MAKING FOREIGN AND DEFENSE POLICY

Foreign policy flows through the same institutional and constitutional structures as domestic policy. Public opinion, interest groups, members of Congress, elections, separation of powers, and federalism all affect the politics of making foreign policy. Yet these structures operate somewhat differently from the way they do in domestic affairs. Of course, international organizations and foreign governments and their embassies also play an important role.

Public Opinion

Different foreign and defense issues evoke different degrees of public interest and involvement. In crisis situations—such as the planning of Operation Desert Storm in Kuwait in 1991—decisions are made by a small group of persons. Yet even in these situations, presidents and their advisers know their decisions will ultimately require support from the public and from Congress.

In noncrisis situations, the public appears to consist of three subcategories. The largest, constituting perhaps as much as 75 percent of the adult population, is the *mass public*. This group knows little about the details of foreign affairs, despite the subject's importance. The mass public concerns itself with foreign affairs mainly in conflict situations, especially those involving the actual or possible use of American troops abroad. The second group is the *attentive public*, constituting perhaps 15 to 20 percent of the population. It maintains an active interest in foreign policy. The *opinion makers* are the third and smallest public; as editors, teachers, writers, political and business leaders, they transmit information and judgments on foreign affairs and mobilize the support of the other two publics.

Still, many people in this country are indifferent or uninformed about foreign and defense policy. Foreign affairs issues are more remote than domestic issues. People have more firsthand information about unemployment, inflation, crime, and hospital costs than about Ukrainian economic reform or Brazilian political problems. The worker in the factory and the boss in the front office know what labor-management relations are about, and they have strong opinions on the subject. They may also have strong opinions about gun control, capital punishment, and abortion. But most Americans have a poor sense of world geography and an even weaker grasp of geopolitics. Sometimes it seems that only when American soldiers or civilians overseas are killed does the mass public become directly concerned with foreign affairs.

Most Americans do recognize that their lives, jobs, and security inevitably reflect international developments. "Contrary to a widely held assumption, their concern does not stop at the water's edge," writes Steven Kull.[19] And a survey of American views on foreign and defense policy concludes that despite the absence of strong White House leadership on foreign affairs, most Americans accept that the United States has serious obligations:

> Relief from the long competition with the Soviet Union and the lack of a clear external threat have made Americans more reluctant to use force abroad and become involved in the affairs of other countries. But they want to maintain current levels of defense in an uncertain world and are committed to diplomatic engagement through alliances and multilateral organizations.[20]

The American public concerns itself with foreign affairs mainly when it involves the use of our troops abroad.

The State and Defense Departments make an effort to keep people informed about those areas of policy they think should be discussed publicly and to keep themselves informed about public opinion. Yet despite occasional talk about open and democratic policy-making processes, most foreign policy negotiations in which our government has a major role are conducted in secret. Even Congress is sometimes kept at a distance, as was the case when the Iranians were encouraged to send arms to Bosnia while President Clinton was assuring Congress that the United States supported the arms embargo.

Special Interests

The mass media can be powerful in shaping public opinion, a fact reflected in frequent disputes between the media and government. Certain reporters and newspapers have helped rally public opinion on behalf of human rights, and press coverage of government treatment of dissidents in China and South Africa put pressure on the White House and Congress to reconsider our policies toward those countries.

It is difficult to generalize about the impact of interest groups on American foreign policies. At moments of international crisis, such as after Iraq invaded Kuwait, a president is usually able to mobilize so much public support that interest groups find it difficult to exert much influence. As a general rule, special interest groups other than major economic interests rarely have a decisive role in the formulation of foreign policy.

Ethnic interest groups, however, can and do play an important role in foreign policy decisions. As a nation of immigrants and the children and grandchildren of immigrants, our citizens often retain a special bond with their country of origin. Thus, Irish Americans, Jewish Americans, African Americans, Asian Americans, Polish Americans, and Greek Americans take a keen interest in decisions affecting Ireland, Israel, South Africa, China, Indonesia, Poland, and Greece. These interest groups sometimes exert powerful pressures on policy makers to support the country to which they are emotionally linked. Congress is attuned to these pressures. And in the 1996 election Asian Americans, and perhaps even Asian countries, made contributions to the election of Bill Clinton and members of Congress.

Foreign Countries and Foreign Companies

Most countries, large and small, have embassies that lobby for their interests in Washington. In addition, some countries like Japan have built up a powerful network of lawyers, lobbyists, and Washington-based publicists who are retained by Japanese companies and trade associations, as well as by the Japanese government, to defend their extensive economic interests in the United States.[21] Lobbyists representing newly industrialized countries like South Korea, Taiwan, Singapore,

Brazil, and Mexico have also expanded their Washington lobbying efforts to fight U.S. protectionism and import quotas on textiles, shoes, and other exports. Whether foreign governments and business interests influence our foreign policy became an issue after large Chinese and Indonesian contributions to Bill Clinton's reelection campaign came to light. The president vigorously denied that contributions buy influence, and the money was returned by the Democratic National Committee.

Political Parties

Political parties do not usually play a major role in shaping foreign and defense policy for two reasons: (1) many Americans still prefer to keep partisan politics out of foreign policy; (2) parties usually take less clear and candid stands on foreign policy than they do on domestic policy. Party platforms often obscure the issues instead of highlighting them, and many members of Congress fail to follow a general party line.

Should parties be concerned with foreign policy? At the end of World War II, sentiment grew stronger for a bipartisan approach to foreign policy. An ambiguous term, **bipartisanship** seems to mean: (1) collaboration between the executive and the congressional foreign policy leaders of both parties; (2) support of presidential foreign policies by both parties in Congress; and (3) downplaying foreign policy issues in national elections and especially in presidential debates. In general, bipartisanship is an attempt to remove the issues of foreign policy from partisan politics.

The Role of Congress

Despite the importance of foreign and defense policy, and even though Congress can block the president's policy and undermine the chief executive's decisions, Congress as an institution seldom makes foreign policy directly. Individual members of Congress, however, are sometimes included within the circle of those who make foreign and defense policy decisions. The power of Congress is mainly consultative, although the legislature has taken the initiative in some trade and foreign economic and military assistance questions. In addition, Congress has attempted to curb presidential war-making powers.[22]

Congress is a crucial link between policy makers and the public. Congress wants a voice—especially "meaningful consultation" with the president in matters of foreign relations. Congress, for example, played an important role in cutting off funds for bombing Cambodia in 1973 and in shaping U.S. foreign policy toward Haiti and Bosnia. But Congress is often divided on issues of foreign and defense policy—as it has been, for example, on the Chemical Weapons Convention, foreign aid, and funding for the United Nations.

For the most part, presidents and their advisers initiate foreign policy, yet members of Congress stimulate, prod, amend, modify, and sometimes block what the White House proposes.

The Potential for a Democratic Foreign Policy

A great paradox exists in conducting the foreign relations of a modern democracy. In the 1830s, Alexis de Tocqueville wrote that foreign relations "demand scarcely any of the qualities which are peculiar to a democracy; they require, on the contrary, the perfect use of all those in which it is deficient."[23] One leading scholar observed more directly that policy makers in our democracy "either . . . must sacrifice what they consider good policy upon the altar of public opinion, or they must by devious means gain support for policies whose true nature is concealed from the public."[24]

"Let me connect you with Edith, our specialist in ethnic conflict in the former Yugoslavia. My expertise happens to be in North Korean intransigence."

Drawing by Handelsman. © 1994 The New Yorker Magazine, Inc.

A democratic foreign policy is one in which policy makers are known and held accountable to the people. That is a tough test for any policy, but it is especially tough for foreign policy because of the need to act with speed, and sometimes with secrecy, the generally low level of information among the general public, the anonymity of most foreign policy leaders, and, of course, the complexity of issues and options. Still, the American public wants to be consulted and informed, and it wants its leaders accountable.

In Vietnam, American policy makers miscalculated the character of the war as well as the commitment of the Vietnamese who opposed the Saigon government. And because these policy makers knew to some extent that they had made mistakes and believed the American people and Congress might not support them in what they thought necessary, they sometimes concealed these difficulties.[25]

A constitutional democracy may not be able to keep leaders from making mistakes, especially when leaders work in secrecy and do not get advance approval for national security decisions. But in a policy area in which big mistakes can be made, the mistakes eventually become public. It is then that the safeguarding agencies of democracy—the opposition party, the press, and dissident opinion—go to work. Changes are demanded, and policies are changed. In the case of Vietnam, public resistance to the war eventually forced the United States to get out. The way in which these agencies of democracy worked in the United States doubtless encouraged the United States to exit from both the Vietnam and Somalia conflicts faster than the Soviets got out of their ill-fated engagement in Afghanistan.

FOREIGN AND DEFENSE POLICY STRATEGIES

How are foreign and defense policies actually implemented? As a major power, the United States can choose a variety of options, but it usually employs the following six, or some combination of them.

Conventional Diplomacy

Much of U.S. foreign policy is conducted by the foreign service and ambassadors in face-to-face discussions in Washington and other capitals, at the United Nations, in Geneva (at arms talks), and elsewhere around the world in regional or international organizations and world conferences. International summit meetings, with their high-profile pomp and drama, are another form of conventional diplomacy. Even though traditional diplomacy appears more subdued and somewhat less vital in this era of personal leader-to-leader communication by telephone, fax, and teleconferencing, it is still an important, if slow, process by which nations can gain information, talk about mutual interests, and try to resolve bilateral and multilateral disputes.

Much of the conventional diplomacy carried out by the State Department and its $5.5 billion budget may not produce important breakthroughs, yet it is difficult to measure the value of diplomatic representation. No price tag can be placed on close personal relations with foreign officials or on information gathered and arguments made to promote American interests around the world. Surely the closing of one embassy or the withdrawal from international organizations is unlikely to cause the United States major setbacks, yet a less active diplomatic corps could mean a less effective foreign policy.

Foreign Aid

The United States regularly grants economic and military assistance to foreign countries, in part for humanitarian reasons and in part to further good relations with other nations. The United States offers aid to more than 100 countries directly

Most American citizens say they would like to have their voice heard more often on major issues. But most political scientists, pollsters, and elected national officials oppose national polls that would in any way bind the national government. Franklin Roosevelt strongly opposed the idea of taking votes on whether to go to war, saying it would be impractical in its application and incompatible with our representative form of government. Political and public opinion analysts also point out that we would never have had a Marshall Plan in the 1940s if we had followed public opinion.

On most issues, the public does not have an opinion in any firm, definitive sense, and to try to discover one may be misguided. Most members of Congress say representatives owe their constituents their judgment, not just slavish deference to temporary passions of the moment. Indeed, critics go so far as to say one of the reasons we do not have a serious foreign policy is because we already pay too much attention to public opinion.

Still, the public would like to be heard, even if its voice is generally not clear on most issues and more likely to be reactive to headlines than the product of careful reflection.

SOURCE: Adapted from Adam Clymer, "Proposing to Eliminate a Polling Gap in Congress," *The New York Times*, May 15, 1994, p. 18.

and to a number of other nations through contributions to various United Nations development funds. Since 1945 we have provided more than $250 billion in economic assistance to foreign countries—a figure that looks and sounds impressive. In 1998, U.S. foreign aid amounted to another $19 billion. Yet the United States devotes less of its gross national product to foreign aid and development than any other industrialized democracy.

Most foreign aid goes to a few countries the United States deems to be of strategic importance—Israel, Egypt, Bosnia, Ukraine, Jordan, India, Russia, South Africa, and Haiti. But much of what constitutes foreign aid is actually spent in the United States, where it pays for the purchase of American services and products being sent to those countries. It thus amounts to a hefty subsidy for American companies and their employees.

Ever since the United States began giving serious amounts of foreign aid after World War II, many Americans and members of Congress have opposed it. Few powerful interest groups or constituencies back foreign aid initiatives. State department officials are invariably the biggest advocates of foreign aid. Presidents also recognize the vital role foreign aid plays in advancing U.S. interests, so presidents keep asking Congress for funds for foreign aid. Successive presidents have all wanted to maintain the leverage with key countries that economic and military assistance aid provides. One of the major debates today is how much economic aid the United States should provide to Russia and the republics that once constituted the Soviet Union.

Despite the assertion by presidents and their secretaries of state that foreign aid—about 1 percent of the federal budget—is an investment to secure our vital national interests and a peaceful future, Congress invariably trims these requests by 15 to 20 percent, saying there is too much waste. Rarely do U.S. policy makers or citizens think much about the basic economic rights of those who live in poor nations. It is fascinating that most discussions of foreign aid are couched in terms of American self-interest rather than authentic humanitarian values.[26]

Economic Sanctions

The United States has frequently practiced the art of economic pressure in response to a nation's unwillingness to abide by what we perceive to be international law or proper relations. The U.S. and U.N. embargo against Haiti in 1994 is a classic example of economic sanctions. Economic sanctions imposed on South Africa helped in encouraging democracy in that nation. But sanctions imposed on Iraq and Cuba have not had much effect on dislodging Saddam Hussein or Fidel Castro.

The popularity of economic sanctions has waxed and waned over the years, yet it is still a potentially important weapon in the arsenal of diplomatic and foreign policy strategies. "Economic sanctions often emerge as the centerpiece when a balance is needed between actions that seem too soft or too strident. In these situations, sanctions are seldom regarded as the 'ideal' weapon; rather they are seen as the 'least bad' alternative."[27] Various evaluations of economic sanctions since World War I find that economic sanctions helped achieve foreign policy goals less than a third of the time.[28]

Sanctions are definitely not popular among the farmers or corporations that have to sacrifice part of their overseas markets to comply with government sanctions or controls. Indeed, business and farm lobbyists try to convince Congress and the White House that unilateral embargoes hurt our economy and produce unwanted results more often than desired ones. Nevertheless, the United States has employed this strategy dozens of times over the past few decades, including current targets of Myanmar, Iran, Iraq, and Libya.

Political Coercion

When relations between nations become especially strained, diplomatic relations are sometimes broken as a means of political coercion. When the United States breaks diplomatic ties, it greatly restricts tourist and business travel to a country and, in effect, curbs political as well as certain economic relations with a nation. The consequences are thus more than merely symbolic.

Breaking off diplomatic relations, however, is a next-to-last resort (force is the last resort), for such action undermines the ability to reason with a nation's leaders or to use other diplomatic strategies to resolve conflicts. The act also undermines our ability to get valuable information about what is going on in a nation and to have a presence in that nation.

Covert Operations

Covert activities are planned and executed to conceal the identity of the sponsor. President Dwight Eisenhower used the Central Intelligence Agency to engage in covert or quasi-military ventures, both to avoid deploying the military and to advance U.S. foreign policy interests. U.S. support for the shah of Iran and the overthrow of the government in Guatemala in the 1950s are examples. During the cold war years, several presidents authorized covert operations in Vietnam and Central America. But covert activities in Cuba, Chile, and elsewhere have backfired, and support for this strategy has cooled in the post–cold war era.[29]

Military Intervention

War, it is said, is not merely an extension of diplomacy; it is also a total breakdown of diplomacy. The United States has intervened militarily in other nations on the average of almost once a year since 1789, although usually in relatively minor or short-term episodes, such as Ronald Reagan's use of troops in Grenada, George Bush's invasion of Panama in 1989, Bill Clinton's peaceful invasion of Haiti in 1994, and peacekeeping efforts with NATO in Bosnia in 1995 and 1996. Of course, these may not be considered minor events by the target nations or by the American families who lost sons in these forays.

Intervention with force is plainly the ultimate strategy—the last resort—in trying to resolve a conflict. Military action by the United States is most successful when it involves small and even medium-sized countries (Grenada, Panama, and Kuwait). But military intervention "often proves ineffective in the context of national civil wars (the United States in Vietnam; Israel in Lebanon)."[30] Lessons from past interventions are one reason Americans were reluctant, if not opposed, to U.S. military intervention in Haiti and Bosnia.

THE UNITED NATIONS

The United States belongs to the 185-nation United Nations and is a member of at least 200 other international organizations. The United Nations was set up in 1945 by the victors of World War II. Its main goal was to promote peace. But when the two superpowers—the United States and the former Soviet Union—became major military rivals, the United Nations was less able to achieve its central objectives.

For most of its first 45 years, the United Nations earned a reputation for ineffectiveness. Critics contend it either ducked or was politically unable to tackle crucial global issues. During much of that time, the U.N. General Assembly, dominated by a combination of Third World and communist nations, was hostile to many U.S. interests. The General Assembly often became a talk shop, passing vague resolutions.

As a result of pressure from the United States, Kofi Annan replaced Boutrous Boutrous Ghali as secretary general of the United Nations in 1996.

But when the cold war ended, the five permanent members of the U.N. Security Council—the United States, China, Russia (which replaced the Soviet Union), Britain, and France—usually worked in harmony. Moreover, the U.N.'s assumption of responsibilities in the Persian Gulf War and its extensive peacekeeping missions in Cyprus and Lebanon won it respect in recent years. U.N. efforts in Cambodia, Somalia, and in Bosnia were less successful (see Table 21–2).

Blue-helmeted U.N. peacekeeping forces are now monitoring cease-fires, elections, and human rights in several areas. These efforts are costly, and the United Nations constantly finds itself pleading with leading nations such as the United States to underwrite the costs of these peace initiatives. Many of the U.N.'s peacekeeping missions are popular, yet as these efforts increase in number and in cost, the negotiations to raise funds for this new international peace army get harder.

Some conservatives have long been skeptical of U.S. involvement in the United Nations, fearing that the United States risks being trapped or outvoted. Critics across the ideological spectrum question whether it makes sense to give every U.N. member an equal vote in the General Assembly, regardless of its size, population, and contribution to the U.N. budget. Critics also worry about creating a standing U.N. army with a large contingent of U.S. troops under foreign command. Some U.S. officials call this current system "taxation without representation." Critics also continue to question the efficiency of the organization's bureaucracy.

Conservatives insist that Congress needs to have a greater say in how the United Nations uses taxpayers' dollars and puts our soldiers' lives at risk. "When the U.N. Security Council votes," said former senator Bob Dole, "American taxpayers should grab their wallets. Once the council approves a peacekeeping operation, the United States is obligated to pay nearly one-third of the cost."[31] Several members of Congress have introduced legislation that would bar U.S. forces from any standing U.N. army and prohibit U.S. troops from serving under foreign command in U.N.

TABLE 21–2

Assessing the United Nations

In general, is the United Nations doing a good job or a poor job in trying to solve the problems it has to face?

Good job	49%
Poor job	38
Don't know	13

We now spend about $270 billion on defense, and our share of U.N. peace operations is about $1 billion. With which do you tend to agree: that U.N. peacekeeping helps preserve peace at an affordable price, or that it imposes burdens that contribute little to our security?

Helps preserve peace affordably	45%
Contributes little to security	45
Depends	3
Don't know	6

Do you think peacekeeping should be a high priority of the U.N. system, somewhat of a priority, or not a priority?

High priority	75%
Somewhat of a priority	17
Not a priority	6
Don't know	2

SOURCE: "Views on National Security," *National Journal,* May 18, 1996, p. 1122.

operations. Many critics, both on the left and right, suggest that the United Nations should be allowed to wither away into irrelevance.[32]

The United Nations has certainly disappointed many of the grander hopes of its ardent founders. The United States, which is assessed 25 percent of the organization's annual budget, is almost always delinquent in its payment. Both the U.S. Congress and recent presidents have urged the United Nations to trim its peacekeeping operations and end its bureaucratic inefficiencies. "The U.N.," said President Clinton, "must be able to show that the money it receives supports saving and enriching people's lives, not unneeded overhead."[33] With mixed success, Clinton worked with Congress to get the United States to pay its back as well as current U.N. dues assessment. Meanwhile, the United Nations significantly reduced its budgets, staff, and peacekeeping operations.

When Secretary of State Madeleine Albright was U.S. ambassador to the United Nations, she defended our U.N. dues and peacekeeping expenses, pointing out that the United Nations is a force multiplier: "When the United States intervenes alone, we pay all of the costs and run all of the risks. When the U.N. acts, we pay one-fourth of the costs, and others provide the vast majority of troops."[34] Our annual U.N. bills, she pointed out, are about equal to the annualized cost of a single aircraft carrier battle group.

The United Nations is an important if not indispensable international instrument for the promotion of peace and the prevention of war. If the United Nations did not exist, however, something else much like it would have to be invented to settle quarrels and decrease the violence among sovereign nations.

U.S. SECURITY AND DEFENSE

The overriding mission of the U.S. defense program is to provide for the physical protection of the country and to protect American interests at home and abroad. We want to deter a nuclear attack against the United States, and we seek to restrain the proliferation of armaments, especially weapons of mass destruction. We are committed to defend our allies and friends from armed aggression. We are also eager to forestall regional conflicts that might threaten the vital interests of the United States or its allies. Further, the United States seeks multilateral alliances such as the United Nations or NATO to provide for the collective security and rule of law among all nations.

The United States has a long history of involvement in world affairs, often by means of military interventions. We have formally declared war by an act of Congress on only five occasions. Although the Persian Gulf War was not declared formally, Congress, in effect, declared war when it authorized the use of troops to repel Iraq. But we have intervened with military forces on about 190 occasions, and military intervention is likely to continue. In this new post–cold war era, "We are the ones who can deter," says General Colin Powell, former chair of the Joint Chiefs of Staff. "We have the overwhelming power, and we have demonstrated the willingness to use it."[35]

Some Americans are concerned the United States will use its military clout unwisely or irresponsibly. Some believe we should resist the temptation to send our military into regional conflicts around the world when other means are available to achieve our objectives.[36] And there is probably widespread agreement that we should not intervene in conflicts unless the action is backed by a broad public consensus and a well-heeled international alliance of nations, similar to the U.N. coalition in the Persian Gulf War. Still, virtually all Americans want to maintain our ability to advance our interests around the globe. They say it would be a grave mistake to forsake our leadership position and abandon our friends and allies at this time of global change.

A Republican, William Cohen, was chosen by Bill Clinton as Secretary of Defense in 1996 to give the cabinet an air of bipartisanship. As a former member of the Senate Armed Forces Committee, Cohen was an advocate of a strong defense posture.

Civilian Control over the Military

One of the bedrock principles of our constitutional democracy is that the president of the United States, the people's elected representative, is the commander in chief. Those in the military have freedom of speech, yet to ensure civilian supremacy, commissioned officers who use "contemptuous words" against a president are subject to punishment. When a two-star general made rude and critical remarks about President Bill Clinton in a speech, he was fined $7,000 and retired from the service. And when a popular World War II hero, General Douglas MacArthur, challenged President Harry Truman's decisions, MacArthur was forced to resign. Constitutional democracy is a remarkable achievement because it is the consent of the governed, not the force of arms, that determines who wields the power of our government.

Defense Organization

The president, Congress, the National Security Council, and the State Department make overall defense policy and attempt to integrate U.S. national security programs. But the day-to-day work of organizing for defense is the job of the Defense Department. Its headquarters, the Pentagon, houses within its miles of corridors 25,000 top military and civilian personnel. The offices of several hundred generals and admirals are there, as is the office of the secretary of defense, which provides civilian control of the armed services.

A major issue in recent decades has been how to organize the Department of Defense to ensure that it can provide both strategic vision and practical coordination among the military services. Prior to 1947 there were two separate military departments, War and Navy. The difficulty of coordinating them during World War II led to demands for unification. In 1947 the Air Force, already an autonomous unit within the War Department, was made an independent department, and all three military departments—Army, Navy, and Air Force—were placed under the general supervision of the secretary of defense. The Unification Act of 1947 was a bundle of compromises between the Army, which favored a tightly integrated department, and the Navy, which wanted a loosely federated structure, but the act at least brought the military services under a common organizational chart.

The Joint Chiefs of Staff (JCS) serves as the principal military adviser to the president, the National Security Council, and the secretary of defense. It includes the military heads of the three armed services, the commandant of the Marine Corps, a chair, and a vice-chair. All the service chiefs are appointed by the president with the consent of the Senate for four-year, nonrenewable terms. The chair of the JCS, a top-ranking military officer from one of the three services or the Marine Corps, is appointed by the president with the consent of the Senate for a two-year term that may be renewed once. Note that their short two-year term is part of the process of ensuring civilian control over the military.

Before 1986 the members of the Joint Chiefs of Staff were, collectively, all powerful. They advised the president and the secretary of defense. Because they functioned as a committee and could not act until unanimous agreement was reached, however, they often produced overly broad decisions. Critics, therefore, viewed much of the work of the Joint Chiefs as wasteful and even dangerous.

The Department of Defense Reorganization Act of 1986 changed that. This legislation shifted considerable power to the chair. Reporting through the secretary of defense, the chair advises the president on military matters, exercises authority over the forces in the field, and is responsible for overall military planning. In theory, the chair of the Joint Chiefs can even make a military decision that the chiefs of the other services oppose. On paper at least, these other chiefs now serve the chair merely as advisers, and even the chair's deputy, the vice-chair, outranks

The Pentagon—headquarters for the Department of Defense and the Joint Chiefs of Staff. It is the world's largest building and has 20 miles of corridors. It houses nearly 25,000 workers, who tell time by 4,200 clocks, drink water from 685 fountains, consume 30,000 cups of coffee daily, and place 200,000 calls a day on 87,000 phones connected by 100,000 miles of cable.

the other service chiefs. It gave the chair a mandate to encourage "jointness" in military education and in other spheres to integrate the services for maximum effectiveness. Disputes still continue, but the chair is now much stronger than was previously the case. The chair of the Joint Chiefs in the 1990s is the most powerful peacetime military officer in U.S. history. The Reorganization Act also strengthened the powers of the theater commanders who actually command forces in various parts of the world.

It is critical to appreciate, however, that the chair of the Joint Chiefs is not the head of the military. The chair and the JCS are the principal advisers to the secretary of defense and the president, but the president can, and has on occasion, disregarded their advice. A president must weigh military action or inaction against the larger foreign and security interests of the nation.

The Confederational Nature of the Defense Bureaucracy

It is common to hear criticisms of the "Pentagon machine" or the "national military establishment." The defense bureaucracy is, however, best understood—as is any bureaucracy—as something less than a monolith. In practice, the Defense Department is comprised of four major components: (1) the Office of the Secretary of Defense and the civilians in the Department of Defense; (2) the Joint Chiefs of Staff; (3) the individual armed services (Army, Navy, Air Force, Marine Corps); and (4) the intelligence community (Defense Intelligence Agency and National Security Agency).

Reflecting the fragmented nature of the larger American political system, defense policy is thrashed out in a day-to-day process of give-and-take among these constituent units in the Defense Department along with officials in the State Department, Central Intelligence Agency, and the National Security Council at the White House. Insiders often stress that this policy-making structure is best thought of as a *confederation*, or bargaining arena, as opposed to a tight chain-of-command hierarchy. In fact, in recent years strong sentiment has emerged for more centralized control and direction of the nation's defense bureaucracy.

A "Military-Industrial Complex"?

By its nature, the defense industry is different from most other large industries in the United States. National defense is what economists call a "public good." There is no way to exclude citizens from "consuming" national defense, whether they wish to pay for it or not. Thus, the government must provide for defense by taxing citizens.

Critics sometimes charge that the military conspires with defense contractors and other strategic elites to maintain a vast network of bases and fleets around the world. They contend that the "military-industrial complex"—the alleged alliance between top military and industrial leaders who have a common interest in arms production—has a life of its own, is too big to be managed or controlled, spends too large a share of our national wealth, and is dedicated to exaggerating what was once "the Soviet menace," or "the Iranian or Iraqi menace," or whatever new enemy might emerge in the post–cold war era.

Military leaders deny the existence of a military-industrial complex. They point to the reduced size of the military and note that since its wartime peak in 1968, the number of military personnel will have dropped from 3.5 million in the late 1960s to about 1.4 million in 1998. Fewer people are in uniform now than at any time since 1950, and fewer U.S. troops are abroad than at any time since 1940. Further, our active fleet has been reduced and will continue to be greatly reduced by the late 1990s.

Although defense contractors and prodefense legislators in Congress still press for major military weapons developments, they are usually outnumbered by those who emphasize domestic and economic policy needs as we shift to a post–cold war economy.

Women now make up over 11 percent of the total enlistment in the armed forces, and during the Persian Gulf War they made up 6 percent of the personnel in the region.

Disputes among military services involve more than professional jealousies. The technological revolution in warfare has rendered obsolete many concepts about military missions, thereby threatening certain roles of some of the services. In the past it made sense to divide command among land, sea, and air forces. Today defense research and development are constantly altering formerly established roles and missions, yet the individual services are reluctant to give up their traditional functions or to serve each other's crucial needs. The Navy, for example, is interested in waging sea warfare, not in running a freight service for the Army. Interservice rivalries erupt when the Army and Air Force quarrel over who should provide air support for ground troops. Each branch also supports weapons that bring it prestige. The Air Force and Navy dispute, for example, over the effectiveness of land-based versus sea-based missiles.

Whether strategic policies are worked out within the Defense Department, the White House, or Congress, the decisions result from a political process in which some measure of consensus is essential. The Joint Chiefs engage in the same type of vote trading used in Congress. On budget issues the chiefs often endorse all the programs desired by each service. When forced to choose on an issue of policy, the chiefs have traditionally compromised among the different service positions rather than attempt to develop a position based on a unified military point of view.

Women in the Military and in Combat

Women constitute 11 percent of the total enlistment in the armed forces; 6 percent of our forces in the Persian Gulf War were female; about 25 percent of Reserve Officer Training Corps (ROTC) cadets are women. The women in Operation Desert Storm piloted troop transport and supply aircraft, helped to operate Patriot antimissile systems, and worked as tank mechanics and military police guarding Iraqi prisoners of war.

Congress has lifted any legal restrictions on Air Force and Navy women becoming combat pilots, and the Pentagon, after prodding by the Clinton administration, has now opened thousands of combat-related positions in the military services for women. The military is redesigning its assignments to ensure equal opportunity exists within its ranks.

A majority of Americans think women should be assigned to ground combat units, but others are still concerned about women in combat situations. According to reports from the Persian Gulf front, few women who served in combat support units recommended the experience. Similarly, many women in the military have said that while they would like to have the right to serve in combat positions, most of them would not opt for these roles.

The difficulty in deciding whether women should participate in combat often comes in defining what is combat. Women working in support units in the Panama conflict of 1989 engaged in fighting. "I find it very difficult to separate this from other jobs where women are at risk, on police and fire departments, as truck drivers," says retired Air Force General Wilma Vaught.[37]

Despite their accomplishments, women in the armed forces have faced countless problems, including sexual harassment and rape, and women officers have complained of men refusing to take orders from them and giving them inappropriate assignments. Female Navy combat pilots complain about "the silent treatment" and gender prejudice.[38] Still, women are generally winning acceptance in the military at all levels and will continue to play increasingly significant roles in virtually all aspects of the armed forces. And just as we have had women ambassadors to the United Nations and a woman secretary of state, some day there will be a woman chair of the Joint Chiefs of Staff or a woman secretary of defense.

SOURCE: Dana Summers. *The Orlando Sentinel.* Tribune Media Services.

The Gay Ban Controversy

Another persisting controversy in the 1990s is whether the military has the right to expel homosexuals from the military services. Even as recently as the mid 1990s, the U.S. military expelled about 1,000 men and women every year because of sexual preference. The Pentagon defended the ban by saying that homosexuals in a military setting create difficulty because there is no privacy, no choice of association or living quarters, and no provision for those who prefer gay and lesbian lifestyles.

Many leaders in Congress and elsewhere criticized the ban, calling it the final bastion of discrimination in the military and saying it reminded them of the army's former official opposition to African Americans in uniform. Bill Clinton called for a complete end to the ban when he campaigned for his first term as president. Once in office, however, he had to settle for a compromise that merely modified the ban. Under a "don't ask, don't tell" policy, military officials are now not permitted to question recruits about their sexual orientation, and gays and lesbians are required to refrain from sexual practices while on duty or assignments. Those who commit homosexual acts are still subject to discharge.

Even after the Clinton compromise was implemented, there was evidence that harassment of gays was still common. "The evidence suggests that some military commanders continue to ask. And under duress, some soldiers continue to tell."[39] The percentage of homosexuals discharged from the military has risen, and many critics believe the new policy is as bad, if not worse, than its predecessors.

Gay and homosexual groups have turned to the courts to try to get the ban and the new Clinton-era regulations overruled as unconstitutional. Some U.S. district courts have ruled that the military may not discharge a person simply because of declared sexual orientation. Yet a 1996 ruling by the U.S. Court of Appeals for the Fourth Circuit upheld the regulations set by the Clinton White House, saying they were properly based on a law enacted by Congress, and that courts are traditionally obligated to defer to the other branches of government, especially when the matter involves military policy.[40]

This constitutional issue is destined for Supreme Court review. The Court will have to balance the seldom-questioned authority of Congress and the president to set the rules for the conduct of the armed forces against constitutional protections of freedom from government interference in individual choices, actions, and speech.

Americans are deeply divided over this issue. Many conservatives are upset that the president and Congress modified the old policy. However, former Republican presidential candidate Barry Goldwater said, "You don't need to be 'straight' to fight and die for your country. You just need to shoot straight."[41]

THE POLITICS OF DEFENSE SPENDING

The U.S. defense budget is over $260 billion a year. Over half the people employed by the national government work in the Defense Department. About three-quarters of federal purchases of goods and services originate in the defense budget; moreover, a few thousand defense installations are scattered across the country. Contracts in excess of $100 billion result in defense-related civilian employment of nearly 2 million workers. More than 1.5 million retired Defense Department personnel draw pensions and other fringe benefits. Thus, the Defense Department's size and impact on our society raise questions about how it can be controlled.

Defense spending in the 1990s decreased, weapons systems were canceled or postponed, bases were closed, ships were retired, and large numbers of troops were brought home from Germany, the Philippines, and elsewhere. This downsizing reflected the end of the cold war, the demise of the Soviet Union, and the lack of support for maintaining defense spending at the 1980s level (see Figure 21–1).

The Draft

Military conscription (the draft) was first instituted by the Confederacy in 1862 and by the Union in 1863 during the Civil War. It was used during World War I, when Congress passed the Selective Service Act. This act called for a draft of males between the ages of 21 and 30, with exemptions for certain public officials and for clergy. In both instances, conscription ended when the conflicts ended. The first peacetime draft began in 1940, with the Selective Service Training Act. By the time of Pearl Harbor in late 1941, men between the ages of 18 and 35 were eligible for the draft. When World War II ended, the draft continued in various forms for almost three decades. Soon after the Vietnam War, the all-volunteer force (AVF) was established by Congress. This force was charged with providing for our peacetime military personnel needs; in time of war, a draft could be reinstated.

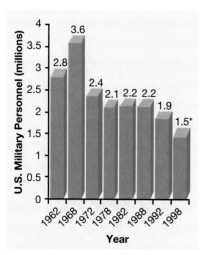

FIGURE 21–1 The Shrinking of the Military: U.S. Personnel in Military Service

SOURCE: *Fiscal Year 1997 Budget of the United States*, Historical Tables (Government Printing Office, 1996), p. 267.

*Estimated.

TABLE 21–3

Public Opinion and Defense Spending

Question: Is the U.S. spending too much, about right, or too little on defense?

Year	Too Much	About Right	Too Little	No Opinion
1995	42%	40%	15%	3%
1993	42	38	17	3
1991	50	36	10	4
1989	49	37	11	3
1987	44	36	14	6
1986	47	36	13	4
1980	14	24	49	13
1976	36	32	22	10
1974	44	32	12	12
1971	49	31	11	9
1969	52	31	8	9

SOURCE: Gallup poll index and 1995 data from polls from Americans Talk Issues Foundation, cited in *National Journal*, September 2, 1995, p. 2185.

Most Americans assumed that once the cold war was won, there would be a huge "peace dividend" and that much of the spending needed to defeat the Soviet Union would be shifted to domestic priorities or tax cuts. Defense spending has declined steadily, and in 1998 it is about 33 percent lower, adjusted for inflation, than it was in 1985. Still, the United States is "now spending more on defense than all of its NATO allies, Japan, Israel and South Korea combined. The U.S. defense budget is more than triple Russia's. And it is higher, in real terms, than it was in 1980."[42]

U.S. military spending now accounts for nearly 40 percent of the world's annual military spending. But many Republican leaders—including John McCain, Newt Gingrich, and Strom Thurmond—say the Clinton administration cut too fast and failed to appreciate the urgent need for an effective ballistic missile defense system.

President Clinton claims he has cut but not gutted the nation's defense preparedness. If we are ever going to even come close to balancing the budget, the military will have to accept its share of cuts, he insists. Clinton vetoed the initial 1996 defense budget authorization bill because it called for too much of an increase in defense technologies and weapons systems. Clinton maintains we are strong militarily. He admits, "We can't be the world's policeman. We can't be everywhere. We can't do everything. But we can make a difference, and when it is consistent with our values and our interests, we have to try. That's what the effort in Bosnia is all about."[43]

It is no secret in Washington that the Pentagon's top military brass would like to see Congress appropriate significantly more funds for new weapons systems, new ships, and new technologies.[44] The 1990s have seen constant U.S. involvement in international peacekeeping and humanitarian relief operations that have strained the military's resources and energy. Yet it is difficult for anyone—defense expert or average citizen, Republican or Democrat—to estimate with any accuracy how much is enough to spend on military preparedness (see Table 21–3).

Pressures to Promote Military Spending and Keep Bases Open

One of the problems with cutting defense spending is that it immediately costs jobs in congressional districts. Weapons systems continue to be protected by members in Congress more concerned with jobs and reelection hopes than with strategic needs.[45] The B-52 Stealth bomber is a notable case in point. After 15 years of design and manufacturing, it has difficulty distinguishing a rainstorm from a mountain. The Pentagon has not asked for more of these billion-dollar planes, yet Congress keeps approving funds for them because cuts in weapons systems and plant closings mean not only that people in the Defense Department and on bases lose their jobs, but also that shopkeepers, bankers, lawyers, doctors, contractors, housekeepers, baby sitters—the list goes on and on—are put out of work.

Weapons are, in fact, a major American industry, and the industry and members of Congress work hard to promote its products. The agreement that operates in other pork-barrel areas works here as well: "You help me in my district, and I'll help you in yours." Even the most antideficit, balance-the-budget conservatives alter their tune when a contract termination hits close to their district. Similarly, the most vigorous antiwar doves in Congress shout the loudest when a base closing is proposed for their home region.

This is not to say that members of Congress cast their vote on military spending solely on whether their district would profit from the decision. An analysis of the relationships between campaign contributors and votes on weapons systems concludes that issues of defense strategy, cost, and a legislator's political philosophy are equally important.[46]

Still, the Defense Department was repeatedly frustrated in its efforts to close no longer needed or uneconomical military bases in the United States. Influential members of Congress went to great lengths lobbying their colleagues that bases in their districts were too important to shut down. Eventually military spokesmen and members of Congress realized that new procedures were needed to handle congressional approval of base closings.

To thwart efforts by legislators to block closings of individual bases, Congress in 1988 set up a blue-ribbon panel to identify military bases that should be closed for budgetary reasons. The panel is appointed by Congress and the president, but it works independently of both branches. It reviews the base-closing suggestions made by the Pentagon and makes recommendations, which have to be accepted in toto or else be rejected by the president. If the president accepts the closings, the package then goes to Congress, where each chamber is allowed 45 days to consider the entire package. Congress also has to accept the entire package or else no closings take place.

This bypass strategy has succeeded. Dozens of bases have now been closed or are in the process of being shut down—and the savings will run into billions of dollars. While there have been predictable grumblings from the big losers and some lawsuits, the federal courts have upheld these procedures, and dozens of additional bases will be closed in the late 1990s.

Military Strategy

A number of major weapons systems whose primary justification was to fight the former Soviet Union have been canceled or their production greatly curtailed in the past few years. All the services have lost personnel and may continue to do so for the next few years. The National Guard and the military reserve have also been cut back about 25 percent.

The nation's primary defense against nuclear attack has been a strategy of *deterrence*, or maintaining the ability to threaten massive retaliation on any nation that attacked us. Effective deterrence is commonly measured by the strength of survivable second-strike force. Thus, the United States has maintained a large, diversified, and well-protected defense system so that a first strike by another nation would not cripple our ability to retaliate decisively.

The United States has sought to prevent a major war by maintaining military forces and demonstrating the determination to use them, if needed, in ways that would persuade opponents that the cost of any attack on our interests would exceed any benefit they could possibly hope to gain. This strategy of "mutual assured destruction" (MAD) is still the core of American defense policy. Pentagon officials claim it has worked (although at a very high cost). At least, they point out, it has succeeded in winning for the United States and our allies more than five decades of peace—a period twice as long as the period between World Wars I and II. But the nature of warfare and the prevention of wars are likely to be considerably different in the twenty-first century.[47]

POLITICS ONLINE

The Internet and the Peruvian Hostage Crisis

For four months in 1997, 72 hostages were held captive in the residence of the Japanese ambassador in Lima, Peru. In the early days of the crisis, the guerrillas from the Tupac Amaru Revolutionary Movement used short-wave radios and the Internet to communicate their grievances and demands. The hostage crisis ended when Peruvian forces stormed the residence. Use of the Internet proved to be an effective way for the terrorists to communicate their complaints about prison conditions in Peru.

One American, Lori Berenson, is serving a life sentence after being convicted of treason by a Peruvian military tribunal. Her family and friends compiled a home page on her case calling for a fair trial:

http://www.tiac.net/users/salem/loriberenson

As the Peruvian hostage crisis illustrates, many different interests can use this new communications tool to press their claims or deliver their demands. Governments can also use the Internet to distribute information about foreign and defense policy:

www.dtic.mil/defenselink

The State Department issues useful travel information, including warnings and information regarding tourist locations, passports, and visa requirements; tips for travelers to all areas of the world, such as how to contact U.S. consuls for help abroad; tips for Americans residing abroad; and business and medical information for travelers. The next time you ate planning a trip overseas, be sure to check out the State Department Web site so you can be fully informed on current conditions and special requirements in foreign countries:

www.whitehouse.gov/WH/Services/Agency/dos.html

SUMMARY

1. American foreign policy from 1945 through 1990 was shaped and at times completely dominated by relations with the superpower rival, the Soviet Union. The competition between these two military giants also dominated world politics. With the passing of the cold war have come new debates over foreign policy goals. The rise of Japan and Europe as economic powers and the increasing importance of economic and trading interests have transformed foreign policy debates as America prepares for the twenty-first century.

2. New foreign policy challenges include population growth in the face of poverty; nuclear, biological, and chemical arms control; the relationship of trade status to human rights violations; aid to former Soviet-bloc nations; the role of NATO and of the U.S. military in a global framework; drug traffic; and the degradation of the global environment.

3. Presidents, Congress, and the American people all become involved in defining our vital national security interests, but they often have contradictory views. Presidents must sometimes act swiftly and decisively. Plainly, the role of the president in foreign affairs was strengthened during the cold war years as the United States developed an enormous standing military capability and an extensive intelligence network. Presidents are often in a good position to see the nation's long-term interests above the tugging of bureaucratic and special interests. But in our constitutional democracy, presidents and their advisers must consult with Congress and inform the

American people. The media and special interests also play a role.

4. U.S. foreign policy interests are advanced by one or a combination of the following strategies: diplomacy, foreign aid, economic sanctions, political coercion (including the breaking off of diplomatic relations), covert action, and military intervention.

5. The United States is an active participant in numerous international organizations, especially the United Nations. The United Nations is likely to play an even greater role in the post–cold war world, even if many Americans, especially conservatives, are highly critical of the way the U.N. works. The primacy of the nation-state is not in question, yet more and more of our global policy problems will be solved through international organizations of one type or another.

6. Our system is designed to provide civilian control over the military. Although the military in any society has enormous potential for direct political involvement, this has not occurred in the United States. The president, Congress, the secretary of defense, and other cabinet officers continually weigh national security against competing claims.

7. Although the 1990s witnessed major reductions in the size of the military and major cuts in military spending, some critics say the defense budget can be cut much further. Critics on the right, however, claim we have seriously weakened our defense preparedness. Yet the nature of warfare and the preventing of wars will no doubt be considerably different in the twenty-first century.

C. Kenneth Allard, *Command Control and the Common Defense* (Yale University Press, 1991).

Stephen E. Ambrose, *Rise to Globalism: American Foreign Policy Since 1938*, 6th ed. (Penguin, 1991).

Christopher Andrew, *For the President's Eyes Only: Secret Intelligence and the American Presidency from Washington to Bush* (HarperCollins, 1995).

James Baker with Thomas M. DeFrank, *The Politics of Diplomacy* (Putnam's Sons, 1995).

Stephen J. Cimbala, *The Politics of Warfare: The Great Powers in the Twentieth Century* (Penn State Press, 1997).

Angelo Codevilla, *Informing Statecraft: Intelligence for a New Century* (Free Press, 1992).

Louis Fisher, *Presidential War Power* (University Press of Kansas, 1995).

John Lewis Gaddis, *The United States and the End of the Cold War* (Oxford University Press, 1992).

Allen E. Goodman, et al., *In from the Cold: Task Force on the Future of U.S. Intelligence* (Twentieth Century Fund, 1996).

Samuel Huntington, *The Clash of Civilization and the Remaking of World Order* (Simon & Schuster, 1996).

Loch K. Johnson, *Secret Agencies: U.S. Intelligence in a Hostile World* (Yale University Press, 1996).

Henry Kissinger, *Diplomacy* (Simon & Schuster, 1994).

Harold Hongju Koh, *The National Security Constitution: Sharing Power after the Iran-Contra Affair* (Yale University Press, 1990).

Kenneth R. Mayer, *The Political Economy of Defense Contracting* (Yale University Press, 1991).

Robert S. McNamara, *In Retrospect: The Tragedy and Lessons of Vietnam* (Times Books, 1995).

Charles C. Moskos and John Sibley Butler, *All That We Can Be: Black Leadership and Racial Integration the Army Way* (Twentieth Century Fund, 1996).

Ralph Nader et al., *The Case Against Free Trade: GATT, NAFTA, and the Globalization of Corporate Power* (Earth Island Press, 1993).

John Prados, *Keepers of the Keys: A History of the National Security Council from Truman to Bush* (William Morrow, 1991).

Rosemary Righter, *Utopia Lost: The United Nations and World Order* (Twentieth Century Fund, 1995).

Craig A. Rimmerman, *Gay Rights, Military Wrongs: Political Perspectives on Lesbians and Gays in the Military* (Garland Publishing, 1996).

Joseph Romm, *Defining National Security: The Nonmilitary Aspect* (Council on Foreign Relations, 1993).

James N. Rosenau, *The United Nations in a Turbulent World* (Lynne Rienner, 1992).

Henry Shue, *Basic Rights: Subsistence, Affluence and U.S. Foreign Policy*, 2d ed. (Princeton University Press, 1996).

George Shultz, *Turmoil and Triumph: My Years as Secretary of State* (Scribner's, 1993).

Ronald Steel, *Temptations of a Superpower* (Harvard University Press, 1995).

Robert W. Tucker and David C. Hendrickson, *The Imperial Temptation: The New World Order and America's Purpose* (Council on Foreign Relations, 1992).

Stephen R. Weissman, *A Culture of Deference: Congress's Failure of Leadership in Foreign Affairs* (Basic Books, 1995).

Bob Woodward, *The Commanders* (Simon & Schuster, 1991).

22

The Democratic Faith

*I*n the 1770s and 1780s America's founding generation fought an eight-year revolution to secure their rights and liberty. Then they faced the challenge of creating a government, first at the Constitutional Convention in 1787 and later in the first Congress, writing a Constitution, and drafting a Bill of Rights that would protect the rights to life, liberty, and self-government for themselves and for those who would come later. But they knew, as we also know, that passive allegiance to ideas and rights is never enough. Every generation must see itself as having a duty to nurture these ideals by actively renewing the community and nation of which it is a part.

The framers knew well the story of Athens. They were familiar with Pericles and his famed funeral oration in which he said that the person who takes no part in public affairs is a useless person, a good-for-nothing. The city's business, as Pericles and many Athenians saw it, was everyone's business. Athens had flourished as a shining beacon of what a civilized city might be, but it foundered when greed, self-centeredness, and smugness set in. As time went on, the Athenians wanted security more than they wanted liberty; they wanted comfort more than they wanted freedom. In the end they lost it all—security, comfort, and freedom. When they asked not what they could do for Athens but rather what Athens could do for them, then Athens ceased to be free. "Responsibility was the price every man must pay for freedom. It was to be had on no other terms."[1]

If we are to be citizens of the United States in the truest meaning of the term, our dreams must go beyond personal ambition and the accumulation of material goods. Our country needs citizens who understand that our well-being is tied to the well-being of our neighbors, community, and country.

As democracy movements around the world gain strength and formerly totalitarian governments topple, we Americans are reminded of our democratic roots. Over the past generation, Chinese students, Polish Solidarity members, East German protesters, Czech patriots, Thai citizens, and Haitian and Burmese democrats have been willing to protest, fight, and even die for the democratic values Thomas Jefferson outlined in the Declaration of Independence. Americans have been pleased and sometimes stunned by the success of most of these movements, but we have also been saddened by the setbacks many of them have encountered. Translating democratic values into a working democratic government is difficult. We in the United States gain renewed appreciation for our system of constitutional democracy as we watch these new republics struggle with social and economic divisions, federalism, the lack of an effective party system, and a poorly developed free press.

Our theme in this last chapter is simple: *Leadership and constitutional structures and protections are important, but an active, committed citizenry that can assume leadership itself is even more important.* Freedom and obligation go together. Liberty and duty go together. The answer to a nation's problems lies not in producing a perfect constitution or a few larger-than-life leaders. The answer lies in educating *a nation of citizen-leaders* who will, regardless of their professional and private ambitions, care about the concerns of the Republic and strive to make democracy work.

We are not complete persons, as the Athenians would remind us, unless we are reacting to and expressing ourselves through *politics*. Citizens should participate in public affairs not solely or primarily because of social or civic duty or the prospect of a particular reward. It is for the completion of self—for our growth and self-

Thomas Jefferson, main author of the Declaration of Independence, first secretary of state, and third president of the United States.

Czech, Chinese, and African Voices on the Democratic Faith

I dream of a republic that is independent, free, and democratic; a republic with economic prosperity yet social justice; a humane republic that serves the individual and therefore hopes that the individual will serve it in turn; a republic of well-rounded people, because without such people, it is impossible to solve any of our problems . . .

Czech President Vaclav Havel
New Year's Day Speech,
January 1, 1990

We have awakened the people
We have seeded democracy
We will win
Our next generation will continue.
It doesn't matter
If we don't succeed.

Poem written by an anonymous democracy demonstrator in China's Tiananmen Square, Spring 1989

During my lifetime I have dedicated myself to this struggle of the African people. I have fought against white domination, and I have fought against black domination. I have cherished the ideal of a democratic and free society in which all persons live together in harmony and with equal opportunities. It is an ideal I hope to live for and to achieve. But if needs be, it is an ideal for which I am prepared to die.

Nelson Mandela
Statement at the Rivonia Trial, 1964

definition in relation to others and as an expression of our concern for those others—that we must act politically.[2]

More than any other form of government, the kind of democracy that has emerged under our Constitution requires a certain kind of faith—and a certain kind of skepticism. It requires faith concerning our common human enterprise, a belief that if the people are informed and caring, they can be trusted with their own self-government, and an optimism that when things begin to go wrong, the people can be relied upon to set them right. But a healthy skepticism is needed as well. Democracy requires us to question our leaders and leadership institutions and never trust any group with too much power. Although we prize majority rule, we must always be skeptical enough to ask whether the majority is right.

Constitutional democracy requires us to be constantly concerned about whether we really tolerate and protect the rights and opinions of others and whether democratic processes are in fact serving the principles of liberty, equality, and justice. In short, the democratic faith rests upon a peculiar blend of faith in the people and skepticism of them.

Thomas Jefferson, one of our best-known champions of the democratic faith, believed in the common sense of the people and in the flowering of the human spirit. Jefferson believed deeply that every government degenerates when it is trusted to its rulers alone. The people themselves, he wrote, are the only safe repositories of government. His was a robust commitment to popular control, to representative processes, and to accountable leadership. But he was no believer in the simple participatory democracy of ancient Greece or revolutionary France. The people, too, must have their power checked and balanced.

Government by the people does not require that everyone be involved in politics and decision-making. Many citizens will always be apathetic toward politics and government. Government by the people, however, does require that a healthy and significant segment of the public be attentive, interested, involved, and willing, at least on occasion, to criticize wrong-headed or harmful public policies and rally in support of sensible policies, programs, and leadership.

Our founders set up a government by *consent of the governed*, and our Bill of Rights specifically denies government authorities any legal opportunity to coerce that consent. Indeed, as Justice Robert H. Jackson wrote in a 1943 Supreme Court decision, *West Virginia Board of Education v Barnette*, "Authority here is to be controlled by public opinion, not public opinion by authority." Jackson added, "If there is any fixed star in our constitutional constellation, it is that no official, high or petty, can prescribe what shall be orthodox in politics, nationalism, religion, or other matters of opinion or force citizens to confess by word or act their faith therein."

With the breakup of the Soviet Union, the liberation of most Eastern European nations, and the strengthening of democracies in parts of Asia and Latin America over the past decade, there may be more people living today under conditions of political freedom than under totalitarian or authoritarian governments. Still, only about 40 percent of the people in the world live in nations considered wholly free. Throughout history, including the present, most governments have been authoritarian or tyrannical. Most people have lived in societies in which a small group at the top have imposed their will on the others. Authoritarian governments justify their actions by saying people are too weak to govern themselves; they need to be ruled. But neither in Castro's Cuba nor in the military regime of North Korea, neither in the People's Republic of China nor in Saudi Arabia, do ordinary people have a voice in the type of decisions we Americans routinely make: Who should go to college, or work in the fields, or serve in the army? How much money should be spent for schools, economic development initiatives, or environmental protection?

THE CASE FOR GOVERNMENT BY THE PEOPLE

The essence of our Constitution is that it both grants power to and withholds power from the national government. Fearing national weakness and popular disorder, the framers wanted to grant the government only enough power to do its basic jobs, such as maintaining national defense and providing financial stability. Valuing above all the principle of individual liberty, the framers wanted to protect the people from too much government. They wanted a *limited government*—but one that would work. The solution was to make government responsive to the people, but at the same time insulate the government from momentary and passionate majorities.

The first step was to *distribute power* among the three branches of government: legislative, executive, and judicial (separation of powers). The second was to *share power* among the branches, to enable them to limit or restrain each other (checks and balances). The third was to *divide power* among state and local governments (federalism). Public officials were also provided with different and competing constituencies. The framers assumed the constituents themselves would be divided (pluralism): northerners versus southerners, rich versus poor, city people versus country people. Finally, in 1791, as additional protection for the individuals' liberties, the members of the first Congress proposed and the state legislatures ratified ten additional amendments known as the Bill of Rights.

Of course, this was not a very efficient system. But efficiency was not the main goal; the framers wanted a *safe* government. They wanted a government that allowed for plenty of deliberation and for consensus building, but that also avoided hasty decision making. It may have been somewhat more efficient than the system under the Articles of Confederation, but the constitutional system was not designed primarily to promote efficiency, and it will rarely measure up well against that standard. Totalitarian governments may get higher marks for efficiency, but Americans have never believed that efficiency was worth that price.

As the decades passed, our national government came under pressure to perform more effectively. The twentieth century brought involvement in vast global wars, depressions, industrialization, and technological changes in transportation, communications, medicine, and education. Huge migrations of Europeans, Hispanics, and Asians into this country as well as migrations of African Americans and other rural people into cities in the North, Midwest, and West changed the makeup of our population. Governments with separation of powers and numerous checks and balances such as ours always have trouble pulling themselves together, but the American experiment had even more trouble. It was too easy for leaders to "pass the buck."

Certain realities also increased the power of political minorities—the influence that comes from campaign contributions to elected officials at every level of government, for example. The power of partisan politics and organized minorities to obstruct action sharpened the whole question of a representative republic. If leaders acting for a majority of people could not act—could not balance the budget, could not pass health care reform or control the senseless killings in our streets and schools—was this really government by the people?

Most Americans want a government that is efficient and effective but also caring. We want to maintain our commitment to liberty and freedom. We want a government that acts for the majority yet also protects minorities. We want to safeguard our nation and our streets in a world full of change and violence. We want to protect the rights of the poor, the elderly, and minorities. Do we expect too much from government? Of course we do!

Constitutional democracy is a system of checks and balances. It balances values and competing dreams. We must balance all individual liberties against the col-

To Protect the Dissenter

When one element in a pluralistic system becomes very powerful in relation to the others, the pluralism of the system itself is in danger. Even with the best of intentions, the dominant element is likely to squeeze out the other elements or render them impotent. . . .

So we have devised a variety of ways to protect the dissenter. Our civil liberties are a part of that system, and so are Robert's Rules of Order, and grievance procedures, and the commonly held view that we should hear both sides of an argument. In short, we have a tradition, a set of attitudes and specific social arrangements designed to ensure that points of view at odds with prevailing doctrine will not be rejected out of hand.

But why be so considerate of dissent and criticism? To answer this question is to state one of the strongest tenets of our political philosophy. We do not expect organizations or societies to be above criticism, nor do we trust the men who run them to be adequately self-critical. We believe that even those aspects of society that are healthy today may deteriorate tomorrow. We believe that power wielded justly today may be wielded corruptly tomorrow. We know that from the ranks of the critics come cranks and troublemakers, but from the same ranks come the saviors and innovators. And since the spirit that welcomes nonconformity is a fragile thing, we have not depended on that spirit alone. We have devised explicit legal and constitutional arrangements to protect the dissenter.

SOURCE: John W. Gardner, *Self-Renewal*, rev. ed. (Norton, 1981), pp. 71–72.

Why People Run for Office

- To solve problems and promote the American Dream—enhancing liberty and justice
- To advance fresh ideas and approaches
- To "throw some rascal out" whose views they dislike
- To gain a voice in policy making
- To serve as a party spokesperson
- To acquire political influence and a platform from which to influence public opinion
- To gain prominence and power
- To satisfy ego needs
- To gain opportunities to learn, grow, travel, and meet all kinds of people
- To be "where the action is"—involved in the thick of government and political life—campaigning, debating, drafting laws, reconciling diverse views, and making the system responsive

Why People Shy Away from Running for Office

- Invasion of privacy
- Less time to spend with families or favorite pastimes
- Less income than in many business or professional occupations
- Exposure to partisan and media criticism
- Involvement in many things most people would rather not do—like marching in countless parades, attending county fairs, and going to endless political dinners, banquets, and service club meetings
- Meager rewards
- Fear that one may have to compromise principles because of the complexity of our adversarial system
- Expense of campaigning
- Aversion to conflict, divisiveness, and ambition
- Concern that the constitutional structure and party system make it nearly impossible to exercise meaningful leadership

lective security and needs of society; we must also balance certain individual liberties against other individual liberties. The question is always: Which rights of which people are to be protected by what means and at what price?

PARTICIPATION AND REPRESENTATION

In essence, the challenge to the future of democracy is whether we can make our representative process work better. No political problem is more complicated than this. For one thing, representation is impossible in the literal sense. Every man and woman has a host of conflicting desires, fears, hopes, and expectations, and no government can represent them all. But even if millions of voters could be represented in their billions of interests, the question of how they would be represented would remain. Through direct representation, such as a New England town meeting? Through economic or professional associations, such as labor unions or political action committees? Through a coalition of minority groups? Through a direct popular majority? Through state and national or even electronic referenda? All these and other alternatives can be defended as proper forms of representation in a constitutional democracy.

Some propose to bypass this thorny problem of representation by vastly increasing the role of direct popular participation in decision making. What many people regard as the most perfect form of democracy exists when every person within a given group has a full and equal opportunity to participate in all decisions and in all processes of influence, persuasion, and discussion that bear on those decisions. Direct participation in decision making, its advocates contend, will serve two major purposes. It will enhance the dignity, self-respect, and understanding of individuals by giving them responsibility for the decisions that shape their lives. And it will act as a safeguard against undemocratic and antidemocratic forms of government and prevent the replacement of democracy by dictatorship or tyranny. This idea rests on a theory of self-protection that says interests can be represented, furthered, and defended best by those whom they concern directly.

Experience with many forms of participatory democracy, however, suggests that it has limitations as a form of decision making. In an age of rapidly growing population, increasingly complex economic and social systems, and enormously wide-ranging decision-making units of government, direct participation can work only in smaller communities or at the neighborhood level. As a practical matter, people simply cannot put in endless hours taking part in every decision that affects their lives.

Participatory democracy still plays an important role in smaller units—in neighborhood associations, local party committees, and the like. And perhaps the idea of participation could be greatly extended, for example, to greater influence of workers in the running of factories and corporations. But we must distinguish between democracy as participation and a greater role for participation in a democracy. One course of action is to enlarge the role of participation in representation; that is, to broaden the power of all people to take part in local decision making and in choosing their representatives in larger units of government. And this brings us back to the hard questions of indirect representation.

If we must have representatives, who shall represent whom? Although this question can be answered in countless ways, in practice there are two basic ways to organize representation. By electing representatives in a multitude of local districts, it is possible to build into representative institutions—the U.S. Congress, for example—most minority interests and attitudes. The other way is through an election system that emphasizes majority representation. This system can be achieved by creating a nationwide electorate that elects one representative (the American president, for example) or by developing a strong two-party system that knits all the local constituencies into coalitions that can elect and sustain national majorities.

A nation does not have to choose between these alternatives. It can have both, as we do in the United States.

Which is better: a government that represents coalitions of minorities or a government that represents a relatively clear-cut majority and has little or no obligation to the minority? The answer depends on what you expect from government. A system that represents coalitions of minorities usually reflects the trading, competition, and compromising that must take place in order to reach agreement among the various groups. Such a government has been called *broker rule*; the government acts essentially as a go-between, as a mediator among organized groups that have definite policy goals. Under broker rule, leaders cannot get too far ahead of the groups; they must tack back and forth, shifting in response to changing group pressures. Instead of acting for a united popular majority with a fairly definite program, either liberal or conservative, the government tries to satisfy all major interests by giving them a voice in decisions and sometimes a veto over actions. In the pushing and hauling of political groups, the government is continually involved in delicate balancing acts.

Some critics believe in broker rule but point out that fair representation has not been achieved in the American system. They point to the extent of nonvoting and other forms of nonparticipation in politics; the fact that low-income persons are less well organized than upper-income persons; the bias of strong organized groups toward the status quo; the lack of competition among much of the news and opinion media, combined with the domination of television and the press by a few corporations; and the virtual monopoly of party politics by the two major parties, which do not always offer the voters meaningful alternatives. In the governmental system itself, critics note devices in Congress like the filibuster and committee control that block majority will and overrepresent certain minorities; the distortion of representation embodied in the Electoral College; and the power of the Supreme Court to invalidate laws demanded by popular majorities acting through the legislative and executive branches.

Such charges may be exaggerated, but they cannot be denied. Those who believe in fairer representation, however, can point to steady improvement in recent years. There have been changes in election laws to simplify voter registration and extend voting and to enforce one-person, one-vote standards. Pressure has been building to regulate campaign finance. And some progress has been made in Congress to strengthen majority rule.

By this point, you undoubtedly appreciate that democracy has to mean much more than popular government and unchecked majority rule. A democracy needs competing politicians with competing views about the public interest. A vital democracy, living and growing, places its faith in the voters, faith that they will elect not just people who will mirror their views but leaders who will exercise their best judgment—"faith that the people will not condemn those whose devotion to principle leads them to unpopular courses, but will reward courage, respect honor, and ultimately recognize right."[3]

The Role of the Politician

Americans today have decidedly mixed views about elected officials. They realize that at their best politicians are skillful at compromising, mediating, negotiating, brokering—and that governing often requires these qualities. But can there be too much of this? Americans also suspect politicians of being ambitious, conniving, unprincipled, opportunistic, and corrupt—"into politics just for what they can get out of it for themselves." Compared to people in other professions, Americans hold most politicians in low esteem.

Still, we often find that certain individual officeholders are responsive, bright, hardworking and friendly (even though we may suspect they are simply trying to

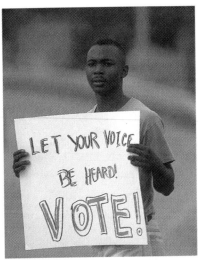

This participant at a Black Voter Awareness Rally in Austin, Texas, is acting on the philosophy expressed by the poster.

Electronic Democracy?

As we enter the twenty-first century, the average American citizen has access to an abundance of information about public affairs. The number of cable television news programs has increased enormously in recent years. Talk-radio regularly airs diverse views on every political controversy. Newspapers and magazines do a fine job of covering national politics, although they do less well at covering state and local public affairs. In half the country, people can vote on many citizen-initiated ballot issues. We also have polls nearly every day on nearly every subject, fascinating technologies that encourage interactive video conferencing, and groups who advocate electronic town meetings.

But we still need institutions such as elected legislatures, which can take the time to digest complicated information and conduct impartial hearings to hear competing points of view. The average citizen rarely has the time or experience to digest all the available information. We are only now beginning to learn how to harness our new electronic technologies to infuse more deliberation into our leadership and public policy making programs.

"Let's run through this once more—and, remember, you choke up at Paragraph Three and brush away the tear at Paragraph Five."

Drawing by D. Reilly. © 1988 The New Yorker Magazine, Inc.

Poking Fun at Politicians

"Don't vote, it only encourages them!"

"Thank God only one of them can win!"

"Old politicians never die, they just evade away."

"A politician is a person who approaches every question with an open mouth."

"Politicians are there when they need you."

"Politicians divide their time between running for office and running for cover."

"Political promises go in one year and out the other."

"In one country it is said that people can rise to public office only when they shoot a rhinoceros. In this country, people can only win public office if they shoot the bull."

get our vote). And our liking sometimes turns into reverence after these same politicians depart or die. Surely George Washington, Abraham Lincoln, Dwight D. Eisenhower, and John F. Kennedy are acclaimed today. Harry Truman liked to joke that a statesman is merely a politician who has been dead for about ten years.

Of course, we must put the problem in perspective. In all democracies the public probably expects too much from politicians. Further, people naturally dislike those who wield power. Public officeholders, after all, tax us, regulate us, and conscript us. We dislike political compromisers and ambitious opportunists—even though we may need such people to get things done.

Why the gap between expectations about the typical and the ideal politician? This gap exists, as we noted back in Chapter 1, because we have such high expectations. We want politicians to be like us but better than us. We want politicians to have all the right answers and all the right values.

When things go wrong in our government or election system, as is often the case, we seldom blame the U.S. Constitution; we revere it too much. "Our belief in popular sovereignty makes us reluctant to blame ourselves. And so we blame the only people left—the politicians. And they, wanting to please us, confirm us in our belief that politicians are at fault by pointing fingers at each other."[4]

But politics is a necessity. Politics is a vital and—at critical times—a noble and crucial leadership activity. As discussed in Chapter 1, politicians are absolutely necessary to help run a democracy—certainly the American republic, whose fragmented powers require politicians to mediate among factions, build coalitions, and compromise among and within branches of government to produce policy and action. But we need more than mainstream regular politicians. We also need political and civic leaders who can rise above everyday "wheeling and dealing" and lead the nation through crises—or, better yet, plan ahead to avert such crises.

Leadership for a Constitutional Democracy

An adequate democratic theory recognizes that constitutional democracy is not self-executing. A democracy needs leaders who have a sense of the past and are willing to share their varying conceptions of the public interest.

Even though one of the most universal cravings of our time is a hunger for creative and compelling leadership, defining creative leadership is a challenge in itself. Leadership can be understood only in the context of both leaders and followers. A leader without followers is a contradiction in terms. Leadership is also situational and contextual; a person is often effective in only one kind of situation. Leadership is not necessarily transferable. James Madison, for example, was a brilliant political and constitutional theorist. He was also a superb politician. Still, he was not a brilliant president. The leadership required to lead a marine platoon up a hill in battle is different from the leadership needed to change racist or sexist attitudes in city governments. The leadership required of a campaign manager differs from that required of a candidate. Leaders of thought are not always effective as leaders of action.

Although leaders are often skilled managers, they need more than just managerial skills. Managers are concerned with doing things the right way; leaders are concerned with doing the right thing. They are more concerned with the future, with the purposes and ends of a society or an organization. Put another way, managers are concerned with efficiency and process, especially routines and standard operating procedures. Leaders, on the other hand, must be concerned with goals and purposes. They must be inventors, risk takers, and entrepreneurs. Further, they must be morale builders who can infuse values into the mission of their community or nation. Indeed, leaders are always defining, defending, and promoting values.

Some leaders have indispensable qualities of contagious self-confidence, unwarranted optimism, and dogged idealism that attract and mobilize others to undertake tasks they never dreamed they could accomplish. In short, they *empower others* and enable many of their followers to become leaders in their own right. Most of the significant breakthroughs in our nation (as well as in our communities) have been made or shaped by people who, while seeing all the complexities and obstacles ahead of them, believed in themselves and in their purposes so much that they refused to be overwhelmed and paralyzed by self-doubts. They were willing to gamble, to take risks, to look at things in a fresh way, and often to invent new rules.[5]

Leaders must recognize the fundamental—unexpressed as well as expressed—wants and needs of potential followers. By bringing followers to a fuller consciousness of their needs, they help convert their hopes and aspirations into practical demands on other leaders, especially leaders in government. Leaders must also sense when people are ready for action. A leader in a democracy consults and listens while educating followers and attempting to renew the goals of an organization.

The whole issue of leadership raises countless questions about participation in and acceptance of power in superior/subordinate, or leader/led, relationships. Leaders must be sensitive to the distinctions between power and authority. *Power* is the strength or raw force to exercise control or coerce someone to do something. *Authority* is power that is accepted as legitimate by subordinates or constituents. How best can leaders earn and sustain moral and social acceptance for their authority? Americans generally prize participation in all kinds of organizations, especially in civic and political life. Yet a part of us yearns for *charismatic* leaders—decisive, attractive, visionary leaders who will simplify problems and relieve us of the burdens of leadership. Ironically, however, savior figures and charismatic leaders often—indeed almost always—create distance, not participation.

Officeholders respond to pressure from movement leaders. Here President John Kennedy meets with organizers of the 1963 March on Washington (left to right): Whitney Young, National Urban League; Dr. Martin Luther King, Jr., Southern Christian Leadership Conference; Rabbi Joachim Prinz, American Jewish Congress; Phillip Randolph, March on Washington director; President Kennedy; Walter Reuther, American Federation of Labor.

On Leadership

Mary Parker Follett wrote a book back in 1923 that summed it up well: "He is a leader who gives form to the inchoate energy in every man. The person who influences me most is not he who does great deeds but he who makes me feel I can do great deeds." That is, the leader guides the group and is at the same time guided by the group. No one can truly lead except from within. Leaders interpret our experience to us. Leaders give form to things vague, things latent, to mere tendencies and aspirations. They integrate, create communities of trust and empower the best in us not by dominating us but by expressing us and our collective energies and ideals and our yearning for liberty, freedom and social justice.

SOURCE: Mary Parker Follett, *The New State* (Longman's, 1923), pp. 229–30.

What Are the Most Important Qualities of a Leader?

No one knows—so much depends on the context, the challenge, and the need. The following qualities or skills are often cited as critically important; none guarantees leadership effectiveness.

- Self-knowledge
- Self-confidence
- Optimism/hope
- Self-discipline
- Sensitivity/empathy
- Stamina/energy
- Tenacity/persistence
- Integrity
- Vision
- Imagination
- Judgment
- Risk taking
- Morale building
- Coalition building
- Negotiating/mediating
- Communicating
- Breadth/creativity
- Concern for results
- Sense of humor
- Enjoyment of people

The Leadership of Kennedy and King

The relationship between John F. Kennedy, a coalition-building office-holder, and Martin Luther King, Jr., movement leader, exemplifies the diversity of leadership. Even though Kennedy raised civil rights issues during his campaign for the presidency in 1960, he never accorded them top priority in his program. Rather, he held off making major civil rights proposals until he could get his economic program through Congress. In the meantime, King and other black movement leaders were protesting, demonstrating, encountering violence, appealing to northern and southern public opinion, and putting intense pressure on Kennedy and other federal officials to protect their civil rights, especially to put through legislation that would protect their right to vote.

As a result of this kind of movement pressure, by 1963 Kennedy was appealing to Congress for civil rights legislation. He worked closely with King and other civil rights leaders through his brother Robert, the attorney general, and at the same time tried to maintain old-time Democratic party coalitions of northerners and white southerners. Movement leaders like King put pressure on the government from the outside—while also working with Robert Kennedy and others from the inside.

After Kennedy's assassination, President Lyndon B. Johnson, together with congressional leaders, built a broad coalition of blacks, liberals, and moderate whites that helped to put the Civil Rights Act of 1964 and the Voting Rights Act of 1965 into law.

There is another type of political leader, one who takes the short rather than the long view, and engages in a short-term bargain: "I'll vote for your bill if you'll vote for mine," or "You raise money for my campaign and I'll help get your daughter a state job after I'm elected." Most political officeholders practice this type of leadership as a practical necessity. It is the common means of doing business.

Leaders in politics can also be defined as agitators or coalition builders. *Agitators*, or *movement leaders*, arouse people's consciousness of their needs and problems, raise their hopes and expectations, organize or take leadership of political and social movements, and mobilize grass-roots pressure on government from the outside. Movement leaders are often considered crusaders or even prophets, whether they be abolitionists, women's suffrage leaders, antislavery leaders, populist proponents of tax and term limits, or environmental crusaders.

Coalition builders are usually intent on winning elections, whereas agitators are more concerned with mobilizing groups of people who may or may not take part in elections. Coalition builders—for example, effective campaign managers—must knit together a variety of groups in order to build a majority that can win elections. Hence, such leaders tend to be power brokers, widening their political appeals as broadly as possible, accommodating single-interest or single-cause groups or movements with intense concerns, and building compromise party platforms that appeal to large numbers of people.

RECONCILING DEMOCRACY AND LEADERSHIP

The American people will never be satisfied with their politicians. Politicians, as well as the people they represent, have different ideas about what is best for the nation. After all, who is really to say what is good for anyone else—let alone for everyone else? That's why we have politicians and politics. To understand this is to better appreciate the delicate and crucial responsibilities entrusted to our elected politicians.

Americans are fond of saying, "It is all politics, you know." This insight is offered as profound. More important, it is intended as a negative, as if things would be improved if we did not have politics and politicians.

But politics is the lifeblood of democracy, and without politics there is no freedom. To conclude that politicians are interested in winning elections is about as profound as to conclude that businesspeople are interested in profits. Of course they are! We do not expect our economy to operate because the shoe store owner is motivated only by a desire to see that people have dry, warm feet. Rather, we harness the shoe store owner's desire to make money as a way to see to it that the largest number of people get the shoes they want at the lowest possible price. So also we harness the elected officials' desire for reelection as the way to ensure that elected officials do what most of the voters want them to do. It is the politician's need to please the voters that is the indispensable link in making democracy work.

Our challenge is to reconcile democracy and leadership. Too often in the past we have held a view of leaders as hierarchical, male, and all-powerful. That conception is antithetical to democratic aspirations. A nation of subservient followers can never be a democratic one. A democratic nation requires educated, skeptical, caring, engaged, and conscientious citizen-leaders. It also requires citizen leaders who will recognize when change is needed and have the courage to bring about necessary reforms and progress.[6]

Such democratic citizen-leaders appreciate that power wielded justly today may be wielded corruptly tomorrow. Democratic citizen-leaders are moved to protest when they know a policy is wrong or when the rights of other citizens are diminished. Such leaders appreciate that criticism of official error is not criticism of our country. Citizen-leaders recognize as well that democracy rests solidly upon a mixed

Four presidents who exhibited very different leadership styles: John F. Kennedy, Lyndon B. Johnson, Dwight D. Eisenhower, and Harry S. Truman. They gathered at the funeral service for Sam Rayburn, former Speaker of the U.S. House of Representatives.

view of human nature. Our capacity for justice, as Reinhold Niebuhr observed, makes democracy possible. But our inclination to injustice makes democracy necessary.

Democratic politics is the forum or arena for excellence and responsibility, where—by acting together—citizens become free. In this sense, politics is not a necessary evil; it is a realistic good. It is the preoccupation of free people, and its existence is a test of freedom.[7]

Thus democratic leadership can be enabling and facilitating. Leadership, thought of as an engagement among equals, a collegial collaboration, can empower and liberate people and enlarge their opinions, choices, and freedoms. The answer for our Republic lies not in producing a handful of great, charismatic, Mount Rushmore leaders, but in educating a citizenry who can boast that we are no longer in need of great leaders or superheroes because we have become a nation of citizens who believe that each of us can make a difference, and that all of us should regularly try.

Leadership is important. However, our system of government is, in many ways, designed to prevent strong and decisive action, lest too much political power be placed in the hands of one or a few people. Thus, while we have emphasized the role of leadership in constitutional democracies in these last few pages, the potential for abuse is checked not only by an involved citizenry but also by the very structure of our constitutional system. Thus the need for those healthy constraints—separation of powers, checks and balances, federalism, bicameral legislatures, and the rule of law so constantly emphasized throughout this book. Equally important, too, are the rights to organize opposition parties and factions and the right to dissent.

THE DEMOCRATIC FAITH

The ultimate test of a democratic system is the legal existence of an officially recognized opposition. A cardinal characteristic of a constitutional democracy is that it not only recognizes the need for the free organization of opposing views but positively encourages this organization. Freedom for political expression and dissent is basic—even freedom for nonsense to be spoken so that good sense not yet recognized gets a chance to be heard.[8]

Proud to Be a Politician

Must a politician gain public office by denouncing the profession? From the tone of many recent congressional races, it would appear that this is a growing trend. Journalist Charles McDowell of the *Richmond Times-Dispatch* noted this trend on the PBS series "The Lawmakers" and suggested that such a tactic "demeans an honorable and essential profession—that of the politician." McDowell proposed that every member of Congress be required to take the following oath:

I affirm that I am a politician. That I am willing to associate with other known politicians. That I have no moral reservations about committing acts of politics. Under the Constitution, I insist that politicians have as much right to indulge in politics as preachers, single-issue zealots, generals, bird-watchers, labor leaders, big business lobbyists, and all other truth-givers.

I confess that, as a politician, I participate in negotiation, compromise, and tradeoffs in order to achieve something that seems reasonable to a majority. And, although I try to be guided by principle, I confess that I often find people of principle on the other side, too.

So help me God.

Crucial to the democratic faith is the belief that a constitutional democracy cherishes the free play of ideas. Only where the safety valve of public discussion is available and where almost any policy is subject to perpetual questioning and challenge can there be the assurance that both minority and majority rights will be served. To be afraid of public debate is to be afraid of self-government. "Rulers always have and always will find it dangerous to their security to permit people to think, believe, talk, write, assemble, and particularly to criticize the government as they please," said former Supreme Court Justice William J. Brennan, "but the language of the First Amendment indicates the framers weighed the risk involved in such freedoms and deliberately chose to stake this government's security and life upon preserving liberty to discuss public affairs intact and untouched by government."[9]

Your authors hold with Thomas Jefferson that there is nothing in the country so radically wrong that it cannot be cured by good newspapers, sound schoolmasters, and a critical reading of history. Inform and educate the citizenry, and a major hurdle is overcome. Jefferson had boundless faith in education. He believed people are rationally endowed by nature with an innate sense of justice; the average person has only to be informed to act wisely. In the long run, said Jefferson, only an educated and enlightened democracy can hope to endure.

Education is one of the best predictors of voting, participation in politics, and knowledge of public affairs. The public may not be equally involved or equally willing to invest in democracy. But the attentive public—frequently those like yourself who have gone to college—has the willingness and self-confidence to see government and politics as necessary and important. An educated public has an understanding of how government works, how individuals can influence decision makers, and how to elect like-minded people. Tolerance for different opinions must be a central part of a civic education.

Recent years have sadly witnessed an increase in racial and ethnic tensions in the United States. These tensions sometimes encourage separation and antagonism toward the larger and more dominant Anglo culture. When carried to the extreme, these tensions promote various ethnicity cults that exaggerate differences, intensify resentments, and drive deep wedges between nationalities and races. "The genius of America" writes historian Arthur M. Schlesinger, Jr., "lies in its capacity to forge a single nation from peoples of remarkably diverse racial, religious, and ethnic origins." Schlesinger acknowledges that our government and society have been more open to some than to others, "but it is more open to all today than it was yesterday and it is likely to be even more open tomorrow than today."[10]

We are a restless, dissatisfied, and searching people. We are our own toughest critics. Our political system is far from perfect, but it still is an open system. People *can* fight city hall. People who disagree with policies in the nation can band together and be heard. We know only too well that the American Dream is never fully attained, and it is certainly not inherited. It must always be achieved. Ultimately, "what joins the Americans one to another is not a common nationality, language, race, or ancestry . . . but rather their complicity in a shared work of the imagination."[11]

Our future will be shaped by those like yourself who care about extending and preserving our political rights and freedoms. Our individual liberties will never be assured unless there are people willing to take responsibility for the progress of the whole community, people willing to exercise their determination and democratic faith. Carved in granite on one of the long corridors in a building on the Harvard University campus are these words of American poet Archibald MacLeish: "How shall freedom be defended? By arms when it is attacked by arms; by truth when it is attacked by lies, by democratic faith when it is attacked by authoritarian dogma. Always, in the final act, by determination and faith."

Millions of Americans visit the great monuments in our nation's capital each year. They admire their beauty and are always impressed by the memorials to Washington, Jefferson, Lincoln, and the Vietnam and Korean War veterans, and by the Capitol, the Supreme Court, and the White House. The strength of the nation, however, resides not in these official buildings but in the hearts, minds, and behavior of citizens. If we lose faith, stop caring, stop participating, and stop believing in the possibilities of self-government, the monuments "will be meaningless piles of stone, and the venture that began with the Declaration of Independence, the venture familiarly known as America will be as lifeless as the stone."[12]

One thing is certain amid all the debates over what constitutional democracy, the Constitution, and the Bill of Rights mean, or should mean. The celebrations and the traumas, the advances and failures, the processes and institutions of "a government by the people"—as contrasted with something called "the state" in other lands—are inseparable from the daily lives and hopes and needs of the 275 million Americans. No one has expressed this belief more eloquently than the noted poet, Walt Whitman:

Walt Whitman, legendary American poet and celebrator of the American experience.

> O I see flashing that this America is only you and me,
>
> Its power, weapons, testimony, are you and me.
>
> Its crimes, lies, thefts, defections, are you and me,
>
> Its Congress is you and me, the officers, capitols, armies, ships, are you and me.
>
> Its endless gestation of new States are you and me,
>
> The war (that war so bloody and grim, the war I will henceforth forget),
>
>   was you and me...
>
> Freedom, language, poems, employments, are you and me,
>
> Past, present, future, are you and me,
>
> I dare not shirk any part of myself,
>
> Nor any part of America good or bad.[13]

Appendix

THE DECLARATION OF INDEPENDENCE

Drafted mainly by Thomas Jefferson, this document adopted by the Second Continental Congress, and signed by John Hancock and fifty-five others, outlined the rights of man and the rights to rebellion and self-government. It declared the independence of the colonies from Great Britain, justified rebellion, and listed the grievances against George the III and his government. What is memorable about this famous document is not only that it declared the birth of a new nation, but that it set forth, with eloquence, our basic philosophy of liberty and representative democracy.

IN CONGRESS, JULY 4, 1776
(The unanimous Declaration of the Thirteen United States of America)

Preamble

When, in the course of human events, it becomes necessary for one people to dissolve the political bands which have connected them with another, and to assume, among the powers of the earth, the separate and equal station to which the laws of nature and of nature's God entitle them, a decent respect to the opinions of mankind requires that they should declare the causes which impel them to the separation.

New Principles of Government

We hold these truths to be self-evident; that all men are created equal, that they are endowed by their Creator with certain unalienable rights, that among these are life, liberty, and the pursuit of happiness.

That, to secure these rights, governments are instituted among men, deriving their just powers from the consent of the governed.

That whenever any form of government becomes destructive of these ends, it is the right of the people to alter or to abolish it, and to institute new government, laying its foundation on such principles, and organizing its powers in such form, as to them shall seem most likely to effect their safety and happiness. Prudence, indeed will dictate that

governments long established should not be changed for light and transient causes; and accordingly all experience hath shown that mankind are more disposed to suffer while evils are sufferable, than to right themselves by abolishing the forms to which they are accustomed. But when a long train of abuses and usurpations, pursuing invariably the same object, evinces a design to reduce them under absolute despotism, it is their right, it is their duty, to throw off such government, and to provide new guards for their future security.

Reasons for Separation

Such has been the patient sufferance of these colonies; and such is now the necessity which constrains them to alter their former systems of government. The history of the present king of Great Britain is a history of repeated injuries and usurpations, all having in direct object the establishment of an absolute tyranny over these states. To prove this, let facts be submitted to a candid world.

He has refused his assent to laws, the most wholesome and necessary for the public good.

He has forbidden his governors to pass laws of immediate and pressing importance unless suspended in their operation till his assent should be obtained; and when so suspended, he has utterly neglected to attend to them.

He has refused to pass other laws for the accommodation of large districts of people, unless those people would relinquish the

right of representation in the legislature, a right inestimable to them, and formidable to tyrants only.

He has called together legislative bodies at places unusual, uncomfortable, and distant for the depository of their public records, for the sole purpose of fatiguing them into compliance with his measures.

He has dissolved representative houses repeatedly, for opposing, with manly firmness, his invasions on the rights of people.

He has refused, for a long time after such dissolutions, to cause others to be elected; whereby the legislative powers incapable of annihilation, have returned to the people at large for their exercise; the state remaining, in the meantime, exposed to all the dangers of invasion from without and convulsions within.

He has endeavored to prevent the population of these states; for that purpose obstructing the laws of naturalization of foreigners, refusing to pass others to encourage their migration hither, and raising the conditions of new appropriations of lands.

He has obstructed the administration of justice, by refusing his assent to laws for establishing judiciary powers.

He has made judges dependent on his will alone for the tenure of their offices, and the amount and payment of their salaries.

He has erected a multitude of new offices, and sent hither swarms of officers to harass our people and eat out their substance.

He has kept among us, in times of peace, standing armies, without the consent of our legislature.

He has affected to render the military independent of, and superior to, the civil power.

He has combined with others to subject us to jurisdiction foreign to our constitution and unacknowledged by our laws, giving his assent to their acts of pretended legislation:

For quartering large bodies of armed troops among us;

For protecting them, by a mock trial, from punishment for any murders which they should commit on the inhabitants of these states;

For cutting off our trade with all parts of the world;

For imposing taxes on us without our consent;

For depriving us, in many cases, of the benefits of trial by jury;

For transporting us beyond seas, to be tried for pretended offenses;

For abolishing the free system of English laws in a neighboring province, establishing therein an arbitrary government, and enlarging its boundaries, so as to render it at once an example and fit instrument for introducing the same absolute rule into these colonies;

For taking away our charters, abolishing our most valuable laws, and altering, fundamentally, the forms of our governments;

For suspending our own legislatures, and declaring themselves invented with power to legislate for us in all cases whatsoever.

He has abdicated government here, by declaring us out of his protection and waging war against us.

He has plundered our seas, ravaged our coasts, burned our towns, and destroyed the lives of our people.

He is at this time transporting large armies of foreign mercenaries to complete the works of death, desolation, and tyranny already begun with circumstances of cruelty and perfidy scarcely paralleled in the most barbarous ages and totally unworthy of the head of a civilized nation.

He has constrained our fellow-citizens, taken captive on the high seas, to bear arms against their country, to become the executioners of their friends and brethren, or to fall themselves by their hands.

He has excited domestic insurrections among us, and has endeavored to bring on the inhabitants of our frontiers the merciless Indian savages, whose known rule of warfare is an undistinguished destruction of all ages, sexes, and conditions.

In every stage of these oppressions we have petitioned for redress in the most humble terms; our repeated petitions have been answered only by repeated injury. A prince whose character is thus marked by every act which may define a tyrant is unfit to be the ruler of a free people.

Nor have we been wanting in attention to our British brethren. We have warned them, from time to time, of attempts by their legislature to extend an unwarrantable juris-diction over us. We have reminded them of the circumstances of our emigration and settlement here. We have appealed to their native justice and magnanimity; and we have conjured them, by the ties of our common kindred, to disavow these usurpations, which would inevitably interrupt our connections and correspondence. They, too, have been deaf to the voice of justice and of consanguinity. We must, therefore, acquiesce in the necessity which denounces our separation, and hold them, as we hold the rest of mankind, enemies in war, in peace, friends.

We, therefore, the representatives of the United States of America, in General Congress assembled, appealing to the Supreme Judge of the world for the rectitude of our intentions, do, in the name and by authority of the good people of these colonies, solemnly publish and declare, that these united colonies are, and of right ought to be, free and independent states; that they are absolved from all allegiance to the British crown, and that all political connection between them and the state of Great Britain is, and ought to be, totally dissolved; and that, as free and independent states, they have full power to levy war, conclude peace, contract alliances, establish commerce, and do all other acts and things which independent states may of a right do. And, for the support of this declaration, with a firm reliance on the protection of Divine Providence, we mutually pledge to each other our lives, our fortunes, and our sacred honor.

THE FEDERALIST, NO. 10, JAMES MADISON

The Federalist, No. 10, written by James Madison soon after the Constitutional Convention, was prepared as one of several dozen newspaper essays aimed at persuading New Yorkers to ratify the proposed constitution. One of the most important basic documents in American political history, it outlines the need for and the general principles of a democratic republic. It also provides a political and economic analysis of the realities of interest group or faction politics.

To the People of the State of New York: Among the numerous advantages promised by a well-constructed union, none deserves to be more accurately developed than its tendency to break and control the violence of faction. The friend of popular governments, never finds himself so much alarmed for their character and fate, as when he contemplates their propensity of this dangerous vice. He will not fail, therefore, to set a due value on any plan which, without violating the principles to which he is attached, provides a proper cure for it. The instability, injustice, and confusion introduced into the public councils, have, in truth, been the mortal diseases under which popular governments have everywhere perished; as they continue to be the favorite and fruitful topics from which the adversaries to liberty derive their most specious declamations. The valuable improvements made by the American constitutions on the popular models, both ancient and modern, cannot certainly be too much admired; but it would be an unwarrantable partiality, to contend that they have as effectually obviated the danger on this side, as was wished and expected. Complaints are everywhere heard from our most considerate and virtuous citizens, equally the friends of public and private faith, and of public and personal liberty, that our governments are too unstable; that the public good is disregarded in the conflicts of rival parties; and that measures are too often decided, not according to the rules of justice, and the rights of the minor party, but by the superior force of an interested and overbearing majority. However anxiously we may wish that these complaints had no foundation, the evidence of known facts will not permit us to deny that they are in some degree true. It will be found, indeed, on a candid review of our situation, that some of the distresses under which we labor have been erroneously charged on the operations of our governments; but it will be found, at the same time, that other causes will not alone account for many of our heaviest misfortunes; and, particularly, for that prevailing and increasing distrust of public engagements, and alarm for private rights, which are echoed from one end of the continent to the other. These must be chiefly, if not wholly, effects of the unsteadiness and injustice, with which a factious spirit has tainted our public administrations.

By a faction, I understand a number of citizens, whether amounting to a majority of the whole, who are united and actuated by some common impulse of passion, or of interest, adverse to the rights of other citizens, or to the permanent and aggregate interests of the community.

There are two methods of curing the mischiefs of faction: the one, by removing its causes; the other, by controlling its effects.

There are again two methods of removing the causes of faction: the one, by destroying the liberty which is essential to its existence; the other, by giving to every citizen the same opinions, the same passions, and the same interests.

It could never be more truly said, than of the first remedy, that it was worse than the disease. Liberty is to faction what air is to fire, an aliment without which it instantly expires. But it could not be a less folly to abolish liberty, which is essential to political life, because it nourishes faction, than it would be to wish the annihilation of air, which is essential to animal life, because it imparts to fire its destructive agency.

The second expedient is as impracticable, as the first would be unwise. As long as the reason of man continues fallible, and he is at liberty to exercise it, different opinions will be formed. As long as the connection subsists between his reason and his self-love, his opinions and his passions will have a reciprocal influence on each other; and the former will be objects to which the latter will attach themselves. The diversity in the faculties of men, from which the rights of property originate, is not less an insuperable obstacle to an uniformity of interests. The protection of these faculties is the first object of government. From the protection of different and unequal faculties of acquiring property, the possession of different degrees and kinds of property immediately results; and from the influence of these on the sentiments and views of the respective

proprietors, ensues a division of the society into different interests and parties.

The latent causes of faction are thus sown in the nature of man; and we see them everywhere brought into different degrees of activity, according to the different circumstances of civil society. A zeal for different opinions concerning religion, concerning government, and many other points, as well of speculation as of practice; an attachment to different leaders ambitiously contending for preeminence and power; or to persons of other descriptions whose fortunes have been interesting to the human passions, have, in turn, divided mankind into parties, inflamed them with mutual animosity, and rendered them much more disposed to vex and oppress each other, than to cooperate for their common good. So strong is this propensity of mankind, to fall into mutual animosities, that where no substantial occasion presents itself, the most frivolous and fanciful distinctions have been sufficient to kindle their unfriendly passions and excite their most violent conflicts. But the most common and durable source of factions, has been the various and unequal distribution of property. Those who hold, and those who are without property, have ever formed distinct interests in society. Those who are creditors, and those who are debtors, fall under a like discrimination. A landed interest, a manufacturing interest, a mercantile interest, a moneyed interest, with many lesser interests, grow up of necessity in civilized nations, and divide them into different classes, actuated by different sentiments and views. The regulation of these various and interfering interests forms the principal task of modern legislation, and involves the spirit of the party and faction in the necessary and ordinary operations of the government.

No man is allowed to be a judge in his own cause; because his interest will certainly bias his judgment, and, not improbably, corrupt his integrity. With equal, nay, with greater reason, a body of men are unfit to be both judges and parties at the same time; yet what are many of the most important acts of legislation, but so many judicial determinations, not indeed concerning the right of single persons, but concerning the rights of large bodies of citizens? And what are the different classes of legislators, but advocates and parties to the causes which they determine? Is a law proposed concerning private debts? It is a questions to which the creditors are parties on one side, and the debtors on the other. Justice ought to hold the balance between them. Yet the parties are, and must be, themselves the judges; and the most numerous party, or, in other words, the most powerful faction, must be expected to prevail. Shall domestic manu-

facturers be encouraged, and in what degree, by restrictions on foreign manufacturers? Are questions which would be differently decided by the landed and the manufacturing classes; and probably by neither with a sole regard to justice and the public good. The apportionment of taxes, on the various descriptions of property, is an act which seems to require the most exact impartiality; yet there is, perhaps, no legislative act, in which greater opportunity and temptation are given to a predominant party to trample on the rules of justice. Every shilling, with which they overburden the inferior number, is a shilling saved to their own pockets.

It is in vain to say, that enlightened statesmen will be able to adjust these clashing interests, and render them all subservient to the public good. Enlightened statesmen will not always be at the helm, nor, in many cases, can such an adjustment be made at all, without taking into view indirect and remote considerations, which will rarely prevail over the immediate interest which one party may find in disregarding the rights of another, or the good of the whole.

The inference to which we are brought is, that the causes of faction cannot be removed; and that relief is only to be sought in the means of controlling its *effects*.

If a faction consists of less than a majority, relief is supplied by the republican principle, which enables the majority to defeat its sinister views, by regular vote. It may clog the administration, it may convulse the society; but it will be unable to execute and mask its violence under the forms of the Constitution. When a majority is included in a faction, the form of popular government, on the other hand, enables it to sacrifice to its ruling passion or interest, both the public good and the rights of other citizens. To secure the public good, and private rights, against the danger of such a faction, and at the same time to preserve the spirit and the form of popular government, is then the great object to which our inquiries are directed. Let me add, that it is the great desideratum, by which alone this form of government can be rescued from the opprobrium under which it has so long laboured, and be recommended to the esteem and adoption of mankind.

By what means is this object attainable? Evidently by one of two only. Either the existence of the same passion or interest in a majority, at the same time, must be prevented; or the majority, having such coexistent passion or interest, must be rendered, by their number and local situation, unable to concert and carry into effect schemes of oppression. If the impulse and the opportunity be suffered to coincide, we well know that neither moral nor religious motives can be relied on as an adequate control. They are not found to be such on the injustice and violence of individuals, and lose their efficacy in proportion to the number combined together; that is, in proportion as their efficacy becomes needful.

From this view of the subject, it may be concluded, that a pure democracy, by which I mean a society consisting of a small number of citizens, who assemble and administer the government in person, can admit of no cure for the mischiefs of faction. A common passion or interest will, in almost every case, be felt by a majority of the whole; a communication and concert, results from the form of government itself; and there is nothing to check the inducements to sacrifice the weaker party, or an obnoxious individual. Hence, it is, that such democracies have ever been spectacles of turbulence and contention; have ever been found incompatible with personal security, or the rights of property; and have in general been as short in their lives, as they have been violent in their deaths. Theoretic politicians, who have patronized this species of government, have erroneously supposed, that by reducing mankind to a perfect equality in their political rights, they would, at the same time be perfectly equalized and assimilated in their possessions, their opinions, and their passions.

A republic, by which I mean a government in which the scheme of representation takes place, opens a different prospect, and promises the cure for which we are seeking. Let us examine the points in which it varies from pure democracy, and we shall comprehend both the nature of the cure and the efficacy which it must derive from the union.

The two great points of difference, between a democracy and a republic, are, first, the delegation of the government, in the latter, to a small number of citizens, elected by the rest; secondly, the greater number of citizens, and greater sphere of country, over which the latter may be extended.

The effect of the first difference is, on the one hand, to refine and enlarge the public views, by passing them through the medium of a chosen body of citizens, whose wisdom may best discern the true interest of their country, and whose patriotism and love of justice, will be least likely to sacrifice it to temporary or partial considerations. Under such a regulation, it may well happen, that the public voice, pronounced by the representatives of the people, will be more consonant to the public good, than if pronounced by the people themselves, convened for the purpose. On the other hand the effect may be inverted. Men of factious tempers, of local prejudices, or of sinis-

ter designs, may by intrigue, by corruption, or by other means, first obtain the suffrages, and then betray the interest of the people. The question resulting is, whether small or extensive republics are most favourable to the election of proper guardians of the public weal; and it is clearly decided in favour of the latter by two obvious considerations.

In the first place, it is to be remarked that, however small the republic may be, the representatives must be raised to a certain number, in order to guard against the cabals of a few; and that however large it may be, they must be limited to a certain number, in order to guard against the confusion of a multitude. Hence, the number of representatives in the two cases not being in proportion to that of the constituents, and being proportionally greatest in the small republic, it follows, that if the proportion of fit characters be not less in the large than in the small republic, the former will present a greater option, and consequently a greater probability of a fit choice.

In the next place, as each representative will be chosen by a greater number of citizens in the large than in the small republic, it will be more difficult for unworthy candidates to practice with success the vicious arts, by which elections are too often carried; and the suffrages of the people being more free, will be more likely to centre in men who possess the most attractive merit, and the most diffusive and established characters.

It must be confessed, that in this, as in most other cases, there is a mean, on both sides of which inconveniences will be found to lie. By enlarging too much the number of electors, you render the representatives too little acquainted with all their local circumstances and lesser interests; as by reducing it too much, you render him unduly attached to these, and too little fit to comprehend and pursue great and national objects. The federal constitution forms a happy combination in this respect; the great and aggregate interests being referred to the national, the local and particular to the state legislatures.

The other point of difference is, the greater number of citizens, and extent of territory, which may be brought within the compass of republican, than of democratic government; and it is this circumstance principally which renders factious combinations less to be dreaded in the former, than in the latter. The smaller the society, the fewer probably will be the distinct parties and interests composing it; the fewer the distinct parties and interests, the more frequently will a majority be found of the same party; and the smaller the number of individuals composing a majority, and the smaller the compass within which they are placed, the more easily

will they concert and execute their plans of oppression. Extend the sphere, and you take in a greater variety of parties and interests; you make it less probable that a majority of the whole will have a common motive to invade the rights of other citizens; or if such a common motive exists, it will be more difficult for all who feel it to discover their own strength, and to act in unison with each other. Besides other impediments, it may be remarked, that where there is a consciousness of unjust or dishonourable purposes, communication is always checked by distrust, in proportion to the number whose concurrence is necessary.

Hence, it clearly appears, that the same advantage, which a republic has over a democracy, in controlling the effects of faction, is enjoyed by a large over a small republic—is enjoyed by the union over the states composing it. Does this advantage consist in the substitution of representatives, whose enlightened views and virtuous sentiments render them superior to local prejudices, and to schemes of injustice? It will not be denied that the representation of the union will be most likely to possess these requisite endowments. Does it consist in the greater security afforded by a greater variety of parties, against the event of any one party being able to outnumber and oppress the rest? In an equal degree does the increased variety of parties, comprised within the union, increase the security? Does it, in fine, consist in the greater obstacles opposed to the concert and accomplishment of the secret wishes of an unjust and interested majority? Here, again, the extent of the union gives it the most palpable advantage.

The influence of factious leaders may kindle a flame within their particular states, but will be unable to spread a general conflagration through the other states; a religious sect may degenerate into a political faction in a part of the confederacy; but the variety of sects dispersed over the entire face of it, must secure the national councils against any danger from that source: a rage for paper money, for an abolition of debts, for an equal division of property, or for any other improper or wicked project, will be less apt to pervade the whole body of the union than a particular member of it; in the same proportion as such a malady is more likely to taint a particular county or district, than an entire state.

In the extent and proper structure of the union, therefore, we behold a republican remedy for the diseases most incident to republican government. And according to the degree of pleasure and pride we feel in being republicans, ought to be our zeal in cherishing the spirit, and supporting the character of federalists.

THE FEDERALIST, NO. 51, JAMES MADISON

The Federalist, No. 51, also written by Madison, is a classic statement in defense of separation of powers and republican processes. Its fourth paragraph is especially famous and is frequently quoted by students of government.

To what expedient, then, shall we finally resort, for maintaining in practice the necessary partition of power among the several departments as laid down in the Constitution? The only answer that can be given is that as all these exterior provisions are found to be inadequate the defect must be supplied, by so contriving the interior structure of the government as that its several constituent parts may, by their mutual relations, be the means of keeping each other in their proper places. Without presuming to undertake a full development of this important idea I will hazard a few general observations which may perhaps place it in a clearer light, and enable us to form a more correct judgment of the principles and structure of the government planned by the convention.

In order to lay a due foundation for that separate and distinct exercise of the different powers of government, which to a certain extent is admitted on all hands to be essential to the preservation of liberty, it is evident that each department should have a will of its own; and consequently should be so constituted that the members of each should have as little agency as possible in the appointment of the members of the others. Were this principle rigorously adhered to, it would require that all the appointments for the supreme executive, legislative, and judiciary magistracies should be drawn from the same fountain of authority, the people, through channels having no communication whatever with one another. Perhaps such a plan of constructing the several departments would be less difficult in practice than it may in contemplation appear. Some difficulties, however, and some additional expense would attend the execution of it. Some deviations, therefore, from the principle must be admitted. In the constitution of the judiciary department in particular, it might be inexpedient to insist rigorously on the principle: first, because peculiar qualifications being essential in the members, the primary consideration ought to be to select that mode of choice which best secures these qualifications; second, because the permanent tenure by which the appointments are held in that department must soon destroy all sense of dependence on the authority conferring them.

It is equally evident that the members of each department should be as little depen-

dent as possible on those of the others for the emoluments annexed to their offices. Were the executive magistrate, or the judges, not independent of the legislature in this particular, their independence in every other would be merely nominal.

But the great security against a gradual concentration of the several powers in the same department consists in giving to those who administer each department the necessary constitutional means and personal motives to resist encroachments of the others. The provision for defense must in this, as in all other cases, be made commensurate to the danger of attack. Ambition must be made to counteract ambition. The interest of the man must be connected with the constitutional rights of the place. It may be a reflection on human nature that such devices should be necessary to control the abuses of government. But what is government itself but the greatest of all reflections on human nature? If men were angels, no government would be necessary. If angels were to govern men, neither external nor internal controls on government would be necessary. In framing a government which is to be administered by men over men, the great difficulty lies in this: you must first enable the government to control the governed; and in the next place oblige it to control itself. A dependence on the people is, no doubt, the primary control on the government; but experience has taught mankind the necessity of auxiliary precautions.

This policy of supplying, by opposite and rival interests, the defect of better motives, might be traced through the whole system of human affairs, private as well as public. We see it particularly displayed in all the subordinate distributions of power, where the constant aim is to divide and arrange the several offices in such a manner as that each may be a check on the other—that the private interest of every individual may be a sentinel over the public rights. These inventions of prudence cannot be less requisite in the distribution of the supreme powers of the State.

But it is not possible to give to each department an equal power of self-defense. In republican government, the legislative authority necessarily predominates. The remedy for this inconveniency is to divide the legislature into different branches; and to render them, by modes of election and different principles of action, as little connected with each other

as the nature of their common functions and their common dependence on the society will admit. It may even be necessary to guard against dangerous encroachments by still further precautions. As the weight of the legislative authority requires that it should be thus divided, the weakness of the executive may require, on the other hand, that it should be fortified. An absolute negative on the legislature appears, at first view, to be the natural defense with which the executive magistrate should be armed. But perhaps it would be neither altogether safe nor alone sufficient. On ordinary occasions it might not be exerted with the requisite firmness, and on extraordinary occasions it might be perfidiously abused. May not this defect of an absolute negative be supplied by some qualified connection between this weaker department and the weaker branch of the stronger department, by which the latter may be led to support the constitutional rights of the former, without being too much detached from the rights of its own department?

If the principles on which these observations are founded be just, as I persuade myself they are, and they be applied as a criterion to the several State constitutions, and to the federal Constitution, it will be found that if the latter does not perfectly correspond with them, the former are infinitely less able to bear such a test.

There are, moreover, two considerations particularly applicable to the federal system of America, which place that system in a very interesting point of view.

First. In a single republic, all the power surrendered by the people is submitted to the administration of a single government; and the usurpations are guarded against by a division of the government into distinct and separate departments. In the compound republic of America, the power surrendered by the people is first divided between two distinct governments, and then the portion allotted to each subdivided among distinct and separate departments. Hence a double security arises to the rights of the people. The different governments will control each other, at the same time that each will be controlled by itself.

Second. It is of great importance in a republic not only to guard the society against the oppression of its rulers, but to guard one part of the society against the injustice of the other part. Different interests necessarily exist in different classes of citizens. If a majority be united by a common interest, the rights of the minority will be insecure. There are but two methods of providing against this evil: the one by creating a will in the community independent of the majority—that is, of the society itself; the other, by comprehending in the society so many separate descriptions of citizens as will render an unjust combination of a majority of the whole very improbable, if not impracticable. The first method prevails in all governments possessing an hereditary or self-appointed authority. This, at best, is but a precarious security; because a power independent of the society may as well espouse the unjust views of the major as the rightful interests of the minor party, and may possibly be turned against both parties. The second method will be exemplified in the federal republic of the United States. Whilst all authority in it will be derived from and dependent on the society, the society itself will be broken into so many parts, interests and classes of citizens, that the rights of individuals, or of the minority, will be in little danger from interested combinations of the majority. In a free government the security for civil rights must be the same as that for religious rights. It consists in the one case in the multiplicity of interests, and in the other in the multiplicity of sects. The degree of security in both cases will depend on the number of interests and sects; and this may be presumed to depend on the extent of country and number of people comprehended under the same government. This view of the subject must particularly recommend a proper federal system to all the sincere and considerate friends of republican government, since it shows that in exact proportion as the territory of the Union may be formed into more circumscribed Confederacies, or States, oppressive combinations of a majority will be facilitated; the best security, under the republican forms, for the rights of every class of citizen, will be diminished; and consequently the stability and independence of some member of the government, the only other security, must be proportionally increased. Justice is the end of government. It is the end of civil society. It ever has been and ever will be pursued until it be obtained, or until liberty be lost in the pursuit. In a society under the forms of which the stronger faction can readily unite and oppress the weaker, anarchy may as truly be said to reign as in a state of nature, where the weaker individual is not secured against the violence of the stronger; and as, in the latter state, even the stronger individuals are prompted, by the uncertainty of their condition, to submit to a government which may protect the weak as well as themselves; so, in the former state, will the more powerful factions or parties be gradually induced, by a like motive, to wish for a government which will protect all parties, the weaker as well as the more powerful. It can be little doubted that if the State of Rhode Island was separated from the Confederacy and left to itself, the insecurity of rights under the popular form of government within such narrow limits would be displayed by such reiterated oppressions of factious majorities that some power altogether independent of the people would soon be called for by the voice of the very factions whose misrule had proved the necessity to it. In the extended republic of the United States, and among the great variety of interests, parties, and sects which it embraces, a coalition of a majority of the whole society could seldom take place on any other principles than those of justice and the general good; whilst there being thus less danger to a minor from the will of a major party, there must be less pretext, also, to provide for the security of the former, by introducing into the government a will not dependent on the latter, or, in other words, a will independent of the society itself. It is no less certain that it is important, notwithstanding the contrary opinions which have been entertained that the larger the society, provided it lie within a practicable sphere, the more duly capable it will be of self-government. And happily for the *republican cause,* the practicable sphere may be carried to a very great extent by a judicious modification and mixture of the *federal principle.*

THE FEDERALIST, NO. 78, ALEXANDER HAMILTON

The Federalist, No. 78, written by Alexander Hamilton, explains and praises the provisions for the judiciary in the newly drafted Constitution. Notice especially how Hamilton asserts that the courts have a key responsibility in determining the meaning of the Constitution as fundamental law. Hamilton is outlining here the doctrine of *judicial review* as we now know it.

We proceed now to an examination of the judiciary department of the proposed government.

In unfolding the defects of the existing Confederation, the utility and necessity of a federal judicature have been clearly pointed out. It is the less necessary to recapitulate the considerations there urged as the propriety of the institution in the abstract is not disputed; the only questions which have been raised being relative to the manner of constituting it, and to its extent. To these points, therefore, our observations shall be confined.

The manner of constituting it seems to embrace these several objects: 1st. The mode of appointing the judges. 2nd. The tenure by which they are to hold their places. 3rd. The partition of the judiciary authority between different courts and their relations to each other.

First. As to the mode of appointing the judges: this is the same with that of appointing the officers of the Union in general and has been so fully discussed in the two last numbers that nothing can be said here which would not be useless repetition.

Second. As to the tenure by which the judges are to hold their places: this chiefly concerns their duration in office, the provisions for their support, the precautions for their responsibility.

According to the plan of the convention, all judges who may be appointed by the United States are to hold their offices *during good behavior;* which is conformable to the most approved of the State constitutions, and among the rest, to that of this State. Its propriety having been drawn into question by the adversaries of that plan is no light symptom of the rage for objection which disorders their imaginations and judgments. The standard of good behavior for the continuance in office of the judicial magistracy is certainly one of the most valuable of the modern improvements in the practice of government. In a monarchy it is an excellent barrier to the despotism of the prince; in a republic it is a no less excellent barrier to the encroachments and oppressions of the representative body. And it is the best expedient which can be devised in any government to secure a steady, upright, and impartial administration of the laws.

Whoever attentively considers the different departments of power must perceive that, in a government in which they are separated from each other, the judiciary, from the nature of its functions, will always be the least dangerous to the political rights of the Constitution; because it will be least in a capacity to annoy or injure them. The executive not only dispenses the honors but holds the sword of the community. The legislature not only commands the purse but prescribes the rules by which the duties and rights of every citizen are to be regulated. The judiciary, on the contrary, has no influence over either the sword or the purse; no direction either of the strength or of the wealth of the society, and can take no active resolution whatever. It may truly be said to have neither FORCE NOR WILL but merely judgment; and must ultimately depend upon the aid of the executive arm even for the efficacy of its judgments.

This simple view of the matter suggests several important consequences. It proves incontestably that the judiciary is beyond comparison the weakest of the three departments of power; that it can never attack with success either of the other two; and that all possible care is requisite to enable it to defend itself against their attacks. It equally proves that though individual oppression may now and then proceed from the courts of justice, the general liberty of the people can never be endangered from that quarter; I mean so long as the judiciary remains truly distinct from both the legislature and the executive. For I agree that "there is no liberty if the power of judging be not separated from the legislative and executive powers." And it proves, in the last place, that as liberty can have nothing to fear from the judiciary alone, but would have everything to fear from its union with either of the other departments, that as all the effects of such a union must ensue from a dependence of the former on the latter, notwithstanding a nominal and apparent separation; that as, from the natural feebleness of the judiciary, it is in continual jeopardy of being overpowered, awed, or influenced by its co-ordinate branches; and that as nothing can contribute so much to its firmness and independence as permanency in office, this quality may therefore be justly regarded as an indispensable ingredient in its constitution, and, in a great measure, as the citadel for the public justice and the public security.

The complete independence of the courts of justice is peculiarly essential in a limited Constitution. By a limited Constitution, I understand one which contains certain specified exceptions to the legislative authority; such, for instance, as that it shall pass no bills of attainder, no *ex post facto* laws, and the like.

Limitations of this kind can be preserved in practice no other way than through the medium of courts of justice, whose duty it must be to declare all acts contrary to the manifest tenor of the Constitution void. Without this, all the reservations of particular rights or privileges would amount to nothing.

Some perplexity respecting the rights of the courts to pronounce legislative acts void, because contrary to the Constitution, has arisen from an imagination that the doctrine would imply a superiority to the judiciary to the legislative power. It is urged that the authority which can declare the acts of another void must necessarily be superior to the one whose acts may be declared void. As this doctrine is of great importance in all the American constitutions, a brief discussion of the grounds on which it rests cannot be unacceptable.

There is no position which depends on clearer principles than that every act of a delegated authority, contrary to the tenor of the commission under which it is exercised, is void. No legislative act, therefore, contrary to the Constitution, can be valid. To deny this would be to affirm that the deputy is greater than his principal; that the servant is above his master; that the representatives of the people are superior to the people themselves; that men acting by virtue of powers do not authorize, but what they forbid.

If it be said that the legislative body are themselves the constitutional judges of their own powers and that the construction they put upon them is conclusive upon the other departments it may be answered that this cannot be the natural presumption where it is not to be collected from any particular provisions in the Constitution. It is not otherwise to be supposed that the Constitution could intend to enable the representatives of the people to substitute their *will* to that of their constituents. It is far more rational to suppose that the courts were designed to be an intermediate body between the people and the legislature in order, among other things, to keep the latter within the limits assigned to their authority. The interpretation of the laws is the proper and peculiar province of the courts. A constitution is, in fact, and must be regarded by the judges as, a fundamental law. It therefore belongs to them to ascertain its meaning as well as the meaning of any particular act proceeding from the legislative body. If there should happen to be an irreconcilable variance between the two, that which has the superior obligation and validity ought, of course, to be preferred; or, in other words, the Constitution ought to be preferred to the statute, the intention of the people to the intention of their agents.

Nor does this conclusion by any means suppose a superiority of the judicial to the legislative power. It only supposes that the power of the people is superior to both, and that where the will of the legislature, declared in its statutes, stands in opposition to that of the people, declared in the Constitution, the judges ought to be governed by the latter rather than the former. They ought to regulate their decisions by the fundamental laws rather than by those which are not fundamental.

This exercise of judicial discretion in determining between two contradictory laws is exemplified in a familiar instance. It not uncommonly happens that there are two statutes existing at one time, clashing in whole or in part with each other and neither of them containing any repealing clause or expression. In such a case, it is the province of the courts to liquidate and fix their meaning and operation. So far as they can, by any fair construction, be reconciled to each other, reason and law conspire to dictate that this should be done; where this is impracticable, it becomes a matter of necessity to give effect to one in exclusion of the other. The rule which has obtained in the courts for determining their relative validity is that the last in order of time shall be preferred to the first. But this is a mere rule of construction, not derived from any positive law but from the nature and reason of the thing. It is a rule not enjoined upon the courts by legislative provision but adopted by themselves, as consonant to truth and propriety, for the direction of their conduct as interpreters of the law. They thought it reasonable that between the interfering acts of an *equal* authority that which was the last indication of its will should have the preference.

But in regard to the interfering acts of a superior and subordinate authority of an original and derivative power, the nature and reason of the thing indicates the converse of that rule as proper to be followed. They teach us that the prior act of a superior ought to be preferred to the subsequent act of an inferior and subordinate authority; and that accordingly, whenever a particular statute contravenes the Constitution, it will be the duty of the judicial tribunals to adhere to the latter and disregard the former.

It can be of no weight to say that the courts, on the pretense of a repugnancy, may substitute their own pleasure to the constitutional intentions of the legislature. This might as well happen in the case of two contradictory statutes; or it might as well happen in every adjudication upon any single statute. The courts must declare the sense of the law; and if they should be disposed to exercise WILL instead of JUDGMENT, the consequence would equally be the substitution of their pleasure to that of the legislative body. The observation, if it prove anything, would prove that there ought to be no judges distinct from that body.

If, then, the courts of justice are to be considered as the bulwarks of a limited Constitution against legislative encroachments, this consideration will afford a strong argument for the permanent tenure of judicial offices, since nothing will contribute so much as this to that independent spirit in the judges which must be essential to the faithful performance of so arduous a duty.

This independence of the judges is equally requisite to guard the Constitution and the rights of individuals from the effects of those ill humors which the arts of designing men, or the influence of particular conjunctures, sometimes disseminate among the people themselves, and which, though they speedily give place to better information, and more deliberate reflection, have a tendency, in the meantime, to occasion dangerous innovations in the government, and serious oppressions of the minor party in the community. Though I trust the friends of the proposed Constitution will never concur with its enemies in questioning that fundamental principal of Republican government which admits the right of the people to alter or abolish the established Constitution whenever they find it inconsistent with their happiness; yet it is not to be inferred from this principle that the representatives of the people, whenever a momentary inclination happens to lay hold of a majority of their constituents incompatible with the provisions in the existing Constitution would, on that account, be justifiable in a violation of those provisions; or that the courts would be under a greater obligation to connive at infractions in this shape than when they had proceeded wholly from the cabals of the representative body. Until the people have, by some solemn and authoritative act, annulled or changed the established form, it is binding upon themselves collectively, as well as individually; and no presumption, or even knowledge of their sentiments, can warrant their representatives in a departure from it prior to such an act. But it is easy to see that it would require an uncommon portion of fortitude in the judges to do their duty as faithful guardians of the Constitution, where legislative invasions of it had been instigated by the major voice of the community.

But it is not with a view to infractions of the Constitution only that the independence of the judges may be an essential safeguard against the effects of occasional ill humors in the society. These sometimes extend no farther than to the injury of the private rights of particular classes of citizens, by unjust and partial laws. Here also the firmness of the judicial magistracy is of vast importance in mitigating the severity and confining the operation of such laws. It not only serves to moderate the immediate mischiefs of those which may have been passed but it operates as a check upon the legislative body in passing them; who, perceiving that obstacles to the success of iniquitous intention are to be expected from the scruples of the courts, are in a manner compelled, by the very motives of the injustice they mediate, to qualify their attempts. This is a circumstance calculated to have more influence upon the character of our governments than but a few may be aware of. The benefits of the integrity and moderation of the judiciary have already been felt in more States than one; and though they may have displeased those whose sinister expectations they may have disappointed, they must have commanded the esteem and applause of all the virtuous and disinterested. Considerate men of every description ought to prize whatever will tend to beget or fortify that temper in the courts; as no man can be sure that he may not be tomorrow the victim of a spirit of injustice, by which he may be a gainer today. And every man must now feel that the inevitable tendency of such a spirit is to sap the foundations of public and private confidence and to introduce in its stead universal distrust and distress.

That inflexible and uniform adherence to the rights of the Constitution, and of individuals, which we perceive to be indispensable in the courts of justice, can certainly not be expected from judges who hold their offices by a temporary commission. Periodical appointments, however regulated, or by whomsoever made, would, in some way or other, be fatal to their necessary independence. If the power of making them was committed either to the executive or legislature there would be danger of an improper complaisance to the branch which possessed it; if to both, there would be an unwillingness to hazard the displeasure of either; if to the people, or to persons chosen by them for the special purpose, there would be too great a disposition to consult popularity to justify a reliance that nothing would be consulted by the Constitution and the laws.

There is yet a further and a weighty reason for the permanency of the judicial offices which is deducible from the nature of the qualifications they require. It has been frequently remarked with great propriety that a voluminous code of laws is one of the inconveniences necessarily connected with the advantages of a free government. To avoid an arbitrary discretion in the courts, it is indispensable that they should be bound down by strict rules and precedents which serve to define and point out their duty in every particular case that comes before them; and it will readily be conceived from the variety of controversies which grow out of the folly and wickedness of mankind that the records of those precedents must unavoidably swell to a very considerable bulk and must demand long and laborious study to acquire a competent knowledge of them. Hence it is that there can be but few men in the society who will have sufficient skill in the laws to qualify them for the stations of judges. And making the proper deductions for the ordinary depravity of human nature, the number must be still smaller of those who unite the requisite integrity with the requisite knowledge. These considerations apprise us that the government can have no great option between fit characters; and that a temporary duration in office which would naturally discourage such characters from quitting a lucrative line of practice to accept a seat on the bench would have a tendency to throw the administration of justice into hands less able and less well qualified to conduct it with utility and dignity. In the present circumstances of this country and in those in which it is likely to be for a long time to come, the disadvantages on this score would be greater than they may at first sight appear; but it must be confessed that they are far inferior to those which present themselves under the other aspects of the subject.

Upon the whole, there can be no room to doubt that the convention acted wisely in copying from the models of those constitutions which have established *good behavior* as the tenure of their judicial offices in point of duration, and that so far from being blamable on this account, their plan would have been inexcusably defective if it had wanted this important feature of good government. The experience of Great Britain affords an illustrious comment on the excellence of the institution.

Presidential Election Results 1789–1996

Year	Candidates	Party	Popular Vote	Electoral Vote
1789	George Washington			69
	John Adams			34
	Others			35
1793	George Washington			132
	John Adams			77
	George Clinton			50
	Others			5
1796	John Adams	Federalist		71
	Thomas Jefferson	Democratic-Republican		68
	Thomas Pinckney	Federalist		59
	Aaron Burr	Democratic-Republican		30
	Others			48
1800	Thomas Jefferson	Democratic-Republican		73
	Aaron Burr	Democratic-Republican		73
	John Adams	Federalist		65
	Charles C. Pinckney	Federalist		64
1804	Thomas Jefferson	Democratic-Republican		162
	Charles C. Pinckney	Federalist		14
1808	James Madison	Democratic-Republican		122
	Charles C. Pinckney	Federalist		47
	George Clinton	Independent-Republican		6
1812	James Madison	Democratic-Republican		128
	DeWitt Clinton	Federalist		89
1816	James Monroe	Democratic-Republican		183
	Rufus King	Federalist		34
1820	James Monroe	Democratic-Republican		231
	John Quincy Adams	Independent-Republican		1
1824	John Quincy Adams	Democratic-Republican	108,740(30.5%)	84
	Andrew Jackson	Democratic-Republican	153,544(43.1%)	99
	Henry Clay	Democratic-Republican	47,136(13.2%)	37
	William H. Crawford	Democratic-Republican	46,618(13.1%)	41
1828	Andrew Jackson	Democratic	647,231(56.0%)	178
	John Quincy Adams	National Republican	509,097(44.0%)	83
1832	Andrew Jackson	Democratic	687,502(55.0%)	219
	Henry Clay	National Republican	530,189(42.4%)	49
	William Wirt	Anti-Masonic		7
	John Floyd	National Republican	33,108(2.6%)	11
1836	Martin Van Buren	Democratic	761,549(50.9%)	170
	William H. Harrison	Whig	549,567(36.7%)	73
	Hugh L. White	Whig	145,396(9.7%)	26
	Daniel Webster	Whig	41,287(2.7%)	14
1840	William H. Harrison	Whig	1,275,017(53.1%)	234
	Martin Van Buren	Democratic	1,128,702(46.9%)	60
1844	James K. Polk	Democratic	1,337,243(49.6%)	170
	Henry Clay	Whig	1,299,068(48.1%)	105
	James G. Birney	Liberty	63,300(2.3%)	
1848	Zachary Taylor	Whig	1,360,101(47.4%)	163
	Lewis Cass	Democratic	1,220,544(42.5%)	127
	Martin Van Buren	Free Soil	291,163(10.1%)	
1852	Franklin Pierce	Democratic	1,601,474(50.9%)	254
	Winfield Scott	Whig	1,386,578(44.1%)	42
1856	James Buchanan	Democratic	1,838,169(45.4%)	174
	John C. Fremont	Republican	1,335,264(33.0%)	114
	Millard Fillmore	American	874,534(21.6%)	8
1860	Abraham Lincoln	Republican	1,865,593(39.8%)	180
	Stephen A. Douglas	Democratic	1,381,713(29.5%)	12
	John C. Breckinridge	Democratic	848,356(18.1%)	72
	John Bell	Constitutional Union	592,906(12.6%)	79
1864	Abraham Lincoln	Republican	2,206,938(55.0%)	212
	George B. McClellan	Democratic	1,803,787(45.0%)	21
1868	Ulysses S. Grant	Republican	3,013,421(52.7%)	214
	Horatio Seymour	Democratic	2,706,829(47.3%)	80
1872	Ulysses S. Grant	Republican	3,596,745(55.6%)	286
	Horace Greeley	Democratic	2,843,446(43.9%)	66
1876	Rutherford B. Hayes	Republican	4,036,571(48.0%)	185
	Samuel J. Tilden	Democratic	4,284,020(51.0%)	184
1880	James A. Garfield	Republican	4,449,053(48.3%)	214
	Winfield S. Hancock	Democratic	4,442,035(48.2%)	155
	James B. Weaver	Greenback-Labor	308,578(3.4%)	
1884	Grover Cleveland	Democratic	4,874,986(48.5%)	219
	James G. Blaine	Republican	4,851,931(48.2%)	182
	Benjamin F. Butler	Greenback-Labor	175,370(1.8%)	

Presidential Election Results 1789–1996

Year	Candidates	Party	Popular Vote	Electoral Vote
1888	Benjamin Harrison	Republican	5,444,337(47.8%)	233
	Grover Cleveland	Democratic	5,540,050(48.6%)	168
1892	Grover Cleveland	Democratic	5,554,414(46.0%)	277
	Benjamin Harrison	Republican	5,190,802(43.0%)	145
	James B. Weaver	Peoples	1,027,329(8.5%)	22
1896	William McKinley	Republican	7,035,638(50.8%)	271
	William J. Bryan	Democratic; Populist	6,467,946(46.7%)	176
1900	William McKinley	Republican	7,219,530(51.7%)	292
	William J. Bryan	Democratic; Populist	6,356,734(45.5%)	155
1904	Theodore Roosevelt	Republican	7,628,834(56.4%)	336
	Alton B. Parker	Democrat	5,084,401(37.6%)	140
	Eugene V. Debs	Socialist	402,460(3.0%)	0
1908	William H. Taft	Republican	7,679,006(51.6%)	321
	William J. Bryan	Democratic	6,409,106(43.1%)	162
	Eugene V. Debs	Socialist	420,820(2.8%)	0
1912	Woodrow Wilson	Democratic	6,286,820(41.8%)	435
	Theodore Roosevelt	Progressive	4,126,020(27.4%)	88
	William H. Taft	Republican	3,483,922(23.2%)	8
	Eugene V. Debs	Socialist	897,011(6.0%)	0
1916	Woodrow Wilson	Democratic	9,129,606(49.3%)	277
	Charles E. Hughes	Republican	8,538,211(46.1%)	254
1920	Warren G. Harding	Republican	16,152,200(61.0%)	404
	James M. Cox	Democratic	9,147,353(34.6%)	127
	Eugene V. Debs	Socialist	919,799(3.5%)	0
1924	Calvin Coolidge	Republican	15,725,016(54.1%)	382
	John W. Davis	Democratic	8,385,586(28.8%)	136
	Robert M. La Follette	Progressive	4,822,856(16.6%)	13
1928	Herbert C. Hoover	Republican	21,392,190(58.2%)	444
	Alfred E. Smith	Democratic	15,016,443(40.8%)	87
1932	Franklin D. Roosevelt	Democratic	22,809,638(57.3%)	472
	Herbert C. Hoover	Republican	15,758,901(39.6%)	59
	Norman Thomas	Socialist	881,951(2.2%)	0
1936	Franklin D. Roosevelt	Democratic	27,751,612(60.7%)	523
	Alfred M. Landon	Republican	16,681,913(36.4%)	8
	William Lemke	Union	891,858(1.9%)	0
1940	Franklin D. Roosevelt	Democratic	27,243,466(54.7%)	449
	Wendell L. Wilkie	Republican	22,304,755(44.8%)	82
1944	Franklin D. Roosevelt	Democratic	25,602,505(52.8%)	432
	Thomas E. Dewey	Republican	22,006,278(44.5%)	99
1948	Harry S. Truman	Democratic	24,105,812(49.5%)	303
	Thomas E. Dewey	Republican	21,970,065(45.1%)	189
	J. Strom Thurmond	States' Rights	1,169,063(2.4%)	39
	Henry A. Wallace	Progressive	1,157,172(2.4%)	0
1952	Dwight D. Eisenhower	Republican	33,936,234(55.2%)	442
	Adlai E. Stevenson	Democratic	27,314,992(44.5%)	89
1956	Dwight D. Eisenhower	Republican	35,590,472(57.4%)	457
	Adlai E. Stevenson	Democratic	26,022,752(42.0%)	73
1960	John F. Kennedy	Democratic	34,227,096(49.9%)	303
	Richard M. Nixon	Republican	34,108,546(49.6%)	219
1964	Lyndon B Johnson	Democratic	43,126,233(61.1%)	486
	Barry Goldwater	Republican	27,174,989(38.5%)	52
1968	Richard M. Nixon	Republican	31,783,783(43.4%)	301
	Hubert H. Humphrey	Democratic	31,271,839(42.7%)	191
	George C. Wallace	American Independent	9,899,557(13.5%)	46
1972	Richard M. Nixon	Republican	46,632,189(61.3%)	520
	George McGovern	Democratic	28,422,015(37.3%)	17
1976	Jimmy Carter	Democratic	40,828,587(50.1%)	297
	Gerald R. Ford	Republican	39,147,613(48.0%)	240
1980	Ronald Reagan	Republican	42,941,145(51.0%)	489
	Jimmy Carter	Democratic	34,663,037(41.0%)	49
	John B. Anderson	Independent	5,551,551(6.6%)	0
1984	Ronald Reagan	Republican	53,428,357(59%)	525
	Walter F. Mondale	Democratic	36,930,923(41%)	13
1988	George Bush	Republican	48,881,011(53%)	426
	Michael Dukakis	Democratic	41,828,350(46%)	111
1992	Bill Clinton	Democratic	38,394,210(43%)	370
	George Bush	Republican	33,974,386(38%)	168
	H. Ross Perot	Independent	16,573,465(19%)	0
1996	Bill Clinton	Democratic	45,628,667(49%)	379
	Bob Dole	Republican	37,869,435(41%)	159
	H. Ross Perot	Reform	7,874,283(8%)	0

Glossary

We have tried to write a readable book about American politics and government. We realize, however, that certain legal terms and political science phrases may not be familiar to some readers. To make such words or phrases (which appear in the text in boldface type) more understandable, we have compiled this glossary.

Administrative law Law relating to the authority and procedures of administrative agencies, as well as to the rules and regulations issued by those agencies.

Advisory opinion An opinion unrelated to a particular case that gives a court's view about a constitutional or legal issue.

Affirmative action Remedial actions—originally relating to employment but now also covering college and university admissions, contracting, and other areas—designed to overcome effects of past societal and individual discrimination against minorities and women.

Amendatory veto State veto power that allows governors to return a bill to the legislature with suggested changes or amendments. The legislators must decide whether to accept the governor's recommendations or attempt to pass the bill in its original form over the veto.

American Dream The widespread belief that individual initiative and hard work can result in economic success, that the next generation can have a better standard of living than the former, and that the United States is a land of opportunity.

Amicus curie ("friend of the court") brief A brief filed by an individual or organization with the permission of the court. It provides arguments in addition to those presented by the immediate parties to the case.

Annapolis Convention A convention held in August 1786 that issued the call to Congress and the states for what became the Constitutional Convention. Attended by delegates from five states, it was called to consider problems of trade and navigation.

Antifederalists Persons opposed to more nationally centralized government in general, and to the ratification of the 1787 Philadelphia Constitution in particular.

Antitrust legislation Federal laws (of which the Sherman Act of 1890 is most prominent), supplemented by state laws, that try to prevent one or a few business firms from dominating a particular market through monopoly or restraint of trade.

Appellate jurisdiction Authority to review decisions of lower courts, administrative tribunals, and some independent regulatory agencies.

Articles of Confederation The first constitution of the newly independent American states. It was drafted in 1777, ratified in 1781, and replaced by the present Constitution in 1789.

Assessment The value a government places on property for purposes of taxation. The assessed value may or may not reflect the real market value.

Assigned counsel Arrangement whereby attorneys are provided for persons accused of crime who are unable to hire their own lawyers. The judge assigns a member of the bar to provide counsel to a particular defendant.

Attentive public Those who follow public affairs fairly carefully, reading newspapers and magazines and watching television news broadcasts to keep informed about politics and world affairs.

Australian ballot A ballot printed by the state, which the voter marks and then places in a ballot box. Also called a **secret ballot.**

Bad tendency doctrine Interpretation of the First Amendment that would permit legislatures to make illegal speech that can reasonably be said to have a tendency to cause people to engage in illegal action.

Bicameralism, Bicameral legislature Two-house legislature; form for 49 of the states as well as for the U.S. Congress.

Bill of attainder Legislative act that inflicts punishment, including deprivation of property without judicial trial, on named individuals or members of a specified group.

Bipartisanship A policy that emphasizes cooperation and a united front between the major political parties, especially on sensitive foreign policy issues.

Block grant Broad grant of funds made by one level of government to another for prescribed activities—for example, health programs or crime prevention—with few strings attached.

Broker rule Government acting essentially as a go-between or mediator among organized groups that have definite policy goals.

Bureau Generally, the largest subunit of a government department or agency.

Bureaucracy Large private or public organizations that are hierarchical in structure, provide each employee with clearly defined responsibility, base actions and decisions on impersonal rules, and hire and promote employees based on skills and training.

Bureaucrat Career government employee, normally one who gains office by appointment rather than election.

Capitalism An economic system characterized by private property, competitive markets, economic incentives, and limited government involvement in the production and pricing of goods and services.

Caucus (legislative) or conference Meeting of the members of a party in a chamber of legislature to select the party leadership in that chamber and to take party positions on pending legislative issues.

Caucus (local party) Meeting of party members in a ward or town to choose party officials and/or candidates for public office and to decide platforms.

Centralists Those who favor national rather than state or local action.

Charter A city "constitution" that outlines the structure of city government, defines the authority of various officials, and provides for their selection.

Checks and balances Constitutional grant of powers that enables each of the three branches of government—legislative, executive, and judicial—to stop some of the acts of the other branches. Ensures each branch a sufficient role in the actions of the others so that no one branch may dominate. The branches must work together if governmental business is to be performed.

City-manager plan See Council-manager plan.

Civil law The legal code regulating conduct between individuals and defining their legal rights. Under civil law, governments provide the forum for the settlement of disputes between private parties in such matters as contracts and business relations. The government can also be a party to a civil action.

Class action suit Lawsuit brought by a person or group of persons on behalf of all persons similarly situated. The class may consist of a few persons or of thousands of persons. An example of a class action would be a suit by one person against an airline, alleging overcharges on behalf of that person and all others charged the same price for the same kind of flight.

Classical liberalism A political philosophy that stresses the importance of the individual and of freedom, equality, private property, limited government, and popular consent.

Clayton Act Act passed by Congress in 1914 that expanded governmental antitrust policy by outlawing specific abuses, such as charging different prices to different buyers in order to destroy a weaker competitor, granting rebates, making false statements about competitors and their products, buying up supplies to stifle competition, and bribing competitors' employees.

Clear and present danger doctrine Interpretation of the First Amendment first announced by Justice Oliver Wendell Holmes. This doctrine would not let laws that directly or indirectly restrict freedom of speech be applied unless the particular speech, article, or book in question presents a clear and present danger that it will lead to acts that the government may make illegal.

Closed primary A primary in which only persons registered in the party holding the primary may vote.

Closed rule A procedural rule in the House of Representatives that prohibits any amendments to bills or provides that only members of the committee reporting the bill may offer amendments.

Closed shop A company in which new employees and retained employees must be union members in good standing.

Cloture Procedure for terminating debate (especially filibusters) in the U.S. Senate.

Coattail effect Influence of a popular or unpopular candidate, especially a presidential candidate, on the electoral success or failure of other candidates on the same party ticket.

Collective bargaining Method whereby representatives of the union and the employer determine wages, hours, and other conditions of employment through direct negotiation.

Commerce clause The clause of the Constitution giving Congress the power to regulate all business activities that cross state lines or affect more than one state, and also prohibiting states from unduly burdening or discriminating against the business activities of other nations or states.

Commission charter Form of city government in which a group of commissioners (usually five) serves as the city council, each commissioner heading a department in the municipal administration.

Common law Body of judge-made law developed as judges decided cases; part of the English and American systems of justice.

Comparable worth The idea that jobs should be paid at the same rate if they require comparable skills and contributions. Advocated by those who believe jobs traditionally dominated by women—nurses, secretaries, and elementary school teachers, for example—are held down in wage rates compared to equivalent type jobs traditionally dominated by men—plumbers and janitors, for example—because of discrimination and role stereotyping.

Comptroller General of the United States Head of the General Accounting Office: appointed by the president with the consent of the Senate for a fifteen-year term to supervise disbursement of funds by government agencies.

Concurrent powers Powers the Constitution gives to both the national and state governments, such as the power to levy taxes.

Concurrent resolution A resolution passed in the same form by both houses of Congress that expresses the "sense" of Congress on some question. Such a resolution is not sent to the president and does not have the force of law.

Concurring opinion An opinion in which a judge explains why he or she agrees with the majority opinion but differs on the reasoning.

Confederation Government created when nation-states, by compact, create a new central government and limit its powers, especially the power to regulate the conduct of individuals directly.

Conference committee Committee appointed by the presiding officers of each house of the legislature to adjust differences on a particular bill. The report of the conference committee back to each chamber cannot be amended but must be accepted or rejected as it stands.

Congressional Budget Office (CBO) An agency of the Congress that analyzes presidential budget recommendations and estimates costs of proposed legislation.

Conglomerate Firm that owns businesses in many unrelated industries.

Connecticut Compromise Agreement by delegates to the Constitutional Convention to give each state two senators, regardless of population. This would offset the decision to allocate representatives in the House of Representatives according to population.

Conservatism Philosophical approach to the role of government that generally favors local or state governmental action over federal governmental action.

Conservative coalition A coalition in Congress of Republicans and southern Democrats who often vote together, at least in recent years, especially on social policy and welfare legislation.

Constitutional Convention The convention in Philadelphia in 1787 (May 25–September 17) that framed the Constitution of the United States. It invented the presidency, electoral college, federalism, and separation of powers—features that are still the central elements of American government. This draft had to be approved by nine states before it was ratified in 1788.

Constitutional democracy A government that enforces recognized limits on those who govern and allows the voice of the people to be heard through free and fair elections.

Constitutional home rule State constitutional authorization for local governmental units to conduct their own affairs.

Constitutionalism The set of arrangements and processes—checks and balances, federalism, separation of powers, rule of law, due process, and a bill of rights—that disperses and limits the power of government officials. Constitutionalism provides for the granting as well as restraining of powers and seeks to ensure that a government's leaders and representatives are accountable to the citizens.

Contract clause Article 1, Section 10, of the Constitution. Originally interpreted to prohibit laws that adversely affected the value of property, but now allows states to make reasonable modifications of contracts to protect public health and safety.

Continuing resolution A bill passed by Congress and agreed to by the president that allows the federal government to continue paying its bills until a new budget is approved.

Council-manager plan Form of city government in which the city council hires a professional administrator to manage city affairs. Also known as the **city-manager plan.**

Cross-cutting cleavages Divisions within society that make groups more heterogeneous or different.

Crossover voting A member of one party voting for a candidate of another party. Open primaries encourage crossover voting and may result in a situation in which nonparty members determine the party's nominee for a particular office.

Cross-pressure A pressure that pulls an individual in different directions, often related to conflicting racial, religious, ethnic, union, or other group values.

Custom Practices of nongovernmental institutions, such as political parties or the electorate, not specified in the Constitution.

Dealignment Dramatic change in the composition of the electorate or its partisan preferences that points to a rejection of both major parties and a move to Independent status.

Decentralists Those who favor state or local action rather than national action.

Debt The accumulated total of federal deficits, minus surpluses, over the years.

Defendant In a civil action, the party defending himself or herself against charges brought by the plaintiff; in a criminal action, the person charged with the offense.

Deficit The difference between the revenues raised from sources of income other than borrowing and the expenditure of government, including paying the interest on past borrowing.

Delegate A view of the role of a member of a legislature which holds that, as delegates, legislators should represent the views of constituents even when personally holding different views.

Demagogue Leader who gains power by means of impassioned appeals to the prejudices and emotions of the masses.

Democracy Government by the people, either directly or indirectly, with free and frequent elections.

Demographics The study of the characteristics of populations.

Deregulation Efforts to reduce or eliminate governmental controls, rules, or regulation of economic activity.

Direct democracy A government in which citizens come together to discuss and pass laws and select rulers. May also refer to the initiative, referendum, and recall.

Direct primary Election open to all members of the party in which voters choose the persons who will be the party's nominees in the general election.

Discharge petition Petition that, if signed by a majority of the members of the House of Representatives, will pry a bill from committee and bring it to the floor for consideration.

Dissenting opinion An opinion in which a judge explains why he or she disagrees with the decision of the majority.

Divided government Governance divided between the parties, as when one controls the White House and the other Congress.

Double jeopardy Trial or punishment for the *same* crime by the *same* government. Such a practice is forbidden by the Constitution.

Due process Established rules and regulations that restrain those who exercise governmental power.

Due process clauses Clauses in the Fifth and Fourteenth Amendments that state that the national (Fifth) and the state (Fourteenth) governments shall not deprive any person of life, liberty, or property without due process of law.

Electoral College The gathering in each state of electors from that state who formally cast their ballots for their parties' candidates for president and vice-president. The electoral college is largely a formality.

Eminent domain Power of governments to take private property for public use. The Constitution requires governments to provide just compensation for property so taken.

Entitlements or entitlement programs Programs such as Social Security, Aid to Families with Dependent Children, Medicare, and unemployment insurance to which qualified citizens are "entitled" by definitions in national legislation.

Environmental impact statement A statement required by federal law from all agencies for any project using federal funds that assesses the potential effect of the proposed project on the environment. Many states also require these statements.

Equal protection clause Clause in the Fourteenth Amendment that forbids any state to deny to any person within its jurisdiction the equal protection of the laws. By interpretation, the Fifth Amendment imposes the same limitation on the national government. This is the major constitutional restraint on the power of governments to discriminate against persons because of race, national origin, or sex.

Equal-time requirement Requirement of Congress and Federal Communications Commission that radio and television licensees must give opposing candidates for public office equal air time.

Establishment clause Clause in the First Amendment that states that Congress shall make no law respecting an establishment of religion. By interpretation, the Fourteenth Amendment imposes the same limitation on state legislatures. It has been interpreted by the Supreme Court to forbid governmental support to any or all religions.

Ethnicity Identification with a group based upon national origin, religion, language, and often race.

Ethnocentrism A selective perception based on individual background, attitudes, and biases that leads one to believe in the superiority of one's nation or ethnic group.

Excise tax Consumer tax on a specific kind of merchandise, such as tobacco.

Exclusionary rule Rule that evidence unconstitutionally obtained cannot be used in a criminal trial as part of the government's main case against persons from whom it was seized.

Executive agreement International agreement made by a president that has the force of a treaty. It does not need the approval of the Senate.

Executive Office of the President Cluster of staff agencies created by the Reorganization Act of 1939 to help the president. Currently the Executive Office includes an Office of Management and Budget, the Council of Economic Advisers, the National Security Council, and a number of specialized offices.

Executive orders Power of presidents or governors to issue orders that have the force of law.

Executive privilege The claim by presidents that they have the discretion to decide that the national interest will be better served if certain information is withheld from the public, including the courts and Congress. In *United States v Nixon* the Supreme Court ruled that even though presidents are entitled to the privilege, the privilege is not unlimited, and its extent is subject to judicial determination.

Ex post facto law Retroactive criminal law that works to the disadvantage of an individual.

Express powers Powers specifically granted to one of the branches of the national government by the Constitution.

Extradition Legal process whereby an alleged criminal offender is surrendered by the officials of one state to officials of the state in which the crime is alleged to have been committed.

Faction What we call "interest groups" today, James Madison called factions. He also thought of political parties as factions.

Fairness doctrine Doctrine interpreted by the Federal Communications Commission that imposed on radio and television licensees an obligation to ensure that differing viewpoints were presented about controversial issues or persons. Repealed by the FCC in 1987.

Federal mandate A requirement imposed by the federal government as a condition of receipt of federal funds.

Federal Reserve System The private-public banking regulatory system created by Congress in 1913 to establish banking practices and regulate currency in circulation and the amount of credit available. It is comprised of 12 regional banks, and its major responsibilities are supervised by a seven-member presidentially appointed Federal Reserve Board of Governors in Washington, D.C.

Federalism Constitutional arrangement whereby power is divided by a constitution between a national government and constituent governments, called states in the United States. The national and the constituent governments both exercise direct authority over individuals.

The Federalist Series of essays favoring the new Constitution, written by Alexander Hamilton, John Jay, and James Madison in 1787 and 1788, during the debate over ratification.

Federalists Persons who supported the Constitution before its ratification in 1787 to 1788. After ratification, a Federalist party developed under the leadership of Alexander Hamilton, George Washington's first secretary of the treasury. Federalists like John Adams and John Marshall generally favored a strong central government and a fiscal policy of assuming state debts and establishing a national bank.

Fee for service System of health care payment in the United States whereby patients choose their own physicians, whose bills are then covered by insurance companies.

Fighting words Words that by their very nature inflict injury upon those to whom they are addressed or cause acts of violence by them.

Filibuster Holding the floor of the U.S. Senate to delay proceedings and thereby prevent a vote on a controversial issue.

Fiscal policy Government policy that attempts to manage the economy by controlling taxing and spending.

Floating debt Short-term borrowing, often by states, to ensure that operating expenses can be met; often consists of bank loans, tax-anticipation warrants, and other notes, all of which are paid for out of current revenues.

Four Freedoms American goals proclaimed by Franklin D. Roosevelt in his message to Congress, January 6, 1941: freedom of speech, freedom of religion, freedom from want, and freedom from fear.

Franchise The right to vote.

Free exercise clause Clause in the First Amendment that states that Congress shall make no law prohibiting the free exercise of religion; extended by the Fourteenth Amendment as a limit on the states.

Free rider An individual who does not join an interest group representing his or her interests, yet receives the benefit of the influence the group achieves.

Full faith and credit clause Clause in the Constitution requiring each state to recognize the civil judgments rendered by the courts of the other states and to accept their public records and acts as valid documents.

Fundamental right Right explicitly or implicitly guaranteed by the U. S. Constitution.

Gender gap The difference between the political opinions or political behavior of men and women.

General Accounting Office (GOA) An independent investigative arm of Congress established in 1921 to check on receipt and disbursement of public funds and review the performance of government agencies.

General Agreement on Tariffs and Taxes (GATT) An international trade organization of over 100 countries, including the United States, to encourage free trade among members by lowering tariffs and other types of trade restrictions.

General property tax Tax levied by local (and some state) governments on real or personal, tangible property, the major portion of which is on the estimated value of one's home and land.

Gerrymandering Drawing an election district in such a way that one party or group has a distinct advantage. The strategy is to provide a close but safe margin in numerous districts while concentrating (and hence wasting) the opposition's vote in a few districts.

Government corporation Cross between a business corporation and a government agency, created to secure greater freedom of action and flexibility for a particular program.

Grand jury A jury comprising 12 to 23 persons who, in private, hear evidence presented by the government to determine whether persons shall be required to stand trial. If the jury believes there is sufficient evidence that a crime was committed, it issues an indictment.

Gross domestic product (GDP) An estimate of the total output of all economic activity in the nation, including goods and services.

Gross national product (GNP) The monetary values of all goods and services in the nation in a given year.

Habeas corpus See Writ of habeas corpus.

Hatch Act Federal statute barring federal employees from active participation in certain kinds of politics and protecting them from being fired on partisan grounds.

Honeymoon A period at the beginning of a new president's term in which the president enjoys generally positive relations with the press and Congress, usually lasting about six months.

Ideology One's basic beliefs about power, political values, and the role of government—beliefs that arise out of educational, economic, and social conditions and experiences.

Impeachment Formal accusation against a public official and the first step in removal from office.

Implied powers Powers given to Congress by the Constitution that allow Congress to do whatever is necessary and proper in order to carry out one of the express powers or any combination of them.

Impoundment Presidential refusal to allow an agency to spend funds authorized and appropriated by Congress.

Independent agency A government agency that is not part of the legislative, executive, or judicial branch. The term also describes a nonregulatory agency that is not part of a cabinet department. Members of regulatory agencies are appointed by the president, confirmed by the Senate, and removable only for some specific "cause." Also called an **independent regulatory agency.**

Independent expenditures Money spent for or against a candidate, usually by an interest group, that is not connected to the campaign of the candidate or his or her opponent.

Industrial policy Government policy that targets specific industries that might be competitive with foreign firms and helps them with tax breaks and financial incentives.

Information affidavit Certification by a public prosecutor that there is evidence to justify bringing named individuals to trial.

Inherent powers Those powers of the national government in the field of foreign affairs that the Supreme Court has declared do not depend upon constitutional grants but rather grow out of the very existence of the national government.

Initiative Procedure whereby a certain number of voters may, by petition, propose a law or constitutional amendment and get it submitted to the people for a vote. Initiatives may be direct (if the proposed law is voted on directly by the people) or indirect (if the proposal is submitted first to the legislature and then to the people, if the legislature rejects it).

Interest group A collection of people who share some common interest or attitude and seek to influence government for specific ends. Interest groups usually work within the framework of government and employ tactics such as lobbying to achieve their goals.

Interested money Financial contributions made by persons or groups in the hopes of influencing the outcome of an election and subsequently influencing policy.

Interlocking directorates Corporations in which an officer or director sits on the board of a competitor

Interstate compacts Agreements among the states. The Constitution requires that most such agreements be approved by Congress.

Iron triangle A mutually supporting relationship among interest groups, congressional committees or subcommittees, and government agencies that share a common policy concern. Also called **Issue network**.

Item veto Authority of the president or the governor of a state to veto specific parts of a legislative bill without having to veto the entire bill. Also known as the **line-item veto.**

Jim Crow laws Laws that required public facilities and places of public accommodation, including those privately owned and operated, to be segregated by race.

Joint committee Committee composed of members of both houses of a legislature. Such committees are intended to speed up legislative action. Some oversee institutions such as the Library of Congress or conduct congressional investigations.

Judicial activism Philosophy proposing that judges cannot decide cases strictly by applying the literal words of the Constitution or by discerning the intention of the framers, but that they could and should openly recognize that judicial decision making is choosing among conflicting values. Judges should so interpret the Constitution as to keep it reflecting the current values of the American people.

Judicial interpretation A method whereby judges can modify a constitutional provision's restrictive force by a narrow interpretation of its meaning.

Judicial restraint Philosophy proposing that, in deciding cases, judges should declare unconstitutional only those legislative actions and executive actions that clearly violate the words of the Constitution or the intent of the framers and that constitutional changes should be left to the formal amendatory process.

Judicial review The power of a court to refuse to enforce a law or government regulation that in the opinion of the judges conflicts with the Constitution. This authority was spelled out by Chief Justice John Marshall in *Marbury v Madison* (1803).

Jurisdictional strike Strike arising from disputes between unions over whose members should perform a particular task.

Justiciable dispute A dispute that grows out of an actual case and is capable of settlement by legal methods. Those constitutional disputes that are political are not justiciable.

Keynesian economics Economic theories based on the principles advocated by John Maynard Keynes: increasing government spending during business slumps and curbing spending during booms.

Labor injunction Court order forbidding specific individuals or groups from performing certain acts, such as striking, that the court considers harmful to the rights and property of an employer or community.

Laissez faire Doctrine opposing governmental interference in economic affairs beyond what is necessary to protect life and property.

Lame duck A politician in office who cannot, or has announced that he or she will not, run again.

Libel Written defamation of another person. Especially in the case of public officials and public figures, the constitutional tests designed to restrict libel actions are very rigid.

Liberalism Philosophical approach to the role of government that generally favors the positive uses of government to bring about justice and equality of opportunity.

Libertarianism Philosophical approach to the role of government that cherishes individual liberty and favors as limited a government as possible. Libertarians believe in free-market economics and a noninterventionist foreign policy.

Literacy test Requirement imposed by some states that prospective voters must prove they understand national and state laws. Now illegal, such tests were used too disqualify blacks from voting in the South.

Lobby/lobbying Activities aimed at influencing public officials, especially legislators, and the policies they enact. This is, of course, part of the citizen's right to petition the government.

Lobbyist Person who is employed by and acts for an organized interest group or corporation to try to influence policy decisions and positions in the executive and legislative branches.

Log rolling Mutual aid and vote trading among legislators.

Lotteries State-sponsored and state-administered gambling used to raise money for public purposes.

Majority leader Legislative position held by an important party member selected by the majority party in caucus or conference. The majority leader helps frame party strategy and tries to keep the membership in line. In the U.S. Senate the majority leader (in consultation with the minority leader) determines the agenda and has strong influence in committee selection.

Majority-minority district A congressional district created to include a substantial number of minority voters. The Supreme Court has ruled that race may be taken into account in drawing district lines, but it must not be the only factor.

Manifest destiny A notion held by many nineteenth-century Americans that the United States was destined to rule the continent, from the Atlantic to the Pacific oceans.

Mass media Means of communication that reach the mass public. The mass media include newspapers and magazines, radio and television (cable and satellite), and films, recordings, and books.

Mayor-council charter The oldest and most common form of city government, consisting of either a weak mayor and city council or a strong mayor and council.

Medicaid Federal program that provides medical benefits for low-income persons.

Medicare National health insurance program for the elderly and disabled.

Melting pot A term used to describe how persons of different nationalities or races are blended or assimilated into American society.

Merit system A system of public employment in which selection and promotion depend on demonstrated performance rather than on political patronage.

Minor party Small political party, more persistent than a third party, and generally composed of ideologues on the right or left.

Minority leader Party leader in each house of a legislature, elected by the minority party as spokesperson for the opposition.

Missouri Plan System for selecting judges that combines features of the appointive and elective methods. The governor makes an initial appointment from a list of persons—usually three—presented by a panel of lawyers and laypersons (the panel is usually appointed by the chief judge of the state court of last resort). After the judge has served for a year, the electorate is asked at the next general election whether or not the judge should be retained in office. If a majority vote yes, the judge serves the rest of the term. At the end of the term, if a judge wishes to serve again, his or her name is once again presented to the electorate.

Monetarism A theory that government should control the money supply to encourage economic growth and restrain inflation.

Monetary policy Government policy that attempts to manage the economy by controlling the money supply.

Monopoly Domination of an industry by one company.

Most-favored nation Trade policy whereby countries give each other the same favorable treatment given to other trade partners.

Movement A large body of people united around a central idea whose goal is to change attitudes or institutions, not only policies.

Movements tend to feel "left out" of government and may sometimes resort to extreme measures to advance their cause.

National Labor Relations Act (1935) Guarantees workers the right to organize and bargain collectively with management. Also known as the **Wagner Act**.

National party convention The national meeting of delegates elected in primaries, caucuses, or state conventions who assemble once every four years for the purpose of nominating candidates for president and vice-president, ratifying the party platform, electing officers, and adopting rules.

National Security Council Planning and advisory board that confers with the president on matters relating to national security. Permanent members include the president, vice-president, secretary of state, secretary of defense, and the chair of the joint chiefs of staff.

National supremacy Constitutional doctrine that whenever conflict occurs between the constitutionally authorized actions of the national government and those of a state or local government, the actions of the national government take priority.

Nationalism A consciousness of the nation-state and of belonging to that entity.

Natural law God or nature's law that defines right from wrong and is higher than human law.

Natural rights Rights of all citizens to dignity and worth; also called **human rights**.

Naturalization Process by which persons acquire citizenship in a country other than the nation of their birth.

Necessary and proper clause Clause of the Constitution setting forth the implied powers of Congress. It states that Congress, in addition to its express powers, has the power to make all laws necessary and proper for carrying out all powers vested by the Constitution in the national government.

Neoconservative A political ideology that accepts some of the welfare state but believes affirmative action has gone too far. Neoconservatives also support military spending to ensure that the United States can defend its global interests.

Neoliberal A political ideology that is distrustful of large bureaucracies and traditional welfare strategies. Neoliberals believe in relying on the marketplace and favor middle-of-the-road tax and defense policies.

New Jersey Plan Plan presented by William Paterson of New Jersey at the Constitutional Convention as a counterproposal to the Virginia Plan. The New Jersey Plan proposed only modifications in the Articles of Confederation and provided for a confederation built around powerful state governments.

New judicial federalism The practice of some state courts of using the bill of rights in their state constitutions to provide more protection for some rights than is provided by Supreme Court interpretation of the Bill of Rights in the Constitution.

North American Free Trade Agreement (NAFTA) Agreement signed by the United

States, Canada, and Mexico in 1992 to form the largest free-trade zone in the world.

Obscenity Quality or state of a work that taken as a whole appeals to a prurient interest in sex by depicting sexual conduct as specifically defined by legislation or judicial interpretation in a patently offensive way and that lacks serious literary, artistic, political, or scientific value.

Office block ballot Method of voting in which all candidates are listed under the office for which they are running. Sometimes called the **Massachusetts ballot**.

Office of Management and Budget (OMB) Presidential staff agency that serves as a clearinghouse for budgetary requests and management improvements. It advises the president in detail about hundreds of government agencies—how much money they should be allotted in the budget and what kind of job they are doing—and it seeks to improve the planning, management, and statistical work of the agencies.

Oligopoly Situation in which a few firms dominate an industry.

Open primary A primary in which any voter, regardless of party, can vote.

Open rule A procedural rule in the House of Representatives that permits floor amendments within the overall time allocated to the bill.

Open shop Labor arrangement in which union membership cannot be required as a condition of employment.

Original jurisdiction The authority of a trial court to hear a case "in the first instance."

Override An action by Congress to try to reverse a presidential veto of legislation by a two-thirds vote in both chambers.

Oversight hearings Congressional committee reviews of how well government agencies are implementing legislation and managing their budgets.

Party column ballot Method of voting in which all candidates are listed under their party designations, making it easy for the voters to cast votes for all the candidates of one party. Sometimes called the **Indiana ballot**.

Party convention A meeting of party delegates to pass on matters of policy and in some cases to select party candidates for public office. Conventions are held on county, state, and national levels.

Party identification Subjective affiliation with a political party, usually acquired in childhood.

Party platform The official statement of party policy.

Party registration The act of declaring party affiliation, in some states required when one registers to vote.

Patronage Dispensing government jobs to persons who belong to the winning political party. Also called **spoils system**.

Petit jury The jury for the trial of a civil or criminal action.

Plea bargaining Negotiations between prosecutor and defendant aimed at getting the defendant to plead guilty in return for the prosecutor's agreeing to reduce the seriousness of the crime for which the defendant will be convicted.

Pocket veto Special veto power exercised by a chief executive after a legislative body has adjourned. Bills that a chief executive does not sign within ten days of adjournment do not become law and are not returned to the chamber of origin for a possible override. In effect, by such an action, a governor or president "puts the bill in his or her pocket," and the bill thus dies.

Police powers Powers of a government to regulate persons and property in order to promote the public health, welfare, safety, and morals. In the United States, the states, but not the national government, have such general police power.

Political action committee (PAC) The political arm of a business, labor, trade association, or other interest group that is legally entitled to raise money on a voluntary basis from members, stockholders, or employees in order to contribute to favored candidates or political parties.

Political culture The widely shared political beliefs, values, and norms concerning the relationship of citizens to government and to one another.

Political question A dispute that requires knowledge of a nonlegal character or the use of techniques not suitable for a court or that are explicitly addressed by the Constitution to Congress or the president. Judges refuse to answer constitutional questions that they declare are political.

Political party An organization that seeks political power by electing people to office so that its positions and philosophy become public policy.

Political socialization The process by which we develop our political attitudes, values, and beliefs.

Poll tax Payment by a person, formerly required in some states, as a condition for voting.

Popular consent The idea that a just government must derive its powers from the consent of the people.

Populists Adherents of a movement and political party of the 1880s and 1890s. Their geographical base was rural—in the Midwest, South, and Southwest especially. Waging "reformist" efforts against the banks, railroads, and other establishments, populists raised issues that influenced the Progressive movement and the Democratic party after 1892.

Pork-barrel Government benefits or programs that help the economy of a member's district—as in "bringing home the bacon."

Preemption The right of a federal law or regulation to preclude enforcement of a state or local law or regulation.

Preferred position doctrine Interpretation of the First Amendment that holds that no law restricting expression is constitutional unless the government can demonstrate convincingly to a court that the law is absolutely necessary to prevent serious injury to the public well-being.

President pro tempore Officer of the U.S. Senate chosen from the ranks—often a junior member of the majority party—who serves as president of the Senate in the absence of the vice-president.

Prior restraint Restraint imposed prior to a speech's being made, a newspaper's being published, or a motion picture's being shown. The restraint may be of various kinds—for example, a requirement that a license be granted or that the approval of a censorship board be given.

Privatization The contracting out to the "for profit" private sector of services that are typically provided by public organizations. Trash collection, ambulance, and fire protection services have been the most common privatizations of public services. The objectives are to obtain the public services at lower costs, and sometimes to shrink the public bureaucracy to encourage additional efficiencies.

Pro bono Term used to refer to the work lawyers (or other professionals) do to serve the public good and for which they either receive no fees or decline fees.

Procedural due process Constitutional requirement that governments proceed by proper methods.

Progressive income tax A tax whereby upper-income citizens pay a larger fraction of their income in taxes than do lower-income citizens; also called a graduated income tax.

Progressives Adherents of a "good government" movement in the first two decades of this century, who advocated measures that would open up the system and weaken party bosses. They favored nonpartisan elections, participatory primaries, and direct elections of senators.

Property rights The rights of an individual to own, use, rent, invest in, buy, and sell property.

Property tax rate Usually a tax per $1,000 of assessed valuation or some other such measure of the value of property.

Proportional representation An election system in which each party running receives the proportion of legislative seats corresponding to its proportion of the vote.

Protectionism The erecting of tariff barriers to protect domestic industry.

Public defender Public official whose job is to provide legal assistance to those persons accused of crimes who are unable to hire their own attorneys.

Public goods Services or commodities that individuals benefit from but that cannot be separately sold or given to individuals. Examples are clean air, national defense, and public safety.

Public opinion Cluster of views and attitudes held by people on a significant issue.

Public policy The substance of what government does. More generally, public policy reflects the intentions of a government and the subsequent actions to implement laws and other decisions of governmental bodies.

Quasi-legislative and quasi-judicial Phrase coined by the Supreme Court to permit non-court and nonlegislative bodies to decide disputes and make rules. Decisions must, however, be subject to court review, and rules must be within the general guidelines established by the legislature.

Race A grouping of human beings with common characteristics presumed to be transmitted genetically. In the United States, race issues focus on African Americans, Asian Americans, and sometimes Hispanics, although, technically, Hispanics can be of any race.

Racial gerrymandering The drawing of election districts so as to ensure that members of a certain race are a minority in all districts.

Random sampling In public opinion polls creating a representative sample through random selection—for example, by shuffling housing tracts and interviewing individuals in every fifth, tenth, or fifteenth house.

Realignment A dramatic change in the composition of the electorate or its partisan preferences, or both.

Recall Election in certain states or communities to determine whether an official should be removed from office before the end of his or her term. A certain number of voters, typically 25 percent of those who voted in the last election, must petition to hold a recall election.

Recidivist One who habitually relapses into crime.

Reconciliation Process by which Congress sets ceilings on what subcommittees can appropriate.

Redistributive policy Governmental policy that seeks to use tax revenues in such a way as to help those who have less. In effect, tax monies from the upper and middle classes are channeled into programs that assist lower income or truly needy people by redistributing some of society's wealth.

Redistricting The redrawing of congressional and other legislative district lines following the census. Also called **reapportionment**.

Reduction veto The power of a governor in a few states to reduce a particular money measure approved by the state legislature.

Referendum Practice of submitting to popular vote measures passed by the legislature or proposed by initiative. Use of the referendum may be required or optional.

Regressive tax A tax whereby lower-income citizens pay a higher fraction of their income in taxes than do higher-income citizens. In other words, a regressive tax is one that weighs most heavily on those least able to pay.

Regulation Governmental order having the force of law and designed to control or govern the behavior of a business, union, or similar organizations and individuals. Governmental regulation seeks to alter the natural workings of the open market to achieve some desired goal.

Regulatory agency, board, or commission Government agency responsible for enforcing particular statutes. Generally such an agency has quasi-legislative and quasi-judicial functions as well as executive powers.

Regulatory taking Government regulation of property so extensive that government is deemed to have taken the property and thus exercised the power of eminent domain, for which it must compensate the property owners.

Reinforcing cleavages Divisions within society that reinforce one another, making groups more homogeneous or similar.

Republic Form of government that derives its powers directly or indirectly from the people. Those chosen to govern are accountable, directly or indirectly, to those whom they govern. In contrast to a direct democracy, in which the people make rules directly, in a republic the people select representatives who make the rules. Also called **representative democracy**.

Restrictive covenant A restriction in a deed limiting to whom property may be sold and how it may be used.

Revenue sharing Program whereby federal funds are provided to state and local governments to be spent largely at the discretion of the receiving governments, subject to few and very general conditions.

Revision commission State commission that recommends changes in the state constitution. The recommendations have no force until acted upon by the state legislature and approved by the voters.

Revolving door The employment cycle in which individuals work, in turn, for governmental agencies regulating interests and then for businesses representing those interests.

Rider A provision that might not have much chance to pass on its own merits but is attached to another bill, often unrelated, to secure its legislative passage. Often bills that have little to do with spending money are attached as riders to appropriations bills, because appropriations bills are rarely defeated or vetoed.

Right of expatriation Right of an individual to choose his or her own nationality.

Right-to-work law Provision in state laws that prohibits arrangements between a union and an employer requiring membership in a union as a condition for getting or keeping a job.

Safe seat Electoral office, usually in legislature, for which the party or the incumbent is so strong that reelection is almost taken for granted.

Sales tax General tax on sales transactions, sometimes exempting food and drugs.

Search warrant A warrant that authorizes the police to search a particular place or person. A search warrant must specify the place to be searched and the objects to be seized in order to protect people from unreasonable government intrusion.

Secondary boycott Efforts by a union involved in a dispute with an employer to place pressure on a third party, who—in response to such pressure—might put pressure on the original offending employer. Such boycotts are forbidden by the 1947 Taft-Hartley Act.

Sedition Attempting to overthrow the government by force or to interrupt its activities by violence.

Select or special committee A congressional committee created for a specific purpose, sometimes to conduct an investigation.

Selective exposure Individuals screening out messages that do not conform to their own biases.

Selective incorporation The doctrine that some, but not all, provisions of the Bill of Rights should be included within the Fourteenth Amendment as a limitation on state and local governments.

Selective perception Individuals perceiving what they want to in media messages and disregarding the rest.

Senatorial courtesy Presidential custom of submitting the names of prospective appointees for approval to senators from the states in which the appointees reside.

Seniority rule A practice in legislatures that assigns the chair of a committee or subcommittee to the member of the majority party who has had the longest continuous service on the committee.

Separation of powers Constitutional division of power among legislative, executive, and judicial branches. The legislative branch is assigned the power to make laws; the executive is charged with the power to apply the laws; and the judiciary receives the power to interpret laws.

Severance tax Tax on the privilege of "severing" natural resources such as coal, oil, and timber, charged to the companies doing the extracting or severing.

Shays' Rebellion Rural rebellion in 1786–87 protesting mortgage foreclosures in western Massachusetts. Led by Daniel Shays, it promoted conservative support for a stronger national government.

Sherman Antitrust Act Act passed by Congress in 1890 that attempted to foster competition and stop the growth of private monopolies by making it unlawful to form a combination that acted to restrain trade.

Shield law Law establishing a legal right for reporters and other representatives of the media to refuse, under certain circumstances, to respond to orders of legislative committees or court subpoenas to reveal sources of information.

Single-member district An electoral rule in which an election determines one representative or official in an electoral district.

Socialism Philosophical approach to the role of government that favors national planning and public ownership of the means of production and exchange.

Social Security A combination of entitlement programs paid for by employer and employee taxes. Includes retirement benefits, health insurance, and support for disabled workers and children of deceased or disabled workers.

Social stratification The division of a community among socioeconomic groups.

Socioeconomic status (SES) A measure of one's standing that combines in one index such factors as education, income, and occupation.

Soft money Money contributed to a state or local political party for nonfederal uses, such as voter registration drives and party mailings, that does not have to be reported under the Federal Election Campaign Act and is often not reported because of tax disclosure laws at that level.

Speaker The presiding officer in the House of Representatives, formally elected by the House but actually selected by the majority party. The Speaker's powers include referring legislation to committees, making appointments to the House Rules Committee, recognizing members who wish to speak, ruling on questions of parliamentary procedure, and appointing special conference committees. There is a similar office in state legislatures.

Split ticket Voting for some of one party's candidates and some candidates from other political parties.

Spoils system Rewarding those who support victorious candidates with profitable contracts or jobs in government; in the nineteenth century often an important incentive for political participation.

Standing committee Permanent legislative committees to which legislation is referred for study; they then report bills and resolutions to their parent chamber.

Stare decisis The rule of precedent, whereby a rule or law contained in a judicial decision is commonly viewed as binding on judges whenever the same question is presented.

State delegation The senators and representatives from the same state, who often help each other secure choice committee assignments, work to promote each other in leadership positions, and watch out for state interests.

Statism Belief in the rights of the state over those of the individual—the opposite of the American tradition that the individual is exalted above the state.

Straight ticket Voting for all of one party's candidates.

Strong mayor-council Form of local government in which the public directly elects the mayor as well as the city council. However, the mayor appoints the department heads with the approval of the council, and in effect serves as the chief executive officer for the city and its administration.

Substantive due process Constitutional requirement that governments act reasonably and that the substance of the laws themselves be fair and reasonable.

Sunset process Process that calls for the termination of a program after a certain number of years, often six or seven, unless it is certified to be doing what it was intended to do. The word comes from the expression that "the sun should set" on programs that have outlived their usefulness.

Supply-side economics Economic strategy of stimulating investment in businesses through tax cuts and reduced governmental regulation that would result in increased employment and eventually increased income tax revenue.

Suspect class Racial or national origin classifications created by law and subject to careful judicial scrutiny. Suspect classifications are likely to be declared unconstitutional unless they can be justified by overwhelmingly desirable state purposes that can be achieved in no other way.

Taft-Hartley Act Act passed by Congress in 1947 that elaborates the terms of labor-management bargaining, the conditions under which strikes can occur, and related aspects of union organization. It worked to restrict some union activities.

Tariff Tax levied on imports to help protect a nation's industries, labor, or farmers from foreign competition. It can also be used merely to raise additional revenue.

Tax expenditure Loss of tax revenue due to provisions of the federal tax laws that allow special exclusions, exemptions, or deductions, or that provide special credit, preferential rates of tax, or deferrals of tax liability.

Third party Temporary political parties that often arise during presidential elections.

Third-party payer System of health care payment in the United States whereby medical bills are paid by an insurance company, or "third party."

Three-fifths compromise North-South agreement at the Constitutional Convention of 1787 to count only three-fifths of the slave population in determining direct taxation and apportionment in the House of Representatives.

Tort law Law, primarily judge made, dealing with damages to compensate people through a civil trial, for legal wrongs done to them, including injuries to person, reputation, or property.

Trade deficit International trading in which the value of imports exceeds the value of exports.

Treason Carefully defined by the Constitution to consist only of levying war against the United States, adhering to its enemies, or giving the latter aid and comfort. No person can be convicted of treason unless the accused confesses in open court or unless two witnesses testify in court that they saw the acts of treason being committed.

Trustee A view of the function of a member of a legislature which holds that legislators may believe that they were sent to Washington or the state capitals to think and vote independently for the general welfare, and not as their constituents determine.

Trusts Monopolies that control goods and services, often in combinations that reduce competition.

Turnout The proportion of the voting-age public that votes.

Two-party system Electoral system in which two major political parties dominate.

Unicameralism, unicameral legislature One-house legislature. Nebraska and almost all cities use this form.

Union shop A company in which new employees must join the union within a stated period of time.

Unit rule Requirement that the whole delegation to a party convention cast its vote as the majority decides.

Unitary system or unitary government Government with power concentrated by the constitution in a central government; also an election system in which voters elect legislators who, in turn, elect the prime minister or head of state.

Usage Long-standing practices of Congress, the president, and the courts not specified in the Constitution.

User charges Fees charged directly to individuals who use certain public services on the basis of service consumed. Sometimes called a **user fee** or **user tax**.

Value-added tax (VAT) A tax on the increased value of a product at each stage of production and distribution rather than just at the point of sale, as with a sales tax.

Veto Rejection of proposed legislation by a president or governor.

Veto session A short session of a state legislature called by the governor to consider vetoed bills.

Virginia Plan Proposal made at the Constitutional Convention by the Virginia delegation that provided for a strong legislature with representation in each house determined by wealth or population. It thus favored the large states.

Voter registration A system designed to reduce voter fraud such as multiple voting and to limit voting to those who have established eligibility by submitting the appropriate form.

Weak mayor–council Form of local government in which the mayor must share most of the executive powers of a city with other elected or appointed boards and commissions. The mayor in weak-mayor cities is often mainly a ceremonial leader.

Whip Party leader who is the liaison between the leadership and the rank-and-file in the legislature.

White primary Under the pretense that it was not governmental action, officials of the Democratic party in the South used to admit only white persons to its primaries. Candidates of the Democratic party were the only ones with any chance of winning in the following general election; blacks were thus excluded from the only election that counted. The white primary in all its various forms was declared unconstitutional by the Supreme Court in *Smith v Allwright* (1944).

Winner-take-all An electoral system in which the candidate with the most votes wins. In American presidential elections, the winner of the popular vote in a state receives all the electoral votes of that state.

Women's suffrage The right of women to vote; denied in federal elections in the United States before passage of the Nineteenth Amendment in 1920.

Writ of certiorari Writ used by the Supreme Court to review decisions of lower courts, federal and state, that are within the discretionary appellate jurisdiction of the Supreme Court. It is a formal device regularly used to bring a case up to the Court.

Writ of habeas corpus Court order requiring explanation to a judge why a prisoner is held in custody.

Writ of mandamus Court order directing an official to perform a nondiscretionary act as required by law.

Yellow-dog contract Contract by an anti-union employer that forces prospective workers to promise they will not join a union after employment.

Notes

CHAPTER 1

1. Robert D. Putnam, *Making Democracy Work: Civic Traditions in Modern Italy* (Princeton University Press, 1993), p. 4.
2. Russell J. Dalton, *Citizen Politics: Public Opinion and Political Parties in Advanced Industrial Democracies*, 2nd ed. (Chatham House, 1996).
3. Herbert Hoover, *American Individualism* (Doubleday, 1922), p.9. See also Michael Sandel, *Democracy's Discontent: America in Search of a Public Philosophy* (Belknap Press of Harvard University Press, 1996).
4. For a major theoretical work on the principle of majority rule, see Robert A. Dahl, *Democracy and Its Critics* (Yale University Press, 1989).
5. James Madison, *The Federalist*, No. 51.
6. Seymor Martin Lipset, "The Social Requisites of Democracy Revisited," *American Sociological Review* 59 (1994), pp. 1–22.
7. For a discussion of the importance for democracy of such overlapping group memberships, see David Truman's seminal work, *The Governmental Process*, 2d ed. (Knopf, 1971).
8. Harry Eckstein, *Lessons for the "Third Wave" from the First* (Center for the Study of Democracy, University of California, Irvine, 1996), p. 20.
9. Robert A. Dahl, *A Preface to Democratic Theory* (University of Chicago Press, 1956), p. 132.
10. Joyce Appleby, "The American Heritage: The Heirs and the Disinherited," *Journal of American History* (December 1987), p. 808.
11. Maryland and Massachusetts documents quoted in Bernard Schwartz, *Roots of the Bill of Rights* (Chelsea House, 1980), 1:68–73.
12. Richard L. Hillard, "Liberalism, Civic Humanism and the American Revolutionary Bills of Rights, 1775–1790," paper presented at the annual meeting of the Organization of American Historians, Reno, Nevada, 1988.
13. Lance Banning, *The Sacred Fire of Liberty: James Madison and the Founding of the Federal Republic* (Cornell University Press, 1995).
14. See the essays in Thomas E. Cronin, ed., *Inventing the American Presidency* (University Press of Kansas, 1989).
15. Charles A. Beard and Mary R. Beard, *A Basic History of the United States* (New Home Library, 1944), p. 136.
16. See Herbert J. Storing, ed., abridgment by Murray Dry, *The Anti-Federalist: Writings by the Opponents of the Constitution* (University of Chicago Press, 1985).
17. Mercy Warren, quoted in Pauline Maier, *The Old Revolutionaries* (Knopf, 1980), p. 284.
18. On the role of the promised bill of rights amendments in the ratification of the Constitution, see Leonard W. Levy, *Constitutional Opinions* (Oxford University Press, 1986), chap. 6.

CHAPTER 2

1. Herbert Storing, "The Constitution and the Bill of Rights," in *Essays on the Constitution of the United States*, ed. M. Judd Harmon (Kennikat Press, 1978), pp. 36–37, points out that many antifederalists remained unsatisfied with the Bill of Rights.
2. Max Lerner, *Ideas for the Ice Age* (Viking, 1991), pp. 241–42. See also *The American Public's Knowledge of the U.S. Constitution: A National Survey of Public Awareness and Personal Opinion* (Hearst Corporation, 1987).
3. Sanford Levinson, *Constitutional Faith* (Princeton University Press, 1988), pp. 9–52.
4. Thomas Jefferson, quoted in Alpheus T. Mason, *The Supreme Court: Palladium of Freedom* (University of Michigan Press, 1962), p. 10.
5. Richard E. Neustadt, *Presidential Power* (Free Press, 1990), p. 29.
6. Robert C. Vipond, *Liberty and Community: Canadian Federalism and the Failure of the Constitution* (State University of New York Press, 1991), p. 192.
7. Edward S. Corwin, "The Constitution as Instrument and as Symbol," *American Political Science Review* (December 1936), p. 1078. J. M. Sosin argues that these earlier precedents do not support the opinion that judicial review was "in the air," in *The Aristocracy of the Long Robe: The Origins of Judicial Review in America* (Greenwood Press, 1989).
8. 1 Cranch 137 (1803).
9. Dumas Malone, *Jefferson the President: First Term, 1801–1805* (Little, Brown, 1970), p. 145.
10. *Dred Scott v Sandford*, 19 Howard 393 (1857).
11. Robert Lowry Clinton, *Marbury v. Madison and Judicial Review* (University Press of Kansas, 1989), pp. 4–42.
12. J. W. Peltason, *Federal Courts in the Political Process* (Random House, 1955).
13. James L. Sundquist, "Needed: A Political Theory for the New Era of Coalition Government in the United States," *Political Science Quarterly* (Winter 1988–89), pp. 613–35; Robert A. Godwin and Art Kaufman, eds., *Separation of Powers: Does It Still Work?* (AEI Press, 1986).
14. Charles O. Jones, "The Separate Presidency," in *The New American Political System*, ed. Anthony King, 2d ed. (AEI Press, 1990), p. 3.
15. Morris P. Fiorina, "An Era of Divided Government," *Political Science Quarterly* 107, no. 3 (1992), p. 407.
16. David R. Mayhew, *Divided We Govern: Party Control, Lawmaking, and Investigations, 1946–1990* (Yale University Press, 1991), p. 4. See also James A. Thurber, ed., *Divided Democracy: Presidents and Congress in Cooperation and Conflict* (Congressional Quarterly, 1991).
17. Charles O. Jones, *Separate But Equal Branches: Congress and the Presidency* (Chatham House, 1995).
18. See Eleanore Bushnell, *Crimes, Follies, and Misfortunes: The Federal Impeachment Trials* (University of Illinois Press, 1992).
19. *Nixon v United States*, 122 L Ed 2d 1 (1993).
20. John R. Labovitz, *Presidential Impeachment* (Yale University Press, 1978).
21. Neustadt, *Presidential Power*, pp. 180–81.
22. Ronald L. Goldfarb, "The 11,000th Amendment: There's a Rush to Amend the Constitution, and It Shows No Signs of Letting Up," *The Washington Post*, National Weekly Edition, November 25–December 1, 1996, p. 22.
23. David E. Kyvig, *Explicit and Authentic Acts: Amending the U.S. Constitution, 1776–1995* (University Press of Kansas, 1996), p. 446.
24. See Committee on the Constitutional System, *A Bicentennial Analysis of the American Political Structure: Report and Recommendations of the Committee on the Constitutional System* (1987), for recommendations of a committee co-chaired by Senator Nancy L. Kassebaum, C. Douglas Dillon, and Lloyd Cutler. For critical comments, see Mark P. Petracca, "To Right What the Constitution Has Wrought or To Wrong What Is Right," presented at annual meeting of the American Political Science Association, Washington, D.C., 1988.
25. Ann Stuart Diamon, "A Convention for Proposing Amendments: The Constitution's Other Method," *Publius* (Summer 1981), pp. 113–46; Wilbur Edel, "Amending the Constitution by Convention: Myths and Realities," *State Government* 55 (1982), pp. 51–56.
26. Russell L. Caplan, *Constitutional Brinksmanship: Amending the Constitution by National Convention* (Oxford University Press, 1988), p. x.
27. Ibid. See also Kyvig, *Explicit and Authentic Acts*, p. 440.
28. For analysis of more than 40 proposals for structural change, see John R. Vile, *Rewriting the United States Constitution: An Examination of Proposals from Reconstruction to the Present* (Praeger, 1991), chap. 8.
29. Samuel S. Freedman and Pamela J. Naughton, *ERA: May a State Change Its Vote?* (Wayne State University Press, 1979).
30. Kyvig, *Explicit and Authentic Acts*, p. 286.
31. Ibid., p. 286; *Dillon v Gloss*, 256 US 368 (1921).

32. William Van Alstyne, "What Do You Think About the Twenty-seventh Amendment," *Constitutional Commentary* 10, no. 1 (University of Minnesota Law School, 1993), p. 15.

33. Gregory A. Caldeira, "Constitutional Change in America: Dynamics of Ratification Under Article V," *Publius* (Fall 1985), p. 29.

34. Janet K. Boles, "Building Support for the ERA: A Case of Too Much, Too Late," *PS: Political Science and Politics* (Fall 1982), p. 572.

35. Mark R. Daniels, Robert Darcy, and Joseph W. Westphal, "The ERA Won—At Least in the Opinion Polls," *PS: Political Science and Politics* (Fall 1982), p. 583.

36. Janet K. Boles, *The Politics of the Equal Rights Amendment: Conflict and Decision-Making Powers* (Longman, 1979), p. 4.

37. Gilbert Y. Steiner, *Constitutional Inequality: The Political Fortunes of the Equal Rights Amendment* (Brookings Institution, 1985), p. 64. See also

Mary Frances Berry, *Why the ERA Failed: Politics, Women's Rights, and the Amending Process of the Constitution* (Indiana University Press, 1986).

38. Margery L. Elfin, "Learning from Failures Present and Past," and Marian L. Palley, "Beyond the Deadline," *PS: Political Science and Politics* (Fall 1982), pp. 582–92. See also Mark R. Daniels and Robert E. Darcy, "As Time Goes By: Arrested Diffusion of the ERA," *Publius* (Fall 1985), p. 51; Joan Hoff-Wilson, ed., *Rights of Passage: The Past and Future of the ERA* (Indiana University Press, 1986).

39. Bill Clinton, quoted in B. Drummond Ayres, Jr., "District of Columbia Is Denied Statehood," *The New York Times*, November 22, 1993, p. A8.

40. Michael Janofsky, "Congress Creates Fiscal Overseer for Washington," *The New York Times*, April 8, 1995, p. A1.

CHAPTER 3

1. For background, see Samuel H. Beer, *To Make a Nation: The Rediscovering of American Federalism* (Harvard University Press, 1993).

2. Ronald L. Watts, "Canadian Federalism in the 1990's: Once More in Question," *Publius* 21 (Summer 1991), pp. 169–90; Robert C. Vipond, "The Canadian Constitutional Crisis: Who's Right on Rights?" *Intergovernmental Perspective* (Fall 1991), pp. 49–52; Vipond, *Liberty and Community: Canadian Federalism and the Failure of the Constitution* (State University of New York Press, 1991).

3. John Darnton, "Nationalist Winds Pick Up Again in Scotland," *The New York Times*, October 17, 1995, p. A1.

4. Both quoted in James M. Perry, "After Years of Trying, GOP Is on the Threshold of Making History by Scaling Back Federalism," *The Wall Street Journal*, October 27, 1995, p. A16.

5. The term "devolution revolution" was coined by Richard P. Nathan in testimony before the Senate Finance Committee, as quoted by Daniel Patrick Moynihan, "The Devolution Revolution," *The New York Times*, August 6, 1995, p. B15.

6. *U.S. Terms Limits, Inc. v Thorton*, 131 L Ed 2d 881 (1995).

7. *United States v Lopez*, 131 L Ed 2d 626 (1995).

8. William H. Stewart, *Concepts of Federalism* (Center for the Study of Federalism and University Press of America, 1984). See also Edward L. Rubin and Malcolm Feeley, "Federalism: Some Notes on a National Neurosis," *UCLA Law Review* 41 (April 1994), pp. 903–52.

9. Daniel J. Elazar, *Exploring Federalism* (University of Alabama Press, 1987), p. 6.

10. See Beer, *To Make a Nation*.

11. William H. Riker, *The Development of American Federalism* (Academic Publishers, 1987), pp. 14–15. Riker contends that not only does federalism not guarantee freedom but that the framers of our federal system, as well as those of other nations, were not animated by considerations of safeguarding freedom but by practical considerations of preserving unity.

12. "Local Governments' Deceptive Charms," *Business Week*, May 1, 1995, p. 166.

13. *Gibbons v Ogden*, 9 Wheaton 1 (1824).

14. *Heart of Atlanta Motel v United States*, 379 US 241 (1964).

15. *United States v Lopez*, 131 L Ed 2d 626 (1995).

16. Nina Totenberg, quoted in Joseph Calve, "Anatomy of a Landmark," *The Recorder*, August 3, 1995, p. 10.

17. *U.S. Steel Corporation v Multistate Tax Commission*, 434 US 452 (1978).

18. *Luther v Borden*, 7 How. 1 (1849).

19. *California v Superior Courts of California*, 482 US 400 (1987).

20. David C. Nice, "State Participation in Interstate Compacts," *Publius* 17 (Spring 1987), p. 70.

21. *McCulloch v Maryland*, 4 Wheaton 316 (1819).

22. *Missouri v Jenkins*, 495 US 33 (1990); *Missouri v Jenkins*, 132 L Ed 263 (1995).

23. *Oklahoma City v Tuttle*, 471 US 808 (1985); *Mainer v Thiboutot*, 488 US (1980); *Monell v New York City Dept. of Social Welfare*, 436 US 658 (1978).

24. David Rapp, "The FEDS: Washington and the States: The Politics of Distrust," *Governing*, September 1, 1992, p. 67; *Florence County School District Four v Carter*, 510 US 7 (1993).

25. Joseph F. Zimmerman, "Federal Preemption Under Reagan's New Federalism," *Publius* 21 (Winter 1991), pp. 7–28.

26. *Webster v Reproductive Health Services*, 492 US 490 (1989); *Planned Parenthood of Southeastern Pa. v Casey*, 505 US 833 (1992).

27. Oliver Wendell Holmes, Jr., *Collected Legal Papers* (Harcourt, 1920), pp. 295–96.

28. *U.S. Terms Limits, Inc. v Thorton*, 131 L Ed 2d 881 (1995).

29. *United States v Darby Lumber Co.*, 312 U.S. 100 (1941).

30. John E. Chubb, "The Political Economy of Federalism," *American Political Science Review* 79 (December 1985), p. 1005.

31. Paul E. Peterson, *The Price of Federalism* (Brookings Institution, 1995), p. 127.

32. William Weld, "The States Won't Be Cruel," *The New York Times*, February 9, 1996, p. A15; *Congressional Quarterly Weekly Report*, August 3, 1996, pp. 2190–96.

33. Donald F. Kettl, *The Regulation of American Federalism* (Johns Hopkins University Press, 1987), pp. 154–55.

34. Norman Beckman, "Developments in Federal-State Relations," *The Book of the States: 1990–91* (Council of State Governments, 1990), p. 528.

35. Joseph F. Zimmerman, "Congressional Regulation of Subnational Governments," *PS: Political Science and Politics* 26 (June 1993), p. 180. See also *Congressional Quarterly Weekly Report*, August 3, 1996, pp. 2190–96.

36. Ron Suskind, "Health-Care Reform May Seem Like a Bitter Pill to Localities Sick of Unfunded Federal Mandates," *The Wall Street Journal*, December 21, 1993.

37. *Congressional Quarterly Weekly Report*, April 15, 1995, p. 1087.

38. *Congressional Quarterly Weekly Report*, November 2, 1996, p. 3119.

39. Scott De Fife, quoted in ibid.

40. Zimmerman, "Congressional Regulation of Subnational Governments," p. 179.

41. Mel Dubnick and Alan Gitelson, "Nationalizing State Policies," in *The Nationalization of State Government*, ed. Jerome J. Hanus (D.C. Heath, 1981), pp. 56–57.

42. Timothy J. Conlan, "And the Beat Goes On: Intergovernmental Mandates and Preemption in an Era of Deregulation," *Publius* 21 (Summer 1991), p. 46.

43. Advisory Commission on Intergovernmental Relations, *Restoring Confidence and Competence* (ACIR, 1981), p. 30.

44. Cynthia Cates Colella, "The Creation, Care and Feeding of the Leviathan: Who and What Makes Government Grow," *Intergovernmental Perspective* (Fall 1979), p. 9.

45. Aaron Wildavsky, "Bare Bones: Putting Flesh on the Skeleton of American Federalism," in Advisory Commission on Intergovernmental Relations, *The Future of Federalism in the 1980s* (ACIR, 1981), p. 79.

46. Paul E. Peterson, *The Price of Federalism* (Brookings Institution, 1995), p. 182.

47. "GOP Confounds Expectations, Expands Federeal Authority," *Congressional Quarterly Weekly Report*, November 2, 1996, p. 3117.

48. Thomas R. Dye, *American Federalism: Competition Among Governments* (Lexington Books, 1990), p. 199.

49. Daniel J. Elazar, *American Federalism: A View from the States*, 3d ed. (Harper and Row, 1984), p. 241.

50. Debra A. Stewart, "State Initiatives in the Federal System: The Politics and Policy of Comparable Worth in 1984," *Publius* (Summer 1985), p. 83.
51. Martha M. Hamilton, "If You Want Something Done Right, Do It Yourself," *Washington Post National Weekly Edition*, September 5–11, 1988, p. 31.
52. Edward Felsenthal, "Firms Ask Congress to Pass Uniform Rules," *The Wall Street Journal*, May 10, 1993, p. B4.
53. John Herbers, "The New Federalism: Unplanned, Innovative, and Here to Stay," *Governing* 1 (October 1987), pp. 28–34.
54. Virginia I. Pastrel, "States' Rights, or Dereliction of Duty?" *Washington Post National Weekly Edition*, July 22–28, 1991, p. 23.
55. Beverly A. Cigler, "Challenges Facing Fiscal Federalism in the 1990s," *PS: Political Science and Politics* 26 (June 1993), p. 183; Ann O'M. Bowman and Michael A. Pagano, "The State of American Federalism, 1989–1990," *Publius* 20 (Fall 1990), p. 7; U.S. General Accounting Office, *Federal-State-Local Relations: Trends of the Past Decade and Emerging Issues* (GAO, March 1990).

56. Robert Pear, "Shifting Where the Buck Stops," *The New York Times*, October 29, 1995, p. E1.
57. Richard P. Nathan, "Federalism: The Great Composition," in *The New American Political System*, ed. Anthony King, 2d ed. (AEI Press, 1990), pp. 234–35.
58. Sam Howe Verhovek, "With Power Shift, State Lawmakers See New Demands," *The New York Times*, September 24, 1995, p. 12.
59. Steven D. Gold, director of the Center for the Study of the States at the State University of New York at Albany, quoted in ibid.
60. Luther Gulick, "Reorganization of the States," *Civil Engineering* (August 1933), pp. 420–21.
61. David E. Osborne, *Laboratories of Democracy* (Harvard Business School Press, 1988), p. 363.
62. Peterson, *Price of Federalism*, p. 195
63. John J. DiIulio, Jr., and Donald F. Kettl, *Fine Print: The Contract with America, Devaluation, and the Administrative Realities of American Federalism* (Brookings Institution, 1995), p. 60.

CHAPTER 4

1. Craig Smith, *To Form a More Perfect Union: The Ratification of the Constitution and the Bill of Rights, 1788–1791* (University Press of America, 1993).
2. *Barron v Baltimore*, 7 Peters 243 (1833).
3. *Gitlow v New York*, 268 US 652 (1925).
4. Ibid.
5. *Richmond Newspapers Inc. v Virginia*, 448 US 555 (1980).
6. "Project Report: Toward an Activist Role for State Bills of Rights," *Harvard Civil Rights-Civil Liberties Law Review* 8 (March 1973), p. 274.
7. Stanley H. Friedelbaum, ed., *Human Rights in the States: New Directions in Constitutional Policy Making* (Greenwood, 1988); Shirley S. Abrahamson and Diane S. Gutmann, "The New Federalism: State Constitutions and State Courts," *Judicature* (August/September 1987), pp. 88–99; Stanley H. Friedelbaum, "Independent State Grounds: Contemporary Invitations to Judicial Activism," in *State Supreme Courts: Policy Makers in the Federal System*, eds. Mary Cornelia Porter and G. Alan Tarr (Greenwood, 1982), p. 46.
8. Peter J. Galie, "State Supreme Courts, Judicial Federalism and the Other Constitutions," *Judicature* (August/September 1987), pp. 100–110. See also Jeff Rosen, "Altered States: Liberals and Forgotten Constitutions," *The New Republic*, July 1, 1991, p. 19; Steven Pressman, "Protecting Rights in State Courts," Editorial Research Reports, *Congressional Quarterly* 1, no. 20 (1988), p. 277; Dorothy Beasley, "State Bills of Rights: Dead or Alive?" *Intergovernmental Perspective* (June 1989), pp. 13–17.
9. Rosen, "Altered States," p. 20.
10. Thanks to Professor Theodore R. Mosch of The University of Tennessee-Martin for calling this to our attention.
11. Miranda S. Spivack, "How States' Rights Can Rectify the Wrongs of the Supreme Court," *The Los Angeles Times*, June 16, 1991, p. M2.
12. Barry Latzer, "The Hidden Conservatism of the State Court 'Revolution,'" *Judicature* (December 1990/January 1991), p. 193.
13. *Lemon v Kurtzman*, 403 US 602 (1971).
14. Dissenting in *Rosenberger v University of Virginia*, 132 L Ed 2d 700 (1995).
15. *Everson v Board of Education*, 333 U.S. 203 (1947); Leonard W. Levy, *The Establishment Clause: Religion and the First Amendment* (Macmillan, 1986).
16. *Walz v Tax Commission*, 397 U.S. 664 (1970); *Lemon v Kurtzman*, 403 U.S. 602 (1971). For a review of these and other cases, see John Swomley, *Religious Liberty and the Secular State: The Constitutional Context* (Prometheus Books, 1987).
17. See their dissenting opinions in *Rosenberger v University of Virginia*, 132 L Ed 2d 700 (1995).
18. *Capital Square Review Board v Pinette*, 132 L Ed 2d 650 (1995).
19. *Lynch v Donnelly* 465 U.S. 669 (1984). *Allegheny County v Greater Pittsburgh ACLU*, 492 US 573 (1989).
20. *Allegheny County v. Greater Pittsburgh ACLU*, 492 US 573 (1989).
21. *Lee v Weisman*, 505 US 577 (1992).

22. *Board of Education of Kiryas Joel Village School District v Grumet*, 512 US 687 (1994).
23. *Harvard Law Review*, "Leading Cases," (November 1995), p 219.
24. *Capital Square Review Board v Pinette*, 132 L Ed 2d 650 (1995).
25. *Bowen v Kendrick*, 487 US 589 (1988); *Texas Monthly, Inc. v Bullock*, 489 U.S. 1 (1989); *Lee v Weisman*, 505 US 577 (1992). *Board of Education of Kiryas Joel Village School District v Grumet*, 512 US 687 (1994).
26. *Engel v Vitale*, 370 US 421 (1962).
27. *Lee v Weisman*, 505 US 577 (1992).
28. *Edwards v Aguillard*, 482 US 578 (1987).
29. *Marsh v Chambers*, 463 US 783 (1983).
30. *Witters v. Washington Department of Service for Blind*, 474 US 481 (1986).
31. Donald L. Brakeman, *Church-State Constitutional Issues: Making Sense of the Establishment Clause* (Greenwood, 1991), p. 125.
32. *Mueller v Allen*, 463 US 388 (1983).
33. *Wolman v Walter*, 433 US 229 (1977).
34. *Zobrest v Catalina Foothills School District*, 509 US 1 (1993).
35. *Walz v Tax Commission*, 397 US 644 (1970).
36. *Board of Education of Westside Community Schools (Dist. 66) v Mergens*, 496 US 226 (1990).
37. *Rosenberger v University of Virginia*, 132 L Ed 2d 700 (1995).
38. *Frazee v Illinois Department of Employment Security*, 489 US 829 (1989).
39. *Wisconsin v Yoder*, 406 US 205 (1972).
40. *Employment Division, Department of Human Resources of Oregon v Smith*, 494 US 872 (1990).
41. *Church of Lukumi Babalu Aye, Inc. v City of Hialeah*, 508 US 384 (1993).
42. *Lamb's Chapel v Center Moriches Union Free School District*, 124 L Ed 2d 352 (1993).
43. *Bob Jones University v United States*, 461 US 574 (1983).
44. *Hernandez v Commissioner*, 489 US 1027 (1989).
45. Jesse H. Choper, *Securing Religious Liberty: Principles for Judicial Interpretation of the Religion Clauses* (University of Chicago Press, 1995), p. 55.
46. *Congressional Record*, 139, no. 65, May 11, 1993.
47. *Weekly Compendium of Presidential Documents* 2377, November 16, 1993.
48. John Stuart Mill, Essay on Liberty (1859), in *The English Philosophers from Bacon to Mill*, ed. Arthur Burtt (Modern Library, 1939), p. 961.
49. *West Virginia State Board of Education v Barnette*, 319 US 624 (1943).
50. *Hustler Magazine v Falwell*, 485 US 46 (1988); *United States v Schriummer*, 279 US 644 (1928).
51. For a thoughtful statement of a somewhat contrary point of view, see Walter Berns, *First Amendment and the Future of American Democracy* (Basic Books, 1976). For a review of the classics and a call for a review of the civil liberties tradition to deal with issues such as the regulation of campaign finance and other matters designed to equalize the competition

in the marketplace of ideas, see Mark A. Graber, *Transforming Free Speech: The Ambiguous Legacy of Civil Libertarianism* (University of California Press, 1991).

52. *R.A.V. v St. Paul*, 505 US 377 (1992).
53. *Gitlow v New York*, 268 US 652 (1925).
54. *Brown v Hartlage*, 456 US 45 (1982), in which the Supreme Court reversed a decision of the Kentucky Court of Appeals based on the bad tendency doctrine.
55. *Schenck v United States*, 249 US 47 (1919).
56. *Whitney v California*, 274 US 357 (1927).
57. *Nebraska Press Association v Stuart*, 427 US 539 (1976). See also Fred W. Friendly, *Minnesota Rag: The Dramatic Story of the Landmark Supreme Court Case That Gave New Meaning to Freedom of the Press* (Random House, 1981).
58. *Hazelwood School District v Kuhlmeier*, 484 US 260 (1988).
59. *Lanzetta v New Jersey*, 306 US 451 (1939).
60. *Winters v New York*, 333 US 507 (1948); *Burstyn v Wilson*, 343 US 495 (1952).
61. *Regan v Time, Inc.*, 468 US 641 (1984).
62. *R.A.V. v St. Paul*, 505 US 377 (1992). See also Edward J. Cleary, *Beyond the Burning Cross: The First Amendment and the Landmark R.A.V. Case* (Random House, 1995) by the attorney for the cross burner.
63. *Dun & Bradstreet v Greenmoss Builders*, 472 US 749 (1985), citing *First National Bank of Boston v Bellotti*, 435 US 765, 766 (1978). See also Edward V. Heck and Albert C. Ringelstein, "The Burger Court and the Primacy of Political Expression," *Western Political Quarterly* 40 (September 1987), pp. 411–23.
64. *Board of Trustees, State University of New York v Fox*, 492 US 469 (1989).
65. Lee C. Bollinger, *Images of a Free Press* (University of Chicago Press, 1991), p. 63.
66. *Lovell v Griffin*, 303 US 444 (1938).
67. *Richmond Newspapers, Inc. v Virginia*, 448 US 555 (1980). For a comprehensive history, see David A. Anderson, "The Origins of the Press Clause," *UCLA Law Review* (February 1983), pp. 455–537.
68. *Philadelphia Newspapers v Hepps*, 475 US 767 (1986); Richard Labunski, *Libel and the First Amendment: Legal History and Practice in Print and Broadcasting* (Transaction Books, 1987).
69. *Cohen v Cowles Media Co.*, 501 US 663 (1991).
70. *Dun & Bradstreet v Greenmoss Builders*, 472 US 749 (1985). See also William W. Van Alstyne, *Interpretations of the First Amendment* (Duke University Press, 1984), pp. 50–67.
71. *Hazelwood School District v Kuhlmeier*, 484 US 260 (1988).
72. *Richmond Newspapers, Inc. v Virginia*, 448 US 555 (1980); David M. O'Brien, *The Public's Right to Know: The Supreme Court and the First Amendment* (Praeger, 1981).
73. *United States v Nixon*, 418 US 683 (1974). See also Daniel N. Hoffman, *Governmental Secrecy and the Founding Fathers: A Study in Constitutional Controls* (Greenwood, 1981).
74. Stephen Labaton, "President Agrees to Release Notes on Whitewater," *New York Times*, December 22, 1995, p. A1.
75. *Gentile v State Bar of Nevada*, 501 US 1030 (1991).
76. Susanna Barber, *News Cameras in the Courtroom: A Free Press-Fair Trial Debate* (Ablex, 1987), p. 9.
77. *Milwaukee Pub. Co. v Burleson*, 255 US 407 (1921).
78. *Lamont v Postmaster General*, 381 US 301 (1965).
79. *Rowan v Post Office Department*, 397 US 728 (1970).
80. *Southeastern Promotions, Ltd. v Conrad*, 420 US 546 (1975).
81. *California v LaRue*, 409 US 109 (1972); see also *Barnes v Glen Theatre, Inc.*, 501 US 560 (1991).
82. *McIntyre v Ohio Election Commission*, 131 L Ed 2d 426 (1995).
83. Ibid.
84. *Burson v Freeman*, 504 US 191 (1992).
85. Lucas A. Powe, Jr., *American Broadcasting and the First Amendment* (University of California Press, 1987).
86. *Federal Communications Commission v League of Women Voters of California*, 468 US 364 (1984).
87. Edmund L. Andres, "Robotic Telephone Sales Calls Come Under Fire in Congress," *New York Times*, October 30, 1991, p. A1.
88. James Barron, "Watch What You Say on the Cordless Phone," *New York Times*, November 9, 1991, p. 9.
89. *Sable Communications v Federal Communications Commission*, 492 US 115 (1989).
90. *Federal Communications Commission v Pacifica Foundation et al.*, 438 US 726 (1978). The Court, however, has refused to review a decision of the Court of Appeals for the District of Columbia, which declared unconstitutional a complete 24-hour ban on the televising of indecent materials.
91. Linda Greenhouse, "Supreme Court Roundup," *The New York Times*, March 3, 1992, p. A2.
92. Barnaby J. Feder, "Toward Defining Free Speech in the Computer Age," *The New York Times*, November 3, 1991, p. E5; Don Oldenburg, "Computers: Rights on the Line," and "The Law: Lost in Cyberspace," *The Washington Post*, October 1, 1991, p. E5. Dan Carney, "TeleCommunications: Conferees Favor 'Indency' Standard," *Congressional Quarterly Weekly Report*, December 9, 1995, p. 3734.
93. Benjamin Wittes, "Taming Cyberspace," *The Recorder*, December 29, 1995, p. 5. See also *The Los Angeles Times*, January 14, 1996, p. M4; also Mark Walsh, "Telecom Fight Just Beginning," *The Recorder*, February 9, 1996, p. 1.
94. On the World Wide Web, see: http//:supct.law.cornell.edu/supct/arcal 97.html
95. *Amalgamated Food Employees v Logan Plaza*, 391 US 308 (1968).
96. *Frisby v Schultz*, 487 US 474 (1988).
97. *Madsen v. Women's Health Center*, 512 US 753 (1994).
98. *Boos v Barry*, 485 US 312 (1988).
99. *United States v O'Brien*, 391 US 367 (1968).
100. *Paris Adult Theatre v Slaton*, 413 US 49 (1973).
101. *United States v O'Brien*, 391 US 367 (1968).
102. *Clark v Community for Creative Non-Violence*, 468 US 288 (1984).
103. *R.A.V. v St. Paul*, 505 US 377 (1992).
104. *Clark v Community for Creative Non-Violence*, 468 US 288 (1984).
105. *Barnes v Glen Theatre, Inc.*, 501 US 560 (1991).
106. *The New York Times v Sullivan*, 376 US 254 (1964). See also Anthony Lewis, *Make No Law: The Sullivan Case and the First Amendment* (Random House, 1991), p. 140.
107. *Harte-Hanks, Inc. v Connaughton*, 491 US 657 (1989).
108. *Hustler Magazine v Falwell*, 485 US 46 (1988).
109. *Masson v New Yorker Magazine, Inc.*, 501 US 496 (1991).
110. Robert Scheer, "Pornography Commissioners Founder on the Limits of Sex," *The Los Angeles Times*, May 1, 1986, p. 19.
111. *Brockett v Spokane Arcades, Inc.*, 472 US 491 (1985).
112. *Miller v California*, 413 US 15 (1973).
113. *Memoirs v Massachusetts*, 383 US 413 (1966).
114. *Jenkins v Georgia*, 418 US 153 (1974).
115. *Young v American Mini Theatres*, 427 US 51 (1976). See also *Renton v Playtime Theatres, Inc.*, 475 US 41 (1986).
116. "From Preamble to Indianapolis City-County Ordinance," cited by Joel B. Grossman, "The First Amendment and the New Anti-Pornography Statutes," *News for Teachers of Political Science* (American Political Science Association, 1985), p. 18. See also Catharine A. MacKinnon, *Only Words* (Harvard University Press, 1993). For a rebuttal to MacKinnon by another feminist, see Nadine Strossen, *Defending Pornography: Free Speech, Sex, and the Fight for Women's Rights* (Scribner's, 1995).
117. Cass R. Sunstein, *The Partial Constitution* (Harvard University Press, 1993), p. 268.
118. Suzanne Stefanac, "Sex and the New Media," *The Recorder*, September 8, 1993, p. 14.
119. Barry Sussman, "With Pornography, It All Depends on Who's Doing the Looking," *Washington Post*-ABC News Poll, *The Washington Post*, National Weekly Edition, March 24, 1986, p. 37.
120. "Anti-Pornography Laws and First Amendment Values," Harvard Law Review 98 (1984), p. 460. See also Donald Alexander Downs, *The New Politics of Pornography* (University of Chicago Press, 1990); Sunstein, *Partial Constitution*, pp. 261–70.
121. *Butler v Her Majesty the Queen* 1 S.C.R. 452 (1992). See also "Pornography, Equality, and a Discrimination-Free Workplace: A Comparative Perspective," *Harvard Law Review* 106 (March 1993), pp. 1075–92; Kent Greenawalt, *Fighting Words* (Princeton University Press, 1995), pp. 113–23.
122. *Hudnut v American Booksellers*, 475 US 1001 (1986); *Sable Communications v Federal Communications Commission*, 492 US 115 (1989).
123. *Chaplinsky v New Hampshire*, 315 US 568 (1942).

124. *Cohen v California*, 403 US 115 (1971). See also *NAACP v Claiborne Hardware Co.*, 458 US 886 (1982); *R.A.V. v St. Paul*, 505 US 377 (1992).

125. *Cohen v California*, 403 US 115 (1971).

126. *United States v Eichman*, 496 US 310 (1990), repeated and reemphasized in *Simon & Schuster v New York State Crime Victims Board*, 502 US 105 (1991).

127. *R.A.V. v St. Paul*, 505 US 377 (1992).

128. David M. Hamlin, "Swastikas and Survivors: Inside the Skokie-Nazi Free Speech Case," *Civil Liberties Review* (March/April 1978).

129. Lee C. Bollinger, *The Tolerant Society: Freedom of Speech and Extremist Speech in America* (Oxford University Press, 1986), pp. 24–32. See also Donald A. Downs, *Nazis in Skokie: Freedom, Community, and the First Amendment* (University of Notre Dame Press, 1985).

130. Bollinger, *Images of a Free Press*.

131. *Walker v Birmingham*, 388 US 307 (1967).

132. "Senate Passes Bill Making Blockades of Abortion Clinics a Federal Crime," *The New York Times*, May 13, 1994, pp. A1, A12.

133. *Madsen v Women's Health Center*, 512 US 753 (1994).

134. *Pruneyard Shopping Center v Robins*, 447 US 74 (1980).

135. *National Association for the Advancement of Colored People v Alabama*, 357 US 449 (1958).

136. *Roberts v United States Jaycees*, 465 US 609 (1984).

137. J. Skelly Wright, "Politics and the Constitution: Is Money Speech?" *Yale Law Journal* 85 (1976), pp. 1001–21.

138. *Buckley v Valeo*, 424 US 1 (1976).

139. *Federal Election Commission v National Political Action Committee*, 470 US 480 (1985).

140. *West Virginia State Board of Education v Barnette*, 319 US 624 (1943).

141. See two works by Leonard W. Levy: *Legacy of Suppression* (Harvard University Press, 1960) and *Freedom of the Press from Zenger to Jefferson* (Bobbs-Merrill, 1966).

142. The Sedition Act of 1798, quoted in James Morton Smith, *Freedom's Fetters: The Alien and Sedition Laws and American Civil Liberties* (Cornell University Press, 1956), p. 442.

143. *Dennis v United States*, 341 US 494 (1950).

144. *Yates v United States*, 354 US 298 (1957).

145. *Brandenburg v Ohio*, 395 US 444 (1969).

CHAPTER 5

1. Sidney Verba and Gary R. Orren, *Equality in America: The View from the Top* (Harvard University Press, 1985), p. 1, on which this section is based.

2. Ellen Carol DuBois, *Feminism and Suffrage: The Emergence of an Independent Women's Movement in America, 1848–1869* (Cornell University Press, 1978); Joan Hoff-Wilson, "Women and the Constitution," *News for Teachers of Political Science* (American Political Science Association), Summer 1985, pp. 10–15.

3. James Vardaman, quoted in Alan P. Grimes, *Democracy and the Amendments to the Constitution* (D. C. Heath, 1979), p. 91. See also Nancy F. Cott, *The Grounding of Modern Feminism* (Yale University Press, 1987).

4. William Borah, quoted in Grimes, *Democracy*, p. 91.

5. Susan M. Hartmann, *From Margin to Mainstream: American Women and Politics since 1960* (Temple University Press, 1989); Susan Gluck Mezey, *In Pursuit of Equality: Women, Public Policy, and the Federal Courts* (St. Martin's Press, 1992).

6. *Plessy v Ferguson*, 163 US 537 (1896).

7. James MacGregor Burns and Stewart Burns, *A People's Charter: The Pursuit of Rights in America* (Knopf, 1991), pp. 305–18.

8. David J. Garrow, *Bearing the Cross: Martin Luther King, Jr., and the Southern Christian Leadership Conference* (Morrow, 1986).

9. Michael R. Belknap, *Federal Law and Southern Order: Racial Violence and Constitutional Conflict in the Post-Brown South* (University of Georgia, 1987), pp. 128–204.

10. Taylor Branch, *Parting the Waters: America in the King Years, 1954–1963* (Simon & Schuster, 1988). See also Harris Wofford, *Of Kennedys and Kings: Making Sense of the Sixties* (Farrar, Strauss and Giroux, 1980).

11. See Robert D. Loevy, *To End All Segregation: The Politics and Passage of the Civil Rights Act of 1964* (University Press of America, 1990).

12. Aldon D. Morris, *The Origins of the Civil Rights Movement: Black Communities Organizing for Change* (Free Press/Macmillan, 1985); James Farmer, *Lay Bare the Heart: An Autobiography of the Civil Rights Movement* (Arbor House, 1985); Branch, *Parting the Waters*.

13. National Advisory Commission on Civil Disorders, *The Kerner Report* (Washington, D.C., Government Printing Office, 1968), p. 1.

14. Charles Murray, *Losing Ground: American Social Policy, 1950–1980* (Basic Books, 1984).

15. Harold L. Hodgkinson, *The Demographics of American Indians: One Percent of the People, Fifty Percent of the Diversity* (Institute for Educational Leadership/Center for Demographic Policy, 1990), pp. 1–5.

16. Charles F. Wilkinson, *American Indians, Times, and the Law* (Yale University Press, 1987), p. 62; Vine Deloria, Jr., and Clifford M. Lytle, *The Nations Within: The Past and Future of American Indian Sovereignty* (Pantheon Books, 1984).

17. *Morton v Mancari*, 417 US 535 (1974); Theodore W. Taylor, *The Bureau of Indian Affairs* (Westview Press, 1984).

18. Office of Technology Assessment, quoted by Spencer Rich in "Native Americans, They Can Still Get Free Health Care If They're Indian Enough," *The Washington Post National Weekly Edition*, July 14, 1986, p. 34.

19. *County of Yakima v Yakima Indian Nation*, 116 L Ed 2d 687 (1992).

20. Theodora Lurie, "Shattering the Myth of the Vanishing American," *The Ford Foundation Letter* 22 (Winter 1991), p. 5.

21. The Bilateral Commission on the Future of the United States—Mexican Relations, *The Challenge of Interdependence* (University Press of America, 1989), p. 99.

22. U.S. Bureau of the Census, *Statistical Abstract of the United States, 1996* (Government Printing Office, 1996), p. 31.

23. Maurilio E. Vigil, *Hispanics in American Politics: Search for Political Power* (University Press of America, 1987).

24. Alan Pifer, *Annual Report of the Carnegie Corporation of New York* (1979), p. 16.

25. *Statistical Abstract, 1996*, p. 286; David Lesher and Gebe Martinez, "Latinos Claim 90s as Their Power Decade at Convention," *Los Angeles Times*, June 29, 1991, p. B9.

26. *1992 National Roster of Hispanic Elected Officials* (Washington, D.C.: National Association of Latino Elected and Appointed Officials, 1992), pp. 164–65.

27. Alfredo Cruz, Southwest Voter Registration and Education Project, quoted in *The Economist*, December 14, 1996, p. 29.

28. National Association of Latino Elected and Appointed Officials, press release, November 13, 1996.

29. Hispanic Link Weekly Report, "Latinas Set Pace as Hispanics Gain 11 Seats in '97," *State Legislatures*, December 2, 1996.

30. Maria Newman, "Latino Meeting in O.C. to Focus on Remapping," *Los Angeles Times*, June 29, 1991, p. A1.

31. Celia W. Dugger, "U.S. Study Says Asian-Americans Face Widespread Discrimination," *The New York Times*, February 29, 1992, p. 1, reporting on U.S. Civil Rights Commission, *Civil Rights Issues Facing Asian Americans in the 1990s*.

32. Won Moo Hurh, *Korean Immigrants in America* (Fairleigh Dickinson University Press, 1984).

33. Antonio J. A. Pido, *The Filipinos in America: Macro/Micro Dimensions of Immigration and Integration* (Center for Migration Studies of New York, 1986).

34. *Minnesota v Clover Leaf Creamery Co.*, 449 US 456 (1981).

35. *San Antonio School District v Rodriguez*, 411 US 1 (1973).

36. *Adarand Constructors Inc. v Pennsylvania*, 132 L Ed 2d, 158 (1995).

37. *Pickett v Brown*, 462 US 1 (1983).

38. *Frontiero v Richardson*, 411 US 677 (1973).

39. *Califano v Webster*, 430 US 313 (1977).

40. *Mississippi University for Women v Hogan*, 458 US 718 (1982).

41. *Rostker v Goldberg*, 453 US 57 (1981).

42. *San Antonio School District v Rodriguez*, 411 US 1 (1973).

43. Sydney P. Freedberg, "Forced Exits? Companies Confront Wave of Age-Discrimination Suits," *The Wall Street Journal*, October 13, 1987, p. 37.

44. *San Antonio School District v Rodriguez*, 411 US 1 (1973).

45. *Washington v Davis*, 426 US 229 (1976). See also *Hunter v Underwood*, 471 US 522 (1985).

46. Justice Sandra Day O'Connor, concurring in *Hernandez v New York*, 500 US 352 (1991).

47. *Personnel Administrator of Massachusetts v Feeney*, 442 US 256 (1979).

48. C. Vann Woodward, *The Strange Career of Jim Crow* (Oxford University Press, 1968).

49. *Plessy v Ferguson*, 163 US 537 (1896).

50. *Brown v Board of Education of Topeka*, 347 US 483 (1954). See also J. W. Peltason, *Fifty-eight Lonely Men: Southern Federal Judges and School Desegregation* (University of Illinois Press, 1971), p. 248.

51. *Brown v Board of Education*, 349 US 294 (1955). For a comprehensive history of the events leading up to Brown, see Richard Kluger, *Simple Justice* (Knopf, 1976); Earl Black, *Southern Governors and Civil Rights: Racial Segregation as a Campaign Issue in the Second Reconstruction* (Harvard University Press, 1977), shows response, reaction, and eventually neutralization of race as a political issue following the *Brown* decision.

52. *Alexander v Board of Education*, 396 US 802 (1969).

53. *Missouri v Jenkins*, 132 L Ed 2d 63 (1995).

54. Alex M. Johnson, Jr., "Bid Whist, Tonk, and *United States v Fordice*: Why Integrationism Fails African-Americans Again," *California Law Review* (December 1993), pp. 1401ff.

55. Gary Orfield, *Must We Bus? Segregated Schools and National Policy* (Brookings Institution, 1979); Jennifer L. Hochschild, *The New American Dilemma: Liberal Democracy and School Desegregation* (Yale University Press, 1984).

56. *Swann v Charlotte-Mecklenburg Board of Education*, 402 US 1 (1971).

57. *Milliken v Bradley*, 418 US 717 (1974); Bernard Schwartz, *The School Busing Case and the Supreme Court* (Oxford University Press, 1986).

58. Gary Orfield, "Separate Societies: Have the Kerner Warnings Come True?" in *Quiet Riots: Race and Poverty in the United States—The Kerner Report Twenty Years Later*, eds. Fred Harris and Roger Wilkins (Pantheon, 1988), p. 116. See also "Segregation's Threat to the Economy," *The New York Times*, December 19, 1993, p. A12.

59. *Missouri v Jenkins*, 495 US 33 (1990).

60. *Missouri v Jenkins*, 132 L Ed 2d 63 (1995).

61. See Gary Orfield, Susan E. Eaton, and the Harvard Project on School Desegregation, *Dismantling Desegregation: The Quiet Reversal of Brown v Board of Education* (New Press, 1996). See also Peter Applebome, "Schools See Reemergence of 'Separate but Equal'," *The New York Times*, April 8, 1997, p. A8.

62. Peter Applebome, "Opponents' Moves Refueling Debate on School Busing," *The New York Times*, September 26, 1995, p. A1.

63. William Celis III, "Study Finds Rising Concentration of Black and Hispanic Students," *The New York Times*, December 14, 1993, p. A1.

64. Raymond Hernandez, "NAACP Suspends Yonkers Leader After Critics of Usefulness of School Busing," *The New York Times*, November 1, 1995, p. A13.

65. Quoted by Peter Applebome, "Opponents' Moves Refueling Debate on School Busing," *The New York Times*, September 26, 1995, p. A1.

66. Quoted in Celis, "Study Finds Rising Concentration," p. A11.

67. V. O. Key, Jr., *Southern Politics* (Knopf, 1949), p. 555. For a history of the rise and fall of black disenfranchisement, see Steven F. Lawson, *Black Ballots: Voting Rights in the South, 1944–1969* (Columbia University Press, 1976).

68. *Smith v Allwright*, 321 US 649 (1944).

69. *Gomillion v Lightfoot*, 364 US 339 (1960).

70. *Harper v Virginia Board of Elections*, 383 US 663 (1966).

71. *Report of the United States Commission on Civil Rights* (Government Printing Office, 1959), pp. 103–4.

72. Harold W. Stanley, *Voter Mobilization and the Politics of Race: The South and Universal Suffrage, 1952–1984* (Praeger, 1987).

73. Abigail M. Thernstrom, *Whose Votes Count? Affirmative Action and Minority Voting Rights* (Harvard University Press, 1987), p. 15.

74. David J. Garrow, *Protest at Selma: Martin Luther King and the Voting Rights Act of 1965* (Yale University Press, 1978).

75. Thernstrom, *Whose Votes Count?* For a contrary view, see Bernard Grofman, Lisa Handley, and Richard Niemi, *Minority Representation and the Quest for Voting Equality* (Cambridge University Press, 1992).

76. *Morse v Republican Party of Virginia*, 134 L Ed 2d 347 (1996).

77. *Presley v Etowah County Commission*, 502 US 491 (1992).

78. *Holder v Hall*, 512 US 874 (1994).

79. Ellen Perlman, "Feds on Remaps: No Go," *City and State*, July 29–August 11, 1991.

80. *Shaw v Reno*, 509 US 630 (1993); see also *Shaw v Reno*, 509 US 874 *Johnson v De Grandy*, 512 US 997 (1994).

81. *Miller v. Johnson*, 132 L Ed 2d 762 (1995).

82. Justice William O. Douglas, dissenting in *Moose Lodge No. 107 v Irvis*, 407 US 163 (1972).

83. *New York State Club Association v New York City*, 487 US 1 (1988).

84. *Civil Rights Cases*, 109 US 3 (1883).

85. *Heart of Atlanta Motel v United States*, 379 US 421 (1964).

86. Paul Burstein, *Discrimination, Jobs, and Politics: The Struggle for Equal Employment Opportunity in the United States since the New Deal* (University of Chicago Press, 1985); Kathanne W. Greene, *Affirmative Action and Principles of Justice* (Greenwood Press, 1989).

87. *Meritor Savings Bank v Vinson*, 477 US 57 (1986); *Harris v Forklift Systems, Inc.*, 510 US 17 (1993).

88. Hanes Walton, Jr., *When the Marching Stopped: The Politics of Civil Rights Regulatory Agencies* (State University of New York Press, 1988).

89. David Rovella, "EEOC Chairman Casellas, 'We Are Being Selective,'" *The National Law Journal*, November 20, 1995, p. 1.

90. John O. Calmore, "To Make Wrong Right: The Necessary and Proper Aspirations of Fair Housing," in *The State of Black America, 1989*, ed. Janet Dewart (National Urban League, 1989), p. 95.

91. Orfield, "Separate Societies," p. 105.

92. Charles M. Lamb, "Housing Discrimination and Segregation," *Catholic University Law Review* (Spring 1981), p. 370.

93. *Shelley v Kraemer*, 334 US 1 (1948).

94. Timothy Noah, "Housing Report Says Racial Bias Remains Prevalent," *The Wall Street Journal*, August 30, 1991, reporting on findings of report prepared by the Urban Institute commissioned by the Department of Housing and Urban Development.

95. Daniel Mitchell quoted in *CQ Researcher, Housing Discrimination*, vol. 5, February 24, 1995, p. 174.

96. "The Racism Next Door: Segregated Housing Is Still a Blight in Most Neighborhoods," *Time*, June 30, 1986, p. 40. See also Alan Finder, "Housing Bias Still Pervades the New York Region," *The New York Times*, March 13, 1989, p. A16.

97. Justice John Marshall Harlan, dissenting in *Plessy v Ferguson*, 163 US 537 (1896).

98. *DeFunis v Odegaard*, 416 US 312 (1974).

99. *University of California Regents v Bakke*, 438 US 265 (1978).

100. Justice Byron White, concurring in *Wygant v Jackson Board of Education*, 476 US 267 (1986).

101. Justice Sandra Day O'Connor, majority opinion, and Justice Thurgood Marshall, dissenting in *Richmond v Croson*, 488 US 469 (1989).

102. Justice William J. Brennan, majority opinion, and Justice Sandra Day O'Connor, dissenting in *Metro Broadcasting v Federal Communications Commission*, 497 US 547 (1990).

103. *Adarand Constructors, Inc. v. Pena*, 132 L Ed 2d 158 (1995).

104. *Shaw v Reno*, 509 US 630 (1993); *Miller v Johnson*, 132 L Ed 2d 676 (1995).

105. *Hopwood v Texas*, 135 L Ed 1095 (1996).

106. Ibid.

107. James Farmer, quoted in Rochelle L. Stanfield, "Black Complaints Haven't Translated into Political Organization and Power," *National Journal*, June 14, 1980, p. 465. Alphonso Pinkey, *The Myth of Black Progress* (Cambridge University Press, 1984), argues that the failure of blacks to make greater progress is due to white racism. William Julius Wilson, *The Declining Significance of Race*, 2d ed. (University of Chicago Press, 1984), argues to the contrary that most of the problems are those of class, not of race. See also Stuart Scheingold, "Constitutional Rights and Social Change: Civil Rights in Perspective," in *Judging the Constitution*, eds. Michael W. McCann and Gerald L. Houseman (Scott, Foresman and Company, 1989), pp. 73–91.

108. National Academy of Science, *A Common Destiny: Blacks and American Society* (National Academy Press, 1989).

109. Orfield, "Separate Societies," p. 103. See also Madeline Landau, "Race, Poverty and the Cities: Hyperinnovation in Complex Policy Systems," Public Affairs Report, *Bulletin of the Institute of Governmental Studies*, University of California, Berkeley, 30 (January 1989), p. 1; Margaret C. Simms, ed., *Black Economic Progress: An Agenda for the 1990's* (Joint Center for Political Studies, 1988); Nicholas Lehmann, *The Promised Land* (Knopf, 1991).

110. Gary Orfield and Carole Ashkinaze, *The Closing Door: Conservative Policy and Black Opportunity* (University of Chicago Press, 1991), p. 26.
111. William J. Wilson, *The Truly Disadvantaged: The Inner City, the Underclass, and Public Policy* (University of Chicago Press, 1987), particularly chap. 5.
112. Orfield and Ashkinaze, *The Closing Door*, pp. 221–34.
113. Edward G. Carmines and James A. Stimson, *Issue Evolution: Race and the Transformation of American Politics* (Princeton University Press, 1989), p. xiii.

CHAPTER 6

1. *Presier v Rodriguez*, 411 US 475 (1973).
2. 28 United States Code 2454.
3. *Stone v Powell*, 428 US 465 (1976); *McCleskey v Zant*, 499 US 467 (1991); *Winthow v Williams*, 507 US 680 (1993). For a review of these decisions, see Jordan Steiker, "Innocence and Federal Habeas," *UCLA Law Review* 41 (December 1993), pp. 303–89.
4. Martin Edelman, *Democratic Theories and the Constitution* (State University of New York Press, 1984), p. 304; Judith N. Shklar, *American Citizenship: The Quest for Inclusion* (Harvard University Press, 1991), p. 3.
5. *Vance v Terrazas*, 444 US 252 (1980).
6. *Slaughter-House Cases* 16 Wallace 36 (1873).
7. Robert Pear, "Governors Limit Revisions Sought in Welfare Law," *The New York Times National Edition*, February 2, 1997, p. A1; Pear, "Legal Immigrants to Get Letters on Welfare Cut," *The New York Times National Edition*, February 6, 1997, p. A16.
8. *Plyer v Doe*, 457 US 202 (1982).
9. Dan Carney, "Law Restricts Illegal Immigration," *Congressional Quarterly Weekly Report*, November 16, 1996, pp. 3287–88.
10. Arnold H. Leibowitz, "The Refugee Act of 1980: Problems and Congressional Concerns," *Annals of the American Academy of Political and Social Sciences* (May 1983), pp. 163–71. See also Gil Loescher and John Scanlan, *Calculated Kindness: Refugees and America's Half-Open Door, 1945 to Present* (Free Press, 1986).
11. *Sale v Haitian Centers Council, Inc.*, 509 US 155 (1993).
12. *Plyer v Doe*, 457 US 202 (1982). See also Paul Yoshihashi, "Employer Sanctions and Illegal Workers," *The Wall Street Journal*, May 26, 1989, p. B1.
13. Eric Schmitt, "Illegal Immigrants Rose to 5 Million in '96," *The New York Times National Edition*, February 8, 1997, p. Y7; Bilateral Commission on the Future of United States–Mexican Relations, *The Challenge of Interdependence: Mexico and the United States* (University Press of America, 1989), p. 185.
14. Belinda Reyes, "Why Return Migration Matters: The Case of Immigration from Western Mexico," Public Policy Institute of California, p. 4, and Belinda Reyes, "Dynamics of Immigration: Return Migration to Western Mexico," Public Policy Institute of California, 1997.
15. *Kleindienst v Mandel*, 408 US 753 (1972).
16. Senator Alan Simpson, quoted by Justice John Paul Stevens in *McNary v Haitian Refugee Center*, 498 US 479 (1991).
17. Bilateral Commission, *Challenge of Interdependence*, p. 77.
18. *Chicago Home Building & Loan Assn. v Blaisdell*, 290 US 398 (1934).
19. *Chicago, Milwaukee, and St. Paul Ry. v Minnesota*, 134 US 418 (1890).
20. Richard A. Epstein, *Taking: Private Property and the Power of Eminent Domain* (Harvard University Press, 1985).
21. *First English Evangelical v Los Angeles County*, 482 US 304 (1987).
22. *United States v 564.54 Acres of Land*, 441 US 506 (1979).
23. Ibid.
24. *Nollan v California Coastal Commission*, 483 US 825 (1987); *Dolan v City of Tigard*, 512 US 374 (1994).
25. *Mathews v Eldridge*, 424 US 319 (1976), restated in *Connecticut v Doeher*, 501 US 1 (1991).
26. *Leary v United States*, 395 US 6 (1969); *Turner v United States*, 369 US 398 (1970).
27. *Meyer v Nebraska*, 262 US 390 (1923).
28. *Meachum v Fano*, 427 US 215 (1976).
29. *Cleveland Board of Education v Loudermill*, 470 US 532 (1985).
30. *Morrissey v Brewer*, 408 US 471 (1972).
31. Philip B. Kurland, *Some Reflections on Privacy and the Constitution* (University of Chicago Center for Policy Study, 1976), p. 9. A classic and influential article about privacy is S. D. Warren and L. D. Brandeis, "The Right to Privacy," *Harvard Law Review*, December 15, 1890, pp. 193–220.
32. *Roe v Wade*, 410 US 113 (1973).
33. *Planned Parenthood of Southeastern Pennsylvania v Casey*, 505 US 833 (1992).
34. *Ohio v Akron Center for Reproductive Health*, 497 US 502 (1990); *Hodgson v Minnesota*, 111 L Ed 2d 344 (1990); *Planned Parenthood of Southeastern Pennsylvania v Casey*, 505 US 833 (1992).
35. *Bowers v Hardwick*, 478 US 186 (1986).
36. *Roemer v Evans*, 134 L Ed 2d 855 (1996).
37. The most comprehensive analysis of these complicated issues is Wayne R. LaFave, *Search and Seizure: A Treatise on the Fourth Amendment*, 2d ed. (West Publishing Co., 1987).
38. *County of Riverside v McLaughlin*, 500 US 44 (1991).
39. *California v Hodari D.*, 499 US 621 (1991).
40. *Mincey v Arizona*, 437 US 385 (1978), reaffirmed in *California v Acevedo*, 500 US 565 (1991).
41. *United States v Ross*, 456 US 798 (1982).
42. *Terry v Ohio*, 392 US 1 (1968); *United States v Sharpe*, 470 US 675 (1985); *Hayes v Florida*, 470 US 811 (1985).
43. *Minnesota v Dickerson*, 508 US 366 (1993).
44. *Adams v Williams*, 407 US 143 (1972).
45. *Chimel v California*, 395 US 752 (1969); *United States v Edward*, 415 US 800 (1974); *Illinois v Lafayette*, 462 US 640 (1983).
46. *Cupp v Murphy*, 412 US 291 (1973).
47. *Florida v Wells*, 495 US 1 (1990).
48. *Schneckloth v Bustamonte*, 412 US 218 (1973); *United States v Matlock*, 415 US 164 (1974).
49. *Almeida-Sanchez v United States*, 413 US 266 (1973); *United States v Ortiz*, 422 US 891 (1975).
50. *United States v Ramsey*, 431 US 606 (1977).
51. *Torres v Puerto Rico*, 442 US 465 (1979).
52. *Coolidge v New Hampshire*, 403 US 443 (1971); *Texas v Brown*, 460 US 730 (1983); *Arizona v Hicks*, 480 US 321 (1987).
53. *Michigan v Tyler*, 436 US 499 (1978); *Mincey v Arizona*, 437 US 385 (1978).
54. Benjamin Wittes, "Ames Case Leads to More Powerful Spy Court," *The Recorder*, November 8, 1994, p. 16.
55. *Tennessee v Garner*, 471 US 1 (1985).
56. *Mapp v Ohio*, 367 US 643 (1961).
57. *United States v Leon*, 468 US 897 (1984).
58. *United States v Payner*, 447 US 727 (1980).
59. *Blau v United States*, 340 US 332 (1951).
60. *Mincey v Arizona*, 437 US 385 (1978).
61. *Miranda v Arizona*, 384 US 436 (1966). Liva Baker, *Miranda: Crime, Law and Politics* (Atheneum, 1983), explores every aspect of the decision, including subsequent controversy about its effects.
62. Felix Frankfurter, dissenting in *United States v Rabinowitz*, 339 US 56 (1950).
63. *Johnson v Zerbst*, 304 US 458 (1938); *Gideon v Wainwright*, 372 US 335 (1963). Anthony Lewis, *Gideon's Trumpet* (Random House, 1964), has become a classic on this issue.
64. *United States v Salerno*, 481 US 739 (1987).
65. *United States v Enterprises, Inc.*, 498 US 292 (1991).
66. *Blanton et al. v North Las Vegas*, 489 US 538 (1989).
67. *J. E. B. v Alabama ex rel T. B.*, 511 US 127 (1994); *Batson v Kentucky*, 476 US 79 (1986); *Powers v Ohio*, 499 US 400 (1991); *Hernandez v New York*, 500 US 352 (1991); *Georgia v McCollum*, 505 US 42 (1990).
68. *Rhodes v Chapman*, 452 US 337 (1981); *Wilson v Seither*, 501 US 294 (1991).
69. *Hutto v Davis*, 454 US 370 (1982).
70. *Solem v Helm*, 463 US 277 (1983).
71. *Benton v Maryland*, 395 US 784 (1969).
72. Jerome Frank, *Courts on Trial* (Princeton University Press, 1949), p. 122. See also Rita James Simon, ed., *The Jury System in America: A Critical*

Overview (Sage Publications, 1975); John Guinther, *The Jury in America* (Facts-on-File Publications, 1988); Steven Brill, *Trial by Jury* (American Lawyer Books/Touchstone, 1989).

73. Laura Mansnerus, "Rewriting the Rules of the Jury System," *The New York Times*, November 4, 1995, p. Y7.

74. See comments of Jeffrey Abramson in *The New York Times*, November 4, 1995, p. Y7.

75. Harry Kalven, Jr., and Hans Zeisel, *The American Jury* (University of Chicago Press, 1971), p. 57. See also Jeffrey Abramson, *We, The Jury: The Jury System and the Ideal of Democracy* (Basic Books, 1994).

76. William O. Douglas, dissenting in *United States v Mara*, 410 US 19 (1973).

77. Bryan Abas, "The Ruckus out of Rocky Flats: Empowering the People Through Grand Juries," *The Recorder*, February 1, 1994, p. 16.

78. "Race and the Criminal Process," *Harvard Law Review* 101 (May 1988), pp. 1493, 1476.

79. Dean Alfred Blumstein and Joan Petersilia, quoted in Norval Morris, "Race and Crime: What Evidence Is There That Race Influences Results in the Criminal Justice System?" *Judicature*, August/September 1988, p. 112.

80. Morris, "Race and Crime," p. 112.

81. Gunnar Myrdal, *An American Dilemma* (Harper and Brothers, 1944).

82. Cassia C. Spohn, "Courts, Sentences, and Prisons," *Daedalus*, "An American Dilemma Revisited," *Journal of the American Academy of Arts and Sciences* (Winter 1995), p. 136.

83. Jonathan Kaufman, Wade Lambert, and Benjamin A. Holden, "Fuhrman's Comments Bolster Black Concerns About Police Conduct," *The Wall Street Journal*, August 31, 1995, p. A1.

84. George Edwards, *The Police on the Urban Frontier* (Institute of Human Relations Press and the American Jewish Committee, 1968), p. 28.

85. Morris, "Race and Crime," p. 113.

86. Associated Press, "Civilian Police-Review Agencies on Rise Nationwide," *The Recorder*, September 9, 1996, p. 8.

87. *West Virginia State Board of Education v Barnette*, 319 US 624 (1943).

88. Robert H. Jackson, *The Supreme Court in the American System of Government* (Harvard University Press, 1955), pp. 81–82.

CHAPTER 7

1. Mihailo Crnobrnja, *The Yugoslav Drama* (McGill-Queens University Press, 1994), p. 23.

2. Chris Hedges, "Bosnia Holds Vote with Few Reports of Real Violence," *The New York Times*, September 15, 1996, p. 1.

3. Clinton Rossiter, *Conservatism in America* (Vintage, 1962), p. 72.

4. *Marbury v Madison*, 1 Cranch 137 (1803).

5. See, generally, Bernard Bailyn, *The Ideological Origins of the American Revolution* (Harvard University Press, 1967).

6. Robert A. Dahl, "Liberal Democracy in the United States," in *A Prospect of Liberal Democracy*, ed. William Livingston (University of Texas Press, 1979), p. 64.

7. Ibid., pp. 59–60.

8. Franklin D. Roosevelt, State of the Union Address, January 11, 1944, *The Public Papers of the President of the United States, 1944* (Government Printing Office, 1962), pp. 371–94.

9. Bill Clinton, Address to Congress on Health Care, *The New York Times*, September 23, 1993, pp. A24–25.

10. Newt Gingrich, *To Renew America* (HarperCollins, 1995), p. 71.

11. Dick Armey, *The Freedom Revolution* (Regnery Publishing, 1995), p.150.

12. For an analysis of one aspect of the underclass, see Paul M. Sniderman and Michael Hagen, *Race and Inequality: A Study in American Values* (Chatham House, 1985).

13. When adjusted using the Consumer Price Index (CPI), the percent of people earning over $75,000 a year has risen from 6.4 percent in 1970 to 12.5 percent in 1993. *Statistical Abstract of the United States, 1995*, Table 723.

14. Harry S Truman, State of the Union Address, 1949, *The Public Papers of the President of the United States, 1949* (Government Printing Office, 1964), pp. 1–7.

15. David Spitz, "A Liberal Perspective on Liberalism and Conservatism," in *Left, Right and Center*, ed. Robert Goldwin (Rand McNally, 1965), p. 31.

16. See also Charles Peters and Philip Keisling, eds., *A New Road for America: The Neoliberal Movement* (University Press of America, 1984); Randall Rothenberg, *The Neoliberals: Creating the New American Politics* (Simon & Schuster, 1984).

17. Armey, *The Freedom Revolution*, pp. 291–93.

18. E. J. Dionne, Jr., *They Only Look Dead: Why Progressives Will Dominate the Next Political Era* (Simon & Schuster, 1996), p. 13. Emphasis in original.

19. Ibid.

20. James Carville, *We're Right, They're Wrong: A Handbook for Spirited Progressives* (Simon & Schuster, 1996), p. 40.

21. Theodore C. Sorensen, *Why I Am a Democrat* (Henry Holt and Company, 1996), pp. 193–94.

22. Kenneth R. Hoover, *Ideology and Political Life* (Brooks/Cole, 1987), p. 34.

23. See Milton Friedman, *Capitalism and Freedom* (University of Chicago Press, 1962); also Friedrich A. Hayek, *The Road to Serfdom* (University of Chicago Press, 1944).

24. Gingrich, *To Renew America*, p. 102.

25. Paula Poundstone, "He Didn't Even Like Girls," *Mother Jones* (May 1993), p. 37.

26. *Romer v Evans*, 116 S. Ct. 1620.

27. Barry Goldwater with Jack Casserly, *Goldwater* (Doubleday, 1988), p. 387.

28. Ronald Reagan, Inaugural Address, 1981, *The Public Papers of the President of the United States, 1981* (Government Printing Office, 1982), p. 1.

29. Kathleen Day, *S & L Hell: The People and the Politics Behind the $1 Trillion Savings and Loan Scandal* (W.W. Norton & Co., 1993).

30. See Edward A. Snyder, "The Effects of Higher Criminal Penalties on Antitrust Enforcement," *Journal of Law and Economics* 33 (October 1990), pp. 439–62; also Brian Burrough and John Helyar, *Barbarians at the Gate: The Fall of RJR Nabisco* (Harper, 1990).

31. Dan Goodman, "Bleeding-Heart Conservatives," *Time*, May 18, 1992, p. 37.

32. Ronald Reagan, Address to the Nation on the Economy, February 5, 1981, *The Public Papers of the President of the United States, 1981* (Government Printing Office, 1982), p. 81.

33. Sylvia Nasar, "Even among the Well-Off, the Rich Get Richer," *The New York Times*, March 5, 1992, p. A1.

34. Karl Marx, "Critique of the Gotha Program," in *Marx Selections*, ed. Allen W. Wood (Macmillan Publishing, 1988), p. 190.

35. Irving Howe, *Socialism and America* (Harcourt, 1985); Michael Harrington, Socialism: Past and Future (Arcade, 1989).

36. Center for Political Studies, University of Michigan, *American National Election Study, 1990: Post Election Survey* (April 1991).

37. Herbert McClosky and Alida Brill, *Dimensions of Tolerance: What Americans Believe about Civil Liberties* (Russell Sage Foundation, 1983), pp. 274–75.

38. Dinesh D'Sousa, *Illiberal Education: The Politics of Race and Sex on Campus* (Free Press, 1991), p. 313.

CHAPTER 8

1. See Clay Robison, "Judge Defends His Order that Mom Speak English," *The Houston Chronicle*, August 30, 1995, p. A1; Scott Parks, "Judge Defends Telling Mom to Speak English to Girl; AG, Others Question Ruling in Custody Case," *The Dallas Morning News*, August 30, 1995, p. A1; and Patty Reinert, "Speak English Only, Judge Orders Mother," *The Houston Chronicle*, August 29, 1995, p. A1.

2. Albert Einstein, quoted in Laurence J. Peter, *Peter's Quotations* (William Morrow, 1977), p. 358.
3. Alexis de Tocqueville, *Democracy in America*, ed. J. P. Mayer, trans. George Lawrence (Doubleday and Company, 1969), p. 278.
4. Ibid., p. 280.
5. U.S. Bureau of the Census, *Statistical Abstract of the United States, 1982–83* (Government Printing Office, 1983), p. 488.
6. U.S. Bureau of the Census, *Statistical Abstract of the United States, 1995* (Government Printing Office, 1995), p. 289.
7. V. O. Key, Jr., *Politics, Parties, and Pressure Groups*, 5th ed. (Thomas Y. Crowell, 1964), p. 232.
8. Earl Black and Merle Black, *The Vital South: How Presidents Are Elected* (Harvard University Press, 1992), p. 4.
9. Joseph A. Pika and Richard A. Watson, *The Presidential Contest*, 5th ed. (Congressional Quarterly Press, 1996), pp. 80–81.
10. Tocqueville, *Democracy in America*, p. 68.
11. Robert S. Erikson, Gerald C. Wright, and John P. McIver, *Statehouse Democracy: Public Opinion and Policy in the American States* (Cambridge University Press, 1993).
12. U.S. Bureau of the Census, *Statistical Abstract of the United States, 1996* (Government Printing Office, 1996), p. 28.
13. Holly Idelson, "Count Adds Seats in Eight States," *Congressional Quarterly Weekly Report* 48 (December 29, 1990), p. 4240.
14. U.S. Bureau of the Census, Release CB 91–24, January 25, 1991.
15. U.S. Bureau of the Census, *Population Profile of the United States, 1993*, U.S. Population Reports P-23, no. 185 (Government Printing Office, 1993), p. 34.
16. *Statistical Abstract, 1996*, pp. 44–46.
17. *Statistical Abstract, 1995*, pp. 41, 45.
18. U.S. Bureau of the Census Home Page: http://www.census.gov/ftp/pub/population/www/metropop.html.
19. *Statistical Abstract, 1996*, p. 14.
20. *Population Profile, 1993*, p. 36.
21. Dale Rogers Marshall, "The Continuing Significance of Race: The Transformation of American Politics," *American Political Science Review* 84 (June 1990), pp. 611–16.
22. Robert D. Ballard, "Introduction: Lure of the New South," in *Search of the New South: The Black Urban Experience in the 1970s and 1980s*, ed. Robert D. Ballard (University of Alabama Press, 1989), p. 5.
23. *Statistical Abstract, 1995*, p. 36 (based on projections for 1995).
24. *Population Profile, 1993*, p. 5.
25. *Statistical Abstract, 1996*, p. 48.
26. U.S. Bureau of the Census, *Household Wealth and Asset Ownership, 1991*, Current Population Reports P-70, no. 34 (Government Printing Office, 1991), table H.
27. *Statistical Abstract, 1996*, p. 461.
28. Ibid., p. 159.
29. Ibid., p. 176.
30. Ibid., pp. 22–23.
31. Mark R. Levy and Michael S. Karmer, *The Ethnic Factor: How America's Minorities Decide Elections* (Simon & Schuster, 1973).
32. Mark Stern, "Democratic Presidency and Voting Rights," in *Blacks in Southern Politics*, eds. Lawrence W. Mooreland, Robert P. Steed, and Todd A. Baker (Praeger, 1987), pp. 50–51.
33. David Bositis, *Blacks and the 1993 Republican National Convention* (Joint Center for Political and Economic Studies, 1992), p. 5; "Portrait of the Electorate," *The New York Times*, November 10, 1996, p. 16.
34. *Statistical Abstract, 1995*, pp. 34–36 (based on projections for 1995).
35. See Frank R. Parker, *Black Votes Count: Political Empowerment in Mississippi after 1965* (University of North Carolina Press, 1990).
36. Black Caucus of State Legislators, Washington, D.C.
37. *Statistical Abstract, 1996*, p. 14.
38. U.S. Bureau of the Census Home Page: http://www.census.gov/ftp/pub/population/socdem/race/api/tab3.txt, March 1994.
39. *Statistical Abstract, 1996*, p. 14.
40. Gary D. Sandefur and Arthur Sakamoto, "American Indian Household Structure and Income," *Demography* 25 (February 1988), p. 74.
41. U.S. Bureau of the Census, *We, The First Americans* (Government Printing Office, 1989), pp. 5–7.
42. Richard Santillan and Carlos Munoz, Jr., "Latinos and the Democratic Party," in *The Democrats Must Lead*, eds. James MacGregor Burns, William Crotty, Lois Lovelace Duke, and Lawrence D. Longley

43. Rodolfo O. de la Garza, Louis DeSipio, F. Chris Garcia, John Garcia, and Angelo Falcon, *Latino Voices: Mexican, Puerto Rican, and Cuban Perspectives on American Politics* (Westview Press, 1992), p. 13.
44. Ibid., p. 14.
45. U.S. Bureau of the Census, *The Hispanic Population in the United States*, Current Population Reports (Government Printing Office, 1992), p. 302.
46. De la Garza et al., *Latino Voices*, p. 14.
47. *Statistical Abstract, 1995*, p. 37.
48. *Statistical Abstract, 1996*, p. 10.
49. James West Davidson, William E. Gienapp, Christine Leigh Heyrman, Mark H. Lytle, and Michael B. Stoff, *Nation of Nations* (McGraw-Hill, 1990), pp. 833–34.
50. G. Thomas Edwards, *Sowing Good Seeds: The Northwest Suffrage Campaigns of Susan B. Anthony* (Oregon Historical Society Press, 1990), p. 136.
51. Paul Kleppner, *Continuity and Change in Electoral Politics, 1893–1928* (Greenwood Press, 1987), p. 172.
52. Carol Mueller, "The Gender Gap and Women's Political Influence," *Annals of the American Academy of Political and Social Sciences* 515 (May 1991), p. 25.
53. Self-reported turnout in the American National Election Studies, 1978–88, shows women voting at 2.2 percent less than men on average.
54. Barbara C. Burrell, *A Woman's Place Is in the House: Campaigning for Congress in the Feminist Era* (University of Michigan Press, 1994).
55. Diane L. Fowlkes, "Feminist Theory: Reconstructing Research and Teaching about American Politics and Government," *News for Teachers of Political Science* (Winter 1987), pp. 6–9. See also Andrea Dworkin, *Right-Wing Women* (Putnam's, 1983); Zillah R. Eisenstein, ed., *Feminism and Sexual Equality: Crisis in Liberal America* (Monthly Review Press, 1984); Ethel Klein, *Gender Politics* (Harvard University Press, 1984); and Rebecca E. Klatch, *Women of the New Right* (Temple University Press, 1987).
56. *Statistical Abstract, 1996*, p. 429.
57. *Statistical Abstract, 1996*, p. 470.
58. *Population Profile, 1993*, p. 27.
59. *Statistical Abstract, 1996*, p. 471.
60. E. J. Dionne, Jr., "Struggle for Work and Family Fueling Women's Movement," *The New York Times*, August 22, 1989, p. A1.
61. Jeffrey Schmalz, "Clinton Carves a Wide Path Deep into Reagan Country," *The New York Times*, November 4, 1992, p. B1.
62. Times Mirror Center for the People and the Press, "Jury Still Out on Clinton's Success" (August 5, 1993), p. 27.
63. For a discussion of the Holocaust, see Leni Yahil, *The Holocaust: The Fate of European Jewry* (Oxford University Press, 1990).
64. Stephen C. LeSuer, *The 1838 Mormon War in Missouri* (University of Missouri Press, 1987), pp. 151–53.
65. John Conway, "An Adapted Organic Tradition," *Daedalus* 117 (Fall 1988), p. 382. For an extended comparison of the impact of religion on politics in the United States and Canada, see Seymour Martin Lipset, *Continental Divide: The Values and Institutions of the United States and Canada* (Routledge, 1990), pp. 74–89.
66. Robert N. Bellah, *Beyond Belief: Essays on Religion in a Post-Traditional World* (University of California Press, 1991), pp. 168–90.
67. National Opinion Research Center, General Social Survey, 1972–94.
68. William H. Flanigan and Nancy H. Zingale, *Political Behavior of the American Electorate*, 8th ed. (CQ Press, 1994), p. 122.
69. Karl Cordell, "The Role of the Evangelical Church in the GDR," *Government and Opposition* 25 (Winter 1990), pp. 48–59.
70. Taylor Branch, *Parting the Waters: America in the King Years, 1954–63* (Simon & Schuster, 1988), p. 3.
71. Kevin Lange, "An Energized Religious Right? Strategies for the Clinton Era," *Christian Century* 110 (February 17, 1993), pp. 177–79.
72. Center for Political Studies, Inter-University Consortium for Political and Social Research, University of Michigan, American National Election Study, 1992.
73. Ibid.
74. Telephone survey of 113,000 households in the 48 contiguous states, April 1989–April 1990, Graduate School of the City University of New York.
75. Raymond E. Wolfinger, Fred I. Greenstein, and Martin Shapiro, *Dynamics of American Politics*, 2d ed. (Prentice Hall, 1980), p. 19.

76. Thomas Jefferson, "Autobiography," in *The Life and Selected Writings of Thomas Jefferson*, eds. Adrienne Koch and William Peden (Modern Library, 1944), p. 38.

77. U.S. Bureau of the Census, *Historical Statistics of the United States, Colonial Times to 1970* (Government Printing Office, 1976), p. 297; *U.S. Bureau of the Census, Statistical Abstract of the United States, 1993* (Government Printing Office, 1994), p. 457.

78. Stanley Fischer, "Symposium on the Slowdown in Productivity Growth," *Journal of Economic Perspectives* 2 (Fall 1988), pp. 3–7.

79. Organization for Economic Cooperation and Development (OECD), *National Accounts*, vol. 1, *Main Aggregates, 1960–89* (OECD, 1991), p. 145.

80. U.S. Department of Education, *Digest of Education Statistics, 1991* (Government Printing Office, 1991), p. 294.

81. U.S. Bureau of the Census, *Preliminary Estimates of Poverty Threshold, 1996* (Government Printing Office, 1997).

82. *Statistical Abstract, 1996*, p. 475.

83. Ibid., p. 473.

84. *Statistical Abstract, 1995*, p. 483.

85. In 1993, there were 32.8 million Americans over the age of 65 and 39.3 million people who fell below the poverty line. *Statistical Abstract, 1995*, pp. 15, 480.

86. Many of those classified as poor at the beginning of the 1980s climbed out of poverty over the course of the decade, but others fell into poverty during the same time. Overall, the proportion of the population classified as in poverty increased during the 1980s. See David Wessel, "Low-Income Mobility Was High in the 1980s," *Wall Street Journal*, June 2, 1992, p. A2.

87. U.S. Census Bureau web site: http://www.census.gov/hhes/income/incineq/p60tb3.html.

88. Stanley Lebergott, *The Americans: An Economic Record* (W.W. Norton, 1984), p. 66.

89. *Statistical Abstract, 1995*, p. 451. "Real" means that inflation has already been taken into account.

90. Daniel Bell, *The Coming of Post-Industrial Society: A Venture in Social Forecasting* (Basic Books, 1973), p. xviii.

91. *Statistical Abstract, 1996*, p. 443.

92. U.S. Department of Education, *Digest of Education Statistics, 1995*, National Center for Education Statistics Web site: http://www.ed.gov/NCES/pubs/D95/dtab004.html.

93. *Statistical Abstract, 1996*, p. 352.

94. *Griggs v Duke Power Company*, 401 US 424 (1971). See also *Wards Cove v Antonio*, 490 US 642 (1989).

95. Joan Biskupic, "Bush Signs Anti-Job Bias Bill amid Furor over Preferences," *Congressional Quarterly Weekly Report* 49 (November 23, 1991), p. 3463.

96. Stephen J. Rose, *American Profile Poster* (Pantheon Books, 1986), p. 9.

97. U.S. Bureau of the Census, *Money, Income and Poverty Status in the United States, 1990*, Current Population Reports P-60, no. 168 (Government Printing Office, 1991), p. 49.

98. Mattei Dogan and Dominique Pelassy, *How to Compare Nations: Strategies in Comparative Politics*, 2d ed. (Chatham House, 1990), p. 47.

99. Responses for subjective social class vary somewhat with wording of the question. The data on Great Britain are from the *Index to International Public Opinion, 1991–92* (Greenwood Press, 1992), p. 462.

100. Lipset, *Continental Divide*, p. 170.

101. *Statistical Abstract, 1995*, pp. 15, 117.

102. U.S. Bureau of the Census, *Voting and Registration in the Election of November 1992*, Current Population Reports P-20, no. 446 (Government Printing Office, 1993).

103. *Statistical Abstract, 1995*, p. 481.

104. *The New York Times*, September 23, 1993, pp. A24–25.

105. Seymour Martin Lipset, *Political Man* (Doubleday, 1963), pp. 283–86.

106. Thomas Jefferson to P. S. du Pont de Nemours, April 24, 1816, *The Writings of Thomas Jefferson*, ed. Paul L. Ford (G. P. Putnam's Sons, 1899), 10:25.

107. *Statistical Abstract, 1995*, p. 151; *Population Profile*, 1993, p. 113.

108. *Statistical Abstract, 1995*, p. 158.

109. U.S. Bureau of the Census Home Page: http://gopher.census.gov:70/0/bureau/pr/subject/income/cb95-185.txt.

110. World Development Report, *The Challenge of Development* (Oxford University Press, 1991), p. 261.

111. *Statistical Abstract, 1996*, pp. 159–60.

112. Jennifer Day and Andrea Curry, Current Population Reports, *Educational Attainment in the United States: March 1995* (U.S. Department of Commerce, 1996), Table 1.

113. Ibid.

114. Herbert McClosky and John Zaller, *The American Ethos: Public Attitudes Toward Capitalism and Democracy* (Harvard University Press, 1984), p. 261.

115. John Gunther, *Inside U.S.A.* (Harper and Brothers, 1947), p. 911.

116. Alan Ehrenhalt, *The United States of Ambition: Politicians, Power, and the Pursuit of Office* (Times Books, 1991), p. 275.

117. Carl N. Degler, *Out of Our Past: The Forces That Shaped Modern America*, 3d ed. (Harper & Row, 1984), p. 322.

CHAPTER 9

1. *Colorado Republican Federal Campaign Committee v FEC*, 116 Sup. Ct. 2309 (1995).

2. Jonathan Weisman, "Union Leaders Predict Victory Even Before Votes Tallied," *Congressional Quarterly Weekly Report*, November 2, 1996, pp. 3163–65; and Federal Elections Commission, "Congressional Spending Up Again in 1996," Press Release, April 14, 1997, p. 7.

3. Quoted in ibid., p. 3164.

4. Alan Greenblatt et al., "House and Senate Report," *Congressional Quarterly Weekly Report*, October 19, 1996, pp. 2970–3041. See also Federal Elections Commission, April 14, 1997, p. 32.

5. John E. Yang and Eric Pianin, "Clinton Wins by Wide Margin; GOP Holding Edge in Congress; House Democrats Chip Away But Fall Short of Goal," *The Washington Post*, November 6, 1996, p. A1.

6. Robin Toner, "GOP Leaders Proclaim Victory over Labor," *The New York Times*, November 7, 1996, p. B3.

7. Factions to James Madison included groups based on ethnic, religious, economic, sectional, and ideological differences. Interest groups today continue to reflect these differences but also include such disparate groups as the League of Women Voters, the Sierra Club, and the National Organization for Women.

8. Robert D. Putnam, *Making Democracy Work: Civic Traditions in Modern Italy* (Princeton University Press, 1993), p. 167. For more discussion of social capital, see James S. Coleman, *Foundations of Social Theory* (Harvard University Press, 1990), pp. 300–321, who credits Glenn Loury with introducing the concept in Glenn Loury, "A Dynamic Theory of Racial Income Differences," in *Women, Minorities, and Employment Discrimination*, eds. P.A. Wallace and A. Le Mund (Lexington Books, 1977). See also Michael J. Sandel, *Democracy's Discontent: America in Search of a Public Philosophy* (Harvard University Press, 1996).

9. Robert D. Pullman, "Bowling Alone: America's Declining Social Capital," *Journal of Democracy* 6 (January 1995), pp. 65–78.

10. Eleanor Flexner, *Century of Struggle* (Harvard University Press, 1975), pp. 7–8, 63–65.

11. Abigail Adams to John Adams, March 31, 1776, in *Feminism: The Essential Historical Writings*, ed. Miriam Schneir (Vintage Books, 1972), p. 3.

12. Milton Cantor and Bruce Laurie, eds., *Class, Sex and the Woman Worker* (Greenwood Press, 1977).

13. *Roe v Wade*, 410 US 113 (1973).

14. For a discussion of the response of established groups and interests to two recent movements, see L. Marvin Querby and Sarah J. Ritichie, "Mobilized Masses and Strategic Opponents: A Resource Mobilization Analysis of the Clean Air and Nuclear Freeze Movements," *Western Political Quarterly* 44 (June 1991), pp. 329–51.

15. Chuck Alston, "Lobbyists Storm Capitol Hill, Clash over Banking Bill," *Congressional Quarterly Weekly Report*, August 24, 1991, pp. 2313–18.

16. James Parks, "COPE Endorsements, 1968–1992," AFL-CIO, Department of Information, personal communication, January 6, 1994.

17. Estimate provided by Robert Biersack of the Federal Election Commission, January 16, 1997.
18. "Union Membership Drops to 16.4 Percent of Employees," *The Wall Street Journal*, February 9, 1990, p. B6; Frank Swoboda, "AFL-CIO Membership Is Shifting: Survey Shows Growing Strength Among Government, Service Unions," *The Washington Post*, October 31, 1991, p. A17.
19. James MacGregor Burns and Stewart Burns, *A People's Charter: The Pursuit of Rights in America* (Knopf, 1991).
20. William R. Donohue, *The Politics of the American Civil Liberties Union* (Transaction, 1985).
21. Michael Lienesch, "Right-wing Religion: Christian Conservatism as a Political Movement," *Political Science Quarterly* 97 (Fall 1982), pp. 403–25.
22. *Public Policy and Foundations: The Role of Politicians in Public Charities* (Center for Responsive Politics, 1987).
23. Anthony Lewis, "The Brazen Speaker," *The New York Times*, January 20, 1997, p. A15.
24. Swoboda, "AFL-CIO Membership Is Shifting," p. A17.
25. There is a debate in the literature about whether group membership has grown. For the view that it has, see Frank R. Baumgartner and Jack L. Walker, "Survey Research and Membership in Voluntary Associations," *American Journal of Political Science* 32 (November 1988), pp. 908–27. For a different perspective, see Tom W. Smith, "Trends in Voluntary Group Membership: Comments on Baumgartner and Walker," *American Journal of Political Science* 34 (August 1990), pp. 646–61, which in turn led to Frank R. Baumgartner and Jack L. Walker, "Measurement Validity and the Continuity of Results in Survey Research," *American Journal of Political Science* 34 (August 1990), pp. 662–70.
26. William P. Browne, "Organized Interests and Their Issue Niches: A Search for Pluralism in a Policy Domain," *Journal of Politics* 52 (May 1990), pp. 477–509.
27. Mancur Olson, *The Logic of Collective Action* (Harvard University Press, 1965), p. 34.
28. Robert Salisbury, "Interest Representation: The Dominance of Institutions," *American Political Science Review* 78 (March 1984), p. 66.
29. Thomas B. Edsall, *The New Politics of Inequality* (Norton, 1984), p. 110.
30. V. O. Key, Jr., *Public Opinion and American Democracy* (Knopf, 1961), pp. 504–7.
31. R. Kenneth Godwin, *One Billion Dollars of Influence: The Direct Marketing of Politics* (Chatham House, 1988).
32. Joan Biskupie, "NRA, Gun-Control Supporters Take Aim at Swing Votes," *Congressional Quarterly Weekly Report*, March 9, 1991, p. 604.
33. Lucius J. Barker, "Third Parties in Litigation: A Systemic View of the Judicial Function," *Journal of Politics* 29 (February 1967), pp. 41–69; Jethro K. Lieberman, *Litigious Society*, rev. ed. (Basic Books, 1983).
34. Gregory A. Calderia and John R. Wright, "Organized Interests and Agenda Setting in the U.S. Supreme Court," *American Political Science Review* 82 (December 1988), pp. 1109–27. See also Gregory A. Calderia and John R. Wright, "Amici Curiae before the Supreme Court: Who Participates, When, and How Much?" *Journal of Politics* 52 (August 1990), pp. 782–806.
35. Karen O'Connor, *Women's Organizations' Use of the Courts* (Lexington Books, 1980).
36. Lee Epstein and C. K. Rowland, "Debunking the Myth of Interest Group Invincibility in the Courts," *American Political Science Review* 85 (March 1991), pp. 205–17.
37. Phil Kuntz, "Cranston Case Ends on Floor with a Murky Plea Bargain," *Congressional Quarterly Weekly Report*, November 23, 1991, pp. 3432–38.
38. Jeffrey H. Birnbaum and Nina Burleigh, "Newt's Cash Machine: GOPAC Was Just a Start; Now Gingrich Is Master of the Beltway Money Game," *Time*, December 18, 1995, p. 39.
39. Ethan Bronner, *Battle for Justice: How the Bork Nomination Shook America* (Norton, 1989), pp. 50–55.
40. Evan Thomas, "Peddling Influence," *Time*, March 3, 1986, p. 28.
41. *Under the Influence: The 1996 Presidential Candidates and their Campaign Advisors* (Center for Public Integrity, 1996), p. 8.
42. David Mayhew, *Congress: The Electoral Connection* (Yale University Press, 1974), p. 45.
43. One indication of the importance of transmitting information may be the frequency of contact by lobbyists. See John R. Wright, "Contributions, Lobbying, and Committee Voting in the U.S. House of Representatives," *American Political Science Review* 84 (June 1990), pp. 418–38.
44. Herbert E. Alexander, *PACs: What They Are, How They Are Changing Political Campaign Financing Patterns* (Grass Roots Guides, 1979), p. 3.
45. For evidence of the impact of PAC expenditures on legislative committee behavior and legislative involvement generally, see Richard L. Hall and Frank W. Wayman, "Buying Time: Moneyed Interests and the Mobilization of Bias in Congressional Committees," *American Political Science Review* 84 (September 1990), pp. 797–820.
46. Factors that predict the formation of PACs include company size and the degree of regulation for corporations. See Craig Humphries, "Corporations, PACs and the Strategic Link between Contributions and Lobbying Activities," *Western Political Quarterly* 44 (June 1991), pp. 353–72.
47. Federal Elections Commission, "PAC Activity Increases in 1995–96 Election Cycle," Press Release, April 22, 1997, p. 5.
48. Edwin M. Epstein, "Business and Labor under the Federal Election Campaign Act of 1971," in *Parties, Interest Groups, and Campaign Finance Laws*, ed. Michael J. Malbin (American Enterprise Institute for Public Policy Research, 1980), p. 112. See also Gary Jacobson, *Money in Congressional Elections* (Yale University Press, 1980).
49. Charles Keating, quoted in David J. Jefferson, "Keating of American Continental Corporation Comes Out Fighting," *The Wall Street Journal*, April 18, 1989, p. B2.
50. Senator Charles C. Mathias, statement in *The New York Times*, February 27, 1986, p. A31.
51. Philip D. Duncan and Christine C. Lawrence, *Politics in America, 1996* (Congressional Quarterly, 1995), pp. 1508–31.
52. Gary J. Andres, "Business Involvement in Campaign Finance: Factors Influencing the Decision to Form a Corporate PAC," *PS: Political Science and Politics* 18 (Spring 1985), p. 213.
53. David B. Magleby and Candice J. Nelson, *The Money Chase: Congressional Campaign Finance Reform* (Brookings, 1990), p. 20. See also Brooks Jackson, *Honest Graft: Big Money and the American Political Process* (Knopf, 1988), p. 131.
54. Serge F. Kovaleski and Susan Schmidt, "Clinton-Lippo Boss Meeting Sought by Huang in Early '93: White House Releases Letter," *The Washington Post*, December 11, 1996, p. A10.
55. "Foreign Firms' U.S. Units Allowed to Operate PACs," *The Wall Street Journal*, June 18, 1991, p. A20.
56. Amy Dockster, "Nice PAC You've Got Here . . . A Pity If Anything Should Happen to It: How Politicians Shake Down the Special Interests," *Washington Monthly*, January 27, 1987, p. 24, quoted in Margaret Cates Nugent and John R. Johannes, eds., *Money, Elections, and Democracy: Reforming Congressional Campaign Finance* (Westview Press, 1990), p. 1.
57. Bernadette A. Budde, quoted in *National Journal*, November 24, 1979, p. 1983.
58. Hall and Wayman, "Buying Time," pp. 797–820. A different study of the House Ways and Means Committee found campaign contributions to be part of the representatives' policy decisions, but even more important was the number of lobbying contacts. See Wright, "Contributions, Lobbying, and Committee Voting," pp. 417–38.
59. For a study of the differences in individual and PAC contributions to incumbents, challengers, and open seat candidates, see Magleby and Nelson, *Money Chase*, chap. 4. See also John Theilmann and Al Wilhite, "The Determinants of Individuals' Campaign Contributions to Congressional Candidates," *American Politics Quarterly* 17 (July 1989), pp. 312–31.
60. Federal Elections Commission, April 22, 1997, p. 1.
61. Federal Commission Press Release, April 29, 1993, p. 3. See also *Buckley v Valeo*, 424 US 1 (1976).
62. Frank J. Sorauf, *Money in American Elections* (Scott, Foresman/Little, Brown, 1988), pp. 64–65.
63. Ronald Reagan, "Remarks to Administration Officials on Domestic Policy," December 13, 1988, *Weekly Compilation of Presidential Documents* 24 (December 1988), pp. 1615–20.
64. Thomas L. Gais, Mark A. Peterson, and Jack L. Walker, "Interest Groups, Iron Triangles, and Representative Institutions in American National Government," *British Journal of Political Science* 14 (April 1984), pp. 161–85.
65. Sylvia Tesh, "In Support of Single-Interest Politics," *Political Science Quarterly* 99 (Spring 1984), pp. 27–44.
66. Alexander, *PACs*, p. 5.

67. Report and Recommendations of the California Commission on Campaign Financing, *The New Gold Rush: Financing California's Legislative Campaigns* (Center for Responsive Government, 1985), pp. 177–97. For a study of state lobby regulation, see Cynthia Opheim, "Explaining the Differences in State Lobby Regulation," *Western Political Quarterly* 44 (June 1991), pp. 405–21.

68. Douglas Jehl and Sara Fritz, "Clinton Team Issues Ethics Rules for Top Appointees," *Los Angeles Times*, December 10, 1992, p. A26.

69. Adam Clymer, "Congress Sends Lobbying Overhaul to Clinton," *The New York Times*, December 16, 1995, sec. 1, p. 36.

70. Magleby and Nelson, *Money Chase*, p. 20. See also Jackson, *Honest Graft*, pp. 72–97.

71. Magleby and Nelson, *Money Chase*, pp. 72–97.

72. See Jackson, *Honest Graft*; Robert Kuttner, "Protection Racket," review of *Honest Graft*, by Brooks Jackson, *The New Republic*, March 16, 1989, pp. 40–42.

73. Gary Jacobson, *The Politics of Congressional Elections*, 3d ed. (HarperCollins, 1992), p. 53. For a different assessment, see Donald P. Green and Jonathan S. Krasno, "Salvation for the Spendthrift Incumbent: Reestimating the Effects of Campaign Spending in House Elections," *American Journal of Political Science* 32 (1988), pp. 884–907.

74. See David Jessup, "Can Political Influence Be Democratized? A Labor Perspective," in *Parties, Interest Groups, and Campaign Finance Laws*, ed., Malbin, pp. 26–55.

CHAPTER 10

1. John E. Mueller, "Choosing Among 133 Candidates," *Public Opinion Quarterly* 34 (Fall 1970), pp. 395–402.

2. E. E. Schattschneider, *Party Government* (Holt, Rinehart and Winston, 1942), p. 1.

3. See, for example, David W. Brady and Charles S. Bullock IV, "Party and Faction Within Legislatures," in *Handbook of Legislative Research*, eds. Gerhard Loewenberg, Samuel C. Patterson, and Malcolm E. Jewell (Harvard University Press, 1985), chap. 4.

4. Charles O. Jones, *The Trusteeship Presidency: Jimmy Carter and the United States Congress* (Louisiana University Press, 1988). See also Charles O. Jones, "Ronald Reagan and the U.S. Congress: Visible Hand Politics," and Paul E. Peterson and Mark Rom, "Lower Taxes, More Spending and Budget Deficits," in *The Reagan Legacy*, ed. Charles O. Jones (Chatham House, 1988), pp. 30–59, 213–40, for discussions of the role of party in Congress during the last two administrations.

5. L. Sandy Maisel, ed., *The Parties Respond: Changes in American Parties and Campaigns* (Westview Press, 1994).

6. Peverill Squire, ed., *The Iowa Caucuses and the Presidential Nominating Process* (Westview Press, 1989).

7. *The Book of the States, 1996–1997* (Council of State Governments, 1996), pp. 157–58.

8. Byron E. Shafer, *Bifurcated Politics* (Harvard University Press, 1988).

9. William H. Riker, "The Two-Party System and Duverger's Law: An Essay on the History of Political Science," *American Political Science Review* 76 (December 1982), pp. 753–66. For a classic analysis, see Schattschneider, *Party Government*.

10. Steven J. Rosenstone, Roy L. Behr, and Edward H. Lazarus, *Third Parties in America: Citizen Response to Major Party Failure* (Princeton University Press, 1984). See also Xandra Kayden and Eddie Mahe, Jr., *The Party Goes On: The Persistence of the Two Party System in the United States* (Basic Books, 1985), pp. 143–144.

11. On the impact of third parties, see Howard R. Penniman, "Presidential Third Parties and the Modern American Two-Party System," in *The Party Symbol*, ed. William J. Crotty (W. H. Freeman, 1980), pp. 101–17. See also Frank Smallwood, *The Other Candidates: Third Parties in Presidential Elections* (University Press of New England, 1983).

12. Benjamin Franklin, George Washington, and Thomas Jefferson, quoted in Richard Hofstadter, *The Idea of a Party System* (University of California Press, 1969), pp. 2, 123.

13. V. O. Key, "A Theory of Critical Elections," *Journal of Politics* 17 (February 1955), pp. 3–18.

14. Walter Dean Burnham, *Critical Elections and the Mainsprings of American Politics* (Norton, 1970), pp. 1–10.

15. E. E. Schattschneider, *The Semisovereign People: A Realist's View of Democracy in America* (Holt, Rinehart and Winston, 1975), pp. 78–80.

16. William E. Gienapp, *The Origins of the Republican Party, 1852–1856* (Oxford University Press, 1987).

17. David W. Brady, "Elections, Congress and Public Policy Changes: 1886–1960," in *Realignment in American Politics: Toward a Theory*, eds. Bruce A. Campbell and Richard Trilling (Texas University Press, 1980), p. 188.

18. Gerald Pomper, "Classification of Presidential Elections," *Journal of Politics* 29 (1967), p. 538.

19. For an examination of American attitudes toward parties over the breadth of American history, see Austin Ranney, *Curing the Mischiefs of Faction: Party Reform in America* (University of California Press, 1975).

20. Federal Election Commission, "Summary of 1989–90 Political Party Finances," March 15, August 6, and October 31, 1991.

21. Paul Allen Beck, *Party Politics in America*, 8th ed. (Longman, 1997), chap. 2.

22. Edmund Burke, "Thoughts on the Cause of the Present Discontents," in *Burke: Select Works*, ed. E. J. Payne (Clarendon Press, 1878), 1:86.

23. Joseph A. Schumpeter, *Capitalism, Socialism and Democracy* (Harper and Row, 1975), p. 283.

24. The early Republican efforts and advantages over the Democrats are well documented in Thomas B. Edsall, *The New Politics of Inequality* (Norton, 1984); Gary C. Jacobson, "The Republican Advantage in Campaign Finances," in *New Direction in American Politics*, eds. Chubb and Peterson, p. 6.

25. See L. Sandy Maisel, *From Obscurity to Oblivion: Running in the Congressional Primary*, rev. ed. (University of Tennessee Press, 1986).

26. John F. Bibby, *Politics, Parties, and Elections in America* (Nelson-Hall, 1992). For further data on these roles, see Cornelius P. Cotter, James L. Gibson, John F. Bibby, and Robert J. Huckshorn, *Party Organizations in American Politics* (Praeger, 1984).

27. See James L. Gibson, Cornelius P. Cotter, John F. Bibby, and Robert J. Huckshorn, "Assessing Party Organizational Strength," *American Journal of Political Science* 27 (May 1983), pp. 193–222; Cotter et al., *Party Organizations in American Politics*.

28. Paul S. Herrnson, *Party Campaigning in the 1980s: Have the National Parties Made a Comeback as Key Players in Congressional Elections?* (Harvard University Press, 1988), p. 122.

29. On the influence of local parties, see Kayden and Mahe, *Party Goes On*.

30. See Bruce E. Keith, David B. Magleby, Candice J. Nelson, Elizabeth Orr, Mark C. Westlye, and Raymond E. Wolfinger, *The Myth of the Independent Voter* (University of California Press, 1992), p. 148.

31. Michael J. Malbin, "The Conventions, Platforms, and Issue Activists," in *The American Elections of 1980*, ed. Austin Ranney (American Enterprise Institute, 1982), pp. 116–41.

32. Katja Bullock, director of information, White House Office of Personnel, interview with David Magleby, April 9, 1992. A listing of many of these positions is presented in a book published by the U.S. Government, *Policy and Supporting Positions* (Government Printing Office, November 9, 1988).

33. See Angus Campbell, Philip E. Converse, Warren E. Miller, and Donald E. Stokes, *The American Voter* (Wiley, 1960); Norman A. Nie, Sidney Verba, and John R. Petrocik, *The Changing American Voter*, enlarged ed. (Harvard University Press, 1979).

34. Campbell et al., *American Voter*, pp. 121–28.

35. Keith et al., *Myth of the Independent Voter*.

36. See Byron E. Shafer, *The End of Realignment: Interpreting American Electoral Eras* (University of Wisconsin Press, 1991).

37. Hedrick Smith, *The Power Game: How Washington Works* (Random House, 1988), p. 671.

38. See Norman R. Luttbeg and Michael M. Gant, *American Electoral Behavior 1952–92*, 2d ed. (Peacock, 1995), p. 39; also Nie et al., *Changing American Voter*, p. 47.

39. Nine percent of all voters were Pure Independents in 1956 and 1960. Keith et al., *Myth of the Independent Voter*, p. 51. In 1992 the same percent were Pure Independents. 1992 American National Election Study.

40. For the "pessimistic view" of the party condition, see Martin P. Wattenberg, *The Decline of American Political Parties, 1952–1992* (Harvard University Press, 1994). See also Alan Ware, *The Breakdown of Democratic Party Organization, 1940–1980* (Clarendon Press, 1985).

41. For the "optimistic view," see Ralph M. Goldman, *Search for Consensus: The Story of the Democratic Party* (Temple University Press, 1979), pp. 366–73; Kayden and Mahe, *Party Goes On*; Larry Sabato, *The Party's Just Begun:*

Shaping Political Parties in America's Future (Scott, Foresman, 1988); Joseph A. Schlesinger, "The New American Political Party," *American Political Science Review* 79 (December 1985), pp. 1152–69; David E. Price, *Bringing Back the Parties* (Congressional Quarterly Press, 1984).

42. "With Democrats in the White House, Partisanship Hits New High," *Congressional Quarterly Weekly Report*, December 18, 1993, pp. 3432–34.

43. "Vote Studies," *Congressional Quarterly Weekly Report*, December 21, 1996, p. 3461.

44. Mark T. Kehoe, "Clinton Veto Tally: Up to 11," *Congressional Quarterly Weekly Report*, January 6, 1996, p. 10.

45. Herrnson, *Party Campaigning in the 1980s*, pp. 80–81.

CHAPTER 11

1. Vanderbilt Television News Archives videotape, Vanderbilt University Library, Nashville, Tenn.

2. "It's Reagan 2 to 1 in Poll by ABC After the Debate," *Chicago Tribune*, October 29, 1980, sec. 1, p. 10.

3. Robert Coles, *The Moral Life of Children* (Atlantic Monthly Press, 1986); Robert Coles, *The Political Life of Children* (Atlantic Monthly Press, 1986).

4. Coles, *Political Life of Children*, pp. 59–60.

5. Pamela Johnston Conover, "The Influence of Group Identifications on Political Perception and Evaluation," *Journal of Politics* 46 (August 1984), pp. 760–85; Henry E. Brady and Paul M. Sniderman, "Attitude Attribution: A Group Basis for Political Reasoning," *American Political Science Review* 79 (December 1985), pp. 1061–78.

6. Shawn W. Rosenberg, "Sociology, Psychology, and the Study of Political Behavior: The Case of the Research on Political Socialization," *Journal of Politics* 47 (May 1985), pp. 715–31.

7. Russell J. Dalton, "Reassessing Parental Socialization: Indicator Unreliability versus Generational Transfer," *American Political Science Review* 74 (June 1980), pp. 421–31.

8. Edgar Litt, "Civic Education Norms and Political Indoctrination," *American Sociological Review* 28 (February 1963), pp. 69–75. See also Elizabeth Leonie Simpson, *Democracy's Stepchildren* (Jossey-Bass, 1971); M. Kent Jennings and Richard G. Niemi, *The Political Character of Adolescence* (Princeton University Press, 1974); Stanley Allen Renshon, "Personality and Family Dynamics in the Political Socialization Process," *American Journal of Political Science* 19 (February 1975), pp. 63–80; Frances Fitzgerald, *America Revised* (Atlantic–Little, Brown, 1979).

9. Kenneth Feldman and Theodore M. Newcomb, *The Impact of College on Students*, vol. 2 (Jossey-Bass, 1969), pp. 16–24, 49–56.

10. Alexander N. Astin et al., *The American Freshmen: National Norms for 1990* (UCLA Graduate School of Education, 1991).

11. See Randall Herbert Balmer, *Mine Eyes Have Seen the Glory: A Journey into the Evangelical Subculture in America* (Oxford University Press, 1993).

12. Suzanne Koprince Sebert, M. Kent Jennings, and Richard G. Niemi, "The Political Texture of Peer Groups," in Jennings and Niemi, *Political Character of Adolescence*, p. 246.

13. Benjamin Page and Robert Shapiro, *The Rational Public* (University of Chicago Press, 1992), p. 237.

14. George J. Church, "What in the World Are We Doing?" *Time*, October 18, 1993, p. 42.

15. Walter Lippmann, *Public Opinion* (Harcourt Brace, 1922; reprint, Macmillan, 1961).

16. David Mayhew, *Congress: The Electoral Connection* (Yale University Press, 1974); Richard F. Fenno, Jr., *Home Style: House Members in Their Districts* (Little Brown, 1978).

17. Warren E. Miller and Donald E. Stokes, "Constituency Influence in Congress," *American Political Science Review* 57 (March 1963), pp. 45–46; Robert S. Erikson and Kent L. Tedin, *American Public Opinion*, 5th ed. (Allyn and Bacon, 1995), p. 279.

18. Everett C. Ladd and John Benson, "The Growth of News Polls in American Politics," in *Media Polls in American Politics*, eds. Thomas Mann and Gary Orren (Washington, D.C.: Brookings Institution, 1992), pp. 19–31.

19. Scott L. Althaus, "The Conservative Nature of Public Opinion," paper presented to the American Political Science Association Annual Meeting, Washington, D.C., 1993, pp. 2–3.

20. Thomas E. Mann and Raymond E. Wolfinger, "Candidates and Parties in Congressional Elections," *American Political Science Review* 74 (September 1980), pp. 617–40.

21. Erikson and Tedin, *American Public Opinion*, p. 304.

22. Neil S. Newhouse and Christine L. Matthews, "NAFTA Revisited: Most Americans Just Weren't Deeply Engaged," *Public Perspective* 5 (January/February 1994), pp. 31–32.

23. 1960–90 American National Election Studies, Center for Political Studies, University of Michigan, Ann Arbor.

24. Frank R. Parker, *Black Votes Count: Political Empowerment in Mississippi After 1965* (University of North Carolina Press, 1990), p. 3.

25. Bernard Grofman and Lisa Handley, "The Impact of the Voting Rights Act on Black Representation in Southern State Legislatures," *Legislative Studies Quarterly* 16 (February 1991), pp. 111–28.

26. G. Bingham Powell, Jr., "American Voter Turnout in Comparative Perspective," *American Political Science Review* 80 (March 1986), p. 38.

27. Raymond E. Wolfinger and Steven J. Rosenstone, "The Effect of Registration Laws on Voter Turnout," *American Political Science Review* 72 (March 1978), p. 24.

28. Raymond E. Wolfinger and Steven J. Rosenstone, *Who Votes?* (Yale University Press, 1980), pp. 78, 88.

29. For a discussion of the differences in the turnout between presidential and midterm elections, see James E. Campbell, "The Presidential Surge and Its Midterm Decline in Congressional Elections, 1868–1988," *Journal of Politics* 53 (May 1991), pp. 477–87.

30. David E. Rosenbaum, "Democrats Keep Solid Hold on Congress," *The New York Times*, November 9, 1988, p. A24.

31. Paula Ries and Anne J. Stone, eds., *The American Women 1992–93: A Status Report* (Women's Research and Education Institute, 1992), p. 415.

32. Congressional Research Service, "Voter Turnout in the Presidential Election of 1992: The States," January 26, 1993, pp. 4–5. See also Powell, "American Voter Turnout," pp. 17–43.

33. Grofman and Handley, "Impact of the Voting Rights Act," pp. 118–22.

34. Ruy A. Teixeira, "Will the Real Nonvoter Please Stand Up?" *Public Opinion*, July/August 1988, pp. 41–59.

35. Raymond E. Wolfinger, David P. Glass, and Peverill Squire, "Predictors of Electoral Turnout: An International Comparison," *Policy Studies Review* 9 (Spring 1990), pp. 567–68. The impact of registration requirements is not greater for poorly educated persons as was once thought. See Jonathan Nogler, "The Effect of Registration Laws on U.S. Voter Turnout," *American Political Science Review* 85 (December 1991), p. 1402.

36. Rosenbaum, "Democrats Keep Solid Hold in Congress," p. A24.

37. Wolfinger and Rosenstone, *Who Votes?* p. 102.

38. Sandra Baxter and Marjorie Lansing, *Women and Politics: The Invisible Majority* (University of Michigan Press, 1980), pp. 106–107.

39. See Angus Campbell, Philip E. Converse, Warren E. Miller, and Donald E. Stokes, *The American Voter* (Wiley, 1960). This volume is a foundation of modern voting analysis despite much new evidence and reinterpretation. See also Norman H. Nie, Sidney Verba, and John R. Petrocik, *The Changing American Voter* (Harvard University Press, 1976); Ruy A. Teixeira, *Why Americans Don't Vote: Turnout Decline in the United States, 1960–1984* (Greenwood, 1987).

40. Wolfinger and Rosenstone, *Who Votes?*

41. Austin Ranney, "Nonvoting Is Not a Social Disease," *Public Opinion*, October/November 1983, pp. 16–19.

42. Thomas Byrne Edsall, *The New Politics of Inequality* (W. W. Norton, 1984), p. 181.
43. Frances Fox Piven and Richard A. Cloward, "Prospects for Voter Registration Reform: A Report on the Experiences of the Human SERVE Campaign," *PS: Political Science and Politics* 18 (Summer 1985), pp. 582–92.
44. Wolfinger and Rosenstone, *Who Votes?* p. 109.
45. 1992 American National Election Study, Center for Political Studies, University of Michigan, Ann Arbor.
46. E. E. Schattschneider, *The Semisovereign People* (Dryden Press, 1975), p. 96.
47. Stephen Earl Bennett and David Resnick, "The Implications of Nonvoting for Democracy in the United States," *American Journal of Political Science* 84 (August 1990), pp. 771–802.
48. Bruce E. Keith, David B. Magleby, Candice J. Nelson, Elizabeth Orr, Mark C. Westlye, and Raymond E. Wolfinger, *The Myth of the Independent Voter* (University of California Press, 1992), pp. 60–75; 1992 American National Election Study, Center for Political Studies, University of Michigan, Ann Arbor.
49. Michael B. MacKuen, Robert S. Erikson, and James A. Stimson, "Macropartisanship," *American Political Science Review* 83 (December 1989), pp. 1125–42.
50. Martin P. Wattenberg, *The Rise of Candidate Centered Politics: Presidential Elections of the 1980s* (Harvard University Press, 1991), p. 1.
51. Ibid.
52. Barry Goldwater, quoted in Theodore H. White, *The Making of the President, 1964* (Athenaeum Publishers, 1965, p. 217.
53. William H. Flanigan and Nancy H. Zingale, *Political Behavior of the American Electorate*, 8th ed. (Congressional Quarterly Press, 1994), p. 173.
54. Roper Center for Public Opinion Research, University of Connecticut, "Public Opinion Online," CBS News/*New York Times* Poll, January 19, 1997.
55. J. Merril Shanks and Warren E. Miller, "Policy Direction and Performance Evaluation: Complementary Explanations of the Reagan Elections," *British Journal of Political Science* 20 (1990), pp. 143–235; Warren E. Miller and J. Merril Shanks, "Alternative Interpretations of the 1988 Election: Policy Direction, Current Conditions, Presidential Performance, and Candidate Traits," paper presented to the American Political Science Association Annual Meeting, Atlanta, 1989.
56. Amihai Glazer, "The Strategy of Candidate Ambiguity," *American Political Science Review* 84 (March 1990), pp. 237–41.
57. Robert S. Erikson and David W. Romero, "Candidate Equilibrium and the Behavioral Model of the Vote," *American Political Science Review* 84 (December 1990), p. 1122.
58. Morris P. Fiorina, *Retrospective Voting in American National Elections* (Yale University Press, 1981).
59. Miller and Shanks, "Alternative Interpretations of the 1988 Election." See also Warren E. Miller and J. Merrill Shanks, *The New American Voter* (Harvard University Press, 1966).
60. Voter Research and Survey, Exit Poll of Voters, November 3, 1992.
61. Gerald H. Kramer, "Short-Term Fluctuations in U.S. Voting Behavior, 1896–1964," *American Political Science Review* 65 (March 1971), pp. 131–43. See also Edward R. Tufte, "Determinants of the Outcomes of Midterm Congressional Elections," *American Political Science Review* 69 (September 1975), pp. 812–26.
62. John R. Hibbing and John R. Alford, "The Educational Impact of Economic Conditions: Who Is Held Responsible?" *American Journal of Political Science* 25 (August 1981), pp. 423–39; Morris P. Fiorina, "Who Is Held Responsible? Further Evidence on the Hibbing-Alford Thesis," *American Journal of Political Science* (February 1983), pp. 158–64.
63. Robert M. Stein, "Economic Voting for Governor and U.S. Senator: The Electoral Consequences of Federalism," *Journal of Politics* 52 (February 1990), pp. 29–53.
64. M. Stephen Weatherford, "Economic Voting and the Symbolic Politics' Argument: A Reinterpretation and Synthesis," *American Political Science Review* 77 (March 1983), pp. 158–74.

CHAPTER 12

1. CNN's *Crossfire*, March 21, 1996, transcript 1609.
2. Quoted in "On Target," *Newsweek*, November 18, 1996, p. 48.
3. Newt Gingrich, speech to Blue Cross/Blue Shield Conference, *The New York Times*, July 20, 1996, p. A8.
4. "On Target," p. 54.
5. *1994 Census of Governments*, vol. 1, no. 2 (Government Printing Office, 1995), p. 1.
6. Washington voters enacted term limits in 1992 after defeating them in 1991.
7. In the 1992 and 1994 National Election Studies, 77–78 percent of Americans favored term limits. Center for Political Studies, University of Michigan.
8. *U.S. Term Limits Inc. v Thornton*, 114 S.Ct. 2703.
9. For an insightful examination of electoral rules, see Bernard Grofman and Arend Lijphart, eds., *Electoral Laws and Their Political Consequences* (Agathon Press, 1986).
10. Arend Lijphart, "The Political Consequences of Electoral Laws, 1945–85," *American Political Science Review* 84 (June 1990), pp. 481–95.
11. George Rabinowitz and Stuart Elaine MacDonald, "The Power of the States in U.S. Presidential Elections," *American Political Science Review* 80 (March 1986), pp. 65–87.
12. Dany M. Adkison and Christopher Elliott, "The Electoral College: A Misunderstood Institution," *PS: Political Science & Politics* 30 (March 1997), pp. 77–80.
13. See, as examples, David Mayhew, *Congress: The Electoral Connection* (Yale University Press, 1974); Richard F. Fenno, Jr., *Home Style: House Members in Their Districts* (Little, Brown, 1978); James E. Campbell, "The Return of Incumbents: The Nature of Incumbency Advantage," *Western Political Science Quarterly* 36 (September 1983), pp. 434–44.
14. Gary King and Andrew Gelman, "Systemic Consequences of Incumbency Advantage in U.S. House Elections," *American Journal of Political Science* 35 (February 1991), pp. 110–37.
15. See Gary C. Jacobson, *The Politics of Congressional Elections*, 4th ed. (Longman, 1997), chap. 6; Alan I. Abramowitz, "Economic Conditions, Presidential Popularity, and Voting Behavior in Midterm Congressional Elections," *Journal of Politics* (February 1985), p. 130.
16. See Edward R. Tufte, *Political Control of the Economy* (Princeton University Press, 1978); see also his "Determinants of the Outcomes of Midterm Congressional Elections," *American Political Science Review* 69 (1975), pp. 812–26. For a more recent discussion of the same subject, see Jacobson, *Politics of Congressional Elections*, pp. 123–78.
17. Alan I. Abramowitz and Jeffrey A. Segal, "Determinants of the Outcomes of U.S. Senate Elections," *Journal of Politics* 48 (1986), pp. 433–39.
18. "Execution at Last Awaits Child Killer," *The Tampa Tribune*, September 28, 1996, p. 12; Kathleen Adams, Charlotte Faltermayer, Janice M. Horowitz, Lina Lofaro, Belinda Luscombe, Jeffrey C. Rubin, Alain L. Sanders, and Sidney Urquhart, "The Election Notebook" (http://allpolitics.com/elections/time.special/notebook.shtml).
19. Judy Walton, "Charges, Money, Time Fly at End: Area Campaigning Heats Up in Final Days," *The Chattanooga Times*, October 31, 1996, p. A1.
20. Alan Ehrenhalt, *The United States of Ambition: Politicians, Power, and the Pursuit of Office* (Times Books, 1991).
21. Mayhew, *Congress*, p. 46.
22. Linda L. Fowler and Robert D. McClure, *Political Ambition: Who Decides to Run for Congress* (Yale University Press, 1989); David T. Canon, "Political Conditions and Experienced Challengers in Congressional Elections, 1972–1984," paper presented to the American Political Science Association Annual Meeting, New Orleans, August 29–September 1, 1985.
23. Keith Krehbiel and John R. Wright, "The Incumbency Effect in Congressional Elections: A Test of Two Explanations," *American Journal of Political Science* 27 (February 1983), p. 140.
24. Juliana Gruenwald and Deborah Kalb, "Despite Push, Democrats Fail to Topple GOP," *Congressional Quarterly Weekly Report*, November 9, 1996, p. 3225.

25. Gary C. Jacobson and Samuel Kernell, *Strategy and Choice in Congressional Elections* (Yale University Press, 1981).

26. David B. Magleby and Candice J. Nelson, *The Money Chase: Congressional Campaign Finance Reform* (Brookings Institution, 1990), p. 37.

27. Politics Now Election Returns: Party Breakdowns (http://pn1.politicsnow.com/campaign/house/resultcharts).

28. Albert D. Cover, "One Good Term Deserves Another: The Advantages of Incumbency in Congressional Elections," *American Journal of Political Science* 21 (August 1977), pp. 523–42; Morris P. Fiorina, *Congress: Keystone of the Washington Establishment* (Yale University Press, 1978); Mayhew, *Congress*, pp. 52–53.

29. Mayhew, *Congress*, p. 61; Richard F. Fenno, Jr., *Congressmen in Committees* (Little, Brown, 1973); Steven S. Smith and Christopher J. Deering, *Committees in Congress*, 3d ed (Congressional Quarterly Press, 1997).

30. See Fenno, *Home Style*.

31. Glenn R. Parker, "The Role of Constituent Trust in Congressional Elections," *Public Opinion Quarterly* 53 (Summer 1989), pp. 175–96.

32. *Thursted v Gregoire* 841 F. Supp. 1068.

33. Candice J. Nelson, "Campaign Finance in Presidential and Congressional Elections," *Political Science Teacher* (Summer 1988), p. 6.

34. Jonathan S. Krasno, *Challengers, Competition, and Reelection: Comparing Senate and House Elections* (Yale University Press, 1994).

35. Alan I. Abramowitz, "Explaining Senate Election Outcomes," *American Political Science Review* 82 (June 1988), pp. 385–403.

36. David B. Magleby, "More Bang for the Buck: Campaign Spending in Small State U.S. Senate Elections," paper presented at the Western Political Science Association Annual Meeting, Salt Lake City, March 30–April 1, 1989.

37. Robert D. Loevy, *The Flawed Path to the Presidency, 1992: Unfairness and Inequality in the Presidential Selection Process* (State University of New York Press, 1994).

38. Rhodes Cook, "GOP Shows Dramatic Growth, Especially in the South," *Congressional Quarterly Weekly Report*, January 13, 1996, pp. 97–100.

39. Paul T. David and James W. Caesar, *Proportional Representation in Presidential Nominating Politics* (University Press of Virginia, 1980).

40. For a discussion of the 1996 primary rules, see Rhodes Cook, "GOP's Rules Favor Dole, If He Doesn't Stumble," *Congressional Quarterly Weekly Report*, January 27, 1996, pp. 228–31.

41. The descriptions of these types of primaries are drawn from James W. Davis, *Presidential Primaries*, rev. ed. (Greenwood Press, 1984), chap. 3. See pp. 56–63 for specifics on each state (and Puerto Rico). This material is used with the permission of the publisher.

42. *The Book of the States, 1996–1997* (Council of State Governments, 1996), pp. 157–58.

43. See John Carmody, "The TV Column," *The Washington Post*, September 2, 1996, p. D4.

44. Stephen J. Wayne, *The Road to the White House 1996: The Politics of Presidential Elections* (St. Martin's Press, 1996), chap. 5.

45. Jeff Fishel, *Presidents and Promises* (Congressional Quarterly Press, 1984).

46. William Safire, "Gore Flattens Perot," *The New York Times*, November 11, 1993, p. A27.

47. Jules Witcover uses the image of a marathon to describe the 1976 presidential campaign in *Marathon: The Pursuit of the Presidency, 1972–1976* (Viking, 1977).

48. Robert S. Erikson, "Economic Conditions and the Presidential Vote," *American Political Science Review* 83 (June 1989), pp. 567–75. Class-based voting has also become more important. See Robert S. Erikson, Thomas O. Lancaster, and David W. Romers, "Group Components of the Presidential Vote, 1952–1984," *Journal of Politics* 51 (May 1989), pp. 337–46.

49. On the key factor of personal attributes in presidential campaigning, see David P. Glass, "Evaluating Presidential Candidates: Who Focuses on Their Personal Attributes?" *Public Opinion Quarterly* 49 (Winter 1985), pp. 517–34. See also Herbert B. Asher, *Presidential Elections and American Politics*, 4th ed. (Dorsey Press, 1988).

50. Sidney Kraus, *The Great Debates: Kennedy vs Nixon, 1960* (Indiana University Press, 1962). See also Myles Martel, *Political Campaign Debates* (Longman, 1983).

51. See Robert Hunter, ed., *Electing the President: A Program for Reform, Final Report of the Commission on National Election* (Center for Strategic and International Studies, 1986); James L. Sundquist, *Constitutional Reform* (Brookings Institution, 1986); Edward N. Kearny, "Presidential Nominations and Representative Democracy: Proposals for Change," *Presidential Studies Quarterly* 14 (Summer 1984), pp. 348–56.

52. Barbara Norrander and Greg W. Smith, "Type of Contest, Candidate Strategy, and Turnout in Presidential Primaries," *American Politics Quarterly* 13 (January 1985), p. 28.

53. Walter Shapiro, "The Primary Lessons of 1988," *Time*, June 20, 1988, p. 19.

54. John G. Geer, "Voting in Presidential Primaries," paper presented to the American Political Science Association Annual Meeting, Washington, D.C., September 1984. See also Albert R. Hunt, "The Media and Presidential Campaigns," in *Elections American Style*, ed. A. James Reichley (Brookings Institution, 1987), pp. 52–74.

55. On the Internet: http://www.fec.gov/pages/96to.htm; also http://www.fec.gov/pages/intro.htm.

56. Steven J. Brams and Peter Fishburn, *Approval Voting* (Birkhauser, 1983).

57. George S. McGovern, "Considerations on Our Political Processes," *Presidential Studies Quarterly* 14 (Summer 1984), pp. 341–47.

58. Gary R. Orren and Nelson W. Polsby, eds., *Media and Momentum: The New Hampshire Primary and Nomination Politics* (Chatham House, 1987).

59. Jonathan D. Salant, "Dole's Outlays May Pose Problems," *Congressional Quarterly Weekly Report*, March 9, 1996, p. 638.

60. American Enterprise Institute memorandum, Spring 1986, p. 10.

61. "A National Agenda for the Eighties," *Report of the President's Commission for a National Agenda for the Eighties* (Government Printing Office, 1980), p. 97, proposes holding only four presidential primaries, scheduled about one month apart.

62. Nelson Polsby, *Consequences of Party Reform* (Oxford University Press, 1983), p. 118.

63. Thomas E. Cronin and Robert Loevy, "The Case for a National Primary Convention Plan," *Public Opinion*, December 1982/January 1983, pp. 50–53.

64. See Judith A. Best, *The Choice of the People? Debating the Electoral College* (Rowman and Littlefield, 1996), and Malcolm S. Forbes, Jr., "Helpful, Useful Antique," *Forbes*, February 6, 1989, p. 27.

65. Neal R. Peirce and Lawrence Longley, *The People's President: The Electoral College in American History and the Direct-Vote Alternative*, 2d ed. (Yale University Press, 1981), describes and advocates the direct-vote alternative. Nelson W. Polsby and Aaron B. Wildavsky, *Presidential Elections: Contemporary Strategies of American Politics*, 9th ed. (Chatham House, 1995), favors the present system.

66. Magleby and Nelson, *Money Chase*, pp. 13–14.

67. Neil O. Staebler, quoted in Herbert E. Alexander and Brian A. Haggerty, *The Federal Election Campaign Act: After a Decade of Political Reform* (Citizen's Research Foundation, 1981), p. 13.

68. *Buckley v Valeo*, 424 US 1 (1976).

69. For a discussion of recent legislation, see Herbert E. Alexander and Monica Bauer, *Financing the 1988 Election* (Westview, 1991); Frank J. Sorauf, *Money in American Elections* (Scott, Foresman, 1988).

70. The Federal Election Commission was late in some payments to 1996 primary candidates because of the heavy early expenditures by several candidates. Eventually, all candidates received their entitlement of FEC money.

71. David Ignatius, "Return of the Fat Cats," *The Washington Post*, November 20, 1988, p. D5; Charles R. Babcock, "$100,000 Donations Plentiful Despite Post-Watergate Restrictions," *The Washington Post*, September 22, 1988, p. A27.

72. Beth Donovan, "Parties Turned Soft Money Law into Hard and Fast Spending," *Congressional Quarterly Weekly Report*, May 15, 1993, pp. 1196–97.

73. David E. Rosenbaum, "In Political Money Game, the Year of Big Loopholes," *The New York Times*, December 26, 1996, p. A1.

74. See *Colorado Republican Federal Campaign Committee vs FEC*, 116 Sup. Ct. 2309 (1995).

75. Herbert Alexander, interview with author, April 5, 1994; Federal Election Commission, press release, March 4, 1993, p. 1. Robert Biersack, Federal Election Commission, interview with author, November 17, 1993.

76. Federal Election Commission, "Congressional Fundraising and Spending Up Again in 1996," press release, April 14, 1997, pp. 32–51.

77. Sorauf, *Money in American Elections*, pp. 64–65.

78. See *Colorado Republican Federal Campaign Committee vs FEC*, 116 Sup. Ct. 2309 (1995).

79. H. Ross Perot, quoted in *Wit and Wisdom of Ross Perot*, ed. Sarah Dana-Hall (Wit and Wisdom Books, 1992), pp. 22–23.

80. Jeffrey Schmalz, "Clinton Carves a Wide Path into Reagan Country," *The New York Times*, November 4, 1992, p. B1.

CHAPTER 13

1. Pew Research Center for the People & the Press, "One in Ten Voters Online for Campaign '96, News Attracts Most Internet Users," press release, December 16, 1996, p. 1.

2. Pew Research Center for the People & the Press, "Fewer Happy with Clinton Victory Than with GOP Congressional Win," press release, December 6, 1996, http://www.people-press.org/postmor.htm.

3. James Fallows, *Breaking the News: How the Media Undermine American Democracy* (Pantheon Books, 1996), p. 3.

4. Pew Center, "Fewer Happy with Clinton Victory."

5. Paul Starobin, "Heeding the Call," *National Journal*, November 30, 1996, pp. 2584–89.

6. William Rivers, *The Other Government* (Universe Books, 1982); Douglas Cater, *The Fourth Branch of Government* (Houghton Mifflin, 1959); Dom Bonafede, "The Washington Press: An Interpreter or a Participant in Policy Making?" *National Journal*, April 24, 1982, pp. 716–21; Michael Ledeen, "Learning to Say 'No' to the Press," *Public Interest* 73 (Fall 1983), p. 113.

7. Leslie G. Moeller, "The Big Four: Mass Media Actualities and Expectations," in *Beyond Media: New Approaches to Mass Communication*, eds. Richard W. Budd and Brent D. Ruben Transaction Books, 1988), p. 15.

8. Times Mirror Center for the People and the Press, "Campaign '92: The Politics of the Economy," press release, January 16, 1992.

9. Ibid.

10. See Ray Hiebert, Donald Ungarait, and Thomas Bohn, *Mass Media VI* (Longman, 1991), chap. 11.

11. See Benjamin I. Page and Jason Tannenbaum, "Populistic Deliberation and Talk Radio," *Journal of Communications* 46, no. 2 (Spring 1996), pp. 33–54; Barry A. Hollander, "Talk Radio," *Journalism and Mass Communications Quarterly* 73 (Spring 1996), pp. 102–13; and Paul Starobin, "Be There or Be Square," *National Journal*, August 3, 1996, pp. 1625–28.

12. Richard Davis and Diana Owen, *New Media and American Politics* (Oxford University Press, forthcoming).

13. Pew Research Center for the People & the Press, "One-in-Ten Voters Online for Campaign '96, News Attracts Most Internet Users," press release, December 16, 1996, p. 1.

14. See Robert A. Rutland, *Newsmongers: Journalism in the Life of the Nation, 1690–1972* (Dial Press, 1973).

15. Frank Luther Mott, *American Journalism*, 3d ed. (Macmillan, 1962), p. 123.

16. See Culver Smith, *The Press, Politics, and Patronage* (University of Georgia Press, 1977).

17. James Pollard, *Presidents and the Press* (Macmillan, 1947), pp. 351–59.

18. Thomas C. Leonard, *The Power of the Press* (Oxford University Press, 1986), p. 93.

19. Whitelaw Reid, quoted in Mott, *American Journalism*, p. 412.

20. Edward W. Chester, *Radio, Television and American Politics* (Sheed and Ward, 1969), p. 62.

21. Frances Perkins, quoted in James MacGregor Burns, *Roosevelt: The Lion and the Fox* (Harcourt Brace, 1956), p. 205.

22. Pew Center, "Fewer Happy with Clinton Victory."

23. Richard Davis, *The Press and American Politics: The New Mediator*, 2nd ed. (Prentice Hall, 1996), p. 75.

24. For a discussion of advocacy journalism, see Morris Janowitz, "Professional Models in Journalism: The Gatekeeper and the Advocate," *Journalism Quarterly* 52 (Winter 1975), pp. 618–26.

25. Peter Stoler, *The War Against the Press: Politics, Pressure, and Intimidation in the 80s* (Dodd, Mead, 1986).

26. Ben H. Bagdikian, *The Media Monopoly* (Beacon Press, 1983).

27. See Doris A. Graber, *Mass Media and American Politics*, 5th ed. (Congressional Quarterly Press, 1997); Gina M. Garramone and Charles K. Atkin, "Mass Communication and Political Socialization: Specifying the Effects," *Public Opinion Quarterly* 50 (Spring 1986), pp. 76–86.

28. Stephanie Storm, "Mergers for Year Approach Record," *The New York Times*, October 31, 1996, p. A1.

29. Geraldine Fabrikant, "The Media Business," *The New York Times*, October 11, 1996.

30. Shanto Iyengar and Donald R. Kinder, *News That Matters* (University of Chicago Press, 1987).

31. William Safire, "Blizzard of Lies," *The New York Times*, January 8, 1996, p. A13.

32. Neil A. Lewis, "White House Says President Would Like to Punch Safire," *The New York Times*, January 10, 1996, p. A11.

33. Harvey G. Zeidenstein, "News Media Perception of White House News Management," *Presidential Studies Quarterly* 24 (Summer 1984), pp. 391–98.

34. See, for example, Jack Dennis, "Preadult Learning of Political Independence: Media and Family Communications Effects," *Communication Research* 13 (July 1987), pp. 401–33; Olive Stevens, *Children Talking Politics* (Martin Robertson, 1982).

35. Elihu Katz and Paul Lazarsfeld, *Personal Influence: The Part Played by People in the Flow of Mass Communications* (Free Press, 1955).

36. See the classic, Angus Campbell, Philip E. Converse, Warren E. Miller, and Donald E. Stokes, *The American Voter* (Wiley, 1960).

37. See other classic works, Paul Lazarsfeld, Bernard Berelson, and Hazel Gaudet, *The People's Choice: How the Voter Makes Up His Mind in a Presidential Campaign*, 3d ed. (Columbia University Press, 1968); Bernard Berelson, Paul Lazarsfeld, and William McPhee, *Voting: A Study of Opinion Formation in a Presidential Campaign* (University of Chicago Press, 1954).

38. Stuart Oskamp, ed., *Television as a Social Issue* (Sage Publications, 1988); James W. Carey, ed., *Media, Myths, and Narratives: Television and the Press* (Sage Publications, 1988).

39. Doris A. Graber, *Processing the News: How People Tame the Information Tide*, 2d ed. (Longman, 1988), pp. 107–13.

40. Times Mirror Center for the People and the Press, "Times Mirror News Interest Index," press releases, January 16 and February 28, 1992.

41. John K. Robinson and Mark R. Levy, eds., *The Main Source: Learning from Television News* (Sage Publications, 1986).

42. Graber, *Processing the News*, p. 115.

43. Times Mirror Center, "Times Mirror News Interest Index," January 16, 1992.

44. Media Studies Center, "Media Get High Marks for Campaign Coverage," press release, November 19, 1996.

45. Fred Smoller, "The Six O'Clock Presidency: Patterns of Network News Coverage of the President," *Presidential Studies Quarterly* 26 (Winter 1986), p. 34.

46. See Nelson Polsby, *Consequences of Party Reform* (Oxford University Press, 1983), pp. 142–46. See also Stanley Rothman and S. Robert Lichter, "Media and Business Elites: Two Classes in Conflict!" *Public Interest* 69 (Fall 1982), pp. 119–25.

47. David Broder, "Beware of the 'Insider' Syndrome: Why Newsmakers and News Reporters Shouldn't Get Too Cozy," *The Washington Post*, December 4, 1988, Outlook Section; see also Broder, "Thin-Skinned Journalists," *The Washington Post*, January 11, 1989, p. A21.

48. See, for example, William A. Rusher, *The Coming Battle for the Media* (William Morrow, 1988).

49. Rush Limbaugh, *See, I Told You So* (Pocket Books, 1993), p. 326.

50. *Public Opinion*, August/September 1985, p. 7.

51. See, for example, Michael Parenti, *Inventing Reality* (St. Martin's Press, 1986); Todd Gitlin, *The Whole World Is Watching: Mass Media in the Making and Unmaking of the New Left* (University of California Press, 1980).

52. Daniel P. Moynihan, "The Presidency and the Press," *Commentary* 51 (March 1971), p. 43.

53. S. Robert Lichter, Stanley Rothman, and Linda S. Lichter, *The Media Elite* (Adler and Adler, 1986).

54. See, for example, Michael J. Robinson and Margaret A. Sheehan, *Over the Wire and on TV: CBS and UPI in Campaign '80* (Russell Sage Foundation, 1983); Lichter, Rothman, and Lichter, *Media Elite*.

55. Among others researching this topic, see Doris A. Graber, "Say It with Pictures: The Impact of Audio-Visual News on Public Opinion Formation," paper presented to the Midwest Political Science Association Annual Meeting, Chicago, April 1987; Benjamin I. Page, Robert Y. Shapiro, and Glenn R. Dempsey, "What Moves Public Opinion?" *American Political Science Review* 76 (March 1987), pp. 23–43.

56. Shanto Iyengar, Mark D. Peters, and Donald R. Kinder, "Experimental Demonstrations of the 'Not-So-Minimal' Consequences of Television News Programs," *American Political Science Review* 76 (December 1982), pp. 848–58.

57. Maxwell E. McCombs and Donald L. Shaw, "The Agenda-Setting Function of the Mass Media," *Public Opinion Quarterly* 36 (1972), pp. 176–87; Iyengar, Peters and Kinder, "Experimental Demonstrations," pp. 848–58; Maxwell E. McCombs and Sheldon Gilbert, "News Influence on Our Pictures of the World," in *Perspectives on Media Effects*, eds. Jennings Bryant and Dolf Gillman (Lawrence Erlbaum, 1986); Iyengar and Kinder, *News That Matters*.

58. Walter Mondale, quoted in Robinson and Sheehan, *Over the Wire and on TV*, p. xiii.

59. Iyengar and Kinder, *News That Matters*.

60. Robert M. Entman, "How the Media Affect What People Think: An Information Processing Approach," *Journal of Politics* 51 (May 1989), pp. 346–70.

61. Shanto Iyengar, "Television News and Citizens' Explanations of National Affairs," *American Political Science Review* 81 (September 1987), pp. 815–32; Iyengar and Kinder, *News That Matters*, pp. 82–89.

62. David B. Magleby, *Direct Legislation: Voting on Ballot Propositions in the United States* (Johns Hopkins University Press, 1984).

63. Steven J. Simmons, *The Fairness Doctrine and the Media* (University of California Press, 1978).

64. Norman E. Issacs, *Untended Gates: The Mismanaged Press* (Columbia University Press, 1985), p. 143.

65. Ibid.

66. S. Robert Lichter and Linda S. Lichter, "Covering the Convention Coverage," *Public Opinion*, September/October 1988, p. 41.

67. Davis, *The Press and American Politics*, p. 279.

68. Frank I. Lutz, *Candidates, Consultants, and Campaigns* (Basil Blackwell, 1988), chap. 7.

69. Michael J. Robinson, "Where's the Beef? Media and Media Elites in 1984," in *The American Elections of 1984*, ed. Austin Ranney (Duke University Press, for the American Enterprise Institute, 1985), pp. 172–77.

70. Richard Armstrong, *The Next Hurrah: The Changing Face of the American Political Process* (Beech Tree Books, 1988), pp. 19–21.

71. See, for example, Kathleen Hall Jamieson, *Packaging the Presidency*, 2d ed. (Oxford University Press, 1992).

72. Frank Rich, "Journal: The Log Cabin Lesson," *The New York Times*, October 21, 1995, p. A21.

73. Larry J. Sabato, *The Rise of Political Consultants* (Basic Books, 1981).

74. Mimi Hall and Judy Keen, "Hillary Clinton's Image Undergoes a Change," *USA Today*, July 16, 1986, p. 16.

75. See, in general, Sabato, *Rise of Political Consultants*; James David Barber, *The Pulse of Politics: Electing Presidents in the Media Age* (Norton, 1980). See also Fred Barnes, "The Myth of Political Consultants," *New Republic*, June 16, 1986, p. 16.

76. Quoted in Sabato, *Rise of Political Consultants*, p. 144.

77. Thomas E. Patterson, *The Mass Media Election: How Americans Choose Their President* (Praeger, 1980), chap. 12.

78. John H. Aldrich, *Before the Convention* (University of Chicago Press, 1980), p. 65. This book is a study of candidates' choices and strategies. See also Patterson, *Mass Media Election*.

79. John Foley et al., *Nominating a President: The Process and the Press* (Praeger, 1980), p. 39. For the press's treatment of incumbents, see James Glen Stovall, "Incumbency and News Coverage of the 1980 Presidential Election Campaign," *Western Political Quarterly* 37 (December 1984), p. 621.

80. Thomas E. Patterson and Robert McClure, *The Myth of Television Power in National Elections* (Putnam, 1976); Patterson, *Mass Media Election*, chap. 13.

81. Edwin Diamond and Stephen Bates, *The Spot: The Rise of Political Advertising on TV* (MIT Press, 1984). For a historical look at political advertising, see Jamieson, *Packaging the Presidency*.

82. Priscilla Southwell, "Voter Turnout in the 1986 Congressional Elections: The Media as Demobilizer?" *American Politics Quarterly* 19 (January 1991), pp. 96–108.

83. David B. Magleby, "Direct Legislation in the American States," in *Referendums Around the World: The Growing Use of Direct Democracy*, eds. David Butler and Austin Ranney (AEI Press, 1994), pp. 218–57.

84. Patterson, *Mass Media Election*, pp. 115–17.

85. Raymond Wolfinger and Peter Linguiti, "Tuning In and Tuning Out," *Public Opinion* 4 (February/March 1981), pp. 56–60.

86. Walter Lippmann, *Public Opinion* (Macmillan, 1938), p. 364.

87. Davis, *The Press and American Politics*, p. 205.

88. Bernard Cohen, *The Press and Foreign Policy* (Princeton University Press, 1963); Gary Orren, "Thinking About the Press and Government," in *Impact: How the Press Affects Federal Policymaking*, ed. Martin Linsky (Norton, 1986), pp. 1–20.

89. Lewis Wolfson, *The Untapped Power of the Press* (Praeger, 1985), p. 79.

90. Stephen Hess, *The Government/Press Connection* (Brookings Institution, 1984), p. 106.

91. Lloyd Cutler, "Foreign Policy on Deadline," *Foreign Policy* 56 (Fall 1984), p. 114.

92. Michael B. Grossman and Martha Joynt Kumar, *Portraying the President* (Johns Hopkins University Press, 1981), pp. 255–63; Smoller, "Six O'Clock Presidency," pp. 31–49.

93. Michael J. Robinson and Kevin R. Appel, "Network News Coverage of Congress," *Political Science Quarterly* 94 (Fall 1979), pp. 407–18; Charles Tidmarch and John C. Pitney, Jr., "Covering Congress," *Polity* 17 (Spring 1984), pp. 463–83.

94. Susan Heilmann Miller, "News Coverage of Congress: The Search for the Ultimate Spokesperson," *Journalism Quarterly* 54 (Autumn 1977), pp. 459–65.

95. See Stephen Hess, *Live From Capitol Hill: Studies of Congress and the Media* (Brookings Institution, 1991), pp. 102–10.

96. Richard Davis, "Whither the Congress and the Supreme Court? The Television News Portrayal of American National Government," *Television Quarterly* 22 (1987), pp. 55–63.

97. For a discussion of the Supreme Court and public opinion, see Thomas R. Marshall, *Public Opinion and the Supreme Court* (Unwin Hyman, 1989); Gregory Caldiera, "Neither the Purse nor the Sword: Dynamics of Public Confidence in the Supreme Court," *American Political Science Review* 80 (December 1986), pp. 1209–28.

98. For a discussion of the relationship between the Supreme Court and the press, see Richard Davis, "Lifting the Shroud: News Media Portrayal of the U.S. Supreme Court," *Communications and the Law* 9 (October 1987), pp. 43–58; Elliot E. Slotnick, "Media Coverage of Supreme Court Decision Making: Problems and Prospects," *Judicature*, October/November 1991, pp. 128–42.

99. Thomas E. Patterson, "The Press and Its Missed Assignment," in *The Elections of 1988*, ed. Michael Nelson (Congressional Quarterly Press, 1989), pp. 107–108.

100. Times Mirror Center, "Campaign '92," January 16, 1992.

101. Theodore White, quoted in Herbert Schmertz, "The Making of the Presidency," *Presidential Studies Quarterly* 16 (Winter 1986), p. 25.

CHAPTER 14

1. Richard F. Fenno, Jr., *Senators on the Campaign Trail: The Politics of Representation* (University of Oklahoma Press, 1996), p. 331.

2. John R. Hibbing and Elizabeth Theiss-Morse, *Congress as Public Enemy: Public Attitudes Toward American Political Institutions* (Cambridge University Press, 1995), p. 147.

3. For an examination of this practice, see Michael Lyons and Peter F. Galderisi, "Incumbency, Reapportionment, and U.S. House Redistricting," *Political Research Quarterly* (December 1995), pp. 857–71.

4. See *Wesberry v Sanders*, 376 US 1 (1964).

5. *Davis v Bandemer*, 478 US 109 (1986).

6. *Shaw v Reno*, 509 US 630 (1993).

7. *Miller v Johnson*, 132 LED 2nd 762 (1995); *Bush v Vera*, 135 L Ed 2nd 248 (1996).

8. Norman I. Ornstein, Thomas E. Mann, and Michael J. Malbin, eds., *Vital Statistics on Congress, 1995–1996* (Congressional Quarterly Books, 1996).

9. Majorie Random Hershey, "The Congressional Elections," in *The Election of 1996*, ed. Gerald M. Pomper (Chatham House, 1997), pp. 230–31.

10. For a brief discussion of the speakership in the 1990s, see Barbara Sinclair, "House Majority Party Leadership in an Era of Legislative Constraint," in *The Postreform Congress*, ed. Roger H. Davison (St. Martin's Press, 1992), pp. 91–111. See also Ronald M. Peters, Jr., ed., *The Speaker: Leadership in the U.S. House of Representatives* (Congressional Quarterly Press, 1995).

11. Quoted in Adam Clymer, "Firebrand Who Got Singed Says Being Speaker Suffices," *The New York Times*, January 22, 1996, p. 1.

12. Newt Gingrich, *To Renew America* (HarperCollins, 1995).

13. See Charles R. Babcock and Ruth Marcus, "The Speaker's About-Face on the Ethics Question," in *The Washington Post National Weekly Edition*, January 6, 1997, pp. 13–14; "The Gingrich Case: The Findings of the Special Counsel," *The New York Times*, January 18, 1997, p. 11.

14. Newt Gingrich, speech recorded by the Associated Press and printed in *Congressional Quarterly*, January 11, 1997, p. 138.

15. For an insightful set of essays on Senate leadership, see Richard A. Baker and Roger H. Davidson, eds., *First Among Equals: Outstanding Senate Leaders of the Twentieth Century* (Congressional Quarterly Books, 1991).

16. For insightful memoirs by three recently retired U.S. Senators, see Bill Bradley, *Time Present, Time Past: A Memoir* (Knopf, 1996); Warren B. Rudman, *Combat: Twelve Years in the U.S. Senate* (Random House, 1996); and Alan K. Simpson, *Right in the Old Kazoo: A Lifetime of Scrapping with the Press* (Morrow, 1997).

17. Sarah A. Binder and Steven S. Smith, *Politics or Principles? Filibustering in the United States Senate* (Brookings Institution, 1997).

18. For a criticism of recent confirmation hearings and various reform proposals, see Stephen L. Carter, *The Confirmation Mess: Cleaning Up the Federal Appointments Process* (Basic Books, 1994).

19. Patrick Fisher, "The Biases of Bicameralism," paper presented to the Western Political Science Association Annual Meeting, San Francisco, March 14–16, 1996, pp. 17–18.

20. See Gingrich, *To Renew America*, p. 121. See also Timothy Penny and Major Garrett, *Common Cents* (Little, Brown, 1995), p. 209.

21. Robert C. Byrd, quoted in David J. Vogler, *The Politics of Congress* (Allyn and Bacon, 1983), p. 77.

22. See the case studies in Fenno, *Senators on the Campaign Trail*.

23. *National Journal*, January 4, 1997, p. 30.

24. Harold W. Stanley and Richard G. Niemi, *Vital Statistics on American Politics*, 4th ed. (Congressional Quarterly Press, 1994), p. 216.

25. See Richard Morrin, "Tuned Out, Turned Off: Millions of Americans Know Little About How Their Government Works," *The Washington Post National Weekly Edition*, February 5–11, 1996, pp. 6–7.

26. Bradley, *Time Past, Time Present*, chap. 4.

27. Dan Carney, "As Hostilities Rage on the Hill, Partisan Vote Rate Soars," *Congressional Quarterly*, January 27, 1996, p. 199.

28. For the president's role in the budget process, see Allen Schick, *The Federal Budget: Politics, Policy, and Process* (Brookings Institution, 1995); see also David G. Adler and Larry N. George, eds., *The Constitution and the Conduct of American Foreign Policy* (University Press of Kansas, 1996).

29. Carroll J. Doherty, "Clinton's Big Comeback Shown in Vote Score," *Congressional Quarterly*, December 21, 1996, pp. 3427–30.

30. Mark A. Peterson, *Legislating Together: The White House and Capital Hill from Eisenhower to Reagan* (Harvard University Press, 1990).

31. For two case studies on the way bills get treated in Congress, see Janet M. Martin, *Lessons from the Hill: The Legislative Journey of an Education Program* (St. Martin's Press, 1993); and Steven Waldman, *The Bill—How Legislation Really Becomes Law: A Case Study of the National Service Bill* (Penguin, 1996).

32. Woodrow Wilson, *Congressional Government* (Houghton, Mifflin & Co., 1885; reprint Johns Hopkins University Press, 1981), p. 69.

33. Christopher J. Deering and Steven S. Smith, *Committees in Congress*, 3d ed. (Congressional Quarterly Press, 1997).

34. Bradley, *Time Past, Time Present*, p. 84.

35. Richard F. Fenno, Jr., *Congressman in Committees* (Little, Brown, 1972). See also Glen R. Parker and Suzanne L. Parker, *Factions in House Committees* (University of Tennessee Press, 1985).

36. Gingrich, *To Renew America*, p. 121.

37. Joel D. Aberbach, *Keeping a Watchful Eye: The Politics of Congressional Oversight* (Brookings Institution, 1990).

38. David J. Vogler, *The Politics of Congress*, 5th ed. (Allyn and Bacon, 1988), p. 213.

39. William S. Cohen, "Why I Am Leaving," *The Washington Post National Weekly Edition*, January 28–February 4, 1996, p. 29.

40. See Schick, *Federal Budget*.

41. John Rhodes, *The Futile System* (EPM Publications, 1976), p. 15. See also Gregg Easterbrook, "What's Wrong with Congress?" *Atlantic Monthly*, December 1984, pp. 57–84.

42. James L. Sundquist, *Constitutional Reform and Effective Government*, rev. ed. (Brookings Institution, 1992); James MacGregor Burns, *The Power To Lead* (Simon & Schuster, 1984). The vast majority of political scientists disagree with these ideas. See, for example, Charles O. Jones, *The Presidency in a Separated System* (Brookings Institution, 1994).

43. "News of the Weak: Why Clinton and Congress Lack The Will To Lead," *The Washington Post National Weekly Edition*, January 13, 1997, p. 21. Journalist David Broder emphasizes this point: "In my view, the most serious of these structural problems is the growing power of interest groups and the declining power of political parties."

44. See Leslie Wayne, "A Special Deal for Lobbyists: A Getaway with Lawmakers," *The New York Times*, January 26, 1997, pp. 1, 12.

45. James Madison, *The Federalist*, No. 57, in *The Federalist*, ed. Jacob E. Cooke (Meridan Books, 1961), p. 385.

CHAPTER 15

1. Glenn A. Phelps, *George Washington and American Constitutionalism* (University Press of Kansas, 1993).

2. It is difficult for the average citizen to assess systematically the psychological health and character of presidential candidates, but voters still try to do so. For a specialist's efforts see Stanley A. Renshon, *The Psychological Assessment of Presidential Candidates* (New York University Press, 1996); and by the same author, *High Hopes: The Clinton Presidency and the Politics of Ambition* (New York University Press, 1996).

3. John Steinbeck, *America and Americans* (Bonanza Books, 1996), p. 46.

4. This theme is developed at length in Thomas E. Cronin and Michael Genovese, *The Paradoxes of the American Presidency* (Oxford University Press, 1997).

5. Charles O. Jones, *The Presidency in a Separated System* (Brookings Institution, 1994), p. 295. See also Jean Reith Schroedl, *Congress, the President, and Policymaking* (M. E. Sharpe, 1994).

6. See, for example, Terry Eastland, *Energy in the Executive* (Free Press, 1992); and Harvey Mansfield, Jr., *Taming the Prince: The Ambivalence of Modern Executive Power* (Free Press, 1989).

7. See Louis Fisher, *Presidential War Power* (University Press of Kansas, 1995); and David Gray Adler and Larry N. George, eds., *The Constitution and the Conduct of American Foreign Policy: Essays on Law and History* (University Press of Kansas, 1996).

8. Louis Fisher, *Constitutional Conflicts Between Congress and the President*, 3d ed. (University Press of Kansas, 1991), p. 285.

9. Gerald Ford, informal talk at the Hinckley Institute of Politics, University of Utah, Salt Lake City, Utah, February 1982.

10. Our analysis here borrows and benefits from ideas in James A. Thurber, "The Roots of Divided Democracy," in *Divided Democracy*, ed. James A. Thurber (Congressional Quarterly Press, 1991).

11. See, for example, former Republican Senator Warren B. Rudman's memoir, *Combat: Twelve Years in the U.S. Senate* (Random House,

1996), chaps. 2, 3. See also former Democratic Congressman Timothy Penny and Major Garrett, *Common Cents* (Little, Brown, 1995).

12. John R. Hibbing and Elizabeth Theiss-Morse, *Congress as Public Enemy: Public Attitudes Toward American Political Institutions* (Cambridge University Press, 1995).

13. Paul Brace and Barbara Hinckley, *Follow the Leader: Opinion Polls and the Modern Presidents* (Basic Books, 1992), p. 87.

14. Roger Davidson and Walter J. Oleszek, *Congress and Its Members*, 5th ed. (Congressional Quarterly Press, 1996), p. 289. See also Mark A. Peterson, *Legislating Together: The White House and Capitol Hill from Eisenhower to Reagan* (Harvard University Press, 1990); David R. Mayhew, *Divided We Govern: Party Control and Investigations, 1946–1990* (Yale University Press, 1991); Burdett A. Loomis, *The Contemporary Congress* (St. Martin's Press, 1996).

15. Clinton Rossiter, *The American Presidency* (Harcourt, Brace and World, 1960), p. 59.

16. See Thomas J. Weko, *The Politicizing Presidency: The White House Personnel Office, 1948–1994* (University Press of Kansas, 1995).

17. "Leadership in Jeopardy: The Fraying of the Presidential Appointments System," *National Academy of Public Administration Report* (November 1985), p. 3.

18. These points are nicely emphasized in James P. Pfiffner, *The Strategic Presidency: Hitting the Ground Running*, 2d ed. (University Press of Kansas, 1996).

19. *United States v Curtiss-Wright Export Corp.*, 299 US 304 (1936).

20. For those who believe the *Curtiss-Wright* ruling was too sweeping, see Harold H. Koh, *The National Security Constitution* (Yale University Press, 1990); Louis Fisher, *Presidential War Power* (University Press of Kansas, 1995); and David Gray Adler and Larry N. George, eds., *The Constitution and the Conduct of American Foreign Policy: Essays on Law and History* (University Press of Kansas, 1996).

21. On the president's major involvement in the budget process, see Allen Schick, *The Federal Budget: Politics, Policy, Process* (Brookings Institution, 1995).

22. See Robert J. Spitzer, *The President and Congress: Executive Hegemony at the Crossroads of American Government* (McGraw-Hill, 1993); Lester G. Seligman and Cary R. Covington, *The Coalition Presidency* (Dorsey Press, 1989).

23. Jon Healey, "Clinton Success Rate Declined to a Record Low in 1995," *Congressional Quarterly*, January 27, 1996, pp. 193–96.

24. *Congressional Quarterly*, December 21, 1996, p. 3455.

25. Warren B. Rudman, *Combat: Twelve Years in the U.S. Senate* (Random House, 1996), p. 251.

26. Robert J. Spitzer, "Regular Veto," in *Encyclopedia of the American Presidency*, eds. Leonard W. Levy and Louis Fisher (Simon & Schuster, 1994), p. 1555.

27. Alison Mitchell, "With Ceremony, Clinton Signs a Line-Item Veto Measure," *The New York Times*, April 10, 1996, p. C20.

28. For a detailed review of the arguments for and against the item veto, see Thomas E. Cronin and Jeffrey Weill, "An Item Veto for Presidents?" *Congress and the Presidency* (Autumn 1985), pp. 127–51.

29. Quoted in Andrew Taylor, "Congress Hands President a Budgetary Scalpel," *Congressional Quarterly*, March 30, 1996, p. 866. See also *Byrd et al. v Raines* (1997), quoted and discussed in Andrew Taylor, "Judge Voids Line-Item Veto Law," *Congressional Quarterly*, April 12, 1997, pp. 833–37.

30. See Kenneth T. Walsh, *Feeding the Beast: The White House versus the Press* (Random House, 1996). See also Richard Morris, *Behind the Oval Office* (Random House, 1997).

31. See also the vigorous criticism of the Washington media and their biases by former U.S. Senator Alan K. Simpson, *Right in the Old Gazoo* (Morrow, 1997).

32. See Sidney Milkis, *The President and the Parties: The Transformation of the American Party System Since the New Deal* (Oxford University Press, 1993); and James W. Davis, *The President as Party Leader* (Praeger, 1992).

33. Information provided to Thomas E. Cronin in a letter, February, 1997, from Ms. Kathryn Hughes, secretary to the Cabinet in the Clinton White House. See also Robert Reich, *Locked in the Cabinet* (Knopf, 1997).

34. One of several publications from this assignment was Al Gore, *Creating a Government That Works Better and Costs Less* (Plume, 1993).

35. There has been a certain amount of controversy about the Twenty-fifth Amendment. See Herbert L. Abrams, *The President Has Been Shot: Confusion, Disability and the Twenty-fifth Amendment* (Stanford University Press, 1994); Laura Myers, "Transfer-of-Power-Rules Urged for Impaired Presidents," *Seattle-Post Intelligencer*, December 4, 1996, p. A3.

36. Former Vice President Dan Quayle's views are of interest, *Standing Firm* (Harper Paperbacks, 1995). Three useful general treatments on the vice-presidency are Jules Witcover, *Crapshoot: Rolling the Dice on the Vice Presidency* (Crown, 1992); Paul Light, *Vice Presidential Power* (Johns Hopkins University Press, 1984); Joel Goldstein, *The Modern Vice Presidency* (Princeton University Press, 1982).

37. See Stephen Skowronek, *The Politics Presidents Make: Leadership from John Adams to George Bush* (Harvard University Press, 1993), chaps. 1–3.

38. Mark Hertsgaard, *On Bended Knee: The Press and the Reagan Presidency* (Farrar, Straus, Giroux, 1988). See also John A. Maltese, *Spin Control: The White House Office of Communications and the Management of Presidential News* (University of North Carolina Press, 1992).

39. Thomas Griffith, "Goodbye to All That," *Time*, April 18, 1988, p. 47.

40. Richard Ellis and Aaron Wildavsky, "Greatness Revisited: Evaluating the Performance of Early American Presidents in Terms of Cultural Dilemmas," *Presidential Studies Quarterly*, Winter 1991, p. 17. See also the book by the same authors, *Dilemmas of Presidential Leadership from Washington through Lincoln* (Transaction Press, 1990).

41. Ellis and Wildavsky, "Greatness Revisited," p.17.

42. Ibid., p. 18.

43. Arthur M. Schlesinger, Jr., "The Ultimate Approval Rating," *The New York Times Magazine*, December 15, 1996, p. 50.

44. Paul Kennedy, *The Rise and Fall of the Great Powers* (Random House, 1987), p. 534.

CHAPTER 16

1. Henry J. Abraham, *The Judicial Process*, 5th ed. (Oxford University Press, 1986), p. 197.

2. Alexis de Tocqueville, *Democracy in America*, ed. Phillips Bradley (Knopf, 1944), 1:278–80.

3. Harold J. Laski, *The American Democracy* (Viking, 1948), p. 110.

4. Joseph F. DiMento and Dean W. Hestermann, "Ordering the Elephants to Dance: Consent Degrees and Organizational Behavior," *Journal of Urban and Contemporary Law* 43 (1993), p. 303.

5. *Luther v Borden*, 7 Howard 1 (1849).

6. *Chicago Grand Trunk Railway Co. v Wellman*, 143 US 339 (1892).

7. Karen Orren, "Standing to Sue, Interest Group Conflict in the Federal Courts," *American Political Science Review* (September 1976), pp. 723–41.

8. Phillip J. Cooper, *Hard Judicial Choices: Federal District Court Judges and State and Local Officials* (Oxford University Press, 1988), p. 15.

9. Jeremiah Smith, quoted in Paul E. Freund, *On Understanding the Supreme Court* (Little, Brown, 1949), p. 3.

10. This discussion is based on H. L. A. Hart, *The Concept of Law* (Oxford University Press, 1961), chap. 7.

11. For one of the great classics, see Benjamin N. Cardozo, *The Nature of the Judicial Process* (Yale University Press, 1921).

12. This discussion is based on Hart, *Concept of Law*, chap. 7.

13. John Marshall Harlan, quoted in ibid., pp. 121–22.

14. C. K. Rowland, "The Federal District Courts," in *The American Courts: A Critical Assessment*, eds. John B. Gates and Charles A. Johnson (Congressional Quarterly Press, 1991), pp. 61–80.

15. Christopher E. Smith, *United States Magistrates in the Federal Courts: Subordinate Judges* (Praeger, 1990); Christopher E. Smith, "From U.S. Magistrates to U.S. Magistrate Judges: Developments Affecting the Federal District Courts' Lower Tier of Judicial Officers," *Judicature*, December 1991/January 1992, pp. 210–15.

16. Dissenting views of Representatives Robert F. Drinan and Thomas N. Kindness, quoted in Smith, *United States Magistrates in the Federal Courts*, p. 183.

17. Steven Puro and Roger Goldman, "U.S. Magistrates: Changing Dimensions of First-Echelon Federal Judicial Officers," in *The Politics of Judicial Reform*, ed. Philip L. Dubois (Heath, 1982). See also Caroll Seron, "Magistrates and the Work of Federal Courts: A New Division of Labor," *Judicature*, April/May 1986, pp. 353–59; Christopher E. Smith, "Who Are the U.S. Magistrates?" *Judicature*, October/November 1987, pp. 143–50.

18. *Peretz v United States*, 501 US 923 (1991).

19. Told to and quoted by C. K. Rowland and Robert A. Carp, *Politics and Judgment in Federal District Courts* (University Press of Kansas, 1996), p. 1.

20. Howard Mintz, "Senate Committee Approves Bill to Split 9th Circuit," *The Recorder*, December 8, 1995, pp. 1, 6; Howard Mintz, "House Weighting Own Proposal to Split Circuit," *The Recorder*, February 13, 1996, p. 3.

21. Editorial, "Short-Circuiting the 9th Circuit," *Los Angeles Times*, November 5, 1995, p. M4. See also Neil A. Lewis, "Partisan Gridlock Blocks Senate Confirmations of Federal Judges," *The New York Times*, November 30, 1995, p. A15.

22. Donald R. Songer, "The Circuit Courts of Appeals," in *American Courts*, eds. Gates and Johnson, pp. 35–37.

23. Deborah J. Barrow and Thomas G. Walker, *A Court Divided: The Fifth Circuit Court of Appeals and the Politics of Judicial Reform* (Yale University Press, 1988); Arthur D. Hellman, ed., *Reconstructing Justice: The Innovations of the Ninth Circuit and the Future of the Federal Courts* (Cornell University Press, 1991).

24. *Bordenkircher v Hayes*, 434 US 357 (1978). See also James Eisenstein, *Counsel for the United States: U.S. Attorneys in the Political and Legal Systems* (Johns Hopkins Press, 1978); *Wayte v United States*, 470 US 598 (1985); *United States v Armstrong*, C.D.O.S., May 13, 1996, p. 3351.

25. Joan Biskupic, "For Court Advocate, a Nominee Who Seeks 'Different Solutions,'" *The Washington Post*, April 19, 1993, p. A21; John G. Roberts, Jr., "The New Solicitor General and the Power of the Amicus," *The Wall Street Journal*, May 5, 1993, p. A21.

26. Karen O'Connor, "The Amicus Curiae Role of the U.S. Solicitor General in Supreme Court Litigation," *Judicature*, December 1982/January 1983, pp. 256–64; Jeffrey A. Segal, "Amicus Curiae Briefs by the Solicitor General During the Warren and Burger Courts," *Western Political Quarterly* 41 (March 1988), pp. 134–44.

27. For a critical analysis, see Lincoln Caplan, *The Tenth Justice: The Solicitor General and the Rule of Law* (Knopf, 1987). For a defense, see former Solicitor General Charles Fried, *Order and Law: Arguing the Reagan Revolution—A Firsthand Account* (Simon & Schuster, 1991). For a more neutral account, see Rebecca Mae Salokar, *The Solicitor General: The Politics of Law* (Temple University Press, 1992).

28. Eva M. Rodriguez, "Senators Train Sights on Solicitor General," *The Recorder*, November 29, 1995, p. 1. See also "Dellinger: New Solicitor General Speaks His Mind," *The Recorder*, September 26, 1996, p. 1.

29. David Leitch, "The Deal for Walter Dellinger," *The Recorder*, June 1993, p. 6.

30. Charley Roberts, "Federal Defender Program to Be Studied," *Los Angeles Daily Journal*, August 19, 1991, p. 7; 61 United States Law Week 2627 (April 20, 1993).

31. Naftali Bendavid, "D-Day for Advocates of the Poor," *The Recorder*, February 22, 1994, p. 10; editorial, "Legal Services Survives, Barely," *The New York Times*, May 6, 1996, p. A14.

32. David Cole, "Confining Compromise: How the Legal Services Corp. Sold Out the Poor," *The Recorder*, February 12, 1997, p. 5.

33. Neil D. McFeeley, *Appointment of Judges: The Johnson Presidency* (University of Texas Press, 1987), p. 1.

34. Stephen LaBaton, "Shifting List of Prospects to Be Justice," *The New York Times*, May 9, 1993, p. A12; Paul M. Barrett, "More Minorities, Women Named to U.S. Courts," *The Wall Street Journal*, December 23, 1993, p. B1.

35. Harold W. Chase, *Federal Judges: The Appointing Process* (University of Minnesota Press, 1972), pp. 3–47; Paul Simon, "The Senate's Role in Judicial Appointments," *Judicature*, June/July 1986, pp. 55–58; Elliot E. Slotnick, "Federal Judicial Recruitment and Selection Research: A Review Essay," *Judicature*, April/May 1988, pp. 317–24.

36. Lettie McSpadden Wenner and Lee F. Dutter, "Contextual Influences on Court Outcomes," *Western Political Quarterly* 41 (March 1988), pp. 115–34; Ronald Stidham and Robert A. Carp, "Exploring Regionalism in

the Federal District Courts," *Los Angeles Daily Journal* 18 (Fall 1988), pp. 113–25.

37. Naftali Bendavid, "Diversity Marks Clinton Judiciary," *The Recorder*, December 30, 1993, p. 11.

38. Naftali Bendavid, "Seeking Diversity, Not Confrontation," *The Recorder*, December 30, 1995, p. 1.

39. Dan Carney, "Battle Looms Between Clinton, GOP Over Court Nominees," *Congressional Quarterly Weekly Report*, February 8, 1997, p. 369.

40. Sheldon Goldman, "Judicial Selection Under Clinton: A Midterm Examination, *Judicature* 78, May/June 1995, p. 281; Carney, "Battle Looms," p. 367.

41. Editorial, "Too Many Federal Court Vacancies," *The New York Times*, February 14, 1997, p. A22. See also Neil Lewis, "Republicans Seek Greater Influence in Naming Judges," *The New York Times*, April 27, 1997, p. A1.

42. Quoted in Stephen Labaton, "Clinton Expected to Change Makeup of Federal Courts," *The New York Times*, March 8, 1993, p. A1; Neil A. Lewis, "Clinton Has a Chance to Shape the Courts," *The New York Times*, February 9, 1997.

43. Edwin Meese III and Rhett DeHart, "The Imperial Judiciary," *Policy Review*, January/February 1997, p. 58.

44. Editorial, "More Doubts About the ABA," *The Wall Street Journal*, April 11, 1989; See also Gordon J. Humphrey, "End ABA Role as Hanging Judge," *The Wall Street Journal*, March 22, 1989, p. A14; *Public Citizen v Department of Justice*, 491 US 440 (1989); Donald Strafes, "Clinton Judges, ABA," *The Recorder*, April 25, 1996.

45. Quoted in Neil A. Lewis, "Head of Senate's Judiciary Committee Reconsiders Advisory Role of A.B.A.," *The New York Times National Edition*, February 19, 1997, p. A11.

46. Daniel Klaidman, "Liberals Hit Clinton on Judge Picks," *The Recorder*, October 27, 1993, pp. 1–14; Neil A. Lewis, "New York City Bar Told to Stop Rating Judges," *The New York Times*, June 4, 1991, p. A14.

47. Charles M. Cameron, Albert D. Cover, and Jeffrey A. Segal, "Senate Voting on Supreme Court Nominees: A Neo-Institutional Model," *American Political Science Review* 84 (June 1990), p. 532.

48. George Watson and John Stookey, "Supreme Court Confirmation Hearings: A View from the Senate," *Judicature*, December 1987/January 1988, p. 193. See also John Massaro, *Supremely Political: The Role of Ideology and Presidential Management in Unsuccessful Supreme Court Nominations* (State University of New York Press, 1990).

49. Sheldon Goldman, "Bush's Judicial Legacy: The Final Imprint," *Judicature*, April/May 1993, p. 291.

50. Quoted in Sheldon Goldman, "Judicial Selection Under Clinton: A Midterm Examination," *Judicature*, May/June 1995, p. 281.

51. Robert A. Carp and C. K. Rowland, *Policymaking and Politics in the Federal District Courts* (University of Tennessee Press, 1983), p. 82.

52. Quoted in J. W. Peltason, *Federal Courts in the Political Process* (Doubleday, 1955), p. 41. See also Laurence H. Tribe, *God Save This Honorable Court: How the Choice of Supreme Court Justices Shapes Our History* (Random House, 1985); Henry J. Abraham, *Justices and Presidents: A Political History of Appointments to the Supreme Court*, 3d ed. (Oxford University Press, 1992).

53. Theodore Roosevelt to Henry Cabot Lodge, *Selections from the Correspondence of Theodore Roosevelt and Henry Cabot Lodge* (Scribner's, 1925), 1:518–19.

54. Sheldon Goldman, "Reagan's Judicial Legacy: Completing the Puzzle and Summing Up," *Judicature*, April/May 1989, pp. 318–30.

55. Leo V. Hennessy, "Redrawing the Political Map? An Impact Analysis of the Reagan Appointments on the U.S. Courts of Appeals," paper presented to the Southern Political Science Association, November 7–9, 1991.

56. Jill Abramson, "Conservative Legal Groups Plan Efforts to Keep Bush Administration on Reagan's Judicial Path," *The Wall Street Journal*, November 21, 1988, p. A16.

57. Robert A. Carp, Donald Songer, C. K. Rowland, Ronald Stidham, and Lisa Richey-Tracey, "The Voting Behavior of Judges Appointed by President Bush," *Judicature*, April/May 1993, pp. 298–302.

58. David G. Savage, *Turning Right: The Making of the Rehnquist Supreme Court* (John Wiley & Sons, 1992), pp. 451–58.

59. William Howard Taft to Horace Taft, November 14, 1929, quoted in Henry Pringle, *The Life and Times of William Howard Taft* (Farrar, 1939), 2:967.

60. Sue Davis, "Federalism and Property Rights: An Examination of Justice Rehnquist's Legal Positivism," *Western Political Quarterly* (June 1986), pp. 250–64.

61. Albert P. Melone, "The Senate's Confirmation Role in Supreme Court Nominations and the Politics of Ideology Versus Impartiality," *Judicature*, August/September 1991, pp. 68–79, argues that the Senate should ask nominees pertinent ideological questions and that nominees have an obligation to be forthcoming. For the contrary view, see William Bradford Reynolds, "The Confirmation Process: Too Much Advice and Too Little Consent," *Judicature*, August/September 1991, pp. 80–82.

62. David M. O'Brien, *Judicial Roulette: Report of the Twentieth Century Fund Task Force on Judicial Selection* (Priority Press Publications, 1988), pp. 10–11.

63. Mark Silverstein, "The People, the Senate and the Court: The Democratization of the Judicial Confirmation System," *Constitutional Commentary* 9 (Winter 1992), p. 58.

64. Donald Santarelli, quoted in Jerry Landauer, "Shaping the Bench," *The Wall Street Journal*, December 10, 1970, p. 1. See also Peltason, *Federal Courts in the Political Process*, p. 32.

65. Michale A. Kahn, "The Appointment of a Supreme Court Justice: A Political Process from Beginning to End," *Presidential Studies Quarterly* 25 (Winter 1995), pp. 26, 39.

66. *Ex parte McCardle*, Wallace 506 (1869).

67. Tony Mauro, "Yipes! Stripes!" *The Recorder*, February 8, 1995, p. 8.

68. Richard Johnson, *The Dynamics of Compliance* (Wiley, 1967), pp. 33–41, as summarized in David Adamany, "Legitimacy, Realigning Elections, and the Supreme Court," *Wisconsin Law Review* (1973), p. 792.

69. Tony Mauro, "Supreme Court Calendar Begs for More Arguments," *The Recorder*, February 13, 1996, p. 1.

70. Tony Mauro, "Jumping into the Pool," *The Recorder*, September 14, 1993, p. 6.

71. Sidney Ulmer, "The Supreme Court's Certiorari Decisions: Conflict as a Predictive Variable," *American Political Science Review* (December 1984), pp. 901–11.

72. Elder Witt, "Reagan Crusade Before Court Unprecedented in Intensity," *Congressional Quarterly Weekly Report*, March 15, 1986, p. 616.

73. Gregory A. Caldeira and John R. Wright, "Organized Interest and Agenda Setting in the U.S. Supreme Court," *American Political Science Review* 82 (December 1988), p. 1110; Donald R. Songer and Reginald S. Sheehan, "Interest Groups' Success in the Courts: Amicus Participation in the Supreme Court," *Political Research Quarterly* 46 (June 1993), pp. 339–54.

74. *University of California Regents v Bakke*, 438 US 265 (1978); *Webster v Reproductive Health Services*, 492 US 490 (1989); *Roe v Wade*, 410 US 113 (1973). See also Susan Behuniak-Long, "Friendly Fire: Amici Curiae and *Webster v Reproductive Health Services*," *Judicature*, February/March 1991, pp. 261–70.

75. *The Recorder*, August 3, 1995. p. 8.

76. Tony Mauro, "The Supreme Court as Quiz Show," *The Recorder*, December 8, 1993, p. 10.

77. Joyce O'Connor, "Selections from Notes Kept on an Internship at the U.S. Supreme Court, Fall 1988," *Law, Courts, and Judicial Process*, newsletter published by Department of Political Science, Purdue University, 6 (Spring 1989), p. 44.

78. Sandra Day O'Connor, quoted in Mauro, "Jumping into the Pool," p. 7.

79. O'Connor, "Selections from Notes Kept on an Internship," p. 46.

80. Mauro, "Yipes! Stripes!" p. 8.

81. Anthony M. Kennedy, Jr., address to Pasadena Bar Association, June 1991, quoted in Richard C. Reuben, "Kennedy Remembers William Brennan," *The Los Angeles Daily Journal*, July 2, 1991, p. 7.

82. William H. Rehnquist, *The Supreme Court: How It Was, How It Is* (William Morrow, 1987), pp. 289–90.

83. This paragraph is condensed from James F. Simon, *The Center Holds: The Power Struggle Inside the Rehnquist Court* (Simon & Schuster, 1995), pp. 270–75.

84. Daniel M. Berman, *It Is So Ordered: The Supreme Court Rules on School Segregation* (Norton, 1986), p. 114; Walter F. Murphy, *Elements of Judicial Strategy* (University of Chicago Press, 1964), p. 66; David M. O'Brien, *Storm Center: The Supreme Court in American Politics*, 2d ed. (W. W. Norton, 1990), pp. 262–72.

85. Clarks Evans Hughes, quoted in Donald E. Lively, *Foreshadows of the Law: Supreme Court Dissents and Constitutional Development* (Praeger, 1992), p. xx.

86. Oliver Wendell Holmes to Harold J. Laski, *Holmes-Laski Letters*, ed. Mark De Wolfe Howe (Atheneum, 1963), 2:124, 125.

87. Simon, *Center Holds*, p. 271.

88. Quoted in John R. Vile, "The Selection and Tenure of Chief Justices," *Judicature*, September/October 1994, p. 98.

89. Robert J. Steamer, *Chief Justice: Leadership and the Supreme Court* (University of South Carolina Press, 1986). See also White Burkett Miller Center of Public Affairs, *The Office of Chief Justice* (University Press of Virginia, 1984).

90. Sue Davis, "The Supreme Court: Rehnquist's or Reagan's," *Western Political Quarterly* 44 (March 1991), p. 98.

91. David G. Savage, "The Rehnquist Court," *Los Angeles Times Magazine*, September 29, 1991, p. 13; David W. Rohde and Harold J. Spaeth, "Ideology, Strategy and Supreme Court Decisions: William Rehnquist as Chief Justice," *Judicature*, December 1988/January 1989, pp. 247–50. See also Joseph F. Kobylka, "Leadership on the Supreme Court of the United States: Chief Justice Burger and the Establishment Clause," *Western Political Quarterly* 42 (December 1989), pp. 545–68.

92. David Danelski, "The Influence of the Chief Justice in the Decisional Process of the Supreme Court," in *The Federal Judicial System: Readings in Process and Behavior*, eds. Thomas P. Jahnige and Sheldon Goldman (Holt, Rinehart and Winston, 1968), p. 148.

93. *Youngstown Sheet and Tube Co. v Sawyer*, 343 US 579 (1952).

94. Stephen L. Wasby, *The Impact of the United States Supreme Court* (Dorsey Press, 1970).

95. J. W. Peltason, *Fifty-Eight Lonely Men: Southern Federal Judges and School Desegregation* (University of Illinois Press, 1971), p. 19.

96. *Immigration and Naturalization Service v Chadha*, 468 US 919 (1983).

97. Cooper, *Hard Judicial Choices*, pp. 347–50.

98. Peter W. Huber, *Liability: The Legal Revolution and Its Consequences* (Basic Books, 1988).

99. Arthur S. Miller, "In Defense of Judicial Activism," in *Supreme Court Activism and Restraint*, eds. Stephen C. Halpern and Charles M. Lamb (Heath, 1982), p. 177. See also, by the chief justice of the West Virginia Supreme Court, Richard Neely, *How Courts Govern America* (Yale University Press, 1981).

100. *United States v Carolene Products*, 304 US 144 (1938). Variations on this basic position have been restated in dozens of recent books. Halpern and Lamb, eds., *Supreme Court Activism and Restraint*, and Mark Tushnet, *Red, White, and Blue: A Critical Analysis of Constitutional Law* (Harvard University Press, 1988), provide balanced analysis from all perspectives. For another analysis of this great debate, see Lief H. Carter, *Contemporary Constitutional Lawmaking* (Pergamon Press, 1985). See also David J. Richards, *Toleration and the Constitution* (Oxford University Press, 1986); Stephen Macedo, *The New Right v the Constitution* (Cato, 1986). Leslie F. Goldstein, "Judicial Review and Democratic Theory: Guardian Democracy vs. Representative Democracy," *Western Political Quarterly* 40 (September 1987), pp. 391–412, also contains a bibliography.

101. Stephen Macedo, "Hurray for Judge Thomas' Conservative Activism," *The Wall Street Journal*, July 11, 1991, p. A11; L. Gordon Crovitz, "Reverse a Precedent, Protect the Constitution," *The Wall Street Journal*, July 10, 1991, p. A13.

102. J. W. Peltason, "The Supreme Court: Transactional or Transformational Leadership," in *Essays in Honor of James MacGregor Burns*, eds. Michael R. Beschloss and Thomas E. Cronin (Prentice Hall, 1988), pp. 165–80; Mark Silverstein and Benjamin Ginsburg, "The Supreme Court and the New Politics of Judicial Power," *Political Science Quarterly* 102 (Fall 1987), pp. 371–88.

103. *Planned Parenthood v Casey*, 505 US 833 (1992).

104. Neil A. Lewis, "Partisan Gridlock Blocks Senate Confirmations of Federal Judges," *The New York Times*, November 30, 1995, p. A14. See also Howard Mintz, "Steering a Center Course: Liberals and Conservatives Alike Assail Clinton's Judicial Appointments," *The Recorder*, March 20, 1996, p. 1.

105. Terry Eastland, "If Clinton Wins, Here's What the Courts Will Look Like," *The Wall Street Journal*, February 28, 1996, p. A10.

106. Quoted in Alison Mitchell, "Clinton Pressing Judge to Relent," *The New York Times*, March 22, 1996, p. B3.

107. Thomas R. Marshall, *Public Opinion and the Supreme Court* (Unwin Hyman, 1989), p. 193. See also Thomas R. Marshall, "The Supreme Court and the Grass Roots: Whom Does the Court Represent Best?" *Judicature*, June/July 1992, pp. 22–28; Michael Comiskey, "The Rehnquist Court and American Values," *Judicature*, March/April 1994, pp. 261–67; William Misler and Reginald S. Sheehan, "The Supreme Court as a Counter-Majoritarian Institution? The Impact of Public Opinion on Supreme Court Decisions," *American Political Science Review* 87 (1993), pp. 87–101; response along with Mishler and Sheehan response, Helmut Norpoth and Jeffrey A. Segal, "Popular Influence on Supreme Court Decisions," *American Political Science Review* 88 (September 1994), pp. 711–24.

108. Quoted by Fred Rodell, *Nine Men: A Political History of the Supreme Court From 1790 to 1995* (Random House, 1955).

109. Gerald N. Rosenberg, *The Hollow Hope: Can Courts Bring About Social Change?* (University of Chicago Press, 1991), p. 343.

110. Rehnquist, *Supreme Court*, p. 98.

CHAPTER 17

1. Bill Clinton, "Second Inaugural Address," *The New York Times*, January 21, 1997, p. A12.

2. See, for example, Kevin Phillips, *Arrogant Capital* (Little, Brown, 1995).

3. See the Republicans blueprint in Steven Moore, ed., *Restoring the Dream: The Bold New Plans by House Republicans* (Times Books, 1995).

4. See the report by Clinton's election strategist, Dick Morris, *Behind the Oval Office* (Random House, 1997).

5. David Osborne and Peter Plastrik, *Banishing Bureaucracy: The Five Strategies for Reinventing Government* (Addison-Wesley, 1997), p. 49.

6. See, for example, Al Gore, *The Best Kept Secrets in Government: How the Clinton Administration Is Reinventing the Way Washington Works* (Random House, 1996). This is one of several reports that have been produced by the national performance review committee Vice-President Gore headed in the mid-1990s.

7. Al Gore, *Creating a Government That Works Better and Costs Less: The Report of the National Performance Review* (Plume-Penguin, 1993).

8. President Clinton, Budget Message, *Budget of U.S. Government for Fiscal Year 1996* (Government Printing Office, 1995), p. 5. See also Gore, *Best Kept Secrets in Government*.

9. Influential writings that helped shape the debate about reforming the bureaucracy include James Q. Wilson, *Bureaucracy: What Government Agencies Do and Why They Do It* (Basic Books, 1989); David Osborne and Ted Gaebler, *Reinventing Government: How the Entrepreneurial Spirit Is Transforming the Public Sector* (Addison-Wesley, 1992); John J. DiIulio, Jr., Gerald Garvey, and Donald F. Kettl, *Improving Government Performance: An Owner's Manual* (Brookings Institution, 1993); and Philip K. Howard, *The Death of Common Sense: How Law Is Suffocating America* (Random House, 1994).

10. Donald F. Kettl, "Building Lasting Reform: Enduring Questions, Missing Answers," in *Inside the Reinvention Machine: Appraising Governmental Reform*, eds. Donald F. Kettl and John J. DiIulio, Jr., (Brookings Institution, 1995), p. 30.

11. Philip K. Howard, *The Death of Common Sense: How Law Is Suffocating America* (Random House, 1994), pp. 9, 11.

12. Sam Brownback, statement as part of a series on "What's Ahead for Conservatives," in *Policy Review*, January/February 1997, pp. 26–27.

13. David E. Rosenbaum, "Corporate Welfare's New Enemies," *The New York Times*, February 2, 1997, p. E1.

14. For a study of bureaucracies and their strategies to keep as much autonomy as possible, see Wilson, *Bureaucracy*.

15. Adapted from Dennis Palumbo and Steven Maynard-Moody, *Contemporary Public Administration* (Longman, 1991), p. 26.

16. See data provided by Gallup polls, *Public Perspective*, December/January 1996, p. 57.

17. For an analysis of the use and abuse of the civil service system in the early twentieth century, see Stephen Skowronek, *Building a New American State* (Cambridge University Press, 1982).

18. See, for example, Dan Baum, *Smoke and Mirrors: The War on Drugs and the Politics of Failure* (Little, Brown, 1996).

19. A history of the old Hatch Act is provided in James Eccles, *The Hatch Act and the American Bureaucracy* (Vantage Press, 1981).

20. For the 1994 revisions of this act, see Jeanne Ponessa, "The Hatch Act Rewrite," *Congressional Quarterly Weekly Report*, November 13, 1993, pp. 3146–47.

21. For an examination of Max Weber's ideas on bureaucracy, see Brian Fry, *Mastering Public Administration: From Max Weber to Dwight Waldo* (Chatham House, 1989).

22. Gore, *Best Kept Secrets in Government*, p. 24.

23. Ibid., p. 31.

24. John W. Gardner, testimony before the U.S. Senate Committee on Government Operations, *Executive Reorganization Proposals, Hearings* (Government Printing Office, 1971), pp. 57–58. See also R. Douglas Arnold, *Congress and the Bureaucracy* (Yale University Press, 1979).

25. Robert J. Samuelson, "Surviving the Guillotine," *Newsweek*, November 20, 1995, p. 65.

26. For the general philosophy of the new congressional Republican leadership, see Newt Gingrich, *To Renew America* (HarperCollins, 1995); and Dick Armey, *The Freedom Revolution* (Regnery, 1995).

27. Jonathan Weisman, "Republicans Showing Less Zeal to Cut Cabinet Departments," *Congressional Quarterly*, January 18, 1997, p. 171.

28. Ibid., p. 172.

29. The strategies used in these places and elsewhere are detailed in Osborne and Gaebler, *Reinventing Government*; and in Osborne and Plastrik, *Banishing Bureaucracy*.

30. B. Don Wood and Richard W. Waterman, *Bureaucractic Dynamics: The Role of Bureaucracy in a Democracy* (Westview Press, 1995), p. 151.

31. E. S. Savas, *Privatization: The Key to Better Government* (Chatham House, 1987).

32. Osborne and Gaebler, *Reinventing Government*, pp. 45–46.

33. Anthony Frank, quoted in interview in *USA Today*, January 8, 1992, p. 7A.

34. Morris P. Fiorina, "Flagellating the Federal Bureaucracy," *Society*, March/April 1983, p. 73.

35. Francis E. Rourke, "Whose Bureaucracy Is This, Anyway?" *PS: Political Science and Politics*, December 1993, p. 691.

36. Wilson, *Bureaucracy*, p. 268. See also James W. Fesler and Donald Kettl, *The Politics of the Administrative Process* (Chatham House, 1991), pp. 99–102.

CHAPTER 18

1. David B. Robertson and Dennis R. Judd, *The Development of American Public Policy* (Scott, Foresman, 1989), p. vii.

2. Murray J. Edelman, *Political Language: Words That Succeed and Policies That Fail* (Academic Press, 1977); Murray J. Edelman, *Politics as Symbolic Action* (Academic Press, 1971).

3. Aaron Wildavsky, *Speaking Truth to Power: The Art and Craft of Policy Analysis* (Little, Brown, 1979), pp. 212–37.

4. Peter Bachrach and Morton Baratz, *Power and Poverty* (Oxford University Press, 1970); Charles E. Lindblom, "Another State of Mind," *American Political Science Review* 76 (March 1982), pp. 9–21.

5. *Budget of the United States Government, Fiscal Year 1997* (Government Printing Office, 1997).

6. *A Citizen's Guide to the Federal Budget* (http:///www.doc. gov/Budget FY 97/guide2.html).

7. For a discussion of the budgetary cycle, see Aaron Wildavsky, *The New Politics of the Budgetary Process* (Scott, Foresman, 1988). See also Howard Shuman, *Politics and the Budget*, 2d ed. (Prentice Hall, 1988).

8. *GAO Indicator of Statistics for 1991* (Government Printing Office, 1991).

9. For a study of changes in the General Accounting Office and its operations, see Wallace Earl Walker, *Changing Organizational Culture: Strategy, Structure and Professionalism in the U.S. General Accounting Office* (University of Tennessee Press, 1986).

10. A lively story of tax reform is told by Jeffrey H. Birnbaum and Alan S. Murray, *Showdown at Gucci Gulch: Lawmakers, Lobbyists, and the Unlikely Triumph of Tax Reform* (Vintage, 1988). See also Timothy J. Conlan, Margaret T. Wrightson, and David R. Beam, *Taxing Choices: The Politics of Tax Reform* (Congressional Quarterly Press, 1990).

11. Joe Drape, "Sinking Job Security," *Atlanta Constitution*, March 13, 1992, p. H1.

12. Bureau of the Census, *Statistical Abstract of the United States 1996* (Government Printing Office, 1996), p. 336, Table 518.

13. Henry J. Aaron and Harvey Galper, *Assessing Tax Reform* (Brookings Institution, 1985), p. 2.

14. Milton Friedman, "Tax Reform Lets Politicians Look for New Donors," *Wall Street Journal*, July 7, 1986, p. 13A.

15. George Hager and David S. Cloud, "Democrats Tie Their Fate to Clinton's Budget Bill," *Congressional Quarterly Weekly Report*, August 7, 1993, p. 2122.

16. For a good overview of the arguments for and against the item veto, see Thomas E. Cronin and Jeffrey J. Weill, "An Item Veto for the President?" *Congress and the Presidency* 12 (Autumn 1985), pp. 127–49; and Ronald C. Moe, *Prospects for the Item Veto at the Federal Level: Lessons from the States* (National Academy of Public Administration, 1988).

17. For a discussion of the "pork" spending argument, see Robert Stein and Kenneth Bickers, *Perpetuating the Pork Barrel* (Cambridge University Press, 1995).

18. Richard Watson, *Presidential Vetoes and Public Policy* (Kansas University Press, 1993).

19. *Congressional Quarterly Weekly Report*, March 30, 1996, p. 864.

20. Watson, *Presidential Vetoes and Public Policy*, pp. 159–60.

21. Benjamin Zycher, "Institutional and Mechanical Control of Federal Spending," in *Proceedings of the Academy of Political Science* 35 (1985), p. 142.

22. Moe, *Prospects for the Item Veto at the Federal Level*.

23. "The Fed: Our Central Bank," issued by the Federal Reserve Bank of Minneapolis (http://woodrow.mpls.frb.fed.us).

24. Milton Friedman and Ann J. Schwartz, *A Monetary History of the United States: 1867–1960* (Princeton University Press, 1963).

25. Thomas F. Cargill, *Money, the Financial System, and Monetary Policy* (Prentice Hall, 1991), p. 10. See also William Greider, *Secrets of the Temple: How the Federal Reserve Runs the Country* (Simon & Schuster, 1987).

26. John R. Wilke, "Showing Its Age: Fed's Huge Empire, Set Up Years Ago, Is Costly and Inefficient," *The Wall Street Journal*, September 12, 1996, p. 1.

27. "The Fed: Our Central Bank," p. 1.

28. Arthur Rolnick, research director at the Minneapolis Fed, quoted by Wilke, "Showing Its Age," p. 2.

29. Quoted in Frederick Lewis Allen, *Since Yesterday* (Harper, 1940), p. 64.

30. W. H. Beveridge, *The Pillars of Security* (Macmillan, 1943), p. 51.

31. The debate over Keynes and his economic theories is still alive in the United States. See, for example, the special issue on Keynes in *The Economist* (American Enterprise Institute, June 1983); see also Robert Eisner, *How Real Is the Federal Deficit?* (Free Press, 1986), and Donald E. Moggridge, *Maynard Keynes: An Economist's Biography* (Routledge, 1992).

32. Lester C. Thurow, *The Zero-Sum Solution: Building a World Class American Economy* (Simon & Schuster, 1983), p. 30. See also Herbert Stein, *Presidential Economics: The Making of Economic Policy from Roosevelt to Reagan and Beyond*, rev. ed. (American Enterprise Institute, 1988).

33. Neil Henderson, "It's Not a Subsidy, Exactly: It's Technical Assistance," *The Washington Post National Weekly Edition*, July 7, 1986, p. 33.

34. Superintendent of Documents, *Annual Report of the United States Patent Office* (Government Printing Office), or on the World Wide Web (http://www.uspto.gov/web/offices/com/annual/annual.html).

35. Clay Chandler, "Doing the Math on Dole's Tax Plan," *The Washington Post National Weekly Edition*, August 26–September 1, 1996, p. 21.

36. "America's Farm Subsidies," *The Economist*, June 27, 1992, p. 21.

37. An important study of agricultural support and political interest is William P. Browne, *Private Interests, Public Policy, and American Agriculture* (University Press of Kansas, 1988).

38. U.S. Bureau of the Census, *Statistical Abstract of the United States, 1996* (Government Printing Office, 1996), p. 786, Table 1284; Patrick G. Marshall, "U.S. Trade Policy," *Congressional Quarterly Weekly Report*, January 29, 1994, pp. 75–88. See also Martin Crutsinger, Associated Press, "U.S. Trade Deficit Improves," February 8, 1996 (http://www.kern.com/tbc/art/BIZ/25688Ahtml).

39. Arlene Wilson, "NAFTA: How Many U.S. Jobs Are at Risk?" *Congressional Research Service Report for Congress*, May 19, 1993, p. 3.

40. Richard W. Stevenson, "NAFTA's Impact on Jobs Has Been Slight, Study Says," *The New York Times*, December 19, 1996, p. C1.

41. Lester Thurow, *Head to Head: The Coming Economic Battle among Japan, Europe, and America* (William Morrow, 1992). See also Jagdish Bhagwati, *The World Trading System at Risk* (Princeton University Press, 1991).

42. *Federal Register*, September 5, 1989, p. 36851.

43. Marin Wolf, "Why Voluntary Export Restraints? An Historical Analysis," *The World Economy* 12, no. 3 (September 1989), p. 284, cited in Bovard, *Fair Trade Fraud*, p. 3.

44. Paul Blustein, "Unfair Traders: Does the U.S. Have Room To Talk?" *The Washington Post*, May 24, 1989, p. F1.

45. The case for industrial policy is well made in Otis Graham, *Losing Time: The Industrial Policy Debate* (Harvard University Press, 1992).

46. For a probing analysis of trade policy, see David B. Yoffie, "American Trade Policy: An Obsolete Bargain?" in *Can the Government Govern?* eds. John E. Chubb and Paul E. Peterson (Brookings Institution, 1989), pp. 100–38.

47. Cordell Hull, *The Memoirs of Cordell Hull* (Macmillan, 1948), quoted in I. M. Destleer, *American Trade Politics: System under Stress* (Institute for Internal Economics, 1986), p. 12.

CHAPTER 19

1. John H. Cushman, Jr., "Surprise Senate Challenge to Pollution Plan," *The New York Times*, December 7, 1996, p. 7. See also Robert Kuttner, *Everything for Sale: The Virtues and Limits of Markets* (Knopf, 1997); Gary Bryner, *Blue Skies, Green Politics: The Clean Air Act of 1990 and Its Interpretation*, 2d ed. (Congressional Quarterly Press, 1995).

2. Stephen Moore, ed., *Restoring the Dream: The Bold New Plan by House Republicans* (Times Books, 1995), p. 156.

3. See Al Gore, *Creating a Government That Works Better and Costs Less* (Plume, 1993); Gore, *The Best Kept Secrets in Government: How the Clinton Administration is Reinventing the Way Washington Works* (Random House, 1996), pp. 76–87.

4. Major debates take place in the field of antitrust policy. And in recent years there have been few court decisions and more negotiated settlements when it comes to mergers and "bigness." See Roger Lowenstein, "Antitrust Enforcers Drop the Ideology, Focus on Economics," *The Wall Street Journal*, February 27, 1997, pp. 1,8. See also Kuttner, *Everything for Sale*, chaps. 5–7.

5. See the fine analysis of clean air legislation and regulations in Bryner, *Blue Skies, Green Politics*.

6. Edward J. Markey, "Promoting Competition and the Public Interest," *Brookings Review* 12 (Winter 1994), pp. 20–21.

7. Michael D. Shear, "New Cable Rates Not a Pretty Picture, Consumer Office Says," *The Washington Post*, July 16, 1993, p. B3.

8. Robert Crandall, "Cable Television Reinventing Regulation," *Brookings Review* 12 (Winter 1994), pp. 12–15.

9. See, for example, Paul W. MacAvoy, *Industry Regulation and the Performance of the American Economy* (W. W. Norton, 1992); Milton Friedman and Rose Friedman, *Free to Choose* (Harcourt Brace Jovanovich, 1980). See also U.S. Senate, Committee on Governmental Affairs, *Benefits of Environmental, Health and Safety Regulation*

(Government Printing Office, 1980); David Bollier and Joan Claybrook, "Regulations That Work," *Washington Monthly*, April 1986, pp. 47–54.

10. On the historical development of, the purpose for, and the underlying reasoning behind antitrust, see George Thompson and Gerald Brady, *Antitrust Fundamentals* (West, 1979).

11. On the origins of the Federal Trade Commission and the role of Louis D. Brandeis, see Thomas K. McCraw, *Prophets of Regulation* (Belknap, 1984), chap. 3.

12. Paul McClure, ed., *Congressional Quarterly's Federal Regulatory Directory*, 8th ed. (Congressional Quarterly Press, 1997), p. 507.

13. Mark Clayton, "Critics Say Justice Department Has Become Too Lax on Antitrust," *Christian Science Monitor*, July 8, 1987, p. 19. See also James B. Stewart, *Den of Thieves* (Simon & Schuster, 1991).

14. See Lowenstein, "Antitrust Enforcers Drop Ideology," pp. 1,8; McClure, ed., *Federal Regulatory Directory, 1997*, p. 180. See also David Whitford, "Sale of the Century," *Fortune*, February 17, 1997, pp. 92–100.

15. McClure, ed., *Federal Regulatory Directory*, p. 221.

16. Matthew A. Crenson, *The Un-Politics of Air Pollution* (Johns Hopkins University Press, 1971), p. 10.

17. Bryner, *Blue Skies, Green Politics*.

18. Allison Pytte, "A Decade's Acrimony Lifts in the Glory of Clean Air," *Congressional Quarterly*, October 2, 1990, pp. 3587–90.

19. Don L. Boroughs with Betsy Carpenter, "Cleaning Up the Environment," *U.S. News and World Report*, March 25, 1991, p. 46.

20. Alissa J. Rubin, "Congress May Break Deadlock on Food Safety Laws," *Congressional Quarterly*, February 15, 1992, pp. 354–56.

21. Michael E. Kraft and Norman J. Vieg, "Environmental Policy in the Reagan Presidency," *Political Science Quarterly* (Fall 1984), pp. 415–39. See also Al Gore, *Earth in the Balance: Ecology and the Human Spirit* (Houghton Mifflin, 1992).

22. McClure, ed., *Federal Regulatory Directory*, p. 240.

23. For a useful history of airline deregulation and its mostly positive results, see Steven A. Morrison and Clifford Winston, *The Evolution of the Airline Industry* (Brookings Institution, 1995).

24. *Economic Report of the President*, transmitted to Congress, February 1991 (Government Printing Office, 1991), p. 171. See also James Barth, *The Great Savings and Loan Debacle* (American Enterprise Institute, 1991).

25. For discussions of the telecommunications industry and its regulatory issues, see Robert W. Crandall and Harold Furchtgott-Roth, *Cable TV: Regulation or Competition?* (Brookings Institution, 1996); Richard Klingler, *The New Information Industry: Regulatory Challenges and the First Amendment* (Brookings Institution, 1996).

26. William G. Laffer III, "How Regulation Is Destroying American Jobs," Heritage Foundation Backgrounder 926, February 16, 1993 (see also http://www.townhall.com/heritage/categories/regulation/bg926.html).

27. Jocelyn White, "Superfund: Pouring Money Down a Hole," *The New York Times*, April 17, 1992, p. A17.

CHAPTER 20

1. Michael B. Katz, *In the Shadow of the Poorhouse: A Social History of Welfare in America* (Basic Books, 1986).

2. *Railroad Retirement Board v Alton Railroad Company*, 295 US 300 (1934).

3. U.S. Bureau of the Census, *Statistical Abstract of the United States, 1996* (Government Printing Office, 1996), p. 332.

4. Social Security Administration home page: http://www.ssa.gov/statistics/highlite.html; Joel Packman, Social Security Administration, personal communication.

5. Martha Derthick, "No More Easy Votes for Social Security," *Brookings Review* 10 (Fall 1992), pp. 50–53.

6. Social Security Administration home page: http://www.ssa.gov/statistics/chart.html. Figures based on January 1997 numbers.

7. Paul Light, *Artful Work: The Politics of Social Security Reform* (Random House, 1985).

8. David S. Cloud, Social Security Funds Not Immune Forever," *Congressional Quarterly Weekly Report*, March 18, 1995, p. 838.

9. Peter Francese, "Social Security Solution," *American Demographics* 15 (February 1993), p. 2.

10. Light, *Artful Work*, p. 89.

11. CNN & Company, transcript, April 20, 1994.

12. *Congress and the Nation, 1945–1964: A Review of Government and Politics* (Congressional Quarterly Press, 1965), 1:49.

13. *Congress and the Nation, 1965–1968: A Review of Government and Politics During the Johnson Years* (Congressional Quarterly Press, 1969), 2:1–13, 625.

14. For examples on both sides of this debate, see John E. Schwartz, *America's Hidden Success: A Reassessment of Twenty Years of Public Policy* (Norton, 1983); Charles Murray, *Losing Ground: American Social Policy, 1950–80* (Basic Books, 1984).

15. William J. Clinton, State of the Union Address, January 23, 1996.

16. William J. Clinton, acceptance speech at the Democratic National Convention, Chicago, 1992.

17. *Budget of the United States Government, Fiscal Year 1995* (Government Printing Office, 1994), p. 12.

18. *Statistical Abstract, 1996*, p. 332.

19. Theodore R. Marmor, Jerry L. Mashaw, and Philip L. Harvey, *America's Misunderstood Welfare State: Persistent Myths, Enduring Realities* (Basic Books, 1990), p. 97.

20. Gertrude Schaffner Goldberg and Eleanor Kremen, eds., *The Feminization of Poverty: Only in America?* (Greenwood Press, 1990).

21. U.S. Bureau of the Census, *Statistical Abstract of the United States, 1971* (Government Printing Office, 1971), p. 299; *Statistical Abstract of the United States, 1993* (Government Printing Office, 1994), p. 371.

22. David Whitman, "Honey, I Shrunk the Welfare Reform Plan," *U.S. News and World Report*, March 21, 1994, p. 37.

23. For a description of issues surrounding Medicaid, see Kathleen N. Lohr and M. Susan Maquis, *Medicare and Medicaid: Past, Present and Future* (Rand Corporation, 1984); Congressional Research Service, *Medicaid Source Book* (Library of Congress, 1993). For a discussion of Medicare generally, see Marmor, Mashaw, and Harvey, *America's Misunderstood Welfare State*.

24. *Statistical Abstract, 1996*, p. 120.

25. *Statistical Abstract, 1993*, p. 108.

26. *Statistical Abstract, 1996*, p. 387.

27. *Statistical Abstract, 1996*, pp. 111, 443; 1995 Health Care Financing Administration web page: http://www.hcfa.gov/news/970127.htm.

28. Sally T. Sonnefeld, Daniel R. Waldo, Jeffery A. Lemieux, and David R. McKusick, "Projections of National Health Expenditures Through the Year 2000," *Health Care Financing Review* 13 (Fall 1991), pp. 1–27.

29. John Greenwald, "Ouch!" *Time*, March 8, 1993, p. 53.

30. *Statistical Abstract, 1993*, p. 430; *Statistical Abstract, 1996*, p. 430.

31. *Statistical Abstract, 1996*, p. 108; Health Care Financing Administration home page: http://www.hcfa.gov/stats/table3.txt.

32. *Statistical Abstract, 1996*, p. 88.

33. Ibid., p. 430.

34. Arnold S. Relman, "Where Does All the Money Go?" *Health Management Quarterly* (Fall 1991), p. 324.

35. Laurene A. Graig, *Health of Nations: An International Perspective on U.S. Health Care Reform* (Congressional Quarterly Press, 1993), p. 20.

36. "Defensive Deliveries," *Time*, February 1, 1993, p. 23.

37. *Statistical Abstract, 1996*, p. 112.

38. Christopher Georges, "Bad Forms," *Washington Monthly* 25 (April 1993), pp. 10–33.

39. Mark M. Hagland, "Physicians Using Computers Show Lower Resource Utilization," *Hospitals*, May 5, 1993, p. 17.

40. Peter C. Coyte, Donald N. Dewees, and Michael Trebilock, "Medical Malpractice: The Canadian Experience," *New England Journal of Medicine*, January 10, 1991, pp. 89–93; *Statistical Abstract, 1996*, p. 125.

41. Associated Press, "Medicare Funds Going Up in Smoke," *Deseret News*, May 17, 1994, p. A1.

42. *Statistical Abstract, 1996*, p. 121.

43. "Health Programs," *Congress and the Nation, 1969–1972: A Review of Government and Politics During Nixon's First Term* (Congressional Quarterly Press, 1973), 3:551.

44. Institute of Medicine, Committee on Employer-Based Health Benefits, *Employment and Health Benefits: A Connection at Risk*, eds. Marilyn J. Field and Harold T. Shapiro (National Academy Press, 1993), p. 5.

45. Beth C. Fuchs and Mark Merlis, "Health Care Reform: Tax System Approaches," *CRS Issue Brief*, October 27, 1993, p. i.

46. Philip B. Kurland and Ralph Lerner, eds., *The Founders' Constitution* (University of Chicago Press, 1987).

47. Mickey Kaus, *The End of Equality* (Basic Books, 1992).

48. Department of Education, National Center for Education Statistics, *Digest of Education Statistics, 1996*: http://www.ed.gov/NICES/pubs/d96/D96T032.html.

49. U.S. Department of Education, "Goals 2000: Increasing Student Achievement Through State and Local Initiatives Report to Congress" (Government Printing Office, April 30, 1996), p. 23.

50. Governor George Allen, "Announcement on Goals 2000" (Commonwealth of Virginia Office of the Governor, January 10, 1997).

51. Representative John A. Boehner (R.-Ohio), quoted in *Congressional Digest*, January 1994, p. 25.

52. B. Guy Peters, *American Public Policy: Promise and Performance*, 4th ed. (Chatham House, 1996), p. 338.

53. Center for Education Reform, "Charter School Highlights and Statistics," updated November 18, 1996, http://edreform.com/pugs/chglance.html.

54. *Congress and the Nation, 1965–68*, 2:309. See also Thomas E. Cronin, Tania Z. Cronin, and Michael E. Milakovich, *U.S. v. Crime in the Streets* (Indiana University Press, 1981).

55. Cronin, Cronin, and Milakovich, *U.S. v. Crime in the Streets*.

CHAPTER 21

1. George F. Kennan, "The Failure in Our Success," *The New York Times*, March 14, 1994, p. A13.

2. Richard Ned Lebow, letter to Prentice Hall, reviewing this chapter for the authors, July 8, 1996, p. 2.

3. William J. Broad, "27 Countries Support New Atom Accord," *The New York Times National Edition*, May 3, 1992, sec. 1, p. 9.

4. Caspar W. Weinberger, "Reelection Plank," *Forbes*, April 22, 1996, p. 33.

5. Michael Mandelbaum, "Lessons of the Next Nuclear War," *Foreign Affairs*, March/April 1995, pp. 22–37.

6. "The Future of Warfare," *The Economist*, March 8, 1997, p. 15.

7. Editorial, "A Dangerous Treaty," *The Wall Street Journal*, February 19, 1997, p. A16. But see Pat Towell, "Clinton Pressures GOP to Act on Chemical Arms Ban," *Congressional Quarterly*, March 11, 1997, pp. 545–50.

8. See, for example, Michael Mandelbaum, *The Dawn of Peace in Europe* (Twentieth Century Fund, 1996).

9. For the views of two recent secretaries of state, see Warren Christopher, "America's Leadership, America's Opportunity," *Foreign Policy* (Spring 1995); and James Baker with Thomas M. DeFrank, *The Politics of Diplomacy* (Putnam's, 1995).

10. For different perspectives on the National Security Council under various presidents, see Harold Hongju Koh, *The National Security Constitution: Sharing Power after the Iran-Contra Affair* (Yale University Press, 1990); and John Prados, *Keepers of the Keys: A History of the National Security Council from Truman to Bush* (William Morrow, 1991).

11. See Tim Zimmerman, "Twilight of the Diplomats," *U.S. News and World Report*, January 27, 1997, pp. 48–49.

12. For a fascinating history of U.S. intelligence operations, see Christopher Andrew, *For the President's Eyes Only: Secret Intelligence and the American Presidency from Washington to Bush* (HarperCollins, 1995).

13. Donna Cassata, "House Backs Increased Budget for CIA, Other Spy Activity," *Congressional Quarterly*, September 16, 1995, p. 2824.

14. See the debate on this in Allen E. Goodman et al., *In from the Cold: Task Force on the Future of U.S. Intelligence* (Twentieth Century Fund, 1996).

15. See Loch K. Johnson, *Secret Agencies: U.S. Intelligence in a Hostile World* (Yale University Press, 1996).

16. Ibid.

17. James Kitfield, "What Now for the Spooks?" *National Journal*, March 1, 1996, p. 597.

18. The full report of this commission headed by Les Aspin and Harold Brown is *Preparing for the 21st Century: An Appraisal of U.S. Intelligence*, Report of the Commission on the Roles and Capabilities of the U.S. Intelligence Community (Government Printing Office, March 1, 1996).

19. Steven Kull, "What the Public Knows That Washington Doesn't," *Foreign Policy* (Winter 1995–96), p. 115.

20. John E. Reilly, ed., *American Public Opinion and U.S. Foreign Policy, 1995* (Chicago Council of Foreign Relations, 1995), p. 40.

21. For an examination of how Japanese companies try to influence foreign policy and trade officials in Washington, see Pat Choate, *Agents of Influence* (Knopf, 1990).

22. For a useful review of how Congress has occasionally challenged and even more often has failed to challenge the White House when it comes to the war power, see Louis Fisher, *Presidential War Power* (University Press of Kansas, 1995).

23. Alexis de Tocqueville, *Democracy in America*, 1835 (Knopf, 1945), pp. 224–25.

24. Hans Morganthau, "The Conduct of American Foreign Policy," *Parliamentary Affairs* (Winter 1949), p. 147.

25. See Robert S. McNamara, *In Retrospect: The Tragedy and Lessons of Vietnam* (Times Books, 1995).

26. But see Henry Shue, *Basic Rights: Subsistance, Affluence and U.S. Foreign Policy*, 2d ed. (Princeton University Press, 1996).

27. Gary Clyde Hufbauer and Jeffrey J. Schott, "Economic Sanctions and Foreign Policy," *PS: Political Science and Politics* (Fall 1985), p. 727.

28. See Dick Kirschten, "Chicken Soup Diplomacy," *National Journal*, January 4, 1997, pp. 13–17.

29. John Prados, *The President's Secret Wars: CIA and Pentagon Covert Operations Since World War II* (Morrow, 1986); Roger Morris, "CIA: Costly, Inept, Anachronistic," *The New York Times*, June 10, 1990, p. E23.

30. Hufbauer and Schott, "Economic Sanctions," p. 278.

31. Bob Dole, "Peacekeepers and Politics," *The New York Times*, January 24, 1994, p. A11. Dole reiterated this general theme in Robert Dole, "Shaping America's Global Future," *Foreign Policy* (Spring 1995), pp. 29–43.

32. See, for example, Michael Lind, "Twilight of the U.N.," *The New Republic*, October 30, 1995, pp. 25–33; Rosemary Righter, *Utopia Lost: The United Nations and World Order* (Twentieth Century Fund, 1995).

33. Bill Clinton, quoted in "The UN at 50," *The New York Times*, October 23, 1995, p. A6. For similar and even stronger views, see Nancy Landon Kassebaum and Lee Hamilton, "Fix the UN," *The Washington Post National Weekly Edition*, July 3–9, 1995, p. 28.

34. Quoted in Tim Zimmerman, "Why the UN Might Be Worth Saving," *U.S. News and World Report*, December 16, 1996, p. 44. See also James Kitfield, "Not-So-United," *National Journal*, January 1, 1997, pp. 69–72.

35. Quoted in Don Oberdorfer, "Strategy for Solo Superpower: The U.S. Plans to Keep Its Powder Dry," *The Washington Post National Weekly Edition*, May 27–June 2, 1991, p. 8.

36. See the provocative arguments in Robert W. Tucker and David C. Hendrickson, *The Imperial Temptation: The New World Order and America's Purpose* (Council on Foreign Relations, 1992). See also Ronald Steel, *Temptations of a Superpower* (Harvard University Press, 1995).

37. Quoted in Genevieve Anton, "Having Women Fight Riddled with Issues," *Colorado Springs Gazette Telegraph*, August 11, 1991, pp. 1, 10.

38. Evan Thomas and Gregory L. Vistica, "Falling Out of the Sky," *Newsweek*, March 17, 1997, p. 26.

39. Philip Shenon, "When 'Don't Ask, Don't Tell' Means Do Ask and Do Tell All," *The New York Times*, March 3, 1996, p. E7.

40. See Neil A. Lewis, "Court Upholds Clinton Policy on Gay Troops," *New York Times*, April 6, 1996, pp. 1, 7.

41. Barry M. Goldwater, "The Gay Ban: Just Plain Un-American," *The Washington Post National Weekly Edition*, June 21–27, 1993, p. 28.

42. Editorial, "Defense Spending, Defense Goals," *The Washington Post National Weekly Edition*, April 1–7, 1996, p. 27. See also Lawrence J. Korb, "The Indefensible Defense Budget," *The Washington Post National Weekly Edition*, July 17–23, 1995, p. 19.

43. Bill Clinton, speech at the McDonnell Douglas plant in Long Beach, Calif., February 23, 1996, reprinted in *Vital Speeches of the Day*, March 15, 1996, p. 323.
44. Tim Weiner, "Military Chiefs Trying to Gain Extra Billions," *The New York Times*, April 11, 1996, pp. A1, A12.
45. See, for example, James Kitfield, "Ships Galore!" *National Journal*, February 10, 1996, pp. 298–302.
46. Kenneth R. Mayer, *The Political Economy of Defense Contracting* (Yale University Press, 1991), p. 223.
47. See John Keegan, *A History of Warfare* (Knopf, 1993); Stephen J. Cimbala, *The Politics of Warfare: The Great Powers in the Twentieth Century* (Penn State Press, 1997); and "The Future of Warfare," *The Economist*, March 8, 1997, pp. 21–24.

CHAPTER 22

1. Edith Hamilton, *The Echo of Greece* (W. W. Norton, 1957), p. 47.
2. Adapted from Kenneth M. Dolbeare and Patricia Dolbeare, *American Ideologies* (Markham Publishing, 1971).
3. John F. Kennedy, *Profiles in Courage* (Pocket Books, 1956), p. 108.
4. Michael Nelson, "Politics as a Vital, and Sometimes Noble, Human Activity," *Chronicle of Higher Education* (August 18, 1995), p. A44.
5. See Thomas E. Cronin, "Thinking and Learning about Leadership," *Presidential Studies Quarterly* (Winter 1984), pp. 22–34. See also Warren Bennis and Patricia Ward Biederman, *Organizing Genius: The Secrets of Creative Collaboration* (Addison-Wesley, 1997).
6. See Kareem Abdul-Jabar and Alan Steinberg, *Black Profiles in Courage* (Morrow, 1996).
7. See Bernard Crick, *In Defense of Politics*, rev. ed. (Pelican Books, 1983); Stimson Bullitt, *To Be a Politician*, rev. ed. (Yale University Press, 1977).
8. See Nat Hentoff, *Free Speech for Me—But Not for Thee: How the American Left and Right Relentlessly Censor Each Other* (Harper Perrenial, 1993).
9. William J. Brennan, commencement address, Brandeis University, Waltham, Mass., May 18, 1986.
10. Arthur M. Schlesinger, Jr., *The Disuniting of America* (W. W. Norton, 1993), p. 134.
11. Lewis H. Lapham, "Who and What Is American?" *Harper's Magazine*, January 1992, p. 48.
12. John W. Gardner, *Self-Renewal*, rev. ed. (Norton, 1981), p. xiv.
13. Walt Whitman, "By Blue Ontario's Shore," *Leaves of Grass*, eds. Harold W. Blodgett and Sculley Bradley (New York University Press, 1965), p. 353.

Photo Credits

Chapter 1: xvi Howard Chandler Christie/The Granger Collection **5** Jeff Widener/AP/Wide World Photos **6** The Granger Collection **9** (*left*) R. Ellis/Sygma (*right*) Dragon Filipovic/AP/Wide World Photos **13** The Granger Collection **14** (*top*) The Granger Collection (*bottom*) The Granger Collection **17** (*top*) The Granger Collection (*bottom*) Corbis-Bettmann **22** Courtesy Louise Turner Arnold

Chapter 2: 24 Wally McNamee/Woodfin Camp & Associates **30** The Granger Collection **31** The Granger Collection **33** Fiona Hanson/AP/Wide World Photos **36** The Granger Collection **37** Ron Edmonds/AP/Wide World Photos **40** (*top*) The Granger Collection (*bottom*) Brown Brothers

Chapter 3: 52 Wilfredo Lee/AP/Wide World Photos **57** Spencer Grant/Photo Researchers, Inc. **59** Corbis-Bettmann **72** Chuck Nacke/Woodfin Camp & Associates

Chapter 4: 78 Eunice Harris/Photo Researchers, Inc. **83** Robert Fried/Stock Boston **85** Vanessa Vick/Photo Researchers, Inc. **87** AP/Wide World Photos **92** (*top*) John Duricka/AP/Wide World Photos (*bottom*) John Spink/Atlanta Journal Constitution/AP/Wide World Photos **96** James Wilson/Woodfin Camp & Associates **98** Charles Tasnadi/AP/Wide World Photos **100** (*left*) Sygma (*right*) Stephen Crowley/New York Times Pictures **103** David Tulis/UPI/Corbis-Bettmann **104** James Nubile/The Image Works

Chapter 5: 108 AP/Wide World Photos **111** Corbis-Bettmann **114** UPI/Corbis-Bettmann **117** Eric Haase/Contact Press Images **119** Chuck Fishman/Woodfin Camp & Associates **124** UPI/Corbis Bettmann **134** Ron Edmonds/Corbis-Bettmann

Chapter 6: 140 Peter Southwick/AP/Wide World Photos **145** Brown Brothers **147** Jeffrey Boan/AP/Wide World Photos **150** Tony Savino **154** Sylvia Johnson/Woodfin Camp & Associates **157** Blair Seitz/Photo Researchers, Inc. **159** James Wilson/Woodfin Camp & Associates **161** Barr/Pool/SIPA Press **162** (*top*) Mingasson/Gamma Liaison, Inc. (*left*) Lee Celano/Reuters/Corbis-Bettmann (*right*) Los Angeles Daily News/Sygma **165** David R. Frazier/Photo Researchers, Inc.

Chapter 7: 170 Spencer Grant /Photo Researchers, Inc. **173** Patrick Robert/Sygma **176** Lewis Hine/Corbis-Bettmann **177** UPI/Corbis-Bettmann **178** Tannen Maury/AP/Wide World Photos **185** (*top*) Reuters/Jim Bourg/Archive Photos (*bottom*) Roberto Borea/AP/Wide World Photos **187** Greg Gibson/AP/Wide World Photos **188** The Libertarian Party **191** Bob Strong/The Image Works

Chapter 8: 194 Robert Frerck/Woodfin Camp and Associates **197** Brown Brothers **202** Alan Carey/The Image Works **204** Elaine Thompson/AP/Wide World Photos **210** (*top*) Chester Higgins, Jr. (*middle*) Nathan Benn/Woodfin Camp & Associates (*bottom*) D. Greco/The Image Works **211** AP/Wide World Photos

Chapter 9: 222 Chris Pizzello/AP/Wide World Photos **225** Library of Congress **226** (*top*) Reuters/Bettmann (*left*) AP/Wide World Photos (*right*) Cynthia Howe/Sygma **229** Michael Heinz/AP/Wide World Photos **235** Paul S. Conklin **236** Kathy Strauss/AP/Wide World Photos **240** (*left*) Corbis-Bettmann (*right*) Roswell Angier/Stock Boston

Chapter 10: 250 Bucci/Nelson/Andrews/Corbis-Bettmann **257** (*left*) Brown Brothers (*middle*) AP/Wide World Photos (*right*) AP/Wide World Photos

259 The Granger Collection **261** Bill Fitzpatrick/The White House Photo Office **262** Denis Paquin/AP/Wide World Photos **263** (*top*) Ed Andrieski/AP/Wide World Photos (*bottom*) Liz Schultz/AP/Wide World Photos

Chapter 11: 278 Bob Daemmrich/Bob Daemmrich Photography **280** Bob Daemmrich/Bob Daemmrich Photography **286** UPI/Corbis-Bettmann **290** Julia Malakie/AP/Wide World Photos **295** Mathew McVay/Stock Boston **296** (*left*) Dale Atkins/AP/Wide World Photos (*right*) Joe Marquette/AP/Wide World Photos

Chapter 12: 302 Reuters/Jim Bourg/Archive Photos **307** Ron Edmonds/AP/Wide World Photos **309** Susan Sterner/AP/Wide World Photos **313** (*top*) Reuters/Fred Prouser/Corbis-Bettmann (*bottom*) Reuters/Sam Mircovich/Corbis-Bettmann **318** (*top*) Joe Burbank/The Orlando Sentinel/AP/Wide World Photos (*bottom*) Greg Gibson/AP/Wide World Photos **324** Jamal A. Wilson/Agence France-Presse **329** Chris Wilkins/Corbis-Bettmann

Chapter 13: 332 Carol Lee/Uniphoto Picture Agency **335** Corinne Dufka/Reuters/Corbis-Bettmann **336** Sam Kittner/Reuters/Corbis-Bettmann **337** National Archives **339** UPI/Corbis-Bettmann **344** Ron Edmnds/AP/Wide World Photos **345** UPI/Corbis-Bettmann **349** Mike Nelson/Agence France Presse/Corbis-Bettmann **354** Trippett/SIPA Press

Chapter 14: 356 Richard Ellis/Sygma **358** (*left*) Corbis-Bettmann (*right*) Corbis Bettmann **359** (*top*) Reuters/Mike Theiler/Corbis-Bettmann (*bottom*) Richard Ellis /Sygma **364** John Duricka/AP/Wide World Photos **370** National Cable Satellite Corporation/C-SPAN **379** John Duricka/AP/Wide World Photos **382** (*top*) Ron Sachs/Consolidated News Pictures, Inc. (*middle*) Barbara Ries/Gamma Liaison, Inc. (*bottom*) B. Markel/Gamma Liaison, Inc.

Chapter 15: 388 Matt Mendelsohn/Corbis-Bettmann **390** The Granger Collection **391** The New York Times Pictures **399** Chesnot/Villard/Witt/SIPA Press **400** Reuters/Win McNamee/Archive Photos **403** AP/Wide World Photos **404** UPI/Corbis Bettmann **408** Greg Gibson/AP/Wide World Photos **411** (*top*) J. Ficara/Sygma (*bottom*) Ron Edmonds/AP/Wide World Photos **412** Rick Bowmer/AP/Wide World Photos

Chapter 16: 418 AP/Wide World Photos **434** (*top*) Clary/UPI/Corbis-Bettmann (*bottom*) Carol T. Powers/AP/Wide World Photos **435** (*top*) Reuters/Corbis-Bettmann (*middle*) Reuters/Gary Hershorn/Corbis-Bettmann (*bottom*)Reuters/Steve Jaffe/Corbis-Bettmann **441** Reuters/Gary Hershorn/Corbis Bettmann

Chapter 17: 446 Reininger/Contact/Woodfin Camp & Associates **448** Larry Downing/Sygma **455** N.R. Rowan/Stock Boston **460** AP/Wide World Photos **466** Robert Giroux/AP/Wide World Photos **471** Doug Mills/AP/Wide World Photos

Chapter 18: 474 Andy Levin **477** Denis Paquin/AP/Wide World Photos **482** Brad Markel/Gamma Liaison, Inc. **485** Robert Visser/Sygma **491** Mike Theiler/Reuters/Corbis-Bettmann **494** Tony Freeman/PhotoEdit **496** Reuters/Lou Dematteis/Corbis-Bettmann

Chapter 19: 500 Porterfield/Chickering/Photo Researchers, Inc. **502** J. Scott Applewhite/AP/Wide World Photos **506** Jack Fields/Photo Researchers, Inc. **510** Leif Skoogfors/Woodfin Camp & Associates **513** (*top*) Ted Spiegel/Black Star (*bottom*) Jeff Mitchell/Reuters/Corbis-Bettmann **514** Robert J. Herko/The Image Bank **517** Alvis Uptis/The Image Bank

Chapter 20: **524** Mark Lennihan/AP/Wide World Photos **526** Mark Lennihan/AP/Wide World Photos **528** Brown Brothers **530** The White House Photo Office **535** John Duricka/AP/Wide World Photos **540** John Duricka/AP/Wide World Photos **541** National Library of Medicine **550** John Ficara/Sygma

Chapter 21: **554** Mark Wilson/AP/Wide World Photos **556** Richard Ellis/Sygma **558** Kimimasa Mayama/Pool/Reuters/Corbis-Bettmann **560** *(top to bottom)* UPI/Corbis-Bettman; Corbis-Bettmann; Corbis-Bettmann; UPI/P. Skingley/Corbis-Bettmann **561** *(top to bottom)* UPI/Corbis-Bettman; UPI/Don Rypka/Corbis-Bettmann; Reuters/Mark Cardwell/Corbis-Bettmann; Reuters/Jeff Mitchell/Corbis-Bettmann **562** Joe Marquette/AP/Wide World Photos **565** UPI/Paul Richards/Corbis-Bettmann **570** UN-DPI, John Isaac/AP/Wide World Photos **572** Joe Marquette/AP/Wide World Photos **573** UPI/Corbis-Bettmann **574** T. Campion/Sygma **575** *(top)* James Montgomery Flagg/The Granger Collection *(bottom)* Howard Chandler Christy/The Granger Collection

Chapter 22: **580** Louis Goldman, Photo Researchers, Inc. **582** Cornelius Tiebout/The Granger Collection **585** Bob Daemmrich Photography **587** UPI/Corbis-Bettmann **589** UPI/Corbis-Bettmann **591** The Granger Collection

Part Identity Photos: I The Granger Collection **II** Andrew Savulich/AP/Wide World Photos **III** Jean-Marc Giboux/Gamma Liaison **IV** John Spragens, Jr. **V** Joe Marquette/Pool **VI** H. Dratch/The Image Works

Index

Jury nullification, 165
Jus sanguinis, 143
Jus soli, 143
Justice, as shared value, 175
Justiciable disputes, 420

Kantor, Mickey, 267
Kasich, John R., 450
Keating, Charles, 237, 323
Keillor, Garrison, 173
Kemp, Jack, 182, 186, 317, 411, 486, 492
Kennedy, Anthony, 65, 66, 82, 154, 438, 439, 463
Kennedy, Edward, 360
Kennedy, John F., 116, 177, 211, 342, 407, 588
Kennedy, Paul, 415
Kerner, Otto, 116
Kerner Commission, 116, 137
Kessler, David, 505
Keynes, John Maynard, 491
Keynesian economics, 491–92
King, Larry, 334, 336
King, Martin Luther, Jr., 102, 103, 115, 116, 210
King, Rodney, 137, 167
Kiser, Samuel C., 195
Klaas, Polly, 310
Knight, Bobby, 62
Knights of Columbus, 233
Knights of Labor, 229
Koppel, Ted, 279
Korean Americans, 120–21
Ku Klux Klan, 127
Kull, Steven, 565

Labor
    current status of, 511
    as interest group, 223, 229–31
Labor injunctions, 510
Labor-management relations, regulation of, 508–11
Laissez-faire policy, 260, 503
Lake, Anthony, 366
Lame duck, 29, 305
Landrieu, Mary, 244
Larry King Live, 32, 318
Laski, Harold, 419, 439
Latency, in public opinion sampling, 282
Laureano, Marta, 195
Law clerks, 437
Law Enforcement Assistance Administration (LEAA), 549–50
Law making, as congressional function, 362
Laws, types of, 420
Leadership
    in constitutional democracy, 415–16, 586–88
    interest group, 236
    of John F. Kennedy, 588
    of Martin Luther King, Jr., 588
    reconciling democracy and, 588–89
Leadership Conference on Civil Rights, 239

League of United Latin American Citizens (LULAC), 120
Least drastic means doctrine, 90
Legal Services Corporation (LSC), 426
Legal tender clause, 149
Legislative branch, 27. *See also* Congress
Legislative courts, 422
Legislators
    attentiveness to constituents, 369
    colleagues' influence on, 369–70
    interest groups' influence on, 372
    as lawmakers, 369–72
    party influence on, 371–72
    policy/philosophical convictions on, 369
    president's influence on, 372
    as representatives, 368
    staffs of, 370–71
Lemon test, 81–82
Lemon v Kurtzman, 81–82
Leno, Jay, 1, 385
Letterman, David, 1, 385
Liability revolution, 426
Libel, 98
Liberalism, 180–84
    criticisms of, 182–84
Libertarianism, 188
Libertarian party, 256, 258
Liberty
    personal, 4, 5
    as shared value, 172
Liddy, G. Gordon, 335
Life-cycle effects, in politics, 217
Limbaugh, Rush, 1, 32, 191, 334, 335, 345, 358
Limited public forums, 103
Lincoln, Abraham, 1, 36, 66, 259, 285, 414, 430
Lippmann, Walter, 285
Lippo Group, 324
Lipset, Seymour Martin, 216
Litigation, by interest groups, 236–37
Livingston, Bob, 378
Lobbying, 240–41
    cooperative, 238–39
    by organized labor, 230–31
Lobbying Disclosure Act (1995), 246–47
Lobbyists, 239–41
Local government, partisanship in, 267
Locke, Gary, 120, 205
Locke, John, 26
Log Cabin Republicans, 350
Log rolling, 370
Lott, Trent, 364, 559

MacArthur, Douglas, 398
MacDougal, James, 166
MacDougal, Susan, 166
MacLeish, Archibald, 590
Madison, Dolly, 410
Madison, James, 3, 16, 20, 21, 25, 26, 29, 55, 167, 210, 212, 224, 367, 415
Magistrates, 422–23
Mails, First Amendment protection of, 93
Major committees, 375–76

Majority leader
    House of Representatives, 363
    Senate, 363
Majority-minority districts, 130
Majority rule, 4, 7, 305
    in British system, 33
Major parties, 256
Malpractice insurance, 541
Managed competition, 542
Mandamus, writ of, 29, 30
Mandates, federal, 60
Mandatory partial preemption, 70
Manifest destiny, 198
Mapp v Ohio, 157
Marble cake federalism, 54
Marbury, William, 29
Marbury v Madison, 28–31, 267, 419
Maritime law, 420
Market Access Program, 450
Mark up of bills, 372
Marshall, John, 29–30, 64–65, 66, 79, 149, 419
Marshall, Thurgood, 134, 432, 434, 437, 438, 439
Marx, Karl, 187
Maryland Act for the Liberties of the People, 13
Mason, George, 20
Mass media, 333–55
    criticism, as presidential constraint, 412–13
    elections and, 347–52
        election night reporting, 352
        electoral campaign, 348–49
        image making, 319, 349–50
        media consultants, 350
        voter choice, 350–52
    family values and, 344
    governance and, 352–54
    influence of, 334–42
        autonomous press and, 337–41
        as linking mechanism, 337
        as new mediator in politics, 341–42
        newspapers, 336
        talk radio, 335–36
        television, 334–35
        World Wide Web, 336–37
    interest groups and, 236
    political socialization and, 284, 343
    public opinion and, 342–47
        agenda setting, 346
        audience, 343–44
        bias, 345–46
        issue framing, 346
        regulation, 347
    as source of political culture, 181
    technology and, 349
Mass public, 564
Mayhew, David R., 31, 240
McCain, John, 559
McCarthy, Eugene, 316
McClosky, Herbert, 191
McCulloch v Maryland, 58, 63–64
McDowell, Charles, 589
McGovern, George, 297

Nuclear arms control, 558–59
Nuclear Regulatory Commission, 504
Nurses Training Act (1964), 531

Objective journalism, 339
Obscenity, 98–99
Occupation, political diversity and, 213–16
Occupational health, regulation of, 509, 515
Occupational safety, regulation of, 509, 515–16
Occupational Safety and Health Act (1970), 509
Occupational Safety and Health Administration (OSHA), 503, 515–16
O'Connor, Sandra Day, 65, 66, 82, 134, 135, 154, 437, 438, 439
Office block ballot, 252
Office of Legal Counsel (OLC), 425
Office of Management and Budget (OMB), 408, 409, 470
  in budget process, 479–80
Office of Personnel Management (OPM), 457
Office of Surface Mining, 504
Off-year elections, 291
Older Americans, 216–17
Older Americans Act (1965), 531
Oligopolies, 507
Omnibus Crime Control and Safe Streets Act (1968), 531
Omnibus Housing Act (1964), 531
Open primaries, 254
Open rule, 363
Open seats, women and, 207
Open shop, 231
Operation Desert Storm, 564, 574
Operation Restore Hope, 285
Opinion makers, 564
Optimism, as shared value, 172, 175
Original jurisdiction, 29
  courts of, 422
  of Supreme Court, 423
Osborne, David, 468
Overbreadth doctrine, 89–90
Override of presidential veto, 374, 406
Overseas Private Investment Corporation, 450
Oversight, congressional, 362, 379
Owens, Steve, 223

Packwood, Bob, 208, 243
PACs
  defined, 225, 241
  effectiveness of, 243–44
  growth of, 241–42
  increasing dependence on, 327–28
  investment of money by, 242–43
  reform and, 247–48
  regulation and, 245–47
Paleoconservatives, 188
Panama, 569
Parks, Rosa, 115

Parochial school aid, 83–84
Partial preemption, 70
Participation
  in constitutional democracy, 584–88
    leadership and, 586–88
    politician's role, 585–86
Part-time citizens, 288
Party activists, 268
Party column ballot, 252
Party identification, 269–70
  voting on basis of, 295–96
Party platforms, 264–65, 266, 271, 317
Party unity score, 274–75
Pasadena, voter participation in, 291, 292
Patent and Trademark Office (PTO), 493
Paterson, William, 18
Patronage, 253
Payner, Jack, 158
Peace Corps, 563
Peace liberals, 182
Pell Grants, 546
Peña, Federico, 119
Penn, Mark, 303
People for the American Way, 428
Percy, Charles, 328
Peremptory challenges, 163
Perkins, Frances, 339
Permissive federalism, 55
Perot, H. Ross, 105, 238, 247, 272, 298, 299, 300, 318, 319, 325, 349, 358, 411
Persian Gulf War, 285, 340, 347
Personal liberty, 4, 5
Personal Responsibility and Work Opportunity Reconciliation Act (1996), 68
Petition, nomination by, 318
Petit juries, 161, 422
Pharmaceutical Manufacturers Association, 543
Picketing, First Amendment protection of, 96–97
Plain-view exception, 157
Planned Parenthood of Southeastern Pennsylvania v Casey, 65, 443
Plato, 4
Plays, First Amendment protection of, 93–94
Plea bargaining, 161, 425
Plessy v Ferguson, 114, 124
Plurality rule, 7, 305
  in British system, 33
Plyler v Doe, 439
Pocket veto, 374, 406
Polarization, 280
Police committees, Senate, 364
Police powers, 149
Policy clarification, as congressional function, 362
Political action committees (PACs), 223
Political activities, as source of political culture, 181
Political coercion, 569

Political culture, 172–80. *See also* Ideology
  American Dream, 178–80
  egalitarian, 414
  hierarchical, 414
  individualistic, 414
  political/economic change, 175–78
  shared values in, 172–75
  sources of, 180–81
Political equality, as shared value, 173
Political involvement, decline in, 12
Political landscape, 195–221
  diversity and, 196–97
  geographical factors
    national identity, 197–98
    place of residence, 201–2
    sectional differences, 198–200
    state/local identity, 200
  personal identity factors
    age, 216–17
    education, 217–19
    gender, 207–8
    occupation, 213–16
    race/ethnicity, 202–7
    religion, 210–12
    sexual orientation, 208–9
    social class, 216
    wealth/income, 212–13
  unity in, 219–20
Political participation. *See* Elections; Interest groups; Political parties; Voting
Political parties, 251–77. *See also* Democrats/Democratic party; Elections; Republicans/Republican party
  American, history of, 258–61
  defined, 262
  demise of, debate over, 274–75
  in electorate, 268–69
  foreign policy and, 566
  functions, 251–53
  in government, 265, 267–68
  influence on legislators, 371–72
  as institutions, 262–64
  interest group formation of, 238
  minor, 256–58
  national, rise of, 31–32
  nomination of candidates by, 253–55
  opposition, 6
  party identification, 269
  party platforms/differences, 264–65, 266, 271, 317
  party systems, 255–56
  public confidence in, 271
  realignment/dealignment, 270, 272–74
  reform/renewal, 275–76
  weak, 394
Political questions, 420
Political socialization, 196, 269, 282
  mass media and, 343
Political speech, centrality of, 90
Politicians, 1–3, 585–86, 589, 590
Politics
  candidate-centered, 310
  confirmation, 365–66

WASHINGTON
Centers of Decision and Landmarks

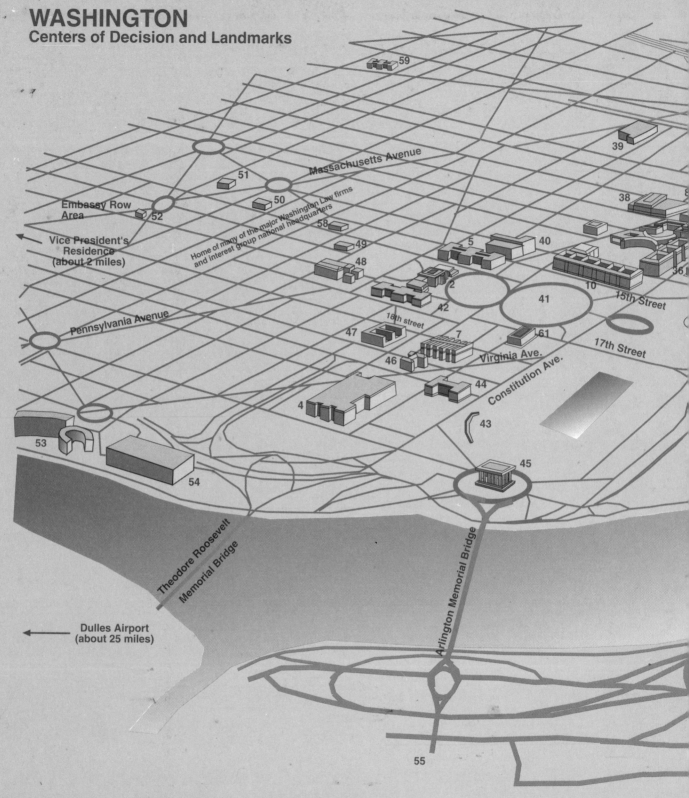

Massachusetts Avenue

Embassy Row Area

← Vice President's Residence (about 2 miles)

Home of many of the major Washington Law firms and interest group national headquarters

Pennsylvania Avenue

18th street

Virginia Ave.

Constitution Ave.

17th Street

15th Street

Theodore Roosevelt Memorial Bridge

Arlington Memorial Bridge

← Dulles Airport (about 25 miles)

1 Congress	12 Dept. of Health and Human Services	21 Republican National Committee
2 The White House	13 Dept. of Housing and Urban Development	22 Congressional Budget Office
3 Supreme Court		23 Food and Drug Administration
4 Dept. of State	14 Dept. of Transportation	24 National Air and Space Museum
5 Dept. of Treasury	15 Dept. of Energy	25 Smithsonian Institution
6 Dept. of Defense	16 Dept. of Education	26 GSA Regional Office
7 Dept. of Interior	17 Senate Office Buildings	27 Bureau of Engraving and Printing
8 Dept. of Justice	18 Hall of States	28 Jefferson Memorial
9 Dept. of Agriculture	19 Library of Congress (Congressional Research Service)	29 Union Station (railroad)
10 Dept. of Commerce		30 National Gallery of Art
11 Dept. of Labor	20 House Office Buildings	31 Federal Trade Commission
		32 National Museum of Natural History

33 Internal Revenue Service	43 Vi
34 National Museum of American History	44 Fe
35 Washington Monument	45 Lin
36 Interstate Commerce Commission	46 Or
37 U.S. Postal Service	47 Ge
38 FBI - Hoover Building	48 Na
39 General Accounting Office	49 W
40 National Press Club	50 W
41 The Ellipse	51 Br
42 Executive Office of the President (Office of Management and Budget) (Council of Economic Advisors) (National Security Council)	52 Ar
	53 W
	54 Jo